GMAT™
Focus Edition

Where do you see yourself in 6 weeks?

You can prep for the GMAT Focus Edition in less time than it takes to catch up on your favorite television shows. Get your FREE 6-Week Study Planner: **mba.com/6-weeks**

- **Start** your prep on the right foot
- **Track** your progress as you learn
- **Keep focused** on your business school journey
- **Gain tools and tips** to achieve your dream score

GMAT™
Focus Edition

GMAT™ Official Guide
2023 – 2024

Your prep begins here. Designed by the makers of the GMAT exam.

The only source of real GMAT questions

What's Included:

✓ Over 650 Practice Questions
✓ Data Insights Review Chapter (**New Section**)
✓ Math and Verbal Review Chapters
✓ Answer Explanations

Plus! Online Exclusive:

✓ **Mobile App** – Study on the Go
✓ Quick Diagnostic to Focus Your Practice
✓ Over 150 Practice Questions
✓ Track Your Progress

 Book + Online + Mobile

 mba.com

 GMAT™ Official Prep

GMAT™ OFFICIAL GUIDE 2023–2024

For general information on our other products and services or to obtain technical support please contact our Customer Care Department within the U.S. at (877) 762-2974, outside the U.S. at (317) 572-3993 or fax (317) 572-4002.

John Wiley & Sons, Inc., also publishes its books in a variety of electronic formats and by print-on-demand. Not all content that is available in standard print versions of this book may appear or be packaged in all book formats. If you have purchased a version of this book that did not include media that is referenced by or accompanies a standard print version, you may request this media by visiting http://booksupport.wiley.com. For more information about Wiley products, visit us at www.wiley.com.

ISBN 978-1-394-16994-8 (pbk); ISBN 978-1-394-16997-9 (ePub)

Printed in the United States of America

SKY10038552_032323

Table of Contents

Dear GMAT™ Test Taker,

Thank you for your interest in graduate management education. Today more than 7,700 graduate programs around the world use the GMAT exam to establish their MBA, business master's, and other graduate-level management degree programs as hallmarks of excellence. Seven out of ten candidates apply to business school with their GMAT exam score.*

By using the *GMAT™ Official Guide* to prepare for the GMAT Focus Edition, you're taking a very important step toward achieving your goals and pursuing admission to the MBA or business master's program that is the best fit for you.

The *GMAT™ Official Guide 2023–2024*, is designed to help you prepare for and build confidence to do your best on exam day. It's the only guide that features real GMAT questions published by the Graduate Management Admission Council (GMAC™), the makers of the GMAT exam. This guide and the other print and digital GMAT™ Official Prep products available at mba.com will give you the confidence to achieve your personal best on the GMAT exam and launch or reinvigorate a rewarding career.

For 70 years, the GMAT exam has helped candidates like you demonstrate their command of the skills needed for success in the classroom and showcase to schools their commitment to pursuing a graduate business degree. Schools use and trust the GMAT exam as part of their admissions process because it's a proven predictor of classroom success and your ability to excel in your chosen program.

The mission of GMAC is to ensure no talent goes undiscovered. We are driven to provide you with the tools and information you need to guide you through your journey in graduate management education, continuously improve the GMAT exam, and help you find and connect with the best-fit schools and programs for you.

We applaud your commitment to educational success and wish you the best on all your future educational and professional endeavors.

Sincerely,

Joy J. Jones

Joy J. Jones
CEO, Graduate Management Admission Council

---

*Top 100 *Financial Times* full-time MBA programs

GMAT™ Official Guide 2023–2024

1.0 What Is the GMAT™ Exam?

1.0 What Is the GMAT™ Exam?

The Graduate Management Admission Test™ (GMAT™) is used in admissions decisions by more than 7,700 graduate management programs at about 2,400 business schools worldwide. It helps both you and these schools gauge how well you can do in graduate-level management studies. Unlike undergraduate grades and courses, whose meanings vary across regions and institutions, your GMAT scores are a standardized, statistically valid, and reliable measure of how well you are likely to do in the core courses of a graduate management program. This guide is for the **GMAT™ Focus Edition.**

The exam has three sections, which test your Verbal Reasoning, Quantitative Reasoning, and Data Insights skills. These skills include critical thinking, data analysis, and problem-solving, which all call for complex judgments. Management faculty and admissions professionals have found that incoming graduate students need these skills. And employers worldwide need their professional staff to have these skills as well.

This chapter gives more details about the GMAT Focus Edition below. You will take the exam on a computer either online or at a test center, always in English. It is not a test of business knowledge, subject mastery, English vocabulary, or advanced computing skills. Nor does it measure other factors helpful in business, such as job experience, leadership ability, motivation, or social skills. Your GMAT score is meant to be an objective, numeric measure of your ability and potential for success. Business schools will use it as part of their holistic admissions processes, which may also consider recommendation letters, essays, interviews, work experiences, and other signs of social and emotional intelligence as well as leadership.

1.1 Why Take the GMAT™ Exam?

Taking the exam helps you stand out as an applicant and show you're ready for and committed to graduate management education. Schools use GMAT scores in choosing the most qualified applicants. They know an applicant who has taken the exam is serious about earning a graduate business degree, and they know the exam scores reliably predict how well applicants can do in graduate business programs.

No matter how you do on the exam, you should contact schools that interest you to learn more about them and to ask how they use GMAT scores and other criteria in admissions decisions. School admissions offices, websites, and publications are key sources of information when you are researching business schools. Note that schools' published GMAT scores are averages of the scores of their admitted students, not minimum scores needed for admission.

> ## *Myth* -vs- **FACT**
>
> *M* – **If I don't get a high GMAT score, I won't get into my top-choice schools.**
>
> F – **There are great schools for students with any GMAT score.**
>
> Few people taking the GMAT exam will get a perfect score of 805, yet many will get into top business-school programs around the world. Admissions officers will use GMAT scores as one factor in admissions decisions along with undergraduate records, application essays, interviews, letters of recommendation, and other information. Visit Program Finder on mba.com to learn which programs and schools are right for you.

To learn more about the exam, test preparation materials, registration, and how to use your GMAT scores in applying to business schools, please visit mba.com/gmatfocus.

1.2 GMAT™ Focus Edition Format

The GMAT™ Focus Edition has three separately timed sections (see the table on the following page). The Data Insights section includes multiple-choice questions along with other kinds of graphical and data analysis questions. The Quantitative Reasoning section and the Verbal Reasoning section have only multiple-choice questions.

All three GMAT sections are computer adaptive. This means the test chooses from a large bank of questions to adjust itself to your ability level, so you will not get many questions that are too hard or too easy for you. The first question will be of medium difficulty. As you answer each question, the computer uses your answer, along with your responses to earlier questions, to choose the next question with the right difficulty level.

Computer-adaptive tests get harder as you answer more questions right. But getting a question that seems easier than the last one doesn't always mean your last answer was wrong. The test must ask you many types of questions on different subjects, so it will not always give you a question of the perfect difficulty level.

A new feature in the GMAT is a bookmark you can use to mark any questions you feel unsure about during the exam. Another new feature lets you review and edit your answers at the end of each section. You can review and edit answers even to questions you have not bookmarked, but bookmarking a question helps you find it again quickly. You can bookmark as many questions as you like. You can review all questions whether or not they are bookmarked, but you can only change your answers to three questions per section. You must finish all your bookmarking, reviewing, and editing within each section's time limit. No extra time is given to use these new features.

Because the computer uses your answers to choose your next question, you cannot skip questions. But at the end of each section, you can go back, review all questions, and edit your answers for up to three questions. If you don't know how to answer a question, try to rule out as many wrong answer choices as possible. Then pick the answer choice you think is best.

Though each test taker gets different questions, the mix of question types is always the same. Your score depends on the difficulty and statistical traits of the questions you answer, as well as on which of your answers are right. By adapting to each test taker, the exam can accurately and efficiently gauge a full range of skill levels, from very high to very low.

The practice questions in this book and the online question bank accessed via mba.com/my-account are formatted and presented differently than questions on the actual exam. The practice questions are organized by question type and from easiest to hardest. But on the test, you may see different types of questions in any order within each section.

Myth -vs- **FACT**

M – **Getting an easier question means I answered the last one wrong.**

F – **Worrying that a question seems too easy isn't helpful.**

Many factors may make the questions easier or harder, so don't waste time worrying if some questions seem easy.

To make sure every test taker gets equivalent content, the test gives specific numbers of questions of each type and about each kind of subject. But sometimes no available question perfectly meets these constraints. In this case, the test chooses the best available question, which may be slightly harder or easier than your next question would normally be. Also, remember you will be stronger in some subjects than in others. Since the test covers the same kinds of subjects for everyone, some items may be harder or easier for you than for other test takers.

Here are six things to know about GMAT questions:

(1) The computer screen shows only one question or question prompt at a time, except for some types of Data Insights questions.

(2) Radio buttons, rather than letters, mark the answer choices for multiple-choice questions.

(3) The Data Insights section gives questions of different types in random order.

(4) You must choose an answer and confirm your choice before moving on to the next question.

(5) You can bookmark questions to remind yourself to review them at the end of the section.

(6) Once you answer all of a section's questions, you may revisit any questions, whether bookmarked or not, and edit up to three answers in the section.

Format of the GMAT™ Focus Edition		
	Questions	Timing
Data Insights Data Sufficiency Multi-Source Reasoning Table Analysis Graphics Interpretation Two-Part Analysis	20	45 min.
Quantitative Reasoning	21	45 min.
Verbal Reasoning Reading Comprehension Critical Reasoning	23	45 min.
	Total Time	135 min.

On exam day, right before you start the exam, you can choose any order in which you will take the three sections. For example, you can choose to start with Verbal Reasoning, then do Quantitative Reasoning, and end with Data Insights. Or, you can choose to do Data Insights first, followed by Verbal Reasoning and then Quantitative Reasoning. Between sections, you can take one optional ten-minute break after either the first section or the second section.

1.3 What Is the Test Experience Like?

You can take the exam either online or at a test center—whichever you prefer. You may feel more comfortable at home with the online delivery format. Or you may prefer the uninterrupted, secure environment of a test center. It is your choice. Both options have the same content, structure, optional ten-minute break, scores, and score scales.

At the Test Center: Over 700 test centers worldwide administer the GMAT exam under standardized conditions. Each test center has proctored testing rooms with individual computer workstations that let you take the exam in a peaceful, quiet setting, with some privacy. You must not take notes or scratch paper into the testing room, but you will get an erasable notepad and marker to use during the test. To learn more about exam day, visit mba.com/gmatfocus.

Online: The GMAT exam delivered online is proctored remotely, so you can take it in the comfort of your home or office. You will need a quiet workspace with a desktop or laptop computer that meets minimum system requirements, a webcam, and a reliable internet connection. For more information about exam day, visit mba.com/gmatfocus.

To learn more about available accommodations for the exam, visit mba.com/accommodations.

1.4 What Is the Test Content Like?

The GMAT exam measures several types of analytical reasoning. The Data Insights section asks you to use diverse reasoning skills to solve realistic problems involving data. It also asks you to interpret and combine data from different sources and in different formats to reach conclusions. The Quantitative Reasoning section gives you basic arithmetic and algebra problems. Some are abstract, while others are realistic word problems.

The test questions are about various subjects, but the exam tells you everything you need to know to answer the questions. You do not need detailed outside knowledge of the subjects. The exam does not test business knowledge, vocabulary, or advanced computer skills. You will need basic math and English skills to do well on the test, but it mainly measures analytical and critical thinking skills.

1.5 Data Insights Section

The GMAT Data Insights section highlights skills that today's business managers need to analyze intricate data and solve complex problems. It tests how well you can assess multiple sources and types of information—graphic, numeric, and verbal—as they relate to one another. It also tests how well you can analyze a practical math problem to tell if enough data is given to solve it. This section asks you to use math, data analysis, and verbal reasoning to analyze complex problems and solve related problems together.

The Data Insights section has five types of questions:

- Multi-Source Reasoning
- Table Analysis
- Graphics Interpretation
- Two-Part Analysis
- Data Sufficiency

Data Insights questions may require math, data analysis, verbal reasoning, or all three. You will have to interpret graphs and sort data tables to answer some questions, but you won't need advanced statistics or spreadsheet skills. For both online and test center exam delivery, you will have access to an on-screen

> ### Myth -vs- FACT
>
> M – **My GMAT score does not predict my success in business school.**
>
> F – **False. The GMAT exam measures your critical thinking skills, which you will need in business school and your career.**
>
> Hundreds of studies across hundreds of schools have proven the GMAT's validity. Together, these studies have shown that performance on the GMAT predicts success in business school even better than undergraduate grades do.
>
> The exam measures how well you reason, solve problems, and analyze data. Some employers may even use the exam to judge your skills in these areas. Even if your program does not require GMAT scores, you can stand out from the crowd by doing well on the exam to show you have the skills to succeed in business school.

calculator with basic functions for the Data Insights section, but *not* for the Quantitative Reasoning section.

In this book, Chapter 5, "Data Insights Review," reviews the basic data analysis skills you need to answer Data Insights questions. Chapter 6, "Data Insights," explains the Data Insights question types and gives test-taking tips.

For practice questions of each type, with full answer explanations, access the Online Question Bank by going to mba.com/my-account and using your unique access code on the inside front cover of this book.

1.6 Quantitative Reasoning Section

The GMAT Quantitative Reasoning section measures how well you solve math problems and interpret graphs. All questions in this section require solving problems using basic arithmetic, algebra, or both. Some are practical word problems, while others are pure math.

In this book, Chapter 3, "Math Review," reviews the basic math you need to answer Quantitative Reasoning questions. Chapter 4, "Quantitative Reasoning," has test-taking tips, practice questions, and answer explanations.

1.7 Verbal Reasoning Section

The GMAT Verbal Reasoning section measures how well you reason, understand what you read, and evaluate arguments. The Verbal Reasoning section includes passages about many topics. Neither the passages nor the questions assume you already know much about the topics discussed. Mingled throughout the section are multiple-choice questions of two main types: Reading Comprehension and Critical Reasoning.

Chapter 7, "Verbal Review," reviews the basic verbal analysis and reasoning skills you need for the Verbal Reasoning section. Chapter 8, "Verbal Reasoning," explains the Verbal Reasoning question subtypes. It also has test-taking tips for each subtype, as well as practice questions and answer explanations.

1.8 How Are Scores Calculated?

The Verbal Reasoning, Quantitative Reasoning, and Data Insights sections are each scored on a scale from 60 to 90, in 1-point increments. You will get four scores: a Data Insights section score, a Verbal Reasoning section score, a Quantitative Reasoning section score, and a Total GMAT Score based on your three section scores. The Total GMAT Score ranges from 205 to 805. Your scores depend on:

- Which questions you answered right
- How many questions you answered
- Each question's difficulty and other statistical characteristics

An algorithm finds your scores based on the factors above. After you answer easier questions correctly, you will get harder questions to answer, letting you earn a higher score. The computer calculates your scores after you finish the exam or when your time runs out.

The following table shows the different types of scores, the scales, and the increments.

Type of Score	Scale	Increments
Total Score	205–805	10
Quantitative Reasoning	60–90	1
Verbal Reasoning	60–90	1
Data Insights	60–90	1

Your GMAT scores are valid for five years from your exam date. Your Total GMAT Score includes a predicted percentile ranking, which shows the percentage of tests taken with scores lower than your score. Visit mba.com to view the most recent predicted percentile rankings tables.

2.0 How to Prepare

2.0 How to Prepare

2.1 How Should I Prepare for the Test?

The GMAT™ Focus Edition has several unique question formats. You should at least know about the test format and these question formats before you take the test. Because the exam is timed, you should also try answering the practice questions in this book. By practicing, you'll learn to pace yourself so that you can finish each section during the exam. You'll also learn about the question formats and the skills you need.

Because the exam assesses reasoning rather than knowledge, memorizing facts probably won't help you. You don't need to study advanced math, but you should know some basic arithmetic and algebra. Likewise, you don't need to study advanced vocabulary words, but you should know English well enough to understand writing at an undergraduate level.

> ## *Myth* -vs- **FACT**
>
> *M* – **You need advanced math skills to get a high GMAT score.**
>
> *F* – **The exam measures your reasoning ability rather than your advanced math skills.**
>
> The exam only requires basic math. You should review the math skills in chapter 3 of this guide and in the *GMAT™ Official Guide Quantitative Review 2023–2024*. GMAT Quantitative Reasoning questions are challenging mainly because of the reasoning skills needed to solve the problems, not the underlying math skills.

2.2 Getting Ready for Exam Day

Whether you take the test online or in a test center, knowing what to expect will help you feel confident and succeed.

Test Center

While checking into a test center, be ready to:

- Show proper identification.
- Give your palm vein scan (where permitted by law).
- Give your digital signature to show that you understand and agree to the Test-Taker Rules and Agreement.
- Have a digital photograph taken.

For more information visit mba.com/gmatfocus.

Online

At least a day before you take your exam online:

- Check your computer—make sure your computer meets the minimum system requirements to run the exam.
- Prepare your workspace—find a quiet place to take your exam, clean your workspace, and remove all objects except your computer and whiteboard.
- Plan ahead—be ready to begin checking in 30 minutes before your scheduled exam time.

For more information visit mba.com/gmatfocus.

2.3 How to Use the *GMAT™ Official Guide 2023–2024*

The *GMAT™ Official Guide* series is the largest official source of actual GMAT questions and has been updated for the GMAT™ Focus Edition. Use this study guide to practice answering the different types of questions. Practice questions of each type are arranged from easy to hard, so we recommend starting at the beginning of each set of practice questions and working through them in order. Some "easy" questions may seem hard to you, and some "hard" questions may seem easy. This is common. Different questions often seem harder to some people and easier to others.

You may also find the questions in this book generally easier or harder than questions you see on the Official Practice Exams or the actual exam. This is expected because, unlike the Official Practice Exams and the actual exam, this guidebook doesn't adjust to your abilities. In this book, about a third of the practice questions are easy, a third are medium, and a third are hard. However, on the actual exam and the Official Practice Exams, you probably won't find such an even mix of difficulty levels. Also, the proportions of questions about different content areas in this book don't reflect the proportions in the actual exam. To find questions of a specific type and difficulty level (for example, easy arithmetic questions), use the index of questions in chapter 9.

> **TIP**
>
> Since the exam is given on a computer, we suggest you practice the questions in this book using the **Online Question Bank** accessed via mba.com/my-account. It includes all the questions in this book, and it lets you create practice sets and track your progress more easily. The Online Question Bank is also available on your mobile device through the GMAT™ Official Practice mobile app. To access the Online Question Bank on your mobile device, first, create an account at mba.com, and then sign into your account on the mobile app.

2.4 How to Use Other GMAT™ Official Prep Products

We recommend using our other GMAT™ Official Prep products along with this guidebook.

- **For a realistic simulation of the exam:** GMAT™ Official Practice Exams 1–6 are the only practice exams that use real exam questions along with the scoring algorithm, user interface, and online whiteboard tool from the real exam. The first two practice exams are free to all test takers at mba.com/gmatprep.

- **For more practice questions:** *GMAT™ Official Guide Data Insights Review 2023–2024*, *GMAT™ Official Guide Verbal Review 2023–2024*, and *GMAT™ Official Guide Quantitative Review 2023–2024* offer more practice questions not included in this book.

For the best results:

1. Learn about the exam and the question types by reading the *GMAT™ Official Guide 2023–2024*.

2. Take the Diagnostic evaluation in the Online Question Bank (access via mba.com/my-account) to gauge your strengths and weaknesses.

3. Practice the questions in the *GMAT™ Official Guide 2023–2024*, focusing on skills you need to improve.

4. Take GMAT™ Focus Official Practice Exam 1. Do not worry about your score on this first practice exam! The goal is to become familiar with the exam and get a baseline score so that you can gauge your progress.

5. As you keep practicing, take more GMAT™ Focus Official Practice Exams to gauge your progress.

6. Before your actual GMAT exam, take a final Official Practice Exam to simulate the real test and see how you score.

The first two GMAT™ Official Practice Exams are in the free GMAT™ Official Starter Kit, which has free practice questions and is available to everyone with an mba.com account. You can buy GMAT™ Focus Official Practice Exams 3 to 6, more GMAT™ Focus Official Practice Questions, and other Official Prep products through mba.com/gmatprep.

2.5 Tips for Taking the Exam

Tips for answering questions of the different types are given later in this book. Here are some general tips to help you do your best on the test.

1. Use your time wisely.
Although the exam stresses accuracy over speed, you should use your time wisely. On average, you have just under two minutes per Verbal Reasoning question, about 2 minutes, 9 seconds per Quantitative Reasoning question, and 2 minutes, 15 seconds per Data Insights question. Once you start the test, an on-screen clock shows how much time you have left. You can hide this display if you want, but by checking the clock periodically, you can make sure to finish in time.

2. Before the actual exam, decide in what order to take the sections.
The exam lets you choose in which order you'll take the sections. Use the GMAT™ Official Practice Exams to practice and find your preferred order. No order is "wrong." Just practice each order and see which one works best for you.

3. Try the practice questions ahead of time.
Timing yourself as you answer the practice questions can give you a sense of how long you will have for each question on the actual test, and whether you are answering them fast enough to finish in time.

> **TIP**
>
> After you've learned about all the question types, use the practice questions in this book and practice them online at mba.com/my-account to prepare for the actual test. Note that most types of Data Insights practice questions are available only online.

4. Study all test directions.
The directions explain exactly what you need to do to answer questions of each type. Study the directions so that you don't miss anything you need to know to answer properly. To review directions during the test, click on the Help icon. But note that your time spent reviewing directions counts against your available time for that section of the test.

5. **Study each question carefully.**
    Before you answer a question, understand exactly what it says. Then pick the best answer choice. Never skim a question or the answer choices. Skimming may make you miss important details or nuances.

6. **Do not spend too much time on any one question.**
    If finding the right answer is taking too long, try to rule out answer choices you know are wrong. Then pick the best of the remaining choices and move on to the next question.

    Not finishing sections or randomly guessing answers can lower your score significantly. As long as you've worked on each section, you will get a score even if you didn't finish one or more sections in time. You don't earn points for questions you never get to see.

7. **Confirm your answers ONLY when you are ready to move on.**
    In the Quantitative Reasoning and Verbal Reasoning sections, once you choose your answer to a question, you are asked to confirm it. As soon as you confirm your response, the next question appears. You can't skip questions. In the Data Insights section, several questions based on the same prompt may appear at once. When more than one question is on a single screen, you can change your answers to any questions on that screen before moving on to the next screen. But until you've reached the end of the section, you can't navigate back to a previous screen to change any answers.

    This book and other study materials from the Graduate Management Admission Council (GMAC) are the ONLY sources of real GMAT questions. All questions that appear or have appeared on the exam are copyrighted and owned by GMAC, which doesn't license them to be reprinted elsewhere. Accessing live GMAT questions in advance or sharing test content while or after you take the test is a serious violation. It could cause your scores to be canceled and schools to be notified. For serious violations, you may be banned from future testing, and other legal remedies may be pursued.

Myth -vs- FACT

M – Avoiding wrong answers is more important than finishing the test.

F – Not finishing can lower your score a lot.

Pacing is important. If a question stumps you, just pick the answer choice that seems best and move on. If you guess wrong, the computer will likely give you an easier question, which you're more likely to answer right. Soon the computer will return to giving you questions matched to your ability. You can bookmark questions you get stuck on, then return to change up to three of your answers if you still have time left at the end of the section. But if you don't finish the section, your score will be reduced. Failing to answer five verbal questions, for example, could lower your score from the 91st percentile to the 77th percentile.

Myth -vs- FACT

M – The first ten questions are critical, so you should spend the most time on them.

F – All questions count.

The test uses each answered question to *initially* estimate how hard your questions should be. As you keep answering questions, the test adjusts by updating the estimate based on all your answers so far. It then chooses questions that closely match its new estimate of your ability. Your final score depends on all your responses and on how hard all the questions you answered were. Taking extra time on the first ten questions won't game the system and might make you run out of time.

3.0 Math Review

3.0 Math Review

This chapter reviews the math you need to answer GMAT™ Quantitative Reasoning questions and some GMAT Data Insights questions. This is only a brief overview, so if you find unfamiliar terms, consult other resources to learn more.

Unlike some math problems you may have solved in school, GMAT math questions ask you to **apply** your math knowledge. For example, rather than asking you to list a number's prime factors to show you understand prime factorization, a GMAT question may ask you to **use** prime factorization and exponents to simplify an algebraic expression with a radical.

To prepare for the GMAT Quantitative Reasoning section and the Data Insights section, first review basic math to make sure you know enough to answer the questions. Then practice using GMAT questions from past exams.

Section 3.1, "Value, Order, and Factors," includes:

1. Numbers and the Number Line
2. Factors, Multiples, Divisibility, and Remainders
3. Exponents
4. Decimals and Place Value
5. Properties of Operations

Section 3.2, "Algebra, Equalities, and Inequalities," includes:

1. Algebraic Expressions and Equations
2. Linear Equations
3. Factoring and Quadratic Equations
4. Inequalities
5. Functions
6. Graphing
7. Formulas and Measurement Conversion

Section 3.3, "Rates, Ratios, and Percents," includes:

1. Ratio and Proportion
2. Fractions
3. Percents
4. Converting Decimals, Fractions, and Percents
5. Working with Decimals, Fractions, and Percents
6. Rate, Work, and Mixture Problems

Section 3.4, "Statistics, Sets, Counting, Probability, Estimation, and Series," includes:

1. Statistics
2. Sets
3. Counting Methods
4. Probability
5. Estimation
6. Sequences and Series

Section 3.5, "Reference Sheets"

3.1 Value, Order, and Factors

1. Numbers and the Number Line

A. All *real numbers* correspond to points on *the number line*, and all points on the number line represent real numbers.

The figure below shows the number line with labeled points standing for the real numbers $-\frac{3}{2}$, 0.2, and $\sqrt{2}$.

The Number Line

B. On a number line, points to the left of zero stand for *negative* numbers, and points to the right of zero stand for *positive* numbers. All real numbers except zero are either positive or negative.

C. For any two numbers on the number line, the number to the left is less than the number to the right. So, as the figure above shows, $-4 < -3 < -\frac{3}{2} < -1$, and $1 < \sqrt{2} < 2$.

D. If a number n is between 1 and 4 on the number line, then $n > 1$ and $n < 4$; that is, $1 < n < 4$. If n is "between 1 and 4, inclusive," then $1 \le n \le 4$.

E. The *absolute value* of a real number x, written as $|x|$, is x if $x \ge 0$ and $-x$ if $x < 0$. A number's absolute value is the distance between that number and zero on the number line. Thus, -3 and 3 have the same absolute value, since each is three units from zero on the number line. The absolute value of any nonzero number is positive.

Examples:

$|-5| = |5| = 5$, $|0| = 0$, and

$\left|\frac{-7}{2}\right| = \frac{7}{2}$.

For any real numbers x and y, $|x + y| \le |x| + |y|$.

Example:

If $x = 10$ and $y = 2$, then $|x + y| = |12| = 12 = |x| + |y|$.

If $x = 10$ and $y = -2$, then $|x + y| = |8| = 8 < 12 = |x| + |y|$.

2. Factors, Multiples, Divisibility, and Remainders

A. An *integer* is any number in the set $\{\ldots -3, -2, -1, 0, 1, 2, 3, \ldots\}$. For any integer n, the numbers in the set $\{n, n + 1, n + 2, n + 3, \ldots\}$ are *consecutive integers*.

B. If x and y are integers and $x \neq 0$, then x is a *divisor* or *factor* of y if $y = xn$ for some integer n. Then y is *divisible* by x and is called a *multiple* of x.

> *Example:*
>
> Since $28 = (7)(4)$, both 4 and 7 are divisors or factors of 28.
>
> But 8 isn't a divisor or factor of 28, since n isn't an integer if $28 = 8n$.

C. Dividing a positive integer y by a positive integer x, and then rounding down to the nearest nonnegative integer, gives the *quotient* of the division.

To find the *remainder* of the division, multiply x by the quotient, then subtract the result from y. The quotient and the remainder are the unique positive integers q and r, respectively, such that $y = xq + r$ and $0 \leq r < x$.

> *Example:*
>
> When 28 is divided by 8, the quotient is 3 and the remainder is 4, because $28 = (8)(3) + 4$.

The remainder r is 0 if and only if y is *divisible* by x. Then x is a divisor or factor of y, and y is a multiple of x.

> *Example:*
>
> Since 32 divided by 8 has a remainder of 0, 32 is divisible by 8. So 8 is a divisor or factor of 32, and 32 is a multiple of 8.

When a smaller integer is divided by a larger integer, the quotient is 0 and the remainder is the smaller integer.

> *Example:*
>
> When 5 is divided by 7, the quotient is 0 and the remainder is 5, since $5 = (7)(0) + 5$.

D. Any integer divisible by 2 is *even*; the set of even integers is $\{\ldots -4, -2, 0, 2, 4, 6, 8, \ldots\}$. Integers not divisible by 2 are *odd*, so $\{\ldots -3, -1, 1, 3, 5, \ldots\}$ is the set of odd integers. For any integer n, the numbers in the set $\{2n, 2n + 2, 2n + 4, \ldots\}$ are *consecutive even integers*, and the numbers in the set $\{2n + 1, 2n + 3, 2n + 5, \ldots\}$ are *consecutive odd integers*.

If a product of integers has at least one even factor, the product is even; otherwise, it's odd. If two integers are both even or both odd, their sum and their difference are even. Otherwise, their sum and their difference are odd.

E. A *prime* number is a positive integer with exactly two positive divisors, 1 and itself. That is, a prime number is divisible by no integer but itself and 1.

> *Example:*
>
> The first six prime numbers are 2, 3, 5, 7, 11, and 13.
>
> But 15 is not a prime number, because it has four positive divisors: 1, 3, 5, and 15.
>
> Nor is 1 a prime number, because it has only one positive divisor: itself.

Every integer greater than 1 is either prime or a product of a unique set of prime factors. A *composite number* is an integer greater than 1 that's not prime.

> *Example:*
>
> $14 = (2)(7)$, $81 = (3)(3)(3)(3)$, and
>
> $484 = (2)(2)(11)(11)$ are composite numbers.

3. Exponents

A. An expression of the form k^n means the nth *power* of k, or k raised to the nth power, where n is the *exponent* and k is the *base*.

B. A positive integer exponent shows how many instances of the base are multiplied together. That is, when n is a positive integer, k^n is the product of n instances of k.

> *Examples:*
>
> x^5 is $(x)(x)(x)(x)(x)$; that is, the product in which x is a factor 5 times and no other factors. We can also say x^5 is the 5th power of x, or x raised to the 5th power.
>
> The second power of 2, also called 2 *squared*, is $2^2 = 2 \times 2 = 4$. The third power of 2, also called 2 *cubed*, is $2^3 = 2 \times 2 \times 2 = 8$.

Squaring a number greater than 1, or raising it to any power greater than 1, gives a larger number.

Squaring a number between 0 and 1 gives a smaller number.

> *Examples:*
>
> $3^2 = 9$, and $9 > 3$.
>
> $(0.1)^2 = 0.01$, and $0.01 < 0.1$.

C. A **square root** of a number n is a number x such that $x^2 = n$. Every positive number has two real square roots, one positive and the other negative. The positive square root of n is written as $\sqrt{n}$ or $n^{\frac{1}{2}}$.

> *Example:*
>
> The two square roots of 9 are $\sqrt{9} = 3$ and $-\sqrt{9} = -3$.

For any x, the nonnegative square root of x^2 equals the absolute value of x; that is, $\sqrt{x^2} = |x|$.

The square root of a negative number is not a real number and is called an **imaginary number**.

D. Every real number r has exactly one real **cube root**, which is the number s such that $s^3 = r$. The real cube root of r is written as $\sqrt[3]{r}$ or $r^{\frac{1}{3}}$.

> *Examples:*
>
> Since $2^3 = 8$, $\sqrt[3]{8} = 2$.
>
> Likewise, $\sqrt[3]{-8} = -2$ because $(-2)^3 = -8$.

4. Decimals and Place Value

A. A **decimal** is a real number written as a series of digits, often with a period called a **decimal point.** The decimal point's position sets the **place values** of the digits.

> *Example:*
>
> The digits in the decimal 7,654.321 have these place values:
>
> | Thousands | | Hundreds | Tens | Ones or units | | Tenths | Hundredths | Thousandths |
> |-----------|---|----------|------|---------------|---|--------|------------|-------------|
> | 7 | , | 6 | 5 | 4 | . | 3 | 2 | 1 |

B. In **scientific notation**, a decimal is written with only one nonzero digit to the decimal point's left, multiplied by a power of 10. To convert a number from scientific notation to regular decimal notation, move the decimal point by the number of places equal to the absolute value of the exponent on the 10. Move the decimal point to the right if the exponent is positive or to the left if the exponent is negative.

Examples:

In scientific notation, 231 is written as 2.31×10^2, and 0.0231 is written as 2.31×10^{-2}.

To convert 2.013×10^4 to regular decimal notation, move the decimal point 4 places to the right, giving 20,130.

Likewise, to convert 1.91×10^{-4} to regular decimal notation, move the decimal point 4 places to the left, giving 0.000191.

C. To add or subtract decimals, line up their decimal points. If one decimal has fewer digits to the right of its decimal point than another, insert zeros to the right of its last digit.

Examples:

To add 17.6512 and 653.27, insert zeros to the right of the last digit in 653.27 to line up the decimal points when the numbers are in a column:

$$
\begin{array}{r}
17.6512 \\
+\,653.2700 \\
\hline
670.9212
\end{array}
$$

Likewise for 653.27 minus 17.6512:

$$
\begin{array}{r}
653.2700 \\
-\,17.6512 \\
\hline
635.6188
\end{array}
$$

D. Multiply decimals as if they were integers, then insert the decimal point in the product so that the number of digits to the right of the decimal point is the sum of the numbers of digits to the right of the decimal points in the numbers being multiplied.

Example:

To multiply 2.09 by 1.3, first multiply the integers 209 and 13 to get 2,717. Since $2 + 1 = 3$ digits to the right of the decimal points in 2.09 and 1.3, put 3 digits in 2,717 to the right of the decimal point to find the product:

$$
\begin{array}{r}
2.09 \quad \text{(2 digits to the right)} \\
\times\,1.3 \quad \text{(1 digit to the right)} \\
\hline
627 \\
2090 \\
\hline
2.717 \quad (2+1 = 3 \text{ digits to the right})
\end{array}
$$

E. To divide a number (the ***dividend***) by a decimal (the ***divisor***), move the divisor's decimal point to the right to make the divisor an integer. Then move the dividend's decimal point the same number of places to the right. Then divide as you would integers. The decimal point in the quotient goes directly above the decimal point in the new dividend.

Example:

To divide 698.12 by 12.4, first move the decimal points in both the divisor 12.4 and the dividend 698.12 one place to the right to make the divisor an integer. That is, replace 698.12/12.4 with 6981.2/124. Then do the long division normally:

$$
\begin{array}{r}
56.3 \\
124\overline{)6981.2} \\
\underline{620} \\
781 \\
\underline{744} \\
372 \\
\underline{372} \\
0
\end{array}
$$

---

5. Properties of Operations

Here are some basic properties of arithmetical operations for any real numbers x, y, and z.

A. Addition and Subtraction

$x + 0 = x = x - 0$

$x - x = 0$

$x + y = y + x$

$x - y = -(y - x) = x + (-y)$

$(x + y) + z = x + (y + z)$

If x and y are both positive, then $x + y$ is also positive.

If x and y are both negative, then $x + y$ is negative.

B. Multiplication and Division

$x \times 1 = x = \dfrac{x}{1}$

$x \times 0 = 0$

If $x \neq 0$, then $\dfrac{x}{x} = 1$

$\dfrac{x}{0}$ is undefined.

$xy = yx$

If $x \neq 0$ and $y \neq 0$, then $\dfrac{x}{y} = \dfrac{1}{\left(\dfrac{y}{x}\right)}$.

$(xy)z = x(yz)$

$xy + xz = x(y + z)$

If $y \neq 0$, then $\left(\dfrac{x}{y}\right) + \left(\dfrac{z}{y}\right) = \dfrac{(x + z)}{y}$.

If x and y are both positive, then xy is also positive.

23

If x and y are both negative, then xy is positive.

If x is positive and y is negative, then xy is negative.

If $xy = 0$, then $x = 0$ or $y = 0$, or both.

C. Exponentiation

$x^1 = x$

$x^0 = 1$

If $x \neq 0$, then $x^{-1} = \frac{1}{x}$

$(x^y)^z = x^{yz} = (x^z)^y$

$x^{y+z} = x^y x^z$

If $x \neq 0$, then $x^{y-z} = \frac{x^y}{x^z}$.

$(xz)^y = x^y z^y$

If $z \neq 0$, then $\left(\frac{x}{z}\right)^y = \frac{x^y}{z^y}$.

If $z \neq 0$, then $x^{\frac{y}{z}} = (x^y)^{\frac{1}{z}} = \left(x^{\frac{1}{z}}\right)^y$.

3.2 Algebra, Equalities, and Inequalities

1. Algebraic Expressions and Equations

A. Algebra is based on arithmetic and on the concept of an **unknown quantity**. Letters like **x** or **n** are **variables** that stand for unknown quantities. Numerical expressions called **constants** stand for known quantities. A combination of variables, constants, and arithmetical operations is an **algebraic expression**.

Solving word problems often requires translating words into algebraic expressions. The table below shows how some words and phrases can be translated as math operations in algebraic expressions:

3.2 Translating Words into Math Operations				
$x + y$	$x - y$	xy	$\frac{x}{y}$	x^y
x added to y *x increased by y* *x more than y* *x plus y* *the sum of x and y* *the total of x and y*	*x decreased by y* *difference of x and y* *y fewer than x* *y less than x* *x minus y* *x reduced by y* *y subtracted from x*	*x multiplied by y* *the product of x and y* *x times y*	*x divided by y* *x over y* *the quotient of x and y* *the ratio of x to y*	*x to the power of y* *x to the yth power*
		If $y = 2$: *double x* *twice x*	If $y = 2$: *half of x* *x halved*	If $y = 2$: *x squared*
		If $y = 3$: *triple x*		If $y = 3$: *x cubed*

B. In an algebraic expression, a *term* is a constant, a variable, or a product of simpler terms that are each a constant or a variable. A variable in a term may be raised to an exponent. A term with no variables is a *constant term*. A constant in a term with one or more variables is a *coefficient*.

> *Example:*
>
> Suppose Pam has 5 more pencils than Fred has. If F is the number of pencils Fred has, then the number of pencils Pam has is $F + 5$. The algebraic expression $F + 5$ has two terms: the variable F and the constant term 5.

C. A *polynomial* is an algebraic expression that's a sum of terms and has exactly one variable. Each term in a polynomial is a variable raised to some power and multiplied by some coefficient. If the highest power a variable is raised to is 1, the expression is a *first degree* (or *linear*) *polynomial* in that variable. If the highest power a variable is raised to is 2, the expression is a *second degree* (or *quadratic*) *polynomial* in that variable.

> *Examples:*
>
> $F + 5$ is a linear polynomial in F, since the highest power of F is 1.
>
> $19x^2 - 6x + 3$ is a quadratic polynomial in x, since the highest power of x is 2.
>
> $\dfrac{3x^2}{(2x - 5)}$ is not a polynomial, because it's not a sum of powers of x multiplied by coefficients.

D. You can simplify many algebraic expressions by factoring or combining *like* terms.

> *Examples:*
>
> The expression $6x + 5x$ is equivalent to $(6 + 5)x$, or $11x$.
>
> In the expression $9x - 3y$, 3 is a factor common to both terms: $9x - 3y = 3(3x - y)$.
>
> The expression $5x^2 + 6y$ has no like terms and no common factors.

E. In a fraction $\dfrac{n}{d}$, n is the *numerator* and d is the *denominator*. In an algebraic expression's numerator and denominator, you can divide out any common factors not equal to zero.

> *Example:*
>
> If $x \neq 3$, then $\dfrac{(x - 3)}{(x - 3)} = 1$.
>
> So $\dfrac{(3xy - 9y)}{(x - 3)} = \dfrac{3y(x - 3)}{(x - 3)} = 3y(1) = 3y$.

F. To multiply two algebraic expressions, multiply each term of one expression by each term of the other.

> *Example:*
>
> $$(3x - 4)(9y + x) = 3x(9y + x) - 4(9y + x)$$
> $$= 3x(9y) + 3x(x) - 4(9y) - 4(x)$$
> $$= 27xy + 3x^2 - 36y - 4x$$

G. To evaluate an algebraic expression, replace its variables with constants.

> *Example:*
>
> If $x = 3$ and $y = -2$, we can evaluate $3xy - x^2 + y$ as
>
> $3(3)(-2) - (3)^2 + (-2) = -18 - 9 - 2 = -29$.

H. An ***algebraic equation*** is an equation with at least one algebraic expression. An algebraic equation's ***solutions*** are the sets of assignments of constant values to its variables that make it true, or "satisfy the equation." An equation may have no solution, one solution, or more than one solution. For equations solved together, the solutions must satisfy all the equations at once. An equation's solutions are also called its ***roots***. To confirm the roots are correct, you can substitute them into the equation.

I. Two equations with the same solution or solutions are ***equivalent***.

> *Examples:*
>
> The equations $2 + x = 3$ and $4 + 2x = 6$ are equivalent, because each has the unique solution $x = 1$. Notice the second equation is the first equation multiplied by 2.
>
> Likewise, the equations $3x - y = 6$ and $6x - 2y = 12$ are equivalent, although each has infinitely many solutions. For any value given to x, giving the value $3x - 6$ to y satisfies both these equations. For example, $x = 2$ with $y = 0$ is a solution to both equations, and so is $x = 5$ with $y = 9$.

2. Linear Equations

A. A ***linear equation*** has a linear polynomial on one side of the equals sign and either a linear polynomial or a constant on the other side—or can be converted to that form. A linear equation with only one variable is a ***linear equation with one unknown***. A linear equation with two variables is ***a linear equation with two unknowns***.

> *Examples:*
>
> $5x - 2 = 9 - x$ is a linear equation with one unknown.
>
> $3x + 1 = y - 2$ is a linear equation with two unknowns.

B. To solve a linear equation with one unknown (that is, to find what value of the unknown satisfies the equation), isolate the unknown on one side of the equation by doing the same operations on both sides. Adding or subtracting the same number from both sides of the equation doesn't change the equality. Likewise, multiplying or dividing both sides by the same nonzero number doesn't change the equality.

Example:

To solve the equation $\frac{5x-6}{3} = 4$, isolate the variable x like this:

$$5x - 6 = 12 \quad \text{multiply both sides by 3}$$
$$5x = 18 \quad \text{add 6 to both sides}$$
$$x = \frac{18}{5} \quad \text{divide both sides by 5}$$

To check the answer $\frac{18}{5}$, substitute it for x in the original equation to confirm it satisfies that equation:

$$\frac{\left(5\left(\frac{18}{5}\right) - 6\right)}{3} = \frac{(18-6)}{3} = \frac{12}{3} = 4$$

So $x = \frac{18}{5}$ is the solution.

C. If two linear equations with the same two unknowns are equivalent, they have infinitely many solutions, as in the example of the equivalent equations $3x - y = 6$ and $6x - 2y = 12$ in section 3.2.1.I above. But if two linear equations with the same two unknowns aren't equivalent, they have at most one solution.

Two linear equations with two unknowns can be solved in several ways. If in solving them you reach a trivial equation like $0 = 0$, the equations are equivalent and have infinitely many solutions. But if you reach a contradiction, the equations have no solution.

Example:

Consider the two equations $3x + 4y = 17$ and $6x + 8y = 35$. Note that $3x + 4y = 17$ implies $6x + 8y = 34$, contradicting the second equation. So, no values of x and y can satisfy both equations at once.

If neither a trivial equation nor a contradiction is reached, a unique solution can be found.

D. To solve two linear equations with two unknowns, you can use one of the equations to express one unknown in terms of the other unknown. Then substitute this result into the second equation to make a new equation with only one unknown. Next, solve this new equation. Substitute the value of its unknown into either of the original equations to find the value of the remaining unknown.

Example:

Let's solve these two equations for x and y:

$$(1) \quad 3x + 2y = 11$$
$$(2) \quad\;\; x - y = 2$$

In equation (2), $x = 2 + y$. So, in equation (1), substitute $2 + y$ for x:

$$3(2 + y) + 2y = 11$$
$$6 + 3y + 2y = 11$$
$$6 + 5y = 11$$
$$5y = 5$$
$$y = 1$$

Since $y = 1$, we find $x - 1 = 2$, so $x = 2 + 1 = 3$.

E. Another way to remove one unknown and solve for x and y is to make the coefficients of one unknown the same in both equations (ignoring the sign). Then either add the equations or subtract one from the other.

Example:

Let's solve the equations:

(1) $6x + 5y = 29$ and

(2) $4x - 3y = -6$

Multiply equation (1) by 3 and equation (2) by 5 to get

$$18x + 15y = 87 \text{ and}$$
$$20x - 15y = -30$$

Add the two equations to remove y. This gives us $38x = 57$, or $x = \dfrac{3}{2}$.

Substituting $\dfrac{3}{2}$ for x in either original equation gives $y = 4$. To check these answers, substitute both values into both the original equations.

3. Factoring and Quadratic Equations

A. Some equations can be solved by *factoring*. To do this, first add or subtract to bring all the expressions to one side of the equation, with 0 on the other side. Then try to express the nonzero side as a product of factors that are algebraic expressions. When that's possible, setting any of these factors equal to 0 makes a simpler equation, because for any x and y, if $xy = 0$, then $x = 0$ or $y = 0$ or both. The solutions of the simpler equations made this way are also solutions of the factored equation.

Example:

Factor to find the solutions of the equation $x^3 - 2x^2 + x = -5(x-1)^2$:

$$x^3 - 2x^2 + x + 5(x-1)^2 = 0$$
$$x(x^2 - 2x + 1) + 5(x-1)^2 = 0$$
$$x(x-1)^2 + 5(x-1)^2 = 0$$
$$(x+5)(x-1)^2 = 0$$
$$x + 5 = 0 \text{ or } x - 1 = 0$$
$$x = -5 \text{ or } x = 1.$$

So, $x = -5$ or $x = 1$.

B. When factoring to solve equations with algebraic fractions, note that a fraction equals 0 if and only if its numerator equals 0 and its denominator doesn't.

Example:

Find the solutions of the equation $\dfrac{x(x-3)(x^2+5)}{x-4} = 0$

The numerator must equal 0: $x(x-3)(x^2+5) = 0$.

Thus, $x = 0$, or $x - 3 = 0$, or $x^2 + 5 = 0$. So, $x = 0$, or $x = 3$, or $x^2 + 5 = 0$.

But $x^2 + 5 = 0$ has no real solution, because $x^2 + 5 = 0$ for every real number x. So, the original equation's solutions are 0 and 3.

C. A *quadratic equation* has the standard form $ax^2 + bx + c = 0$, where a, b, and c are real numbers and $a \neq 0$.

Examples:

$$x^2 + 6x + 5 = 0$$
$$3x^2 - 2x = 0, \text{ and}$$
$$x^2 + 4 = 0$$

D. Some quadratic equations are easily solved by factoring.

Example (1):

$$x^2 + 6x + 5 = 0$$
$$(x+5)(x+1) = 0$$
$$x + 5 = 0 \text{ or } x + 1 = 0$$
$$x = -5 \text{ or } x = -1$$

Example (2):

$$3x^2 - 3 = 8x$$
$$3x^2 - 8x - 3 = 0$$
$$(3x+1)(x-3) = 0$$
$$3x + 1 = 0 \text{ or } x - 3 = 0$$
$$x = -\frac{1}{3} \text{ or } x = 3$$

E. A quadratic equation has at most two real roots but may have just one or even no root.

> *Examples:*
>
> The equation $x^2 - 6x + 9 = 0$ can be written as $(x - 3)^2 = 0$ or $(x - 3)(x - 3) = 0$. So, its only root is 3.
>
> The equation $x^2 + 4 = 0$ has no real root. Since any real number squared is greater than or equal to zero, $x^2 + 4$ must be greater than zero if x is a real number.

F. An expression of the form $a^2 - b^2$ can be factored as $(a - b)(a + b)$.

> *Example:*
>
> We can solve the quadratic equation $9x^2 - 25 = 0$ like this:
> $$(3x - 5)(3x + 5) = 0$$
> $$3x - 5 = 0 \text{ or } x + 5 = 0$$
> $$x = \frac{5}{3} \text{ or } x = -\frac{5}{3}$$

G. If a quadratic expression isn't easily factored, we can still find its roots with the **quadratic formula:** If $ax^2 + bx + c = 0$ and $a \neq 0$, the roots are
$$x = \frac{-b + \sqrt{b^2 - 4ac}}{2a} \text{ and } x = \frac{-b - \sqrt{b^2 - 4ac}}{2a}$$

These roots are two distinct real numbers unless $b^2 - 4ac \leq 0$.

If $b^2 - 4ac = 0$, the two root expressions both equal $-\frac{b}{2a}$, so the equation has only one root.

If $b^2 - 4ac < 0$, then $\sqrt{b^2 - 4ac}$ is not a real number, so the equation has no real root.

4. Inequalities

A. An *inequality* is a statement with one of these symbols:

$\neq$ is not equal to

$>$ is greater than

$\geq$ is greater than or equal to

$<$ is less than

$\leq$ is less than or equal to

> *Example:*
>
> $5x - 3 < 9$ and $6x \geq y$

B. Solve a linear inequality with one unknown like you solve a linear equation: isolate the unknown on one side. As with an equation, the same number can be added to or subtracted from both sides of the inequality. And you can multiply or divide both sides by a positive number without changing the order of the inequality. However, multiplying or dividing an inequality by a negative number reverses the order of the inequality. Thus, $6 > 2$, but $(-1)(6) < (-1)(2)$.

Example (1):

To solve the inequality $3x - 2 > 5$ for x, isolate x:

$$3x - 2 > 5$$

$$3x > 7 \quad \text{(add 2 to both sides)}$$

$$x > \frac{7}{3} \quad \text{(divide both sides by 3)}$$

Example (2):

To solve the inequality $\dfrac{5x - 1}{-2} < 3$ for x, isolate x:

$$\frac{5x - 1}{-2} < 3$$

$$5x - 1 > -6 \quad \text{(multiply both sides by } -2)$$

$$5x > -5 \quad \text{(add 1 to both sides)}$$

$$x > -1 \quad \text{(divide both sides by 5)}$$

---

5. Functions

A. An algebraic expression in one variable can define a *function* of that variable. A function is written as a letter like f or g along with the variable in the expression. Function notation is a short way to express a value's substitution for a variable.

Examples:

(i) The expression $x^3 - 5x^2 + 2$ can define a function f written as $f(x) = x^3 - 5x^2 + 2$.

(ii) The expression $\dfrac{2z + 7}{\sqrt{z + 1}}$ can define a function g written as $g(z) = \dfrac{2z + 7}{\sqrt{z + 1}}$.

In these examples, the symbols "$f(x)$" and "$g(z)$" don't stand for products. Each is just a symbol for an algebraic expression, and is read "f of x" or "g of z."

The substitution of 1 for x in the first expression can be written as $f(1) = -2$. Then $f(1)$ is called the "value of f at $x = 1$."

Likewise, in the second expression the value of g at $z = 0$ is $g(0) = 7$.

B. Once a function $f(x)$ is defined, think of x as an input and $f(x)$ as the output. In any function, any one input gives at most one output. But different inputs can give the same output.

Example:

If $h(x) = |x + 3|$, then $h(-4) = 1 = h(-2)$.

C. The set of all allowed inputs for a function is the function's *domain*. In the examples in section 3.2.5.A above, the domain of f is the set of all real numbers, and the domain of g is the set of all numbers greater than -1.

Any function's definition can restrict the function's domain. For example, the definition "$a(x) = 9x - 5$ for $0 \le x \le 10$" restricts the domain of a to real numbers greater than or equal to 0 but less than or equal to 10. If the definition has no restrictions, the domain is the set of all values of x that each give a real output when input into the function.

D. The set of a function's outputs is the function's **range**.

> *Examples:*
>
> (i) For the function $h(x) = |x + 3|$ in the example in section 3.2.5.B above, the range is the set of all numbers greater than or equal to 0.
>
> (ii) For the function $a(x) = 9x - 5$ for $0 \le x \le 10$ defined in section 3.2.5.C above, the range is the set of every value y such that $-5 \le y \le 85$.

6. Graphing

A. The figure below shows the rectangular **coordinate plane**. The horizontal line is the **x–axis** and the vertical line is the **y-axis**. These two axes intersect at the **origin**, called *O*. The axes divide the plane into four quadrants, I, II, III, and IV, as shown.

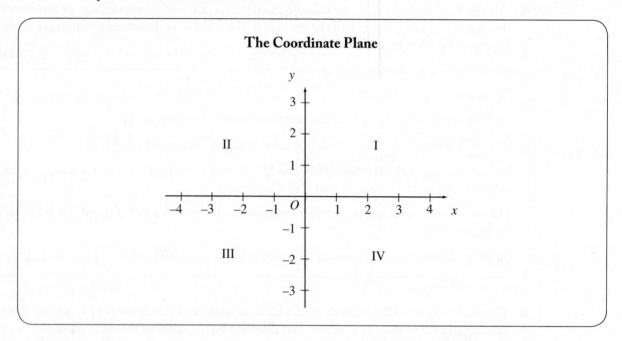

The Coordinate Plane

B. Any ordered pair (x, y) of real numbers defines a point in the coordinate plane. The point's **x-coordinate** is the first number in this pair. It shows how far the point is to the right or left of the y-axis. If the x-coordinate is positive, the point is to the right of the y-axis. If it's negative, the point is to the left of the y-axis. If it's 0, the point is on the axis. The point's **y-coordinate** is the second number in the ordered pair. It shows how far the point is above or below the x-axis. If the y-coordinate is positive, the point is above the x-axis. If it's negative, the point is below the x-axis. If it's 0, the point is on the axis.

Example:

In the graph below, the (x,y) coordinates of point P are $(2,3)$. P is 2 units to the right of the y-axis, so $x = 2$. Since P is 3 units above the x-axis, $y = 3$.

Likewise, the (x,y) coordinates of point Q are $(-4,-3)$. The origin O has coordinates $(0,0)$.

C. The coordinates of each point on a line in the coordinate plane satisfy a linear equation of the form $y = mx + b$ (or the form $x = a$ if the line is vertical).

In the equation $y = mx + b$, the coefficient m is the line's *slope*, and the constant term b is the line's *y-intercept*.

The y-intercept is the y-coordinate of the point where the line intersects the y-axis. Likewise, the *x-intercept* is the x-coordinate of the point where the line intersects the x-axis.

For any two points on the line, the slope is the ratio of the difference in their y-coordinates to the difference in their x-coordinates. To find the slope, subtract one point's y-coordinate from that of the others. Then subtract the former point's x-coordinate from the latter's—not the other way around!

If a line's slope is negative, the line slants down from left to right.

If its slope is positive, the line slants up.

If the slope is 0, the line is horizontal. A horizontal line's equation has the form $y = b$, since $m = 0$.

For a vertical line, the slope is not defined.

Example:

In the graph below, each point on the line satisfies the equation $y = -\frac{1}{2}x + 1$. To check this for the points $(-2,2)$, $(2,0)$, and $(0,1)$, substitute each point's coordinates for x and y in the equation.

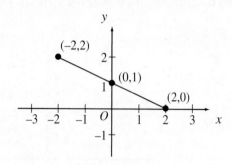

You can use the points $(-2, 2)$ and $(2, 0)$ to find the line's slope:

$$\frac{\text{the difference in the } y\text{-coordinates}}{\text{the difference in the } x\text{-coordinates}} = \frac{0-2}{2-(-2)} = \frac{-2}{4} = -\frac{1}{2}.$$

The y-intercept is 1. That's the value of y when x is set to 0 in $y = -\frac{1}{2}x + 1$.

To find the x-intercept, set y to 0 in the same equation:

$$-\frac{1}{2}x + 1 = 0$$
$$-\frac{1}{2}x = -1$$
$$x = 2.$$

Thus, the x-intercept is 2.

D. You can use the definition of slope to find the equation of a line through two points (x_1, y_1) and (x_2, y_2) with $x_1 \neq x_2$. The slope is $m = \frac{y_2 - y_1}{x_2 - x_1}$. Given the known point (x_1, y_1) and the slope m, any other point (x, y) on the line must satisfy the equation $m = \frac{(y - y_1)}{(x - x_1)}$, or equivalently $(y - y_1) = m(x - x_1)$. Using (x_2, y_2) instead of (x_1, y_1) as the known point gives an equivalent equation.

Example:

The graph below shows points (−2,4) and (3,−3).

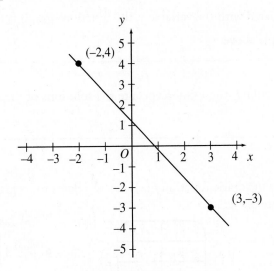

The line's slope is $\dfrac{(-3-4)}{(3-(-2))} = -\dfrac{7}{5}$. To find an equation of this line, let's use the point (3,−3):

$$y - (-3) = \left(-\frac{7}{5}\right)(x - 3)$$

$$y + 3 = \left(-\frac{7}{5}\right)x + \frac{21}{5}$$

$$y = \left(-\frac{7}{5}\right)x + \frac{6}{5}$$

So, the y-intercept is $\dfrac{6}{5}$.

Find the x-intercept like this:

$$0 = -\frac{7}{5}x + \frac{6}{5}$$

$$\frac{7}{5}x = \frac{6}{5}$$

$$x = \frac{6}{7}$$

The graph shows both these intercepts.

E. If two linear equations with unknowns x and y have a unique solution, their graphs are two lines intersecting at the point that is the solution.

If two linear equations are equivalent, they both stand for the same line and have infinitely many solutions.

Two linear equations with no solution stand for parallel lines that don't intersect.

F. Graph any function $f(x)$ in the coordinate plane by equating y with the function's value: $y = f(x)$. For any x in the function's domain, the point $(x, f(x))$ is on the function's graph. For every point in the graph, the y-coordinate is the function's value at the x-coordinate.

Example:

Consider the function $f(x) = -\frac{7}{5}x + \frac{6}{5}$.

If $f(x)$ is equated with the variable y, the function's graph is the graph of the equation $y = -\frac{7}{5}x + \frac{6}{5}$ in the example above.

G. For any function f, the x-intercepts are the solutions of the equation $f(x) = 0$. The y-intercept is the value $f(0)$.

Example:

To see how a quadratic function $f(x) = x^2 - 1$ relates to its graph, let's plot some points $(x, f(x))$ in the coordinate plane:

x	$f(x)$
−2	3
−1	0
0	−1
1	0
2	3

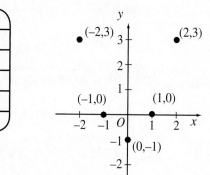

The graph below shows all the points for $-2 \leq x \leq 2$:

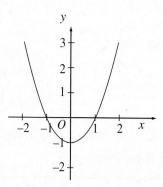

The roots of this equation $f(x) = x^2 - 1 = 0$ are $x = 1$ and $x = -1$. They match the x-intercepts, since x-intercepts are found by setting $y = 0$ and solving for x.

The y-intercept is $f(0) = -1$, because that's the value of y for $x = 0$.

7. Formulas and Measurement Conversion

A. A *formula* is an algebraic equation whose variables have specific meanings. To use a formula, assign quantities to its variables to match these meanings.

> *Example:*
>
> In the physics formula $F = ma$, the variable F stands for force, the variable m stands for mass, and the variable a stands for acceleration. The standard metric unit of force, the newton, is just enough force to accelerate a mass of 1 kilogram by 1 meter/second^2.
>
> So, if we know a rock with a mass of 2 kilograms is accelerating at 5 meters/second^2, we can use the formula $F = ma$ by setting the variable m to 2 kilograms, and the variable a to 5 meters/second^2. Then we find that 10 newtons of force F are pushing the rock.
>
> Note: You don't need to learn physics formulas or terms like this to prepare for the GMAT, but some specific GMAT questions may give you the formulas and terms you need to solve them.

B. Any quantitative relationship between units of measure can be written as a formula.

> *Examples:*
>
> (i) Since 1 kilometer is 1,000 meters, the formula $m = 1000k$ can stand for the relationship between kilometers (k) and meters (m).
>
> (ii) The formula $C = \frac{5}{9}(F - 32)$ can stand for the relationship between temperature measurements in degrees Celsius (C) and degrees Fahrenheit (F).

C. Except for units of time, a GMAT question that requires converting one unit of measure to another will give the relationship between those units.

> *Example:*
>
> A train travels at a constant 25 meters per second. How many kilometers does it travel in 5 minutes? (1 kilometer = 1,000 meters)
>
> *Solution:* In 1 minute the train travels $(25)(60) = 1,500$ meters, so in 5 minutes it travels 7,500 meters. Since 1 kilometer = 1,000 meters, we find 7,500 meters = 7.5 kilometers.

3.3 Rates, Ratios, and Percents

1. Ratio and Proportion

A. The *ratio* of a number x to a nonzero number y may be written as $x : y$, or $\frac{x}{y}$, or x to y. The order of a ratio's terms is important. Unless the absolute values of x and y are equal, $\frac{x}{y} \neq \frac{y}{x}$.

Examples:

The ratio of 2 to 3 may be written as 2:3, or $\frac{2}{3}$, or 2 to 3.

The ratio of the number of months with exactly 30 days to the number of months with exactly 31 days is 4:7, not 7:4.

B. A *proportion* is an equation between two ratios.

Example:

2:3 = 8:12 is a proportion.

C. One way to solve for an unknown in a proportion is to cross multiply, then solve the resulting equation.

Example:

To solve for n in the proportion $\frac{2}{3} = \frac{n}{12}$, cross multiply to get $3n = 24$, then divide both sides by 3 to find $n = 8$.

D. Some word problems can be solved using ratios.

Example:

If 5 shirts cost a total of $44, then what is the total cost of 8 shirts at the same cost per shirt?

Solution: If c is the cost of the 8 shirts, then $\frac{5}{44} = \frac{8}{c}$. Cross multiplying gives $5c = 8 \times 44 = 352$, so $c = \frac{352}{5} = 70.4$. Thus, the 8 shirts cost a total of $70.40.

2. Fractions

A. In a fraction $\frac{n}{d}$, n is the **numerator** and d is the **denominator**. A fraction's denominator can never be 0, because division by 0 is undefined.

B. *Equivalent* fractions stand for the same number. To check whether two fractions are equivalent, divide each fraction's numerator and denominator by the largest factor common to that numerator and that denominator, their **greatest common divisor** (gcd). This is called **reducing each fraction to its lowest terms**. Two fractions are equivalent if and only if reducing each to its lowest terms makes them identical.

Example:

To check whether $\frac{8}{36}$ and $\frac{14}{63}$ are equivalent, first reduce each to its lowest terms. In the first fraction, 4 is the gcd of the numerator 8 and the denominator 36. Dividing both the numerator and the denominator of $\frac{8}{36}$ by 4 gives $\frac{2}{9}$. In the second fraction, 7 is the gcd of the numerator 14 and the denominator 63. Dividing both the numerator and the denominator of $\frac{14}{63}$ by 7 also gives $\frac{2}{9}$. Since reducing $\frac{8}{36}$ and $\frac{14}{63}$ to their lowest terms makes them identical, they're equivalent.

C. To add or subtract two fractions with the same denominator, just add or subtract the numerators, leaving the denominators the same.

Examples:

$\frac{3}{5} + \frac{4}{5} = \frac{3+4}{5} = \frac{7}{5}$ and

$\frac{5}{7} - \frac{2}{7} = \frac{5-2}{7} = \frac{3}{7}$

D. To add or subtract two fractions with different denominators, first express them as fractions with the same denominator.

Example:

To add $\frac{3}{5}$ and $\frac{4}{7}$, multiply the numerator and denominator of $\frac{3}{5}$ by 7 to get $\frac{21}{35}$. Then multiply the numerator and denominator of $\frac{4}{7}$ by 5 to get $\frac{20}{35}$. Since both fractions now have the same denominator 35, you can easily add them: $\frac{3}{5} + \frac{4}{7} = \frac{21}{35} + \frac{20}{35} = \frac{41}{35}$

E. To multiply two fractions, multiply their numerators, and also multiply their denominators.

Example:

$\frac{2}{3} \times \frac{4}{7} = \frac{2 \times 4}{3 \times 7} = \frac{8}{21}$

F. The **reciprocal** of a fraction $\frac{n}{d}$ is $\frac{d}{n}$ if n and d are not 0.

Example:

The reciprocal of $\frac{4}{7}$ is $\frac{7}{4}$

G. To divide by a fraction, multiply by its reciprocal.

> *Example:*
>
> $$\frac{2}{3} \div \frac{4}{7} = \frac{2}{3} \times \frac{7}{4} = \frac{14}{12} = \frac{7}{6}$$

H. A *mixed number* is written as an integer next to a fraction. It equals the integer plus the fraction.

> *Example:*
>
> The mixed number $7\frac{2}{3} = 7 + \frac{2}{3}$

I. To write a mixed number as a fraction, multiply the integer part of the mixed number by the denominator of the fractional part. Add this product to the numerator. Then put this sum over the denominator.

> *Example:*
>
> $$7\frac{2}{3} = \frac{(7 \times 3) + 2}{3} = \frac{23}{3}$$

3. Percents

A. The word *percent* means *per hundred* or *number out of 100*.

> *Example:*
>
> Saying that 37 percent, or 37%, of the houses in a city are painted blue means that 37 houses per 100 in the city are painted blue.

B. A percent may be greater than 100.

> *Example:*
>
> Saying that the number of blue houses in a city is 150% of the number of red houses means the city has 150 blue houses for every 100 red houses. Since 150:100 = 3:2, this is the same as saying the city has 3 blue houses for every 2 red houses.

C. A percent need not be an integer.

> *Example:*
>
> Saying that the number of pink houses in a city is 0.5% of the number of blue houses means the city has 0.5 of a pink house for every 100 blue houses. Since 0.5:100 = 1:200, this is the same as saying the city has 1 pink house for every 200 blue houses.
>
> Likewise, saying that the number of orange houses is 12.5% of the number of blue houses means the ratio of orange houses to blue houses is 12.5:100 = 1:8. Therefore, there is 1 orange house for every 8 blue houses.

4. Converting Decimals, Fractions, and Percents

A. Decimals can be rewritten as fractions or sums of fractions.

> *Examples:*
>
> $$0.321 = \frac{3}{10} + \frac{2}{100} + \frac{1}{1,000} = \frac{321}{1,000}$$
>
> $$0.0321 = \frac{0}{10} + \frac{3}{100} + \frac{2}{1,000} + \frac{1}{10,000} = \frac{321}{10,000}$$
>
> $$1.56 = 1 + \frac{5}{10} + \frac{6}{100} = \frac{156}{100}$$

B. To rewrite a percent as a fraction, write the percent number as the numerator over a denominator of 100. To rewrite a percent as a decimal, move the decimal point in the percent two places to the left and drop the percent sign. To rewrite a decimal as a percent, move the decimal point two places to the right, then add a percent sign.

> *Examples:*
>
> $$37\% = \frac{37}{100} = 0.37$$
>
> $$300\% = \frac{300}{100} = 3$$
>
> $$0.5\% = \frac{0.5}{100} = 0.005$$

C. To find a certain percent of a number, multiply the number by the percent expressed as a fraction or decimal.

Examples:

20% of 90 = $90\left(\dfrac{20}{100}\right) = 90\left(\dfrac{1}{5}\right) = \dfrac{90}{5} = 18$

20% of 90 = $90\,(0.2) = 18$

250% of 80 = $80\left(\dfrac{250}{100}\right) = 80\,(2.5) = 200$

0.5% of 12 = $12\left(\dfrac{0.5}{100}\right) = 12(0.005) = 0.06$

5. Working with Decimals, Fractions, and Percents

A. To find the percent increase or decrease from one quantity to another, first find the amount of increase or decrease. Then divide this amount by the original quantity. Write this quotient as a percent.

Examples:

Suppose a price increases from $24 to $30. To find the percent increase, first find the amount of increase: $30 − $24 = $6. Divide this $6 by the original price of $24 to find the percent increase: $\dfrac{6}{24} = 0.25 = 25\%$.

Now suppose a price falls from $30 to $24. The amount of decrease is $30 − $24 = $6. So, the percent decrease is $\dfrac{6}{30} = 0.20 = 20\%$.

Notice the percent **increase** from 24 to 30 (25%) doesn't equal the percent **decrease** from 30 to 24 (20%).

A percent increase or decrease may be greater than 100%.

Example:

Suppose a house's price in 2018 was 300% of its price in 2003. By what percent did the price increase?

Solution: If n is the price in 2003, the percent increase is $\left|\dfrac{(3n - n)}{n}\right| = \left|\dfrac{2n}{n}\right| = 2$, or 200%.

B. A price discounted by *n* percent is $(100 - n)$ percent of the original price.

> *Example:*
>
> A customer paid $24 for a dress. If the customer got a 25% discount off the original price of the dress, what was the original price before the discount?
>
> *Solution:* The discounted price is $(100 - 25 = 75)$% of the original price. So, if p is the original price, $0.75p = \$24$ is the discounted price. Thus, $p = (\$24 / 0.75) = \$32$, the original price before the discount.

Two discounts can be combined to make a larger discount.

> *Example:*
>
> A price is discounted 20%. Then this reduced price is discounted another 30%. These two discounts together make an overall discount of what percent?
>
> *Solution:* If p is the original price, then $0.8p$ is the price after the first discount. The price after the second discount is $(0.7)(0.8)\, p = 0.56p$. The overall discount is $100\% - 56\% = 44\%$.

C. *Gross profit* equals revenues minus expenses, or selling price minus cost.

> *Example:*
>
> A certain appliance costs a merchant $30. At what price should the merchant sell the appliance to make a gross profit of 50% of the appliance's cost?
>
> *Solution:* The merchant should sell the appliance for a price s such that $s - 30 = (0.5)(30)$. So, $s = \$30 + \$15 = \$45$.

D. *Simple annual interest* on a loan or investment is based only on the original loan or investment amount (the ***principal***). It equals (principal) × (interest rate) × (time).

> *Example:*
>
> If $8,000 is invested at 6% simple annual interest, how much interest is earned after 3 months?
>
> *Solution:* Since the annual interest rate is 6%, the interest for 1 year is $(0.06)(\$8,000) = \$480$.
> A year has 12 months, so the interest earned in 3 months is $\left(\dfrac{3}{12}\right)(\$480) = \$120$.

E. *Compound interest* is based on the principal plus any interest already earned.

Compound interest over *n* periods = (principal) × (1 + interest per period)^n − principal.

Example:

If $10,000 is invested at 10% annual interest, compounded every 6 months, what is the balance after 1 year?

Solution: Since the interest is compounded every 6 months, or twice a year, the interest rate for each 6-month period is 5%, half the 10% annual rate. So, the balance after the first 6 months is 10,000 + (10,000)(0.05) = $10,500.

For the second 6 months, the interest is based on the $10,500 balance after the first 6 months. So, the balance after 1 year is 10,500 + (10,500)(0.05) = $11,025.

The balance after 1 year can also be written as $10,000 \times \left(1 + \dfrac{0.10}{2}\right)^2$ dollars.

F. To solve some word problems with percents and fractions, you can organize the information in a table.

Example:

In a production lot, 40% of the toys are red, and the rest are green. Half of the toys are small, and half are large. If 10% of the toys are red and small, and 40 toys are green and large, how many of the toys are red and large?

Solution: First make a table to organize the information:

	Red	Green	Total
Small	10%		50%
Large			50%
Total	40%	60%	100%

Then fill in the missing percents so that the "Red" and "Green" percents in each row add up to that row's total, and the "Small" and "Large" percents in each column add up to that column's total:

	Red	Green	Total
Small	10%	40%	50%
Large	30%	20%	50%
Total	40%	60%	100%

The number of large green toys, 40, is 20% of the total number of toys (*n*), so 0.20*n* = 40. Thus, the total number of toys *n* = 200. So, 30% of the 200 toys are red and large. Since (0.3)(200) = 60, we find that 60 of the toys are red and large.

---

6. Rate, Work, and Mixture Problems

A. The distance an object travels is its average speed multiplied by the time it takes to travel that distance. That is, ***distance = rate × time.***

> *Example:*
>
> How many kilometers did a car travel in 4 hours at an average speed of 70 kilometers per hour?
>
> *Solution:* Since distance = rate × time, multiply 70 km/hour × 4 hours to find that the car went 280 kilometers.

B. To find an object's average travel speed, divide the total travel distance by the total travel time.

> *Example:*
>
> On a 600-kilometer trip, a car went half the distance at an average speed of 60 kilometers per hour (kph), and the other half at an average speed of 100 kph. The car didn't stop between the two halves of the trip. What was the car's average speed over the whole trip?
>
> *Solution:* First find the total travel time. For the first 300 kilometers, the car went at 60 kph, taking $\frac{300}{60}$ = 5 hours. For the second 300 kilometers, the car went at 100 kph, taking $\frac{300}{100}$ = 3 hours. So, the total travel time was 5 + 3 = 8 hours. The car's average speed was $\frac{600 \text{ kilometers}}{8 \text{ hours}}$ = 75 kph.
>
> Notice the average speed was not $\frac{(60 + 100)}{2}$ = 80 kph.

C. A ***work problem*** usually says how fast certain individuals work and asks you to find how fast they work together, or vice versa.

The basic formula for work problems is $\frac{1}{r} + \frac{1}{s} = \frac{1}{h}$, where r is how long an amount of work takes a certain individual, s is how long that much work takes a different individual, and h is how long that much work takes both individuals working at the same time.

> *Example:*
>
> Suppose one machine takes 4 hours to make 1,000 bolts, and a second machine takes 5 hours to make 1,000 bolts. How many hours do both machines working at the same time take to make 1,000 bolts?
>
> *Solution:*
>
> $$\frac{1}{4} + \frac{1}{5} = \frac{1}{h}$$
>
> $$\frac{5}{20} + \frac{4}{20} = \frac{1}{h}$$
>
> $$\frac{9}{20} = \frac{1}{h}$$
>
> $$9h = 20$$
>
> $$h = \frac{20}{9} = 2\frac{2}{9}$$
>
> Working together, the two machines can make 1,000 bolts in $2\frac{2}{9}$ hours.

Use the same formula to find how long it takes one individual to do an amount of work alone.

Example:

Suppose Art and Rita both working at the same time take 4 hours to do an amount of work, and Art alone takes 6 hours to do that much work. Then how many hours does Rita alone take to do that much work?

Solution:

$$\frac{1}{6} + \frac{1}{R} = \frac{1}{4}$$

$$\frac{1}{R} = \frac{1}{4} - \frac{1}{6} = \frac{1}{12}$$

$$R = 12$$

Rita alone takes 12 hours to do that much work.

D. In *mixture problems*, substances with different properties are mixed, and you must find the mixture's properties.

Example:

If 6 kilograms of nuts that cost $1.20 per kilogram are mixed with 2 kilograms of nuts that cost $1.60 per kilogram, how much does the mixture cost per kilogram?

Solution: The 8 kilograms of nuts cost a total of 6($1.20) + 2($1.60) = $10.40. So, the cost per kilogram is $\frac{\$10.40}{8}$ = $1.30.

Some mixture problems use percents.

Example:

How many liters of a solution that is 15% salt must be added to 5 liters of a solution that is 8% salt to make a solution that is 10% salt?

Solution: Let n be the needed number of liters of the 15% solution. The amount of salt in n liters of 15% solution is $0.15n$. The amount of salt in the 5 liters of 8% solution is $(0.08)(5)$. These amounts add up to the amount of salt in the 10% mixture, which is $0.10(n + 5)$. So,

$$0.15n + 0.08(5) = 0.10(n + 5)$$

$$15n + 40 = 10n + 50$$

$$5n = 10$$

$$n = 2 \text{ liters}$$

So, 2 liters of the 15% salt solution must be added to the 8% solution to make the 10% solution.

3.4 Statistics, Sets, Counting, Probability, Estimation, and Series

1. Statistics

A. A common statistical measure is the ***average*** or ***(arithmetic) mean,*** a type of center for a set of numbers. The average or mean of n numbers is the sum of the n numbers divided by n.

> *Example:*
>
> The average of the 5 numbers 6, 4, 7, 10, and 4 is $\dfrac{(6 + 4 + 7 + 10 + 4)}{5} = \dfrac{31}{5} = 6.2$.

B. The ***median*** is another type of center for a set of numbers. To find the median of n numbers, order the numbers from least to greatest. If n is odd, the median is the middle number in the list. But if n is even, the median is the average of the two middle numbers. The median may be less than, equal to, or greater than the mean of the same numbers.

> *Example:*
>
> To find the median of the 5 numbers 6, 4, 7, 10, and 4, order them from least to greatest: 4, 4, 6, 7, 10. The median is 6, the middle number in this list.
>
> The median of the 6 numbers 4, 6, 6, 8, 9, 12 is $\dfrac{(6 + 8)}{2} = 7$. But the mean of these 6 numbers is $\dfrac{(4 + 6 + 6 + 8 + 9 + 12)}{6} = \dfrac{45}{6} = 7.5$.

Often about half the numbers in a set are less than the median, and about half are greater than the median. But not always.

> *Example:*
>
> For the 15 numbers 3, 5, 7, 7, 7, 7, 7, 7, 8, 9, 9, 9, 9, 10, and 10, the median is 7. Only $\dfrac{2}{15}$ of the numbers are less than the median.

C. The ***mode*** of a list of numbers is the number that occurs most often in the list.

> *Example:*
>
> The mode of the list of numbers 1, 3, 6, 4, 3, 5 is 3, since 3 is the only number that occurs more than once in the list.

A list of numbers may have more than one mode.

Example:

The list 1, 2, 3, 3, 3, 5, 7, 10, 10, 10, 20 has two modes, 3 and 10.

D. There are many ways to measure how spread out or dispersed numerical data are. The simplest measure of dispersion is the *range*, which is the greatest value in the data minus the least value.

Example:

The range of the 5 numbers 11, 10, 5, 13, 21 is 21 − 5 = 16. Notice the range depends on only 2 of the numbers.

E. Another common measure of dispersion is the ***standard deviation.*** Generally, the farther the numbers spread away from the mean, the greater the standard deviation. To find the standard deviation of n numbers:

(1) Find their arithmetic mean,

(2) Find the differences between the mean and each of the n numbers,

(3) Square each difference,

(4) Find the average of the squared differences, and

(5) Take the nonnegative square root of this average.

Examples:

Let's use the table below to find the standard deviation of the 5 numbers 0, 7, 8, 10, 10, which have the mean 7.

x	$x - 7$	$(x - 7)^2$
0	−7	49
7	0	0
8	1	1
10	3	9
10	3	9
	Total	68

The standard deviation is $\sqrt{\dfrac{68}{5}} \approx 3.7$

The standard deviation depends on every number in the set, but more on those farther from the mean. This is why the standard deviation is smaller for a set of data grouped closer around its mean.

As a second example, consider the numbers 6, 6, 6.5, 7.5, 9, which also have the mean 7. These numbers are grouped closer around the mean 7 than the numbers in the first example. That makes the standard deviation in this second example only about 1.1, far below the standard deviation of 3.7 in the first example.

F. How many times a value occurs in a data set is its *frequency* in the set. When different data values have different frequencies, a *frequency distribution* can help show how the values are distributed.

Example:

Consider this data set of 20 numbers:

$$-4 \quad 0 \quad 0 \quad -3 \quad -2 \quad -1 \quad -1 \quad 0 \quad -1 \quad -4$$
$$-1 \quad -5 \quad 0 \quad -2 \quad 0 \quad -5 \quad -2 \quad 0 \quad 0 \quad -1$$

We can show its frequency distribution in a table listing each data value x and x's frequency f:

Data Value x	Frequency f
−5	2
−4	2
−3	1
−2	3
−1	5
0	7
Total	20

This frequency distribution table makes computing statistical measures easier:

Mean: $= \dfrac{(-5)(2) + (-4)(2) + (-3)(1) + (-2)(3) + (-1)(5) + (0)(7)}{20} = -1.6$

Median: −1 (the average of the 10th and 11th numbers)

Mode: 0 (the number that occurs most often)

Range: $0 - (-5) = 5$

Standard deviation: $\sqrt{\dfrac{(-5 + 1.6)^2(2) + (-4 + 1.6)^2(2) + \ldots + (0 + 1.6)^2(7)}{20}} \approx 1.7$

---

2. Sets

A. In math, a *set* is a collection of numbers or other things. The things in the set are its *elements*. A list of a set's elements in a pair of braces stands for the set. The list's order doesn't matter.

Example:

$\{-5, 0, 1\}$ is the same set as $\{0, 1, -5\}$. That is, $\{-5, 0, 1\} = \{0, 1, -5\}$.

B. The number of elements in a finite set S is written as $|S|$.

> *Example:*
>
> $S = \{-5, 0, 1\}$ is a set with $|S| = 3$.

C. If all the elements in a set S are also in a set T, then S is a ***subset*** of T. This is written as $S \subseteq T$ or $T \supseteq S$.

> *Example:*
>
> $\{-5, 0, 1\}$ is a subset of $\{-5, 0, 1, 4, 10\}$. That is, $\{-5, 0, 1\} \subseteq \{-5, 0, 1, 4, 10\}$.

D. The ***union*** of two sets A and B is the set of all elements that are each in A or in B or both. The union is written as $A \cup B$.

> *Example:*
>
> $\{3, 4\} \cup \{4, 5, 6\} = \{3, 4, 5, 6\}$

E. The ***intersection*** of two sets A and B is the set of all elements that are each in **both** A and B. The intersection is written as $A \cap B$.

> *Example:*
>
> $\{3, 4\} \cap \{4, 5, 6\} = \{4\}$

F. Two sets sharing no elements are ***disjoint*** or ***mutually exclusive.***

> *Example:*
>
> $\{-5, 0, 1\}$ and $\{4, 10\}$ are disjoint.

G. A ***Venn diagram*** shows how two or more sets are related. Suppose sets S and T aren't disjoint, and neither is a subset of the other. The Venn diagram below shows their intersection $S \cap T$ as a shaded area.

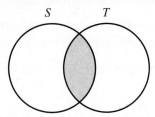

A Venn Diagram of Two Intersecting Sets

S T

A Venn diagram of sets S and T, with their intersection $S \cap T$ shaded.

H. The number of elements in the union of two finite sets S and T is the number of elements in S, plus the number of elements in T, minus the number of elements in the intersection of S and T. That is, $|S \cup T| = |S| + |T| - |S \cap T|$. This is the ***general addition rule for two sets.***

Example:

$$|\{3, 4\} \cup \{4, 5, 6\}| = |\{3, 4\}| + |\{4, 5, 6\}| - |\{3, 4\} \cap \{4, 5, 6\}| =$$

$$|\{3, 4\}| + |\{4, 5, 6\}| - |\{4\}| = 2 + 3 - 1 = 4.$$

If S and T are disjoint, then $|S \cup T| = |S| + |T|$, since $|S \cap T| = 0$.

I. You can often solve word problems involving sets by using Venn diagrams and the general addition rule.

Example:

Each of 25 students is taking history, mathematics, or both. If 20 of them are taking history and 18 of them are taking mathematics, how many of them are taking both history and mathematics?

Solution: Separate the 25 students into three disjoint sets: the students taking history only, those taking mathematics only, and those taking both history and mathematics. This gives us the Venn diagram below, where n is the number of students taking both courses, $20 - n$ is the number taking history only, and $18 - n$ is the number taking mathematics only.

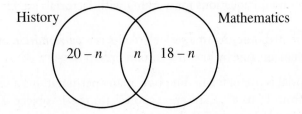

History   Mathematics

$20 - n$ n $18 - n$

Since there are 25 students total, $(20 - n) + n + (18 - n) = 25$, so $n = 13$. So, 13 students are taking both history and mathematics. Notice $20 + 18 - 13 = 25$ is an example of the general addition rule for two sets.

3. Counting Methods

A. To count sets of elements without listing them, you can sometimes use this *multiplication principle*:

If an object will be chosen from a set of *m* objects, and another object will be chosen from a different set of *n* objects, then *mn* different choices are possible.

Example:

Suppose a meal at a restaurant must include exactly 1 entree and 1 dessert. The entree can be any 1 of 5 options, and the dessert can be any 1 of 3 options. Then $5 \times 3 = 15$ different meals are available.

B. Here is a more general version of the multiplication principle: the number of possible choices of 1 object apiece out of any number of sets is the product of the numbers of objects in those sets. For example, when choosing 1 object apiece out of 3 sets with *x*, *y*, and *z* elements, respectively, *xyz* different choices are possible. The general multiplication principle also means that when choosing 1 object apiece out of *n* different sets of exactly *m* objects apiece, m^n different choices are possible.

Example:

Each time a coin is flipped, the 2 possible results are heads and tails. In a set of 8 consecutive coin flips, think of each flip as a set of those 2 possible results. The 8 flips give us 8 of these 2-element sets. So, the set of 8 flips has a total of 2^8 possible results.

C. A concept often used with the multiplication principle is the *factorial.* For any integer $n > 1$, *n* factorial is written as *n*! and is the product of all the integers from 1 through *n*. Also, by definition, $0! = 1! = 1$.

Examples:

$2! = 2 \times 1 = 2$

$3! = 3 \times 2 \times 1 = 6$

$4! = 4 \times 3 \times 2 \times 1 = 24$, etc.

Two other useful equations for working with factorials are $n! = (n-1)!(n)$ and $(n + 1)! = (n!)(n + 1)$.

D. Any sequential ordering of a set's elements is a *permutation* of the set. A permutation is a way to choose elements one by one in a certain order.

The factorial is useful for finding how many permutations a set has. If a set of *n* objects is being ordered from 1st to n^{th}, there are *n* choices for the 1st object, $n - 1$ choices left for the 2nd object, $n - 2$ choices left for the 3rd object, and so on, until only 1 choice is left for the nth object. So, by the multiplication principle, a set of *n* objects has $n(n-1)(n-2) \ldots (3)(2)(1) = n!$ permutations.

Example:

The set of letters A, B, and C has $3! = 6$ permutations: ABC, ACB, BAC, BCA, CAB, and CBA.

E. When $0 \le k \le n$, each possible choice of k objects out of n objects is a ***combination*** of n objects taken k at a time. The number of these combinations is written as $\binom{n}{k}$. This is also the number of k-element subsets of a set with n elements, since the combinations simply are these subsets. It can be calculated as $\binom{n}{k} = \dfrac{n!}{k!(n-k)!}$. Note that $\binom{n}{k} = \binom{n}{n-k}$.

Example:

The 2-element subsets of $S = \{A, B, C, D, E\}$ are the combinations of the 5 letters in S taken 2 at a time. There are $\binom{5}{2} = \dfrac{5!}{2!3!} = \dfrac{120}{(2)(6)} = 10$ of these subsets: $\{A, B\}, \{A, C\}, \{A, D\}, \{A, E\}, \{B, C\}$, $\{B, D\}, \{B, E\}, \{C, D\}, \{C, E\}$, and $\{D, E\}$.

For each of its 2–element subsets, a 5-element set also has exactly one 3-element subset containing the elements not in that 2-element subset. For example, in S the 3-element subset $\{C, D, E\}$ contains the elements not in the 2-element subset $\{A, B\}$, the 3-element subset $\{B, D, E\}$ contains the elements not in the 2-element subset $\{A, C\}$, and so on. This shows a 5-element set like S has exactly as many 2-element subsets as 3-element subsets, so $\binom{5}{2} = 10 = \binom{5}{3}$.

---

4. Probability

A. Sets and counting methods are also important to ***discrete probability***. Discrete probability involves ***experiments*** with finitely many possible ***outcomes***. An ***event*** is a set of an experiment's possible outcomes.

Example:

Rolling a 6-sided die with faces numbered 1 to 6 is an experiment with 6 possible outcomes. Let's call these outcomes 1, 2, 3, 4, 5, and 6, each number being the one facing up after the roll. One event in this experiment is that the outcome is 4. This event is written as $\{4\}$.

Another event in the experiment is that the outcome is an odd number. This event has the three outcomes 1, 3, and 5. It is written as $\{1, 3, 5\}$.

B. The probability of an event E is written as $P(E)$ and is a number between 0 and 1, inclusive. If E is an empty set of no possible outcomes, then E is ***impossible***, and $P(E) = 0$. If E is the set of all possible outcomes of the experiment, then E is ***certain***, and $P(E) = 1$. Otherwise, E is possible but uncertain, and $0 < P(E) < 1$. If F is a subset of E, then $P(F) \le P(E)$.

C. If the probabilities of two or more outcomes of an experiment are equal, those outcomes are ***equally likely***. For an experiment whose outcomes are all equally likely, the probability of an event E is

$$P(E) = \frac{\text{the number of outcomes in } E}{\text{the total number of possible outcomes}}.$$

Example:

In the earlier example of a 6-sided die rolled once, suppose the die is fair so that all 6 outcomes are equally likely. Then each outcome's probability is $\dfrac{1}{6}$. The probability that the outcome is an odd number is $P(\{1, 3, 5\}) = \dfrac{|\{1, 3, 5\}|}{6} = \dfrac{3}{6} = \dfrac{1}{2}$.

D. Given two events E and F in an experiment, these further events are defined:

(i) "not E" is the set of outcomes not in E;

(ii) "E or F" is the set of outcomes in E or F or both, that is, $E \cup F$;

(iii) "E and F" is the set of outcomes in both E and F, that is, $E \cup F$.

The probability that E doesn't occur is $P(\text{not } E) = 1 - P(E)$.

The probability that "E or F" occurs is $P(E \text{ or } F) = P(E) + P(F) - P(E \text{ and } F)$. This is based on the general addition rule for two sets, given above in section 3.4.2.H.

Example:

In the example above of a 6-sided die rolled once, let E be the event $\{1, 3, 5\}$ that the outcome is an odd number. Let F be the event $\{2, 3, 5\}$ that the outcome is a prime number. Then

$P(E \text{ and } F) = P(E \cap F) = P(\{3, 5\}) = \dfrac{|\{3, 5\}|}{6} = \dfrac{2}{6} = \dfrac{1}{3}$. So $P(E \text{ or } F) = P(E) + P(F) -$

$P(E \text{ and } F) = \dfrac{3}{6} + \dfrac{3}{6} - \dfrac{2}{6} = \dfrac{4}{6} = \dfrac{2}{3}$.

The event "E or F" is $E \cup F = \{1, 2, 3, 5\}$, so $P(E \text{ or } F) = \dfrac{|\{1, 2, 3, 5\}|}{6} = \dfrac{4}{6} = \dfrac{2}{3}$.

Events E and F are **mutually exclusive** if no outcomes are in $E \cap F$. Then the event "E and F" is impossible: $P(E \text{ and } F) = 0$. The special addition rule for the probability of two mutually exclusive events is $P(E \text{ or } F) = P(E) + P(F)$.

E. Two events A and B are **independent** if neither changes the other's probability. The multiplication rule for independent events E and F is $P(E \text{ and } F) = P(E)P(F)$.

Example:

In the example above of the 6-sided die rolled once, let A be the event $\{2, 4, 6\}$ and B be the event $\{5, 6\}$. Then A's probability is $P(A) = \dfrac{|A|}{6} = \dfrac{3}{6} = \dfrac{1}{2}$. The probability of A occurring **if B occurs** is $\dfrac{|A \cap B|}{|B|} = \dfrac{|\{6\}|}{|\{5, 6\}|} = \dfrac{1}{2}$, the same as $P(A)$.

Likewise, B's probability is $P(B) = \dfrac{|B|}{6} = \dfrac{2}{6} = \dfrac{1}{3}$. The probability of B occurring **if A occurs** is $\dfrac{|B \cap A|}{|A|} = \dfrac{\{6\}}{|\{2, 4, 6\}|} = \dfrac{1}{3}$, the same as $P(B)$.

So, neither event changes the other's probability. Thus, A and B are independent. Therefore, by the multiplication rule for independent events, $P(A \text{ and } B) = P(A)P(B) = \left(\dfrac{1}{2}\right)\left(\dfrac{1}{3}\right) = \dfrac{1}{6}$.

Notice the event "A and B" is $A \cap B = \{6\}$, so $P(A \text{ and } B) = P(\{6\}) = \dfrac{1}{6}$.

The general addition rule and the multiplication rule discussed above provide that if E and F are independent, $P(E \text{ or } F) = P(E) + P(F) - P(E)P(F)$.

F. An event A is ***dependent*** on an event B if B changes the probability of A.

The probability of A occurring if B occurs is written as $P(A|B)$. So, the statement that A is dependent on B can be written as $P(A|B) \neq P(A)$.

A general multiplication rule for any dependent or independent events A and B is $P(A \text{ and } B) = P(A|B)P(B)$.

Example:

In the example of the 6-sided die rolled once, let A be the event $\{4, 6\}$ and B be the event $\{4, 5, 6\}$. Then the probability of A is $P(A) = \dfrac{|A|}{6} = \dfrac{2}{6} = \dfrac{1}{3}$. But the probability that A occurs **if B occurs** is

$P(A|B) = \dfrac{|A \cap B|}{|B|} = \dfrac{|\{4, 6\}|}{|\{4, 5, 6\}|} = \dfrac{2}{3}$. Thus, $P(A|B) \neq P(A)$, so A is dependent on B.

Likewise, the probability that B occurs is $P(B) = \dfrac{|B|}{6} = \dfrac{3}{6} = \dfrac{1}{2}$. But the probability that B occurs **if**

A occurs is $P(B|A) = \dfrac{|B \cap A|}{|A|} = \dfrac{|\{4, 6\}|}{|\{4, 6\}|} = 1$. Thus, $P(B|A) \neq P(B)$, so B is dependent on A.

In this example, by the general multiplication rule for events,

$P(A \text{ and } B) = P(A|B)P(B) = \left(\dfrac{2}{3}\right)\left(\dfrac{1}{2}\right) = \dfrac{1}{3}$. Likewise, $P(A \text{ and } B) = P(B|A)P(A) = (1)\left(\dfrac{1}{3}\right) = \dfrac{1}{3}$.

Notice the event "A and B" is $A \cap B = \{4, 6\} = A$, so $P(A \text{ and } B) = P(\{4, 6\}) = \dfrac{1}{3} = P(A)$.

G. The rules above can be combined for more complex probability calculations.

Example:

In an experiment with events A, B, and C, suppose $P(A) = 0.23$, $P(B) = 0.40$, and $P(C) = 0.85$. Also suppose events A and B are mutually exclusive, and events B and C are independent. Since A and B are mutually exclusive, $P(A \text{ or } B) = P(A) + P(B) = 0.23 + 0.40 = 0.63$.

Since B and C are independent, $P(B \text{ or } C) = P(B) + P(C) - P(B)P(C) = 0.40 + 0.85 - (0.40)(0.85) = 0.91$.

$P(A \text{ or } C)$ and $P(A \text{ and } C)$ can't be found from the information given. But we can find that $P(A) + P(C) = 1.08 > 1$. So $P(A) + P(C)$ can't equal $P(A \text{ or } C)$, which like any probability must be less than or equal to 1. This means that A and C can't be mutually exclusive, and that $P(A \text{ and } C) \geq 0.08$.

Since $A \cap B$ is a subset of A, we can also find that $P(A \text{ and } C) \leq P(A) = 0.23$.

And C is a subset of $A \cup C$, so $P(A \text{ or } C) \geq P(C) = 0.85$.

Thus, we've found that $0.85 \leq P(A \text{ or } C) \leq 1$ and that $0.08 \leq P(A \text{ and } C) \leq 0.23$.

---

5. Estimation

A. Calculating exact answers to complex math questions is often too hard or too slow. Estimating the answers by simplifying the questions may be easier and faster.

One way to estimate is to **round** the numbers in the original question: replace each number with a nearby number that has fewer digits. Often a number is rounded to a nearby multiple of some power of 10.

For any integer n and real number m, you can **round m down** to a multiple of 10^n by deleting all of m's digits to the right of the digit that stands for multiples of 10^n.

To **round m up** to a multiple of 10^n, first add 10^n to m, then round the result down.

To **round m to the nearest** 10^n, first find the digit in m that stands for a multiple of 10^{n-1}. If this digit is 5 or higher, round m up to a multiple of 10^n. Otherwise, round m down to a multiple of 10^n.

Examples:

(i) To round 7651.4 to the nearest hundred (multiple of 10^2), first notice the digit standing for tens (multiples of 10^1) is 5.

Since this digit is 5 or higher, round up:

First add 100 to the original number: 7651.4 + 100 = 7751.4.

Then drop all the digits to the right of the one standing for multiples of 100 to get 7700.

Notice that 7700 is closer to 7651.4 than 7600 is, so 7700 is the nearest 100.

(ii) To round 0.43248 to the nearest thousandth (multiple of 10^{-3}), first notice the digit standing for ten-thousandths (multiples of 10^{-4}) is 4. Since $4 < 5$, round down: just drop all the digits to the right of the digit standing for thousandths to get 0.432.

B. Rounding can simplify complex arithmetical calculations and give rough answers. If you keep more digits of the original numbers, the answers are usually more exact, but the calculations take longer.

Example:

You can roughly estimate the value of $\dfrac{(298.534 + 58.296)}{1.4822 + 0.937 + 0.014679}$ by rounding the numbers in the dividend to the nearest 10 and the numbers in the divisor to the nearest 0.1:

$$\frac{(298.534 + 58.296)}{1.4822 + 0.937 + 0.014679} \approx \frac{300 + 60}{1.5 + 0.9 + 0} = \frac{360}{2.4} = 150$$

C. Sometimes it is easier to estimate by rounding to a multiple of a number other than 10, like the nearest square or cube of an integer.

Examples:

(i) You can roughly estimate the value of $\dfrac{2447.16}{11.9}$ by noting first that both the dividend and the divisor are near multiples of 12: 2448 and 12. So $\dfrac{2447.16}{11.9} \approx \dfrac{2448}{12} = 204$.

(ii) You can roughly estimate the value of $\sqrt{\dfrac{8.96}{24.82 \times 4.057}}$ by noting first that each decimal number in the expression is near the square of an integer: $8.96 \approx 9 = 3^2$, $24.82 \approx 25 = 5^2$, and $4.057 \approx 4 = 2^2$. So $\sqrt{\dfrac{8.96}{24.82 \times 4.057}} \approx \sqrt{\dfrac{3^2}{5^2 \times 2^2}} = \sqrt{\dfrac{3^2}{10^2}} = \dfrac{3}{10}$.

D. Sometimes finding a *range* of possible values for an expression is more useful than finding a single estimated value. The range's *upper bound* is the smallest number found to be greater than (or greater than or equal to) the expression's value. The range's *lower bound* is the largest number found to be less than (or less than or equal to) the expression's value.

Example:

In the equation $x = \dfrac{2.32^2 - 2.536}{2.68^2 + 2.79}$, each decimal is greater than 2 and less than 3. So, $\dfrac{2^2 - 3}{3^2 + 3} < x < \dfrac{3^2 - 2}{2^2 + 2}$. Simplifying these fractions, we find that x is in the range $\dfrac{1}{12} < x < \dfrac{7}{6}$. The range's lower bound is $\dfrac{1}{12}$, and the upper bound is $\dfrac{7}{6}$.

6. Sequences and Series

A. A *sequence* is an algebraic function whose domain includes only positive integers. A function $a(n)$ that is a sequence can be written as a_n. The domain of an *infinite sequence* is the set of all positive integers. For any positive integer n, the domain of a *finite sequence of length* n is the set of the first n positive integers.

Example:

(i) The function $a(n) = n^2 + \left(\dfrac{n}{5}\right)$ is an infinite sequence a_n whose domain is the set of all positive integers $n = 1, 2, 3, \ldots$. Its value at $n = 3$ is $a_3 = 3^2 + \dfrac{3}{5} = 9.6$.

(ii) The same function $a(n) = n^2 + \left(\dfrac{n}{5}\right)$ restricted to the domain $\{1, 2, 3\}$ is a finite sequence of length 3 whose range is $\{1.2, 4.4, 9.6\}$.

(iii) An infinite sequence like $b_n = (-1)^n(n!)$ can be written out by listing its values in the order $b_1, b_2, b_3, \ldots, b_n, \ldots$: that is, $-1, 2, -6, \ldots, (-1)^n(n!), \ldots$

The value $(-1)^n(n!)$ is the nth term of the sequence.

B. A *series* is the sum of a sequence's terms.

For an infinite sequence $a(n)$, the **infinite series** $\sum_{n=1}^{\infty} a(n)$ is the sum of the sequence's infinitely many terms, $a_1 + a_2 + a_3 + \ldots$

The sum of the first k terms of sequence a_n is called a **partial sum**. It is written as $\sum_{i=1}^{k} a_i$, or $a_1 + \ldots + a_k$.

Example:

The infinite series based on the function $a(n) = n^2 + \left(\frac{n}{5}\right)$ is $\sum_{i=1}^{\infty} n^2 + \left(\frac{n}{5}\right)$. It's the sum of the infinitely many terms $\left(1^2 + \frac{1}{5}\right) + \left(2^2 + \frac{2}{5}\right) + \left(3^2 + \frac{3}{5}\right) + \ldots$

The partial sum of the first three terms of the same function $a(n) = n^2 + \left(\frac{n}{5}\right)$ is
$$\sum_{i=1}^{3} a_i = \left(1^2 + \frac{1}{5}\right) + \left(2^2 + \frac{2}{5}\right) + \left(3^2 + \frac{3}{5}\right) = 1.2 + 4.4 + 9.6 = 15.2.$$

3.5   Reference Sheets

Arithmetic and Decimals

ABSOLUTE VALUE:

$|x|$ is x if $x \geq 0$ and $-x$ if $x < 0$.

For any x and y, $|x + y| \leq |x| + |y|$.

$\sqrt{x^2} = |x|$.

EVEN AND ODD NUMBERS:

Even × Even = Even	Even × Odd = Even
Odd × Odd = Odd	Even + Even = Even
Even + Odd = Odd	Odd + Odd = Even

ADDITION AND SUBTRACTION:

$x + 0 = x = x - 0$

$x - x = 0$

$x + y = y + x$

$x - y = -(y - x) = -y + x$

$(x + y) + z = x + (y + z)$

If x and y are both positive, then $x + y$ is also positive.

If x and y are both negative, then $x + y$ is negative.

DECIMALS:

Add or subtract decimals by lining up their decimal points:

17.6512	653.2700
+ 653.2700	−17.6512
670.9212	635.6188

To multiply decimal A by decimal B:

First, ignore the decimal points, and multiply A and B as if they were integers.

Next, if decimal A has n digits to the right of its decimal point, and decimal B has m digits to the right of its decimal point, place the decimal point in $A \times B$ so it has $m + n$ digits to its right.

To divide decimal A by decimal B, first move the decimal points of A and B equally many digits to the right until B is an integer, then divide as you would integers.

QUOTIENTS AND REMAINDERS:

The quotient q and the remainder r of dividing positive integer x by positive integer y are unique positive integers such that

$y = xq + r$ and $0 \leq r < x$.

The remainder r is 0 if and only if y is divisible by x. Then x is a factor of y.

MULTIPLICATION AND DIVISION:

$x \times 1 = x = \dfrac{x}{1}$

$x \times 0 = 0$

If $x \neq 0$, then $\dfrac{x}{x} = 1$.

$\dfrac{x}{0}$ is undefined.

$xy = yx$

If $x \neq 0$ and $y \neq 0$, then $\dfrac{x}{y} = \dfrac{1}{\left(\frac{y}{x}\right)}$.

$(xy)z = x(yz)$

$xy + xz = x(y + z)$

If $y \neq 0$, then $\left(\dfrac{x}{y}\right) + \left(\dfrac{z}{y}\right) = \dfrac{(x + z)}{y}$

If x and y are both positive, then xy is also positive.

If x and y are both negative, then xy is positive.

If x is positive and y is negative, then xy is negative.

If $xy = 0$, then $x = 0$ or $y = 0$, or both.

SCIENTIFIC NOTATION:

To convert a number in scientific notation $A \times 10^n$ into regular decimal notation, move A's decimal point n places to the right if n is positive, or $|n|$ places to the left if n is negative.

To convert a decimal to scientific notation, move the decimal point n spaces so that exactly one nonzero digit is to its left. Multiply the result by 10^n if you moved the decimal point to the left or by 10^{-n} if you moved it to the right.

Exponents

SQUARES, CUBES, AND SQUARE ROOTS:

Every positive number has two real square roots, one positive and the other negative. The table below shows the positive square roots rounded to the nearest hundredth.

n	n^2	n^3	$\sqrt{n}$
1	1	1	1
2	4	8	1.41
3	9	27	1.73
4	16	64	2
5	25	125	2.24
6	36	216	2.45
7	49	343	2.65
8	64	512	2.83
9	81	729	3
10	100	1,000	3.16

EXPONENTIATION:

Formula	Example
$x^1 = x$	$2^1 = 2$
$x^0 = 1$	$2^0 = 1$
If $x \neq 0$, then $x^{-1} = \frac{1}{x}$.	$2^{-1} = \frac{1}{2}$
If $x > 1$ and $y > 1$, then $x^y > x$.	$2^3 = 8 > 2$
If $0 < x < 1$ and $y > 1$, then $x^y < x$.	$0.2^3 = 0.008 < 0.2$
$(x^y)^z = x^{yz} = (x^z)^y$	$(2^3)^4 = 2^{12} = (2^4)^3$
$x^{y+z} = x^y x^z$	$2^7 = 2^3 2^4$
If $x \neq 0$, then $x^{y-z} = \frac{x^y}{x^z}$.	$2^{5-3} = \frac{2^5}{2^3}$
$(xz)^y = x^y z^y$	$6^4 = 2^4 3^4$
If $z \neq 0$, then $\left(\frac{x}{z}\right)^y = \frac{x^y}{z^y}$	$\left(\frac{3}{4}\right)^2 = \frac{3^2}{4^2} = \frac{9}{16}$
If $z \neq 0$, then $x^{\frac{y}{z}} = (x^y)^{\frac{1}{z}} = (x^{\frac{1}{z}})^y$.	$4^{\frac{2}{3}} = (4^2)^{\frac{1}{3}} = (4^{\frac{1}{3}})^2$

Algebraic Expressions and Linear Equations

TRANSLATING WORDS INTO MATH OPERATIONS:

$x + y$	$x - y$	xy	$\dfrac{x}{y}$	x^y
x added to y *x increased by y* *x more than y* *x plus y* *the sum of x and y* *the total of x and y*	*x decreased by y* *difference of x and y* *y fewer than x* *y less than x* *x minus y* *x reduced by y* *y subtracted from x*	*x multiplied by y* *the product of x and y* *x times y*	*x divided by y* *x over y* *the quotient of x and y* *the ratio of x to y*	*x to the power of y* *x to the y^(th) power*
		If $y = 2$: *double x* *twice x*	If $y = 2$: *half of x* *x halved*	If $y = 2$: *x squared*
		If $y = 3$: *triple x*		If $y = 3$: *x cubed*

MANIPULATING ALGEBRAIC EXPRESSIONS:

Technique	Example
Factor to combine like terms	$3xy - 9y = 3y(x - 3)$
Divide out common factors	$\dfrac{(3xy - 9y)}{(x - 3)} = \dfrac{3y(x - 3)}{(x - 3)} = 3y(1) = 3y$
Multiply two expressions by multiplying each term of one expression by each term of the other	$\begin{aligned}(3x - 4)(9y + x) &= 3x(9y + x) - 4(9y + x) \\ &= 3x(9y) + 3x(x) + -4(9y) + -4(x) \\ &= 27xy + 3x^2 - 36y - 4x\end{aligned}$
Substitute constants for variables	If $x = 3$ and $y = -2$, then $3xy - x^2 + y$ can be evaluated as $3(3)(-2) - (3)^2 + (-2) = -18 - 9 - 2 = -29$.

SOLVING LINEAR EQUATIONS:

Technique	Example
Isolate a variable on one side of an equation by doing the same operations on both sides of the equation.	Solve the equation $\frac{(5x - 6)}{3} = 4$ like this: (1) Multiply both sides by 3 to get $5x - 6 = 12$. (2) Add 6 to both sides to get $5x = 18$. (3) Divide both sides by 5 to get $x = \frac{18}{5}$.
To solve two equations with two variables x and y: (1) Express x in terms of y using one of the equations. (2) Substitute that expression for x to make the second equation have only the variable y. (3) Solve the second equation for y. (4) Substitute the solution for y into the first equation to solve for x.	Solve the equations A: $x - y = 2$ and B: $3x + 2y = 11$: (1) From A, $x = 2 + y$. (2) In B, substitute $2 + y$ for x to get $3(2 + y) + 2y = 11$. (3) Solve B for y: $6 + 3y + 2y = 11$ $\qquad 6 + 5y = 11$ $\qquad\quad 5y = 5$ $\qquad\quad\ y = 1$. (4) Since $y = 1$, from A we find $x = 2 + 1 = 3$.
Alternative technique: (1) Multiply both sides of one equation or both equations so that the coefficients on y have the same absolute value in both equations. (2) Add or subtract the two equations to remove y and solve for x. (3) Substitute the solution for x into the first equation to find the value of y.	Solve the equations A: $x - y = 2$ and B: $3x + 2y = 11$: (1) Multiply both sides of A by 2 to get $2x - 2y = 4$. (2) Add the equation in (1) to equation B: $\quad 2x - 2y + 3x + 2y = 4 + 11$ $\qquad\qquad 5x = 15$ $\qquad\qquad\ x = 3$. (3) Since $x = 3$, from A we find $3 - y = 2$, so $y = 1$.

Factoring, Quadratic Equations, and Inequalities

SOLVING EQUATIONS BY FACTORING:

Techniques	Example
(1) Start with a polynomial equation. (2) Add or subtract expressions until 0 is on one side of the equation. (3) Write the nonzero side as a product of factors. (4) Set each factor to 0 to find a simple equation giving a solution to the original equation.	$x^3 - 2x^2 + x = -5(x - 1)^2$ $x^3 - 2x^2 + x + 5(x - 1)^2 = 0$ (i) $x(x^2 - 2x + 1) + 5(x - 1)^2 = 0$ (ii) $x(x - 1)^2 + 5(x - 1)^2 = 0$ (iii) $(x + 5)(x - 1)^2 = 0$ $x + 5 = 0$ or $x - 1 = 0$. So, $x = -5$ or $x = 1$.

FORMULAS FOR FACTORING:

$a^2 - b^2 = (a - b)(a + b)$

$a^2 + 2ab + b^2 = (a + b)(a + b)$

$a^2 - 2ab + b^2 = (a - b)(a - b)$

THE QUADRATIC FORMULA:

For any quadratic equation $ax^2 + bx + c = 0$ with $a \neq 0$, the roots are

$$x = \frac{-b + \sqrt{b^2 - 4ac}}{2a} \text{ and } x = \frac{-b - \sqrt{b^2 - 4ac}}{2a}$$

These roots are two distinct real numbers unless $b^2 - 4ac \leq 0$.

If $b^2 - 4ac = 0$, the equation has only one root: $\frac{-b}{2a}$.

If $b^2 - 4ac < 0$, the equation has no real roots.

SOLVING INEQUALITIES:

Explanation	Example
As in solving an equation, the same number can be added to or subtracted from both sides of the inequality, or both sides can be multiplied or divided by a positive number, without changing the order of the inequality. But multiplying or dividing an inequality by a negative number reverses the order of the inequality. Thus, $6 > 2$, but $(-1)(6) < (-1)(2)$.	To solve the inequality $\frac{(5x - 1)}{-2} < 3$ for x, isolate x: (1) $5x - 1 > -6$ (multiplying both sides by -2, reversing the order of the inequality) (2) $5x > -5$ (add 1 to both sides) (3) $x > -1$ (divide both sides by 5)

LINES IN THE COORDINATE PLANE:

An equation $y = mx + b$ defines a line with slope m whose y–intercept is b.

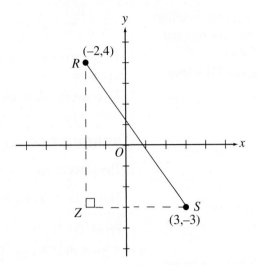

For a line through two points (x_1, y_1) and (x_2, y_2) with $x_1 \neq x_2$, the slope is $m = \frac{(y_2 - y_1)}{(x_2 - x_1)}$. Given the known point (x_1, y_1) and the slope m, any other point (x, y) on the line satisfies the equation $m = \frac{(y - y_1)}{(x - x_1)}$.

Above, the line's slope is $\frac{(-3 - 4)}{(3 - (-2))} = \frac{7}{5}$. To find an equation of the line, we can use the point $(3, -3)$:

$$y - (-3) = \left(-\frac{7}{5}\right)(x - 3)$$

$$y + 3 = \left(-\frac{7}{5}\right)x + \frac{21}{5}$$

$$y = \left(-\frac{7}{5}\right)x + \frac{6}{5}$$

So, the y–intercept is $\frac{6}{5}$.

Find the x–intercept like this:

$$0 = \left(-\frac{7}{5}\right)x + \frac{6}{5}$$

$$\left(\frac{7}{5}\right)x = \frac{6}{5}$$

$$x = \frac{6}{7}$$

The graph shows both these intercepts.

Rates, Ratios, and Percents

FRACTIONS:

Equivalent or Equal Fractions:
Two fractions stand for the same number if dividing each fraction's numerator and denominator by their greatest common divisor makes the fractions identical.

Adding, Subtracting, Multiplying, and Dividing Fractions:

$$\frac{a}{b} + \frac{c}{d} = \frac{ad}{bd} + \frac{bc}{bd}; \frac{a}{b} - \frac{c}{d} = \frac{ad}{bd} - \frac{bc}{bd}$$

$$\frac{a}{b} \times \frac{c}{d} = \frac{ac}{bd}; \frac{a}{b} \div \frac{c}{d} = \frac{ad}{bc}$$

MIXED NUMBERS:

A mixed number of the form $a\frac{b}{c}$ equals the fraction $\frac{ac + b}{c}$.

RATE:

distance = rate × time

PROFIT:

Gross profit = Revenues − Expenses, or

Gross profit = Selling price − Cost.

INTEREST:

Simple annual interest =

(principal) × (interest rate) × (time)

Compound interest over n periods =

(principal) × (1 + interest per period)^n − principal

PERCENTS:

$x\% = \frac{x}{100}$.

$x\%$ of y equals $\frac{xy}{100}$.

To convert a percent to a decimal, drop the percent sign, then move the decimal point two digits left.

To convert a decimal to a percent, add a percent sign, then move the decimal point two digits right.

PERCENT INCREASE OR DECREASE:

The percent increase from x to y is $100\left(\frac{y - x}{x}\right)\%$.

The percent decrease from x to y is $100\left(\frac{x - y}{x}\right)\%$.

DISCOUNTS:

A price discounted by n percent becomes $(100 - n)$ percent of the original price.

A price discounted by n percent and then by m percent becomes $(100 - n)(100 - m)$ percent of the original price.

WORK:

$\frac{1}{r} + \frac{1}{s} = \frac{1}{h}$, where r is how long one individual takes to do an amount of work, s is how long a second individual takes to do that much work, and h is how long they take to do that much work when both are working at the same time.

MIXTURES:

	Number of units of a substance or mixture	Amount of an ingredient per unit of the substance or mixture	Total amount of that ingredient in the substance or mixture
Substance A	X	M	X × M
Substance B	Y	N	Y × N
Mixture of A and B	X + Y	$\frac{(X \times M) + (Y \times N)}{X + Y}$	(X × M) + (Y × N)

Statistics, Sets, and Counting Methods

STATISTICS:

Concept	Definition for a set of n numbers ordered from least to greatest	Example with data set $\{4, 4, 5, 7, 10\}$
Mean	The sum of the n numbers, divided by n	$\dfrac{(4 + 4 + 5 + 7 + 10)}{5} = \dfrac{30}{5} = 6$
Median	The middle number if n is odd; The mean of the two middle numbers if n is even.	5 is the middle number in $\{4, 4, 5, 7, 10\}$.
Mode	The number that appears most often in the set	4 is the only number that appears more than once in $\{4, 4, 5, 7, 10\}$.
Range	The largest number in the set minus the smallest	$10 - 4 = 6$
Standard Deviation	Calculate like this: (1) Find the arithmetic mean, (2) Find the differences between each of the n numbers and the mean, (3) Square each of the differences, (4) Find the average of the squared differences, and (5) Take the nonnegative square root of this average.	(1) The mean is 6. (2) $-2, -2, -1, 1, 4$ (3) $4, 4, 1, 1, 16$ (4) $\dfrac{26}{5} = 5.2$ (5) $\sqrt{5.2}$

SETS:

Concept	Notation for finite sets S and T	Example
Number of elements	$\lvert S \rvert$	$S = \{-5, 0, 1\}$ is a set with $\lvert S \rvert = 3$.
Subset	$S \subseteq T$ (S is a subset of T); $S \supseteq T$ (T is a subset of S)	$\{-5, 0, 1\}$ is a subset of $\{-5, 0, 1, 4, 10\}$.
Union	$S \cup T$	$\{3, 4\} \cup \{4, 5, 6\} = \{3, 4, 5, 6\}$
Intersection	$S \cap T$	$\{3, 4\} \cap \{4, 5, 6\} = \{4\}$
The general addition rule for two sets	$\lvert S \cup T \rvert = \lvert S \rvert + \lvert T \rvert - \lvert S \cap T \rvert$	$\lvert \{3, 4\} \cup \{4, 5, 6\} \rvert =$ $\lvert \{3, 4\} \rvert + \lvert \{4, 5, 6\} \rvert - \lvert \{3, 4\} \cap \{4, 5, 6\} \rvert =$ $\lvert \{3, 4\} \rvert + \lvert \{4, 5, 6\} \rvert - \lvert \{4\} \rvert = 2 + 3 - 1 = 4$.

COUNTING METHODS:

Concept and Equations	Examples
Multiplication Principle: The number of possible choices of 1 element apiece from the sets $A_1, A_2, \ldots, A_n$ is $\lvert A_1 \rvert \times \lvert A_2 \rvert \times \ldots \times \lvert A_n \rvert$.	The number of possible choices of 1 element apiece from the sets $S = \{-5, 0, 1\}$, $T = \{3, 4\}$, and $U = \{3, 4, 5, 6\}$ is $\lvert S \rvert \times \lvert T \rvert \times \lvert U \rvert = 3 \times 2 \times 4 = 24$.
Factorial: $n! = n \times (n-1) \times \ldots \times 1$ $0! = 1! = 1$ $n! = (n-1)!(n)$	$4! = 4 \times 3 \times 2 \times 1 = 24$ $4! = 3! \times 4$
Permutations: A set of n objects has $n!$ permutations	The set of letters A, B, and C has $3! = 6$ permutations: ABC, ACB, BAC, BCA, CAB, and CBA.
Combinations: The number of possible choices of k objects from a set of n objects is $\binom{n}{k} = \dfrac{n!}{k!(n-k)!}$.	The number of 2-element subsets of set $\{A, B, C, D, E\}$ is $$\binom{5}{2} = \frac{5!}{2!3!} = \frac{120}{(2)(6)} = 10.$$ The 10 subsets are: $\{A, B\}$, $\{A, C\}$, $\{A, D\}$, $\{A, E\}$, $\{B, C\}$, $\{B, D\}$, $\{B, E\}$, $\{C, D\}$, $\{C, E\}$, and $\{D, E\}$.

Probability, Sequences, and Partial Sums

PROBABILITY:

Concept	Definition, Notation, and Equations	Example: Rolling a die with 6 numbered sides once
Event	A set of outcomes of an experiment	The event of the outcome being an odd number is the set $\{1, 3, 5\}$.
Probability	The probability $P(E)$ of an event E is a number between 0 and 1, inclusive. If each outcome is equally likely, $P(E) =$ $\dfrac{\text{(the number of possible outcomes in E)}}{\text{(the total number of possible outcomes)}}$.	If the 6 outcomes are equally likely, the probability of each outcome is $\dfrac{1}{6}$. The probability that the outcome is an odd number is $P(\{1, 3, 5\}) =$ $\dfrac{\|\{1, 3, 5\}\|}{6} = \dfrac{3}{6} = \dfrac{1}{2}$.
Conditional Probability	The probability that E occurs if F occurs is $P(E\|F) = \dfrac{\|E \cap F\|}{\|F\|}$.	$P(\{1, 3, 5\}\|\{1, 2\}) = \dfrac{\|\{1\}\|}{\|\{1, 2\}\|} = \dfrac{1}{2}$
Not E	The set of outcomes not in event E: $P(\text{not } E) = 1 - P(E)$.	$P(\text{not}\{3\}) = \dfrac{6-1}{6} = \dfrac{5}{6}$
E and F	The set of outcomes in both E and F, that is, $E \cap F$; $P(E \text{ and } F) = P(E \cap F) = P(E\|F)P(F)$.	For $E = \{1, 3, 5\}$ and $F = \{2, 3, 5\}$: $P(E \text{ and } F) = P(E \cap F) = P(\{3, 5\}) =$ $\dfrac{\|\{3, 5\}\|}{6} = \dfrac{2}{6} = \dfrac{1}{3}$
E or F	The set of outcomes in E or F or both, that is, $E \cup F$; $P(E \text{ or } F) = P(E) + P(F) - P(E \text{ and } F)$.	For $E = \{1, 3, 5\}$ and $F = \{2, 3, 5\}$: $P(E \text{ or } F) = P(E) + P(F) - P(E \text{ and } F)$ $= \dfrac{3}{6} + \dfrac{3}{6} - \dfrac{2}{6} = \dfrac{4}{6} = \dfrac{2}{3}$.
Dependent and Independent Events	E is dependent on F if $P(E\|F) \neq P(E)$. E and F are independent if neither is dependent on the other. If E and F are independent, $P(E \text{ and } F) = P(E)P(F)$.	For $E = \{2, 4, 6\}$ and $F = \{5, 6\}$: $P(E\|F) = P(E) = \dfrac{1}{2}$, and $P(F\|E) = P(F) = \dfrac{1}{3}$, so E and F are independent. Thus $P(E \text{ and } F) = P(E)P(F) = \left(\dfrac{1}{2}\right)\left(\dfrac{1}{3}\right) = \dfrac{1}{6}$.

SEQUENCE:

An algebraic function whose domain contains only positive integers.

Example: Function $a(n) = n^2 + \left(\dfrac{n}{5}\right)$ with the domain of all positive integers $n = 1, 2, 3, \ldots$ is an infinite sequence a_n.

PARTIAL SUM:

The sum $\displaystyle\sum_{i=1}^{k} a_i$ of the first k terms of series a_n is a partial sum of the series.

Example: For the function $a(n) = n^2 + \left(\dfrac{n}{5}\right)$, the partial sum of the first three terms is

$$\sum_{i=1}^{3} a_i = \left(1^2 + \dfrac{1}{5}\right) + \left(2^2 + \dfrac{2}{5}\right) + \left(3^2 + \dfrac{3}{5}\right).$$

To register for the GMAT™ exam go to www.mba.com/register

4.0 Quantitative Reasoning

4.0 Quantitative Reasoning

The Quantitative Reasoning section of the GMAT™ exam tests your math skills in the areas reviewed in Chapter 3, "Math Review": Value, Order, Factors, Algebra, Equalities, Inequalities, Rates, Ratios, Percents, Statistics, Sets, Counting, Probability, Estimation, and Series. Quantitative Reasoning questions also test how well you reason quantitatively, solve math problems, and interpret graphic data. All the math needed to answer the questions is generally taught in secondary school (or high school) math classes.

To answer a Quantitative Reasoning question, you pick one of five given answer choices. First study the question to see what information it gives and what it's asking you to do with that information. Then, scan the answer choices. If the problem seems simple, try to find the answer quickly. Then, check your answer against the choices. If your answer isn't among the choices, or if the problem is complicated, think again about what the problem is asking you to do, and try to rule out some of the choices. If you still can't narrow down the answer to a single choice, reread the question. It gives all the information you need to find the right answer. If you already know about the topic, don't use that knowledge to answer. Use only the information given.

You have 45 minutes to answer the 21 questions in the section. That's an average of about two minutes, nine seconds per question. You may run out of time if you spend too long on any one question. If you find yourself stuck on a question, it may be wise to simply pick the answer that seems best, even if you're not sure. Guessing is not usually the best way to score high on the GMAT, but making an educated guess is better than not answering.

Below are tips for solving Quantitative Reasoning questions, directions for the section, and sample questions with an answer key and explanations for the answers. These explanations also show strategies that may help you solve other Quantitative Reasoning questions.

4.1 Tips for Answering Quantitative Reasoning Questions

1. **Pace yourself.**

   Check the on-screen timer to see how much time you have left. Work carefully, but don't take too long double-checking an answer or struggling with a hard problem.

2. **Use the erasable notepad provided.**

   Solving a problem step by step on the notepad may help you avoid mistakes. If the problem doesn't show a diagram, drawing your own may be helpful.

3. **Study each question to understand what it's asking.**

   Approach word problems one step at a time. Read each sentence. When it's useful, translate the problem into math expressions.

4. **Scan all the answer choices before working on the problem.**

   By scanning the answer choices, you can avoid finding the answer in the wrong form. For example, if the choices are all fractions like $\frac{1}{4}$, you know to work out the answer as a fraction, not as a decimal like 0.25. Similarly, if the choices are all estimates, you can often take shortcuts. For example, you may be able to estimate by rounding 48% to 50% if every answer choice is an estimate.

5. **Don't waste time on a problem that's too hard for you.**

   Make your best guess. Then, move on to the next question.

4.2 Section Instructions

Go to www.mba.com/tutorial to read instructions for the section and get a feel for what the test center screens look like on the actual GMAT exam.

4.3 Practice Questions

Solve the problem and pick the best answer choice given.

Numbers: All numbers used are real numbers.

Figures: A figure in a Quantitative Reasoning question gives information useful in solving the problem. Figures are drawn as accurately as possible, except as noted. Lines shown as straight are straight. Lines that look jagged may also be straight. Points, angles, regions, etc., are positioned as shown. All figures are flat unless otherwise noted.

Questions 1 to 87 - Difficulty: Easy

1. The numbers of cars sold at a certain dealership on six of the last seven business days were 4, 7, 2, 8, 3, and 6, respectively. If the number of cars sold on the seventh business day was either 2, 4, or 5, for which of the three values does the average (arithmetic mean) number of cars sold per business day, for the seven business days, equal the median number of cars sold per day for the seven days?

   I.   2
   II. 4
   III. 5

   (A) II only
   (B) III only
   (C) I and II only
   (D) II and III only
   (E) I, II, and III

Performance Time	Ticket Price	Number of Tickets Sold
Thursday night	$40	200
Friday night	$50	240
Saturday afternoon	$40	220
Saturday night	$50	300

2. The table shows a summary of the ticket sales from four performances of a certain play. What is the difference between the maximum and the minimum ticket-sale revenue from a single performance?

   (A) $4,000
   (B) $5,100
   (C) $6,200
   (D) $7,000
   (E) $9,600

3. During a trip that they took together, Carmen, Juan, Maria, and Rafael drove an average (arithmetic mean) of 80 miles each. Carmen drove 72 miles, Juan drove 78 miles, and Maria drove 83 miles. How many miles did Rafael drive?

   (A) 80
   (B) 82
   (C) 85
   (D) 87
   (E) 89

4. Each week, a clothing salesperson receives a commission equal to 15 percent of the first $500 in sales and 20 percent of all additional sales that week. What commission would the salesperson receive on total sales for the week of $1,300 ?

    (A) $195
    (B) $227
    (C) $235
    (D) $260
    (E) $335

5. A certain restaurant that regularly advertises through the mail has 1,040 cover letters and 3,000 coupons in stock. In its next mailing, each envelope will contain 1 cover letter and 2 coupons. If all of the cover letters in stock are used, how many coupons will remain in stock after this mailing?

    (A)   920
    (B)   1,040
    (C)   1,500
    (D)   1,960
    (E)   2,080

6. List S consists of 10 consecutive odd integers, and list T consists of 5 consecutive even integers. If the least integer in S is 7 more than the least integer in T, how much greater is the average (arithmetic mean) of the integers in S than the average of the integers in T?

    (A)   2
    (B)   7
    (C)   8
    (D)   12
    (E)   22

7. The price of a coat in a certain store is $500. If the price of the coat is to be reduced by $150, by what percent is the price to be reduced?

    (A)   10%
    (B)   15%
    (C)   20%
    (D)   25%
    (E)   30%

8. $\left(\dfrac{1}{2}-\dfrac{1}{3}\right)+\left(\dfrac{1}{3}-\dfrac{1}{4}\right)+\left(\dfrac{1}{4}-\dfrac{1}{5}\right)+\left(\dfrac{1}{5}-\dfrac{1}{6}\right)=$

    (A) $-\dfrac{1}{6}$
    (B)   0
    (C) $\dfrac{1}{3}$
    (D) $\dfrac{1}{2}$
    (E) $\dfrac{2}{3}$

9. While a family was away on vacation, they paid a neighborhood boy $11 per week to mow their lawn and $4 per day to feed and walk their dog. If the family was away for exactly 3 weeks, how much did they pay the boy for his services?

    (A) $45
    (B) $54
    (C) $71
    (D) $95
    (E) $117

10. Last year $48,000 of a certain store's profit was shared by its 2 owners and their 10 employees. Each of the 2 owners received 3 times as much as each of their 10 employees. How much did each owner receive from the $48,000 ?

    (A) $12,000
    (B) $9,000
    (C) $6,000
    (D) $4,000
    (E) $3,000

11. On a vacation, Rose exchanged $500.00 for euros at an exchange rate of 0.80 euro per dollar and spent $\frac{3}{4}$ of the euros she received. If she exchanged the remaining euros for dollars at an exchange rate of $1.20 per euro, what was the dollar amount she received?

(A) $60.00
(B) $80.00
(C) $100.00
(D) $120.00
(E) $140.00

| x | x | x | y | y | v |
| v | x | x | y | w | w |

12. Each of the 12 squares shown is labeled x, y, v, or w. What is the ratio of the number of these squares labeled x or y to the number of these squares labeled v or w?

(A) 1:2
(B) 2:3
(C) 4:3
(D) 3:2
(E) 2:1

Number of Solid-Colored Marbles in Three Jars

Jar	Number of red marbles	Number of green marbles	Total number of red and green marbles
P	x	y	80
Q	y	z	120
R	x	z	160

13. In the table above, what is the number of green marbles in Jar R?

(A) 70
(B) 80
(C) 90
(D) 100
(E) 110

14. Bouquets are to be made using white tulips and red tulips, and the ratio of the number of white tulips to the number of red tulips is to be the same in each bouquet. If there are 15 white tulips and 85 red tulips available for the bouquets, what is the greatest number of bouquets that can be made using all the tulips available?

(A) 3
(B) 5
(C) 8
(D) 10
(E) 13

15. Over the past 7 weeks, the Smith family had weekly grocery bills of $74, $69, $64, $79, $64, $84, and $77. What was the Smiths' average (arithmetic mean) weekly grocery bill over the 7-week period?

(A) $64
(B) $70
(C) $73
(D) $74
(E) $85

16. 125% of 5 =

(A) 5.125
(B) 5.25
(C) 6
(D) 6.125
(E) 6.25

17. During a recent storm, 9 neighborhoods experienced power failures of durations 34, 29, 27, 46, 18, 25, 12, 35, and 16 minutes, respectively. For these 9 neighborhoods, what was the median duration, in minutes, of the power failures?

(A) 34
(B) 29
(C) 27
(D) 25
(E) 18

18. When traveling at a constant speed of 32 miles per hour, a certain motorboat consumes 24 gallons of fuel per hour. What is the fuel consumption of this boat at this speed measured in miles traveled per gallon of fuel?

(A) $\dfrac{2}{3}$

(B) $\dfrac{3}{4}$

(C) $\dfrac{4}{5}$

(D) $\dfrac{4}{3}$

(E) $\dfrac{3}{2}$

19. A technician makes a round-trip to and from a certain service center by the same route. If the technician completes the drive to the center and then completes 10 percent of the drive from the center, what percent of the round-trip has the technician completed?

(A) 5%

(B) 10%

(C) 25%

(D) 40%

(E) 55%

20. From 2000 to 2003, the number of employees at a certain company increased by a factor of $\dfrac{1}{4}$. From 2003 to 2006, the number of employees at this company decreased by a factor of $\dfrac{1}{3}$. If there were 100 employees at the company in 2006, how many employees were there at the company in 2000 ?

(A) 200

(B) 120

(C) 100

(D) 75

(E) 60

21. Which of the following statements must be true about the average (arithmetic mean) and the median of 5 consecutive integers?

   I.   The average is one of the integers.

   II.   The median is one of the integers.

   III.   The median equals the average.

(A) I only

(B) II only

(C) III only

(D) I and II only

(E) I, II, and III

22. A collection of 16 coins, each with a face value of either 10 cents or 25 cents, has a total face value of $2.35. How many of the coins have a face value of 25 cents?

(A) 3

(B) 5

(C) 7

(D) 9

(E) 11

23. A retailer purchased eggs at $2.80 per dozen and sold the eggs at 3 eggs for $0.90. What was the retailer's gross profit from purchasing and selling 5 dozen eggs? (1 dozen eggs = 12 eggs)

(A) $0.90

(B) $2.40

(C) $4.00

(D) $11.30

(E) $12.00

24. In a set of 24 cards, each card is numbered with a different positive integer from 1 to 24. One card will be drawn at random from the set. What is the probability that the card drawn will have either a number that is divisible by both 2 and 3 or a number that is divisible by 7 ?

(A) $\dfrac{3}{24}$

(B) $\dfrac{4}{24}$

(C) $\dfrac{7}{24}$

(D) $\dfrac{8}{24}$

(E) $\dfrac{17}{24}$

25. As a salesperson, Phyllis can choose one of two methods of annual payment: either an annual salary of $35,000 with no commission or an annual salary of $10,000 plus a 20% commission on her total annual sales. What must her total annual sales be to give her the same annual pay with either method?

(A) $100,000
(B) $120,000
(C) $125,000
(D) $130,000
(E) $132,000

26. If $1 < x < y < z$, which of the following has the greatest value?

(A) $z(x + 1)$
(B) $z(y + 1)$
(C) $x(y + z)$
(D) $y(x + z)$
(E) $z(x + y)$

27. Set X consists of eight consecutive integers. Set Y consists of all the integers that result from adding 4 to each of the integers in set X and all the integers that result from subtracting 4 from each of the integers in set X. How many more integers are there in set Y than in set X?

(A) 0
(B) 4
(C) 8
(D) 12
(E) 16

28. Of the following, which is the closest to $\dfrac{60.2}{1.03 \times 4.86}$?

(A) 10
(B) 12
(C) 13
(D) 14
(E) 15

29. Thabo owns exactly 140 books, and each book is either paperback fiction, paperback nonfiction, or hardcover nonfiction. If he owns 20 more paperback nonfiction books than hardcover nonfiction books, and twice as many paperback fiction books as paperback nonfiction books, how many hardcover nonfiction books does Thabo own?

(A) 10
(B) 20
(C) 30
(D) 40
(E) 50

30. If the average (arithmetic mean) of the four numbers 3, 15, 32, and $(N + 1)$ is 18, then $N =$

(A) 19
(B) 20
(C) 21
(D) 22
(E) 29

31. If $x > 0$, $\dfrac{x}{50} + \dfrac{x}{25}$ is what percent of x ?

    (A)   6%
    (B)   25%
    (C)   37%
    (D)   60%
    (E)   75%

32. During a certain time period, Car X traveled north along a straight road at a constant rate of 1 mile per minute and used fuel at a constant rate of 5 gallons every 2 hours. During this time period, if Car X used exactly 3.75 gallons of fuel, how many miles did Car X travel?

    (A)   36
    (B)   37.5
    (C)   40
    (D)   80
    (E)   90

33. Cheryl purchased 5 identical hollow pine doors and 6 identical solid oak doors for the house she is building. The regular price of each solid oak door was twice the regular price of each hollow pine door. However, Cheryl was given a discount of 25% off the regular price of each solid oak door. If the regular price of each hollow pine door was $40, what was the total price of all 11 doors?

    (A) $320
    (B) $540
    (C) $560
    (D) $620
    (E) $680

34. A certain store will order 25 crates of apples. The apples will be of three different varieties—McIntosh, Rome, and Winesap—and each crate will contain apples of only one variety. If the store is to order more crates of Winesap than crates of McIntosh and more crates of Winesap than crates of Rome, what is the least possible number of crates of Winesap that the store will order?

    (A)   7
    (B)   8
    (C)   9
    (D)   10
    (E)   11

35. A bicycle store purchased two bicycles, one for $250 and the other for $375, and sold both bicycles at a total gross profit of $250. If the store sold one of the bicycles for $450, which of the following could be the store's gross profit from the sale of the other bicycle?

    (A) $75
    (B) $100
    (C) $125
    (D) $150
    (E) $175

36. If $k^2 = m^2$, which of the following must be true?

    (A) $k = m$
    (B) $k = -m$
    (C) $k = |m|$
    (D) $k = -|m|$
    (E) $|k| = |m|$

37. Makoto, Nishi, and Ozuro were paid a total of $780 for waxing the floors at their school. Each was paid in proportion to the number of hours he or she worked. If Makoto worked 15 hours, Nishi worked 20 hours, and Ozuro worked 30 hours, how much was Makoto paid?

    (A) $52
    (B) $117
    (C) $130
    (D) $180
    (E) $234

38. If x is a positive integer and $4^x - 3 = y$, which of the following CANNOT be a value of y?

    (A)   1
    (B)   7
    (C)   13
    (D)   61
    (E)   253

39. If $(1 - 1.25)N = 1$, then $N =$

    (A)   −400
    (B)   −140
    (C)   −4
    (D)   4
    (E)   400

40. The quotient when a certain number is divided by $\frac{2}{3}$ is $\frac{9}{2}$. What is the number?

    (A) $\frac{4}{27}$
    (B) $\frac{1}{3}$
    (C)   3
    (D)   6
    (E) $\frac{27}{4}$

41. The price of gasoline at a service station increased from $1.65 per gallon last week to $1.82 per gallon this week. Sally paid $26.40 for gasoline last week at the station. How much more will Sally pay this week at the station for the same amount of gasoline?

    (A) $1.70
    (B) $2.55
    (C) $2.64
    (D) $2.72
    (E) $2.90

Monthly Charge for Low-Use Telephone
Contract Offered by Company X

Monthly rate (up to 75 message units)	20% less than standard rate of $10.00
Per unit in excess of 75 message units	$0.065

42. Based on the rates above, how much would Company X charge a customer with a low-use contract for using 95 message units in a month?

    (A) $9.30
    (B) $11.30
    (C) $12.88
    (D) $14.88
    (E) $16.18

43. If $2x + y = 7$ and $x + 2y = 5$, then $\dfrac{x + y}{3} =$

    (A)   1
    (B) $\frac{4}{3}$
    (C) $\frac{17}{5}$
    (D) $\frac{18}{5}$
    (E)   4

44. City X has a population 4 times as great as the population of City Y, which has a population twice as great as the population of City Z. What is the ratio of the population of City X to the population of City Z?

    (A)   1:8
    (B)   1:4
    (C)   2:1
    (D)   4:1
    (E)   8:1

Tides at Bay Cove on July 13

45. The graph above shows the height of the tide, in feet, above or below a baseline. Which of the following is closest to the difference, in feet, between the heights of the highest and lowest tides on July 13 at Bay Cove?

   (A)   1.7
   (B)   1.9
   (C)   2.2
   (D)   2.5
   (E)   2.7

46. If $S = 1 + \dfrac{1}{2^2} + \dfrac{1}{3^2} + \dfrac{1}{4^2} + \dfrac{1}{5^2} + \dfrac{1}{6^2} + \dfrac{1}{7^2} + \dfrac{1}{8^2} + \dfrac{1}{9^2} + \dfrac{1}{10^2}$, which of the following is true?

   (A) $S > 3$
   (B) $S = 3$
   (C) $2 < S < 3$
   (D) $S = 2$
   (E) $S < 2$

47. A manufacturer of a certain product can expect that between 0.3 percent and 0.5 percent of the units manufactured will be defective. If the retail price is $2,500 per unit and the manufacturer offers a full refund for defective units, how much money can the manufacturer expect to need to cover the refunds on 20,000 units?

   (A)   Between $15,000 and $25,000
   (B)   Between $30,000 and $50,000
   (C)   Between $60,000 and $100,000
   (D)   Between $150,000 and $250,000
   (E)   Between $300,000 and $500,000

48. Which of the following is closest to $\sqrt{\dfrac{4.2(1,590)}{15.7}}$?

   (A)   20
   (B)   40
   (C)   60
   (D)   80
   (E)   100

49. The sum of the weekly salaries of 5 employees is $3,250. If each of the 5 salaries is to increase by 10 percent, then the average (arithmetic mean) weekly salary per employee will increase by

   (A) $52.50
   (B) $55.00
   (C) $57.50
   (D) $62.50
   (E) $65.00

50. Last week Chris earned x dollars per hour for the first 40 hours worked plus 22 dollars per hour for each hour worked beyond 40 hours. If last week Chris earned a total of 816 dollars by working 48 hours, what is the value of x ?

   (A)   13
   (B)   14
   (C)   15
   (D)   16
   (E)   17

51. The value of $\dfrac{\frac{7}{8} + \frac{1}{9}}{\frac{1}{2}}$ is closest to which of the following?

   (A)   2
   (B) $\dfrac{3}{2}$
   (C)   1
   (D) $\dfrac{1}{2}$
   (E)   0

52. The positive two-digit integers x and y have the same digits, but in reverse order. Which of the following must be a factor of $x + y$?

(A) 6
(B) 9
(C) 10
(D) 11
(E) 14

53. In a certain sequence of 8 numbers, each number after the first is 1 more than the previous number. If the first number is –5, how many of the numbers in the sequence are positive?

(A) None
(B) One
(C) Two
(D) Three
(E) Four

54. A total of s oranges are to be packaged in boxes that will hold r oranges each, with no oranges left over. When n of these boxes have been completely filled, what is the number of boxes that remain to be filled?

(A) $s - nr$
(B) $s - \dfrac{n}{r}$
(C) $rs - n$
(D) $\dfrac{s}{n} - r$
(E) $\dfrac{s}{r} - n$

55. If $0 < a < b < c$, which of the following statements must be true?

I. $2a > b + c$
II. $c - a > b - a$
III. $\dfrac{c}{a} < \dfrac{b}{a}$

(A) I only
(B) II only
(C) III only
(D) I and II
(E) II and III

	Monday	Tuesday	Wednesday	Thursday
Company A	45	55	50	50
Company B	10	30	30	10
Company C	34	28	28	30
Company D	39	42	41	38
Company E	50	60	60	70

56. The table shows the numbers of packages shipped daily by each of five companies during a 4-day period. The standard deviation of the numbers of packages shipped daily during the period was greatest for which of the five companies?

(A) A
(B) B
(C) C
(D) D
(E) E

57. Company Q plans to make a new product next year and sell each unit of this new product at a selling price of $2. The variable costs per unit in each production run are estimated to be 40% of the selling price, and the fixed costs for each production run are estimated to be $5,040. Based on these estimated costs, how many units of the new product will Company Q need to make and sell in order for their revenue to equal their total costs for each production run?

(A) 4,200
(B) 3,150
(C) 2,520
(D) 2,100
(E) 1,800

58. A small business invests $9,900 in equipment to produce a product. Each unit of the product costs $0.65 to produce and is sold for $1.20. How many units of the product must be sold before the revenue received equals the total expense of production, including the initial investment in equipment?

    (A) 12,000
    (B) 14,500
    (C) 15,230
    (D) 18,000
    (E) 20,000

Estimated Number of Home-Schooled
Students by State, January 2001

State	Number (in thousands)
A	181
B	125
C	103
D	79
E	72

59. According to the table shown, the estimated number of home-schooled students in State A is approximately what percent greater than the number in State D ?

    (A) 25%
    (B) 55%
    (C) 100%
    (D) 125%
    (E) 155%

60. When n liters of fuel were added to a tank that was already $\frac{1}{3}$ full, the tank was filled to $\frac{7}{9}$ of its capacity. In terms of n, what is the capacity of the tank, in liters?

    (A) $\frac{10}{9}n$

    (B) $\frac{4}{3}n$

    (C) $\frac{3}{2}n$

    (D) $\frac{9}{4}n$

    (E) $\frac{7}{3}n$

61. Kevin invested $8,000 for one year at a simple annual interest rate of 6 percent and invested $10,000 for one year at an annual interest rate of 8 percent compounded semiannually. What is the total amount of interest that Kevin earned on the two investments?

    (A) $880
    (B) $1,088
    (C) $1,253
    (D) $1,280
    (E) $1,296

62. The harvest yield from a certain apple orchard was 350 bushels of apples. If x of the trees in the orchard each yielded 10 bushels of apples, what fraction of the harvest yield was from these x trees?

    (A) $\frac{x}{35}$

    (B) $1 - \frac{x}{35}$

    (C) $10x$

    (D) $35 - x$

    (E) $350 - 10x$

63. In a certain fraction, the denominator is 16 greater than the numerator. If the fraction is equivalent to 80 percent, what is the denominator of the fraction?

    (A) 32
    (B) 64
    (C) 72
    (D) 80
    (E) 120

64. Greg assembles units of a certain product at a factory. Each day he is paid $2.00 per unit for the first 40 units that he assembles and $2.50 for each additional unit that he assembles that day. If Greg assembled at least 30 units on each of two days and was paid a total of $180.00 for assembling units on the two days, what is the greatest possible number of units that he could have assembled on one of the two days?

    (A) 48
    (B) 52
    (C) 56
    (D) 60
    (E) 64

65. Which of the following is greatest?

    (A) $10\sqrt{3}$
    (B) $9\sqrt{4}$
    (C) $8\sqrt{5}$
    (D) $7\sqrt{6}$
    (E) $6\sqrt{7}$

66. Al and Ben are drivers for SD Trucking Company. One snowy day, Ben left SD at 8:00 a.m. heading east and Al left SD at 11:00 a.m. heading west. At a particular time later that day, the dispatcher retrieved data from SD's vehicle tracking system. The data showed that, up to that time, Al had averaged 40 miles per hour and Ben had averaged 20 miles per hour. It also showed that Al and Ben had driven a combined total of 240 miles. At what time did the dispatcher retrieve data from the vehicle tracking system?

    (A) 1:00 p.m.
    (B) 2:00 p.m.
    (C) 3:00 p.m.
    (D) 5:00 p.m.
    (E) 6:00 p.m.

67. Of the land owned by a farmer, 90 percent was cleared for planting. Of the cleared land, 40 percent was planted with soybeans and 50 percent of the cleared land was planted with wheat. If the remaining 720 acres of cleared land was planted with corn, how many acres did the farmer own?

    (A) 5,832
    (B) 6,480
    (C) 7,200
    (D) 8,000
    (E) 8,889

68. At the start of an experiment, a certain population consisted of 3 animals. At the end of each month after the start of the experiment, the population size was double its size at the beginning of that month. Which of the following represents the population size at the end of 10 months?

    (A) 2^3
    (B) 3^2
    (C) $2(3^{10})$
    (D) $3(2^{10})$
    (E) $3(10^2)$

69. If $\left(\dfrac{1}{3} + \dfrac{1}{4} + \dfrac{1}{5} + \dfrac{1}{6}\right) = r\left(\dfrac{1}{9} + \dfrac{1}{12} + \dfrac{1}{15} + \dfrac{1}{18}\right)$, then $r =$

    (A) $\dfrac{1}{3}$
    (B) $\dfrac{4}{3}$
    (C) 3
    (D) 4
    (E) 12

70. If x and y are positive integers such that y is a multiple of 5 and $3x + 4y = 200$, then x must be a multiple of which of the following?

    (A) 3
    (B) 6
    (C) 7
    (D) 8
    (E) 10

71. Which of the following expressions can be written as an integer?

    I. $\left(\sqrt{82} + \sqrt{82}\right)^2$

    II. $(82)\left(\sqrt{82}\right)$

    III. $\dfrac{\left(\sqrt{82}\right)\left(\sqrt{82}\right)}{82}$

    (A)   None
    (B)   I only
    (C)   III only
    (D)   I and II
    (E)   I and III

72. Pumping alone at their respective constant rates, one inlet pipe fills an empty tank to $\frac{1}{2}$ of capacity in 3 hours and a second inlet pipe fills the same empty tank to $\frac{2}{3}$ of capacity in 6 hours. How many hours will it take both pipes, pumping simultaneously at their respective constant rates, to fill the empty tank to capacity?

    (A)   3.25
    (B)   3.6
    (C)   4.2
    (D)   4.4
    (E)   5.5

73. If $x^2 - 2 < 0$, which of the following specifies all the possible values of x ?

    (A) $0 < x < 2$
    (B) $0 < x < \sqrt{2}$
    (C) $-\sqrt{2} < x < \sqrt{2}$
    (D) $-2 < x < 0$
    (E) $-2 < x < 2$

Book Number	Pages in Book	Total Pages Read
1	253	253
2	110	363
3	117	480
4	170	650
5	155	805
6	50	855
7	205	1,060
8	70	1,130
9	165	1,295
10	105	1,400
11	143	1,543
12	207	1,750

74. Shawana made a schedule for reading books during 4 weeks (28 days) of her summer vacation. She has checked out 12 books from the library. The number of pages in each book and the order in which she plans to read the books are shown in the table above. She will read exactly 50 pages each day. The only exception will be that she will never begin the next book on the same day that she finishes the previous one, and therefore on some days she may read fewer than 50 pages. At the end of the 28th day, how many books will Shawana have finished?

    (A)   7
    (B)   8
    (C)   9
    (D)   10
    (E)   11

75. In Western Europe, x bicycles were sold in each of the years 1990 and 1993. The bicycle producers of Western Europe had a 42 percent share of this market in 1990 and a 33 percent share in 1993. Which of the following represents the decrease in the annual number of bicycles produced and sold in Western Europe from 1990 to 1993 ?

(A)   9% of $\dfrac{x}{100}$

(B)   14% of $\dfrac{x}{100}$

(C)   75% of $\dfrac{x}{100}$

(D)   9% of x

(E)   14% of x

76. If k is a positive integer, what is the remainder when $(k + 2)(k^3 - k)$ is divided by 6 ?

(A)   0
(B)   1
(C)   2
(D)   3
(E)   4

77. Which of the following fractions is closest to $\dfrac{1}{2}$?

(A) $\dfrac{4}{7}$

(B) $\dfrac{5}{9}$

(C) $\dfrac{6}{11}$

(D) $\dfrac{7}{13}$

(E) $\dfrac{9}{16}$

78. If $p \neq 0$ and $p - \dfrac{1 - p^2}{p} = \dfrac{r}{p}$, then $r =$

(A) $p + 1$
(B) $2p - 1$
(C) $p^2 + 1$
(D) $2p^2 - 1$
(E) $p^2 + p - 1$

79. If the range of the six numbers 4, 3, 14, 7, 10, and x is 12, what is the difference between the greatest possible value of x and the least possible value of x ?

(A)   0
(B)   2
(C)   12
(D)   13
(E)   15

80. What number is 108 more than two-thirds of itself?

(A)   72
(B)   144
(C)   162
(D)   216
(E)   324

81. A service provider charges c dollars for the first 50 hours of service used per month and 40 cents for each 30 minutes in excess of 50 hours used during the month. If x is an integer greater than 50, which of the following expressions gives this service provider's charge, in dollars, for a month in which x hours of service were used?

(A) $c + 0.40x$
(B) $c + 0.80x$
(C) $c + 0.40(x - 50)$
(D) $c + 0.80(x - 50)$
(E) $c + 0.40(2x - 50)$

82. A salesperson who had been driving at a speed of 100 kilometers per hour slowed down to a speed of 47 kilometers per hour. Approximately how many miles per hour was the speed reduced? (1 kilometer ≈ 0.625 mile)

(A)   29
(B)   33
(C)   53
(D)   63
(E)   75

83. Company P had 15 percent more employees in December than it had in January. If Company P had 460 employees in December, how many employees did it have in January?

    (A) 391
    (B) 400
    (C) 410
    (D) 423
    (E) 445

	Recording Time	Viewing Time
Tuesday	4 hours	None
Wednesday	None	1 to 2 hours
Thursday	2 hours	None
Friday	None	2 to 3 hours

84. The table above shows the numbers of hours of television programs that Jane recorded last week and the numbers of hours she spent viewing these recorded programs. No recorded program was viewed more than once. If h is the number of hours of recorded programs she had not yet viewed by the end of Friday, which of the following intervals represents all of the possible values of h ?

    (A) $0 \le h \le 1$
    (B) $1 \le h \le 2$
    (C) $2 \le h \le 3$
    (D) $0 \le h \le 2$
    (E) $1 \le h \le 3$

85. A dance troupe has a total of 50 dancers split into 2 groups. The costumes worn by Group A cost $80 each, and those worn by Group B cost $90 each. If the total cost of all the costumes is $4,270, what is the total cost of the costumes worn by Group B ?

    (A) $1,840
    (B) $2,070
    (C) $2,135
    (D) $2,160
    (E) $2,430

86. A doctor prescribed 18 cubic centimeters of a certain drug to a patient whose body weight was 120 pounds. If the typical dosage is 2 cubic centimeters per 15 pounds of body weight, by what percent was the prescribed dosage greater than the typical dosage?

    (A) 8%
    (B) 9%
    (C) 11%
    (D) 12.5%
    (E) 14.8%

87. The function f is defined by $f(x) = \sqrt{x} - 10$ for all positive numbers x. If $u = f(t)$ for some positive numbers t and u, what is t in terms of u ?

    (A) $\sqrt{\sqrt{u} + 10}$
    (B) $\left(\sqrt{u} + 10\right)^2$
    (C) $\sqrt{u^2 + 10}$
    (D) $(u + 10)^2$
    (E) $(u^2 + 10)^2$

Questions 88 to 145 - Difficulty: Medium

88. The average distance between the Sun and a certain planet is approximately 2.3×10^{14} inches. Which of the following is closest to the average distance between the Sun and the planet, in kilometers? (1 kilometer is approximately 3.9×10^4 inches.)

    (A) 7.1×10^8
    (B) 5.9×10^9
    (C) 1.6×10^{10}
    (D) 1.6×10^{11}
    (E) 5.9×10^{11}

89. If m is the average (arithmetic mean) of the first 10 positive multiples of 5 and if M is the median of the first 10 positive multiples of 5, what is the value of $M - m$?

    (A) −5
    (B) 0
    (C) 5
    (D) 25
    (E) 27.5

90. According to a survey of 200 people, 60 enjoy skiing and 80 enjoy skating. If the number of people who enjoy neither skiing nor skating is 2 times the number of people who enjoy both skiing and skating, how many people surveyed enjoy neither skiing nor skating?

(A) 20
(B) 40
(C) 50
(D) 80
(E) 120

$$m \oplus p = n$$
$$n \oplus r = m$$
$$n \oplus q = q$$
$$p \oplus q = p$$
$$q \oplus p = r$$

91. If the relations shown hold for the operation $\oplus$ and the numbers m, n, p, q, and r, then $[(m \oplus p) \oplus q] \oplus p =$

(A) m
(B) n
(C) p
(D) q
(E) r

92. To rent a tractor, it costs a total of x dollars for the first 24 hours, plus y dollars per hour for each hour in excess of 24 hours. Which of the following represents the cost, in dollars, to rent a tractor for 36 hours?

(A) $x + 12y$
(B) $x + 36y$
(C) $12x + y$
(D) $24x + 12y$
(E) $24x + 36y$

93. If the mass of 1 cubic centimeter of a certain substance is 7.3 grams, what is the mass, in kilograms, of 1 cubic meter of this substance? (1 cubic meter = 1,000,000 cubic centimeters; 1 kilogram = 1,000 grams)

(A) 0.0073
(B) 0.73
(C) 7.3
(D) 7,300
(E) 7,300,000

94. If $z \neq 0$ and $z + \dfrac{1 - 2z^2}{z} = \dfrac{w}{z}$, then $w =$

(A) $z + 1$
(B) $z^2 + 1$
(C) $-z^2 + 1$
(D) $-z^2 + z + 1$
(E) $-2z^2 + 1$

95. For all real numbers a, b, c, d, e, and f, the operation $\ominus$ is defined by the equation $(a, b, c) \ominus (d, e, f) = ad + be + cf$. What is the value of $(1, -2, 3) \ominus \left(1, -\dfrac{1}{2}, \dfrac{1}{3}\right)$?

(A) -1
(B) $\dfrac{5}{6}$
(C) 1
(D) $\dfrac{5}{2}$
(E) 3

96. If m and p are positive integers and $m^2 + p^2 < 100$, what is the greatest possible value of mp?

(A) 36
(B) 42
(C) 48
(D) 49
(E) 51

97. If $\dfrac{x}{y} = \dfrac{c}{d}$ and $\dfrac{d}{c} = \dfrac{b}{a}$, which of the following must be true?

I. $\dfrac{y}{x} = \dfrac{b}{a}$

II. $\dfrac{x}{a} = \dfrac{y}{b}$

III. $\dfrac{y}{a} = \dfrac{x}{b}$

(A) I only
(B) II only
(C) I and II only
(D) I and III only
(E) I, II, and III

98. If k is an integer and $(0.0025)(0.025)(0.00025) \times 10^k$ is an integer, what is the least possible value of k?

(A) −12
(B) −6
(C) 0
(D) 6
(E) 12

99. If $a(a + 2) = 24$ and $b(b + 2) = 24$, where $a \neq b$, then $a + b =$

(A) −48
(B) −2
(C) 2
(D) 46
(E) 48

100. In a recent election, Ms. Robbins received 8,000 votes cast by independent voters, that is, voters not registered with a specific political party. She also received 10 percent of the votes cast by those voters registered with a political party. If N is the total number of votes cast in the election and 40 percent of the votes cast were cast by independent voters, which of the following represents the number of votes that Ms. Robbins received?

(A) $0.06N + 3,200$
(B) $0.1N + 7,200$
(C) $0.4N + 7,200$
(D) $0.1N + 8,000$
(E) $0.06N + 8,000$

101. The profit P, in dollars, for any given month at a certain company is defined by $P = I - C$, where I represents total income, in dollars, and C represents total costs, in dollars, for the month. For each of the first 4 months of the year, $C = I + 32,000$; and for each of the next 3 months, $I = C + 36,000$. If $I = C + 10,000$ for each of the 5 remaining months of the year, what was the company's total profit for the 12-month year?

(A) $10,000
(B) $30,000
(C) $40,000
(D) $50,000
(E) $70,000

102. A manufacturer makes and sells 2 products, P and Q. The revenue from the sale of each unit of P is $20.00 and the revenue from the sale of each unit of Q is $17.00. Last year the manufacturer sold twice as many units of Q as P. What was the manufacturer's average (arithmetic mean) revenue per unit sold of these 2 products last year?

(A) $28.50
(B) $27.00
(C) $19.00
(D) $18.50
(E) $18.00

103. A worker carries jugs of liquid soap from a production line to a packing area, carrying 4 jugs per trip. If the jugs are packed into cartons that hold 7 jugs each, how many jugs are needed to fill the last partially filled carton after the worker has made 17 trips?

(A) 1
(B) 2
(C) 4
(D) 5
(E) 6

104. Last year a state senate consisting of only Republican and Democrat members had 20 more Republican members than Democrat members. This year the senate has the same number of members as last year, but it has 2 fewer Republican members than last year. If this year the number of Republican members is $\frac{2}{3}$ the number of senate members, how many members does the senate have this year?

(A) 33
(B) 36
(C) 42
(D) 45
(E) 48

105. Sam has $800 in his account. He will deposit $1 in his account one week from now, $2 two weeks from now, and each week thereafter he will deposit an amount that is $1 greater than the amount that he deposited one week before. If there are no other transactions, how much money will Sam have in his account 50 weeks from now?

(A) $850
(B) $1,200
(C) $1,675
(D) $2,075
(E) $3,350

106. A certain state's milk production was 980 million pounds in 2007 and 2.7 billion pounds in 2014. Approximately how many more million <u>gallons</u> of milk did the state produce in 2014 than in 2007 ? (1 billion = 10^9 and 1 gallon = 8.6 pounds.)

(A) 100
(B) 200
(C) 1,700
(D) 8,200
(E) 14,800

107. Working simultaneously and independently at an identical constant rate, four machines of a certain type can produce a total of x units of product P in 6 days. How many of these machines, working simultaneously and independently at this constant rate, can produce a total of 3x units of product P in 4 days?

(A) 24
(B) 18
(C) 16
(D) 12
(E) 8

108. The symbol Δ denotes one of the four arithmetic operations: addition, subtraction, multiplication, or division. If $6 \Delta 3 \le 3$, which of the following must be true?

I. $2 \Delta 2 = 0$
II. $2 \Delta 2 = 1$
III. $4 \Delta 2 = 2$

(A) I only
(B) II only
(C) III only
(D) I and II only
(E) I, II, and III

109. If $mn \ne 0$ and 25 percent of n equals $37\frac{1}{2}$ percent of m, what is the value of $\frac{12n}{m}$?

(A) 18
(B) $\frac{32}{3}$
(C) 8
(D) 3
(E) $\frac{9}{8}$

110. Last year Joe grew 1 inch and Sally grew 200 percent more than Joe grew. How many inches did Sally grow last year?

(A) 0
(B) 1
(C) 2
(D) 3
(E) 4

Technique	Percent of Consumers
Television ads	35%
Coupons	22%
Store displays	18%
Samples	15%

111. The table shows <u>partial</u> results of a survey in which consumers were asked to indicate which one of six promotional techniques most influenced their decision to buy a new food product. Of those consumers who indicated one of the four techniques listed, what fraction indicated either coupons or store displays?

(A) $\dfrac{2}{7}$

(B) $\dfrac{1}{3}$

(C) $\dfrac{2}{5}$

(D) $\dfrac{4}{9}$

(E) $\dfrac{1}{2}$

112. If 65 percent of a certain firm's employees are full-time and if there are 5,100 more full-time employees than part-time employees, how many employees does the firm have?

(A) 8,250
(B) 10,200
(C) 11,050
(D) 16,500
(E) 17,000

113. The cost C, in dollars, to remove p percent of a certain pollutant from a pond is estimated by using the formula $C = \dfrac{100,000p}{100 - p}$. According to this estimate, how much more would it cost to remove 90 percent of the pollutant from the pond than it would cost to remove 80 percent of the pollutant?

(A) $500,000
(B) $100,000
(C) $50,000
(D) $10,000
(E) $5,000

114. If $xy \neq 0$ and $x^2y^2 - xy = 6$, which of the following could be y in terms of x?

I. $\dfrac{1}{2x}$

II. $-\dfrac{2}{x}$

III. $\dfrac{3}{x}$

(A) I only
(B) II only
(C) I and II
(D) I and III
(E) II and III

115. $\sqrt{4.8 \times 10^9}$ is closest in value to

(A) 2,200
(B) 70,000
(C) 220,000
(D) 7,000,000
(E) 22,000,000

116. In a certain high school, 80 percent of the seniors are taking calculus, and 60 percent of the seniors who are taking calculus are also taking physics. If 10 percent of the seniors are taking neither calculus nor physics, what percent of the seniors are taking physics?

(A) 40%
(B) 42%
(C) 48%
(D) 58%
(E) 80%

117. If the units digit of $\dfrac{5,610.37}{10^k}$ is 6, what is the value of k?

(A)   3
(B)   2
(C)   1
(D)   −1
(E)   −2

118. Three printing presses, R, S, and T, working together at their respective constant rates, can do a certain printing job in 4 hours. S and T, working together at their respective constant rates, can do the same job in 5 hours. How many hours would it take R, working alone at its constant rate, to do the same job?

(A)   8
(B)   10
(C)   12
(D)   15
(E)   20

Results of a Poll

Company	Number Who Own Stock in the Company
AT&T	30
IBM	48
GM	54
FORD	75
US Air	83

119. In a poll, 200 subscribers to *Financial Magazine X* indicated which of five specific companies they own stock in. The results are shown in the table above. If 15 of the 200 own stock in both IBM and AT&T, how many of those polled own stock in neither company?

(A)   63
(B)   93
(C)   107
(D)   122
(E)   137

120. The sum of all the integers k such that −26 < k < 24 is

(A)   0
(B)   −2
(C)   −25
(D)   −49
(E)   −51

121. The number line shown contains three points R, S, and T, whose coordinates have absolute values r, s, and t, respectively. Which of the following equals the average (arithmetic mean) of the coordinates of the points R, S, and T?

(A) s
(B) $s + t - r$
(C) $\dfrac{r - s - t}{3}$
(D) $\dfrac{r + s + t}{3}$
(E) $\dfrac{s + t - r}{3}$

122. Mark and Ann together were allocated n boxes of cookies to sell for a club project. Mark sold 10 boxes less than n and Ann sold 2 boxes less than n. If Mark and Ann have each sold at least one box of cookies, but together they have sold less than n boxes, what is the value of n?

(A)   11
(B)   12
(C)   13
(D)   14
(E)   15

$$\begin{array}{r} 3P5 \\ + 4QR \\ \hline 8S4 \end{array}$$

123. In the correctly worked addition problem shown, *P*, *Q*, *R*, and *S* are digits. If *Q* = 2*P*, which of the following could be the value of *S* ?

(A) 3
(B) 4
(C) 5
(D) 7
(E) 9

124. A certain high school has 5,000 students. Of these students, *x* are taking music, *y* are taking art, and *z* are taking both music and art. How many students are taking neither music nor art?

(A) 5,000 – *z*
(B) 5,000 – *x* – *y*
(C) 5,000 – *x* + *z*
(D) 5,000 – *x* – *y* – *z*
(E) 5,000 – *x* – *y* + *z*

125. Each person who attended a company meeting was either a stockholder in the company, an employee of the company, or both. If 62 percent of those who attended the meeting were stockholders and 47 percent were employees, what percent were stockholders who were NOT employees?

(A) 34%
(B) 38%
(C) 45%
(D) 53%
(E) 62%

Accounts	Amount Budgeted	Amount Spent
Payroll	$110,000	$117,000
Taxes	40,000	42,000
Insurance	2,500	2,340

126. The table shows the amount budgeted and the amount spent for each of three accounts in a certain company. For which of these accounts did the amount spent differ from the amount budgeted by more than 6 percent of the amount budgeted?

(A) Payroll only
(B) Taxes only
(C) Insurance only
(D) Payroll and Insurance
(E) Taxes and Insurance

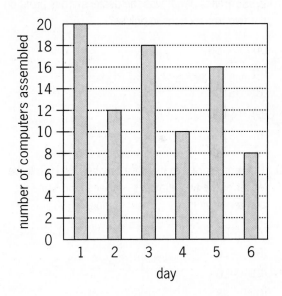

127. The graph shows the number of computers assembled during each of 6 consecutive days. From what day to the next day was the percent change in the number of computers assembled the greatest in magnitude?

(A) From Day 1 to Day 2
(B) From Day 2 to Day 3
(C) From Day 3 to Day 4
(D) From Day 4 to Day 5
(E) From Day 5 to Day 6

128. If $n = 20! + 17$, then n is divisible by which of the following?

   I.   15
   II. 17
   III. 19

   (A)   None
   (B)   I only
   (C)   II only
   (D)   I and II
   (E)   II and III

129. Exchange Rates in a Particular Year

$$\$1 = 5.3 \text{ francs}$$
$$\$1 = 1.6 \text{ marks}$$

   An American dealer bought a table in Germany for 480 marks and sold the same table in France for 2,385 francs. What was the dealer's gross profit on the two transactions in dollars?

   (A) $0
   (B) $50
   (C) $100
   (D) $150
   (E) $200

130. The product of two negative numbers is 160. If the lesser of the two numbers is 4 less than twice the greater, what is the greater number?

   (A)   −20
   (B)   −16
   (C)   −10
   (D)   −8
   (E)   −4

131. According to a certain estimate, the depth $N(t)$, in centimeters, of the water in a certain tank at t hours past 2:00 in the morning is given by $N(t) = -20(t - 5)^2 + 500$ for $0 \leq t \leq 10$. According to this estimate, at what time in the morning does the depth of the water in the tank reach its maximum?

   (A)   5:30
   (B)   7:00
   (C)   7:30
   (D)   8:00
   (E)   9:00

132. After driving to a riverfront parking lot, Bob plans to run south along the river, turn around, and return to the parking lot, running north along the same path. After running 3.25 miles south, he decides to run for only 50 minutes more. If Bob runs at a constant rate of 8 minutes per mile, how many miles farther south can he run and still be able to return to the parking lot in 50 minutes?

   (A)   1.5
   (B)   2.25
   (C)   3.0
   (D)   3.25
   (E)   4.75

133. Alex deposited x dollars into a new account that earned 8 percent annual interest, compounded annually. One year later Alex deposited an additional x dollars into the account. If there were no other transactions and if the account contained w dollars at the end of two years, which of the following expresses x in terms of w?

   (A) $\dfrac{w}{1 + 1.08}$

   (B) $\dfrac{w}{1.08 + 1.16}$

   (C) $\dfrac{w}{1.16 + 1.24}$

   (D) $\dfrac{w}{1.08 + (1.08)^2}$

   (E) $\dfrac{w}{(1.08)^2 + (1.08)^3}$

134. M is the sum of the reciprocals of the consecutive integers from 201 to 300, inclusive. Which of the following is true?

   (A) $\dfrac{1}{3} < M < \dfrac{1}{2}$

   (B) $\dfrac{1}{5} < M < \dfrac{1}{3}$

   (C) $\dfrac{1}{7} < M < \dfrac{1}{5}$

   (D) $\dfrac{1}{9} < M < \dfrac{1}{7}$

   (E) $\dfrac{1}{12} < M < \dfrac{1}{9}$

135. Working simultaneously at their respective constant rates, Machines A and B produce 800 nails in x hours. Working alone at its constant rate, Machine A produces 800 nails in y hours. In terms of x and y, how many hours does it take Machine B, working alone at its constant rate, to produce 800 nails?

   (A) $\dfrac{x}{x+y}$

   (B) $\dfrac{y}{x+y}$

   (C) $\dfrac{xy}{x+y}$

   (D) $\dfrac{xy}{x-y}$

   (E) $\dfrac{xy}{y-x}$

136. Carol purchased one basket of fruit consisting of 4 apples and 2 oranges and another basket of fruit consisting of 3 apples and 5 oranges. Carol is to select one piece of fruit at random from each of the two baskets. What is the probability that one of the two pieces of fruit selected will be an apple and the other will be an orange?

   (A) $\dfrac{1}{4}$

   (B) $\dfrac{1}{2}$

   (C) $\dfrac{1}{24}$

   (D) $\dfrac{5}{24}$

   (E) $\dfrac{13}{24}$

137. Last year Brand X shoes were sold by dealers in 403 different regions worldwide, with an average (arithmetic mean) of 98 dealers per region. If last year these dealers sold an average of 2,488 pairs of Brand X shoes per dealer, which of the following is closest to the total number of pairs of Brand X shoes sold last year by the dealers worldwide?

   (A) 10^4

   (B) 10^5

   (C) 10^6

   (D) 10^7

   (E) 10^8

10, 4, 26, 16

138. What is the median of the numbers shown?

   (A) 10

   (B) 13

   (C) 14

   (D) 15

   (E) 16

	Number of Marbles in Each of Three Bags	Percent of Marbles in Each Bag That Are Blue (to the nearest tenth)
Bag P	37	10.8%
Bag Q	x	66.7%
Bag R	32	50.0%

139. If $\dfrac{1}{3}$ of the total number of marbles in the three bags listed in the table above are blue, how many marbles are there in bag Q?

   (A) 5

   (B) 9

   (C) 12

   (D) 23

   (E) 46

Age Category (in years)	Number of Employees
Less than 20	29
20–29	58
30–39	36
40–49	21
50–59	10
60–69	5
70 and over	2

140. The table above gives the age categories of the 161 employees at Company X and the number of employees in each category. According to the table, if m is the median age, in years, of the employees at Company X, then m must satisfy which of the following?

    (A) $20 \leq m \leq 29$
    (B) $25 \leq m \leq 34$
    (C) $30 \leq m \leq 39$
    (D) $35 \leq m \leq 44$
    (E) $40 \leq m \leq 49$

141. If k and n are positive integers such that $n > k$, then $k! + (n - k) \cdot (k - 1)!$ is equivalent to which of the following?

    (A) $k \cdot n!$
    (B) $k! \cdot n$
    (C) $(n - k)!$
    (D) $n \cdot (k + 1)!$
    (E) $n \cdot (k - 1)!$

142. Ron is 4 inches taller than Amy, and Barbara is 1 inch taller than Ron. If Barbara's height is 65 inches, what is the median height, in inches, of these three people?

    (A)   60
    (B)   61
    (C)   62
    (D)   63
    (E)   64

143. If x and y are positive numbers such that $x + y = 1$, which of the following could be the value of $100x + 200y$?

    I.   80
    II.   140
    III.   199

    (A)   II only
    (B)   III only
    (C)   I and II
    (D)   I and III
    (E)   II and III

144. If X is the hundredths digit in the decimal $0.1X$ and if Y is the thousandths digit in the decimal $0.02Y$, where X and Y are nonzero digits, which of the following is closest to the greatest possible value of $\dfrac{0.1X}{0.02Y}$?

    (A)   4
    (B)   5
    (C)   6
    (D)   9
    (E)   10

145. If each of the 12 teams participating in a certain tournament plays exactly one game with each of the other teams, how many games will be played?

    (A)   144
    (B)   132
    (C)   66
    (D)   33
    (E)   23

146. The cost to rent a small bus for a trip is x dollars, which is to be shared equally among the people taking the trip. If 10 people take the trip rather than 16, how many more dollars, in terms of x, will it cost per person?

    (A) $\dfrac{x}{6}$

    (B) $\dfrac{x}{10}$

    (C) $\dfrac{x}{16}$

    (D) $\dfrac{3x}{40}$

    (E) $\dfrac{3x}{80}$

147. Clarissa will create her summer reading list by randomly choosing 4 books from the 10 books approved for summer reading. She will list the books in the order in which they are chosen. How many different lists are possible?

    (A)   6
    (B)   40
    (C)   210
    (D)   5,040
    (E)   151,200

148. If n is a positive integer and the product of all the integers from 1 to n, inclusive, is divisible by 990, what is the least possible value of n?

    (A)   8
    (B)   9
    (C)   10
    (D)   11
    (E)   12

149. The probability that event M will NOT occur is 0.8 and the probability that event R will NOT occur is 0.6. If events M and R CANNOT both occur, which of the following is the probability that either event M or event R will occur?

    (A) $\dfrac{1}{5}$

    (B) $\dfrac{2}{5}$

    (C) $\dfrac{3}{5}$

    (D) $\dfrac{4}{5}$

    (E) $\dfrac{12}{25}$

150. The total cost for Company X to produce a batch of tools is $10,000 plus $3 per tool. Each tool sells for $8. The gross profit earned from producing and selling these tools is the total income from sales minus the total production cost. If a batch of 20,000 tools is produced and sold, then Company X's gross profit per tool is

    (A) $3.00
    (B) $3.75
    (C) $4.50
    (D) $5.00
    (E) $5.50

151. If Q is an odd number and the median of Q consecutive integers is 120, what is the largest of these integers?

    (A) $\dfrac{Q-1}{2}+120$

    (B) $\dfrac{Q}{2}+119$

    (C) $\dfrac{Q}{2}+120$

    (D) $\dfrac{Q+119}{2}$

    (E) $\dfrac{Q+120}{2}$

152. If there are fewer than 8 zeros between the decimal point and the first nonzero digit in the decimal expansion of $\left(\dfrac{t}{1,000}\right)^4$, which of the following numbers could be the value of t?

   I.   3
   II. 5
   III. 9

(A) None
(B) I only
(C) II only
(D) III only
(E) II and III

153. A three-digit code for certain locks uses the digits 0, 1, 2, 3, 4, 5, 6, 7, 8, 9 according to the following constraints. The first digit cannot be 0 or 1, the second digit must be 0 or 1, and the second and third digits cannot both be 0 in the same code. How many different codes are possible?

(A) 144
(B) 152
(C) 160
(D) 168
(E) 176

154. Jackie has two solutions that are 2 percent sulfuric acid and 12 percent sulfuric acid by volume, respectively. If these solutions are mixed in appropriate quantities to produce 60 liters of a solution that is 5 percent sulfuric acid, approximately how many liters of the 2 percent solution will be required?

(A) 18
(B) 20
(C) 24
(D) 36
(E) 42

155. If Jake loses 8 pounds, he will weigh twice as much as his sister. Together they now weigh 278 pounds. What is Jake's present weight, in pounds?

(A) 131
(B) 135
(C) 139
(D) 147
(E) 188

156. For each student in a certain class, a teacher adjusted the student's test score using the formula $y = 0.8x + 20$, where x is the student's original test score and y is the student's adjusted test score. If the standard deviation of the original test scores of the students in the class was 20, what was the standard deviation of the adjusted test scores of the students in the class?

(A) 12
(B) 16
(C) 28
(D) 36
(E) 40

157. Last year 26 members of a certain club traveled to England, 26 members traveled to France, and 32 members traveled to Italy. Last year no members of the club traveled to both England and France, 6 members traveled to both England and Italy, and 11 members traveled to both France and Italy. How many members of the club traveled to at least one of these three countries last year?

(A) 52
(B) 67
(C) 71
(D) 73
(E) 79

158. A store reported total sales of $385 million for February of this year. If the total sales for the same month last year was $320 million, approximately what was the percent increase in sales?

(A) 2%
(B) 17%
(C) 20%
(D) 65%
(E) 83%

159. When positive integer x is divided by positive integer y, the remainder is 9. If $\dfrac{x}{y} = 96.12$, what is the value of y?

    (A)   96
    (B)   75
    (C)   48
    (D)   25
    (E)   12

160. If $x(2x + 1) = 0$ and $\left(x + \dfrac{1}{2}\right)(2x - 3) = 0$, then $x =$

    (A) -3
    (B) $-\dfrac{1}{2}$
    (C) 0
    (D) $\dfrac{1}{2}$
    (E) $\dfrac{3}{2}$

161. A certain experimental mathematics program was tried out in 2 classes in each of 32 elementary schools and involved 37 teachers. Each of the classes had 1 teacher and each of the teachers taught at least 1, but not more than 3, of the classes. If the number of teachers who taught 3 classes is n, then the least and greatest possible values of n, respectively, are

    (A)   0 and 13
    (B)   0 and 14
    (C)   1 and 10
    (D)   1 and 9
    (E)   2 and 8

162. For the positive numbers, n, $n + 1$, $n + 2$, $n + 4$, and $n + 8$, the mean is how much greater than the median?

    (A)   0
    (B)   1
    (C) $n + 1$
    (D) $n + 2$
    (E) $n + 3$

163. The present ratio of students to teachers at a certain school is 30 to 1. If the student enrollment were to increase by 50 students and the number of teachers were to increase by 5, the ratio of students to teachers would then be 25 to 1. What is the present number of teachers?

    (A)   5
    (B)   8
    (C)   10
    (D)   12
    (E)   15

164. What is the smallest integer n for which $25^n > 5^{12}$?

    (A)   6
    (B)   7
    (C)   8
    (D)   9
    (E)   10

165. Sixty percent of the members of a study group are women, and 45 percent of those women are lawyers. If one member of the study group is to be selected at random, what is the probability that the member selected is a woman lawyer?

    (A)   0.10
    (B)   0.15
    (C)   0.27
    (D)   0.33
    (E)   0.45

166. Each year for 4 years, a farmer increased the number of trees in a certain orchard by $\dfrac{1}{4}$ of the number of trees in the orchard the preceding year. If all of the trees thrived and there were 6,250 trees in the orchard at the end of the 4-year period, how many trees were in the orchard at the beginning of the 4-year period?

    (A)   1,250
    (B)   1,563
    (C)   2,250
    (D)   2,560
    (E)   2,752

Number of Shipments of Manufactured Homes
in the United States, 1990–2000

167. According to the chart shown, which of the following is closest to the median annual number of shipments of manufactured homes in the United States for the years from 1990 to 2000, inclusive?

    (A) 250,000
    (B) 280,000
    (C) 310,000
    (D) 325,000
    (E) 340,000

168. For the positive integers a, b, and k, $a^k \| b$ means that a^k is a divisor of b, but a^{k+1} is not a divisor of b. If k is a positive integer and $2^k \| 72$, then k is equal to

    (A) 2
    (B) 3
    (C) 4
    (D) 8
    (E) 18

169. A certain characteristic in a large population has a distribution that is symmetric about the mean m. If 68 percent of the distribution lies within one standard deviation d of the mean, what percent of the distribution is less than $m + d$?

    (A) 16%
    (B) 32%
    (C) 48%
    (D) 84%
    (E) 92%

170. Four extra-large sandwiches of exactly the same size were ordered for m students, where $m > 4$. Three of the sandwiches were evenly divided among the students. Since 4 students did not want any of the fourth sandwich, it was evenly divided among the remaining students. If Carol ate one piece from each of the four sandwiches, the amount of sandwich that she ate would be what fraction of a whole extra-large sandwich?

    (A) $\dfrac{m+4}{m(m-4)}$
    (B) $\dfrac{2m-4}{m(m-4)}$
    (C) $\dfrac{4m-4}{m(m-4)}$
    (D) $\dfrac{4m-8}{m(m-4)}$
    (E) $\dfrac{4m-12}{m(m-4)}$

171. Which of the following equations has $1 + \sqrt{2}$ as one of its roots?

    (A) $x^2 + 2x - 1 = 0$
    (B) $x^2 - 2x + 1 = 0$
    (C) $x^2 + 2x + 1 = 0$
    (D) $x^2 - 2x - 1 = 0$
    (E) $x^2 - x - 1 = 0$

172. In Country C, the unemployment rate among construction workers dropped from 16 percent on September 1, 1992, to 9 percent on September 1, 1996. If the number of construction workers was 20 percent greater on September 1, 1996, than on September 1, 1992, what was the approximate percent change in the number of unemployed construction workers over this period?

    (A) 50% decrease
    (B) 30% decrease
    (C) 15% decrease
    (D) 30% increase
    (E) 55% increase

173. In a box of 12 pens, a total of 3 are defective. If a customer buys 2 pens selected at random from the box, what is the probability that neither pen will be defective?

(A) $\frac{1}{6}$

(B) $\frac{2}{9}$

(C) $\frac{6}{11}$

(D) $\frac{9}{16}$

(E) $\frac{3}{4}$

174. At a certain fruit stand, the price of each apple is 40 cents and the price of each orange is 60 cents. Mary selects a total of 10 apples and oranges from the fruit stand, and the average (arithmetic mean) price of the 10 pieces of fruit is 56 cents. How many oranges must Mary put back so that the average price of the pieces of fruit that she keeps is 52 cents?

(A) 1
(B) 2
(C) 3
(D) 4
(E) 5

175. A pharmaceutical company received $3 million in royalties on the first $20 million in sales of the generic equivalent of one of its products and then $9 million in royalties on the next $108 million in sales. By approximately what percent did the ratio of royalties to sales decrease from the first $20 million in sales to the next $108 million in sales?

(A) 8%
(B) 15%
(C) 45%
(D) 52%
(E) 56%

Times at Which the Door
Opened from 8:00 to 10:00

8:00	8:06	8:30	9:05
8:03	8:10	8:31	9:11
8:04	8:18	8:54	9:29
8:04	8:19	8:57	9:31

176. The light in a restroom operates with a 15-minute timer that is reset every time the door opens as a person goes in or out of the room. Thus, after someone enters or exits the room, the light remains on for only 15 minutes unless the door opens again and resets the timer for another 15 minutes. If the times listed above are the times at which the door opened from 8:00 to 10:00, approximately how many minutes during this two-hour period was the light off?

(A) 10
(B) 25
(C) 35
(D) 40
(E) 70

177. If p is the product of the integers from 1 to 30, inclusive, what is the greatest integer k for which 3^k is a factor of p?

(A) 10
(B) 12
(C) 14
(D) 16
(E) 18

178. If $n = 3^8 - 2^8$, which of the following is NOT a factor of n?

(A) 97
(B) 65
(C) 35
(D) 13
(E) 5

179. Club X has more than 10 but fewer than 40 members. Sometimes the members sit at tables with 3 members at one table and 4 members at each of the other tables, and sometimes they sit at tables with 3 members at one table and 5 members at each of the other tables. If they sit at tables with 6 members at each table except one and fewer than 6 members at that one table, how many members will be at the table that has fewer than 6 members?

    (A) 1
    (B) 2
    (C) 3
    (D) 4
    (E) 5

180. In order to complete a reading assignment on time, Terry planned to read 90 pages per day. However, she read only 75 pages per day at first, leaving 690 pages to be read during the last 6 days before the assignment was to be completed. How many days in all did Terry have to complete the assignment on time?

    (A) 15
    (B) 16
    (C) 25
    (D) 40
    (E) 46

181. If $s > 0$ and $\sqrt{\dfrac{r}{s}} = s$, what is r in terms of s?

    (A) $\dfrac{1}{s}$
    (B) $\sqrt{s}$
    (C) $s\sqrt{s}$
    (D) s^3
    (E) $s^2 - s$

182. If $3 < x < 100$, for how many values of x is $\dfrac{x}{3}$ the square of a prime number?

    (A) Two
    (B) Three
    (C) Four
    (D) Five
    (E) Nine

183. A researcher plans to identify each participant in a certain medical experiment with a code consisting of either a single letter or a pair of distinct letters written in alphabetical order. What is the least number of letters that can be used if there are 12 participants, and each participant is to receive a different code?

    (A) 4
    (B) 5
    (C) 6
    (D) 7
    (E) 8

184. An object thrown directly upward is at a height of h feet after t seconds, where $h = -16(t - 3)^2 + 150$. At what height, in feet, is the object 2 seconds after it reaches its maximum height?

    (A)   6
    (B)   86
    (C) 134
    (D) 150
    (E) 166

185. Which of the following is equivalent to the pair of inequalities $x + 6 > 10$ and $x - 3 \le 5$?

    (A) $2 \le x < 16$
    (B) $2 \le x < 4$
    (C) $2 < x \le 8$
    (D) $4 < x \le 8$
    (E) $4 \le x < 16$

186. David has d books, which is 3 times as many as Jeff and $\dfrac{1}{2}$ as many as Paula. How many books do the three of them have altogether, in terms of d?

    (A) $\dfrac{5}{6}d$
    (B) $\dfrac{7}{3}d$
    (C) $\dfrac{10}{3}d$
    (D) $\dfrac{7}{2}d$
    (E) $\dfrac{9}{2}d$

187. There are 8 teams in a certain league and each team plays each of the other teams exactly once. If each game is played by 2 teams, what is the total number of games played?

    (A)   15
    (B)   16
    (C)   28
    (D)   56
    (E)   64

188. At his regular hourly rate, Don had estimated the labor cost of a repair job as $336 and he was paid that amount. However, the job took 4 hours longer than he had estimated and, consequently, he earned $2 per hour less than his regular hourly rate. What was the time Don had estimated for the job, in hours?

    (A)   28
    (B)   24
    (C)   16
    (D)   14
    (E)   12

189. If $\dfrac{p}{q} < 1$, and p and q are positive integers, which of the following must be greater than 1 ?

    (A) $\sqrt{\dfrac{p}{q}}$

    (B) $\dfrac{p}{q^2}$

    (C) $\dfrac{p}{2q}$

    (D) $\dfrac{q}{p^2}$

    (E) $\dfrac{q}{p}$

190. To mail a package, the rate is x cents for the first pound and y cents for each additional pound, where $x > y$. Two packages weighing 3 pounds and 5 pounds, respectively, can be mailed separately or combined as one package. Which method is cheaper, and how much money is saved?

    (A)   Combined, with a savings of $x - y$ cents
    (B)   Combined, with a savings of $y - x$ cents
    (C)   Combined, with a savings of x cents
    (D)   Separately, with a savings of $x - y$ cents
    (E)   Separately, with a savings of y cents

191. If money is invested at r percent interest, compounded annually, the amount of the investment will double in approximately $\dfrac{70}{r}$ years. If Pat's parents invested $5,000 in a long-term bond that pays 8 percent interest, compounded annually, what will be the approximate total amount of the investment 18 years later, when Pat is ready for college?

    (A) $20,000
    (B) $15,000
    (C) $12,000
    (D) $10,000
    (E) $9,000

192. On a recent trip, Cindy drove her car 290 miles, rounded to the nearest 10 miles, and used 12 gallons of gasoline, rounded to the nearest gallon. The actual number of miles per gallon that Cindy's car got on this trip must have been between

    (A) $\dfrac{290}{12.5}$ and $\dfrac{290}{11.5}$

    (B) $\dfrac{295}{12}$ and $\dfrac{285}{11.5}$

    (C) $\dfrac{285}{12}$ and $\dfrac{295}{12}$

    (D) $\dfrac{285}{12.5}$ and $\dfrac{295}{11.5}$

    (E) $\dfrac{295}{12.5}$ and $\dfrac{285}{11.5}$

193. Which of the following inequalities is an algebraic expression for the shaded part of the number line above?

(A) $|x| \le 3$

(B) $|x| \le 5$

(C) $|x - 2| \le 3$

(D) $|x - 1| \le 4$

(E) $|x + 1| \le 4$

194. In a small snack shop, the average (arithmetic mean) revenue was $400 per day over a 10-day period. During this period, if the average daily revenue was $360 for the first 6 days, what was the average daily revenue for the last 4 days?

(A) $420

(B) $440

(C) $450

(D) $460

(E) $480

195. If y is the smallest positive integer such that 3,150 multiplied by y is the square of an integer, then y must be

(A) 2

(B) 5

(C) 6

(D) 7

(E) 14

196. If $[x]$ is the greatest integer less than or equal to x, what is the value of $[-1.6] + [3.4] + [2.7]$?

(A) 3

(B) 4

(C) 5

(D) 6

(E) 7

197. In the first week of the year, Nancy saved $1. In each of the next 51 weeks, she saved $1 more than she had saved in the previous week. What was the total amount that Nancy saved during the 52 weeks?

(A) $1,326

(B) $1,352

(C) $1,378

(D) $2,652

(E) $2,756

198. In a certain sequence, the term x_n is given by the formula $x_n = 2x_{n-1} - \frac{1}{2}(x_{n-2})$ for all $n \ge 2$. If $x_0 = 3$ and $x_1 = 2$, what is the value of x_3?

(A) 2.5

(B) 3.125

(C) 4

(D) 5

(E) 6.75

199. During a trip, Francine traveled x percent of the total distance at an average speed of 40 miles per hour and the rest of the distance at an average speed of 60 miles per hour. In terms of x, what was Francine's average speed for the entire trip?

(A) $\dfrac{180 - x}{2}$

(B) $\dfrac{x + 60}{4}$

(C) $\dfrac{300 - x}{5}$

(D) $\dfrac{600}{115 - x}$

(E) $\dfrac{12,000}{x + 200}$

200. If $n = (33)^{43} + (43)^{33}$, what is the units digit of n?

(A) 0

(B) 2

(C) 4

(D) 6

(E) 8

201. Team A and Team B are competing against each other in a game of tug-of-war. Team A, consisting of 3 males and 3 females, decides to line up male, female, male, female, male, female. The lineup that Team A chooses will be one of how many different possible lineups?

    (A) 9
    (B) 12
    (C) 15
    (D) 36
    (E) 720

202. If $d = \dfrac{1}{2^3 \times 5^7}$ is expressed as a terminating decimal, how many nonzero digits will d have?

    (A) One
    (B) Two
    (C) Three
    (D) Seven
    (E) Ten

203. For any positive integer n, the sum of the first n positive integers equals $\dfrac{n(n+1)}{2}$. What is the sum of all the even integers between 99 and 301 ?

    (A) 10,100
    (B) 20,200
    (C) 22,650
    (D) 40,200
    (E) 45,150

204. November 16, 2001, was a Friday. If each of the years 2004, 2008, and 2012 had 366 days, and the remaining years from 2001 through 2014 had 365 days, what day of the week was November 16, 2014 ?

    (A) Sunday
    (B) Monday
    (C) Tuesday
    (D) Wednesday
    (E) Thursday

205. How many prime numbers between 1 and 100 are factors of 7,150 ?

    (A) One
    (B) Two
    (C) Three
    (D) Four
    (E) Five

206. A sequence of numbers a_1, a_2, a_3, ... is defined as follows: $a_1 = 3$, $a_2 = 5$, and every term in the sequence after a_2 is the product of all terms in the sequence preceding it, e.g., $a_3 = (a_1)(a_2)$ and $a_4 = (a_1)(a_2)(a_3)$. If $a_n = t$ and $n > 2$, what is the value of a_{n+2} in terms of t ?

    (A) $4t$
    (B) t^2
    (C) t^3
    (D) t^4
    (E) t^8

207. Last year the price per share of Stock X increased by k percent and the earnings per share of Stock X increased by m percent, where k is greater than m. By what percent did the ratio of price per share to earnings per share increase, in terms of k and m ?

    (A) $\dfrac{k}{m}\%$
    (B) $(k - m)\%$
    (C) $\dfrac{100(k - m)}{100 + k}\%$
    (D) $\dfrac{100(k - m)}{100 + m}\%$
    (E) $\dfrac{100(k - m)}{100 + k + m}\%$

208. Of the 300 subjects who participated in an experiment using virtual-reality therapy to reduce their fear of heights, 40 percent experienced sweaty palms, 30 percent experienced vomiting, and 75 percent experienced dizziness. If all of the subjects experienced at least one of these effects and 35 percent of the subjects experienced exactly two of these effects, how many of the subjects experienced only one of these effects?

   (A)   105
   (B)   125
   (C)   130
   (D)   180
   (E)   195

209. If $m^{-1} = -\dfrac{1}{3}$, then m^{-2} is equal to

   (A)   −9
   (B)   −3
   (C) $-\dfrac{1}{9}$
   (D) $\dfrac{1}{9}$
   (E)   9

210. A photography dealer ordered 60 Model X cameras to be sold for $250 each, which represents a 20 percent markup over the dealer's initial cost for each camera. Of the cameras ordered, 6 were never sold and were returned to the manufacturer for a refund of 50 percent of the dealer's initial cost. What was the dealer's approximate profit or loss as a percent of the dealer's initial cost for the 60 cameras?

   (A)   7% loss
   (B)   13% loss
   (C)   7% profit
   (D)   13% profit
   (E)   15% profit

211. Seven pieces of rope have an average (arithmetic mean) length of 68 centimeters and a median length of 84 centimeters. If the length of the longest piece of rope is 14 centimeters more than 4 times the length of the shortest piece of rope, what is the maximum possible length, in centimeters, of the longest piece of rope?

   (A)   82
   (B)   118
   (C)   120
   (D)   134
   (E)   152

212. What is the difference between the sixth and the fifth terms of the sequence 2, 4, 7, … whose n^{th} term is $n + 2^{n-1}$?

   (A)   2
   (B)   3
   (C)   6
   (D)   16
   (E)   17

213. From the consecutive integers −10 to 10, inclusive, 20 integers are randomly chosen with repetitions allowed. What is the least possible value of the product of the 20 integers?

   (A) $(-10)^{20}$
   (B) $(-10)^{10}$
   (C)   0
   (D) $-(10)^{19}$
   (E) $-(10)^{20}$

214. The letters D, G, I, I, and T can be used to form 5-letter strings such as DIGIT or DGIIT. Using these letters, how many 5-letter strings can be formed in which the two occurrences of the letter I are separated by at least one other letter?

   (A)   12
   (B)   18
   (C)   24
   (D)   36
   (E)   48

215. $\dfrac{0.99999999}{1.0001} - \dfrac{0.99999991}{1.0003} =$

    (A) 10^{-8}
    (B) $3(10^{-8})$
    (C) $3(10^{-4})$
    (D) $2(10^{-4})$
    (E) 10^{-4}

216. Last Sunday a certain store sold copies of Newspaper A for $1.00 each and copies of Newspaper B for $1.25 each, and the store sold no other newspapers that day. If r percent of the store's revenue from newspaper sales was from Newspaper A and if p percent of the newspapers that the store sold were copies of Newspaper A, which of the following expresses r in terms of p ?

    (A) $\dfrac{100p}{125 - p}$

    (B) $\dfrac{150p}{250 - p}$

    (C) $\dfrac{300p}{375 - p}$

    (D) $\dfrac{400p}{500 - p}$

    (E) $\dfrac{500p}{625 - p}$

217. For the past n days, the average (arithmetic mean) daily production at a company was 50 units. If today's production of 90 units raises the average to 55 units per day, what is the value of n ?

    (A) 30
    (B) 18
    (C) 10
    (D) 9
    (E) 7

218. If a two-digit positive integer has its digits reversed, the resulting integer differs from the original by 27. By how much do the two digits differ?

    (A) 3
    (B) 4
    (C) 5
    (D) 6
    (E) 7

219. In an electric circuit, two resistors with resistances x and y are connected in parallel. In this case, if r is the combined resistance of these two resistors, then the reciprocal of r is equal to the sum of the reciprocals of x and y. What is r in terms of x and y ?

    (A) xy
    (B) $x + y$

    (C) $\dfrac{1}{x + y}$

    (D) $\dfrac{xy}{x + y}$

    (E) $\dfrac{x + y}{xy}$

220. Xavier, Yvonne, and Zelda each try independently to solve a problem. If their individual probabilities for success are $\dfrac{1}{4}$, $\dfrac{1}{2}$, and $\dfrac{5}{8}$, respectively, what is the probability that Xavier and Yvonne, but not Zelda, will solve the problem?

    (A) $\dfrac{11}{8}$

    (B) $\dfrac{7}{8}$

    (C) $\dfrac{9}{64}$

    (D) $\dfrac{5}{64}$

    (E) $\dfrac{3}{64}$

221. If $\dfrac{1}{x} - \dfrac{1}{x+1} = \dfrac{1}{x+4}$, then x could be

    (A) 0
    (B) −1
    (C) −2
    (D) −3
    (E) −4

222. $\left(\dfrac{1}{2}\right)^{-3}\left(\dfrac{1}{4}\right)^{-2}\left(\dfrac{1}{16}\right)^{-1}=$

(A) $\left(\dfrac{1}{2}\right)^{-48}$

(B) $\left(\dfrac{1}{2}\right)^{-11}$

(C) $\left(\dfrac{1}{2}\right)^{-6}$

(D) $\left(\dfrac{1}{8}\right)^{-11}$

(E) $\left(\dfrac{1}{8}\right)^{-6}$

223. List T consists of 30 positive decimals, none of which is an integer, and the sum of the 30 decimals is S. The estimated sum of the 30 decimals, E, is defined as follows. Each decimal in T whose tenths digit is even is rounded up to the nearest integer, and each decimal in T whose tenths digit is odd is rounded down to the nearest integer; E is the sum of the resulting integers. If $\dfrac{1}{3}$ of the decimals in T have a tenths digit that is even, which of the following is a possible value of $E - S$?

I.   −16

II.   6

III.   10

(A)   I only

(B)   I and II only

(C)   I and III only

(D)   II and III only

(E)   I, II, and III

224. If $5-\dfrac{6}{x}=x$, then x has how many possible values?

(A)   None

(B)   One

(C)   Two

(D)   A finite number greater than two

(E)   An infinite number

225. Seed mixture X is 40 percent ryegrass and 60 percent bluegrass by weight; seed mixture Y is 25 percent ryegrass and 75 percent fescue. If a mixture of X and Y contains 30 percent ryegrass, what percent of the weight of the mixture is X?

(A)   10%

(B) $33\dfrac{1}{3}$%

(C)   40%

(D)   50%

(E) $66\dfrac{2}{3}$%

226. How many of the integers that satisfy the inequality $\dfrac{(x+2)(x+3)}{x-2}\geq 0$ are less than 5?

(A)   1

(B)   2

(C)   3

(D)   4

(E)   5

227. Of the 150 houses in a certain development, 60 percent have air-conditioning, 50 percent have a sunporch, and 30 percent have a swimming pool. If 5 of the houses have all three of these amenities and 5 have none of them, how many of the houses have exactly two of these amenities?

(A)   10

(B)   45

(C)   50

(D)   55

(E)   65

228. The value of $\dfrac{2^{-14}+2^{-15}+2^{-16}+2^{-17}}{5}$ is how many times the value of $2^{(-17)}$?

(A) $\dfrac{3}{2}$

(B) $\dfrac{5}{2}$

(C)   3

(D)   4

(E)   5

4.4 Answer Key

1.	B	33.	C	65.	B	97.	C	129.	D
2.	D	34.	C	66.	B	98.	E	130.	D
3.	D	35.	E	67.	D	99.	B	131.	B
4.	C	36.	E	68.	D	100.	E	132.	A
5.	A	37.	D	69.	C	101.	B	133.	D
6.	D	38.	B	70.	E	102.	E	134.	A
7.	E	39.	C	71.	E	103.	B	135.	E
8.	C	40.	C	72.	B	104.	E	136.	E
9.	E	41.	D	73.	C	105.	D	137.	E
10.	B	42.	A	74.	B	106.	B	138.	B
11.	D	43.	B	75.	D	107.	B	139.	B
12.	E	44.	E	76.	A	108.	C	140.	A
13.	D	45.	E	77.	D	109.	A	141.	E
14.	B	46.	E	78.	D	110.	D	142.	E
15.	C	47.	D	79.	D	111.	D	143.	E
16.	E	48.	A	80.	E	112.	E	144.	D
17.	C	49.	E	81.	D	113.	A	145.	C
18.	D	50.	D	82.	B	114.	E	146.	E
19.	E	51.	A	83.	B	115.	B	147.	D
20.	B	52.	D	84.	E	116.	D	148.	D
21.	E	53.	C	85.	E	117.	B	149.	C
22.	B	54.	E	86.	D	118.	E	150.	C
23.	C	55.	B	87.	D	119.	E	151.	A
24.	C	56.	B	88.	B	120.	D	152.	A
25.	C	57.	A	89.	B	121.	E	153.	B
26.	E	58.	D	90.	E	122.	A	154.	E
27.	C	59.	D	91.	E	123.	A	155.	E
28.	B	60.	D	92.	A	124.	E	156.	B
29.	B	61.	E	93.	D	125.	D	157.	B
30.	C	62.	A	94.	C	126.	D	158.	C
31.	A	63.	D	95.	E	127.	D	159.	B
32.	E	64.	C	96.	D	128.	C	160.	B

161.	A	175.	C	189.	E	203.	B	217.	E
162.	B	176.	B	190.	A	204.	A	218.	A
163.	E	177.	C	191.	A	205.	D	219.	D
164.	B	178.	C	192.	D	206.	D	220.	E
165.	C	179.	E	193.	E	207.	D	221.	C
166.	D	180.	B	194.	D	208.	D	222.	B
167.	C	181.	D	195.	E	209.	D	223.	B
168.	B	182.	B	196.	A	210.	D	224.	C
169.	D	183.	B	197.	C	211.	D	225.	B
170.	E	184.	B	198.	C	212.	E	226.	D
171.	D	185.	D	199.	E	213.	E	227.	D
172.	B	186.	C	200.	A	214.	D	228.	C
173.	C	187.	C	201.	D	215.	D		
174.	E	188.	B	202.	B	216.	D		

4.5 Answer Explanations

The following discussion is intended to familiarize you with the most efficient and effective approaches to the kinds of problems common to Quantitative Reasoning questions. The particular questions in this chapter are generally representative of the kinds of Quantitative Reasoning questions you will encounter on the GMAT exam. Remember that it is the problem solving strategy that is important, not the specific details of a particular question.

Questions 1 to 87 - Difficulty: Easy

1. The numbers of cars sold at a certain dealership on six of the last seven business days were 4, 7, 2, 8, 3, and 6, respectively. If the number of cars sold on the seventh business day was either 2, 4, or 5, for which of the three values does the average (arithmetic mean) number of cars sold per business day, for the seven business days, equal the median number of cars sold per day for the seven days?

    I.   2
    II. 4
    III. 5
    (A) II only
    (B) III only
    (C) I and II only
    (D) II and III only
    (E) I, II, and III

Arithmetic Statistics

Listed in numerical order, the given numbers are 2, 3, 4, 6, 7, and 8. If the 7th number were 2 or 4, then the numbers in numerical order would be 2, 2, 3, 4, 6, 7, and 8 or 2, 3, 4, 4, 6, 7, and 8. In either case the median would be 4 and the average would be $\dfrac{2 + 2 + 3 + 4 + 6 + 7 + 8}{7} =$ $\dfrac{32}{7}$ or $\dfrac{2 + 3 + 4 + 4 + 6 + 7 + 8}{7} = \dfrac{34}{7}$, neither of which equals 4. So, for neither of the values in I or II does the average equal the median. If the 7th number were 5, then the

numbers in numerical order would be 2, 3, 4, 5, 6, 7, and 8. The median would be 5 and the average would be $\dfrac{2 + 3 + 4 + 5 + 6 + 7 + 8}{7} = \dfrac{35}{7} = 5$. Thus, for the value in III, the average equals the mean.

The correct answer is B.

Performance Time	Ticket Price	Number of Tickets Sold
Thursday night	$40	200
Friday night	$50	240
Saturday afternoon	$40	220
Saturday night	$50	300

2. The table shows a summary of the ticket sales from four performances of a certain play. What is the difference between the maximum and the minimum ticket-sale revenue from a single performance?

    (A) $4,000
    (B) $5,100
    (C) $6,200
    (D) $7,000
    (E) $9,600

Arithmetic Interpretation of Tables

For each performance, the product of the ticket price and the number of tickets sold is the ticket-sale revenue. The following table shows these values.

Performance Time	Ticket-sale Revenue
Thursday night	200($40) = $8,000
Friday night	240($50) = $12,000
Saturday afternoon	220($40) = $8,800
Saturday night	300($50) = $15,000

From these values it follows that for a single performance, the maximum ticket-sale revenue is $15,000 and the minimum ticket-sale revenue is $8,000, and therefore the difference between these two revenues is $15,000 − $8,000 = $7,000.

The correct answer is D.

3. During a trip that they took together, Carmen, Juan, Maria, and Rafael drove an average (arithmetic mean) of 80 miles each. Carmen drove 72 miles, Juan drove 78 miles, and Maria drove 83 miles. How many miles did Rafael drive?

   (A) 80
   (B) 82
   (C) 85
   (D) 87
   (E) 89

Arithmetic Statistics

Let $C, J, M,$ and R be the numbers of miles, respectively, that Carmen, Juan, Maria, and Rafael drove. Since the average of the numbers of miles they drove is 80, it follows that

$$\frac{C + J + M + R}{4} = 80 \text{, or } C + J + M + R = 4(80)$$

= 320. It is given that $C = 72, J = 78,$ and $M = 83.$ Therefore, $72 + 78 + 83 + R = 320,$ or $R = 87.$

The correct answer is D.

4. Each week, a clothing salesperson receives a commission equal to 15 percent of the first $500 in sales and 20 percent of all additional sales that week. What commission would the salesperson receive on total sales for the week of $1,300 ?

   (A) $195
   (B) $227
   (C) $235
   (D) $260
   (E) $335

Arithmetic Applied Problems

The commission on the total sales can be calculated as follows:

$$\begin{array}{c} \text{commission on} \\ \text{first \$500} \end{array} + \begin{array}{c} \text{commission on} \\ \text{amount over \$500} \end{array}$$

$$= \quad (0.15)(\$500) + (0.20)(\$1{,}300 - \$500)$$

$$= \quad \$75 + \$160$$

Therefore, the commission on the total sales is $75 + $160 = $235.

The correct answer is C.

5. A certain restaurant that regularly advertises through the mail has 1,040 cover letters and 3,000 coupons in stock. In its next mailing, each envelope will contain 1 cover letter and 2 coupons. If all of the cover letters in stock are used, how many coupons will remain in stock after this mailing?

   (A) 920
   (B) 1,040
   (C) 1,500
   (D) 1,960
   (E) 2,080

Arithmetic Applied Problems

In the next mailing there will be 1,040 cover letters and 2(1,040) = 2,080 coupons. Therefore, after the next mailing the number of coupons remaining in stock will be 3,000 − 2,080 = 920.

The correct answer is A.

6. List S consists of 10 consecutive odd integers, and list T consists of 5 consecutive even integers. If the least integer in S is 7 more than the least integer in T, how much greater is the average (arithmetic mean) of the integers in S than the average of the integers in T?

(A)   2
(B)   7
(C)   8
(D)   12
(E)   22

Arithmetic Statistics

Let the integers in S be $s, s + 2, s + 4, \ldots, s + 18$, where s is odd. Let the integers in T be $t, t + 2, t + 4, t + 6, t + 8$, where t is even. Given that $s = t + 7$, it follows that $s - t = 7$. The average of the integers in S is $\dfrac{10s + 90}{10} = s + 9$, and, similarly, the average of the integers in T is $\dfrac{5t + 20}{5} = t + 4$. The difference in these averages is $(s + 9) - (t + 4) = (s - t) + (9 - 4) = 7 + 5 = 12$. Thus, the average of the integers in S is 12 greater than the average of the integers in T.

The correct answer is D.

7. The price of a coat in a certain store is $500. If the price of the coat is to be reduced by $150, by what percent is the price to be reduced?

(A)   10%
(B)   15%
(C)   20%
(D)   25%
(E)   30%

Arithmetic Percents

A reduction of $150 from $500 represents a percent decrease of $\left(\dfrac{150}{500} \times 100 \right)\% = 30\%$.

Therefore, the price of the coat was reduced by 30%.

The correct answer is E.

8. $\left(\dfrac{1}{2} - \dfrac{1}{3} \right) + \left(\dfrac{1}{3} - \dfrac{1}{4} \right) + \left(\dfrac{1}{4} - \dfrac{1}{5} \right) + \left(\dfrac{1}{5} - \dfrac{1}{6} \right) =$

(A) $-\dfrac{1}{6}$
(B)   0
(C) $\dfrac{1}{3}$
(D) $\dfrac{1}{2}$
(E) $\dfrac{2}{3}$

Arithmetic Operations on Rational Numbers

The parentheses can be removed without any change of signs, and after doing this most of the terms can be additively cancelled as shown below.

$$\frac{1}{2} - \frac{1}{3} + \frac{1}{3} - \frac{1}{4} + \frac{1}{4} - \frac{1}{5} + \frac{1}{5} - \frac{1}{6} = \frac{1}{2} - \frac{1}{6}$$
$$= \frac{1}{3}$$

The correct answer is C.

9. While a family was away on vacation, they paid a neighborhood boy $11 per week to mow their lawn and $4 per day to feed and walk their dog. If the family was away for exactly 3 weeks, how much did they pay the boy for his services?

(A) $45
(B) $54
(C) $71
(D) $95
(E) $117

Arithmetic Applied Problems

A period of exactly 3 weeks consists of exactly $3(7) = 21$ days. Therefore, the boy was paid for 3 weeks of mowing the lawn and for 21 days of feeding and walking the dog, for a total pay of $3(\$11) + 21(\$4) = \$33 + \$84 = \$117$.

The correct answer is E.

10. Last year $48,000 of a certain store's profit was shared by its 2 owners and their 10 employees. Each of the 2 owners received 3 times as much as each of their 10 employees. How much did each owner receive from the $48,000?

    (A) $12,000
    (B) $9,000
    (C) $6,000
    (D) $4,000
    (E) $3,000

    Algebra First-Degree Equations

    Let A be the amount received by each owner and let B be the amount received by each employee. From the given information it follows that $A = 3B$ and $2A + 10B = 48,000$. Thus, $2(3B) + 10B = 48,000$, or $16B = 48,000$, or $B = 3,000$. Therefore, the amount received by each owner was $A = 3B = 3(\$3,000) = \$9,000$.

    The correct answer is B.

11. On a vacation, Rose exchanged $500.00 for euros at an exchange rate of 0.80 euro per dollar and spent $\frac{3}{4}$ of the euros she received. If she exchanged the remaining euros for dollars at an exchange rate of $1.20 per euro, what was the dollar amount she received?

    (A) $60.00
    (B) $80.00
    (C) $100.00
    (D) $120.00
    (E) $140.00

    Arithmetic Operations with Rational Numbers

    At the exchange rate of 0.80 euro per dollar, Rose exchanged $500.00 for $(0.80)(500) =$ 400 euros. She spent $\frac{3}{4}(400) = 300$ euros, had $400 - 300 = 100$ euros left, and exchanged them for dollars at the exchange rate of $1.20 per euro. Therefore, the dollar amount she received was $(1.20)(100) = \$120.00$.

    The correct answer is D.

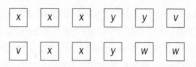

12. Each of the 12 squares shown is labeled x, y, v, or w. What is the ratio of the number of these squares labeled x or y to the number of these squares labeled v or w?

    (A) 1:2
    (B) 2:3
    (C) 4:3
    (D) 3:2
    (E) 2:1

    Arithmetic Ratio and Proportion

    By a direct count, there are 8 squares labeled x or y (5 labeled x, 3 labeled y) and there are 4 squares labeled v or w (2 labeled v, 2 labeled w). Therefore, the ratio of the number of squares labeled x or y to the number of squares labeled v or w is 8:4, which reduces to 2:1.

    The correct answer is E.

Number of Solid-Colored Marbles in Three Jars			
Jar	Number of red marbles	Number of green marbles	Total number of red and green marbles
P	x	y	80
Q	y	z	120
R	x	z	160

13. In the table above, what is the number of green marbles in Jar R?

    (A) 70
    (B) 80
    (C) 90
    (D) 100
    (E) 110

    Arithmetic; Algebra Interpretation of Tables; Applied Problems

    First, set up an equation to find the total number of marbles in the three jars as follows:

    $$x + y + y + z + x + z = 80 + 120 + 160$$
    $$2x + 2y + 2z = 360 \text{ combine the like terms}$$
    $$x + y + z = 180 \text{ divide both sides by 2}$$

Then, since it can be seen from the table that the number of green marbles in Jar R is z, solve for z to answer the problem. To do this most efficiently, use the information from the table for Jar P, which is that $x + y = 80$.

$$x + y + z = 180$$

$$80 + z = 180 \text{ substitute 80 for } x + y$$

$$z = 100$$

The correct answer is D.

14. Bouquets are to be made using white tulips and red tulips, and the ratio of the number of white tulips to the number of red tulips is to be the same in each bouquet. If there are 15 white tulips and 85 red tulips available for the bouquets, what is the greatest number of bouquets that can be made using all the tulips available?

(A) 3
(B) 5
(C) 8
(D) 10
(E) 13

Arithmetic Applied Problems; Properties of Numbers

Because all the tulips are to be used and the same number of white tulips will be in each bouquet, the number of white tulips in each bouquet times the number of bouquets must equal the total number of white tulips, or 15. Thus, the number of bouquets must be a factor of 15, and so the number must be 1, 3, 5, or 15. Also, the number of red tulips in each bouquet times the number of bouquets must equal the total number of red tulips, or 85. Thus, the number of bouquets must be a factor of 85, and so the number must be 1, 5, 17, or 85. Since the number of bouquets must be 1, 3, 5, or 15, and the number of bouquets must be 1, 5, 17, or 85, it follows that the number of bouquets must be 1 or 5, and thus the greatest number of bouquets that can be made is 5. Note that each of the 5 bouquets will have 3 white tulips, because $(5)(3) = 15$, and each of the 5 bouquets will have 17 red tulips, because $(5)(17) = 85$.

The correct answer is B.

15. Over the past 7 weeks, the Smith family had weekly grocery bills of $74, $69, $64, $79, $64, $84, and $77. What was the Smiths' average (arithmetic mean) weekly grocery bill over the 7-week period?

(A) $64
(B) $70
(C) $73
(D) $74
(E) $85

Arithmetic Statistics

The average weekly grocery bill over the 7-week period can be calculated by dividing the total of the 7 weekly grocery bills by 7.

$$= \frac{\$74 + \$69 + \$64 + \$79 + \$64 + \$84 + \$77}{7}$$

$$= \frac{\$511}{7} = \$73$$

An alternate method is suggested by the fact that the bills, in dollars, are close to 70. Note that if all the bills were 70, then the average would be 70. This method makes use of the amount by which the bills are over 70 or under 70.

bill	amount over 70	amount under 70
74	4	*
69	*	1
64	*	6
79	9	*
64	*	6
84	14	*
77	7	*
total	34	13

Therefore, since $34 > 13$, the average is over 70 by $\frac{34 - 13}{7} = \frac{21}{7} = 3$, so 73.

Tip: When calculating an average value where the values are roughly clustered together, it is often quicker to pick a fixed value and add to this fixed value the average of the signed differences from the fixed value. In the solution above, the fixed value was 70 and the signed differences are 4, –1, –6, 9, –6, 14, and 7.

Additional Example: Calculate the average of 99, 102, 101, 98, and 96. Letting 100 be the fixed value, the average can be calculated as follows:

$$100 + \frac{-1 + 2 + 1 - 2 - 4}{5} = 100 - \frac{4}{5}$$
$$= 100 - 0.8 = 99.2$$

Note that these values cluster more closely to 99 than to 100, but 100 is probably simpler to work with.

The correct answer is C.

16. 125% of 5 =

(A) 5.125
(B) 5.25
(C) 6
(D) 6.125
(E) 6.25

Arithmetic Percents

125% of 5 represents $\frac{125}{100} \times 5$, or $1.25 \times 5 = 6.25$.

The correct answer is E.

17. During a recent storm, 9 neighborhoods experienced power failures of durations 34, 29, 27, 46, 18, 25, 12, 35, and 16 minutes, respectively. For these 9 neighborhoods, what was the median duration, in minutes, of the power failures?

(A) 34
(B) 29
(C) 27
(D) 25
(E) 18

Arithmetic Statistics

To determine the median of these 9 numbers, put the numbers in numerical order in a list and determine the middle value in the list:

12, 16, 18, 25, **27**, 29, 34, 35, 46

From this list it follows that the median is 27.

The correct answer is C.

18. When traveling at a constant speed of 32 miles per hour, a certain motorboat consumes 24 gallons of fuel per hour. What is the fuel consumption of this boat at this speed measured in miles traveled per gallon of fuel?

(A) $\frac{2}{3}$

(B) $\frac{3}{4}$

(C) $\frac{4}{5}$

(D) $\frac{4}{3}$

(E) $\frac{3}{2}$

Arithmetic Operations With Rational Numbers

If the motorboat consumes 24 gallons of fuel in 1 hour, then it consumes 1 gallon of fuel in $\frac{1}{24}$ hour. If the motorboat travels 32 miles in 1 hour, then it travels $\frac{32}{24} = \frac{4}{3}$ miles in $\frac{1}{24}$ hour, which is the length of time it takes to consume 1 gallon of fuel. Thus, the motorboat travels $\frac{4}{3}$ miles per gallon of fuel.

The correct answer is D.

19. A technician makes a round-trip to and from a certain service center by the same route. If the technician completes the drive to the center and then completes 10 percent of the drive from the center, what percent of the round-trip has the technician completed?

(A) 5%
(B) 10%
(C) 25%
(D) 40%
(E) 55%

Arithmetic Percents

In completing the drive to the service center, the technician has completed 50% of the round-trip. The drive from the center is the other 50% of the round-trip. In completing 10% of the drive from the center, the technician has completed an additional 10% of 50%, or 5% of the round-trip. Thus, the technician has completed 50% + 5% = 55% of the round-trip.

The correct answer is E.

20. From 2000 to 2003, the number of employees at a certain company increased by a factor of $\frac{1}{4}$. From 2003 to 2006, the number of employees at this company decreased by a factor of $\frac{1}{3}$. If there were 100 employees at the company in 2006, how many employees were there at the company in 2000 ?

   (A)   200
   (B)   120
   (C)   100
   (D)   75
   (E)   60

Algebra First-Degree Equations

Let N be the number of employees in 2000. In 2003 there were $\frac{1}{4}(\text{number in 2000}) = \frac{1}{4}N$ more employees than in 2000, for a total of $N + \frac{1}{4}N = \frac{5}{4}N$ employees. In 2006 there were $\frac{1}{3}(\text{number in 2003}) = \frac{1}{3}\left(\frac{5}{4}\right)N$ fewer employees than in 2003, for a total of $\frac{5}{4}N - \frac{1}{3}\left(\frac{5}{4}N\right) = \frac{5}{6}N$ employees. It is given that there were 100 employees in 2006, so $\frac{5}{6}N = 100$, or $N = \frac{6}{5}(100) = 120$.

The correct answer is B.

21. Which of the following statements must be true about the average (arithmetic mean) and the median of 5 consecutive integers?

   I.   The average is one of the integers.
   II.   The median is one of the integers.
   III. The median equals the average.

   (A)   I only
   (B)   II only
   (C)   III only
   (D)   I and II only
   (E)   I, II, and III

Algebra Statistics

If n is the least of the 5 consecutive integers then, in increasing order, the integers are

$$n,\ n+1,\ n+2,\ n+3,\ n+4.$$

Statement I must be true because the average of the integers is $\dfrac{n+(n+1)+(n+2)+(n+3)+(n+4)}{5}$, or $\dfrac{5n+10}{5} = n+2$, and $n+2$ is one of the integers.

Statement II must be true because the median is the middle number in the list, which is $n+2$, and $n+2$ is one of the integers.

Statement III must be true because $n+2$ is both the average and the median.

The correct answer is E.

22. A collection of 16 coins, each with a face value of either 10 cents or 25 cents, has a total face value of $2.35. How many of the coins have a face value of 25 cents?

   (A)   3
   (B)   5
   (C)   7
   (D)   9
   (E)   11

Algebra First-Degree Equations

Let x represent the number of coins each with a face value of 25 cents. Then, since there are 16 coins in all, $16 - x$ represents the number of coins each with a face value of 10 cents. The total face value of the coins is $2.35 or 235 cents so,

$25x + 10(16 - x) = 235$ given
$25x + 160 - 10x = 235$ distributive property
$15x + 160 = 235$ combine like terms
$15x = 75$ subtract 160 from both sides
$x = 5$ divide both sides by 15

Therefore, 5 of the coins have a face value of 25 cents.

The correct answer is B.

23. A retailer purchased eggs at $2.80 per dozen and sold the eggs at 3 eggs for $0.90. What was the retailer's gross profit from purchasing and selling 5 dozen eggs? (1 dozen eggs = 12 eggs)

   (A) $0.90
   (B) $2.40
   (C) $4.00
   (D) $11.30
   (E) $12.00

Arithmetic Applied Problems

The retailer's cost was $2.80 per dozen eggs and the retailer's revenue was $0.90 per 3 eggs, or 4($0.90) = $3.60 per dozen eggs. Therefore, the retailer's profit for 5 dozen eggs—revenue minus cost for 5 dozen eggs—was 5($3.60 − $2.80) = 5($0.80) = $4.00.

The correct answer is C.

24. In a set of 24 cards, each card is numbered with a different positive integer from 1 to 24. One card will be drawn at random from the set. What is the probability that the card drawn will have either a number that is divisible by both 2 and 3 or a number that is divisible by 7 ?

   (A) $\dfrac{3}{24}$

   (B) $\dfrac{4}{24}$

   (C) $\dfrac{7}{24}$

   (D) $\dfrac{8}{24}$

   (E) $\dfrac{17}{24}$

Arithmetic Probability

The desired probability is N divided by 24, where N is the number of positive integers from 1 through 24 that are either divisible by both 2 and 3, or divisible by 7. Since an integer is divisible by both 2 and 3 if and only if the integer is divisible by 6, it follows that N is the number of positive integers from 1 through 24 that are either divisible by 6 or divisible by 7. There are 4 numbers from 1 through 24 that are divisible by 6, namely 6, 12,

18, and 24. There are 3 numbers from 1 through 24 that are divisible by 7, namely 7, 14, and 21. Since these numbers are all different from each other, it follows that $N = 4 + 3 = 7$ and the desired probability is $\dfrac{N}{24} = \dfrac{7}{24}$.

The correct answer is C.

25. As a salesperson, Phyllis can choose one of two methods of annual payment: either an annual salary of $35,000 with no commission or an annual salary of $10,000 plus a 20% commission on her total annual sales. What must her total annual sales be to give her the same annual pay with either method?

   (A) $100,000
   (B) $120,000
   (C) $125,000
   (D) $130,000
   (E) $132,000

Algebra Applied Problems

Letting s be Phyllis's total annual sales needed to generate the same annual pay with either method, the given information can be expressed as $35,000 = 10,000 + 0.2s$. Solve this equation for s.

   $\$35,000 = \$10,000 + 0.2s$

   $\$25,000 = 0.2s$

   $\$125,000 = s$

The correct answer is C.

26. If $1 < x < y < z$, which of the following has the greatest value?

   (A) $z(x + 1)$
   (B) $z(y + 1)$
   (C) $x(y + z)$
   (D) $y(x + z)$
   (E) $z(x + y)$

Algebra Inequalities

This problem can be solved by calculating each of the options for a fixed and appropriate choice of values of the variables. For example, if $x = 2$, $y = 3$, and $z = 4$, then $1 < x < y < z$ and the values of the options are as follows:

(A) $z(x + 1) = 4(2 + 1) = 12$

(B) $z(y + 1) = 4(3 + 1) = 16$

(C) $x(y + z) = 2(3 + 4) = 14$

(D) $y(x + z) = 3(2 + 4) = 18$

(E) $z(x + y) = 4(2 + 3) = 20$

Alternatively, this problem can also be solved algebraically.

E is greater than each of A and B:

$$z(x + 1) = zx + z \quad < \quad zx + zy = z(x + y)$$
$$\quad\text{A} \qquad\qquad \text{use } 1 < y \qquad\qquad \text{E}$$

$$z(y + 1) = zy + z \quad < \quad zy + zx = z(y + x)$$
$$\quad\text{B} \qquad\qquad \text{use } 1 < x \qquad\qquad \text{E}$$

E is greater than each of C and D:

$$x(y + z) = xy + xz \quad < \quad zy + xz = z(y + x)$$
$$\quad\text{C} \qquad\qquad \text{use } x < z \qquad\qquad \text{E}$$

$$y(x + z) = yx + yz \quad < \quad zx + yz = z(x + y)$$
$$\quad\text{D} \qquad\qquad \text{use } y < z \qquad\qquad \text{E}$$

The correct answer is E.

27. Set X consists of eight consecutive integers. Set Y consists of all the integers that result from adding 4 to each of the integers in set X and all the integers that result from subtracting 4 from each of the integers in set X. How many more integers are there in set Y than in set X?

(A) 0

(B) 4

(C) 8

(D) 12

(E) 16

Arithmetic Operations with Integers

Since the 8 consecutive integers in Set X are not specified, let Set $X = \{3, 4, 5, 6, 7, 8, 9, 10\}$. The following table shows Set X and Set Y whose elements were obtained by adding 4 to each

element of Set X and subtracting 4 from each element of Set X. The elements of Set Y that are also in Set X are marked with an asterisk, *. There are 8 unmarked elements in Set Y, so Set Y has 8 more elements than Set X.

Set X	Set Y	
	Add 4	Subtract 4
3	7*	−1
4	8*	0
5	9*	1
6	10*	2
7	11	3*
8	12	4*
9	13	5*
10	14	6*

The correct answer is C.

28. Of the following, which is the closest to $\dfrac{60.2}{1.03 \times 4.86}$?

(A) 10

(B) 12

(C) 13

(D) 14

(E) 15

Arithmetic Estimation

Replace the three numbers appearing in the expression with three nearby integers that allow the arithmetic operations to be carried out easily to get an approximation.

$$\frac{60.2}{1.03 \times 4.86} \approx \frac{\overset{12}{\cancel{60}}}{1 \times \underset{1}{\cancel{5}}} = \frac{12}{1 \times 1} = 12$$

The correct answer is B.

29. Thabo owns exactly 140 books, and each book is either paperback fiction, paperback nonfiction, or hardcover nonfiction. If he owns 20 more paperback nonfiction books than hardcover nonfiction books, and twice as many paperback fiction books as paperback nonfiction books, how many hardcover nonfiction books does Thabo own?

(A) 10

(B) 20

(C) 30

(D) 40

(E) 50

Algebra Simultaneous First-Degree Equations

Let F represent the number of paperback fiction books that Thabo owns; N_p, the number of paperback nonfiction books; and N_h, the number of hardcover nonfiction books. It is given that $F + N_p + N_h = 140$, $N_p = N_h + 20$, and $F = 2N_p = 2(N_h + 20)$. It follows that

$$F + N_p + N_h = 140 \text{ given}$$
$$2(N_h + 20) + (N_h + 20) + N_h = 140 \text{ by substitution}$$
$$4N_h + 60 = 140 \text{ combine like terms}$$
$$4N_h = 80 \text{ subtract 60 from both sides}$$
$$N_h = 20 \text{ divide both sides by 4}$$

The correct answer is B.

30. If the average (arithmetic mean) of the four numbers 3, 15, 32, and $(N + 1)$ is 18, then $N =$

(A) 19

(B) 20

(C) 21

(D) 22

(E) 29

Arithmetic Statistics

From the given information and the definition of average, it follows that
$$\frac{3 + 15 + 32 + (N + 1)}{4} = 18, \text{ or } \frac{51 + N}{4} = 18.$$
Multiplying both sides of the last equation by 4 gives $51 + N = 72$. Therefore, $N = 72 - 51 = 21$.

The correct answer is C.

31. If $x > 0$, $\dfrac{x}{50} + \dfrac{x}{25}$ is what percent of x?

(A) 6%

(B) 25%

(C) 37%

(D) 60%

(E) 75%

Algebra Arithmetic; Simplifying Algebraic Expressions; Percents

Because we want a percent, use a common denominator of 100 to combine the two terms.
$\dfrac{x}{50} + \dfrac{x}{25} = \dfrac{2x}{100} + \dfrac{4x}{100} = \dfrac{6x}{100} = \left(\dfrac{6}{100}\right)x$, which is 6% of x.

The correct answer is A.

32. During a certain time period, Car X traveled north along a straight road at a constant rate of 1 mile per minute and used fuel at a constant rate of 5 gallons every 2 hours. During this time period, if Car X used exactly 3.75 gallons of fuel, how many miles did Car X travel?

(A) 36

(B) 37.5

(C) 40

(D) 80

(E) 90

Arithmetic Applied Problems

The car used fuel at the rate of 5 gallons every 2 hours, and thus after using 3.75 gallons of fuel, the car had traveled for $(3.75)\left(\dfrac{2}{5}\right)$ hours.

One way to obtain this value is indicated by the calculations in following table.

5 gal	corresponds to	2 hr	Given
1 gal	corresponds to	$\dfrac{2}{5}$ hr	Divide by 5
3.75 gal	corresponds to	$(3.75)\left(\dfrac{2}{5}\right)$ hr	Multiply by 3.75

Since $(3.75)\left(\dfrac{2}{5}\right) = \left(\dfrac{15}{4}\right)\left(\dfrac{2}{5}\right) = \dfrac{3}{2}$ hours = 90 minutes, the car drove for 90 minutes at a rate of 1 mile per minute. Therefore, the total distance the car drove was

distance = rate × time = $\left(1\,\dfrac{\text{mi}}{\text{min}}\right)$ (90 min) = 90 miles.

The correct answer is E.

33. Cheryl purchased 5 identical hollow pine doors and 6 identical solid oak doors for the house she is building. The regular price of each solid oak door was twice the regular price of each hollow pine door. However, Cheryl was given a discount of 25% off the regular price of each solid oak door. If the regular price of each hollow pine door was $40, what was the total price of all 11 doors?

(A) $320
(B) $540
(C) $560
(D) $620
(E) $680

Algebra Applied Problems; Percents

The price of each pine door is $40, so the price of 5 pine doors is 5($40) = $200. The price of each oak door is twice that of a pine door, and thus $80, which becomes (0.75)($80) = $60 when the 25% discount is applied. Therefore, the price of 6 oak doors at the 25% discount is 6($60) = $360, and hence the total price of all 11 doors is $200 + $360 = $560.

The correct answer is C.

34. A certain store will order 25 crates of apples. The apples will be of three different varieties—McIntosh, Rome, and Winesap—and each crate will contain apples of only one variety. If the store is to order more crates of Winesap than crates of McIntosh and more crates of Winesap than crates of Rome, what is the least possible number of crates of Winesap that the store will order?

(A) 7
(B) 8
(C) 9
(D) 10
(E) 11

Arithmetic Applied Problems

Let M, R, and W be the numbers of crates, respectively, of McIntosh, Rome, and Winesap apples. From the given information it follows that $M + R + W = 25$ and $M \le R < W$. Find the least possible value of W such that positive integer values of M, R, and W satisfy these two conditions.

Since the values 8, 8, and 9 for M, R, and W satisfy these two conditions, $W = 9$ is possible. Thus, the least possible value of W is less than or equal to 9. It is not possible for the value of W to be less than 9, since if the value of W were less than 9, then $M + R + W < 25$. This is because in this case, the greatest possible values of M, R, and W would be 7, 7, and 8, which have a sum less than 25. Therefore, the least possible value of W is 9.

The correct answer is C.

35. A bicycle store purchased two bicycles, one for $250 and the other for $375, and sold both bicycles at a total gross profit of $250. If the store sold one of the bicycles for $450, which of the following could be the store's gross profit from the sale of the other bicycle?

(A) $75
(B) $100
(C) $125
(D) $150
(E) $175

Arithmetic Profit and Loss

Let $450 and $R be the individual revenues from selling the two bicycles. Then the unknown profit from selling one of the bicycles is either $R − $250 or $R − $375.

$$\text{total profit} = (\text{total revenue}) - (\text{total cost})$$
$$\$250 = (\$450 + \$R) - (\$250 + \$375)$$
$$\$250 = \$R - \$175$$
$$\$425 = \$R$$

From this it follows that the unknown profit is either $425 − $250 = $175 or $425 − $375 = $50.

The correct answer is E.

36. If $k^2 = m^2$, which of the following must be true?

(A) $k = m$

(B) $k = -m$

(C) $k = |m|$

(D) $k = -|m|$

(E) $|k| = |m|$

Algebra Simplifying Algebraic Expressions

One method of solving this problem is to take the nonnegative square root of both sides of the equation $k^2 = m^2$ and then since $\sqrt{u^2} = |u|$ for all real numbers u, it follows that $|k| = \sqrt{k^2} = \sqrt{m^2} = |m|$.

The table below shows that each of the other answer choices can be true but can also be false. For each pair of values for k and m, it is true that $k^2 = m^2$.

	True for		False for	
	k	m	k	m
A $k = m$	3	3	3	−3
B $k = -m$	−3	3	3	3
C $k = |m|$	3	−3	−3	−3
D $k = -|m|$	−3	−3	3	−3

The correct answer is E.

37. Makoto, Nishi, and Ozuro were paid a total of $780 for waxing the floors at their school. Each was paid in proportion to the number of hours he or she worked. If Makoto worked 15 hours, Nishi worked 20 hours, and Ozuro worked 30 hours, how much was Makoto paid?

(A) $52

(B) $117

(C) $130

(D) $180

(E) $234

Arithmetic Ratio and Proportion

Makoto, Nishi, and Ozuro worked a total of $15 + 20 + 30 = 65$ hours and were paid a total of $780. Since Makoto worked 15 of the 65 hours and he was paid in proportion to the number of hours he worked, his pay was $\frac{15}{65}(\$780)$. To determine which of the answer choices equals this amount of money, note that $\frac{15}{65}$ can be reduced to $\frac{3}{13}$ by dividing the numerator and denominator by 5. Also note that 780 can be factored as $(10)(78) = (10)(2)(39) = (10)(2)(3)(13)$. Then calculate $\frac{3}{\cancel{13}}(10)(2)(3)(\cancel{13}) = (3)(10)(2)(3) = 180$.

Tip: In problems requiring calculations with fractions, it can be helpful to reduce fractions and utilize cancellation, as much as possible.

The correct answer is D.

38. If x is a positive integer and $4^x - 3 = y$, which of the following CANNOT be a value of y?

(A) 1

(B) 7

(C) 13

(D) 61

(E) 253

Arithmetic Exponents

This can be solved by calculating the value of $4^x - 3$ for the first few positive integer values of x.

x	4^x	$4^x - 3$	answer choice
1	4	1	A
2	16	13	C
3	64	61	D
4	256	253	E

Alternatively, this can be solved by observing that 4^x always has units digit 4 or 6—the product of two integers with units digit 4 has units digit 6, the product of two integers with units digit 6 has units digit 4, etc.—and therefore any integer that does not have units digit $4 - 3 = 1$ or $6 - 3 = 3$ cannot be the value of $4^x - 3$ for some positive integer value of x.

The correct answer is B.

39. If $(1 - 1.25)N = 1$, then $N =$

   (A)   −400
   (B)   −140
   (C)   −4
   (D)   4
   (E)   400

Algebra Operations with Rational Numbers

Since $(1 - 1.25)N = -0.25N = -\dfrac{1}{4}N$, the equation becomes $-\dfrac{1}{4}N = 1$, which has solution $N = -4$.

The correct answer is C.

40. The quotient when a certain number is divided by $\dfrac{2}{3}$ is $\dfrac{9}{2}$. What is the number?

   (A) $\dfrac{4}{27}$

   (B) $\dfrac{1}{3}$

   (C)   3

   (D)   6

   (E) $\dfrac{27}{4}$

Arithmetic Operations with Rational Numbers

Let N be the unknown number. The quotient when N is divided by $\dfrac{2}{3}$ is $N \div \dfrac{2}{3}$, which equals $N \times \dfrac{3}{2} = \dfrac{3}{2}N$ (invert and multiply). Since this

quotient equals $\dfrac{9}{2}$, it follows that $\dfrac{3}{2}N = \dfrac{9}{2}$.

Therefore, $N = \left(\dfrac{9}{2}\right)\left(\dfrac{2}{3}\right) = 3$.

Tip: Sometimes a correct method of calculation will be intuitively evident if difficult-to-conceptualize numbers are replaced with easy-to-conceptualize numbers. For example, if the first sentence had instead been "The quotient when a certain number is divided by 2 is 3" (i.e., after dividing a certain number by 2, the result is 3), then it may be intuitively evident that the number can be obtained by multiplying 2 and 3. Thus, for this problem, the number can be obtained by multiplying $\dfrac{2}{3}$ and $\dfrac{9}{2}$.

The correct answer is C.

41. The price of gasoline at a service station increased from $1.65 per gallon last week to $1.82 per gallon this week. Sally paid $26.40 for gasoline last week at the station. How much more will Sally pay this week at the station for the same amount of gasoline?

   (A) $1.70
   (B) $2.55
   (C) $2.64
   (D) $2.72
   (E) $2.90

Arithmetic Applied Problems

Since $1.82 − $1.65 = $0.17, Sally paid $0.17 per gallon more this week than last week. Therefore, the total additional amount that Sally paid this week over last week is the number of gallons Sally purchased times $0.17.

Number of gallons purchased last week:
$$\frac{\text{total paid last week}}{\text{price per gallon last week}} = \frac{26.40}{1.65}$$

Number of gallons purchased this week: $\dfrac{26.40}{1.65}$

Total additional amount paid this week:
$$(\$0.17)\frac{26.40}{1.65} = (\$0.17)(16) = \$2.72.$$

One way to lessen the arithmetic computations is to work with integers and factor.

$$0.17\left(\frac{26.4}{1.65}\right) = \frac{(17)(264)}{1,650}$$ multiply numerator and denominator by 1,000 for ease of calculation

$$= \frac{(17)(3 \times 8 \times 11)}{3 \times 5 \times 11 \times 10}$$ factor

$$= \frac{(17)(\cancel{3} \times 8 \times \cancel{11})}{\cancel{3} \times 5 \times \cancel{11} \times 10}$$ identify common factors

$$= \frac{17 \times 8}{50}$$ cancel common factors

$$= \frac{136}{50}$$ multiply

$$= \frac{13.6}{5}$$ divide numerator and denominator by 10

$$= 2.72$$ divide

The correct answer is D.

Monthly Charge for Low-Use Telephone Contract Offered by Company X

Monthly rate (up to 75 message units)	20% less than standard rate of $10.00
Per unit in excess of 75 message units	$0.065

42. Based on the rates above, how much would Company X charge a customer with a low-use contract for using 95 message units in a month?

(A) $9.30
(B) $11.30
(C) $12.88
(D) $14.88
(E) $16.18

Arithmetic Interpretation of Tables

The low-use contract charge for using 95 message units in a month is the monthly rate plus the charge for messages in excess of 75.

Monthly rate	+ Charge for excess	= Total charge
$(100\% - 20\%)(\$10)$	$+ (95 - 75)(\$0.065)$	=
$(0.8)(\$10)$	$+ (20)(\$0.065)$	=
$8.00	+ $1.30	= $9.30

Note that the product $(20)(0.065)$ can be obtained by multiplying 0.065 by 10 and then doubling the result.

The correct answer is A.

43. If $2x + y = 7$ and $x + 2y = 5$, then $\frac{x+y}{3} =$

(A) 1

(B) $\frac{4}{3}$

(C) $\frac{17}{5}$

(D) $\frac{18}{5}$

(E) 4

Algebra Simultaneous Equations

Adding the equations $2x + y = 7$ and $x + 2y = 5$ gives $3x + 3y = 12$, or $x + y = 4$. Dividing both sides of the last equation by 3 gives $\frac{x+y}{3} = \frac{4}{3}$.

The correct answer is B.

44. City X has a population 4 times as great as the population of City Y, which has a population twice as great as the population of City Z. What is the ratio of the population of City X to the population of City Z?

(A) 1:8
(B) 1:4
(C) 2:1
(D) 4:1
(E) 8:1

Arithmetic Ratio and Proportion

Let X, Y, and Z be the populations of Cities X, Y, and Z, respectively. It is given that $X = 4Y$, and $Y = 2Z$ or $Z = \frac{Y}{2}$. Then, $\frac{X}{Z} = \frac{4Y}{\frac{Y}{2}} = (4Y)\left(\frac{2}{Y}\right) = \frac{8}{1}$.

The correct answer is E.

Tides at Bay Cove on July 13

45. The graph above shows the height of the tide, in feet, above or below a baseline. Which of the following is closest to the difference, in feet, between the heights of the highest and lowest tides on July 13 at Bay Cove?

(A) 1.7
(B) 1.9
(C) 2.2
(D) 2.5
(E) 2.7

Arithmetic Interpretation of Graphs and Tables

From the graph, the highest tide is 2.2 ft above the baseline and the lowest tide is 0.5 ft below the baseline. Therefore, the difference between the heights of the highest tide and the lowest tide is $[2.2 - (-0.5)]$ ft $= (2.2 + 0.5)$ ft $= 2.7$ ft.

The correct answer is E.

46. If $S = 1 + \dfrac{1}{2^2} + \dfrac{1}{3^2} + \dfrac{1}{4^2} + \dfrac{1}{5^2} + \dfrac{1}{6^2} + \dfrac{1}{7^2} + \dfrac{1}{8^2} + \dfrac{1}{9^2} + \dfrac{1}{10^2}$, which of the following is true?

(A) $S > 3$
(B) $S = 3$
(C) $2 < S < 3$
(D) $S = 2$
(E) $S < 2$

Arithmetic Estimation

Because $\dfrac{1}{3^2}$ is less than $\dfrac{1}{2^2}$ and each of $\dfrac{1}{5^2}$,

$\dfrac{1}{6^2}, \dfrac{1}{7^2}, \dfrac{1}{8^2}, \dfrac{1}{9^2}$, and $\dfrac{1}{10^2}$ is less than $\dfrac{1}{4^2}$,

$$1 + \underbrace{\dfrac{1}{2^2} + \dfrac{1}{3^2}}_{< 1 + 2\left(\dfrac{1}{2^2}\right) = 1\dfrac{1}{2}} + \underbrace{\dfrac{1}{4^2} + \dfrac{1}{5^2} + \dfrac{1}{6^2} + \dfrac{1}{7^2} + \dfrac{1}{8^2} + \dfrac{1}{9^2} + \dfrac{1}{10^2}}_{+ 7\left(\dfrac{1}{4^2}\right) = \dfrac{7}{16}}$$

Therefore, $S < 1\dfrac{1}{2} + \dfrac{7}{16} < 2$.

The correct answer is E.

47. A manufacturer of a certain product can expect that between 0.3 percent and 0.5 percent of the units manufactured will be defective. If the retail price is $2,500 per unit and the manufacturer offers a full refund for defective units, how much money can the manufacturer expect to need to cover the refunds on 20,000 units?

(A) Between $15,000 and $25,000
(B) Between $30,000 and $50,000
(C) Between $60,000 and $100,000
(D) Between $150,000 and $250,000
(E) Between $300,000 and $500,000

Arithmetic Applied Problems

The expected number of defective units is between 0.3% and 0.5% of 20,000, or between $(0.003)(20,000) = 60$ and $(0.005)(20,000) = 100$. Since each unit has a retail price of $2,500, the amount of money needed to cover the refunds for the expected number of defective units is between $60($2,500)$ and $100($2,500)$, or between $150,000 and $250,000.

The correct answer is D.

48. Which of the following is closest to $\sqrt{\dfrac{4.2(1,590)}{15.7}}$?

    (A)   20
    (B)   40
    (C)   60
    (D)   80
    (E)   100

Arithmetic Estimation

Replace the numbers that appear with nearly equal values that are perfect squares and then evaluate the resulting expression:

$$\sqrt{\frac{4(1,600)}{16}} = \sqrt{\frac{4 \times \cancel{16} \times 100}{\cancel{16}}} = \sqrt{4 \times 100}$$

$$= \sqrt{4} \times \sqrt{100} = 2 \times 10 = 20$$

The correct answer is **A**.

49. The sum of the weekly salaries of 5 employees is $3,250. If each of the 5 salaries is to increase by 10 percent, then the average (arithmetic mean) weekly salary per employee will increase by

    (A) $52.50
    (B) $55.00
    (C) $57.50
    (D) $62.50
    (E) $65.00

Arithmetic Applied Problems; Percents

Let S_1, S_2, S_3, S_4, and S_5 be the salaries, in dollars, of the 5 employees. Since the sum of the 5 salaries is 3,250, then $S_1 + S_2 + S_3 + S_4 + S_5 = 3,250$ and the average salary is $\dfrac{S_1 + S_2 + S_3 + S_4 + S_5}{5} = \dfrac{3,250}{5} = 650$.

After each salary is increased by 10%, the salaries will be $(1.1)S_1$, $(1.1)S_2$, $(1.1)S_3$, $(1.1)S_4$, and $(1.1)S_5$ and the average salary, in dollars, will be

$$\frac{(1.1)S_1 + (1.1)S_2 + (1.1)S_3 + (1.1)S_4 + (1.1)S_5}{5} =$$

$$1.1 \times \left(\frac{S_1 + S_2 + S_3 + S_4 + S_5}{5} \right) = 1.1 \times 650 = 715.$$

Therefore, the increase in the average salary is $715 − $650 = $65.

The correct answer is **E**.

50. Last week Chris earned x dollars per hour for the first 40 hours worked plus 22 dollars per hour for each hour worked beyond 40 hours. If last week Chris earned a total of 816 dollars by working 48 hours, what is the value of x ?

    (A)   13
    (B)   14
    (C)   15
    (D)   16
    (E)   17

Algebra Applied Problems

Chris worked 40 hours at a rate of $x per hour, $48 − 40 = 8$ hours at a rate of $22 per hour, and earned a total of $816.

$40x + 8(22) = 816$	given information
$40x + 176 = 816$	multiply 8 and 22
$40x = 640$	subtract 176 from both sides
$x = 16$	divide both sides by 40

The correct answer is **D**.

51. The value of $\dfrac{\dfrac{7}{8} + \dfrac{1}{9}}{\dfrac{1}{2}}$ is closest to which of the following?

    (A)   2
    (B) $\dfrac{3}{2}$
    (C)   1
    (D) $\dfrac{1}{2}$
    (E)   0

Arithmetic Estimation

First, note that division by $\dfrac{1}{2}$ is the same as multiplication by $\dfrac{2}{1}$ (invert and multiply), so, $\left(\dfrac{7}{8} + \dfrac{1}{9} \right) \div \dfrac{1}{2} = \left(\dfrac{7}{8} + \dfrac{1}{9} \right) \times \dfrac{2}{1} = \left(\dfrac{7}{8} + \dfrac{1}{9} \right) \times 2$. Then, because the question asks for the value "closest to" and not the exact value, estimate $\left(\dfrac{7}{8} + \dfrac{1}{9} \right) \times 2 \approx \left(\dfrac{7}{8} + \dfrac{1}{8} \right) \times 2$ and calculate $\left(\dfrac{7 + 1}{8} \right) \times 2 = \dfrac{8}{8} \times 2 = 2$.

Alternatively, calculate $\frac{7}{8}+\frac{1}{9}$ using the common denominator of 72, $\frac{7}{8}+\frac{1}{9}=\frac{63}{72}+\frac{8}{72}=\frac{71}{72}$, then estimate $\frac{71}{72}\approx\frac{72}{72}=1$, then calculate $1(2)=2$.

The correct answer is A.

52. The positive two-digit integers x and y have the same digits, but in reverse order. Which of the following must be a factor of $x + y$?

(A) 6
(B) 9
(C) 10
(D) 11
(E) 14

Arithmetic Properties of Numbers

Let m and n be digits. If $x = 10m + n$, then $y = 10n + m$. Adding x and y gives $x + y = (10m + n) + (10n + m) = 11m + 11n = 11(m + n)$, and therefore 11 is a factor of $x + y$.

The correct answer is D.

53. In a certain sequence of 8 numbers, each number after the first is 1 more than the previous number. If the first number is −5, how many of the numbers in the sequence are positive?

(A) None
(B) One
(C) Two
(D) Three
(E) Four

Arithmetic Sequences

The sequence consists of eight consecutive integers beginning with −5:

$$-5,\ -4,\ -3,\ -2,\ -1,\ 0,\ 1,\ 2$$

In this sequence exactly two of the numbers are positive.

The correct answer is C.

54. A total of s oranges are to be packaged in boxes that will hold r oranges each, with no oranges left over. When n of these boxes have been completely filled, what is the number of boxes that remain to be filled?

(A) $s - nr$

(B) $s - \dfrac{n}{r}$

(C) $rs - n$

(D) $\dfrac{s}{n} - r$

(E) $\dfrac{s}{r} - n$

Algebra Algebraic Expressions

If s oranges are packed r oranges to a box with no oranges left over, then the number of boxes that will be filled is $\dfrac{s}{r}$. If n of these boxes are already filled, then $\dfrac{s}{r} - n$ boxes remain to be filled.

The correct answer is E.

55. If $0 < a < b < c$, which of the following statements must be true?

I. $2a > b + c$

II. $c - a > b - a$

III. $\dfrac{c}{a} < \dfrac{b}{a}$

(A) I only
(B) II only
(C) III only
(D) I and II
(E) II and III

Algebra Inequalities

Given $0 < a < b < c$, Statement I is not necessarily true. If, for example, $a = 1$, $b = 2$, and $c = 3$, then $0 < a < b < c$, but $2a = 2(1) < 2 + 3 = b + c$.

Given $0 < a < b < c$, then $c > b$, and subtracting a from both sides gives $c - a > b - a$. Therefore, Statement II is true.

Given $0 < a < b < c$, Statement III is not necessarily true. If, for example, $a = 1$, $b = 2$, and $c = 3$, then $0 < a < b < c$, but $\dfrac{c}{a} = \dfrac{3}{1} > \dfrac{2}{1} = \dfrac{b}{a}$.

The correct answer is B.

	Monday	Tuesday	Wednesday	Thursday
Company A	45	55	50	50
Company B	10	30	30	10
Company C	34	28	28	30
Company D	39	42	41	38
Company E	50	60	60	70

56. The table shows the numbers of packages shipped daily by each of five companies during a 4-day period. The standard deviation of the numbers of packages shipped daily during the period was greatest for which of the five companies?

   (A) A
   (B) B
   (C) C
   (D) D
   (E) E

Arithmetic Statistics

Since the standard deviation of a data set is a measure of how widely the data are scattered about their mean, find the mean number of packages shipped by each company and then calculate the deviations of the company's data from its mean.

For Company A, the mean number of packages shipped is $\dfrac{45 + 55 + 2(50)}{4} = 50$ and the deviations from this mean are -5, 5, 0, and 0. Note that the numbers of packages allow for quick calculations of the means. For example, for Company A the total number of packages is the sum of $45 + 55 = 100$ and $50 + 50 = 100$, and for Company D the total number of packages is the sum of $39 + 41 = 80$ and $42 + 38 = 80$.

The following table shows the means and deviations for the 5 companies.

	mean	deviations from mean
Company A	50	-5, 5, 0, 0
Company B	**20**	**-10, 10, 10, -10**
Company C	30	4, -2, -2, 0
Company D	40	-1, 2, 1, -2
Company E	60	-10, 0, 0, 10

This table shows that the magnitude of each of the 4 deviations for Company B is greater than or equal to the magnitude of any of the other deviations, which strongly suggests that the standard deviation is greatest for Company B.

For those interested, the standard deviations can be calculated as $\sqrt{\dfrac{\text{sum of (deviations)}^2}{4}}$. However, since we only wish to determine which company has the greatest standard deviation, it suffices to calculate the values of "sum of (deviations)^2", because dividing these values by 4 followed by taking a square root will not change their order (that is, the greatest will still be the greatest).

	(deviations)^2	sum of (deviations)^2
Company A	25, 25, 0, 0	50
Company B	**100, 100, 100, 100**	**400**
Company C	16, 4, 4, 0	24
Company D	1, 4, 1, 4	10
Company E	100, 0, 0, 100	200

The correct answer is B.

57. Company Q plans to make a new product next year and sell each unit of this new product at a selling price of $2. The variable costs per unit in each production run are estimated to be 40% of the selling price, and the fixed costs for each production run are estimated to be $5,040. Based on these estimated costs, how many units of the new product will Company Q need to make and sell in order for their revenue to equal their total costs for each production run?

   (A) 4,200
   (B) 3,150
   (C) 2,520
   (D) 2,100
   (E) 1,800

Algebra Applied Problems

Let x be the desired number of units to be sold at a price of $2 each. Then the revenue for selling these units is $2x$, and the total cost for selling these units is $(40\%)(\$2.00)x = \$0.80x$ plus a fixed cost of $5,040.

revenue = total cost   given requirement

$2x = 0.8x + 5,040$ given information

$1.2x = 5,040$ subtract $0.8x$ from both sides

$x = 4,200$ divide both sides by 1.2

The correct answer is A.

58. A small business invests $9,900 in equipment to produce a product. Each unit of the product costs $0.65 to produce and is sold for $1.20. How many units of the product must be sold before the revenue received equals the total expense of production, including the initial investment in equipment?

    (A) 12,000
    (B) 14,500
    (C) 15,230
    (D) 18,000
    (E) 20,000

Arithmetic Rate

Let n be the number of units desired. Then, in dollars, the revenue received is $1.2n$ and the total expense is $9,900 + 0.65n$. These two amounts are equal when $1.2n = 9,900 + 0.65n$, or $0.55n = 9,900$. Therefore,

$$n = \frac{9,900}{0.55} = \frac{990,000}{55} = \frac{90,000}{5} = 18,000.$$

The correct answer is D.

Estimated Number of Home-Schooled
Students by State, January 2001

State	Number (in thousands)
A	181
B	125
C	103
D	79
E	72

59. According to the table shown, the estimated number of home-schooled students in State A is approximately what percent greater than the number in State D?

    (A) 25%
    (B) 55%
    (C) 100%
    (D) 125%
    (E) 155%

Arithmetic Percents

The percent increase from the number in State D to the number in State A is

$$= \left(\frac{181,000 - 79,000}{79,000} \times 100 \right)\% \quad \text{expression for percent increase}$$

$$= \left(\frac{181 - 79}{79} \times 100 \right)\% \quad \text{reduce fraction}$$

$$= \left(\frac{102}{79} \times 100 \right)\% \quad \text{subtract}$$

$$\approx \left(\frac{100}{80} \times 100 \right)\% \quad \text{approximate}$$

$$= (1.25 \times 100)\% \quad \text{divide}$$

$$= 125\% \quad \text{multiply}$$

The correct answer is D.

60. When n liters of fuel were added to a tank that was already $\frac{1}{3}$ full, the tank was filled to $\frac{7}{9}$ of its capacity. In terms of n, what is the capacity of the tank, in liters?

    (A) $\frac{10}{9}n$

    (B) $\frac{4}{3}n$

    (C) $\frac{3}{2}n$

    (D) $\frac{9}{4}n$

    (E) $\frac{7}{3}n$

Algebra Applied Problems

Let C represent the capacity of the tank, in liters. It follows that

$$\frac{1}{3}C + n = \frac{7}{9}C \quad \text{given}$$

$$n = \frac{7}{9}C - \frac{1}{3}C \quad \text{subtract } \frac{1}{3}C \text{ from both sides}$$

$$n = \frac{4}{9}C \quad \text{combine like terms}$$

$$\frac{9}{4}n = C \quad \text{divide both sides by } \frac{4}{9}$$

The correct answer is D.

61. Kevin invested $8,000 for one year at a simple annual interest rate of 6 percent and invested $10,000 for one year at an annual interest rate of 8 percent compounded semiannually. What is the total amount of interest that Kevin earned on the two investments?

    (A) $880
    (B) $1,088
    (C) $1,253
    (D) $1,280
    (E) $1,296

Arithmetic Applied Problems

Interest on $8,000 investment: For simple interest, recall that the amount of interest is

(Principal) × (Interest rate) × (Time)	=	($8,000)(0.06)(1)
	=	$480

Interest on $10,000 investment: For compound interest, recall that the amount of interest is the final investment value minus the principal, which is equal to $P\left(1+\dfrac{r}{n}\right)^{nt} - P$, where

P	=	principal	=	$10,000
r	=	annual interest rate	=	0.08
n	=	periods per year	=	2
t	=	number of years	=	1

Substitute these values and calculate the result:

$$10{,}000\left(1+\dfrac{0.08}{2}\right)^{(2)(1)} - 10{,}000$$

$10{,}000(1.04)^2 - 10{,}000$	arithmetic
$10{,}000(1.04^2 - 1)$	factor out 10,000
$10{,}000(1.0816 - 1)$	square 1.04
$10{,}000(0.0816)$	subtract
816	multiply

Therefore, the total amount of interest on the two investments is $480 + $816 = $1,296.

Tip: The algebraic identity $(a + b)^2 = a^2 + 2ab + b^2$ is sometimes useful in squaring numbers quickly. For example, $1.04^2 = (1 + 0.04)^2$ can be obtained by adding the following three numbers: square of 1, double the product of 1 and 0.04, and square of 0.04. Another example is $305^2 = (300 + 5)^2$.

a	b	a^2	$2ab$	b^2
1	0.04	1	0.08	0.0016
300	5	90,000	3,000	25

Thus, 1.04^2 can be calculated by $1 + 0.08 + 0.0016$ and 305^2 can be calculated by $90{,}000 + 3{,}000 + 25$. The additions are especially easy when, as is the case with these examples, the nonzero digits of the numbers being added all have different place values. This is often the case when b is relatively small compared to a.

The correct answer is E.

62. The harvest yield from a certain apple orchard was 350 bushels of apples. If x of the trees in the orchard each yielded 10 bushels of apples, what fraction of the harvest yield was from these x trees?

    (A) $\dfrac{x}{35}$

    (B) $1 - \dfrac{x}{35}$

    (C) $10x$

    (D) $35 - x$

    (E) $350 - 10x$

Algebra Algebraic Expressions

Since each of the x trees yielded 10 bushels, the total number of bushels yielded by these trees was $10x$. Since the yield of the entire orchard was 350 bushels, $\dfrac{10x}{350} = \dfrac{x}{35}$ was the fraction of the total yield from these x trees.

The correct answer is A.

63. In a certain fraction, the denominator is 16 greater than the numerator. If the fraction is equivalent to 80 percent, what is the denominator of the fraction?

    (A) 32
    (B) 64
    (C) 72
    (D) 80
    (E) 120

Algebra First-Degree Equations

Let n be the numerator of the fraction. Then $n + 16$ is the denominator of the fraction.

From the given information it follows that $\frac{n}{n+16} = 80\%$, which is solved below.

$$\frac{n}{n+16} = \frac{4}{5} \qquad \text{convert 80\% to a fraction}$$

$$5n = 4(n+16) \qquad \text{clear fractions}$$
$$5n = 4n + 64 \qquad \text{simplify}$$
$$n = 64 \qquad \text{subtract } 4n \text{ from both sides}$$

Therefore, the denominator of the fraction is $n + 16 = 64 + 16 = 80$.

The correct answer is D.

64. Greg assembles units of a certain product at a factory. Each day he is paid $2.00 per unit for the first 40 units that he assembles and $2.50 for each additional unit that he assembles that day. If Greg assembled at least 30 units on each of two days and was paid a total of $180.00 for assembling units on the two days, what is the greatest possible number of units that he could have assembled on one of the two days?

(A) 48

(B) 52

(C) 56

(D) 60

(E) 64

Arithmetic Applied Problems

Since the task is to find the greatest number of units Greg could have assembled on one of the days, start by checking the answer choice with the greatest value (in this case, E).

E Number of units assembled on day with greatest number: 64

Pay: 40($2.00) + 24($2.50) = $80.00 + $60.00 = $140.00

Pay for other day: $180.00 − $140.00 = $40

Number of units assembled on other day: $\frac{\$40}{\$2} = 20$

Conclusion: Because 20 < 30, the greatest number is NOT 64.

D Number of units assembled on day with greatest number: 60

Pay: 40($2.00) + 20($2.50) = $80.00 + $50.00 = $130.00

Pay for other day: $180.00 − $130.00 = $50

Number of units assembled on other day: $\frac{\$50}{\$2} = 25$

Conclusion: Because 25 < 30, the greatest number is NOT 60.

C Number of units assembled on day with greatest number: 56

Pay: 40($2.00) + 16($2.50) = $80.00 + $40.00 = $120.00

Pay for other day: $180.00 − $120.00 = $60

Number of units assembled on other day: $\frac{\$60}{\$2} = 30$

Conclusion: Because $30 \geq 30$, the greatest number IS 56.

Note that neither 48 nor 52 can be the greatest because 56 > 48 and 56 > 52.

The correct answer is C.

65. Which of the following is greatest?

(A) $10\sqrt{3}$

(B) $9\sqrt{4}$

(C) $8\sqrt{5}$

(D) $7\sqrt{6}$

(E) $6\sqrt{7}$

Arithmetic Operations on Radical Expressions

Since all the expressions represent positive numbers, the expression that has the greatest squared value will be the expression that has the greatest value.

$\left(10\sqrt{3}\right)^2 = 100 \times 3 = 300$ (not greatest)

$\left(9\sqrt{4}\right)^2 = 81 \times 4 = 324$ (greatest)

$\left(8\sqrt{5}\right)^2 = 64 \times 5 = 320$ (not greatest)

$\left(7\sqrt{6}\right)^2 = 49 \times 6 = 294$ (not greatest)

$\left(6\sqrt{7}\right)^2 = 36 \times 7 = 252$ (not greatest)

The correct answer is B.

66. Al and Ben are drivers for SD Trucking Company. One snowy day, Ben left SD at 8:00 a.m. heading east and Al left SD at 11:00 a.m. heading west. At a particular time later that day, the dispatcher retrieved data from SD's vehicle tracking system. The data showed that, up to that time, Al had averaged 40 miles per hour and Ben had averaged 20 miles per hour. It also showed that Al and Ben had driven a combined total of 240 miles. At what time did the dispatcher retrieve data from the vehicle tracking system?

   (A)   1:00 p.m.
   (B)   2:00 p.m.
   (C)   3:00 p.m.
   (D)   5:00 p.m.
   (E)   6:00 p.m.

Algebra Applied Problems

Let t be the number of hours after 8:00 a.m. that Ben drove. Then Al, who began 3 hours after Ben began and thus drove 3 hours less than Ben, drove $(t - 3)$ hours. First, find the total distance each drove in terms of t.

	rate	time	distance = rate × time
Al	40	$t - 3$	$40(t - 3)$
Ben	20	t	$20t$

Since the combined total distance that Al and Ben drove was 240 miles, it follows that $40(t - 3) + 20t = 240$. Solve for t.

$$
\begin{aligned}
40(t - 3) + 20t &= 240 && \text{given} \\
60t - 120 &= 240 && \text{expand and combine like terms} \\
60t &= 360 && \text{add 120 to both sides} \\
t &= 6 && \text{divide both sides by 60}
\end{aligned}
$$

Therefore, the data was retrieved 6 hours after 8:00 a.m., which was 2:00 p.m.

The correct answer is B.

67. Of the land owned by a farmer, 90 percent was cleared for planting. Of the cleared land, 40 percent was planted with soybeans and 50 percent of the cleared land was planted with wheat. If the remaining 720 acres of cleared land was planted with corn, how many acres did the farmer own?

   (A)   5,832
   (B)   6,480
   (C)   7,200
   (D)   8,000
   (E)   8,889

Arithmetic Applied Problems; Percents

Corn was planted on $100\% - (40\% + 50\%) = 10\%$ of the cleared land, and the cleared land represents 90% of the farmer's land. Therefore, corn was planted on 10% of 90%, or $(0.10)(0.90) = 0.09 = 9\%$, of the farmer's land. It is given that corn was planted on 720 acres, so if x is the number of acres the farmer owns, then $0.09x = 720$ and $x = \dfrac{720}{0.09} = 8,000$.

The correct answer is D.

68. At the start of an experiment, a certain population consisted of 3 animals. At the end of each month after the start of the experiment, the population size was double its size at the beginning of that month. Which of the following represents the population size at the end of 10 months?

   (A) 2^3
   (B) 3^2
   (C) $2(3^{10})$
   (D) $3(2^{10})$
   (E) $3(10^2)$

Arithmetic Applied Problems; Sequences

The population doubles each month, so multiply the previous month's population by 2 to get the next month's population. Thus, at the end of the 1st month the population will be $(3)(2)$, at the end of the 2nd month the population will be $(3)(2)(2)$, at the end of the 3rd month the population will be $(3)(2)(2)(2)$, and so on. Therefore, at the end of the 10th month the population will be the product of 3 and ten factors of 2, which equals $3(2^{10})$.

The correct answer is D.

69. If $\left(\dfrac{1}{3}+\dfrac{1}{4}+\dfrac{1}{5}+\dfrac{1}{6}\right)=r\left(\dfrac{1}{9}+\dfrac{1}{12}+\dfrac{1}{15}+\dfrac{1}{18}\right)$, then $r=$

   (A) $\dfrac{1}{3}$

   (B) $\dfrac{4}{3}$

   (C) 3

   (D) 4

   (E) 12

Arithmetic Operations with Rational Numbers

$$\left(\frac{1}{3}+\frac{1}{4}+\frac{1}{5}+\frac{1}{6}\right) = r\left(\frac{1}{9}+\frac{1}{12}+\frac{1}{15}+\frac{1}{18}\right)$$

$$\left(\frac{1}{3}+\frac{1}{4}+\frac{1}{5}+\frac{1}{6}\right) = r\left(\frac{1}{3}\right)\left(\frac{1}{3}+\frac{1}{4}+\frac{1}{5}+\frac{1}{6}\right)$$

$$1 = r\left(\frac{1}{3}\right)$$

$$3 = r$$

Alternatively,

$$\left(\frac{1}{3}+\frac{1}{4}+\frac{1}{5}+\frac{1}{6}\right) = r\left(\frac{1}{9}+\frac{1}{12}+\frac{1}{15}+\frac{1}{18}\right)$$

$$\left(\frac{20}{60}+\frac{15}{60}+\frac{12}{60}+\frac{10}{60}\right) = r\left(\frac{20}{180}+\frac{15}{180}+\frac{12}{180}+\frac{10}{180}\right)$$

$$\left(\frac{20+15+12+10}{60}\right) = r\left(\frac{20+15+12+10}{180}\right)$$

$$\left(\frac{20+15+12+10}{60}\right)\left(\frac{20+15+12+10}{60}\right)$$
$$\times\left(\frac{180}{20+15+12+10}\right) \times\left(\frac{180}{20+15+12+10}\right) = r$$

$$\frac{180}{60} = r$$

$$3 = r$$

The correct answer is C.

70. If x and y are positive integers such that y is a multiple of 5 and $3x + 4y = 200$, then x must be a multiple of which of the following?

   (A) 3

   (B) 6

   (C) 7

   (D) 8

   (E) 10

Arithmetic Properties of Numbers

Since y is a multiple of 5, consider the following table:

y	$4y$	$3x =$ $200 - 4y$	$x = \dfrac{200 - 4y}{3}$	Is x a positive integer?
5	20	180	60	**yes**
10	40	160	$\dfrac{160}{3}$	no
15	60	140	$\dfrac{140}{3}$	no
20	80	120	40	**yes**
25	100	100	$\dfrac{100}{3}$	no
30	120	80	$\dfrac{80}{3}$	no
35	140	60	20	**yes**
40	160	40	$\dfrac{40}{3}$	no
45	180	20	$\dfrac{20}{3}$	no
50	200	0	0	no

The only positive integers x that satisfy the $3x + 4y = 200$, where y is a multiple of 5, are 60, 40, and 20; each is a multiple of 10.

Note: It is not necessary to perform all of the calculations shown here, nor is it necessary to fill out the table completely. Using "number sense" to see the patterns (e.g., numbers in the second column increase by 20 while numbers in the third column decrease by 20) will shorten the work considerably.

The correct answer is E.

71. Which of the following expressions can be written as an integer?

 I. $\left(\sqrt{82}+\sqrt{82}\right)^2$

 II. $(82)\left(\sqrt{82}\right)$

 III. $\dfrac{\left(\sqrt{82}\right)\left(\sqrt{82}\right)}{82}$

 (A)   None
 (B)   I only
 (C)   III only
 (D)   I and II
 (E)   I and III

Arithmetic Operations with Radical Expressions

Expression I represents an integer because $\left(\sqrt{82}+\sqrt{82}\right)^2 = \left(2\sqrt{82}\right)^2 = (4)(82)$.

Expression II does not represent an integer because $(82)\sqrt{82} = \sqrt{82^3}$ and $82^3 = 2^3 \times 41^3$ is not a perfect square. Regarding this last assertion, note that the square of any integer has the property that each of its distinct prime factors is repeated an even number of times. For example, $24^2 = (2^3 \times 3)^2 = 2^6 \times 3^2$ has the prime factor 2 repeated 6 times and the prime factor 3 repeated twice. Expression III represents an integer, because $\dfrac{\left(\sqrt{82}\right)\left(\sqrt{82}\right)}{82} = \dfrac{82}{82} = 1$.

The correct answer is E.

72. Pumping alone at their respective constant rates, one inlet pipe fills an empty tank to $\dfrac{1}{2}$ of capacity in 3 hours and a second inlet pipe fills the same empty tank to $\dfrac{2}{3}$ of capacity in 6 hours. How many hours will it take both pipes, pumping simultaneously at their respective constant rates, to fill the empty tank to capacity?

 (A)   3.25
 (B)   3.6
 (C)   4.2
 (D)   4.4
 (E)   5.5

Arithmetic Applied Problems

The first pipe can fill $\dfrac{1}{2}$ of the tank in 3 hours, which is equivalent to the rate of filling $\dfrac{1}{2} \div 3 = \dfrac{1}{6}$ of the tank per hour. The second pipe can fill $\dfrac{2}{3}$ of the tank in 6 hours, which is equivalent to the rate of filling $\dfrac{2}{3} \div 6 = \dfrac{1}{9}$ of the tank per hour. Together, they can fill the tank at a rate of $\dfrac{1}{6} + \dfrac{1}{9} = \dfrac{5}{18}$ of the tank per hour. Thus, when both pipes are used at the same time, they will fill the tank in $\dfrac{18}{5} = 3.6$ hours.

The correct answer is B.

73. If $x^2 - 2 < 0$, which of the following specifies all the possible values of x?

 (A) $0 < x < 2$
 (B) $0 < x < \sqrt{2}$
 (C) $-\sqrt{2} < x < \sqrt{2}$
 (D) $-2 < x < 0$
 (E) $-2 < x < 2$

Algebra Inequalities

The corresponding equality $x^2 - 2 = 0$ has two solutions, $x = \sqrt{2}$ and $x = -\sqrt{2}$, and thus there are three intervals to test for inclusion in the solution of the inequality: $x < -\sqrt{2}, -\sqrt{2} < x < \sqrt{2}$, and $x > \sqrt{2}$, labeled I_1, I_2, and I_3, respectively, in the figure below.

Next, choose a value from each of these intervals to test whether the inequality holds:

From I_1, for example, choose $x = -2$; the inequality becomes $(-2)^2 - 2 < 0$ (False).

From I_2, for example, choose $x = 0$; the inequality becomes $(0)^2 - 2 < 0$ (True).

From I_3, for example, choose $x = 2$; the inequality becomes $(2)^2 - 2 < 0$ (False).

Therefore, the solution consists of only values in I_2.

Alternatively, the expression $x^2 - 2$ can be factored as $(x - \sqrt{2})(x + \sqrt{2})$. The value of the factor $(x - \sqrt{2})$ is 0 at $x = \sqrt{2}$, negative for values of x less than $\sqrt{2}$, and positive for values of x greater than $\sqrt{2}$. Similarly, the value of the factor $(x + \sqrt{2})$ is 0 at $x = -\sqrt{2}$, negative for values of x less than $-\sqrt{2}$, and positive for values of x greater than $-\sqrt{2}$. Using the number line, this information can be summarized as shown below:

Then, as shown below, vertical lines through the zeros partition the number line into three intervals I_1, I_2, and I_3.

I_1: $x < -\sqrt{2}$, where both factors are negative, so the product
$(x - \sqrt{2})(x + \sqrt{2})$ is positive.

I_2: $-\sqrt{2} < x < \sqrt{2}$, where one factor is positive and the other is negative, so the
product $(x - \sqrt{2})(x + \sqrt{2})$ is negative.

I_3: $x > \sqrt{2}$, where both factors are positive, so the product
$(x - \sqrt{2})(x + \sqrt{2})$ is positive.

Therefore, the solution consists of only values in I_2.

The correct answer is C.

Book Number	Pages in Book	Total Pages Read
1	253	253
2	110	363
3	117	480
4	170	650
5	155	805
6	50	855
7	205	1,060
8	70	1,130
9	165	1,295
10	105	1,400
11	143	1,543
12	207	1,750

74. Shawana made a schedule for reading books during 4 weeks (28 days) of her summer vacation. She has checked out 12 books from the library. The number of pages in each book and the order in which she plans to read the books are shown in the table above. She will read exactly 50 pages each day. The only exception will be that she will never begin the next book on the same day that she finishes the previous one, and therefore on some days she may read fewer than 50 pages. At the end of the 28th day, how many books will Shawana have finished?

(A) 7

(B) 8

(C) 9

(D) 10

(E) 11

Arithmetic Operations with Integers

Book 1: 6 days—50 pages on each of Days 1–5, 3 pages on Day 6 [5(50) + 3 = 253]

Book 2: 3 days—50 pages on each of Days 7 and 8, 10 pages on Day 9 [2(50) + 10 = 110]

Book 3: 3 days—50 pages on each of Days 10 and 11, 17 pages on Day 12 [2(50) + 17 = 117]

Book 4: 4 days—50 pages on each of Days 13–15, 20 pages on Day 16 [3(50) + 20 = 170]

Book 5: 4 days—50 pages on each of Days 17–19, 5 pages on Day 20 [3(50) + 5 = 155]

Book 6: 1 day—50 pages on Day 21 [1(50) = 50]

Book 7: 5 days—50 pages on each of Days 22–25, 5 pages on Day 26 [4(50) + 5 = 205]

Book 8: 2 days—50 pages on Day 27, 20 pages on Day 28 [50 + 20 = 70]

At this point, Shawana has read on a total of 28 days and has finished 8 books.

The correct answer is B.

75. In Western Europe, x bicycles were sold in each of the years 1990 and 1993. The bicycle producers of Western Europe had a 42 percent share of this market in 1990 and a 33 percent share in 1993. Which of the following represents the decrease in the annual number of bicycles produced and sold in Western Europe from 1990 to 1993?

(A) 9% of $\dfrac{x}{100}$

(B) 14% of $\dfrac{x}{100}$

(C) 75% of $\dfrac{x}{100}$

(D) 9% of x

(E) 14% of x

Arithmetic Percents

Of the x bicycles sold in Western Europe in 1990, 42% of them were produced in Western Europe. It follows that the number of bicycles produced and sold in Western Europe in 1990 was 0.42x. Similarly, of the x bicycles sold in Western Europe in 1993, 33% were produced in Western Europe. It follows that the number of bicycles produced and sold in Western Europe in 1993 was 0.33x. Therefore, the decrease in the annual number of bicycles produced and sold in Western Europe from 1990 to 1993 was 0.42x − 0.33x = 0.09x, which is 9% of x.

The correct answer is D.

76. If k is a positive integer, what is the remainder when $(k + 2)(k^3 − k)$ is divided by 6 ?

(A) 0

(B) 1

(C) 2

(D) 3

(E) 4

Algebra Properties of Numbers

Since k can be any positive integer, the remainder must be the same regardless of the value of k. If $k = 2$, for example, then $(k + 2)(k^3 − k) = (2 + 2)(2^3 − 2) = (4)(6)$, which is a multiple of 6, and therefore, the remainder when divided by 6 is 0.

Alternatively, factor the given expression:

$$(k + 2)(k^3 − k) = (k + 2)(k)(k^2 − 1)$$
$$= (k + 2)(k)(k + 1)(k − 1)$$

Now, rearrange the factors in ascending order $(k − 1)(k)(k + 1)(k + 2)$, and observe that for any positive integer k, the factors are four consecutive integers, two of which are even and one of which is divisible by 3. Therefore, $(k + 2)(k^3 − k)$ is divisible by both 2 and 3. Thus, $(k + 2)(k^3 − k)$ is divisible by 6 with 0 remainder.

The correct answer is A.

77. Which of the following fractions is closest to $\dfrac{1}{2}$?

(A) $\dfrac{4}{7}$

(B) $\dfrac{5}{9}$

(C) $\dfrac{6}{11}$

(D) $\dfrac{7}{13}$

(E) $\dfrac{9}{16}$

Arithmetic Fractions

A fraction equals $\dfrac{1}{2}$ if its numerator is half its denominator. Thus, to compare the answer choices with $\dfrac{1}{2}$, rewrite $\dfrac{1}{2}$ to have the same denominators as the answer choices. This will allow for an easy determination of the distance to $\frac{1}{2}$.

answer choice	value	rewrite of $\frac{1}{2}$	distance to $\frac{1}{2}$
A	$\frac{4}{7}$	$\frac{3.5}{7}$	$\frac{0.5}{7}$
B	$\frac{5}{9}$	$\frac{4.5}{9}$	$\frac{0.5}{9}$
C	$\frac{6}{11}$	$\frac{5.5}{11}$	$\frac{0.5}{11}$
D	$\frac{7}{13}$	$\frac{6.5}{13}$	$\frac{0.5}{13}$
E	$\frac{9}{16}$	$\frac{8}{16}$	$\frac{1}{16}$

Clearly, $\frac{0.5}{13}$ is smaller than each of $\frac{0.5}{7}$, $\frac{0.5}{9}$, and $\frac{0.5}{11}$ because the numerators are equal, and thus larger denominators correspond to smaller values. Also, $\frac{0.5}{13} = \frac{1}{26}$ is smaller than $\frac{1}{16}$. Therefore, $\frac{7}{13}$ is closest to $\frac{1}{2}$.

The correct answer is D.

78. If $p \neq 0$ and $p - \dfrac{1-p^2}{p} = \dfrac{r}{p}$, then $r =$

(A) $p + 1$
(B) $2p - 1$
(C) $p^2 + 1$
(D) $2p^2 - 1$
(E) $p^2 + p - 1$

Algebra Simplifying Algebraic Expressions

$p - \dfrac{1-p^2}{p} = \dfrac{r}{p}$	given
$p^2 - (1 - p^2) = r$	multiply both sides by p
$2p^2 - 1 = r$	combine like terms

The correct answer is D.

79. If the range of the six numbers 4, 3, 14, 7, 10, and x is 12, what is the difference between the greatest possible value of x and the least possible value of x ?

(A) 0
(B) 2
(C) 12
(D) 13
(E) 15

Arithmetic Statistics

The range of the six numbers 3, 4, 7, 10, 14, and x is 12. If x were neither the greatest nor the least of the six numbers, then the greatest and least of the six numbers would be 14 and 3. But, this cannot be possible because the range of the six numbers would be $14 - 3 = 11$ and not 12 as stated. Therefore, x must be either the greatest or the least of the six numbers. If x is the greatest of the six numbers, then 3 is the least, and $x - 3 = 12$. It follows that $x = 15$. On the other hand, if x is the least of the six numbers, then 14 is the greatest, and $14 - x = 12$. It follows that $x = 2$. Thus, there are only two possible values of x, namely 15 and 2, and so the difference between the greatest and least possible values of x is $15 - 2 = 13$.

The correct answer is D.

80. What number is 108 more than two-thirds of itself?

(A) 72
(B) 144
(C) 162
(D) 216
(E) 324

Algebra First-Degree Equations

Let x be the number that is 108 more than two-thirds of itself. Then, $108 + \frac{2}{3}x = x$. Solve for x as follows:

$$108 + \frac{2}{3}x = x$$

$$108 = \frac{1}{3}x$$

$$324 = x$$

The correct answer is E.

81. A service provider charges c dollars for the first 50 hours of service used per month and 40 cents for each 30 minutes in excess of 50 hours used during the month. If x is an integer greater than 50, which of the following expressions gives this service provider's charge, in dollars, for a month in which x hours of service were used?

(A) $c + 0.40x$

(B) $c + 0.80x$

(C) $c + 0.40(x - 50)$

(D) $c + 0.80(x - 50)$

(E) $c + 0.40(2x - 50)$

Algebra Algebraic Expressions

For x hours of service used in the month, the charge is c dollars for the first 50 hours used, leaving $(x - 50)$ hours to be charged at 40 cents per half hour, which is equivalent to 80 cents per hour. Therefore, the total charge, in dollars, for a month in which x hours of service were used is $c + 0.80(x - 50)$.

The correct answer is D.

82. A salesperson who had been driving at a speed of 100 kilometers per hour slowed down to a speed of 47 kilometers per hour. Approximately how many miles per hour was the speed reduced? (1 kilometer ≈ 0.625 mile)

(A)   29

(B)   33

(C)   53

(D)   63

(E)   75

Arithmetic Measurement Conversion

$$(100 - 47)\ \frac{\text{km}}{\text{hr}} \qquad \text{amount of reduction}$$

$$53\ \frac{\text{km}}{\text{hr}} \qquad \text{subtract}$$

$$\left(53\ \frac{\text{km}}{\text{hr}}\right)\left(0.625\ \frac{\text{mi}}{\text{km}}\right) \qquad 1\ \text{km} = 0.625\ \text{mi}$$

$$(50)(0.6)\ \frac{\text{mi}}{\text{hr}} \qquad \text{estimate}$$

$$30\ \frac{\text{mi}}{\text{hr}} \qquad \text{multiply}$$

From the calculations it follows that speed was reduced, in miles per hour, by a little more than 30; among the answer choices, only 33 is a reasonable choice. The exact value is 33.125, and this can be found by multiplying 53 and 0.625 or, since $(53)\left(\dfrac{625}{1{,}000}\right) = (53)\left(\dfrac{5}{8}\right) = \dfrac{265}{8}$, dividing 265 by 8.

The correct answer is B.

83. Company P had 15 percent more employees in December than it had in January. If Company P had 460 employees in December, how many employees did it have in January?

(A)   391

(B)   400

(C)   410

(D)   423

(E)   445

Arithmetic Percents

It is given that 460 is 115% of the number of employees in January. Therefore, the number of employees in January was

$$\frac{460}{1.15} = \frac{460}{1.15}\left(\frac{100}{100}\right) = \left(\frac{460}{115}\right)(100) = (4)(100) = 400.$$

The correct answer is B.

	Recording Time	Viewing Time
Tuesday	4 hours	None
Wednesday	None	1 to 2 hours
Thursday	2 hours	None
Friday	None	2 to 3 hours

84. The table above shows the numbers of hours of television programs that Jane recorded last week and the numbers of hours she spent viewing these recorded programs. No recorded program was viewed more than once. If h is the number of hours of recorded programs she had not yet viewed by the end of Friday, which of the following intervals represents all of the possible values of h?

(A) $0 \le h \le 1$

(B) $1 \le h \le 2$

(C) $2 \le h \le 3$

(D) $0 \le h \le 2$

(E) $1 \le h \le 3$

Arithmetic Inequalities

By the end of Friday Jane had recorded a total of $4 + 2 = 6$ hours of programs, and she had viewed between $1 + 2 = 3$ hours and $2 + 3 = 5$ hours of these programs. Therefore, the number of hours of recorded programs that Jane had not yet viewed by the end of Friday was between $6 - 5 = 1$ and $6 - 3 = 3$.

The correct answer is E.

85. A dance troupe has a total of 50 dancers split into 2 groups. The costumes worn by Group A cost $80 each, and those worn by Group B cost $90 each. If the total cost of all the costumes is $4,270, what is the total cost of the costumes worn by Group B ?

(A) $1,840

(B) $2,070

(C) $2,135

(D) $2,160

(E) $2,430

Algebra Applied Problems; First-Degree Equations

Let n be the number of dancers in Group B. Then the number of dancers in Group A is $50 - n$, and we are given that $(50 - n)(\$80) + (n)(\$90) = \$4,270$.

$(50 - n)(80) + 90n = 4{,}270$	given
$(50 - n)(8) + 9n = 427$	divide both sides by 10
$400 - 8n + 9n = 427$	distributive law
$n = 27$	combine like terms and subtract 400 from each side

Therefore, the total cost of the costumes worn by Group B is $27(\$90) = \$2,430$.

The correct answer is E.

86. A doctor prescribed 18 cubic centimeters of a certain drug to a patient whose body weight was 120 pounds. If the typical dosage is 2 cubic centimeters per 15 pounds of body weight, by what percent was the prescribed dosage greater than the typical dosage?

(A) 8%

(B) 9%

(C) 11%

(D) 12.5%

(E) 14.8%

Arithmetic Percents

If the typical dosage is 2 cubic centimeters per 15 pounds of body weight, then the typical dosage for a person who weighs 120 pounds is $2\left(\dfrac{120}{15}\right) = 2(8) = 16$ cubic centimeters. The prescribed dosage of 18 cubic centimeters is, therefore, $\left(\left(\dfrac{18 - 16}{16}\right) \times 100\right)\%$ or 12.5% greater than the typical dosage.

The correct answer is D.

87. The function f is defined by $f(x) = \sqrt{x} - 10$ for all positive numbers x. If $u = f(t)$ for some positive numbers t and u, what is t in terms of u ?

(A) $\sqrt{\sqrt{u} + 10}$

(B) $\left(\sqrt{u} + 10\right)^2$

(C) $\sqrt{u^2 + 10}$

(D) $(u + 10)^2$

(E) $(u^2 + 10)^2$

Algebra Functions

Because $f(x) = \sqrt{x} - 10$ it follows that $f(t) = \sqrt{t} - 10$. The problem states that $u = f(t)$, so by substitution $u = \sqrt{t} - 10$. To express t in terms of u, isolate t on one side of the equation:

u	$=$	$\sqrt{t} - 10$	given
$u + 10$	$=$	$\sqrt{t}$	add 10 to both sides
$(u + 10)^2$	$=$	t	square both sides

Therefore, t in terms of u is $(u + 10)^2$.

The correct answer is D.

88. The average distance between the Sun and a certain planet is approximately 2.3×10^{14} inches. Which of the following is closest to the average distance between the Sun and the planet, in kilometers? (1 kilometer is approximately 3.9×10^4 inches.)

(A) 7.1×10^8

(B) 5.9×10^9

(C) 1.6×10^{10}

(D) 1.6×10^{11}

(E) 5.9×10^{11}

Arithmetic Measurement Conversion

Convert to kilometers and then estimate.

$$(2.3 \times 10^{14} \text{ in})\left(\frac{1 \text{ km}}{3.9 \times 10^4 \text{ in}}\right) = \frac{2.3 \times 10^{14}}{3.9 \times 10^4} \text{ km}$$

$$= \frac{2.3}{3.9} \times 10^{14-4} \text{ km}$$

$$\approx \frac{2}{4} \times 10^{10}$$

$$= 0.5 \times 10^{10}$$

$$= 5 \times 10^9$$

The correct answer is B.

89. If m is the average (arithmetic mean) of the first 10 positive multiples of 5 and if M is the median of the first 10 positive multiples of 5, what is the value of $M - m$?

(A) -5

(B) 0

(C) 5

(D) 25

(E) 27.5

Arithmetic Statistics

The first 10 positive multiples of 5 are 5, 10, 15, 20, 25, 30, 35, 40, 45, and 50. From this, the average of the 10 multiples, that is, $\frac{\text{sum of values}}{\text{number of values}}$, can be calculated:

$$m = \frac{5+10+15+20+25+30+35+40+45+50}{10}$$

$$= \frac{275}{10} = 27.5.$$

Since there is an even number of multiples, the median, M, is the average of the middle two numbers, 25 and 30:

$$M = \frac{25+30}{2} = 27.5 .$$

Therefore, the median minus the average is:

$$M - m = 27.5 - 27.5 = 0.$$

This problem can also be solved as follows. Since the values can be grouped in pairs (i.e., 5 and 50, 10 and 45, 15 and 40, etc.), each of which is symmetric with respect to the median, it follows that the mean and median are equal.

The correct answer is B.

90. According to a survey of 200 people, 60 enjoy skiing and 80 enjoy skating. If the number of people who enjoy neither skiing nor skating is 2 times the number of people who enjoy both skiing and skating, how many people surveyed enjoy neither skiing nor skating?

(A) 20

(B) 40

(C) 50

(D) 80

(E) 120

Algebra Sets

Determine the number of people who enjoy neither skiing nor skating.

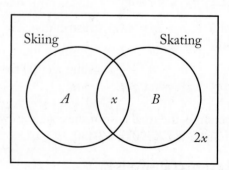

Consider the Venn diagram above, where A represents the number of people who enjoy skiing only, B represents the number of people who enjoy skating only, and x is the number of people who enjoy both skiing and skating. As stated, the number of people who enjoy neither is twice the number who enjoy both, so $2x$ represents the number of people who enjoy neither skiing nor skating. From the given information, it follows that $60 = A + x$, $80 = B + x$, and $200 = A + x + B + 2x = (A + x) + (B + x) + x$. By substitution, $200 = 60 + 80 + x$, so $x = 60$ and $2x = 120$.

The correct answer is E.

$$m \oplus p = n$$
$$n \oplus r = m$$
$$n \oplus q = q$$
$$p \oplus q = p$$
$$q \oplus p = r$$

91. If the relations shown hold for the operation $\oplus$ and the numbers m, n, p, q, and r, then $[(m \oplus p) \oplus q] \oplus p =$

(A) m

(B) n

(C) p

(D) q

(E) r

Algebra Formulas

$$[(m \oplus p) \oplus q] \oplus p \quad \text{given}$$
$$[n \oplus q] \oplus p \quad m \oplus p = n$$
$$q \oplus p \quad n \oplus q = q$$
$$r \quad q \oplus p = r$$

The correct answer is E.

92. To rent a tractor, it costs a total of x dollars for the first 24 hours, plus y dollars per hour for each hour in excess of 24 hours. Which of the following represents the cost, in dollars, to rent a tractor for 36 hours?

(A) $x + 12y$

(B) $x + 36y$

(C) $12x + y$

(D) $24x + 12y$

(E) $24x + 36y$

Algebra Algebraic Expressions

Determine the cost to rent a tractor for 36 hours if the cost is x dollars for the first 24 hours and y dollars for each hour in excess of 24 hours.

The cost will be x dollars for the first 24 hours plus y dollars for each of $36 - 24 = 12$ hours. Thus the total cost of renting the tractor for 36 hours is $(x + 12y)$ dollars.

The correct answer is A.

93. If the mass of 1 cubic centimeter of a certain substance is 7.3 grams, what is the mass, in kilograms, of 1 cubic meter of this substance? (1 cubic meter = 1,000,000 cubic centimeters; 1 kilogram = 1,000 grams)

(A) 0.0073

(B) 0.73

(C) 7.3

(D) 7,300

(E) 7,300,000

Arithmetic Measurement Conversion

Determine the mass, in kilograms, of 1 cubic meter of a substance if the mass of 1 cubic centimeter of this substance is 7.3 grams.

1 cubic meter is 1,000,000 cubic centimeters and each cubic centimeter has a mass of 7.3 grams, so 1 cubic meter has a mass of $7.3(1,000,000) = 7,300,000$ grams. Then, since 1 kilogram = 1,000 grams,

$$7,300,000 \text{ grams} = \frac{7,300,000}{1,000}$$
$$= 7,300 \text{ kilograms.}$$

The correct answer is D.

94. If $z \neq 0$ and $z + \dfrac{1 - 2z^2}{z} = \dfrac{w}{z}$, then $w =$

(A) $z + 1$

(B) $z^2 + 1$

(C) $-z^2 + 1$

(D) $-z^2 + z + 1$

(E) $-2z^2 + 1$

Algebra Simplifying Algebraic Expressions

Multiplying both sides of $\frac{w}{z} = z + \frac{1-2z^2}{z}$ by z

gives $w = z\left(z + \frac{1-2z^2}{z}\right) = z^2 + (1 - 2z^2) = 1 - z^2$.

The correct answer is C.

95. For all real numbers a, b, c, d, e, and f, the operation Θ is defined by the equation $(a, b, c) \Theta (d, e, f) = ad + be + cf$. What is the value of $(1, -2, 3) \Theta \left(1, -\frac{1}{2}, \frac{1}{3}\right)$?

(A) -1

(B) $\frac{5}{6}$

(C) 1

(D) $\frac{5}{2}$

(E) 3

Algebra Formulas

By definition, $(1, -2, 3) \Theta \left(1, -\frac{1}{2}, \frac{1}{3}\right) =$

$(1)(1) + (-2)\left(-\frac{1}{2}\right) + (3)\left(\frac{1}{3}\right) = 1 + 1 + 1 = 3$.

The correct answer is E.

96. If m and p are positive integers and $m^2 + p^2 < 100$, what is the greatest possible value of mp ?

(A) 36

(B) 42

(C) 48

(D) 49

(E) 51

Arithmetic Operations with Integers

Trying various integer values for m and corresponding values of p that satisfy $m^2 + p^2 < 100$ might be the quickest way to solve this problem. First, $m < 10$ and $p < 10$; otherwise, $m^2 + p^2 < 100$ is not true.

If $m = 9$, then for $m^2 + p^2 < 100$ to be true, $p < \sqrt{100-81} = \sqrt{19}$, so $p \leq 4$, and the greatest possible value for mp is $(9)(4) = 36$.

Similarly, if $m = 8$, then $p < \sqrt{100-64} = \sqrt{36}$, so $p \leq 5$, and the greatest possible value for mp is $(8)(5) = 40$.

If $m = 7$, then $p < \sqrt{100-49} = \sqrt{51}$, so $p \leq 7$, and the greatest possible value for mp is $(7)(7) = 49$.

If $m = 6$, then $p < \sqrt{100-36} = \sqrt{64}$, so $p \leq 7$, and the greatest possible value for mp is $(6)(7) = 42$.

If $m \leq 5$ and $p \leq 9$, it follows that $mp \leq 45$.

Thus, the greatest possible value for mp is 49.

The correct answer is D.

97. If $= \frac{x}{y} = \frac{c}{d}$ and $\frac{d}{c} = \frac{b}{a}$, which of the following must be true?

I. $\frac{y}{x} = \frac{b}{a}$

II. $\frac{x}{a} = \frac{y}{b}$

III. $\frac{y}{a} = \frac{x}{b}$

(A) I only

(B) II only

(C) I and II only

(D) I and III only

(E) I, II, and III

Algebra Ratio and Proportion

Equation I is true:

$\frac{x}{y} = \frac{c}{d}$	given
$\frac{y}{x} = \frac{d}{c}$	take reciprocals
$\frac{d}{c} = \frac{b}{a}$	given
$\frac{y}{x} = \frac{b}{a}$	use last two equations

Equation II is true:

$\frac{y}{x} = \frac{b}{a}$	Equation I (shown true)

$$y = \frac{bx}{a} \qquad \text{multiply both sides by } x$$

$$\frac{y}{b} = \frac{x}{a} \qquad \text{divide both sides by } b$$

Equation III is false, since otherwise it would follow that:

$$y = \frac{bx}{a} \qquad \text{from earlier}$$

$$\frac{y}{a} = \frac{bx}{a^2} \qquad \text{divide both sides by } a$$

$$\frac{x}{b} = \frac{bx}{a^2} \qquad \text{use Equation III (assumed true)}$$

$$x = \frac{b^2 x}{a^2} \qquad \text{multiply both sides by } b$$

From this it follows that Equation III will hold only if $\frac{b^2}{a^2} = 1$, which can be false. For example, if $x = a = c = 1$ and $y = b = d = 2$ (a choice of values for which $\frac{x}{y} = \frac{c}{d}$ and $\frac{d}{c} = \frac{b}{a}$ are true), then $\frac{b^2}{a^2} \neq 1$ and Equation III is $\frac{2}{1} = \frac{1}{2}$, which is false.

The correct answer is C.

98. If k is an integer and $(0.0025)(0.025)(0.00025) \times 10^k$ is an integer, what is the least possible value of k ?

(A)   −12
(B)   −6
(C)   0
(D)   6
(E)   12

Arithmetic Properties of Numbers

Let $N = (0.0025)(0.025)(0.00025) \times 10^k$. Rewriting each of the decimals as an integer times a power of 10 gives $N = (25 \times 10^{-4})(25 \times 10^{-3})(25 \times 10^{-5}) \times 10^k = (25)^3 \times 10^{k-12}$. Since the units digit of $(25)^3$ is 5, it follows that if $k = 11$, then the tenths digit of N would be 5, and thus N would not be an integer; and if $k = 12$, then N would be $(25)^3 \times 10^0 = (25)^3$, which is an integer. Therefore, the least value of k such that N is an integer is 12.

The correct answer is E.

99. If $a(a + 2) = 24$ and $b(b + 2) = 24$, where $a \neq b$, then $a + b =$

(A)   −48
(B)   −2
(C)   2
(D)   46
(E)   48

Algebra Second-Degree Equations

$$a(a + 2) = 24 \qquad \text{given}$$
$$a^2 + 2a = 24 \qquad \text{use distributive property}$$
$$a^2 + 2a - 24 = 0 \qquad \text{subtract 24 from both sides}$$
$$(a + 6)(a - 4) = 0 \qquad \text{factor}$$

So, $a + 6 = 0$, which means that $a = -6$, or $a - 4 = 0$, which means $a = 4$. The equation with the variable b has the same solutions, and so $b = -6$ or $b = 4$.

Since $a \neq b$, then $a = -6$ and $b = 4$, which means $a + b = -6 + 4 = -2$, or $a = 4$ and $b = -6$, which means that $a + b = 4 + (-6) = -2$

The correct answer is B.

100. In a recent election, Ms. Robbins received 8,000 votes cast by independent voters, that is, voters not registered with a specific political party. She also received 10 percent of the votes cast by those voters registered with a political party. If N is the total number of votes cast in the election and 40 percent of the votes cast were cast by independent voters, which of the following represents the number of votes that Ms. Robbins received?

(A) $0.06N + 3,200$
(B) $0.1N + 7,200$
(C) $0.4N + 7,200$
(D) $0.1N + 8,000$
(E) $0.06N + 8,000$

Algebra Percents

If N represents the total number of votes cast and 40% of the votes cast were cast by independent voters, then 60% of the votes cast, or $0.6N$ votes, were cast by voters registered with a political party. Ms. Robbins received 10% of these, and so Ms. Robbins received $(0.10)(0.6N) = 0.06N$ votes cast by voters registered with a political party.

Thus, Ms. Robbins received 0.06*N* votes cast by voters registered with a political party and 8,000 votes cast by independent voters, so she received 0.06*N* + 8,000 votes in all.

The correct answer is E.

101. The profit *P*, in dollars, for any given month at a certain company is defined by *P* = *I* − *C*, where *I* represents total income, in dollars, and *C* represents total costs, in dollars, for the month. For each of the first 4 months of the year, *C* = *I* + 32,000; and for each of the next 3 months, *I* = *C* + 36,000. If *I* = *C* + 10,000 for each of the 5 remaining months of the year, what was the company's total profit for the 12-month year?

    (A) $10,000
    (B) $30,000
    (C) $40,000
    (D) $50,000
    (E) $70,000

Arithmetic Applied Problems

For each of the first 4 months, total costs exceeded total income by $32,000, and hence for each of 4 months total profit was −$32,000. Also, for each of the next 3 months, total income exceeded total costs by $36,000, and hence for each of 3 months total profit was $36,000. Finally, for each of the remaining 5 months, total income exceeded total costs by $10,000, and hence for each of 5 months total profit was $10,000. Therefore, the total profit for the 12-month year was 4(−$32,000) + 3($36,000) + 5($10,000) = $30,000.

Alternatively, the given equations can be easily manipulated to obtain the values of *I* − *C* for each month, as shown below.

Given Equation	Value of *I* − *C*	Number of Months	Net Profit
C = *I* + 32,000	*I* − *C* = −32,000	4	−$128,000
I = *C* + 36,000	*I* − *C* = 36,000	3	$108,000
I = *C* + 10,000	*I* − *C* = 10,000	5	$50,000

Adding the values in the right-most column gives the total profit for the 12-month year: −$128,000 + $108,000 + $50,000 = $30,000.

The correct answer is B.

102. A manufacturer makes and sells 2 products, P and Q. The revenue from the sale of each unit of P is $20.00 and the revenue from the sale of each unit of Q is $17.00. Last year the manufacturer sold twice as many units of Q as P. What was the manufacturer's average (arithmetic mean) revenue per unit sold of these 2 products last year?

    (A) $28.50
    (B) $27.00
    (C) $19.00
    (D) $18.50
    (E) $18.00

Arithmetic Statistics

Let *x* represent the number of units of Product P the manufacturer sold last year. Then 2*x* represents the number of units of Product Q the manufacturer sold last year, and *x* + 2*x* = 3*x* represents the total number of units of Products P and Q the manufacturer sold last year. The total revenue from the sale of Products P and Q was $(20*x*) + $(17(2*x*)) = $(54*x*), so the average revenue per unit sold was $\frac{\$(54x)}{3x}$ = $18.

The correct answer is E.

103. A worker carries jugs of liquid soap from a production line to a packing area, carrying 4 jugs per trip. If the jugs are packed into cartons that hold 7 jugs each, how many jugs are needed to fill the last partially filled carton after the worker has made 17 trips?

    (A) 1
    (B) 2
    (C) 4
    (D) 5
    (E) 6

Arithmetic Remainders

Carrying 4 jugs per trip, the worker carries a total of 4(17) = 68 jugs in 17 trips. At 7 jugs per carton, these jugs will completely fill 9 cartons with 5 jugs left over since $(9)(7) + 5 = 68$. To fill the 10th carton, $7 - 5 = 2$ jugs are needed.

The correct answer is B.

104. Last year a state senate consisting of only Republican and Democrat members had 20 more Republican members than Democrat members. This year the senate has the same number of members as last year, but it has 2 fewer Republican members than last year. If this year the number of Republican members is $\frac{2}{3}$ the number of senate members, how many members does the senate have this year?

    (A)   33

    (B)   36

    (C)   42

    (D)   45

    (E)   48

Algebra First-Degree Equations

Let D be the number of Democrat members last year. Then $D + 20$ is the number of Republican members last year and $(D + 20) - 2 = D + 18$ is the number of Republican members this year. Since the total number of members this year is the same as last year, it follows that there are 2 more Democrat members this year than last year, and so the number of Democrat members this year is $D + 2$ and the total number of members this year is $2D + 20$. Using the fact that this year the number of Republican members is $\frac{2}{3}$ the total number of members, the value of D can be found.

$D + 18 = \frac{2}{3}(2D + 20)$	given
$3(D + 18) = 2(2D + 20)$	multiply both sides by 3
$3D + 54 = 4D + 40$	distributive law
$D = 14$	subtract both $3D$ and 40 from both sides

Therefore, the total number of members this year is $2D + 20 = 2(14) + 20 = 48$.

The correct answer is E.

105. Sam has $800 in his account. He will deposit $1 in his account one week from now, $2 two weeks from now, and each week thereafter he will deposit an amount that is $1 greater than the amount that he deposited one week before. If there are no other transactions, how much money will Sam have in his account 50 weeks from now?

    (A) $850

    (B) $1,200

    (C) $1,675

    (D) $2,075

    (E) $3,350

Arithmetic Series and Sequences

Determine the amount Sam will have in his account after 50 weeks if the account starts with $800 and Sam deposits $1 more each week than he deposited the week before.

Sam's deposits over the 50-week period will be $1 + 2 + 3 + \ldots + 48 + 49 + 50 = (1 + 50) + (2 + 49) + (3 + 48) + \ldots + (25 + 26) = (25)(51) = \$1,275$. Thus, after 50 weeks Sam will have $\$800 + \$1,275 = \$2,075$.

The correct answer is D.

106. A certain state's milk production was 980 million pounds in 2007 and 2.7 billion pounds in 2014. Approximately how many more million <u>gallons</u> of milk did the state produce in 2014 than in 2007? (1 billion $= 10^9$ and 1 gallon $= 8.6$ pounds.)

    (A)   100

    (B)   200

    (C)   1,700

    (D)   8,200

    (E)   14,800

Arithmetic Measurement Conversion

Using 2.7 billion $= 2,700$ million, the amount of increase in millions of gallons can be calculated as follows.

The amount of increase is:
$(2,700 - 980)$ million pounds $= 1,720$ million pounds

To convert pounds into gallons:

$$(1{,}720 \text{ million } \cancel{\text{pounds}})\left(\frac{1 \text{ gallon}}{8.6 \ \cancel{\text{pounds}}}\right)$$

$$= 200 \text{ million gallons}$$

The correct answer is B.

107. Working simultaneously and independently at an identical constant rate, 4 machines of a certain type can produce a total of x units of product P in 6 days. How many of these machines, working simultaneously and independently at this constant rate, can produce a total of $3x$ units of product P in 4 days?

(A)   24

(B)   18

(C)   16

(D)   12

(E)   8

Algebra Applied Problems

Define a *machine day* as 1 machine working for 1 day. Then, 4 machines each working 6 days is equivalent to $(4)(6) = 24$ machine days. Thus, x units of product P were produced in 24 machine days, and $3x$ units of product P will require $(3)(24) = 72$ machine days, which is equivalent to $\frac{72}{4} = 18$ machines working independently and simultaneously for 4 days.

The correct answer is B.

108. The symbol Δ denotes one of the four arithmetic operations: addition, subtraction, multiplication, or division. If $6 \Delta 3 \leq 3$, which of the following must be true?

  I. $2 \Delta 2 = 0$

  II. $2 \Delta 2 = 1$

  III. $4 \Delta 2 = 2$

(A)   I only

(B)   II only

(C)   III only

(D)   I and II only

(E)   I, II, and III

Arithmetic Operations with Integers

If Δ represents addition, subtraction, multiplication, or division, then $6 \Delta 3$ is equal to either $6 + 3 = 9$, or $6 - 3 = 3$, or $6 \times 3 = 18$, or $6 \div 3 = 2$. Since it is given that $6 \Delta 3 \leq 3$, Δ represents either subtraction or division.

Statement I is true for subtraction since $2 - 2 = 0$ but not true for division since $2 \div 2 = 1$.

Statement II is not true for subtraction since $2 - 2 = 0$ but is true for division since $2 \div 2 = 1$.

Statement III is true for subtraction since $4 - 2 = 2$ and is true for division since $4 \div 2 = 2$. Therefore, only Statement III must be true.

The correct answer is C.

109. If $mn \neq 0$ and 25 percent of n equals $37\frac{1}{2}$ percent of m, what is the value of $\frac{12n}{m}$?

(A)   18

(B) $\frac{32}{3}$

(C)   8

(D)   3

(E) $\frac{9}{8}$

Algebra Percents; First-Degree Equations

It is given that $(25\%)n = (37.5\%)m$, or $0.25n = 0.375m$. The value of $\frac{12n}{m}$ can be found by first finding the value of $\frac{n}{m}$ and then multiplying the result by 12. Doing this gives $\frac{12n}{m} = \left(\frac{0.375}{0.25}\right)(12) = 18$. Alternatively, the numbers involved allow for a series of simple equation transformations to be carried out, such as the following:

$0.25n = 0.375m$	given
$25n = 37.5m$	multiply both sides by 100
$50n = 75m$	multiply both sides by 2
$2n = 3m$	divide both sides by 25
$12n = 18m$	multiply both sides by 6
$\frac{12n}{m} = 18$	divide both sides by m

The correct answer is A.

110. Last year Joe grew 1 inch and Sally grew 200 percent more than Joe grew. How many inches did Sally grow last year?

    (A) 0
    (B) 1
    (C) 2
    (D) 3
    (E) 4

Arithmetic Percents

Joe grew 1 inch last year and Sally grew 200 percent more than Joe grew, so Sally grew 1 inch plus 200 percent of 1 inch or $1 + 2(1) = 3$ inches.

The correct answer is D.

Technique	Percent of Consumers
Television ads	35%
Coupons	22%
Store displays	18%
Samples	15%

111. The table shows partial results of a survey in which consumers were asked to indicate which one of six promotional techniques most influenced their decision to buy a new food product. Of those consumers who indicated one of the four techniques listed, what fraction indicated either coupons or store displays?

    (A) $\dfrac{2}{7}$

    (B) $\dfrac{1}{3}$

    (C) $\dfrac{2}{5}$

    (D) $\dfrac{4}{9}$

    (E) $\dfrac{1}{2}$

Arithmetic Percents; Ratio and Proportion

Let T be the total number of consumers who were asked. Then the table shows $35\% + 22\% + 18\% + 15\% = 90\%$ of this total, or $0.9T$ consumers. Also, the number of consumers

who indicated either coupons or store displays was $0.22T + 0.18T = 0.4T$. Therefore, the number of consumers who indicated either coupons or store displays divided by the number of consumers shown in the table is $\dfrac{0.4T}{0.9T} = \dfrac{4}{9}$.

The correct answer is D.

112. If 65 percent of a certain firm's employees are full-time and if there are 5,100 more full-time employees than part-time employees, how many employees does the firm have?

    (A)   8,250
    (B)   10,200
    (C)   11,050
    (D)   16,500
    (E)   17,000

Algebra Simultaneous Equations

Let T represent the total number of employees the firm has; F, the number of full-time employees; and P, the number of part-time employees. Since 65 percent of the firm's employees are full-time, it follows that 35 percent are part-time. Thus, $F = 0.65T$ and $P = 0.35T$. However, $F = P + 5,100$, so $0.65T = 0.35T + 5,100$, so $0.30T = 5,100$, and $T = \dfrac{5,100}{0.30} = 17,000$.

The correct answer is E.

113. The cost C, in dollars, to remove p percent of a certain pollutant from a pond is estimated by using the formula $C = \dfrac{100,000p}{100 - p}$. According to this estimate, how much more would it cost to remove 90 percent of the pollutant from the pond than it would cost to remove 80 percent of the pollutant?

    (A) $500,000
    (B) $100,000
    (C) $50,000
    (D) $10,000
    (E) $5,000

Algebra; Arithmetic Simplifying Algebraic Expressions; Operations on Rational Numbers

Removing 90% of the pollutant from the pond would cost $\dfrac{(100,000)(90)}{100-90} = \dfrac{9,000,000}{10} =$ 900,000 dollars, and removing 80% of the pollutant would cost $\dfrac{(100,000)(80)}{100-80} =$ $\dfrac{8,000,000}{20} = 400,000$ dollars. The difference is, then, $900,000 - \$400,000 = \$500,000$.

The correct answer is A.

114. If $xy \neq 0$ and $x^2y^2 - xy = 6$, which of the following could be y in terms of x?

I. $\dfrac{1}{2x}$

II. $-\dfrac{2}{x}$

III. $\dfrac{3}{x}$

(A) I only
(B) II only
(C) I and II
(D) I and III
(E) II and III

Algebra Second-Degree Equations

$$x^2y^2 - xy = 6 \quad \text{given}$$
$$x^2y^2 - xy - 6 = 0 \quad \text{subtract 6 from both sides}$$
$$(xy + 2)(xy - 3) = 0 \quad \text{factor}$$

So, $xy + 2 = 0$, which means $xy = -2$ and $y = -\dfrac{2}{x}$, or $xy - 3 = 0$, which means that $xy = 3$ and $y = \dfrac{3}{x}$. Thus, y in terms of x could be given by the expressions in II or III.

The correct answer is E.

115. $\sqrt{4.8 \times 10^9}$ is closest in value to

(A) 2,200
(B) 70,000
(C) 220,000
(D) 7,000,000
(E) 22,000,000

Arithmetic Operations on Radical Expressions

$$\sqrt{4.8} \times \sqrt{10^9} = \sqrt{48 \times 10^8} \quad \text{substitute } 48 \times 10^8 \text{ for } 4.8 \times 10^9$$

$$= \sqrt{48} \times \sqrt{10^8} \quad \sqrt{ab} = \sqrt{a} \times \sqrt{b}$$

$$\approx \sqrt{49} \times \sqrt{10^8} \quad 49 \approx 48$$

and then

$$\sqrt{49} \times \sqrt{10^8} = 7 \times 10^4 \quad \sqrt{49} = 7,\ \sqrt{10^8} = \sqrt{(10^4)^2} = 10^4$$

$$= 70,000$$

The correct answer is B.

116. In a certain high school, 80 percent of the seniors are taking calculus, and 60 percent of the seniors who are taking calculus are also taking physics. If 10 percent of the seniors are taking neither calculus nor physics, what percent of the seniors are taking physics?

(A) 40%
(B) 42%
(C) 48%
(D) 58%
(E) 80%

Arithmetic Sets

Determine what percent of the seniors at a certain high school are taking physics.

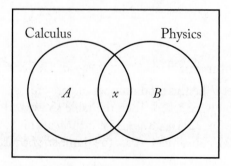

Consider the prior Venn diagram, where A represents the percent of the seniors who are taking calculus only, B represents the percent of the seniors who are taking physics only, and x is the percent of the seniors who are taking both calculus and physics. As stated, 80 percent of the seniors are taking calculus, so $A + x = 0.8$, and 60 percent of the seniors taking calculus are taking physics, so $x = (0.8)(0.6) = 0.48$. Also, $A + x + B = 0.9$ since 10 percent of the seniors are taking neither calculus nor physics. It follows that $B = 0.9 - (A + x) = 0.9 - 0.8 = 0.1$. Therefore, the percent of the seniors who are taking physics is given by $B + x = 0.1 + 0.48 = 0.58$ or 58 percent.

The correct answer is D.

117. If the units digit of $\dfrac{5,610.37}{10^k}$ is 6, what is the value of k?

    (A)   3
    (B)   2
    (C)   1
    (D)   −1
    (E)   −2

Arithmetic Exponents

As shown in the table below, the units digit of $\dfrac{5,610.37}{10^k}$ is 6 when $k = 2$.

$$\frac{5,610.37}{10^{-2}} = \frac{5,610.37}{0.01} = 561,03\mathbf{7}$$

$$\frac{5,610.37}{10^{-1}} = \frac{5,610.37}{0.1} = 56,103.7$$

$$\frac{5,610.37}{10^{0}} = \frac{5,610.37}{1} = 5,61\mathbf{0}.37$$

$$\frac{5,610.37}{10^{1}} = \frac{5,610.37}{10} = 56\mathbf{1}.037$$

$$\frac{5,610.37}{10^{2}} = \frac{5,610.37}{100} = 5\mathbf{6}.1037$$

$$\frac{5,610.37}{10^{3}} = \frac{5,610.37}{1,000} = \mathbf{5}.61037$$

The correct answer is B.

118. Three printing presses, R, S, and T, working together at their respective constant rates, can do a certain printing job in 4 hours. S and T, working together at their respective constant rates, can do the same job in 5 hours. How many hours would it take R, working alone at its constant rate, to do the same job?

    (A)   8
    (B)   10
    (C)   12
    (D)   15
    (E)   20

Algebra Applied Problems

Let r be the portion of the job that printing press R, working alone, completes in 1 hour; and let s and t be the corresponding portions, respectively, for printing press S and printing press T. From the given information, it follows that $r + s + t = \dfrac{1}{4}$ and $s + t = \dfrac{1}{5}$. Subtracting these two equations gives $r = \dfrac{1}{4} - \dfrac{1}{5} = \dfrac{1}{20}$. It follows that printing press R, working alone, will complete $\dfrac{1}{20}$ of the job in 1 hour, and therefore printing press R, working alone, will complete the job in 20 hours.

The correct answer is E.

Results of a Poll

Company	Number Who Own Stock in the Company
AT&T	30
IBM	48
GM	54
FORD	75
US Air	83

119. In a poll, 200 subscribers to *Financial Magazine X* indicated which of five specific companies they own stock in. The results are shown in the table above. If 15 of the 200 own stock in both IBM and AT&T, how many of those polled own stock in neither company?

(A)   63
(B)   93
(C)   107
(D)   122
(E)   137

Arithmetic Sets; Interpretation of Tables

Since 48 of the 200 subscribers polled own stock in IBM and 15 of these 48 subscribers also own stock in AT&T, it follows that 48 − 15 = 33 subscribers own stock in IBM but not in AT&T, as shown in the Venn diagram below. Similarly, 30 − 15 = 15 of the 200 subscribers own stock in AT&T but not in IBM. Therefore, if n is the number of those polled who do not own stock in either IBM or AT&T, then 33 + 15 + 15 + n = 200, or n = 137.

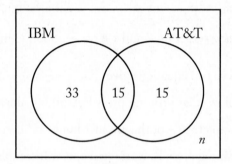

The correct answer is E.

---

120. The sum of all the integers k such that −26 < k < 24 is

(A)   0
(B)   −2
(C)   −25
(D)   −49
(E)   −51

Arithmetic Operations on Integers

In the sum of all integers k such that −26 < k < 24, the positive integers from 1 through 23 can be paired with the negative integers from −1 through −23. The sum of these pairs is 0 because $a + (-a) = 0$ for all integers a. Therefore, the sum of all integers k such that −26 < k < 24 is −25 + (−24) + (23)(0) = −49.

The correct answer is D.

---

121. The number line shown contains three points R, S, and T, whose coordinates have absolute values r, s, and t, respectively. Which of the following equals the average (arithmetic mean) of the coordinates of the points R, S, and T?

(A) s
(B) $s + t - r$
(C) $\dfrac{r - s - t}{3}$
(D) $\dfrac{r + s + t}{3}$
(E) $\dfrac{s + t - r}{3}$

Arithmetic Absolute Value; Number Line

Because point R is to the left of 0 on the number line, the coordinate of R is negative. It is given that r is the absolute value of the coordinate of R and so the coordinate of R is $-r$. Because points S and T are to the right of 0 on the number line, their coordinates are positive. It is given that s and t are the absolute values of the coordinates of S and T, and so the coordinates of S and T are s and t. The arithmetic mean of the coordinates of R, S, and T is $\dfrac{s + t - r}{3}$.

The correct answer is E.

---

122. Mark and Ann together were allocated n boxes of cookies to sell for a club project. Mark sold 10 boxes less than n and Ann sold 2 boxes less than n. If Mark and Ann have each sold at least one box of cookies, but together they have sold less than n boxes, what is the value of n?

(A)   11
(B)   12
(C)   13
(D)   14
(E)   15

Algebra Inequalities

Mark sold $n - 10$ boxes and Ann sold $n - 2$ boxes. Because each person sold at least one box, it follows that $n - 10 \geq 1$ and $n - 2 \geq 1$, which implies that

$n \geq 11$. On the other hand, together they sold less than n boxes, so $(n - 10) + (n - 2) < n$, which implies that $n < 12$. Therefore, n is an integer such that $n \geq 11$ and $n < 12$, which implies that $n = 11$.

The correct answer is A.

$$
\begin{array}{r}
3P5 \\
+\ 4QR \\
\hline
8S4
\end{array}
$$

123. In the correctly worked addition problem shown, P, Q, R, and S are digits. If $Q = 2P$, which of the following could be the value of S?

(A) 3
(B) 4
(C) 5
(D) 7
(E) 9

Arithmetic Place Value

Step 1: Analysis of the units column.

By considering the sum of the unit digits, $5 + R = 4$ or $5 + R = 14$. Since $R \geq 0$, we have $5 + R \geq 5$, and thus $5 + R = 4$ is not possible. Therefore, $5 + R = 14$. It follows that $R = 9$ and 1 is carried to the tens column.

Step 2: Analysis of the tens and hundreds columns.

Since $3 + 4 = 7$ and the hundreds digit of $8S4$ is 8, it follows that 1 must have been carried from the tens column to the hundreds column. Therefore, the sum of the tens digits must be $S + 10$, and hence $1 + P + Q = S + 10$, where the 1 was carried from the units column.

Step 3: Apply the assumption $Q = 2P$ to rule out answer choices B, C, and D.

Substituting $2P$ for Q in the equation $1 + P + Q = S + 10$ gives $1 + P + 2P = S + 10$, which can be rewritten as $S = 3P - 9 = 3(P - 3)$. This shows that S is divisible by 3, and therefore, answer choices B, C, and D can NOT be correct.

Step 4: Show that $S = 9$ is not possible.

If $S = 9$, then we have $9 = 3(P - 3)$. Solving this equation gives $P = 6$. However, from $Q = 2P$, it follows that $Q = 12$, which is not a digit. Therefore, $S = 9$ is not possible and answer choice E is NOT correct.

The only possibility remaining is $S = 3$. Although it is not necessary to verify that $S = 3$ is consistent, one can show that $S = 3$ leads to the following for the sum:

$$
\begin{array}{r}
345 \\
+\ 489 \\
\hline
834
\end{array}
$$

The correct answer is A.

124. A certain high school has 5,000 students. Of these students, x are taking music, y are taking art, and z are taking both music and art. How many students are taking neither music nor art?

(A) $5{,}000 - z$
(B) $5{,}000 - x - y$
(C) $5{,}000 - x + z$
(D) $5{,}000 - x - y - z$
(E) $5{,}000 - x - y + z$

Algebra Sets

Since x students are taking music, y students are taking art, and z students are taking both music and art, the number of students taking only music is $x - z$, and the number of students taking only art is $y - z$, as illustrated by the following Venn diagram.

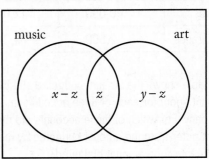

Therefore, the number of students taking neither music nor art is
$5,000 - [(x - z) + z + (y - z)] = 5,000 - x - y + z.$

The correct answer is E.

125. Each person who attended a company meeting was either a stockholder in the company, an employee of the company, or both. If 62 percent of those who attended the meeting were stockholders and 47 percent were employees, what percent were stockholders who were <u>NOT</u> employees?

    (A)   34%
    (B)   38%
    (C)   45%
    (D)   53%
    (E)   62%

Arithmetic Sets

Let M represent the number of meeting attendees. Then, since 62% of M or $0.62M$ were stockholders and 47% of M or $0.47M$ were employees, it follows that $0.62M + 0.47M = 1.09M$ were either stockholders, employees, or both. Since $1.09M$ exceeds M, the excess $1.09M - M = 0.09M$ must be the number of attendees who were both stockholders and employees, leaving the rest $0.62M - 0.09M = 0.53M$, or 53%, of the meeting attendees to be stockholders but not employees.

The correct answer is D.

Accounts	Amount Budgeted	Amount Spent
Payroll	$110,000	$117,000
Taxes	40,000	42,000
Insurance	2,500	2,340

126. The table shows the amount budgeted and the amount spent for each of three accounts in a certain company. For which of these accounts did the amount spent differ from the amount budgeted by more than 6 percent of the amount budgeted?

    (A)   Payroll only
    (B)   Taxes only
    (C)   Insurance only
    (D)   Payroll and Insurance
    (E)   Taxes and Insurance

Arithmetic Percents

For Payroll, 6% of the budgeted amount is $(0.06)(\$110,000) = \$6,600$. Since $\$117,000 - \$110,000 = \$7,000 > \$6,600$, the amount spent differed from the amount budgeted by more than 6%.

For Taxes, 6% of the budgeted amount is $(0.06)(\$40,000) = \$2,400$. Since $\$42,000 - \$40,000 = \$2,000 < \$2,400$, the amount spent did not differ from the amount budgeted by more than 6%.

For Insurance, 6% of the budgeted amount is $(0.06)(\$2,500) = \$150$. Since $\$2,500 - \$2,340 = \$160 > \$150$, the amount spent differed from the amount budgeted by more than 6%.

Thus, the amount spent differed from the amount budgeted by more than 6% for Payroll and Insurance.

The correct answer is D.

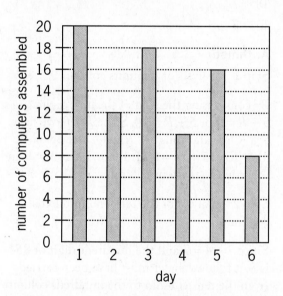

127. The graph shows the number of computers assembled during each of 6 consecutive days. From what day to the next day was the percent change in the number of computers assembled the greatest in magnitude?

    (A)   From Day 1 to Day 2
    (B)   From Day 2 to Day 3
    (C)   From Day 3 to Day 4
    (D)   From Day 4 to Day 5
    (E)   From Day 5 to Day 6

Arithmetic Percents

The following table shows the percent change from each day to the next and the magnitude of the percent change.

Time Period	Percent Change	Magnitude of Percent Change
From Day 1 to Day 2	$\left(\dfrac{12-20}{20} \times 100\right)\% = \left(-\dfrac{8}{20} \times 100\right)\% = -40\%$	40
From Day 2 to Day 3	$\left(\dfrac{18-12}{12} \times 100\right)\% = \left(\dfrac{6}{12} \times 100\right)\% = 50\%$	50
From Day 3 to Day 4	$\left(\dfrac{10-18}{18} \times 100\right)\% = \left(-\dfrac{8}{18} \times 100\right)\% \approx -44\%$	44
From Day 4 to Day 5	$\left(\dfrac{16-10}{10} \times 100\right)\% = \left(\dfrac{6}{10} \times 100\right)\% = 60\%$	60
From Day 5 to Day 6	$\left(\dfrac{8-16}{16} \times 100\right)\% = \left(-\dfrac{8}{16} \times 100\right)\% = -50\%$	50

The correct answer is D.

128. If $n = 20! + 17$, then n is divisible by which of the following?

   I.   15
   II.   17
   III. 19

(A)   None
(B)   I only
(C)   II only
(D)   I and II
(E)   II and III

Arithmetic Properties of Numbers

Because 20! is the product of all integers from 1 through 20, it follows that 20! is divisible by each integer from 1 through 20. In particular, 20! is divisible by each of the integers 15, 17, and 19. Since 20! and 17 are both divisible by 17, their sum is divisible by 17, and hence the correct answer will include II. If n were divisible by 15, then $n - 20!$ would be divisible by 15. But, $n - 20! = 17$ and 17 is not divisible by 15. Therefore, the correct answer does not include I. If n were divisible by 19, then $n - 20!$ would be divisible by 19. But, $n - 20! = 17$ and 17 is not divisible by 19. Therefore, the correct answer does not include III.

The correct answer is C.

129. Exchange Rates in a Particular Year

       \$1 = 5.3 francs
       \$1 = 1.6 marks

An American dealer bought a table in Germany for 480 marks and sold the same table in France for 2,385 francs. What was the dealer's gross profit on the two transactions in dollars?

(A)   \$0
(B)   \$50
(C)   \$100
(D)   \$150
(E)   \$200

Arithmetic Measurement Conversion

Given that \$1 = 1.6 marks, it follows that $\dfrac{\$1}{1.6} = 1$ mark and 480 marks $= 480\left(\dfrac{\$1}{1.6}\right) = \$300$. Similarly, given that \$1 = 5.3 francs, it follows that $\dfrac{\$1}{5.3} = 1$ franc and 2,385 francs $= 2,385\left(\dfrac{\$1}{5.3}\right) = \$450$. The gross profit on the two transactions is $\$450 - \$300 = \$150$.

The correct answer is D.

130. The product of two negative numbers is 160. If the lesser of the two numbers is 4 less than twice the greater, what is the greater number?

    (A) −20
    (B) −16
    (C) −10
    (D) −8
    (E) −4

Algebra Second-Degree Equations

Let x and y be the two numbers, where x is the lesser of the two numbers and y is the number desired. From the given information it follows that $xy = 160$ and $x = 2y - 4$, from which it follows that $(2y - 4)y = 160$. Dividing both sides of the last equation by 2 gives $(y - 2)y = 80$. Thus, 80 is to be written as a product of two negative numbers, one that is 2 less than the other. Trying simple factorizations of 80 quickly leads to the value of y: $(-40)(-2) = 80$, $(-20)(-4) = 80$, $(-10)(-8) = 80$. Therefore, $y = -8$. Note that because −8 is one of the answer choices, it is not necessary to ensure there are no other negative solutions to the equation $(y - 2)y = 80$.

Alternatively, $(y - 2)y = 80$ can be written as $y^2 - 2y - 80 = 0$. Factoring the left side gives $(y + 8)(y - 10) = 0$, and $y = -8$ is the only negative solution.

The correct answer is D.

131. According to a certain estimate, the depth $N(t)$, in centimeters, of the water in a certain tank at t hours past 2:00 in the morning is given by $N(t) = -20(t - 5)^2 + 500$ for $0 \le t \le 10$. According to this estimate, at what time in the morning does the depth of the water in the tank reach its maximum?

    (A) 5:30
    (B) 7:00
    (C) 7:30
    (D) 8:00
    (E) 9:00

Algebra Functions

When $t = 5$, the value of $-20(t - 5)^2 + 500$ is 500. For all values of t between 0 and 10, inclusive, except $t = 5$, the value of $-20(t - 5)^2$ is negative

and $-20(t - 5)^2 + 500 < 500$. Therefore, the tank reaches its maximum depth 5 hours after 2:00 in the morning, which is 7:00 in the morning.

The correct answer is B.

132. After driving to a riverfront parking lot, Bob plans to run south along the river, turn around, and return to the parking lot, running north along the same path. After running 3.25 miles south, he decides to run for only 50 minutes more. If Bob runs at a constant rate of 8 minutes per mile, how many miles farther south can he run and still be able to return to the parking lot in 50 minutes?

    (A) 1.5
    (B) 2.25
    (C) 3.0
    (D) 3.25
    (E) 4.75

Algebra Applied Problems

After running 3.25 miles south, Bob has been running for $(3.25 \text{ miles})\left(8\dfrac{\text{minutes}}{\text{mile}}\right) = 26$ minutes. Thus, if t is the number of additional minutes that Bob can run south before turning around, then the number of minutes that Bob will run north, after turning around, will be $t + 26$. Since Bob will be running a total of 50 minutes after the initial 26 minutes of running, it follows that $t + (t + 26) = 50$, or $t = 12$. Therefore, Bob can run south an additional

$$\dfrac{12 \text{ minutes}}{8 \dfrac{\text{minutes}}{\text{mile}}} = 1.5 \text{ miles before turning around.}$$

The correct answer is A.

133. Alex deposited x dollars into a new account that earned 8 percent annual interest, compounded annually. One year later Alex deposited an additional x dollars into the account. If there were no other transactions and if the account contained w dollars at the end of two years, which of the following expresses x in terms of w?

    (A) $\dfrac{w}{1 + 1.08}$

    (B) $\dfrac{w}{1.08 + 1.16}$

(C) $\dfrac{w}{1.16+1.24}$

(D) $\dfrac{w}{1.08+(1.08)^2}$

(E) $\dfrac{w}{(1.08)^2+(1.08)^3}$

Algebra Applied Problems

At the end of the first year, the value of Alex's initial investment was $x(1.08)$ dollars, and after he deposited an additional x dollars into the account, its value was $[x(1.08)+x]$ dollars. At the end of the second year, the value was w dollars, where $w=[x(1.08)+x](1.08)=x(1.08)^2+x(1.08)=x[(1.08)^2+1.08]$. Thus, $x=\dfrac{w}{1.08+(1.08)^2}$.

The correct answer is D.

134. M is the sum of the reciprocals of the consecutive integers from 201 to 300, inclusive. Which of the following is true?

(A) $\dfrac{1}{3}<M<\dfrac{1}{2}$

(B) $\dfrac{1}{5}<M<\dfrac{1}{3}$

(C) $\dfrac{1}{7}<M<\dfrac{1}{5}$

(D) $\dfrac{1}{9}<M<\dfrac{1}{7}$

(E) $\dfrac{1}{12}<M<\dfrac{1}{9}$

Arithmetic Estimation

M	$=\dfrac{1}{201}+\dfrac{1}{202}+\dfrac{1}{203}+\ldots+\dfrac{1}{298}+\dfrac{1}{299}+\dfrac{1}{300}$	Given
	$>\dfrac{1}{300}+\dfrac{1}{300}+\dfrac{1}{300}+\ldots+\dfrac{1}{300}+\dfrac{1}{300}+\dfrac{1}{300}$	See Note 1 below

Note 1: 300 is greater than each of 201, 202, 203, …, 298, and 299, so the reciprocal of 300 is less than the reciprocal of each of 201, 202, 203, …, 298, and 299 and the sum in line 2 of the table above, $(100)\left(\dfrac{1}{300}\right)=\dfrac{1}{3}$, is less than the sum of line 1. Thus, $\dfrac{1}{3}<M$.

M	$=\dfrac{1}{201}+\dfrac{1}{202}+\dfrac{1}{203}+\ldots+\dfrac{1}{298}+\dfrac{1}{299}+\dfrac{1}{300}$	Given
	$<\dfrac{1}{200}+\dfrac{1}{200}+\dfrac{1}{200}+\ldots+\dfrac{1}{200}+\dfrac{1}{200}+\dfrac{1}{200}$	See Note 2 below

Note 2: 200 is less than each of 201, 202, 203, …, 298, and 299, so the reciprocal of 200 is greater than the reciprocal of each of 201, 202, 203, …, 298, and 299 and the sum in line 2 of the table above, $(100)\left(\dfrac{1}{200}\right)=\dfrac{1}{2}$, is greater than the sum of line 1. Thus, $\dfrac{1}{2}>M$ or $M<\dfrac{1}{2}$. Combining the results $\dfrac{1}{3}<M$ and $M<\dfrac{1}{2}$ gives $\dfrac{1}{3}<M<\dfrac{1}{2}$.

The correct answer is A.

135. Working simultaneously at their respective constant rates, Machines A and B produce 800 nails in x hours. Working alone at its constant rate, Machine A produces 800 nails in y hours. In terms of x and y, how many hours does it take Machine B, working alone at its constant rate, to produce 800 nails?

(A) $\dfrac{x}{x+y}$

(B) $\dfrac{y}{x+y}$

(C) $\dfrac{xy}{x+y}$

(D) $\dfrac{xy}{x-y}$

(E) $\dfrac{xy}{y-x}$

Algebra Applied Problems

Let R_A and R_B be the constant rates, in nails per hour, at which Machines A and B work, respectively. Then it follows from the given information that $R_A+R_B=\dfrac{800}{x}$ and $R_A=\dfrac{800}{y}$.

Hence, $\dfrac{800}{y}+R_B=\dfrac{800}{x}$, or

$$R_B=\dfrac{800}{x}-\dfrac{800}{y}=800\left(\dfrac{1}{x}-\dfrac{1}{y}\right)=800\left(\dfrac{y-x}{xy}\right).$$

Therefore, the time, in hours, it would take Machine B to produce 800 nails is given by

$$\dfrac{800}{800\left(\dfrac{y-x}{xy}\right)}=\dfrac{xy}{y-x}.$$

The correct answer is E.

136. Carol purchased one basket of fruit consisting of 4 apples and 2 oranges and another basket of fruit consisting of 3 apples and 5 oranges. Carol is to select one piece of fruit at random from each of the two baskets. What is the probability that one of the two pieces of fruit selected will be an apple and the other will be an orange?

(A) $\dfrac{1}{4}$

(B) $\dfrac{1}{2}$

(C) $\dfrac{1}{24}$

(D) $\dfrac{5}{24}$

(E) $\dfrac{13}{24}$

Arithmetic Probability

There are 6 pieces of fruit in the first basket and 8 pieces of fruit in the second basket. By the multiplication principle, the number of selections of a piece of fruit from the first basket and a piece of fruit from the second basket is $(6)(8) = 48$. Of these selections, $(4)(5) = 20$ are such that an apple is selected from the first basket and an orange is selected from the second basket, and $(2)(3) = 6$ are such that an orange is selected from the first basket and an apple is selected from the second basket. Therefore, there is a total of $20 + 6 = 26$ selections in which one apple is chosen and one orange is chosen, and hence the probability of such a selection is $\dfrac{26}{48} = \dfrac{13}{24}$.

Alternatively, the desired probability is the sum of the probabilities of two disjoint events. In the first event, an apple is selected from the first basket and an orange is selected from the second basket; the probability of this event is $\left(\dfrac{4}{6}\right)\left(\dfrac{5}{8}\right) = \dfrac{20}{48}$.

In the second event, an orange is selected from the first basket and an apple is selected from the second basket; the probability of this event is $\left(\dfrac{2}{6}\right)\left(\dfrac{3}{8}\right) = \dfrac{6}{48}$. Therefore, the desired probability is $\dfrac{20}{48} + \dfrac{6}{48} = \dfrac{26}{48} = \dfrac{13}{24}$.

The correct answer is E.

137. Last year Brand X shoes were sold by dealers in 403 different regions worldwide, with an average (arithmetic mean) of 98 dealers per region. If last year these dealers sold an average of 2,488 pairs of Brand X shoes per dealer, which of the following is closest to the total number of pairs of Brand X shoes sold last year by the dealers worldwide?

(A) 10^4

(B) 10^5

(C) 10^6

(D) 10^7

(E) 10^8

Arithmetic Estimation; Exponents

Since the average number of dealers per region is 98, it follows that $\dfrac{\text{number of dealers}}{403} = 98$, and thus the number of dealers is $(98)(403)$. Also, since the average number of pairs sold per dealer is 2,488, it follows that $\dfrac{\text{number of pairs sold}}{(98)(403)} = 2{,}488$, and thus the number of pairs sold is $(98)(403)(2{,}488)$, which is approximately $(100)(400)(2500) = (10^2)(4 \times 10^2)(25 \times 10^2)$. Therefore, the total number of pairs sold is approximately $(4)(25) \times 10^{2+2+2} = 100 \times 10^6 = 10^8$.

The correct answer is E.

10, 4, 26, 16

138. What is the median of the numbers shown?

(A) 10

(B) 13

(C) 14

(D) 15

(E) 16

Arithmetic Statistics

To determine the median of these 4 numbers, put the numbers in numerical order in a list and determine the average of the two middle values in the list:

4, **10**, **16**, 26

From this list it follows that the median is the average of 10 and 16, which is $\frac{10+16}{2} = 13$.

The correct answer is B.

	Number of Marbles in Each of Three Bags	Percent of Marbles in Each Bag That Are Blue (to the nearest tenth)
Bag P	37	10.8%
Bag Q	×	66.7%
Bag R	32	50.0%

139. If $\frac{1}{3}$ of the total number of marbles in the three bags listed in the table above are blue, how many marbles are there in bag Q ?

(A)   5
(B)   9
(C)   12
(D)   23
(E)   46

Algebra Percents

What is the value of x, the number of marbles in bag Q ? From the given information and rounded to the nearest integer, bag P has $(37)(0.108) = 4$ blue marbles, bag Q has $(x)(0.667) = \frac{2}{3}x$ blue marbles, and bag R has $(32)(0.5) = 16$ blue marbles. Therefore, the total number of blue marbles is equal to $4 + \frac{2}{3}x + 16 = 20 + \frac{2}{3}x$. It is given that $\frac{1}{3}$ of the total number of marbles are blue, so the total number of blue marbles is also equal to $\frac{1}{3}(37 + x + 32) = \frac{1}{3}x + 23$. It follows that $20 + \frac{2}{3}x = \frac{1}{3}x + 23$, or $\frac{1}{3}x = 3$, or $x = 9$.

The correct answer is B.

Age Category (in years)	Number of Employees
Less than 20	29
20–29	58
30–39	36
40–49	21
50–59	10
60–69	5
70 and over	2

140. The table above gives the age categories of the 161 employees at Company X and the number of employees in each category. According to the table, if m is the median age, in years, of the employees at Company X, then m must satisfy which of the following?

(A) $20 \leq m \leq 29$
(B) $25 \leq m \leq 34$
(C) $30 \leq m \leq 39$
(D) $35 \leq m \leq 44$
(E) $40 \leq m \leq 49$

Arithmetic Statistics

The median of 161 ages is the 81st age when the ages are listed in order. Since 29 of the ages are less than 20, the median age must be greater than or equal to 20. Since 58 of the ages are between 20 and 29, a total of $29 + 58 = 87$ of the ages are less than or equal to 29, and thus the median age is less than or equal to 29. Therefore, the median age is greater than or equal to 20 and less than or equal to 29.

The correct answer is A.

141. If k and n are positive integers such that $n > k$, then $k! + (n - k) \cdot (k - 1)!$ is equivalent to which of the following?

(A) $k \cdot n!$
(B) $k! \cdot n$
(C) $(n - k)!$
(D) $n \cdot (k + 1)!$
(E) $n \cdot (k - 1)!$

Algebra Simplifying Algebraic Expressions

$k! + (n-k) \cdot (k-1)!$	given
$k \cdot (k-1)! + (n-k) \cdot (k-1)!$	$k! = k \cdot (k-1)!$
$[k + (n-k)] \cdot (k-1)!$	factor out $(k-1)!$
$n \cdot (k-1)!$	combine like terms

The correct answer is E.

142. Ron is 4 inches taller than Amy, and Barbara is 1 inch taller than Ron. If Barbara's height is 65 inches, what is the median height, in inches, of these three people?

(A) 60
(B) 61
(C) 62
(D) 63
(E) 64

Arithmetic Operations with Integers

Let R, A, and B be the heights, respectively and in inches, of Ron, Amy, and Barbara. It is given that $R = 4 + A$, $B = 1 + R$, and $B = 65$. Therefore, $R = B - 1 = 65 - 1 = 64$ and $A = R - 4 = 64 - 4 = 60$. From this it follows that the three heights, in inches, are 60, 64, and 65. The median of these three heights is 64.

The correct answer is E.

143. If x and y are positive numbers such that x + y = 1, which of the following could be the value of 100x + 200y?

I.   80
II. 140
III. 199

(A) II only
(B) III only
(C) I and II
(D) I and III
(E) II and III

Algebra Simultaneous Equations; Inequalities

Since $x + y = 1$, then $y = 1 - x$ and $100x + 200y$ can be expressed as $100x + 200(1 - x) = 200 - 100x$. Test each value.

I. If $200 - 100x = 80$, then $x = \dfrac{200 - 80}{100} = 1.2$ and $y = 1 - 1.2 = -0.2$.

Since y must be positive, 80 cannot be a value of $100x + 200y$.

II. If $200 - 100x = 140$, then $x = \dfrac{200 - 140}{100} = 0.6$ and $y = 1 - 0.6 = 0.4$, so 140 can be a value of $100x + 200y$.

III. If $200 - 100x = 199$, then $x = \dfrac{200 - 199}{100} = 0.01$ and $y = 1 - 0.01 = 0.99$, so 199 can be a value of $100x + 200y$.

The correct answer is E.

144. If X is the hundredths digit in the decimal 0.1X and if Y is the thousandths digit in the decimal 0.02Y, where X and Y are nonzero digits, which of the following is closest to the greatest possible value of $\dfrac{0.1x}{0.02y}$?

(A) 4
(B) 5
(C) 6
(D) 9
(E) 10

Arithmetic Operations with Decimals; Place Value

The greatest possible value of $\dfrac{0.1X}{0.02Y}$ will occur when 0.1X has the greatest possible value and 0.02Y has the least possible value. Since X and Y are nonzero digits, this means than X must be 9 and Y must be 1. The greatest possible value of $\dfrac{0.1X}{0.02Y}$ is then $\dfrac{0.19}{0.021} \approx 9.05$, which is closest to 9.

The correct answer is D.

145. If each of the 12 teams participating in a certain tournament plays exactly one game with each of the other teams, how many games will be played?

(A) 144
(B) 132
(C) 66
(D) 33
(E) 23

Arithmetic Elementary Combinatorics

Since each of the 12 teams will play exactly one game with each of the other teams,

the number of games that will be played is
equal to the number of selections of 2 teams,
without regard to order, from 12 teams.
This is the number of combinations of
12 teams taken 2 at a time, which is equal to

$$\binom{12}{2} = \frac{12!}{2!(12-2)!} = \frac{(10!)(11)(12)}{(2)(10!)} = 66.$$

Alternatively, each of the 12 teams will play each
of the 11 other teams. The product $(12)(11)$ counts
each of the games twice since, for example, this
product separately counts "Team A plays Team B"
and "Team B plays Team A". Therefore, the number
of games that will be played is $\frac{(12)(11)}{2} = 66$.

The correct answer is C.

Questions 146 to 228 - Difficulty: Hard

146. The cost to rent a small bus for a trip is *x* dollars,
which is to be shared equally among the people taking
the trip. If 10 people take the trip rather than 16,
how many more dollars, in terms of *x*, will it cost per
person?

   (A) $\frac{x}{6}$

   (B) $\frac{x}{10}$

   (C) $\frac{x}{16}$

   (D) $\frac{3x}{40}$

   (E) $\frac{3x}{80}$

Algebra Applied Problems

If 16 people take the trip, the cost per person
would be $\frac{x}{16}$ dollars. If 10 people take the
trip, the cost would be $\frac{x}{10}$ dollars. (Note
that the lowest common multiple of 10 and
16 is 80.) Thus, if 10 people take the trip,
the increase in dollars per person would be
$\frac{x}{10} - \frac{x}{16} = \frac{8x}{80} - \frac{5x}{80} = \frac{3x}{80}$.

The correct answer is E.

147. Clarissa will create her summer reading list by
randomly choosing 4 books from the 10 books
approved for summer reading. She will list the books in
the order in which they are chosen. How many different
lists are possible?

   (A) 6
   (B) 40
   (C) 210
   (D) 5,040
   (E) 151,200

Arithmetic Elementary Combinatorics

Any of the 10 books can be listed first. Any of the
9 books remaining after the first book is listed can
be listed second. Any of the 8 books remaining
after the first and second books are listed can be
listed third. Any of the 7 books remaining after
the first, second, and third books are listed can
be listed fourth. By the multiplication principle,
there are $(10)(9)(8)(7) = 5,040$ different lists
possible.

The correct answer is D.

148. If *n* is a positive integer and the product of all the
integers from 1 to *n*, inclusive, is divisible by 990,
what is the least possible value of *n* ?

   (A) 8
   (B) 9
   (C) 10
   (D) 11
   (E) 12

Arithmetic Properties of Numbers

For convenience, let *N* represent the product of
all integers from 1 through *n*. Then, since *N* is
divisible by 990, every prime factor of 990 must
also be a factor of *N*. The prime factorization of
990 is $2 \times 3^2 \times 5 \times 11$, and therefore, 11 must be
a factor of *N*. Then, the least possible value of *N*
with factors of 2, 5, 3^2, and 11 is $1 \times 2 \times 3 \times \cdots \times 11$,
and the least possible value of *n* is 11.

The correct answer is D.

149. The probability that event M will NOT occur is 0.8 and the probability that event R will NOT occur is 0.6. If events M and R CANNOT both occur, which of the following is the probability that either event M or event R will occur?

(A) $\dfrac{1}{5}$

(B) $\dfrac{2}{5}$

(C) $\dfrac{3}{5}$

(D) $\dfrac{4}{5}$

(E) $\dfrac{12}{25}$

Arithmetic Probability

Let $P(M)$ be the probability that event M will occur, let $P(R)$ be the probability that event R will occur, and let $P(M \text{ and } R)$ be the probability that events M and R both occur. Then the probability that either event M or event R will occur is $P(M) + P(R) - P(M \text{ and } R)$. From the given information, it follows that $P(M) = 1.0 - 0.8 = 0.2$, $P(R) = 1.0 - 0.6 = 0.4$, and $P(M \text{ and } R) = 0$. Therefore, the probability that either event M or event R will occur is

$0.2 + 0.4 - 0 = 0.6 = \dfrac{3}{5}$.

The correct answer is C.

150. The total cost for Company X to produce a batch of tools is $10,000 plus $3 per tool. Each tool sells for $8. The gross profit earned from producing and selling these tools is the total income from sales minus the total production cost. If a batch of 20,000 tools is produced and sold, then Company X's gross profit per tool is

(A) $3.00
(B) $3.75
(C) $4.50
(D) $5.00
(E) $5.50

Arithmetic Applied Problems

The total cost to produce 20,000 tools is $10,000 + $3(20,000) = $70,000. The revenue resulting from the sale of 20,000 tools is $8(20,000) = $160,000. The gross profit is

$160,000 − $70,000 = $90,000, and the gross profit per tool is $\dfrac{\$90{,}000}{20{,}000} = \$4.50$.

The correct answer is C.

151. If Q is an odd number and the median of Q consecutive integers is 120, what is the largest of these integers?

(A) $\dfrac{Q-1}{2} + 120$

(B) $\dfrac{Q}{2} + 119$

(C) $\dfrac{Q}{2} + 120$

(D) $\dfrac{Q+119}{2}$

(E) $\dfrac{Q+120}{2}$

Arithmetic Statistics

For an odd number of data values, the median is the middle number. Thus, 120 is the middle number, and so half of the $Q - 1$ remaining values are at most 120 and the other half of the $Q - 1$ remaining values are at least 120. In particular, $\dfrac{Q-1}{2}$ data values lie to the right of 120 when the data values are listed in increasing order from left to right, and so the largest data value is $120 + \dfrac{Q-1}{2}$. Alternatively, it is evident that (B), (C), or (E) cannot be correct since these expressions do not have an integer value when Q is odd. For the list consisting of the single number 120 (i.e., if $Q = 1$), (D) fails because $\dfrac{Q+119}{2} = \dfrac{1+119}{2} = 60 \neq 120$ and (A) does not fail because $\dfrac{Q-1}{2} + 120 = \dfrac{1-1}{2} + 120 = 120$.

The correct answer is A.

152. If there are fewer than 8 zeros between the decimal point and the first nonzero digit in the decimal expansion of $\left(\dfrac{t}{1{,}000}\right)^4$, which of the following numbers could be the value of t?

    I.   3
    II.   5
    III. 9

    (A) None
    (B) I only
    (C) II only
    (D) III only
    (E) II and III

Arithmetic Properties of Numbers; Decimals

Since $\left(\dfrac{t}{1{,}000}\right)^4 = \left(t \times \dfrac{1}{1{,}000}\right)^4 = t^4 \times \left(\dfrac{1}{1{,}000}\right)^4 =$

$t^4 \times \dfrac{1}{1{,}000^4}$ and $(1{,}000)^4 = (10^3)^4 = 10^{12}$, it

follows that $\left(\dfrac{t}{1{,}000}\right)^4 = t^4 \times \dfrac{1}{10^{12}} = t^4 \times 10^{-12}$.

The following table illustrates the effect that multiplication by 10^{-1}, 10^{-2}, 10^{-3}, and 10^{-4} has on the placement of the decimal point of 52.7, a number chosen only for illustrative purposes.

multiplication by	resulting number	placement of decimal point
10^{-1}	5.27	1 place left of original
10^{-2}	0.527	2 places left of original
10^{-3}	0.0527	3 places left of original
10^{-4}	0.00527	4 places left of original

Therefore, the decimal point of $t^4 \times 10^{-12}$ is 12 positions to the left of the decimal point of t^4. Now consider the value of $t^4 \times 10^{-12}$ for the three given values of t.

t	t^4	$t^4 \times 10^{-12}$	# zeros after decimal point
3	81	0.000000000081	10
5	625	0.000000000625	9
9	6,561	0.000000006561	8

From the prior table it follows that NONE of these values of t is such that $t^4 \times 10^{-12}$ has fewer than 8 zeros between the decimal point and the first nonzero digit.

The correct answer is A.

153. A three-digit code for certain locks uses the digits 0, 1, 2, 3, 4, 5, 6, 7, 8, 9 according to the following constraints. The first digit cannot be 0 or 1, the second digit must be 0 or 1, and the second and third digits cannot both be 0 in the same code. How many different codes are possible?

    (A) 144
    (B) 152
    (C) 160
    (D) 168
    (E) 176

Arithmetic Elementary Combinatorics

Since the first digit cannot be 0 or 1, there are 8 digits possible for the first digit. Since the second digit must be 0 or 1, there are 2 digits possible for the second digit. If there were no other restrictions, all 10 digits would be possible for the third digit, making the total number of possible codes $8 \times 2 \times 10 = 160$. But, the additional restriction that the second and third digits cannot both be 0 in the same code eliminates the 8 codes 2-0-0, 3-0-0, 4-0-0, 5-0-0, 6-0-0, 7-0-0, 8-0-0, and 9-0-0. Therefore, there are $160 - 8 = 152$ possible codes.

The correct answer is B.

154. Jackie has two solutions that are 2 percent sulfuric acid and 12 percent sulfuric acid by volume, respectively. If these solutions are mixed in appropriate quantities to produce 60 liters of a solution that is 5 percent sulfuric acid, approximately how many liters of the 2 percent solution will be required?

    (A) 18
    (B) 20
    (C) 24
    (D) 36
    (E) 42

Algebra Simultaneous Equations

Let x represent the quantity of the 2% sulfuric acid solution in the mixture, from which it follows that the 2% sulfuric acid solution contributes $0.02x$ liters of sulfuric acid to the mixture. Let y represent the quantity of the 12% sulfuric acid solution in the mixture, from which it follows that the 12% sulfuric acid solution contributes $0.12y$ liters of sulfuric acid to the mixture. Since there are 60 liters of the mixture, $x + y = 60$. The quantity of sulfuric acid in the mixture, which is 5% sulfuric acid, is then $(0.05)(60) = 3$ liters. Therefore, $0.02x + 0.12y = 3$. Substituting $60 - x$ for y gives $0.02x + 0.12(60 - x) = 3$. Then,

$0.02x + 0.12(60 - x) = 3$	given
$0.02x + 7.2 - 0.12x = 3$	use distributive property
$7.2 - 0.1x = 3$	combine like terms
$-0.1x = -4.2$	subtract 7.2 from both sides
$x = 42$	divide both sides by −0.1

The correct answer is E.

155. If Jake loses 8 pounds, he will weigh twice as much as his sister. Together they now weigh 278 pounds. What is Jake's present weight, in pounds?

(A)   131
(B)   135
(C)   139
(D)   147
(E)   188

Algebra Systems of Equations

Let J represent Jake's weight and S represent his sister's weight. Then $J - 8 = 2S$ and $J + S = 278$. Solve the second equation for S and get $S = 278 - J$. Substituting the expression for S into the first equation gives

$$J - 8 = 2(278 - J)$$
$$J - 8 = 556 - 2J$$
$$J + 2J = 556 + 8$$
$$3J = 564$$
$$J = 188$$

The correct answer is E.

156. For each student in a certain class, a teacher adjusted the student's test score using the formula $y = 0.8x + 20$, where x is the student's original test score and y is the student's adjusted test score. If the standard deviation of the original test scores of the students in the class was 20, what was the standard deviation of the adjusted test scores of the students in the class?

(A)   12
(B)   16
(C)   28
(D)   36
(E)   40

Arithmetic Statistics

The solution to this problem relies on the statistical properties summarized in the following table:

Data Set Values	Mean	Standard Deviation
x	μ	σ
$ax + b$	$a\mu + b$	$a\sigma$

The standard deviation of the original test scores was 20. Therefore, when the teacher multiplied each student's score by 0.8 and then added 20, the standard deviation of the set of adjusted scores is $0.8(20) = 16$.

The correct answer is B.

157. Last year 26 members of a certain club traveled to England, 26 members traveled to France, and 32 members traveled to Italy. Last year no members of the club traveled to both England and France, 6 members traveled to both England and Italy, and 11 members traveled to both France and Italy. How many members of the club traveled to at least one of these three countries last year?

(A)   52
(B)   67
(C)   71
(D)   73
(E)   79

Arithmetic Applied Problems

The numbers in the following diagram represent the numbers of members of the club who traveled to the indicated countries, and these numbers can be determined as follows. Since no members traveled to both England and France, both regions that form the overlap of England and France are labeled with 0. It follows that none of the 6 members who traveled to both England and Italy traveled to France, and so the region corresponding to England and Italy only is labeled with 6. It also follows that none of the 11 members who traveled to both France and Italy traveled to England, and so the region corresponding to France and Italy only is labeled with 11. At this point it can be determined that $26 - 6 = 20$ members traveled to England only, $26 - 11 = 15$ members traveled to France only, and $32 - (6 + 11) = 15$ members traveled to Italy only.

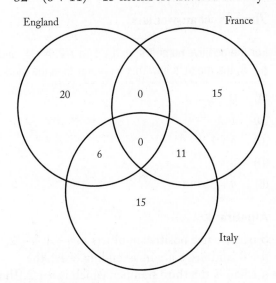

From the diagram it follows that $20 + 15 + 6 + 11 + 15 = 67$ members traveled to at least one of these three countries.

The correct answer is B.

158. A store reported total sales of $385 million for February of this year. If the total sales for the same month last year was $320 million, approximately what was the percent increase in sales?

(A) 2%
(B) 17%
(C) 20%
(D) 65%
(E) 83%

Arithmetic Percents

The percent increase in sales from last year to this year is 100 times the quotient of the difference in sales for the two years divided by the sales last year. Thus, the percent increase is

$$\frac{385 - 320}{320} \times 100 = \frac{65}{320} \times 100$$

$$= \frac{13}{64} \times 100$$

$$\approx \frac{13}{65} \times 100$$

$$= \frac{1}{5} \times 100$$

$$= 20\%$$

The correct answer is C.

159. When positive integer x is divided by positive integer y, the remainder is 9. If $\dfrac{x}{y} = 96.12$, what is the value of y?

(A) 96
(B) 75
(C) 48
(D) 25
(E) 12

Arithmetic Properties of Numbers

The remainder is 9 when x is divided by y, so $x = yq + 9$ for some positive integer q. Dividing both sides by y gives $\dfrac{x}{y} = q + \dfrac{9}{y}$.

But, $\dfrac{x}{y} = 96.12 = 96 + 0.12$. Equating the two expressions for $\dfrac{x}{y}$ gives $q + \dfrac{9}{y} = 96 + 0.12$.

Thus, $q = 96$ and $\dfrac{9}{y} = 0.12$.

$$9 = 0.12\,y$$

$$y = \frac{9}{0.12}$$

$$y = 75$$

The correct answer is B.

160. If $x(2x + 1) = 0$ and $\left(x + \dfrac{1}{2}\right)(2x - 3) = 0$, then $x =$

   (A) -3

   (B) $-\dfrac{1}{2}$

   (C) 0

   (D) $\dfrac{1}{2}$

   (E) $\dfrac{3}{2}$

Algebra Second-Degree Equations; Simultaneous Equations

Setting each factor equal to 0, it can be seen that the solution set to the first equation is $\left\{0, -\dfrac{1}{2}\right\}$ and the solution set to the second equation is $\left\{-\dfrac{1}{2}, \dfrac{3}{2}\right\}$. Therefore, $-\dfrac{1}{2}$ is the solution to both equations.

The correct answer is B.

161. A certain experimental mathematics program was tried out in 2 classes in each of 32 elementary schools and involved 37 teachers. Each of the classes had 1 teacher and each of the teachers taught at least 1, but not more than 3, of the classes. If the number of teachers who taught 3 classes is n, then the least and greatest possible values of n, respectively, are

   (A)   0 and 13

   (B)   0 and 14

   (C)   1 and 10

   (D)   1 and 9

   (E)   2 and 8

Algebra Simultaneous Equations; Inequalities

It is given that $2(32) = 64$ classes are taught by 37 teachers. Let k, m, and n be the number of teachers who taught, respectively, 1, 2, and 3 of the classes. Then $k + m + n = 37$ and $k + 2m + 3n = 64$. Subtracting these two equations gives $m + 2n = 64 - 37 = 27$, or $2n = 27 - m$, and therefore $2n \leq 27$. Because n is an integer, it follows that $n \leq 13$ and B cannot be the answer. Since $n = 0$ is possible, which can be seen by using $m = 27$ and $k = 10$ (obtained by solving $2n = 27 - m$ with $n = 0$, then by solving $k + m + n = 37$ with $n = 0$ and $m = 27$), the answer must be A.

It is not necessary to ensure that $n = 13$ is possible to answer the question. However, it is not difficult to see that $k = 23$, $m = 1$, and $n = 13$ satisfy the given conditions.

The correct answer is A.

162. For the positive numbers, n, $n + 1$, $n + 2$, $n + 4$, and $n + 8$, the mean is how much greater than the median?

   (A)   0

   (B)   1

   (C) $n + 1$

   (D) $n + 2$

   (E) $n + 3$

Algebra Statistics

Since the five positive numbers n, $n + 1$, $n + 2$, $n + 4$, and $n + 8$ are in ascending order, the median is the third number, which is $n + 2$. The mean of the five numbers is

$$\frac{n + (n + 1) + (n + 2) + (n + 4) + (n + 8)}{5}$$

$$= \frac{5n + 15}{5}$$

$$= n + 3$$

Since $(n + 3) - (n + 2) = 1$, the mean is 1 greater than the median.

The correct answer is B.

163. The present ratio of students to teachers at a certain school is 30 to 1. If the student enrollment were to increase by 50 students and the number of teachers were to increase by 5, the ratio of students to teachers would then be 25 to 1. What is the present number of teachers?

    (A) 5
    (B) 8
    (C) 10
    (D) 12
    (E) 15

Algebra Applied Problems

After noting that $\dfrac{\text{number of students}}{\text{number of teachers}} = \dfrac{30}{1}$ implies that the number of students is 30 times the number of teachers, this problem can be solved with arithmetic, as shown in the table below, by guessing the present number of teachers, increasing the numbers of students and teachers as specified, then checking to see if the resulting ratio is equal to $\dfrac{25}{1}$.

Present Number of Teachers	Present Number of Students	Teachers Increased by 5	Students Increased by 50	Resulting Ratio	Equal to $\frac{25}{1}$?
5	150	10	200	$\dfrac{200}{10} = \dfrac{20}{1}$	no
8	240	13	290	$\dfrac{290}{13} = \dfrac{22\frac{4}{13}}{1}$	no
10	300	15	350	$\dfrac{350}{15} = \dfrac{23\frac{1}{3}}{1}$	no
12	360	17	410	$\dfrac{410}{17} = \dfrac{24\frac{2}{17}}{1}$	no
15	450	20	500	$\dfrac{500}{20} = \dfrac{25}{1}$	yes

Therefore, the present number of teachers is 15.

Alternatively, the problem can be solved using algebra.

The following table summarizes the given information, where s represents the present number of students and t represents the present number of teachers:

	Number of Students	Number of Teachers	$\dfrac{\text{Students}}{\text{Teachers}}$	Equation After Cross Multiplying
Present	s	t	$\dfrac{s}{t} = \dfrac{30}{1}$	$s = 30t$
After Increases	$s + 50$	$t + 5$	$\dfrac{s+50}{t+5} = \dfrac{25}{1}$	$s + 50 = 25(t + 5)$

Determine the value of t using $s = 30t$ (Equation 1) and $s + 50 = 25(t + 5) = 25t + 125$ (Equation 2).

$s + 50$	$=$	$25t + 125$	equation 2
$30t + 50$	$=$	$25t + 125$	substitution from Equation 1
$5t + 50$	$=$	125	subtract $25t$ from both sides
$5t$	$=$	75	subtract 50 from both sides
t	$=$	15	divide both sides by 5

Therefore, the present number of teachers is 15.

The correct answer is E.

164. What is the smallest integer n for which $25^n > 5^{12}$?

   (A)   6
   (B)   7
   (C)   8
   (D)   9
   (E)   10

Arithmetic Operations with Rational Numbers

Because $5^2 = 25$, a common base is 5. Rewrite the left side with 5 as a base: $25^n = (5^2)^n = 5^{2n}$. It follows that the desired integer is the least integer n for which $5^{2n} > 5^{12}$. This will be the least integer n for which $2n > 12$, or the least integer n for which $n > 6$, which is 7.

The correct answer is B.

165. Sixty percent of the members of a study group are women, and 45 percent of those women are lawyers. If one member of the study group is to be selected at random, what is the probability that the member selected is a woman lawyer?

   (A)   0.10
   (B)   0.15
   (C)   0.27
   (D)   0.33
   (E)   0.45

Arithmetic Probability

For simplicity, suppose there are 100 members in the study group. Since 60 percent of the members are women, there are 60 women in the group. Also, 45 percent of the women are lawyers so there are $0.45(60) = 27$ women lawyers in the study group. Therefore the probability of selecting a woman lawyer is $\dfrac{27}{100} = 0.27$.

The correct answer is C.

166. Each year for 4 years, a farmer increased the number of trees in a certain orchard by $\dfrac{1}{4}$ of the number of trees in the orchard the preceding year. If all of the trees thrived and there were 6,250 trees in the orchard at the end of the 4-year period, how many trees were in the orchard at the beginning of the 4-year period?

   (A)   1,250
   (B)   1,563
   (C)   2,250
   (D)   2,560
   (E)   2,752

Arithmetic Operations on Rational Numbers

Let N be the number of trees in the orchard at the beginning of the 4-year period. Since the number of trees increases by a factor of $\dfrac{1}{4}$ each year, the number of trees after the first year is $N + \dfrac{1}{4}N = \dfrac{5}{4}N$. Note that this shows algebraically that an increase by a factor of $\dfrac{1}{4}$ corresponds to multiplication by $\dfrac{5}{4}$. Therefore, the number of trees after the second year is $\dfrac{5}{4}$ times $\dfrac{5}{4}N$, which equals $\left(\dfrac{5}{4}\right)^2 N$. Similarly, the number of trees after the third year is $\left(\dfrac{5}{4}\right)^3 N$ and the number of trees after the fourth year is $\left(\dfrac{5}{4}\right)^4 N$. Since the number of trees after the fourth year is 6,250, it follows that $\left(\dfrac{5}{4}\right)^4 N = 6,250$. Next, solve for N:

$\left(\dfrac{5}{4}\right)^4 N$	$=$	$6{,}250$	given
$\left(\dfrac{5^4}{4^4}\right) N$	$=$	$6{,}250$	property of exponents
N	$=$	$6{,}250 \div \dfrac{5^4}{4^4}$	divide both sides by $\dfrac{5^4}{4^4}$
N	$=$	$6{,}250 \times \dfrac{4^4}{5^4}$	invert and multiply
N	$=$	$2 \times 5^5 \times \dfrac{4^4}{5^4}$	factor $6{,}250$
N	$=$	$2 \times 5 \times 4^4$	cancel common factors
N	$=$	$2{,}560$	multiply

The correct answer is D.

Number of Shipments of Manufactured Homes
in the United States, 1990–2000

167. According to the chart shown, which of the following is closest to the median annual number of shipments of manufactured homes in the United States for the years from 1990 to 2000, inclusive?

(A)   250,000
(B)   280,000
(C)   310,000
(D)   325,000
(E)   340,000

Arithmetic Interpretation of Graphs and Tables; Statistics

From the chart, the approximate numbers of shipments are as follows:

Year	Number of Shipments
1990	190,000
1991	180,000
1992	210,000
1993	270,000
1994	310,000
1995	350,000
1996	380,000
1997	370,000
1998	390,000
1999	360,000
2000	270,000

Since there are 11 entries in the table and 11 is an odd number, the median of the numbers of shipments is the 6th entry when the numbers of shipments are arranged in order from least to greatest. In order, from least to greatest, the first 6 entries are:

Number of Shipments
180,000
190,000
210,000
270,000
270,000
310,000

The 6th entry is 310,000.

The correct answer is C.

168. For the positive integers a, b, and k, $a^k \| b$ means that a^k is a divisor of b, but a^{k+1} is not a divisor of b. If k is a positive integer and $2^k \| 72$, then k is equal to

(A)   2
(B)   3
(C)   4
(D)   8
(E)   18

Arithmetic Property of Numbers

Since $72 = (2^3)(3^2)$, it follows that 2^3 is a divisor of 72 and 2^4 is not a divisor of 72. Therefore, $2^3 \| 72$, and hence $k = 3$.

The correct answer is B.

169. A certain characteristic in a large population has a distribution that is symmetric about the mean m. If 68 percent of the distribution lies within one standard deviation d of the mean, what percent of the distribution is less than $m + d$?

(A) 16%
(B) 32%
(C) 48%
(D) 84%
(E) 92%

Arithmetic Statistics

Since 68% lies between $m - d$ and $m + d$, a total of $(100 - 68)\% = 32\%$ lies to the left of $m - d$ and to the right of $m + d$. Because the distribution is symmetric about m, half of the 32% lies to the right of $m + d$. Therefore, 16% lies to the right of $m + d$, and hence $(100 - 16)\% = 84\%$ lies to the left of $m + d$.

The correct answer is D.

170. Four extra-large sandwiches of exactly the same size were ordered for m students, where $m > 4$. Three of the sandwiches were evenly divided among the students. Since 4 students did not want any of the fourth sandwich, it was evenly divided among the remaining students. If Carol ate one piece from each of the four sandwiches, the amount of sandwich that she ate would be what fraction of a whole extra-large sandwich?

(A) $\dfrac{m+4}{m(m-4)}$

(B) $\dfrac{2m-4}{m(m-4)}$

(C) $\dfrac{4m-4}{m(m-4)}$

(D) $\dfrac{4m-8}{m(m-4)}$

(E) $\dfrac{4m-12}{m(m-4)}$

Algebra Applied Problems

Since each of 3 of the sandwiches was evenly divided among m students, each piece was $\dfrac{1}{m}$ of a sandwich. Since the fourth sandwich was evenly divided among $m - 4$ students, each piece was

$\dfrac{1}{m-4}$ of the fourth sandwich. Carol ate 1 piece from each of the four sandwiches, so she ate a total of

$$(3)\frac{1}{m} + \frac{1}{m-4} = \frac{3(m-4)+m}{m(m-4)} = \frac{4m-12}{m(m-4)}$$

The correct answer is E.

171. Which of the following equations has $1 + \sqrt{2}$ as one of its roots?

(A) $x^2 + 2x - 1 = 0$
(B) $x^2 - 2x + 1 = 0$
(C) $x^2 + 2x + 1 = 0$
(D) $x^2 - 2x - 1 = 0$
(E) $x^2 - x - 1 = 0$

Algebra Second-Degree Equations

This problem can be solved by working backwards to construct a quadratic equation with $1 + \sqrt{2}$ as a root that does not involve radicals.

$$
\begin{aligned}
x &= 1 + \sqrt{2} &&\text{set } x \text{ to the desired value} \\
x - 1 &= \sqrt{2} &&\text{subtract 1 from both sides} \\
(x-1)^2 &= 2 &&\text{square both sides} \\
x^2 - 2x + 1 &= 2 &&\text{expand the left side} \\
x^2 - 2x - 1 &= 0 &&\text{subtract 2 from both sides}
\end{aligned}
$$

The correct answer is D.

172. In Country C, the unemployment rate among construction workers dropped from 16 percent on September 1, 1992, to 9 percent on September 1, 1996. If the number of construction workers was 20 percent greater on September 1, 1996, than on September 1, 1992, what was the approximate percent change in the number of unemployed construction workers over this period?

(A) 50% decrease
(B) 30% decrease
(C) 15% decrease
(D) 30% increase
(E) 55% increase

Arithmetic Percents

Letting N represent the number of construction workers on September 1, 1992, the information given in the problem is as follows:

(1) On September 1, 1992, the unemployment rate among construction workers was 16 percent, so the **number** of unemployed construction workers on September 1, 1992, was **0.16N**.

(2) On September 1, 1996, the **number** of construction workers was 20 percent greater than on September 1, 1992, so the **number** of construction workers on September 1, 1996, was **1.2N**.

(3) On September 1, 1996, the unemployment rate among construction workers was 9 percent, so the **number** of unemployed construction workers on September 1, 1996, was **0.09(1.2N)**.

As a fraction, the percent change in the **number** of unemployed construction workers from September 1, 1992, to September 1, 1996, is given by:

$$\frac{\text{number in 1996} - \text{number in 1992}}{\text{number in 1992}} = \frac{0.09(1.2N) - 0.16N}{0.16N} \quad \text{substitution of expressions from (1) and (3)}$$

$$= \frac{(0.09)(1.2) - 0.16}{0.16} \quad \text{divide numerator and denominator by } N$$

$$= \frac{9(12) - 160}{160} \quad \text{multiply numerator and denominator by 1,000 for ease of calculation}$$

$$= \frac{108 - 160}{160} \quad \text{multiply}$$

$$= -\frac{52}{160} \quad \text{subtract}$$

$$= -\frac{13}{40} \quad \text{divide numerator and denominator by 4}$$

$$\approx -\frac{13}{39} \quad 39 \approx 40$$

$$\approx -\frac{1}{3} \quad \text{divide numerator and denominator by 13}$$

Then, as a percent, $-\frac{1}{3}$ represents a decrease of about 30%.

The correct answer is B.

173. In a box of 12 pens, a total of 3 are defective. If a customer buys 2 pens selected at random from the box, what is the probability that neither pen will be defective?

(A) $\frac{1}{6}$

(B) $\frac{2}{9}$

(C) $\frac{6}{11}$

(D) $\frac{9}{16}$

(E) $\frac{3}{4}$

Arithmetic Probability

The probability that the first pen selected is not defective is $\frac{9}{12} = \frac{3}{4}$ (9 pens are not defective out of a total of 12 pens). Assuming the first pen selected is not defective, the probability that the second pen is not defective is $\frac{8}{11}$ (this time 8 pens are not defective out of a total of 11 pens). Therefore, using the multiplication rule for dependent events, the probability that both pens are not defective is $\left(\frac{3}{4}\right)\left(\frac{8}{11}\right) = \frac{6}{11}$.

Alternatively, by a direct count using the number of combinations of n objects taken k at a time (see section 3.4.3 *Counting Methods* in the Math Review chapter), there are

$$\binom{9}{2} = \frac{(9)(8)}{2} = 36 \text{ ways to select 2 non-defective}$$

pens from the 9 non-defective pens, and there are $\binom{12}{2} = \dfrac{(12)(11)}{2} = 66$ ways to select 2 pens from the 12 pens. Therefore, the probability that the 2 pens selected are not defective is

$$\frac{\text{number of ways to select 2 non-defective pens}}{\text{number of ways to select 2 pens}} = \frac{36}{66} = \frac{6}{11}.$$

The correct answer is C.

174. At a certain fruit stand, the price of each apple is 40 cents and the price of each orange is 60 cents. Mary selects a total of 10 apples and oranges from the fruit stand, and the average (arithmetic mean) price of the 10 pieces of fruit is 56 cents. How many oranges must Mary put back so that the average price of the pieces of fruit that she keeps is 52 cents?

(A) 1
(B) 2
(C) 3
(D) 4
(E) 5

Algebra Statistics

This problem can be solved using arithmetic or algebra.

<u>With algebra</u>

Let x be the number of oranges Mary selected originally. It follows that the number of apples Mary selected is $10 - x$ since the number of pieces of fruit she selected originally was 10. The average price of the 10 pieces of fruit is 56 cents so,

$\dfrac{40(10-x)+60x}{10} = 56$	given
$40(10-x)+60x = 560$	multiply both sides by 10
$400 - 40x + 60x = 560$	distributive property
$400 + 20x = 560$	combine like terms
$20x = 160$	subtract 400 from each term
$x = 8$	divide both sides by 20

Thus, Mary originally selected 8 oranges and 2 apples.

If y represents the number of oranges that Mary must put back, then $8 - y$ is the number of oranges she keeps. So, with the 2 apples, the total number of pieces of fruit she keeps is $2 + (8 - y)$. The average price of these $2 + (8 - y)$ pieces of fruit is 52 cents so,

$\dfrac{40(2)+60(8-y)}{2+(8-y)} = 52$	given
$40(2)+60(8-y) = 52[2+(8-y)]$	multiply both sides by $2 + (8-y)$
$40(2)+60(8-y) = 52(10-y)$	combine like terms
$80 + 480 - 60y = 520 - 52y$	distributive property
$560 - 60y = 520 - 52y$	combine like terms
$560 = 520 + 8y$	add $60y$ to both sides
$40 = 8y$	subtract 520 from both sides
$5 = y$	divide both sides by 8

Therefore, Mary must put back 5 oranges so that the average price of the 2 apples and 3 oranges she keeps is $\dfrac{40(2)+60(3)}{5} = \dfrac{260}{5} = 52$ cents.

<u>With arithmetic</u>

In order to know how many oranges Mary should put back to decrease the average price of the pieces of fruit she is buying to 52 cents, the number of oranges she originally selected needs to be determined. Consider the following table:

Number of apples	Number of oranges	Average price (cents)	Average = 56 cents?
1	9	$\dfrac{1(40)+9(60)}{10} = \dfrac{580}{10} = 58$	no
2	8	$\dfrac{2(40)+8(60)}{10} = \dfrac{560}{10} = 56$	**yes**

Thus, Mary originally selected 2 apples and 8 oranges.

Next, determine how many oranges Mary must put back so that the average price of the pieces of fruit she keeps is 52 cents, consider the following table:

Number of apples	Number of oranges put back	Number of oranges kept	Average price (cents)	Average = 52 cents?
2	1	7	$\dfrac{2(40)+7(60)}{9}=\dfrac{500}{9}=55\dfrac{5}{9}$	no
2	2	6	$\dfrac{2(40)+6(60)}{8}=\dfrac{440}{8}=55$	no
2	3	5	$\dfrac{2(40)+5(60)}{7}=\dfrac{380}{7}=54\dfrac{2}{7}$	no
2	4	4	$\dfrac{2(40)+4(60)}{6}=\dfrac{320}{6}=53\dfrac{1}{3}$	no
2	5	3	$\dfrac{2(40)+3(60)}{5}=\dfrac{260}{5}=52$	**yes**

Therefore, Mary must put back 5 oranges.

Note: It is not necessary to perform all of the calculations shown here. It should be obvious, for example, that $\dfrac{500}{9}, \dfrac{380}{7}$, and $\dfrac{320}{6}$ are not whole numbers and therefore cannot equal 52. Nor is it necessary to increment the number of oranges she must put back by 1. For this problem, a good guess might be 4, thinking she might need to put back half the oranges she selected originally. Since putting back 4 oranges doesn't bring the average price down enough, the only other choice is 5, which is the correct answer.

Note that the steps are explained in great detail here. Having good algebraic manipulation skills would make most of the steps fairly automatic.

The correct answer is E.

175. A pharmaceutical company received $3 million in royalties on the first $20 million in sales of the generic equivalent of one of its products and then $9 million in royalties on the next $108 million in sales. By approximately what percent did the ratio of royalties to sales decrease from the first $20 million in sales to the next $108 million in sales?

(A) 8%
(B) 15%
(C) 45%
(D) 52%
(E) 56%

Arithmetic Percents

The ratio of royalties to sales for the first $20 million in sales is $\dfrac{3}{20}$, and the ratio of royalties to sales for the next $108 million in sales is $\dfrac{9}{108} = \dfrac{1}{12}$. Now calculate the percent decrease from $\dfrac{3}{20}$ to $\dfrac{1}{12}$.

$$\dfrac{\dfrac{1}{12}-\dfrac{3}{20}}{\dfrac{3}{20}} \times 100 = \left(\dfrac{1}{12}-\dfrac{3}{20}\right) \times \dfrac{20}{3} \times 100$$

$$= \left(\dfrac{1 \times 20}{12 \times 3} - \dfrac{3 \times 20}{20 \times 3}\right) \times 100$$

$$= \left(\dfrac{5}{9} - 1\right) \times 100$$

$$= -\dfrac{4}{9} \times 100$$

$$\approx -0.44 \times 100$$

$$\approx 45\% \text{ decrease}$$

An alternate way to calculate the percent decrease from $\dfrac{3}{20}$ to $\dfrac{1}{12}$ is to scale the values up until they are integers, which allows for a simpler calculation. Multiplying each of these values by 60 gives $60 \times \dfrac{3}{20} = 9$ and $60 \times \dfrac{1}{12} = 5$, respectively, so the problem reduces to calculating the percent decrease from 9 to 5. Therefore, $\dfrac{5-9}{9} \times 100 = -\dfrac{4}{9} \times 100 \approx -0.44 \times 100 \approx 45\%$ decrease.

The correct answer is C.

Times at Which the Door
Opened from 8:00 to 10:00

8:00	8:06	8:30	9:05
8:03	8:10	8:31	9:11
8:04	8:18	8:54	9:29
8:04	8:19	8:57	9:31

176. The light in a restroom operates with a 15-minute timer that is reset every time the door opens as a person goes in or out of the room. Thus, after someone enters or exits the room, the light remains on for only 15 minutes unless the door opens again and resets the timer for another 15 minutes. If the times listed above are the times at which the door opened from 8:00 to 10:00, approximately how many minutes during this two-hour period was the light off?

(A) 10
(B) 25
(C) 35
(D) 40
(E) 70

Arithmetic Operations with Integers

In the table given above, read down the columns looking for pairs of consecutive times that are more than 15 minutes apart. The following table shows all such pairs:

Consecutive times more than 15 minutes apart	Minutes between times door opens	Minutes that light is on	Minutes that light is off
8:31 and 8:54	$54 - 31 = 23$	15	$23 - 15 = 8$
9:11 and 9:29	$29 - 11 = 18$	15	$18 - 15 = 3$
9:31 and 10:00	$60 - 31 = 29$	15	$29 - 15 = 14$
Total time light is off			25

The correct answer is B.

177. If p is the product of the integers from 1 to 30, inclusive, what is the greatest integer k for which 3^k is a factor of p?

(A) 10
(B) 12
(C) 14
(D) 16
(E) 18

Arithmetic Properties of Numbers

The table below shows the numbers from 1 to 30, inclusive, that have at least one factor of 3 and how many factors of 3 each has.

Multiples of 3 Between 1 and 30	Number of Factors of 3
3	1
$6 = 2 \times 3$	1
$9 = 3 \times 3$	2
$12 = 2 \times 2 \times 3$	1
$15 = 3 \times 5$	1
$18 = 2 \times 3 \times 3$	2
$21 = 3 \times 7$	1
$24 = 2 \times 2 \times 2 \times 3$	1
$27 = 3 \times 3 \times 3$	3
$30 = 2 \times 3 \times 5$	1

The sum of the numbers in the right column is 14. Therefore, 3^{14} is the greatest power of 3 that is a factor of the product of the first 30 positive integers.

The correct answer is C.

178. If $n = 3^8 - 2^8$, which of the following is NOT a factor of n?

    (A) 97
    (B) 65
    (C) 35
    (D) 13
    (E)   5

Arithmetic Properties of Numbers

Since $3^8 - 2^8$ is the difference of the perfect squares $(3^4)^2$ and $(2^4)^2$, then $3^8 - 2^8 = (3^4 + 2^4)(3^4 - 2^4)$. But $3^4 - 2^4$ is also the difference of the perfect squares $(3^2)^2$ and $(2^2)^2$ so $3^4 - 2^4 = (3^2 + 2^2)(3^2 - 2^2)$ and therefore $3^8 - 2^8 = (3^4 + 2^4)(3^2 + 2^2)(3^2 - 2^2)$. It follows that $3^8 - 2^8$ can be factored as $(81 + 16)(9 + 4)(9 - 4) = (97)(13)(5)$. Therefore, 7 is not a factor of $3^8 - 2^8$, and hence $35 = 5 \times 7$ is not a factor of $3^8 - 2^8$. It is easy to see that each of 97, 13, and 5 is a factor of $3^8 - 2^8$, and so is 65, since $65 = 5 \times 13$, although this additional analysis is not needed to arrive at the correct answer.

The correct answer is C.

179. Club X has more than 10 but fewer than 40 members. Sometimes the members sit at tables with 3 members at one table and 4 members at each of the other tables, and sometimes they sit at tables with 3 members at one table and 5 members at each of the other tables. If they sit at tables with 6 members at each table except one and fewer than 6 members at that one table, how many members will be at the table that has fewer than 6 members?

    (A) 1
    (B) 2
    (C) 3
    (D) 4
    (E) 5

Arithmetic Properties of Numbers

Let n be the number of members that Club X has. Since the members can be equally divided into groups of 4 each with 3 left over, and the members can be equally divided into groups of 5 each with 3 left over, it follows that $n - 3$ is divisible by both 4 and 5. Therefore, $n - 3$ must be

a multiple of $(4)(5) = 20$. Also, because the only multiple of 20 that is greater than 10 and less than 40 is 20, it follows that $n - 3 = 20$, or $n = 23$. Finally, when these 23 members are divided into the greatest number of groups of 6 each, there will be 5 members left over, since $23 = (3)(6) + 5$.

The correct answer is E.

180. In order to complete a reading assignment on time, Terry planned to read 90 pages per day. However, she read only 75 pages per day at first, leaving 690 pages to be read during the last 6 days before the assignment was to be completed. How many days in all did Terry have to complete the assignment on time?

    (A) 15
    (B) 16
    (C) 25
    (D) 40
    (E) 46

Algebra Applied Problems

Let n be the number of days that Terry read at the slower rate of 75 pages per day. Then $75n$ is the number of pages Terry read at this slower rate, and $75n + 690$ is the total number of pages Terry needs to read. Also, $n + 6$ is the total number of days that Terry will spend on the reading assignment. The requirement that Terry average 90 pages per day is equivalent to $\dfrac{75n + 690}{n + 6} = 90$.

Then

$$\frac{75n + 690}{n + 6} = 90$$
$$75n + 690 = 90n + 540$$
$$150 = 15n$$
$$10 = n$$

Therefore, the total number of days that Terry has to complete the assignment on time is $n + 6 = 10 + 6 = 16$.

The correct answer is B.

181. If $s > 0$ and $\sqrt{\dfrac{r}{s}} = s$, what is r in terms of s ?

(A) $\dfrac{1}{s}$

(B) $\sqrt{s}$

(C) $s\sqrt{s}$

(D) s^3

(E) $s^3 - s$

Algebra Equations

Solve the equation for r as follows:

$$\sqrt{\frac{r}{s}} = s$$

$\dfrac{r}{s} = s^2$ square both sides of the equation

$r = s^3$ multiply both sides by s

The correct answer is D.

182. If $3 < x < 100$, for how many values of x is $\dfrac{x}{3}$ the square of a prime number?

(A) Two

(B) Three

(C) Four

(D) Five

(E) Nine

Arithmetic Properties of Numbers

If $\dfrac{x}{3}$ is the square of a prime number, then possible values of $\dfrac{x}{3}$ are $2^2, 3^2, 5^2, 7^2, \ldots$. Therefore, possible values of x are $3 \times 2^2 = 12$, $3 \times 3^2 = 27$, $3 \times 5^2 = 75$, $3 \times 7^2 = 147$, …. Since only three of these values, namely 12, 27, and 75, are between 3 and 100, there are three values of x such that $\dfrac{x}{3}$ is the square of a prime number.

The correct answer is B.

183. A researcher plans to identify each participant in a certain medical experiment with a code consisting of either a single letter or a pair of distinct letters written in alphabetical order. What is the least number of letters that can be used if there are 12 participants, and each participant is to receive a different code?

(A) 4

(B) 5

(C) 6

(D) 7

(E) 8

Arithmetic Elementary Combinatorics

None of the essential aspects of the problem is affected if the letters are restricted to be the first n letters of the alphabet, for various positive integers n. With the 3 letters a, b, and c, there are 6 codes: a, b, c, ab, ac, and bc. With the 4 letters a, b, c, and d, there are 10 codes: a, b, c, d, ab, ac, ad, bc, bd, and cd. Clearly, more than 12 codes are possible with 5 or more letters, so the least number of letters that can be used is 5.

The correct answer is B.

184. An object thrown directly upward is at a height of h feet after t seconds, where $h = -16(t - 3)^2 + 150$. At what height, in feet, is the object 2 seconds after it reaches its maximum height?

(A) 6

(B) 86

(C) 134

(D) 150

(E) 166

Algebra Applied Problems

Since $(t - 3)^2$ is positive when $t \neq 3$ and zero when $t = 3$, it follows that the *minimum* value of $(t - 3)^2$ occurs when $t = 3$. Therefore, the *maximum* value of $-16(t - 3)^2$, and also the maximum value of $-16(t - 3)^2 + 150$, occurs when $t = 3$. Hence, the height 2 seconds after the maximum height is the value of h when $t = 5$, or $-16(5 - 3)^2 + 150 = 86$.

The correct answer is B.

185. Which of the following is equivalent to the pair of inequalities $x + 6 > 10$ and $x - 3 \le 5$?

    (A) $2 \le x < 16$
    (B) $2 \le x < 4$
    (C) $2 < x \le 8$
    (D) $4 < x \le 8$
    (E) $4 \le x < 16$

Algebra Inequalities

Solve the inequalities separately and combine the results.

$$x + 6 > 10$$
$$x > 4$$

$$x - 3 \le 5$$
$$x \le 8$$

Since $x > 4$, then $4 < x$. Combining $4 < x$ and $x \le 8$ gives $4 < x \le 8$.

The correct answer is D.

186. David has d books, which is 3 times as many as Jeff and $\frac{1}{2}$ as many as Paula. How many books do the three of them have altogether, in terms of d ?

    (A) $\frac{5}{6}d$

    (B) $\frac{7}{3}d$

    (C) $\frac{10}{3}d$

    (D) $\frac{7}{2}d$

    (E) $\frac{9}{2}d$

Algebra Applied Problems; Simultaneous Equations

Let J be the number of books that Jeff has, and let P be the number of books Paula has. Then, the given information about David's books can be expressed as $d = 3J$ and $d = \frac{1}{2}P$. Solving these

two equations for J and P gives $\frac{d}{3} = J$ and $2d = P$.

Thus, $d + J + P = d + \frac{d}{3} + 2d = 3\frac{1}{3}d = \frac{10}{3}d$.

The correct answer is C.

187. There are 8 teams in a certain league and each team plays each of the other teams exactly once. If each game is played by 2 teams, what is the total number of games played?

    (A)   15
    (B)   16
    (C)   28
    (D)   56
    (E)   64

Arithmetic Operations on Rational Numbers

Since no team needs to play itself, each team needs to play 7 other teams. In addition, each game needs to be counted only once, rather than once for each team that plays that game. Since two teams play each game, $\frac{8 \times 7}{2} = 28$ games are needed.

The correct answer is C.

188. At his regular hourly rate, Don had estimated the labor cost of a repair job as $336 and he was paid that amount. However, the job took 4 hours longer than he had estimated and, consequently, he earned $2 per hour less than his regular hourly rate. What was the time Don had estimated for the job, in hours?

    (A)   28
    (B)   24
    (C)   16
    (D)   14
    (E)   12

Algebra Second-Degree Equations

For ease of calculation later, note that $336 = 6 \times 7 \times 8$.

To avoid fairly extensive algebraic manipulation, consider starting with the answer choices by checking to see which one satisfies the conditions of the problem.

Estimated		Actual	
Number of hours	Per hour pay†	Number of hours	Per hour pay
A 28	$\dfrac{\$336}{28} = \$12^*$	32	$\dfrac{\$336}{32} \neq \$10^{**}$
B 24	$\dfrac{\$336}{24} = \$14$	28	$\dfrac{\$336}{28} = \$12$
C 16	$\dfrac{\$336}{16} = \$21$	20	$\dfrac{\$336}{20} \neq \$19$
D 14	$\dfrac{\$336}{14} = \$24$	18	$\dfrac{\$336}{18} \neq \$22$
E 12	$\dfrac{\$336}{12} = \$28$	16	$\dfrac{\$336}{16} \neq \$26$

† Note that Don used his regular hourly rate to estimate the labor cost of the repair job, so if he estimated $336 for his labor for a t-hour job, then his regular hourly rate was $\dfrac{\$336}{t}$.

*Cancel wherever possible

$$\frac{336}{28} = \frac{6 \times \cancel{7} \times \cancel{8}^2}{\cancel{7} \times \cancel{4}} = 12$$

**This would need to be $12 − $2 = $10 in order for (A) 28 to be correct.

The correct answer is B.

189. If $\dfrac{p}{q} < 1$, and p and q are positive integers, which of the following must be greater than 1 ?

(A) $\sqrt{\dfrac{p}{q}}$

(B) $\dfrac{p}{q^2}$

(C) $\dfrac{p}{2q}$

(D) $\dfrac{q}{p^2}$

(E) $\dfrac{q}{p}$

Arithmetic Properties of Numbers

Since p and q are positive integers, $0 < \dfrac{p}{q} < 1$.

A   Since $\dfrac{p}{q} < 1$, then $q > p$. Taking the square root of both sides of the inequality gives $\sqrt{q} > \sqrt{p}$. Then, $\sqrt{\dfrac{p}{q}} = \dfrac{\sqrt{p}}{\sqrt{q}}$, so here the denominator will still be larger than the numerator. CANNOT be greater than 1.

B   Squaring the denominator increases the denominator, which decreases the value of the fraction. CANNOT be greater than 1.

C   Multiplying the denominator by 2 increases the denominator, which decreases the value of the fraction. CANNOT be greater than 1.

D   Since $\dfrac{p}{q} < 1$, then $q > p$. When $p^2 < q$, this expression will be greater than 1, but p^2 need not be less than q. For example, if $p = 2$ and $q = 100$, $\dfrac{p}{q} = \dfrac{2}{100}$ and $\dfrac{q}{p^2} = \dfrac{100}{2^2} = \dfrac{100}{4} = 25 > 1$. However, if $p = 3$ and $q = 4$, then $\dfrac{p}{q} = \dfrac{3}{4}$ and $\dfrac{q}{p^2} = \dfrac{4}{3^2} = \dfrac{4}{9} < 1$. NEED NOT be greater than 1.

E   Again, since $\dfrac{p}{q} < 1$, then $q > p$. Thus, the reciprocal, $\dfrac{q}{p}$, always has a value greater than 1 because the numerator will always be a larger positive integer than the denominator. MUST be greater than 1.

The correct answer is E.

190. To mail a package, the rate is x cents for the first pound and y cents for each additional pound, where $x > y$. Two packages weighing 3 pounds and 5 pounds, respectively, can be mailed separately or combined as one package. Which method is cheaper, and how much money is saved?

    (A) Combined, with a savings of $x - y$ cents
    (B) Combined, with a savings of $y - x$ cents
    (C) Combined, with a savings of x cents
    (D) Separately, with a savings of $x - y$ cents
    (E) Separately, with a savings of y cents

    Algebra Applied Problems

    Shipping the two packages separately would cost $1x + 2y$ for the 3-pound package and $1x + 4y$ for the 5-pound package. Shipping them together (as a single 8-pound package) would cost $1x + 7y$. By calculating the sum of the costs for shipping the two packages separately minus the cost for shipping the one combined package, it is possible to determine the difference in cost, as shown.

    $\big((1x + 2y) + (1x + 4y)\big) - (1x + 7y)$ (cost for 3 lb. + cost for 5 lb.) − cost for 8 lb.

    $= (2x + 6y) - (1x + 7y)$ combine like terms

    $= 2x + 6y - 1x - 7y$ distribute the negative

    $= x - y$ combine like terms

    Since $x > y$, this value is positive, which means it costs more to ship two packages separately. Thus it is cheaper to mail one combined package at a cost savings of $x - y$ cents.

    The correct answer is A.

191. If money is invested at r percent interest, compounded annually, the amount of the investment will double in approximately $\dfrac{70}{r}$ years. If Pat's parents invested $5,000 in a long-term bond that pays 8 percent interest, compounded annually, what will be the approximate total amount of the investment 18 years later, when Pat is ready for college?

    (A) $20,000
    (B) $15,000
    (C) $12,000
    (D) $10,000
    (E) $9,000

    Algebra Applied Problems

    Since the investment will double in $\dfrac{70}{r} = \dfrac{70}{8} = 8.75 \approx 9$ years, the value of the investment over 18 years can be approximated by doubling its initial value twice. Therefore, the approximate value will be $(\$5,000)(2)(2) = \$20,000$.

    The correct answer is A.

192. On a recent trip, Cindy drove her car 290 miles, rounded to the nearest 10 miles, and used 12 gallons of gasoline, rounded to the nearest gallon. The actual number of miles per gallon that Cindy's car got on this trip must have been between

    (A) $\dfrac{290}{12.5}$ and $\dfrac{290}{11.5}$

    (B) $\dfrac{295}{12}$ and $\dfrac{285}{11.5}$

    (C) $\dfrac{285}{12}$ and $\dfrac{295}{12}$

    (D) $\dfrac{285}{12.5}$ and $\dfrac{295}{11.5}$

    (E) $\dfrac{295}{12.5}$ and $\dfrac{285}{11.5}$

    Arithmetic Estimation

    The lowest number of miles per gallon can be calculated using the lowest possible miles and the highest amount of gasoline. Also, the highest number of miles per gallon can be calculated using the highest possible miles and the lowest amount of gasoline.

    Since the miles are rounded to the nearest 10 miles, the number of miles is between 285 and 295. Since the gallons are rounded to the nearest gallon, the number of gallons is between 11.5 and 12.5. Therefore, the lowest number of miles per gallon is $\dfrac{\text{lowest miles}}{\text{highest gallons}} = \dfrac{285}{12.5}$

and the highest number of miles per gallon is

$$\frac{\text{highest miles}}{\text{lowest gallons}} = \frac{295}{11.5}$$

The correct answer is D.

193. Which of the following inequalities is an algebraic expression for the shaded part of the number line above?

(A) $|x| \leq 3$

(B) $|x| \leq 5$

(C) $|x-2| \leq 3$

(D) $|x-1| \leq 4$

(E) $|x+1| \leq 4$

Algebra Inequalities

The number line above shows $-5 \leq x \leq 3$. To turn this into absolute value notation, as all the choices are written, the numbers need to be opposite signs of the same value.

Since the distance between –5 and 3 is 8 $(3 - (-5) = 8)$, that distance needs to be split in half with –4 to one side and 4 to the other. Each of these two values is 1 more than the values in the inequality above, so adding 1 to all terms in the inequality gives $-4 \leq x+1 \leq 4$, which is the same as $|x+1| \leq 4$.

The correct answer is E.

194. In a small snack shop, the average (arithmetic mean) revenue was $400 per day over a 10-day period. During this period, if the average daily revenue was $360 for the first 6 days, what was the average daily revenue for the last 4 days?

(A) $420

(B) $440

(C) $450

(D) $460

(E) $480

Arithmetic; Algebra Statistics; Applied Problems

Let x be the average daily revenue for the last 4 days. Using the formula

$$\text{average} = \frac{\text{sum of values}}{\text{number of values}}, \text{ the information}$$

regarding the average revenues for the 10-day and 6-day periods can be expressed as follows and solved for x:

$$\$400 = \frac{6(\$360)+4x}{10}$$

$\$4,000 = \$2,160 + 4x$ multiply both sides by 10

$\$1,840 = 4x$ subtract $2,160 from both sides

$\$460 = x$ divide both sides by 4

The correct answer is D.

195. If y is the smallest positive integer such that 3,150 multiplied by y is the square of an integer, then y must be

(A) 2

(B) 5

(C) 6

(D) 7

(E) 14

Arithmetic Properties of Numbers

To find the smallest positive integer y such that $3,150y$ is the square of an integer, first find the prime factorization of 3,150 by a method similar to the following:

$3,150 = 10 \times 315$

$\qquad = (2 \times 5) \times (3 \times 105)$

$\qquad = 2 \times 5 \times 3 \times (5 \times 21)$

$\qquad = 2 \times 5 \times 3 \times 5 \times (3 \times 7)$

$\qquad = 2 \times 3^2 \times 5^2 \times 7$

To be a perfect square, $3,150y$ must have an even number of each of its prime factors. At a minimum, y must have one factor of 2 and one factor of 7 so that $3,150y$ has two factors of each of the primes 2, 3, 5, and 7. The smallest positive integer value of y is then $(2)(7) = 14$.

The correct answer is E.

196. If [x] is the greatest integer less than or equal to x, what is the value of $[-1.6]+[3.4]+[2.7]$?

    (A)   3
    (B)   4
    (C)   5
    (D)   6
    (E)   7

    Arithmetic Profit and Loss

    The greatest integer that is less than or equal to −1.6 is −2. It cannot be −1 because −1 is greater than −1.6. The greatest integer that is less than or equal to 3.4 is 3. It cannot be 4 because 4 is greater than 3.4. The greatest integer that is less than or equal to 2.7 is 2. It cannot be 3 because 3 is greater than 2.7. Therefore, $[-1.6]+[3.4]+[2.7]=-2+3+2=3$.

    The correct answer is A.

197. In the first week of the year, Nancy saved $1. In each of the next 51 weeks, she saved $1 more than she had saved in the previous week. What was the total amount that Nancy saved during the 52 weeks?

    (A) $1,326
    (B) $1,352
    (C) $1,378
    (D) $2,652
    (E) $2,756

    Arithmetic Operations on Rational Numbers

    In dollars, the total amount saved is the sum of 1, (1 + 1), (1 + 1 + 1), and so on, up to and including the amount saved in the 52nd week, which was $52. Therefore, the total amount saved in dollars was 1 + 2 + 3 + … + 50 + 51 + 52. This sum can be easily evaluated by grouping the terms as (1 + 52) + (2 + 51) + (3 + 50) + … + (26 + 27), which results in the number 53 added to itself 26 times. Therefore, the sum is (26)(53) = 1,378.

    Alternatively, the formula for the sum of the first n positive integers is $\dfrac{n(n+1)}{2}$. Therefore, the sum of the first 52 positive integers is $\dfrac{52(53)}{2}=26(53)=1,378$.

    The correct answer is C.

198. In a certain sequence, the term x_n is given by the formula $x_n = 2x_{n-1} - \dfrac{1}{2}(x_{n-2})$ for all $n \geq 2$. If $x_0 = 3$ and $x_1 = 2$, what is the value of x_3 ?

    (A)   2.5
    (B)   3.125
    (C)   4
    (D)   5
    (E)   6.75

    Algebra Simplifying Algebraic Expressions

    Given the formula $x_n = 2x_{n-1} - \dfrac{1}{2}(x_{n-2})$ with $x_0 = 3$ and $x_1 = 2$, then

    $$x_2 = 2x_1 - \frac{1}{2}x_0$$
    $$= 2(2) - \frac{1}{2}(3)$$
    $$= \frac{5}{2}$$
    $$x_3 = 2x_2 - \frac{1}{2}x_1$$
    $$= 2\left(\frac{5}{2}\right) - \frac{1}{2}(2)$$
    $$= 5 - 1$$
    $$= 4$$

    The correct answer is C.

199. During a trip, Francine traveled x percent of the total distance at an average speed of 40 miles per hour and the rest of the distance at an average speed of 60 miles per hour. In terms of x, what was Francine's average speed for the entire trip?

    (A) $\dfrac{180-x}{2}$

    (B) $\dfrac{x+60}{4}$

    (C) $\dfrac{300-x}{5}$

    (D) $\dfrac{600}{115-x}$

    (E) $\dfrac{12,000}{x+200}$

    Algebra Applied Problems

    Assume for simplicity that the total distance of Francine's trip is 100 miles. Then the following table gives all of the pertinent information.

Distance	Rate	Time = $\dfrac{\text{Distance}}{\text{Rate}}$
x	40	$\dfrac{x}{40}$
$100 - x$	60	$\dfrac{100 - x}{60}$

The total time for Francine's trip is

$$\frac{x}{40} + \frac{100 - x}{60} = \frac{3x}{120} + \frac{2(100 - x)}{120}$$

$$= \frac{3x + 2(100 - x)}{120}$$

$$= \frac{3x + 200 - 2x}{120}$$

$$= \frac{x + 200}{120}$$

Francine's average speed over the entire trip is

$$\frac{\text{total distance}}{\text{total time}} = \frac{100}{\dfrac{x + 200}{120}} = \frac{12{,}000}{x + 200}.$$

The correct answer is E.

200. If $n = (33)^{43} + (43)^{33}$, what is the units digit of n?

(A) 0
(B) 2
(C) 4
(D) 6
(E) 8

Arithmetic Properties of Numbers

When a polynomial is raised to a power, the last term in the expression is the last term of the polynomial raised to that power. For example, $(a + b)^2 = a^2 + 2ab + b^2$. We can think of 33 as the binomial $10 \cdot 3 + 3$ whose last term is the units digit 3. Thus, the units digit of 33^2 is $3^2 = 9$. Similarly, for 33^3 we have $3^3 = 27$, so the units digit of 33^3 is 7. The patterns for powers of 33 and 43 are shown in the following table.

power of 33	units digit	power of 43	units digit
33^1	3	43^1	3
33^2	9	43^2	9
33^3	7	43^3	7
33^4	1	43^4	1
33^5	3	43^5	3
33^6	9	43^6	9
33^7	7	43^7	7
33^8	1	43^8	1
$\vdots$	$\vdots$	$\vdots$	$\vdots$
33^{32}	1	43^{32}	1
33^{33}	3	43^{33}	3
$\vdots$	$\vdots$		
33^{40}	1		
33^{41}	3		
33^{42}	9		
33^{43}	7		

From the table above, the units digit of 3^{43} is 7 and the units digit of 43^{33} is 3. Since $7 + 3 = 10$, the units digit of $33^{43} + 43^{33}$ is 0.

The correct answer is A.

201. Team A and Team B are competing against each other in a game of tug-of-war. Team A, consisting of 3 males and 3 females, decides to line up male, female, male, female, male, female. The lineup that Team A chooses will be one of how many different possible lineups?

(A) 9
(B) 12
(C) 15
(D) 36
(E) 720

Arithmetic Elementary Combinatorics

Any of the 3 males can be first in the line, and any of the 3 females can be second. Either of the 2 remaining males can be next, followed by either of the 2 remaining females. The last 2 places in the line are filled with the only male left followed by the only female left. By the multiplication principle, there are $3 \times 3 \times 2 \times 2 \times 1 \times 1 = 36$ different lineups possible.

The correct answer is D.

202. If $d = \dfrac{1}{2^3 \times 5^7}$ is expressed as a terminating decimal, how many nonzero digits will d have?

    (A) One
    (B) Two
    (C) Three
    (D) Seven
    (E) Ten

Arithmetic Operations on Rational Numbers

It will be helpful to use the fact that a factor that is an integer power of 10 has no effect on the number of nonzero digits a terminating decimal has.

$$\frac{1}{2^3 \times 5^7} = \frac{1}{2^3 \times 5^3} \times \frac{1}{5^4}$$

$$= \left(\frac{1}{2 \times 5}\right)^3 \times \left(\frac{1}{5}\right)^4$$

$$= \left(\frac{1}{10}\right)^3 \times \left(\frac{1}{5}\right)^4$$

$$= 10^{-3} \times (0.2)^4$$

$$= 10^{-3} \times (0.0016)$$

$$= 0.0000016$$

The correct answer is B.

203. For any positive integer n, the sum of the first n positive integers equals $\dfrac{n(n+1)}{2}$. What is the sum of all the even integers between 99 and 301 ?

    (A) 10,100
    (B) 20,200
    (C) 22,650
    (D) 40,200
    (E) 45,150

Algebra Simplifying Expressions; **Arithmetic** Computation with Integers

Note: The following approach does not rely on the given formula.

To determine how many integers are to be summed, consider the following:

5 even integers have 10 as their first two digits, namely 100, 102, 104, 106, 108; 5 even integers have 11 as their first two digits, namely 110, 112, 114, 116, 118;

$\vdots$

5 even integers have 28 as their first two digits, namely 280, 282, 284, 286, 288;

5 even integers have 29 as their first two digits, namely 290, 292, 294, 296, 298.

The first two digits range from 10 through 29, so there are $29 - 10 + 1 = 20$ such pairs of two digits. Thus there are $20(5) = 100$ even integers between 100 and 298. Including 300, there are 101 even integers between 99 and 301.

These even integers are listed below.

1st	2nd	3rd	4th	...	50th	51st	52nd	...	98th	99th	100th	101st
100	102	104	106	...	198	200	202	...	294	296	298	300

To sum, pair the integers

1st and 101st	$100 + 300 = 400$	
2nd and 100th	$102 + 298 = 400$	
3rd and 99th	$104 + 296 = 400$	$50(400) = 20{,}000$
4th and 98th	$106 + 294 = 400$	
$\vdots$		
50th and 52nd	$198 + 202 = 400$	
51st	$= 200$	$+\qquad 200$

$$\overline{\qquad\qquad\qquad 20{,}200}$$

Alternatively, let S represent the sum. Then,

$$S = 100 + 102 + 104 + \ldots + 296 + 298 + 300$$
next, rewrite the sum

$$S = 300 + 298 + 296 + \ldots + 104 + 102 + 100$$
then add the two equations

$$2S = 400 + 400 + 400 + \ldots + 400 + 400 + 400$$
now divide by 2

$$S = 200 + 200 + 200 + \ldots + 200 + 200 + 200$$
there are 101 terms in S, so

$$S = 101(200) = 20{,}200.$$

The correct answer is B.

204. November 16, 2001, was a Friday. If each of the years 2004, 2008, and 2012 had 366 days, and the remaining years from 2001 through 2014 had 365 days, what day of the week was November 16, 2014 ?

    (A) Sunday
    (B) Monday
    (C) Tuesday
    (D) Wednesday
    (E) Thursday

Arithmetic Operations with Integers

The number of days between November 16, 2001, and November 16, 2014, is $10(365) + 3(366) = 4,748$ and, because $4,748 = 7(678) + 2$, it follows that 4,748 days is 678 weeks plus 2 days. Then, 678 weeks from Friday, November 16, 2001, is Friday, November 14, 2014, and 2 days from Friday, November 14, 2014, is Sunday, November 16, 2014.

The correct answer is A.

205. How many prime numbers between 1 and 100 are factors of 7,150 ?

    (A) One
    (B) Two
    (C) Three
    (D) Four
    (E) Five

Arithmetic Rate

To find the number of prime numbers between 1 and 100 that are factors of 7,150, find the prime factorization of 7,150 using a method similar to the following:

$7,150 = 10 \times 715$

$\quad\quad = (2 \times 5) \times (5 \times 143)$

$\quad\quad = 2 \times 5 \times 5 \times (11 \times 13)$

Thus, 7,150 has four prime factors: 2, 5, 11, and 13.

The correct answer is D.

206. A sequence of numbers a_1, a_2, a_3, ... is defined as follows: $a_1 = 3$, $a_2 = 5$, and every term in the sequence after a_2 is the product of all terms in the sequence preceding it, e.g., $a_3 = (a_1)(a_2)$ and $a_4 = (a_1)(a_2)(a_3)$. If $a_n = t$ and $n > 2$, what is the value of a_{n+2} in terms of t ?

    (A) $4t$
    (B) t^2
    (C) t^3
    (D) t^4
    (E) t^8

Algebra Sequences

It is given that $a_n = (a_1)(a_2) \ldots (a_{n-1})$ and $a_n = t$. Therefore, $a_{n+1} = (a_1)(a_2) \ldots (a_{n-1})(a_n) = (a_n)(a_n) = t^2$ and $a_{n+2} = (a_1)(a_2) \ldots (a_n)(a_{n+1}) = (a_{n+1})(a_{n+1}) = (t^2)(t^2) = t^4$.

The correct answer is D.

207. Last year the price per share of Stock X increased by k percent and the earnings per share of Stock X increased by m percent, where k is greater than m. By what percent did the ratio of price per share to earnings per share increase, in terms of k and m ?

    (A) $\dfrac{k}{m}\%$
    (B) $(k - m)\%$
    (C) $\dfrac{100(k-m)}{100+k}\%$
    (D) $\dfrac{100(k-m)}{100+m}\%$
    (E) $\dfrac{100(k-m)}{100+k+m}\%$

Algebra Percents

Although this problem can be solved algebraically, the answer can also be identified by choosing numerical values for the variables, calculating the percent increase in the ratio, and comparing the result with the corresponding numerical values of the answer choices. To this end, let the original price per share be \$1,000 and earnings per share be \$200, where $k = 10$ and $m = 5$. Note that $k > m$ for these values.

	Before increase	After increase
price	$1,000	1.1($1,000) = $1,100
earnings	$200	1.05($200) = $210
$\frac{\text{price}}{\text{earnings}}$	$\frac{1,000}{200} = 5$	$\frac{1,100}{210} = \frac{110}{21}$

Therefore, the percent increase in the ratio of price per share to earnings per share is

$$\left(\frac{\frac{110}{21} - 5}{5} \times 100 \right)\% = \left(\frac{110 - 105}{(5)(21)} \times 100 \right)\% = \frac{500}{105}\%$$

Now substitute $k = 10$ and $m = 5$ into the answer choices to determine which answer choice gives $\frac{500}{105}\%$.

A $\frac{10}{5}\%$ **NO**

B $(10 - 5)\%$ **NO**

C $\frac{100(5)}{100 + 10}\% = \frac{500}{110}\%$ **NO**

D $\frac{100(5)}{100 + 5}\% = \frac{500}{105}\%$ **YES**

E $\frac{100(5)}{100 + 10 + 5}\% = \frac{500}{115}\%$ **NO**

The correct answer is D.

208. Of the 300 subjects who participated in an experiment using virtual-reality therapy to reduce their fear of heights, 40 percent experienced sweaty palms, 30 percent experienced vomiting, and 75 percent experienced dizziness. If all of the subjects experienced at least one of these effects and 35 percent of the subjects experienced exactly two of these effects, how many of the subjects experienced only one of these effects?

(A) 105
(B) 125
(C) 130
(D) 180
(E) 195

Arithmetic Applied Problems

Let a be the number who experienced only one of the effects, b be the number who experienced exactly two of the effects, and c be the number

who experienced all three of the effects. Then $a + b + c = 300$, since each of the 300 participants experienced at least one of the effects. From the given information, $b = 105$ (35% of 300), which gives $a + 105 + c = 300$, or $a + c = 195$ (Eq. 1). Also, if the number who experienced sweaty palms (40% of 300, or 120) is added to the number who experienced vomiting (30% of 300, or 90), and this sum is added to the number who experienced dizziness (75% of 300, or 225), then each participant who experienced only one of the effects is counted exactly once, each participant who experienced exactly two of the effects is counted exactly twice, and each participant who experienced all three of the effects is counted exactly 3 times. Therefore, $a + 2b + 3c = 120 + 90 + 225 = 435$. Using $b = 105$, it follows that $a + 2(105) + 3c = 435$, or $a + 3c = 225$ (Eq. 2). Then solving the system defined by Eq. 1 and Eq. 2,

$$\begin{cases} a + c = 195 \\ a + 3c = 225 \end{cases} \quad \text{multiply 1st equation by } -3$$

$$\begin{cases} -3a - 3c = -585 \\ a + 3c = 225 \end{cases} \quad \text{add equations}$$

$-2a = -360$, or $a = 180$

The correct answer is D.

209. If $m^{-1} = -\frac{1}{3}$, then m^{-2} is equal to

(A) -9
(B) -3
(C) $-\frac{1}{9}$
(D) $\frac{1}{9}$
(E) 9

Arithmetic Negative Exponents

Using rules of exponents, $m^{-2} = m^{-1 \times 2} = \left(m^{-1}\right)^2$, and since $m^{-1} = -\frac{1}{3}$, $m^{-2} = \left(-\frac{1}{3}\right)^2 = \frac{1}{9}$.

The correct answer is D.

210. A photography dealer ordered 60 Model X cameras to be sold for $250 each, which represents a 20 percent markup over the dealer's initial cost for each camera. Of the cameras ordered, 6 were never sold and were returned to the manufacturer for a refund of 50 percent of the dealer's initial cost. What was the dealer's approximate profit or loss as a percent of the dealer's initial cost for the 60 cameras?

(A) 7% loss
(B) 13% loss
(C) 7% profit
(D) 13% profit
(E) 15% profit

Arithmetic Percents

Given that $250 is 20% greater than a camera's initial cost, it follows that the initial cost for each camera was $\left(\$\dfrac{250}{1.2}\right)$. Therefore, the initial cost for the 60 cameras was $60\left(\$\dfrac{250}{1.2}\right)$. The total revenue is the sum of the amount obtained from selling $60 - 6 = 54$ cameras for $250 each and the $\left(\dfrac{1}{2}\right)\left(\$\dfrac{250}{1.2}\right)$ refund for each of 6 cameras, or $(54)(\$250)+(6)\left(\dfrac{1}{2}\right)\left(\$\dfrac{250}{1.2}\right)$. The total profit, as a percent of the total initial cost, is

$$\left(\dfrac{(\text{total revenue})-(\text{total initial cost})}{(\text{total initial cost})}\times 100\right)\% =$$

$$\left(\left(\dfrac{(\text{total revenue})}{(\text{total initial cost})}-1\right)\times 100\right)\%. \text{ Using}$$

the numerical expressions obtained above,

$$\dfrac{(\text{total revenue})}{(\text{total initial cost})}-1$$

$$=\dfrac{(54)(250)+6\left(\dfrac{1}{2}\right)\left(\dfrac{250}{1.2}\right)}{(60)\left(\dfrac{250}{1.2}\right)}-1 \quad \text{by substitution}$$

$$=\dfrac{54+3\left(\dfrac{1}{1.2}\right)}{(60)\left(\dfrac{1}{1.2}\right)}-1 \quad \text{by canceling 250s}$$

$$=\dfrac{54(1.2)+3}{60}-1 \quad \begin{array}{l}\text{by multiplying}\\ \text{top and bottom by 1.2}\\ \text{and then canceling 1.2}\end{array}$$

$$=\dfrac{67.8}{60}-1$$

$$=1.13-1$$

$$=0.13$$

Finally, $(0.13 \times 100)\% = 13\%$, which represents a profit since it is positive.

The correct answer is D.

211. Seven pieces of rope have an average (arithmetic mean) length of 68 centimeters and a median length of 84 centimeters. If the length of the longest piece of rope is 14 centimeters more than 4 times the length of the shortest piece of rope, what is the maximum possible length, in centimeters, of the longest piece of rope?

(A) 82
(B) 118
(C) 120
(D) 134
(E) 152

Algebra Statistics

Let $a, b, c, d, e, f,$ and g be the lengths, in centimeters, of the pieces of rope, listed from least to greatest. From the given information it follows that $d = 84$ and $g = 4a + 14$. Therefore, listed from least to greatest, the lengths are $a, b, c, 84, e, f,$ and $4a + 14$. The maximum value of $4a + 14$ will occur when the maximum value of a is used, and this will be the case only if the shortest 3 pieces all have the same length. Therefore, listed from least to greatest, the lengths are $a, a, a, 84, e, f$, and $4a + 14$. The maximum value for $4a + 14$ will occur when e and f are as small as possible. Since e and f are to the right of the median, they must be at least 84 and so 84 is the least possible value for each of e and f. Therefore, listed from least to greatest, the lengths are $a, a, a, 84, 84, 84$, and $4a + 14$. Since the average length is 68, it follows that

$$\frac{a+a+a+84+84+84+(4a+14)}{7} = 68, \text{ or } a = 30.$$

Hence, the maximum length of the longest piece is $(4a + 14) = [4(30) + 14] = 134$ centimeters.

The correct answer is D.

212. What is the difference between the sixth and the fifth terms of the sequence 2, 4, 7, … whose nth term is $n + 2^{n-1}$?

(A) 2
(B) 3
(C) 6
(D) 16
(E) 17

Algebra Simplifying Algebraic Expressions

According to the given formula, the sixth term of the sequence is $6 + 2^{6-1} = 6 + 2^5$ and the fifth term is $5 + 2^{5-1} = 5 + 2^4$. Then,

$$\left(6 + 2^5\right) - \left(5 + 2^4\right) = \left(6 - 5\right) + \left(2^5 - 2^4\right)$$

$$= 1 + 2^4\left(2 - 1\right)$$

$$= 1 + 2^4$$

$$= 1 + 16$$

$$= 17$$

The correct answer is E.

213. From the consecutive integers –10 to 10, inclusive, 20 integers are randomly chosen with repetitions allowed. What is the least possible value of the product of the 20 integers?

(A) $(-10)^{20}$
(B) $(-10)^{10}$
(C) 0
(D) $-(10)^{19}$
(E) $-(10)^{20}$

Arithmetic Properties of Numbers

If –10 is chosen an odd number of times and 10 is chosen the remaining number of times (for example, choose –10 once and choose 10 nineteen times, or choose –10 three times and choose 10 seventeen times), then the product of the 20 chosen numbers will be $-(10)^{20}$. Note that $-(10)^{20}$ is less than $-(10)^{19}$, the only other negative value among the answer choices.

The correct answer is E.

214. The letters D, G, I, I, and T can be used to form 5-letter strings such as DIGIT or DGIIT. Using these letters, how many 5-letter strings can be formed in which the two occurrences of the letter I are separated by at least one other letter?

(A) 12
(B) 18
(C) 24
(D) 36
(E) 48

Arithmetic Elementary Combinatorics

There are 6 ways to select the locations of the 2 occurrences of the letter I, and this number can be determined by listing all such ways as shown below, where the symbol * is used in place of the letters D, G, and T:

$$I^*I^{**}, I^{**}I^*, I^{***}I, {}^*I^*I^*, {}^*I^{**}I, {}^{**}I^*I$$

Alternatively, the number of ways to select the locations of the 2 occurrences of the letter I can be determined by using $\binom{5}{2} - 4 =$

$\dfrac{5!}{(2!)(3!)} - 4 = 10 - 4 = 6$, which is the number of ways to select 2 of the 5 locations minus the 4 ways in which the 2 selected locations are adjacent.

For each of these 6 ways to select the locations of the 2 occurrences of the letter I, there are 6 ways to select the locations of the letters D, G, and T, which can be determined by using 3! = 6 or by listing all such ways:

$$DGT, DTG, GDT, GTD, TDG, TGD$$

It follows that the number of ways to select the locations of the 5 letters to form 5-letter strings is $(6)(6) = 36$.

The correct answer is D.

215. $\dfrac{0.99999999}{1.0001} - \dfrac{0.99999991}{1.0003} =$

(A) 10^{-8}
(B) $3(10^{-8})$
(C) $3(10^{-4})$
(D) $2(10^{-4})$
(E) 10^{-4}

Arithmetic Operations on Rational Numbers

Calculations with lengthy decimals can be avoided by writing 0.99999999 as $1 - 10^{-8}$, 0.99999991 as $1 - 9(10^{-8})$, 1.0001 as $1 + 10^{-4}$, and 1.0003 as $1 + 3(10^{-4})$. Doing this gives

$$\frac{1-10^{-8}}{1+10^{-4}} - \frac{1-9(10^{-8})}{1+3(10^{-4})}$$

$$= \frac{\left[1+10^{-4}\right]\left[1-10^{-4}\right]}{1+10^{-4}} - \frac{1-9(10^{-8})}{1+3(10^{-4})}$$

$$= \frac{1-10^{-4}}{1} - \frac{1-9(10^{-8})}{1+3(10^{-4})}$$

$$= \frac{\left[1-10^{-4}\right]\left[1+3(10^{-4})\right]-\left[1-9(10^{-8})\right]}{1+3(10^{-4})}$$

$$= \frac{1+3(10^{-4})-10^{-4}-3(10^{-8})-1+9(10^{-8})}{1+3(10^{-4})}$$

$$= \frac{2(10^{-4})+6(10^{-8})}{1+3(10^{-4})}$$

$$= \frac{\left[2(10^{-4})\right]\left[1+3(10^{-4})\right]}{1+3(10^{-4})}$$

$$= 2(10^{-4})$$

The correct answer is D.

216. Last Sunday a certain store sold copies of Newspaper A for $1.00 each and copies of Newspaper B for $1.25 each, and the store sold no other newspapers that day. If r percent of the store's revenue from newspaper sales was from Newspaper A and if p percent of the newspapers that the store sold were copies of Newspaper A, which of the following expresses r in terms of p?

(A) $\dfrac{100p}{125-p}$

(B) $\dfrac{150p}{250-p}$

(C) $\dfrac{300p}{375-p}$

(D) $\dfrac{400p}{500-p}$

(E) $\dfrac{500p}{625-p}$

Algebra Percents

Because the number of newspapers sold at the store last Sunday is not given, assume for simplicity that number is 1,000. Also, the value of p is not given, so choose a convenient value to work with, say $p = 60$. In the table that follows, the chosen numbers are in **boldface**.

	Newspaper A	Newspaper B	Total
Percent of papers sold	$p =$ **60**	40	100
Number sold	600	400	**1,000**
Revenue	600($1) = $600	400($1.25) = $500	$1,100
Percent of revenue (r)	$\dfrac{600}{1,100} \times 100 = \dfrac{600}{11}$		

Now, check the answer choices using $p = 60$ to see which one yields $\frac{600}{11}$.

(A) $\frac{100p}{125-p} = \frac{100(60)}{125-60} = \frac{6,000}{65}$

No (65 doesn't have 11 as a factor)

(B) $\frac{150p}{250-p} = \frac{150(60)}{250-60} = \frac{9,000}{190}$

No (190 doesn't have 11 as a factor)

(C) $\frac{300p}{375-p} = \frac{300(60)}{375-60} = \frac{18,000}{315}$

No (315 doesn't have 11 as a factor)

(D) $\frac{400p}{500-p} = \frac{400(60)}{500-60} = \frac{24,000}{440}$

Yes (440 has 11 as a factor) $\frac{24,000}{440} = \frac{600}{11}$

(E) $\frac{500p}{625-p} = \frac{500(60)}{625-60} = \frac{30,000}{565}$

No (565 doesn't have 11 as a factor)

The correct answer is D.

217. For the past n days, the average (arithmetic mean) daily production at a company was 50 units. If today's production of 90 units raises the average to 55 units per day, what is the value of n?

(A) 30
(B) 18
(C) 10
(D) 9
(E) 7

Arithmetic; Algebra Statistics; Applied Problems; Simultaneous Equations

Let x be the total production of the past n days.

Using the formula $\text{average} = \frac{\text{sum of values}}{\text{number of values}}$, the information in the problem can be expressed in the following two equations

$50 = \frac{x}{n}$ — daily average of 50 units over the past n days

$55 = \frac{x+90}{n+1}$ — increased daily average when including today's 90 units

Solving the first equation for x gives $x = 50n$. Then substituting $50n$ for x in the second equation gives the following that can be solved for n:

$55 = \frac{50n+90}{n+1}$

$55(n+1) = 50n + 90$ — multiply both sides by $(n+1)$

$55n + 55 = 50n + 90$ — distribute the 55

$5n = 35$ — subtract $50n$ and 55 from both sides

$n = 7$ — divide both sides by 5

The correct answer is E.

218. If a two-digit positive integer has its digits reversed, the resulting integer differs from the original by 27. By how much do the two digits differ?

(A) 3
(B) 4
(C) 5
(D) 6
(E) 7

Algebra Applied Problems

Let the one two-digit integer be represented by $10t + s$, where s and t are digits, and let the other integer with the reversed digits be represented by $10s + t$. The information that the difference between the integers is 27 can be expressed in the following equation, which can be solved for the answer.

$(10s + t) - (10t + s) = 27$

$10s + t - 10t - s = 27$ — distribute the negative

$9s - 9t = 27$ — combine like terms

$s - t = 3$ — divide both sides by 9

Thus, it is seen that the two digits s and t differ by 3.

The correct answer is A.

219. In an electric circuit, two resistors with resistances x and y are connected in parallel. In this case, if r is the combined resistance of these two resistors, then the reciprocal of r is equal to the sum of the reciprocals of x and y. What is r in terms of x and y?

(A) xy

(B) $x + y$

(C) $\dfrac{1}{x + y}$

(D) $\dfrac{xy}{x + y}$

(E) $\dfrac{x + y}{xy}$

Algebra Applied Problems

Note that two numbers are reciprocals of each other if and only if their product is 1. Thus the reciprocals of r, x, and y are $\dfrac{1}{r}$, $\dfrac{1}{x}$, and $\dfrac{1}{y}$, respectively. So, according to the problem, $\dfrac{1}{r} = \dfrac{1}{x} + \dfrac{1}{y}$. To solve this equation for r, begin by creating a common denominator on the right side by multiplying the first fraction by $\dfrac{y}{y}$ and the second fraction by $\dfrac{x}{x}$:

$$\frac{1}{r} = \frac{1}{x} + \frac{1}{y}$$

$$\frac{1}{r} = \frac{y}{xy} + \frac{x}{xy}$$

$$\frac{1}{r} = \frac{x + y}{xy} \quad \text{combine the fractions on the right side}$$

$$r = \frac{xy}{x + y} \quad \text{invert the fractions on both sides}$$

The correct answer is D.

220. Xavier, Yvonne, and Zelda each try independently to solve a problem. If their individual probabilities for success are $\dfrac{1}{4}$, $\dfrac{1}{2}$, and $\dfrac{5}{8}$, respectively, what is the probability that Xavier and Yvonne, but not Zelda, will solve the problem?

(A) $\dfrac{11}{8}$

(B) $\dfrac{7}{8}$

(C) $\dfrac{9}{64}$

(D) $\dfrac{5}{64}$

(E) $\dfrac{3}{64}$

Arithmetic Probability

Since the individuals' probabilities are independent, they can be multiplied to figure out the combined probability. The probability of Xavier's success is given as $\dfrac{1}{4}$, and the probability of Yvonne's success is given as $\dfrac{1}{2}$. Since the probability of Zelda's success is given as $\dfrac{5}{8}$, then the probability of her NOT solving the problem is $1 - \dfrac{5}{8} = \dfrac{3}{8}$.

Thus, the combined probability is

$$\left(\frac{1}{4}\right)\left(\frac{1}{2}\right)\left(\frac{3}{8}\right) = \frac{3}{64}.$$

The correct answer is E.

221. If $\dfrac{1}{x} - \dfrac{1}{x + 1} = \dfrac{1}{x + 4}$, then x could be

(A) 0

(B) −1

(C) −2

(D) −3

(E) −4

Algebra Second-Degree Equations

Solve the equation for x. Begin by multiplying all the terms by $x(x+1)(x+4)$ to eliminate the denominators.

$$\frac{1}{x} - \frac{1}{x+1} = \frac{1}{x+4}$$

$$(x+1)(x+4) - x(x+4) = x(x+1)$$

$$(x+4)(x+1-x) = x(x+1) \quad \text{factor the } (x+4) \text{ out front on the left side}$$

$$(x+4)(1) = x(x+1) \quad \text{simplify}$$

$$(x+4) = x^2 + x \quad \text{distribute the } x \text{ on the right side}$$

$$4 = x^2 \quad \text{subtract } x \text{ from both sides}$$

$$\pm 2 = x \quad \text{take the square root of both sides}$$

Both -2 and 2 are square roots of 4 since $(-2^2) = 4$ and $(2^2) = 4$. Thus, x could be -2.

This problem can also be solved as follows. Rewrite the left side as, $\dfrac{(x+1)-x}{x(x+1)} = \dfrac{1}{x(x+1)}$, then set equal to the right side to get

$\dfrac{1}{x(x+1)} = \dfrac{1}{x+4}$. Next, cross multiply:

$(1)(x+4) = x(x+1)(1)$. Therefore, $x+4 = x^2 + x$, or $x^2 = 4$, so $x = \pm 2$.

The correct answer is C.

222. $\left(\dfrac{1}{2}\right)^{-3} \left(\dfrac{1}{4}\right)^{-2} \left(\dfrac{1}{16}\right)^{-1} =$

(A) $\left(\dfrac{1}{2}\right)^{-48}$

(B) $\left(\dfrac{1}{2}\right)^{-11}$

(C) $\left(\dfrac{1}{2}\right)^{-6}$

(D) $\left(\dfrac{1}{8}\right)^{-11}$

(E) $\left(\dfrac{1}{8}\right)^{-6}$

Arithmetic Operations on Rational Numbers

It is clear from the answer choices that all three factors need to be written with a common denominator, and they thus become

$$\left(\frac{1}{2}\right)^{-3} = \left(\frac{1}{2}\right)^{-3}$$

$$\left(\frac{1}{4}\right)^{-2} = \left(\left(\frac{1}{2}\right)^2\right)^{-2} = \left(\frac{1}{2}\right)^{-4}$$

$$\left(\frac{1}{16}\right)^{-1} = \left(\left(\frac{1}{2}\right)^4\right)^{-1} = \left(\frac{1}{2}\right)^{-4}$$

So, $\left(\dfrac{1}{2}\right)^{-3} \left(\dfrac{1}{4}\right)^{-2} \left(\dfrac{1}{16}\right)^{-1} =$

$$\left(\frac{1}{2}\right)^{-3}\left(\frac{1}{2}\right)^{-4}\left(\frac{1}{2}\right)^{-4} = \left(\frac{1}{2}\right)^{-3-4-4} = \left(\frac{1}{2}\right)^{-11}.$$

The correct answer is B.

223. List T consists of 30 positive decimals, none of which is an integer, and the sum of the 30 decimals is S. The estimated sum of the 30 decimals, E, is defined as follows. Each decimal in T whose tenths digit is even is rounded up to the nearest integer, and each decimal in T whose tenths digit is odd is rounded down to the nearest integer; E is the sum of the resulting integers.

If $\dfrac{1}{3}$ of the decimals in T have a tenths digit that is even, which of the following is a possible value of $E - S$?

  I. -16

  II.   6

  III.   10

(A) I only

(B) I and II only

(C) I and III only

(D) II and III only

(E) I, II, and III

Arithmetic Operations on Rational Numbers

First, consider $E - S$ as the total of the "contributions" made by the decimals in T with even tenths digits and the "contributions" made by the decimals in T with odd tenths digits, as shown in the following tables.

	Decimals with even tenth digit	Example
Number that occurs in T	$\frac{1}{3}(30)=10$	
Max possible tenth digit	8	14.89999
Contribution each makes to $E-S$	Greater than 0.1	$15-14.89999$ $=0.10001$
Total contribution to $E-S$	Greater than $10(0.1)$ $=1$	
Min possible tenth digit	0	14.00001
Contribution each makes to $E-S$	Less than 1	$15-14.00001$ $=0.99999$
Total contribution to $E-S$	Less than $10(1)=10$	
Summary	$1<$ (evens' contribution to $E-S$) <10	

	Decimals with odd tenth digit	Example
Number that occurs in T	$\frac{2}{3}(30)=20$	
Max possible tenth digit	9	14.9999
Contribution each makes to $E-S$	Greater than -1	$14-14.9999$ $=-0.9999$
Total contribution to $E-S$	Greater than $20(-1)$ $=-20$	
Min possible tenth digit	1	14.1
Contribution each makes to $E-S$	Less than or equal to -0.1	$14-14.1$ $=-0.1$
Total contribution to $E-S$	Less than or equal to $20(-0.1)=-2$	
Summary	$-20<$ (odds' contribution to $E-S$) ≤-2	

Adding the summary inequalities from the tables gives

$1+(-20)<$ (evens' contribution to $E-S$) $+$ (odds' contribution to $E-S$) $<10+(-2)$ or $-19<E-S<8$. Thus, the possible values of $E-S$ include -16 and 6, but not 10.

Note that if T contains 10 repetitions of 1.8 and 20 repetitions of 1.9, then $S=10(1.8)+20(1.9)=18+38=56$, $E=10(2)+20(1)=20+20=40$, and $E-S=40-56=-16$.

However, if T contains 10 repetitions of 1.2 and 20 repetitions of 1.1, then $S=10(1.2)+20(1.1)=12+22=34$, $E=10(2)+20(1)=20+20=40$, and $E-S=40-34=6$.

The correct answer is B.

224. If $5-\dfrac{6}{x}=x$, then x has how many possible values?

(A) None

(B) One

(C) Two

(D) A finite number greater than two

(E) An infinite number

Algebra Second-Degree Equations

Solve the equation to determine how many values are possible for x.

$$5-\frac{6}{x}=x$$
$$5x-6=x^2$$
$$0=x^2-5x+6$$
$$0=(x-3)(x-2)$$
$$x=3 \text{ or } 2$$

The correct answer is C.

225. Seed mixture X is 40 percent ryegrass and 60 percent bluegrass by weight; seed mixture Y is 25 percent ryegrass and 75 percent fescue. If a mixture of X and Y contains 30 percent ryegrass, what percent of the weight of the mixture is X ?

(A)   10%

(B) $33\frac{1}{3}\%$

(C)   40%

(D)   50%

(E) $66\frac{2}{3}\%$

Algebra Applied Problems

Let X be the amount of seed mixture X in the final mixture, and let Y be the amount of seed mixture Y in the final mixture. The final mixture of X and Y needs to contain 30 percent ryegrass seed, so any other kinds of grass seed are irrelevant to the solution to this problem. The information about the ryegrass percentages for X, Y, and the final mixture can be expressed in the following equation and solved for X.

$0.40X + 0.25Y = 0.30(X + Y)$

$0.40X + 0.25Y = 0.30X + 0.30Y$ distribute the 0.30 on the right side

$\qquad 0.10X = 0.05Y$ subtract $0.30X$ and $0.25Y$ from both sides

$\qquad\qquad X = 0.5Y$ divide both sides by 0.10

Using this, the percent of the weight of the combined mixture $(X + Y)$ that is X is

$$\frac{X}{X+Y} = \frac{0.5Y}{0.5Y + Y} = \frac{0.5Y}{1.5Y} = \frac{0.5}{1.5} = 0.33\overline{3} = 33\frac{1}{3}\%$$

The correct answer is B.

226. How many of the integers that satisfy the inequality $\dfrac{(x+2)(x+3)}{x-2} \geq 0$ are less than 5 ?

(A)   1

(B)   2

(C)   3

(D)   4

(E)   5

Algebra Inequalities

Note: This explanation is very detailed. However, many of the steps should become more automatic with additional practice in solving nonlinear inequalities.

The expression $\dfrac{(x+2)(x+3)}{x-2}$ contains three binomials, namely $x + 2$, $x + 3$, and $x - 2$, that determine for what values of x each binomial is zero, negative, and positive. The table below summarizes these values.

Binomial	Zero for	Negative for	Positive for
$x + 3$	$x = -3$	$x < -3$	$x > -3$
$x + 2$	$x = -2$	$x < -2$	$x > -2$
$x - 2$	$x = 2$	$x < 2$	$x > 2$

Note that, although $x - 2 = 0$ when $x = 2$, $\dfrac{(x+2)(x+3)}{x-2}$ is undefined for $x = 2$. However, $\dfrac{(x+2)(x+3)}{x-2} = 0$ when $x = -3$ and when $x = -2$. Both of these values are integers less than 5. (i)

The following number line shows the information in the table above. The vertical segments at $x = -3$, $x = -2$, and $x = 2$ partition the number line into 4 intervals:

I_1, where $x < -3$

I_2, where $-3 < x < -2$

I_3, where $-2 < x < 2$

I_4, where $x > 2$.

I_1: All three binomials are negative, so the inequality $\dfrac{(x+2)(x+3)}{x-2} \geq 0$ is NOT satisfied.

I_2: Contains no integers, so need not be considered further.

I_3: Two binomials are positive, one is negative so the inequality $\dfrac{(x+2)(x+3)}{x-2} \geq 0$ is NOT satisfied.

I_4: All three binomials are positive, so the inequality $\dfrac{(x+2)(x+3)}{x-2} \geq 0$ is satisfied. The integers in this interval that are less than 5 are 3 and 4. (ii)

From (i) and (ii), there are 4 integers, namely −3, −2, 3, and 4, for which $\dfrac{(x+2)(x+3)}{x-2} \geq 0$.

The correct answer is D.

227. Of the 150 houses in a certain development, 60 percent have air-conditioning, 50 percent have a sunporch, and 30 percent have a swimming pool. If 5 of the houses have all three of these amenities and 5 have none of them, how many of the houses have exactly two of these amenities?

   (A)   10
   (B)   45
   (C)   50
   (D)   55
   (E)   65

Arithmetic Sets

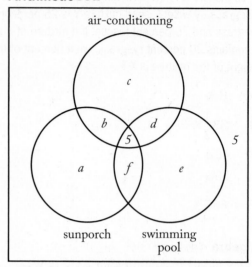

Since 60% of the 150 houses have air-conditioning, $b + c + d + 5 = 0.6(150) = 90$, so $b + c + d = 85$ (i). Similarly, since 50% have a sunporch, $a + b + f + 5 = 0.5(150) = 75$, so $a + b + f = 70$ (ii). Likewise, since 30% have a swimming pool, $d + e + f + 5 = 0.3(150) = 45$, so $d + e + f = 40$ (iii). Adding equations (i), (ii), and (iii) gives $(b + c + d) + (a + b + f) + (d + e + f) = 195$, or $a + 2b + c + 2d + e + 2f = 195$ (iv). But $a + b + c + d + e + f + 5 + 5 = 150$, or $a + b + c + d + e + f = 140$ (v). Subtracting equation (v) from equation (iv) gives $b + d + f = 55$, so 55 houses have exactly two of the amenities.

The correct answer is D.

228. The value of $\dfrac{2^{-14} + 2^{-15} + 2^{-16} + 2^{-17}}{5}$ is how many times the value of $2^{(-17)}$?

   (A) $\dfrac{3}{2}$

   (B) $\dfrac{5}{2}$

   (C)   3

   (D)   4

   (E)   5

Arithmetic Negative Exponents

If the value of $\dfrac{2^{-14} + 2^{-15} + 2^{-16} + 2^{-17}}{5}$ is x times

the value of 2^{-17}, then

$$x(2^{-17}) = \frac{2^{-14} + 2^{-15} + 2^{-16} + 2^{-17}}{5}$$

$$x = \frac{\dfrac{2^{-14} + 2^{-15} + 2^{-16} + 2^{-17}}{5}}{2^{-17}}$$

$$= \frac{2^{-14} + 2^{-15} + 2^{-16} + 2^{-17}}{5} \times 2^{17}$$

$$= \frac{\left(2^{-14} + 2^{-15} + 2^{-16} + 2^{-17}\right) \times 2^{17}}{5}$$

$$= \frac{2^{-14+17} + 2^{-15+17} + 2^{-16+17} + 2^{-17+17}}{5}$$

$$= \frac{2^{3} + 2^{2} + 2^{1} + 2^{0}}{5}$$

$$= \frac{8 + 4 + 2 + 1}{5}$$

$$= 3$$

The correct answer is C.

To register for the GMAT™ exam go to www.mba.com/register

5.0 Data Insights Review

5.0 Data Insights Review

To prepare for the Data Insights section of the GMAT™ and succeed in graduate business programs, you need basic skills in analyzing data. This chapter is about the kinds of data shown in tables and charts. It's only a brief overview, so if you find unfamiliar terms, consult outside resources to learn more. Before reading this chapter, you may want to read this guidebook's Section 3.4.1, "Statistics," and Section 7.2.2, "Generalizations and Predictions," to review basic statistics and inductive generalization.

Section 5.1, "Data Sets and Types," includes these topics:

1. Data Sets
2. Qualitative Data
3. Quantitative Data

Section 5.2, "Data Displays," includes these topics:

1. Tables
2. Qualitative Charts
3. Quantitative Charts

Section 5.3, "Data Patterns" includes these topics:

1. Distributions
2. Trends and Correlations

5.1 Data Sets and Types

1. Data Sets

A. A *data set* is an organized collection of data about a specific topic. A data set can be shown with one or more tables, charts, or both.

> *Example:*
>
> One data set might have data about all the employees in a company's human resources division, such as their first names, last names, home addresses, phone numbers, positions, salaries, hiring dates, and full-time or part-time statuses.

B. A *case* is an individual or thing about which data is collected. Often the same types of data about many cases together form a data set. Then a table or chart can show those types of data for all the cases.

> *Example:*
>
> In the example above, each employee in the human resources department is a case.

C. A *variable* is any specific type of data collected about a set of cases. For each case in a data set, the variable has a *value*.

> *Example:*
>
> In the example above, each type of data collected about the employees is a variable: *first name* is one variable, *home address* is another variable, *phone number* is a third variable, and so on. If Zara is an employee in the human resources department, one value of the variable *first name* is "Zara."

In a simple table, the top row often names the variables. Each column shows one variable's values for all the cases. In a chart, labels usually say which variables are shown.

D. The value of a ***dependent variable*** depends on the values of one or more other variables in the data set. An ***independent variable*** is not dependent.

> *Example:*
>
> In a data set of revenues, expenses, and profits, *revenue* and *expense* are independent variables. But *profit* is a dependent variable because profit is calculated as revenue minus expense. For each case, the value of the variable *profit* depends on the values of the variable's *revenue* and *expense*.

E. A ***data point*** gives the value of a specific variable in a specific case. A cell in a table usually stands for a data point.

> *Example:*
>
> In the example above, one data point might be that Zara's position is assistant manager. That is, the data point gives the value "assistant manager" for the variable *position* in Zara's case.

F. A ***record*** is a list of the data points for one case. A row in a table usually shows one record. In a chart, a record might be shown as a point, a line, a bar, or a small shape with a specific position or length.

> *Example:*
>
> In the example above, one record might list Zara's first name, last name, home address, phone number, position, salary, hiring date, and full-time or part-time status.

2. Qualitative Data

A. ***Qualitative data*** is any type of data that doesn't use numbers to stand for a quantity. Statements, words, names, letters, symbols, algebraic expressions, colors, images, sounds, computer files, and web links are all qualitative data. Even data that looks numeric is qualitative if the numbers don't stand for quantities.

> *Example:*
>
> Phone numbers are qualitative data. That's because they don't stand for quantities and aren't used in math—for example, they are generally not summed, multiplied, or averaged.

B. ***Nominal data*** is any type of qualitative data that's not ordered in any relevant way. The statistical measures of mean, median, and range don't apply to nominal data because those measures need an ordering that nominal data lacks. But even in a set of nominal data, some values may appear more often than others. So, the statistical measure of mode does apply to nominal data because the mode is simply the value that appears most often. To review these statistical terms, refer to Section 3.4.1, "Statistics."

Example:

In the example above, the first names of the human resource department's employees are nominal data if their alphabetical order doesn't matter in the data set. Suppose three of the employees share the first name "Amy," but no more than two of the employees share any other first name. Then "Amy" is the mode of the first names of the department's employees because it's the first name that appears most often in the data set.

C. **Ordinal data** is qualitative data ordered in a way that matters in the data set. Because ordinal data is qualitative, its values can't be added, subtracted, multiplied, or divided. So, the statistical measures of mean and range do not apply to ordinal data because they're calculated with those arithmetic operations. However, the statistical measure of median does apply to ordinal data because finding a median only requires putting the values in an order. The statistical measure of mode also applies, just as it does for nominal data.

Example:

In a data set for a weekly schedule of appointments, the weekdays Monday, Tuesday, Wednesday, Thursday, and Friday are ordinal data. These days are in an order that matters to the schedule, but they're not numbers and don't measure quantities. Suppose the data set lists seven appointments: two on Monday, two on Tuesday, and three on Thursday. The fourth appointment is the median in the schedule because three appointments are before it and three are after it. The fourth appointment is on Tuesday, so "Tuesday" is the median value of the variable *weekday* for the appointments in this data set. "Thursday" is the mode, because more of the appointments are on Thursday than on any other day.

D. **Binary data** takes only two values, like "true" and "false." Binary data is ordinal if the order of the two values matters, but nominal otherwise. Tables may show binary values with two words like "yes" and "no," or with two letters like "T" and "F," or simply with a check mark or "X" standing for one of the two values, and a blank space standing for the other.

Example:

In the example above of the data set of employees in a human resource department, their employment status is a binary variable with two values: "full time" and "part time." A table might show the employment status data in a column simply titled "Full Time," with a checkmark for each full-time employee and a blank for each part-time employee.

E. **Partly ordered data** has an order among some cases but not among others. The statistical measure of median does not apply to a set of partly ordered values, though it might apply to a subset whose values are all fully ordered.

Example:

Suppose a family tree shows how people over several generations were related as parents, children, and siblings, but doesn't show when each person was born. This tree lets us partly order the family members by the variable *age*. For example, suppose the family tree shows that Haruto's children were Honoka and Akari and Honoka's child was Minato. Since we know that all parents are older than their children, we can tell that Haruto was older than Honoka and Akari, and that Honoka was older than Minato. That also means Haruto was older than Minato. But we cannot determine whether Akari is older or younger than her sister Honoka. We can't even deduce with certainty whether Akari is older or younger than her nephew Minato. So, the family tree only partly orders the family members by age.

3. Quantitative Data

A. *Quantitative data* is data about quantities measured in numbers. Quantitative values can be added, multiplied, averaged, and so on. The statistical measures of mean, median, mode, range, and standard deviation all apply to quantitative data.

Example:

In the example above of the data set of the employees in the human resource department, the salaries are quantitative data. They're amounts of money shown as numbers.

B. Quantitative data is *continuous* if it measures something that can be infinitely divided.

Examples:

Temperatures are continuous data. That's because for any two different temperatures, some third temperature is between them—warmer than one and cooler than the other. Likewise, altitudes are continuous data. For any two different altitudes, some third altitude is higher than one and lower than the other.

A set of continuous quantitative values rarely has a mode. Because infinitely many of these values are possible, usually no two of them in a data set are exactly alike.

C. Quantitative data that isn't continuous is *discrete*.

Examples:

The numbers of students taking different university courses are discrete data, because they're whole numbers. A course normally can't have a fractional number of students.

As another example, prices in a currency are discrete data, because they can't be divided beyond the currency's smallest denomination. Suppose one price in euros is €3.00, and another is €3.01. No price in euros is larger than the first and smaller than the second, because the currency has no denomination below one euro cent (1/100 of a euro). That means you can't have a price of €3.005, for example. The prices in euros aren't continuous, so they're discrete.

Counted numbers of people, objects, or events are generally discrete data.

D. *Interval data* uses a measurement scale whose number zero doesn't stand for a complete absence of the factor measured. So, for interval data, a measurement above zero doesn't show how much greater than nothing the measured quantity is. Because of this, the ratio of two measurements in interval data isn't the ratio of the two measured quantities.

Examples:

Dates given in years are interval data. In different societies' calendars, the year "0" stands for different years. The year 0 in the Gregorian calendar was roughly the year 3760 in the Hebrew calendar, −641 in the Islamic calendar, and −78 in the Indian National calendar. In none of these calendars does 0 stand for the very first year ever. This means, for example, that the ratio of the numbers in the two years 500 CE and 1500 CE in the Gregorian calendar isn't the ratio of two amounts: the year 500 CE isn't 1/3 the amount of the year 1500 CE.

As another example, temperatures given in degrees Celsius or Fahrenheit are also interval data. The temperature 0 degrees Celsius is 32 degrees Fahrenheit. In neither temperature scale does 0 degrees mean absolute 0, the complete absence of heat. This means, for example, that the ratio of the numbers in the temperatures 30°F and 60°F isn't the ratio of two amounts of heat. Thus, 60°F isn't twice as hot as 30°F.

In a measurement scale for interval data, each unit stands for the same amount. That is, any two measurements that differ by the same number of units stand for two quantities that differ by the same amount.

Examples:

In the example above of dates given in years, the year 1500 CE was 1000 years after 500 CE, because 1500 − 500 = 1000. Likewise, the year 1600 CE was 1000 years after 600 CE, because 1600 − 600 = 1000. Although you can't divide one year by another to find a real ratio, you can subtract one year from another to find a real-time interval—in this case, 1000 years.

Likewise, 60°F is the same amount warmer than 40°F as it is cooler than 80°F. A 20°F difference in two measured temperatures always stands for the same real difference in heat between those temperatures.

E. *Ratio data* uses a measurement scale whose number zero stands for the absence of the measured factor. In ratio data, as in interval data, the difference between two measurements stands for the actual difference between the measured amounts. However, in ratio data, unlike interval data, the ratio of two measurements also stands for the actual ratio of the measured amounts.

Examples:

Measured weights are ratio data, whether they're in kilograms or pounds. That's because 0 kilograms stands for a complete absence of weight, as does 0 pounds. So, the ratio of 10 kilograms to 5 kilograms is a ratio of two real weights. Because the ratio of 10 to 5 is 2 to 1, 10 kilograms is twice as heavy as 5 kilograms, and 10 pounds is twice as heavy as 5 pounds.

As another example, temperatures measured in degrees Kelvin are ratio data. That's because 0°K stands for absolute zero, the complete absence of heat. Thus, 200°K is really twice as hot as 100°K. As explained above, this isn't the case with temperatures measured in degrees Celsius or Fahrenheit, which are interval data.

F. ***Logarithmic data*** use a measurement scale whose higher values stand for amounts exponentially farther apart. For logarithmic data, as for ratio data, the number zero stands for a complete absence. But in logarithmic data, the higher two measurements a certain number of units apart are, the greater the real difference between the measured amounts is.

> *Example:*
>
> Noise measured in decibels is logarithmic data. Although 0 decibels indicates complete silence, a noise of 30 decibels is 10 times as loud as a noise of 20 decibels, not just 1.5 times as loud. And the real difference in loudness between 40 decibels and 30 decibels is 10 times the real difference in loudness between 30 decibels and 20 decibels, even though the first difference and the second difference are each 10 decibels.

Because the units at higher levels on a logarithmic scale stand for greater amounts of difference, you can't just sum and divide logarithmic data to find a statistical mean. Nor can you subtract one logarithmic measurement from another to find a statistical range. Finding the mean and range require more complex calculations, which you won't have to do on the GMAT.

5.2 Data Displays

1. Tables

A. A ***table*** shows data in rows and columns. In a simple table, the top row shows the names of the variables and is called the ***header***. Below the header, usually each row shows one record, each column shows one variable, and each cell shows one data point. Sometimes another row above the header has the table's title or description. Sometimes a column or a few rows within the table are used only to group the records by category. Likewise, a row or a few columns within the table are sometimes used only to group the variables by category. Sometimes a row or column shows totals, averages, or other operations on the values in other rows or columns.

Example:

The table below shows revenues, expenses, and profits for two branches of Village Shoppe for one year. The top row is the header listing the independent variables *revenue* and *expense* and the dependent variable *profit*. In each row, the profit is just the revenue minus the expense.

The table has only four rows of records. These are the third row showing the Mapleton branch's January-June finances, the fourth row showing the Mapleton branch's April-December finances, the sixth row showing the Elmville branch's January-June finances, and the seventh row showing the Elmville branch's April-December finances. The second row "Mapleton branch" serves to group the third and fourth rows together. Likewise, the fifth row "Elmville branch" serves to group the sixth and seventh rows together. The bottom row "Annual grand totals" doesn't show a record, but rather sums the values in the four records for each of the three variables.

Village Shoppe	Revenue	Expense	Profit
Mapleton branch			
January-June	125000	40000	85000
April-December	90000	35000	55000
Elmville branch			
January-June	85000	30000	55000
April-December	115000	25000	90000
Annual grand totals	**415000**	**130000**	**285000**

B. Sometimes a table's title or description explains the data shown. To understand the data, always study any title or description.

Example:

In the table below, the title says the populations are in **thousands**. So, to find the total population aged 44 and under, add 63,376 thousand and 86,738 thousand. This gives 150,114 thousand, which is 150,114,000. If you only read the numbers without noticing the title, you'll get the wrong result for the total population aged 44 and under.

Population by Age Group (in thousands)	
Age	Population
17 years and under	63,376
18–44 years	86,738
45–64 years	43,845
65 years and over	24,051

2. Qualitative Charts

A. Many different types of charts show qualitative data. This book's Section 3.4.2, "Sets," discusses one type of qualitative chart, the **Venn diagram**. Here we describe a few other common types. But the GMAT may also challenge you with unfamiliar types of charts this book doesn't discuss. To understand any type of chart, study its labels. The labels will tell you how to read the chart's various points, lines, shapes, symbols, and colors. Several labels may be together, sometimes inside a rectangle on the chart, to make a **legend**.

B. A *network diagram* has lines connecting small circles or other shapes. Each small shape is a *node* standing for an individual, and each line stands for a relationship between two individuals. In some network diagrams, the lines are one-way or two-way arrows standing for one-way or two-way relationships.

Example:

In the network diagram below, the lettered nodes stand for six pen pals: Alice, Ben, Cathy, Dave, Ellen, and Frank. The arrows show who got a letter from whom in the past month. Each arrow points from the pen pal who sent the letter to the one who got it. A two-way arrow means both the pen pals got letters from each other. This diagram tells us many facts about the pen pals and their relationships over the past month. For example, it shows who got the most letters (Cathy received three) and who got the fewest (Frank received none).

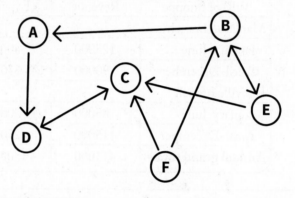

C. A *tree diagram* is a type of network diagram that shows partly ordered data like organizational structures, ancestral relationships, or conditional probabilities. In a tree diagram, each relationship is one way.

Example:

Expanding on the example in 5.1.2.E above, the tree diagram below shows how all of Haruto's descendants are related. Each line connects a parent above to his or her child below. The diagram shows how Haruto has two children, four grandchildren, and one great-grandchild. From the diagram we can tell that Akari is older than her grandchild Mei, and that Himari and Minato are cousins. However, we can't tell whether Akari, Mei, or Himari is older than Minato.

D. In a *flowchart*, each node stands for a step in a process. Arrows direct you from each step to the next. An arrow pointing back to an earlier step tells you to repeat that step. A flowchart usually has at least three types of nodes. *Process nodes* stand for actions to take and are usually rectangles. *Decision nodes* show questions to answer and are usually diamond shaped. At least two labeled arrows lead from each decision node to show how choosing the next step depends on how you answer the question. *Terminal nodes* show the start or end of the process and are usually oval.

Example:

The flowchart below shows a simple process for getting cereal from a store. The top oval shows the first step, going to the store. The arrow below it then takes us to a process node saying to look for a cereal we like. For the third step, we reach a decision node asking us whether we found the cereal we wanted. If we did, we follow the node's "Yes" arrow to another process node telling us to buy the cereal we found, then move on to the bottom terminal node telling us to go home. Otherwise, we follow the node's "No" arrow to a second decision node asking whether the store offers other good cereal choices. If it doesn't, we follow another "No" arrow telling us to give up and go home. But if the store does offer other good cereal choices, we follow a "Yes" arrow taking us back to the "look for a cereal you like" step to peruse the choices again. We repeat the loop until we either find a cereal we want to buy or decide the store has no more good cereal choices. Since the store won't have infinitely many cereals to consider, we eventually end at the bottom terminal node and go home.

3. Quantitative charts

A. Here we discuss a few common types of charts that normally show quantitative data. The GMAT may also use rarer types this book doesn't discuss. To understand any type of quantitative chart, study the description and any labels to find out what cases and variables are shown, and how. Also notice any axes, these show the measurement scales used. Some quantitative charts have no axes, while others have one, two, or, rarely, three or more. For each axis, notice whether it shows 0 and any negative values, or whether it starts above 0. Study the numbers on the axes and note any named units the numbers stand for. You must read the axes correctly to read the data shown.

Example:

In the chart below, labels say the scale on the left is for the temperature data, and the scale on the right is for the precipitation data. The bottom axis shows four months of the year, spaced three months apart. The chart's title tells us each data point gives the **average** temperature or precipitation in City X during a given month. This implies that the temperatures and precipitations shown are averages over many years. Suppose we're asked to find the average temperature and precipitation in City X in April. To do this, we don't have to calculate averages of any of the values shown. Those values are **already** averages. So, to find the average temperature for April, we simply read the April temperature data point by noting it's slightly lower than the 15 on the temperature scale at the left. Likewise, to find the average precipitation for April, we read the April precipitation data point by noticing it's about as high as the 8 on the precipitation scale on the right. This means the chart says that in April, the average temperature is about 14° Celsius and the average precipitation about 8 centimeters. Since the question is only about April, the data shown for January, July, and October are irrelevant.

**AVERAGE TEMPERATURE AND
PRECIPITATION IN CITY X**

B. A *pie chart* has a circle divided into sections like pie slices. The sections make up the whole circle without overlapping. They stand for parts that together make up some whole amount. Usually, each section is sized in proportion to the part it stands for, and labeled with that part's fraction, or percent, of the whole amount. You can use these fractions, or percents, in calculations. Refer to Section 3.3, "Rates, Ratios, and Percents," to review how.

Example:

In the pie chart below, the sections are sized in proportion to their percent amounts. These percents add up to 100%. Suppose we're told that Al's weekly net salary is $350 and asked how many of the categories shown each individually took at least $80 of that $350. To answer, first we find that $\frac{\$80}{\$350}$ is about 23%, which means $80 or more of Al's salary went to a category, if and only if, at least 23% went to that category. So, the graph shows exactly two categories that each took at least $80 of Al's salary: the category *Savings* took 25% of his salary and *Rent and Utilities* took 30%.

DISTRIBUTION OF AL'S WEEKLY NET SALARY

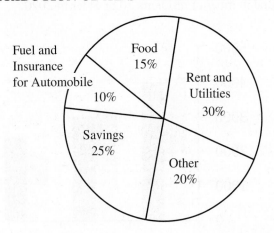

C. A *bar chart* has a series of vertical or horizontal bars standing for a set of cases. A simple bar chart has only one quantitative variable. The bars' different heights or lengths show that variable's values for different cases.

A *grouped* bar chart may have more than one quantitative variable. Its bars are grouped together. Each group either shows the values of different variables for one case, or else the values of related cases for one variable.

And in a *stacked* bar chart, segments are stacked into bars. Each segment inside a bar stands for part of an amount, and the whole bar stands for the whole amount.

Example:

The bar chart below is both grouped and stacked. Each pair of grouped bars shows population figures for one of three towns. In each pair, the bar on the left shows the town's population in 2010, and the bar on the right shows the town's population in 2020. Inside each bar, the lower segment shows how many people in the town were under age 30, and the upper segment shows how many were age 30 or older. For example, the chart's fifth bar shows that in 2010 Ceburg's population was around 2,000, including about 1,100 people under 30 and 900 people 30 or older. And the chart's sixth bar shows that by 2020, Ceburg's population had grown to around 2,400, including about 1,200 people under 30 and 1,200 people 30 or older. By reading the chart this way to find the amounts shown, we can also estimate various other amounts, like the three towns' combined total number of residents 30 or older in 2020.

D. A *histogram* looks like a vertical bar chart but works differently. In a histogram, each bar stands for a range of values that the same quantitative variable can take. These ranges don't overlap. Together they usually include every value the variable can take, or at least every value it does take in some population. The bars are in order left to right, from the one standing for the lowest range of values to the one standing for the highest range. Each bar's height shows the number or proportion of times the variable's value is in the range the bar stands for. A bar chart makes it easy to see how the values are distributed.

Example:

The histogram below shows the measured weights of 31 gerbils. Each bar's height shows how many gerbils were in a specific weight range. For example, the bar farthest left says 3 gerbils each weighed from 60 to 65 grams. The histogram doesn't show any individual gerbil's weight. However, it does give us some statistical information. For example, by adding the numbers of gerbils in the different weight ranges, we can tell that the 16th-heaviest of the 31 gerbils weighed between 75 and 80 grams. This means the gerbils' median weight was in that range. The histogram also shows that the gerbils mainly weighed between 70 and 85 grams apiece, though several weighed less or more.

E. A *line chart* often shows how the values of one or more quantitative variables change over time. Typically, the horizontal axis has the time scale, and the vertical axis has one or more scales for the variable or variables. One or more lines connect the data points. Different lines may stand either for different variables or for a single variable applied to different cases. Line charts make it easy to see trends and correlations.

Some line charts show probability distributions instead of changes over time, as we'll see in section 5.3.1 below.

Examples:

In section 5.2.3.A above, the chart of average monthly temperatures and precipitations is a line chart whose two variables have two separate scales, one on the left and one on the right.

The line chart below shows how many toasters of each of three different brands were sold each year from 2017 to 2022. Each sloping line shows how sales changed for one of the three brands during that period. The legend on the bottom says which line stands for which toaster brand. All three lines use the scale on the left, whose numbers stand for thousands of units sold annually. The chart shows that over the six years, annual sales of Crispo toasters increased dramatically, while annual sales of Brownita toasters declined to almost zero, and annual sales of Toastador toasters fluctuated.

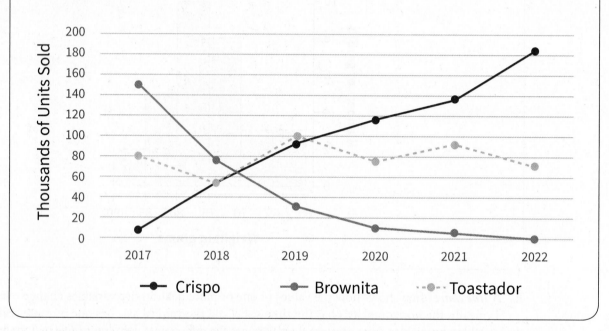

F. A *scatterplot* has at least two quantitative variables, one on each axis. For each case in the data, a dot's position shows the variables' values. No lines connect the scattered dots, but a straight or curved line through the scatterplot may show an overall trend in the data. Sometimes the dots have a few different shapes or colors to show they stand for cases in different categories. And in scatterplots called ***bubble charts***, the dots have different sizes standing for values of a third variable.

Scatterplots are useful for showing correlations. They also show how much individual cases fit an overall correlation or deviate from it.

Example:

The scatterplot below shows measured widths and lengths of leaves on two plants. Each dot stands for one leaf. The dot's position stands for the leaf's width and length in centimeters, as the scatterplot's two axes show. The legend says how one set of dots stand for leaves on the first plant, and another set for leaves on the second. The scatterplot shows that in general, the longer leaves tend to be wider, and vice versa. It also shows how leaves on the second plant tend to be somewhat longer and wider than those on the first, with some exceptions.

5.3 Data Patterns

1. Distributions

A. A data *distribution* is a pattern in how often different values appear in data. How data in a sample is distributed can tell you how likely different values are to appear in the same population outside the sample. In this book, Section 7.2.2, "Generalizations and Predictions," discusses generalizations and predictions based on samples.

B. A distribution is *uniform* when each value occurs more or less equally often. It's less uniform when the differences between how frequently the values occur are greater. The more uniform a distribution is for a sample, the better it supports the conclusion that the distribution for other cases in the population is likewise uniform.

Example:

Suppose the six faces on a die are numbered 1 to 6. And suppose that when rolled sixty times, the die comes up 1 eleven times, 2 nine times, 3 ten times, 4 eleven times, 5 ten times, and 6 nine times. This isn't a **perfectly** uniform distribution, because the six values 1 to 6 didn't occur exactly ten times apiece. However, because each value did occur between nine and eleven times, the distribution is **fairly** uniform. This suggests that each of the six values is about equally likely to occur again when the die is rolled, and that the distribution of the values for future rolls will stay fairly uniform.

C. A variable's values are often distributed unevenly. Sometimes one central value occurs most often, with other values occurring less often the farther they are from the central value. When this type of distribution is ***normal***, each value below the central value occurs just as often as the value equally far above the central value. For a perfectly normal distribution, the central value is the mean, the median, and the mode. When plotted on a chart, a normal distribution is bell shaped, with a central hump tapering off equally into tails on both sides. But a distribution with a larger tail on one side of the hump than the other is not normal but ***skewed***. For a skewed distribution, the mean is often farther out on the larger tail than the median is.

Example:

The two charts below show distributions of lengths for two beetle species. The chart on the left shows that the lengths of species A beetles have roughly a normal distribution. The central hump is symmetrical, with equal tails on both sides. By looking at the chart, we can tell that the mode, the median, and the mean of the lengths for species A are all around 5 millimeters. However, the chart on the right shows that the lengths of species B beetles have a skewed distribution. The tail on the right side of the hump is larger than the tail on the left side, which means more beetles of species B have lengths above the mode than below it. As a result, the median length for species B is above the mode, and the mean is above the median.

D. The more tightly clustered a distribution is around a central value, the higher and narrower the hump is, and the smaller the tails are. A more tightly clustered distribution also has a smaller standard deviation, as discussed in Section 3.4.1, "Statistics." The more tightly clustered a distribution is for an observed sample, the more likely a new case from the population outside that sample is to have a value near the distribution's central value.

Example:

For each of three tasks, the chart below shows how frequently it takes workers different lengths of time in minutes to complete that task. Even though the bottom axis shows times from 1 to 5 minutes, it doesn't stand for a single period starting at 1 minute and ending at 5 minutes. Instead, it stands for a range of lengths of task completion times.

Notice how the chart uses smooth curves to show the frequencies of different completion times. That suggests it shows trends idealized from the observed data points, which could be shown more precisely as separate dots or bars.

For each task, the distribution of completion times is uniform, with a mode, median, and mean of 3 minutes. But the completion times are most tightly clustered around 3 minutes for Task A, and least tightly clustered for Task C. That means the standard deviation of the completion times is lowest for Task A and highest for Task C. It also means the probability is higher that an individual worker will take close to 3 minutes to complete Task A than to complete Task C. A worker's completion time for Task C is less predictable and likely to be farther from 3 minutes. So, the chart gives **stronger evidence** for the conclusion that finishing Task A will take a worker between 2 and 4 minutes than for the conclusion that finishing Task C will take that worker between 2 and 4 minutes.

E. Data distributions take many other shapes too. Some have two or more humps, and others have random variations in frequency among adjacent values. In general, the less the values in a sample cluster around one central hump, the larger the standard deviation is, and the less predictable the values are for cases in the population outside the observed sample.

2. Trends and Correlations

A. Charts often show trends over time. They may show that a variable's values increase, decrease, fluctuate, or change in cycles. They may also show values of different plotted variables changing the same ways or opposite ways.

Other things equal, an observed trend over a period is evidence that the same trend extends at least slightly before and after that period. This evidence is stronger the longer the observed trend has lasted and the more varied the conditions it's lasted through. Generalizing from a longer observed period with more varied conditions is like generalizing from a larger sample, as discussed in Section 7.2.2,

"Generalizations and Predictions." But the odds increase of other factors disrupting the observed trend at times more distant from the observed period, and in situations whose conditions differ more from those observed.

> *Example:*
>
> The line chart in section 5.2.3.E above shows that annual sales of Crispo toasters rose from fewer than 10,000 in 2017 to over 180,000 in 2022. If this trend continues another year, even more than 180,000 Crispo toasters will be sold in 2023. However, many factors might disrupt Crispo's surging popularity. For example, another company might start making better or cheaper toasters, drawing consumers away from Crispo toasters. Or broader social, economic, or technological changes might reduce demand for toasters altogether. The more years pass outside the observed period of 2017 through 2022, the more likely such disruptions become. So, the observed trend gives stronger evidence that annual Crispo toaster sales will be over 180,000 in 2023 than it gives that they'll still be over 180,000 in 2050.

B. Two quantitative or ordinal variables are ***positively correlated*** if they both tend to be higher in the same cases. They're ***negatively correlated*** if one tends to be higher in cases where the other is lower.

> *Examples:*
>
> If warmer days tend to be rainier in a certain region, then temperature and precipitation are positively correlated there.
>
> But if warmer days tend to be drier in a different region, then temperature and precipitation are negatively correlated in that second region.

C. On a line chart, the lines standing for positively correlated variables tend to slope up or down together. The more consistently the slopes match, the stronger the positive correlation. But when two variables are negatively correlated, the line standing for one tends to slope up where the other slopes down, and vice versa. The more consistently the lines slope in opposite directions, the stronger the negative correlation.

> *Examples:*
>
> The chart in section 5.2.3.A shows a positive correlation between average monthly temperature and precipitation in City X. The temperature and precipitation lines both slope up together from January through July, and then slope down together.
>
> The chart in section 5.2.3.E shows a negative correlation between annual sales of Crispo toasters and annual sales of Brownita toasters. Throughout this chart, the line standing for Crispo toaster sales slopes up and the line standing for Brownita toaster sales slopes down. However, the chart shows no clear positive or negative correlation of Crispo or Brownita toaster sales with Toastador toaster sales. The line standing for Toastador toaster sales fluctuates, sometimes sloping up and sometimes down. It shows no consistent trend relative to the other two lines. So, the chart doesn't clearly support a prediction that in future years Toastador sales will increase or decrease as Crispo or Brownita sales do the same or the opposite.

D. When a scatterplot shows a positive correlation, the dots tend to cluster around a line that slopes up. When it shows a negative correlation, they tend to cluster around a line that slopes down. The stronger the correlation, the more tightly the dots cluster around the sloped line. If the dots spread farther away from the sloped line, or cluster around a line with a less consistent slope, the correlation is weaker or non-existent.

> *Example:*
>
> The scatterplot in section 5.2.3.F shows leaf width as positively correlated with leaf length for both plants. The dots mostly cluster around a line sloping up, which means wider leaves tend to be longer and vice versa. Thus, the scatterplot supports a prediction that if another leaf on one of the plants is measured, it too will probably be wider if it's longer. However, the correlation in the scatterplot isn't perfect. For example, the dot farthest to the right is lower than each of about a dozen dots to its left. That dot farthest to the right stands for a leaf that's both longer and thinner than any of the leaves those other dozen dots stand for. This inconsistency in the correlation somewhat weakens the scatterplot's support for the prediction that another leaf measured on one of the plants will be wider if it's longer.

E. Values of a nominal variable may also be associated with higher or lower values of an ordinal or quantitative variable. Different values of two nominal variables can also be associated with each other.

> *Examples:*
>
> Species is a nominal variable. Individuals of some species tend to weigh more than individuals of other species, so different values of the nominal variable species are associated with higher or lower values of the quantitative variable weight.
>
> As another example, university students majoring in certain subjects like physics are more likely to take certain courses like statistics than university students majoring in other subjects like theater are, even though university major and enrollment in a course are both nominal variables.

An association involving a nominal variable like species isn't a positive or negative correlation because nominal variables aren't ordered; one species isn't greater or less than another. Still, these nominal associations can be shown in qualitative charts and tables and can support predictions. Knowing an animal's species gives you some evidence about roughly how much it will likely weigh and knowing a university student's major gives you some evidence about what courses they're most likely to take.

6.0 Data Insights

6.0 Data Insights

This chapter describes the Data Insights section of the GMAT™ exam, explains what it measures, discusses the five types of Data Insights questions, and offers strategies for answering them.

Because most Data Insights questions are interactive, you must use a computer to access them fully. Among Data Insights questions, only the Data Sufficiency questions can be fully shown on paper. So, those are the only Data Insights practice questions in this book.

> **For additional Data Insights practice questions, go to** mba.com/my-account **and access the Online Question Bank using the code from the inside front cover.**

Overview of the Data Insights Section

The Data Insights section measures your skill at analyzing data shown in formats often used in real business situations. You'll need this skill to make informed decisions as a future business leader. Data Insights questions ask you to assess multiple sources and types of information—graphic, numeric, and verbal—as they relate to one another.

This section asks you to:

- Use math, verbal reasoning, and data analysis,

- Solve connected problems together, and

- Give answers in different formats, not just traditional multiple choice.

Many Data Insights questions ask you to study graphs and sort tables to find information. These questions don't require advanced statistics or spreadsheet expertise. Other Data Insights questions ask you to tell whether given data is enough to solve a math problem, but don't ask you to solve it. You may also use an approved calculator.

You have 45 minutes to answer the 20 questions in the Data Insights section, an average of two minutes, fifteen seconds per question. Throughout the section are questions of five types. Some need multiple responses. A question may use math, data analysis, verbal reasoning, or all three. Questions involving math require knowing the topics reviewed in Chapter 3, "Math Review": Value, Order, Factors, Algebra, Equalities, Inequalities, Rates, Ratios, Percents, Statistics, Sets, Counting, Probability, Estimation, and Series. Questions involving data analysis require understanding different types of data shown in tables or graphs, finding patterns in that data, and using other skills reviewed in Chapter 5, "Data Insights Review." Questions involving verbal reasoning require understanding texts, reasoning, evaluating arguments, and using other skills reviewed in Chapter 7, "Verbal Review."

To prepare for the Data Insights section, first review basic math, data analysis, and verbal reasoning skills to make sure you know enough to answer the questions. Then practice on GMAT questions from past exams.

Special Features:

- Unlike the GMAT exam's Quantitative Reasoning and Verbal Reasoning sections, the Data Insights section is not computer adaptive. This means that answering questions correctly or incorrectly doesn't affect which questions appear next.

- Unlike the other sections of the GMAT exam, the Data Insights section sometimes shows two or more questions on a single screen. When it does, you can change your answers before clicking

"Next" to go on to the next screen. But once you're on a new screen, you can't return to the previous screen.

- The Data Insights section uses some math, but it doesn't ask you to calculate by hand. An onscreen calculator with basic functions is available for this section. For more information, please go to mba.com/calculator-policy.

6.1 What Is Measured

The Data Insights section measures how well you use data to solve problems. Specifically, it tests the skills described below:

Skill Category	Details	Examples
Apply	Understand principles, rules, or other concepts. Use them in a new context or predict what would follow if new information were added.	• Tell whether new examples follow or break given rules • Tell how new situations would affect a trend • Use given principles to draw conclusions about new data
Evaluate	Judge the quality of given information	• Tell whether information from one source supports or weakens a claim in another source • Tell whether given information is enough to justify a course of action • Judge how well evidence supports an argument or plan • Find errors or gaps in given information
Infer	Draw unstated conclusions from given information	• Calculate an outcome's probability using given data • Tell whether statements follow logically from the information given • Say what a term means in a given context • Find a rate of change in data gathered over time
Recognize	Identify information given explicitly, including specific facts, details, or relationships between pieces of information	• Find agreements and disagreements between information sources • Find how strongly two variables are correlated • Give a ranking based on a table by combining categories (for example, saying which product maximizes revenue and minimizes costs) • Tell which data is given as evidence in an argument
Strategize	Find ways to work toward a goal given specific needs or constraints	• Choose a plan that minimizes risks and maximizes value • Identify trade-offs needed to reach a goal • Tell which math formula gives the desired result • Decide which ways of completing a task meet given needs

6.2 Question Types and Test-Taking Strategies

The Data Insights section has five types of questions: Multi-Source Reasoning, Table Analysis, Graphics Interpretation, Two-Part Analysis, and Data Sufficiency. We describe each below.

1. Multi-Source Reasoning

What you see:

- Two or three tabs on the left side of your screen. Each tab shows a written passage, a table, a graph, or another form of information. The different tabs may show information in different forms. You click on the tabs to see what's on them and find what you need to answer the questions.

Example of information sources presented on multiple tabs:

For outside laboratory tests, the museum's first-year budget for the Kaxna collection allows unlimited IRMS testing, and a total of $7,000—equal to the cost of 4 TL tests plus 15 radiocarbon tests, or the cost of 40 ICP-MS tests—for all other tests. For each technique applied by an outside lab, the museum is charged a fixed price per artifact.

- A question with answer choices on the right side of your screen. With each set of tabs, three questions appear one at a time.

The response type:

- Some questions are traditional multiple choice, with five answer choices.

- Others are "conditional statement" questions. Each question gives a condition. Below that are three rows with content such as sentences, phrases, words, numbers, or formulas. For each row, mark "yes" or "true" if the row's contents meet the given condition, and "no" or "false" otherwise.

  - Mark one answer PER ROW.

  - You must mark all three rows correctly to get credit for the question.

Example of a conditional statement question:

For each of the following artifacts in the museum's Kaxna collection, select *Yes* if, based on the museum's assumptions, a range of dates for the object's creation can be obtained using one of the techniques in the manner described. Otherwise, select *No*.

Yes   No

○   ○   Bronze statue of a deer

○   ○   Fired-clay pot

○   ○   Wooden statue of a warrior

Tips for Answering Multi-Source Reasoning Questions

- **Answer using only the information given.**

  The tabs show all the information you need to answer correctly. If you already know about the topic, don't use that knowledge to answer. Use only the information in the tabs.

- **Analyze each source of information.**

  As you read a text passage, note each statement's role. Refer to Section 7.1, "Analyzing Passages," for explanation.

Notice labels and scales to understand the data shown in tables and graphs. Refer to Chapter 5, "Data Insights Review," for explanation.

- **Read the whole question.**

    You need to understand what each question is asking you to do. For example, some questions ask you to spot conflicts between the information sources. Others ask you to draw conclusions by combining information from different sources. There are also questions that ask you to judge which information sources are relevant to a question.

    While answering the questions, you can always click on the tabs to review any of the information.

2. Table Analysis

What you see:

- A data table like a spreadsheet. You can sort it by each data column.

Example of data table with sorting drop-down menu:

The table displays data on *Brazilian agricultural* products in 2009.

Sort By: | Production, world share (%) ▼ |

Commodity	Production, world share (%)	Production, world rank	Exports, world share (%)	Exports, world rank
Pork	4	4	12	4
Cotton	5	5	10	4
Corn	8	4	10	2
Chickens	15	3	38	1
Beef	16	2	22	1
Sugar	21	1	44	1
Soybeans	27	2	40	2
Coffee	40	1	32	1
Orange juice	56	1	82	1

The response type:

- The questions are in "conditional statement" form. Each question gives a condition. Below that are three rows with contents such as sentences, phrases, words, numbers, or formulas. For each row, mark "yes" or "true" if the row's contents meet the condition, and "no" or "false" otherwise.

- Mark one answer PER ROW.

- You must mark all three rows correctly to get credit for the question.

Example of a conditional statement question:

For each of the following statements, select *Yes* if the statement can be shown to be true based on the information in the table. Otherwise select *No*.

Yes	No	
○	○	No individual country produces more than one-fourth of the world's sugar.
○	○	If Brazil produces less than 20% of the world's supply of any commodity listed in the table, Brazil is not the world's top exporter of that commodity.
○	○	Of the commodities in the table for which Brazil ranks first in world exports, Brazil produces more than 20% of the world's supply.

Tips for Answering Table Analysis Questions

- **Study the table and any text around it to learn what kind of data it shows.**

  Knowing what kind of data is in the table helps you find the information you need.

- **Study the condition in the question.**

  The question gives a condition like *"is consistent with the information provided"* or *"can be inferred from the information provided."* Understanding that condition helps you understand how to mark each row.

- **Read each answer row to decide how to sort the table.**

  Often an answer row's contents hint at how to sort the table by one or more columns to make the data you need easier to find.

- **Judge whether each answer row's contents meet the given condition.**

  In each row, you can only mark one of the two answer choices, and only one is right. Think about whether the row's contents meet the condition in the question.

3. Graphics Interpretation

What you see:

- A graph or other image. Section 5.2, "Data Displays," explains some kinds of graphics you might see.

- One or more statements with missing parts. Each missing part has a drop-down menu.

Example of graphics:

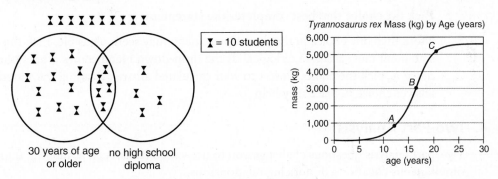

Example of statement with blank/missing information and drop-down menus:

Use the drop-down menus to complete each statement according to the information presented in the diagram.

If one student is selected at random from the 300 surveyed, the chance that the student will be under 30 or a high school graduate or both is [Select... ▼]

If one student is selected at random from the 300 surveyed, the chance that the student will be both under 30 and high school graduate is [1 out of 3 ▼]

Select...

1 out of 6

1 out of 3

2 out of 3

5 out of 6

The response type:

- Each drop-down menu shows a list of choices such as words, phrases, or numbers. Pick the best choice in the drop-down menu to fill in the missing part of the statement.

  - If the question has two or more drop-down menus, you must pick the best choices in all of them to get credit for the question.

Tips for Answering Graphics Interpretation Questions

- **Study the graphic.**

  Find the information in the graphic. Notice any marked values on the axes. Also notice any differences between units in the graphic and units the text discusses. Don't assume the graphic is drawn to scale.

- **Read any text around the graphic.**

  Text near the graphic may clarify what the graphic means. The text may also give information that's not in the graphic but is needed to answer the question.

- **Study the statements with drop-down menus.**

  Studying these statements helps you understand what the question is asking you to do. Graphics interpretation questions may ask you to interpret and connect data, to find how different pieces of data are related, or to draw conclusions from a data set. You may have to do some math, for example to find or compare rates of change.

- **Read all the choices in each drop-down menu.**

  The menu choices may have clues about how to answer the question.

- **Pick the choice that best completes the statement.**

  More than one choice in the drop-down menu may seem plausible. Pick the one that makes the statement most accurate or logical. If the drop-down menu comes after a phrase like *nearest to* or *closest to*, pick the choice closest to your calculated answer. Reading the statement again with your answer choice in place may help.

4. Two-Part Analysis

Two-part analysis questions challenge you to use varied skills, such as judging trade-offs, solving simultaneous equations, or noticing relationships.

What you see:

- A written scenario.

- Instructions asking you to use the scenario to make two choices that together or separately meet one or more conditions.

- A response table with three columns.

Example of a written scenario:

A literature department at a small university in an English-speaking country is organizing a two-day festival in which it will highlight the works of ten writers who have been the subjects of recent scholarly work by the faculty. Five writers will be featured each day. To reflect the department's strengths, the majority of writers scheduled for one of the days will be writers whose primary writing language is not English. On the other day of the festival, at least four of the writers will be women. Neither day should have more than two writers from the same country. Departmental members have already agreed on a schedule for eight of the writers. That schedule showing names, along with each writer's primary writing language and country of origin, is shown.

- Day 1:

    Achebe (male, English, Nigeria)

    Weil (female, French, France)

    Gavalda (female, French, France)

    Barrett Browning (female, English, UK)

- Day 2:

    Rowling (female, English, UK)

    Austen (female, English, UK)

    Ocantos (male, Spanish, Argentina)

    Lu Xun (male, Chinese, China)

Example of a response based on passage information:

Select a writer who could be added to the schedule for either day. Then select a writer who could be added to the schedule for neither day. Make only two selections, one in each column.

Either day	Neither day	Writer
⊚	⊚	LeGuin (female, English, USA)
⊚	⊚	Longfellow (make, English, USA)
⊚	⊚	Murasaki (female, Japanese, Japan)
⊚	⊚	Colette (female, French, France)
⊚	⊚	Vargas Llosa (male, Spanish, Peru)
⊚	⊚	Zola (male, French, France)

The response type:

- In the response table, the top row labels the columns. Below that, the first two columns have buttons you click to choose from a list in the third column.

- Pick one answer PER COLUMN, not per row.

    - To get credit for the question, you must pick one correct answer in the first column, and one in the second column.

    - You can pick the same answer in both columns.

Tips for Answering Two-Part Analysis Questions

- **Answer using only the information given.**

    The question tells you everything you need to know to pick the right answers. If you already know about the topic, do not use that knowledge to answer the question. Rely on the information provided to answer the question.

- **Read the instructions below the written scenario.**

    The table's top row may not fully explain the tasks in the first two columns. Carefully read how the instructions describe the tasks.

- **Make exactly two choices.**

    Pick one answer in the first column and one answer in the second column.

- **Read all the answer choices before picking any.**

  Before you pick answers in the first two columns, read all the answer choices in the third column.

- **Notice if the instructions say the two answers depend on each other.**

  Some two-part analysis questions ask you to make two independent choices. Others ask you to pick two answers that combine into a single correct response. Follow the instructions to make sure your two answer choices combine the right way.

- **Pick the same answer in both columns if it is the best choice for both.**

  Sometimes the same answer is the best choice for both columns.

5. Data Sufficiency

Like Quantitative Reasoning questions, Data Sufficiency questions use the basic math reviewed in Chapter 3, "Math Review." A Data Sufficiency question asks you to analyze a math problem, decide whether given information is relevant, and tell if enough information is given to solve the problem. But it doesn't ask you to find the problem's solution. Instead, you classify the problem by picking one of five answer choices. These five choices are the same for each question.

What you see:

- A math problem, sometimes with background information.
- Two statements labeled (1) and (2).

Example of a Data Sufficiency Math Problem and Statements

In Mr. Smith's class, what is the ratio of the number of boys to the number of girls?

(1) There are 3 times as many girls as boys in Mr. Smith's class.

(2) The number of boys is $\frac{1}{4}$ of the total number of boys and girls in Mr. Smith's class.

The response type:

- Each question is multiple choice, always with these five answer choices:

  (A) Statement (1) ALONE is sufficient, but statement (2) alone is not sufficient.

  (B) Statement (2) ALONE is sufficient, but statement (1) alone is not sufficient.

  (C) BOTH statements TOGETHER are sufficient, but NEITHER statement ALONE is sufficient.

  (D) EACH statement ALONE is sufficient.

  (E) Statements (1) and (2) TOGETHER are NOT sufficient.

Pick exactly one of these answer choices. To answer correctly, you must judge whether statement (1) alone gives enough information to solve the math problem, and whether statement (2) alone does. If neither statement alone gives enough information to solve the problem, you must judge whether both do.

Tips for Answering Data Sufficiency Questions

- **Analyze the math problem and the two statements step by step.**

  First read the math problem and any background information. Then read statement (1). Decide whether it gives enough information to solve the problem. Now go on to statement (2). Ignore statement (1) while you decide whether statement (2) alone gives enough information to solve the problem. If you have found that either statement alone gives enough information to solve the problem, you now know enough to pick the right answer choice from among (A), (B), and (D).

  If you find that neither statement alone gives enough information to solve the problem, decide whether both give enough information together. If so, the right answer choice is (C). Otherwise, it's (E).

  Here's a flowchart showing how to find the right answer choice step by step.

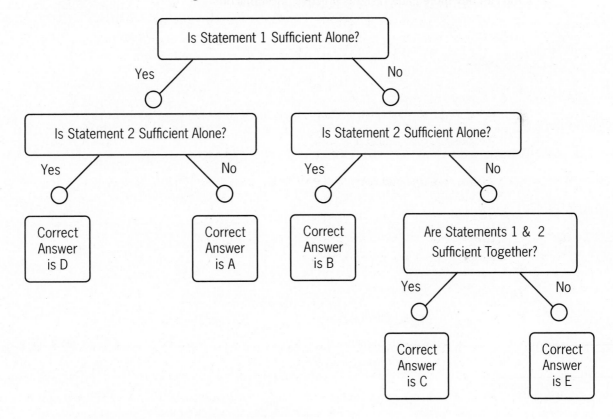

- **Don't waste time solving the math problem.**

  You only have to decide whether the two statements give enough information to solve it.

- **Check whether there's enough information to solve the exact problem given.**

  For example, suppose the problem is to find the value of a variable y. Then you have to decide whether each statement gives enough information to find **one and only one** value for y. Here, the question is not whether the statements give enough information to find an equation like $y = x + 2$. Nor is it whether they give enough information to find a range of values rather than y's exact value. So, ignore those irrelevant questions.

- **Don't assume any images are drawn to scale.**

  They may not be. For example, if a figure described as a rectangle looks like a square, that doesn't mean it is a square.

6.3 Section Instructions

Go to www.mba.com/tutorial to read instructions for the section and get a feel for what the test center screens look like on the actual GMAT exam.

More Data Insights Samples

For more sample questions of each type, visit: mba.com/ir-questions

More Data Insights Practice

Below are Data Insights practice questions. Use your unique access code from the inside front cover of this book to access additional practice questions with answer explanations at mba.com/my-account. You can buy more Data Insights practice questions on mba.com/gmatprep.

6.4 Practice Questions

Questions 229 to 268 - Difficulty: Easy

229. What is the number of pages of a certain journal article?

   (1)   The size of each page is $5\frac{1}{2}$ inches by 8 inches.
   (2)   The average (arithmetic mean) number of words per page is 250.

230. If a certain vase contains only roses and tulips, how many tulips are there in the vase?

   (1)   The number of roses in the vase is 4 times the number of tulips in the vase.
   (2)   There is a total of 20 flowers in the vase.

231. The cost of 10 pounds of apples and 2 pounds of grapes was $12. What was the cost per pound of apples?

   (1)   The cost per pound of grapes was $2.
   (2)   The cost of 2 pounds of apples was less than the cost of 1 pound of grapes.

232. What was the median annual salary for the employees at Company X last year?

   (1)   Last year there were 29 employees at Company X.
   (2)   Last year 12 employees at Company X had an annual salary of $24,000.

233. How many basic units of currency X are equivalent to 250 basic units of currency Y?

   (1)   100 basic units of currency X are equivalent to 625 basic units of currency Y.
   (2)   2,000 basic units of currency X are equivalent to 12,500 basic units of currency Y.

234. A company bought 3 printers and 1 scanner. What was the price of the scanner?

   (1)   The total price of the printers and the scanner was $1,300.
   (2)   The price of each printer was 4 times the price of the scanner.

235. Each of the 256 solid-colored marbles in a box is either blue, green, or purple. What is the ratio of the number of blue marbles to the number of purple marbles in the box?

   (1)   The number of green marbles in the box is 4 times the number of blue marbles in the box.
   (2)   There are 192 green marbles in the box.

236. A certain mixture of paint requires blue, yellow, and red paints in ratios of 2:3:1, respectively, and no other ingredients. If there are ample quantities of the blue and red paints available, is there enough of the yellow paint available to make the desired amount of the mixture?

    (1) Exactly 20 quarts of the mixture are needed.
    (2) Exactly 10 quarts of the yellow paint are available.

237. There are 2 groups of students who took a history test. Was the average (arithmetic mean) score of the students in Group A higher than the average score of the students in Group B who took the test?

    (1) Of the students who took the test, 10 were in Group A and 12 were in Group B.
    (2) On the test, the highest score achieved was achieved by a Group B student and the lowest score achieved was achieved by a Group A student.

238. The research funds of a certain company were divided among three departments, X, Y, and Z. Which one of the three departments received the greatest proportion of the research funds?

    (1) The research funds received by departments X and Y were in the ratio 3 to 5, respectively.
    (2) The research funds received by departments X and Z were in the ratio 2 to 1, respectively.

239. In a certain class, some students donated cans of food to a local food bank. What was the average (arithmetic mean) number of cans donated per student in the class?

    (1) The students donated a total of 56 cans of food.
    (2) The total number of cans donated was 40 greater than the total number of students in the class.

240. Each of the n employees at a certain company has a different annual salary. What is the median of the annual salaries of the n employees?

    (1) When the annual salaries of the n employees are listed in increasing order, the median is the 15th salary.
    (2) The sum of the annual salaries of the n employees is $913,500.

241. In a recent town election, what was the ratio of the number of votes in favor of a certain proposal to the number of votes against the proposal?

    (1) There were 60 more votes in favor of the proposal than against the proposal.
    (2) There were 240 votes in favor of the proposal.

242. How many men are in a certain company's vanpool program?

    (1) The ratio of men to women in the program is 3 to 2.
    (2) The men and women in the program fill 6 vans.

243. Each of the marbles in a jar is either red or white or blue. If one marble is to be selected at random from the jar, what is the probability that the marble will be blue?

    (1) There are a total of 24 marbles in the jar, 8 of which are red.
    (2) The probability that the marble selected will be white is $\frac{1}{2}$.

244. Last semester, Professor K taught two classes, A and B. Each student in class A handed in 7 assignments, and each student in class B handed in 5 assignments. How many students were in class A ?

    (1) The students in both classes combined handed in a total of 85 assignments.
    (2) There were 10 students in class B.

245. Was the amount of John's heating bill for February greater than it was for January?

    (1) The ratio of the amount of John's heating bill for February to that for January was $\frac{26}{25}$.
    (2) The sum of the amounts of John's heating bills for January and February was $183.60.

246. Machine R and machine S work at their respective constant rates. How much time does it take machine R, working alone, to complete a certain job?

    (1) The amount of time that it takes machine S, working alone, to complete the job is $\frac{3}{4}$ the amount of time that it takes machine R, working alone, to complete the job.

    (2) Machine R and machine S, working together, take 12 minutes to complete the job.

247. What was the range of the selling prices of the 30 wallets sold by a certain store yesterday?

    (1) $\frac{1}{3}$ of the wallets had a selling price of $24 each.

    (2) The lowest selling price of the wallets was $\frac{1}{3}$ the highest selling price of the wallets.

248. Three houses are being sold through a real estate agent. What is the asking price for the house with the second-largest asking price?

    (1) The difference between the greatest and the least asking price is $130,000.

    (2) The difference between the two greater asking prices is $85,000.

249. How many people in a group of 50 own neither a fax machine nor a laser printer?

    (1) The total number of people in the group who own a fax machine or a laser printer or both is less than 50.

    (2) The total number of people in the group who own both a fax machine and a laser printer is 15.

250. A certain investment earned a fixed rate of 4 percent interest per year, compounded annually, for five years. The interest earned for the third year of the investment was how many dollars greater than that for the first year?

    (1) The amount of the investment at the beginning of the second year was $4,160.00.

    (2) The amount of the investment at the beginning of the third year was $4,326.40.

251. For a certain car repair, the total charge consisted of a charge for parts, a charge for labor, and a 6 percent sales tax on both the charge for parts and the charge for labor. If the charge for parts, excluding sales tax, was $50.00, what was the total charge for the repair?

    (1) The sales tax on the charge for labor was $9.60.

    (2) The total sales tax was $12.60.

252. George has a total of B books in his library, 25 of which are hardcover fiction books. What is the value of B?

    (1) 40 of the B books are fiction and the rest are nonfiction.

    (2) 60 of the B books are hardcovers and the rest are paperbacks.

253. In each of the last five years, Company K donated p percent of its annual profits to a certain scholarship fund. Did Company K donate more than $10,000 to the scholarship fund last year?

    (1) Two years ago, Company K had annual profits of $3 million and donated $15,000 to the scholarship fund.

    (2) Last year, Company K had annual profits of $2.5 million.

254. The people in a line waiting to buy tickets to a show are standing one behind the other. Adam and Beth are among the people in the line, and Beth is standing behind Adam with a number of people between them. If the number of people in front of Adam plus the number of people behind Beth is 18, how many people in the line are behind Beth?

    (1) There are a total of 32 people in the line.

    (2) 23 people in the line are behind Adam.

255. In a certain group of 50 people, how many are doctors who have a law degree?

    (1) In the group, 36 people are doctors.

    (2) In the group, 18 people have a law degree.

256. Of a group of 50 households, how many have at least one cat or at least one dog, but not both?

    (1) The number of households that have at least one cat and at least one dog is 4.
    (2) The number of households that have no cats and no dogs is 14.

257. Robin invested a total of $12,000 in two investments, X and Y, so that the investments earned the same amount of simple annual interest. How many dollars did Robin invest in investment Y ?

    (1) Investment X paid 3 percent simple annual interest, and investment Y paid 6 percent simple annual interest.
    (2) Robin invested more than $1,000 in investment X.

258. In a real estate office that employs n salespeople, f of them are females and x of the females are new employees. What is the value of n ?

    (1) If an employee were randomly selected from the n employees, the probability of selecting a female would be $\frac{2}{3}$.
    (2) If an employee were randomly selected from the f female employees, the probability of selecting a new employee would be $\frac{1}{2}$.

259. Do at least 60 percent of the students in Pat's class walk to school?

    (1) At least 60 percent of the female students in Pat's class walk to school.
    (2) The number of students in Pat's class who walk to school is twice the number of students who do not walk to school.

260. A certain plumber charges $92 for each job completed in 4 hours or less and $23 per hour for each job completed in more than 4 hours. If it took the plumber a total of 7 hours to complete two separate jobs, what was the total amount charged by the plumber for the two jobs?

    (1) The plumber charged $92 for one of the two jobs.
    (2) The plumber charged $138 for one of the two jobs.

261. If x and y are positive numbers, is $\frac{x+1}{y+1} > \frac{x}{y}$?

    (1) $x > 1$
    (2) $x < y$

262. Every object in a box is either a sphere or a cube, and every object in the box is either red or green. How many objects are in the box?

    (1) There are six cubes and five green objects in the box.
    (2) There are two red spheres in the box.

263. A certain truck uses $\frac{1}{12} + kv^2$ gallons of fuel per mile when its speed is v miles per hour, where k is a constant. At what speed should the truck travel so that it uses $\frac{5}{12}$ gallon of fuel per mile?

    (1) The value of k is $\frac{1}{10,800}$.
    (2) When the truck travels at 30 miles per hour, it uses $\frac{1}{6}$ gallon of fuel per mile.

264. If a school district paid a total of $35 per desk for x desks and a total of $30 per table for y tables, what was the total amount that the district paid for these desks and tables?

    (1) The total amount the district paid for the y tables was $900.
    (2) $x = 90$, and the total amount the district paid for the x desks was 3.5 times the total amount the district paid for the y tables.

265. Three children inherited a total of X dollars. If the oldest child inherited $7,000 more than the youngest child, and the youngest child inherited $9,000 less than the middle child, what is the value of X ?

    (1) The middle child inherited $27,000.
    (2) The youngest child and the middle child together inherited a total of $45,000.

266. If a building has 6,000 square meters of floor space, how many offices are in the building?

    (1) Exactly $\frac{1}{4}$ of the floor space is not used for offices.
    (2) There are exactly 20 executive offices and each of these occupies 3 times as much floor space as the average for all of the remaining offices.

267. For which type of investment, J or K, is the annual rate of return greater?

    (1) Type J returns $115 per $1,000 invested for any one-year period and type K returns $300 per $2,500 invested for any one-year period.
    (2) The annual rate of return for an investment of type K is 12%.

268. If Car X followed Car Y across a certain bridge that is a $\frac{1}{2}$ mile long, how many seconds did it take Car X to travel across the bridge?

    (1) Car X drove onto the bridge exactly 3 seconds after Car Y drove onto the bridge and drove off the bridge exactly 2 seconds after Car Y drove off the bridge.
    (2) Car Y traveled across the bridge at a constant speed of 30 miles per hour.

Questions 269 to 301 - Difficulty: Medium

269. What is the total number of executives at Company P?

    (1) The number of male executives is $\frac{3}{5}$ the number of female executives.
    (2) There are 4 more female executives than male executives.

270. Jack picked 76 apples. Of these, he sold $4y$ apples to Juanita and $3t$ apples to Sylvia. If he kept the remaining apples, how many apples did he keep? (t and y are positive integers.)

    (1) $y \geq 15$ and $t = 2$
    (2) $y = 17$

271. The total price of 5 pounds of regular coffee and 3 pounds of decaffeinated coffee was $21.50. What was the price of the 5 pounds of regular coffee?

    (1) If the price of the 5 pounds of regular coffee had been reduced 10 percent and the price of the 3 pounds of decaffeinated coffee had been reduced 20 percent, the total price would have been $18.45.
    (2) The price of the 5 pounds of regular coffee was $3.50 more than the price of the 3 pounds of decaffeinated coffee.

272. A certain painting job requires a mixture of yellow, green, and white paint. If 12 quarts of paint are needed for the job, how many quarts of green paint are needed?

    (1) The ratio of the amount of green paint to the amount of yellow and white paint combined needs to be 1 to 3.
    (2) The ratio of the amount of yellow paint to the amount of green paint needs to be 3 to 2.

273. A company produces a certain toy in only 2 sizes, small or large, and in only 2 colors, red or green. If, for each size, there are equal numbers of red and green toys in a certain production lot, what fraction of the total number of green toys is large?

    (1) In the production lot, 400 of the small toys are green.
    (2) In the production lot, $\frac{2}{3}$ of the toys produced are small.

274. Jones has worked at Firm X twice as many years as Green, and Green has worked at Firm X four years longer than Smith. How many years has Green worked at Firm X?

    (1) Jones has worked at Firm X 9 years longer than Smith.
    (2) Green has worked at Firm X 5 years less than Jones.

275. On June 1, Mary paid Omar $360 for rent and utilities for the month of June. Mary moved out early, and Omar refunded the money she paid for utilities, but not for rent, for the days in June after she moved out. How many dollars did Omar refund to Mary?

    (1) Mary moved out on June 24.
    (2) The amount Mary paid for utilities was less than $\frac{1}{5}$ the amount Mary paid for rent.

276. The 10 students in a history class recently took an examination. What was the maximum score on the examination?

    (1) The mean of the scores was 75.
    (2) The standard deviation of the scores was 5.

277. Last school year, each of the 200 students at a certain high school attended the school for the entire year. If there were 8 cultural performances at the school during the last school year, what was the average (arithmetic mean) number of students attending each cultural performance?

    (1) Last school year, each student attended at least one cultural performance.
    (2) Last school year, the average number of cultural performances attended per student was 4.

278. A clothing manufacturer makes jackets that are wool or cotton or a combination of wool and cotton. The manufacturer has 3,000 pounds of wool and 2,000 pounds of cotton on hand. Is this enough wool and cotton to make at least 1,000 jackets?

    (1) Each wool jacket requires 4 pounds of wool, and no cotton.
    (2) Each cotton jacket requires 6 pounds of cotton, and no wool.

279. Each month, Jim receives a base salary plus a 10 percent commission on the price of each car he sells that month. If Jim sold 15 cars last month, what was the total amount of base salary and commissions that Jim received that month?

    (1) Last month, Jim's base salary was $3,000.
    (2) Last month, Jim sold 3 cars whose prices totaled $60,000 and 5 cars whose prices totaled $120,000.

280. By what percentage was the price of a certain television set discounted for a sale?

    (1) The price of the television set before it was discounted for the sale was 25 percent greater than the discounted price.
    (2) The price of the television set was discounted by $60 for the sale.

281. A paint mixture was formed by mixing exactly 3 colors of paint. By volume, the mixture was x% blue paint, y% green paint, and z% red paint. If exactly 1 gallon of blue paint and 3 gallons of red paint were used, how many gallons of green paint were used?

    (1) $x = y$
    (2) $z = 60$

282. For a basic monthly fee of F yen (¥F), Naoko's first cell phone plan allowed him to use a maximum of 420 minutes on calls during the month. Then, for each of x additional minutes he used on calls, he was charged ¥M, making his total charge for the month ¥T, where $T = F + xM$. What is the value of F?

    (1) Naoko used 450 minutes on calls the first month and the total charge for the month was ¥13,755.
    (2) Naoko used 400 minutes on calls the second month and the total charge for the month was ¥13,125.

283. Is the sum of the prices of the 3 books that Shana bought less than $48?

    (1) The price of the most expensive of the 3 books that Shana bought is less than $17.
    (2) The price of the least expensive of the 3 books that Shana bought is exactly $3 less than the price of the second most expensive book.

284. A company makes and sells two products, P and Q. The costs per unit of making and selling P and Q are $8.00 and $9.50, respectively, and the selling prices per unit of P and Q are $10.00 and $13.00, respectively. In one month the company sold a total of 834 units of these products. Was the total profit on these items more than $2,000.00?

    (1) During the month, more units of P than units of Q were sold.
    (2) During the month, at least 100 units of Q were sold.

285. Jill has applied for a job with each of two different companies. What is the probability that she will get job offers from both companies?

    (1) The probability that she will get a job offer from neither company is 0.3.

    (2) The probability that she will get a job offer from exactly one of the two companies is 0.5.

286. A certain computer company produces two different monitors, P and Q. In 2010, what was the net profit from the sale of the two monitors?

    (1) Of the company's expenses in 2010, rent and utilities totaled $500,000.

    (2) In 2010, the company sold 50,000 units of monitor P at $300 per unit and 30,000 units of monitor Q at $650 per unit.

287. A conveyor belt moves bottles at a constant speed of 120 centimeters per second. If the conveyor belt moves a bottle from a loading dock to an unloading dock, is the distance that the conveyor belt moves the bottle less than 90 meters? (1 meter = 100 centimeters)

    (1) It takes the conveyor belt less than 1.2 minutes to move the bottle from the loading dock to the unloading dock.

    (2) It takes the conveyor belt more than 1.1 minutes to move the bottle from the loading dock to the unloading dock.

288. In a product test of a common cold remedy, x percent of the patients tested experienced side effects from the use of the drug and y percent experienced relief of cold symptoms. What percent of the patients tested experienced both side effects and relief of cold symptoms?

    (1) Of the 1,000 patients tested, 15 percent experienced neither side effects nor relief of cold symptoms.

    (2) Of the patients tested, 30 percent experienced relief of cold symptoms without side effects.

289. Three roommates—Bela, Gyorgy, and Janos—together saved money for a trip. The amount that Bela saved was equal to 8% of his monthly income. The amount that Gyorgy saved was exactly $\frac{1}{3}$ of the total amount saved by all 3 roommates. What was the total amount saved for the trip by all 3 roommates?

    (1) Bela had a monthly income of $2,000.

    (2) Janos saved 1.5 times as much for the trip as Bela.

290. In each game of a certain tournament, a contestant either loses 3 points or gains 2 points. If Pat had 100 points at the beginning of the tournament, how many games did Pat play in the tournament?

    (1) At the end of the tournament, Pat had 104 points.

    (2) Pat played fewer than 10 games.

291. At the beginning of the year, the Finance Committee and the Planning Committee of a certain company each had n members, and no one was a member of both committees. At the end of the year, 5 members left the Finance Committee and 3 members left the Planning Committee. How many members did the Finance Committee have at the beginning of the year?

    (1) The ratio of the total number of members who left at the end of the year to the total number of members at the beginning of the year was 1:6.

    (2) At the end of the year, 21 members remained on the Planning Committee.

292. Max purchased a guitar for a total of $624, which consisted of the price of the guitar and the sales tax. Was the sales tax rate greater than 3 percent?

    (1) The price of the guitar that Max purchased was less than $602.

    (2) The sales tax for the guitar that Max purchased was less than $30.

293. Was the number of books sold at Bookstore X last week greater than the number of books sold at Bookstore Y last week?

    (1) Last week, more than 1,000 books were sold at Bookstore X on Saturday and fewer than 1,000 books were sold at Bookstore Y on Saturday.

    (2) Last week, less than 20 percent of the books sold at Bookstore X were sold on Saturday and more than 20 percent of the books sold at Bookstore Y were sold on Saturday.

294. From May 1 to May 30 in the same year, the balance in a checking account increased. What was the balance in the checking account on May 30 ?

    (1) If, during this period of time, the increase in the balance in the checking account had been 12 percent, then the balance in the account on May 30 would have been $504.

    (2) During this period of time, the increase in the balance in the checking account was 8 percent.

295. A merchant discounted the sale price of a coat and the sale price of a sweater. Which of the two articles of clothing was discounted by the greater dollar amount?

    (1) The percent discount on the coat was 2 percentage points greater than the percent discount on the sweater.

    (2) Before the discounts, the sale price of the coat was $10 less than the sale price of the sweater.

296. If the positive integer n is added to each of the integers 69, 94, and 121, what is the value of n ?

    (1) $69 + n$ and $94 + n$ are the squares of two consecutive integers.

    (2) $94 + n$ and $121 + n$ are the squares of two consecutive integers.

297. If a merchant purchased a sofa from a manufacturer for $400 and then sold it, what was the selling price of the sofa?

    (1) The selling price of the sofa was greater than 140 percent of the purchase price.

    (2) The merchant's gross profit from the purchase and sale of the sofa was $\frac{1}{3}$ of the selling price.

298. Last year, in a certain housing development, the average (arithmetic mean) price of 20 new houses was $160,000. Did more than 9 of the 20 houses have prices that were less than the average price last year?

    (1) Last year the greatest price of one of the 20 houses was $219,000.

    (2) Last year the median of the prices of the 20 houses was $150,000.

299. For a certain city's library, the average cost of purchasing each new book is $28. The library receives $15,000 from the city each year; the library also receives a bonus of $2,000 if the total number of items checked out over the course of the year exceeds 5,000. Did the library receive the bonus last year?

    (1) The library purchased an average of 50 new books each month last year and received enough money from the city to cover this cost.

    (2) The lowest number of items checked out in one month was 459.

$$7, 9, 6, 4, 5, x$$

300. If x is a number in the list above, what is the median of the list?

    (1) $x > 7$

    (2) The median of the list equals the arithmetic mean of the list.

301. Three dice, each of which has its 6 sides numbered 1 through 6, are tossed. The sum of the 3 numbers that are facing up is 12. Is at least 1 of these numbers 5 ?

    (1) None of the 3 numbers that are facing up is divisible by 3.

    (2) Of the numbers that are facing up, 2, but not all 3, are equal.

Questions 302 to 332 - Difficulty: Hard

302. Did the population of Town C increase by at least 100 percent from the year 2000 to the year 2010 ?

    (1) The population of Town C in 2000 was $\frac{2}{3}$ of the population in 2005.

    (2) The population of Town C increased by a greater number of people from 2005 to 2010 than it did from 2000 to 2005.

303. In a survey of 200 college graduates, 30% said they had received student loans during their college careers, and 40% said they had received scholarships. What percent of those surveyed said that they had received neither student loans nor scholarships during their college careers?

    (1) 25% of those surveyed said that they had received scholarships but no loans.

    (2) 50% of those surveyed who said that they had received loans also said that they had received scholarships.

304. Stores L and M each sell a certain product at a different regular price. If both stores discount their regular price of the product, is the discount price at Store M less than the discount price at Store L ?

    (1) At Store L the discount price is 10 percent less than the regular price; at Store M the discount price is 15 percent less than the regular price.

    (2) At Store L the discount price is $5 less than the regular store price; at Store M the discount price is $6 less than the regular price.

305. A box contains only red chips, white chips, and blue chips. If a chip is randomly selected from the box, what is the probability that the chip will be either white or blue?

    (1) The probability that the chip will be blue is $\frac{1}{5}$.

    (2) The probability that the chip will be red is $\frac{1}{3}$.

306. Did the sum of the prices of three shirts exceed $60 ?

    (1) The price of the most expensive of the shirts exceeded $30.

    (2) The price of the least expensive of the shirts exceeded $20.

307. What is the total number of coins that Bert and Claire have?

    (1) Bert has 50 percent more coins than Claire.

    (2) The total number of coins that Bert and Claire have is between 21 and 28.

308. A telephone station has x processors, each of which can process a maximum of y calls at any particular time, where x and y are positive integers. If 500 calls are sent to the station at a particular time, can the station process all of the calls?

    (1) $x = 600$

    (2) $100 < y < 200$

	Price per Flower
Roses	$1.00
Daisies	$0.50

309. Kim and Sue each bought some roses and some daisies at the prices shown above. If Kim bought the same total number of roses and daisies as Sue, was the price of Kim's purchase of roses and daisies higher than the price of Sue's purchase of roses and daisies?

    (1) Kim bought twice as many daisies as roses.

    (2) Kim bought 4 more roses than Sue bought.

310. Jazz and blues recordings accounted for 6 percent of the $840 million revenue from the sales of recordings in Country Y in 2000. What was the revenue from the sales of jazz and blues recordings in Country Y in 1998 ?

    (1) Jazz and blues recordings accounted for 5 percent of the revenue from the sales of recordings in Country Y in 1998.

    (2) The revenue from the sales of jazz and blues recordings in Country Y increased by 40 percent from 1998 to 2000.

311. On a certain nonstop trip, Marta averaged x miles per hour for 2 hours and y miles per hour for the remaining 3 hours. What was her average speed, in miles per hour, for the entire trip?

    (1) $2x + 3y = 280$

    (2) $y = x + 10$

312. A group consisting of several families visited an amusement park where the regular admission fees were ¥5,500 for each adult and ¥4,800 for each child. Because there were at least 10 people in the group, each paid an admission fee that was 10% less than the regular admission fee. How many children were in the group?

    (1) The total of the admission fees paid for the adults in the group was ¥29,700.

    (2) The total of the admission fees paid for the children in the group was ¥4,860 more than the total of the admission fees paid for the adults in the group.

313. What is the ratio of the average (arithmetic mean) height of students in class X to the average height of students in class Y?

    (1) The average height of the students in class X is 120 centimeters.

    (2) The average height of the students in class X and class Y combined is 126 centimeters.

314. Each week a certain salesman is paid a fixed amount equal to $300, plus a commission equal to 5 percent of the amount of his sales that week over $1,000. What is the total amount the salesman was paid last week?

    (1) The total amount the salesman was paid last week is equal to 10 percent of the amount of his sales last week.

    (2) The salesman's sales last week totaled $5,000.

315. At a bakery, all donuts are priced equally and all bagels are priced equally. What is the total price of 5 donuts and 3 bagels at the bakery?

    (1) At the bakery, the total price of 10 donuts and 6 bagels is $12.90.

    (2) At the bakery, the price of a donut is $0.15 less than the price of a bagel.

316. Last year, if Arturo spent a total of $12,000 on his mortgage payments, real estate taxes, and home insurance, how much did he spend on his real estate taxes?

    (1) Last year, the total amount that Arturo spent on his real estate taxes and home insurance was $33\frac{1}{3}$ percent of the amount that he spent on his mortgage payments.

    (2) Last year, the amount that Arturo spent on his real estate taxes was 20 percent of the total amount he spent on his mortgage payments and home insurance.

317. Is the number of members of Club X greater than the number of members of Club Y?

    (1) Of the members of Club X, 20 percent are also members of Club Y.

    (2) Of the members of Club Y, 30 percent are also members of Club X.

318. The only articles of clothing in a certain closet are shirts, dresses, and jackets. The ratio of the number of shirts to the number of dresses to the number of jackets in the closet is 9:4:5, respectively. If there are more than 7 dresses in the closet, what is the total number of articles of clothing in the closet?

    (1) The total number of shirts and jackets in the closet is less than 30.

    (2) The total number of shirts and dresses in the closet is 26.

319. Material A costs $3 per kilogram, and Material B costs $5 per kilogram. If 10 kilograms of Material K consists of x kilograms of Material A and y kilograms of Material B, is $x > y$?

    (1) $y > 4$

    (2) The cost of the 10 kilograms of Material K is less than $40.

320. At what speed was a train traveling on a trip when it had completed half of the total distance of the trip?

    (1) The trip was 460 miles long and took 4 hours to complete.

    (2) The train traveled at an average rate of 115 miles per hour on the trip.

321. Tom, Jane, and Sue each purchased a new house. The average (arithmetic mean) price of the three houses was $120,000. What was the median price of the three houses?

    (1) The price of Tom's house was $110,000.
    (2) The price of Jane's house was $120,000.

322. A certain bookcase has 2 shelves of books. On the upper shelf, the book with the greatest number of pages has 400 pages. On the lower shelf, the book with the least number of pages has 475 pages. What is the median number of pages for all of the books on the 2 shelves?

    (1) There are 25 books on the upper shelf.
    (2) There are 24 books on the lower shelf.

323. In planning for a car trip, Joan estimated both the distance of the trip, in miles, and her average speed, in miles per hour. She accurately divided her estimated distance by her estimated average speed to obtain an estimate for the time, in hours, that the trip would take. Was her estimate within 0.5 hour of the actual time that the trip took?

    (1) Joan's estimate for the distance was within 5 miles of the actual distance.
    (2) Joan's estimate for her average speed was within 10 miles per hour of her actual average speed.

Shipment	S1	S2	S3	S4	S5	S6
Fraction of the Total Value of the Six Shipments	$\frac{1}{4}$	$\frac{1}{5}$	$\frac{1}{6}$	$\frac{3}{20}$	$\frac{2}{15}$	$\frac{1}{10}$

324. Six shipments of machine parts were shipped from a factory on two trucks, with each shipment entirely on one of the trucks. Each shipment was labeled either S1, S2, S3, S4, S5, or S6. The table shows the value of each shipment as a fraction of the total value of the six shipments. If the shipments on the first truck had a value greater than $\frac{1}{2}$ of the total value of the six shipments, was S3 shipped on the first truck?

    (1) S2 and S4 were shipped on the first truck.
    (2) S1 and S6 were shipped on the second truck.

	Favorable	Unfavorable	Not Sure
Candidate M	40	20	40
Candidate N	30	35	35

325. The table above shows the results of a survey of 100 voters who each responded "Favorable" or "Unfavorable" or "Not Sure" when asked about their impressions of Candidate M and of Candidate N. What was the number of voters who responded "Favorable" for both candidates?

    (1) The number of voters who did not respond "Favorable" for either candidate was 40.
    (2) The number of voters who responded "Unfavorable" for both candidates was 10.

326. A school administrator will assign each student in a group of n students to one of m classrooms. If $3 < m < 13 < n$, is it possible to assign each of the n students to one of the m classrooms so that each classroom has the same number of students assigned to it?

    (1) It is possible to assign each of $3n$ students to one of m classrooms so that each classroom has the same number of students assigned to it.
    (2) It is possible to assign each of $13n$ students to one of m classrooms so that each classroom has the same number of students assigned to it.

327. At a certain clothing store, customers who buy 2 shirts pay the regular price for the first shirt and a discounted price for the second shirt. The store makes the same profit from the sale of 2 shirts that it makes from the sale of 1 shirt at the regular price. For a customer who buys 2 shirts, what is the discounted price of the second shirt?

    (1) The regular price of each of the 2 shirts the customer buys at the clothing store is $16.
    (2) The cost to the clothing store of each of the 2 shirts the customer buys is $12.

328. What is the median number of employees assigned per project for the projects at Company Z?

    (1) 25 percent of the projects at Company Z have 4 or more employees assigned to each project.
    (2) 35 percent of the projects at Company Z have 2 or fewer employees assigned to each project.

329. Last year, a certain company began manufacturing product X and sold every unit of product X that it produced. Last year the company's total expenses for manufacturing product X were equal to $100,000 plus 5 percent of the company's total revenue from all units of product X sold. If the company made a profit on product X last year, did the company sell more than 21,000 units of product X last year?

    (1) The company's total revenue from the sale of product X last year was greater than $110,000.

    (2) For each unit of product X sold last year, the company's revenue was $5.

330. Beginning in January of last year, Carl made deposits of $120 into his account on the 15th of each month for several consecutive months and then made withdrawals of $50 from the account on the 15th of each of the remaining months of last year. There were no other transactions in the account last year. If the closing balance of Carl's account for May of last year was $2,600, what was the range of the monthly closing balances of Carl's account last year?

    (1) Last year the closing balance of Carl's account for April was less than $2,625.

    (2) Last year the closing balance of Carl's account for June was less than $2,675.

331. What amount did Jean earn from the commission on her sales in the first half of 1988 ?

    (1) In 1988 Jean's commission was 5 percent of the total amount of her sales.

    (2) The amount of Jean's sales in the second half of 1988 averaged $10,000 per month more than in the first half.

332. In a certain business, production index p is directly proportional to efficiency index e, which is in turn directly proportional to investment index i. What is p if $i = 70$?

    (1) $e = 0.5$ whenever $i = 60$.

    (2) $p = 2.0$ whenever $i = 50$.

6.5 Answer Key

229.	E	250.	D	271.	D	292.	A	313.	E
230.	C	251.	D	272.	A	293.	C	314.	D
231.	A	252.	E	273.	B	294.	C	315.	A
232.	E	253.	C	274.	D	295.	E	316.	B
233.	D	254.	C	275.	E	296.	D	317.	C
234.	C	255.	E	276.	E	297.	B	318.	D
235.	C	256.	C	277.	B	298.	B	319.	B
236.	C	257.	A	278.	C	299.	D	320.	E
237.	E	258.	E	279.	E	300.	A	321.	B
238.	C	259.	B	280.	A	301.	C	322.	C
239.	C	260.	B	281.	D	302.	C	323.	E
240.	E	261.	B	282.	B	303.	D	324.	B
241.	C	262.	E	283.	C	304.	C	325.	A
242.	E	263.	D	284.	E	305.	B	326.	B
243.	C	264.	B	285.	C	306.	B	327.	B
244.	C	265.	D	286.	E	307.	C	328.	C
245.	A	266.	E	287.	A	308.	A	329.	B
246.	C	267.	A	288.	E	309.	B	330.	C
247.	E	268.	C	289.	C	310.	B	331.	E
248.	E	269.	C	290.	E	311.	A	332.	B
249.	E	270.	C	291.	D	312.	C		

6.6 Answer Explanations

The following discussion of Data Insights is intended to familiarize you with the most efficient and effective approaches to the kinds of problems common to Data Insights. The particular questions in this chapter are generally representative of the kinds of Data Insights questions you will encounter on the GMAT exam. Remember that it is the problem solving strategy that is important, not the specific details of a particular question.

Questions 229 to 268 - Difficulty: Easy

229. What is the number of pages of a certain journal article?

    (1)   The size of each page is $5\frac{1}{2}$ inches by 8 inches.

    (2)   The average (arithmetic mean) number of words per page is 250.

Arithmetic Applied Problems

(1)   Given that each page is $5\frac{1}{2}$ inches by 8 inches, any positive integer can be the number of pages of the journal article. For example, it is possible that the journal article consists of 10 pages, each $5\frac{1}{2}$ inches by 8 inches. However, it is also possible that the journal article consists of 20 pages, each $5\frac{1}{2}$ inches by 8 inches. Therefore, the number of pages cannot be determined; NOT sufficient.

(2)   Given that the average number of words per page is 250, any positive integer can be the number of pages of the journal article. For example, it is possible that the journal article consists of 10 pages and contains a total of 10(250) = 2,500 words, and in this case the average number of words per page is $\frac{2,500}{10}$ = 250. However, it is also possible that the journal article consists of 20 pages and contains a total of 20(250) = 5,000 words, and in this case the average number of words per page is also $\frac{5,000}{20}$ = 250. Therefore, the number of pages cannot be determined; NOT sufficient.

Taking (1) and (2) together, it is still not possible to determine the number of pages because

each of the examples used above satisfies both (1) and (2).

The correct answer is E; both statements together are still not sufficient.

230. If a certain vase contains only roses and tulips, how many tulips are there in the vase?

    (1)   The number of roses in the vase is 4 times the number of tulips in the vase.

    (2)   There is a total of 20 flowers in the vase.

Arithmetic Ratio and Proportion

The task is to determine the number of tulips in the vase.

(1)   This says that for every tulip in the vase, there are 4 roses so the ratio of roses to tulips is 4:1. Because there could be 4 roses and 1 tulip or there could be 20 roses and 5 tulips, the number of tulips cannot be uniquely determined; NOT sufficient.

(2)   This says the total number of roses and tulips in the vase is 20. Because there could be 10 roses and 10 tulips or there could be 15 roses and 5 tulips, the number of tulips cannot be uniquely determined; NOT sufficient.

From (1), the ratio of roses to tulips is 4:1 so $\frac{1}{5}$ of the flowers in the vase are tulips. From (2), there are 20 flowers in the vase. So, taking (1) and (2) together, the number of tulips in the vase is $\frac{1}{5}(20) = 4$.

The correct answer is C; both statements together are sufficient.

231. The cost of 10 pounds of apples and 2 pounds of grapes was $12. What was the cost per pound of apples?

    (1)   The cost per pound of grapes was $2.
    (2)   The cost of 2 pounds of apples was less than the cost of 1 pound of grapes.

Arithmetic Applied Problems

Determine the cost per pound of apples.

    (1)   The cost per pound of grapes was $2. The cost of 2 pounds of grapes was 2($2) = $4. The cost of the 10 pounds of apples was $12 − $4 = $8. The cost per pound of the apples was $\frac{\$8}{10}$ = $0.80; SUFFICIENT.
    (2)   Intuitively, since (2) involves an inequality, it seems as if it wouldn't give enough information to determine the unique cost per pound of apples. A good strategy might be to guess multiple values for the costs per pound of apples and grapes that satisfy the condition given in the problem (the cost of 10 pounds of apples and 2 pounds of grapes is $12) and look for values that also meet the condition in (2), namely that the cost of 2 pounds of apples is less than the cost of 1 pound of grapes. For example:

Cost per pound of apples	Cost per pound of grapes	Total cost of 10 pounds of apples and 2 pounds of grapes, in dollars	Is total cost $12?	Is the cost of 2 pounds of apples less than the cost of 1 pound of grapes?
$1	$1	10(1) + 2(1)	yes	No, 2(1) ≮ 1
$0.50	$3.50	10(0.5) + 2(3.5)	yes	Yes, 2(0.50) < 3.50
$0.60	$3.00	10(0.6) + 2(3)	yes	Yes, 2(0.60) < 3.00

As shown in the table, the cost per pound of apples could be $0.50 or $0.60, so the cost per pound of apples cannot be uniquely determined; NOT sufficient.

The correct answer is A; statement 1 alone is sufficient.

232. What was the median annual salary for the employees at Company X last year?

    (1)   Last year there were 29 employees at Company X.
    (2)   Last year 12 employees at Company X had an annual salary of $24,000.

Arithmetic Statistics

    (1)   Given that there were 29 employees, the median salary is the 15th salary in a list of 29 positive numbers, but we cannot determine the value of any of the numbers; NOT sufficient.

    (2)   Given that 12 employees had an annual salary of $24,000, the median salary is the median of a list of 12 or more positive numbers, of which 12 are equal to $24,000. If there were only 12 employees, then the median salary would be $24,000. However, if there were more than 2(12) = 24 employees and all but 12 of the employees had an annual salary of $30,000, then the median salary would be $30,000; NOT sufficient.

Taking (1) and (2) together, if 12 employees had an annual salary of $24,000 and the remaining 17 employees had an annual salary of $20,000, then the median salary would be $20,000. However, if 12 employees had an annual salary of $24,000 and the remaining 17 employees had an annual salary of $30,000, then the median salary would be $30,000.

Tip: If more than half the numbers in a list of numbers have the same value, then the median of the list will be that value, regardless of the values of the remaining numbers.

The correct answer is E; both statements together are still not sufficient.

233. How many basic units of currency X are equivalent to 250 basic units of currency Y ?

    (1)   100 basic units of currency X are equivalent to 625 basic units of currency Y.
    (2)   2,000 basic units of currency X are equivalent to 12,500 basic units of currency Y.

Arithmetic Ratio and Proportion

(1) The equivalency of 100 basic units of currency X and 625 basic units of currency Y means that 1 basic unit of currency Y is equivalent to $\frac{100}{625}$ basic units of currency X. Therefore, 250 basic units of currency Y are equivalent to $(250)\left(\frac{100}{625}\right)$ basic units of currency X; SUFFICIENT.

(2) The equivalency of 2,000 basic units of currency X and 12,500 basic units of currency Y means that 1 basic unit of currency Y is equivalent to $\frac{2{,}000}{12{,}500}$ basic units of currency X. Therefore, 250 basic units of currency Y are equivalent to $(250)\left(\frac{2{,}000}{12{,}500}\right)$ basic units of currency X; SUFFICIENT.

Tip: For Data Insights questions in which the task is to determine a specific value, there is no need to perform calculations to get the value in its simplest form. The goal is to determine whether the value can be uniquely determined, not to find the actual value in its simplest form.

The correct answer is D; each statement alone is sufficient.

234. A company bought 3 printers and 1 scanner. What was the price of the scanner?

    (1) The total price of the printers and the scanner was $1,300.

    (2) The price of each printer was 4 times the price of the scanner.

Algebra Simultaneous Equations

Let P_1, P_2, and P_3 be the prices, in dollars, of the 3 printers and let S be the price, in dollars, of the scanner. What is the value of S?

(1) Given that $P_1 + P_2 + P_3 + S = 1{,}300$, it is clear that the value of S cannot be determined; NOT sufficient.

(2) Given that $P_1 = P_2 = P_3 = 4S$, it is possible that $P_1 = P_2 = P_3 = 400$ and $S = 100$. On the other hand, it is also possible that $P_1 = P_2 = P_3 = 800$ and $S = 200$; NOT sufficient.

Taking (1) and (2) together, substituting $P_1 = 4S$, $P_2 = 4S$, and $P_3 = 4S$ into $P_1 + P_2 + P_3 + S = 1{,}300$ gives $4S + 4S + 4S + S = 1{,}300$, or $13S = 1{,}300$, and therefore $S = 100$.

The correct answer is C; both statements together are sufficient.

235. Each of the 256 solid-colored marbles in a box is either blue, green, or purple. What is the ratio of the number of blue marbles to the number of purple marbles in the box?

    (1) The number of green marbles in the box is 4 times the number of blue marbles in the box.

    (2) There are 192 green marbles in the box.

Arithmetic Ratio and Proportion

Let B, G, and P be the numbers of marbles, respectively, that are blue, green, and purple. From the given information it follows that $B + G + P = 256$. What is the value of $\frac{B}{P}$?

(1) Given that $G = 4B$, it is possible that $\frac{B}{P} = \frac{1}{251}$ (choose $B = 1$, $G = 4$, and $P = 251$) and it is possible that $\frac{B}{P} = \frac{1}{123}$ (choose $B = 2$, $G = 8$, and $P = 246$); NOT sufficient.

(2) Given that $G = 192$, it is possible that $\frac{B}{P} = \frac{1}{63}$ (choose $B = 1$, $G = 192$, and $P = 63$) and it is possible that $\frac{B}{P} = \frac{1}{31}$ (choose $B = 2$, $G = 192$, and $P = 62$); NOT sufficient.

Taking (1) and (2) together, it follows from $G = 4B$ and $G = 192$ that $192 = 4B$, or $B = 48$. Thus, $B + G + P = 256$ becomes $48 + 192 + P = 256$, and so $P = 256 - 48 - 192 = 16$. Therefore, $\frac{B}{P} = \frac{48}{16}$.

The correct answer is C; both statements together are sufficient.

236. A certain mixture of paint requires blue, yellow, and red paints in ratios of 2:3:1, respectively, and no other ingredients. If there are ample quantities of the blue and red paints available, is there enough of the yellow paint available to make the desired amount of the mixture?

(1) Exactly 20 quarts of the mixture are needed.

(2) Exactly 10 quarts of the yellow paint are available.

Arithmetic Ratios

Given that the mixture requires blue paint, yellow paint, and red paint in the ratios 2:3:1, it follows that $\dfrac{3}{2+3+1} = \dfrac{1}{2}$ of the mixture will be yellow paint. Determining whether there is enough yellow paint available depends on how much of the mixture is needed and how much yellow paint is available.

(1) This indicates that exactly 20 quarts of the paint mixture are needed, so $\dfrac{1}{2}(20)$ = 10 quarts of yellow paint are needed. However, there is no information about how much yellow paint is available; NOT sufficient.

(2) This indicates that exactly 10 quarts of yellow paint are available, but there is no information about how much of the mixture or how much yellow paint is needed; NOT sufficient.

Taking (1) and (2) together, 10 quarts of yellow paint are needed and 10 quarts are available.

The correct answer is C; both statements together are sufficient.

237. There are 2 groups of students who took a history test. Was the average (arithmetic mean) score of the students in Group A higher than the average score of the students in Group B who took the test?

(1) Of the students who took the test, 10 were in Group A and 12 were in Group B.

(2) On the test, the highest score achieved was achieved by a Group B student and the lowest score achieved was achieved by a Group A student.

Arithmetic Statistics

(1) Given that 10 of the scores were by students in Group A and 12 of the scores were by students in Group B, the following table shows two possibilities.

A scores	B scores	A average	B average	A average > B average?
10 scores of 8	12 scores of 1	8	1	yes
10 scores of 1	12 scores of 8	1	8	no

Therefore, it is not possible to determine whether the average score of the students in Group A is higher than the average score of the students in Group B; NOT sufficient.

(2) Given that the highest score achieved was achieved by a Group B student and the lowest score achieved was achieved by a Group A student, the following table shows two possibilities.

A scores	B scores	A average	B average	A average > B average?
1, 7, 7	2, 2, 8	5	4	yes
1, 1, 1	8, 8, 8	1	8	no

Therefore, it is not possible to determine whether the average score of the students in Group A is higher than the average score of the students in Group B; NOT sufficient.

Taking (1) and (2) together, the table below shows that it is not possible to determine whether the average score of the students in Group A is higher than the average score of the students in Group B.

A scores		B scores		A average	B average	A average > B average?
score	frequency	score	frequency			
2	1	3	11	4.7	4	yes
5	9	15	1			
score	frequency	score	frequency			
2	1	6	12	4.7	6	no
5	9					

The correct answer is E; both statements together are still not sufficient.

238. The research funds of a certain company were divided among three departments, X, Y, and Z. Which one of the three departments received the greatest proportion of the research funds?

    (1) The research funds received by departments X and Y were in the ratio 3 to 5, respectively.

    (2) The research funds received by departments X and Z were in the ratio 2 to 1, respectively.

Algebra Order; Ratio

Let x, y, and z be the research funds, respectively, of departments X, Y, and Z. Which of

$$\frac{x}{x+y+z}, \frac{y}{x+y+z}, \text{ or } \frac{z}{x+y+z} \text{ is the greatest,}$$

or respectively, which of x, y, or z is the greatest?

    (1) Given that $\frac{x}{y} = \frac{3}{5}$ where x and y are positive, it follows that $x < y$. However, nothing is known about z other than z is positive, so it cannot be determined which of x, y, or z is the greatest; NOT sufficient.

    (2) Given that $\frac{x}{z} = \frac{2}{1}$ where x and z are positive, it follows that $z < x$. However, nothing is known about y other than y is positive, so it cannot be determined which of x, y, or z is the greatest; NOT sufficient.

Taking (1) and (2) together, it follows from (1) that $x < y$ and it follows from (2) that $z < x$. Therefore, $z < x < y$ and y is the greatest.

The correct answer is C; both statements together are sufficient.

239. In a certain class, some students donated cans of food to a local food bank. What was the average (arithmetic mean) number of cans donated per student in the class?

    (1) The students donated a total of 56 cans of food.

    (2) The total number of cans donated was 40 greater than the total number of students in the class.

Arithmetic Statistics

Let s be the number of students and let c be the number of cans. What is the value of $\frac{c}{s}$?

    (1) Given that $c = 56$, it is not possible to determine the value of $\frac{c}{s}$ because nothing is known about the value of s other than s is a positive integer; NOT sufficient.

    (2) Given that $c = 40 + s$, it is not possible to determine the value of $\frac{c}{s}$. For example, if $c = 40$ and $s = 40$, then $\frac{c}{s} = 1$. However, if $c = 80$ and $s = 40$, then $\frac{c}{s} = 2$; NOT sufficient.

Taking (1) and (2) together, it follows that $40 + s = c = 56$, or $s = 56 - 40 = 16$. Therefore, $c = 56$, $s = 16$, and $\frac{c}{s} = \frac{56}{16}$.

The correct answer is C; both statements together are sufficient.

240. Each of the n employees at a certain company has a different annual salary. What is the median of the annual salaries of the n employees?

    (1) When the annual salaries of the n employees are listed in increasing order, the median is the 15th salary.

    (2) The sum of the annual salaries of the n employees is $913,500.

Arithmetic Statistics

    (1) Given that the median is the 15th salary and all n salaries are different, it follows that there are 14 salaries less than the 15th salary and 14 salaries greater than the 15th salary, for a total of 29 employee salaries. However, there is no information about what any of the salaries actually are, so the median of the salaries cannot be determined; NOT sufficient.

    (2) Given that the sum of the annual salaries is $913,500, the median salary cannot be uniquely determined. To determine more than one possible value for the median salary, use common divisibility rules to find factors of $913,500.

    For example, 913,500 is divisible by 5 because it ends in 0. Then, because 913,500 = 5(182,700), there could be 5 salaries, each $182,700. But the salaries must be all different, so we need 5 different salaries that total $913,500. They could be the salaries shown in the table below. Note that the pattern starts with the 3rd (middle) salary of $182,700, then the 2nd and 4th salaries are "paired" in that one is decreased and the other is increased by the same amount from $182,700. Likewise, for the 1st and 5th salaries. The median is $182,700.

Salary #	Salary
1	$182,698
2	$182,699
3	**$182,700**
4	$182,701
5	$182,702
Total	$913,500

Also, 913,500 is divisible by 9 because the sum of its digits is divisible by 9 and $913,500 = 9(101,500)$. Using ideas similar to those used in the first example, there could be 9 different salaries that total $913,500. Using the same technique as in the first example, these salaries could be those shown below. All 9 salaries are listed to reinforce the technique. They need not be written out as part of the solution.

Salary #	Salary
1	$101,496
2	$101,497
3	$101,498
4	$101,499
5	**$101,500**
6	$101,501
7	$101,502
8	$101,503
9	$101,504
Total	$913,500

Therefore, the median salary could be $182,700 or $101,500; NOT sufficient.

Taking (1) and (2) together, there are 29 different salaries and their sum is $913,500, but this information is not sufficient to uniquely determine the median.

Salary number	Salary (Example I)	Salary (Example II)
1	$30,100	$30,100
2	$30,200	$30,200
3	$30,300	$30,300
⋮	⋮	⋮
14	$31,400	$31,380
15	**$31,500**	**$31,540**
16	$31,600	$31,580
⋮	⋮	⋮
27	$32,700	$32,700
28	$32,800	$32,800
29	$32,900	$32,900
Total	$913,500	$913,500

Note that $913,500 = 29(31,500)$. The table above shows two examples, each consisting of 29 different salaries (not all are shown, however) that were obtained using techniques similar to those used in the previous examples. Note that, in both examples, the 1st salary is $1,400 less than $31,500 and the 29th is $1,400 more than $31,500, the 2nd salary is $1,300 less than $31,500 and the 28th is $1,300 more than $31,500, and so on. The salary columns in both examples are identical except for the 14th, 15th, and 16th salaries, which were used to obtain different medians.

In each example, the median is the 15th salary, so (1) is satisfied, and the sum of the salaries is $913,500, so (2) is satisfied. But the median in one case is $31,500 and the median in the other case is $31,540.

The correct answer is E;
both statements together are still not sufficient.

241. In a recent town election, what was the ratio of the number of votes in favor of a certain proposal to the number of votes against the proposal?

(1) There were 60 more votes in favor of the proposal than against the proposal.

(2) There were 240 votes in favor of the proposal.

Arithmetic Ratio and Proportion

Let F be the number of votes in favor and let A be the number of votes against. What is the value of $\frac{F}{A}$?

(1) Given that $F = 60 + A$, it is possible that $\frac{F}{A} = 2$ (choose $F = 120$ and $A = 60$) and it is possible that $\frac{F}{A} = 3$ (choose $F = 90$ and $A = 30$); NOT sufficient.

(2) Given that $F = 240$, it is possible that $\frac{F}{A} = 1$ (choose $F = 240$ and $A = 240$) and it is possible that $\frac{F}{A} = 2$ (choose $F = 240$ and $A = 120$); NOT sufficient.

Taking (1) and (2) together, substitute $F = 240$ into $F = 60 + A$ to get $240 = 60 + A$, or $A = 180$. Therefore, $\frac{F}{A} = \frac{240}{180}$.

The correct answer is C; both statements together are sufficient.

242. How many men are in a certain company's vanpool program?

(1) The ratio of men to women in the program is 3 to 2.

(2) The men and women in the program fill 6 vans.

Arithmetic Applied Problems

Let m be the number of men in the program and let w be the number of women in the program. What is the value of m ?

(1) Given that $\frac{m}{w} = \frac{3}{2}$, it is not possible to determine the value of m. For example, if $m = 3$ and $w = 2$, then $\frac{m}{w} = \frac{3}{2}$ is true; and if $m = 6$ and $w = 4$, then $\frac{m}{w} = \frac{3}{2}$ is true; NOT sufficient.

(2) Given that the men and women fill 6 vans, it is clearly not possible to determine the value of m; NOT sufficient.

Taking (1) and (2) together, it is still not possible to determine the value of m. Even if it is assumed that each van has the same maximum capacity, it is possible that $m = 18$ and $w = 12$ (a total of

30 people, which would fill 6 vans each having a capacity of 5 people) and it is possible that $m = 36$ and $w = 24$ (a total of 60 people, which would fill 6 vans each having a capacity of 10 people).

The correct answer is E; both statements together are still not sufficient.

243. Each of the marbles in a jar is either red or white or blue. If one marble is to be selected at random from the jar, what is the probability that the marble will be blue?

(1) There are a total of 24 marbles in the jar, 8 of which are red.

(2) The probability that the marble selected will be white is $\frac{1}{2}$.

Arithmetic Probability

This problem can be solved by determining the number of marbles in the jar and the number that are blue.

(1) This indicates that there are 24 marbles in the jar and 8 of them are red. The number of marbles that are blue is not known; NOT sufficient.

(2) This indicates neither the number of marbles in the jar nor the number that are blue; NOT sufficient.

Taking (1) and (2) together, there are 24 marbles in the jar, 8 of which are red and $\frac{1}{2}(24) = 12$ of which are white. Then, the number of blue marbles is $24 - 8 - 12 = 4$, and the probability that one marble selected at random will be blue is $\frac{4}{24} = \frac{1}{6}$.

The correct answer is C; both statements together are sufficient.

244. Last semester, Professor K taught two classes, A and B. Each student in class A handed in 7 assignments, and each student in class B handed in 5 assignments. How many students were in class A ?

(1) The students in both classes combined handed in a total of 85 assignments.

(2) There were 10 students in class B.

Algebra Simultaneous Equations

Let a be the number of students in class A and let b be the number of students in class B. Then the students in class A handed in a total of $7a$ assignments and the students in class B handed in a total of $5b$ assignments. What is the value of a ?

(1) Given that $7a + 5b = 85$, it is not possible to determine the value of a. For example, it is possible that $a = 5$ and $b = 10$, since $7(5) + 5(10) = 85$. On the other hand, it is also possible that $a = 10$ and $b = 3$, since $7(10) + 5(3) = 85$; NOT sufficient.

(2) Given that $b = 10$, it is not possible to determine the value of a. For example, it is possible that $a = b = 10$; and it is also possible that $a = 5$ and $b = 10$; NOT sufficient.

Taking (1) and (2) together, substituting $b = 10$ into $7a + 5b = 85$ gives $7a + 5(10) = 85$, or $7a = 35$, or $a = 5$.

**The correct answer is C;
both statements together are sufficient.**

245. Was the amount of John's heating bill for February greater than it was for January?

(1) The ratio of the amount of John's heating bill for February to that for January was $\frac{26}{25}$.

(2) The sum of the amounts of John's heating bills for January and February was $183.60.

Arithmetic Applied Problems

Let J and F be the amounts, respectively and in dollars, of the heating bills for January and February. Is $F > J$?

(1) Given that $\frac{F}{J} = \frac{26}{25}$, it follows that $\frac{F}{J} > 1$. Multiplying both sides of the inequality $\frac{F}{J} > 1$ by the positive quantity J gives $F > J$; SUFFICIENT.

(2) Given that $J + F = 183.60$, it is not possible to determine whether $F > J$. For example, if $J = 83.60$ and $F = 100.00$, then $J + F = 183.60$ and $F > J$. On the other hand, if $J = 100.00$ and $F = 83.60$, then $J + F = 183.60$ and $F < J$; NOT sufficient.

**The correct answer is A;
statement 1 alone is sufficient.**

246. Machine R and machine S work at their respective constant rates. How much time does it take machine R, working alone, to complete a certain job?

(1) The amount of time that it takes machine S, working alone, to complete the job is $\frac{3}{4}$ the amount of time that it takes machine R, working alone, to complete the job.

(2) Machine R and machine S, working together, take 12 minutes to complete the job.

Algebra Applied Problems

(1) Given that machine S takes $\frac{3}{4}$ as long as machine R to complete the job, if the rate of each machine were doubled, then machine S would still take $\frac{3}{4}$ as long as machine R to complete the job and machine R, working alone, would then take half as long to complete the job as compared to before the rates were doubled; NOT sufficient.

(2) Given that machine R and machine S, working together, take 12 minutes to complete the job, if machine S is extremely slow and thus contributes very little when the machines are working together, then it would take machine R, working alone, only a little more than 12 minutes to complete the job. However, if machine S, working alone, takes only a few seconds less than 12 minutes to complete the job, and thus machine R contributes very little when the machines are working together, then it would take machine R, working alone, a long time to complete the job; NOT sufficient.

Taking (1) and (2) together, let t be the time it takes for machine R, working alone, to complete the job. Then the time it takes machine S, working alone, to complete the job is $\frac{3}{4}t$. Thus, the individual constant rates of machines R and S are, respectively, $\frac{1}{t}$ and $\frac{1}{\frac{3}{4}t} = \left(\frac{4}{3}\right)\frac{1}{t}$, and their combined rate is $\left(1 + \frac{4}{3}\right)\frac{1}{t} = \frac{7}{3t}$. Since it takes 12 minutes to complete the job when the machines are working together, it follows that $\left(\dfrac{7}{3t}\right)(12) = 1$, which can be solved for t.

The correct answer is C; both statements together are sufficient.

247. What was the range of the selling prices of the 30 wallets sold by a certain store yesterday?

    (1) $\dfrac{1}{3}$ of the wallets had a selling price of $24 each.

    (2) The lowest selling price of the wallets was $\dfrac{1}{3}$ the highest selling price of the wallets.

Arithmetic Statistics

Since the range of a data set is the greatest value in the data set minus the least value in the data set, this problem can be solved if the least selling price and the greatest selling price of the wallets sold by the store yesterday can be determined.

    (1) This indicates that 10 of the wallets had a selling price of $24 each, but does not indicate the least selling price or the greatest selling price of the wallets sold by the store yesterday; NOT sufficient.

    (2) This indicates that $L = \dfrac{1}{3} G$, where L represents the least selling price and G represents the greatest selling price, but does not give enough information to determine $G - L$; NOT sufficient.

Taking (1) and (2) together, the least and greatest selling prices of the wallets sold by the store yesterday could be $10 and $30 for a range of $30 - $10 = $20, or the least and greatest selling prices of the wallets sold by the store yesterday could be $20 and $60 for a range of $60 - $20 = $40.

The correct answer is E; both statements together are still not sufficient.

248. Three houses are being sold through a real estate agent. What is the asking price for the house with the second-largest asking price?

    (1) The difference between the greatest and the least asking price is $130,000.

    (2) The difference between the two greater asking prices is $85,000.

Algebra Simultaneous Equations

Let x, y, and z, where $x \le y \le z$, be the asking prices of the three houses. This problem can be solved by determining the value of y.

    (1) This indicates that $z - x = $130,000$, but does not give the value of y; NOT sufficient.

    (2) This indicates that $z - y = $85,000$, but does not give the value of y; NOT sufficient.

Taking (1) and (2) together, x, y, and z could be $100,000, $145,000, and $230,000, respectively, in which case the second highest selling price is $145,000, or they could be $200,000, $245,000, and $330,000, respectively, in which case the second highest selling price is $245,000.

The correct answer is E; both statements together are still not sufficient.

249. How many people in a group of 50 own neither a fax machine nor a laser printer?

    (1) The total number of people in the group who own a fax machine or a laser printer or both is less than 50.

    (2) The total number of people in the group who own both a fax machine and a laser printer is 15.

Algebra Sets

    (1) This indicates that the total number who own either a fax machine or a laser printer or both is less than 50, but does not indicate how much less than 50 the total number is. Thus, the number of people in the group who own neither a fax machine nor a laser printer cannot be determined; NOT sufficient.

    (2) This indicates that, of the 50 people, 15 own both a fax machine and a laser printer, but does not indicate how many own one or the other. Thus, the number of people in the group who own neither a fax machine nor a laser printer cannot be determined; NOT sufficient.

Taking (1) and (2) together, it is known that 15 people own both a fax machine and a laser printer and that the total number who own either a fax machine or a laser printer or both is less than 50, but the exact number who own neither still cannot be determined. For example, if 20 people own only a fax machine and 10 people own only a laser printer, then both (1) and (2) are true and the number of people who own neither a fax machine nor a laser printer is $50 - 20 - 10 - 15 = 5$. However, if 10 people own only a fax machine and 10 people own only a laser printer, then both (1) and (2) are true and the number of people who own neither a fax machine nor a laser printer is $50 - 10 - 10 - 15 = 15$.

The correct answer is E;
both statements together are still not sufficient.

250. A certain investment earned a fixed rate of 4 percent interest per year, compounded annually, for five years. The interest earned for the third year of the investment was how many dollars greater than that for the first year?

(1) The amount of the investment at the beginning of the second year was $4,160.00.

(2) The amount of the investment at the beginning of the third year was $4,326.40.

Arithmetic Applied Problems; Percents

This problem can be solved by determining the dollar amount of the interest earned for the third year minus the dollar amount of interest earned in the first year, or, in symbols, $[A(1.04)^3 - A(1.04)^2] - [A(1.04)^1 - A]$, where A represents the dollar amount of the investment. This can be determined if the value of A can be determined.

(1) This indicates that $A(1.04)^1 = \$4,160.00$, since the amount of the investment at the beginning of the second year is the same as the amount of the investment at the end of the first year. Thus, the value of A can be determined by dividing 4,160.00 by 1.04; SUFFICIENT.

(2) This indicates that $A(1.04)^2 = \$4,326.40$, since the amount of the investment at the beginning of the third year is the same as the amount of the investment at the end of the second year. Thus, the value of A can be

determined by dividing 4,326.40 by $(1.04)^2$; SUFFICIENT.

The correct answer is D;
each statement alone is sufficient.

251. For a certain car repair, the total charge consisted of a charge for parts, a charge for labor, and a 6 percent sales tax on both the charge for parts and the charge for labor. If the charge for parts, excluding sales tax, was $50.00, what was the total charge for the repair?

(1) The sales tax on the charge for labor was $9.60.

(2) The total sales tax was $12.60.

Arithmetic Applied Problems; Percents

To find the total charge, T, for the repair, requires determining the value, in dollars, of $T = (1.06)(50 + L) = 53 + 1.06L$, where L represents the charge, in dollars, for labor. This value can be determined if the value of L can be determined.

(1) This indicates that $0.06L = 9.60$, from which L can be determined by dividing 9.60 by 0.06; SUFFICIENT.

(2) This indicates that $(0.06)(50 + L) = 12.60$. So, $3.00 + 0.06L = 12.60$ or $0.06L = 9.60$, which is the same as the equation in (1); SUFFICIENT.

The correct answer is D;
each statement alone is sufficient.

252. George has a total of B books in his library, 25 of which are hardcover fiction books. What is the value of B?

(1) 40 of the B books are fiction and the rest are nonfiction.

(2) 60 of the B books are hardcovers and the rest are paperbacks.

Arithmetic Applied Problems

Since 25 of George's B books are hardcover fiction, it is reasonable to assume that some of George's books might be paperback and some might be nonfiction. Therefore, the following table might be useful in determining, if possible, the value of B.

Fiction		Nonfiction		B
Hardcover	Paperback	Hardcover	Paperback	
25				

(1) If 40 of the *B* books are fiction, then
40 − 25 = 15 are paperback fiction. This
information is shown in the following table.

Fiction		Nonfiction		B
Hardcover	Paperback	Hardcover	Paperback	
25	15			

The rest are nonfiction, but there is no
indication how many are nonfiction. Note
that the table has two blank cells under
Nonfiction and these can be filled with any
numbers, which implies that the value of
B cannot be uniquely determined; NOT
sufficient.

(2) If 60 of the *B* books are hardcovers, then
60 − 25 = 35 are hardcover nonfiction. This
information is shown in the following table.

Fiction		Nonfiction		B
Hardcover	Paperback	Hardcover	Paperback	
25		35		

The rest are paperbacks, but there is no
indication of how many are paperbacks. The
table has two blank cells under paperback,
and these can be filled with any numbers,
which implies that the value of *B* cannot be
uniquely determined; NOT sufficient.

Taking the information from both (1) and (2),
shown in the following table, is still not sufficient
to uniquely determine the value of *B*.

Fiction		Nonfiction		B
Hardcover	Paperback	Hardcover	Paperback	
25	15	35		

The table has one blank cell under Paperback that
can be filled with any number, which implies that
the value of *B* cannot be uniquely determined.

**The correct answer is E;
both statements together are still not sufficient.**

253. In each of the last five years, Company K donated
p percent of its annual profits to a certain scholarship

fund. Did Company K donate more than $10,000 to
the scholarship fund last year?

(1) Two years ago, Company K had annual profits
of $3 million and donated $15,000 to the
scholarship fund.

(2) Last year, Company K had annual profits of
$2.5 million.

Arithmetic Applied Problems; Percents

(1) Although the given information allows
the value of *p* to be determined (see
further below), no information is available
about Company K's profit last year; NOT
sufficient.

(2) It is given that Company K's profit last
year was $2.5 million. However, no
information is available about the value of
p or how much Company K donated to the
scholarship fund last year; NOT sufficient.

Taking (1) and (2) together, from (1) it follows
that 15,000 is *p*% of 3 million, so $15{,}000 = \left(\dfrac{p}{100}\right)$
$(3{,}000{,}000)$, or $p = \dfrac{(100)(15{,}000)}{3{,}000{,}000} = \dfrac{15}{30} = 0.5$.

Using the value of *p* and (2), it follows that the
amount Company K donated to the scholarship
fund last year was (0.5%)($2.5 million) = (0.005)
($2,500,000) = $12,500. Therefore, Company K
donated more than $10,000 to the scholarship
fund last year.

Tip: If a Data Insights problem asks a question
about the value of something, it is not necessary
to determine a specific decimal, a reduced fraction,
or any other representation for this value if it is
known that only one such value exists. Thus, in
the previous paragraph, it is not necessary to solve
for *p* (it is enough to know that a unique value of
p can be found) and it is not necessary to evaluate
the product (*p*%)($2.5 million), since whatever the
product is, it will either be greater than $10,000,
and the answer to the question will be "yes," or
not be greater than $10,000, and the answer to the
question will be "no."

**The correct answer is C;
both statements together are sufficient.**

254. The people in a line waiting to buy tickets to a show
are standing one behind the other. Adam and Beth

are among the people in the line, and Beth is standing behind Adam with a number of people between them. If the number of people in front of Adam plus the number of people behind Beth is 18, how many people in the line are behind Beth?

(1)   There are a total of 32 people in the line.
(2)   23 people in the line are behind Adam.

Arithmetic Order

Beth is standing in line behind Adam with a number of people between them. Let x be the number of people ahead of Adam, let y be the number of people between Adam and Beth, and let z be the number of people behind Beth. It is given that $x + z = 18$. Determine z.

(1)   This indicates that there are 32 people in the line. Two of these people are Adam and Beth, so there are 30 other people in line besides Adam and Beth. Therefore, $x + y + z = 30$ and $x + z = 18$. From this, $y = 12$, but z cannot be determined uniquely. For example, if $x = 5$, then $z = 13$, but if $x = 10$, then $z = 8$; NOT sufficient.

(2)   This indicates that $y + 1 + z = 23$ because the people behind Adam consist of the people between Adam and Beth, Beth herself, and the people behind Beth. If, for example, $y = 4$, then $z = 18$, but if $y = 9$, then $z = 13$; NOT sufficient.

Taking (1) and (2) together, $y = 12$ from (1) and $y + z = 22$ from (2). Therefore, $z = 10$, and there are 10 people in line behind Beth.

The correct answer is C; both statements together are sufficient.

255. In a certain group of 50 people, how many are doctors who have a law degree?

(1)   In the group, 36 people are doctors.
(2)   In the group, 18 people have a law degree.

Arithmetic Sets

(1)   Given that there are 36 people who are doctors, there is no information about how many of the 36 people have a law degree, and therefore it cannot be determined how many of the 36 people are doctors with a law degree; NOT sufficient.

(2)   Given that there are 18 people who have a law degree, there is no information about how many of the 18 people are doctors, and therefore it cannot be determined how many of the 18 people are doctors with a law degree; NOT sufficient.

Taking (1) and (2) together, if n is the number of doctors with a law degree, the contingency table below shows that more than one value of n is possible by assigning appropriate values in the column labeled "not a doctor."

	doctor	not a doctor	total
law degree	n		18
no law degree	$36 - n$		32
total	36	14	50

For example, the first table below gives $n = 10$ and the second table below gives $n = 12$.

	doctor	not a doctor	total
law degree	n	8	18
no law degree	$36 - n$	6	32
total	36	14	50

	doctor	not a doctor	total
law degree	n	6	18
no law degree	$36 - n$	8	32
total	36	14	50

The correct answer is E; both statements together are still not sufficient.

256. Of a group of 50 households, how many have at least one cat or at least one dog, but not both?

(1)   The number of households that have at least one cat and at least one dog is 4.
(2)   The number of households that have no cats and no dogs is 14.

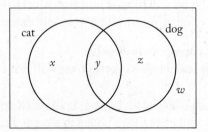

Arithmetic Sets

Using the labels on the Venn diagram, $w + x + y + z = 50$. Determine the value of $x + z$.

(1) This indicates that $y = 4$, so $w + x + z = 46$, but the value of $x + z$ cannot be uniquely determined; NOT sufficient.

(2) This indicates that $w = 14$, so $x + y + z = 36$, but the value of $x + z$ cannot be uniquely determined; NOT sufficient.

Taking (1) and (2) together, $14 + x + 4 + z = 50$, so $x + z = 50 - 14 - 4 = 32$.

The correct answer is C; both statements together are sufficient.

257. Robin invested a total of $12,000 in two investments, X and Y, so that the investments earned the same amount of simple annual interest. How many dollars did Robin invest in investment Y ?

(1) Investment X paid 3 percent simple annual interest, and investment Y paid 6 percent simple annual interest.

(2) Robin invested more than $1,000 in investment X.

Algebra Applied Problems

For investments X and Y, let r_X and r_Y be the annual percentage interest rates, respectively, and let x and y be the investment amounts, respectively and in dollars. Then $x + y = 12{,}000$ and $r_X \cdot x = r_Y \cdot y$. What is the value of y ?

(1) Given that $r_X = 3$ and $r_Y = 6$, then from $r_X \cdot x = r_Y \cdot y$ it follows that $3x = 6y$, or $x = 2y$. Therefore, $x + y = 12{,}000$ becomes $2y + y = 12{,}000$, or $3y = 12{,}000$, or $y = 4{,}000$; SUFFICIENT.

(2) Given that $x > 1{,}000$, it is not possible to determine the value of y. For example, $y = 4{,}000$ is possible (choose $r_X = 3$, $r_Y = 6$, and $x = 8{,}000$) and $y = 6{,}000$ is possible (choose $r_X = 3$, $r_Y = 3$, and $x = 6{,}000$); NOT sufficient.

The correct answer is A; statement 1 alone is sufficient.

258. In a real estate office that employs n salespeople, f of them are females and x of the females are new employees. What is the value of n ?

(1) If an employee were randomly selected from the n employees, the probability of selecting a female would be $\frac{2}{3}$.

(2) If an employee were randomly selected from the f female employees, the probability of selecting a new employee would be $\frac{1}{2}$.

Arithmetic Probability

(1) Given that $\frac{f}{n} = \frac{2}{3}$, it is possible that $n = 3$ (choose $f = 2$ and $x = 1$) and it is possible that $n = 6$ (choose $f = 4$ and $x = 2$); NOT sufficient.

(2) Given that $\frac{x}{f} = \frac{1}{2}$, the value of n cannot be determined because $\frac{x}{f} = \frac{1}{2}$ is true for each of the two choices of values of n, f, and x that were used in (1); NOT sufficient.

Taking (1) and (2) together is still not sufficient because both (1) and (2) hold for each of the two choices of values of n, f, and x that were used in (1).

The correct answer is E; both statements together are still not sufficient.

259. Do at least 60 percent of the students in Pat's class walk to school?

(1) At least 60 percent of the female students in Pat's class walk to school.

(2) The number of students in Pat's class who walk to school is twice the number of students who do not walk to school.

Arithmetic Percents

This problem can be solved by determining the total number of students in Pat's class and the number who walk to school.

(1) This indicates that at least 60% of the female students in Pat's class walk to school. However, it does not give any information about the other students in Pat's class; NOT sufficient.

(2) Letting x represent the number of students in Pat's class who do not walk to school, this indicates that $2x$ students in Pat's class walk to school and that the total number of students in Pat's class is $x + 2x = 3x$. From this, the percent of students in Pat's class who walk to school is $\left[\frac{2x}{3x}100\right]\% = \left[\frac{2}{3}(100)\right]\%$; SUFFICIENT.

**The correct answer is B;
statement 2 alone is sufficient.**

260. A certain plumber charges $92 for each job completed in 4 hours or less and $23 per hour for each job completed in more than 4 hours. If it took the plumber a total of 7 hours to complete two separate jobs, what was the total amount charged by the plumber for the two jobs?

(1) The plumber charged $92 for one of the two jobs.

(2) The plumber charged $138 for one of the two jobs.

Arithmetic Applied Problems

Find the total amount charged for two jobs lasting a total of 7 hours if the plumber charges $92 for a job lasting 4 hours or less and $23 per hour for a job lasting more than 4 hours.

(1) This indicates that one of the two jobs lasted 4 hours or less. If that job lasted 2 hours, then the other job lasted 5 hours, and the charge for that job would be ($23)(5) = $115, making the total for the two jobs $92 + $115 = $207. However, if the jobs lasted 1 hour and 6 hours, respectively, then the total charge for the two jobs would be $92 + (6)($23) = $92 + $138 = $230; NOT sufficient.

(2) This indicates that one job lasted $\frac{\$138}{\$23}$ = 6 hours. Therefore, the other job lasted for 1 hour and the charge for that job was $92, making the total charge for the two jobs $92 + $138 = $230; SUFFICIENT.

**The correct answer is B;
statement 2 alone is sufficient.**

261. If x and y are positive numbers, is $\frac{x+1}{y+1} > \frac{x}{y}$?

(1) $x > 1$

(2) $x < y$

Algebra Inequalities

Since y is positive, multiplying both sides of the inequality $\frac{x+1}{y+1} > \frac{x}{y}$ by $y(y+1)$ gives $y(x+1) > x(y+1)$ or $xy + y > xy + x$, which is equivalent to $y > x$. So, determining whether the inequality $\frac{x+1}{y+1} > \frac{x}{y}$ is true is equivalent to determining whether the inequality $y > x$ is true.

(1) This indicates that $x > 1$. If, for example, $x = 3$ and $y = 4$, then $y > x$ is true. However, if $x = 4$ and $y = 3$, then $y > x$ is not true; NOT sufficient.

(2) This indicates that $x < y$, so $y > x$ is true; SUFFICIENT.

**The correct answer is B;
statement 2 alone is sufficient.**

262. Every object in a box is either a sphere or a cube, and every object in the box is either red or green. How many objects are in the box?

(1) There are six cubes and five green objects in the box.

(2) There are two red spheres in the box.

Arithmetic Sets

This problem can be solved using a contingency table set up as shown below, where T represents the number to be determined.

	cube	sphere	total
red			
green			
total			T

(1) The following table displays the information that there are 6 cubes and 5 green objects:

	cube	sphere	total
red			
green			5
total	6		T

It is obvious that there is not enough information to determine a unique value for T; NOT sufficient.

(2) The following table displays the information that there are 2 red spheres:

	cube	sphere	total
red		2	
green			
total			T

It is obvious that there is not enough information to determine a unique value for T; NOT sufficient.

The following table displays the information from (1) and (2) taken together:

	cube	sphere	total
red		2	
green			5
total	6		T

It is obvious that there is still not enough information to determine a unique value for T.

**The correct answer is E;
both statements together are still not sufficient.**

263. A certain truck uses $\frac{1}{12} + kv^2$ gallons of fuel per mile when its speed is v miles per hour, where k is a constant. At what speed should the truck travel so that it uses $\frac{5}{12}$ gallon of fuel per mile?

(1) The value of k is $\frac{1}{10,800}$.

(2) When the truck travels at 30 miles per hour, it uses $\frac{1}{6}$ gallon of fuel per mile.

Algebra Applied Problems

This problem can be solved by determining the positive value of v so that $\frac{1}{12} + kv^2 = \frac{5}{12}$.

(1) This indicates the value of k and so the value of v can be determined by solving $\frac{1}{12} + \frac{1}{10,800} v^2 = \frac{5}{12}$ for v; SUFFICIENT.

(2) This indicates that $\frac{1}{12} + k(30)^2 = \frac{1}{6}$. The value of k can be determined by solving this equation for k. Then that value of k can be substituted into $\frac{1}{12} + kv^2 = \frac{5}{12}$, which can then be solved for the value of v; SUFFICIENT.

**The correct answer is D;
each statement alone is sufficient.**

264. If a school district paid a total of $35 per desk for x desks and a total of $30 per table for y tables, what was the total amount that the district paid for these desks and tables?

(1) The total amount the district paid for the y tables was $900.

(2) $x = 90$, and the total amount the district paid for the x desks was 3.5 times the total amount the district paid for the y tables.

Algebra Simultaneous Equations

Determine the value of $35x + 30y$.

(1) Given that $30y = 900$, it follows that $y = 30$. However, it is not possible to determine the value of $35x + 30y = 35x + 900$ because more than one possible value of x is possible; NOT sufficient.

(2) Given that $x = 90$ and $35x = 3.5(30y)$, it follows that $(35)(90) = (3.5)(30)y$, or $y = \frac{35}{3.5} \times \frac{90}{30} = 10 \times 3 = 30$, and therefore $35x + 30y = 35(90) + 30(30)$; SUFFICIENT.

**The correct answer is B;
statement 2 alone is sufficient.**

265. Three children inherited a total of X dollars. If the oldest child inherited $7,000 more than the youngest child, and the youngest child inherited $9,000 less than the middle child, what is the value of X?

(1) The middle child inherited $27,000.

(2) The youngest child and the middle child together inherited a total of $45,000.

Algebra Simultaneous Equations

Let A, B, and C be the amounts inherited, respectively and in dollars, of the oldest, middle, and youngest child. It is given that $A = 7,000 + C$ and $C = B - 9,000$. Then $A = 7,000 + (B - 9,000) = B - 2,000$. Determine the value of $A + B + C$, or equivalently, determine the value of $(B - 2,000) + B + (B - 9,000) = 3B - 11,000$.

(1) Given that $B = 27,000$, it follows that $3B - 11,000 = 70,000$; SUFFICIENT.

(2) Given that $B + C = 45,000$, then using $C = B - 9,000$ it follows that $B + (B - 9,000) = 45,000$, which can be solved to obtain $B = 27,000$. Therefore, $3B - 11,000 = 70,000$; SUFFICIENT.

The correct answer is D; each statement alone is sufficient.

266. If a building has 6,000 square meters of floor space, how many offices are in the building?

(1) Exactly $\frac{1}{4}$ of the floor space is not used for offices.

(2) There are exactly 20 executive offices and each of these occupies 3 times as much floor space as the average for all of the remaining offices.

Algebra Simultaneous Equations

(1) This says that exactly $\frac{3}{4}(6,000) = 4,500$ square meters of floor space are used for offices since exactly $\frac{1}{4}(6,000) = 1,500$ square meters of the floor space are not used for offices. No information is given about the configuration of the 4,500 square meters used for offices. Therefore, the number of offices in the building cannot be determined; NOT sufficient.

(2) While this says there are exactly 20 executive offices and each occupies 3 times the average space of the other offices, no information is given about how much of the 6,000 square meters of floor space in the building is used for offices nor how the offices are configured. Therefore, the number of offices in the building cannot be determined; NOT sufficient.

Taking (1) and (2) together, 4,500 square meters of space are used for offices which include 20 executive offices, and each executive office occupies 3 times as much floor space as the average of all of the remaining offices. However, no information is given about the actual size of an executive office or about the actual average size of the remaining offices. Therefore, the number of offices in the building cannot be determined. The examples in the table verify this:

Non-executive		Executive			
Number	Size (m²)	Number	Size (m²)	Total number of offices	Total space used for offices
30	50	20	150	30 + 20 = 50	30(50) + 20(150) = 4,500
15	60	20	180	15 + 20 = 35	15(60) + 20(180) = 4,500

The correct answer is E; both statements together are still not sufficient.

267. For which type of investment, J or K, is the annual rate of return greater?

(1) Type J returns $115 per $1,000 invested for any one-year period and type K returns $300 per $2,500 invested for any one-year period.

(2) The annual rate of return for an investment of type K is 12%.

Arithmetic Percents

Compare the annual rates of return for Investments J and K.

(1) For Investment J, the annual rate of return is $115 per $1,000 for any one-year period, which can be converted to a percent. For Investment K, the annual rate of return is $300 per $2,500 for any one-year period, which can also be converted to a percent. These two percents can be compared to determine which is greater; SUFFICIENT.

(2) Investment K has an annual rate of return of 12%, but no information is given about the annual rate of return for Investment J; NOT sufficient.

The correct answer is A; statement 1 alone is sufficient.

268. If Car X followed Car Y across a certain bridge that is a $\frac{1}{2}$ mile long, how many seconds did it take Car X to travel across the bridge?

    (1) Car X drove onto the bridge exactly 3 seconds after Car Y drove onto the bridge and drove off the bridge exactly 2 seconds after Car Y drove off the bridge.

    (2) Car Y traveled across the bridge at a constant speed of 30 miles per hour.

Arithmetic Rate Problem

Find the number of seconds that it took Car X to cross the $\frac{1}{2}$-mile bridge.

    (1) If Car X drove onto the bridge 3 seconds after Car Y and drove off the bridge 2 seconds after Car Y, then Car X took 1 second less to cross the bridge than Car Y. Since there is no information on how long Car Y took to cross the bridge, there is no way to determine how long Car X took to cross the bridge; NOT sufficient.

    (2) If the speed of Car Y was 30 miles per hour, it took Car Y $\frac{1}{60}$ hour = 1 minute = 60 seconds to cross the bridge. However, there is no information on how long Car X took to cross the bridge; NOT sufficient.

Taking (1) and (2) together, Car X took 1 second less than Car Y to cross the bridge and Car Y took 60 seconds to cross the bridge, so Car X took $60 - 1 = 59$ seconds to cross the bridge.

The correct answer is C; both statements together are sufficient.

Questions 269 to 301 - Difficulty: Medium

269. What is the total number of executives at Company P ?

    (1) The number of male executives is $\frac{3}{5}$ the number of female executives.

    (2) There are 4 more female executives than male executives.

Algebra Simultaneous Equations

Let M be the number of male executives at Company P and let F be the number of female executives at Company P. Determine the value of $M + F$.

    (1) Given that $M = \frac{3}{5}F$, it is not possible to determine the value of $M + F$. For example, if $M = 3$ and $F = 5$, then $M = \frac{3}{5}F$ and $M + F = 8$. However, if $M = 6$ and $F = 10$, then $M = \frac{3}{5}F$ and $M + F = 16$; NOT sufficient.

    (2) Given that $F = M + 4$, it is not possible to determine the value of $M + F$. For example, if $M = 3$ and $F = 7$, then $F = M + 4$ and $M + F = 10$. However, if $M = 4$ and $F = 8$, then $F = M + 4$ and $M + F = 12$; NOT sufficient.

Taking (1) and (2) together, then $F = M + 4$ and $M = \frac{3}{5}F$, so $F = \frac{3}{5}F + 4$. Now solve for F to get $\frac{2}{5}F = 4$ and $F = 10$. Therefore, using $F = 10$ and $F = M + 4$, it follows that $M = 6$, and hence $M + F = 6 + 10 = 16$.

The correct answer is C; both statements together are sufficient.

270. Jack picked 76 apples. Of these, he sold $4y$ apples to Juanita and $3t$ apples to Sylvia. If he kept the remaining apples, how many apples did he keep? (t and y are positive integers.)

    (1) $y \geq 15$ and $t = 2$
    (2) $y = 17$

Algebra Simultaneous Equations

Determine the value of the nonnegative integer $76 - 4y - 3t$.

    (1) Given that $y \geq 15$ and $t = 2$, it follows that $76 - 4y - 3t = 76 - 4y - 6 = 70 - 4y$ could have the value $70 - 4(15) = 10$, $70 - 4(16) = 6$, or $70 - 4(17) = 2$; NOT sufficient.

    (2) Given that $y = 17$, it follows that $76 - 4y - 3t = 76 - 68 - 3t = 8 - 3t$ could

have the value $8 - 3(1) = 5$ or $8 - 3(2) = 2$; NOT sufficient.

Taking (1) and (2) together, it follows that $76 - 4y - 3t = 76 - 4(17) - 3(2) = 2$.

The correct answer is C; both statements together are sufficient.

271. The total price of 5 pounds of regular coffee and 3 pounds of decaffeinated coffee was $21.50. What was the price of the 5 pounds of regular coffee?

    (1) If the price of the 5 pounds of regular coffee had been reduced 10 percent and the price of the 3 pounds of decaffeinated coffee had been reduced 20 percent, the total price would have been $18.45.

    (2) The price of the 5 pounds of regular coffee was $3.50 more than the price of the 3 pounds of decaffeinated coffee.

Algebra Simultaneous Equations

Let $x be the price of 5 pounds of regular coffee and let $y be the price of 3 pounds of decaffeinated coffee. Then $x + y = 21.5$, or $y = 21.5 - x$. Determine the value of x.

    (1) Given that $0.9x + 0.8y = 18.45$, the value of x can be determined because substituting $y = 21.5 - x$ into $0.9x + 0.8y = 18.45$ gives a single equation with unknown x, and that equation can be solved for a unique value of x; SUFFICIENT.

    Alternatively (see the Tip below), $y = 21.5 - x$ and $0.9x + 0.8y = 18.45$ are equations of nonparallel lines in the coordinate plane and thus have a single point of intersection. One way to ensure that the lines are not parallel is to solve each equation for y in terms of x and note that the coefficients of x are different. In this case, $y = 21.5 - x$ gives a coefficient of x equal to -1 and $0.9x + 0.8y = 18.45$ gives a coefficient of x equal to $-\dfrac{0.9}{0.8}$.

    (2) Given that $x = 3.5 + y$, the value of x can be determined because substituting $y = 21.5 - x$ into $x = 3.5 + y$ gives a single equation with unknown x, and that equation can be solved for a unique value of x; SUFFICIENT.

Alternatively (see the Tip below), $y = 21.5 - x$ and $x = 3.5 + y$ are equations of nonparallel lines in the coordinate plane and thus have a single point of intersection. One way to ensure that the lines are not parallel is to solve each equation for y in terms of x and note that the coefficients of x are different. In this case, $y = 21.5 - x$ gives a coefficient of x equal to -1 and $x = 3.5 + y$ gives a coefficient of x equal to 1.

Tip: Data Insights problems involving simultaneous equations usually do not have to be solved. Instead, it is typically enough to determine whether no solution exists, exactly one solution exists, or more than one solution exists, and this can often be accomplished by graphical methods.

The correct answer is D; each statement alone is sufficient.

272. A certain painting job requires a mixture of yellow, green, and white paint. If 12 quarts of paint are needed for the job, how many quarts of green paint are needed?

    (1) The ratio of the amount of green paint to the amount of yellow and white paint combined needs to be 1 to 3.

    (2) The ratio of the amount of yellow paint to the amount of green paint needs to be 3 to 2.

Algebra Ratios; Simultaneous Equations

This problem involves 3 quantities:

The number of quarts of yellow paint, represented by Y; the number of quarts of green paint, represented by G; and the number of quarts of white paint, represented by W.

It is given that $Y + G + W = 12$.

The task is to uniquely determine the value of G, which is possible only if there is enough information to eliminate Y and W from $Y + G + W = 12$, so that only G is left.

    (1) Using the variables introduced above, this gives $\dfrac{G}{Y + W} = \dfrac{1}{3}$ or $3G = Y + W$. Substituting $3G$ for $Y + W$ in $Y + G + W = 12$ gives $4G = 12$, which yields a unique value of G; SUFFICIENT.

(2) Using the variables introduced above, this gives $\frac{Y}{G} = \frac{3}{2}$ or $Y = \frac{3}{2}G$. Then, by substitution, $\frac{3}{2}G + G + W = 12$. Because the value of W can vary, the value of G cannot be uniquely determined; NOT sufficient.

The correct answer is A; statement 1 alone is sufficient.

273. A company produces a certain toy in only 2 sizes, small or large, and in only 2 colors, red or green. If, for each size, there are equal numbers of red and green toys in a certain production lot, what fraction of the total number of green toys is large?

(1) In the production lot, 400 of the small toys are green.

(2) In the production lot, $\frac{2}{3}$ of the toys produced are small.

Algebra Ratios

Let x be the number of small toys of each color, and let y be the number of large toys of each color. The contingency table below gives a summary of the information given. Determine the value of $\frac{y}{x+y}$.

	small	large	total
red	x	y	$x + y$
green	x	y	$x + y$
total	$2x$	$2y$	$2x + 2y$

(1) Given that $x = 400$, it is clearly not possible to determine the value of $\frac{y}{x+y} = \frac{y}{400+y}$; NOT sufficient.

(2) Given that $\frac{2}{3}$ of the toys are small, then because there are $(2x + 2y)$ toys altogether and $2x$ small toys, it follows that $\frac{2x}{2x + 2y} = \frac{2}{3}$. Therefore, $3(2x) = 2(2x + 2y)$, or $x = 2y$, and hence $\frac{y}{x+y} = \frac{y}{2y+y} = \frac{y}{3y} = \frac{1}{3}$; SUFFICIENT.

The correct answer is B; statement 2 alone is sufficient.

274. Jones has worked at Firm X twice as many years as Green, and Green has worked at Firm X four years longer than Smith. How many years has Green worked at Firm X ?

(1) Jones has worked at Firm X 9 years longer than Smith.

(2) Green has worked at Firm X 5 years less than Jones.

Algebra Simultaneous Equations

Let J, G, and S be the number of years Jones, Green, and Smith, respectively, have worked at Firm X. Then $J = 2G$ and $G = 4 + S$. What is the value of G ?

(1) Given that $J = 9 + S$, then from $J = 2G$ it follows that $2G = 9 + S$. From $G = 4 + S$ it follows that $S = G - 4$, and therefore $G - 4$ can be substituted for S in the equation $2G = 9 + S$ to obtain $2G = 9 + (G - 4)$, or $G = 5$; SUFFICIENT.

(2) Given that $G = J - 5$, it follows from $J = 2G$ that $G = 2G - 5$, or $G = 5$; SUFFICIENT.

The correct answer is D; each statement alone is sufficient.

275. On June 1, Mary paid Omar $360 for rent and utilities for the month of June. Mary moved out early, and Omar refunded the money she paid for utilities, but not for rent, for the days in June after she moved out. How many dollars did Omar refund to Mary?

(1) Mary moved out on June 24.

(2) The amount Mary paid for utilities was less than $\frac{1}{5}$ the amount Mary paid for rent.

Algebra Applied Problems; Proportions

This problem could be solved by making a table of possible amounts Mary could have paid for rent and utilities for the month of June, such that they total $360, as shown below.

Rent	Utilities
$300	$60
$310	$50
$320	$40
$330	$30
$340	$20
$350	$10

(1) Given that Mary moved out on June 24, Omar refunded the amount she paid for 6 days of utilities or $\frac{6}{30} = \frac{1}{5}$ of the amount she paid for the whole month. As seen from the table, this amount varies, so $\frac{1}{5}$ of the total amount varies. Therefore, the amount Omar refunded to Mary cannot be uniquely determined; NOT sufficient.

Note that a third column, as shown below, could be added to the table to confirm that $\frac{1}{5}$ of the amount she paid for utilities for the whole month varies. Adding this column will aid in determining whether (1) and (2) together are sufficient. Amounts shown in **boldface** satisfy (1).

Rent	Utilities	$\frac{1}{5}$ Utilities
$300	$60	**$12**
$310	$50	**$10**
$320	$40	**$8**
$330	$30	**$6**
$340	$20	**$4**
$350	$10	**$2**

(2) Given that the amount Mary paid for utilities was less than $\frac{1}{5}$ the amount she paid for rent, the amount Omar refunded to Mary cannot be uniquely determined. To verify this, another column can be added to the table to show $\frac{1}{5}$ the amount Mary paid for rent and to show the amounts she paid for utilities that are less than $\frac{1}{5}$ the amount she paid for rent. Amounts shown *underlined* in the table below satisfy (2); NOT sufficient.

Rent	Utilities	$\frac{1}{5}$ Utilities	$\frac{1}{5}$ Rent
$300	$60	**$12**	$60
$310	$50	**$10**	$62
$320	$40	**$8**	$64
$330	$30	**$6**	$66
$340	$20	**$4**	$68
$350	$10	**$2**	$70

Taking (1) and (2) together, observe that there are several amounts in boldface in the third column that satisfy (1) and corresponding amounts underlined in the second column that satisfy (2). Therefore, the amount Omar refunded to Mary cannot be uniquely determined.

**The correct answer is E;
both statements together are still not sufficient.**

276. The 10 students in a history class recently took an examination. What was the maximum score on the examination?

(1) The mean of the scores was 75.
(2) The standard deviation of the scores was 5.

Arithmetic Statistics

(1) Given that the mean of the scores was 75, then all 10 scores could have been 75 and the maximum score would be 75. However, it is also possible that the scores were 74, 76, and 8 scores of 75, and the maximum score would be 76; NOT sufficient.

(2) Given that the standard deviation of the scores was 5, it is not possible to determine the maximum score because adding a fixed nonzero number to each of the scores will not change the standard deviation but doing this will change the maximum score; NOT sufficient.

Taking (1) and (2) together, it seems reasonable that the maximum still cannot be determined, but since the method used in (2) above changes the mean, something more explicit is needed. The standard deviation of the 10 scores is $\sqrt{\dfrac{\text{sum of (deviations)}^2}{10}}$, where each "deviation" is the (unsigned) difference between the score and 75 (the mean of the scores). Thus, the standard deviation of the 10 scores will be 5 if the sum of squares of the deviations is 250. The following table shows two possibilities for the 10 scores, each with a mean of 75 and a standard deviation of 5.

Scores	Deviations from 75	Sum of (deviations)^2
70, 70, 70, 70, 70 80, 80, 80, 80, 80	5, 5, 5, 5, 5 5, 5, 5, 5, 5	$10(5^2) = 250$
70, 70, 70, 70, 75 75, 75, 80, 80, 85	5, 5, 5, 5, 0 0, 0, 5, 5, 10	$6(5^2) + 10^2 = 250$

Since the maximum of the upper list of scores is 80 and the maximum of the lower list of scores is 85, it follows that the maximum score cannot be determined.

Tip: For any list of numbers, the sum of the *signed* deviations from the mean is 0. This allows for an easy verification that the mean of each list above is 75. For example, the signed deviations for the second list are −5, −5, −5, −5, 0, 0, 0, 5, 5, and 10, which add to 0. This idea is also useful in constructing various lists of numbers that have the same mean, such as the two lists above.

**The correct answer is E;
both statements together are still not sufficient.**

277. Last school year, each of the 200 students at a certain high school attended the school for the entire year. If there were 8 cultural performances at the school during the last school year, what was the average (arithmetic mean) number of students attending each cultural performance?

    (1) Last school year, each student attended at least one cultural performance.

    (2) Last school year, the average number of cultural performances attended per student was 4.

Arithmetic Statistics

Determine the average number of students attending each of 8 cultural performances at a school that has 200 students.

    (1) This indicates that each student attended at least one cultural performance, but the average number of students attending each performance cannot be uniquely determined. It could be as low as $\frac{200}{8} = 25$ students if each student attended exactly one performance, or it could be as high as $\frac{200}{1} = 200$ if each student attended every performance; NOT sufficient.

    (2) This indicates that, since the average number of performances attended per student was 4, $\frac{\text{total attendance at performances}}{\text{total number of students}} = 4$, so the total attendance at the performances is $(4)(200) = 800$ students. It follows that the average number of students attending each performance is $\frac{800}{8} = 100$; SUFFICIENT.

**The correct answer is B;
statement 2 alone is sufficient.**

278. A clothing manufacturer makes jackets that are wool or cotton or a combination of wool and cotton. The manufacturer has 3,000 pounds of wool and 2,000 pounds of cotton on hand. Is this enough wool and cotton to make at least 1,000 jackets?

    (1) Each wool jacket requires 4 pounds of wool, and no cotton.

    (2) Each cotton jacket requires 6 pounds of cotton, and no wool.

Arithmetic Applied Problems

    (1) Given that each wool jacket requires 4 pounds of wool and no cotton, then at most a total of 750 wool jackets can be made (because $\frac{3,000}{4} = 750$), and possibly no other jackets. Therefore, it is possible that there is enough wool and cotton to make at least 1,000 jackets (for example, if there is enough cotton to make 250 cotton jackets) and it is possible that there is not enough wool and cotton to make at least 1,000 jackets (for example, if there is less than the amount of cotton needed to make 250 cotton jackets); NOT sufficient.

    (2) Given that each cotton jacket requires 6 pounds of cotton and no wool, then at most a total of 333 cotton jackets can be made (because rounding $\frac{2,000}{6}$ down to the nearest integer gives 333), and possibly no other jackets. Therefore, it is possible that there is enough wool and cotton to make at least 1,000 jackets (for example, if there is enough wool to make 667 wool jackets), and it is possible that there is not enough wool

and cotton to make at least 1,000 jackets (for example, if there is less than the amount of wool needed to make 667 wool jackets); NOT sufficient.

Taking (1) and (2) together, there is enough wool and cotton to make 750 wool jackets and 333 cotton jackets for a total of 1,083 jackets.

The correct answer is C; both statements together are sufficient.

279. Each month, Jim receives a base salary plus a 10 percent commission on the price of each car he sells that month. If Jim sold 15 cars last month, what was the total amount of base salary and commissions that Jim received that month?

   (1) Last month, Jim's base salary was $3,000.
   (2) Last month, Jim sold 3 cars whose prices totaled $60,000 and 5 cars whose prices totaled $120,000.

Arithmetic Applied Problems

Determine the total of Jim's base salary plus a 10% commission on the price of each of the 15 cars he sold last month.

   (1) This indicates that Jim's base salary was $3,000 but gives no information about the prices of the 15 cars he sold last month; NOT sufficient.

   (2) This indicates that Jim's commission on 8 cars that he sold last month can be determined but gives no information about his base salary or about the prices of the other 7 cars he sold last month; NOT sufficient.

Taking (1) and (2) together gives Jim's base salary and information about the prices of 8 of the 15 cars he sold last month, but does not provide information about the selling prices of the other 7 cars he sold.

The correct answer is E; both statements together are still not sufficient.

280. By what percent was the price of a certain television set discounted for a sale?

   (1) The price of the television set before it was discounted for the sale was 25 percent greater than the discounted price.

   (2) The price of the television set was discounted by $60 for the sale.

Arithmetic Percents

Let B represent the price, in dollars, for the television before the sale and let D represent the discounted price, in dollars. The percent by which B was discounted to obtain D can be determined if the value of $\dfrac{B-D}{B}$ can be determined.

   (1) This indicates that B is 25% greater than D or that $B = 1.25D$. Then,
   $$\dfrac{B-D}{B} = \dfrac{1.25D-D}{1.25D} = \dfrac{0.25}{1.25} = 0.2 \text{ or } 20\%;$$
   SUFFICIENT.

   (2) This indicates that $D = B - 60$, but B is unknown. For example, B could be 100 and the value of $\dfrac{B-D}{B}$ would be $\dfrac{60}{100}$, or B could be 500 and the value of $\dfrac{B-D}{B}$ would be $\dfrac{60}{500}$; NOT sufficient.

The correct answer is A; statement 1 alone is sufficient.

281. A paint mixture was formed by mixing exactly 3 colors of paint. By volume, the mixture was $x\%$ blue paint, $y\%$ green paint, and $z\%$ red paint. If exactly 1 gallon of blue paint and 3 gallons of red paint were used, how many gallons of green paint were used?

   (1) $x = y$
   (2) $z = 60$

Algebra First-Degree Equations

Letting T represent the total number of gallons of the paint in the mixture, and B, G, and R the amounts of blue paint, green paint, and red paint, respectively, in the mixture, then $B = \dfrac{x}{100}T$, $G = \dfrac{y}{100}T$, and $R = \dfrac{z}{100}T$. It is given that $\dfrac{x}{100}T = 1$ and $\dfrac{z}{100}T = 3$, from which it follows that $z = 3x$. Also, since there are exactly three colors of paint, $x + y + z = 100$ and $B + G + R = T$. Determine the value of G, or equivalently, the value $\dfrac{y}{100}T$.

(1)   Given that $x = y$ and $\dfrac{x}{100}T = 1$, it follows that $\dfrac{y}{100}T = 1$; SUFFICIENT.

(2)   Given that $z = 60$ and $\dfrac{z}{100}T = 3$, it follows that $T = 5$. Knowing that the total amount of paint in the mixture is 5 gallons of which 1 gallon is blue paint and 3 gallons are red paint, the amount of green paint can be determined; SUFFICIENT.

The correct answer is D; each statement alone is sufficient.

282. For a basic monthly fee of F yen (¥F), Naoko's first cell phone plan allowed him to use a maximum of 420 minutes on calls during the month. Then, for each of x additional minutes he used on calls, he was charged ¥M, making his total charge for the month ¥T, where $T = F + xM$. What is the value of F ?

    (1)   Naoko used 450 minutes on calls the first month and the total charge for the month was ¥13,755.

    (2)   Naoko used 400 minutes on calls the second month and the total charge for the month was ¥13,125.

Algebra Simultaneous Equations

(1)   Given that Naoko used 450 minutes and was charged ¥13,125, it follows that $F + (450 - 420)M = 13,755$, or $F + 30M = 13,755$. However, the value of F cannot be determined. For example, $F = 13,005$ and $M = 25$ is possible, and $F = 13,035$ and $M = 24$ is possible; NOT sufficient.

(2)   Given that Naoko used 400 minutes and was charged ¥13,125, it follows that $F = 13,125$, since Naoko did not use more than 420 minutes; SUFFICIENT.

The correct answer is B; statement 2 alone is sufficient.

283. Is the sum of the prices of the 3 books that Shana bought less than $48 ?

    (1)   The price of the most expensive of the 3 books that Shana bought is less than $17.

    (2)   The price of the least expensive of the 3 books that Shana bought is exactly $3 less than the price of the second most expensive book.

Arithmetic Operations with Integers; Order

Let B_1, B_2, and B_3 be the prices, in dollars and in numerical order, of the 3 books. Thus, $B_1 \le B_2 \le B_3$. Determine whether $B_1 + B_2 + B_3 < 48$.

(1)   Given that $B_3 < 17$, it is possible that $B_1 + B_2 + B_3 < 48$ (choose $B_1 = B_2 = 15$ and $B_3 = 16$) and it is possible that $B_1 + B_2 + B_3 > 48$ (choose $B_1 = B_2 = 16$ and $B_3 = 16.5$); NOT sufficient.

(2)   Given that $B_1 = B_2 - 3$, it is possible that $B_1 + B_2 + B_3 < 48$ (choose $B_1 = 3$, $B_2 = 6$, and $B_3 = 10$) and it is possible that $B_1 + B_2 + B_3 > 48$ (choose $B_1 = 3$, $B_2 = 6$, and $B_3 = 48$); NOT sufficient.

Taking (1) and (2) together, from (1) and the information given it follows that $B_3 < 17$ and $B_2 \le B_3 < 17$, or $B_2 < 17$. Also, from $B_2 < 17$ and (2), it follows that $B_1 < 17 - 3$, or $B_1 < 14$. Therefore, $B_1 + B_2 + B_3$ is the sum of 3 numbers—a number less than 14, a number less than 17, and a number less than 17—and thus $B_1 + B_2 + B_3 < 14 + 17 + 17 = 48$.

The correct answer is C; both statements together are sufficient.

284. A company makes and sells two products, P and Q. The costs per unit of making and selling P and Q are $8.00 and $9.50, respectively, and the selling prices per unit of P and Q are $10.00 and $13.00, respectively. In one month the company sold a total of 834 units of these products. Was the total profit on these items more than $2,000.00 ?

    (1)   During the month, more units of P than units of Q were sold.

    (2)   During the month, at least 100 units of Q were sold.

Arithmetic Applied Problems

It is given that the profit on each unit of P is $10.00 - $8.00 = $2.00, and the profit on each unit of Q is $13.00 - $9.50 = $3.50. Also if p and q represent the number of units of Products P and Q made and sold, then it is given that $p + q = 834$. Determining if the total profit on these items was more than $2,000 requires determining how many units of at least one of the products were sold.

(1) This indicates that $p > q$, but does not give a specific value for p or q; NOT sufficient.

(2) This indicates that $q \geq 100$, but does not give a specific value for q; NOT sufficient.

Taking (1) and (2) together, $p > q$ and $q \geq 100$, so $p > 100$, but a specific value for p or q cannot be determined.

The correct answer is E;
both statements together are still not sufficient.

285. Jill has applied for a job with each of two different companies. What is the probability that she will get job offers from both companies?

(1) The probability that she will get a job offer from neither company is 0.3.

(2) The probability that she will get a job offer from exactly one of the two companies is 0.5.

Arithmetic Probability

Let $P(2)$ be the probability that she will get a job offer from both companies, $P(1)$ be the probability that she will get a job offer from exactly one of the companies, and $P(0)$ be the probability that she will get a job offer from neither company. Then $P(2) + P(1) + P(0) = 1$. What is the value of $P(2)$?

(1) Given that $P(0) = 0.3$, it follows that $P(2) + P(1) + 0.3 = 1$, or $P(2) + P(1) = 0.7$. However, the value of $P(2)$ cannot be determined, since nothing is known about the value of $P(1)$ other than $0 \leq P(1) \leq 0.7$; NOT sufficient.

(2) (2) Given that $P(1) = 0.5$, it follows that $P(2) + 0.5 + P(0) = 1$, or $P(2) + P(0) = 0.5$. However, the value of $P(2)$ cannot be determined, since nothing is known about the value of $P(0)$ other than $0 \leq P(1) \leq 0.5$; NOT sufficient.

Taking (1) and (2) together, it follows that $P(2) + 0.5 + 0.3 = 1$, or $P(2) = 0.2$.

The correct answer is C;
both statements together are sufficient.

286. A certain computer company produces two different monitors, P and Q. In 2010, what was the net profit from the sale of the two monitors?

(1) Of the company's expenses in 2010, rent and utilities totaled $500,000.

(2) In 2010, the company sold 50,000 units of monitor P at $300 per unit and 30,000 units of monitor Q at $650 per unit.

Arithmetic Applied Problems

The net profit from the sale of the two monitors is the total revenue, $\$R$, from the sale of the two monitors minus the total cost, $\$C$, of the two monitors, or $\$R - \$C$. Determine the value of $R - C$.

(1) Given that the rent and utilities totaled $500,000, it is not possible to determine the value of $R - C$ because we only know that $C \geq 500,000$ and we do not know anything about the value of R; NOT sufficient.

(2) Given that $\$R = 50,000(\$300) + 30,000(\$650)$, it is not possible to determine the value of $R - C$ because we do not know anything about the value of C; NOT sufficient.

Taking (1) and (2) together, it is not possible to determine the value of $R - C$ because from (2) the value of R is fixed and from both (1) and (2) we can only conclude that $C \geq 500,000$, and therefore more than one value of $R - C$ is possible.

The correct answer is E;
both statements together are still not sufficient.

287. A conveyor belt moves bottles at a constant speed of 120 centimeters per second. If the conveyor belt moves a bottle from a loading dock to an unloading dock, is the distance that the conveyor belt moves the bottle less than 90 meters? (1 meter = 100 centimeters)

(1) It takes the conveyor belt less than 1.2 minutes to move the bottle from the loading dock to the unloading dock.

(2) It takes the conveyor belt more than 1.1 minutes to move the bottle from the loading dock to the unloading dock.

Arithmetic Applied Problems

Since the rate at which the conveyor belt moves is given as 120 centimeters per second, which is equivalent to $\dfrac{120}{100} = 1.2$ meters per second, the conveyor will move less than 90 meters if it moves for less than $\dfrac{90}{1.2} = 75$ seconds.

(1) This indicates that the length of time the conveyor belt moves is less than 1.2 minutes, which is equivalent to $(1.2)(60) = 72$ seconds and $72 < 75$; SUFFICIENT.

(2) This indicates that the length of time the conveyor belt moves is more than 1.1 minutes, which is equivalent to $(1.1)(60) = 66$ seconds, but does not indicate how much more than 66 seconds the conveyor moves. If the conveyor moves for 70 seconds $(70 > 66)$, for example, it moves less than 90 meters since $70 < 75$. However, if the conveyor belt moves for 80 seconds $(80 > 66)$, then it moves more than 90 meters since $80 > 75$; NOT sufficient.

The correct answer is A; statement 1 alone is sufficient.

288. In a product test of a common cold remedy, x percent of the patients tested experienced side effects from the use of the drug and y percent experienced relief of cold symptoms. What percent of the patients tested experienced both side effects and relief of cold symptoms?

(1) Of the 1,000 patients tested, 15 percent experienced neither side effects nor relief of cold symptoms.

(2) Of the patients tested, 30 percent experienced relief of cold symptoms without side effects.

Algebra Sets

The Venn diagram below represents the numbers of patients who experienced neither, one, or both side effects and relief. In the diagram,

a = number who experienced side effects only,
b = number who experienced both,
c = number who experienced relief only,
d = number who experienced neither,

where $T = a + b + c + d$ is the total number of patients. Note that $a + b = \dfrac{x}{100}T$ and $b + c = \dfrac{y}{100}T$. Determine the value of $\dfrac{b}{T}$.

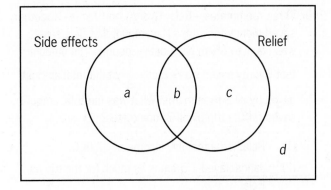

(1) Given that 1,000 patients were tested and $(0.15)(1,000) = 150$ patients experienced neither side effects nor relief, it follows that $a + b + c + d = 1,000$ and $d = 150$. Therefore, $a + b + c + 150 = 1,000$, or $a + b + c = 850$. However, there is no information about how the remaining 850 patients are assigned to the other categories. Thus, the percent of patients who experienced both side effects and relief could be any value between 0% and 85%; NOT sufficient.

(2) Given that 30% of the patients experienced relief without side effects, there is no information about how the remaining 70% of the patients are assigned to the other categories. Thus, the percent of patients who experienced both side effects and relief could be any value between 0% and 70%; NOT sufficient.

Taking (1) and (2) together, it follows that 150 patients experienced neither side effects nor relief and $(0.3)(1,000) = 300$ patients experienced relief only. Therefore, from $a + b + c + d = T$ it follows that $a + b + 300 + 150 = 1,000$, or $a + b = 550$. However, it is still not possible to determine a unique value of $\dfrac{b}{T} = \dfrac{b}{1,000}$, the percent of patients who experienced both side effects and relief. For example, it is possible that $a = 300$ and $b = 250$ (that is, the percent who experienced both could be 25%), and it is possible that $a = 250$ and $b = 300$ (that is, the percent who experienced both could be 30%).

The correct answer is E; both statements together are still not sufficient.

289. Three roommates—Bela, Gyorgy, and Janos—together saved money for a trip. The amount that Bela saved was equal to 8% of his monthly income. The amount that Gyorgy saved was exactly $\frac{1}{3}$ of the total amount saved by all 3 roommates. What was the total amount saved for the trip by all 3 roommates?

    (1) Bela had a monthly income of $2,000.
    (2) Janos saved 1.5 times as much for the trip as Bela.

Algebra First-Degree Equations

Letting B, G, and J represent the amounts saved by Bela, Gyorgy, and Janos, respectively, then $B = 0.08I$, where I represents Bela's monthly income, $G = \frac{1}{3}(B + G + J)$, and $G = \frac{1}{2}(B + J)$. Determine the value of $B + G + J$.

    (1) This allows the value of B to be determined, but gives no information about the values of G or J; NOT sufficient.
    (2) This gives the relationship between the values of J and B, but no information to determine the value of either B or J; NOT sufficient.

Taking (1) and (2) together, the values of both B and J can be determined as can the value of G since $G = \frac{1}{2}(B + J)$. Thus, the value of $B + G + J$ can be determined.

**The correct answer is C;
both statements together are sufficient.**

290. In each game of a certain tournament, a contestant either loses 3 points or gains 2 points. If Pat had 100 points at the beginning of the tournament, how many games did Pat play in the tournament?

    (1) At the end of the tournament, Pat had 104 points.
    (2) Pat played fewer than 10 games.

Arithmetic Computation with Integers

Pat either lost 3 points or gained 2 points in each game she played. Therefore, since she had 100 points at the beginning of the tournament, her score at the end of the tournament was $100 - 3x + 2y$, where x and y represent, respectively, the number of games in which she lost 3 points and the number of games in which she gained 2 points. Determine the value of $x + y$.

    (1) This indicates that $100 - 3x + 2y = 104$, but no information is given about the values of x or y. For example, the values of x and y could be 0 and 2, respectively, so that $x + y = 2$ or the values of x and y could be 2 and 5, respectively, so that $x + y = 7$; NOT sufficient.
    (2) This indicates that Pat played fewer than 10 games, but in each of the examples above, Pat played fewer than 10 games; NOT sufficient.

Since the examples given satisfy both (1) and (2), taking (1) and (2) together does not give enough information to determine the value of $x + y$.

**The correct answer is E;
both statements together are still not sufficient.**

291. At the beginning of the year, the Finance Committee and the Planning Committee of a certain company each had n members, and no one was a member of both committees. At the end of the year, 5 members left the Finance Committee and 3 members left the Planning Committee. How many members did the Finance Committee have at the beginning of the year?

    (1) The ratio of the total number of members who left at the end of the year to the total number of members at the beginning of the year was 1:6.
    (2) At the end of the year, 21 members remained on the Planning Committee.

Algebra Applied Problems

    (1) It is given that $\frac{8}{2n} = \frac{1}{6}$, since a total of $3 + 5 = 8$ members left at the end of the year and there were a total of $n + n = 2n$ members at the beginning of the year. It follows that $(8)(6) = (2n)(1)$, or $n = 24$; SUFFICIENT.
    (2) It is given that $n - 3 = 21$, since 3 members from the original n members left the Planning Committee at the end of the year. It follows that $n = 21 + 3 = 24$; SUFFICIENT.

**The correct answer is D;
each statement alone is sufficient.**

292. Max purchased a guitar for a total of $624, which consisted of the price of the guitar and the sales tax. Was the sales tax rate greater than 3 percent?

    (1) The price of the guitar that Max purchased was less than $602.

    (2) The sales tax for the guitar that Max purchased was less than $30.

Arithmetic Applied Problems; Percents

Letting P be the price, in dollars, of the guitar and $r\%$ be the sales tax rate, it is given that $P\left(1+\dfrac{r}{100}\right)=624$. Determine if $r>3$.

(1) Given that $P<602$, then $624 = P\left(1+\dfrac{r}{100}\right) < 602\left(1+\dfrac{r}{100}\right)$, and so

$1+\dfrac{r}{100}>\dfrac{624}{602}$. Therefore, $\dfrac{r}{100}>$

$\dfrac{624}{602}-1=\dfrac{22}{602}=\dfrac{11}{301}>\dfrac{3}{100}$, because

$(11)(100)>(3)(301)$, and so

$r>100\left(\dfrac{3}{100}\right)=3$; SUFFICIENT.

(2) Given that the sales tax was less than $30, it is not possible to determine whether the sales tax rate was greater than 3%. Since $(0.03)(\$624)=\$18.72$, a 3% sales tax rate on the price corresponds to a sales tax that is less than $18.72, since the price is less than $624. Therefore, it is possible that the sales tax is less than $30 and the sales tax rate is less than 3%, since any sales tax rate less than 3% would give a sales tax that is less than $18.72 (and hence less than $30).

However, it is also possible that the sales tax is less than $30 and the sales tax rate is 4% (which is greater than 3%), since a 4% sales tax rate implies $P\left(1+\dfrac{4}{100}\right)=624$, or $P=\dfrac{62,400}{104}=600$, and thus the sales tax would be $0.04(\$600)=\$24<\$30$; NOT sufficient.

The correct answer is A; statement 1 alone is sufficient.

293. Was the number of books sold at Bookstore X last week greater than the number of books sold at Bookstore Y last week?

    (1) Last week, more than 1,000 books were sold at Bookstore X on Saturday and fewer than 1,000 books were sold at Bookstore Y on Saturday.

    (2) Last week, less than 20 percent of the books sold at Bookstore X were sold on Saturday and more than 20 percent of the books sold at Bookstore Y were sold on Saturday.

Arithmetic Inequalities

Determine if Bookstore X sold more books last week than Bookstore Y.

(1) This indicates that Bookstore X sold more books on Saturday than Bookstore Y, but it gives no information about the numbers of books sold by the two bookstores on the other days of last week; NOT sufficient.

(2) This gives information about the percents of the books sold last week that were sold on Saturday, but it gives no information about the actual numbers of books sold at the two bookstores last week. Therefore, a comparison of the numbers of books sold last week by Bookstore X and Bookstore Y is not possible; NOT sufficient.

Taking (1) and (2) together, if x represents the number of books that Bookstore X sold on Saturday and T_X represents the total number of books that Bookstore X sold last week, then $x>1,000$ and $x<0.2T_X$. It follows that $1,000<0.2T_X$ and so $T_X>5,000$. Similarly, if y represents the number of books that Bookstore Y sold on Saturday and T_Y represents the total number of books that Bookstore Y sold last week, then $y<1,000$ and $y>0.2T_Y$. It follows that $0.2T_Y<1,000$, and so $T_Y<5,000$. Combining the inequalities gives $T_Y<5,000<T_X$, and so $T_Y<T_X$, which means that Bookstore X sold more books last week than Bookstore Y.

The correct answer is C; both statements together are sufficient.

294. From May 1 to May 30 in the same year, the balance in a checking account increased. What was the balance in the checking account on May 30 ?

(1) If, during this period of time, the increase in the balance in the checking account had been 12 percent, then the balance in the account on May 30 would have been $504.

(2) During this period of time, the increase in the balance in the checking account was 8 percent.

Arithmetic Applied Problems; Percents

(1) Given that the amount on May 30 would have been $504 if the increase had been 12%, it follows that the amount on May 1 was $\$\dfrac{504}{1.12} = \$450$. However, the balance on May 30 cannot be determined because the (actual) percent increase is not given. For example, if the increase had been 10%, then the balance on May 30 would have been $(1.1)(\$450) = \$495$, which is different from $504; NOT sufficient.

(2) Given that the increase was 8%, the amount on May 30 could be $108 (if the amount on May 1 was $100) and the amount on May 30 could be $216 (if the amount on May 1 was $200); NOT sufficient.

Taking (1) and (2) together, it follows that the amount on May 30 was $(\$450)(1.08) = \$486$.

The correct answer is C; both statements together are sufficient.

295. A merchant discounted the sale price of a coat and the sale price of a sweater. Which of the two articles of clothing was discounted by the greater dollar amount?

(1) The percent discount on the coat was 2 percentage points greater than the percent discount on the sweater.

(2) Before the discounts, the sale price of the coat was $10 less than the sale price of the sweater.

Arithmetic Applied Problems; Percents

(1) Given that the discount on the coat was 2 percentage points greater than the discount on the sweater, the sweater could have been discounted by the greater dollar amount ($30 sweater with 10% discount is a

discount of $3; $20 coat with 12% discount is a discount of $2.40) and the coat could have been discounted by the greater dollar amount ($110 sweater with 10% discount is a discount of $11; $100 coat with 12% discount is a discount of $12); NOT sufficient.

(2) Given that the coat's sale price was $10 less than the sweater's sale price, the same examples used to show that (1) is not sufficient can be used for (2); NOT sufficient.

Taking (1) and (2) together is of no more help than either (1) or (2) taken separately because the same examples used to show that (1) is not sufficient also show that (2) is not sufficient.

The correct answer is E; both statements together are still not sufficient.

296. If the positive integer n is added to each of the integers 69, 94, and 121, what is the value of n ?

(1) $69 + n$ and $94 + n$ are the squares of two consecutive integers.

(2) $94 + n$ and $121 + n$ are the squares of two consecutive integers.

Algebra Computation with Integers

(1) Given that $69 + n$ and $94 + n$ are squares of consecutive integers and differ by 25 (that is, $(94 + n) - (69 + n) = 25$), look for consecutive integers whose squares differ by 25. It would be wise to start with $10^2 = 100$ since $94 + n$ will be greater than 94.

$$10^2 = 100$$
$$\quad\quad\quad\quad \}\text{ difference is } 21$$
$$11^2 = 121$$
$$\quad\quad\quad\quad \}\text{ difference is } 23$$
$$12^2 = 144$$
$$\quad\quad\quad\quad \}\text{ difference is } 25$$
$$13^2 = 169$$

Then, the consecutive integers whose squares differ by 25 are $69 + n = 144$ and $94 + n = 169$. The value of n can be determined from either equation.

To be sure that the value for n is unique, consider algebraically that the difference of the squares of consecutive integers is 25. So, $(x + 1)^2 - x^2 = 25$, from which it follows that $x^2 + 2x + 1 - x^2 = 25$ and $2x + 1 = 25$. This equation has a unique solution; SUFFICIENT.

(2)   Given that $94 + n$ and $121 + n$ are squares of consecutive integers and differ by 27 (that is, $(121 + n) - (94 + n) = 27$), look for consecutive integers whose squares differ by 27. It would be wise to start with $12^2 = 144$ since $121 + n$ will be greater than 121.

$12^2 = 144$
      } difference is 25
$13^2 = 169$
      } difference is 27
$14^2 = 196$

Then, the consecutive integers whose squares differ by 27 are $94 + n = 169$ and $121 + n = 196$. The value of n can be determined from either equation; SUFFICIENT.

Tip: Since this and other such problems can be solved quickly using numbers, it might be helpful to have rapid recall of the perfect squares, possibly through 20^2.

**The correct answer is D;
each statement alone is sufficient.**

297. If a merchant purchased a sofa from a manufacturer for $400 and then sold it, what was the selling price of the sofa?

(1)   The selling price of the sofa was greater than 140 percent of the purchase price.

(2)   The merchant's gross profit from the purchase and sale of the sofa was $\frac{1}{3}$ of the selling price.

Algebra Applied Problems

Letting s represent the selling price of the sofa, in dollars, determine the value of s.

(1)   The condition that the selling price of the sofa was greater than 140 percent of the purchase price is equivalent to $s > 1.4(400)$, from which it is not possible to determine the selling price; NOT sufficient.

(2)   Given that the gross profit from the purchase and sale of the sofa was $\frac{1}{3}$ of the selling price, it follows that $s - 400 = \frac{1}{3}s$ since gross profit is defined to be the selling price minus the purchase price. From this, a unique value of s can be determined; SUFFICIENT.

**The correct answer is B;
statement 2 alone is sufficient.**

298. Last year, in a certain housing development, the average (arithmetic mean) price of 20 new houses was $160,000. Did more than 9 of the 20 houses have prices that were less than the average price last year?

(1)   Last year the greatest price of one of the 20 houses was $219,000.

(2)   Last year the median of the prices of the 20 houses was $150,000.

Arithmetic Statistics

(1)   Given that the greatest of the prices was $219,000, the table below shows two possibilities in which the average price was $160,000.

Example I		Example II	
price	frequency	price	frequency
$101,000	1	$119,000	1
$160,000	18	$159,000	18
$219,000	1	$219,000	1

In Example I, note that $101,000 + 219,000 = 320,000 = 160,000 + 160,000$, so the sum of the prices is 20($160,000) and the average price is $160,000. Example II is then obtained from Example I by transferring $1,000 from each of the $160,000 prices to the $101,000 price, and thus the sum of the prices in Example II is also 20($160,000).

Example I shows that only 1 of the prices could have been less than the average price, and Example II shows that 19 of the prices could have been less than the average price; NOT sufficient.

(2)   Given that the median of the 20 prices was $150,000, then when the prices are listed

in numerical order from least to greatest, the average of the 10th and 11th prices is $150,000. Therefore, the 10th price must be less than or equal to $150,000, since if the 10th price was greater than $150,000, then both prices would be greater than $150,000 and their average would be greater than $150,000 (the median), contrary to what is given. Moreover, since the first 9 prices are less than or equal to the 10th price, it follows that the first 10 prices are each less than or equal to $150,000. Therefore, at least 10 of the prices are less than the average price; SUFFICIENT.

**The correct answer is B;
statement 2 alone is sufficient.**

299. For a certain city's library, the average cost of purchasing each new book is $28. The library receives $15,000 from the city each year; the library also receives a bonus of $2,000 if the total number of items checked out over the course of the year exceeds 5,000. Did the library receive the bonus last year?

(1) The library purchased an average of 50 new books each month last year and received enough money from the city to cover this cost.

(2) The lowest number of items checked out in one month was 459.

Arithmetic Applied Problems

(1) Given that the library purchased an average of 50 new books each month, for the entire year the library purchased a total of $(50)(12) = 600$ books for a total cost of $(600)(\$28) = \$16,800$. Excluding any possible bonus, the library received $15,000 from the city. Since this amount received from the city is not enough to cover the cost of the books, and the information provided in (1) says that the total amount received from the city was enough to cover the cost of the books, it follows that the library received a bonus; SUFFICIENT.

(2) Given that the least number of books checked out in one month was 459, it follows that the total number of books checked out for the year was at least $(12)(459) = 5,508$. Since this is greater than

5,000, it follows that the total number of books checked out for the year was greater than 5,000 and the library received a bonus; SUFFICIENT.

**The correct answer is D;
each statement alone is sufficient.**

7, 9, 6, 4, 5, x

300. If x is a number in the list above, what is the median of the list?

(1) $x > 7$

(2) The median of the list equals the arithmetic mean of the list.

Arithmetic Statistics

(1) The given numbers in the list, in order, are $4, 5, 6, 7, 9$. From (1), $x > 7$, so the list could be $4, 5, 6, 7, x, 9$ or the list could be $4, 5, 6, 7, 9, x$. In either case, the two middle numbers are 6 and 7 and the median is $\frac{6+7}{2} = \frac{13}{2}$; SUFFICIENT.

(2) The mean of the list is $\frac{7+9+6+4+5+x}{6} = \frac{31+x}{6}$, which depends on the value of x. Likewise, the median depends on the value of x. If $x = 2$, then the list is $2, 4, 5, 6, 7, 9$, which has median $\frac{5+6}{2} = \frac{11}{2}$ and arithmetic mean $\frac{31+2}{6} = \frac{33}{6} = \frac{11}{2}$, thereby satisfying (2). However, if $x = 8$, then the list is $4, 5, 6, 7, 8, 9$, which has median $\frac{6+7}{2} = \frac{13}{2}$ and arithmetic mean $\frac{31+8}{6} = \frac{39}{6} = \frac{13}{2}$, thereby satisfying (2); NOT sufficient.

**The correct answer is A;
statement 1 alone is sufficient.**

301. Three dice, each of which has its 6 sides numbered 1 through 6, are tossed. The sum of the 3 numbers that are facing up is 12. Is at least 1 of these numbers 5 ?

(1) None of the 3 numbers that are facing up is divisible by 3.

(2)   Of the numbers that are facing up, 2, but not all
      3, are equal.

Arithmetic Properties of Integers

When three dice, each with its 6 faces numbered
1 through 6, are tossed and the sum of the three
integers facing up is 12, the possible outcomes are
$\{1, 5, 6\}$, $\{2, 4, 6\}$, $\{2, 5, 5\}$, $\{3, 3, 6\}$, $\{3, 4, 5\}$, and
$\{4, 4, 4\}$. Determine if, in the outcome described,
at least one of the numbers is 5.

(1)   This indicates that none of the numbers
      is divisible by three. The outcome could
      be $\{4, 4, 4\}$. In this case, none of the three
      numbers is 5. On the other hand, the
      outcome could be $\{2, 5, 5\}$. In this case,
      at least one of the numbers is 5;
      NOT sufficient.

(2)   This indicates that two of the numbers,
      but not all three, are equal. The outcome
      could be $\{3, 3, 6\}$. In this case, none of the
      three numbers is 5. On the other hand, the
      outcome could be $\{2, 5, 5\}$. In this case,
      at least one of the numbers is 5; NOT
      sufficient.

Taking (1) and (2) together, of the possible
outcomes $\{1, 5, 6\}$, $\{2, 4, 6\}$, $\{3, 3, 6\}$, and $\{3, 4, 5\}$
are eliminated because they do not satisfy (1), and
$\{4, 4, 4\}$ is eliminated because it does not satisfy
(2). This leaves only $\{2, 5, 5\}$, and at least one
number is 5.

**The correct answer is C;
both statements together are sufficient.**

Questions 302 to 332 - Difficulty: Hard

302. Did the population of Town C increase by at least
      100 percent from the year 2000 to the year 2010 ?

      (1)   The population of Town C in 2000 was $\frac{2}{3}$ of the
            population in 2005.

      (2)   The population of Town C increased by a greater
            number of people from 2005 to 2010 than it did
            from 2000 to 2005.

Algebra Percents

Determine whether the population of Town C
increased by at least 100 percent from the year
2000 to the year 2010.

(1)   Given that the population of Town C in
      2000 was $\frac{2}{3}$ of the population in 2005,
      it is impossible to determine whether the
      population of Town C increased by at least
      100 percent from the year 2000 to the year
      2010 because no information is given that
      helps to determine the population in 2010;
      NOT sufficient.

(2)   Given that the population of Town C
      increased by a greater number of people
      from 2005 to 2010 than it did from 2000 to
      2005, it is not possible to determine whether
      the population of Town C increased by at
      least 100 percent from the year 2000 to the
      year 2010 because no information is given
      that helps determine the increase from 2000
      to 2005; NOT sufficient.

Taking (1) and (2) together, from (1) the
population in 2000 was $\frac{2}{3}$ of the population in
2005, so if P represents the population in 2005,
then the population increase from 2000 to 2005 is
$P - \frac{2}{3}P = \frac{1}{3}P$. From (2), the population increase
from 2005 to 2010 was greater than $\frac{1}{3}P$, so
the population increase from 2000 to 2010
was greater than $\frac{1}{3}P + \frac{1}{3}P = \frac{2}{3}P$. Thus, the
percent increase from 2000 to 2010 is given by
$\frac{\text{increase in population from 2000 to 2010}}{\text{population in 2000}}$, which
is greater than $\dfrac{\frac{2}{3}P}{\frac{2}{3}P} = 1$ or 100%.

**The correct answer is C;
both statements together are sufficient.**

303. In a survey of 200 college graduates, 30% said
      they had received student loans during their college
      careers, and 40% said they had received scholarships.
      What percent of those surveyed said that they had
      received neither student loans nor scholarships during
      their college careers?

      (1)   25% of those surveyed said that they had
            received scholarships but no loans.

(2) 50% of those surveyed who said that they had received loans also said that they had received scholarships.

Arithmetic Sets

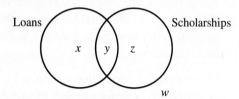

Using the variables shown on the Venn diagram above, determine the value of w. According to the information given, 30% had received student loans, so $x + y = 0.3(200) = 60$ and $x = 60 - y$. Also, 40% had received scholarships, so $y + z = 0.4(200) = 80$ and $z = 80 - y$. Then, since $x + y + z + w = 200$, $w = 200 - x - y - z = 200 - (60 - y) - y - (80 - y) = 60 + y$. Thus, if the value of y can be determined, then the value of w can be determined.

(1) Since 25% received scholarships but no loans, $z = 80 - y = 0.25(200) = 50$ and $y = 30$; SUFFICIENT.

(2) Since 50% of those who had received loans had also received scholarships, $0.5(x + y) = y$ and so $0.5(60) = 30 = y$; SUFFICIENT.

The correct answer is D; each statement alone is sufficient.

304. Stores L and M each sell a certain product at a different regular price. If both stores discount their regular price of the product, is the discount price at Store M less than the discount price at Store L?

(1) At Store L the discount price is 10 percent less than the regular price; at Store M the discount price is 15 percent less than the regular price.

(2) At Store L the discount price is $5 less than the regular store price; at Store M the discount price is $6 less than the regular price.

Arithmetic Percents

Let L_r and L_d be the regular and discounted prices, respectively, at Store L, and let M_r and M_d be the regular and discounted prices, respectively, at Store M. Determine if $M_d < L_d$.

(1) Knowing that $L_d = (1 - 0.10)L_r = 0.90L_r$ and that $M_d = (1 - 0.15)M_r = 0.85M_r$ gives no information for comparing M_d and L_d; NOT sufficient.

(2) Knowing that $L_d = L_r - 5$ and that $M_d = M_r - 6$ gives no information for comparing M_d and L_d; NOT sufficient.

Taking (1) and (2) together gives $0.90L_r = L_r - 5$ and $0.85 M_r = M_r - 6$, from which it follows that $0.10L_r = 5$ or $L_r = 50$ and $0.15M_r = 6$ or $M_r = 40$. Then $L_d = 50 - 5 = 45$ and $M_d = 40 - 6 = 34$. Therefore, $M_d < L_d$.

The correct answer is C; both statements together are sufficient.

305. A box contains only red chips, white chips, and blue chips. If a chip is randomly selected from the box, what is the probability that the chip will be either white or blue?

(1) The probability that the chip will be blue is $\frac{1}{5}$.

(2) The probability that the chip will be red is $\frac{1}{3}$.

Arithmetic Probability

(1) Since the probability of drawing a blue chip is known, the probability of drawing a chip that is not blue (in other words, a red or white chip) can also be found. However, the probability of drawing a white or blue chip cannot be determined from this information; NOT sufficient.

(2) The probability that the chip will be either white or blue is the same as the probability that it will NOT be red. Thus, the probability is $1 - \left(\frac{1}{3}\right) = \left(\frac{2}{3}\right)$; SUFFICIENT.

The correct answer is B; statement 2 alone is sufficient.

306. Did the sum of the prices of three shirts exceed $60?

(1) The price of the most expensive of the shirts exceeded $30.

(2) The price of the least expensive of the shirts exceeded $20.

Arithmetic Applied Problems

(1) Given that the price of the most expensive shirt exceeded $30, the sum of the prices of the shirts can be under $60 (if the prices were $10, $10, and $35) and the sum of the prices of the shirts can be over $60 (if the prices were $10, $10, and $50); NOT sufficient.

(2) Given that the price of the least expensive shirt exceeded $20, it follows that the sum of the prices of the shirts exceeds 3($20) = $60; SUFFICIENT.

**The correct answer is B;
statement 2 alone is sufficient.**

307. What is the total number of coins that Bert and Claire have?

(1) Bert has 50 percent more coins than Claire.

(2) The total number of coins that Bert and Claire have is between 21 and 28.

Arithmetic Computation with Integers

Determine the total number of coins Bert and Claire have. If B represents the number of coins that Bert has and C represents the number of coins that Claire has, determine $B + C$.

(1) Bert has 50% more coins than Claire, so $B = 1.5C$, and $B + C = 1.5C + C = 2.5C$, but the value of C can vary; NOT sufficient.

(2) The total number of coins Bert and Claire have is between 21 and 28, so $21 < B + C < 28$ and, therefore, $B + C$ could be 22, 23, 24, 25, 26, or 27; NOT sufficient.

Taking (1) and (2) together, $21 < 2.5C < 28$ and then $\frac{21}{2.5} < C < \frac{28}{2.5}$ or $8.4 < C < 11.2$.
If $C = 9$, then $B = (1.5)(9) = 13.5$; if $C = 10$, then $B = (1.5)(10) = 15$; and if $C = 11$, then $B = (1.5)(11) = 16.5$. Since B represents a number of coins, B is an integer. Therefore, $B = 15$, $C = 10$, and $B + C = 25$.

**The correct answer is C;
both statements together are sufficient.**

308. A telephone station has x processors, each of which can process a maximum of y calls at any particular time, where x and y are positive integers. If 500 calls are sent to the station at a particular time, can the station process all of the calls?

(1) $x = 600$

(2) $100 < y < 200$

Algebra Applied Problems

At a particular time, the telephone station can process a maximum of xy calls, where x and y are positive integers. Determine whether $xy \geq 500$.

(1) Given that $x = 600$, it follows that $xy \geq 600$ since $y \geq 1$ (y is a positive integer); SUFFICIENT.

(2) Given that $100 < y < 200$, $xy < 500$ is possible (if $x = 3$ and $y = 150$) and $xy \geq 500$ is possible (if $x = 10$ and $y = 150$); NOT sufficient.

**The correct answer is A;
statement 1 alone is sufficient.**

	Price per Flower
Roses	$1.00
Daisies	$0.50

309. Kim and Sue each bought some roses and some daisies at the prices shown above. If Kim bought the same total number of roses and daisies as Sue, was the price of Kim's purchase of roses and daisies higher than the price of Sue's purchase of roses and daisies?

(1) Kim bought twice as many daisies as roses.

(2) Kim bought 4 more roses than Sue bought.

Algebra Applied Problems

Let R_K be the number of roses that Kim bought, let R_S be the number of roses that Sue bought, and let T be the total number of roses and daisies each bought. Then Kim bought $(T - R_K)$ daisies and Sue bought $(T - R_S)$ daisies. For the roses and daisies, Kim paid a total of $\$[R_K + \frac{1}{2}(T - R_K)] = \$\frac{1}{2}(R_K + T)$ and Sue paid a total of $\$[R_S + \frac{1}{2}(T - R_S)] = \$\frac{1}{2}(R_S + T)$.

Determine whether $\frac{1}{2}(R_K + T) > \frac{1}{2}(R_S + T)$, or equivalently, determine whether $R_K > R_S$.

(1) Given that $T - R_K = 2R_K$, or $T = 3R_K$, it is not possible to determine whether $R_K > R_S$ because no information is provided about the value of R_S; NOT sufficient.

(2) Given that $R_K = R_S + 4$, it follows that $R_K > R_S$; SUFFICIENT.

The correct answer is B; statement 2 alone is sufficient.

310. Jazz and blues recordings accounted for 6 percent of the $840 million revenue from the sales of recordings in Country Y in 2000. What was the revenue from the sales of jazz and blues recordings in Country Y in 1998?

(1) Jazz and blues recordings accounted for 5 percent of the revenue from the sales of recordings in Country Y in 1998.

(2) The revenue from the sales of jazz and blues recordings in Country Y increased by 40 percent from 1998 to 2000.

Arithmetic Percents

It is given that jazz and blues recordings accounted for 6% of the $840 million revenue of recordings in Country Y in 2000. Determine the revenue from the sales of jazz and blues recordings in 1998.

(1) This indicates that jazz and blues recordings accounted for 5% of the revenue from the sales of recordings in Country Y in 1998. However, no information is given to indicate what the revenue from the sales of recordings was in 1998. Therefore, the revenue from sales of jazz and blues recordings in 1998 cannot be determined; NOT sufficient.

(2) This indicates that the revenue from the sales of jazz and blues recordings in Country Y increased by 40% from 1998 to 2000. Letting R_{1998} and R_{2000} represent the revenue from the sales of jazz and blues recordings in 1998 and 2000, respectively, then $R_{2000} = 1.4R_{1998}$, and so $(0.06)(\$840 \text{ million}) = 1.4R_{1998}$, from which R_{1998} can be determined; SUFFICIENT.

The correct answer is B; statement 2 alone is sufficient.

311. On a certain nonstop trip, Marta averaged x miles per hour for 2 hours and y miles per hour for the remaining 3 hours. What was her average speed, in miles per hour, for the entire trip?

(1) $2x + 3y = 280$

(2) $y = x + 10$

Algebra Rate Problems

Marta traveled a total of $(2x + 3y)$ miles in $2 + 3 = 5$ hours for an average speed of $\left(\dfrac{2x + 3y}{5}\right)$ miles per hour. Determine the value of $\dfrac{2x + 3y}{5}$.

(1) Given that $2x + 3y = 280$, it follows that $\dfrac{2x + 3y}{5} = \dfrac{280}{5}$; SUFFICIENT.

(2) Given that $y = x + 10$, it follows that $\dfrac{2x + 3y}{5} = \dfrac{2x + 3(x + 10)}{5} = x + 6$. Therefore, the value of $\dfrac{2x + 3y}{5}$ can be 56 (if $x = 50$ and $y = 60$) and the value of $\dfrac{2x + 3y}{5}$ can be 61 (if $x = 55$ and $y = 65$); NOT sufficient.

The correct answer is A; statement 1 alone is sufficient.

312. A group consisting of several families visited an amusement park where the regular admission fees were ¥5,500 for each adult and ¥4,800 for each child. Because there were at least 10 people in the group, each paid an admission fee that was 10% less than the regular admission fee. How many children were in the group?

(1) The total of the admission fees paid for the adults in the group was ¥29,700.

(2) The total of the admission fees paid for the children in the group was ¥4,860 more than the total of the admission fees paid for the adults in the group.

Arithmetic Simultaneous Equations

Determine the number of children in a group of at least 10 people who visited an amusement park.

(1) This indicates that $(0.9)(5,500)A = 29,700$, where A represents the number of adults in the group. From this, the number of adults

can be determined. However, the number of children in the group cannot be determined without additional information about the exact number of people in the group; NOT sufficient.

(2) If C and A represent the numbers of children and adults, respectively, in the group, this indicates that $(0.9)(4,800)C = (0.9)(5,500)A + 4,860$, or $48C = 55A + 54$, or $48C - 55A = 54$, which is a single equation with two variables from which unique values of C and A cannot be determined, even under the assumptions that C and A are integers such that $C + A \geq 10$. For example, the values of C and A could be 8 and 6, respectively, since $(48)(8) - (55)(6) = 54$, or the values of C and A could be 63 and 54, respectively, since $(48)(63) - (55)(54) = 54$; NOT sufficient.

Taking (1) and (2) together, it follows that

$$A = \frac{29,700}{(0.9)(5,500)} = 6 \text{ and}$$

$$C = \frac{(0.9)(5,500)(6) + 4,860}{(0.9)(4,800)} = 8.$$

The correct answer is C;
both statements together are sufficient.

313. What is the ratio of the average (arithmetic mean) height of students in class X to the average height of students in class Y ?

(1) The average height of the students in class X is 120 centimeters.

(2) The average height of the students in class X and class Y combined is 126 centimeters.

Arithmetic Statistics

(1) Given that the average height of the students in class X is 120 cm, but given no information about the average height of the students in class Y, the desired ratio cannot be determined; NOT sufficient.

(2) Given that the average height of the students in class X and class Y combined is 126 cm, the ratio of the averages of the individual classes cannot be determined. For example, if class X consists of 10 students, each of whom has height 120 cm, and

class Y consists of 10 students, each of whom has height 132 cm, then the average height of the students in class X and class Y combined is $\frac{10(120) + 10(132)}{20} = 126$ cm and the ratio of the averages of the individual classes is $\frac{120}{132}$. However, if class X consists of 10 students, each of whom has height 120 cm and class Y consists of 20 students, each of whom has height 129 cm, then the average height of the students in class X and class Y combined is $\frac{10(120) + 20(129)}{30} = 126$ cm and the ratio of the averages of the individual classes is $\frac{120}{129}$; NOT sufficient.

Taking (1) and (2) together is of no more help than either (1) or (2) taken separately because the same examples used to show that (2) is not sufficient include the information from (1).

The correct answer is E;
both statements together are still not sufficient.

314. Each week a certain salesman is paid a fixed amount equal to $300, plus a commission equal to 5 percent of the amount of his sales that week over $1,000. What is the total amount the salesman was paid last week?

(1) The total amount the salesman was paid last week is equal to 10 percent of the amount of his sales last week.

(2) The salesman's sales last week totaled $5,000.

Algebra Applied Problems

Let P be the salesman's pay for last week and let S be the amount of his sales last week. Then $P = 300 + 0.05(S - 1,000)$. Determine the value of P.

(1) Given $P = 0.10S$, then $0.10S = 300 + 0.05(S - 1,000)$. This equation can be solved for a unique value of S, from which the value of P can be determined; SUFFICIENT.

(2) Given $S = 5,000$, then $P = 300 + 0.05(5,000 - 1,000)$; SUFFICIENT.

The correct answer is D;
each statement alone is sufficient.

315. At a bakery, all donuts are priced equally and all bagels are priced equally. What is the total price of 5 donuts and 3 bagels at the bakery?

    (1) At the bakery, the total price of 10 donuts and 6 bagels is $12.90.
    (2) At the bakery, the price of a donut is $0.15 less than the price of a bagel.

Algebra Simultaneous Equations

Let x be the price, in dollars, of each donut and let y be the price, in dollars, of each bagel. Find the value of $5x + 3y$.

    (1) Given that $10x + 6y = 12.90$, since
    $5x + 3y = \frac{1}{2}(10x + 6y)$, it follows that
    $5x + 3y = \frac{1}{2}(12.90)$; SUFFICIENT.

    (2) Given that $x = y - 0.15$, then $5x + 3y = 5(y - 0.15) + 3y = 8y - 0.75$, which varies as y varies; NOT sufficient.

**The correct answer is A;
statement 1 alone is sufficient.**

316. Last year, if Arturo spent a total of $12,000 on his mortgage payments, real estate taxes, and home insurance, how much did he spend on his real estate taxes?

    (1) Last year, the total amount that Arturo spent on his real estate taxes and home insurance was $33\frac{1}{3}$ percent of the amount that he spent on his mortgage payments.
    (2) Last year, the amount that Arturo spent on his real estate taxes was 20 percent of the total amount he spent on his mortgage payments and home insurance.

Arithmetic Applied Problems

Let M, R, and H be the amounts that Arturo spent last year on mortgage payments, real estate taxes, and home insurance, respectively. Given that $M + R + H = 12,000$, determine the value of R.

    (1) Given that $R + H = \frac{1}{3}M$ and $M + R + H = 12,000$, then $M + \frac{1}{3}M = 12,000$, or $M = 9,000$. However, the value of R cannot

be determined, since it is possible that $R = 2,000$ (use $M = 9,000$ and $H = 1,000$) and it is possible that $R = 1,000$ (use $M = 9,000$ and $H = 2,000$); NOT sufficient.

    (2) Given that $R = \frac{1}{5}(M + H)$, or $5R = M + H$ and $M + R + H = 12,000$, which can be rewritten as $(M + H) + R = 12,000$, then $5R + R = 12,000$, or $R = 2,000$; SUFFICIENT.

**The correct answer is B;
statement 2 alone is sufficient.**

317. Is the number of members of Club X greater than the number of members of Club Y ?

    (1) Of the members of Club X, 20 percent are also members of Club Y.
    (2) Of the members of Club Y, 30 percent are also members of Club X.

Arithmetic Sets

    (1) Given that 20 percent of the members of Club X are also members of Club Y, these 20 percent could be the only members of Club Y, in which case all the members of Club Y belong to Club X and Club X would have a greater number of members than Club Y. However, these 20 percent could form only a tiny portion of the members of Club Y and Club Y would have a greater number of members than Club X; NOT sufficient.

    (2) Given that 30 percent of the members of Club Y are also members of Club X, these 30 percent could be the only members of Club X, in which case all the members of Club X belong to Club Y and Club Y would have a greater number of members than Club X. However, these 30 percent could form only a tiny portion of the members of Club X and Club X would have a greater number of members than Club Y; NOT sufficient.

Taking (1) and (2) together, the Venn diagram below shows the numbers of members in one or both of Club X and Club Y. For example, b is the number of members of Club X that are also members of Club Y, and b is the number of members of Club Y that are also members of Club X. We are to determine whether $a + b$, the number of members of Club X, is greater than $b + c$, the number of members of Club Y.

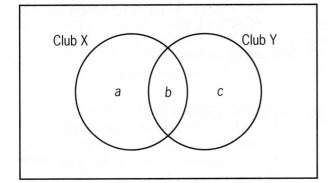

$$b = \frac{1}{5}(a + b) \quad \text{from (1) and } 20\% = \frac{1}{5}$$

$$5b = a + b \quad \text{multiply both sides by 5}$$

$$b = \frac{3}{10}(b + c) \quad \text{from (2) and } 30\% = \frac{3}{10}$$

$$\frac{10}{3}b = b + c \quad \text{multiply both sides by } \frac{10}{3}$$

The 2nd equation above says that the number of members of Club X is $5b$ and the 4th equation above says that the number of members of Club Y is $\frac{10}{3}b$. Since 5 is greater than $\frac{10}{3}$, it follows that the number of members of Club X is greater than the number of members of Club Y.

**The correct answer is C;
both statements together are sufficient.**

318. The only articles of clothing in a certain closet are shirts, dresses, and jackets. The ratio of the number of shirts to the number of dresses to the number of jackets in the closet is 9:4:5, respectively. If there are more than 7 dresses in the closet, what is the total number of articles of clothing in the closet?

   (1) The total number of shirts and jackets in the closet is less than 30.
   (2) The total number of shirts and dresses in the closet is 26.

Arithmetic Ratio and Proportion

Letting s, d, and j represent, respectively, the numbers of shirts, dresses, and jackets in the closet, then $s = 9x$, $d = 4x$, and $j = 5x$, where x is

a positive integer. It is given that $4x > 7$, and so $4x \geq 8$ or $x \geq 2$ since x is an integer. Determine the value of $9x + 4x + 5x = 18x$.

   (1) This indicates that $9x + 5x < 30$, and so $14x \leq 28$ or $x \leq 2$ since x is an integer. It follows from $x \geq 2$ and $x \leq 2$ that $x = 2$ and $18x = 36$; SUFFICIENT.

   (2) This indicates that $9x + 4x = 26$ or $13x = 26$, or $x = 2$. It follows that $18x = 36$; SUFFICIENT.

**The correct answer is D;
each statement alone is sufficient.**

319. Material A costs \$3 per kilogram, and Material B costs \$5 per kilogram. If 10 kilograms of Material K consists of x kilograms of Material A and y kilograms of Material B, is $x > y$?

   (1) $y > 4$
   (2) The cost of the 10 kilograms of Material K is less than \$40.

Algebra Inequalities

Since $x + y = 10$, the relation $x > y$ is equivalent to $x > 10 - x$, or $x > 5$.

   (1) The given information is consistent with $x = 5.5$ and $y = 4.5$, and the given information is also consistent with $x = y = 5$. Therefore, it is possible for $x > y$ to be true and it is possible for $x > y$ to be false; NOT sufficient.

   (2) Given that $3x + 5y < 40$, or $3x + 5(10 - x) < 40$, then $3x - 5x < 40 - 50$. It follows that $-2x < -10$, or $x > 5$; SUFFICIENT.

**The correct answer is B;
statement 2 alone is sufficient.**

320. At what speed was a train traveling on a trip when it had completed half of the total distance of the trip?

   (1) The trip was 460 miles long and took 4 hours to complete.
   (2) The train traveled at an average rate of 115 miles per hour on the trip.

Arithmetic Applied Problems

Determine the speed of the train when it had completed half the total distance of the trip.

(1) Given that the train traveled 460 miles in 4 hours, the train could have traveled at the constant rate of 115 miles per hour for 4 hours, and thus it could have been traveling 115 miles per hour when it had completed half the total distance of the trip. However, the train could have traveled 150 miles per hour for the first 2 hours (a distance of 300 miles) and 80 miles per hour for the last 2 hours (a distance of 160 miles), and thus it could have been traveling 150 miles per hour when it had completed half the total distance of the trip; NOT sufficient.

(2) Given that the train traveled at an average rate of 115 miles per hour, each of the possibilities given in the explanation for (1) could occur, since 460 miles in 4 hours gives an average speed of $\frac{460}{4} = 115$ miles per hour; NOT sufficient.

Assuming (1) and (2), each of the possibilities given in the explanation for (1) could occur. Therefore, (1) and (2) together are not sufficient.

**The correct answer is E;
both statements together are still not sufficient.**

321. Tom, Jane, and Sue each purchased a new house. The average (arithmetic mean) price of the three houses was $120,000. What was the median price of the three houses?

(1) The price of Tom's house was $110,000.
(2) The price of Jane's house was $120,000.

Arithmetic Statistics

Let T, J, and S be the purchase prices for Tom's, Jane's, and Sue's new houses. Given that the average purchase price is 120,000, or $T + J + S = 3(120,000)$, determine the median purchase price.

(1) Given $T = 110,000$, the median could be 120,000 (if $J = 120,000$ and $S = 130,000$) or 125,000 (if $J = 125,000$ and $S = 125,000$); NOT sufficient.

(2) Given $J = 120,000$, the following two cases include every possibility consistent with $T + J + S = (3)(120,000)$, or $T + S = (2)(120,000)$.

    (i) $T = S = 120,000$

(ii) One of T or S is less than 120,000 and the other is greater than 120,000.

In each case, the median is clearly 120,000; SUFFICIENT.

**The correct answer is B;
statement 2 alone is sufficient.**

322. A certain bookcase has 2 shelves of books. On the upper shelf, the book with the greatest number of pages has 400 pages. On the lower shelf, the book with the least number of pages has 475 pages. What is the median number of pages for all of the books on the 2 shelves?

(1) There are 25 books on the upper shelf.
(2) There are 24 books on the lower shelf.

Arithmetic Statistics

(1) The information given says nothing about the number of books on the lower shelf. If there are fewer than 25 books on the lower shelf, then the median number of pages will be the number of pages in one of the books on the upper shelf or the average number of pages in two books on the upper shelf. Hence, the median will be at most 400. If there are more than 25 books on the lower shelf, then the median number of pages will be the number of pages in one of the books on the lower shelf or the average number of pages in two books on the lower shelf. Hence, the median will be at least 475; NOT sufficient.

(2) An analysis very similar to that used in (1) shows the information given is not sufficient to determine the median; NOT sufficient.

Given both (1) and (2), it follows that there is a total of 49 books. Therefore, the median will be the 25th book when the books are ordered by number of pages. Since the 25th book in this ordering is the book on the upper shelf with the greatest number of pages, the median is 400. Therefore, (1) and (2) together are sufficient.

**The correct answer is C;
both statements together are sufficient.**

323. In planning for a trip, Joan estimated both the distance of the trip, in miles, and her average speed, in miles per hour. She accurately divided her estimated

distance by her estimated average speed to obtain an estimate for the time, in hours, that the trip would take. Was her estimate within 0.5 hour of the actual time that the trip took?

(1) Joan's estimate for the distance was within 5 miles of the actual distance.

(2) Joan's estimate for her average speed was within 10 miles per hour of her actual average speed.

Arithmetic Applied Problems; Estimating

(1) Given that the estimate for the distance was within 5 miles of the actual distance, it is not possible to determine whether the estimate of the time (that is, the estimated distance divided by the estimated average speed) was within 0.5 hour of the actual time because nothing is known about the estimated average speed; NOT sufficient.

(2) Given that the estimate for the average speed was within 10 miles per hour of the actual average speed, it is not possible to determine whether the estimate of the time (that is, the estimated distance divided by the estimated average speed) was within 0.5 hour of the actual time because nothing is known about the estimated distance; NOT sufficient.

Taking (1) and (2) together, the table below shows two possibilities for the estimated distance, estimated average speed, actual distance, and actual average speed that are consistent with the information given in (1) and (2).

estimated distance	estimated speed	actual distance	actual speed
20 miles	$20 \frac{\text{miles}}{\text{hour}}$	20 miles	$20 \frac{\text{miles}}{\text{hour}}$
20 miles	$20 \frac{\text{miles}}{\text{hour}}$	20 miles	$10 \frac{\text{miles}}{\text{hour}}$

In the first row of the table, the estimate of the time and the actual time are each equal to 1 hour, and so the estimate of the time is within 0.5 hour of the actual time. In the second row of the table, the estimate of the time is 1 hour and the actual time is $\frac{20}{10} = 2$ hours, and so the estimate of the time is not within 0.5 hour of the actual time.

The correct answer is E; both statements together are still not sufficient

Shipment	S1	S2	S3	S4	S5	S6
Fraction of the Total Value of the Six Shipments	$\frac{1}{4}$	$\frac{1}{5}$	$\frac{1}{6}$	$\frac{3}{20}$	$\frac{2}{15}$	$\frac{1}{10}$

324. Six shipments of machine parts were shipped from a factory on two trucks, with each shipment entirely on one of the trucks. Each shipment was labeled either S1, S2, S3, S4, S5, or S6. The table shows the value of each shipment as a fraction of the total value of the six shipments. If the shipments on the first truck had a value greater than $\frac{1}{2}$ of the total value of the six shipments, was S3 shipped on the first truck?

(1) S2 and S4 were shipped on the first truck.

(2) S1 and S6 were shipped on the second truck.

Arithmetic Operations on Rational Numbers

Given that the shipments on the first truck had a value greater than $\frac{1}{2}$ of the total value of the 6 shipments, determine if S3 was shipped on the first truck.

To avoid dealing with fractions, it will be convenient to create scaled values of the shipments by multiplying each fractional value by 60, which is the least common denominator of the fractions. Thus, the scaled values associated with S1, S2, S3, S4, S5, and S6 are 15, 12, 10, 9, 8, and 6, respectively. The given information is that the scaled value of the shipments on the first truck is greater than $\left(\frac{1}{2}\right)(60) = 30$.

(1) Given that the first truck includes shipments with scaled values 12 and 9, it may or may not be the case that S3 (the shipment with scaled value 10) is on the first truck. For example, the first truck could contain only S2, S3, and S4, for a total scaled value $12 + 10 + 9 = 31 > 30$. Or, the first truck could contain only S1, S2, and S4, for a total scaled value $15 + 12 + 9 = 36 > 30$; NOT sufficient.

(2) Given that the second truck includes shipments with scaled values 15 and 6, the

second truck cannot contain S3. Otherwise, the second truck would contain shipments with scaled values 15, 6, and 10, for a total scaled value $15 + 6 + 10 = 31$, leaving at most a total scaled value 29 (which is not greater than 30) for the first truck; SUFFICIENT.

The correct answer is B; statement 2 alone is sufficient.

	Favorable	Unfavorable	Not Sure
Candidate M	40	20	40
Candidate N	30	35	35

325. The table above shows the results of a survey of 100 voters who each responded "Favorable" or "Unfavorable" or "Not Sure" when asked about their impressions of Candidate M and of Candidate N. What was the number of voters who responded "Favorable" for both candidates?

   (1) The number of voters who did not respond "Favorable" for either candidate was 40.

   (2) The number of voters who responded "Unfavorable" for both candidates was 10.

Arithmetic Sets

Let x, y, and z, respectively, be the numbers of voters who responded "Favorable," "Unfavorable," and "Not Sure" to both candidates. The table below gives a more complete tabulation of the survey results. For example, since 20 voters responded "Unfavorable" for Candidate M and y of those 20 voters also responded "Unfavorable" for Candidate N, it follows that $20 - y$ of those 20 voters responded "Unfavorable" for Candidate M only. Determine the value of x, the number of voters who responded "Favorable" for both candidates.

	Favorable	Unfavorable	Not Sure
M and N	x	y	z
M only	$40 - x$	$20 - y$	$40 - z$
N only	$30 - x$	$35 - y$	$35 - z$

   (1) It is given that the number of voters who did not respond "Favorable" for either candidate was 40. Also, from the table

above the number of voters who responded "Favorable" for at least one candidate was $(40 - x) + (30 - x) + x = 70 - x$. Since there were 100 voters, it follows that $(70 - x) + 40 = 100$, which can be solved for a unique value of x; SUFFICIENT.

   (2) It is given that the number of voters who responded "Unfavorable" for both candidates was 10, or $y = 10$. However, there is not enough information to determine the value of x. This can be seen by choosing different integer values for x between 0 and 30, inclusive, and using each value to complete the table above (choose $z = 5$ for completeness, for example); NOT sufficient.

The correct answer is A; statement 1 alone is sufficient.

326. A school administrator will assign each student in a group of n students to one of m classrooms. If $3 < m < 13 < n$, is it possible to assign each of the n students to one of the m classrooms so that each classroom has the same number of students assigned to it?

   (1) It is possible to assign each of $3n$ students to one of m classrooms so that each classroom has the same number of students assigned to it.

   (2) It is possible to assign each of $13n$ students to one of m classrooms so that each classroom has the same number of students assigned to it.

Arithmetic Properties of Numbers

Determine if n is divisible by m.

   (1) Given that $3n$ is divisible by m, then n is divisible by m if $m = 9$ and $n = 27$ (note that $3 < m < 13 < n$, $3n = 81$, and $m = 9$, so $3n$ is divisible by m) and n is not divisible by m if $m = 9$ and $n = 30$ (note that $3 < m < 13 < n$, $3n = 90$, and $m = 9$, so $3n$ is divisible by m); NOT sufficient.

   (2) Given that $13n$ is divisible by m, then $13n = qm$, or $\dfrac{n}{m} = \dfrac{q}{13}$, for some integer q.

   Since 13 is a prime number that divides qm (because $13n = qm$) and 13 does not divide m (because $m < 13$), it follows that 13 divides q.

Therefore, $\dfrac{q}{13}$ is an integer, and since $\dfrac{n}{m} = \dfrac{q}{13}$, then $\dfrac{n}{m}$ is an integer. Thus, n is divisible by m; SUFFICIENT.

**The correct answer is B;
statement 2 alone is sufficient.**

327. At a certain clothing store, customers who buy 2 shirts pay the regular price for the first shirt and a discounted price for the second shirt. The store makes the same profit from the sale of 2 shirts that it makes from the sale of 1 shirt at the regular price. For a customer who buys 2 shirts, what is the discounted price of the second shirt?

   (1) The regular price of each of the 2 shirts the customer buys at the clothing store is $16.
   (2) The cost to the clothing store of each of the 2 shirts the customer buys is $12.

Arithmetic Applied Problems

Solving this problem relies on the definition of profit: profit = selling price − cost.

   (1) Given that the regular price of each of the 2 shirts is $16, the discounted price cannot be uniquely determined because no information is given about the rate of discount, the amount of discount, or the cost; NOT sufficient.

   (2) Recall that profit = selling price − cost. Since the store makes the same profit from the sale of 2 shirts as it makes from the sale of 1 shirt at the regular price, the profit from the second shirt is $0. It follows that the selling price (that is, the discounted price) of the second shirt equals its cost.

   Given that the cost of each of the shirts is $12, it follows that the discounted price of the second shirt is $12; SUFFICIENT.

**The correct answer is B;
statement 2 alone is sufficient.**

328. What is the median number of employees assigned per project for the projects at Company Z ?

   (1) 25 percent of the projects at Company Z have 4 or more employees assigned to each project.
   (2) 35 percent of the projects at Company Z have 2 or fewer employees assigned to each project.

Arithmetic Statistics

   (1) Although 25 percent of the projects have 4 or more employees, there is essentially no information about the middle values of the numbers of employees per project. For example, if there were a total of 100 projects, then the median could be 2 (75 projects that have exactly 2 employees each and 25 projects that have exactly 4 employees each) or the median could be 3 (75 projects that have exactly 3 employees each and 25 projects that have exactly 4 employees each); NOT sufficient.

   (2) Although 35 percent of the projects have 2 or fewer employees, there is essentially no information about the middle values of the numbers of employees per project. For example, if there were a total of 100 projects, then the median could be 3 (35 projects that have exactly 2 employees each and 65 projects that have exactly 3 employees each) or the median could be 4 (35 projects that have exactly 2 employees each and 65 projects that have exactly 4 employees each); NOT sufficient.

Given both (1) and (2), $100 - (25 + 35)$ percent = 40 percent of the projects have exactly 3 employees. Therefore, when the numbers of employees per project are listed from least to greatest, 35 percent of the numbers are 2 or less and $(35 + 40)$ percent = 75 percent are 3 or less, and hence the median is 3.

**The correct answer is C;
both statements together are sufficient.**

329. Last year, a certain company began manufacturing product X and sold every unit of product X that it produced. Last year the company's total expenses for manufacturing product X were equal to $100,000 plus 5 percent of the company's total revenue from all units of product X sold. If the company made a profit

on product X last year, did the company sell more than 21,000 units of product X last year?

(1) The company's total revenue from the sale of product X last year was greater than $110,000.

(2) For each unit of product X sold last year, the company's revenue was $5.

Algebra Applied Problems

Recall that Profit = Revenue – Expenses and for this company the profit on product X last year was positive. Then, letting R represent total revenue, in dollars, from all units of product X sold, profit = $R - (100,000 + 0.05R) = 0.95R - 100,000$. So,

$$0.95R - 100,000 > 0.$$

(1) This says $R > 110,000$, but gives no information on how many units were sold or the price at which they were sold. Therefore, whether the company sold more than 21,000 units cannot be determined; NOT sufficient.

number sold	unit price	R, in dollars	number sold > 21,000 ?
1,200	$100	120,000	no
22,000	$10	220,000	yes

Note that a calculator is not needed to verify that the profit (which is given in dollars by 95% of $R - 100,000$) is positive for each of these two values of R. For example,

10% of 120,000	=	12,000	move decimal point 1 place to the left
5% of 120,000	=	6,000	5% is $\frac{1}{2}$ of 10%
120,000 – 6,000	=	114,000	$R - 5\%$ of $R =$ 95% of R
114,000 – 100,000	=	14,000	95% of $R - 100,000$

(2) This says the unit price was $5. If x represents the number of units sold, then $R = 5x$ and, by substitution, the requirement that the profit is positive becomes $0.95(5x) - 100,000 > 0$.

$0.95(5x) - 100,000$	>	0	given
$0.95(5x)$	>	100,000	add 100,000 to both sides
$0.95x$	>	20,000	divide both sides by 5
x	>	$\dfrac{20,000}{0.95}$	divide both sides by 0.95
x	>	$\dfrac{20,000}{\frac{19}{20}}$	$0.95 = \dfrac{95}{100} = \dfrac{19}{20}$
x	>	$(20,000)\left(\dfrac{20}{19}\right)$	invert divisor and multiply
x	>	$20,000 + (20,000)\left(\dfrac{1}{19}\right)$	$\dfrac{20}{19} = 1 + \dfrac{1}{19}$
x	>	$20,000 + 1,000$	$\dfrac{1}{19} > \dfrac{1}{20}, (20,000)\dfrac{1}{20} = 1,000$
x	>	21,000	add

Therefore, the company sold more than 21,000 units; SUFFICIENT.

The correct answer is B; statement 2 alone is sufficient.

330. Beginning in January of last year, Carl made deposits of $120 into his account on the 15th of each month for several consecutive months and then made withdrawals of $50 from the account on the 15th of each of the remaining months of last year. There were no other transactions in the account last year. If the

closing balance of Carl's account for May of last year was $2,600, what was the range of the monthly closing balances of Carl's account last year?

(1) Last year the closing balance of Carl's account for April was less than $2,625.

(2) Last year the closing balance of Carl's account for June was less than $2,675.

Arithmetic Statistics

It is given that the closing balance for May was $2,600 and the closing balance for each month either increases by $120 or decreases by $50 relative to the closing balance for the previous month, depending on when the withdrawals began. Therefore, the closing balance for June was either $2,720 or $2,550, and the closing balance for April was either $2,480 or $2,650. The table below shows these possibilities for 5 of the months that the withdrawals could have begun. The values in the last two rows of the table remain the same for later months that the withdrawals could have begun.

Withdrawals began	Close April	Close May	Close June
Apr 15	$2,650	$2,600	$2,550
May 15	$2,650	$2,600	$2,550
Jun 15	$2,480	$2,600	$2,550
Jul 15	$2,480	$2,600	$2,720
Aug 15	$2,480	$2,600	$2,720

(1) Given that the closing balance for April was less than $2,625, it follows from the table above that the withdrawals could have begun in June or in any later month. For each of these possibilities, the balance at the beginning of January was $2,600 − 5($120) = $2,000, since each of the 5 transactions made before the end of May were $120 deposits. Therefore, the range of the monthly closing balances of the account can vary because the range will depend on how many of the transactions made after May were $120 deposits and how many were $50 withdrawals; NOT sufficient.

(2) Given that the closing balance for June was less than $2,675, it follows from the table above that the withdrawals could have begun in June or in any earlier

month. For each of these possibilities, the balance at the end of December was $2,600 − 7($50) = $2,250, since each of the 7 transactions made after the end of May were $50 withdrawals. Therefore, the range of the monthly closing balances of the account can vary because the range will depend on how many of the transactions made before May were $120 deposits and how many were $50 withdrawals; NOT sufficient.

Taking (1) and (2) together, withdrawals started in June or later by (1) and withdrawals started in June or earlier by (2), so withdrawals started in June. Therefore, each of the monthly closing balances of the account is known, and thus the range of these monthly closing balances can be determined.

The correct answer is C; both statements together are sufficient.

331. What amount did Jean earn from the commission on her sales in the first half of 1988 ?

(1) In 1988 Jean's commission was 5 percent of the total amount of her sales.

(2) The amount of Jean's sales in the second half of 1988 averaged $10,000 per month more than in the first half.

Arithmetic Applied Problems

Let A be the amount of Jean's sales in the first half of 1988. Determine the value of A.

(1) If the amount of Jean's sales in the first half of 1988 was $10,000, then her commission in the first half of 1988 would have been (5%)($10,000) = $500. On the other hand, if the amount of Jean's sales in the first half of 1988 was $100,000, then her commission in the first half of 1988 would have been (5%)($100,000) = $5,000; NOT sufficient.

(2) No information is given that relates the amount of Jean's sales to the amount of Jean's commission; NOT sufficient.

Given (1) and (2), from (1) the amount of Jean's commission in the first half of 1988 is (5%)A. From (2) the amount of Jean's sales in the second half of 1988 is A + $60,000. Both statements together do not give information to determine the value of A.

**The correct answer is E;
both statements together are still not sufficient.**

332. In a certain business, production index p is directly proportional to efficiency index e, which is in turn directly proportional to investment index i. What is p if $i = 70$?

(1)　$e = 0.5$ whenever $i = 60$.

(2)　$p = 2.0$ whenever $i = 50$.

Arithmetic Proportions

(1)　This gives only values for e and i, and, while p is directly proportional to e, the nature of this proportion is unknown. Therefore, p cannot be determined; NOT sufficient.

(2)　Since p is directly proportional to e, which is directly proportional to i, then p is directly

proportional to i. Therefore, the following proportion can be set up: $\dfrac{p}{i} = \dfrac{2.0}{50}$.
If $i = 70$, then $\dfrac{p}{70} = \dfrac{2.0}{50}$. Through cross multiplying, this equation yields $50p = 140$, or $p = 2.8$; SUFFICIENT.

The preceding approach is one method that can be used. Another approach is as follows: It is given that $p = Ke = K(Li) = (KL)i$, where K and L are the proportionality constants, and the value of $70KL$ is to be determined. Statement (1) allows us to determine the value of L, but gives nothing about K, and thus (1) is not sufficient. Statement (2) allows us to determine the value of KL, and thus (2) is sufficient.

**The correct answer is B;
statement 2 alone is sufficient.**

7.0 Verbal Review

7.0 Verbal Review

To prepare for the Verbal Reasoning section as well as the Data Insights section of the GMAT™ exam, and to succeed in graduate business programs, you need basic skills in analyzing and evaluating texts and the ideas they express. This chapter explains concepts to help you develop these skills. This is only a brief overview, so if you find unfamiliar terms or concepts, consult outside resources to learn more.

The sections below can help you develop skills you need for the Verbal Reasoning and Data Insights sections of the GMAT exam.

Section 7.1, "Analyzing Passages," includes these topics:

1. Arguments
2. Explanations and Plans
3. Narratives and Descriptions

Section 7.2, "Inductive Reasoning," includes these topics:

1. Inductive Arguments
2. Generalizations and Predictions
3. Causal Reasoning
4. Analogies

Section 7.3, "Deductive Reasoning," includes these topics:

1. Deductive Arguments
2. Logical Operators
3. Reasoning with Logical Operators
4. Necessity, Probability, and Possibility
5. Quantifiers
6. Reasoning with Quantifiers

7.1 Analyzing Passages

1. Arguments

A. An *argument* gives one or more ideas as reasons to accept one or more other ideas. Often some of these ideas are implied but not stated.

> *Example:*
>
> The sidewalk is dry, so it must not have rained last night.
>
> This argument gives the observation that the sidewalk is dry as a reason to accept that it didn't rain last night. The argument implies but doesn't say that rain typically leaves sidewalks wet.

B. A *premise* is an idea that an argument gives as a reason to accept another idea. An argument can have any number of premises.

The words and phrases below often mark premises:

after all	for one thing	moreover
because	furthermore	seeing that
for	given that	since
for the reason that	in light of the fact that	whereas

Example:

Our mayor shouldn't support the proposal to expand the freeway because the expansion's benefits wouldn't justify the costs. Furthermore, most voters oppose the expansion.

This is an argument with two stated premises. The word ***because*** marks the first premise, that the expansion's benefits wouldn't justify the costs. The word ***furthermore*** marks the second premise, that most voters oppose the expansion. These premises are given as reasons the mayor shouldn't support the proposal.

C. A *conclusion* is an idea an argument supports with one or more premises. An ***intermediate conclusion*** is a conclusion the argument uses to support another conclusion. A ***main conclusion*** is a conclusion the argument doesn't use to support any other conclusion.

The words and phrases below often mark conclusions:

clearly	*it follows that*	*suggests that*
entails that	*proves*	*surely*
hence	*shows that*	*therefore*
implies that	*so*	*thus*

Example:

Julia just hiked fifteen kilometers, so she must have burned a lot of calories. Surely, she's hungry now.

This argument has a premise, an intermediate conclusion, and a main conclusion. The word ***so*** marks the intermediate conclusion, that Julia must have burned a lot of calories. The word ***surely*** marks the main conclusion: that Julia is hungry now. The premise that Julia just hiked fifteen kilometers is used to support the intermediate conclusion, which in turn is used to support the main conclusion.

Conclusions may be stated before, between, or after premises. Sometimes no marker words mark which statements are premises, and which are conclusions. To find premises and conclusions without marker words, consider which statements the author gives as reasons to accept which other statements. The reasons given are the premises. The ideas the author tries to persuade readers to accept are the conclusions.

Example:

For healthy eating, Healthful Brand Donuts are the best donuts you can buy. Unlike any other donuts on the market, Healthful Brand Donuts have plenty of fiber and natural ingredients.

In this argument, the author tries to persuade the reader that Healthful Brand Donuts are the best donuts to buy for healthy eating. So, the first sentence is the conclusion. The statement about Healthful Brand Donuts' ingredients is a premise because it's given as a reason to accept the conclusion. Since the author's intent is clear, no marker words are needed.

D. A *valid* argument is one whose conclusions follow from its premises. A valid argument can have false premises and conclusions. In a valid argument with false premises, the conclusion *would* follow if the premises *were* true.

A *sound* argument is a valid argument with true premises. Since a sound argument's premises are true, and its conclusions follow from those premises, its conclusions must also be true.

Examples:

(i) Everyone who tries fried eggplant is guaranteed to love the taste. So, if you try it, you'll love the taste too.

In example (i), the premise is false: not everyone who tries fried eggplant is guaranteed to love the taste. So, example (i) is not a sound argument. But it is a valid argument because if everyone who tried fried eggplant *were* guaranteed to love the taste, it would follow that you, too, would love the taste if *you* tried it.

(ii) Some people who try fried eggplant dislike the taste. So, if you try it, you'll probably dislike the taste too.

In example (ii), the premise is true: some people who try fried eggplant do dislike the taste. However, example (ii) is an invalid argument, so it's not sound. *Some* people dislike the taste of fried eggplant, but that does not mean *you personally* will *probably* dislike the taste.

E. An *assumption* is an idea taken for granted. An assumption may be a premise in an argument, a claim about a cause or effect in a causal explanation, a condition a plan relies on, or any other type of idea taken for granted in a passage. A conclusion is never an assumption—an argument doesn't take a conclusion for granted, but rather gives reasons to accept it.

A passage may also have *implicit assumptions* the author considers too obvious to state. These unstated ideas fill logical gaps between the passage's statements. An argument or explanation with implausible implicit assumptions is weak and vulnerable to criticism.

F. A *necessary assumption* of an argument is an idea that must be true for the argument's stated premises to be good enough reasons to accept its conclusions. That is, a necessary assumption is one the argument needs in order to work.

Example:

Mario has booked a flight scheduled to arrive at 5:00 p.m.—which should let him get here by around 6:30 p.m. So, by 7:00 p.m. we'll be going out to dinner with Mario.

In this argument, one necessary assumption is that the flight Mario booked will arrive not much later than scheduled. A second necessary assumption is that Mario caught his flight. Unless these and all the argument's other necessary assumptions are true, the argument's stated premises aren't good enough reasons to accept the conclusion.

G. A *sufficient assumption* of an argument is an idea whose truth would make the argument's main conclusion follow from the stated premises.

Example:

The study of poetry is entirely without value since poetry has no practical use.

In this argument, one sufficient assumption is that studying anything with no practical use is entirely without value. This assumption, together with the argument's stated premise, is enough to make the conclusion follow: if both the premise and the assumption are true, the conclusion must also be true. A second, narrower sufficient assumption is that studying literature with no practical use is entirely without value, and poetry is literature. Neither of these sufficient assumptions is a necessary assumption.

H. Arguments are often classified based on what kinds of conclusions they're used to support.

i. A *prescriptive* argument supports a conclusion about what should or shouldn't be done. Prescriptive arguments may advocate adopting or rejecting policies, procedures, strategies, goals, laws, or ethical norms.

Example:

Our company's staff is too small to handle our upcoming project. So, to make sure the project succeeds, the company should hire more employees.

The example above in section 7.1.1.B is also a prescriptive argument because it concludes that the mayor ***should not*** support the proposed freeway expansion.

---

ii. An *evaluative* argument supports a conclusion that something is good or bad, desirable or undesirable, without advocating any particular policy or actions.

Example:

This early novel is clearly one of the greatest of all time. Not only did it pioneer brilliantly innovative narrative techniques, but it did so with exceptional grace, subtlety, and sophistication.

---

iii. An *interpretive* argument supports a conclusion about something's underlying significance. An interpretive argument may support or oppose an account of the meaning, importance, or implications of observations, a theory, an artistic or literary work, or a historical event.

Example:

Many famous authors have commented emphatically on this early novel, either praising or condemning it. This suggests the novel has had an enormous influence on later fiction.

---

iv. A *causal* argument supports a conclusion that one or more factors did or did not contribute to one or more effects. A causal argument may support or oppose an account of the causes, reasons, or motivations for an event, condition, decision, or outcome. For example, a causal argument may support or oppose an account of the influences behind a literary or artistic style or movement.

Example:

Our houseplant started to thrive only when we moved it to a sunny window. So, probably the reason it was sickly before then was that it wasn't getting enough sunlight.

Another causal argument can be found in the example in section 7.1.1.C above, which concludes that Julia must be hungry now.

---

v. A basic *factual* argument supports a factual conclusion that doesn't fit in any other category explained above.

Example:

All dogs are mammals. Rover is a dog. Therefore, Rover is a mammal.

---

2. Explanations and Plans

A. A *causal explanation* **claims** that one or more factors contribute to one or more effects. A causal explanation might not be an argument. It might have no premises or conclusions. But a causal explanation can be a premise or conclusion in an argument.

The words and phrases below often mark a causal explanation:

as a result	*due to*	*results in*
because	*leads to*	*that's why*
causes	*produces*	*thereby*
contributes to	*responsible for*	*thus*

Some of these words also mark premises or conclusions in arguments. To tell how the words are used, you may have to judge whether the author is giving reasons to accept a conclusion or saying what causes an effect. If the author is saying what causes an effect, without trying to persuade the reader that the effect is real, the passage is a causal explanation but not an argument.

Just as an argument may have premises, intermediate conclusions, and main conclusions, a causal explanation may claim that one or more factors cause one or more intermediate effects that, in turn, cause further effects.

> *Example:*
>
> Julia just hiked fifteen kilometers, thereby burning a lot of calories. That's why she's hungry now.
>
> This is a causal explanation claiming that a factor (Julia's fifteen-kilometer hike) caused an intermediate effect (Julia burning a lot of calories) that, in turn, caused another effect (Julia being hungry now). The word ***thereby*** marks the intermediate effect, and the phrase ***that's why*** marks the final effect. This explanation doesn't try to convince the reader that Julia's hungry. It just explains what made her hungry. So, it's not an argument.

B. An ***observation*** is a claim that something was observed or is otherwise directly known. In the example of a causal explanation above, the claims that Julia just hiked fifteen kilometers and that she's hungry are observations. But if her burning of calories was not directly known or observed, the claim that she burned a lot of calories is not an observation.

C. A ***hypothesis*** is a tentative idea neither known nor assumed to be true. A hypothesis can be an argument's conclusion. Causal explanations are often hypotheses. A passage may discuss ***alternative hypotheses***, such as competing explanations for the same observation. Sometimes a passage gives pros and cons of alternative hypotheses without arguing for any particular hypothesis as a conclusion.

> *Example:*
>
> A bush in our yard just died. The invasive insects we have seen around the yard lately might be the cause. Or the bush might not have gotten enough water. It's been a dry summer.
>
> This example presents two alternative hypotheses. The first hypothesis gives the observation that invasive insects have been in the yard as a possible causal explanation for the bush's observed death. This hypothesis assumes the insects can hurt bushes like the one in the yard. The second hypothesis provides the observation that it's been a dry summer as an alternative causal explanation for the bush's observed death. This hypothesis assumes dry weather can result in bushes getting too little water. The passage presents observations to tentatively support each hypothesis. But it doesn't argue for either hypothesis as a conclusion.

D. A ***plan*** describes an imagined set of actions meant to work together to achieve one or more goals. A plan is not itself an argument. Its actions aren't proposed as reasons to accept a goal, but rather as ways to reach it. A prescriptive argument may recommend or oppose a plan. A plan may also be among an argument's premises.

Just as an argument may have premises, intermediate conclusions, and main conclusions, a plan may suggest actions to reach intermediate goals that, in turn, are meant to help achieve main goals. And like an argument, a plan may have assumptions, including necessary and sufficient assumptions. A necessary assumption of a plan is one that must be true for the plan to achieve its goals. And a sufficient assumption of a plan is one whose truth guarantees the plan would achieve its goals if followed.

A plan is not a causal explanation. The actions a plan suggests haven't been done yet, so they can't have caused anything else to happen. However, any plan does assume possible future causal links between its proposed actions and its goals.

Example:

To repaint our house, we will need to buy gallons of paint. To do that, we could go to the hardware store.

In this plan, going to the hardware store is an action imagined to help reach the intermediate goal of getting gallons of paint. The intermediate goal is imagined to help reach the main goal of repainting the house. This plan isn't itself an argument, but combined with the premise that we *should* repaint the house, the plan could be part of a prescriptive argument that we *should* go to the hardware store.

3. Narratives and Descriptions

A. A *narrative* describes a sequence of related events. A narrative is not an argument, an explanation, or a plan. But it may contain one or more arguments, causal explanations, or plans—or be contained in them.

The words and phrases below often show narrative sequence:

after	*earlier*	*then*
afterwards	*later*	*thereafter*
before	*previously*	*until*
beforehand	*since*	*while*
during	*subsequently*	*when*

Example:

While Julia was hiking fifteen kilometers, she burned a lot of calories. Afterwards, she felt hungry.

This narrative describes a sequence of three events. The word *while* shows Julia's hike and her burning of calories happened at the same time. The word *afterwards* shows that her hunger arose soon after the first two events. Although you can reasonably assume these events were causally linked, the narrative doesn't say they were. So, it's not an explicit causal explanation. And since the narrative doesn't report the events as reasons to accept a particular conclusion, it's not an argument either.

B. Not all passages are arguments, causal explanations, plans, or narratives. Some passages report on views, findings, innovations, places, societies, artistic works, devices, organisms, etc., without arguing for a conclusion, explaining what caused what, suggesting actions to reach a goal, or narrating what happened.

C. Likewise, not all statements in passages are premises, conclusions, observations to be explained, hypotheses, or reports of events. Statements in passages can also:

- Give background information to help the reader understand the rest of the passage
- Describe details of something the passage is discussing
- Express the author's attitude toward material in the passage
- Provide examples to illustrate general statements
- Summarize ideas the passage is arguing against

7.2 Inductive Reasoning

1. Inductive Arguments

A. In an ***inductive argument***, the premises are meant to support a conclusion but not to fully prove it. For example, the premises may just be meant to give evidence that the conclusion is **probably** true, leaving a chance that the conclusion is false despite that evidence.

B. An inductive argument may be ***strengthened*** by adding reasons that directly support the conclusion or reasons that help the argument's premises better support the conclusion. Conversely, an inductive argument may be ***weakened*** by adding reasons that directly cast doubt on the argument's conclusion, or that make the argument's premises less effective at supporting the conclusion. Below, we discuss how various types of inductive arguments are evaluated, strengthened, and weakened.

2. Generalizations and Predictions

A. An argument by ***generalization*** often uses premises about a sample of a population to support a conclusion about the whole population.

> *Example:*
>
> Six of the eight apartments available for lease in this building are studio apartments. So, probably about $\frac{3}{4}$ of all the apartments in the building are studio apartments.
>
> In this example, the apartments available for lease are a ***sample*** of the ***population*** of all apartments in the building. Since six of the eight apartments available for lease are studio apartments, $\frac{3}{4}$ of the apartments in the sample are studio apartments. The argument generalizes from this by assuming the whole population is probably like the sample. It concludes that as in the sample, probably about $\frac{3}{4}$ of the apartments in the population are studio apartments.

B. A ***related*** argument by generalization uses premises about a whole population to support a conclusion about part of that population.

> *Example:*
>
> About $\frac{3}{4}$ of all the apartments in the building are studio apartments. So, probably about $\frac{3}{4}$ of the apartments on the building's second floor are studio apartments.
>
> This example uses a premise about the proportion of studio apartments in the population (all the apartments in the building) to support the conclusion that there's a similar proportion of studio apartments in just a part of the population (the apartments on the second floor).

C. A ***predictive*** argument by generalization uses a premise about the sample observed so far in a population to support a conclusion about another part of the population.

Example:

Of the eight apartments I've visited in this building so far, six have been studio apartments. So, probably about six out of the next eight apartments I visit in the building will also be studio apartments.

In this example, the apartments the author has visited so far are a sample of the total population of apartments in the building. The observation about the proportion of studio apartments in the sample is used to support a prediction that roughly the same proportion of studio apartments will be found in another part of the population—the next eight apartments the author will visit in the building.

D. The strength of an argument by generalization partly depends on how similar the sample is to the overall population, or to the unobserved part of the population a prediction is about. A sample chosen in a way likely to make it relevantly different than that of the population is a ***biased sample***. An argument using a biased sample is flawed.

Example:

In a telephone survey of our city's residents, about four out of every five respondents said they usually answer the phone when it rings. So, about four out of every five residents of our city usually answer the phone when it rings.

In this example, the sample is the respondents to the telephone survey. People who usually answer the phone when it rings are more likely than other people to respond to telephone surveys. Because the sample was selected through a telephone survey, probably a greater proportion of the sample than of all city residents usually answer the phone when it rings. So, the argument is flawed because the sample is biased.

E. The strength of an argument generalizing from a sample also partly depends on the sample's size. The smaller the sample, the weaker the argument. This is because a smaller sample is statistically likely to differ more from the populations' average traits. An argument by generalization that uses too small a sample to justify its conclusion is flawed by ***hasty generalization***.

Example:

A coin came up heads five of the eight times Beth flipped it. This suggests the coin she flipped is weighted to make it come up heads more often than tails.

In this argument, the sample is the eight flips of the coin, and the population is all the potential flips of the same coin. The sample is probably not biased because Beth's flips of the coin are probably no more likely than anyone else's flips of the same coin to come up heads or tails. However, the sample is too small to justify the conclusion that the coin is weighted to favor heads. A fair, unweighted coin flipped eight times usually comes up heads more or fewer than exactly four times—just by chance. So, this argument is flawed by hasty generalization. If Beth and other people flipped the coin thousands or millions of times, and still saw it come up heads in five out of every eight flips, that would strengthen the argument. But no matter how many times the coin was flipped to confirm this pattern, a tiny chance would be left that the coin was not weighted to favor heads and that the results had been purely random.

F. An argument by generalization is weaker when its conclusion is more precise, and stronger when its conclusion is vaguer, given the same premises. That's because a sample usually doesn't precisely match the population it's extracted from. A more precise conclusion allowing a smaller range of potential mismatches between sample and population is less likely to be true, given the same evidence. An argument whose conclusion is too precise for its premises to justify is flawed by the *fallacy of specificity*.

Example:

Biologists carefully caught, weighed, and released fifty frogs out of the hundreds in a local lake. These fifty frogs weighed an average of 32.86 grams apiece. So, the frogs in the lake must also weigh an average of 32.86 grams apiece.

In this example, the sample might be biased because frogs of certain types might have been easier for the biologists to catch. But even if the biologists avoided any sampling bias, the average weight of the fifty sampled frogs probably wouldn't exactly match the average weight of the hundreds of frogs in the lake. The conclusion is too precise, and the argument suffers from the fallacy of specificity. A stronger argument might use the same evidence to conclude less precisely that the frogs in the lake weigh on average between 25 and 40 grams apiece. This less precise conclusion would still be true even if the average weight of the sampled frogs didn't exactly match the average weight of all the frogs in the lake. Since the less precise conclusion is more likely to be true given the same evidence, that evidence justifies it better. That means the argument for the less precise conclusion is stronger.

---

3. Causal Reasoning

A. Causal arguments use premises about correlations or causal links to support conclusions about causes and effects. Causal reasoning is hard because causal links can't be directly observed. And there's no scientific or philosophical consensus about what causality is. But saying that one type of situation causally contributes to another usually implies that after a situation of the first type, situations of the second type are more likely. It also implies that situations of the first type help to reasonably explain situations of the second type.

Example:

Bushes of the species in our yard tend to die after several weeks without water. So, they must need water at least every few weeks to survive.

In this example, the premise is that after situations of one type (bushes of a certain species getting no water for several weeks), situations of another type become more likely (the bushes dying). The conclusion is basically that the first type of situation causes the second: getting no water for several weeks causes bushes of that species to die.

B. A causal argument may use a general correlation to support the conclusion that a situation of one type caused a situation of another type.

> *Example:*
>
> A bush in our yard just died. There's been no rain this summer, and no one has been watering the yard. Bushes of the species in our yard tend to die after several weeks without water. So, probably the bush died because it didn't get enough water.
>
> In this example, the first premise says that a *specific* situation of one type (a bush of a specific species dying) followed a specific situation of another type (the bush going without water for weeks). The final premise says that *in general*, situations of the first type (bushes of that species dying) follow situations of the second type (bushes of that species getting no water for weeks). These premises together support the conclusion that the lack of water caused the bush to die.

C. Causal arguments can be weakened by observations that suggest alternative causal explanations. A way to check which of two competing explanations is stronger is to look at situations that include the possible cause from one explanation but not the possible cause from the other.

> *Example:*
>
> **Explanation 1:** Bushes of this species tend to die after several weeks without water. Maybe the lack of water kills the bushes.
>
> **Explanation 2:** Bushes of this species grow only in a region where long dry spells are always very hot. Maybe the heat alone kills these bushes during weeks without water.
>
> To check which of these two hypothetical explanations is stronger, we can run two experiments. Each experiment creates a situation with one of the two proposed causes but not the other.
>
> **Experiment 1:** Water some of the bushes often during weeks of extreme heat and see how well they survive.
>
> **Experiment 2:** Keep some of the bushes dry in cooler weather and see how well they survive.
>
> Finding that the bushes survive well in Experiment 1 but not in Experiment 2 would support Explanation 1 and cast doubt on Explanation 2.
>
> Finding that the bushes survive well in Experiment 2 but not in Experiment 1 would support Explanation 2 and cast doubt on Explanation 1.
>
> Finding that the bushes always die in both experiments would support both explanations, suggesting either heat or drought alone can kill the bushes.
>
> Finding that the bushes survive well in both experiments would cast doubt on both explanations. It would suggest that something other than drought or heat is killing the bushes—or that drought and heat must occur together to kill the bushes.

D. Experiments to test causal hypotheses shouldn't add or remove possible causal factors other than those tested for.

> *Examples:*
>
> (i) To run Experiment 1 above, a scientist planted some of the bushes in a tropical rainforest where very hot days are usually rainy.
>
> (ii) To run Experiment 2 above, a scientist planted some of the bushes under an awning where rain couldn't reach them in cooler weather.
>
> These versions of the two experiments are problematic because they add other possible causal factors. In example (i), the rainforest's soil type, insects, or humidity might make it harder or easier for the bushes to survive, regardless of the heat and rainfall. In example (ii), putting the bushes under an awning would likely help keep them shaded. That too might make it easier or harder for the bushes to survive, regardless of the heat and rainfall. These experimental design flaws cast doubt on any argument that cites these versions of the experiments as evidence to support Explanation 1 or Explanation 2.

Testing a hypothesis through experiments usually means reasoning by generalization: a conclusion about a whole population is reached by observing a sample in the experiment. Causal arguments based on experiments can have the flaws discussed above in Section 7.2.2, "Generalizations and Predictions." A causal argument is weak if it generalizes from a sample that's too small or chosen in a biased way. In small or biased samples, correlations between factors that aren't causally linked often appear just by chance or because of outside factors.

E. Even when two factors clearly are causally linked, it can be hard to tell which causes which, or whether a third, underlying factor causes them both.

> *Example:*
>
> One type of earthworm is far more often found in soil under healthy bushes of a certain species than in soil under sickly bushes of that same species.
>
> Even if the earthworms' presence is causally linked to the bushes' health, the causal link could be that:
>
> (i) the earthworms improve the bushes' health, or
>
> (ii) healthier bushes attract the earthworms, or
>
> (iii) certain soil conditions both improve the bushes' health and attract the earthworms.
>
> More than one of these causal links, and others, may hold at once. A way to untangle the causal links is to find out:
>
> (i) how healthy the bushes are in the same soil conditions without earthworms;
>
> (ii) how attracted the earthworms are to those soil conditions without the bushes; and
>
> (iii) whether the earthworms tend to appear around healthier bushes even in different soil conditions.

F. Even reliable correlations sometimes arise just by chance. One way to check whether a correlation between two types of situations is just a coincidence is to test whether stopping situations of the first type also stops situations of the other type. Even when no test is possible, you can consider whether there's any plausible way either type of situation could cause the other.

Example:

For years, Juan has arrived at work at a hair salon every weekday at exactly 8 a.m. Five hundred miles to the north, over the same years, Ashley has arrived at work at a car dealership every weekday at exactly 8:01 a.m. So, Juan's daily arrival at his work must make Ashley arrive at her work a minute later.

In this example, even though for years Ashley has always arrived at work a minute after Juan has, the argument is absurdly weak. That's because Juan's arrival at his work has no apparent way to affect when Ashley arrives at her work. But we could still test the hypothesis in the argument's conclusion. For example, we could persuade Juan to vary his arrival times, then see whether Ashley's arrival times change to match. With no plausible link between the two workers' arrival times, we'd need a lot of evidence like this to reasonably overcome the suspicion that the correlation is pure coincidence. However, finding out that Juan and Ashley know each other and have reasons to coordinate their work schedules could give us a plausible causal link between their arrival times. That would greatly strengthen the argument that their arrival times are indeed causally linked.

---

4. Analogies

A. An argument by *analogy* starts by saying two or more things are alike in certain ways. The argument then gives a claim about one of those two things as a reason to accept a similar claim about the other.

Example:

Laotian cuisine and Thai cuisine use many of the same ingredients and cooking techniques. Ahmed enjoys Thai cuisine. So, if he tried Laotian cuisine, he'd probably enjoy it.

This example starts by saying how Laotian cuisine and Thai cuisine are alike: they use similar ingredients and cooking techniques. The argument then makes a claim about Thai cuisine: that Ahmed enjoys it. By analogy, these premises support a similar claim about Laotian cuisine: Ahmed would enjoy it if he tried it.

B. For an argument by analogy to work well, the noted similarities must be *relevant* to whether the two things are also similar in the way the conclusion claims. The argument in the example above meets this standard. A cuisine's ingredients and cooking techniques usually affect how much a specific person would enjoy it. Noting that Laotian cuisine and Thai cuisine have similar ingredients and cooking techniques is relevant to whether Ahmed is likely to similarly enjoy the two cuisines.

An argument by analogy is weaker if its premises only note similarities that are less relevant to its conclusion.

Example:

Laotian cuisine and Latvian cuisine both come from nations whose English names start with the letter **L**. Ahmed enjoys Latvian cuisine. If he tried Laotian cuisine, he'd probably enjoy it.

This example notes that Laotian cuisine and Latvian cuisine are similar with respect to the English names of the nations they're from. Since the spelling of a nation's name almost never affects how much anyone enjoys that nation's cuisine, this similarity is irrelevant to whether Ahmed would similarly enjoy the two cuisines. The analogy is absurd, and the argument is flawed. To save the argument, we'd need a good reason why the noted similarity is relevant after all— for example, evidence that Ahmed is an unusual person whose enjoyment of different cuisines depends on English spellings.

C. A reasonable argument by analogy can be strengthened by noting other relevant similarities between the things compared or weakened by noting relevant dissimilarities.

Example:

Beth and Alan are children living on the same block in the Hazelfern School District. Beth attends Tubman Primary School. Therefore, Alan probably does as well.

Noting that Beth and Alan are both in the same grade would strengthen this moderately reasonable argument because that similarity increases the odds that they attend the same school. However, noting that Beth is eight years older than Alan would weaken the argument because that dissimilarity suggests Alan may be too young to attend the school Beth attends.

7.3 Deductive Reasoning

1. Deductive Arguments

A. The premises of a *deductive argument* are given to fully prove its conclusion. A valid deductive argument with only true premises **must** have a true conclusion. An argument presented as deductive is flawed if its premises can all be true while its conclusion is false. However, a flawed deductive argument might still work well as an inductive argument if the author doesn't wrongly present the premises as **proving** the conclusion.

2. Logical Operators

A. A *logical operator* shows how the truth or falsehood of one or more statements affect the truth or falsehood of a larger statement made from them and the operator. The basic logical operators are *negations*, *logical conjunctions*, *disjunctions*, and *implications*.

B. A statement's *negation* is true just when the statement is false. Words and phrases like *not*, *it is false that*, and *it is not the case that* often mark negation.

Statements are often vague, ambiguous, context-sensitive, or subjective. They may be true in one sense and false in another, they may be only partly true, or their truth may be indefinite. If a statement is only true in one way or to a limited degree, its negation is false in the same way and to the same degree.

> *Example:*
>
> "The cat is on the mat" can have the negation "The cat is not on the mat." Either of these statements is true if the other is false—but only when both are about the same cat and the same mat, in the same sense and the same context. If you make the first statement while the cat is sleeping on the mat, but then the cat wakes up and leaves before you make the second statement, the context has changed. Then your second statement isn't the negation of your first. If the cat is only partly on the mat when both statements are made, then the second statement is ***partly*** false just as much as the first is partly true, and in just the same way.

C. A *logical conjunction* of two statements is true just when both are true. The words and phrases below can mark a logical conjunction of statements *A* and *B*:

A and B	*A even though B*	*not only A but also B*
Although A, B	*A. Furthermore, B.*	*A, whereas B*
A but B	*A, however, B*	

The conjunction markers ***and***, ***furthermore***, and ***not only . . . but also*** usually imply that *A* and *B* are relevant to each other or mentioned for similar reasons—for example, that both are premises supporting the same conclusion. On the other hand, the conjunction markers ***although***, ***but***, ***even though***, ***however***, and ***whereas*** suggest tension between *A* and *B*—for example, that it's surprising *A* and *B* are both true, or that *A* and *B* support conflicting conclusions, or that *A* and *B* differ in some other unexpected way.

> *Examples:*
>
> (i) Raul has worked for this company a long time, and he's searching for another job.
>
> (ii) Although Raul has worked for this company a long time, he's searching for another job.
>
> Both these examples say that Raul has worked for the company a long time, and that he's searching for another job. But in example (ii), ***although*** suggests Raul's search for another job is ***surprising***, given that he's worked for the company a long time. In contrast, the ***and*** in example (i) suggests Raul's search for another job is ***unsurprising*** now that he's worked for the company a long time.

D. A *disjunction* of two statements is true only when one of them is true. The words and phrases *A or B*, *either A or B*, and *A unless B* often mark a disjunction of *A* and *B*.

There are two kinds of disjunction. An ***inclusive disjunction*** of two statements is true when **at least** one of them is true, and **also** when both are. An ***exclusive disjunction*** of two statements is true just when **exactly** one of them is true—**not** when both are. English disjunctions often aren't clearly inclusive or clearly exclusive. But *A or B or both* clearly means inclusive disjunction. And *A or B but not both* clearly means exclusive disjunction.

Examples:

(i) It will either rain or snow tomorrow.

(ii) It will rain tomorrow unless it snows.

These examples both say that at least one of the statements "It will rain tomorrow" and "It will snow tomorrow" is true. But neither example clearly says whether or not it might **both** rain **and** snow tomorrow. To clarify, we can say:

(iii) Tomorrow, it will rain or snow—or both. (***inclusive disjunction***)

or

(iv) Tomorrow, it will either rain or snow, but not both. (***exclusive disjunction***)

E. A ***conditional says*** that for one statement to be true, another must be true. In other words, a conditional means the first statement entails the second. The words and phrases below all mark the same conditional link between statements **A** and **B**:

A would mean that B	*B if A*	*A only if B*
If A, then B	*Not A unless B*	*B provided that A*

Conditionals of these forms do not mean that **A** is true, nor that **B** is. They do not give **A** as a reason to accept **B**. So, in a conditional, **A** isn't a premise and **B** isn't a conclusion. That is, a conditional is not an argument. However, the conditional ***if A then B*** does mean that correctly assuming **A** as a premise lets you correctly reach **B** as a conclusion.

Examples:

(i) It will snow tonight only if the temperature falls below 5 degrees Celsius.

(ii) It won't snow tonight unless the temperature falls below 5 degrees Celsius.

(iii) If it snows tonight, it'll mean the temperature has fallen below 5 degrees Celsius.

These three conditionals all mean the same thing. Each says that snow tonight would require temperatures below 5 degrees Celsius. They do not say that it **will** snow tonight, nor that temperatures **will** be below 5 degrees Celsius. They do suggest, for example, that seeing it snow tonight would tell you the temperature must be below 5 degrees Celsius.

Although conditionals often make or suggest causal claims, their meaning isn't always causal. The examples above do not mean that snow tonight would ***cause*** the temperature to fall below 5 degrees Celsius.

None of these examples imply that it ***must*** snow if the temperature falls below 5 degrees Celsius tonight. A conditional ***if A, then B*** does not imply that ***if B, then A***.

F. Two *logically equivalent* statements *A and B* are always both true or both false under the same conditions. Each implies the other. That is, *if A then B*, and *if B then A*. These two conditionals can be combined as *A if and only if B*.

3. Reasoning with Logical Operators

A. Here's a list of some types of logically equivalent statements made with logical operators. In this list, *not* means negation, *and* means logical conjunction, *or* means inclusive disjunction, and *if . . . then* means conditional implication.

Logical Equivalences with Logical Operators		
A and B	is logically equivalent to	*B and A*
not (A and B)	is logically equivalent to	*not-A or not-B*
A or B	is logically equivalent to	*B or A*
not (A or B)	is logically equivalent to	*not-A and not-B* (in other words, neither *A* nor *B*)
if A then B	is logically equivalent to	*if not-B then not-A*
if A then (B and C)	is logically equivalent to	*(if A then B) and (if A then C)*
if A then (B or C)	is logically equivalent to	*(if A then B) or (if A then C)*
if (A or B) then C	is logically equivalent to	*(if A then C) and (if B then C)*

B. Of any two logically equivalent statements, either can be a premise supporting the other as a conclusion in a valid argument. For any line in the list above, a valid argument has a premise of the form on one side and a logically equivalent conclusion of the form on the other side.

Examples:

The second line in the list above says that for any statements *A* and *B*, the statement *not (A and B)* is logically equivalent to *not-A or not-B*. This gives us two valid arguments:

(i) *not (A and B), therefore not-A or not-B*

and

(ii) *not-A or not-B, therefore not (A and B)*

For example, the statement *Ashley and Tim don't both live in this neighborhood* is logically equivalent to *Either Ashley doesn't live in this neighborhood or Tim doesn't*. This lets us make two valid arguments:

(iii) Ashley and Tim don't both live in this neighborhood. Therefore, either Ashley doesn't live in this neighborhood or Tim doesn't.

and

(iv) Either Ashley doesn't live in this neighborhood or Tim doesn't. Therefore, Ashley and Tim don't both live in this neighborhood.

C. Here's a list of some other valid argument forms with logical operators, and of invalid forms often confused with them.

Valid and Invalid Inferences with Logical Operators	
Valid: *A and B, therefore A*	**Invalid:** *A, therefore A and B*
Valid: *A, therefore A or B*	**Invalid:** *A or B, therefore A*
Valid: *not-A and not-B, therefore not (A and B)*	**Invalid:** *not (A and B), therefore not-A and not-B*
Valid: *not (A or B), therefore not-A or not-B*	**Invalid:** *not-A or not-B, therefore not (A or B)*
Valid: *if A, then B; and A; therefore B*	**Invalid:** *if A, then B; and B; therefore A*
Valid: *if A, then B; and not-B; therefore not-A*	**Invalid:** *if A, then B; and not-A; therefore not-B*

Examples:

The third line in the table above says that ***not-A and not-B, therefore not (A and B)*** is valid, but ***not (A and B), therefore not-A and not-B*** is invalid. A simple example of a **valid** argument is:

(i) Ashley doesn't live in this neighborhood, and Tim doesn't either. Therefore, Ashley and Tim don't both live in this neighborhood.

Swapping argument (i)'s premise with its conclusion makes this **invalid** argument:

(ii) Ashley and Tim don't both live in this neighborhood. Therefore, Ashley doesn't live in this neighborhood and Tim doesn't either.

As another example, the table's fifth line says that ***if A, then B; and A; therefore B*** is valid, but ***if A, then B; and B; therefore, A*** is invalid. Another **valid** argument is:

(iii) If Ashley lives in this neighborhood, so does Tim. Ashley does live in this neighborhood. Therefore, Tim also lives in this neighborhood.

However, swapping argument (iii)'s second premise with its conclusion makes this **invalid** argument:

(iv) If Ashley lives in this neighborhood, so does Tim. Tim does live in this neighborhood. Therefore, Ashley lives in this neighborhood.

4. Necessity, Probability, and Possibility

A. Some words and phrases mark how likely a statement is to be true. For example, they may mean that:

- The statement is ***necessarily*** true; that is, there's a 100 percent chance the statement is true; or

- The statement is ***probably*** true; that is, there's a good chance the statement is true;

- The statement is ***possibly*** true; that is, the odds are greater than 0 percent that the statement is true.

Saying a claim is possibly true or probably true usually implies it's not necessarily true.

B. The table below shows three categories of words and phrases that can stand for degrees of probability:

Words Standing for Necessity, Probability, and Possibility		
Necessity	*Probability*	*Possibility*
certainly	*probably*	*can*
clearly	*likely*	*could*
definitely	*more likely than not*	*may*
must		*maybe*
necessarily		*might*
surely		*perhaps*
		possibly

The words *probably* and *likely* sometimes mean high probability, like a 95 percent chance. Other times they mean a medium chance, even one below 50 percent. Don't give these terms any exact meanings when you find them on the GMAT exam.

C. The table below lists some valid argument forms with necessity, probability, and possibility, as well as invalid forms often confused with them.

Valid and Invalid Inferences with Necessity, Probability, and Possibility	
Valid: *Probably A, therefore possibly A*	**Invalid:** *Possibly A, therefore probably A*
Valid: *Possibly (A and B), therefore possibly A and possibly B*	**Invalid:** *Possibly A and possibly B, therefore possibly (A and B)*
Valid: *Probably (A and B), therefore probably A and probably B*	**Invalid:** *Probably A and probably B, therefore probably (A and B)*
Valid: *Probably A or probably B, therefore probably (A or B)*	**Invalid:** *Probably (A or B), therefore probably A or probably B*
Valid: *Necessarily A or necessarily B, therefore necessarily (A or B)*	**Invalid:** *Necessarily (A or B), therefore necessarily A or necessarily B*

Examples:

The table's second line says that *possibly (A and B), therefore possibly A and possibly B* is valid, while *possibly A and possibly B, therefore possibly (A and B)* is invalid. A simple **valid** argument is:

(i) Possibly Tim and Ashley both live in this house. So, possibly Tim lives in this house, and possibly Ashley does.

Swapping argument (i)'s premise with its conclusion gives us this **invalid** argument:

(ii) Possibly Tim lives in this house, and possibly Ashley does. So, possibly both Tim and Ashley live in this house.

To see that argument (ii) is invalid, suppose you know only one person lives in the house, but you don't know whether that person is Tim, Ashley, or someone else. Then argument (ii)'s premise would be true, but its conclusion would be false.

5. Quantifiers

A. A *quantifier* is a word or phrase for a proportion, number, or amount. Some basic quantifiers are *all*, *most*, *some*, and *none*.

    i. A quantifier like *all* means 100 percent of the individuals in a category, or the whole of an amount.

    ii. A quantifier like *most* usually means more than half the individuals in a category, or more than half of a whole. *Most* usually implies *not all*, but not always. Writing *most but not all*, or else *most or all*, can clarify the meaning.

    iii. A quantifier like *some* often means one or more individuals in a category, or part of a whole. *Some* usually but not always implies *not all*. However, *only some* clearly does imply *not all*, while *at least some* clearly doesn't. *Some* with a plural usually means *more than one*. In contrast, *some* with a singular usually means *exactly one*. For example, "some dogs" usually means "more than one dog," while "some dog" usually means "exactly one dog." But "some dog or dogs" means "at least one dog."

    iv. A quantifier like *no* or *none of* means something is being denied about all the individuals in a category, or about all of some whole.

    v. Other common quantifiers have more nuanced meanings. For example, *a few* vaguely means a small number more than two. The upper limit of what counts as *a few* depends on context. For example, *a few Europeans* might mean thousands of people (still a tiny part of Europe's population). But *a few residents in our building* might mean only three or four people if the building has only fifteen residents.

B. The table below classifies some quantifier words by their meanings.

"All" and similar quantifier words	**"Most" and similar quantifier words**	**"Some" and similar quantifier words**	**"No" and similar quantifier words**
all	*generally*	*a number*	*never*
always	*a majority*	*a portion*	*no*
any	*most*	*any*	*none*
both	*more than half*	*at least one*	*not any*
each	*usually*	*occasionally*	*not one*
every		*one or more*	*nowhere*
everywhere		*some*	
whenever		*sometimes*	
wherever		*somewhere*	

Notice the table shows *any* both as a quantifier like *all* and as a quantifier like *some*. That's because *any* can have either meaning. For example, *Any of the students would prefer chocolate ice cream* means *Each of the students would prefer chocolate ice cream*. However, *I don't know if any of the students would prefer chocolate ice cream* means *I don't know if even one of the students would prefer chocolate ice cream*.

C. A quantifier used with a category usually implies the category isn't empty. This doesn't always hold in hypothetical statements, in conditionals, or with the quantifier *any*.

Examples:

(i) All life forms native to planets other than Earth are carbon-based.

(ii) Any life forms native to planets other than Earth would be carbon-based.

In (i), the words *all* and *are* show the author is claiming there really are life forms native to planets other than Earth. However, in (ii), the words *any* and *would be* show the author is carefully avoiding that claim.

D. Statements with two or more quantifiers sometimes look alike but differ in meaning because of word order and phrasing.

Example:

(i) Some beverage must be the favorite of every student in the class.

(ii) Each student in the class must have some favorite beverage.

Statement (i) suggests that every student in the class must have ***the same*** favorite beverage. In contrast, statement (ii) can be true even if each student has a ***different*** favorite beverage.

6. Reasoning with Quantifiers

A. Here's a list of some logically equivalent statement forms with quantifiers. In this list, *some* means *one or more*. The forms in the list use plurals, but similar equivalences can hold without plurals. For example, *No water is fire* is logically equivalent to *No fire is water*, even though those two statements don't have plurals like the forms in the list do.

Logical Equivalences with Quantifiers		
All As are Bs	is logically equivalent to	*No As are not Bs.*
Some As are Bs	is logically equivalent to	*Some Bs are As.*
No As are Bs	is logically equivalent to	*No Bs are As.*
Some As are not Bs	is logically equivalent to	*Not all As are Bs.*

However, ***All As are Bs*** is **not** equivalent to ***All Bs are As***. ***Some As are not Bs*** is **not** equivalent to ***Some Bs are not As***.

Examples:

(i) The true statement, ***All ostriches are birds***, is not equivalent to the false statement, ***All birds are ostriches***.

(ii) The true statement, ***Some birds are not ostriches***, is not equivalent to the false statement, ***Some ostriches are not birds***.

B. As explained above, either of two logically equivalent statements can be a premise supporting the other as a conclusion in a valid argument. This works for equivalences with quantifiers just like it does for equivalences with logical operators.

C. A *syllogism* is a type of simple argument whose two premises have one quantifier apiece, and whose conclusion also has one quantifier.

Here's a list of some valid syllogism forms along with invalid forms that they are sometimes confused with. As above, in this list, **some** means **one or more**.

Valid and Invalid Syllogisms
Valid: *All As are Bs. All Bs are Cs. So, all As are Cs.*
Invalid: *All As are Bs. All Bs are Cs. So, all Cs are As.*
Invalid: *All As are Bs. All Cs are Bs. So, all As are Cs.*
Invalid: *All Bs are As. All Bs are Cs. So, all As are Cs.*
Valid: *Some As are Bs. All Bs are Cs. So, some As are Cs.*
Invalid: *All As are Bs. Some Bs are Cs. So, some As are Cs.*
Invalid: *Some As are Bs. Some Bs are Cs. So, some As are Cs.*
Valid: *All As are Bs. No Bs are Cs. So, no As are Cs.*
Invalid: *No As are Bs. All Bs are Cs. So, no As are Cs.*
Invalid: *No As are Bs. No Bs are Cs. So, all As are Cs.*
Invalid: *No As are Bs. All Bs are Cs. So, some As are not Cs.*

Examples:

The list's first line says that **All As are Bs. All Bs are Cs. So, all As are Cs** is valid. And here's a **valid** syllogism of that form:

(i) All the trees in the local park were planted by the town arborist. All the trees the arborist planted have been labeled by her. So, all the trees in the park must have been labeled by the arborist.

A similar looking but **invalid** syllogism has the form **All As are Bs. All Bs are Cs. So, all Cs are As** from the list's second line:

(ii) All the trees in the local park were planted by the town arborist. All the trees the arborist planted have been labeled by her. So, all the trees the arborist has labeled must be in the park.

To see that argument (ii) is invalid, notice that even if both premises are true, the arborist might also have labeled trees outside the park—maybe even trees she didn't plant.

Another **invalid** syllogism has the form **All As are Bs. All Cs are Bs. So, all As are Cs** from the list's third line:

(iii) All the trees in the local park were planted by the town arborist. All the trees the arborist has labeled are trees she planted. So, all the trees in the park must have been labeled by the arborist.

To see that argument (iii) is invalid, notice that even if both premises are true, the arborist might not have labeled every tree she planted, nor even every tree she planted in the park.

The form in the list's fourth line (**All Bs are As. All Bs are Cs. So, all As are Cs**) gives us yet another **invalid** syllogism:

(iv) All the trees the town arborist has planted are in the local park. All the trees the arborist planted have been labeled by her. So, all the trees in the park must have been labeled by the arborist.

To see that argument (iv) is invalid, notice that even if both premises are true, the park might have many trees that the arborist neither planted nor labeled.

D. Some quantifier words in the table "Basic Quantifier Words" in Section 7.3.5.B above refer to time or place. For example, *whenever* means *every time*, *usually* means *most times*, and *never* means *at no time*. Understanding these meanings can help you rewrite arguments using these words into standard syllogisms to check their validity.

Example:

Max never goes running when the sidewalks are icy. The sidewalks are usually icy on January mornings, so Max does not go running on most January mornings.

We can rewrite this argument in the valid syllogism form *No As are Bs. Most Cs are Bs. So, most Cs are not As*:

No occasions when Max goes running are occasions when the sidewalks are icy. Most January mornings are occasions when the sidewalks are icy. So, most January mornings are not occasions when Max goes running.

Since arguments in this syllogism form are valid, we can tell that the argument in this example is valid.

To register for the GMAT™ exam go to www.mba.com/register

8.0 Verbal Reasoning

8.0 Verbal Reasoning

The Verbal Reasoning section of the GMAT™ exam uses multiple-choice questions to measure your skill in reasoning, understanding what you read, and evaluating arguments. This section has passages about many topics, but it doesn't assume you already know about the topics. Mingled throughout the section are questions of two main types of questions: Reading Comprehension and Critical Reasoning.

Reading Comprehension questions are based on passages of around 200 to 350 words. With each passage are several questions asking you to understand, analyze, apply, and evaluate that passage's information and concepts. On the left side of your screen, the passage stays visible as you answer the questions about it. On the right side of your screen, one question appears at a time, along with its answer choices. Different passages may have different numbers of questions.

Critical Reasoning questions are based on passages usually of fewer than 100 words. Unlike Reading Comprehension passages, each Critical Reasoning passage has just one question. This question asks you to logically analyze, evaluate, or reason about an argument, situation, or plan the passage presents. Only one passage and its single question appear at a time.

You have 45 minutes to answer the 23 questions in the Verbal Reasoning section, an average of just under two minutes per question.

To prepare for the Verbal Reasoning section, first review basic concepts of text analysis and logical reasoning to make sure you know enough to answer the questions. Refer to Chapter 7, "Verbal Review," which briefly covers these concepts. After reviewing, practice on questions from past GMAT exams.

8.1 What Is Measured

The Verbal Reasoning section measures how well you understand, analyze, apply, evaluate, and reason about information and ideas in texts. Specifically, it tests the following skills:

Skill Category	Details	Examples
Recognize stated ideas	Understand, restate, and summarize information	• Find a passage's overall theme or point • Find a specific detail • Summarize a set of statements • Tell if an idea is stated or implied • Tell what a word or phrase means in context
Analyze reasoning structure	Identify premises, conclusions, explanations, argument techniques, reasons for plans, and background information	• Tell what argument technique someone uses • Tell a statement's role in a passage
Apply ideas in new contexts	Use general ideas in new situations the passage doesn't discuss	• Decide which new situation is most like one in the passage • Tell which new action would follow or break a rule in the passage • Decide which new example would best illustrate an idea in the passage

Skill Category	Details	Examples
Infer	Draw an unstated conclusion from information given	• Decide which conclusion a passage most strongly supports • Tell what follows logically from information given • Decide what a stated opinion implies • Recognize an author's attitude from word choices in a passage
Identify unstated assumptions	Find an assumption that fills a logical gap in an argument, explanation, or plan	• Find an assumption an argument depends on • Find an assumption that makes an argument's conclusion follow logically • Tell what must happen for a plan to succeed
Evaluate hypotheses	Judge explanations for a situation	• Decide what would most help explain why a plan failed • Decide what most likely caused an observed effect
Resolve discrepancies	Explain or justify an apparent conflict between two statements or situations	• Explain why a factor didn't cause its usual effect • Decide which principle resolves a conflict between two opinions
Strengthen or weaken reasoning	Identify new information that either supports or undermines an argument, explanation, or claim	• Tell which discovery would cast the most doubt on an argument's reasoning • Tell what added evidence would best support a causal explanation
Identify reasoning flaws	Identify mistakes such as confusing correlation with causation or confusing a sufficient assumption with a necessary one	• Decide which observation points to a reasoning flaw • Tell which criticism an argument is most vulnerable to
Identify points of disagreement	Tell what two parties disagree about, based on their statements	• Find the main implied point of disagreement in a dialogue between two people
Solve a practical problem	Recognize a good strategy for solving a problem	• Find a way of sampling a population accurately despite an obstacle

8.2 Question Types

Reading Comprehension and Critical Reasoning are the two main Verbal Reasoning question types. Each has several subtypes. During the test, the subtypes aren't labeled. Each question tells you what you need to do.

1. Reading Comprehension

The five Reading Comprehension question subtypes are Main Idea, Supporting Idea, Inference, Application, and Evaluation. Each tests a different main skill, but sometimes the skills overlap. For example, to find a passage's main idea, you must understand the passage's logical and rhetorical structure. To make inferences or apply ideas from a passage, you often must find its main and supporting ideas.

Below, we discuss the Reading Comprehension question subtypes.

A. Main Idea

- In each passage, the individual sentences and paragraphs develop one central point and share one overall purpose. A Main Idea question asks you to find this central point or purpose. Sometimes the passage tells you its central point. Other times you must infer it from the passage's overall structure and content.

- A Main Idea question may ask which answer option best restates the central point, best explains the author's main goal in writing the passage, or works best as a title for the passage.

- Main Idea questions use phrases like these:

  . . . most accurately expresses the main idea . . . ,

  The primary purpose of the passage as a whole is to . . . , or

  In the passage, the author seeks primarily to . . . .

- The right answer to a Main Idea question about an argumentative passage often restates or describes the main conclusion of the main argument. To find the main conclusion, you must find which statements in the passage are given as reasons to accept which other statements. The main conclusion is an idea that the whole passage gives reasons to accept, but that isn't in turn given as a reason to accept some further conclusion.

- When the passage isn't argumentative, the right answer to a Main Idea question usually says the passage's overall theme or purpose. The overall theme is often an idea repeated in different paragraphs. The overall purpose is usually a goal toward which all the paragraphs work. If the passage has no overall theme or purpose, the right answer may just summarize the passage. For example, the right answer to a Main Idea question about a narrative passage might summarize the events described or state their overall outcome.

- Wrong answer choices often repeat passage details that aren't the main point, make claims that look like the main point but are different, or state ideas not mentioned in the passage but related to it.

B. Supporting Idea

- Supporting Idea questions may ask you about anything the passage states except for the main point. To answer a Supporting Idea question, you must understand individual statements and their roles in the passage.

- Answers to Supporting Idea questions almost never directly quote the passage. They usually rephrase statements from the passage or describe them abstractly. A Supporting Idea question may ask which statement plays a specific role in the passage. For example, it may ask you to find a premise, an intermediate conclusion, a described viewpoint, an objection, an example or counterexample, a causal claim, background information, descriptive detail, or part of an explanation or narrative. It may also ask what a word or phrase means in the context of the passage.

- Supporting Idea questions often use phrases like these:

    According to the passage . . . ,

    Which of the following does the author cite as . . . ,

    Which of the following does the author offer as an objection to . . . ,

    The passage compares . . . ,

    The passage mentions . . . , or

    Which of the following does the author propose . . . .

C. Inference

- Inference questions ask about ideas the passage suggests or supports but doesn't state. Some of these questions ask about ideas the author clearly meant the passage to imply. Others ask about logical implications, which the author may not have noticed.

- An Inference question may ask you to find:

    a likely cause or effect of a situation the passage describes,

    a specific implication of a generalization in the passage, or

    a statement that someone discussed in the passage would likely accept or reject.

- Sometimes the inference follows from one small part of the passage. Other times it depends on several statements scattered through different paragraphs. Sometimes the question says where to look in the passage, but not always.

- Inference questions often use phrases like these:

    Which of the following statements about . . . is most strongly supported by . . . ,

    It can be inferred from the passage that . . . ,

    If the claims about . . . are true, which of the following is most likely also true?

    The passage implies that . . . , or

    The information in the passage suggests that . . . .

- Wrong answer choices may be true, and related to the passage, but not supported by it. Conversely, the right answer choice may be false but follow logically from false statements in the passage. For example, even if the passage rightly says a theory is mistaken, a question might ask what would follow if the theory were true.

D. Application

- Application questions ask how situations or ideas the passage discusses relate to other situations or ideas the passage doesn't mention.

- Application questions may use words like *would, could, might,* or *should,* or phrases like *most clearly exemplifies, most similar to,* or *most likely ruled out by.*

- Some Application questions ask you to reason by analogy. They may ask which of several roles, methods, goals, or relationships is most like one the passage mentions. Refer to Section 7.2.4, "Analogies," which explains reasoning by analogy.

- Other Application questions ask you to apply general rules. For example, they may ask:

    which rule's enforcement would help achieve a goal the passage mentions, which principle a judgment in the passage relies on,

which action would break or follow a rule the passage states,

which generalization the evidence in the passage best fits, or

which general strategy could solve a problem the passage describes.

- The third type of Application question asks you to extend the discussion in the passage. Questions of this type may ask for:

the best topic for a new paragraph added to the end of the passage,

a good example of a point the author makes, or

the author's most likely response to a possible objection.

- The fourth type of Application question asks about "what-if" scenarios. These questions may ask:

how different experimental results might affect a researcher's conclusions,

how a trend the passage mentions might be disrupted, or

how events might have gone differently if a situation had never occurred.

- Don't rule out answer choices just because they're not about the passage. Because Application questions relate the passage to topics outside its scope, the right answers are often about topics the passage never mentions. For instance, the right answer to an analogy question about the passage's explanation of a water-treatment process might be about book publishing.

E. Evaluation

- Evaluation questions ask you to assess the passage's organization and logic.

- They often use phrases like these:

The purpose of . . . ,

. . . most accurately describes the structure of . . . ,

. . . most strengthens . . . ,

. . . would most justify . . . ,

. . . is most vulnerable to the objection that . . . , or

Which . . . additional information would most help. . . .

- An Evaluation question's answer choices are often abstract. They may not use specific words or ideas from the passage. For example, a question about a paragraph's function might have this answer choice: *It rejects a theory presented in the preceding paragraph and offers some criteria that an alternative theory would need to meet.*

- Some Evaluation questions ask about the roles of different parts of the passage. They may ask:

how the whole passage or part of it is structured,

why the author put a specific detail in the passage,

what purpose a statement in the passage serves,

how the author tries to persuade readers to accept a claim, or

what attitude most likely motivated an opinion the passage mentions.

- Other Evaluation questions ask about:

  the strengths, weaknesses, relevance, or effectiveness of parts of the passage,

  implicit assumptions in the passage,

  what would best resolve apparent conflicts between parts of the passage, or

  potential objections, justifications, supporting evidence, or counterexamples. These questions are often similar to Critical Reasoning questions, discussed below.

2. Critical Reasoning

The four subtypes of Critical Reasoning question are Analysis, Construction, Critique, and Plan. We discuss each below.

A. Analysis

- Analysis questions ask about a passage's logical structure and the roles that statements play in it.

- Analysis questions often use phrases like these:

  . . . the two portions in boldface play which of the following roles?

  The argument proceeds by . . .

  A technique used in the argument is to . . .

  . . . responds to . . . by . . .

  The statements above can best serve as part of an argument against . . .

  Which of the following is the main point of disagreement between . . .

- Some Analysis questions ask about the logical or rhetorical roles of one or two statements in the passage. Often the passage shows these statements in boldface.

- Other Analysis questions ask about an argumentative method in the passage. Sometimes the passage itself is an argument, and the question asks how it works. Other times, the passage is a dialogue, and the question asks what argumentative technique one speaker uses in replying to the other.

- Another type of Analysis question asks about an unstated point in the passage. This point may be a conclusion the passage is clearly meant to support. It may also be a point of agreement or disagreement between the two speakers in a dialogue.

B. Construction

- Construction questions ask how to best complete partial arguments or explanations.

- Construction questions often use phrases like these:

  . . . most logically completes . . .

  If the statements above are true . . .

  . . . most strongly support . . .

  . . . best explains the discrepancy . . .

  . . . depends on the assumption that . . .

  . . . enables the conclusion to be properly drawn?

  . . . provides the strongest justification for . . .

- Some Construction questions ask what conclusion a set of premises best supports. These questions may ask for a conclusion that logically follows from the premises, or for a conclusion that the premises merely give evidence for.

- Other Construction questions ask for a missing premise to support a given conclusion. A question like this usually says whether the premise must be a necessary assumption, a sufficient assumption, a relevant observation, or a justification for a position. The passage may state only the conclusion, or it may also give other premises to combine with the missing premise.

- Another type of Construction question asks what would best explain either an observation or a puzzling discrepancy between observations.

C. Critique

- Critique questions ask you to judge reasoning in passages, find its strengths or weaknesses, and decide how it could be improved.

- Critique questions often use phrases like these:

  . . . most vulnerable to the criticism that . . .

  . . . logically flawed in that . . .

  . . . most seriously weakens . . .

  . . . casts the most serious doubt on . . .

  . . . most strengthens . . .

  . . . most strongly supports . . .

  . . . would be most useful to know in order to evaluate . . .

- Some Critique questions ask how an argument is logically flawed or unacceptably weak. These questions are often about arguments with standard reasoning flaws, like the flaws discussed in Sections 7.2, "Inductive Reasoning," and 7.3, "Deductive Reasoning." In other cases, the arguments have no standard flaw but don't work because they rely on some obviously implausible assumption.

- Other Critique questions ask what new evidence would most strengthen or weaken an argument. The arguments in these cases are always inductive because evidence can't strengthen or weaken a deductive argument. Section 7.2, "Inductive Reasoning," explains what kinds of evidence can strengthen and weaken arguments.

- Finally, some Critique questions ask you what would be most helpful to know in order to assess a hypothesis or inductive argument in the passage. The answer choices for these questions start with the word *Whether*, followed by an idea whose truth is unknown. The right answer choice gives the idea whose truth or falsehood would be most helpful to know in order to decide whether the hypothesis in the passage is true. The wrong answer choices give ideas that, whether true or false, are less relevant to the hypothesis.

D. Plan

- Plan questions ask you to construct or judge reasoning about proposed courses of action, or plans. Section 7.1.2.D briefly explains reasoning about plans.

- Plan questions use many of the same phrases found in Construction and Critique questions, but the questions are always about plans, strategies, or courses of action.

- Plan questions may ask:

  what must be true for a plan to succeed,

what conditions would make a plan more or less likely to succeed,

what would be most helpful to know in order to judge a plan,

what evidence would best support someone's opinion about a plan,

how a plan is flawed,

what strategy would most help overcome a problem,

what policy would most help reach a goal under certain conditions, or

why a plan succeeded, failed, or had some unexpected effect.

8.3 Tips for Answering Verbal Reasoning Questions

1. Answer using only the information given and common knowledge.

The passages and common knowledge tell you everything you need to answer correctly. If you already know about the passage topic, don't use that knowledge to answer. Answer based on what the passage states or implies, and on common knowledge. For example, if the passage says something happened during a snowstorm, you can use common knowledge about snowstorms to infer that the weather wasn't hot.

2. Look for cue words marking statements' roles.

Section 7.1, "Analyzing Passages," explains how certain cue words often mark premises, conclusions, causal explanations, and narrative sequences. These cue words often tell you what roles statements near them play. Also notice transition words marking where the passage moves from one topic to another, and how they suggest those topics are related. Often you can tell a statement's role even without a cue word. For example, if the passage clearly gives one statement as a reason to accept another, you don't need cue words to tell that the first statement is a premise and the second a conclusion.

3. Analyze the passage's structure and purpose.

Once you know the roles individual statements play, you can find the passage's overall structure and purpose. Does the passage mainly report facts and events? Does it argue for a conclusion? Does it discuss competing causal explanations? Does it comment on situations or other writers' views? Notice which premises are given to support which conclusions, and which causes are said to produce which effects. Notice also if the passage uses intermediate conclusions to support a main conclusion. Finally, notice any clear but unstated implications of the passage.

4. Use basic principles of good reasoning to judge the passage's reasoning.

Section 7.2, "Inductive Reasoning," and 7.3, "Deductive Reasoning," review some principles of good reasoning. When a question asks you to judge the reasoning in the passage, use these basic principles. You don't need advanced knowledge of logic or any other subject to answer correctly.

5. **Notice exactly what the question asks.**

Often the wrong answer to one question would be the right answer to another question that looks similar. You need to pick the right answer that specifically answers the question asked. That means you must focus on the question. For example, if the question asks about a specific part of the passage, don't pick an answer choice about some other part of the passage. As another example, these two questions could easily be confused:

i) Which of the following crops is grown by *the most farms* in Nation X?

ii) Farms in Nation X grow *the most of* which of the following crops?

The nation's farms may grow the most of a crop that's not the one grown by the most farms. If many small farms grow potatoes while a few huge farms grow wheat, the right answer to (i) could be *potatoes* even if the right answer to (ii) is *wheat*.

6. **Read all the answer choices before picking one.**

Verbal Reasoning questions often ask you to pick the best answer choice of those given. To tell which answer choice is best, you must read them all.

7. **If you're not sure which answer choice is right, try ruling out some that are clearly wrong.**

Ruling out some clearly wrong answer choices can help you find the right answer choice. If you're still undecided between two answer choices, study the passage again for clues you may have missed.

8. **Pace yourself.**

You have less than two minutes per question. You need to spend much of that time reading the passages. To avoid running out of time, don't spend too long on any one question. If you get stuck on a question for a couple of minutes after ruling out some of the answer choices, just pick the remaining choice that seems best. Then go to the next question.

8.4 Section Instructions

Go to www.mba.com/tutorial to read instructions for the section and get a feel for what the test center screens look like on the actual GMAT exam.

To register for the GMAT™ exam go to www.mba.com/register

8.5 Practice Questions: Reading Comprehension

Each of the Reading Comprehension questions is based on the content of a passage. After reading the passage answer all questions pertaining to it on the basis of what is stated or implied in the passage. For each question, select the best answer of the choices given. On the actual GMAT exam, you will see no more than four questions per passage.

Questions 333–377 - Difficulty: Easy

Questions 333–335 refer to the passage.

Line   Scientists long believed that two nerve clusters in the human hypothalamus, called suprachiasmatic nuclei (SCNs), were what controlled our circadian rhythms. Those rhythms are the biological cycles
(5)   that recur approximately every 24 hours in synchronization with the cycle of sunlight and darkness caused by Earth's rotation. Studies have demonstrated that in some animals, the SCNs control daily fluctuations in blood pressure, body
(10)   temperature, activity level, and alertness, as well as the nighttime release of the sleep-promoting agent melatonin. Furthermore, cells in the human retina dedicated to transmitting information about light levels to the SCNs have recently been discovered.
(15)   Four critical genes governing circadian cycles have been found to be active in every tissue, however, not just the SCNs, of flies, mice, and humans. In addition, when laboratory rats that usually ate at will were fed only once a day, peak
(20)   activity of a clock gene in their livers shifted by 12 hours, whereas the same clock gene in the SCNs remained synchronized with light cycles. While scientists do not dispute the role of the SCNs in controlling core functions such as the regulation of
(25)   body temperature and blood pressure, scientists now believe that circadian clocks in other organs and tissues may respond to external cues other than light—including temperature changes—that recur regularly every 24 hours.

333. The primary purpose of the passage is to

(A)   challenge recent findings that appear to contradict earlier findings

(B)   present two sides of an ongoing scientific debate

(C)   report answers to several questions that have long puzzled researchers

(D)   discuss evidence that has caused a long-standing belief to be revised

(E)   attempt to explain a commonly misunderstood biological phenomenon

334. The passage mentions each of the following as a function regulated by the SCNs in some animals EXCEPT

(A)   activity level

(B)   blood pressure

(C)   alertness

(D)   vision

(E)   temperature

335. The author of the passage would probably agree with which of the following statements about the SCNs?

    (A) The SCNs are found in other organs and tissues of the body besides the hypothalamus.

    (B) The SCNs play a critical but not exclusive role in regulating circadian rhythms.

    (C) The SCNs control clock genes in a number of tissues and organs throughout the body.

    (D) The SCNs are a less significant factor in regulating blood pressure than scientists once believed.

    (E) The SCNs are less strongly affected by changes in light levels than they are by other external cues.

Line   In their study of whether offering a guarantee of service quality will encourage customers to visit a particular restaurant, Tucci and Talaga have found that the effect of such guarantees is mixed. For
(5)   higher-priced restaurants, there is some evidence that offering a guarantee increases the likelihood of customer selection, probably reflecting the greater financial commitment involved in choosing an expensive restaurant. For lower-priced restaurants,
(10)   where one expects less assiduous service, Tucci and Talaga found that a guarantee could actually have a negative effect: a potential customer might think that a restaurant offering a guarantee is worried about its service. Moreover, since customers understand a
(15)   restaurant's product and know what to anticipate in terms of service, they are empowered to question its quality. This is not generally true in the case of skilled activities such as electrical work, where, consequently, a guarantee might have greater customer appeal.
(20)   For restaurants generally, the main benefit of a service guarantee probably lies not so much in customer appeal as in managing and motivating staff. Staff members would know what service standards are expected of them and also know that the success
(25)   of the business relies on their adhering to those standards. Additionally, guarantees provide some basis for defining the skills needed for successful service in areas traditionally regarded as unskilled, such as waiting tables.

336. The primary purpose of the passage is to

(A)   question the results of a study that examined the effect of service-quality guarantees in the restaurant industry

(B)   discuss potential advantages and disadvantages of service-quality guarantees in the restaurant industry

(C)   examine the conventional wisdom regarding the effect of service-quality guarantees in the restaurant industry

(D)   argue that only certain restaurants would benefit from the implementation of service-quality guarantees

(E)   consider the impact that service-quality guarantees can have on the service provided by a restaurant

337. It can be inferred that the author of the passage would agree with which of the following statements about the appeal of service guarantees to customers?

(A)   Such guarantees are likely to be somewhat more appealing to customers of restaurants than to customers of other businesses.

(B)   Such guarantees are likely to be more appealing to customers who know what to anticipate in terms of service.

(C)   Such guarantees are likely to have less appeal in situations where customers are knowledgeable about a business's product or service.

(D)   In situations where a high level of financial commitment is involved, a service guarantee is not likely to be very appealing.

(E)   In situations where customers expect a high level of customer service, a service guarantee is likely to make customers think that a business is worried about its service.

338. According to the passage, Tucci and Talaga found that service guarantees, when offered by lower-priced restaurants, can have which of the following effects?

    (A) Customers' developing unreasonably high expectations regarding service

    (B) Customers' avoiding such restaurants because they fear that the service guarantee may not be fully honored

    (C) Customers' interpreting the service guarantee as a sign that management is not confident about the quality of its service

    (D) A restaurant's becoming concerned that its service will not be assiduous enough to satisfy customers

    (E) A restaurant's becoming concerned that customers will be more emboldened to question the quality of the service they receive

Line　One proposal for preserving rain forests is
to promote the adoption of new agricultural
technologies, such as improved plant varieties and
use of chemical herbicides, which would increase
(5)　productivity and slow deforestation by reducing
demand for new cropland. Studies have shown
that farmers in developing countries who have
achieved certain levels of education, wealth, and
security of land tenure are more likely to adopt such
(10)　technologies. But these studies have focused on
villages with limited land that are tied to a market
economy rather than on the relatively isolated, self-
sufficient communities with ample land characteristic
of rain-forest regions. A recent study of the Tawahka
(15)　people of the Honduran rain forest found that farmers
with some formal education were more likely to
adopt improved plant varieties but less likely to
use chemical herbicides and that those who spoke
Spanish (the language of the market economy) were
(20)　more likely to adopt both technologies. Nonland
wealth was also associated with more adoption of
both technologies, but availability of uncultivated land
reduced the incentive to employ the productivity-
enhancing technologies. Researchers also measured
(25)　land-tenure security: in Tawahka society, kinship ties
are a more important indicator of this than are legal
property rights, so researchers measured it by a
household's duration of residence in its village. They
found that longer residence correlated with more
(30)　adoption of improved plant varieties but less adoption
of chemical herbicides.

339. The passage suggests that in the study mentioned in
line 14 the method for gathering information about
security of land tenure reflects which of the following
pairs of assumptions about Tawahka society?

(A)　The security of a household's land tenure
depends on the strength of that household's
kinship ties, and the duration of a household's
residence in its village is an indication of the
strength of that household's kinship ties.

(B)　The ample availability of land makes security of
land tenure unimportant, and the lack of a need
for secure land tenure has made the concept of
legal property rights unnecessary.

(C)　The strength of a household's kinship ties is
a more reliable indicator of that household's
receptivity to new agricultural technologies than
is its quantity of nonland wealth, and the duration
of a household's residence in its village is a more
reliable indicator of that household's security of
land tenure than is the strength of its kinship ties.

(D)　Security of land tenure based on kinship ties
tends to make farmers more receptive to the use
of improved plant varieties, and security of land
tenure based on long duration of residence in a
village tends to make farmers more receptive to
the use of chemical herbicides.

(E)　A household is more likely to be receptive to the
concept of land tenure based on legal property
rights if it has easy access to uncultivated land,
and a household is more likely to uphold the
tradition of land tenure based on kinship ties
if it possesses a significant degree of nonland
wealth.

340. According to the passage, the proposal mentioned in line 1 is aimed at preserving rain forests by encouraging farmers in rain-forest regions to do each of the following EXCEPT

(A) adopt new agricultural technologies

(B) grow improved plant varieties

(C) decrease their use of chemical herbicides

(D) increase their productivity

(E) reduce their need to clear new land for cultivation

Line   The argument for "monetizing"—or putting a
monetary value on—ecosystem functions may be
stated thus: Concern about the depletion of natural
resources is widespread, but this concern, in the
(5)   absence of an economic argument for conservation,
has not translated into significant conservational
progress. Some critics blame this impasse on
environmentalists, whom they believe fail to address
the economic issues of environmental degradation.
(10)   Conservation can appear unprofitable when compared
with the economic returns derived from converting
natural assets (pristine coastlines, for example) into
explicitly commercial ones (such as resort hotels).
But according to David Pearce, that illusion stems
(15)   from the fact that "services" provided by ecological
systems are not traded on the commodities market,
and thus have no readily *quantifiable* value. To
remedy this, says Pearce, one has to show that all
ecosystems have economic value—indeed, that all
(20)   ecological services are economic services. Tourists
visiting wildlife preserves, for example, create
jobs and generate income for national economies;
undisturbed forests and wetlands regulate water
runoff and act as water-purifying systems, saving
(25)   millions of dollars worth of damage to property
and to marine ecosystems. In Gretchen Daily's
view, monetization, while unpopular with many
environmentalists, reflects the dominant role that
economic considerations play in human behavior,
(30)   and the expression of economic value in a common
currency helps inform environmental decision-making
processes.

Questions 341–344 refer to the passage.

341. Information in the passage suggests that David Pearce
would most readily endorse which of the following
statements concerning monetization?

(A)   Monetization represents a strategy that is
attractive to both environmentalists and their
critics.

(B)   Monetization is an untested strategy,
but it is increasingly being embraced by
environmentalists.

(C)   Monetization should at present be restricted to
ecological services and should only gradually
be extended to such commercial endeavors as
tourism and recreation.

(D)   Monetization can serve as a means of
representing persuasively the value of
environmental conservation.

(E)   Monetization should inform environmental
decision-making processes only if it is accepted
by environmentalist groups.

342. Which of the following most clearly represents an
example of an "ecological service" as that term is used
in line 20 ?

(A)   A resort hotel located in an area noted for its
natural beauty

(B)   A water-purifying plant that supplements natural
processes with nontoxic chemicals

(C)   A wildlife preserve that draws many international
travelers

(D)   A nonprofit firm that specializes in restoring
previously damaged ecosystems

(E)   A newsletter that keeps readers informed of
ecological victories and setbacks

343. According to the passage, Daily sees monetization as an indication of which of the following?

    (A) The centrality of economic interests to people's actions

    (B) The reluctance of the critics of environmentalism to acknowledge the importance of conservation

    (C) The inability of financial interests and ecological interests to reach a common ideological ground

    (D) The inevitability of environmental degradation

    (E) The inevitability of the growth of ecological services in the future

344. Which of the following can be inferred from the passage concerning the environmentalists mentioned in line 8 ?

    (A) They are organized in opposition to the generation of income produced by the sale of ecological services.

    (B) They are fewer in number but better organized and better connected to the media than their opponents.

    (C) They have sometimes been charged with failing to use a particular strategy in their pursuit of conservational goals.

    (D) They have been in the forefront of publicizing the extent of worldwide environmental degradation.

    (E) They define environmental progress differently and more conservatively than do other organized groups of environmentalists.

Line Much research has been devoted to investigating what motivates consumers to try new products. Previous consumer research suggests that both the price of a new product and the way it is advertised

(5) affect consumers' perceptions of the product's performance risk (the possibility that the product will not function as consumers expect and/or will not provide the desired benefits). Some of this research has concluded that a relatively high price will reduce

(10) a consumer's perception of the performance risk associated with purchasing a particular product, while other studies have reported that price has little or no effect on perceived performance risk. These conflicting findings may simply be due to the nature

(15) of product advertisements: a recent study indicates that the presentation of an advertised message has a marked effect on the relationship between price and perceived performance risk.

 Researchers have identified consumers' perception

(20) of the credibility of the source of an advertised message—i.e., the manufacturer—as another factor affecting perceived performance risk: one study found that the greater the source credibility, the lower the consumer's perception of the risk of purchasing

(25) an advertised new product. However, past research suggests that the relationship between source credibility and perceived performance risk may be more complex: source credibility may interact with price in a subtle way to affect consumers' judgments

(30) of the performance risk associated with an advertised product.

345. According to the passage, the studies referred to in line 12 reported which of the following about the effect of price on consumers' perception of the performance risk associated with a new product?

 (A) Although most consumers regard price as an important factor, their perception of the performance risk associated with a new product is ultimately determined by the manufacturer's reputation.

 (B) Price interacts with the presentation of an advertised message to affect perceived performance risk.

 (C) Price does not significantly affect consumers' perception of the performance risk associated with a new product.

 (D) Consumers tend to regard price as more important than the manufacturer's credibility when they are buying from that manufacturer for the first time.

 (E) Consumers are generally less concerned about a new product's performance risk when that product is relatively expensive.

346. The "past research" mentioned in line 25 suggests which of the following about perceived performance risk?

 (A) The more expensive a new product is, the more likely consumers may be to credit advertised claims about that product.

 (B) The more familiar consumers are with a particular manufacturer, the more willing they may be to assume some risk in the purchase of a new product being advertised by that manufacturer.

 (C) Consumers' perception of the performance risk associated with a new product being advertised may be influenced by an interplay between the product's price and the manufacturer's credibility.

 (D) Consumers may be more likely to believe that a product will function as it is advertised to do when they have bought products from a particular manufacturer before.

 (E) The price of a particular advertised product may have less impact than the manufacturer's credibility on consumers' assessment of the performance risk associated with that product.

347. The passage is primarily concerned with

    (A) challenging the implications of previous research into why consumers try new products

    (B) suggesting new marketing strategies for attracting consumers to new products

    (C) reconciling two different views about the effect of price on consumers' willingness to try new products

    (D) describing a new approach to researching why consumers try new products

    (E) discussing certain findings regarding why consumers try new products

348. Which of the following, if true, would most tend to weaken the conclusion drawn from "some of this research" (line 8)?

    (A) In a subsequent study, consumers who were asked to evaluate new products with relatively low prices had the same perception of the products' performance risk as did consumers who were shown the same products priced more expensively.

    (B) In a subsequent study, the quality of the advertising for the products that consumers perceived as having a lower performance risk was relatively high, while the quality of the advertising for the products that consumers perceived as having a higher performance risk was relatively poor.

    (C) In a subsequent study, the products that consumers perceived as having a lower performance risk were priced higher than the highest priced products in the previous research.

    (D) None of the consumers involved in this research had ever before bought products from the manufacturers involved in the research.

    (E) Researchers found that the higher the source credibility for a product, the more consumers were willing to pay for it.

Line   Historians remain divided over the role of banks in facilitating economic growth in the United States in the late eighteenth and early nineteenth centuries. Some scholars contend
(5)   that banks played a minor role in the nation's growing economy. Financial institutions, they argue, appeared only after the economy had begun to develop, and once organized, followed conservative lending practices, providing aid to
(10)   established commercial enterprises but shunning those, such as manufacturing and transportation projects, that were more uncertain and capital-intensive (i.e., requiring greater expenditures in the form of capital than in
(15)   labor).

A growing number of historians argue, in contrast, that banks were crucial in transforming the early national economy. When state legislatures began granting more bank charters
(20)   in the 1790s and early 1800s, the supply of credit rose accordingly. Unlike the earliest banks, which had primarily provided short-term loans to well-connected merchants, the banks of the early nineteenth century issued credit widely. As Paul
(25)   Gilje asserts, the expansion and democratization of credit in the early nineteenth century became the driving force of the American economy, as banks began furnishing large amounts of capital to transportation and industrial enterprises. The
(30)   exception, such historians argue, was in the South; here, the overwhelmingly agrarian nature of the economy generated outright opposition to banks, which were seen as monopolistic institutions controlled by an elite group of
(35)   planters.

Questions 349–353 refer to the passage.

349. The primary purpose of the passage is to

   (A)   compare the economic role played by southern banks with the economic role played by banks in the rest of the United States during the late eighteenth and early nineteenth centuries

   (B)   reevaluate a conventional interpretation of the role played by banks in the American economy during the late eighteenth and early nineteenth centuries

   (C)   present different interpretations of the role played by banks in the American economy during the late eighteenth and early nineteenth centuries

   (D)   analyze how the increasing number of banks in the late eighteenth and early nineteenth centuries affected the American economy

   (E)   examine how scholarly opinion regarding the role played by banks in the American economy during the late eighteenth and early nineteenth centuries has changed over time

350. The passage suggests that the scholars mentioned in line 4 would argue that the reason banks tended not to fund manufacturing and transportation projects in the late eighteenth and early nineteenth centuries was that

   (A)   these projects, being well established and well capitalized, did not need substantial long-term financing from banks

   (B)   these projects entailed a level of risk that was too great for banks' conservative lending practices

   (C)   banks preferred to invest in other, more speculative projects that offered the potential for higher returns

   (D)   bank managers believed that these projects would be unlikely to contribute significantly to economic growth in the new country

   (E)   bank managers believed funding these projects would result in credit being extended to too many borrowers

351. The passage suggests that Paul Gilje would be most likely to agree with which of the following claims about the lending practices of the "earliest banks" (see line 21)?

    (A)   These lending practices were unlikely to generate substantial profits for banks.

    (B)   These lending practices only benefited a narrow sector of the economy.

    (C)   The restrictive nature of these lending practices generated significant opposition outside of the South.

    (D)   The restrictive nature of these lending practices forced state legislatures to begin granting more bank charters by the early nineteenth century.

    (E)   These lending practices were likely to be criticized by economic elites as being overly restrictive.

352. The passage suggests that the opposition to banks in the South in the early nineteenth century stemmed in part from the perception that banks

    (A)   did not benefit more than a small minority of the people

    (B)   did not support the interests of elite planters

    (C)   were too closely tied to transportation and industrial interests

    (D)   were unwilling to issue the long-term loans required by agrarian interests

    (E)   were too willing to lend credit widely

353. Which of the following statements best describes the function of the last sentence of the passage?

    (A)   It provides evidence tending to undermine the viewpoint of the scholars mentioned in line 5.

    (B)   It resolves a conflict over the role of banks summarized in the first paragraph.

    (C)   It clarifies some of the reasons state legislatures began granting more bank charters.

    (D)   It qualifies a claim made earlier in the passage about the impact of banks on the American economy in the early nineteenth century.

    (E)   It supports a claim made earlier in the passage about how the expansion of credit affected the economy.

Line　　In recent years, Western business managers have been heeding the exhortations of business journalists and academics to move their companies toward long-term, collaborative "strategic partnerships" with
(5)　　their external business partners (e.g., suppliers). The experts' advice comes as a natural reaction to numerous studies conducted during the past decade that compared Japanese production and supply practices with those of the rest of the world. The
(10)　　link between the success of a certain well-known Japanese automaker and its effective management of its suppliers, for example, has led to an unquestioning belief within Western management circles in the value of strategic partnerships. Indeed, in the automobile
(15)　　sector all three United States manufacturers and most of their European competitors have launched programs to reduce their total number of suppliers and move toward having strategic partnerships with a few.
(20)　　However, new research concerning supplier relationships in various industries demonstrates that the widespread assumption of Western managers and business consultants that Japanese firms manage their suppliers primarily through strategic
(25)　　partnerships is unjustified. Not only do Japanese firms appear to conduct a far smaller proportion of their business through strategic partnerships than is commonly believed, but they also make extensive use of "market-exchange" relationships, in which
(30)　　either party can turn to the marketplace and shift to different business partners at will, a practice usually associated with Western manufacturers.

Questions 354–357 refer to the passage.

354. The passage is primarily concerned with

(A) examining economic factors that may have contributed to the success of certain Japanese companies

(B) discussing the relative merits of strategic partnerships as compared with those of market-exchange relationships

(C) challenging the validity of a widely held assumption about how Japanese firms operate

(D) explaining why Western companies have been slow to adopt a particular practice favored by Japanese companies

(E) pointing out certain differences between Japanese and Western supplier relationships

355. According to the passage, the advice referred to in line 6 was a response to which of the following?

(A) A recent decrease in the number of available suppliers within the United States automobile industry

(B) A debate within Western management circles during the past decade regarding the value of strategic partnerships

(C) The success of certain European automobile manufacturers that have adopted strategic partnerships

(D) An increase in demand over the past decade for automobiles made by Western manufacturers

(E) Research comparing Japanese business practices with those of other nations

356. The author mentions "the success of a certain well-known Japanese automaker" in lines 10–11, most probably in order to

    (A) demonstrate some of the possible reasons for the success of a certain business practice

    (B) cite a specific case that has convinced Western business experts of the value of a certain business practice

    (C) describe specific steps taken by Western automakers that have enabled them to compete more successfully in a global market

    (D) introduce a paradox about the effect of a certain business practice in Japan

    (E) indicate the need for Western managers to change their relationships with their external business partners

357. Which of the following is cited in the passage as evidence supporting the author's claim about what the new research referred to in line 20 demonstrates?

    (A) The belief within Western management circles regarding the extent to which Japanese firms rely on strategic partnerships

    (B) The surprising number of European and United States businesses that have strategic partnerships with their suppliers

    (C) The response of Western automobile manufacturers to the advice that they adopt strategic partnerships with their suppliers

    (D) The prevalence of "market-exchange" relationships between Japanese firms and their suppliers

    (E) The success of a particular Japanese automobile manufacturer that favors strategic partnerships with its suppliers

Line

In an effort to explain why business acquisitions often fail, scholars have begun to focus on the role of top executives of acquired companies. Acquired companies that retain their top executives tend to

(5) have more successful outcomes than those that do not. Furthermore, existing research suggests that retaining the highest-level top executives, such as the CEO (chief executive officer) and COO (chief operating officer), is related more positively to postacquisition

(10) success than retaining lower-ranked top executives. However, this explanation, while insightful, suffers from two limitations. First, the focus on positional rank does not recognize the variation in length of service that may exist in top executive posts across companies,

(15) nor does it address which particular top executives (with respect to length of service) should be retained to achieve a successful acquisition outcome. Second, the relationship between retained top executives and acquisition outcomes offered by existing research

(20) is subject to opposing theoretical explanations related to length of service. The resource-based view (RBV) suggests that keeping acquired company top executives with longer organizational tenure would lead to more successful outcomes, as those executives

(25) have idiosyncratic and nontransferable knowledge of the acquired company that would be valuable for the effective implementation of the acquisition. The opposing position, offered by the upper echelons perspective (UEP), suggests that retaining top

(30) executives having short organizational tenure would lead to more successful outcomes, as they would have the adaptability to manage most effectively during the uncertainty of the acquisition process.

Responding to these limitations, Bergh conducted

(35) a study of executive retention and acquisition outcome that focused on the organizational tenure of retained company top executives in 104 acquisitions, followed over 5 years. Bergh considered the acquisition successful if the acquired company was

(40) retained and unsuccessful if it was divested. Bergh's findings support the RBV position. Apparently, the benefits of long organizational tenure lead to more successful outcomes than the benefits of short organizational tenure. While longer tenured top

(45) executives may have trouble adapting to change, it appears that their perspectives and knowledge bases offer unique value after the acquisition. Although from the UEP position it seems sensible to retain less tenured executives and allow more tenured

(50) ones to leave, such a strategy appears to lower the probability of acquisition success.

Questions 358–361 refer to the passage.

358. According to the passage, the research mentioned in line 6 suggests which of the following about lower-ranked top executives and postacquisition success?

(A) Given that these executives are unlikely to contribute to postacquisition success, little effort should be spent trying to retain them.

(B) The shorter their length of service, the less likely it is that these executives will play a significant role in postacquisition success.

(C) These executives are less important to postacquisition success than are more highly ranked top executives.

(D) If they have long tenures, these executives may prove to be as important to postacquisition success as are more highly ranked top executives.

(E) Postacquisition success is unlikely if these executives are retained.

359. The resource-based view, as described in the passage, is based on which of the following ideas?

(A) The managerial skills of top executives become strongest after the first five years of their tenure.

(B) Company-specific knowledge is an important factor in the success of an acquisition process.

(C) The amount of nontransferable knowledge possessed by long-tenured top executives tends to be underestimated.

(D) Effective implementation of an acquisition depends primarily on the ability of executives to adapt to change.

(E) Short-tenured executives are likely to impede the implementation of a successful acquisition strategy.

360. The passage suggests that Bergh and a proponent of the upper echelons perspective would be most likely to disagree over which of the following?

    (A) Whether there is a positive correlation between short organizational tenure and managerial adaptability

    (B) Whether there is a positive correlation between long organizational tenure and the acquisition of idiosyncratic and nontransferable knowledge

    (C) Whether adaptability is a useful trait for an executive who is managing an acquisition process

    (D) Whether retaining less-tenured top executives of an acquired company is an optimal strategy for achieving postacquisition success

    (E) Whether retaining highest-level top executives of acquired companies is more important than retaining lower-ranked top executives

361. According to the passage, prior to Bergh's study, research on the role of top executives of acquired companies in business acquisition success was limited in which of the following ways?

    (A) It did not address how the organizational tenure of top executives affects postacquisition success.

    (B) It did not address why some companies have longer-tenured CEOs than others.

    (C) It did not consider strategies for retaining long-tenured top executives of acquired companies.

    (D) It failed to differentiate between the contribution of highest-level top executives to postacquisition success and that of lower-ranked top executives.

    (E) It underestimated the potential contribution that lower-level top executives can make to postacquisition success.

Line   When Jamaican-born social activist Marcus
        Garvey came to the United States in 1916, he
        arrived at precisely the right historical moment.
        What made the moment right was the return of
(5)   African American soldiers from the First World War
        in 1918, which created an ideal constituency for
        someone with Garvey's message of unity, pride,
        and improved conditions for African American
        communities.
(10)   Hoping to participate in the traditional American
        ethos of individual success, many African American
        people entered the armed forces with enthusiasm,
        only to find themselves segregated from white
        troops and subjected to numerous indignities. They
(15)   returned to a United States that was as segregated
        as it had been before the war. Considering similar
        experiences, anthropologist Anthony F. C. Wallace
        has argued that when a perceptible gap arises
        between a culture's expectations and the reality of
(20)   that culture, the resulting tension can inspire a
        revitalization movement: an organized, conscious
        effort to construct a culture that fulfills long-
        standing expectations.
            Some scholars have argued that Garvey created
(25)   the consciousness from which he built, in the 1920s,
        the largest revitalization movement in
        African American history. But such an argument only
        tends to obscure the consciousness of
        identity, strength, and sense of history that already
(30)   existed in the African American community. Garvey
        did not create this consciousness; rather, he gave
        this consciousness its political expression.

362. According to the passage, which of the following
     contributed to Marcus Garvey's success?

   (A)   He introduced cultural and historical
         consciousness to the African American
         community.

   (B)   He believed enthusiastically in the traditional
         American success ethos.

   (C)   His audience had already formed a
         consciousness that made it receptive to his
         message.

   (D)   His message appealed to critics of African
         American support for United States military
         involvement in the First World War.

   (E)   He supported the movement to protest
         segregation that had emerged prior to his arrival
         in the United States.

363. The passage suggests that many African American
     people responded to their experiences in the armed
     forces in which of the following ways?

   (A)   They maintained as civilians their enthusiastic
         allegiance to the armed forces.

   (B)   They questioned United States involvement in the
         First World War.

   (C)   They joined political organizations to protest the
         segregation of African American troops and the
         indignities they suffered in the military.

   (D)   They became aware of the gap between their
         expectations and the realities of American
         culture.

   (E)   They repudiated Garvey's message of pride and
         unity.

364. It can be inferred from the passage that the "scholars" mentioned in line 24 believe which of the following to be true?

    (A) Revitalization resulted from the political activism of returning African American soldiers following the First World War.

    (B) Marcus Garvey had to change a number of prevailing attitudes in order for his mass movement to find a foothold in the United States.

    (C) The prevailing sensibility of the African American community provided the foundation of Marcus Garvey's political appeal.

    (D) Marcus Garvey hoped to revitalize consciousness of cultural and historical identity in the African American community.

    (E) The goal of the mass movement that Marcus Garvey helped bring into being was to build on the pride and unity among African Americans.

365. According to the passage, many African American people joined the armed forces during the First World War for which of the following reasons?

    (A) They wished to escape worsening economic conditions in African American communities.

    (B) They expected to fulfill ideals of personal attainment.

    (C) They sought to express their loyalty to the United States.

    (D) They hoped that joining the military would help advance the cause of desegregation.

    (E) They saw military service as an opportunity to fulfill Marcus Garvey's political vision.

Line   Arboria is floundering in the global marketplace, incurring devastating losses in market position and profits. The problem is not Arboria's products, but Arboria's trade policy. Arboria faces the prospect

(5)   of continuing economic loss until Arborian business and political leaders recognize the fundamental differences between Arborian and foreign economic systems. Today the key trade issue is not free trade versus protectionism but diminishing trade versus

(10)   expanding trade.

Arboria is operating with an obsolete trade policy, an artifact of the mid-1940s when Arboria and Whorfland dominated the global economy, tariffs were the principal obstacle to trade, and Arborian

(15)   supremacy was uncontested in virtually all industries. In the intervening decades, economic circumstances have shifted radically. Arborian trade policy has not.

Today, Arboria's trade policy seems paralyzed by the relentless conflict between proponents of

(20)   "free" and "fair" trade. The free traders argue that Arborian markets should be open, and the movement of goods and services across national borders unrestrained. The fair traders assert that access to Arborian markets should be restricted until Arborian

(25)   businesses are granted equal access to foreign markets. They contend that free trade is impossible while other nations erect barriers to Arborian exports.

Both are correct: fair trade requires equal access and equal access leads to free trade. But both sides

(30)   base their positions on the same two outdated premises:

1. Global commerce is conducted under the terms of the General Agreement on Tariffs and Trade (GATT) and dominated by Arboria and similar economic

(35)   systems abroad.

2. Multilateral negotiations are the most effective way to resolve pressing trade issues.

Both assumptions are wrong. The 40-year-old GATT

(40)   now covers less than 7 percent of global commerce. World trade is no longer dominated by the free-trade economies; nearly 75 percent is conducted by economic systems operating with principles at odds with those of Arboria. Forging a multilateral

(45)   trade policy consensus among so many diverse economic systems has become virtually impossible. And while multilateral talks drag on, Arboria misses opportunities for trade expansion.

366. Which of the following best states the difference between free trade and fair trade, as explained in the passage?

(A)   Free trade requires no trade tariffs whatsoever, whereas fair trade assumes multilateral agreement on tariffs for goods of equal worth.

(B)   Free trade is based on the unrestricted movement of goods across all national boundaries, whereas fair trade is based on a nation's restriction of commerce with each nation that erects trade barriers to the first nation's exports.

(C)   The trade policies of countries like Arboria are based on the principles of free trade, whereas the trade policies of other types of world economies are based on fair trade.

(D)   Free-trade nations negotiate individual trade agreements with each of their trading partners, whereas fair-trade nations conduct multilateral trade negotiations.

(E)   Free trade assumes a constant level of global commerce, whereas fair trade promotes a steady expansion of international trade.

367. It can be inferred that the author of the passage would most likely agree with which of the following statements about multilateral trade negotiations?

(A)   They are the most effective way to resolve trade problems.

(B)   They are most effective in dealing with fair-trade issues between nations.

(C)   They have only recently begun to make an impact on world trade.

(D)   Arborian reliance on multilateral trade negotiations, while appropriate in the past, is inadequate for today's global marketplace.

(E)   The principles of multilateral trade negotiations are incompatible with current Arborian foreign trade policy.

368. Which of the following statements best summarizes the author's opinion of "free traders" and "fair traders"?

(A) The free and the fair traders' continuing debate provides a healthy and effective forum for examining Arborian trade policy.

(B) The proponents of fair trade are essentially correct, while those who advocate free trade are not.

(C) The proponents of free trade are better able to deal with current economic problems than are the fair traders.

(D) Neither the free nor the fair traders can come up with a workable trade policy because neither takes multilateral negotiations into account.

(E) The proponents of both free and fair trade have based their positions on out-of-date premises that do not reflect current economic conditions.

369. The author mentions all of the following as characteristic of world trade in the mid-1940s EXCEPT:

(A) Arboria played a major role in the global marketplace.

(B) Whorfland played a major role in the global marketplace.

(C) Tariffs were the main obstacle to trade.

(D) Fair-trade economies dominated international trade.

(E) Arborian manufacturers were unsurpassed in most industries.

370. In presenting the argument in the passage, the author uses all of the following EXCEPT:

(A) statistical information about global commerce

(B) definitions of terms concerning world trade

(C) generalizations about Arboria's economic system

(D) historical background of Arborian trade policy

(E) an example of an economic system whose principles differ from those of Arboria

371. The author asserts which of the following about Arboria's trade policy?

(A) A dramatic revision of Arboria's trade policy will be necessary unless Arborian manufacturers improve the quality of their goods.

(B) The most crucial issue facing Arborian trade policymakers is that of free trade versus protectionism.

(C) Arboria's current trade policy was essentially developed during the 1940s and has changed little since that time.

(D) Arboria's trade policy is widely emulated throughout the world, to the extent that most international commerce is modeled on Arboria's principles.

(E) Arboria's trade policy has evolved gradually over the last eighty years, constantly readjusting itself in response to shifts in global commerce.

372. The passage is primarily concerned with

(A) illustrating the erosion of Arboria's position in the world marketplace

(B) examining the differences between "free" and "fair" traders

(C) advocating a reassessment of Arboria's trade policy

(D) criticizing the terms of the General Agreement on Tariffs and Trade (GATT)

(E) comparing the different economic circumstances of Arboria's trade partners

373. The author implies that the main obstacle to a truly effective Arborian trade policy is the

(A) weak position that Arboria currently holds in the global marketplace

(B) inability of Arborian leaders to recognize that foreign economic systems are based on principles fundamentally different from their own

(C) dominance of the supporters of free trade in the conflict between free-trade and fair-trade advocates

(D) apparent inability of Arborian industries to produce goods that are competitive in the world market

(E) protectionism that characterizes the foreign trade policies of so many of Arboria's trade partners

Line   Biologists have advanced two theories to explain
          why schooling of fish occurs in so many fish species.
          Because schooling is particularly widespread among
          species of small fish, both theories assume that
(5)   schooling offers the advantage of some protection
          from predators.
              Proponents of theory A dispute the assumption
          that a school of thousands of fish is highly visible.
          Experiments have shown that any fish can be seen,
(10)   even in very clear water, only within a sphere of
          200 meters in diameter. When fish are in a compact
          group, the spheres of visibility overlap. Thus the
          chance of a predator finding the school is only
          slightly greater than the chance of the predator
(15)   finding a single fish swimming alone. Schooling
          is advantageous to the individual fish because a
          predator's chance of finding any particular fish
          swimming in the school is much smaller than its
          chance of finding at least one of the same group of
(20)   fish if the fish were dispersed throughout an area.
              However, critics of theory A point out that some
          fish form schools even in areas where predators
          are abundant and thus little possibility of escaping
          detection exists. They argue that the school continues
(25)   to be of value to its members even after detection.
          They advocate theory B, the "confusion effect," which
          can be explained in two different ways.
              Sometimes, proponents argue, predators simply
          cannot decide which fish to attack. This indecision
(30)   supposedly results from a predator's preference
          for striking prey that is distinct from the rest of the
          school in appearance. In many schools the fish are
          almost identical in appearance, making it difficult for
          a predator to select one. The second explanation
(35)   for the "confusion effect" has to do with the sensory
          confusion caused by a large number of prey moving
          around the predator. Even if the predator makes the
          decision to attack a particular fish, the movement
          of other prey in the school can be distracting. The
(40)   predator's difficulty can be compared to that of a
          tennis player trying to hit a tennis ball when two are
          approaching simultaneously.

Questions 374–377 refer to the passage.

374. According to the passage, theory B states that which of the following is a factor that enables a schooling fish to escape predators?

(A) The tendency of fish to form compact groups

(B) The movement of other fish within the school

(C) The inability of predators to detect schools

(D) The ability of fish to hide behind one another in a school

(E) The great speed with which a school can disperse

375. According to the passage, both theory A and theory B have been developed to explain how

(A) fish hide from predators by forming schools

(B) forming schools functions to protect fish from predators

(C) schooling among fish differs from other protective behaviors

(D) small fish are able to make rapid decisions

(E) small fish are able to survive in an environment densely populated by large predators

376. According to one explanation of the "confusion effect," a fish that swims in a school will have greater advantages for survival if it

(A) tends to be visible for no more than 200 meters

(B) stays near either the front or the rear of a school

(C) is part of a small school rather than a large school

(D) is very similar in appearance to the other fish in the school

(E) is medium-sized

377. The author is primarily concerned with

(A) discussing different theories

(B) analyzing different techniques

(C) defending two hypotheses

(D) refuting established beliefs

(E) revealing new evidence

Line

In *Winters v. United States* (1908), the Supreme Court held that the right to use waters flowing through or adjacent to the Fort Berthold Indian Reservation was reserved to American Indians by the treaty
(5) establishing the reservation. Although this treaty did not mention water rights, the Court ruled that the federal government, when it created the reservation, intended to deal fairly with American Indians by reserving for them the waters without which their
(10) lands would have been useless. Later decisions, citing Winters, established that courts can find federal rights to reserve water for particular purposes if (1) the land in question lies within an enclave under exclusive federal jurisdiction; (2) the land has been
(15) formally withdrawn from federal public lands—i.e., withdrawn from the stock of federal lands available for private use under federal land use laws—and set aside or reserved; and (3) the circumstances reveal the government intended to reserve water as well as
(20) land when establishing the reservation.

Some American Indian tribes have also established water rights through the courts based on their traditional diversion and use of certain waters prior to the United States' acquisition of sovereignty. For
(25) example, the Rio Grande pueblos already existed when the United States acquired sovereignty over New Mexico in 1848. Although they at that time became part of the United States, the pueblo lands never formally constituted a part of federal public
(30) lands; in any event, no treaty, statute, or executive order has ever designated or withdrawn the pueblos from public lands as American Indian reservations. This fact, however, has not barred application of the Winters doctrine. What constitutes an American Indian
(35) reservation is a question of practice, not of legal definition, and the pueblos have always been treated as reservations by the United States. This pragmatic approach is buttressed by *Arizona v. California* (1963), wherein the Supreme Court indicated that
(40) the manner in which any type of federal reservation is created does not affect the application to it of the Winters doctrine. Therefore, the reserved water rights of Pueblo Indians have priority over other citizens' water rights as of 1848, the year in which pueblos
(45) must be considered to have become reservations.

378. According to the passage, which of the following was true of the treaty establishing the Fort Berthold Indian Reservation?

(A) It was challenged in the Supreme Court a number of times.

(B) It was rescinded by the federal government, an action that gave rise to the Winters case.

(C) It cited American Indians' traditional use of the land's resources.

(D) It failed to mention water rights to be enjoyed by the reservation's inhabitants.

(E) It was modified by the Supreme Court in *Arizona v. California.*

379. The passage suggests that, if the criteria discussed in lines 10–20 of the text were the only criteria for establishing a reservation's water rights, which of the following would be true?

(A) The water rights of the inhabitants of the Fort Berthold Indian Reservation would not take precedence over those of other citizens.

(B) Reservations established before 1848 would be judged to have no water rights.

(C) There would be no legal basis for the water rights of the Rio Grande pueblos.

(D) Reservations other than American Indian reservations could not be created with reserved water rights.

(E) Treaties establishing reservations would have to mention water rights explicitly in order to reserve water for a particular purpose.

380. Which of the following most accurately summarizes the relationship between *Arizona v. California*, as that decision is described in the passage, and the criteria discussed in lines 10–20?

(A) *Arizona v. California* abolishes these criteria and establishes a competing set of criteria for applying the Winters doctrine.

(B) *Arizona v. California* establishes that the Winters doctrine applies to a broader range of situations than those defined by these criteria.

(C) *Arizona v. California* represents the sole example of an exception to the criteria as they were set forth in the Winters doctrine.

(D) *Arizona v. California* does not refer to the Winters doctrine to justify water rights, whereas these criteria do rely on the Winters doctrine.

(E) *Arizona v. California* applies the criteria derived from the Winters doctrine only to federal lands other than American Indian reservations.

381. The "pragmatic approach" mentioned in lines 37–38 of the passage is best defined as one that

(A) grants recognition to reservations that were never formally established but that have traditionally been treated as such

(B) determines the water rights of all citizens in a particular region by examining the actual history of water usage in that region

(C) gives federal courts the right to reserve water along with land even when it is clear that the government originally intended to reserve only the land

(D) bases the decision to recognize the legal rights of a group on the practical effect such a recognition is likely to have on other citizens

(E) dictates that courts ignore precedents set by such cases as *Winters v. United States* in deciding what water rights belong to reserved land

382. It can be inferred from the passage that the Winters doctrine has been used to establish which of the following?

(A) A rule that the government may reserve water only by explicit treaty or agreement

(B) A legal distinction between federal lands reserved for American Indians and federal lands reserved for other purposes

(C) Criteria governing when the federal government may set land aside for a particular purpose

(D) The special status of American Indian tribes' rights to reserved land

(E) The federal right to reserve water implicitly as well as explicitly under certain conditions

383. The author cites the fact that the Rio Grande pueblos were never formally withdrawn from public lands primarily in order to do which of the following?

(A) Suggest why it might have been argued that the Winters doctrine ought not to apply to pueblo lands

(B) Imply that the United States never really acquired sovereignty over pueblo lands

(C) Argue that the pueblo lands ought still to be considered part of federal public lands

(D) Support the argument that the water rights of citizens other than American Indians are limited by the Winters doctrine

(E) Suggest that federal courts cannot claim jurisdiction over cases disputing the traditional diversion and use of water by Pueblo Indians

384. The primary purpose of the passage is to

(A) trace the development of laws establishing American Indian reservations

(B) explain the legal bases for the water rights of American Indian tribes

(C) question the legal criteria often used to determine the water rights of American Indian tribes

(D) discuss evidence establishing the earliest date at which the federal government recognized the water rights of American Indians

(E) point out a legal distinction between different types of American Indian reservations

385. The passage suggests that the legal rights of citizens other than American Indians to the use of water flowing into the Rio Grande pueblos are

(A) guaranteed by the precedent set in *Arizona v. California*

(B) abolished by the Winters doctrine

(C) deferred to the Pueblo Indians whenever treaties explicitly require this

(D) guaranteed by federal land-use laws

(E) limited by the prior claims of the Pueblo Indians

Line   In corporate purchasing, competitive scrutiny is
typically limited to suppliers of items that are directly
related to end products. With "indirect" purchases
(such as computers, advertising, and legal services),
(5)   which are not directly related to production,
corporations often favor "supplier partnerships"
(arrangements in which the purchaser forgoes the
right to pursue alternative suppliers), which can
inappropriately shelter suppliers from rigorous
(10)   competitive scrutiny that might afford the purchaser
economic leverage. There are two independent
variables—availability of alternatives and ease of
changing suppliers—that companies should use
to evaluate the feasibility of subjecting suppliers of
(15)   indirect purchases to competitive scrutiny. This can
create four possible situations.
    In Type 1 situations, there are many alternatives
and change is relatively easy. Open pursuit of
alternatives—by frequent competitive bidding, if
(20)   possible—will likely yield the best results. In Type 2
situations, where there are many alternatives but
change is difficult—as for providers of employee
health-care benefits—it is important to continuously
test the market and use the results to secure
(25)   concessions from existing suppliers. Alternatives
provide a credible threat to suppliers, even if the
ability to switch is constrained. In Type 3 situations,
there are few alternatives, but the ability to switch
without difficulty creates a threat that companies
(30)   can use to negotiate concessions from existing
suppliers. In Type 4 situations, where there are few
alternatives and change is difficult, partnerships may
be unavoidable.

Questions 386–390 refer to the passage.

386. Which of the following can be inferred about supplier
partnerships, as they are described in the passage?

   (A)   They cannot be sustained unless the goods or
          services provided are available from a large
          number of suppliers.

   (B)   They can result in purchasers paying more
          for goods and services than they would in a
          competitive-bidding situation.

   (C)   They typically are instituted at the urging of the
          supplier rather than the purchaser.

   (D)   They are not feasible when the goods or services
          provided are directly related to the purchasers'
          end products.

   (E)   They are least appropriate when the purchasers'
          ability to change suppliers is limited.

387. Which of the following best describes the relation of
the second paragraph to the first?

   (A)   The second paragraph offers proof of an
          assertion made in the first paragraph.

   (B)   The second paragraph provides an explanation
          for the occurrence of a situation described in the
          first paragraph.

   (C)   The second paragraph discusses the application
          of a strategy proposed in the first paragraph.

   (D)   The second paragraph examines the scope of a
          problem presented in the first paragraph.

   (E)   The second paragraph discusses the
          contradictions inherent in a relationship
          described in the first paragraph.

388. It can be inferred that the author of the passage would be most likely to make which of the following recommendations to a company purchasing health care benefits for its employees?

   (A) Devise strategies for circumventing the obstacles to replacing the current provider of health care benefits.

   (B) Obtain health care benefits from a provider that also provides other indirect products and services.

   (C) Obtain bids from other providers of health care benefits in order to be in a position to negotiate a better deal with the current provider.

   (D) Switch providers of health care benefits whenever a different provider offers a more competitive price.

   (E) Acknowledge the difficulties involved in replacing the current provider of health care benefits and offer to form a partnership with the provider.

389. Which of the following is one difference between Type 2 situations and Type 4 situations, as they are described in the passage?

   (A) The number of alternative suppliers available to the purchaser

   (B) The most effective approach for the purchaser to use in obtaining competitive bids from potential suppliers

   (C) The degree of difficulty the purchaser encounters when changing suppliers

   (D) The frequency with which each type of situation occurs in a typical business environment

   (E) The likelihood that any given purchase will be an indirect purchase

390. According to the passage, which of the following factors distinguishes an indirect purchase from other purchases?

   (A) The ability of the purchasing company to subject potential suppliers of the purchased item to competitive scrutiny

   (B) The number of suppliers of the purchased item available to the purchasing company

   (C) The methods of negotiation that are available to the purchasing company

   (D) The relationship of the purchased item to the purchasing company's end product

   (E) The degree of importance of the purchased item in the purchasing company's business operations

Line   Carotenoids, a family of natural pigments, form
an important part of the colorful signals used by
many animals. Animals acquire carotenoids either
directly (from the plants and algae that produce
(5)   them) or indirectly (by eating insects) and store them
in a variety of tissues. Studies of several animal
species have shown that when choosing mates,
females prefer males with brighter carotenoid-based
coloration. Owens and Olson hypothesize that the
(10)   presence of carotenoids, as signaled by coloration,
would be meaningful in the context of mate selection
if carotenoids were either rare or required for
health. The conventional view is that carotenoids
are meaningful because they are rare: healthier
(15)   males can forage for more of the pigments than
can their inferior counterparts. Although this may be
true, there is growing evidence that carotenoids are
meaningful also because they are required: they are
used by the immune system and for detoxification
(20)   processes that are important for maintaining health.
It may be that males can use scarce carotenoids
either for immune defense and detoxification or for
attracting females. Males that are more susceptible
to disease and parasites will have to use their
(25)   carotenoids to boost their immune systems, whereas
males that are genetically resistant will use fewer
carotenoids for fighting disease and will advertise
this by using the pigments for flashy display instead.

391. According to the "conventional view" referred to in
line 13 of the passage, brighter carotenoid-based
coloration in certain species suggests that an
individual

(A)   lives in a habitat rich in carotenoid-bearing plants
and insects

(B)   has efficient detoxification processes

(C)   has a superior immune system

(D)   possesses superior foraging capacity

(E)   is currently capable of reproducing

392. The idea that carotenoid-based coloration is significant
partly because carotenoids are required for health
suggests that a lack of bright coloration in a male is
most likely to indicate which of the following?

(A)   Inefficient detoxification processes

(B)   Immunity to parasite infestation

(C)   Low genetic resistance to disease

(D)   Lack of interest in mating

(E)   Lack of carotenoid-storing tissues

393. The passage suggests that relatively bright carotenoid-
based coloration is a signal of which of the following
characteristics in males of certain animal species?

(A)   Readiness for mating behavior

(B)   Ability to fight

(C)   Particular feeding preferences

(D)   Recovery from parasite infestation

(E)   Fitness as a mate

394. The passage implies which of the following about the
insects from which animals acquire carotenoids?

(A)   They do not produce carotenoids themselves.

(B)   They use carotenoids primarily for coloration.

(C)   They maintain constant levels of carotenoids in
their tissues.

(D)   They are unable to use carotenoids to boost
their immune system.

(E)   They are available in greater abundance than are
carotenoid-bearing plants.

395. Information in the passage suggests that which of the following is true of carotenoids that a male animal uses for detoxification processes?

    (A) They were not acquired directly from plants and algae.

    (B) They cannot be replenished through foraging.

    (C) They cannot be used simultaneously to brighten coloration.

    (D) They do not affect the animal's susceptibility to parasites.

    (E) They increase the chances that the animal will be selected as a mate.

Line   Linda Kerber argued in the mid-1980s that after
          the American Revolution (1775–1783), an ideology
          of "republican motherhood" resulted in a surge of
          educational opportunities for women in the United
(5)   States. Kerber maintained that the leaders of
          the new nation wanted women to be educated in
          order to raise politically virtuous sons. A virtuous
          citizenry was considered essential to the success
          of the country's republican form of government;
(10)   virtue was to be instilled not only by churches and
          schools, but by families, where the mother's role
          was crucial. Thus, according to Kerber, motherhood
          became pivotal to the fate of the republic, providing
          justification for an unprecedented attention to female
(15)   education.
              Introduction of the "republican motherhood"
          thesis dramatically changed historiography. Prior
          to Kerber's work, educational historians barely
          mentioned women and girls; Thomas Woody's
(20)   1929 work is the notable exception. Examining
          newspaper advertisements for academies, Woody
          found that educational opportunities increased for
          both girls and boys around 1750. Pointing to "An
          Essay on Woman" (1753) as reflecting a shift in
(25)   view, Woody also claimed that practical education
          for females had many advocates before the
          Revolution. Woody's evidence challenges the notion
          that the Revolution changed attitudes regarding
          female education, although it may have accelerated
(30)   earlier trends. Historians' reliance on Kerber's
          "republican motherhood" thesis may have obscured
          the presence of these trends, making it difficult
          to determine to what extent the Revolution really
          changed women's lives.

Questions 396–400 refer to the passage.

396. According to the passage, Kerber maintained that
     which of the following led to an increase in educational
     opportunities for women in the United States after the
     American Revolution?

     (A)   An unprecedented demand by women for
           greater educational opportunities in the decades
           following the Revolution

     (B)   A new political ideology calling for equality of
           opportunity between women and men in all
           aspects of life

     (C)   A belief that the American educational system
           could be reformed only if women participated
           more fully in that system

     (D)   A belief that women needed to be educated if
           they were to contribute to the success of the
           nation's new form of government

     (E)   A recognition that women needed to be educated
           if they were to take an active role in the nation's
           schools and churches

397. According to the passage, within the field of
     educational history, Thomas Woody's 1929 work was

     (A)   innovative because it relied on newspaper
           advertisements as evidence

     (B)   exceptional in that it concentrated on the period
           before the American Revolution

     (C)   unusual in that it focused on educational
           attitudes rather than on educational practices

     (D)   controversial in its claims regarding educational
           opportunities for boys

     (E)   atypical in that it examined the education of girls

398. The passage suggests that Woody would have agreed with which of the following claims regarding "An Essay on Woman"?

    (A) It expressed attitudes concerning women's education that were reflected in new educational opportunities for women after 1750.

    (B) It persuaded educators to offer greater educational opportunities to women in the 1750s.

    (C) It articulated ideas about women's education that would not be realized until after the American Revolution.

    (D) It offered one of the most original arguments in favor of women's education in the United States in the eighteenth century.

    (E) It presented views about women's education that were still controversial in Woody's own time.

399. The passage suggests that, with regard to the history of women's education in the United States, Kerber's work differs from Woody's primarily concerning which of the following?

    (A) The extent to which women were interested in pursuing educational opportunities in the eighteenth century

    (B) The extent of the support for educational opportunities for girls prior to the American Revolution

    (C) The extent of public resistance to educational opportunities for women after the American Revolution

    (D) Whether attitudes toward women's educational opportunities changed during the eighteenth century

    (E) Whether women needed to be educated in order to contribute to the success of a republican form of government

400. According to the passage, Kerber argued that political leaders thought that the form of government adopted by the United States after the American Revolution depended on which of the following for its success?

    (A) Women assuming the sole responsibility for instilling political virtue in children

    (B) Girls becoming the primary focus of a reformed educational system that emphasized political virtue

    (C) The family serving as one of the primary means by which children were imbued with political virtue

    (D) The family assuming many of the functions previously performed by schools and churches

    (E) Men and women assuming equal responsibility for the management of schools, churches, and the family

Line   In the Sonoran Desert of northwestern Mexico and
southern Arizona, the flowers of several species of
columnar cacti—cardon, saguaro, and organ
pipe—were once exclusively pollinated at night by
(5)   nectar-feeding bats, as their close relatives in arid
tropical regions of southern Mexico still are. In these
tropical regions, diurnal (daytime) visitors to columnar
cactus flowers are ineffective pollinators because,
by sunrise, the flowers' stigmas become unreceptive
(10)   or the flowers close. Yet the flowers of the Sonoran
Desert cacti have evolved to remain open after sunrise,
allowing pollination by such diurnal visitors as bees and
birds. Why have these cacti expanded their range of
pollinators by remaining open and receptive in daylight?
(15)   This development at the northernmost range of
columnar cacti may be due to a yearly variation in the
abundance—and hence the reliability—of migratory
nectar-feeding bats. Pollinators can be unreliable
for several reasons. They can be dietary generalists
(20)   whose fidelity to a particular species depends on
the availability of alternative food sources. Or, they
can be dietary specialists, but their abundance may
vary widely from year to year, resulting in variable
pollination of their preferred food species. Finally, they
(25)   may be dietary specialists, but their abundance may
be chronically low relative to the availability of flowers.
Recent data reveals that during spring in the
Sonoran Desert, the nectar-feeding bats are
specialists feeding on cardon, saguaro, and
(30)   organpipe flowers. However, whereas cactus-flower
abundance tends to be high during spring, bat
population densities tend to be low except near
maternity roosts. Moreover, in spring, diurnal cactus-
pollinating birds are significantly more abundant in
(35)   this region than are the nocturnal bats. Thus, with bats
being unreliable cactus-flower pollinators, and daytime
pollinators more abundant and therefore more reliable,
selection favors the cactus flowers with traits that
increase their range of pollinators. While data suggest
(40)   that population densities of nectar-feeding bats are
also low in tropical areas of southern Mexico, where
bats are the exclusive pollinators of many species
of columnar cacti, cactus-flower density and bat
population density appear to be much more evenly
(45)   balanced there: compared with the Sonoran Desert's
cardon and saguaro, columnar cacti in southern Mexico
produce far fewer flowers per night. Accordingly,
despite their low population density, bats are able to
pollinate nearly 100 percent of the available flowers.

Questions 401–403 refer to the passage.

401. The primary purpose of the passage is to

(A)   compare the adaptive responses of several
species of columnar cacti in the Sonoran Desert
with those in the arid tropical regions of southern
Mexico

(B)   discuss some of the possible causes of the
relatively low abundance of migratory nectar-
feeding bats in the Sonoran Desert

(C)   provide a possible explanation for a particular
evolutionary change in certain species of
columnar cacti in the Sonoran Desert

(D)   present recent findings that challenge a
particular theory as to why several species
of columnar cacti in the Sonoran Desert have
expanded their range of pollinators

(E)   compare the effectiveness of nocturnal and
diurnal pollination for several different species of
columnar cacti in the Sonoran Desert

402. According to the passage, which of the following types
of nectar-feeding pollinators is likely to be an unreliable
pollinator of a particular cactus flower?

(A)   A dietary specialist whose abundance is typically
high in relation to that of the flower

(B)   A dietary specialist whose abundance is at times
significantly lower than that of the flower

(C)   A dietary generalist for whom that flower's
nectar is not a preferred food but is the most
consistently available food

(D)   A dietary generalist for whom that flower's nectar
is slightly preferred to other available foods

(E)   A dietary generalist that evolved from a species
of dietary specialists

403. According to the passage, present-day columnar cacti in the Sonoran Desert differ from their close relatives in southern Mexico in that the Sonoran cacti

(A) have flowers that remain open after sunset

(B) are pollinated primarily by dietary specialists

(C) can be pollinated by nectar-feeding bats

(D) have stigmas that are unreceptive to pollination at night

(E) are sometimes pollinated by diurnal pollinators

Line   Manufacturers have to do more than build large
manufacturing plants to realize economies of scale.
It is true that as the capacity of a manufacturing
operation rises, costs per unit of output fall as plant
(5)   size approaches "minimum efficient scale," where the
cost per unit of output reaches a minimum,
determined roughly by the state of existing technology
and size of the potential market. However, minimum
efficient scale cannot be fully realized unless a steady
(10)   "throughput" (the flow of materials through a plant) is
attained. The throughput needed to maintain the
optimal scale of production requires careful
coordination not only of the flow of goods through the
production process, but also of the flow of input from
(15)   suppliers and the flow of output to wholesalers and
final consumers. If throughput falls below a critical
point, unit costs rise sharply and profits disappear. A
manufacturer's fixed costs and "sunk costs" (original
capital investment in the physical plant) do not
(20)   decrease when production declines due to inadequate
supplies of raw materials, problems on the factory
floor, or inefficient sales networks. Consequently,
potential economies of scale are based on the
physical and engineering characteristics of the
(25)   production facilities—that is, on tangible capital—but
realized economies of scale are operational and
organizational, and depend on knowledge, skills,
experience, and teamwork—that is, on organized
human capabilities, or intangible capital.
(30)   The importance of investing in intangible capital
becomes obvious when one looks at what happens in
new capital-intensive manufacturing industries. Such
industries are quickly dominated, not by the first firms
to acquire technologically sophisticated plants of
(35)   theoretically optimal size, but rather by the first to
exploit the full potential of such plants. Once some
firms achieve this, a market becomes extremely hard
to enter. Challengers must construct comparable
plants and do so after the first movers have already
(40)   worked out problems with suppliers or with new
production processes. Challengers must create
distribution networks and marketing systems in
markets where first movers have all the contacts and
know-how. And challengers must recruit management
(45)   teams to compete with those that have already
mastered these functional and strategic activities.

Questions 404–408 refer to the passage.

404. The passage suggests that in order for a manufacturer
in a capital-intensive industry to have a decisive
advantage over competitors making similar products,
the manufacturer must

(A) be the first in the industry to build production
facilities of theoretically optimal size

(B) make every effort to keep fixed and sunk costs
as low as possible

(C) be one of the first to operate its manufacturing
plants at minimum efficient scale

(D) produce goods of higher quality than those
produced by direct competitors

(E) stockpile raw materials at production sites in
order to ensure a steady flow of such materials

405. The passage suggests that which of the following is
true of a manufacturer's fixed and sunk costs?

(A) The extent to which they are determined
by market conditions for the goods being
manufactured is frequently underestimated.

(B) If they are kept as low as possible, the
manufacturer is very likely to realize significant
profits.

(C) They are the primary factor that determines
whether a manufacturer will realize economies of
scale.

(D) They should be on a par with the fixed and sunk
costs of the manufacturer's competitors.

(E) They are not affected by fluctuations in a
manufacturing plant's throughput.

406. In the context of the passage as a whole, the second
paragraph serves primarily to

(A) provide an example to support the argument
presented in the first paragraph

(B) evaluate various strategies discussed in the first
paragraph

(C) introduce evidence that undermines the
argument presented in the first paragraph

(D) anticipate possible objections to the argument
presented in the first paragraph

(E) demonstrate the potential dangers of a
commonly used strategy

407. The passage LEAST supports the inference that a manufacturer's throughput could be adversely affected by

   (A) a mistake in judgment regarding the selection of a wholesaler

   (B) a breakdown in the factory's machinery

   (C) a labor dispute on the factory floor

   (D) an increase in the cost per unit of output

   (E) a drop in the efficiency of the sales network

408. The primary purpose of the passage is to

   (A) point out the importance of intangible capital for realizing economies of scale in manufacturing

   (B) show that manufacturers frequently gain a competitive advantage from investment in large manufacturing facilities

   (C) argue that large manufacturing facilities often fail because of inadequate investment in both tangible and intangible capital

   (D) suggest that most new industries are likely to be dominated by firms that build large manufacturing plants early

   (E) explain why large manufacturing plants usually do not help manufacturers achieve economies of scale

Line
A small number of the forest species of lepidoptera (moths and butterflies, which exist as caterpillars during most of their life cycle) exhibit regularly recurring patterns of population growth
(5) and decline—such fluctuations in population are known as population cycles. Although many different variables influence population levels, a regular pattern such as a population cycle seems to imply a dominant, driving force. Identification of that driving
(10) force, however, has proved surprisingly elusive despite considerable research. The common approach of studying causes of population cycles by measuring the mortality caused by different agents, such as predatory birds or parasites, has been
(15) unproductive in the case of lepidoptera. Moreover, population ecologists' attempts to alter cycles by changing the caterpillars' habitat and by reducing caterpillar populations have not succeeded. In short, the evidence implies that these insect populations, if
(20) not self-regulating, may at least be regulated by an agent more intimately connected with the insect than are predatory birds or parasites.

Recent work suggests that this agent may be a virus. For many years, viral disease had been reported
(25) in declining populations of caterpillars, but population ecologists had usually considered viral disease to have contributed to the decline once it was underway rather than to have initiated it. The recent work has been made possible by new techniques of molecular
(30) biology that allow viral DNA to be detected at low concentrations in the environment. Nuclear polyhedrosis viruses are hypothesized to be the driving force behind population cycles in lepidoptera in part because the viruses themselves follow an
(35) infectious cycle in which, if protected from direct sunlight, they may remain virulent for many years in the environment, embedded in durable crystals of polyhedrin protein. Once ingested by a caterpillar, the crystals dissolve, releasing the virus to infect
(40) the insect's cells. Late in the course of the infection, millions of new virus particles are formed and enclosed in polyhedrin crystals. These crystals reenter the environment after the insect dies and decomposes, thus becoming available to infect
(45) other caterpillars.

One of the attractions of this hypothesis is its broad applicability. Remarkably, despite significant differences in habitat and behavior, many species of lepidoptera have population cycles of similar length, between eight
(50) and eleven years. Nuclear polyhedrosis viral infection is one factor these disparate species share.

Questions 409–414 refer to the passage.

409. The primary purpose of the passage is to

(A) describe the development of new techniques that may help to determine the driving force behind population cycles in lepidoptera

(B) present evidence that refutes a particular theory about the driving force behind population cycles in lepidoptera

(C) present a hypothesis about the driving force behind population cycles in lepidoptera

(D) describe the fluctuating patterns of population cycles in lepidoptera

(E) question the idea that a single driving force is behind population cycles in lepidoptera

410. It can be inferred from the passage that the mortality caused by agents such as predatory birds or parasites was measured in an attempt to

(A) develop an explanation for the existence of lepidoptera population cycles

(B) identify behavioral factors in lepidoptera that affect survival rates

(C) identify possible methods for controlling lepidoptera population growth

(D) provide evidence that lepidoptera populations are self-regulating

(E) determine the life stages of lepidoptera at which mortality rates are highest

411. Which of the following, if true, would most weaken the author's conclusion in lines 18–22 ?

(A) New research reveals that the number of species of birds and parasites that prey on lepidoptera has dropped significantly in recent years.

(B) New experiments in which the habitats of lepidoptera are altered in previously untried ways result in the shortening of lepidoptera population cycles.

(C) Recent experiments have revealed that the nuclear polyhedrosis virus is present in a number of predators and parasites of lepidoptera.

(D) Differences among the habitats of lepidoptera species make it difficult to assess the effects of weather on lepidoptera population cycles.

(E) Viral disease is typically observed in a large proportion of the lepidoptera population.

412. According to the passage, before the discovery of new techniques for detecting viral DNA, population ecologists believed that viral diseases

(A) were not widely prevalent among insect populations generally

(B) affected only the caterpillar life stage of lepidoptera

(C) were the driving force behind lepidoptera population cycles

(D) attacked already declining caterpillar populations

(E) infected birds and parasites that prey on various species of lepidoptera

413. According to the passage, nuclear polyhedrosis viruses can remain virulent in the environment only when

(A) the polyhedrin protein crystals dissolve

(B) caterpillar populations are in decline

(C) they are present in large numbers

(D) their concentration in a particular area remains low

(E) they are sheltered from direct sunlight

414. It can be inferred from the passage that while inside its polyhedrin protein crystals, the nuclear polyhedrosis virus

(A) is exposed to direct sunlight

(B) is attractive to predators

(C) cannot infect caterpillars' cells

(D) cannot be ingested by caterpillars

(E) cannot be detected by new techniques of molecular biology

Line   Resin is a plant secretion that hardens when exposed to air; fossilized resin is called amber. Although Pliny in the first century recognized that amber was produced from "marrow discharged by

(5)   trees," amber has been widely misunderstood to be a semiprecious gem and has even been described in mineralogy textbooks. Confusion also persists surrounding the term "resin," which was defined before rigorous chemical analyses were available.

(10)   Resin is often confused with gum, a substance produced in plants in response to bacterial infections, and with sap, an aqueous solution transported through certain plant tissues. Resin differs from both gum and sap in that scientists have not determined a

(15)   physiological function for resin.

    In the 1950s, entomologists posited that resin may function to repel or attract insects. Fraenkel conjectured that plants initially produced resin in nonspecific chemical responses to insect attack

(20)   and that, over time, plants evolved that produced resin with specific repellent effects. But some insect species, he noted, might overcome the repellent effects, actually becoming attracted to the resin. This might induce the insects to feed on those

(25)   plants or aid them in securing a breeding site. Later researchers suggested that resin mediates the complex interdependence, or "coevolution," of plants and insects over time. Such ideas led to the development of the specialized discipline of chemical

(30)   ecology, which is concerned with the role of plant chemicals in interactions with other organisms and with the evolution and ecology of plant antiherbivore chemistry (plants' chemical defenses against attack by herbivores such as insects).

Questions 415–418 refer to the passage.

415. According to the passage, which of the following is true of plant antiherbivore chemistry?

(A) Changes in a plant's antiherbivore chemistry may affect insect feeding behavior.

(B) A plant's repellent effects often involve interactions between gum and resin.

(C) A plant's antiherbivore responses assist in combating bacterial infections.

(D) Plant antiherbivore chemistry plays only a minor role in the coevolution of plants and insects.

(E) Researchers first studied repellent effects in plants beginning in the 1950s.

416. Of the following topics, which would be most likely to be studied within the discipline of chemical ecology as it is described in the passage?

(A) Seeds that become attached to certain insects, which in turn carry away the seeds and aid in the reproductive cycle of the plant species in question

(B) An insect species that feeds on weeds detrimental to crop health and yield, and how these insects might aid in agricultural production

(C) The effects of deforestation on the life cycles of subtropical carnivorous plants and the insect species on which the plants feed

(D) The growth patterns of a particular species of plant that has proved remarkably resistant to herbicides

(E) Insects that develop a tolerance for feeding on a plant that had previously been toxic to them, and the resultant changes within that plant species

417. The author refers to "bacterial infections" (see line 11) most likely in order to

    (A) describe the physiological function that gum performs in plants

    (B) demonstrate that sap is not the only substance that is transported through a plant's tissues

    (C) explain how modern chemical analysis has been used to clarify the function of resin

    (D) show that gum cannot serve as an effective defense against herbivores

    (E) give an example of how confusion has arisen with regard to the nature of resin

418. The author of the passage refers to Pliny most probably in order to

    (A) give an example of how the nature of amber has been misunderstood in the past

    (B) show that confusion about amber has long been more pervasive than confusion about resin

    (C) make note of the first known reference to amber as a semiprecious gem

    (D) point out an exception to a generalization about the history of people's understanding of amber

    (E) demonstrate that Pliny believed amber to be a mineral

Line   During the 1980s, many economic historians
        studying Latin America focused on the impact of
        the Great Depression of the 1930s. Most of these
        historians argued that although the Depression
(5)   began earlier in Latin America than in the United
        States, it was less severe in Latin America and did
        not significantly impede industrial growth there.
        The historians' argument was grounded in national
        government records concerning tax revenues and
(10)   exports and in government-sponsored industrial
        censuses, from which historians have drawn
        conclusions about total manufacturing output
        and profit levels across Latin America. However,
        economic statistics published by Latin American
(15)   governments in the early twentieth century are
        neither reliable nor consistent; this is especially
        true of manufacturing data, which were gathered
        from factory owners for taxation purposes and
        which therefore may well be distorted. Moreover,
(20)   one cannot assume a direct correlation between
        the output level and the profit level of a given
        industry as these variables often move in opposite
        directions. Finally, national and regional economies
        are composed of individual firms and industries,
(25)   and relying on general, sweeping economic
        indicators may mask substantial variations among
        these different enterprises. For example, recent
        analyses of previously unexamined data on textile
        manufacturing in Brazil and Mexico suggest that the
(30)   Great Depression had a more severe impact on this
        Latin American industry than scholars
        had recognized.

419. The primary purpose of the passage is to

    (A)   compare the impact of the Great Depression
           on Latin America with its impact on the United
           States

    (B)   criticize a school of economic historians for
           failing to analyze the Great Depression in Latin
           America within a global context

    (C)   illustrate the risks inherent in comparing different
           types of economic enterprises to explain
           economic phenomena

    (D)   call into question certain scholars' views
           concerning the severity of the Great Depression
           in Latin America

    (E)   demonstrate that the Great Depression had
           a more severe impact on industry in Latin
           America than in certain other regions

420. Which of the following conclusions about the Great
     Depression is best supported by the passage?

    (A)   It did not impede Latin American industrial
           growth as much as historians had previously
           thought.

    (B)   It had a more severe impact on the Brazilian and
           the Mexican textile industries than it had on Latin
           America as a region.

    (C)   It affected the Latin American textile industry
           more severely than it did any other industry in
           Latin America.

    (D)   The overall impact on Latin American industrial
           growth should be reevaluated by economic
           historians.

    (E)   Its impact on Latin America should not be
           compared with its impact on the United States.

421. Which of the following, if true, would most strengthen the author's assertion regarding economic indicators in lines 25–27 ?

    (A) During an economic depression, European textile manufacturers' profits rise while their industrial output remains steady.

    (B) During a national economic recession, United States microchips manufacturers' profits rise sharply while United States steel manufacturers' profits plunge.

    (C) During the years following a severe economic depression, textile manufacturers' output levels and profit levels increase in Brazil and Mexico but not in the rest of Latin America.

    (D) Although Japanese industry as a whole recovers after an economic recession, it does not regain its previously high levels of production.

    (E) While European industrial output increases in the years following an economic depression, total output remains below that of Japan or the United States.

Line   Among the myths taken as fact by the environmental managers of most corporations is the belief that environmental regulations affect all competitors in a given industry uniformly. In reality,
(5)   regulatory costs—and therefore compliance— fall unevenly, economically disadvantaging some companies and benefiting others. For example, a plant situated near a number of larger noncompliant competitors is less likely to attract
(10)   the attention of local regulators than is an isolated plant, and less attention means lower costs.
    Additionally, large plants can spread compliance costs such as waste treatment across a larger revenue base; on the other hand, some smaller
(15)   plants may not even be subject to certain provisions such as permit or reporting requirements by virtue of their size. Finally, older production technologies often continue to generate toxic wastes that were not regulated when the
(20)   technology was first adopted. New regulations have imposed extensive compliance costs on companies still using older industrial coal-fired burners that generate high sulfur dioxide and nitrogen oxide outputs, for example, whereas new
(25)   facilities generally avoid processes that would create such waste products. By realizing that they have discretion and that not all industries are affected equally by environmental regulation, environmental managers can help their companies
(30)   to achieve a competitive edge by anticipating regulatory pressure and exploring all possibilities for addressing how changing regulations will affect their companies specifically.

Questions 422–425 refer to the passage.

422. It can be inferred from the passage that a large plant might have to spend more than a similar but smaller plant on environmental compliance because the larger plant is

(A) more likely to attract attention from local regulators

(B) less likely to be exempt from permit and reporting requirements

(C) less likely to have regulatory costs passed on to it by companies that supply its raw materials

(D) more likely to employ older production technologies

(E) more likely to generate wastes that are more environmentally damaging than those generated by smaller plants

423. According to the passage, which of the following statements about sulfur dioxide and nitrogen oxide outputs is true?

(A) Older production technologies cannot be adapted so as to reduce production of these outputs as waste products.

(B) Under the most recent environmental regulations, industrial plants are no longer permitted to produce these outputs.

(C) Although these outputs are environmentally hazardous, some plants still generate them as waste products despite the high compliance costs they impose.

(D) Many older plants have developed innovative technological processes that reduce the amounts of these outputs generated as waste products.

(E) Since the production processes that generate these outputs are less costly than alternative processes, these less expensive processes are sometimes adopted despite their acknowledged environmental hazards.

424. Which of the following best describes the relationship of the statement about large plants (lines 12–17) to the passage as a whole?

    (A)   It presents a hypothesis that is disproved later in the passage.

    (B)   It highlights an opposition between two ideas mentioned in the passage.

    (C)   It provides examples to support a claim made earlier in the passage.

    (D)   It exemplifies a misconception mentioned earlier in the passage.

    (E)   It draws an analogy between two situations described in the passage.

425. The primary purpose of the passage is to

    (A)   address a widespread environmental management problem and suggest possible solutions

    (B)   illustrate varying levels of compliance with environmental regulation among different corporations

    (C)   describe the various alternatives to traditional methods of environmental management

    (D)   advocate increased corporate compliance with environmental regulation

    (E)   correct a common misconception about the impact of environmental regulations

Line Findings from several studies on corporate mergers and acquisitions during the 1970s and 1980s raise questions about why firms initiate and consummate such transactions. One study showed,
(5) for example, that acquiring firms were on average unable to maintain acquired firms' pre-merger levels of profitability. A second study concluded that post-acquisition gains to most acquiring firms were not adequate to cover the premiums paid to obtain
(10) acquired firms. A third demonstrated that, following the announcement of a prospective merger, the stock of the prospective acquiring firm tends to increase in value much less than does that of the firm for which it bids. Yet mergers and acquisitions remain common,
(15) and bidders continue to assert that their objectives are economic ones. Acquisitions may well have the desirable effect of channeling a nation's resources efficiently from less to more efficient sectors of its economy, but the individual executives arranging
(20) these deals must see them as advancing either their own or their companies' private economic interests. It seems that factors having little to do with corporate economic interests explain acquisitions. These factors may include the incentive compensation of
(25) executives, lack of monitoring by boards of directors, and managerial error in estimating the value of firms targeted for acquisition. Alternatively, the acquisition acts of bidders may derive from modeling: a manager does what other managers do.

Questions 426–429 refer to the passage.

426. The primary purpose of the passage is to

(A) review research demonstrating the benefits of corporate mergers and acquisitions and examine some of the drawbacks that acquisition behavior entails

(B) contrast the effects of corporate mergers and acquisitions on acquiring firms and on firms that are acquired

(C) report findings that raise questions about a reason for corporate mergers and acquisitions and suggest possible alternative reasons

(D) explain changes in attitude on the part of acquiring firms toward corporate mergers and acquisitions

(E) account for a recent decline in the rate of corporate mergers and acquisitions

427. It can be inferred from the passage that the author would be most likely to agree with which of the following statements about corporate acquisitions?

(A) Their known benefits to national economies explain their appeal to individual firms during the 1970s and 1980s.

(B) Despite their adverse impact on some firms, they are the best way to channel resources from less to more productive sectors of a nation's economy.

(C) They are as likely to occur because of poor monitoring by boards of directors as to be caused by incentive compensation for managers.

(D) They will be less prevalent in the future, since their actual effects will gain wider recognition.

(E) Factors other than economic benefit to the acquiring firm help to explain the frequency with which they occur.

428. The author of the passage mentions the effect of acquisitions on national economies most probably in order to

(A) provide an explanation for the mergers and acquisitions of the 1970s and 1980s overlooked by the findings discussed in the passage

(B) suggest that national economic interests played an important role in the mergers and acquisitions of the 1970s and 1980s

(C) support a noneconomic explanation for the mergers and acquisitions of the 1970s and 1980s that was cited earlier in the passage

(D) cite and point out the inadequacy of one possible explanation for the prevalence of mergers and acquisitions during the 1970s and 1980s

(E) explain how modeling affected the decisions made by managers involved in mergers and acquisitions during the 1970s and 1980s

429. The author of the passage implies that which of the following is a possible partial explanation for acquisition behavior during the 1970s and 1980s?

(A) Managers wished to imitate other managers primarily because they saw how financially beneficial other firms' acquisitions were.

(B) Managers miscalculated the value of firms that were to be acquired.

(C) Lack of consensus within boards of directors resulted in their imposing conflicting goals on managers.

(D) Total compensation packages for managers increased during that period.

(E) The value of bidding firms' stock increased significantly when prospective mergers were announced.

Line   Two works published in 1984 demonstrate
contrasting approaches to writing the history of
United States women. Buel and Buel's biography
of Mary Fish (1736–1818) makes little effort to
(5) place her story in the context of recent
historiography on women. Lebsock, meanwhile,
attempts not only to write the history of women in
one southern community, but also to redirect two
decades of historiographical debate as to
(10) whether women gained or lost status in the
nineteenth century as compared with the
eighteenth century. Although both books offer the
reader the opportunity to assess this controversy
regarding women's status, only Lebsock's deals with
(15) it directly. She examines several different aspects
of women's status, helping to refine and resolve the
issues. She concludes that while
women gained autonomy in some areas,
especially in the private sphere, they lost it in
(20) many aspects of the economic sphere. More
importantly, she shows that the debate itself
depends on frame of reference: in many respects,
women lost power in relation to men, for example,
as certain jobs (delivering babies, supervising
(25) schools) were taken over by men. Yet women also
gained power in comparison with their previous
status, owning a higher proportion of real estate,
for example. In contrast, Buel and Buel's
biography provides ample raw material for
(30) questioning the myth, fostered by some
historians, of a colonial golden age in the
eighteenth century but does not give the reader
much guidance in analyzing the controversy over
women's status.

430. The primary purpose of the passage is to

(A) examine two sides of a historiographical debate

(B) call into question an author's approach to a historiographical debate

(C) examine one author's approach to a historiographical debate

(D) discuss two authors' works in relationship to a historiographical debate

(E) explain the prevalent perspective on a historiographical debate

431. The author of the passage mentions the supervision of schools primarily in order to

(A) remind readers of the role education played in the cultural changes of the nineteenth century in the United States

(B) suggest an area in which nineteenth-century American women were relatively free to exercise power

(C) provide an example of an occupation for which accurate data about women's participation are difficult to obtain

(D) speculate about which occupations were considered suitable for United States women of the nineteenth century

(E) illustrate how the answers to questions about women's status depend on particular contexts

432. With which of the following characterizations of Lebsock's contribution to the controversy concerning women's status in the nineteenth-century United States would the author of the passage be most likely to agree?

(A) Lebsock has studied women from a formerly neglected region and time period.

(B) Lebsock has demonstrated the importance of frame of reference in answering questions about women's status.

(C) Lebsock has addressed the controversy by using women's current status as a frame of reference.

(D) Lebsock has analyzed statistics about occupations and property that were previously ignored.

(E) Lebsock has applied recent historiographical methods to the biography of a nineteenth-century woman.

433. According to the passage, Lebsock's work differs from Buel and Buel's work in that Lebsock's work

(A) uses a large number of primary sources

(B) ignores issues of women's legal status

(C) refuses to take a position on women's status in the eighteenth century

(D) addresses larger historiographical issues

(E) fails to provide sufficient material to support its claims

434. The passage suggests that Lebsock believes that compared to nineteenth-century American women, eighteenth-century American women were

(A) in many respects less powerful in relation to men

(B) more likely to own real estate

(C) generally more economically independent

(D) more independent in conducting their private lives

(E) less likely to work as school superintendents

435. The passage suggests that Buel and Buel's biography of Mary Fish provides evidence for which of the following views of women's history?

(A) Women have lost power in relation to men since the colonial era.

(B) Women of the colonial era were not as likely to be concerned with their status as were women in the nineteenth century.

(C) The colonial era was not as favorable for women as some historians have believed.

(D) Women had more economic autonomy in the colonial era than in the nineteenth century.

(E) Women's occupations were generally more respected in the colonial era than in the nineteenth century.

Line   Acting on the recommendation of a British
government committee investigating the high
incidence in white lead factories of illness among
employees, most of whom were women, the Home
(5)   Secretary proposed in 1895 that Parliament enact
legislation that would prohibit women from holding
most jobs in white lead factories. Although the
Women's Industrial Defence Committee (WIDC),
formed in 1892 in response to earlier legislative
(10)   attempts to restrict women's labor, did not discount
the white lead trade's potential health dangers, it
opposed the proposal, viewing it as yet another
instance of limiting women's work opportunities.
    Also opposing the proposal was the Society for
(15)   Promoting the Employment of Women (SPEW),
which attempted to challenge it by investigating the
causes of illness in white lead factories. SPEW
contended, and WIDC concurred, that controllable
conditions in such factories were responsible for
(20)   the development of lead poisoning. SPEW provided
convincing evidence that lead poisoning could be
avoided if workers were careful and clean and if
already extant workplace safety regulations were
stringently enforced. However, the Women's Trade
(25)   Union League (WTUL), which had ceased in the late
1880s to oppose restrictions on women's labor,
supported the eventually enacted proposal, in part
because safety regulations were generally not being
enforced in white lead factories, where there were
(30)   no unions (and little prospect of any) to pressure
employers to comply with safety regulations.

Questions 436–438 refer to the passage.

436. The passage suggests that WIDC differed from WTUL
      in which of the following ways?

      (A)   WIDC believed that the existing safety regulations
             were adequate to protect women's health,
             whereas WTUL believed that such regulations
             needed to be strengthened.

      (B)   WIDC believed that unions could not succeed
             in pressuring employers to comply with such
             regulations, whereas WTUL believed that unions
             could succeed in doing so.

      (C)   WIDC believed that lead poisoning in white
             lead factories could be avoided by controlling
             conditions there, whereas WTUL believed that
             lead poisoning in such factories could not
             be avoided no matter how stringently safety
             regulations were enforced.

      (D)   At the time that the legislation concerning white
             lead factories was proposed, WIDC was primarily
             concerned with addressing health conditions
             in white lead factories, whereas WTUL was
             concerned with improving working conditions in
             all types of factories.

      (E)   At the time that WIDC was opposing legislative
             attempts to restrict women's labor, WTUL had
             already ceased to do so.

437. Which of the following, if true, would most clearly support the contention attributed to SPEW in lines 17–20 ?

   (A) Those white lead factories that most strongly enforced regulations concerning worker safety and hygiene had the lowest incidences of lead poisoning among employees.

   (B) The incidence of lead poisoning was much higher among women who worked in white lead factories than among women who worked in other types of factories.

   (C) There were many household sources of lead that could have contributed to the incidence of lead poisoning among women who also worked outside the home in the late nineteenth century.

   (D) White lead factories were more stringent than were certain other types of factories in their enforcement of workplace safety regulations.

   (E) Even brief exposure to the conditions typically found in white lead factories could cause lead poisoning among factory workers.

438. The passage is primarily concerned with

   (A) presenting various groups' views of the motives of those proposing certain legislation

   (B) contrasting the reasoning of various groups concerning their positions on certain proposed legislation

   (C) tracing the process whereby certain proposed legislation was eventually enacted

   (D) assessing the success of tactics adopted by various groups with respect to certain proposed legislation

   (E) evaluating the arguments of various groups concerning certain proposed legislation

Line   It is an odd but indisputable fact that the
seventeenth-century English women who are
generally regarded as among the forerunners of
modern feminism are almost all identified with the
(5)   Royalist side in the conflict between Royalists and
Parliamentarians known as the English Civil Wars.
Since Royalist ideology is often associated with the
radical patriarchalism of seventeenth-century
political theorist Robert Filmer—a patriarchalism
(10)   that equates family and kingdom and asserts the
divinely ordained absolute power of the king and,
by analogy, of the male head of the household—
historians have been understandably puzzled by the
fact that Royalist women wrote the earliest
(15)   extended criticisms of the absolute subordination
of women in marriage and the earliest systematic
assertions of women's rational and moral equality
with men. Some historians have questioned the
facile equation of Royalist ideology with Filmerian
(20)   patriarchalism; and indeed, there may have been
no consistent differences between Royalists and
Parliamentarians on issues of family organization
and women's political rights, but in that case one
would expect early feminists to be equally divided
(25)   between the two sides.
        Catherine Gallagher argues that Royalism
engendered feminism because the ideology of
absolute monarchy provided a transition to an
ideology of the absolute self. She cites the example
(30)   of the notoriously eccentric author Margaret
Cavendish (1626–1673), duchess of Newcastle.
Cavendish claimed to be as ambitious as any
woman could be, but knowing that as a woman she
was excluded from the pursuit of power in the real
(35)   world, she resolved to be mistress of her own
world, the "immaterial world" that any person can
create within her own mind—and, as a writer, on
paper. In proclaiming what she called her
"singularity," Cavendish insisted that she was a
(40)   self-sufficient being within her mental empire, the
center of her own subjective universe rather than a
satellite orbiting a dominant male planet. In
justifying this absolute singularity, Cavendish
repeatedly invoked the model of the absolute
(45)   monarch, a figure that became a metaphor for the
self-enclosed, autonomous nature of the individual
person. Cavendish's successors among early
feminists retained her notion of woman's sovereign
self, but they also sought to break free from the
(50)   complete political and social isolation that her
absolute singularity entailed.

Questions 439–444 refer to the passage.

439. The author of the passage refers to Robert Filmer (see line 9) primarily in order to

    (A) show that Royalist ideology was somewhat more radical than most historians appear to realize

    (B) qualify the claim that patriarchalism formed the basis of Royalist ideology

    (C) question the view that most early feminists were associated with the Royalist faction

    (D) highlight an apparent tension between Royalist ideology and the ideas of early feminists

    (E) argue that Royalists held conflicting opinions on issues of family organization and women's political rights

440. The passage suggests which of the following about the seventeenth-century English women mentioned in line 2 ?

    (A) Their status as forerunners of modern feminism is not entirely justified.

    (B) They did not openly challenge the radical patriarchalism of Royalist Filmerian ideology.

    (C) Cavendish was the first among these women to criticize women's subordination in marriage and assert women's equality with men.

    (D) Their views on family organization and women's political rights were diametrically opposed to those of both Royalist and Parliamentarian ideology.

    (E) Historians would be less puzzled if more of them were identified with the Parliamentarian side in the English Civil Wars.

441. The passage suggests that Margaret Cavendish's decision to become an author was motivated, at least in part, by a desire to

    (A) justify her support for the Royalist cause
    (B) encourage her readers to work toward eradicating Filmerian patriarchalism
    (C) persuade other women to break free from their political and social isolation
    (D) analyze the causes for women's exclusion from the pursuit of power
    (E) create a world over which she could exercise total control

442. The phrase "a satellite orbiting a dominant male planet" (lines 41–42) refers most directly to

    (A) Cavendish's concept that each woman is a sovereign self
    (B) the complete political and social isolation of absolute singularity
    (C) the immaterial world that a writer can create on paper
    (D) the absolute subordination of women in a patriarchal society
    (E) the metaphorical figure of the absolute monarch

443. The primary purpose of the passage is to

    (A) trace the historical roots of a modern sociopolitical movement
    (B) present one scholar's explanation for a puzzling historical phenomenon
    (C) contrast two interpretations of the ideological origins of a political conflict
    (D) establish a link between the ideology of an influential political theorist and that of a notoriously eccentric writer
    (E) call attention to some points of agreement between opposing sides in an ideological debate

444. Which of the following, if true, would most clearly undermine Gallagher's explanation of the link between Royalism and feminism?

    (A) Because of their privileged backgrounds, Royalist women were generally better educated than were their Parliamentarian counterparts.
    (B) Filmer himself had read some of Cavendish's early writings and was highly critical of her ideas.
    (C) Cavendish's views were highly individual and were not shared by the other Royalist women who wrote early feminist works.
    (D) The Royalist and Parliamentarian ideologies were largely in agreement on issues of family organization and women's political rights.
    (E) The Royalist side included a sizable minority faction that was opposed to the more radical tendencies of Filmerian patriarchalism.

Line   Frazier and Mosteller assert that medical research could be improved by a move toward larger, simpler clinical trials of medical treatments. Currently, researchers collect far more background information
(5)   on patients than is strictly required for their trials—substantially more than hospitals collect—thereby escalating costs of data collection, storage, and analysis. Although limiting information collection could increase the risk that researchers will overlook
(10)   facts relevant to a study, Frazier and Mosteller contend that such risk, never entirely eliminable from research, would still be small in most studies. Only in research on entirely new treatments are new and unexpected variables likely to arise.
(15)   Frazier and Mosteller propose not only that researchers limit data collection on individual patients but also that researchers enroll more patients in clinical trials, thereby obtaining a more representative sample of the total population with
(20)   the disease under study. Often researchers restrict study participation to patients who have no ailments besides those being studied. A treatment judged successful under these ideal conditions can then be evaluated under normal conditions. Broadening the
(25)   range of trial participants, Frazier and Mosteller suggest, would enable researchers to evaluate a treatment's efficacy for diverse patients under various conditions and to evaluate its effectiveness for different patient subgroups. For example, the value
(30)   of a treatment for a progressive disease may vary according to a patient's stage of disease. Patients' ages may also affect a treatment's efficacy.

445.   The passage is primarily concerned with

(A)   identifying two practices in medical research that may affect the accuracy of clinical trials

(B)   describing aspects of medical research that tend to drive up costs

(C)   evaluating an analysis of certain shortcomings of current medical research practices

(D)   describing proposed changes to the ways in which clinical trials are conducted

(E)   explaining how medical researchers have traditionally conducted clinical trials and how such trials are likely to change

446.   Which of the following can be inferred from the passage about a study of the category of patients referred to in lines 20–22 ?

(A)   Its findings might have limited applicability.

(B)   It would be prohibitively expensive in its attempt to create ideal conditions.

(C)   It would be the best way to sample the total population of potential patients.

(D)   It would allow researchers to limit information collection without increasing the risk that important variables could be overlooked.

(E)   Its findings would be more accurate if it concerned treatments for a progressive disease than if it concerned treatments for a nonprogressive disease.

447. It can be inferred from the passage that a study limited to patients like those mentioned in lines 20–22 would have which of the following advantages over the kind of study proposed by Frazier and Mosteller?

    (A) It would yield more data and its findings would be more accurate.

    (B) It would cost less in the long term, though it would be more expensive in its initial stages.

    (C) It would limit the number of variables researchers would need to consider when evaluating the treatment under study.

    (D) It would help researchers to identify subgroups of patients with secondary conditions that might also be treatable.

    (E) It would enable researchers to assess the value of an experimental treatment for the average patient.

448. The author mentions patients' ages (line 32) primarily in order to

    (A) identify the most critical variable differentiating subgroups of patients

    (B) cast doubt on the advisability of implementing Frazier and Mosteller's proposals about medical research

    (C) indicate why progressive diseases may require different treatments at different stages

    (D) illustrate a point about the value of enrolling a wide range of patients in clinical trials

    (E) substantiate an argument about the problems inherent in enrolling large numbers of patients in clinical trials

449. According to the passage, which of the following describes a result of the way in which researchers generally conduct clinical trials?

    (A) They expend resources on the storage of information likely to be irrelevant to the study they are conducting.

    (B) They sometimes compromise the accuracy of their findings by collecting and analyzing more information than is strictly required for their trials.

    (C) They avoid the risk of overlooking variables that might affect their findings, even though doing so raises their research costs.

    (D) Because they attempt to analyze too much information, they overlook facts that could emerge as relevant to their studies.

    (E) In order to approximate the conditions typical of medical treatment, they base their methods of information collection on those used by hospitals.

Line   There are recent reports of apparently drastic
declines in amphibian populations and of extinctions
of a number of the world's endangered amphibian
species. These declines, if real, may be signs of a
(5)   general trend toward extinction, and many
environmentalists have claimed that immediate
environmental action is necessary to remedy
this "amphibian crisis," which, in their view, is an
indicator of general and catastrophic environmental
(10)   degradation due to human activity.
     To evaluate these claims, it is useful to make a
preliminary distinction that is far too often ignored.
A declining population should not be confused with
an endangered one. An endangered population is
(15)   always rare, almost always small, and, by definition,
under constant threat of extinction even without a
proximate cause in human activities. Its disappearance,
however unfortunate, should come as no great
surprise. Moreover, chance events—which may
(20)   indicate nothing about the direction of trends in
population size—may lead to its extinction. The
probability of extinction due to such random factors
depends on the population size and is independent of
the prevailing direction of change in that size.
(25)   For biologists, population declines are potentially
more worrisome than extinctions. Persistent
declines, especially in large populations, indicate a
changed ecological context. Even here, distinctions
must again be made among declines that are only
(30)   apparent (in the sense that they are part of habitual
cycles or of normal fluctuations), declines that take
a population to some lower but still acceptable
level, and those that threaten extinction (e.g., by
taking the number of individuals below the minimum
(35)   viable population). Anecdotal reports of population
decreases cannot distinguish among these
possibilities, and some amphibian populations have
shown strong fluctuations in the past.
     It is indisputably true that there is simply not
(40)   enough long-term scientific data on amphibian
populations to enable researchers to identify real
declines in amphibian populations. Many fairly
common amphibian species declared all but extinct
after severe declines in the 1950s and 1960s
(45)   have subsequently recovered, and so might
the apparently declining populations that have
generated the current appearance of an amphibian
crisis. Unfortunately, long-term data will not soon
be forthcoming, and postponing environmental
(50)   action while we wait for it may doom species and
whole ecosystems to extinction.

Questions 450–455 refer to the passage.

450. The primary purpose of the passage is to

     (A)   assess the validity of a certain view

     (B)   distinguish between two phenomena

     (C)   identify the causes of a problem

     (D)   describe a disturbing trend

     (E)   allay concern about a particular phenomenon

451. It can be inferred from the passage that the author
believes which of the following to be true of the
environmentalists mentioned in lines 5–6 ?

     (A)   They have wrongly chosen to focus on anecdotal
reports rather than on the long-term data that
are currently available concerning amphibians.

     (B)   Their recommendations are flawed because
their research focuses too narrowly on a single
category of animal species.

     (C)   Their certainty that population declines in general
are caused by environmental degradation is not
warranted.

     (D)   They have drawn premature conclusions
concerning a crisis in amphibian populations
from recent reports of declines.

     (E)   They have overestimated the effects of chance
events on trends in amphibian populations.

452. It can be inferred from the passage that the author
believes which of the following to be true of the
amphibian extinctions that have recently been
reported?

     (A)   They have resulted primarily from human
activities causing environmental degradation.

     (B)   They could probably have been prevented if
timely action had been taken to protect the
habitats of amphibian species.

     (C)   They should not come as a surprise, because
amphibian populations generally have been
declining for a number of years.

     (D)   They have probably been caused by a
combination of chance events.

     (E)   They do not clearly constitute evidence of
general environmental degradation.

453. According to the passage, each of the following is true of endangered amphibian species EXCEPT:

   (A) They are among the rarest kinds of amphibians.
   (B) They generally have populations that are small in size.
   (C) They are in constant danger of extinction.
   (D) Those with decreasing populations are the most likely candidates for immediate extinction.
   (E) They are in danger of extinction due to events that sometimes have nothing to do with human activities.

454. Which of the following most accurately describes the organization of the passage?

   (A) A question is raised, a distinction regarding it is made, and the question is answered.
   (B) An interpretation is presented, its soundness is examined, and a warning is given.
   (C) A situation is described, its consequences are analyzed, and a prediction is made.
   (D) Two interpretations of a phenomenon are described, and one of them is rejected as invalid.
   (E) Two methods for analyzing a phenomenon are compared, and further study of the phenomenon is recommended.

455. Which of the following best describes the function of the sentence in lines 35–38 ?

   (A) To give an example of a particular kind of study
   (B) To cast doubt on an assertion made in the previous sentence
   (C) To raise an objection to a view presented in the first paragraph
   (D) To provide support for a view presented in the first paragraph
   (E) To introduce an idea that will be countered in the following paragraph

Line While the most abundant and dominant species within a particular ecosystem is often crucial in perpetuating the ecosystem, a "keystone" species, here defined as one whose effects are much larger

(5) than would be predicted from its abundance, can also play a vital role. But because complex species interactions may be involved, identifying a keystone species by removing the species and observing changes in the ecosystem is problematic. It might

(10) seem that certain traits would clearly define a species as a keystone species; for example, *Pisaster ochraceus* is often a keystone predator because it consumes and suppresses mussel populations, which in the absence of this starfish

(15) can be a dominant species. But such predation on a dominant or potentially dominant species occurs in systems that do as well as in systems that do not have species that play keystone roles. Moreover, whereas *P. ochraceus* occupies an unambiguous

(20) keystone role on wave-exposed rocky headlands, in more wave-sheltered habitats the impact of *P. ochraceus* predation is weak or nonexistent, and at certain sites sand burial is responsible for eliminating mussels. Keystone status appears to

(25) depend on context, whether of particular geography or of such factors as community diversity (for example, a reduction in species diversity may thrust more of the remaining species into keystone roles) and length of species

(30) interaction (since newly arrived species in particular may dramatically affect ecosystems).

Questions 456–459 refer to the passage.

456. The passage mentions which of the following as a factor that affects the role of *P. ochraceus* as a keystone species within different habitats?

(A) The degree to which the habitat is sheltered from waves

(B) The degree to which other animals within a habitat prey on mussels

(C) The fact that mussel populations are often not dominant within some habitats occupied by *P. ochraceus*

(D) The size of the *P. ochraceus* population within the habitat

(E) The fact that there is great species diversity within some habitats occupied by *P. ochraceus*

457. Which of the following hypothetical experiments most clearly exemplifies the method of identifying species' roles that the author considers problematic?

(A) A population of seals in an Arctic habitat is counted in order to determine whether it is the dominant species in that ecosystem.

(B) A species of fish that is a keystone species in one marine ecosystem is introduced into another marine ecosystem to see whether the species will come to occupy a keystone role.

(C) In order to determine whether a species of monkey is a keystone species within a particular ecosystem, the monkeys are removed from that ecosystem and the ecosystem is then studied.

(D) Different mountain ecosystems are compared to determine how geography affects a particular species' ability to dominate its ecosystem.

(E) In a grassland experiencing a changing climate, patterns of species extinction are traced in order to evaluate the effect of climate changes on keystone species in that grassland.

458. Which of the following, if true, would most clearly support the argument about keystone status advanced in the last sentence of the passage (lines 24–31) ?

(A) A species of bat is primarily responsible for keeping insect populations within an ecosystem low, and the size of the insect population in turn affects bird species within that ecosystem.

(B) A species of iguana occupies a keystone role on certain tropical islands, but does not play that role on adjacent tropical islands that are inhabited by a greater number of animal species.

(C) Close observation of a savannah ecosystem reveals that more species occupy keystone roles within that ecosystem than biologists had previously believed.

(D) As a keystone species of bee becomes more abundant, it has a larger effect on the ecosystem it inhabits.

(E) A species of moth that occupies a keystone role in a prairie habitat develops coloration patterns that camouflage it from potential predators.

459. The passage suggests which of the following about the identification of a species as a keystone species?

(A) Such an identification depends primarily on the species' relationship to the dominant species.

(B) Such an identification can best be made by removing the species from a particular ecosystem and observing changes that occur in the ecosystem.

(C) Such an identification is likely to be less reliable as an ecosystem becomes less diverse.

(D) Such an identification seems to depend on various factors within the ecosystem.

(E) Such an identification can best be made by observing predation behavior.

Line   Conodonts, the spiky phosphatic remains (bones and teeth composed of calcium phosphate) of tiny marine animals that probably appeared about 520 million years ago, were once among the most
(5)   controversial of fossils. Both the nature of the organism to which the remains belonged and the function of the remains were unknown. However, since the 1981 discovery of fossils preserving not just the phosphatic elements but also other remains
(10)   of the tiny soft-bodied animals (also called conodonts) that bore them, scientists' reconstructions of the animals' anatomy have had important implications for hypotheses concerning the development of the vertebrate skeleton.
(15)   The vertebrate skeleton had traditionally been regarded as a defensive development, champions of this view postulating that it was only with the much later evolution of jaws that vertebrates became predators. The first vertebrates, which were soft-
(20)   bodied, would have been easy prey for numerous invertebrate carnivores, especially if these early vertebrates were sedentary suspension feeders. Thus, traditionalists argued, these animals developed coverings of bony scales or plates, and teeth were
(25)   secondary features, adapted from the protective bony scales. Indeed, external skeletons of this type are common among the well-known fossils of ostracoderms, jawless vertebrates that existed from approximately 500 to 400 million years ago.
(30)   However, other paleontologists argued that many of the definitive characteristics of vertebrates, such as paired eyes and muscular and skeletal adaptations for active life, would not have evolved unless the first vertebrates were predatory. Teeth were more
(35)   primitive than external armor according to this view, and the earliest vertebrates were predators.
    The stiffening notochord along the back of the body, V-shaped muscle blocks along the sides, and posterior tail fins help to identify conodonts as
(40)   among the most primitive of vertebrates. The lack of any mineralized structures apart from the elements in the mouth indicates that conodonts were more primitive than the armored jawless fishes such as the ostracoderms. It now appears that the hard parts that
(45)   first evolved in the mouth of an animal improved its efficiency as a predator, and that aggression rather than protection was the driving force behind the origin of the vertebrate skeleton.

Questions 460–462 refer to the passage.

460. According to the passage, the anatomical evidence provided by the preserved soft bodies of conodonts led scientists to conclude that

   (A) conodonts had actually been invertebrate carnivores

   (B) conodonts' teeth were adapted from protective bony scales

   (C) conodonts were primitive vertebrate suspension feeders

   (D) primitive vertebrates with teeth appeared earlier than armored vertebrates

   (E) scientists' original observations concerning the phosphatic remains of conodonts were essentially correct

461. The second paragraph in the passage serves primarily to

   (A) outline the significance of the 1981 discovery of conodont remains to the debate concerning the development of the vertebrate skeleton

   (B) contrast the traditional view of the development of the vertebrate skeleton with a view derived from the 1981 discovery of conodont remains

   (C) contrast the characteristics of the ostracoderms with the characteristics of earlier soft-bodied vertebrates

   (D) explain the importance of the development of teeth among the earliest vertebrate predators

   (E) present the two sides of the debate concerning the development of the vertebrate skeleton

462. It can be inferred that on the basis of the 1981 discovery of conodont remains, paleontologists could draw which of the following conclusions?

   (A)   The earliest vertebrates were sedentary suspension feeders.

   (B)   Ostracoderms were not the earliest vertebrates.

   (C)   Defensive armor preceded jaws among vertebrates.

   (D)   Paired eyes and adaptations for activity are definitive characteristics of vertebrates.

   (E)   Conodonts were unlikely to have been predators.

Line   Jon Clark's study of the effect of the modernization
          of a telephone exchange on exchange maintenance
          work and workers is a solid contribution to a debate
          that encompasses two lively issues in the history and
(5)   sociology of technology: technological determinism
          and social constructivism.
               Clark makes the point that the characteristics of a
          technology have a decisive influence on job skills and
          work organization. Put more strongly, technology can
(10)   be a primary determinant of social and managerial
          organization. Clark believes this possibility has
          been obscured by the recent sociological fashion,
          exemplified by Braverman's analysis, that emphasizes
          the way machinery reflects social choices. For
(15)   Braverman, the shape of a technological system is
          subordinate to the manager's desire to wrest control
          of the labor process from the workers. Technological
          change is construed as the outcome of negotiations
          among interested parties who seek to incorporate
(20)   their own interests into the design and configuration
          of the machinery. This position represents the new
          mainstream called social constructivism.
               The constructivists gain acceptance by
          misrepresenting technological determinism:
(25)   technological determinists are supposed to believe,
          for example, that machinery imposes appropriate
          forms of order on society. The alternative to
          constructivism, in other words, is to view technology
          as existing outside society, capable of directly
(30)   influencing skills and work organization.
               Clark refutes the extremes of the constructivists
          by both theoretical and empirical arguments.
          Theoretically he defines "technology" in terms of
          relationships between social and technical variables.
(35)   Attempts to reduce the meaning of technology to
          cold, hard metal are bound to fail, for machinery is
          just scrap unless it is organized functionally and
          supported by appropriate systems of operation and
          maintenance. At the empirical level Clark shows how
(40)   a change at the telephone exchange from
          maintenance-intensive electromechanical switches
          to semielectronic switching systems altered work
          tasks, skills, training opportunities, administration,
          and organization of workers. Some changes Clark
(45)   attributes to the particular way management and
          labor unions negotiated the introduction of the
          technology, whereas others are seen as arising from
          the capabilities and nature of the technology itself.
          Thus Clark helps answer the question: "When is
(50)   social choice decisive and when are the concrete
          characteristics of technology more important?"

Questions 463–470 refer to the passage.

463. The primary purpose of the passage is to

    (A) advocate a more positive attitude toward
         technological change

    (B) discuss the implications for employees of the
         modernization of a telephone exchange

    (C) consider a successful challenge to the
         constructivist view of technological change

    (D) challenge the position of advocates of
         technological determinism

    (E) suggest that the social causes of technological
         change should be studied in real situations

464. Which of the following statements about the
     modernization of the telephone exchange is supported
     by information in the passage?

    (A) The new technology reduced the role of
         managers in labor negotiations.

    (B) The modernization was implemented without the
         consent of the employees directly affected by it.

    (C) The modernization had an impact that went
         significantly beyond maintenance routines.

    (D) Some of the maintenance workers felt victimized
         by the new technology.

    (E) The modernization gave credence to the view of
         advocates of social constructivism.

465. Which of the following most accurately describes
     Clark's opinion of Braverman's position?

    (A) He respects its wide-ranging popularity.

    (B) He disapproves of its misplaced emphasis on the
         influence of managers.

    (C) He admires the consideration it gives to the
         attitudes of the workers affected.

    (D) He is concerned about its potential to impede
         the implementation of new technologies.

    (E) He is sympathetic to its concern about the
         impact of modern technology on workers.

466. The information in the passage suggests that which of the following statements from hypothetical sociological studies of change in industry most clearly exemplifies the social constructivists' version of technological determinism?

(A) It is the available technology that determines workers' skills, rather than workers' skills influencing the application of technology.

(B) All progress in industrial technology grows out of a continuing negotiation between technological possibility and human need.

(C) Some organizational change is caused by people; some is caused by computer chips.

(D) Most major technological advances in industry have been generated through research and development.

(E) Some industrial technology eliminates jobs, but educated workers can create whole new skills areas by the adaptation of the technology.

467. The information in the passage suggests that Clark believes that which of the following would be true if social constructivism had not gained widespread acceptance?

(A) Businesses would be more likely to modernize without considering the social consequences of their actions.

(B) There would be greater understanding of the role played by technology in producing social change.

(C) Businesses would be less likely to understand the attitudes of employees affected by modernization.

(D) Modernization would have occurred at a slower rate.

(E) Technology would have played a greater part in determining the role of business in society.

468. According to the passage, constructivists employed which of the following to promote their argument?

(A) Empirical studies of business situations involving technological change

(B) Citation of managers supportive of their position

(C) Construction of hypothetical situations that support their view

(D) Contrasts of their view with a misstatement of an opposing view

(E) Descriptions of the breadth of impact of technological change

469. The author of the passage uses the expression "are supposed to" in line 25 primarily in order to

(A) suggest that a contention made by constructivists regarding determinists is inaccurate

(B) define the generally accepted position of determinists regarding the implementation of technology

(C) engage in speculation about the motivation of determinists

(D) lend support to a comment critical of the position of determinists

(E) contrast the historical position of determinists with their position regarding the exchange modernization

470. Which of the following statements about Clark's study of the telephone exchange can be inferred from information in the passage?

(A) Clark's reason for undertaking the study was to undermine Braverman's analysis of the function of technology.

(B) Clark's study suggests that the implementation of technology should be discussed in the context of conflict between labor and management.

(C) Clark examined the impact of changes in the technology of switching at the exchange in terms of overall operations and organization.

(D) Clark concluded that the implementation of new switching technology was equally beneficial to management and labor.

(E) Clark's analysis of the change in switching systems applies only narrowly to the situation at the particular exchange that he studied.

Line   Because the framers of the United States
        Constitution (written in 1787) believed that protecting
        property rights relating to inventions would encourage
        the new nation's economic growth, they gave
(5)   Congress—the national legislature—a constitutional
        mandate to grant patents for inventions. The resulting
        patent system has served as a model for those in
        other nations. Recently, however, scholars have
        questioned whether the American system helped
(10)   achieve the framers' goals. These scholars have
        contended that from 1794 to roughly 1830, American
        inventors were unable to enforce property rights
        because judges were "antipatent" and routinely
        invalidated patents for arbitrary reasons. This
(15)   argument is based partly on examination of court
        decisions in cases where patent holders ("patentees")
        brought suit alleging infringement of their patent
        rights. In the 1820s, for instance, 75 percent
        of verdicts were decided against the patentee.
(20)   The proportion of verdicts for the patentee began to
        increase in the 1830s, suggesting to these scholars
        that judicial attitudes toward patent rights began
        shifting then.
        Not all patent disputes in the early nineteenth
(25)   century were litigated, however, and litigated
        cases were not drawn randomly from the
        population of disputes. Therefore the rate of
        verdicts in favor of patentees cannot be used
        by itself to gauge changes in judicial attitudes
(30)   or enforceability of patent rights. If early judicial
        decisions were prejudiced against patentees, one
        might expect that subsequent courts—allegedly
        more supportive of patent rights—would reject
        the former legal precedents. But pre-1830
(35)   cases have been cited as frequently as later
        decisions, and they continue to be cited today,
        suggesting that the early decisions, many of
        which clearly declared that patent rights were
        a just recompense for inventive ingenuity,
(40)   provided a lasting foundation for patent law.
        The proportion of judicial decisions in favor of
        patentees began to increase during the 1830s
        because of a change in the underlying population
        of cases brought to trial. This change was partly
(45)   due to an 1836 revision to the patent system:
        an examination procedure, still in use today, was
        instituted in which each application is scrutinized
        for its adherence to patent law. Previously,
        patents were automatically granted upon payment
(50)   of a $30 fee.

Questions 471–475 refer to the passage.

471. The passage implies that which of the following was
     a reason that the proportion of verdicts in favor of
     patentees began to increase in the 1830s ?

     (A)   Patent applications approved after 1836 were
            more likely to adhere closely to patent law.

     (B)   Patent laws enacted during the 1830s better
            defined patent rights.

     (C)   Judges became less prejudiced against
            patentees during the 1830s.

     (D)   After 1836, litigated cases became less
            representative of the population of patent
            disputes.

     (E)   The proportion of patent disputes brought to trial
            began to increase after 1836.

472. The passage implies that the scholars mentioned in
     line 8 would agree with which of the following criticisms
     of the American patent system before 1830 ?

     (A)   Its definition of property rights relating to
            inventions was too vague to be useful.

     (B)   Its criteria for the granting of patents were not
            clear.

     (C)   It made it excessively difficult for inventors to
            receive patents.

     (D)   It led to excessive numbers of patent-
            infringement suits.

     (E)   It failed to encourage national economic growth.

473. It can be inferred from the passage that the frequency
     with which pre-1830 cases have been cited in court
     decisions is an indication that

     (A)   judicial support for patent rights was strongest in
            the period before 1830

     (B)   judicial support for patent rights did not increase
            after 1830

     (C)   courts have returned to judicial standards that
            prevailed before 1830

     (D)   verdicts favoring patentees in patent-infringement
            suits did not increase after 1830

     (E)   judicial bias against patentees persisted after
            1830

474. It can be inferred from the passage that the author and the scholars referred to in line 21 disagree about which of the following aspects of the patents defended in patent-infringement suits before 1830 ?

    (A) Whether the patents were granted for inventions that were genuinely useful

    (B) Whether the patents were actually relevant to the growth of the United States economy

    (C) Whether the patents were particularly likely to be annulled by judges

    (D) Whether the patents were routinely invalidated for reasons that were arbitrary

    (E) Whether the patents were vindicated at a significantly lower rate than patents in later suits

475. The author of the passage cites which of the following as evidence challenging the argument referred to in lines 14–15 ?

    (A) The proportion of cases that were decided against patentees in the 1820s

    (B) The total number of patent disputes that were litigated from 1794 to 1830

    (C) The fact that later courts drew upon the legal precedents set in pre-1830 patent cases

    (D) The fact that the proportion of judicial decisions in favor of patentees began to increase during the 1830s

    (E) The constitutional rationale for the 1836 revision of the patent system

Line   Jacob Burckhardt's view that Renaissance European women "stood on a footing of perfect equality" with Renaissance men has been repeatedly cited by feminist scholars as a prelude to their

(5)   presentation of rich historical evidence of women's inequality. In striking contrast to Burckhardt, Joan Kelly in her famous 1977 essay, "Did Women Have a Renaissance?" argued that the Renaissance was a period of economic and social decline for women

(10)   relative both to Renaissance men and to medieval women. Recently, however, a significant trend among feminist scholars has entailed a rejection of both Kelly's dark vision of the Renaissance and Burckhardt's rosy one. Many recent works by these

(15)   scholars stress the ways in which differences among Renaissance women—especially in terms of social status and religion—work to complicate the kinds of generalizations both Burckhardt and Kelly made on the basis of their observations about

(20)   upper-class Italian women.

    The trend is also evident, however, in works focusing on those middle- and upper-class European women whose ability to write gives them disproportionate representation in the historical

(25)   record. Such women were, simply by virtue of their literacy, members of a tiny minority of the population, so it is risky to take their descriptions of their experiences as typical of "female experience" in any general sense. Tina Krontiris, for example, in

(30)   her fascinating study of six Renaissance women writers, does tend at times to conflate "women" and "women writers," assuming that women's gender, irrespective of other social differences, including literacy, allows us to view women as a homogeneous

(35)   social group and make that group an object of analysis. Nonetheless, Krontiris makes a significant contribution to the field and is representative of those authors who offer what might be called a cautiously optimistic assessment of Renaissance

(40)   women's achievements, although she also stresses the social obstacles Renaissance women faced when they sought to raise their "oppositional voices." Krontiris is concerned to show women intentionally negotiating some power for themselves

(45)   (at least in the realm of public discourse) against potentially constraining ideologies, but in her sober and thoughtful concluding remarks, she suggests that such verbal opposition to cultural stereotypes was highly circumscribed; women seldom attacked

(50)   the basic assumptions in the ideologies that oppressed them.

Questions 476–482 refer to the passage.

476. The author of the passage discusses Krontiris primarily to provide an example of a writer who

(A)   is highly critical of the writings of certain Renaissance women

(B)   supports Kelly's view of women's status during the Renaissance

(C)   has misinterpreted the works of certain Renaissance women

(D)   has rejected the views of both Burckhardt and Kelly

(E)   has studied Renaissance women in a wide variety of social and religious contexts

477. According to the passage, Krontiris's work differs from that of the scholars mentioned in line 12 in which of the following ways?

(A)   Krontiris's work stresses the achievements of Renaissance women rather than the obstacles to their success.

(B)   Krontiris's work is based on a reinterpretation of the work of earlier scholars.

(C)   Krontiris's views are at odds with those of both Kelly and Burkhardt.

(D)   Krontiris's work focuses on the place of women in Renaissance society.

(E)   Krontiris's views are based exclusively on the study of a privileged group of women.

478. According to the passage, feminist scholars cite Burckhardt's view of Renaissance women primarily for which of the following reasons?

    (A) Burckhardt's view forms the basis for most arguments refuting Kelly's point of view.

    (B) Burckhardt's view has been discredited by Kelly.

    (C) Burckhardt's view is one that many feminist scholars wish to refute.

    (D) Burckhardt's work provides rich historical evidence of inequality between Renaissance women and men.

    (E) Burckhardt's work includes historical research supporting the arguments of the feminist scholars.

479. It can be inferred that both Burckhardt and Kelly have been criticized by the scholars mentioned in line 12 for which of the following?

    (A) Assuming that women writers of the Renaissance are representative of Renaissance women in general

    (B) Drawing conclusions that are based on the study of an atypical group of women

    (C) Failing to describe clearly the relationship between social status and literacy among Renaissance women

    (D) Failing to acknowledge the role played by Renaissance women in opposing cultural stereotypes

    (E) Failing to acknowledge the ways in which social status affected the creative activities of Renaissance women

480. The author of the passage suggests that Krontiris incorrectly assumes that

    (A) social differences among Renaissance women are less important than the fact that they were women

    (B) literacy among Renaissance women was more prevalent than most scholars today acknowledge

    (C) during the Renaissance, women were able to successfully oppose cultural stereotypes relating to gender

    (D) Renaissance women did not face many difficult social obstacles relating to their gender

    (E) in order to attain power, Renaissance women attacked basic assumptions in the ideologies that oppressed them

481. The last sentence in the passage serves primarily to

    (A) suggest that Krontiris's work is not representative of recent trends among feminist scholars

    (B) undermine the argument that literate women of the Renaissance sought to oppose social constraints imposed on them

    (C) show a way in which Krontiris's work illustrates a "cautiously optimistic" assessment of Renaissance women's achievements

    (D) summarize Krontiris's view of the effect of literacy on the lives of upper- and middle-class Renaissance women

    (E) illustrate the way in which Krontiris's study differs from the studies done by Burckhardt and Kelly

482. The author of the passage implies that the women studied by Krontiris are unusual in which of the following ways?

    (A) They faced obstacles less formidable than those faced by other Renaissance women.

    (B) They have been seen by historians as more interesting than other Renaissance women.

    (C) They were more concerned about recording history accurately than were other Renaissance women.

    (D) Their perceptions are more likely to be accessible to historians than are those of most other Renaissance women.

    (E) Their concerns are likely to be of greater interest to feminist scholars than are the ideas of most other Renaissance women.

Line   When asteroids collide, some collisions cause
an asteroid to spin faster; others slow it down. If
asteroids are all monoliths—single rocks—undergoing
random collisions, a graph of their rotation rates
(5)   should show a bell-shaped distribution with statistical
"tails" of very fast and very slow rotators. If asteroids
are rubble piles, however, the tail representing the
very fast rotators would be missing, because any
loose aggregate spinning faster than once every few
(10)   hours (depending on the asteroid's bulk density)
would fly apart. Researchers have discovered that
all but five observed asteroids obey a strict limit on
rate of rotation. The exceptions are all smaller than
200 meters in diameter, with an abrupt cutoff for
(15)   asteroids larger than that.

The evident conclusion—that asteroids larger than
200 meters across are multicomponent structures or
rubble piles—agrees with recent computer modeling
of collisions, which also finds a transition at that
(20)   diameter. A collision can blast a large asteroid to bits,
but after the collision those bits will usually move
slower than their mutual escape velocity. Over several
hours, gravity will reassemble all but the fastest
pieces into a rubble pile. Because collisions among
(25)   asteroids are relatively frequent, most large bodies
have already suffered this fate. Conversely, most
small asteroids should be monolithic, because impact
fragments easily escape their feeble gravity.

Questions 483–486 refer to the passage.

483. The passage implies which of the following about the
five asteroids mentioned in line 12 ?

   (A)   Their rotation rates are approximately the same.

   (B)   They have undergone approximately the same
          number of collisions.

   (C)   They are monoliths.

   (D)   They are composed of fragments that have
          escaped the gravity of larger asteroids.

   (E)   They were detected only recently.

484. The discovery of which of the following would call into
question the conclusion mentioned in line 16 ?

   (A)   An asteroid 100 meters in diameter rotating at a
          rate of once per week

   (B)   An asteroid 150 meters in diameter rotating at a
          rate of 20 times per hour

   (C)   An asteroid 250 meters in diameter rotating at a
          rate of once per week

   (D)   An asteroid 500 meters in diameter rotating at a
          rate of once per hour

   (E)   An asteroid 1,000 meters in diameter rotating at
          a rate of once every 24 hours

485. According to the passage, which of the following is a prediction that is based on the strength of the gravitational attraction of small asteroids?

(A) Small asteroids will be few in number.

(B) Small asteroids will be monoliths.

(C) Small asteroids will collide with other asteroids very rarely.

(D) Most small asteroids will have very fast rotation rates.

(E) Almost no small asteroids will have very slow rotation rates.

486. The author of the passage mentions "escape velocity" (see line 22) in order to help explain which of the following?

(A) The tendency for asteroids to become smaller rather than larger over time

(B) The speed with which impact fragments reassemble when they do not escape an asteroid's gravitational attraction after a collision

(C) The frequency with which collisions among asteroids occur

(D) The rotation rates of asteroids smaller than 200 meters in diameter

(E) The tendency for large asteroids to persist after collisions

Line   Most attempts by physicists to send particles
faster than the speed of light involve a remarkable
phenomenon called quantum tunneling, in which
particles travel through solid barriers that appear
(5)   to be impenetrable. If you throw a ball at a wall,
you expect it to bounce back, not to pass straight
through it. Yet subatomic particles perform the
equivalent feat. Quantum theory says that there is a
distinct, albeit small, probability that such a particle
(10)   will tunnel its way through a barrier; the probability
declines exponentially as the thickness of the
barrier increases. Though the extreme rapidity of
quantum tunneling was noted as early as 1932,
not until 1955 was it hypothesized—by Wigner and
(15)   Eisenbud—that tunneling particles sometimes
travel faster than light. Their grounds were
calculations that suggested that the time it takes a
particle to tunnel through a barrier increases with
the thickness of the barrier until tunneling time
(20)   reaches a maximum; beyond that maximum, tunneling
time stays the same regardless of barrier thickness.
This would imply that once maximum tunneling time
is reached, tunneling speed will increase without
limit as barrier thickness increases. Several recent
(25)   experiments have supported this hypothesis that
tunneling particles sometimes reach superluminal
speed. According to measurements performed by
Raymond Chiao and colleagues, for example, photons
can pass through an optical filter at 1.7 times the
(30)   speed of light.

487. The author of the passage mentions calculations about
tunneling time and barrier thickness in order to

(A)   suggest that tunneling time is unrelated to
barrier thickness

(B)   explain the evidence by which Wigner and
Eisenbud discovered the phenomenon of
tunneling

(C)   describe data recently challenged by Raymond
Chiao and colleagues

(D)   question why particles engaged in quantum
tunneling rarely achieve extremely high speeds

(E)   explain the basis for Wigner and Eisenbud's
hypothesis

488. The passage implies that if tunneling time reached no
maximum in increasing with barrier thickness, then

(A)   tunneling speed would increase with barrier
thickness

(B)   tunneling speed would decline with barrier
thickness

(C)   tunneling speed would vary with barrier thickness

(D)   tunneling speed would not be expected to
increase without limit

(E)   successful tunneling would occur even less
frequently than it does

489. Which of the following statements about the earliest
scientific investigators of quantum tunneling can be
inferred from the passage?

(A)   They found it difficult to increase barrier
thickness continually.

(B)   They anticipated the later results of Chiao and
his colleagues.

(C)   They did not suppose that tunneling particles
could travel faster than light.

(D)   They were unable to observe instances of
successful tunneling.

(E)   They made use of photons to study the
phenomenon of tunneling.

8.6 Answer Key: Reading Comprehension

#	Ans	#	Ans	#	Ans	#	Ans	#	Ans
333.	D	365.	B	397.	E	429.	B	461.	E
334.	D	366.	B	398.	A	430.	D	462.	B
335.	B	367.	D	399.	B	431.	E	463.	C
336.	B	368.	E	400.	C	432.	B	464.	C
337.	C	369.	D	401.	C	433.	D	465.	B
338.	C	370.	E	402.	B	434.	C	466.	A
339.	A	371.	C	403.	E	435.	C	467.	B
340.	C	372.	C	404.	C	436.	E	468.	D
341.	D	373.	B	405.	E	437.	A	469.	A
342.	C	374.	B	406.	A	438.	B	470.	C
343.	A	375.	B	407.	D	439.	D	471.	A
344.	C	376.	D	408.	A	440.	E	472.	E
345.	C	377.	A	409.	C	441.	E	473.	B
346.	C	378.	D	410.	A	442.	D	474.	D
347.	E	379.	C	411.	B	443.	B	475.	C
348.	A	380.	B	412.	D	444.	C	476.	D
349.	C	381.	A	413.	E	445.	D	477.	E
350.	B	382.	E	414.	C	446.	A	478.	C
351.	B	383.	A	415.	A	447.	C	479.	B
352.	A	384.	B	416.	E	448.	D	480.	A
353.	D	385.	E	417.	A	449.	A	481.	C
354.	C	386.	B	418.	D	450.	A	482.	D
355.	E	387.	C	419.	D	451.	D	483.	C
356.	B	388.	C	420.	D	452.	E	484.	D
357.	D	389.	A	421.	B	453.	D	485.	B
358.	C	390.	D	422.	B	454.	B	486.	E
359.	B	391.	D	423.	C	455.	C	487.	E
360.	D	392.	C	424.	C	456.	A	488.	D
361.	A	393.	E	425.	E	457.	C	489.	C
362.	C	394.	A	426.	C	458.	B		
363.	D	395.	C	427.	E	459.	D		
364.	B	396.	D	428.	D	460.	D		

8.7 Answer Explanations: Reading Comprehension

The following discussion of Reading Comprehension is intended to familiarize you with the most efficient and effective approaches to the kinds of problems common to Reading Comprehension. The particular questions in this chapter are generally representative of the kinds of Reading Comprehension questions you will encounter on the GMAT exam. Remember that it is the problem solving strategy that is important, not the specific details of a particular question.

Questions 333–377 - Difficulty: Easy

Questions 333–335 refer to the passage on page 318.

333. The primary purpose of the passage is to

   (A) challenge recent findings that appear to contradict earlier findings

   (B) present two sides of an ongoing scientific debate

   (C) report answers to several questions that have long puzzled researchers

   (D) discuss evidence that has caused a long-standing belief to be revised

   (E) attempt to explain a commonly misunderstood biological phenomenon

Main Idea

This question depends on understanding the passage as a whole. The passage begins by describing a long-held belief regarding humans' circadian rhythms: that the SCNs control them. It then goes on to explain that new findings have led scientists to believe that other organs and tissues may be involved in regulating the body's circadian rhythms as well.

A   The passage does not challenge the more-recent findings. Furthermore, the recent findings that the passage recounts do not contradict earlier findings; rather, when placed alongside those earlier findings, they have led scientists to reach additional conclusions.

B   The passage does not discuss a two-sided debate; no findings or conclusions are disputed by any figures in the passages.

C   There is only one question at issue in the passage: whether the SCN alone control human circadian rhythms. Furthermore, nothing in the passage suggests that researchers have been puzzled for a long time about this.

D   Correct. The new evidence regarding circadian rhythm–related gene activity in all the body's tissue has led scientists to revise their long–standing belief that the SCN alone control circadian rhythms.

E   The biological phenomenon of circadian rhythms is not, at least as far as the passage is concerned, misunderstood. Its causes are being investigated and refined.

The correct answer is D.

334. The passage mentions each of the following as a function regulated by the SCNs in some animals EXCEPT

   (A) activity level

   (B) blood pressure

   (C) alertness

   (D) vision

   (E) temperature

Supporting Idea

This question asks about what is NOT specifically mentioned in the passage with regard to functions regulated by the SCN. Those functions, as identified in the passage, are blood pressure, body temperature, activity level, alertness, and the release of melatonin.

A   The passage includes activity level in its list of functions regulated by the SCN.

B   The passage includes blood pressure in its list of functions regulated by the SCN.

C   The passage includes alertness in its list of functions regulated by the SCN.

D   Correct. While the passage does say that cells in the human retina transmit information to the SCN, there is no suggestion that the SCN reciprocally control vision.

E   The passage includes temperature in its list of functions regulated by the SCN.

The correct answer is D.

335. The author of the passage would probably agree with which of the following statements about the SCNs?

(A)   The SCNs are found in other organs and tissues of the body besides the hypothalamus.

(B)   The SCNs play a critical but not exclusive role in regulating circadian rhythms.

(C)   The SCNs control clock genes in a number of tissues and organs throughout the body.

(D)   The SCNs are a less significant factor in regulating blood pressure than scientists once believed.

(E)   The SCNs are less strongly affected by changes in light levels than they are by other external cues.

Application

The author of the passage states in the second paragraph, *Four critical genes governing circadian cycles have been found to be active in every tissue, however, not just in the SCNs, of flies, mice, and humans.* The author goes on in that paragraph to point out that though scientists still accept the role of SCNs in *controlling core functions,* they *now believe that circadian clocks in other organs and tissues may respond to external cues other than light . . . that recur regularly every 24 hours.* The author nowhere disputes these beliefs, and so it is reasonable to conclude that the author of the passage agrees that these beliefs are true.

A   The author states that the SCNs are nerve clusters in the hypothalamus, and nothing in the passage contradicts or undermines the supposition that they are only in the hypothalamus.

B   Correct. The author indicates in the second paragraph that while scientists still believe that the SCNs control core circadian function, they also believe that circadian clocks found elsewhere in the body have an effect as well. Because the author nowhere disputes these beliefs, it is reasonable to conclude that the author would agree that SCNs play a critical but not exclusive role in regulating circadian rhythms.

C   The evidence offered in the second paragraph about the activity of the clock gene in rat livers suggests that these clock genes are not under the SCNs' control. The passage does not suggest that the SCNs control any of the non-SCN controllers of circadian rhythms.

D   The author states in the second paragraph that scientists do not dispute the idea that the SCNs regulate blood pressure.

E   The first paragraph indicates that the SCNs respond to light levels; clock genes in other tissues are the ones that may respond to other external cues.

The correct answer is B.

Questions 336–338 refer to the passage on page 320.

336. The primary purpose of the passage is to

   (A) question the results of a study that examined the effect of service-quality guarantees in the restaurant industry

   (B) discuss potential advantages and disadvantages of service-quality guarantees in the restaurant industry

   (C) examine the conventional wisdom regarding the effect of service-quality guarantees in the restaurant industry

   (D) argue that only certain restaurants would benefit from the implementation of service-quality guarantees

   (E) consider the impact that service-quality guarantees can have on the service provided by a restaurant

Main Idea

This question depends on understanding the passage as a whole. The first paragraph describes Tucci and Talaga's findings regarding the effect of service-quality guarantees: that they have different, more positive results for higher-priced restaurants than for lower-priced ones, which could be affected negatively. The second paragraph explains that a particular benefit from service guarantees could accrue to restaurants generally.

A   The passage does not question the results of Tucci and Talaga's study; rather, the passage appears to accept the results of the study as accurate.

B   **Correct.** The potential advantages involve the management and motivation of service staff, as well as, for higher-priced restaurants, a greater likelihood of being selected by customers over other restaurants. Potential disadvantages for lower-priced restaurants include the possibility that potential customers may believe that such restaurants are concerned about the quality of their service.

C   The passage does not indicate whether there is any conventional wisdom regarding service-quality guarantees in the restaurant industry.

D   The second paragraph of the passage suggests that restaurants in general could potentially enjoy some benefits from the implementation of service-quality guarantees. For lower-priced restaurants, these benefits could offset the possible negative effects of service-quality guarantees described in the first paragraph.

E   The second paragraph of the passage indicates an effect that service-quality guarantees could have on a restaurant's staff and the service that the staff provides, but this is only one of the subsidiary points contributing to the focus of the passage as a whole. The first is more concerned with the question of what effect these guarantees would have on whether customers choose to patronize that restaurant.

The correct answer is B.

337. It can be inferred that the author of the passage would agree with which of the following statements about the appeal of service guarantees to customers?

   (A) Such guarantees are likely to be somewhat more appealing to customers of restaurants than to customers of other businesses.

   (B) Such guarantees are likely to be more appealing to customers who know what to anticipate in terms of service.

   (C) Such guarantees are likely to have less appeal in situations where customers are knowledgeable about a business's product or service.

   (D) In situations where a high level of financial commitment is involved, a service guarantee is not likely to be very appealing.

   (E) In situations where customers expect a high level of customer service, a service guarantee is likely to make customers think that a business is worried about its service.

Inference

This question asks for an inference from the passage about the author's view of why and how service guarantees would appeal to customers. The question does not ask specifically about service guarantees in the context of restaurants, but rather service guarantees in general. The end of the first paragraph addresses this general question: a service guarantee may appeal most to customers in the case of activities whose quality they are less likely to know how to question.

A   The author states that a service guarantee might have greater appeal in the case of skilled activities than it would for restaurant customers.

B   According to the author, customers who know what to expect in terms of service—a group that includes restaurant customers—would likely find service guarantees less appealing.

C   **Correct.** The author makes clear that service guarantees would be less appealing to restaurant customers when they know what to expect in terms of the quality of service.

D   The passage provides some evidence that where a high level of financial commitment is involved, a service guarantee may be more rather than less appealing than in other situations. In discussing higher-priced restaurants, which require a relatively high level of financial commitment, the author states that Tucci and Talaga found evidence that a service guarantee would likely appeal to customers.

E   The author implies that customers of higher-priced restaurants expect a high level of service, certainly a level higher than that expected by customers of lower-priced restaurants. But it is at lower-priced restaurants that Tucci and Talaga found that a service guarantee makes customers think a given restaurant is concerned about its service.

The correct answer is C.

338. According to the passage, Tucci and Talaga found that service guarantees, when offered by lower-priced restaurants, can have which of the following effects?

(A)   Customers' developing unreasonably high expectations regarding service

(B)   Customers' avoiding such restaurants because they fear that the service guarantee may not be fully honored

(C)   Customers' interpreting the service guarantee as a sign that management is not confident about the quality of its service

(D)   A restaurant's becoming concerned that its service will not be assiduous enough to satisfy customers

(E)   A restaurant's becoming concerned that customers will be more emboldened to question the quality of the service they receive

Supporting Idea

This question requires identifying Tucci and Talaga's findings regarding service guarantees offered by lower-priced restaurants. The passage states directly that these researchers found in these situations that a guarantee could lead potential customers to think that the restaurant has concerns about its service.

A   The passage does not report that Tucci and Talaga found that service guarantees create unreasonably high expectations regarding service.

B   The passage does not report that Tucci and Talaga found that customers doubted that service guarantees would be honored.

C   **Correct.** The passage explicitly indicates that Tucci and Talaga found that potential customers of lower-priced restaurants could interpret service guarantees as indicating worries about the quality of service.

D   The passage indicates that Tucci and Talaga found that customers might think that lower-priced restaurants are offering service guarantees because they are concerned that the quality of their service is too low, but the passage does not indicate that service guarantees lead such restaurants to have concerns about the quality of their service, and in fact it may be that such guarantees could lead to improvements in service.

E   The passage indicates that service guarantees offered at lower-priced restaurants may empower customers to question the quality of service, but it does not indicate that service guarantees lead restaurants to have concerns about this.

The correct answer is C.

Questions 339–340 refer to the passage on page 322.

Main Idea Summary

The passage primarily reports some research findings regarding the extent to which farmers in certain types of rain forest regions are likely to adopt technologies that would increase productivity and slow deforestation by reducing demand for new cropland. It begins by noting that some studies have not included the types of farming communities that are characteristic of rainforest regions. The latter part of the passage describes some research regarding these previously omitted communities. The findings of that research provide evidence of how various factors may influence whether farmers in those communities adopt improved plant varieties and/or chemical herbicides.

339. The passage suggests that in the study mentioned in line 14 the method for gathering information about security of land tenure reflects which of the following pairs of assumptions about Tawahka society?

(A) The security of a household's land tenure depends on the strength of that household's kinship ties, and the duration of a household's residence in its village is an indication of the strength of that household's kinship ties.

(B) The ample availability of land makes security of land tenure unimportant, and the lack of a need for secure land tenure has made the concept of legal property rights unnecessary.

(C) The strength of a household's kinship ties is a more reliable indicator of that household's receptivity to new agricultural technologies than is its quantity of nonland wealth, and the duration of a household's residence in its village is a more reliable indicator of that household's security of land tenure than is the strength of its kinship ties.

(D) Security of land tenure based on kinship ties tends to make farmers more receptive to the use of improved plant varieties, and security of land tenure based on long duration of residence in a village tends to make farmers more receptive to the use of chemical herbicides.

(E) A household is more likely to be receptive to the concept of land tenure based on legal property rights if it has easy access to uncultivated land, and a household is more likely to uphold the tradition of land tenure based on kinship ties if it possesses a significant degree of nonland wealth.

Evaluation

In discussing the study, the passage notes that the strength of kinship ties is a more important indicator of land-tenure security than are legal property rights. The researchers, knowing this, measured land-tenure security by indirectly measuring the strength of kinship ties. How long a household had resided in its village was taken as an indicator of the strength of kinship ties, and indirectly, of the household's degree of land-tenure security.

A   **Correct.** This summarizes two assumptions that the passage suggests were made by the researchers.

B   The passage notes that ample availability of land is characteristic of rain-forest communities, which presumably includes the Tawahka people on whom the study focused. However, based on the information in the passage, the study did not assume that land-tenure security was unimportant in that community.

C   The passage reports that the study took a household's duration of residence in its village as a reliable indicator of the strength of the household's kinship ties. Thus, the researchers did not assume that duration of residence was a more reliable measure of land-tenure security than kinship ties.

D   The passage does not indicate that the researchers assumed this. As already stated, the researchers in effect equated a household's strength of kinship ties with its length of residence in its village. Though only the latter was directly measured, both were regarded as guarantors and indicators of land-tenure security. According to the passage, the researchers found that "longer residence correlated with more adoption of improved plant varieties but with less adoption of chemical herbicides." This was a finding based on research data, not an assumption.

E   The passage does not attribute to the researchers an assumption that "a household is more likely to be receptive to the concept of land tenure based on legal property rights if it has easy access to uncultivated land."

The correct answer is A.

340. According to the passage, the proposal mentioned in line 1 is aimed at preserving rain forests by encouraging farmers in rain-forest regions to do each of the following EXCEPT

(A)   adopt new agricultural technologies

(B)   grow improved plant varieties

(C)   decrease their use of chemical herbicides

(D)   increase their productivity

(E)   reduce their need to clear new land for cultivation

Supporting Idea

The goal of the proposal is to help preserve rain forests by encouraging the adoption of new agricultural technologies, including use of chemical herbicides. The latter would presumably help improve crop yields on existing land, reducing the need to clear portions of rain forest to expand agricultural production.

A   The proposal aims to encourage farmers to adopt new agricultural technologies.

B   The proposal aims to encourage farmers to grow improved plant varieties.

C   **Correct.** The proposal aims to encourage farmers to adopt new agricultural technologies, such as increased use of chemical herbicides. So persuading farmers to reduce their use of chemical herbicides is not part of the proposal.

D   The proposal aims to encourage farmers to increase their productivity.

E   The proposal aims to encourage farmers to reduce their need to clear rain-forest land for cultivation.

The correct answer is C.

Questions 341–344 refer to the passage on page 324.

Main Idea Summary

The passage as a whole functions as an introduction to the notion of monetizing (i.e., putting a monetary value on) ecosystem functions. The passage begins by considering the argument for monetizing such functions and then considers David Pearce's claim that all ecosystems have economic value and that, by showing this, we can help overcome the illusion that conservation is relatively unprofitable. The passage concludes with Gretchen Daily's view that monetization will help inform environmental decision making.

341. Information in the passage suggests that David Pearce would most readily endorse which of the following statements concerning monetization?

(A)   Monetization represents a strategy that is attractive to both environmentalists and their critics.

(B)   Monetization is an untested strategy, but it is increasingly being embraced by environmentalists.

(C)   Monetization should at present be restricted to ecological services and should only gradually be extended to such commercial endeavors as tourism and recreation.

(D)   Monetization can serve as a means of representing persuasively the value of environmental conservation.

(E)   Monetization should inform environmental decision-making processes only if it is accepted by environmentalist groups.

Inference

This question requires an understanding of David Pearce's view of monetization. According to the passage, Pearce finds the idea that conservation is unprofitable to be an illusion. He argues for showing the economic value of ecosystems in order to make progress in conserving those ecosystems.

A   The passage attributes to Gretchen Daily the view that monetization is unpopular with environmentalists. The passage gives no reason to believe that Pearce would endorse the idea that environmentalists currently find monetization attractive.

B   The passage gives no indication that monetization is increasingly being embraced by environmentalists, even if Pearce thinks it should be.

C   The passage indicates Pearce's belief that some types of tourism are also types of ecological services that have economic value and that they should be monetized.

D   **Correct.** Pearce believes that monetization quantifies the value of the services provided by ecological systems—and if that value is quantified, people are more likely to be persuaded to conserve those systems.

E   Pearce is arguing, against some environmentalists, that monetization should inform the decision-making process with regard to preserving ecosystems.

The correct answer is D.

342. Which of the following most clearly represents an example of an "ecological service" as that term is used in line 20 ?

(A)   A resort hotel located in an area noted for its natural beauty

(B)   A water-purifying plant that supplements natural processes with nontoxic chemicals

(C)   A wildlife preserve that draws many international travelers

(D)   A nonprofit firm that specializes in restoring previously damaged ecosystems

(E)   A newsletter that keeps readers informed of ecological victories and setbacks

Application

Based on the passage, *ecological services* are services provided by natural assets that have not been converted into commercial assets. Thus any example of such an ecological service requires that the area providing it is natural.

A   The passage mentions resort hotels as an example of explicitly commercial assets. Although some hotels might be situated in ecologically valuable natural environments, any ecological services in such cases would be contributed by the natural environments, not by the hotels themselves.

B   Water purifying is *an ecological* service if it is supplied by *undisturbed forests and wetlands*. The word *plant* here must mean a technological installation, not a botanical organism, because it is said to supplement—not to be part of—the natural processes. Thus it is not a natural asset and therefore does not provide an ecological service as described in the passage.

C   **Correct.** The passage states that a wildlife preserve that creates jobs and generates income would be providing an ecological service.

D   A nonprofit firm that restores damaged ecosystems would be performing a valuable ecology-related service, but it would not itself be an example of a natural asset providing an ecological service.

E   Environmentalists and others would most likely find such a newsletter informative, but it would not be an ecological service, because it is not a service provided by a natural asset.

The correct answer is C.

343. According to the passage, Daily sees monetization as an indication of which of the following?

   (A) The centrality of economic interests to people's actions

   (B) The reluctance of the critics of environmentalism to acknowledge the importance of conservation

   (C) The inability of financial interests and ecological interests to reach a common ideological ground

   (D) The inevitability of environmental degradation

   (E) The inevitability of the growth of ecological services in the future

Supporting Idea

This question asks about Daily's view of monetization, and according to the passage, she sees monetization as a practice that *reflects the dominant role that economic decisions play in human behavior.*

A   Correct. According to the passage, Daily believes that economic interests are central to people's actions, and monetization of ecological services would take that central role realistically into account.

B   The passage gives no evidence of this. It says nothing about how the concept of monetization relates to critics of environmentalism or about what Daily's opinion regarding such a relationship might be. It is reasonable to suppose that some critics of environmentalism would oppose the move to monetize the values of ecosystem functions because they believe that many ecosystem functions do not have true monetary value. However, the passage mentions Daily's views on the topic only as they relate to environmentalists, not to critics of environmentalism.

C   This is the opposite of what, according to the passage, Daily says can be a benefit of monetization. For Daily, monetization represents a way for financial interests and ecological interests to reach a common ground; by using this common currency, both sides can make good decisions about the environment.

D   Monetization, in Daily's view, would help to prevent environmental degradation; the passage does not suggest that she regards such degradation as at all inevitable.

E   Daily does not see monetization as inevitably spurring the growth of ecological services but as more likely preventing their decline by leaving those services undisturbed.

The correct answer is A.

344. Which of the following can be inferred from the passage concerning the environmentalists mentioned in line 8 ?

   (A) They are organized in opposition to the generation of income produced by the sale of ecological services.

   (B) They are fewer in number but better organized and better connected to the media than their opponents.

   (C) They have sometimes been charged with failing to use a particular strategy in their pursuit of conservational goals.

   (D) They have been in the forefront of publicizing the extent of worldwide environmental degradation.

   (E) They define environmental progress differently and more conservatively than do other organized groups of environmentalists.

Inference

The sentence in question states that critics blame environmentalists for their failure *to address the economic issues of environmental degradation.*

A   The passage states that, in the absence of monetization, conservation can appear unprofitable. But this does not mean that the environmentalists in question are opposed to conservation generating income.

B   The passage does not address the issue of the number of environmentalists in question, the number of those opposed to them, or whether either group is better connected to the media.

C   Correct. The passage indicates that critics of the environmentalists in question believe environmentalists are to blame for not using an effective economics-based strategy to promote conservation.

D   Although it may be the case that the environmentalists in question have been prominent in publicizing worldwide environmental degradation, the passage does not provide grounds for inferring that the possibility is necessarily true.

E   The passage suggests that certain critics consider environmentalists in general to be at fault for failing to address economic issues. In this respect, the passage makes no distinctions among different environmentalist groups, organized or otherwise, yet this answer choice is based on the assumption that the passage has made this distinction. Therefore, this answer choice cannot be inferred from the passage.

The correct answer is C.

Questions 345–348 refer to the passage on page 326.

Main Idea Summary

The passage consists of a brief overview of some research into a question related to marketing: how do various factors influence consumers' perceptions of performance risk (the possibility that a product will not function as consumers expect and/or will not provide the desired benefits)? The first paragraph reports some purported findings about the effects of price and advertising on such perceptions. The second paragraph reports some research into the ways in which perceptions of manufacturers' credibility may influence perceptions of performance risk. It then briefly discusses the possibility that some of the factors may interact with one another in more complex ways.

345. According to the passage, the studies referred to in line 12 reported which of the following about the effect of price on consumers' perception of the performance risk associated with a new product?

(A)   Although most consumers regard price as an important factor, their perception of the performance risk associated with a new product

is ultimately determined by the manufacturer's reputation.

(B)   Price interacts with the presentation of an advertised message to affect perceived performance risk.

(C)   Price does not significantly affect consumers' perception of the performance risk associated with a new product.

(D)   Consumers tend to regard price as more important than the manufacturer's credibility when they are buying from that manufacturer for the first time.

(E)   Consumers are generally less concerned about a new product's performance risk when that product is relatively expensive.

Supporting Idea

The question asks about information explicitly provided in the passage. The first paragraph explains that there are *conflicting findings* in the research about how the price of a product affects a consumer's perception of the performance risk of that product. Some studies have found that higher priced products reduce the perception of performance risk. The *other studies* referred to in line 12, however, have found little or no connection between price and perceived performance risk.

A   The passage does not mention that these studies consider the manufacturer's reputation.

B   The passage does not mention that these studies consider advertising messages.

C   **Correct.** The passage indicates that these studies have found little or no connection between relative price and consumers' perception of performance risk.

D   The passage does not mention that these studies consider the manufacturer's credibility.

E   Although some studies have found that a relatively high price reduces the perception of performance risk, the passage explains that the studies referred to in line 12 have not confirmed that finding.

The correct answer is C.

346. The "past research" mentioned in line 25 suggests which of the following about perceived performance risk?

(A) The more expensive a new product is, the more likely consumers may be to credit advertised claims about that product.

(B) The more familiar consumers are with a particular manufacturer, the more willing they may be to assume some risk in the purchase of a new product being advertised by that manufacturer.

(C) Consumers' perception of the performance risk associated with a new product being advertised may be influenced by an interplay between the product's price and the manufacturer's credibility.

(D) Consumers may be more likely to believe that a product will function as it is advertised to do when they have bought products from a particular manufacturer before.

(E) The price of a particular advertised product may have less impact than the manufacturer's credibility on consumers' assessment of the performance risk associated with that product.

Supporting Idea

The question asks about information explicitly provided in the passage. The second paragraph explains that, according to some research, consumers perceive a product as having less performance risk when they trust the source of advertising about that product. *Past research*, however, suggests that performance risk is affected not merely by the credibility of the source, but by an interaction between source credibility and the price of the product.

A   The passage does not indicate that the past research addressed the question of how the price of a product affects consumers' perception of advertised claims. It only says that the research suggests that the two factors *interact*.

B   Although the passage discusses consumers' perception of how risky a purchase might be, it does not address the relationship between familiarity and willingness to assume risk.

C   **Correct.** The *past research* suggests that performance risk is affected by an

interaction between the price of the product and the credibility of the source of the advertising about the product—in other words, the manufacturer.

D   The *past research* suggests that consumers' beliefs about a product's performance are affected not merely by their perception of the manufacturer, but by an interplay between source credibility and product price. The passage does not mention any possible role of prior experience in this interplay.

E   The passage does not discuss whether price or the manufacturer's credibility has more of an effect on perceived performance risk.

The correct answer is C.

347. The passage is primarily concerned with

(A) challenging the implications of previous research into why consumers try new products

(B) suggesting new marketing strategies for attracting consumers to new products

(C) reconciling two different views about the effect of price on consumers' willingness to try new products

(D) describing a new approach to researching why consumers try new products

(E) discussing certain findings regarding why consumers try new products

Main Idea

The question depends on understanding the passage as a whole. The passage begins with a statement explaining that much research has investigated *what motivates consumers to try new products*. It then defines one such motivating factor—perception of performance risk. The remainder of the passage summarizes research into how price and a manufacturer's advertising affect consumers' perception of performance risk.

A   The passage summarizes research findings that conflict with one another but does not support some findings over others.

B   The passage does not suggest any new marketing strategies.

C The first paragraph mentions a study that could reconcile two conflicting findings, but this is only a supporting point in the passage's larger purpose of summarizing research.

D The passage does not describe new research approaches.

E **Correct.** The passage discusses studies about performance risk, which is a factor that motivates consumers to try new products.

The correct answer is E.

348. Which of the following, if true, would most tend to weaken the conclusion drawn from "some of this research" (line 8)?

(A) In a subsequent study, consumers who were asked to evaluate new products with relatively low prices had the same perception of the products' performance risk as did consumers who were shown the same products priced more expensively.

(B) In a subsequent study, the quality of the advertising for the products that consumers perceived as having a lower performance risk was relatively high, while the quality of the advertising for the products that consumers perceived as having a higher performance risk was relatively poor.

(C) In a subsequent study, the products that consumers perceived as having a lower performance risk were priced higher than the highest priced products in the previous research.

(D) None of the consumers involved in this research had ever before bought products from the manufacturers involved in the research.

(E) Researchers found that the higher the source credibility for a product, the more consumers were willing to pay for it.

Evaluation

The question depends on evaluating the reasoning behind the conclusion of some research and deciding which evidence would weaken that conclusion. The research concludes that higher prices reduce consumers' perception of performance risk associated with a particular product. This conclusion involves a claim of cause and effect, so evidence showing that higher prices do not cause that effect would weaken the argument.

A **Correct.** If lowering prices has no effect on consumers' perception of performance risk, the conclusion of the research is called into question.

B Without further information, an observed correlation between quality of advertising and perceived performance risk would hardly be relevant to the research conclusion about the effects of price. We are given no information about whether there is any significant correlation between advertising quality and price and no evidence that the correlation between advertising quality and perceptions of performance risk indicates a causal connection. Even if advertising quality caused perceptions of lower performance risk, this would be theoretically compatible with the conclusion about the effect of price; the studies concluded that higher prices cause perceptions of lower performance risk, not that they are the only thing that causes such perceptions.

C This answer choice provides no basis for comparison among prices within the subsequent study. For all we can tell, the prices that correlated with higher perceived performance risk in the subsequent study may have been lower than those that correlated with lower perceived risk. In that case, the subsequent study would tend to strengthen, not weaken, the conclusion drawn from the earlier research.

D This indirectly suggests one type of reasoning to consider in checking whether the conclusion is well-founded, but its relevance is only remote. If the research involved only people who had never before bought products from the manufacturers involved in the research, this would raise the question of whether the sample might have been unrepresentative of consumers in general. However, we are given no reason to suppose that consumers who had previously bought from the manufacturers might be affected differently from the other group by differences in price.

E Credibility of the source of advertisements is discussed as a separate issue in the second paragraph. We are given no information about how source credibility might relate to price or about how the prices that consumers are willing to pay might relate to the advertised prices of the products. Therefore, the relevance of this answer choice to the conclusion is only conjectural at best.

The correct answer is A.

Questions 349–353 refer to the passage on page 328.

349. The primary purpose of the passage is to

(A) compare the economic role played by southern banks with the economic role played by banks in the rest of the United States during the late eighteenth and early nineteenth centuries

(B) reevaluate a conventional interpretation of the role played by banks in the American economy during the late eighteenth and early nineteenth centuries

(C) present different interpretations of the role played by banks in the American economy during the late eighteenth and early nineteenth centuries

(D) analyze how the increasing number of banks in the late eighteenth and early nineteenth centuries affected the American economy

(E) examine how scholarly opinion regarding the role played by banks in the American economy during the late eighteenth and early nineteenth centuries has changed over time

Main Idea

Answering this question correctly depends on understanding the passage as a whole. The passage describes two contrasting views about the role banks played in the economic growth of the United States around the turn of the nineteenth century. The first paragraph describes the view that banks played only a small role. The second paragraph describes the contrasting view that banks played a critical role.

A   The mention of banks in the South is a small part of a larger discussion about the role of banks in the country as a whole.

B   The passage describes two major views held by historians; it does not reevaluate either of those views.

C   **Correct.** The passage describes two different views about the role that banks played in America's growing economy.

D   The passage does not analyze any aspect of the relationship between the increasing number of banks and the economy. It alludes to the increase in numbers only within a broader description of two contrasting views about how banks affected the economy.

E   Although the passage does indicate that a growing number of historians hold one of the two views it describes, the primary purpose of the passage is not to examine how scholarly opinion has changed, but rather to describe in some detail those two views.

The correct answer is C.

350. The passage suggests that the scholars mentioned in line 4 would argue that the reason banks tended not to fund manufacturing and transportation projects in the late eighteenth and early nineteenth centuries was that

(A) these projects, being well established and well capitalized, did not need substantial long-term financing from banks

(B) these projects entailed a level of risk that was too great for banks' conservative lending practices

(C) banks preferred to invest in other, more speculative projects that offered the potential for higher returns

(D) bank managers believed that these projects would be unlikely to contribute significantly to economic growth in the new country

(E) bank managers believed funding these projects would result in credit being extended to too many borrowers

Inference

The question asks about information implied by the passage. According to the scholars' view described in the first paragraph, banks *followed conservative lending practices*: they shunned projects that were uncertain and that required substantial investments in capital. It follows that, according to those scholars, the reason banks chose not to fund certain projects was that the projects entailed too great a risk.

A   The passage indicates that manufacturing and transportation projects were less well established than those the banks preferred to fund, not more so.

B   **Correct.** Because the projects were uncertain and required a great deal of capital, banks considered them too risky.

C   The passage does not indicate that the scholars argue that banks preferred to invest in more speculative projects. In fact, it suggests that they argue the opposite: the banks avoided investing not only in manufacturing and transportation projects but also in any projects that were at least as risky as those.

D   The passage does not mention bank managers' beliefs about economic growth, and it does not provide any basis for inferring that the scholars in question held any particular views regarding such beliefs.

E   The passage does not mention, or provide a basis for inferences about, bank managers' concerns about numbers of borrowers.

The correct answer is B.

351. The passage suggests that Paul Gilje would be most likely to agree with which of the following claims about the lending practices of the "earliest banks" (see line 21)?

(A)   These lending practices were unlikely to generate substantial profits for banks.

(B)   These lending practices only benefited a narrow sector of the economy.

(C)   The restrictive nature of these lending practices generated significant opposition outside of the South.

(D)   The restrictive nature of these lending practices forced state legislatures to begin granting more bank charters by the early nineteenth century.

(E)   These lending practices were likely to be criticized by economic elites as being overly restrictive.

Inference

This question asks about conclusions that can be logically inferred from information provided in the passage. According to the second paragraph, Paul Gilje believes that a driving force in American economic growth in the early nineteenth century was banks' lending to a larger and more diverse group of borrowers. The question asks what this would imply about Gilje's view toward earlier banks—which, the passage explains, offered credit only to *well-connected merchants*.

A   The profitability of banks' lending practices is not at issue in the discussion.

B   **Correct.** The passage says that the earliest banks had primarily made loans only to a narrow sector—well-connected merchants—and that they began lending more broadly in the early nineteenth century. It then cites Gilje's view to corroborate and explicate this claim. This strongly suggests that Gilje agrees with the claim.

C   Opposition to the earliest banks is not mentioned or alluded to in the discussion.

D   The passage provides no basis for inferring that Gilje held any particular view as to why legislatures began granting more bank charters.

E   The passage does not mention or provide a basis for inference about the views of economic elites regarding the lending practices of the earliest banks in the United States. It thus provides no basis for inferring that Gilje would have any particular opinion on this topic.

The correct answer is B.

352. The passage suggests that the opposition to banks in the South in the early nineteenth century stemmed in part from the perception that banks

(A)   did not benefit more than a small minority of the people

(B)   did not support the interests of elite planters

(C)   were too closely tied to transportation and industrial interests

(D)   were unwilling to issue the long-term loans required by agrarian interests

(E)   were too willing to lend credit widely

Inference

The question asks about statements that can be inferred from information provided in the passage. The second paragraph explains that people who opposed banks in the South saw them as monopolies controlled by elite planters. This would imply that those who opposed banks believed that most people in the South did not benefit from them.

A   Correct. Since people opposed the banks on the grounds that they were monopolies controlled by an elite group of planters, they likely thought banks did not benefit most of the population.

B   The passage states *the overwhelmingly agrarian nature of the economy generated outright opposition to banks, which were seen as monopolistic institutions controlled by an elite group of planters.* That statement implies that people believed the banks did serve the interests of elite planters, the opposite of what this answer choice states.

C   The passage indicates that people believed banks in the South were tied to planters, not to transportation and industrial interests.

D   Southern banks' willingness to provide long-term loans is not discussed or alluded to in the passage.

E   The passage does not imply that anyone believed banks in the South were willing to lend credit widely. Since people believed the banks were controlled by the elite, they more likely thought banks were unwilling to lend credit widely.

The correct answer is A.

---

353. Which of the following statements best describes the function of the last sentence of the passage?

(A)   It provides evidence tending to undermine the viewpoint of the scholars mentioned in line 5.

(B)   It resolves a conflict over the role of banks summarized in the first paragraph.

(C)   It clarifies some of the reasons state legislatures began granting more bank charters.

(D)   It qualifies a claim made earlier in the passage about the impact of banks on the American economy in the early nineteenth century.

(E)   It supports a claim made earlier in the passage about how the expansion of credit affected the economy.

Evaluation

This question asks about the function of the last sentence in relation to the rest of the passage. The first paragraph describes the view of one set of historians. The second paragraph describes the contrasting view of a second set of historians. The last sentence of the passage points out an exception mentioned by the second set of historians.

A   The last sentence pertains to the view of historians described in the second paragraph, not those described in the first paragraph.

B   The conflict between the two differing views is not resolved by the passage.

C   The passage does not explain why legislatures began granting more bank charters.

D   Correct. The second set of historians claim banks spurred American economic growth at the turn of the nineteenth century, but the last sentence adds an exception to that claim.

E   The last sentence does not support the claim made by the second set of historians, but rather serves as an exception to that claim.

The correct answer is D.

Questions 354–357 refer to the passage on page 330.

354. The passage is primarily concerned with

(A) examining economic factors that may have contributed to the success of certain Japanese companies

(B) discussing the relative merits of strategic partnerships as compared with those of market-exchange relationships

(C) challenging the validity of a widely held assumption about how Japanese firms operate

(D) explaining why Western companies have been slow to adopt a particular practice favored by Japanese companies

(E) pointing out certain differences between Japanese and Western supplier relationships

Main Idea

This question asks for an assessment of what the passage as a whole is doing. The passage discusses how Western business managers have been following the advice of academics and journalists to pursue strategic partnerships with their suppliers. The advice is based on studies comparing Japanese production and supply practices with those of the rest of the world. Newer research, however, indicates that Japanese practices actually differ from those indicated in the earlier studies and are not significantly different from practices associated with Western manufacturers.

A The passage is not primarily concerned with economic factors contributing to the success of Japanese companies, but rather with whether Japanese relationships with suppliers conform to the practices recently adopted by Western business manufacturers.

B Although the passage discusses strategic partnerships and market-exchange relationships, it does not discuss their relative merits.

C **Correct.** The passage does question the view promoted by several studies regarding the relationship Japanese firms have with their suppliers.

D The passage does not indicate that Western companies have been slow to adopt any particular practice favored by Japanese companies.

E Rather than pointing out differences between Japanese and Western supplier relationships, it actually suggests that they are more similar than generally realized.

The correct answer is C.

355. According to the passage, the advice referred to in line 6 was a response to which of the following?

(A) A recent decrease in the number of available suppliers within the United States automobile industry

(B) A debate within Western management circles during the past decade regarding the value of strategic partnerships

(C) The success of certain European automobile manufacturers that have adopted strategic partnerships

(D) An increase in demand over the past decade for automobiles made by Western manufacturers

(E) Research comparing Japanese business practices with those of other nations

Supporting Idea

This question is concerned with identifying what the passage says about certain experts' advice. The passage indicates that the experts' advice is based on numerous studies carried out over the previous decade that compared Japanese manufacturing and supply practices with those of the rest of the world.

A The passage indicates that the major automobile manufacturers in the United States have decreased the number of suppliers they deal with, but the experts' advice was not in response to such a decrease; rather, the decrease was in response to the manufacturers' adoption of the experts' advice.

B The passage does not say anything about a debate within Western management circles regarding management partnerships.

C   The passage mentions that European manufacturers have adopted strategic partnerships, but it does not indicate how successful those manufacturers have been.

D   The passage does not indicate whether demand for automobiles has increased over the past decade.

E   **Correct.** The passage indicates that the experts' advice was made in reaction to studies that compared Japanese business practices regarding production and suppliers with those of other companies.

The correct answer is E.

356. The author mentions "the success of a certain well-known Japanese automaker" in lines 10–11, most probably in order to

(A)   demonstrate some of the possible reasons for the success of a certain business practice

(B)   cite a specific case that has convinced Western business experts of the value of a certain business practice

(C)   describe specific steps taken by Western automakers that have enabled them to compete more successfully in a global market

(D)   introduce a paradox about the effect of a certain business practice in Japan

(E)   indicate the need for Western managers to change their relationships with their external business partners

Evaluation

The question requires the test-taker to determine the author's reason for mentioning *the success of a certain well-known Japanese automaker*. Most likely, the author wishes to present a specific case that was crucial in leading Western management circles to value strategic partnerships.

A   The passage does not discuss reasons for the success of the business practice.

B   **Correct.** The well-known success of a certain Japanese automaker is offered as a reason for Western management circles to believe in the value of the business practice of forming strategic partnerships.

C   Although the passage does indicate that Western automakers have adopted strategic partnerships with suppliers, it does not indicate whether this has enabled them to become more successful globally.

D   The passage does not specifically discuss any paradox related to the effects of Japanese business practices.

E   Although the passage does give reason to think that the changes adopted by Western managers may have made their relationships with external business partners less, rather than more, like the relationships Japanese managers have, the passage does not indicate whether the Western managers need to make any further changes.

The correct answer is B.

357. Which of the following is cited in the passage as evidence supporting the author's claim about what the new research referred to in line 20 demonstrates?

(A)   The belief within Western management circles regarding the extent to which Japanese firms rely on strategic partnerships

(B)   The surprising number of European and United States businesses that have strategic partnerships with their suppliers

(C)   The response of Western automobile manufacturers to the advice that they adopt strategic partnerships with their suppliers

(D)   The prevalence of "market-exchange" relationships between Japanese firms and their suppliers

(E)   The success of a particular Japanese automobile manufacturer that favors strategic partnerships with its suppliers

Supporting Idea

To answer this question, you must identify what evidence is cited in the passage regarding the author's claim that new research casts doubt on the widespread view that Japanese firms primarily manage their supplier relationships through strategic partnerships. To support this claim regarding the new research, the author points out that Japanese firms make extensive use of "market-exchange relationships," which are alternatives to the strategic relationships discussed in the preceding paragraph.

A   This is the belief that the author claims that the new research casts doubt on, so it would not make sense for the author to cite this as evidence for the author's claim.

B   This is cited as a result of the belief that the author claims the new research casts doubt on, not as evidence for the author's claim.

C   The new research undermines the basis of the advice referred to here—advice that the Western automobile manufacturers heed—so it would make little sense for the author to cite this as evidence in support of the author's claim about the new research.

D   Correct. The passage does cite this prevalence as evidence for the author's claim that the new research casts doubt on the widely held view about Japanese firms.

E   Citing this firm's success would tend to support the widespread view about Japanese firms, not undermine that view.

The correct answer is D.

Questions 358–361 refer to the passage on page 332.

Main Idea Summary

The passage primarily addresses a question about what a company should do when it has acquired another company and needs to lay off some of the upper management team of the acquired company. *Is the acquisition more likely to be successful if top executives with longer experience in the acquired company are retained or if those with less experience in the company are retained?* The passage introduces the topic by way of a related discussion about which top executive positions should be retained. It then discusses some theoretical considerations in favor of two opposing views about whether longer-tenured executives or shorter-tenured executives should be retained. The final paragraph describes a study designed to help decide the issue. The main idea of the passage is that this study supports the view that acquisitions are more likely to succeed if longer-tenured top executives in the acquired company are retained than if shorter-tenured top executives are retained.

358. According to the passage, the research mentioned in line 6 suggests which of the following about lower-ranked top executives and postacquisition success?

(A)   Given that these executives are unlikely to contribute to postacquisition success, little effort should be spent trying to retain them.

(B)   The shorter their length of service, the less likely it is that these executives will play a significant role in postacquisition success.

(C)   These executives are less important to postacquisition success than are more highly ranked top executives.

(D)   If they have long tenures, these executives may prove to be as important to postacquisition success as are more highly ranked top executives.

(E)   Postacquisition success is unlikely if these executives are retained.

Supporting Idea

The question asks about information provided by the passage. According to the third sentence, research suggests that retaining the highest-level top executives in an acquisition is more strongly associated with success than retaining lower-ranked top executives—which suggests, in turn, that lower-ranked top executives are less important than top-level executives to postacquisition success, though it does not suggest that they are unimportant to such success.

A   The research indicates that lower-ranked top executives are less strongly associated with success than are higher-ranked executives but does not provide advice about retention efforts.

B   The research mentioned in the third sentence does not consider length of service.

C   Correct. The research indicates that lower-ranked top executives are less strongly associated with postacquisition success than are the highest-ranked executives.

D   The research mentioned in the third sentence does not consider length of service.

E   The research suggests that lower-ranked top
     executives are less strongly associated with
     postacquisition success but does not suggest
     that they decrease the likelihood of success.

The correct answer is C.

359. The resource-based view, as described in the passage,
     is based on which of the following ideas?

     (A) The managerial skills of top executives become
          strongest after the first five years of their tenure.

     (B) Company-specific knowledge is an important
          factor in the success of an acquisition process.

     (C) The amount of nontransferable knowledge
          possessed by long-tenured top executives tends
          to be underestimated.

     (D) Effective implementation of an acquisition
          depends primarily on the ability of executives to
          adapt to change.

     (E) Short-tenured executives are likely to impede
          the implementation of a successful acquisition
          strategy.

Evaluation

This question requires analysis of the reasoning
underlying one of the two explanations described
in the passage. The resource-based view (RBV)
holds that retaining high-level executives with
long tenure will contribute to success because
those people have important company-specific
knowledge. This view rests on the assumption
that company-specific knowledge is valuable to
postacquisition success.

A   In RBV, executives with long tenure are
     valuable not specifically for their managerial
     skills but for their knowledge about the
     acquired company. The passage does not
     restrict to five years the period in which this
     knowledge is gained.

B   Correct. RBV values executives' knowledge
     of the acquired company and is based on the
     belief that company-specific knowledge is
     valuable for postacquisition success.

C   The passage does not indicate that RBV claims
     that executives' company-specific knowledge
     is generally undervalued. But the passage does
     indicate that RBV regards such knowledge as
     valuable to postacquisition success.

D   In RBV, executives with long tenure are
     valuable not for their ability to adapt to
     change, but for their knowledge about the
     acquired company.

E   RBV does not suggest that short-tenured
     executives impede postacquisition success,
     only that they are less important to success
     than the highest-ranked executives.

The correct answer is B.

360. The passage suggests that Bergh and a proponent of
     the upper echelons perspective would be most likely to
     disagree over which of the following?

     (A) Whether there is a positive correlation between
          short organizational tenure and managerial
          adaptability

     (B) Whether there is a positive correlation between
          long organizational tenure and the acquisition of
          idiosyncratic and nontransferable knowledge

     (C) Whether adaptability is a useful trait for an
          executive who is managing an acquisition
          process

     (D) Whether retaining less-tenured top executives of
          an acquired company is an optimal strategy for
          achieving postacquisition success

     (E) Whether retaining highest-level top executives
          of acquired companies is more important than
          retaining lower-ranked top executives

Inference

The question asks about conclusions that can
reasonably be drawn from the information
provided in the passage. Bergh's study supports
the resource-based view (RBV), which suggests
that top executives with long tenure are more
valuable to postacquisition success than other
executives. The upper echelons perspective
(UEP), in contrast, suggests that top executives
with shorter tenure are more valuable to
postacquisition success. Thus, Bergh and a
proponent of UEP would likely disagree about
whether long or short tenure top executives
are more valuable to a positive outcome in a
postacquisition situation.

A   The passage does not provide sufficiently
     specific information about statistical
     relationships to determine whether Bergh

and proponents of UEP would agree or disagree about whether there is such a positive correlation.

B   There is a weak suggestion in the passage that Bergh believes such a positive correlation exists, but there is no indication that a proponent of UEP would question such a correlation.

C   The passage does not indicate that Bergh would disagree with proponents of UEP that adaptability is a valuable trait in an executive who is managing an acquisition.

D   Correct. The passage suggests that proponents of UEP believe that retaining less-tenured top executives during and after an acquisition is a better strategy, while Bergh believes that retaining longer-tenured top executives is better.

E   The passage suggests that Bergh and proponents of UEP agree that retaining the highest-level top executives is more important to postacquisition success than is retaining lower-ranked top executives.

The correct answer is D.

361. According to the passage, prior to Bergh's study, research on the role of top executives of acquired companies in business acquisition success was limited in which of the following ways?

(A)   It did not address how the organizational tenure of top executives affects postacquisition success.

(B)   It did not address why some companies have longer-tenured CEOs than others.

(C)   It did not consider strategies for retaining long-tenured top executives of acquired companies.

(D)   It failed to differentiate between the contribution of highest-level top executives to postacquisition success and that of lower-ranked top executives.

(E)   It underestimated the potential contribution that lower-level top executives can make to postacquisition success.

Supporting Idea

This question asks about information explicitly provided in the passage. The first paragraph summarizes research indicating that retaining

highest-level top executives during and after an acquisition is more strongly associated with successful outcomes than retaining lower-ranking top executives. The paragraph then states that this research has limitations, including failing to take into account how long the highest-ranking executives have worked for the company. The second paragraph explains that Bergh's study responds to those limitations by analyzing the role of tenure (length of service in the organization).

A   Correct. The passage indicates that the research about the role of highest-level executives in acquisitions is limited by its failure to consider tenure.

B   The passage does not portray the failure of the research to address this as a limitation of the research in question.

C   The passage does not portray the failure of the research to consider this as a limitation of the research in question.

D   The passage indicates that the research does, in fact, differentiate between the respective contributions of these two groups of top executives.

E   Undervaluing the contributions of lower-level top executives is not one of the limitations mentioned in the passage.

The correct answer is A.

Questions 362–365 refer to the passage on page 334.

Main Idea Summary

The passage is primarily concerned with Marcus Garvey's role in the African American revitalization movement of the early twentieth century. The passage's first paragraph states that the return of African American soldiers from the First World War created an ideal constituency for Garvey's message of pride and unity among African Americans. The second paragraph describes the disillusionment of these soldiers upon their return and discusses Anthony F. C. Wallace's idea that the tension between a culture's expectations and reality can inspire a revitalization movement. The final paragraph argues that Garvey did not create the consciousness on which he built his movement, but merely gave it its political expression.

362. According to the passage, which of the following contributed to Marcus Garvey's success?

(A) He introduced cultural and historical consciousness to the African American community.

(B) He believed enthusiastically in the traditional American success ethos.

(C) His audience had already formed a consciousness that made it receptive to his message.

(D) His message appealed to critics of African American support for United States military involvement in the First World War.

(E) He supported the movement to protest segregation that had emerged prior to his arrival in the United States.

Supporting Idea

To answer this question, find what the passage states explicitly about how Marcus Garvey achieved his success. The passage begins by stating that Garvey arrived at the right time: that returning African American soldiers were primed to receive what he had to say about the African American community. These soldiers already held strong beliefs about their rights to opportunities for success; the passage concludes that the divide between the soldiers' expectations and their experiences led to Garvey's success.

A   The passage states that African American people were in possession of a strong cultural and historical consciousness prior to Garvey's arrival in the United States.

B   The passage attributes belief in the traditional American success ethos to African American people who joined the armed forces; it does not mention Garvey's beliefs on this subject.

C   **Correct.** African American soldiers who had experienced segregation during the First World War were ready to hear what Garvey had to say.

D   Critics of African American support for United States involvement in the First World War are not mentioned in the passage.

E   While Garvey most likely would have supported a movement to protest

segregation, such a movement is not discussed in the passage.

The correct answer is C.

363. The passage suggests that many African American people responded to their experiences in the armed forces in which of the following ways?

(A) They maintained as civilians their enthusiastic allegiance to the armed forces.

(B) They questioned United States involvement in the First World War.

(C) They joined political organizations to protest the segregation of African American troops and the indignities they suffered in the military.

(D) They became aware of the gap between their expectations and the realities of American culture.

(E) They repudiated Garvey's message of pride and unity.

Inference

According to the passage, African Americans enthusiastically joined the armed services but were confronted with continued segregation, both in the military and when they returned home. The passage does not explicitly state their response to these experiences, but a response can be inferred. The second paragraph refers to anthropologist Anthony F. C. Wallace, who argued that a revitalization movement may be brought about by the perception of a gap between expectations and reality, and such a revitalization did occur in African American communities following the First World War; thus, many African American people may have become aware of a gap such as Wallace described.

A   The passage states that African American troops experienced segregation and other indignities while in the military; these experiences could reasonably be inferred to have dampened their enthusiasm for the armed forces. Regardless, the passage does not suggest an enthusiastic allegiance.

B   The passage describes African American people's enthusiasm about joining the military. Although they experienced segregation and other indignities while in the military, the passage does not suggest that their opinion about involvement in the war changed.

C   While African American troops may have joined political organizations, the passage does not provide any actual evidence of this having occurred.

D   Correct. The fact that, as the passage states, a revitalization movement occurred in the African American community following the First World War suggests that the returning soldiers did become aware of the gap between their expectations of an improved situation with regard to segregation and the reality of continued segregation in the United States.

E   The passage does not suggest that African American troops repudiated Garvey's message. On the contrary, it states that Garvey built *the largest revitalization movement in African American history*. This suggests that the members of the African American community, including the returning soldiers, were extremely receptive to Garvey's message.

The correct answer is D.

364. It can be inferred from the passage that the "scholars" mentioned in line 24 believe which of the following to be true?

(A)   Revitalization resulted from the political activism of returning African American soldiers following the First World War.

(B)   Marcus Garvey had to change a number of prevailing attitudes in order for his mass movement to find a foothold in the United States.

(C)   The prevailing sensibility of the African American community provided the foundation of Marcus Garvey's political appeal.

(D)   Marcus Garvey hoped to revitalize consciousness of cultural and historical identity in the African American community.

(E)   The goal of the mass movement that Marcus Garvey helped bring into being was to build on the pride and unity among African Americans.

Inference

To determine what it is logical to infer regarding the scholars discussed in the third paragraph,

look at the context in which they are mentioned. According to the passage, these scholars argue that Garvey was responsible for creating a particular consciousness within the African American community, a consciousness that the passage identifies as *identity, strength, and* [a] *sense of history*. Unlike the passage author, these scholars believe strongly in Garvey's responsibility for this consciousness, so they would most likely reject any suggestion that it existed prior to his arrival and activism.

A   According to the passage, the scholars believe that Garvey was responsible for the creation of the consciousness that led to revitalization, which suggests that revitalization resulted from Garvey's activism, not soldiers' activism.

B   Correct. According to the passage, the scholars believe that Garvey created the consciousness that led to his revitalization movement. This suggests that he had to change prevailing attitudes in order to foster this new consciousness.

C   According to the passage, the scholars believe that Garvey created a new consciousness in the African American community; thus, the prevailing sensibility could not have provided a foundation for his appeal.

D   According to the passage, the scholars believe that Garvey built his revitalization movement on a new consciousness of cultural and historical identity, not a previously existing one.

E   According to the passage, the scholars' position is that Garvey's movement was built on a new sense of pride and unity that he provided, and that that sense did not precede Garvey's work.

The correct answer is B.

365. According to the passage, many African American people joined the armed forces during the First World War for which of the following reasons?

(A)   They wished to escape worsening economic conditions in African American communities.

(B)   They expected to fulfill ideals of personal attainment.

(C)   They sought to express their loyalty to the United States.

(D)   They hoped that joining the military would help advance the cause of desegregation.

(E)   They saw military service as an opportunity to fulfill Marcus Garvey's political vision.

Supporting Idea

This question depends on identifying what the passage states directly about African American people's reasons for joining the armed forces. The reason offered by the passage is that the African American people who entered the armed forces did so because they were *hoping to participate in the traditional American ethos of individual success.*

A   Although this is a plausible reason for entering the armed forces, the passage does not discuss economic conditions.

B   **Correct.** The passage states that African American people who joined the armed forces during the First World War wanted to achieve individual success.

C   The passage does not discuss African American people's loyalty to the United States.

D   The passage states that African American troops experienced segregation, but it does not suggest that they had hoped their joining the military would promote desegregation.

E   The passage suggests that African American troops did not become aware of Marcus Garvey's political vision until after they returned from the First World War.

The correct answer is B.

Questions 366–373 refer to the passage on page 336.

366.   Which of the following best states the difference between free trade and fair trade, as explained in the passage?

(A)   Free trade requires no trade tariffs whatsoever, whereas fair trade assumes multilateral agreement on tariffs for goods of equal worth.

(B)   Free trade is based on the unrestricted movement of goods across all national boundaries, whereas fair trade is based on a nation's restriction of commerce with each nation that erects trade barriers to the first nation's exports.

(C)   The trade policies of countries like Arboria are based on the principles of free trade, whereas the trade policies of other types of world economies are based on fair trade.

(D)   Free-trade nations negotiate individual trade agreements with each of their trading partners, whereas fair-trade nations conduct multilateral trade negotiations.

(E)   Free trade assumes a constant level of global commerce, whereas fair trade promotes a steady expansion of international trade.

Evaluation

This question requires you to understand how the passage explains the difference between free trade and fair trade. The passage discusses international trade as viewed from the perspective of the nation of Arboria. The distinction between free trade and fair trade is discussed in the third paragraph. Free trade between two countries is understood as free movement of goods in each direction across countries' borders. From the Arborian perspective, fair trade is understood as mutually beneficial trading arrangements, where access to the Arborian market is granted only to nations that allow Arborian exports equal access to their own markets.

A   The distinction between free trade and fair trade in the passage does not hinge on the absence or presence of tariffs in a trading regime, even though the passage implies that asymmetric application of tariffs would render a trading regime unfair.

B   **Correct.** As explained above, free trade implies open access to markets; fair trade implies that each of any two trading partner nations should allow the same level of access for imports from the other nation.

C   Whether true or false, this is a claim of a factual kind, and does not provide anything resembling a definition of the two terms, *free trade* and *fair trade*. The passage suggests that Arboria has a free-trade economy and many other nations do not.

D   The passage tells us that both the free-trade advocates and the fair-trade advocates base their positions, in part, on the idea that multilateral negotiations are the most effective way of resolving pressing trade issues.

E   The passage suggests that free trade without fair trade would hinder the expansion of trade (especially Arborian trade) and that fair trade would eventually lead to free trade. But the passage also suggests that international trade between two countries can be simultaneously free and fair. As presented in the passage, the distinction between the two aspects of trade does not hinge on whether the regime promotes a steady expansion of international trade.

The correct answer is B.

367. It can be inferred that the author of the passage would most likely agree with which of the following statements about multilateral trade negotiations?

(A)   They are the most effective way to resolve trade problems.

(B)   They are most effective in dealing with fair-trade issues between nations.

(C)   They have only recently begun to make an impact on world trade.

(D)   Arborian reliance on multilateral trade negotiations, while appropriate in the past, is inadequate for today's global marketplace.

(E)   The principles of multilateral trade negotiations are incompatible with current Arborian foreign trade policy.

Inference

Answering this question requires you to infer from the given information what claim about multilateral trade negotiations the author would most likely agree with. According to the passage, the advocates of free trade and the advocates of fair trade both assume that multilateral negotiations are the most effective way to resolve trading issues. But the passage claims that this assumption is wrong and outdated for current trading conditions. The passage argues that nearly 75 percent of trade is conducted by widely divergent economic systems in countries not subscribing to the same trading principles as Arboria and that this makes negotiation of multilateral trade agreements virtually impossible.

A   As explained above, the author of the passage takes a position opposed to this.

B   According to the passage, it is virtually impossible to negotiate multilateral agreements with countries that do not accept the same trading principles as Arboria and that therefore may have differing notions of what makes trade fair.

C   The passage suggests that the assumption concerning multilateral trade negotiations had for 40 years been accepted by the free-trade countries that dominated world trade—as well as possibly by other trading countries.

D   **Correct.** As explained above, this is a part of the argument in the passage.

E   The passage does not argue that a principle concerning multilateral approaches in negotiating trade policy, long accepted by Arborian trading authorities, was incompatible with "current" foreign-trade policy. Rather, the passage suggests that that principle and the associated policy should be questioned and rejected, with a view to formulating a policy more relevant to current conditions.

The correct answer is D.

368. Which of the following statements best summarizes the author's opinion of "free traders" and "fair traders"?

(A)   The free and the fair traders' continuing debate provides a healthy and effective forum for examining Arborian trade policy.

(B)   The proponents of fair trade are essentially correct, while those who advocate free trade are not.

(C)   The proponents of free trade are better able to deal with current economic problems than are the fair traders.

(D)   Neither the free nor the fair traders can come up with a workable trade policy because neither takes multilateral negotiations into account.

(E)   The proponents of both free and fair trade have based their positions on out-of-date premises that do not reflect current economic conditions.

Supporting Idea

This question requires an understanding of what the author has to say about "free traders" and "fair traders." The final paragraph of the passage states that "both sides," i.e. the proponents of free trade and the proponents of fair trade, base their positions on two assumptions that, according to the passage, are outdated. The passage attributes this outdatedness to changes that have occurred in the composition of international trade.

A   The passage implies that the debate between the free traders and the fair traders is unlikely to make progress because of two outdated assumptions that both sides make.

B   The passage implies that fair trade ultimately leads to free trade. The passage implies that trade can be both free and fair.

C   The passage indicates that assumptions on which the free traders and the fair traders rely are incompatible with the current realities of international trade.

D   The passage argues that both free traders and fair traders wrongly assume that the best way to resolve trade issues is through the use of multilateral negotiations.

E   **Correct.** This is a claim that is central to the argument in the passage, as explained above.

The correct answer is E.

369.   The author mentions all of the following as characteristic of world trade in the mid-1940s EXCEPT:

(A)   Arboria played a major role in the global marketplace.

(B)   Whorfland played a major role in the global marketplace.

(C)   Tariffs were the main obstacle to trade.

(D)   Fair-trade economies dominated international trade.

(E)   Arborian manufacturers were unsurpassed in most industries.

Supporting Idea

The word "mentions" in the question is to be taken as meaning "explicitly states" (as opposed to implies or suggests), so this question requires that you recognize what is and is NOT explicitly

stated in the passage regarding world trade in the mid-1940s. The passage states that Arboria and Whorfland dominated the global economy for a long period, but no longer do so. It also states that tariffs were the main obstacle to trade during the time of Arboria's trade supremacy and that in most industries, Arboria had no close competitors. The passage neither states nor implies that at that time fair-trade economies dominated world trade.

A   The passage states that this was so in the mid-1940s.

B   This is stated in the passage.

C   The passage states: "tariffs were the principal obstacle to trade."

D   **Correct.** The passage does NOT mention this; it neither states nor implies that in the mid-1940s, fair-trade economies dominated world trade.

E   The passage states: "Arborian supremacy was uncontested in virtually all industries."

The correct answer is D.

370.   In presenting the argument in the passage, the author uses all of the following EXCEPT:

(A)   statistical information about global commerce

(B)   definitions of terms concerning world trade

(C)   generalizations about Arboria's economic system

(D)   historical background of Arborian trade policy

(E)   an example of an economic system whose principles differ from those of Arboria

Evaluation

This question concerns rhetorical techniques used in the passage, and we are asked to identify a technique that is NOT used.

A   The passage gives some statistical information about global commerce: e.g., 75% of world trade involves countries with divergent economic systems that differ from those of Arboria.

B   The passage defines free trade and fair trade.

C   The passage states that the supremacy of Arboria in most industries was for a long time uncontested.

D   The passage indicates how the trade regime in which Arboria participates was established 40 years previously.

E   **Correct.** No individual economic system besides that of Whorfland—which has adopted the same trading principles as Arboria—is cited in the passage.

The correct answer is E.

371.   The author asserts which of the following about Arboria's trade policy?

(A)   A dramatic revision of Arboria's trade policy will be necessary unless Arborian manufacturers improve the quality of their goods.

(B)   The most crucial issue facing Arborian trade policymakers is that of free trade versus protectionism.

(C)   Arboria's current trade policy was essentially developed during the 1940s and has changed little since that time.

(D)   Arboria's trade policy is widely emulated throughout the world, to the extent that most international commerce is modeled on Arboria's principles.

(E)   Arboria's trade policy has evolved gradually over the last eighty years, constantly readjusting itself in response to shifts in global commerce.

Supporting Idea

This question asks us to identify something stated in the passage—though not necessarily in the exact words given. We should look for the statement that is the most precise paraphrase of a statement made in the passage.

A   Although the passage indicates that some revision of Arborian trade policy is needed, the passage does not indicate that such a revision would be unnecessary if the quality of Arborian manufactures improved.

B   The passage states: "Today the key trade issue is not free trade versus protectionism."

C   **Correct.** The passage states that the current trade policy is obsolete and "an artifact of the mid-1940s," and adds that although ecoomic circumstances have changed, Arborian trade policy has not.

D   The passage states: "nearly 75 percent [of world trade] is conducted by economic systems operating with principles at odds with those of Arboria."

E   The passage does not state that this is so; in fact, it emphasizes the lack of change over the previous 40 years in Arborian trade policy and the absence of readjustment in response to significant changes in conditions affecting global trade.

The correct answer is C.

372.   The passage is primarily concerned with

(A)   illustrating the erosion of Arboria's position in the world marketplace

(B)   examining the differences between "free" and "fair" traders

(C)   advocating a reassessment of Arboria's trade policy

(D)   criticizing the terms of the General Agreement on Tariffs and Trade (GATT)

(E)   comparing the different economic circumstances of Arboria's trade partners

Main Idea

We are asked here to select the phrase that most accurately identifies the topic that is the central theme of the passage. The discussion revolves around trade policy—specifically the way in which it has affected the interests of the nation of Arboria. In the course of exploring this central topic, several issues are touched on: the loss of Arborian dominance in global trade; the distinction between free trade and fair trade; the impact of GATT on the governance of global trade; and the percentage of total trade conducted by countries other than Arboria and Whorfland.

A   Illustrating something generally involves providing a specific example. But the passage gives no example to show how the Arborian trade position has declined relative to that of other countries.

B   The distinction between free trade and fair trade, as understood by the advocates of each of these, is explained in the broader context of considering Arborian trade policy. But the passage emphasizes the common assumptions relied on by both free traders and fair traders.

C **Correct.** This is the theme of the passage, which advocates a reconsideration of Arborian trade policy and the longstanding assumptions on which it has been based. This central concern prompts the discussion of other relevant, but subsidiary, topics.

D The individual terms of GATT are not examined or criticized in any detail, but the relevance of GATT to current global trade is minimized.

E No such comparison is made, even though the divergence of economic systems involved in world trade is emphasized with a view to demonstrating the difficulty in negotiating multilateral trade deals and the obsolescence of the multilateral approach.

The correct answer is C.

373. The author implies that the main obstacle to a truly effective Arborian trade policy is the

(A) weak position that Arboria currently holds in the global marketplace

(B) inability of Arborian leaders to recognize that foreign economic systems are based on principles fundamentally different from their own

(C) dominance of the supporters of free trade in the conflict between free-trade and fair-trade advocates

(D) apparent inability of Arborian industries to produce goods that are competitive in the world market

(E) protectionism that characterizes the foreign trade policies of so many of Arboria's trade partners

Inference

Correctly answering this question requires you to infer from the given information what the main obstacle to an effective Arborian trade policy is. The correct response is to be found in the first

paragraph of the passage, which contains the following sentence: "Arboria faces the prospect of continuing economic loss until Arborian business and political leaders recognize the fundamental differences between Arborian and foreign economic systems." The phrase *continuing economic loss* indicates, from the author's perspective, an ineffective trade policy. The *until*-clause signifies that a necessary condition of improving the situation is a recognition by leaders that Arborian and foreign economic systems are fundamentally different. The final paragraph emphasizes that such differences exist: "75 percent [of world trade] is conducted by economic systems operating with principles at odds with those of Arboria."

A The passage does not state or imply that Arboria has a "weak position" in global trade; rather, it emphasizes that Arboria can gain a much stronger position and "misses opportunities for trade expansion."

B **Correct.** See the detailed analysis given above.

C The passage nowhere states or implies that the free-trade advocates are dominant in the dispute with fair-trade advocates, even though the passage suggests that developed economies such as Arboria and Whorfland have long practiced free trade and been dominant in global trade.

D The passage neither states nor implies that the goods produced by Arborian industries are deficient in quality or are overpriced, but it does suggest that some countries that export to Arboria have trade barriers, such as tariffs, that impede importation of Arborian products.

E The passage suggests that some trading partners of Arboria have trade barriers impeding imports from Arboria, but the passage asserts the following: "Today the key trade issue is not free trade versus protectionism but diminishing trade versus expanding trade."

The correct answer is B.

Questions 374–377 refer to the passage on page 338.

374. According to the passage, theory B states that which of the following is a factor that enables a schooling fish to escape predators?

A) The tendency of fish to form compact groups

(B) The movement of other fish within the school

(C) The inability of predators to detect schools

(D) The ability of fish to hide behind one another in a school

(E) The great speed with which a school can disperse

Supporting Idea

This question depends on understanding what the passage states about theory B, the "confusion effect." One element of theory B is that predators may experience sensory confusion created by large numbers of moving fish in a school.

A   The compactness of groups of schooling fish is an element of theory A, not theory B.

B   **Correct.** It is the movement of schooling fish around a predator that creates sensory confusion in the predator; this movement may distract the predator and help to protect individual fish in the school.

C   According to the passage's description of theory A, predators are actually slightly more likely to detect schools than they are to detect individual fish.

D   Theory B does not involve fish hiding behind one another, but rather moving around the predator.

E   The passage does not discuss the speed of dispersal of schools of fish.

The correct answer is B.

375. According to the passage, both theory A and theory B have been developed to explain how

(A) fish hide from predators by forming schools

(B) forming schools functions to protect fish from predators

(C) schooling among fish differs from other protective behaviors

(D) small fish are able to make rapid decisions

(E) small fish are able to survive in an environment densely populated by large predators

Supporting Idea

The passage states in its first paragraph that two theories were developed to explain why schooling occurs in so many fish species and that they both assume that schooling helps protect fish from predators.

A   While theory A involves an explanation of how schooling makes an individual fish less likely to be found by predators, theory B explains how schooling protects fish even when they are detected by predators.

B   **Correct.** Both theory A and theory B begin with the assumption that schooling provides protection from predators, and each theory offers a different explanation for how that protection occurs.

C   The passage does not discuss protective behaviors other than schooling.

D   The decision-making ability of predators, not schooling fish, is discussed in the passage; schooling is presented as an instinctive behavior.

E   The passage suggests that only theory B helps explain schooling behavior in environments where many predators, large or otherwise, are found, and that theory A explains schooling in areas where predators are not as abundant.

The correct answer is B.

376. According to one explanation of the "confusion effect," a fish that swims in a school will have greater advantages for survival if it

(A) tends to be visible for no more than 200 meters

(B) stays near either the front or the rear of a school

(C) is part of a small school rather than a large school

(D) is very similar in appearance to the other fish in the school

(E) is medium-sized

Inference

The "confusion effect" is discussed in the third and fourth paragraphs. The first explanation of the "confusion effect" proposes that because predators prefer to select distinctive prey, they find it difficult to select one fish from among many that look the same.

A   The 200-meter visibility of fish is part of the explanation for theory A, not theory B (the "confusion effect").

B   The location of an individual fish within a school is not discussed in the passage as being important to the "confusion effect."

C   The size of a school of fish is not discussed as an element of the "confusion effect."

D   **Correct.** Because predators, according to the "confusion effect," prefer to select prey that is distinct from the rest of the school, a fish that is similar in appearance to the other fish in its school would most likely enjoy a survival advantage.

E   The size of a fish relative to the other fish in its school would most likely contribute to its ability to survive: that is, if it resembled other fish in size, it would be safer, based on what the passage says about the "confusion effect." Furthermore, the passage gives no reason to think that merely being medium-sized would confer any advantage (unless the other fish were medium-sized as well).

The correct answer is D.

377. The author is primarily concerned with

(A)   discussing different theories
(B)   analyzing different techniques
(C)   defending two hypotheses
(D)   refuting established beliefs
(E)   revealing new evidence

Main Idea

Determining the author's primary concern depends on understanding the focus of the passage as a whole. The author presents two theories that purport to account for why fish, particularly small fish, tend to school, and

explains the arguments of proponents of each theory.

A   **Correct.** The author discusses two theories—identified as theory A and theory B—that account for the tendency of fish to school.

B   The author is not concerned with different techniques in the passage.

C   The two theories of why fish school could be referred to as hypotheses, but the author is not primarily concerned with defending them; rather, the passage explains how each attempts to account for the phenomenon in question.

D   The author presents, rather than refutes, beliefs about why fish tend to school.

E   The author reveals no evidence, new or otherwise, in the passage. The passage is a general discussion of scientific opinions based on existing evidence.

Questions 378–429 - Difficulty: Medium

Questions 378–385 refer to the passage on page 339.

378. According to the passage, which of the following was true of the treaty establishing the Fort Berthold Indian Reservation?

(A)   It was challenged in the Supreme Court a number of times.
(B)   It was rescinded by the federal government, an action that gave rise to the Winters case.
(C)   It cited American Indians' traditional use of the land's resources.
(D)   It failed to mention water rights to be enjoyed by the reservation's inhabitants.
(E)   It was modified by the Supreme Court in *Arizona v. California*.

Supporting Idea

This question depends on recognizing what the passage says about the treaty that established the Fort Berthold Indian Reservation. The passage indicates that the treaty does not mention water rights, but the federal government had intended, according to the Supreme Court, to reserve for the inhabitants of the reservation the waters that were essential to the usefulness of the land.

A   The passage does discuss Supreme Court cases, but it does not explicitly mention any challenges in the Supreme Court to the treaty.

B   The passage does not state that the federal government rescinded the treaty.

C   The passage does not indicate that the treaty made any reference to the traditional use of the land's resources.

D   Correct. The passage indicates that the treaty does not mention water rights.

E   The passage's reference to *Arizona v. California* relates to the treaty that established the Fort Berthold Indian Reservation only in that *Arizona v. California* refers to the Winters doctrine, which was established in a case regarding that treaty; *Arizona v. California* does not modify that treaty in any way.

The correct answer is D.

379. The passage suggests that, if the criteria discussed in lines 10–20 of the text were the only criteria for establishing a reservation's water rights, which of the following would be true?

(A)   The water rights of the inhabitants of the Fort Berthold Indian Reservation would not take precedence over those of other citizens.

(B)   Reservations established before 1848 would be judged to have no water rights.

(C)   There would be no legal basis for the water rights of the Rio Grande pueblos.

(D)   Reservations other than American Indian reservations could not be created with reserved water rights.

(E)   Treaties establishing reservations would have to mention water rights explicitly in order to reserve water for a particular purpose.

Inference

The question requires you to make an inference based on a hypothetical situation in which the criteria discussed in lines 10–20 are the only criteria relevant to establishing a reservation's water rights. These criteria relate to any reservation that has been formally withdrawn from federal public lands, in which the circumstances of that withdrawal make clear that the government had intended to reserve both water and land when the reservation was established. Because the Rio Grande pueblos never formally constituted a part of federal public lands, they were never formally withdrawn from these lands, and so this set of criteria does not apply to these pueblos. Thus, if these were the only legal criteria for establishing water rights, then there would be no legal basis for water rights for the Rio Grande pueblos.

A   The criteria, which were established on the precedent set in the *Winters v. United States* ruling, all apply to the Fort Berthold Indian Reservation.

B   Although in actual fact there were no Indian reservations formally established before 1848, nothing in the passage suggests that there were not any, or that none would have met the criteria.

C   Correct. If the criteria were the only criteria relevant for establishing water rights, then the passage suggests that, because the Rio Grande pueblos were never formally withdrawn from federal public lands, there would be no legal basis for water rights for these pueblos.

D   The criteria as expressed in the passage do not restrict the type of reservation covered to American Indian reservations.

E   The criteria are meant to cover any circumstances in which the government intended to reserve water rights, whether water rights are explicitly mentioned or not.

The correct answer is C.

380. Which of the following most accurately summarizes the relationship between *Arizona v. California,* as that decision is described in the passage, and the criteria discussed in lines 10–20?

(A) *Arizona v. California* abolishes these criteria and establishes a competing set of criteria for applying the Winters doctrine.

(B) *Arizona v. California* establishes that the Winters doctrine applies to a broader range of situations than those defined by these criteria.

(C) *Arizona v. California* represents the sole example of an exception to the criteria as they were set forth in the Winters doctrine.

(D) *Arizona v. California* does not refer to the Winters doctrine to justify water rights, whereas these criteria do rely on the Winters doctrine.

(E) *Arizona v. California* applies the criteria derived from the Winters doctrine only to federal lands other than American Indian reservations.

Evaluation

This question requires you to determine how *Arizona v. California,* as it is described in the passage, relates to the criteria discussed in lines 10–20. Those criteria, which were established in various decisions based on the precedent of *Winters v. United States,* lay down conditions under which courts can uphold federal rights to reserve water. One of the criteria is related to land formally withdrawn from federal public lands. *Arizona v. California* establishes that the Winters doctrine—which stipulates that water rights need not have been granted explicitly—applies to a broader range of situations than those defined by the criteria. For instance, the doctrine can apply in cases in which the land in question was never formally withdrawn from public lands.

A   The passage does not indicate that *Arizona v. California* abolishes these criteria. It merely indicates that *Arizona v. California* recognizes further situations to which the Winters doctrine can apply.

B   **Correct.** The passage indicates that *Arizona v. California* applies the Winters doctrine to a situation that falls outside these criteria.

C   The passage does not indicate that there are no other exceptions besides *Arizona v. California* to these criteria.

D   The passage indicates that *Arizona v. California* does refer to the Winters doctrine to justify water rights.

E   The passage does not indicate that *Arizona v. California* applies these criteria at all; instead, *Arizona v. California* broadens the range of situations to which the Winters doctrine applies.

The correct answer is B.

381. The "pragmatic approach" mentioned in lines 37–38 of the passage is best defined as one that

(A) grants recognition to reservations that were never formally established but that have traditionally been treated as such

(B) determines the water rights of all citizens in a particular region by examining the actual history of water usage in that region

(C) gives federal courts the right to reserve water along with land even when it is clear that the government originally intended to reserve only the land

(D) bases the decision to recognize the legal rights of a group on the practical effect such a recognition is likely to have on other citizens

(E) dictates that courts ignore precedents set by such cases as *Winters v. United States* in deciding what water rights belong to reserved land

Evaluation

This question depends on determining how the term *pragmatic approach* is used in lines 37–38. The passage states that what constitutes an American Indian reservation is a matter not of legal definition, but of practice. The Rio Grande pueblos, though they were never formally established by a withdrawal from federal public lands, have always been treated in practice as reservations. This is what is described in the passage as a *pragmatic approach.*

A   **Correct.** The passage refers to the idea that *[w]hat constitutes an American Indian reservation is a question of practice, not of legal definition* as a *pragmatic approach.* Thus, the pragmatic approach does not require that a reservation has been formally established, but only that it has been traditionally treated as such.

B The passage does not concern itself with the water rights of all citizens.

C The passage clearly indicates that determining whether the government intended to reserve water along with the land is crucial for courts.

D The passage does not specifically consider the likely practical effect of recognizing a particular group's legal rights on other citizens.

E The passage indicates that the pragmatic approach is supported by *Arizona v. California,* which used, and expanded on, the precedent set by *Winters v. United States.*

The correct answer is A.

382. It can be inferred from the passage that the Winters doctrine has been used to establish which of the following?

(A) A rule that the government may reserve water only by explicit treaty or agreement

(B) A legal distinction between federal lands reserved for American Indians and federal lands reserved for other purposes

(C) Criteria governing when the federal government may set land aside for a particular purpose

(D) The special status of American Indian tribes' rights to reserved land

(E) The federal right to reserve water implicitly as well as explicitly under certain conditions

Inference

This question requires you to make an inference based on facts the passage cites regarding the Winters doctrine. The passage indicates that the Supreme Court ruled in *Winters v. United States* that, despite the fact that the treaty establishing the Berthold Indian Reservation made no explicit mention of water rights, the federal government had intended to reserve such rights to the American Indians living on that reservation. Later court rulings that cited the Winters ruling as precedent further refined this doctrine such that water rights can be reserved implicitly if

circumstances reveal [that] the government intended to reserve water as well as land when establishing the reservation.

A The passage states that the Winters doctrine ruled that even if a treaty has not explicitly reserved water, water may be reserved if conditions reveal that the reservation of water had been intended.

B The passage indicates that the Winters doctrine presupposes such a legal distinction; it does not establish it.

C The passage does not give any information that suggests that the Winters doctrine has been used to establish any criteria governing when the federal government may set land aside for a particular purpose.

D The passage indicates that the Winters doctrine gives special status to the water flowing through reserved lands, but it does not suggest that the doctrine has been used to establish any special status of American Indian tribes' rights to those lands.

E **Correct.** The passage provides information suggesting that the Winters doctrine has been used to establish a federal right to implicitly reserve water under certain conditions.

The correct answer is E.

383. The author cites the fact that the Rio Grande pueblos were never formally withdrawn from public lands primarily in order to do which of the following?

(A) Suggest why it might have been argued that the Winters doctrine ought not to apply to pueblo lands

(B) Imply that the United States never really acquired sovereignty over pueblo lands

(C) Argue that the pueblo lands ought still to be considered part of federal public lands

(D) Support the argument that the water rights of citizens other than American Indians are limited by the Winters doctrine

(E) Suggest that federal courts cannot claim jurisdiction over cases disputing the traditional diversion and use of water by Pueblo Indians

Evaluation

The passage in the first paragraph outlines a set of criteria that, through various court decisions using the Winters decision as precedent, refined what came to be known as the Winters doctrine. These decisions established that courts can uphold federal rights to reserve water (specifically, for use by American Indians) if, among other conditions, *the land has been formally withdrawn from federal public lands*. Because the Rio Grande pueblos never formally constituted a part of federal public lands, it might appear that the Winters doctrine would not apply to them. The passage indicates, however, that *Arizona v. California* established that this doctrine did apply to them.

A   **Correct.** Because the Rio Grande pueblo lands were never formally withdrawn from federal public lands—because they never were a part of federal public lands—it might have appeared that the Winters doctrine did not apply to them, because that doctrine had traditionally been taken to apply only to land that had been formally withdrawn from federal public lands.

B   The passage does suggest that the federal government never acquired sovereignty over the Rio Grande pueblos. But the passage indicates this not by citing the fact that the pueblos were never formally withdrawn from public lands, but by pointing out that these pueblos were never part of federal public lands in the first place.

C   The passage states that the pueblo lands were never considered to be part of federal public lands.

D   It is not the fact that these lands were never withdrawn from federal public lands that is cited in support of this argument; it is, rather, the fact that these lands were never part of federal public lands that is cited for this purpose.

E   The passage actually suggests the opposite of what this says, namely, that federal courts can claim jurisdiction over such cases.

The correct answer is A.

384. The primary purpose of the passage is to

(A)   trace the development of laws establishing American Indian reservations

(B)   explain the legal bases for the water rights of American Indian tribes

(C)   question the legal criteria often used to determine the water rights of American Indian tribes

(D)   discuss evidence establishing the earliest date at which the federal government recognized the water rights of American Indians

(E)   point out a legal distinction between different types of American Indian reservations

Main Idea

Answering this question requires identifying the primary purpose of the passage. The passage is mainly concerned with describing the legal bases of American Indian tribal water rights.

A   The passage does not discuss the development of laws establishing reservations. It is concerned with American Indian water rights.

B   **Correct.** The passage's primary concern is to discuss certain principles relating to American Indian water rights established in various court cases.

C   The passage does not question the legal criteria it discusses.

D   The passage indicates that a groundbreaking Supreme Court ruling regarding the water rights of American Indians was handed down in 1908, but that ruling suggested that the federal government had intended at an earlier stage, in the treaty establishing the Fort Berthold Indian Reservation, to recognize water rights; the passage gives no indication, though, of the date of that treaty, nor whether that treaty would have been the first recognition in law of such rights. The passage is concerned with the legal bases of American Indian water rights, not with when the federal government first recognized them.

E   The passage does discuss both lands that have been explicitly created as reservations by treaty and lands that have been treated as reservations although they had never been legally constituted as such; however, (1) the passage indicates that in crucial ways there are no legal distinctions between these two different types of American reservation, and (2) this is not the primary focus of the passage, which, instead, concerns the legal bases of American Indian water rights.

The correct answer is B.

385. The passage suggests that the legal rights of citizens other than American Indians to the use of water flowing into the Rio Grande pueblos are

(A) guaranteed by the precedent set in *Arizona v. California*

(B) abolished by the Winters doctrine

(C) deferred to the Pueblo Indians whenever treaties explicitly require this

(D) guaranteed by federal land-use laws

(E) limited by the prior claims of the Pueblo Indians

Inference

The question requires you to make an inference regarding the legal rights of citizens other than American Indians to the use of water flowing into the Rio Grande pueblos. The second paragraph of the passage discusses the Rio Grande pueblos, the rights to the water flowing into them, and the legal bases regarding those rights. Most relevantly to this question, the final sentence of the passage indicates that *the reserved water rights of Pueblo Indians have priority over other citizens' water rights.*

A The passage indicates that the precedent set in *Arizona v. California* declares that the Winters doctrine applies to the pueblos, despite their never having been explicitly set aside as a reservation. This gave the inhabitants of the pueblos priority rights to water. Thus, the legal rights of citizens other than American Indians are not guaranteed by the precedent set in that ruling.

B The passage does not rule out the possibility that citizens other than American Indians may have some rights to the water; their

rights are merely limited by the prior claims of the Pueblo Indians.

C The passage does not explicitly discuss treaties to which Pueblo Indians are a party.

D The passage gives no indication that federal land-use laws guarantee the legal rights of citizens other than American Indians to water flowing into the Rio Grande pueblos.

E **Correct.** The passage explicitly states that the reserved water rights of Pueblo Indians have priority over other citizens' water rights.

The correct answer is E.

Questions 386–390 refer to the passage on page 341.

Main Idea Summary

The passage seeks to provide guidance about when companies should subject their suppliers to "competitive scrutiny" (readily comparing suppliers to provide the purchaser with economic leverage) and when they should accept "supplier partnerships" (arrangements in which the purchaser forgoes the right to pursue alternative suppliers). It does this primarily by distinguishing among four types of situations, each with its own set of implications for which approach is likely to be more advantageous.

386. Which of the following can be inferred about supplier partnerships, as they are described in the passage?

(A) They cannot be sustained unless the goods or services provided are available from a large number of suppliers.

(B) They can result in purchasers paying more for goods and services than they would in a competitive-bidding situation.

(C) They typically are instituted at the urging of the supplier rather than the purchaser.

(D) They are not feasible when the goods or services provided are directly related to the purchasers' end products.

(E) They are least appropriate when the purchasers' ability to change suppliers is limited.

Inference

According to the passage, in supplier partnerships a corporate purchaser forgoes the right to pursue alternative suppliers for certain goods or services. This tends to reduce or eliminate the threat of competition for the supplier in the partnership. It can be inferred that the corporate purchaser in a supplier partnership risks paying more for goods or services than it would if the supplier had to compete for the business.

A   The passage suggests something incompatible with this, i.e., that availability of the relevant goods or services from many suppliers would undermine rather than strengthen a supplier partnership.

B   Correct. The passage indicates that supplier partnerships, by definition, reduce the supplier's exposure to competition, and it can be inferred from this that a purchaser in such a partnership could sometimes pay more for the supplied goods or services than if not in the partnership.

C   The passage is silent on how supplier partnerships are initiated, and the passage gives no reason to believe that these would usually be initiated by suppliers.

D   The passage indicates that supplier partnerships are usually instituted for the supply of goods or services that do not contribute directly to the company's end products, though the passage gives no reason to believe that such partnerships would never make sense for supply of items directly related to end products.

E   The passage states that where alternative suppliers for certain goods or services are few and change from an existing supplier is difficult, partnerships may be "unavoidable." This seems to imply that in such cases, supplier partnerships are the most appropriate.

The correct answer is B.

387. Which of the following best describes the relation of the second paragraph to the first?

(A)   The second paragraph offers proof of an assertion made in the first paragraph.

(B)   The second paragraph provides an explanation for the occurrence of a situation described in the first paragraph.

(C)   The second paragraph discusses the application of a strategy proposed in the first paragraph.

(D)   The second paragraph examines the scope of a problem presented in the first paragraph.

(E)   The second paragraph discusses the contradictions inherent in a relationship described in the first paragraph.

Evaluation

The first paragraph recommends that a corporate purchaser of certain categories of goods and services should consider two variables to evaluate how, if at all, it might exert pressure on a supplier to gain economic advantage. Applying the two variables, the second paragraph identifies four different scenarios and, for each scenario, explains how the purchaser can gain some economic advantage.

A   The second paragraph is not focused on proving anything; rather it conducts an analysis of the ways in which, under various conditions, a corporate purchaser can gain economic advantage from a supplier.

B   The second paragraph conducts an analysis of various situations affecting the feasibility of a purchaser's exerting pressure to gain economic advantage from a supplier; it is not focused on explaining what causes the occurrence of any situation mentioned in the first paragraph.

C   Correct. The first paragraph recommends that corporate purchasers consider two variables in analyzing the feasibility of exerting pressure on suppliers with a view to economic advantage; the second paragraph shows how purchasers can apply those variables to identify four different types of situations affecting the degree to which economic advantage can be gained by exerting competitive pressure.

D   The first paragraph is not focused on presenting a problem, but rather on indicating an approach that purchasers might use in evaluating the feasibility of exerting economic pressure on suppliers with a view to economic advantage. The second paragraph elaborates on the suggested approach.

E   The second paragraph does not characterize as contradictory any relationship involved in the four types of situations it discusses. The first paragraph discusses supplier partnerships and identifies a disadvantage that they sometimes involve for purchasers; but the discussion in the second paragraph does not focus exclusively on situations that involve a supplier partnership.

The correct answer is C.

388.   It can be inferred that the author of the passage would be most likely to make which of the following recommendations to a company purchasing health care benefits for its employees?

(A)   Devise strategies for circumventing the obstacles to replacing the current provider of health care benefits.

(B)   Obtain health care benefits from a provider that also provides other indirect products and services.

(C)   Obtain bids from other providers of health care benefits in order to be in a position to negotiate a better deal with the current provider.

(D)   Switch providers of health care benefits whenever a different provider offers a more competitive price.

(E)   Acknowledge the difficulties involved in replacing the current provider of health care benefits and offer to form a partnership with the provider.

Inference

In the passage, health care benefits are used as an example of a Type 2 situation, where there are many competing providers, but where changing from one provider to another is difficult. In Type 2 situations, the author of the passage

recommends that the corporate purchaser examine the alternative providers to provide leverage in bargaining with the existing provider.

A   Presumably handling any obstacles to replacement would be necessary if a corporate purchaser had decided to change providers. The author of the passage does not preclude the possibility that this may sometimes be a reasonable decision but does not recommend it.

B   The author of the passage does not consider such a possibility, and does not even recommend switching from the existing provider in a Type 2 situation.

C   **Correct.** The recommendation offered in the passage is to review competitive alternatives to the existing provider, with a view to bargaining effectively for better terms with the existing provider.

D   As already noted, the author of the passage does not recommend switching from the existing provider, but recommends reviewing competitive alternatives to exert pressure on the existing provider to grant more favorable terms.

E   The author of the passage does not recommend this course of action in a Type 2 situation, which the corporate purchase of health care benefits exemplifies. The only situation in which the author views a supplier partnership as possibly the best of a set of bad options is a Type 4 situation, where there are few competitive alternatives available and change is difficult.

The correct answer is C.

389.   Which of the following is one difference between Type 2 situations and Type 4 situations, as they are described in the passage?

(A)   The number of alternative suppliers available to the purchaser

(B)   The most effective approach for the purchaser to use in obtaining competitive bids from potential suppliers

(C)   The degree of difficulty the purchaser encounters when changing suppliers

(D)   The frequency with which each type of situation occurs in a typical business environment

(E)   The likelihood that any given purchase will be an indirect purchase

Evaluation

According to the passage, Type 2 situations are those where there are several competitive alternative suppliers available but where changing from the existing supplier would be difficult. Type 4 situations are those where there are few competitive alternative suppliers and changing from the existing supplier would be difficult.

A   **Correct.** The two types of situations differ in the number of competitive alternatives to the existing supplier that are available: in Type 2 situations there are several; in Type 4 situations there are few.

B   How should the prospective purchaser ensure that potential suppliers submit truly competitive bids, or can a prospective purchaser even ensure it? The passage gives no answer to such questions that helps to identify a difference between the two types of situations.

C   In both types of situations as described in the passage, changing to a new supplier is difficult, and no difference in the degree of difficulty is mentioned.

D   How frequently each of the two types of situations typically occur is not addressed in the passage.

E   Indirect purchases, as described in the passage, are goods or services that are not embodied in the corporation's end products. Many corporate producers currently make indirect purchases such as computers or business consultancy services. The passage does not compare the proportion of a corporation's total purchases that are indirect (the proportion would presumably vary widely depending on the nature of a corporation's production); so the passage provides no rational basis for estimating a universally applicable likelihood that a given purchase would be indirect.

The correct answer is A.

390.   According to the passage, which of the following factors distinguishes an indirect purchase from other purchases?

(A)   The ability of the purchasing company to subject potential suppliers of the purchased item to competitive scrutiny

(B)   The number of suppliers of the purchased item available to the purchasing company

(C)   The methods of negotiation that are available to the purchasing company

(D)   The relationship of the purchased item to the purchasing company's end product

(E)   The degree of importance of the purchased item in the purchasing company's business operations

Supporting Idea

The passage characterizes a purchase of goods or services as indirect when the goods or services are not directly related to the end products of the purchasing corporation. Examples given are computers, advertising, and legal services. By implication, direct purchases by an automobile manufacturer could include steel, batteries, and tires: these would obviously be inputs embodied in the final products.

A   The passage suggests that "competitive scrutiny" is typically applied only to suppliers of direct purchases, but makes the case that it could be applied also to suppliers of indirect purchases. The exposure to competitive scrutiny is not the characteristic that the passage uses to distinguish direct from indirect purchases.

B   The number of available suppliers clearly can vary for both direct purchases and indirect purchases, and the passage provides no reason to think otherwise.

C   The passage provides no information about the methods of negotiation that are available for direct purchases. The passage does not base the distinction between direct and indirect purchases on differences in methods of negotiation.

D   **Correct.** The passage defines direct purchases as those directly related to the purchasing firm's end products; indirect purchases are purchases that are not related to the end products.

E   The type of purchase—direct or indirect—is not, according to the passage, determined by the degree of importance of the purchase in facilitating the purchasing firm's business operations. For example, purchase of advertising by an accounting firm could be critically important for success of the firm's business operations, but such a purchase would likely count as indirect, given the way the passage defines indirect purchases.

The correct answer is D.

Questions 391–395 refer to the passage on page 343.

Main Idea Summary

The passage serves primarily to support the notion that carotenoids are meaningful in the context of mate selection not only because they are rare but because they are required. The passage begins with a discussion of carotenoids and the role they play in mate selection among animals. The passage then considers the question of why they play this role. The traditional view is that they do so because they are rare, but the passage asserts that there is growing evidence that they also do so because they are required for health. Males that are genetically resistant to disease and parasites can use carotenoids for flashy display instead of using them entirely for fighting disease.

391. According to the "conventional view" referred to in line 13 of the passage, brighter carotenoid-based coloration in certain species suggests that an individual

(A)   lives in a habitat rich in carotenoid-bearing plants and insects

(B)   has efficient detoxification processes

(C)   has a superior immune system

(D)   possesses superior foraging capacity

(E)   is currently capable of reproducing

Supporting Idea

According to the passage, the conventional view is that carotenoids in a male animal—recognizable by brighter coloration—are meaningful in the context of mate selection

because they are rare and not easily acquired. A male that displays brighter coloration than other males would appear to a female of the species to have foraged more effectively and would therefore seem healthier, and more eligible as a mate, than some less brightly colored males.

A   Male animals in a carotenoid-rich environment might, on average, have brighter coloration, but the passage does not imply that this is part of the conventional view. The passage represents the conventional view as emphasizing the rarity of carotenoids, and the consequent difficulty of finding them.

B   The conventional view holds that a brightly colored male might appear healthier than less brightly colored males to a female of the species. If the male were healthier, this would presumably require having efficient detoxification processes. But the passage does not treat this as part of the conventional view.

C   If a male animal is healthier than other males of the species, presumably that male has a superior immune system, but the passage does not represent this as part of the conventional view.

D   Correct. The passage represents the conventional view as holding that more brightly colored males seem to females to be more effective foragers, and therefore healthier.

E   The passage does not represent the conventional view as holding that brighter coloration in a male animal would be taken by a female of the species as indicating a current ability to reproduce.

The correct answer is D.

392. The idea that carotenoid-based coloration is significant partly because carotenoids are required for health suggests that a lack of bright coloration in a male is most likely to indicate which of the following?

(A)   Inefficient detoxification processes

(B)   Immunity to parasite infestation

(C)   Low genetic resistance to disease

(D)   Lack of interest in mating

(E)   Lack of carotenoid-storing tissues

Inference

The passage states that carotenoids are used by the immune system and for detoxification processes that help maintain health. Males that are more susceptible to disease and parasites, i.e., males that lack high genetic resistance to such things, must use up the carotenoids they accumulate to boost their immune systems. The passage suggests that consequently male animals perceived by females of the species as having used up their carotenoids would be perceived as having relatively low genetic resistance to disease and parasites.

A   Even if an animal has efficient detoxification processes, the passage suggests that carotenoids would be used up in such processes. Thus, having relatively less bright coloration (and therefore less carotenoids) would not necessarily indicate inefficient detoxification processes.

B   The information in the passage suggests that having low genetic resistance to parasite infections is consistent with having immunity to at least some parasite infections, because carotenoids can be used to boost immunity. But this comes at the cost of lacking bright coloration.

C   **Correct.** The passage indicates that a male's having relatively bright coloration could indicate relatively high genetic resistance to disease, and having relatively less bright coloration could indicate relatively low genetic resistance, because the carotenoids that create bright coloration would have been used to boost immunity or aid detoxification processes.

D   The passage does not suggest that male animals lacking bright coloration would be perceived by a female of the species as lacking interest in mating.

E   The passage does not address the issue of whether carotenoid-storing tissues may be lacking in a male of a species that would normally have such tissues. The passage only states that "many" animal species use colorful signals made possible by carotenoids.

The correct answer is C.

393. The passage suggests that relatively bright carotenoid-based coloration is a signal of which of the following characteristics in males of certain animal species?

(A)   Readiness for mating behavior
(B)   Ability to fight
(C)   Particular feeding preferences
(D)   Recovery from parasite infestation
(E)   Fitness as a mate

Application

According to the passage, "studies of several animal species have shown that when choosing mates, females prefer males with brighter, carotenoid-based coloration." The passage examines two mechanisms by which carotenoid-based coloration might affect mate selection: either signaling good health or signaling high genetic resistance to infection. It is implicit in the discussion that whichever mechanism is in question, bright coloration would function to signal fitness as a mate.

A   The passage discusses how bright carotenoid-based coloration may affect mate selection but does not cite perceived bright coloration as signaling readiness for mating behavior.

B   The passage suggests that bright carotenoid-based coloration tends to signal good health or genetic resistance to factors that cause illness. The passage does not refer to ability to fight.

C   The passage does not refer to feeding preferences, but only indicates that animals with bright carotenoid-based coloration would have consumed organisms that are rich in carotenoids.

D   The passage explores the possibility that bright carotenoid-based coloration could signal high genetic resistance to infection, but implies that recovery from infection could arise from strong immune resistance rather than from high genetic resistance, and could be signaled by lack of carotenoid-based brightness.

E   **Correct.** The passage discussion indicates that, whatever the precise mechanism, bright carotenoid-based coloration in males of certain species functions to signal fitness as a mate.

The correct answer is E.

394. The passage implies which of the following about the insects from which animals acquire carotenoids?

(A) They do not produce carotenoids themselves.

(B) They use carotenoids primarily for coloration.

(C) They maintain constant levels of carotenoids in their tissues.

(D) They are unable to use carotenoids to boost their immune system.

(E) They are available in greater abundance than are carotenoid-bearing plants.

Inference

The passage says that animals "acquire carotenoids either directly (from the plants and algae that produce them) or indirectly (by eating insects)."

A **Correct.** The passage indicates that the phrase *acquire . . . . directly* signifies in this context acquisition from the ultimate source of carotenoids, so the phrase *acquire . . . indirectly* signifies an acquisition that is not from the ultimate source. This implies that insects do not produce their own carotenoids, but derive them by consuming plants, algae, or other insects.

B This may well be true of some insects, but no information in the passage implies it.

C No information in the passage implies that carotenoid levels in insect tissue remain constant over time.

D The passage contains no information that relates to the immune system of any insect species.

E Even if this is true, the passage contains no information that implies it.

The correct answer is A.

395. Information in the passage suggests that which of the following is true of carotenoids that a male animal uses for detoxification processes?

(A) They were not acquired directly from plants and algae.

(B) They cannot be replenished through foraging.

(C) They cannot be used simultaneously to brighten coloration.

(D) They do not affect the animal's susceptibility to parasites.

(E) They increase the chances that the animal will be selected as a mate.

Inference

The passage states that carotenoids are used by the immune system and for detoxification processes. To the extent that any carotenoids are used for these purposes, the passage suggests, they would not also be available for bright-colored display to potential mates.

A The passage states that animals can acquire carotenoids from insects, as well as from plants and algae. Nothing indicates that a male animal's use of the carotenoids would determine which of these sources they are acquired from.

B No information in the passage suggests this. The passage tells us that males acquire carotenoids by foraging.

C **Correct.** The passage implies that the quantity of carotenoids used for detoxification is no longer available for any other purpose, such as display of bright coloration.

D The passage suggests that carotenoids could benefit immune response; this implies the possibility of better resistance to parasitic infections.

E The passage conjectures that a male animal's use of carotenoids for detoxification processes could reduce the chances of being selected as a mate.

The correct answer is C.

Questions 396–400 refer to the passage on page 345.

Main Idea Summary

The passage is a discussion of historian Linda Kerber's "republican motherhood" thesis, according to which the American Revolution led to an increase in educational opportunities for women and girls in the United States in the late eighteenth century. Kerber's work was influential at least partly because she explored a topic (female education) that historians had largely ignored. However, the passage cites an earlier historian who had provided evidence that the trend toward greater educational opportunities for women and girls had begun decades before the American Revolution. The main idea of the passage is that the influence of the "republican motherhood" thesis may have led historians to overlook evidence that the trend Kerber describes was already underway before the American Revolution.

396. According to the passage, Kerber maintained that which of the following led to an increase in educational opportunities for women in the United States after the American Revolution?

(A) An unprecedented demand by women for greater educational opportunities in the decades following the Revolution

(B) A new political ideology calling for equality of opportunity between women and men in all aspects of life

(C) A belief that the American educational system could be reformed only if women participated more fully in that system

(D) A belief that women needed to be educated if they were to contribute to the success of the nation's new form of government

(E) A recognition that women needed to be educated if they were to take an active role in the nation's schools and churches

Supporting Idea

The passage ascribes to Linda Kerber the claim that there was "a surge of educational opportunities for women in the United States" after the American Revolution, and that this surge resulted from a new ideology of "republic motherhood." According to the passage, Kerber argued that the nation's leaders advocated education for women to equip them, in their family role, to raise politically virtuous sons.

A The passage attributes no claim to Kerber concerning a demand by women for education.

B The passage attributes no claim to Kerber concerning a new ideology calling for equality between women and men.

C Kerber's argument as represented in the passage did not claim that an increase in education opportunities for women resulted from a belief that such an increase was required for successful reform of the American educational system.

D Correct. According to the passage, Kerber argued that educational opportunities for women increased because the nation's leaders believed that successful democratic government would require that women raise politically virtuous sons within their families, and that women could do so only if they had access to education themselves.

E According to the passage, Kerber's thesis primarily concerns the roles that it was believed educated women could play in raising politically virtuous sons in the context of the family, not in the nation's schools or churches.

The correct answer is D.

397. According to the passage, within the field of educational history, Thomas Woody's 1929 work was

(A) innovative because it relied on newspaper advertisements as evidence

(B) exceptional in that it concentrated on the period before the American Revolution

(C) unusual in that it focused on educational attitudes rather than on educational practices

(D) controversial in its claims regarding educational opportunities for boys

(E) atypical in that it examined the education of girls

Supporting Idea

According to the passage, Woody's work was a "notable exception" as contrast to the work of other educational historians, who "barely mentioned women and girls."

A Other historians prior to Woody's 1929 work may have used newspaper advertisements as evidence, but the passage provides no information as to whether this was so.

B The passage is silent as to whether educational historians besides Woody concentrated on the period before the American Revolution.

C   The passage does not provide information as to the extent to which either Woody or other historians focused on educational attitudes as opposed to educational practices.

D   According to the passage, Woody noted that educational opportunities increased for both girls and boys around 1750. But the passage does not indicate that this claim, or any other claim Woody may have made about educational opportunities for boys, was controversial.

E   **Correct.** As stated above, the passage describes Woody's work as a "notable exception," i.e., atypical, with respect to his discussion of education for girls.

The correct answer is E.

398.   The passage suggests that Woody would have agreed with which of the following claims regarding "An Essay on Woman"?

(A)   It expressed attitudes concerning women's education that were reflected in new educational opportunities for women after 1750.

(B)   It persuaded educators to offer greater educational opportunities to women in the 1750s.

(C)   It articulated ideas about women's education that would not be realized until after the American Revolution.

(D)   It offered one of the most original arguments in favor of women's education in the United States in the eighteenth century.

(E)   It presented views about women's education that were still controversial in Woody's own time.

Application

According to the passage, Woody characterized "An Essay on Woman" (1753) as reflecting a shift in view, and the context indicates that this shift concerned new attitudes that accompanied increased opportunities after 1750 for girls to become educated women.

A   **Correct.** Based on the passage, this is a claim with which Woody would likely have agreed.

B   The passage represents Woody as claiming that "An Essay on Woman" reflected changes that had already occurred around 1750. The passage does not indicate whether Woody would have agreed with this claim about a persuasive effect on educators.

C   Nothing in the passage represents Woody as thinking that "An Essay on Woman" had ideas about women's education that did not come to fruition until after the American Revolution. The tenor of Woody's thinking, as the passage represents it, is that the essay reflected changes already occurring.

D   The passage indicates that Woody characterizes "An Essay on Woman" as "reflecting" a view that had already gained some currency; so it is unlikely that Woody saw the essay as offering any highly original arguments in favor of women's education.

E   It may be true that "An Essay on Woman" presented some views that were at least somewhat controversial even around 1929, but the passage provides no information that addresses this point.

The correct answer is A.

399.   The passage suggests that, with regard to the history of women's education in the United States, Kerber's work differs from Woody's primarily concerning which of the following?

(A)   The extent to which women were interested in pursuing educational opportunities in the eighteenth century

(B)   The extent of the support for educational opportunities for girls prior to the American Revolution

(C)   The extent of public resistance to educational opportunities for women after the American Revolution

(D)   Whether attitudes toward women's educational opportunities changed during the eighteenth century

(E)   Whether women needed to be educated in order to contribute to the success of a republican form of government

Evaluation

The passage represents Kerber as claiming that the American Revolution led to a surge in educational opportunities for women because the nation's leaders believed women needed to be educated if they were to raise politically virtuous sons. Woody, however, is represented as claiming that there was a significant increase in such opportunities and significant advocacy for women's education well before the Revolution.

A   The passage does not represent either Kerber or Woody as addressing the extent to which women were interested in pursuing educational opportunities in the eighteenth century.

B   Correct. The passage attributes to Woody the view that "practical education for females had many advocates before the Revolution," notably in the 1750s, and that the Revolution at most accelerated an earlier trend of changing attitudes. This is contrary to the views attributed to Kerber.

C   The passage gives no information as to whether Kerber or Woody addresses this issue, nor does it discuss to what extent, if any, such resistance may have occurred.

D   The passage indicates that Kerber and Woody hold that there was a change in attitudes toward women's educational opportunities during the eighteenth century, disagreeing, however, as to whether the most significant change occurred before or after the Revolution.

E   Neither Kerber nor Woody is represented by the passage as holding divergent views on this point, and it would be reasonable to think that they may have agreed.

The correct answer is B.

400. According to the passage, Kerber argued that political leaders thought that the form of government adopted by the United States after the American Revolution depended on which of the following for its success?

(A)   Women assuming the sole responsibility for instilling political virtue in children

(B)   Girls becoming the primary focus of a reformed educational system that emphasized political virtue

(C)   The family serving as one of the primary means by which children were imbued with political virtue

(D)   The family assuming many of the functions previously performed by schools and churches

(E)   Men and women assuming equal responsibility for the management of schools, churches, and the family

Supporting Idea

The passage attributes to Kerber the claim that the nation's leaders believed a virtuous citizenry was essential to the success of the nation's republican form of government, and that women would play a primary role in raising future citizens who would be politically virtuous.

A   According to the passage, Kerber indicates that the nation's leaders believed churches and schools, as well as families, would work to imbue political virtue, though they emphasized the crucial role of families.

B   Kerber argues that the educational system underwent reform in the sense that educational opportunities for women increased; but does not claim that schools or families would change focus to imbue girls with political virtue.

C   Correct. Kerber argues that political leaders emphasized the family as the primary means by which future citizens would be imbued with political virtue.

D   Kerber does not claim the nation's leaders proposed that the family would take over functions previously fulfilled by schools and churches.

E   Kerber does not attribute to the nation's leaders the view that men and women would exercise equal roles in managing schools, churches, and the family.

The correct answer is C.

Questions 401–403 refer to the passage on page 347.

401. The primary purpose of the passage is to

(A) compare the adaptive responses of several species of columnar cacti in the Sonoran Desert with those in the arid tropical regions of southern Mexico

(B) discuss some of the possible causes of the relatively low abundance of migratory nectar-feeding bats in the Sonoran Desert

(C) provide a possible explanation for a particular evolutionary change in certain species of columnar cacti in the Sonoran Desert

(D) present recent findings that challenge a particular theory as to why several species of columnar cacti in the Sonoran Desert have expanded their range of pollinators

(E) compare the effectiveness of nocturnal and diurnal pollination for several different species of columnar cacti in the Sonoran Desert

Main Idea

This question depends on understanding the passage as a whole. The first paragraph discusses an evolutionary change undergone by columnar cacti in the Sonoran Desert with regard to pollination. The second paragraph offers a possible reason for this change—migratory nectar-feeding bats are unreliable pollinators—and the third paragraph goes on to provide evidence that supports the reason given in the second paragraph.

A   The passage does compare the adaptations of cacti in the Sonoran Desert with those of cacti in southern Mexico, but it does so in support of a larger point about the Sonoran Desert cacti.

B   The relatively low abundance of migratory nectar-feeding bats in the Sonoran Desert is important to the passage in that it provides a reason why the columnar cacti in that region have made certain adaptations. But the passage does not explain why the bats are not particularly abundant.

C   **Correct.** The flowers of the columnar cacti in the Sonoran Desert have evolved to remain open after sunrise, and the passage is primarily concerned with explaining why this change may have taken place.

D   The passage presents recent findings that support, rather than challenge, a theory as to why the columnar cacti of the Sonoran Desert have expanded their range of pollinators. The passage does not allude to any competing theory that may be challenged by the findings.

E   Any comparison of the effectiveness of nocturnal and diurnal pollination for columnar cacti in the Sonoran Desert is made in support of the passage's primary concern: explaining why these cacti have come to remain open and receptive to pollination in daylight.

The correct answer is C.

402. According to the passage, which of the following types of nectar-feeding pollinators is likely to be an unreliable pollinator of a particular cactus flower?

(A) A dietary specialist whose abundance is typically high in relation to that of the flower

(B) A dietary specialist whose abundance is at times significantly lower than that of the flower

(C) A dietary generalist for whom that flower's nectar is not a preferred food but is the most consistently available food

(D) A dietary generalist for whom that flower's nectar is slightly preferred to other available foods

(E) A dietary generalist that evolved from a species of dietary specialists

Supporting Idea

This question depends on recognizing the qualities of an unreliable pollinator, as described in the passage. The second paragraph addresses this issue: it explains that the unreliability of pollinators can arise in any of three ways: they may be dietary generalists with alternative sources of food; they may be dietary specialists whose own abundance varies; or they may be dietary specialists whose abundance is chronically low in relation to the flowers.

A   A dietary specialist whose abundance is high in relation to the flowers on which it feeds would likely be a reliable pollinator.

B   **Correct.** A dietary specialist whose abundance is at times significantly lower than that of the flower it pollinates would be, according to the passage, unreliable.

C   A dietary generalist who finds the flower of a particular species more consistently available than other suitable food sources would most likely be a reliable pollinator of that flower.

D   A dietary generalist who prefers the flower's nectar would likely be a reliable pollinator of that flower compared to other flowers.

E   The passage provides no reason to believe that the evolution of a pollinator's dietary preference has any bearing on its reliability as a pollinator.

The correct answer is B.

403. According to the passage, present-day columnar cacti in the Sonoran Desert differ from their close relatives in southern Mexico in that the Sonoran cacti

(A)   have flowers that remain open after sunset

(B)   are pollinated primarily by dietary specialists

(C)   can be pollinated by nectar-feeding bats

(D)   have stigmas that are unreceptive to pollination at night

(E)   are sometimes pollinated by diurnal pollinators

Supporting Idea

This question depends on identifying a difference noted in the passage between columnar cacti in the Sonoran Desert and their relatives in southern Mexico. The first paragraph states that in southern Mexico, columnar cactus flowers are not receptive to pollination by diurnal pollinators, whereas in the Sonoran Desert, the flowers have evolved to allow diurnal pollination.

A   The cacti in both the Sonoran Desert and southern Mexico have flowers that remain open after sunset, because cacti in both locations can be pollinated nocturnally.

B   Sonoran Desert cacti are pollinated, at least partially, by nectar-feeding bats, which are dietary specialists. But the cacti in southern Mexico are pollinated by these specialists, too.

C   Sonoran Desert cacti can be pollinated by nectar-feeding bats—but so can cacti in southern Mexico.

D   Cacti in the Sonoran Desert have stigmas that have evolved to be receptive to pollination both at night and during the day.

E   **Correct.** The distinction between cacti in the Sonoran Desert and those in southern Mexico is that Sonoran Desert cacti have evolved to allow pollination during the day—that is, pollination by diurnal pollinators.

The correct answer is E.

Questions 404–408 refer to the passage on page 349.

404. The passage suggests that in order for a manufacturer in a capital-intensive industry to have a decisive advantage over competitors making similar products, the manufacturer must

(A)   be the first in the industry to build production facilities of theoretically optimal size

(B)   make every effort to keep fixed and sunk costs as low as possible

(C)   be one of the first to operate its manufacturing plants at minimum efficient scale

(D)   produce goods of higher quality than those produced by direct competitors

(E)   stockpile raw materials at production sites in order to ensure a steady flow of such materials

Inference

This question asks for an inference about what a manufacturer in a capital-intensive industry must do to have an advantage over competitors making similar products. The passage addresses this question by stating that advantage accrues to those firms that are the first to exploit the full potential of optimally sized, technologically sophisticated plants. In this context, exploiting the full potential of such plants means operating them at *minimum efficient scale*. Based on the definition in the first paragraph, this means that the plant must have an output of such a size that the cost per unit of output is at a minimum.

A   The passage says that for new capital-intensive firms to dominate the market, it is not enough for them to have optimally sized plants; the plants must also be operated in a way that fully exploits their potential.

B   While keeping fixed and sunk costs low would obviously help keep overall costs low, the passage does not suggest that this is decisive in enabling a firm to have an advantage over competitors.

C   **Correct.** Being among the first
     manufacturers to operate plants at minimum
     efficient scale means that those plants
     are being exploited to their full potential.
     This strategy would most likely give such
     manufacturers a decisive advantage over new
     firms hoping to compete effectively.

D   The passage does not discuss the quality of
     goods made by manufacturers.

E   The passage does not suggest that stockpiling
     raw materials is the most efficient way to
     ensure a steady flow of raw materials into the
     manufacturing process, though the passage
     states that such a steady flow is a factor in
     achieving minimum efficient scale.

The correct answer is C.

405. The passage suggests that which of the following is
     true of a manufacturer's fixed and sunk costs?

     (A) The extent to which they are determined
          by market conditions for the goods being
          manufactured is frequently underestimated.

     (B) If they are kept as low as possible, the manufacturer
          is very likely to realize significant profits.

     (C) They are the primary factor that determines
          whether a manufacturer will realize economies of
          scale.

     (D) They should be on a par with the fixed and sunk
          costs of the manufacturer's competitors.

     (E) They are not affected by fluctuations in a
          manufacturing plant's throughput.

Inference

This question asks about what the passage implies
about fixed and sunk costs. The passage states that
when production declines due to certain factors,
such costs remain at the same level (which
may be high), and the cost per unit produced
(*unit costs*) rises sharply.

A   The passage discusses the impact of market
     conditions on determining what the optimal
     size of a manufacturing plant is (which
     affects fixed and sunk costs). But it makes
     no claim about the frequency with which
     such an impact is "underestimated."

B   The passage emphasizes that failing to
     keep throughput at an efficiently high level
     reduces profitability because that failure

results in increased cost per unit (to which,
of course, the plant's fixed and sunk costs
contribute). But the passage does not claim
that keeping aggregate fixed and sunk costs
very low is necessary in order to have the
most competitive production operation.

C   The passage emphasizes that the crucial
     factor in achieving economies of scale
     is efficient operation of the production
     facilities, not the size of the firm's fixed
     and sunk costs (even though such costs are
     clearly in part determined by the size and
     design of the production facilities).

D   While a manufacturer's fixed and sunk
     costs may be on a par with those of the
     manufacturer's competitors, the passage
     provides no grounds for inferring that there
     is any need for them to be (for example,
     physical plants that employ different
     technologies may have different price tags).

E   **Correct.** According to the passage,
     "throughput" refers to the flow of materials
     through a plant. This flow can vary as a
     result of various factors, but fixed and
     sunk costs—financial resources already
     committed—remain the same regardless of
     such variation.

The correct answer is E.

406. In the context of the passage as a whole, the second
     paragraph serves primarily to

     (A) provide an example to support the argument
          presented in the first paragraph

     (B) evaluate various strategies discussed in the first
          paragraph

     (C) introduce evidence that undermines the
          argument presented in the first paragraph

     (D) anticipate possible objections to the argument
          presented in the first paragraph

     (E) demonstrate the potential dangers of a
          commonly used strategy

Evaluation

This question asks about the rhetorical function of
the second paragraph. While the first paragraph
argues that a crucial factor in achieving economies
of scale is intangible capital, or organized human
capabilities, the second paragraph uses the example

of new capital-intensive manufacturing industries to help show that this is indeed the case.

A **Correct.** The second paragraph provides an example that illustrates the claims made in the first paragraph. It discusses the way in which intangible capital—e.g., distribution networks, marketing systems, smooth production processes, and qualified management teams—enables manufacturers in new capital-intensive manufacturing industries to realize economies of scale and achieve market dominance.

B The second paragraph does, in a sense, "evaluate" investment in intangible capital: it suggests that such investment is necessary. However, investment in intangible capital is the only strategy it discusses.

C The second paragraph supports rather than undermines the first paragraph's argument.

D Nothing in the second paragraph suggests that there are, or could be, any objections to the first paragraph's argument.

E The second paragraph discusses the potential positive outcomes of investing in intangible capital. It suggests that there might be negative consequences to not making such investments, but it does not indicate that avoiding such investments is a commonly used strategy.

The correct answer is A.

407. The passage LEAST supports the inference that a manufacturer's throughput could be adversely affected by

(A) a mistake in judgment regarding the selection of a wholesaler

(B) a breakdown in the factory's machinery

(C) a labor dispute on the factory floor

(D) an increase in the cost per unit of output

(E) a drop in the efficiency of the sales network

Application

This question may be best approached by using an elimination strategy—first finding the four choices that can reasonably be inferred from the passage, and then checking to make sure that the remaining choice cannot reasonably be inferred. This requires understanding the information the passage gives about throughput, then making inferences about what can cause throughput to drop. The passage defines throughput generally as *the flow of materials through a plant* and goes on to explain that it involves coordination of the production process itself, as well as obtaining materials from suppliers and marketing and distributing the manufactured products. Anything that damages this flow of materials and products would be said to have an adverse effect on throughput.

A Making a poor judgment about a wholesaler would most likely have an adverse effect on throughput, in that it could affect *the flow of output to wholesalers and final consumers.*

B A breakdown in machinery would likely fall into the category of *problems on the factory floor* mentioned in the passage and would likely prove damaging to throughput because of its effect on the production process itself.

C A labor dispute would also likely fall into the category of *problems on the factory floor* mentioned in the passage and would probably cause a decline in production and thus adversely affect throughput.

D **Correct.** The passage emphasizes that changes in throughput can cause increases or decreases in costs per unit. But the passage is not committed to any claims about how changes in costs per unit might affect throughput.

E The passage suggests that inefficient sales networks could cause a decline in production. Thus a decrease in sales efficiency would most likely adversely affect a manufacturer's ability to provide goods to consumers, and thus would create problems with throughput.

The correct answer is D.

408. The primary purpose of the passage is to

(A) point out the importance of intangible capital for realizing economies of scale in manufacturing

(B) show that manufacturers frequently gain a competitive advantage from investment in large manufacturing facilities

(C) argue that large manufacturing facilities often fail because of inadequate investment in both tangible and intangible capital

(D) suggest that most new industries are likely to be dominated by firms that build large manufacturing plants early

(E) explain why large manufacturing plants usually do not help manufacturers achieve economies of scale

Main Idea

This question depends on understanding the passage as a whole. In general, it makes an argument for investing in intangible capital as a way for manufacturers to realize economies of scale, and it supports its argument with an example.

A **Correct.** The passage focuses on intangible capital as a crucial factor in realizing economies of scale.

B According to the passage, manufacturers gain competitive advantage by building plants of optimal size that they then fully exploit; nothing in the passage suggests that large plants are frequently optimal.

C The passage assumes that manufacturers invest appropriately in tangible capital and argues that it is important for them to invest in intangible capital as well.

D The passage states that new capital-intensive manufacturing industries are dominated not by firms that are the first to build large plants, but by firms that exploit the full potential of their plants.

E The passage indicates that economies of scale can be achieved in plants of optimal size. The passage does not suggest that large plants cannot be optimal.

The correct answer is A.

Questions 409–414 refer to the passage on page 351.

409. The primary purpose of the passage is to

(A) describe the development of new techniques that may help to determine the driving force behind population cycles in lepidoptera

(B) present evidence that refutes a particular theory about the driving force behind population cycles in lepidoptera

(C) present a hypothesis about the driving force behind population cycles in lepidoptera

(D) describe the fluctuating patterns of population cycles in lepidoptera

(E) question the idea that a single driving force is behind population cycles in lepidoptera

Main Idea

This question depends on understanding the passage as a whole in order to identify its purpose. The first paragraph defines population cycles of lepidoptera and discusses some ways those cycles have been studied. It suggests that a particular agent may regulate these cycles. The second paragraph describes a candidate for this agent: nuclear polyhedrosis viruses. The third paragraph explains why this hypothesis is compelling.

A The passage mentions new techniques in molecular biology, but it does so in order to explain why a particular candidate for the agent behind population cycles has come to light.

B The theory the passage presents is that there is a driving force behind lepidoptera population cycles. It does not refute this theory; rather, it offers a convincing case for nuclear polyhedrosis viruses as that force. It also discusses some previous approaches to seeking plausible hypotheses but does not focus on refuting any particular hypothesis.

C **Correct.** The passage is primarily concerned with presenting the hypothesis that nuclear polyhedrosis viruses are the driving force behind lepidoptera population cycles.

D The first paragraph describes the fluctuating patterns of lepidoptera population cycles, but it does so to explain what population cycles are, so that it can then go on to attempt to account for those cycles.

E The passage is concerned with making a case for nuclear polyhedrosis viruses as the driving force behind at least some lepidoptera population cycles, not with questioning the idea that there is a driving force.

The correct answer is C.

410. It can be inferred from the passage that the mortality caused by agents such as predatory birds or parasites was measured in an attempt to

(A) develop an explanation for the existence of lepidoptera population cycles

(B) identify behavioral factors in lepidoptera that affect survival rates

(C) identify possible methods for controlling lepidoptera population growth

(D) provide evidence that lepidoptera populations are self-regulating

(E) determine the life stages of lepidoptera at which mortality rates are highest

Inference

The passage states that mortality caused by various agents, birds and parasites among them, was measured because this was the common approach to studying causes of population cycles. This in turn suggests that those scientists engaged in such measuring in the case of lepidoptera were attempting to come up with a definitive explanation for why those lepidoptera population cycles occurred.

A   **Correct.** Measuring mortality caused by various agents was part of the attempt to determine the driving force behind lepidoptera population cycles.

B   The passage does not indicate that behavioral factors in lepidoptera are related to their mortality as caused by agents such as predatory birds or parasites.

C   The passage is concerned not with controlling lepidoptera population growth, but rather with determining why population cycles occur.

D   According to the information in the passage, scientists sought to measure mortality caused by particular agents in order to determine the driving force behind lepidoptera population cycles. In suggesting that mortality caused by these agents is not that force, the measurements may have indicated that the cycles could be self-regulating, but they were not undertaken in order to provide such evidence.

E   The passage discusses mortality primarily in the caterpillar stage and does not suggest that any research was directed toward

comparing caterpillar mortality rates with mortality rates in other life stages of the insects.

The correct answer is A.

411. Which of the following, if true, would most weaken the author's conclusion in lines 18–22 ?

(A) New research reveals that the number of species of birds and parasites that prey on lepidoptera has dropped significantly in recent years.

(B) New experiments in which the habitats of lepidoptera are altered in previously untried ways result in the shortening of lepidoptera population cycles.

(C) Recent experiments have revealed that the nuclear polyhedrosis virus is present in a number of predators and parasites of lepidoptera.

(D) Differences among the habitats of lepidoptera species make it difficult to assess the effects of weather on lepidoptera population cycles.

(E) Viral disease is typically observed in a large proportion of the lepidoptera population.

Evaluation

The sentence in question presents the author's conclusion that lepidoptera populations may be self-regulating or regulated by something more closely connected to the insects than predatory birds or parasites are. To weaken that conclusion requires weakening its support, namely, that mortality caused by predators and parasites seems not to affect population cycles, and that changing habitats and reducing populations has not altered population cycles either.

A   A drop in birds and parasites preying on lepidoptera would not weaken the author's conclusion; mortality caused by these predators has not affected population cycles.

B   **Correct.** New experiments involving changes in habitat that did succeed in altering population cycles would suggest that the populations are not in fact self-regulating, and that the search for another cycle-altering agent may be unnecessary.

C   This finding would support the idea that the nuclear polyhedrosis virus is responsible for population cycles—that is, that the virus is the closely connected agent the author concludes is responsible.

D   The suggestion that the effects of weather may not have been adequately assessed is remotely relevant to the author's conclusion, but the mere difficulty of assessing the effects provides no positive reason to suppose that weather may be the cause of the cycles. On the other hand, answer choice B does offer evidence for an alternative explanation.

E   Viral disease is what the author ultimately suggests is the agent that drives the lepidoptera population cycles in question. The wide presence of viruses in lepidoptera could help support the author's conclusion.

The correct answer is B.

412. According to the passage, before the discovery of new techniques for detecting viral DNA, population ecologists believed that viral diseases

(A)   were not widely prevalent among insect populations generally

(B)   affected only the caterpillar life stage of lepidoptera

(C)   were the driving force behind lepidoptera population cycles

(D)   attacked already declining caterpillar populations

(E)   infected birds and parasites that prey on various species of lepidoptera

Supporting Idea

This question addresses what the passage states directly about population ecologists' beliefs regarding viral diseases prior to the discovery of new viral DNA–detection techniques. The second paragraph of the passage states that these ecologists believed viral disease contributed to population decline that was already underway rather than initiating it.

A   The second paragraph states that viral disease had been reported; thus, population ecologists were aware of its existence in insect populations. The passage is consistent with ecologists having believed that it was prevalent.

B   The passage focuses mainly on the caterpillar life stage of lepidoptera, but there is nothing to suggest that scientists held

particular beliefs regarding viral diseases' restriction to that life stage.

C   It is after, not before, the discovery of new techniques for detecting viral DNA when populations ecologists came to believe that such diseases were the driving force behind the population cycles.

D   **Correct.** As stated in the passage, population ecologists believed that viral diseases contributed to already occurring population decline.

E   The passage does not discuss whether viral diseases may infect any lepidoptera predators.

The correct answer is D.

413. According to the passage, nuclear polyhedrosis viruses can remain virulent in the environment only when

(A)   the polyhedrin protein crystals dissolve

(B)   caterpillar populations are in decline

(C)   they are present in large numbers

(D)   their concentration in a particular area remains low

(E)   they are sheltered from direct sunlight

Supporting Idea

The passage states in the second paragraph that these viruses remain virulent for many years if they are protected from direct sunlight. They are embedded in crystals of polyhedrin protein.

A   The viruses remain virulent partially because of their being contained in polyhedrin protein crystals. They would most likely not remain virulent if those crystals dissolved.

B   The viruses remain virulent even when caterpillar populations are not in decline; that is how the viruses initiate new population declines.

C   According to the passage, viral DNA has been detected in the environment at low concentrations, yet the viruses are still virulent. Thus, they need not be present in large numbers.

D   Nothing in the passage indicates that the concentration of these viruses must be low for them to be virulent.

E   **Correct.** The passage says that if the viruses are protected from direct sunlight, they remain virulent for many years. The context strongly suggests that if they are not so protected, they do not remain virulent.

The correct answer is E.

414. It can be inferred from the passage that while inside its polyhedrin protein crystals, the nuclear polyhedrosis virus

(A) is exposed to direct sunlight

(B) is attractive to predators

(C) cannot infect caterpillars' cells

(D) cannot be ingested by caterpillars

(E) cannot be detected by new techniques of molecular biology

Inference

The passage indicates that the polyhedrin protein crystals protect the nuclear polyhedrosis virus when it is in the environment. When a caterpillar ingests those crystals, they dissolve. That releases the virus, whereupon it infects the caterpillar's cells. Thus it is reasonable to infer that the virus must be released from the crystals before it can infect the caterpillar.

A   The passage states that nuclear polyhedrosis viruses remain embedded in polyhedrin protein crystals if protected from direct sunlight, not that the virus is exposed to light when it is in the protein crystals.

B   Nothing in the passage indicates that any organism preys on the virus itself or that it attracts predators to caterpillars that it infects.

C   **Correct.** The virus must be released from the crystals before it can infect caterpillars' cells.

D   The passage states that caterpillars ingest the polyhedrin protein crystals.

E   According to the passage, new techniques of molecular biology enable the detection of viral DNA in the environment. The nuclear polyhedrosis virus persists in the environment inside protein crystals. The passage suggests that the new techniques are able to detect the virus inside its crystals but does not provide any evidence about whether they detect it directly or infer its presence indirectly.

The correct answer is C.

Questions 415–418 refer to the passage on page 353.

Main Idea Summary

The primary purpose of the passage is to describe resin and discuss a theory on its biological function. The first paragraph identifies some of the characteristics of resin and distinguishes it from gum and sap; one way in which resin differs from these two substances is that its physiological function is not clearly understood. The second paragraph considers whether resin may function to repel or attract insects, and indicates that the consideration of such issues led to the development of the discipline of chemical ecology.

415. According to the passage, which of the following is true of plant antiherbivore chemistry?

(A) Changes in a plant's antiherbivore chemistry may affect insect feeding behavior.

(B) A plant's repellent effects often involve interactions between gum and resin.

(C) A plant's antiherbivore responses assist in combating bacterial infections.

(D) Plant antiherbivore chemistry plays only a minor role in the coevolution of plants and insects.

(E) Researchers first studied repellent effects in plants beginning in the 1950s.

Supporting Idea

This question addresses what the information in the passage indicates about plant antiherbivore chemistry—that is, plants' chemical defenses against herbivore attacks. The second paragraph of the passage cites the views of various scientists regarding the possible role of resin in antiherbivore chemistry; plants could have evolved resin specifically to repel insects.

A   **Correct.** According to the second paragraph, various scientists have suggested that a change in antiherbivore chemistry, here specifically involving resin, could repel insects; alternatively, some insects could have been attracted to resin, feeding more heavily on plants that produced it. Other researchers have suggested that even if resin does not directly repel or attract insects, it may indirectly affect insect-feeding behavior by mediating changes in plants' antiherbivore chemistry.

B   The first paragraph states that plants produce gum in response to bacterial infections. Although this does not rule out the hypothesis that gum also contributes to plants' antiherbivore chemistry, the passage provides no evidence that it does so.

C   According to the passage, a plant's antiherbivore responses have developed to combat predators, such as insects, that eat plants. The passage provides no evidence that such responses also combat bacterial infections.

D   The second paragraph indicates that plant antiherbivore chemistry plays a major role in the discipline of chemical ecology, and chemical ecology concerns itself with coevolution of plants and insects.

E   According to the passage, it was in the 1950s that entomologists began discussing resin's possible role in repelling and attracting insects. The passage does not suggest that this marked the beginning of their study of repellent effects more generally.

The correct answer is A.

416.   Of the following topics, which would be most likely to be studied within the discipline of chemical ecology as it is described in the passage?

(A)   Seeds that become attached to certain insects, which in turn carry away the seeds and aid in the reproductive cycle of the plant species in question

(B)   An insect species that feeds on weeds detrimental to crop health and yield, and how these insects might aid in agricultural production

(C)   The effects of deforestation on the life cycles of subtropical carnivorous plants and the insect species on which the plants feed

(D)   The growth patterns of a particular species of plant that has proved remarkably resistant to herbicides

(E)   Insects that develop a tolerance for feeding on a plant that had previously been toxic to them, and the resultant changes within that plant species

Application

The discipline of chemical ecology, as it is described in the passage, deals with how plants use chemicals to interact with other organisms—in particular, how they defend against attack—and how those interactions have evolved. To be studied within that discipline, a specific topic would need to address some aspect of that chemical interaction.

A   The passage provides no reason to suppose that the topic of seeds and how they travel would be studied within chemical ecology, given that it does not discuss how chemicals might be involved in the reproductive cycle.

B   The passage provides no indication that chemical ecology would be concerned with how weed-destroying insects would aid agricultural production.

C   The passage provides no indication that deforestation would involve plant chemicals or that its effects would be studied in chemical ecology.

D   The passage provides no indication that a plant's resistance to herbicides would be studied in chemical ecology, but the passage does suggest that the focus of chemical ecology is on how plants chemically interact with other organisms.

E   **Correct.** Chemical ecology developed to deal with the interdependence between plants and insects. Insects' developing a tolerance for feeding on a once-toxic plant, and the plants' resultant changes, is a situation of just such interdependence: plants and insects coevolving.

The correct answer is E.

417.   The author refers to "bacterial infections" (see line 11) most likely in order to

(A)   describe the physiological function that gum performs in plants

(B)   demonstrate that sap is not the only substance that is transported through a plant's tissues

(C) explain how modern chemical analysis has been used to clarify the function of resin

(D) show that gum cannot serve as an effective defense against herbivores

(E) give an example of how confusion has arisen with regard to the nature of resin

Evaluation

The author mentions *bacterial infections* in the first paragraph as the reason why plants produce the substance known as gum.

A **Correct.** The author states directly that plants produce gum in response to bacterial infections.

B The author states directly that sap is transported through plant tissues. The passage does not address the question of whether bacterial infections or anything related to them are similarly transported.

C The passage indicates that rigorous chemical analysis is now available, but scientists still do not know resin's function. The reference to bacterial infections is related to gum, not resin.

D The reference to bacterial infections indicates the actual purpose served by gum; it does not function to show ways in which gum is inadequate.

E Gum itself serves as an example of the confusion surrounding the nature of resin; bacterial infections, to which gum production is a response, do not serve as that example.

The correct answer is A.

418. The author of the passage refers to Pliny most probably in order to

(A) give an example of how the nature of amber has been misunderstood in the past

(B) show that confusion about amber has long been more pervasive than confusion about resin

(C) make note of the first known reference to amber as a semiprecious gem

(D) point out an exception to a generalization about the history of people's understanding of amber

(E) demonstrate that Pliny believed amber to be a mineral

Evaluation

The passage states generally that *amber has been widely misunderstood* but cites Pliny as noting correctly, in the first century, that amber resulted from a substance discharged by trees.

A Pliny's observation was, according to the author, accurate and not a misunderstanding.

B The author equates confusion about amber with confusion about resin; the reference to Pliny does not indicate which of the two, amber or resin, has been more widely misunderstood.

C The author indicates that others, not Pliny, mischaracterized amber as a semiprecious gem—and when that mischaracterization first occurred is not identified.

D **Correct.** Pliny's recognition that amber came from a substance discharged by trees stands, in the author's account, as an exception to the widespread incorrect identifications of the substance.

E Others held the belief that amber was a mineral. The passage indicates that Pliny recognized that amber came from trees but provides no evidence that he also considered it a mineral.

The correct answer is D.

Questions 419–421 refer to the passage on page 355.

419. The primary purpose of the passage is to

(A) compare the impact of the Great Depression on Latin America with its impact on the United States

(B) criticize a school of economic historians for failing to analyze the Great Depression in Latin America within a global context

(C) illustrate the risks inherent in comparing different types of economic enterprises to explain economic phenomena

(D) call into question certain scholars' views concerning the severity of the Great Depression in Latin America

(E) demonstrate that the Great Depression had a more severe impact on industry in Latin American than in certain other regions

Main Idea

This question depends on understanding the passage as a whole. The passage first describes the view of many economic historians of the 1980s. It next describes the evidence on which that view is based. The remainder of the passage raises issues about the rationale for that view.

A   The comparison between Latin America and the United States is only a small part of a larger argument analyzing studies of the Great Depression in Latin America.

B   The passage does not discuss a global context for the Great Depression.

C   The passage does not primarily aim to illustrate risks that may be generally inherent in explaining economic phenomena.

D   Correct. The passage claims that certain scholars underestimate the severity of the Great Depression in Latin America.

E   The passage does not claim that the impact of the Great Depression on Latin American industry was generally more severe than its impact on industry elsewhere.

The correct answer is D.

420. Which of the following conclusions about the Great Depression is best supported by the passage?

(A)   It did not impede Latin American industrial growth as much as historians had previously thought.

(B)   It had a more severe impact on the Brazilian and the Mexican textile industries than it had on Latin America as a region.

(C)   It affected the Latin American textile industry more severely than it did any other industry in Latin America.

(D)   The overall impact on Latin American industrial growth should be reevaluated by economic historians.

(E)   Its impact on Latin America should not be compared with its impact on the United States.

Inference

This question asks which conclusion is most strongly supported by the passage. The passage presents the rationale of some historians for their

conclusion that the Great Depression did not significantly interfere with economic growth in Latin America. It then critiques that rationale and conclusion. By questioning the historians' claims, the passage suggests that a reevaluation of the Great Depression's effect on Latin America is needed.

A   The passage does not significantly support this. The passage indicates that, in fact, the Great Depression impeded Latin American economic development more than some historians had thought.

B   The passage does not significantly support this. The passage does not compare the impact on the Brazilian and Mexican textile industries to the impact on the Latin American region.

C   The passage does not significantly support this. The passage does not compare the effect of the Great Depression on the textile industry to its effect on other industries.

D   Correct. As presented in the passage, the passage author's critique of the historians' rationale for their claims provides significant support for the conclusion that their claims should be reevaluated.

E   The passage does not significantly support the claim that the comparison in question should not be made.

The correct answer is D.

421. Which of the following, if true, would most strengthen the author's assertion regarding economic indicators in lines 25–27 ?

(A)   During an economic depression, European textile manufacturers' profits rise while their industrial output remains steady.

(B)   During a national economic recession, United States microchips manufacturers' profits rise sharply while United States steel manufacturers' profits plunge.

(C)   During the years following a severe economic depression, textile manufacturers' output levels and profit levels increase in Brazil and Mexico but not in the rest of Latin America.

(D)   Although Japanese industry as a whole recovers after an economic recession, it does not regain its previously high levels of production.

(E)   While European industrial output increases in the years following an economic depression, total output remains below that of Japan or the United States.

Application

The question involves applying information from outside the passage to a claim made by the author. The text in lines 25–27 asserts that broad economic indicators pertaining to a nation or region can obscure differences between individual firms or industries within that nation or region. The question asks which evidence would most strengthen the support for that conclusion.

A   This refers only to the relationship between a single industry's profits and its output, not to general economic indicators.

B   **Correct.** The phrase *a national recession* refers to a general economic indicator. Suppose that in a situation described as a national recession, one industry (microchip manufacturing) prospers while another industry (steel manufacturing) does not. This would provide some additional support, over and above that given in the passage, for the assertion that broad economic indicators may mask differences between industries.

C   Economic differences between countries do not strengthen the support for the author's assertion regarding variations among different firms and industries in one country or region.

D   This has no obvious bearing on how sweeping economic indicators can mask differences between industries or enterprises in a single country or region.

E   A comparison of different countries does not pertain to the assertion regarding variation among firms and industries in the same country.

The correct answer is B.

Questions 422–425 refer to the passage on page 357.

422. It can be inferred from the passage that a large plant might have to spend more than a similar but smaller plant on environmental compliance because the larger plant is

(A)   more likely to attract attention from local regulators

(B)   less likely to be exempt from permit and reporting requirements

(C)   less likely to have regulatory costs passed on to it by companies that supply its raw materials

(D)   more likely to employ older production technologies

(E)   more likely to generate wastes that are more environmentally damaging than those generated by smaller plants

Inference

This item depends on understanding the implications of the passage's discussion of differences between large and small plants. It asks what might be true of a larger plant that would compel it to spend more than a smaller plant on environmental compliance. The passage addresses this issue by stating that smaller plants are often not subject to the same permit or reporting requirements that larger plants are.

A   The likelihood of attracting regulatory attention is discussed only in the context of comparing plants that are *isolated* with small plants that are near large noncompliant ones. The passage does not suggest that size is generally the crucial determining factor in attracting regulatory attention.

B   **Correct.** According to the passage, certain permit or reporting requirements may not apply to smaller plants; this suggests that larger plants are less likely than smaller plants to be exempt from these requirements, and thus that the larger plants would have to spend more to comply.

C   The passage does not discuss the passing on of regulatory costs from suppliers to plants.

D   The passage does not suggest that larger plants are any more likely than smaller plants to employ older production technologies.

E   The passage does not distinguish between the types of wastes emitted by larger plants and those emitted by smaller plants.

The correct answer is B.

423. According to the passage, which of the following statements about sulfur dioxide and nitrogen oxide outputs is true?

(A)   Older production technologies cannot be adapted so as to reduce production of these outputs as waste products.

(B)   Under the most recent environmental regulations, industrial plants are no longer permitted to produce these outputs.

(C)   Although these outputs are environmentally hazardous, some plants still generate them as waste products despite the high compliance costs they impose.

(D)   Many older plants have developed innovative technological processes that reduce the amounts of these outputs generated as waste products.

(E)   Since the production processes that generate these outputs are less costly than alternative processes, these less expensive processes are sometimes adopted despite their acknowledged environmental hazards.

Supporting Idea

This item depends on identifying what the passage states explicitly about outputs of sulfur dioxide and nitrogen oxide. The passage says that plants that produce these outputs are those that use older industrial coal-fired burners, and that such plants are subject to extensive compliance costs imposed by new regulations.

A   The passage does not address the question of whether older production technologies might be adapted to reduce outputs of sulfur dioxide and nitrogen oxide.

B   The passage states that new regulations have imposed high compliance costs on companies

that produce sulfur dioxide and nitrogen oxide outputs, not that these outputs are prohibited.

C   **Correct.** The passage states that some companies are still using the older kinds of burners that generate sulfur dioxide and nitrogen oxide outputs, and that new regulations have imposed high compliance costs on these companies.

D   The passage does not address the question of whether older plants have developed new processes to reduce the amounts of sulfur dioxide and nitrogen oxide they produce.

E   Sulfur dioxide and nitrogen oxide outputs, the passage suggests, are produced only by older industrial coal-fired burners; newer facilities (using alternative processes) do not employ this technology, the expense of which is not mentioned in the passage.

The correct answer is C.

424. Which of the following best describes the relationship of the statement about large plants (lines 12–17) to the passage as a whole?

(A)   It presents a hypothesis that is disproved later in the passage.

(B)   It highlights an opposition between two ideas mentioned in the passage.

(C)   It provides examples to support a claim made earlier in the passage.

(D)   It exemplifies a misconception mentioned earlier in the passage.

(E)   It draws an analogy between two situations described in the passage.

Evaluation

This question asks about the role played in the passage by the following statement: *Additionally, large plants can spread compliance costs such as waste treatment across a larger revenue base; on the other hand, some smaller plants may not even be subject to certain provisions such as permit or reporting requirements by virtue of their size.* This statement describes situations in which compliance costs for plants of different sizes may differ, which serve as evidence in support of the passage's main claim: that environmental regulations do *not* affect all competitors in a given industry uniformly.

A   The statement in question is not a hypothesis; rather, it reports factors that are known to affect the varying impact of environmental regulations.

B   This is too vague to be a good description of the kind of relationship the question asks about. The statement in question does present a contrast—it suggests that larger plants' compliance costs are lower under some circumstances, while smaller plants' compliance costs are lower under other circumstances. But this purports to state two facts rather than mere *ideas*; they are contrasting facts but not in any meaningful sense *opposed*, since they can easily coexist.

C   **Correct.** The statement provides examples to support the initial claim made in the passage that regulatory costs fall unevenly on competitors in an industry: large plants can spread compliance costs around, and smaller plants may not even have to pay certain costs.

D   This statement helps to dispel, not exemplify, a misconception mentioned earlier in the passage—i.e., the myth that environmental regulations affect all companies in an industry the same way.

E   The statement does not suggest that the situation of larger and smaller plants is similar (or analogous) to any other situation mentioned in the passage.

The correct answer is C.

425. The primary purpose of the passage is to

(A) address a widespread environmental management problem and suggest possible solutions

(B) illustrate varying levels of compliance with environmental regulation among different corporations

(C) describe the various alternatives to traditional methods of environmental management

(D) advocate increased corporate compliance with environmental regulation

(E) correct a common misconception about the impact of environmental regulations

Main Idea

This question depends on understanding the passage as a whole. Its first sentence indicates its main purpose: to dispel a myth about environmental regulations that is often taken as fact.

A   The passage is not about the management of any environmental problem, which would be a problem about how to prevent or undo damage to the environment. The passage primarily aims to dispel a belief that the passage says is widely held by environmental managers.

B   The passage refers to variations in firms' levels of compliance with environmental regulations, but its primary purpose is not to illustrate those varying levels, nor does it do so.

C   The passage suggests that most environmental managers are mistaken about a key concept; its primary purpose is not to describe traditional methods of environmental management or alternatives to those traditional methods, nor does it do so.

D   The passage takes no position on whether companies should increase their compliance with environmental regulation.

E   **Correct.** The passage primarily aims to dispel the belief that environmental regulations affect all companies in an industry uniformly.

The correct answer is E.

Questions 426–429 refer to the passage on page 359.

426. The primary purpose of the passage is to

(A) review research demonstrating the benefits of corporate mergers and acquisitions and examine some of the drawbacks that acquisition behavior entails

(B) contrast the effects of corporate mergers and acquisitions on acquiring firms and on firms that are acquired

(C) report findings that raise questions about a reason for corporate mergers and acquisitions and suggest possible alternative reasons

(D) explain changes in attitude on the part of acquiring firms toward corporate mergers and acquisitions

(E) account for a recent decline in the rate of corporate mergers and acquisitions

Main Idea

This question requires understanding what the passage as a whole is trying to do. The passage begins by citing three studies that demonstrate that when firms acquire other firms, there is not necessarily a worthwhile economic gain. The passage then cites economic interests as the reason given by firms when they acquire other firms but calls into question the veracity of this reasoning. The passage then goes on to speculate as to why mergers and acquisitions occur.

A The research cited in the passage calls into question whether mergers and acquisitions are beneficial to firms.

B The passage is not concerned with comparing the relative effects of mergers and acquisitions on the acquired and acquiring firms.

C **Correct.** The passage surveys reports that question the reason given by firms when they acquire other firms and suggests other reasons for these acquisitions.

D The passage does not indicate that there has been a change in the attitude of acquiring firms toward mergers and acquisitions.

E The passage does not indicate that there has been a decline in the rate of mergers and acquisitions.

The correct answer is C.

427. It can be inferred from the passage that the author would be most likely to agree with which of the following statements about corporate acquisitions?

(A) Their known benefits to national economies explain their appeal to individual firms during the 1970s and 1980s.

(B) Despite their adverse impact on some firms, they are the best way to channel resources from less to more productive sectors of a nation's economy.

(C) They are as likely to occur because of poor monitoring by boards of directors as to be caused by incentive compensation for managers.

(D) They will be less prevalent in the future, since their actual effects will gain wider recognition.

(E) Factors other than economic benefit to the acquiring firm help to explain the frequency with which they occur.

Inference

This question requires understanding what view the author has about a particular issue. The three studies cited by the passage all suggest that mergers and acquisitions do not necessarily bring economic benefit to the acquiring firms. The author concludes therefore that *factors having little to do with corporate economic interests explain acquisitions* and then goes on to speculate as to what the reasons may actually be.

A The passage indicates that while mergers and acquisitions may benefit the national economy, the appeal of mergers and acquisitions must be tied to companies' *private economic interests.*

B The passage makes no judgment as to the best way for firms to channel resources from less to more efficient economic sectors.

C The passage makes no comparison between the influence of poor monitoring by boards and that of executive incentives.

D The passage makes no prediction as to future trends in the market for mergers and acquisitions.

E **Correct.** The passage states that factors other than economic interests drive mergers and acquisitions.

The correct answer is E.

428. The author of the passage mentions the effect of acquisitions on national economies most probably in order to

(A) provide an explanation for the mergers and acquisitions of the 1970s and 1980s overlooked by the findings discussed in the passage

(B)   suggest that national economic interests played an important role in the mergers and acquisitions of the 1970s and 1980s

(C)   support a noneconomic explanation for the mergers and acquisitions of the 1970s and 1980s that was cited earlier in the passage

(D)   cite and point out the inadequacy of one possible explanation for the prevalence of mergers and acquisitions during the 1970s and 1980s

(E)   explain how modeling affected the decisions made by managers involved in mergers and acquisitions during the 1970s and 1980s

Evaluation

This question requires understanding why a piece of information is included in the passage. After the passage cites the results of the three studies on mergers and acquisitions, which call into question the economic benefits of acquisitions, it indicates that firms nonetheless claim that their objectives are economic. The passage then states that while acquisitions *may well have* a desirable effect on national economies, the results of the studies suggest that factors other than economic interest must drive executives to arrange mergers and acquisitions.

A   The passage does not mention national economies as part of an explanation for the occurrence of mergers and acquisitions.

B   The passage suggests that the effect of acquisitions on national economies is not tied to any explanations for why acquisitions occur.

C   The effect of acquisitions on national economies is not mentioned in the passage as an explanation for why acquisitions occur.

D   **Correct.** The passage uses the mention of national economies as part of a larger point questioning the stated motivations behind firms' efforts to acquire other firms.

E   In the passage, modeling is unrelated to the idea that acquisitions may have a desirable effect on national economies.

The correct answer is D.

429.   The author of the passage implies that which of the following is a possible partial explanation for acquisition behavior during the 1970s and 1980s?

(A)   Managers wished to imitate other managers primarily because they saw how financially beneficial other firms' acquisitions were.

(B)   Managers miscalculated the value of firms that were to be acquired.

(C)   Lack of consensus within boards of directors resulted in their imposing conflicting goals on managers.

(D)   Total compensation packages for managers increased during that period.

(E)   The value of bidding firms' stock increased significantly when prospective mergers were announced.

Inference

This question requires recognizing what can be inferred from the information in the passage. After providing the results of the studies of mergers and acquisitions, the author concludes that even though acquiring firms state that their objectives are economic, *factors having little to do with corporate economic interests explain acquisitions* (lines 10–11). Among alternative explanations, the author points to *managerial error in estimating the value of firms targeted for acquisition* (lines 12–13) as possibly contributing to acquisition behavior in the 1970s and 1980s.

A   While the passage indicates that managers may have modeled their behavior on other managers, it does not provide a reason for why this would be so.

B   **Correct.** The author states that one explanation for acquisition behavior may be that managers erred when they estimated the value of firms being acquired.

C   The author discusses a lack of monitoring by boards of directors but makes no mention of consensus within these boards.

D   The author does not discuss compensation packages for managers.

E   The passage does not state how significantly the value of the bidding firm's stock increased upon announcing a merger but only that it increased less in value than did the stock of the prospective firm being acquired.

The correct answer is B.

Questions 430–489 - Difficulty: Hard

Questions 430–435 refer to the passage on page 361.

430. The primary purpose of the passage is to

(A)   examine two sides of a historiographical debate

(B)   call into question an author's approach to a historiographical debate

(C)   examine one author's approach to a historiographical debate

(D)   discuss two authors' works in relationship to a historiographical debate

(E)   explain the prevalent perspective on a historiographical debate

Main Idea

This question requires understanding what the passage as a whole is attempting to do. The passage opens by introducing two books published in 1984 that both concern the history of women in the United States. The passage then makes it clear that one book deals *directly* (line 15) with the issue of women's status, while the other does not. The passage then goes on to discuss the perspective that each book takes and what each book has to offer for an assessment of women's status in the eighteenth and nineteenth centuries.

A   The two books discussed in the passage do not take different sides on a particular debate but rather are described as being more or less useful to the debate itself.

B   The passage focuses on how two different books contain information useful to a particular historiographical debate but does not call into question the approach of either book.

C   The passage focuses on two authors' works, not one.

D   **Correct.** The passage discusses what two different books have to offer in relation to a particular historiographical debate.

E   The passage does not describe any perspective on a particular historiographical debate as being more prevalent than any other.

The correct answer is D.

431. The author of the passage mentions the supervision of schools primarily in order to

(A)   remind readers of the role education played in the cultural changes of the nineteenth century in the United States

(B)   suggest an area in which nineteenth-century American women were relatively free to exercise power

(C)   provide an example of an occupation for which accurate data about women's participation are difficult to obtain

(D)   speculate about which occupations were considered suitable for United States women of the nineteenth century

(E)   illustrate how the answers to questions about women's status depend on particular contexts

Evaluation

Answering this question depends on understanding what role a particular piece of information plays in the passage as a whole. The author implicitly supports Lebsock's contention (beginning at line 20) that different frames of reference can produce different perspectives on the debate about women's status in the eighteenth and nineteenth centuries. The author then summarizes different contexts cited by Lebsock to support the contention about frames of reference. As part of this summary, the author refers to *supervising schools* (lines 24–25) as an example of a job that apparently showed women losing power.

A   The passage does not discuss the role of education in the nineteenth century.

B   The passage does mention some ways in which, according to Lebsock, *women . . . gained power* (lines 25–26) in the nineteenth century, but *supervising schools* is not among them.

C   The passage does not discuss the difficulty of obtaining data about particular occupations.

D   The passage makes no judgments about
the suitability for women of any jobs in the
nineteenth century.

E   **Correct.** The passage mentions supervising
schools as part of an illustration of Lebsock's
claim that the debate about women's status
depends on the context being examined.

The correct answer is E.

432. With which of the following characterizations of
Lebsock's contribution to the controversy concerning
women's status in the nineteenth-century United States
would the author of the passage be most likely to agree?

(A)   Lebsock has studied women from a formerly
neglected region and time period.

(B)   Lebsock has demonstrated the importance of
frame of reference in answering questions about
women's status.

(C)   Lebsock has addressed the controversy by using
women's current status as a frame of reference.

(D)   Lebsock has analyzed statistics about occupations
and property that were previously ignored.

(E)   Lebsock has applied recent historiographical
methods to the biography of a nineteenth-century
woman.

Supporting Idea

Answering this question requires recognizing
information explicitly given in the passage. The
passage introduces the work of Lebsock in line 6
and then goes on to describe several characteristics
of Lebsock's book. In lines 20–22, the author
introduces Lebsock's claim that the historiographical
debate about women's status is dependent on frame
of reference and calls that claim important; the
passage then gives an example showing how frame
of reference affects views of women's status. In so
doing, the author displays an implicit agreement
with Lebsock's discussion on this point.

A   The author of the passage portrays neither the
place nor time period that Lebsock focuses on
as having been neglected by historians.

B   **Correct.** The author describes as important
Lebsock's idea that frame of reference
informs the debate about women's status.

C   According to the passage, Lebsock's book
deals with women's status in the eighteenth

and nineteenth centuries, not the present
status of women.

D   The passage does not mention or imply that
Lebsock analyzed statistics in writing her book.

E   Although the passage does describe
Lebsock's book as pertaining to an ongoing
historiographical debate, it identifies the book's
topic as *women in one southern community* (lines
7–8), not the life of a single woman.

The correct answer is B.

433. According to the passage, Lebsock's work differs from
Buel and Buel's work in that Lebsock's work

(A)   uses a large number of primary sources

(B)   ignores issues of women's legal status

(C)   refuses to take a position on women's status in
the eighteenth century

(D)   addresses larger historiographical issues

(E)   fails to provide sufficient material to support its
claims

Supporting Idea

This question asks for recognition of information
contained in the passage. In the first sentence,
the passage states that Buel and Buel's work and
Lebsock's work have *contrasting approaches*. The
passage then proceeds, using descriptions of each
work's approach, to illustrate how the works differ.
The passage notes that Buel and Buel's work *makes
little effort* to place its biographical subject *in the
context of recent historiography on women* (lines 5–6),
whereas Lebsock's work attempts *to redirect two
decades of historiographical debate* about women's status.

A   Primary sources are not mentioned in the
passage in relation to either work discussed.

B   The legal status of women is not mentioned
in the passage.

C   Lebsock's work is described in the passage
as attempting to redirect the debate about
women's status in the eighteenth and
nineteenth centuries.

D   **Correct.** The passage suggests that by
not placing its subject's story in the
context of historiography, Buel and Buel's
work does not therefore address larger
historiographical issues, as Lebsock's does.

E   The passage tends to support Lebsock's views and does not refer to any lack of support for the claims made in Lebsock's work.

The correct answer is D.

434. The passage suggests that Lebsock believes that compared to nineteenth-century American women, eighteenth-century American women were

(A)   in many respects less powerful in relation to men
(B)   more likely to own real estate
(C)   generally more economically independent
(D)   more independent in conducting their private lives
(E)   less likely to work as school superintendents

Inference

This question requires making an inference based on information given in the passage. As part of the passage's description of Lebsock's contribution to the historiographical debate about women's status in the eighteenth and nineteenth centuries, Lebsock's conclusions about women's autonomy are described. As part of this description, the passage cites Lebsock's conclusion that nineteenth-century women lost economic autonomy when compared to eighteenth-century women (lines 17–20).

A   The passage states that in many ways women in the nineteenth century *lost power in relation to men* (line 23), which would imply that in those respects eighteenth-century women had more power in relation to men, not less. The only increase mentioned in nineteenth-century women's power is associated with owning more real estate.
B   The passage states that more nineteenth-century women owned real estate.
C   **Correct.** As the passage states, Lebsock concluded that nineteenth-century women lost economic autonomy compared to eighteenth-century women.
D   The passage states that nineteenth-century women gained more independence in their private lives.
E   The passage cites school superintendents as an example of an occupation more likely to be held by eighteenth-century women.

The correct answer is C.

435. The passage suggests that Buel and Buel's biography of Mary Fish provides evidence for which of the following views of women's history?

(A)   Women have lost power in relation to men since the colonial era.
(B)   Women of the colonial era were not as likely to be concerned with their status as were women in the nineteenth century.
(C)   The colonial era was not as favorable for women as some historians have believed.
(D)   Women had more economic autonomy in the colonial era than in the nineteenth century.
(E)   Women's occupations were generally more respected in the colonial era than in the nineteenth century.

Inference

This question requires understanding what the passage implies. The approach that Buel and Buel's work takes is specifically described in lines 3–6 and again in lines 28–34. In lines 29–32, the passage states that Buel and Buel's work *provides ample raw material for questioning the myth . . . of a colonial golden age in the eighteenth century*, referring to a myth about women's status. In describing this golden age as a myth fostered by some historians, the passage suggests that this era was not as favorable to women as these historians suggest.

A   The passage describes Lebsock's work as providing such evidence, not Buel and Buel's work.
B   The passage does not pertain to the level of concern women had for their status.
C   **Correct.** The final paragraph of the passage describes Buel and Buel's work as providing material that calls into question claims that the eighteenth century was especially favorable to women.
D   The passage refers to the economic autonomy of women in relation to Lebsock's work, not Buel and Buel's work.
E   The passage does not refer to whether any particular occupations held by women were more respected at one time or another.

The correct answer is C.

Questions 436–438 refer to the passage on page 363.

436. The passage suggests that WIDC differed from WTUL in which of the following ways?

(A) WIDC believed that the existing safety regulations were adequate to protect women's health, whereas WTUL believed that such regulations needed to be strengthened.

(B) WIDC believed that unions could not succeed in pressuring employers to comply with such regulations, whereas WTUL believed that unions could succeed in doing so.

(C) WIDC believed that lead poisoning in white lead factories could be avoided by controlling conditions there, whereas WTUL believed that lead poisoning in such factories could not be avoided no matter how stringently safety regulations were enforced.

(D) At the time that the legislation concerning white lead factories was proposed, WIDC was primarily concerned with addressing health conditions in white lead factories, whereas WTUL was concerned with improving working conditions in all types of factories.

(E) At the time that WIDC was opposing legislative attempts to restrict women's labor, WTUL had already ceased to do so.

Inference

To answer this question you need to understand the differences between WIDC and WTUL as they are described in the passage. The only information about WTUL in the passage is that it had stopped opposing restrictions on women's labor in the late 1880s, and that, because existing safety regulations were not being enforced, it supported the proposal to prohibit women from working in white lead factories. WIDC, on the other hand, was formed in 1892 specifically to oppose restrictions on women's labor, and it opposed the proposal.

A   According to the passage, WIDC did believe that existing safety regulations, if enforced, could prevent lead poisoning. WTUL may or may not have believed that the safety regulations needed to be strengthened; all the passage states is that WTUL did not believe that the safety regulations were likely to be enforced.

B   The passage states that WTUL believed that because there were no unions to pressure employers, the employers would not comply with safety regulations. The passage does not present any information on which to base a conclusion about WIDC's beliefs regarding union pressure on employers.

C   Based on information in the passage, both WIDC and SPEW believed that enforcing safety regulations could protect women against lead poisoning. WIDC supported SPEW's position on the matter. WTUL believed that safety regulations were unlikely to be enforced because of the lack of unions.

D   The passage states that WIDC viewed the proposal to restrict women's employment in white lead factories as an instance of legislation designed to limit women's work opportunities—precisely the legislation that WIDC was formed to oppose. Thus, WIDC was not primarily concerned with the factories' health conditions.

E   **Correct.** WIDC began opposing legislative attempts to restrict women's labor in 1892 and continued to do so through at least 1895, when the Home Secretary proposed prohibiting women from working in white lead factories. WTUL stopped opposing restrictions on women's labor in the late 1880s, before WIDC was even founded. Thus, the passage suggests that WTUL had stopped opposing restrictions on women's labor well before WIDC worked to oppose such legislation.

The correct answer is E.

437. Which of the following, if true, would most clearly support the contention attributed to SPEW in lines 17–20 ?

(A) Those white lead factories that most strongly enforced regulations concerning worker safety and hygiene had the lowest incidences of lead poisoning among employees.

(B)   The incidence of lead poisoning was much higher among women who worked in white lead factories than among women who worked in other types of factories.

(C)   There were many household sources of lead that could have contributed to the incidence of lead poisoning among women who also worked outside the home in the late nineteenth century.

(D)   White lead factories were more stringent than were certain other types of factories in their enforcement of workplace safety regulations.

(E)   Even brief exposure to the conditions typically found in white lead factories could cause lead poisoning among factory workers.

Evaluation

This question requires the reader to find a statement that would provide additional support for the contention made in the following statement: *SPEW contended, and WIDC concurred, that controllable conditions in such factories were responsible for the development of lead poisoning.* Information suggesting that when conditions were controlled, lead poisoning was less likely to develop would provide support for SPEW's contention.

A   Correct. If incidences of lead poisoning were low in those factories that enforced hygiene and safety regulations, that would suggest that lead poisoning was not an inevitable result of working in a white lead factory—but rather that lead poisoning was the result of poor hygiene and safety practices.

B   It would not be particularly surprising for the incidence of lead poisoning to be higher among women working in white lead factories than among women working in other kinds of factories—but such a finding would say nothing about whether controllable conditions had any effect on the development of lead poisoning.

C   The existence of household sources of lead that might contribute to lead

poisoning would weaken, not support, SPEW's contention that controllable factory conditions were responsible for the development of lead poisoning.

D   If white lead factories enforced workplace safety regulations more stringently than did some other types of factories, it might be the case that SPEW's contention was incorrect: that even controlled conditions could not prevent a high incidence of lead poisoning.

E   If the conditions typically found in white lead factories were particularly bad with regard to safety and hygiene, it could conceivably be the case that SPEW's contention was true— that is, that the conditions that caused lead poisoning were controllable. But it might also be the case that an uncontrollable aspect of those conditions caused lead poisoning. Thus, this neither supports nor undermines SPEW's contention clearly.

The correct answer is A.

438.   The passage is primarily concerned with

(A)   presenting various groups' views of the motives of those proposing certain legislation

(B)   contrasting the reasoning of various groups concerning their positions on certain proposed legislation

(C)   tracing the process whereby certain proposed legislation was eventually enacted

(D)   assessing the success of tactics adopted by various groups with respect to certain proposed legislation

(E)   evaluating the arguments of various groups concerning certain proposed legislation

Main Idea

Answering this question depends on identifying the overall point of the passage. The passage is mainly concerned with explaining the reasons behind the positions taken by WIDC and SPEW, which opposed the proposal to enact legislation prohibiting women from holding most white lead factory jobs, and the reasoning of WTUL, which supported the proposal.

A   The passage explains how WIDC viewed the proposal, but it does not indicate what any of the groups believed about the motivations of the Home Secretary, who made the proposal.

B Correct. The passage contrasts the reasoning of the WIDC and SPEW, both of which believed that enforcing safety regulations would make the proposed legislation unnecessary, with the reasoning of WTUL, which thought that safety regulations were unlikely to be enforced and thus supported the proposal.

C The passage simply states that the proposal was eventually enacted; it does not trace the process by which this occurred.

D The passage implies that WIDC and SPEW were unsuccessful in their opposition to the proposed legislation, but it identifies only one tactic used in opposition to it: SPEW's attempt to challenge it by investigating the causes of lead poisoning.

E The passage does not evaluate the groups' arguments concerning the proposed legislation; rather, it presents those arguments without comment on their quality or value.

The correct answer is B.

Questions 439–444 refer to the passage on page 365.

439. The author of the passage refers to Robert Filmer (see line 9) primarily in order to

(A) show that Royalist ideology was somewhat more radical than most historians appear to realize

(B) qualify the claim that patriarchalism formed the basis of Royalist ideology

(C) question the view that most early feminists were associated with the Royalist faction

(D) highlight an apparent tension between Royalist ideology and the ideas of early feminists

(E) argue that Royalists held conflicting opinions on issues of family organization and women's political rights

Evaluation

This question asks about the role of Filmer in the passage. The author states that Filmer's radical patriarchalism is associated with Royalist ideology and then goes on to define radical patriarchalism

as an ideology that asserts the power of the king and the male head of the household. Early feminists, however, questioned the subordination of women in marriage. Thus, there seems to be a conflict between these two sets of ideas.

A Although the passage refers to Filmer's view as *radical patriarchalism*, it provides no evidence regarding any differences in the degrees to which historians consider that view, or Royalism in general, to be radical.

B Filmer's work supports the claim that patriarchalism was the basis of Royalist ideology; it does not qualify such a claim.

C That Filmer's approach was one of radical patriarchalism makes it surprising that early feminists were associated with the Royalist faction, but it does not provide any grounds for questioning whether they were so associated.

D Correct. There is apparent tension between Filmer's radical patriarchalism, if that is indeed essential to Royalist ideology, and the ideas of early feminists, who questioned such patriarchalism.

E The author refers to Filmer in order to suggest, initially, a uniformity among Royalists regarding family and women; it is only later in the passage that this view becomes more complicated.

The correct answer is D.

440. The passage suggests which of the following about the seventeenth-century English women mentioned in line 2?

(A) Their status as forerunners of modern feminism is not entirely justified.

(B) They did not openly challenge the radical patriarchalism of Royalist Filmerian ideology.

(C) Cavendish was the first among these women to criticize women's subordination in marriage and assert women's equality with men.

(D) Their views on family organization and women's political rights were diametrically opposed to those of both Royalist and Parliamentarian ideology.

(E) Historians would be less puzzled if more of them were identified with the Parliamentarian side in the English Civil Wars.

Inference

The first sentence of the passage refers to women who are both regarded as forerunners of modern feminism and identified as Royalists. The passage goes on to suggest that, given Royalist ideology's association with Filmer's radical patriarchalism (equating absolute power of the king with absolute power of the male head of household), it is surprising that feminism would find any footing within such an ideology.

A Nothing in the passage disputes the idea that the seventeenth-century English women in question should be considered the forerunners of modern feminism.

B Gallagher provides the example of Margaret Cavendish as a writer who did openly challenge radical patriarchalism—albeit only in her writings.

C The passage states that Cavendish had successors among early feminists, but it does not indicate whether she herself was the first seventeenth-century English woman to assert women's equality.

D The passage does not indicate what the Parliamentarian view of family organization and women's political rights was, so there is no way to determine whether the Royalist forerunners of modern feminism were opposed to that view.

E **Correct.** The basic puzzle the passage sets out to solve is why the forerunners of modern feminism would have been associated with the Royalist side, which seems to have been based on radical patriarchalism. Historians would most likely have been less surprised if these women had been identified with the Parliamentarian side, which presumably did not embrace radical patriarchalism.

The correct answer is E.

441. The passage suggests that Margaret Cavendish's decision to become an author was motivated, at least in part, by a desire to

(A) justify her support for the Royalist cause

(B) encourage her readers to work toward eradicating Filmerian patriarchalism

(C) persuade other women to break free from their political and social isolation

(D) analyze the causes for women's exclusion from the pursuit of power

(E) create a world over which she could exercise total control

Inference

This question asks about Margaret Cavendish's reasons for becoming an author. The second paragraph describes her as someone who *insisted that she was a self-sufficient being*; she understood that, given the real-world strictures in place, she could achieve this self-sufficiency in her own mind and on paper as a writer. So her decision to become a writer can be inferred to be motivated by her desire to exercise power and control.

A The passage states that Cavendish justified her being the center of her own universe by invoking the Royalist figure of the absolute monarch; there is no suggestion in the passage that Cavendish felt the need to justify any support for the actual Royalist cause.

B The passage gives no direct indication that Cavendish was even aware of Filmerian patriarchalism.

C The second paragraph states that Cavendish's idea of absolute singularity carried with it the idea of social and political isolation; Cavendish was most likely not motivated by a desire to persuade other women to break free from such isolation.

D Cavendish took the exclusion of women from the pursuit of power for granted; the passage does not suggest that she was concerned with its causes.

E **Correct.** According to the passage, Cavendish considered herself a self-sufficient being who was at the center of her own universe; in her writing, she wanted to create a world in which this was also true.

The correct answer is E.

442. The phrase "a satellite orbiting a dominant male planet" (lines 41–42) refers most directly to

(A) Cavendish's concept that each woman is a sovereign self

(B) the complete political and social isolation of absolute singularity

(C) the immaterial world that a writer can create on paper

(D) the absolute subordination of women in a patriarchal society

(E) the metaphorical figure of the absolute monarch

Evaluation

The phrase in question is *a satellite orbiting a dominant male planet*. The passage states that this was the idea that Cavendish was reacting against; she preferred instead the idea that she was the center of her own universe, her own sovereign, subject to no one.

A The idea of a satellite orbiting a dominant male planet refers not to Cavendish's idea that each woman is a sovereign self, but rather to the idea directly opposed to that: each woman must submit to a dominant male.

B A *satellite orbiting a dominant male planet* is by definition not isolated, nor is it singular.

C According to the passage, Cavendish wished to create her own world as a writer so that she did not have to be a *satellite*.

D **Correct.** The phrase refers to the idea that in a patriarchal society, women are as satellites to men, who are the dominant planets.

E While radical patriarchy does equate the monarch with the male head of the household, the in question phrase is most directly about the relationship, under patriarchy, between women and men.

The correct answer is D.

443. The primary purpose of the passage is to

(A) trace the historical roots of a modern sociopolitical movement

(B) present one scholar's explanation for a puzzling historical phenomenon

(C) contrast two interpretations of the ideological origins of a political conflict

(D) establish a link between the ideology of an influential political theorist and that of a notoriously eccentric writer

(E) call attention to some points of agreement between opposing sides in an ideological debate

Main Idea

This question asks about the passage as a whole. The passage is mainly concerned with outlining Catherine Gallagher's attempt to explain why, given Royalist ideology's apparent association with radical patriarchalism, Royalist women offered feminist critiques of women's subordination in marriage and asserted their equality with men.

A The passage makes no connection between early feminism and its modern form.

B **Correct.** The passage presents a puzzling historical phenomenon, that Royalist women critiqued patriarchalism, in the first paragraph, and then presents Catherine Gallagher's explanation for that phenomenon in the second paragraph.

C While the passage discusses the political conflict between the Royalists and Parliamentarians in the English Civil Wars in the first paragraph, neither this conflict, nor its ideological origins are the focus of the passage. Furthermore, the passage does not offer any interpretations of the origins of the conflict.

D The passage attempts to unlink the ideology of political theorist Robert Filmer and the eccentric author Margaret Cavendish by suggesting that Filmer's radical patriarchalism was not the only way of understanding Royalist ideology. Cavendish provided a different understanding entirely.

E While both sides of the ideological debate did agree on the absolute monarchy, the passage as a whole does not focus on this agreement, but rather on the disagreement about where, theoretically, the idea of absolute monarchy leads.

The correct answer is B.

444. Which of the following, if true, would most clearly undermine Gallagher's explanation of the link between Royalism and feminism?

(A) Because of their privileged backgrounds, Royalist women were generally better educated than were their Parliamentarian counterparts.

(B)   Filmer himself had read some of Cavendish's early writings and was highly critical of her ideas.

(C)   Cavendish's views were highly individual and were not shared by the other Royalist women who wrote early feminist works.

(D)   The Royalist and Parliamentarian ideologies were largely in agreement on issues of family organization and women's political rights.

(E)   The Royalist side included a sizable minority faction that was opposed to the more radical tendencies of Filmerian patriarchalism.

Inference

This question asks about how to undermine the way in which Gallagher connects Royalism and feminism. According to Gallagher, Cavendish's work exemplifies the connection between these ideas, because Cavendish took the idea of absolute monarchy and extended that to the idea of absolute self, an idea that should, Cavendish believed, apply to women as well as men.

A   Gallagher's explanation of the link between Royalism and feminism does not depend on the education level of Royalist women relative to Parliamentarian women.

B   Filmer most likely would have been critical of Cavendish's ideas, had he encountered them, but the passage does not indicate that Gallagher's argument had anything to do with whether Filmer read Cavendish's writings.

C   **Correct.** Gallagher uses Cavendish's work to explain how Royalism gave rise to feminism, but if Cavendish's views were completely atypical of other Royalist women, then those views cannot explain the link as Gallagher suggests they do.

D   The passage states in the first paragraph that if the Royalists and Parliamentarians were in agreement *on issues of family organization and women's political rights*, then feminists should have been divided between the two sides—but they were not. So this idea, if true, would undermine that statement, but not Gallagher's argument about the link between Royalists and feminists.

E   If more Royalists were opposed to Filmer's radical patriarchalism, then Cavendish's writings would seem to be more

representative of tendencies in Royalist ideology, thus making Gallagher's case stronger, not weaker.

The correct answer is C.

Questions 445–449 refer to the passage on page 367.

445.   The passage is primarily concerned with

(A)   identifying two practices in medical research that may affect the accuracy of clinical trials

(B)   describing aspects of medical research that tend to drive up costs

(C)   evaluating an analysis of certain shortcomings of current medical research practices

(D)   describing proposed changes to the ways in which clinical trials are conducted

(E)   explaining how medical researchers have traditionally conducted clinical trials and how such trials are likely to change

Main Idea

This question requires an understanding of what the passage as a whole is doing. The passage introduces Frazier and Mosteller as proposing changes to the ways clinical trials in medical research are currently conducted. The rest of the passage then describes these proposed changes together with the support Frazier and Mosteller provide for adopting these changes.

A   The passage identifies practices in medical research to help illustrate the basis for Frazier and Mosteller's proposed changes.

B   The passage mentions medical research costs as one example within the larger description of Frazier and Mosteller's proposed changes.

C   The passage is not concerned with evaluating Frazier and Mosteller's proposed changes.

D   **Correct.** The passage describes the changes proposed by Frazier and Mosteller to the way clinical trials are conducted.

E   The passage is not concerned with establishing the likelihood of any changes to the way medical research is conducted.

The correct answer is D.

446. Which of the following can be inferred from the passage about a study of the category of patients referred to in lines 20–22 ?

(A) Its findings might have limited applicability.

(B) It would be prohibitively expensive in its attempt to create ideal conditions.

(C) It would be the best way to sample the total population of potential patients.

(D) It would allow researchers to limit information collection without increasing the risk that important variables could be overlooked.

(E) Its findings would be more accurate if it concerned treatments for a progressive disease than if it concerned treatments for a nonprogressive disease.

Inference

This question requires drawing an inference from information given in the passage. In describing the proposals put forth by Frazier and Mosteller, the passage states in lines 15–20 that they propose using more patients in clinical trials than are currently being used, and that the trials would thereby obtain *a more representative sample of the total population with the disease under study.* The passage then states that researchers often *restrict* (lines 20–22) their trials to certain types of patients, therefore limiting the applicability of their findings.

A **Correct.** The passage states that the researchers preferred to restrict the types of patients used in their studies, thereby using a less representative sample than if they used a more inclusive group of patients.

B The passage mentions the added expense of clinical trials only in relation to data storage, collection, and analysis.

C The passage describes the category of patients referred to as restricted and therefore unrepresentative of the total population.

D While the passage does mention the amount of data collected about an individual patient, that topic is not connected to the category of patients referred to in lines 20–22.

E The passage does not suggest that a study using the category of patients referred to would be more effective in investigating progressive diseases.

The correct answer is A.

447. It can be inferred from the passage that a study limited to patients like those mentioned in lines 20–22 would have which of the following advantages over the kind of study proposed by Frazier and Mosteller?

(A) It would yield more data and its findings would be more accurate.

(B) It would cost less in the long term, though it would be more expensive in its initial stages.

(C) It would limit the number of variables researchers would need to consider when evaluating the treatment under study.

(D) It would help researchers to identify subgroups of patients with secondary conditions that might also be treatable.

(E) It would enable researchers to assess the value of an experimental treatment for the average patient.

Inference

This question requires understanding what the information in the passage implies. The passage explains that Frazier and Mosteller's proposal involves enrolling more patients in clinical trials (lines 18–19) than is the case with the category of patients referred to. The passage then explains that broadening the range of trial participants would allow an evaluation of particular treatments *under various conditions* and *for different patient subgroups* (line 29). This strongly suggests that limiting the patients used to those described in the referred text would limit the number of variables researchers would need to consider.

A The passage suggests that not limiting the patients used in clinical trials will yield more data than restricting them will.

B The passage refers to the costs of clinical trials only as they concern the collection, storage, and analysis of data collected from participants.

C **Correct.** By limiting the patients used to those having the ailment under study, the passage suggests that researchers need to consider fewer variables in their assessment of a treatment.

D The passage suggests that *not* limiting the types of patients used in clinical trials will better allow researchers to evaluate subgroups.

E   The passage suggests that limiting the types of patients available for clinical trials results in data for specific, rather than average, populations.

The correct answer is C.

448. The author mentions patients' ages (line 32) primarily in order to

(A) identify the most critical variable differentiating subgroups of patients

(B) cast doubt on the advisability of implementing Frazier and Mosteller's proposals about medical research

(C) indicate why progressive diseases may require different treatments at different stages

(D) illustrate a point about the value of enrolling a wide range of patients in clinical trials

(E) substantiate an argument about the problems inherent in enrolling large numbers of patients in clinical trials

Evaluation

Answering this question requires understanding how a particular piece of information functions in the passage as a whole. The passage is concerned with describing the proposals of Frazier and Mosteller. One of these proposals, described in the second paragraph, involves broadening the range of participants used in clinical trials. The passage states that in following this proposal, Frazier and Mosteller suggest that the effectiveness of treatments can be assessed for different patient subgroups. To affirm the value of broadening the range of participants, the passage then cites two examples of criteria by which relevant subgroups might be identified: disease stages and patients' ages.

A   The passage makes no judgment as to the value of the subgroups it refers to in relation to broadened participation in clinical trials.

B   The passage does not call into question the potential effectiveness of Frazier and Mosteller's proposals.

C   The passage's example of patients' ages is not intended to be causally connected to its previous example regarding progressive diseases.

D   **Correct.** Patients' ages are referred to in the passage to identify subgroups that could be evaluated if the range of participants in clinical trials were broadened.

E   The passage refers to patients' ages in support of Frazier and Mosteller's proposal that more patients be used in clinical trials.

The correct answer is D.

449. According to the passage, which of the following describes a result of the way in which researchers generally conduct clinical trials?

(A) They expend resources on the storage of information likely to be irrelevant to the study they are conducting.

(B) They sometimes compromise the accuracy of their findings by collecting and analyzing more information than is strictly required for their trials.

(C) They avoid the risk of overlooking variables that might affect their findings, even though doing so raises their research costs.

(D) Because they attempt to analyze too much information, they overlook facts that could emerge as relevant to their studies.

(E) In order to approximate the conditions typical of medical treatment, they base their methods of information collection on those used by hospitals.

Supporting Idea

This question asks for an identification of specific information given in the passage. The passage describes the proposals of Frazier and Mosteller as attempting to improve the way clinical trials have generally been conducted. In describing how current trials are generally conducted, the passage states that researchers *collect far more background information on patients than is strictly required for their trials* (lines 4–6) and that they therefore escalate the costs of the trials.

A   **Correct.** The passage states that researchers generally collect more information than they need to perform their clinical trials, which drives up the costs of the trials.

B   The passage makes no judgment about the accuracy of the information collected by researchers who currently hold clinical trials.

C   The passage states that the risk of overlooking relevant information in clinical trials is *never entirely eliminable* (line 11).

D   The passage states that researchers generally collect more information than is relevant, not that they overlook relevant information.

E   The passage states that, in general, researchers currently collect more information than hospitals do (line 6).

The correct answer is A.

Questions 450–455 refer to the passage on page 369.

450. The primary purpose of the passage is to

(A)   assess the validity of a certain view

(B)   distinguish between two phenomena

(C)   identify the causes of a problem

(D)   describe a disturbing trend

(E)   allay concern about a particular phenomenon

Main Idea

This question requires understanding, in general terms, the purpose of the passage as a whole. The first paragraph identifies an area of concern: declines in amphibian populations may constitute a crisis, one that indicates humans' catastrophic effects on the environment. The rest of the passage then goes on to evaluate, as the second paragraph states, whether claims of crisis-level extinctions as a result of human activity are valid. In making this evaluation, the passage discusses the possible causes of extinctions, biologists' prioritization of population declines over extinctions, and the fact that we lack extensive long-term data on amphibian populations.

A   **Correct.** The passage's main purpose is to assess whether the view that humans are causing crisis-level declines in amphibian populations is valid.

B   The passage takes care, particularly in the third paragraph, to distinguish between population declines and extinctions, but this is not its primary purpose.

C   The passage makes clear that it is difficult to identify the real extent of the problem facing amphibian populations, much less identify its causes.

D   The first paragraph notes what may seem to be a disturbing trend—the decline in amphibian populations—but the rest of the passage is concerned not with describing that trend in greater detail, but rather with determining whether it is in fact occurring.

E   While the passage provides possible grounds for concluding that concern about declining amphibian populations is overblown, it concludes by suggesting that we might, because we lack data, doom species and ecosystems to extinction. Thus, the overall purpose is not to allay concern.

The correct answer is A.

451. It can be inferred from the passage that the author believes which of the following to be true of the environmentalists mentioned in lines 5–6 ?

(A)   They have wrongly chosen to focus on anecdotal reports rather than on the long-term data that are currently available concerning amphibians.

(B)   Their recommendations are flawed because their research focuses too narrowly on a single category of animal species.

(C)   Their certainty that population declines in general are caused by environmental degradation is not warranted.

(D)   They have drawn premature conclusions concerning a crisis in amphibian populations from recent reports of declines.

(E)   They have overestimated the effects of chance events on trends in amphibian populations.

Inference

This question asks about the author's view of the environmentalists mentioned in the first paragraph. These environmentalists have claimed, based on amphibian population declines, that the situation is a crisis and that immediate action must be taken. The author, however, states that the declines are only *apparently* drastic and questions whether they are real, thus suggesting that the environmentalists are drawing conclusions in the absence of a complete consideration of the situation.

A   The passage indicates that anecdotal reports are insufficient, but so too are other resources. The fourth paragraph of the passage makes clear that there is not enough long-term data available on which to base conclusions about amphibian populations.

B   The passage does not indicate that the environmentalists under discussion have conducted research on any animal species.

C   The passage does not indicate that the environmentalists in question hold, with certainty, any particular view regarding population declines in general.

D   **Correct.** The author argues that the recent declines may have several different causes, and that environmentalists have jumped to a conclusion about the cause of the declines as well as their significance.

E   The environmentalists, in attributing population declines to intentional human activity, have more likely underestimated than overestimated the effects of chance events on amphibian populations.

The correct answer is D.

452.   It can be inferred from the passage that the author believes which of the following to be true of the amphibian extinctions that have recently been reported?

(A)   They have resulted primarily from human activities causing environmental degradation.

(B)   They could probably have been prevented if timely action had been taken to protect the habitats of amphibian species.

(C)   They should not come as a surprise, because amphibian populations generally have been declining for a number of years.

(D)   They have probably been caused by a combination of chance events.

(E)   They do not clearly constitute evidence of general environmental degradation.

Inference

The author suggests throughout the passage that recently reported amphibian extinctions may have several different causes: they may be due to any number of chance events, for example, or may simply be the result of a small population that finds itself unable to continue under difficult conditions, whatever causes those conditions.

A   The author states in the second paragraph that extinctions may occur without a proximate cause in human activities and does not make a commitment to any particular explanation of the amphibian extinctions.

B   That chance events can cause extinctions suggests that even if habitats had been protected, extinctions still might have occurred.

C   In the second paragraph, the author says that extinctions *should come as no great surprise*, but this option is imprecise. The amphibian populations have not generally *been declining for a number of years*. The author says in the third paragraph that amphibian populations show strong fluctuations; further, in the fourth paragraph, the author says that there is insufficient long-term data to conclude that amphibian populations have been, or are, in decline.

D   The author suggests that the extinctions may have been caused by chance events, but there is not enough data to know whether or not this is probable.

E   **Correct.** The reported extinctions could have resulted from several different causes; thus, they are not clear evidence of general environmental degradation.

The correct answer is E.

453.   According to the passage, each of the following is true of endangered amphibian species EXCEPT:

(A)   They are among the rarest kinds of amphibians.

(B)   They generally have populations that are small in size.

(C)   They are in constant danger of extinction.

(D)   Those with decreasing populations are the most likely candidates for immediate extinction.

(E)   They are in danger of extinction due to events that sometimes have nothing to do with human activities.

Application

This question asks what the passage does not say is true of endangered amphibian species. The second paragraph discusses endangered species, stating that they are *always rare, almost always small, and, by definition, under constant threat of extinction*, which may be caused by chance events. The possibility of their extinction, the passage states, depends only on the population size, and not whether that population is increasing or decreasing.

A   The second paragraph mentions rarity as a characteristic of endangered amphibian species.

B   According to the second paragraph, endangered amphibian species are generally those of small populations.

C   The second paragraph states that an endangered population is under constant threat of extinction.

D   Correct. The last sentence of the second paragraph states that the probability of extinction due to chance events is independent of how a population changes in size. Immediate extinction would more likely come from such events, whereas population decline is gradual, even if fairly rapid.

E   Endangered species, according to the second paragraph, may become extinct due to chance events—that is, events that have nothing to do with human activities.

The correct answer is D.

454. Which of the following most accurately describes the organization of the passage?

(A)   A question is raised, a distinction regarding it is made, and the question is answered.

(B)   An interpretation is presented, its soundness is examined, and a warning is given.

(C)   A situation is described, its consequences are analyzed, and a prediction is made.

(D)   Two interpretations of a phenomenon are described, and one of them is rejected as invalid.

(E)   Two methods for analyzing a phenomenon are compared, and further study of the phenomenon is recommended.

Evaluation

This question asks about the organization of the passage as a whole. In the first paragraph, the author tells about a situation that has

been interpreted in a particular way by environmentalists. The passage then proceeds to consider whether that interpretation is valid, and while it does not come to a definitive conclusion on that point, the final paragraph warns about the possible consequences of not taking the action recommended by the environmentalists.

A   The passage does initially raise a question regarding whether the environmentalists' interpretation of events is valid, but it does not answer that question, for the appropriate long-term data are not available.

B   Correct. The passage presents environmentalists' interpretation of recent news regarding amphibians, then examines the soundness of that interpretation. Finally, the author warns that postponing environmental action may have disastrous consequences.

C   The first paragraph describes a situation of possibly drastic declines in amphibian populations but does not follow this description with an analysis of its consequences.

D   The passage suggests that apparent declines in amphibian populations may or may not constitute a crisis, but it does not reject either idea.

E   While the passage does imply, in its final paragraph, that long-term data on amphibian populations should be collected, the passage does not compare two methods for analyzing amphibian populations or population declines in those populations.

The correct answer is B.

455. Which of the following best describes the function of the sentence in lines 35–38 ?

(A)   To give an example of a particular kind of study

(B)   To cast doubt on an assertion made in the previous sentence

(C)   To raise an objection to a view presented in the first paragraph

(D)   To provide support for a view presented in the first paragraph

(E)   To introduce an idea that will be countered in the following paragraph

Evaluation

The sentence in question discusses the way in which anecdotal reports of population decreases cannot help biologists determine whether those decreases are normal fluctuations, take populations to lower levels that are not actually worrisome, or actually threaten extinctions. This indicates that the view mentioned in the first paragraph—reports of declines indicate a catastrophic crisis—may be mistaken.

A   The sentence does not address a particular kind of study; it objects to the use of anecdotal reports in place of actual study.
B   The previous sentence describes the possibilities referred to in the sentence in question. The sentence does not cast doubt on any of those possibilities.
C   **Correct.** The view that reports of amphibian population declines indicate a crisis, as presented in the first paragraph, is countered by the objection here that there are several possible causes for population declines, and anecdotal reports cannot distinguish among those possibilities.
D   The first paragraph is concerned with articulating the view that amphibian population declines constitute a crisis. This sentence does not support that view; instead, it offers reason to question it.
E   The sentence introduces the idea that amphibian populations have fluctuated in the past, and the following paragraph supports this idea by stating that several amphibian species that appeared almost extinct in the 1950s and 1960s have recovered. Thus, the paragraph does not counter the sentence.

The correct answer is C.

Questions 456–459 refer to the passage on page 371.

Main Idea Summary

The main idea of the passage is that attempts to identify keystone species are complicated by multiple factors, including the difficulty of directly testing for keystone status with controlled experiments and the fact that keystone status appears to depend in complex ways on the contexts in which the species are found. The passage defines a keystone species as one whose effects on its ecosystem *are much larger than would be predicted from its abundance*. It notes that testing for keystone status by removing species from their environment and observing the effects of their absence is problematic. It then discusses one species of starfish to exemplify the difficulties inherent in determining whether a species is a keystone one. Drawing on those examples, the passage describes some ways in which keystone status depends on species' contexts.

456.   The passage mentions which of the following as a factor that affects the role of *P. ochraceus* as a keystone species within different habitats?

(A)   The degree to which the habitat is sheltered from waves
(B)   The degree to which other animals within a habitat prey on mussels
(C)   The fact that mussel populations are often not dominant within some habitats occupied by *P. ochraceus*
(D)   The size of the *P. ochraceus* population within the habitat
(E)   The fact that there is great species diversity within some habitats occupied by *P. ochraceus*

Supporting Idea

This question depends on recognizing what the passage states about the factors affecting *P. ochraceus*'s role as a keystone species, which is different in different habitats. According to the passage, *P. ochraceus* consumes and suppresses mussel populations in some habitats—specifically, those that are wave-exposed—making it a keystone predator in those habitats. But in wave-sheltered habitats, *P. ochraceus* does not play the same role in suppressing mussel populations.

A   **Correct.** The passage clearly states that *P. ochraceus*'s role in wave-exposed habitats differs from its role in wave-sheltered habitats.
B   The passage says that the impact of *P. ochraceus* predation on mussels is not strong in wave-sheltered habitats, but this is

not—at least not at all sites—because other animals are preying on the mussels; rather, at least at some sites, it is because mussels are controlled by sand burial.

C   The passage does not suggest that mussel populations are dominant in any habitats occupied by *P. ochraceus*.

D   The size of the *P. ochraceus* population affects the size of the mussel population within wave-exposed habitats, but the passage does not suggest that *P. ochraceus*'s role as a keystone species depends on the size of its population within those habitats.

E   The only other species the passage mentions in conjunction with *P. ochraceus* habitats is the mussel; the passage does not address species diversity in these habitats.

The correct answer is A.

457. Which of the following hypothetical experiments most clearly exemplifies the method of identifying species' roles that the author considers problematic?

(A)   A population of seals in an Arctic habitat is counted in order to determine whether it is the dominant species in that ecosystem.

(B)   A species of fish that is a keystone species in one marine ecosystem is introduced into another marine ecosystem to see whether the species will come to occupy a keystone role.

(C)   In order to determine whether a species of monkey is a keystone species within a particular ecosystem, the monkeys are removed from that ecosystem and the ecosystem is then studied.

(D)   Different mountain ecosystems are compared to determine how geography affects a particular species' ability to dominate its ecosystem.

(E)   In a grassland experiencing a changing climate, patterns of species extinction are traced in order to evaluate the effect of climate changes on keystone species in that grassland.

Application

Answering this question depends on recognizing what the author says about identifying species' roles in habitats and then extending that to another situation. The author considers a particular method of studying keystone species problematic: removing a suspected keystone species from

its habitat and observing what happens to the ecosystem. The author finds this problematic because interactions among species are complex.

A   The author does not discuss counting the members of a population as a problematic way of determining whether that population is a dominant species.

B   The method that the author finds problematic has to do with observing what happens to an ecosystem when a keystone species is removed from it, not with observing what happens to a different ecosystem when the species is introduced into it.

C   **Correct.** The author states explicitly that removing a species from a habitat in order to determine its keystone status is problematic. Removing the monkeys from their habitat is a clear example of this problematic practice.

D   Comparison of habitats in order to determine geography's effect on a particular species' dominance would most likely find favor with the author, for this is the approach the author seems to advocate in investigating *P. ochraceus*'s keystone status.

E   The author does not discuss tracing patterns of extinction or changing climates in the passage.

The correct answer is C.

458. Which of the following, if true, would most clearly support the argument about keystone status advanced in the last sentence of the passage (lines 24–31)?

(A)   A species of bat is primarily responsible for keeping insect populations within an ecosystem low, and the size of the insect population in turn affects bird species within that ecosystem.

(B)   A species of iguana occupies a keystone role on certain tropical islands, but does not play that role on adjacent tropical islands that are inhabited by a greater number of animal species.

(C)   Close observation of a savannah ecosystem reveals that more species occupy keystone roles within that ecosystem than biologists had previously believed.

(D)   As a keystone species of bee becomes more abundant, it has a larger effect on the ecosystem it inhabits.

(E)   A species of moth that occupies a keystone role in a prairie habitat develops coloration patterns that camouflage it from potential predators.

Evaluation

To answer this question, focus on the argument advanced in the last sentence of the passage and identify what information would support that argument. In the last sentence of the passage, the author claims that keystone status depends on context. The author then offers three contextual factors that may affect a species' keystone status: geography, community diversity (i.e., the number of species in a given habitat), and length of species interaction. Evidence supporting this argument would show that context is important to a species' keystone status.

A   This scenario does not indicate anything about keystone status; this is simply a description of how species populations in a single ecosystem affect one another.

B   **Correct.** That the iguana is a keystone species in a location that has limited species diversity but not a keystone species in a location that has greater species diversity suggests that keystone status does indeed depend on context. Thus, this example supports the author's argument in the last sentence of the passage.

C   That biologists were mistaken about keystone species in a particular ecosystem does not have a bearing on whether keystone status is context dependent.

D   It is not surprising that an increase in a species' population would lead to that species having a larger effect on its ecosystem—but this does not speak directly to the question of whether keystone status itself depends on context.

E   A keystone species enhancing its ability to survive in a single ecosystem does not lend any support to the idea that keystone status depends on context. The moth's keystone status would have to undergo some change for this to have a bearing on the question of context.

The correct answer is B.

459.   The passage suggests which of the following about the identification of a species as a keystone species?

(A)   Such an identification depends primarily on the species' relationship to the dominant species.

(B)   Such an identification can best be made by removing the species from a particular ecosystem and observing changes that occur in the ecosystem.

(C)   Such an identification is likely to be less reliable as an ecosystem becomes less diverse.

(D)   Such an identification seems to depend on various factors within the ecosystem.

(E)   Such an identification can best be made by observing predation behavior.

Inference

Answering this question requires identifying how the passage suggests that keystone species should be identified. The passage identifies a particular way in which keystone status should *not* be determined: removing a species and observing what happens to the ecosystem. The passage also argues that keystone status depends strongly on context: that is, an ecosystem's characteristics, including its geography and inhabitants, determine its keystone species.

A   While the passage uses an example of a keystone species, *P. ochraceus*, which preys on a species that would, in the keystone species' absence, be dominant, there is nothing to suggest that a keystone species *must* have a particular relationship with the dominant, or potentially dominant, species in an ecosystem.

B   The passage explicitly states that this method of identification would be problematic.

C   A reduction in an ecosystem's diversity might alter which species occupy keystone roles in that ecosystem, the passage suggests, but there is no indication that identifying such species would become more difficult.

D   **Correct.** If, as the passage suggests, keystone status for any given species depends on the context of the ecosystem in which it lives, then it is likely that identifying keystone species depends strongly on understanding what factors of the ecosystem contribute to creating keystone status. The passage lists such factors as geography, community diversity, and species interaction.

E While the passage uses a predator, *P. ochraceus*, as its example of a keystone species, there is no indication that predation is an essential component of the actual definition of keystone species (*one whose effects are much larger than would be predicted from its abundance*).

The correct answer is D.

Questions 460–462 refer to the passage on page 373.

Main Idea Summary

The first paragraph of the passage indicates that the 1981 discovery of fossil remains of the tiny soft-bodied animals known as conodonts shed light on hypotheses regarding the development of vertebrate skeletons. The second paragraph states that the traditional view was that the vertebrate skeleton had developed as a defensive mechanism and that teeth were secondary features. The paragraph mentions, however, that other paleontologists argued that certain characteristics of vertebrates would not have evolved had the vertebrates not been predators and that teeth were more primitive than external armor. The final paragraph argues that certain features of conodonts suggest that hard parts first evolved in the mouth to improve predation, and aggression rather than protection drove the origin of the vertebrate skeleton. Supporting these latter claims is the primary purpose of the passage.

460. According to the passage, the anatomical evidence provided by the preserved soft bodies of conodonts led scientists to conclude that

(A) conodonts had actually been invertebrate carnivores

(B) conodonts' teeth were adapted from protective bony scales

(C) conodonts were primitive vertebrate suspension feeders

(D) primitive vertebrates with teeth appeared earlier than armored vertebrates

(E) scientists' original observations concerning the phosphatic remains of conodonts were essentially correct

Supporting Idea

This question depends on understanding how a particular type of evidence—the preserved soft bodies of conodonts—supports a particular conclusion stated in the passage. The third paragraph makes this relationship explicit, explaining that certain features of conodonts show them to be more primitive than other vertebrates. Further, those features indicate that they came before ostracoderms and other armored jawless fishes. These remains support the conclusion stated in the second paragraph regarding teeth being more primitive than external armor.

A The passage states explicitly that conodonts were not invertebrates but rather vertebrates.

B This view is attributed to certain traditionalists but is contradicted by other paleontological evidence presented in the second and third paragraphs. According to the third paragraph, the evidence provided by the preserved soft bodies of conodonts undermines this traditional view.

C The final sentence of the passage indicates that the evidence in question supports the conclusion that conodonts were predators rather than suspension feeders.

D Correct. The third paragraph explains how conodonts' remains support the conclusion that teeth were more primitive than external armor.

E The second paragraph explains that originally, scientists thought that early vertebrates were not predators—but the remainder of the passage indicates that this idea is inconsistent with more recent evidence described in the passage.

The correct answer is D.

461. The second paragraph in the passage serves primarily to

    (A) outline the significance of the 1981 discovery of conodont remains to the debate concerning the development of the vertebrate skeleton

    (B) contrast the traditional view of the development of the vertebrate skeleton with a view derived from the 1981 discovery of conodont remains

    (C) contrast the characteristics of the ostracoderms with the characteristics of earlier soft-bodied vertebrates

    (D) explain the importance of the development of teeth among the earliest vertebrate predators

    (E) present the two sides of the debate concerning the development of the vertebrate skeleton

Evaluation

This question depends on understanding the second paragraph in the context of the passage as a whole. The second paragraph begins by noting the traditional view of the vertebrate skeleton—that it was a defense against predators—and then goes on to explain that other paleontologists argued against this idea, claiming instead that vertebrates began as predators and that teeth were a more primary feature than external armor.

A   The second paragraph focuses on describing the debate rather than on the distinctive contribution of the 1981 discovery to that debate.

B   The second paragraph does not explicitly indicate whether the opposition to the traditional view originally rested on the 1981 discovery of conodont remains. In fact, the surrounding discussion, in the first and third paragraphs, suggests that the discovery in 1981 turned out to support the opposing view, which some paleontologists already held at that time.

C   The mention of ostracoderms in the second paragraph merely serves to indicate how the traditionalists' arguments might have seemed plausible. The paragraph as a whole is not devoted to contrasting the ostracoderms with earlier soft-bodied vertebrates.

D   The development of teeth figures in the second paragraph, but this development is mentioned first as a feature that some believed to have been adapted from protective scales; only the final sentence of the paragraph connects teeth to early vertebrate predators.

E   **Correct.** According to the passage, the debate concerning the development of the vertebrate skeleton hinges on whether vertebrates began as predators, with teeth, or whether skeletal defenses such as external armor evolved first. The primary purpose of the second paragraph is to distinguish these two sides.

The correct answer is E.

462. It can be inferred that on the basis of the 1981 discovery of conodont remains, paleontologists could draw which of the following conclusions?

    (A) The earliest vertebrates were sedentary suspension feeders.

    (B) Ostracoderms were not the earliest vertebrates.

    (C) Defensive armor preceded jaws among vertebrates.

    (D) Paired eyes and adaptations for activity are definitive characteristics of vertebrates.

    (E) Conodonts were unlikely to have been predators.

Inference

What could paleontologists conclude, based on the 1981 discovery of conodont remains? That discovery, according to the passage, supported the view of certain paleontologists that the earliest vertebrates were predators with teeth—unlike the ostracoderms, which had no jaws.

A   According to the second paragraph, traditionalists believed that early vertebrates were sedentary suspension feeders. But the 1981 discovery supported instead the hypothesis that early vertebrates were predators instead.

B   **Correct.** According to the third paragraph, the conodonts' body structures indicated that they were more primitive than the ostracoderms, so the ostracoderms must not have been the earliest vertebrates.

C   Traditionalists argued that teeth were adapted from bony scales that provided defensive armor, but the 1981 discovery suggested that teeth preceded such scales.

D   Paleontologists knew prior to the 1981 discovery that paired eyes and other adaptations are characteristics of vertebrates. They used this knowledge to help them interpret the 1981 discovery.

E   The third paragraph indicates that conodonts, given their teeth, were most likely predators.

The correct answer is B.

Questions 463–470 refer to the passage on page 375.

463. The primary purpose of the passage is to

(A)   advocate a more positive attitude toward technological change

(B)   discuss the implications for employees of the modernization of a telephone exchange

(C)   consider a successful challenge to the constructivist view of technological change

(D)   challenge the position of advocates of technological determinism

(E)   suggest that the social causes of technological change should be studied in real situations

Main Idea

This question asks for an assessment of what the passage as a whole is doing. The passage introduces Clark's study as a *solid contribution* (line 3) to the debate between technological determinists and social constructivists. In the second paragraph, Braverman is introduced as holding a position of social constructivism, a position that Clark takes issue with. In the final paragraph, the passage holds that *Clark refutes the extremes of the constructivists* (line 31), and Clark's arguments challenging social constructivism are then described.

A   The passage takes no position on the merits of technological change but is concerned only with the role of such change in society.

B   The passage mentions telephone exchange workers as an example that helps illustrate the more central debate between determinists and constructivists.

C   **Correct.** The passage is mainly concerned with portraying Clark's view as a successful challenge to constructivism.

D   The passage describes Clark's view as a successful challenge to social constructivism, not technological determinism.

E   The passage is concerned with describing a challenge to social constructivism and not with suggesting the context in which technological change ought to be studied.

The correct answer is C.

464. Which of the following statements about the modernization of the telephone exchange is supported by information in the passage?

(A)   The new technology reduced the role of managers in labor negotiations.

(B)   The modernization was implemented without the consent of the employees directly affected by it.

(C)   The modernization had an impact that went significantly beyond maintenance routines.

(D)   Some of the maintenance workers felt victimized by the new technology.

(E)   The modernization gave credence to the view of advocates of social constructivism.

Supporting Idea

This question requires recognizing information contained in the passage. The passage states in the first paragraph that Clark's study focused on the modernization of a telephone exchange and the effect this had on maintenance work and workers. After describing Braverman's analysis in the second paragraph as being at odds with Clark's views, the passage discusses Clark's views in more detail in the final paragraph. As part of this discussion, the passage notes that Clark shows how a change from *maintenance-intensive electromechanical switches to semielectronic switching systems* at the telephone exchange *altered work tasks, skills, training opportunities, administration, and organization of workers* (lines 42–44). Thus, the passage shows that the modernization of the telephone exchange affected much more than maintenance routines.

A   The passage does not discuss whether new technology reduces the role of managers in labor negotiations.
B   The passage does not discuss the role of employee consent in the modernization of the telephone exchange.
C   **Correct.** The passage states that the modernization of the telephone exchange affected tasks, skills, training, administration, and the organization of workers.
D   The passage does not suggest that maintenance workers felt victimized by the modernization of the telephone exchange.
E   The passage describes modernization as a fact viewable from a perspective of social constructivism or technological determinism, but that does not in itself support either view.

The correct answer is C.

465. Which of the following most accurately describes Clark's opinion of Braverman's position?

(A)   He respects its wide-ranging popularity.
(B)   He disapproves of its misplaced emphasis on the influence of managers.
(C)   He admires the consideration it gives to the attitudes of the workers affected.
(D)   He is concerned about its potential to impede the implementation of new technologies.
(E)   He is sympathetic to its concern about the impact of modern technology on workers.

Inference

Answering this question requires inferring what the passage's author likely believes. The passage describes Braverman's position as one of mainstream social constructivism (lines 23–24), a position that Clark takes issue with. Although it describes Braverman's position, the rest of the passage is devoted to showing how Clark's position takes issue with Braverman's.

In the second paragraph, the passage describes Clark as holding that *technology can be a primary determinant of social and managerial organization* (lines 9–11), which suggests that managers are sometimes subordinate to technological change. In lines 15–17, however, Braverman is described as holding that *the shape of a technological system is subordinate to the manager's desire to wrest control of the labor process from the workers*, which shows that Clark and Braverman are at odds on this point.

A   Since the passage says that Clark believes an important insight *has been obscured by the recent sociological fashion* that Braverman's views exemplify (lines 11–14), one cannot infer that Clark respects the popularity of Braverman's views.
B   **Correct.** The passage shows that Clark believes managers to have less influence over how technology affects an organization than Braverman claims that they have.
C   The passage does not indicate that Clark admires any aspect of Braverman's position.
D   The passage does not indicate that Clark considers impediments to modernization.
E   The passage does not indicate that Clark is sympathetic to any concerns attributed to Braverman.

The correct answer is B.

466. The information in the passage suggests that which of the following statements from hypothetical sociological studies of change in industry most clearly exemplifies the social constructivists' version of technological determinism?

(A)   It is the available technology that determines workers' skills, rather than workers' skills influencing the application of technology.
(B)   All progress in industrial technology grows out of a continuing negotiation between technological possibility and human need.
(C)   Some organizational change is caused by people; some is caused by computer chips.
(D)   Most major technological advances in industry have been generated through research and development.

(E) Some industrial technology eliminates jobs, but educated workers can create whole new skills areas by the adaptation of the technology.

Application

This question requires understanding different points of view discussed in the passage. In the first paragraph, the passage mentions the debate involving technological determinism and social constructivism. In the second and third paragraphs, the passage uses Braverman's analysis to illustrate the social constructivists' position and in the third paragraph suggests that the constructivists are *misrepresenting technological determinism* (line 24). In lines 29–30, the constructivists are reported to hold that technological determinism views technology as *existing outside society, capable of directly influencing skills and work organization.*

A **Correct.** This statement is consistent with the constructivists' view that technological determinism sees technology as outside of society, influencing workers' skills.

B The passage states that the constructivists hold that *technological determinists are supposed to believe . . . that machinery imposes appropriate forms of order on society* (lines 25–27), suggesting that no negotiation is present.

C According to the description of them in the passage, constructivists portray technological determinists as believing that technology, not people, drives organizational change.

D The passage does not portray either constructivists or determinists as being concerned with technological research and development.

E The passage does not portray either constructivists or determinists as being concerned with technology-driven job elimination or creation.

The correct answer is A.

467. The information in the passage suggests that Clark believes that which of the following would be true if social constructivism had not gained widespread acceptance?

(A) Businesses would be more likely to modernize without considering the social consequences of their actions.

(B) There would be greater understanding of the role played by technology in producing social change.

(C) Businesses would be less likely to understand the attitudes of employees affected by modernization.

(D) Modernization would have occurred at a slower rate.

(E) Technology would have played a greater part in determining the role of business in society.

Inference

Answering this question involves understanding a point of view as it is described in the passage. The passage aligns Clark's study closely with the technological determinists, summarizing his view in lines 9–11: *technology can be a primary determinant of social and managerial organization.* In the following sentence, the passage states that Clark believes that *this possibility is obscured by the recent sociological fashion, exemplified by Braverman's analysis* (lines 11–13). After illustrating Braverman's analysis, the passage then states that it represents *social constructivism.*

A According to the passage, Clark holds that constructivists obscure how modernization might have social consequences.

B **Correct.** According to the passage, Clark sees constructivism as obscuring the possibility that technology plays a primary role in social change.

C The passage does not discuss how the attitudes of employees are perceived by their employers.

D The passage describes a debate about the history and sociology of technology; it does not suggest that sociological analyses affect the pace of modernization.

E The passage describes a debate about the history and sociology of technology; it does not suggest that sociological analyses affect the role that technology plays in business.

The correct answer is B.

468. According to the passage, constructivists employed which of the following to promote their argument?

(A) Empirical studies of business situations involving technological change

(B) Citation of managers supportive of their position

(C) Construction of hypothetical situations that support their view

(D) Contrasts of their view with a misstatement of an opposing view

(E) Descriptions of the breadth of impact of technological change

Supporting Idea

Answering this question involves recognizing information given in the passage. The passage indicates that a debate exists between technological determinists and social constructivists, suggesting that these views are in opposition. The passage goes on to state that *constructivists gain acceptance by misrepresenting technological determinism* (lines 23–24). This misrepresentation is presented as the *alternative to constructivism* (lines 27–28), suggesting that constructivists promoted their own view by contrasting it with a misrepresentation of determinists' views.

A   The passage mentions empirical studies in relation to Clark's study but not Braverman's analysis.

B   The passage does not mention that managers were supportive of any particular point of view within the sociology of technology.

C   The passage does not mention any hypothetical situations as being used by the constructivists in support of their view.

D   **Correct.** The passage indicates that the constructivists have come into fashion by contrasting their own views with a misrepresentation of the views of technological determinists.

E   The passage does not describe the constructivists as making determinations regarding the degree of impact that technological change has on social or managerial organization.

The correct answer is D.

469. The author of the passage uses the expression "are supposed to" in line 25 primarily in order to

(A) suggest that a contention made by constructivists regarding determinists is inaccurate

(B) define the generally accepted position of determinists regarding the implementation of technology

(C) engage in speculation about the motivation of determinists

(D) lend support to a comment critical of the position of determinists

(E) contrast the historical position of determinists with their position regarding the exchange modernization

Evaluation

This question requires understanding how a particular phrase functions in the passage as a whole. In the third paragraph the passage states that *constructivists gain acceptance by misrepresenting technological determinism* (lines 23–24) and follows this claim with an example of this misrepresentation, stating that *technological determinists are supposed to believe, for example* (lines 25–26). This line implies that the constructivist view of the determinists is inaccurate.

A   **Correct.** The passage uses the expression in part to provide an example of the constructivists' misrepresentation of the determinists.

B   The passage indicates that the view attributed to the determinists is a misrepresentation, not one that is generally accepted by determinists.

C   The expression in the passage is part of a discussion about the motivation of constructivists, not determinists.

D   The expression in the passage is part of a discussion that is critical of the constructivists, not the determinists.

E   The passage does not describe either the historical position of determinists or their position on the exchange modernization.

The correct answer is A.

470. Which of the following statements about Clark's study of the telephone exchange can be inferred from information in the passage?

(A) Clark's reason for undertaking the study was to undermine Braverman's analysis of the function of technology.

(B) Clark's study suggests that the implementation of technology should be discussed in the context of conflict between labor and management.

(C) Clark examined the impact of changes in the technology of switching at the exchange in terms of overall operations and organization.

(D) Clark concluded that the implementation of new switching technology was equally beneficial to management and labor.

(E) Clark's analysis of the change in switching systems applies only narrowly to the situation at the particular exchange that he studied.

Inference

This question requires understanding what the passage implies in its discussion of a point of view. The details of Clark's views are discussed primarily in the final paragraph. The passage states that on an empirical level, Clark demonstrates that technological change regarding switches at the telephone exchange *altered work tasks, skills, training opportunities, administration, and organization of workers* (lines 42–44). The passage goes on to state Clark's contention that these changes even influenced negotiations between management and labor unions.

A   The passage indicates that Clark's study addressed the extremes of both technological determinism and social constructivism. It cites Braverman as a proponent of social constructivism but provides no evidence that Clark's motivation in beginning his study was specifically to target an analysis offered by Braverman.

B   The passage indicates that Clark attributed some organizational change to the way labor and management negotiated the introduction of technology but does not mention conflict between them.

C   **Correct.** According to the passage, Clark concludes that changes to the technology of switches had an influence on several aspects

of the overall operations and organization of the telephone exchange.

D   The passage does not indicate that Clark assesses the benefits of technological change to either labor or management.

E   The passage indicates that Clark believes the change in switching technology influenced many aspects of the overall operations of the telephone exchange.

The correct answer is C.

Questions 471–475 refer to the passage on page 377.

Main Idea Summary

The central question addressed by the passage is whether, during the period 1794 to 1830, judges in the United States were prejudiced against patent holders. After a brief introduction to the history of patents, the author presents some purported evidence that the courts during this period had an antipatent bias. The passage then presents some considerations that weigh against such a conclusion. The main idea of the passage, implied in the chain of reasoning in the second paragraph but not explicitly stated, is that the pattern of judgments against patentees during the period in question was probably due to the fact that many patents had been awarded without merit rather than to an antipatent bias of the judges.

471. The passage implies that which of the following was a reason that the proportion of verdicts in favor of patentees began to increase in the 1830s ?

(A) Patent applications approved after 1836 were more likely to adhere closely to patent law.

(B) Patent laws enacted during the 1830s better defined patent rights.

(C) Judges became less prejudiced against patentees during the 1830s.

(D) After 1836, litigated cases became less representative of the population of patent disputes.

(E) The proportion of patent disputes brought to trial began to increase after 1836.

Inference

The question asks which statement can be reasonably inferred, from information provided in the passage, to be a reason for the increase in proportion of verdicts favoring patentees, starting in the 1830s. The second paragraph argues that what changed in that decade was not judges' attitudes toward patent law, but the types of patent cases that were litigated. It explains that a law passed in 1836 required that, for the first time in U.S. history, applications for patents had to be examined for their adherence to patent law before a patent would be issued. This information implies that patents granted after 1836 were more likely to adhere to patent law and were thus more likely to be upheld in court.

A **Correct.** The passage implies that patents granted after the 1836 law went into effect were more likely to adhere to patent law.

B The passage does not indicate that any law mentioned made changes to the definition of patent rights; rather, the passage indicates that the patent system was revised to require that patent applications be reviewed for adherence to existing law.

C The passage rejects the explanation that judges' attitudes toward patent rights became more favorable.

D The passage indicates that the population of disputes that were litigated changed after 1836, but it does not suggest that the population of litigated disputes differed from that of patent disputes as a whole.

E The passage does not indicate any change in the proportion of patent disputes brought to trial.

The correct answer is A.

472. The passage implies that the scholars mentioned in line 8 would agree with which of the following criticisms of the American patent system before 1830?

(A) Its definition of property rights relating to inventions was too vague to be useful.

(B) Its criteria for the granting of patents were not clear.

(C) It made it excessively difficult for inventors to receive patents.

(D) It led to excessive numbers of patent-infringement suits.

(E) It failed to encourage national economic growth.

Inference

This question asks about a statement implied by the passage. The scholars mentioned in line 8 question whether U.S. patent law achieved its goal. That goal is described in the first sentence of the passage: to encourage America's economic growth. Thus, it is reasonable to conclude that the scholars would criticize the pre-1830 patent system for failing to encourage economic growth.

A The scholars contend that judges rejected patents for arbitrary reasons, not because the definition of property rights was vague.

B The passage does not indicate that the scholars were critical of the criteria for granting patents.

C The scholars are concerned with inventors' attempts to protect their patents, not the difficulty of acquiring a patent in the first place.

D The passage does not imply that the scholars in question believed that too many patent-infringement suits were brought to court, but rather that too few succeeded.

E **Correct.** The scholars doubt that patent law helped to achieve its goal, which was to encourage economic growth.

The correct answer is E.

473. It can be inferred from the passage that the frequency with which pre-1830 cases have been cited in court decisions is an indication that

(A) judicial support for patent rights was strongest in the period before 1830

(B) judicial support for patent rights did not increase after 1830

(C) courts have returned to judicial standards that prevailed before 1830

(D) verdicts favoring patentees in patent-infringement suits did not increase after 1830

(E) judicial bias against patentees persisted after 1830

Inference

The question asks what is indicated by the frequency with which pre-1830 cases have been cited in court decisions. The second paragraph rejects some scholars' claims that judges prior to the 1830s were *antipatent*, while judges after that time were more accepting of patent rights. The passage supports its critique by pointing out that decisions made by judges before the 1830s have been cited as precedents by later judges just as frequently as post-1830s decisions have been. This implies that later judges' attitudes toward patent rights were similar to those of pre-1830s judges. Thus, there is no reason to believe judges' attitudes toward patent rights changed at that time.

A   The passage argues that judicial support for patents did not change in the 1830s.

B   Correct. Pre-1830s court decisions have been cited as frequently as later decisions, suggesting no change in judges' attitudes.

C   The passage does not indicate that judicial standards changed from, and then returned to, those that prevailed before 1830.

D   Although actual numbers of favorable verdicts are not mentioned, the passage indicates that the proportion of verdicts decided in favor of patentees did, in fact, increase beginning in the 1830s.

E   The passage rejects the notion that judges were biased against patentees either before or after 1830.

The correct answer is B.

474. It can be inferred from the passage that the author and the scholars referred to in line 21 disagree about which of the following aspects of the patents defended in patent-infringement suits before 1830?

(A)   Whether the patents were granted for inventions that were genuinely useful

(B)   Whether the patents were actually relevant to the growth of the United States economy

(C)   Whether the patents were particularly likely to be annulled by judges

(D)   Whether the patents were routinely invalidated for reasons that were arbitrary

(E)   Whether the patents were vindicated at a significantly lower rate than patents in later suits

Inference

The question depends on recognizing differences between two explanations—one favored by the scholars mentioned in line 21, the other favored by the author—for the frequency with which patents were invalidated in U.S. courts prior to 1830. The first paragraph describes the scholars' view that judges before 1830 were *antipatent* and rejected patentees' claims for *arbitrary reasons*. The author of the passage rejects that view. As an alternate explanation, the author in the second paragraph implies that earlier patents often violated copyright law; this view is supported with reference to an 1836 revision to the patent system which instituted a procedure by which patent applications were inspected to ensure adherence to patent law.

A   The author and the scholars are both focused on protecting inventors' property rights, not with their inventions' utility.

B   Although the passage suggests that the scholars thought America's patent system did not help encourage economic growth, there is no suggestion that either the scholars or the author believes actual patents defended in court were irrelevant to economic growth.

C   Both the scholars and the author believe that patents defended in court prior to 1830 were more likely to be invalidated than were patents in later legal disputes.

D   Correct. The scholars claim that judges before 1830 decided against patentees for arbitrary reasons, but the passage suggests that the patents may have been invalidated because they failed to adhere to patent law.

E   Both the scholars and the author accept that patents were upheld in court less often before 1830 than after.

The correct answer is D.

475. The author of the passage cites which of the following as evidence challenging the argument referred to in lines 14–15 ?

(A)   The proportion of cases that were decided against patentees in the 1820s

(B)   The total number of patent disputes that were litigated from 1794 to 1830

(C)   The fact that later courts drew upon the legal precedents set in pre-1830 patent cases

(D) The fact that the proportion of judicial decisions in favor of patentees began to increase during the 1830s

(E) The constitutional rationale for the 1836 revision of the patent system

Supporting Idea

The question asks what evidence the author brings to bear against the argument referred to in lines 14–15. In the first paragraph, the author summarizes scholars' arguments to the conclusion that judges' attitudes toward patent rights shifted in the 1830s, based on the fact that judges earlier had routinely ruled against patentees in lawsuits whereas judges after that time provided more protection for patent rights. In the second paragraph the author challenges the claim that judges' attitudes shifted. The author provides evidence that judges after the 1830s cited legal precedents set in pre-1830s cases, suggesting that their views had not changed.

A   The proportion of cases decided against patentees in the 1920s is cited as evidence that supports the scholars' argument in the first paragraph, not as evidence challenging their views.

B   The total number of disputes litigated is not mentioned in the passage.

C   Correct. The fact that judges after 1830 cited earlier cases as precedents is used as evidence to challenge scholars' claims that judges' attitudes shifted around 1830.

D   The change in the proportion of decisions in favor of patentees is a fact that both the scholars and the author of the passage attempt to explain.

E   No constitutional rationale for the 1836 law is mentioned in the passage.

The correct answer is C.

Questions 476–482 refer to the passage on page 379.

Main Idea Summary

The passage is primarily concerned with surveying various views of the social standing of European women during the Renaissance. The first paragraph discusses Jacob Burckhardt's view that the Renaissance was a period in which women had equality with men; Joan Kelly's contrary view that the Renaissance was a period in which women's status relative both to men and to medieval women was in decline; and a more complex view, held by various feminist scholars, who suggest that Burckhardt and Kelly each drew too heavily on observations of upper-class Italian women. The second paragraph warns of the risks of conflating "women" and "women writers" in studying the status of Renaissance women, but, despite such a caveat regarding Tina Krontiris's research, praises her contributions to the field. The author sees her as representative of a cautiously optimistic assessment of Renaissance women's achievements while stressing the social obstacles Renaissance women faced and the caution they exercised when opposing cultural stereotypes.

476. The author of the passage discusses Krontiris primarily to provide an example of a writer who

(A) is highly critical of the writings of certain Renaissance women

(B) supports Kelly's view of women's status during the Renaissance

(C) has misinterpreted the works of certain Renaissance women

(D) has rejected the views of both Burckhardt and Kelly

(E) has studied Renaissance women in a wide variety of social and religious contexts

Evaluation

This question focuses on the author's reason for mentioning Krontiris's work. The passage states that Krontiris, in her discussion of six Renaissance women writers, is an example of scholars who are optimistic about women's achievements but also suggest that these women faced significant obstacles. She is a writer who, in other words, agrees with neither Kelly's negative views nor Burckhardt's positive approach.

A   The passage indicates that Krontiris uses the Renaissance women writers' works as historical evidence, not that she offered any criticism of the works themselves.

B   Krontiris's work, according to the author, is cautiously optimistic about women's achievements during the Renaissance. This contradicts Kelly's view that the status of women declined during this time.

C   The author suggests that Krontiris may have erred in taking her six subjects as representative of all women during the Renaissance, not that she made any misinterpretations of their actual writing.

D   Correct. The author uses Krontiris as an example of those feminist scholars who have rejected the overgeneralized approaches of both Kelly and Burckhardt.

E   The author makes clear that Krontiris's study focuses on literate Renaissance women, who constituted a small minority.

The correct answer is D.

477. According to the passage, Krontiris's work differs from that of the scholars mentioned in line 12 in which of the following ways?

(A)   Krontiris's work stresses the achievements of Renaissance women rather than the obstacles to their success.

(B)   Krontiris's work is based on a reinterpretation of the work of earlier scholars.

(C)   Krontiris's views are at odds with those of both Kelly and Burkhardt.

(D)   Krontiris's work focuses on the place of women in Renaissance society.

(E)   Krontiris's views are based exclusively on the study of a privileged group of women.

Supporting Idea

This question asks what the passage directly states about the difference between Krontiris's work and the feminist scholars mentioned in the first paragraph. The feminist scholars mentioned in the first paragraph explore differences among Renaissance women, particularly their social status and religion, and thus complicate Burckhardt's and Kelly's generalizations. Krontiris's work, on the other hand, focuses on Renaissance women writers, who are a distinctly privileged and small social group.

A   The second paragraph makes clear that Krontiris addresses the obstacles faced by Renaissance women.

B   The passage does not suggest that Krontiris is reinterpreting or drawing on reinterpretations of the work of earlier scholars.

C   The second paragraph shows that Krontiris's work does complicate both Burckhardt's and Kelly's views, but in this, she is in agreement with the feminist scholars mentioned in the first paragraph.

D   Both Krontiris and the feminist scholars mentioned in the first paragraph are concerned with the place of women in Renaissance society.

E   Correct. The feminist scholars mentioned in the first paragraph are concerned with women of different social classes and religions, whereas Krontiris's work focuses on a limited social group.

The correct answer is E.

478. According to the passage, feminist scholars cite Burckhardt's view of Renaissance women primarily for which of the following reasons?

(A)   Burckhardt's view forms the basis for most arguments refuting Kelly's point of view.

(B)   Burckhardt's view has been discredited by Kelly.

(C)   Burckhardt's view is one that many feminist scholars wish to refute.

(D)   Burckhardt's work provides rich historical evidence of inequality between Renaissance women and men.

(E)   Burckhardt's work includes historical research supporting the arguments of the feminist scholars.

Supporting Idea

This question asks what the passage says explicitly about why feminist scholars reference Burckhardt's view of Renaissance women. The first paragraph states that Burckhardt's view is that Renaissance women enjoyed *perfect equality* with men, and then follows that by noting how feminist scholars have *repeatedly cited* this view to contrast it with extensive evidence of women's inequality during the Renaissance.

A   The passage does not indicate that any feminist scholars cite Burckhardt to refute Kelly's view. It uses Krontiris as an example of scholars who refute Kelly's point of view to a certain degree, but Krontiris does not use Burckhardt's view as her basis for doing so; Krontiris argues against Burckhardt as well.

B   According to the first paragraph, Kelly's work was in certain ways inconsistent with Burckhardt's view, but that is not a reason why Burckhardt's view is cited by feminist scholars. Rather, according to the passage, they cite it in order to argue against it.

C   **Correct.** Many feminist scholars wish to refute Burckhardt's view that Renaissance women and men were equal.

D   As the first paragraph makes clear, Burckhardt's work emphasizes equality, not inequality, between Renaissance women and men.

E   The passage does not discuss the historical research on which Burckhardt based his work.

The correct answer is C.

479. It can be inferred that both Burckhardt and Kelly have been criticized by the scholars mentioned in line 12 for which of the following?

(A)   Assuming that women writers of the Renaissance are representative of Renaissance women in general

(B)   Drawing conclusions that are based on the study of an atypical group of women

(C)   Failing to describe clearly the relationship between social status and literacy among Renaissance women

(D)   Failing to acknowledge the role played by Renaissance women in opposing cultural stereotypes

(E)   Failing to acknowledge the ways in which social status affected the creative activities of Renaissance women

Inference

Line 12 refers to feminist scholars who have rejected both Kelly's and Burckhardt's views of the status of Renaissance women. The next sentence states that the feminist scholars use class and religious differences among Renaissance women to argue against Kelly's and Burckhardt's generalizations, which were based on upper-class Italian women.

A   The second paragraph suggests that Krontiris at times conflates Renaissance women writers and women in general, but the passage does not indicate that the feminist scholars believe this of Kelly or Burckhardt.

B   **Correct.** The feminist scholars mentioned study different types of Renaissance women and so reject Kelly's and Burckhardt's conclusions that were based on a group that was not in fact typical.

C   Krontiris, not Kelly and Burckhardt, is the scholar who, according to the passage, fails to address the relationship between literacy and social status.

D   The passage provides no grounds for determining whether Kelly, Burckhardt, or the feminist scholars mentioned in the first paragraph dealt with Renaissance women's opposition to cultural stereotypes; Krontiris's work is concerned with this question.

E   The first paragraph suggests that feminist scholars criticized Kelly and Burckhardt for failing to acknowledge the ways in which social status complicates any generalizations that can be made about Renaissance women's lives, not their creative activities specifically.

The correct answer is B.

480. The author of the passage suggests that Krontiris incorrectly assumes that

(A)   social differences among Renaissance women are less important than the fact that they were women

(B)   literacy among Renaissance women was more prevalent than most scholars today acknowledge

(C)   during the Renaissance, women were able to successfully oppose cultural stereotypes relating to gender

(D)   Renaissance women did not face many difficult social obstacles relating to their gender

(E)   in order to attain power, Renaissance women attacked basic assumptions in the ideologies that oppressed them

Inference

The first statement the author makes about Krontiris, in the second paragraph, concerns what the author characterizes as a problem with Krontiris's work. Krontiris takes the Renaissance women writers she studies as representative of all Renaissance women; the author says that designating *women* as the most important grouping fails to consider whether other social differences might make for differences in experience.

A **Correct.** The author indicates that Krontiris's error lies in assuming that women's identity as women trumps social and other differences.

B The author does not suggest that Krontiris assumes inappropriate literacy levels among Renaissance women, but rather that Krontiris does not give sufficient consideration to the idea that women who could read and write most likely led lives very different from those of women who could not read and write.

C The author says that Krontiris suggests that there were many cultural stereotypes that women were not able to oppose effectively.

D Krontiris, according to the author, acknowledges the many social obstacles faced by women on the basis of their gender.

E According to the author, Krontiris's concluding remarks suggest that Renaissance women *seldom attacked the basic assumptions in the ideologies that oppressed them.*

The correct answer is A.

481. The last sentence in the passage serves primarily to

(A) suggest that Krontiris's work is not representative of recent trends among feminist scholars

(B) undermine the argument that literate women of the Renaissance sought to oppose social constraints imposed on them

(C) show a way in which Krontiris's work illustrates a "cautiously optimistic" assessment of Renaissance women's achievements

(D) summarize Krontiris's view of the effect of literacy on the lives of upper- and middle-class Renaissance women

(E) illustrate the way in which Krontiris's study differs from the studies done by Burckhardt and Kelly

Evaluation

The function of the final sentence of the passage is to indicate how Krontiris's work takes neither a completely positive nor completely negative view of Renaissance women's experiences—i.e., how her work is representative of those authors who are cautiously optimistic about the achievements of Renaissance women.

A The passage discusses Krontiris's work as an example of the trend described in the latter part of the first paragraph and mentioned in the first line of the second paragraph. The last sentence in the passage shows that Krontiris's work is in fact representative of recent trends among feminist scholars.

B The last sentence in the passage states that Renaissance women's opposition to cultural stereotypes was circumscribed, but it also suggests that these women did gain some power for themselves. Thus, the sentence does not serve primarily to undermine the argument that the women sought to oppose social constraints.

C **Correct.** Krontiris's work illustrates the "cautiously optimistic" view by embracing both the idea that Renaissance women could gain a certain amount of power and the idea that the extent of their opposition was limited.

D The last sentence in the passage summarizes Krontiris's view, but that view does not, according to the passage, take into account the effect of literacy on the members of a particular social class.

E The main function of the final sentence of the passage is to take up the idea of the *cautiously optimistic* assessment offered in the penultimate sentence. This does mark a significant departure from both Burckhardt and Kelly, but the distinction between their work and that of other feminist scholars is marked more clearly earlier in the passage.

The correct answer is C.

482. The author of the passage implies that the women studied by Krontiris are unusual in which of the following ways?

    (A) They faced obstacles less formidable than those faced by other Renaissance women.

    (B) They have been seen by historians as more interesting than other Renaissance women.

    (C) They were more concerned about recording history accurately than were other Renaissance women.

    (D) Their perceptions are more likely to be accessible to historians than are those of most other Renaissance women.

    (E) Their concerns are likely to be of greater interest to feminist scholars than are the ideas of most other Renaissance women.

Inference

The women Krontiris studied are unusual, the author suggests, because they were literate, thus putting them among the minority of Renaissance women. That they could write, however, means that their written reflections are part of the historical record, whereas the direct impressions of experiences had by Renaissance women who could not write about their lives are lost to history.

A The author implies that the obstacles faced by Krontiris's subjects may have been different from those faced by other women, not that they were less formidable.

B The author does not imply that the women studied by Krontiris are seen as more interesting; rather, the author indicates that their work is that which is available for study.

C The women Krontiris studies were able to record their own history because they, unlike most other Renaissance women, were literate. This does not imply that they were more concerned with recording history accurately.

D **Correct.** Because Krontiris's subjects were literate, they were able to write down, and thus preserve for historians, their perceptions in a way that most other Renaissance women were not.

E The author does not suggest that feminist scholars in general are more interested in the concerns of middle- and upper-class literate women than they are with women of other classes.

The correct answer is D.

Questions 483–486 refer to the passage on page 381.

Main Idea Summary

The main idea of the passage is that observations of asteroid collisions and computer simulations of such collisions indicate that most observed asteroids are loose collections of rocks and only small asteroids are individual, solid rocks. The passage begins by describing how, in theory, one could determine the structure of asteroids by observing the rates at which they spin after collisions. The passage then reports that, using this method, scientists have found that most observed asteroids spin in ways that are inconsistent with their being solid rocks. The second paragraph indicates that the conclusions are supported by computer modeling and then presents a causal explanation for the observed phenomena.

483. The passage implies which of the following about the five asteroids mentioned in line 12 ?

    (A) Their rotation rates are approximately the same.

    (B) They have undergone approximately the same number of collisions.

    (C) They are monoliths.

    (D) They are composed of fragments that have escaped the gravity of larger asteroids.

    (E) They were detected only recently.

Inference

In line 12, *five observed asteroids*, refers to the five asteroids whose rotation rates are exceptions to the strict limit on the rate of rotation found in all other observed asteroids. These five asteroids all have diameters smaller than 200 meters. The passage indicates that if asteroids were all monoliths—that is, single rocks—then their rotation rates would form a bell curve when graphed, but if asteroids were piles of rubble, the tail of the bell curve indicating very fast rotation rates would be missing. Among asteroids larger than 200 meters, this tail is missing, and only the five asteroids described as exceptions have rotation rates falling at the very high end of the bell curve.

A   All that the passage states about the rotation rates of these five asteroids is that they do not obey a strict limit. The passage does not rule out that their rates of rotation are significantly different from one another.

B   According to the passage, frequent collisions occur among asteroids. But the passage does not suggest that asteroids that are of similar sizes, or that have particularly high rotation rates, will be similar in terms of the number of collisions that they have undergone to reach those distinctive states.

C   **Correct.** The second paragraph states that *most small asteroids* should be monolithic, and the five observed asteroids are all smaller than 200 meters in diameter.

D   The five asteroids are most likely not composed of fragments because, as the passage states, small asteroids should be monoliths.

E   The passage notes that researchers have observed these five asteroids, along with others, but it does not indicate when these asteroids were originally detected.

The correct answer is C.

484. The discovery of which of the following would call into question the conclusion mentioned in line 16 ?

(A)   An asteroid 100 meters in diameter rotating at a rate of once per week

(B)   An asteroid 150 meters in diameter rotating at a rate of 20 times per hour

(C)   An asteroid 250 meters in diameter rotating at a rate of once per week

(D)   An asteroid 500 meters in diameter rotating at a rate of once per hour

(E)   An asteroid 1,000 meters in diameter rotating at a rate of once every 24 hours

Application

The conclusion that the text in line 16 points to is that asteroids with diameters greater than 200 meters are *multicomponent structures or rubble piles*. To call that conclusion into question, an observation would have to suggest that asteroids larger than 200 meters across are not such multicomponent structures. According to the first paragraph, rubble piles cannot be fast rotators: spinning faster than once every few hours would make them fly apart.

A   Nothing in the passage suggests that the behavior of an asteroid 100 meters in diameter is relevant to a conclusion about the behavior of asteroids greater than 200 meters in diameter.

B   Nothing in the passage suggests that the behavior of an asteroid 150 meters in diameter would have any effect on a conclusion about the constitution of asteroids with diameters greater than 200 meters.

C   An asteroid 250 meters in diameter rotating at a rate of once per week would be rotating at a slow enough rate to hold together a pile of rubble. Thus, this observation would be entirely consistent with the conclusion about asteroids larger than 200 meters in diameter.

D   **Correct.** Assuming that an asteroid composed of a pile of rubble is of a great enough density, a rotation rate greater than one revolution every few hours would make it fly apart. So a 500-meter asteroid rotating at a rate of once per hour—that is, faster than the crucial speed—would fly apart if it were not a monolith. The conclusion states that all asteroids larger than 200 meters are multicomponent structures (that is, are not monoliths), so the discovery of a 500-meter asteroid rotating at a rate of once an hour would call into question that conclusion.

E   An asteroid rotating at a rate of once every 24 hours would, regardless of size, be rotating much more slowly than the *once every few hours* that the passage claims would make a pile of rubble of a sufficient density fly apart. So an asteroid with a diameter of 1,000 meters that rotated once per day could be a pile of rubble and not conflict with the conclusion.

The correct answer is D.

485. According to the passage, which of the following is a prediction that is based on the strength of the gravitational attraction of small asteroids?

(A) Small asteroids will be few in number.

(B) Small asteroids will be monoliths.

(C) Small asteroids will collide with other asteroids very rarely.

(D) Most small asteroids will have very fast rotation rates.

(E) Almost no small asteroids will have very slow rotation rates.

Supporting Idea

Regarding small asteroids, the second paragraph states that they have feeble gravity. Any fragments from impacts would escape that gravity, and thus, the passage states, the small asteroids *should be monolithic*.

A   Small asteroids could be few in number, but the passage does not offer such a prediction.

B   Correct. This prediction is offered in the second paragraph, based on the fact that small asteroids do not have strong gravitational attraction. Any impact fragments will easily escape the weak gravitational attraction of the small asteroids.

C   The passage discusses large asteroids collisions in more detail than small-asteroid collisions, but it provides no basis for predicting how often large and small asteroids will, comparatively, be involved in such collisions.

D   The first paragraph indicates that the rotation rates of small asteroids can exceed the upper limit on the rotation rates of large asteroids, but it does not indicate that most small asteroids have rotation rates that exceed this upper limit.

E   The passage only indicates that there are few observed exceptions to the upper limit on rotation rates of large asteroids, and these exceptions are all smaller than 200 meters in diameter; the passage does not indicate that there are few small asteroids that have very slow rotation rates.

The correct answer is B.

486. The author of the passage mentions "escape velocity" (see line 22) in order to help explain which of the following?

(A) The tendency for asteroids to become smaller rather than larger over time

(B) The speed with which impact fragments reassemble when they do not escape an asteroid's gravitational attraction after a collision

(C) The frequency with which collisions among asteroids occur

(D) The rotation rates of asteroids smaller than 200 meters in diameter

(E) The tendency for large asteroids to persist after collisions

Evaluation

This question asks about the purpose of the author's use of the phrase *escape velocity* in the second paragraph. The author is discussing what occurs after an asteroid collision, in which a large asteroid might be blasted to bits. The bits, according to the author, will move slower than their *mutual escape velocity*—that is, the speed at which they would have to move to get away from each other and not reassemble, under the influence of gravity, into a rubble pile.

A   The author is emphasizing the asteroid bits that do not escape rather than those that do. Asteroids may become smaller over time, but the fact that most bits move slower than their escape velocity would not help to explain this shrinkage.

B   That the bits of asteroid move slower than their escape velocity helps explain why the fragments reassemble, but it does not help explain the speed with which they reassemble.

C   According to the author, asteroid collisions occur frequently, but the escape velocity of the resulting fragments does not help to explain that frequency.

D   The concept of escape velocity may help explain why small asteroids are monoliths, but it has no relevance, at least as far as the passage indicates, to those asteroids' rotation rates.

E   **Correct.** After a collision, it is the asteroid fragments' failure to reach escape velocity that allows the fragments' gravitational pull to reassemble them into a rubble pile.

The correct answer is E.

Questions 487–489 refer to the passage on page 383.

Main Idea Summary

The primary purpose of the passage is to discuss the theory underlying attempts to get particles to travel faster than the speed of light by means of quantum tunneling. The passage states that quantum theory implies that there is a small probability that a particle can tunnel through a solid barrier. The time it takes a particle to tunnel through a barrier increases as the thickness of the barrier increases, but only up to a maximum amount of time; beyond that maximum, the amount of time does not vary no matter the thickness of the barrier. This implies that, given a certain thickness, the particle will exceed the speed of light, and this has received some empirical support.

487. The author of the passage mentions calculations about tunneling time and barrier thickness in order to

(A)   suggest that tunneling time is unrelated to barrier thickness

(B)   explain the evidence by which Wigner and Eisenbud discovered the phenomenon of tunneling

(C)   describe data recently challenged by Raymond Chiao and colleagues

(D)   question why particles engaged in quantum tunneling rarely achieve extremely high speeds

(E)   explain the basis for Wigner and Eisenbud's hypothesis

Evaluation

This question asks why the author discusses calculations about tunneling time and barrier thickness. According to the passage, these calculations provided the grounds for Wigner and Eisenbud's hypothesis that tunneling particles may travel faster than light.

A   The passage states that tunneling time is related to barrier thickness, up to the point at which tunneling time reaches a maximum.

B   The passage indicates that the phenomenon of tunneling was noted at least as early as 1932. It provides no evidence that Wigner and Eisenbud discovered it.

C   The passage uses Chiao's work to support the idea that tunneling particles may move faster than light, not challenge it.

D   The author describes calculations about tunneling time and barrier thickness in order to explain that particles engaged in quantum tunneling may in fact achieve extremely high speeds, not to explain the rarity of the phenomenon.

E   **Correct.** The calculations about tunneling time and barrier thickness supported Wigner and Eisenbud's hypothesis that quantum tunneling could occur at speeds faster than that of light.

The correct answer is E.

488. The passage implies that if tunneling time reached no maximum in increasing with barrier thickness, then

(A)   tunneling speed would increase with barrier thickness

(B)   tunneling speed would decline with barrier thickness

(C)   tunneling speed would vary with barrier thickness

(D)   tunneling speed would not be expected to increase without limit

(E)   successful tunneling would occur even less frequently than it does

Inference

The passage states that because tunneling time reaches a maximum, then tunneling speed must increase as barrier thickness increases. But if tunneling time did not reach such a maximum, then speed need not increase without limit; the particle could have as low a speed in thicker barriers as in thinner ones and take longer to tunnel through a barrier.

A   If tunneling time could not reach a maximum, then speed might increase, decrease, or remain the same as barrier thickness increases.

B   If tunneling time could not reach a maximum, then speed might increase, decrease, or remain the same as barrier thickness increases.

C   Tunneling speed could vary with barrier thickness if tunneling time could not reach a maximum, but there is no basis in the passage on which to conclude that this is definitely so.

D   Correct. The tunneling particle could have as low a speed in thicker barriers as in thinner ones and simply take longer to make its way through a thicker barrier.

E   The passage states that the probability of successful tunneling declines as the thickness of the barrier increases. However, it does not address the issue of whether the differences in probability of successful tunneling are due to the greater time required to go through thicker barriers.

The correct answer is D.

489. Which of the following statements about the earliest scientific investigators of quantum tunneling can be inferred from the passage?

(A)   They found it difficult to increase barrier thickness continually.

(B)   They anticipated the later results of Chiao and his colleagues.

(C)   They did not suppose that tunneling particles could travel faster than light.

(D)   They were unable to observe instances of successful tunneling.

(E)   They made use of photons to study the phenomenon of tunneling.

Inference

This question asks about the earliest investigators of quantum tunneling. The passage notes that quantum tunneling's *extreme rapidity* was observed in 1932; thus, the earliest investigators of this phenomenon knew of its existence at that time. Not until 1955 did Wigner and Eisenbud hypothesize that the particles traveled faster than light. Thus, it is logical to infer that the earliest investigators did not imagine such a speed.

A   There is nothing in the passage to suggest that the earliest investigators of quantum tunneling had difficulty manipulating barrier thickness.

B   The passage states that Chiao and his colleagues measured photons moving at 1.7 times the speed of light—but the passage does not provide evidence that the earliest investigators anticipated such speeds.

C   **Correct.** The passage suggests that prior to 1955, investigators of quantum tunneling had not hypothesized that the particles could travel faster than the speed of light.

D   The passage indicates that by 1932, investigators had noted the rapidity of quantum tunneling; although this does not entail that they observed the phenomenon, it is consistent with their having been able to do so.

E   The passage indicates that Chiao's work involves photons, but it does not indicate the type of particles used or observed by the earliest investigators of the phenomenon.

The correct answer is C.

To register for the GMAT™ exam go to www.mba.com/register

8.8 Practice Questions: Critical Reasoning

Each of the Critical Reasoning questions is based on a short argument, a set of statements, or a plan of action. For each question, select the best answer of the choices given.

490. Arts advocate: Few universities require that students who are specializing in science and technology take many art courses. However, real progress in science and technology requires an element of creativity, which the arts foster. Thus, to help science and technology students succeed in their careers, universities should increase the number of art courses required for them.

Which of the following would, if true, most strengthen the argument above?

(A) Universities required more art courses for science and technology students in the past.

(B) Participation in art courses increases students' creative thinking in their science and technology courses.

(C) More students who are interested in art would specialize in science and technology if the number of art courses required for those programs were increased.

(D) Some of the most prominent scientists began their careers as artists.

(E) Discussion of science and technology topics in art courses increases creative thinking among students in those courses.

491. Ramirez: The film industry claims that pirated DVDs, which are usually cheaper than legitimate DVDs and become available well before a film's official DVD release date, adversely affect its bottom line. But the industry should note what the spread of piracy indicates: consumers want lower prices and faster DVD releases. Lowering prices of DVDs and releasing them sooner would mitigate piracy's negative effect on film industry profits.

The argument above relies on which of the following assumptions?

(A) Releasing legitimate DVDs earlier would not cause any reduction in the revenue the film industry receives from the films' theatrical release.

(B) Some people who would otherwise purchase pirated DVDs would be willing to purchase legitimate DVDs if they were less expensive and released earlier than they are now.

(C) The film industry will in the future be able to produce DVDs more cheaply than is currently the case.

(D) Some current sellers of pirated DVDs would likely discontinue their businesses if legitimate DVDs were released faster and priced lower.

(E) Current purchasers of pirated DVDs are aware that those DVDs are not authorized by the film industry.

492. Harunia Province has a relatively dry climate and is attracting a fast-growing population that has put increasing demands on its water supply. The two companies that supply water to the region have struggled to keep up with demand and still remain profitable. Yet now they are asking Harunian authorities to write residential water-use regulations that could reduce their revenues and restrict their future flexibility in supplying water profitably.

Which of the following would, if true, most logically help explain why the water-supply companies are asking the authorities to regulate residential water use?

(A) The companies are planning large water-transportation and irrigation systems that require the approval of neighboring provinces.

(B) The companies believe regulation is inevitable and that having it in place now will allow better planning and thus future profitability.

(C) Few, if any, Harunian government officials have investments in the companies or serve on their boards of directors.

(D) The companies believe that the population is not likely to continue to grow.

(E) Long-term climate projections suggest that greater rainfall will eventually increase the amount of water available.

493. Loss of the Gocha mangrove forests has caused coastal erosion, reducing fish populations and requiring the Gocha Fishing Cooperative (GFC) to partially fund dredging and new shore facilities. However, as part of its subsidiary businesses, the GFC has now invested in a program to replant significant parts of the coast with mangrove trees. Given income from a controlled harvest of wood with continuing replanting, the mangrove regeneration effort makes it more likely that the cooperative will increase its net income.

Which of the following, if true, would most strengthen the argument that mangrove replanting will increase the Gocha cooperative's net income?

(A) The cost of dredging and shore facilities was shared with the local government.

(B) The GFC will be able to hire local workers to assist with the mangrove replanting.

(C) The GFC derives 10 percent of its revenue from salt-production facilities in an area previously cleared of mangroves.

(D) Mangrove forests tend to increase the commercial fish populations in coastal fishing grounds.

(E) A controlled harvesting of mangrove wood by the GFC would have little effect on coastal erosion.

494. Executives at the Fizzles Beverage Company plan to boost profits in Country X on their range of fruit-flavored drinks by introducing new flavors based on tropical fruits that are little known there. The executives reason that since the fruit drinks of other companies have none of these flavors, Fizzles will not have to compete for customers and thus will be able to sell the drinks at a higher price.

Which of the following, if true, presents the most serious potential weakness of the plan?

(A) The new fruit drinks would be priced significantly higher than other Fizzles fruit drinks with more conventional flavors.

(B) In a telephone survey, at least one of the consumers contacted said that they preferred many of the new flavors to all of the more familiar flavors.

(C) To build widespread demand for the new flavors, Fizzles would have to launch an advertising campaign to familiarize consumers with them.

(D) Consumers choosing among fruit-flavored drinks of different brands generally buy on the basis of name recognition and price rather than the specific fruit flavor.

(E) Few consumers who are loyal to a specific brand of fruit-flavored drinks would willingly switch to another brand that costs more.

495. Economist: In 2015, the average per-person amount paid for goods and services purchased by consumers in Country X was the equivalent of $17,570 in United States dollars, just 30 percent of the corresponding figure of $58,566 for Country Y. Yet in 2015, there was already a substantial middle class in Country X that had discretionary income for middle-class consumer goods such as new vehicles, computers, or major household appliances, while a significant portion of the middle class in Country Y did not have sufficient income to purchase such items.

Which of the following, if true, most helps explain the discrepancy in the relationships described by the economist?

(A) There are many consumer goods, such as household appliances, that are produced in Country X to be sold in the Country Y market.

(B) The volume of trade between Country X and Country Y is increasing rapidly in both directions.

(C) The economy of Country Y is recovering from a downturn that affected both Country Y and Country X.

(D) Country X residents pay much less than their Country Y counterparts for housing, transportation, and child care.

(E) In Country Y as well as in Country X, there are few assembly-line jobs in factories that pay a middle-class wage.

496. Neuroscientist: Memory evolved to help animals react appropriately to situations they encounter by drawing on the past experience of similar situations. But this does not require that animals perfectly recall every detail of all their experiences. Instead, to function well, memory should generalize from past experiences that are similar to the current one.

The neuroscientist's statements, if true, most strongly support which of the following conclusions?

(A) At least some animals perfectly recall every detail of at least some past experiences.

(B) Perfectly recalling every detail of all their past experiences could help at least some animals react more appropriately than they otherwise would to new situations they encounter.

(C) Generalizing from past experiences requires clear memories of most if not all the details of those experiences.

(D) Recalling every detail of all past experiences would be incompatible with any ability to generalize from those experiences.

(E) Animals can often react more appropriately than they otherwise would to situations they encounter if they draw on generalizations from past experiences of similar situations.

497. In Country X's last election, the Reform Party beat its main opponent, the Conservative Party, although pollsters, employing in-person interviews shortly before the vote, had projected a Conservative Party victory. Afterwards, the pollsters determined that, unlike Conservative Party supporters, Reform Party supporters were less likely to express their party preference during in-person interviews than they were during telephone interviews. Therefore, using only telephone interviews instead would likely result in more accurate projections for the next election.

Which of the following statements, if true, would most support the argument in the passage?

(A) The number of voters in Country X's next election will be significantly larger than the number of voters in the last election.

(B) The Conservative Party will win the next election.

(C) For each person interviewed in telephone polls before the next election, pollsters will be able to reasonably determine the likelihood of that person voting.

(D) People who expressed no party preference during the in-person interviews shortly before Country X's last election did not outnumber the people who expressed a preference for the Conservative Party.

(E) In the next election, pollsters will be able to conduct more in-person interviews than telephone interviews.

498. A company that manufactures plastic products from recyclable plastic is, surprisingly, unconcerned that economic conditions may worsen, despite analysts' belief that consumers would then consider ecofriendly plastic products an expensive luxury. But the company reasons that it will be able to lower its prices because, in a weakened economy, other ecofriendly plastic manufacturers are likely to fail. Demand among manufacturers for recyclable plastics as raw materials would then plummet, creating an oversupply of such materials, making them less expensive for the manufacturer to purchase and thus lowering the company's costs.

Which of the following, if true, most weakens the company's reasoning?

(A) Smaller ecofriendly plastic manufacturers are more likely to fail in a weakened economy than larger ecofriendly manufacturers are.

(B) Some retailers whose sales include various companies' ecofriendly plastic products have struggled in recent years despite the overall good economy.

(C) Consumers would likely soon learn of the oversupply of recyclable plastics and cease recycling them, significantly raising manufacturers' raw-material costs.

(D) Retailers, including retailers that cater to consumers seeking certain types of ecofriendly products, may lose some business if economic conditions worsen.

(E) The plastics used by the company in its products were, after a recent investigation by a regulatory body, declared to be safe for consumers.

499. Researchers asked volunteers to imagine they were running a five-kilometer race against 50 people and then against 500 people, races in each of which the top 10 percent would receive a $1,000 prize. Asked about the effort they would apply in the respective cases, the volunteers indicated, on average, that they would run slower in the race against the greater number of people. A likely explanation of this result is that those of the volunteers who were most *comparatively inclined*— those who most tended to compare themselves with others in the social environment—determined (perhaps unconsciously) that extreme effort would not be worthwhile in the 500-competitor race.

Which of the following would, if known to be true, most help justify the explanation offered above?

(A) The volunteers who were most comparatively inclined were also those that had the greatest desire to win a $1,000 prize.

(B) The volunteers who were the least comparatively inclined had no greater desire to win the $1,000 than those who were the most comparatively inclined.

(C) The volunteers who were most comparatively inclined were likely to indicate that they would run the two races at the same speed.

(D) The most comparatively inclined volunteers believed that they were significantly less likely to finish in the top 10 percent in the race against 500 than in the race against 50.

(E) Volunteers were chosen for participation in the study on the basis of answers to various questions designed to measure the degree to which the volunteers were comparatively inclined.

500. According to a study, after a week of high-altitude living, twenty men had slimmed down. The men, middle-aged residents of low-altitude areas, had been taken to a research station at 2,650 meters (8,694 feet) above sea level. They had unrestricted access to food and were forbidden vigorous exercise, yet they lost an average of 1.5 kilograms (3.3 pounds) during their one-week stay. Clearly, the lower availability of oxygen at higher altitudes, or hypobaric hypoxia, can be said to have caused the weight loss, since

_____.

Which of the following would, if true, most logically complete the argument?

(A) a decrease in oxygen intake has been shown to depress appetite

(B) the men all participated in the same kinds of exercise during their stay

(C) the foods available to the men had fewer calories than the foods they usually ate

(D) exercise at higher altitudes is more difficult than exercise at lower altitudes is

(E) several weeks after returning home, the men still weighed less than they had before the study

501. Editorial: Our city's public transportation agency is facing a budget shortfall. The fastest growing part of the budget has been employee retirement benefits, which are exceptionally generous. Unless the budget shortfall is resolved, transportation service will be cut, and many transportation employees will lose their jobs. Thus, it would be in the employees' best interest for their union to accept cuts in retirement benefits.

Which of the following is an assumption the editorial's argument requires?

(A) The transportation employees' union should not accept cuts in retirement benefits if doing so would not be in the employees' best interest.

(B) The only feasible way for the agency to resolve the budget shortfall would involve cutting transportation service and eliminating jobs.

(C) Other things being equal, it is in the transportation employees' interest to have exceptionally generous retirement benefits.

(D) Cutting the retirement benefits would help resolve the agency's budget shortfall.

(E) The transportation employees' union will not accept cuts in retirement benefits if doing so will not allow more transportation employees to keep their jobs.

502. Researchers hope to find clues about the A'mk peoples who lived in the Kaumpta region about one thousand years ago but who left few obvious traces. The researchers plan to hire the few remaining shamans of the modern-day indigenous people in Kaumpta, who are believed to be descended from the A'mk, to lead them to ancestral sites that may be the remains of A'mk buildings or ceremonial spaces. The shamans were taught the location of such sites as part of their traditional training as youths, and their knowledge of traditional Kaumpta customs may help determine the nature of any sites the researchers find.

Which of the following is an assumption on which the success of the plan depends?

(A) The researchers have reliable evidence that the A'mk of one thousand years ago built important ceremonial spaces.

(B) The shamans have a reasonably accurate memory of A'mk sites they learned about as youths.

(C) Kaumpta shamans are generally held in high esteem for their traditional knowledge.

(D) Modern technologies available to the researchers are likely to be able to find some A'mk sites easily.

(E) Most or all A'mk sites are likely to be found within the Kaumpta region.

503. Astronomer: Most stars are born in groups of thousands, each star in a group forming from the same parent cloud of gas. Each cloud has a unique, homogeneous chemical composition. Therefore, whenever two stars have the same chemical composition as each other, they must have originated from the same cloud of gas.

Which of the following, if true, would most strengthen the astronomer's argument?

(A) In some groups of stars, not every star originated from the same parent cloud of gas.

(B) Clouds of gas of similar or identical chemical composition may be remote from each other.

(C) Whenever a star forms, it inherits the chemical composition of its parent cloud of gas.

(D) Many stars in vastly different parts of the universe are quite similar in their chemical compositions.

(E) Astronomers can at least sometimes precisely determine whether a star has the same chemical composition as its parent cloud of gas.

504. With employer-paid training, workers have the potential to become more productive not only in their present employment but also in any number of jobs with different employers. To increase the productivity of their workforce, many firms are planning to maintain or even increase their investments in worker training. But some training experts object that if a trained worker is hired away by another firm, the employer that paid for the training has merely subsidized a competitor. They note that such hiring has been on the rise in recent years.

Which of the following would, if true, contribute most to defeating the training experts' objection to the firms' strategy?

(A) Firms that promise opportunities for advancement to their employees get, on average, somewhat larger numbers of job applications from untrained workers than do firms that make no such promise.

(B) In many industries, employees who take continuing-education courses are more competitive in the job market.

(C) More and more educational and training institutions are offering reduced tuition fees to firms that subsidize worker training.

(D) Research shows that workers whose training is wholly or partially subsidized by their employer tend to get at least as much training as do workers who pay for all their own training.

(E) For most firms that invest in training their employees, the value added by that investment in employees who stay exceeds the value lost through other employees' leaving to work for other companies.

505. In emerging economies in Africa and other regions, large foreign banks that were set up during the colonial era have long played a major economic role. These institutions have tended to confine their business to the wealthier of banks' potential customers. But development of these countries' economies requires financing of the small businesses that dominate their manufacturing, farming, and services sectors. So economic growth will be likely to occur if local banks take on this portion of the financial services markets, since _____.

Which of the following completions would produce the strongest argument?

(A) local banks tend not to strive as much as large foreign banks to diversify their investments

(B) small farming and manufacturing businesses contribute to economic growth if they obtain adequate investment capital

(C) large foreign banks in emerging economies could, with local employees and appropriate local consultation, profitably expand their business to less wealthy clients

(D) some small businesses are among the wealthier customers of foreign banks in emerging economies

(E) local banks in emerging economies tend to be less risk-averse than foreign banks

506. Exporters in Country X are facing lower revenues due to a shortage of the large metal shipping containers in which they send their goods by sea to other countries. Fewer containers arrive in Country X due to reductions in imports. This has meant lost orders, costly delays, and a scramble for alternatives, such as air freight, all of which are costlier. Moreover, the revenues of exporters in Country X will probably continue to decline in the near future. This is because other countries are likely to find it increasingly unprofitable to export their goods to Country X, and because _____.

Which of the following would most logically complete the passage?

(A) production of shipping containers in Country X is growing rapidly as a response to the shortage

(B) shipping companies are willing to move containers from country to country only when the containers are full

(C) the cost of shipping alternatives such as air freight is likely to stabilize in the near future

(D) consumers in Country X are purchasing more products than ever before

(E) the worldwide demand for goods made in Country X has only recently begun to rise after a long decline

507. Candle Corporation's television stations are likely to have more income from advertisers than previously. This is because advertisers prefer to reach people in the 18- to 49-year-old age group and the number of people in that group watching Candle television is increasing. Furthermore, among Candle viewers, the percentage of viewers 18 to 49 years old is increasing.

Which of the following, if true, would most strengthen the argument that Candle Corporation will receive more income from advertisers?

(A) Advertisers carefully monitor the demographic characteristics of television audiences and purchase advertising time to reach the audiences they prefer to reach.

(B) Among people over 49 years old, fewer viewers of Candle stations buy products advertised on television than do viewers of other stations.

(C) There will be increasingly more advertisements on television that are directed at viewers who are over 49 years old.

(D) Candle stations plan to show reruns of television shows during hours when other stations run shows for the first time.

(E) People 18 to 49 years old generally have less disposable income to spend than do people over 49 years old.

508. A provincial government plans to raise the gasoline tax to give people an incentive to drive less, reducing traffic congestion in the long term. However, skeptics point out that most people in the province live in areas where cars are the only viable transportation to jobs and stores and therefore cannot greatly change their driving habits in response to higher gasoline prices.

In light of the skeptics' objection, which of the following, if true, would most logically support the prediction that the government's plan will achieve its goal of reducing traffic congestion?

(A) The revenue from the tax will be used to make public transportation a viable means of transportation to jobs and stores for far more people.

(B) The tax will encourage many residents to switch to more fuel-efficient cars, reducing air pollution and other problems.

(C) Because gasoline has been underpriced for decades, the province has many neighborhoods where cars are the only viable means of transportation.

(D) Most residents who cannot greatly change their driving habits could compensate for high gasoline prices by reducing other expenses.

(E) Traffic congestion is an especially serious problem for people for whom cars are the only viable means of transportation.

509. Editorial: The roof of Northtown's municipal equipment-storage building collapsed under the weight of last week's heavy snowfall. The building was constructed recently and met local building-safety codes in every particular, except that the nails used for attaching roof supports to the building's columns were of a smaller size than the codes specify for this purpose. Clearly, this collapse exemplifies how even a single, apparently insignificant departure from safety standards can have severe consequences.

Which of the following, if true, most seriously weakens the editorial's argument?

(A) The only other buildings to suffer roof collapses from the weight of the snowfall were older buildings constructed according to less exacting standards than those in the codes.

(B) The amount of snow that accumulated on the roof of the equipment-storage building was greater than the predicted maximum that was used in drawing up the safety codes.

(C) Because the equipment-storage building was not intended for human occupation, some safety-code provisions that would have applied to an office building did not apply to it.

(D) The municipality of Northtown itself has the responsibility for ensuring that buildings constructed within its boundaries meet the provisions of the building-safety codes.

(E) Because the equipment-storage building was used for storing snow-removal equipment, the building was almost completely empty when the roof collapsed.

510. Political theorist: Even with the best spies, area experts, and satellite surveillance, foreign policy assessments can still lack important information. In such circumstances intuitive judgment is vital. A national leader with such judgment can make good decisions about foreign policy even when current information is incomplete, since _____.

Which of the following, if true, most logically completes the argument?

(A) the central reason for failure in foreign policy decision making is the absence of critical information

(B) those leaders whose foreign policy decisions have been highly ranked have also been found to have good intuitive judgment

(C) both intuitive judgment and good information are required for sound decision making

(D) good foreign policy decisions often lead to improved methods of gathering information

(E) intuitive judgment can produce good decisions based on past experience, even when there are important gaps in current information

511. Supply shortages and signs of growing demand are driving cocoa prices upward. Unusually severe weather in cocoa-producing regions—too much rain in Brazil and too little in West Africa—has limited production. Further, Europe and North America recently reported stronger demand for cocoa. In the first quarter, grinding of cocoa beans—the first stage in processing cocoa for chocolate—rose 8.1 percent in Europe and 16 percent

in North America. Analysts have concluded that cocoa's price will continue to rise at least into the near future.

Which of the following would, if true, most strengthen the reasoning above?

(A) Ground cocoa beans can be stored for long periods before they spoil.

(B) Several European and North American manufacturers that use cocoa have recently improved their processing capacity.

(C) It takes new cocoa trees five or six years before they start bearing fruit.

(D) Governments in Europe and North America are likely to change current restrictions on cocoa imports.

(E) Historically, cocoa production has varied widely from year to year.

512. During the earliest period of industrialization in Britain, steam engines were more expensive to build and operate than either windmills or water mills, the other practicable sources of power for factories. Yet despite their significant cost disadvantage, steam-powered factories were built in large numbers well before technical improvements brought their cost down. Furthermore, they were built even in regions where geographical conditions permitted the construction of wind- and water-powered factories close to major markets.

Which of the following, if true, most helps to explain the proliferation of steam-powered factories during the earliest period of industrialization in Britain?

(A) In many areas of Britain, there were fewer steam-powered factories than wind- or water-powered factories in the earliest period of industrialization.

(B) Unlike wind- or water-powered factories, steam-powered factories were fueled with coal, which sometimes had to be transported significant distances from the mine to the site of the factory.

(C) It was both difficult and expensive to convert a factory from wind power or water power to steam power.

(D) In the early period of industrialization, many goods sold in towns and cities could not be mass-produced in factories.

(E) In Britain, the number of sites where a wind- or water-powered factory could be built was insufficient to provide for all of the demand for factory-produced goods at the time.

513. Snowmaking machines work by spraying a mist that freezes immediately on contact with cold air. Because the sudden freezing kills bacteria, QuickFreeze is planning to market a wastewater purification system that works on the same principle. The process works only when temperatures are cold, however, so municipalities using it will still need to maintain a conventional system. Which of the following, if true, provides the strongest grounds for a prediction that municipalities will buy QuickFreeze's purification system despite the need to maintain a conventional purification system as well?

(A) Bacteria are not the only impurities that must be removed from wastewater.

(B) Many municipalities have old wastewater purification systems that need to be replaced.

(C) Conventional wastewater purification systems have not been fully successful in killing bacteria at cold temperatures.

(D) During times of warm weather, when it is not in use, QuickFreeze's purification system requires relatively little maintenance.

(E) Places where the winters are cold rarely have a problem of water shortage.

514. **Plant scientists have used genetic engineering on seeds to produce crop plants that are highly resistant to insect damage**. Unfortunately, the seeds themselves are quite expensive, and the plants require more fertilizer and water to grow well than normal ones. Accordingly, **for most farmers the savings on pesticides would not compensate for the higher seed costs and the cost of additional fertilizer**. However, since consumer demand for grains, fruits, and vegetables grown without the use of pesticides continues to rise, the use of genetically engineered seeds of this kind is likely to become widespread.

In the argument given, the two portions in **boldface** play which of the following roles?

(A) The first supplies a context for the argument; the second is the argument's main conclusion.

(B) The first introduces a development that the argument predicts will have a certain outcome; the second is a state of affairs that, according to the argument, contributes to bringing about that outcome.

(C) The first presents a development that the argument predicts will have a certain outcome; the second acknowledges a consideration that tends to weigh against that prediction.

(D) The first provides evidence to support a prediction that the argument seeks to defend; the second is that prediction.

(E) The first and the second each provide evidence to support the argument's main conclusion.

515. Which of the following most logically completes the passage?

Leptin, a protein occurring naturally in the blood, appears to regulate how much fat the body carries by speeding up the metabolism and decreasing the appetite when the body has too much fat. Mice that do not naturally produce leptin have more fat than other mice, but lose fat rapidly when they are given leptin injections. Unfortunately, however, leptin cannot be used as a dietary supplement to control fat, since _____.

(A) the digestive system breaks down proteins before they can enter the bloodstream

(B) there are pharmaceuticals already available that can contribute to weight loss by speeding up the metabolism

(C) people with unusually low levels of leptin in their blood tend to have a high percentage of body fat

(D) the mice that do not naturally produce leptin were from a specially bred strain of mice

(E) mice whose bodies did produce leptin also lost some of their body fat when given leptin injections

516. Suncorp, a new corporation with limited funds, has been clearing large sections of the tropical Amazon forest for cattle ranching. This practice continues even though greater profits can be made from rubber tapping, which does not destroy the forest, than from cattle ranching, which does destroy the forest.

Which of the following, if true, most helps to explain why Suncorp has been pursuing the less profitable of the two economic activities mentioned above?

(A) The soil of the Amazon forest is very rich in nutrients that are important in the development of grazing lands.

(B) Cattle-ranching operations that are located in tropical climates are more profitable than cattle-ranching operations that are located in cold-weather climates.

(C) In certain districts, profits made from cattle ranching are more heavily taxed than profits made from any other industry.

(D) Some of the cattle that are raised on land cleared in the Amazon are killed by wildcats.

(E) The amount of money required to begin a rubber-tapping operation is twice as high as the amount needed to begin a cattle ranch.

517. Archaeologists use technology to analyze ancient sites. It is likely that this technology will advance considerably in the near future, allowing archaeologists to gather more information than is currently possible. If they study certain sites now, they risk contaminating or compromising them for future studies. Therefore, in order to maximize the potential for gathering knowledge in the long run, a team of archaeologists plans to delay the examination of a newly excavated site.

Which of the following would be most useful to investigate for the purpose of evaluating the plan's prospects for achieving its goal?

(A) Whether any of the contents of the site will significantly deteriorate before the anticipated technology is available

(B) Whether there will continue to be improvements on the relevant technology

(C) Whether the team can study a site other than the newly excavated site for the time being

(D) Whether the site was inhabited by a very ancient culture

(E) Whether the anticipated technology will damage objects under study

518. More and more law firms specializing in corporate taxes are paid on a contingency-fee basis. Under this arrangement, if a case is won, the firm usually receives more than it would have received if it had been paid on the alternate hourly rate basis. If the case is lost, the firm receives nothing. Most firms are likely to make more under the contingency-fee arrangement.

Which of the following, if true, would most strengthen the prediction above?

(A) Firms that work exclusively under the hourly rate arrangement spend, on average, fewer hours on cases that are won than on cases that are lost.

(B) Some litigation can last for years before any decision is reached, and, even then, the decision may be appealed.

(C) Firms under the contingency-fee arrangement still pay their employees on an hourly basis.

(D) Since the majority of firms specialize in certain kinds of cases, they are able to assess accurately their chances of winning each potential case.

(E) Firms working under the contingency-fee arrangement take in fewer cases per year than do firms working under the hourly rate arrangement.

519. Pretzel Vendor: The new license fee for operating a pretzel stand outside the art museum is prohibitively expensive. Charging typical prices, I would need to sell an average of 25 pretzels per hour to break even. At my stand outside City Hall, with about as many passers-by as at the art museum, I average only 15 per hour. So I could not break even running a stand outside the art museum, much less turn a profit.

Which of the following, if true, most seriously weakens the pretzel vendor's argument?

(A) The pretzel vendor does not sell anything other than pretzels.

(B) People who visit the art museum are more likely to buy pretzels than are people who go to City Hall.

(C) The license fee for operating a pretzel stand outside City Hall will not increase.

(D) People who buy pretzels at pretzel stands are more likely to do so during the lunch hour than at other times.

(E) The city will grant more licenses for pretzel stands outside the art museum than the number it grants for stands outside City Hall.

520. Beginning in 1966 all new cars sold in Morodia were required to have safety belts and power steering. Previously, most cars in Morodia were without these features. Safety belts help to prevent injuries in collisions, and power steering helps to avoid collisions in the first place. But even though in 1966 one-seventh of the cars in Morodia were replaced with new cars, the number of car collisions and collision-related injuries did not decline.

Which of the following, if true about Morodia, most helps to explain why the number of collisions and collision-related injuries in Morodia failed to decline in 1966?

(A)   Because of a driver-education campaign, most drivers and passengers in cars that did have safety belts used them in 1966.

(B)   Most of the new cars bought in 1966 were bought in the months of January and February.

(C)   In 1965, substantially more than one-seventh of the cars in Morodia were replaced with new cars.

(D)   An excessive reliance on the new safety features led many owners of new cars to drive less cautiously in 1966 than before.

(E)   The seat belts and power steering put into new cars sold in 1966 had to undergo strict quality-control inspections by manufacturers, whether the cars were manufactured in Morodia or not.

521.   Manufacturers of mechanical pencils make most of their profit on pencil leads rather than on the pencils themselves. The Write Company, which cannot sell its leads as cheaply as other manufacturers can, plans to alter the design of its mechanical pencil so that it will accept only a newly designed Write Company lead, which will be sold at the same price as the Write Company's current lead.

Which of the following, if true, most strongly supports the Write Company's projection that its plan will lead to an increase in its sales of pencil leads?

(A)   The new Write Company pencil will be introduced at a price higher than the price the Write Company charges for its current model.

(B)   In the foreseeable future, manufacturers of mechanical pencils will probably have to raise the prices they charge for mechanical pencils.

(C)   The newly designed Write Company lead will cost somewhat more to manufacture than the Write Company's current lead does.

((D)   A rival manufacturer recently announced similar plans to introduce a mechanical pencil that would accept only the leads produced by that manufacturer.

(E)   In extensive test marketing, mechanical-pencil users found the new Write Company pencil markedly superior to other mechanical pencils they had used.

522.   Enterprise Bank currently requires customers with checking accounts to maintain a minimum balance or pay a monthly fee. Enterprise plans to offer accounts with no monthly fee and no minimum-balance requirement; to cover their projected administrative costs of $3 per account per month they plan to charge $30 for overdrawing an account. Since each month on average slightly more than 10 percent of Enterprise's customers overdraw their accounts, bank officials predict the new accounts will generate a profit.

Which of the following, if true, most strongly supports the bank officials' prediction?

(A)   Some of Enterprise Bank's current checking account customers are expected to switch to the new accounts once they are offered.

(B)   One third of Enterprise Bank's revenues are currently derived from monthly fees tied to checking accounts.

(C)   Many checking account customers who occasionally pay a fee for not maintaining a minimum balance in their account generally maintain a balance well above the minimum.

(D)   Customers whose checking accounts do not have a minimum-balance requirement are more likely than others to overdraw their checking accounts.

(E)   Customers whose checking accounts do not have a minimum-balance requirement are more likely than others to write checks for small amounts.

523.   Highway Official: When resurfacing our concrete bridges, we should use electrically conductive concrete (ECC) rather than standard concrete. In the winter, ECC can be heated by passing an electric current through it, thereby preventing ice buildup. The cost of the electricity needed is substantially lower than the cost of the deicing salt we currently use.

Taxpayer: But ECC is vastly more expensive than standard concrete, so your proposal is probably not justifiable on economic grounds.

Which of the following, if true, could best be used by the highway official to support the official's proposal in the face of the taxpayer's objection?

(A)   The use of deicing salt causes corrosion of reinforcing steel in concrete bridge decks and damage to the concrete itself, thereby considerably shortening the useful life of concrete bridges.

(B)   Severe icing conditions can cause power outages and slow down the work of emergency crews trying to get power restored.

(C)   In weather conditions conducive to icing, ice generally forms on the concrete surfaces of bridges well before it forms on parts of the roadway that go over solid ground.

(D) Aside from its potential use for deicing bridges, ECC might also be an effective means of keeping other concrete structures such as parking garages and airport runways ice free.

(E) If ECC were to be used for a bridge surface, the electric current would be turned on only at times at which ice was likely to form.

524. In virtually any industry, technological improvements increase labor productivity, which is the output of goods and services per person-hour worked. In Parland's industries, labor productivity is significantly higher than it is in Vergia's industries. Clearly, therefore, Parland's industries must, on the whole, be further advanced technologically than Vergia's are.

The argument is most vulnerable to which of the following criticisms?

(A) It offers a conclusion that is no more than a paraphrase of one of the pieces of information provided in its support.

(B) It presents as evidence in support of a claim information that is inconsistent with other evidence presented in support of the same claim.

(C) It takes one possible cause of a condition to be the actual cause of that condition without considering any other possible causes.

(D) It takes a condition to be the effect of something that happened only after the condition already existed.

(E) It makes a distinction that presupposes the truth of the conclusion that is to be established.

525. Chaco Canyon, a settlement of the ancient Anasazi culture in North America, had massive buildings. **It must have been a major Anasazi center**. Analysis of wood samples shows that some of the timber for the buildings came from the Chuska and San Mateo mountains, 50 miles from Chaco Canyon. **Only a major cultural center would have the organizational power to import timber from 50 miles away**.

In the argument given, the two portions in **boldface** play which of the following roles?

(A) The first is a premise used to support the argument's main conclusion; the second is the argument's main conclusion.

(B) The first is the argument's main conclusion; the second is a premise used to support that conclusion.

(C) The first is one of two premises used to support the argument's main conclusion; the second is the other of those two premises.

(D) The first is a premise used to support the argument's main conclusion; the second is a premise used to support another conclusion drawn in the argument.

(E) The first is inferred from another statement in the argument; the second is inferred from the first.

526. The Maxilux car company's design for its new luxury model, the Max 100, included a special design for the tires that was intended to complement the model's image. The winning bid for supplying these tires was submitted by Rubco. Analysts concluded that the bid would only just cover Rubco's costs on the tires, but Rubco executives claim that winning the bid will actually make a profit for the company.

Which of the following, if true, most strongly justifies the claim made by Rubco's executives?

(A) In any Maxilux model, the spare tire is exactly the same make and model as the tires that are mounted on the wheels.

(B) Rubco holds exclusive contracts to supply Maxilux with the tires for a number of other models made by Maxilux.

(C) The production facilities for the Max 100 and those for the tires to be supplied by Rubco are located very near each other.

(D) When people who have purchased a carefully designed luxury automobile need to replace a worn part of it, they almost invariably replace it with a part of exactly the same make and type.

(E) When Maxilux awarded the tire contract to Rubco, the only criterion on which Rubco's bid was clearly ahead of its competitors' bids was price.

527. Which of the following most logically completes the passage?

Most bicycle helmets provide good protection for the top and back of the head, but little or no protection for the temple regions on the sides of the head. A study of head injuries resulting from bicycle accidents showed that a large proportion were caused by blows to the temple area. Therefore, if bicycle helmets protected this area, the risk of serious head injury in bicycle accidents would be greatly reduced, especially since _____.

(A) among the bicyclists included in the study's sample of head injuries, only a very small proportion had been wearing a helmet at the time of their accident

(B) even those bicyclists who regularly wear helmets have a poor understanding of the degree and kind of protection that helmets afford

(C) a helmet that included protection for the temples would have to be somewhat larger and heavier than current helmets

(D) the bone in the temple area is relatively thin and impacts in that area are thus very likely to cause brain injury

(E) bicyclists generally land on their arm or shoulder when they fall to the side, which reduces the likelihood of severe impacts on the side of the head

528. Which of the following most logically completes the argument?

In a typical year, Innovair's airplanes are involved in 35 collisions while parked or being towed in airports, with a resulting yearly cost of $1,000,000 for repairs.

To reduce the frequency of ground collisions, Innovair will begin giving its ground crews additional training, at an annual cost of $500,000. Although this will cut the number of ground collisions by about half at best, the drop in repair costs can be expected to be much greater, since _____.

(A) most ground collisions happen when ground crews are rushing to minimize the time a delayed airplane spends on the ground

(B) a ground collision typically occurs when there are no passengers on the airplane

(C) the additional training will focus on helping ground crews avoid those kinds of ground collisions that cause the most costly damage

(D) the $500,000 cost figure for the additional training of ground crews includes the wages that those crews will earn during the time spent in actual training

(E) most ground collisions have been caused by the least experienced ground-crew members

529. Many agriculturally intensive areas of the world are beginning to encounter water scarcity problems. As a result, many farmers in these areas are likely to reduce their output as the water supply they need in order to maintain production shrinks. However, one group of farmers in such a region plans to increase their production by implementing techniques for water conservation.

Which of the following, if true, would most strongly support the prediction that the group's plan will succeed?

(A) Farmers that can gain a larger share of the food market in their regions will be better positioned to control more water resources.

(B) Most agricultural practices in areas with water shortages are water-intensive.

(C) Other regions of the world not facing water shortages are likely to make up for the reduction in agricultural output.

(D) Demand for agricultural products in the group's region is not expected to decline.

(E) More than half the water used for agriculture in the farmers' region is lost to evaporation or leakage from irrigation channels.

530. Hollywood restaurant is replacing some of its standard tables with tall tables and stools. The restaurant already fills every available seat during its operating hours, and the change in seating arrangements will not result in an increase in the restaurant's seating capacity. Nonetheless, the restaurant's management expects revenue to increase as a result of the seating change without any concurrent change in menu, prices, or operating hours.

Which of the following, if true, provides the best reason for the expectation?

(A) One of the taller tables takes up less floor space than one of the standard tables.

(B) Diners seated on stools typically do not linger over dinner as long as diners seated at standard tables.

(C) Since the restaurant will replace only some of its standard tables, it can continue to accommodate customers who do not care for the taller tables.

(D) Few diners are likely to avoid the restaurant because of the new seating arrangement.

(E) The standard tables being replaced by tall tables would otherwise have to be replaced with new standard tables at a greater expense.

531. A major network news organization experienced a drop in viewership in the week following the airing of a controversial report on the economy. The network also received a very large number of complaints regarding the report. The network, however, maintains that negative reactions to the report had nothing to do with its loss of viewers.

Which of the following, if true, most strongly supports the network's position?

(A) The other major network news organizations reported similar reductions in viewership during the same week.

(B) The viewers who registered complaints with the network were regular viewers of the news organization's programs.

(C) Major network news organizations publicly attribute drops in viewership to their own reports only when they receive complaints about those reports.

(D) This was not the first time that this network news organization has aired a controversial report on the economy that has inspired viewers to complain to the network.

(E) Most network news viewers rely on network news broadcasts as their primary source of information regarding the economy.

532. Only a reduction of 10 percent in the number of scheduled flights using Greentown's airport will allow the delays that are so common there to be avoided. Hevelia airstrip, 40 miles away, would, if upgraded and expanded, be an attractive alternative for fully 20 percent of the passengers using Greentown airport. Nevertheless, experts reject the claim that turning Hevelia into a full-service airport would end the chronic delays at Greentown.

Which of the following, if true, most helps to justify the experts' position?

(A) Turning Hevelia into a full-service airport would require not only substantial construction at the airport itself, but also the construction of new access highways.

(B) A second largely undeveloped airstrip close to Greentown airport would be a more attractive alternative than Hevelia for many passengers who now use Greentown.

(C) Hevelia airstrip lies in a relatively undeveloped area but would, if it became a full-service airport, be a magnet for commercial and residential development.

(D) If an airplane has to wait to land, the extra jet fuel required adds significantly to the airline's costs.

(E) Several airlines use Greentown as a regional hub, so that most flights landing at Greentown have many passengers who then take different flights to reach their final destinations.

533. Farmer: Worldwide, just three grain crops—rice, wheat, and corn—account for most human caloric intake. To maintain this level of caloric intake and also keep pace with global population growth, yields per acre from each of these crops will have to increase at least 1.5 percent every year, given that the supply of cultivated land is diminishing. Therefore, the government should increase funding for research into new ways to improve yields.

Which of the following is an assumption on which the farmer's argument depends?

(A) It is solely the government's responsibility to ensure that the amount of rice, wheat, and corn produced worldwide keeps pace with global population growth.

(B) Increasing government funding for research into new ways to improve the yields per acre of rice, wheat, and corn crops would help to increase total worldwide annual production of food from these crops.

(C) Increasing the yields per acre of rice, wheat, and corn is more important than increasing the yields per acre of other crops.

(D) Current levels of funding for research into ways of improving grain crop yields per acre have enabled grain crop yields per acre to increase by more than 1.5 percent per year worldwide.

(E) In coming decades, rice, wheat, and corn will become a minor part of human caloric intake, unless there is government-funded research to increase their yields per acre.

534. The air quality board recently informed Coffee Roast, a small coffee roasting firm, of a complaint regarding the smoke from its roaster. Recently enacted air quality regulations require machines roasting more than 10 pounds of coffee to be equipped with expensive smoke-dissipating afterburners. The firm, however, roasts only 8 pounds of coffee at a time. Nevertheless, the company has decided to purchase and install an afterburner.

Which of the following, if true, most strongly supports the firm's decision?

(A) Until settling on the new air quality regulations, the board had debated whether to require afterburners for machines roasting more than 5 pounds of coffee at a time.

(B) Coffee roasted in a machine equipped with an afterburner has its flavor subtly altered.

(C) The cost to the firm of an afterburner is less than the cost of replacing its roaster with a smaller one.

(D) Fewer complaints are reported in areas that maintain strict rules regarding afterburners.

(E) The firm has reason to fear that negative publicity regarding the complaints could result in lost sales.

535. People who do regular volunteer work tend to live longer, on average, than people who do not. It has been found that "doing good," a category that certainly includes volunteer work, releases endorphins, the brain's natural opiates, which induce in people a feeling of well-being. Clearly, there is a connection: Regular releases of endorphins must in some way help to extend people's lives.

Which of the following, if true, most seriously undermines the force of the evidence given as support for the hypothesis that endorphins promote longevity?

(A) People who do regular volunteer work are only somewhat more likely than others to characterize the work they do for a living as "doing good."

(B) Although extremely high levels of endorphins could be harmful to health, such levels are never reached as a result of the natural release of endorphins.

(C) There are many people who have done some volunteer work but who do not do such work regularly.

(D) People tend not to become involved in regular volunteer work unless they are healthy and energetic to begin with.

(E) Releases of endorphins are responsible for the sense of well-being experienced by many long-distance runners while running.

536. A study compared a sample of Swedish people older than 75 who needed in-home assistance with a similar sample of Israeli people. The people in the two samples received both informal assistance, provided by family and friends, and formal assistance, professionally provided. Although Sweden and Israel have equally well-funded and comprehensive systems for providing formal assistance, the study found that the people in the Swedish sample received more formal assistance, on average, than those in the Israeli sample.

Which of the following, if true, does most to explain the difference that the study found?

(A) A companion study found that among children needing special in-home care, the amount of formal assistance they received was roughly the same in Sweden as in Israel.

(B) More Swedish than Israeli people older than 75 live in rural areas where formal assistance services are sparse or nonexistent.

(C) Although in both Sweden and Israel much of the funding for formal assistance ultimately comes from the central government, the local structures through which assistance is delivered are different in the two countries.

(D) In recent decades, the increase in life expectancy of someone who is 75 years old has been greater in Israel than in Sweden.

(E) In Israel, people older than 75 tend to live with their children, whereas in Sweden people of that age tend to live alone.

537. Film Director: It is true that certain characters and plot twists in my newly released film *The Big Heist* are similar to characters and plot twists in *Thieves*, a movie that came out last year. Pointing to these similarities, the film studio that produced *Thieves* is now accusing me of taking ideas from that film. The accusation is clearly without merit. All production work on *The Big Heist* was actually completed months before *Thieves* was released.

Which of the following, if true, provides the strongest support for the director's position?

(A) Before *Thieves* began production, its script had been circulating for several years among various film studios, including the studio that produced *The Big Heist*.

(B) The characters and plot twists that are most similar in the two films have close parallels in many earlier films of the same genre.

(C) The film studio that produced *Thieves* seldom produces films in this genre.

(D) The director of *Thieves* worked with the director of *The Big Heist* on several earlier projects.

(E) Production work on *Thieves* began before production work on *The Big Heist* was started.

538. In Mernia commercial fossil hunters often sell important fossils they have found, not to universities or museums, but to individual collectors, who pay much better but generally do not allow researchers access to their collections. To increase the number of fossils available for research, some legislators propose requiring all fossils that are found in Mernia to be sold only to universities or museums.

Which of the following, if true, most strongly indicates that the legislators' proposal will fail to achieve its goal?

(A) Some fossil hunters in Mernia are not commercial fossil hunters, but rather are amateurs who keep the fossils that they find.

(B) Most fossils found in Mernia are common types that have little scientific interest.

(C) Commercial fossil hunters in Mernia currently sell some of the fossils they find to universities and museums.

(D) Many universities in Mernia do not engage in fossil research.

(E) Most fossils are found by commercial fossil hunters, and they would give up looking for fossils if they were no longer allowed to sell to individual collectors.

539. Economist: Tropicorp, which constantly seeks profitable investment opportunities, has been buying and clearing sections of tropical forest for cattle ranching, although pastures newly created there become useless for grazing after just a few years. The company has not gone into rubber tapping, even though greater profits can be made from rubber tapping, which leaves the forest intact. Thus, some environmentalists argue that **Tropicorp's actions do not serve even its own economic interest**. However, the initial investment required for a successful rubber-tapping operation is larger than that needed for a cattle ranch; there is a shortage of workers employable in rubber-tapping operations; and taxes are higher on profits from rubber tapping than on profits from cattle ranching. Consequently, **the environmentalists' conclusion is probably wrong**.

In the economist's argument, the two **boldface** portions play which of the following roles?

(A) The first supports the conclusion of the economist's argument; the second calls that conclusion into question.

(B) The first states the conclusion of the economist's argument; the second supports that conclusion.

(C) The first supports the conclusion of the environmentalists' argument; the second states that conclusion.

(D) The first states the conclusion of the environmentalists' argument; the second states the conclusion of the economist's argument.

(E) Each supports the conclusion of the economist's argument.

540. Brown tides are growths of algae on the sea's surface that prevent sunlight from reaching marine plants below, thereby destroying not only the plants but also the shellfish that live off these plants. Biologists recently isolated a virus that, when added to seawater, kills the algae that cause brown tides. Adding large quantities of this virus to waters affected by brown tides will therefore make it possible to save the populations of shellfish that inhabit those waters.

Which of the following, if true, provides the most support for the conclusion of the argument?

(A) When applied in large quantities, the virus not only kills the algae that cause brown tides but also many harmless kinds of algae.

(B) Marine animals that prey on shellfish avoid areas of the sea in which brown tides are occurring.

(C) The number of different kinds of virus present in seawater is far greater than many marine biologists had, until recently, believed.

(D) The presence of large quantities of the virus in seawater does not adversely affect the growth of marine plants.

(E) The amount of the virus naturally present in seawater in which brown tides occur is neither significantly greater nor significantly less than the amount present in seawater in which brown tides do not occur.

541. In persons with astigmatism, the clear outer layer of the eye is deformed in a way that impairs and sometimes distorts vision. The elongated figures in the paintings of El Greco (1541–1614) were so unusual that some critics sought to explain them by hypothesizing that, without knowing it, El Greco had an astigmatism that caused everything to appear to him in the distorted way that was characteristic of his painted figures.

The proposed explanation is most vulnerable to the criticism that it fails to

(A) establish that during the period in which El Greco lived, there was any correction available to those who did realize their vision was distorted

(B) provide evidence that astigmatism was common in the 1500s and 1600s

(C) consider that the critics who proposed the explanation might have suffered from astigmatism

(D) consider the effect of the hypothesized astigmatism on El Greco's perception of his own paintings

(E) allow for the possibility that artists see the world differently than do nonartists

542. Marketing executive for Magu Corporation: Whenever Magu opens a manufacturing facility in a new city, the company should sponsor, or make donations to, a number of nonprofit organizations in that city. Doing so would improve Magu's image in the community, and thus the money spent on such charitable ventures would lead to increased sales.

Which statement would, if true, point to the most serious weakness in the marketing executive's advice?

(A) Magu sells its products internationally, so sales in any one city represent only a small portion of total revenue.

(B) Spending on charitable ventures would require Magu to decrease direct advertisements, which are the most effective means of reaching its target customers.

(C) If market conditions change, Magu may have to close any such facility or relocate it.

(D) Some nonprofit organizations are poorly organized, so money donated to them would be of little benefit to the community.

(E) If workers at the manufacturing facility believed their wages or working conditions were poor, their complaints would outweigh any good impressions generated by Magu's donations or sponsorships.

543. In the last few years, plant scientists have been able to genetically engineer seeds to produce crops highly resistant to insect damage. Farmers growing crops with these seeds will be able to spend significantly less on pesticides. This cost reduction would more than make up for the higher cost of the genetically engineered seeds. Clearly, therefore, farmers who grow crops from genetically engineered seeds will be able to reduce their costs by using them.

Which of the following, if true, most weakens the argument?

(A) Plant scientists have not yet developed insect-resistant strains of every crop that is currently grown commercially.

(B) The cost of several commonly used pesticides is expected to rise in the next few years.

(C) Crops grown from the genetically engineered seeds require significantly more fertilizer and water to grow well than do crops grown from nonengineered seeds.

(D) In the future, the cost of genetically engineered seeds is likely to fall to the level of nonengineered seeds.

(E) The crops that now require the greatest expenditure on pesticides are not the ones for which genetically engineered seeds will become available.

544. Educational Theorist: Recent editorials have called for limits on the amount of homework assigned to schoolchildren younger than 12. They point out that free-time activities play an important role in childhood development and that homework in large quantities can severely restrict children's free time, hindering their development. But the actual average homework time for children under 12—little more than 30 minutes per night—leaves plenty of free time. In reality, therefore, the editorials' rationale cannot justify the restriction they advocate.

Which of the following, if true, would most seriously call into question the educational theorist's conclusion?

(A)   Some teachers give as homework assignments work of a kind that research suggests is most effective educationally when done in class.

(B)   For children younger than 12, regularly doing homework in the first years of school has no proven academic value, but many educators believe that it fosters self-discipline and time management.

(C)   Some homework assignments are related to free-time activities that children engage in, such as reading or hobbies.

(D)   A substantial proportion of schoolchildren under 12, particularly those in their first few years of school, have less than 10 minutes of homework assigned per night.

(E)   Some free-time activities teach children skills or information that they later find useful in their schoolwork.

545. Thyrian lawmaker: Thyria's Cheese Importation Board inspects all cheese shipments to Thyria and rejects shipments not meeting specified standards. Yet only one percent is ever rejected. Therefore, since the health consequences and associated economic costs of not rejecting that one percent are negligible, whereas the board's operating costs are considerable, for economic reasons alone the board should be disbanded.

Consultant: I disagree. The threat of having their shipments rejected deters many cheese exporters from shipping substandard product.

The consultant responds to the lawmaker's argument by

(A)   rejecting the lawmaker's argument while proposing that the standards according to which the board inspects imported cheese should be raised

(B)   providing evidence that the lawmaker's argument has significantly overestimated the cost of maintaining the board

(C)   objecting to the lawmaker's introducing into the discussion factors that are not strictly economic

(D)   pointing out a benefit of maintaining the board which the lawmaker's argument has failed to consider

(E)   shifting the discussion from the argument at hand to an attack on the integrity of the cheese inspectors

546. The tulu, a popular ornamental plant, does not reproduce naturally, and is only bred and sold by specialized horticultural companies. Unfortunately, the tulu is easily devastated by a contagious fungal rot. The government ministry plans to reassure worried gardeners by requiring all tulu plants to be tested for fungal rot before being sold. However, infected plants less than 30 weeks old have generally not built up enough fungal rot in their systems to be detected reliably. And many tulu plants are sold before they are 24 weeks old.

Which of the following, if performed by the government ministry, could logically be expected to overcome the problem with their plan to test for the fungal rot?

(A)   Releasing a general announcement that tulu plants less than 30 weeks old cannot be effectively tested for fungal rot

(B)   Requiring all tulu plants less than 30 weeks old to be labeled as such

(C)   Researching possible ways to test tulu plants less than 24 weeks old for fungal rot

(D)   Ensuring that tulu plants are not sold before they are 30 weeks old

(E)   Quarantining all tulu plants from horticultural companies at which any case of fungal rot has been detected until those tulu plants can be tested for fungal rot

547. While many people think of genetic manipulation of food crops as being aimed at developing larger and larger plant varieties, some plant breeders have in fact concentrated on discovering or producing dwarf varieties, which are roughly half as tall as normal varieties.

Which of the following would, if true, most help to explain the strategy of the plant breeders referred to above?

(A)   Plant varieties used as food by some are used as ornamentals by others.

(B)   The wholesale prices of a given crop decrease as the supply of it increases.

(C)   Crops once produced exclusively for human consumption are often now used for animal feed.

(D)   Short plants are less vulnerable to strong wind and heavy rains.

(E)   Nations with large industrial sectors tend to consume more processed grains.

548. Airline Representative: The percentage of flight delays caused by airline error decreased significantly this year. This indicates that airlines listened to complaints about preventable errors and addressed the problems. Although delays caused by weather and other uncontrollable factors will always be part of travel, preventable delays are clearly decreasing.

Which of the following most clearly points to a logical flaw in the representative's reasoning?

(A) Airlines may be motivated by financial concerns to underreport the percentage of flight delays caused by airline error.

(B) The delays caused by uncontrollable factors could have led to an increase in complaints to airlines.

(C) Complaints may not be the most reliable measure of how many errors occurred in a given year.

(D) Delays caused by weather and other uncontrollable factors could have increased dramatically during the year under discussion.

(E) Airline customers might not believe that particular delays were caused by uncontrollable factors rather than airline error.

549. Although the school would receive financial benefits if it had soft drink vending machines in the cafeteria, we should not allow them. Allowing soft drink machines there would not be in our students' interest. If our students start drinking more soft drinks, they will be less healthy.

The argument depends on which of the following?

(A) If the soft drink vending machines were placed in the cafeteria, students would consume more soft drinks as a result.

(B) The amount of soft drinks that most students at the school currently drink is not detrimental to their health.

(C) Students are apt to be healthier if they do not drink soft drinks at all than if they just drink small amounts occasionally.

(D) Students will not simply bring soft drinks from home if the soft drink vending machines are not placed in the cafeteria.

(E) The school's primary concern should be to promote good health among its students.

550. Many athletes inhale pure oxygen after exercise in an attempt to increase muscular reabsorption of oxygen. Measured continuously after exercise, however, the blood lactate levels of athletes who inhale pure oxygen are practically identical, on average, to those of athletes who breathe normal air. The lower the blood lactate level is, the higher the muscular reabsorption of oxygen is.

If the statements above are all true, they most strongly support which of the following conclusions?

(A) Athletes' muscular reabsorption of oxygen is not increased when they inhale pure oxygen instead of normal air.

(B) High blood lactate levels cannot be reduced.

(C) Blood lactate levels are a poor measure of oxygen reabsorption by muscles.

(D) The amount of oxygen reabsorbed by an athlete's muscles always remains constant.

(E) The inhaling of pure oxygen has no legitimate role in athletics.

551. Historian: Fifteenth-century advances in mapmaking contributed to the rise of modern nation-states. In medieval Europe (from the fifth to the fifteenth century), sovereignty centered in cities and towns and radiated outward, with boundaries often ambiguously defined. The conceptual shift toward the modern state began in the late fifteenth century, when mapmakers learned to reflect geography accurately by basing maps on latitude-longitude grids. By the mid-seventeenth century, nearly all maps showed boundary lines.

Which of the following would, if true, most strengthen the historian's reasoning?

(A) Borders did not become codified in Europe until certain treaties were signed in the early nineteenth century.

(B) During the medieval period, various authorities in Europe claimed power over collections of cities and towns, not contiguous territories.

(C) Many members of the political elite collected maps as a hobby during the late sixteenth and early seventeenth centuries.

(D) Seventeenth-century treatises and other sources of political authority describe areas of sovereignty rather than illustrate them using maps.

(E) During the fifteenth century in Europe, mapmakers simplified the borders of sovereignty by drawing clear lines of demarcation between political powers.

552. Sascha: The attempt to ban parliament's right to pass directed-spending bills—bills that contain provisions specifically funding the favorite projects of some powerful politicians—is antidemocratic. Our nation's constitution requires that money be drawn from our treasury only when so stipulated by laws passed by parliament, the branch of government most directly representative of the citizens. This requirement is based on the belief that exercising the power to spend public resources involves the ultimate exercise of state authority and that therefore _____.

Which of the following most logically completes Sascha's argument?

(A) designating funding specifically for the favorite projects of some powerful politicians should be considered antidemocratic

(B) the right to exercise such a power should belong exclusively to the branch of government most directly representative of the citizens

(C) exercising the power to spend public resources is in most cases—but not all—protected by the constitution

(D) modifications to any spending bills should be considered expenditures authorized by law

(E) only officials who are motivated by concerns for reelection should retain that power

553. Boreal owls range over a much larger area than do other owls of similar size. Scientists have hypothesized that **it is scarcity of prey that leads the owls to range so widely**. This hypothesis would be hard to confirm directly, since it is not possible to produce a sufficiently accurate count of the populations of small mammals inhabiting the forests where boreal owls live. Careful study of owl behavior has, however, shown that **boreal owls do range over larger areas when they live in regions where food of the sort eaten by small mammals is comparatively sparse**. This indicates that the scientists' hypothesis is not sheer speculation.

In the argument given, the two **boldfaced** portions play which of the following roles?

(A) The first presents an explanatory hypothesis; the second states the main conclusion of the argument.

(B) The first presents an explanatory hypothesis; the second presents evidence tending to support this hypothesis.

(C) The first presents an explanatory hypothesis; the second presents evidence to support an alternative explanation.

(D) The first describes a position that the argument opposes; the second presents evidence to undermine the support for the position being opposed.

(E) The first describes a position that the argument opposes; the second states the main conclusion of the argument.

554. Cognitive scientist: Using the pioneering work of comparative psychologist Gordon Gallup as a model, several studies have investigated animals' capacity for mirror self-recognition (MSR). Most animals exposed to a mirror respond only with social behavior, such as aggression. However, in the case of the great apes, repeated exposure to mirrors leads to self-directed behaviors, such as exploring the inside of the mouth, suggesting that these animals recognize the reflection as an image of self. The implication of these studies is that the great apes have a capacity for self-awareness unique among nonhuman species.

The cognitive scientist makes which of the following assumptions in the argument above?

(A) Gallup's work has established that the great apes have a capacity for MSR unique among nonhuman species.

(B) If an animal does not have the capacity for MSR, it does not have the capacity for self-awareness.

(C) If a researcher exposes an animal to a mirror and that animal exhibits social behavior, that animal is incapable of being self-aware.

(D) When exposed to a mirror, all animals display either social behavior or self-directed behavior.

(E) Animals that do not exhibit MSR may demonstrate a capacity for self-awareness in other ways.

555. Last year a record number of new manufacturing jobs were created. Will this year bring another record? Well, any new manufacturing job is created either within an existing company or by the start-up of a new company. **Within existing firms, new jobs have been created this year at well below last year's record pace**. At the same time, there is considerable evidence that the number of new companies starting up will be no higher this year than it was last year and **there is no reason to think that the new companies starting up this year will create more jobs per company than did last year's start-ups**. So clearly, the number of new jobs created this year will fall short of last year's record.

In the argument given, the two portions in **boldface** play which of the following roles?

(A) The first is a claim that the argument challenges; the second is an explicit assumption on which that challenge is based.

(B) The first is a claim that the argument challenges; the second is a judgment advanced in support of the main conclusion of the argument.

(C) The first provides evidence in support of the main conclusion of the argument; the second is an objection that has been raised against that main conclusion.

(D) The first provides evidence in support of the main conclusion of the argument; the second is a judgment advanced in support of that main conclusion.

(E) The first and the second are each claims that have been advanced in support of a position that the argument opposes.

556. A study of ticket sales at a summer theater festival found that people who bought tickets to individual plays had a no-show rate of less than 1 percent, while those who paid in advance for all ten plays being performed that summer had a no-show rate of nearly 30 percent. This may be at least in part because the greater the awareness customers retain about the cost of an item, the more likely they are to use it.

Which of the following would, if true, best serve as an alternative explanation of the results of the study?

(A) The price per ticket was slightly cheaper for those who bought all ten tickets in advance.

(B) Many people who attended the theater festival believed strongly that they should support it financially.

(C) Those who attended all ten plays became eligible for a partial refund.

(D) Usually, people who bought tickets to individual plays did so immediately prior to each performance that they attended.

(E) People who arrived just before the performance began could not be assured of obtaining seats in a preferred location.

557. Although there is no record of poet Edmund Spenser's parentage, we do know that as a youth Spenser attended the Merchant Tailors' School in London for a period between 1560 and 1570. Records from this time indicate that the Merchant Tailors' Guild then had only three members named Spenser: Robert Spenser, listed as a gentleman; Nicholas Spenser, elected the Guild's Warden in 1568; and John Spenser, listed as a "journeyman cloth-maker." Of these, the last was likely the least affluent of the three—and most likely Edmund's father, since school accounting records list Edmund as a scholar who attended the school at a reduced fee.

Which of the following is an assumption on which the argument depends?

(A) Anybody in sixteenth-century London who made clothing professionally would have had to be a member of the Merchant Tailors' Guild.

(B) The fact that Edmund Spenser attended the Merchant Tailors' School did not necessarily mean that he planned to become a tailor.

(C) No member of the Guild could become Guild warden in sixteenth-century London unless he was a gentleman.

(D) Most of those whose fathers were members of the Merchant Tailors' Guild were students at the Merchant Tailors' School.

(E) The Merchant Tailors' School did not reduce its fees for the children of the more affluent Guild members.

558. Hea Sook: One should not readily believe urban legends. Most legends are propagated because the moral lesson underlying them supports a political agenda. People will repeat a tale if it fits their purpose. They may not deliberately spread untruths, but neither are they particularly motivated to investigate deeply to determine if the tale they are telling is true.

Kayla: But people would not repeat stories that they did not believe were true. Therefore, one can safely assume that if a story has been repeated by enough people then it is more likely to be true.

Kayla's reply is most vulnerable to the criticism that it

(A) does not specify how many people need to repeat a story before someone is justified believing it

(B) overstates the significance of political agendas in the retelling of stories

(C) fails to address the claim that people will not verify the truth of a story that fits their purpose

(D) implicitly supports the claim that the people repeating legends are not deliberately spreading untruths

(E) cannot distinguish people's motivations for repeating urban legends from their motivations for repeating other types of story

559. Rainwater contains hydrogen of a heavy form called deuterium. The deuterium content of wood reflects the deuterium content of rainwater available to trees during their growth. Wood from trees that grew between 16,000 and 24,000 years ago in North America contains significantly more deuterium than wood from trees growing today. But water trapped in several North American caves that formed during that same early period contains significantly less deuterium than rainwater in North America contains today.

Which of the following, if true, most helps to reconcile the two findings?

(A) There is little deuterium in the North American caves other than the deuterium in the water trapped there.

(B) Exposure to water after a tree has died does not change the deuterium content of the wood.

(C) Industrialization in North America over the past 100 years has altered the deuterium content of rain.

(D) Trees draw on shallow groundwater from rain that falls during their growth, whereas water trapped in caves may have fallen as rainwater thousands of years before the caves formed.

(E) Wood with a high deuterium content is no more likely to remain preserved for long periods than is wood with a low deuterium content.

560. Enforcement of local speed limits through police monitoring has proven unsuccessful in the town of Ardane. In many nearby towns, speed humps (raised areas of pavement placed across residential streets, about 300 feet apart) have reduced traffic speeds on residential streets by 20 to 25 percent. In order to reduce traffic speed and thereby enhance safety in residential neighborhoods, Ardane's transportation commission plans to install multiple speed humps in those neighborhoods.

Which of the following, if true, identifies a potentially serious drawback to the plan for installing speed humps in Ardane?

(A) On residential streets without speed humps, many vehicles travel at speeds more than 25 percent above the posted speed limit.

(B) Because of their high weight, emergency vehicles such as fire trucks and ambulances must slow almost to a stop at speed humps.

(C) The residential speed limit in Ardane is higher than that of the nearby towns where speed humps were installed.

(D) Motorists who are not familiar with the streets in Ardane's residential districts would be likely to encounter the speed humps unawares unless warned by signs and painted indicators.

(E) Bicyclists generally prefer that speed humps be constructed so as to leave a space on the side of the road where bicycles can travel without going over the humps.

561. Which of the choices most logically completes the following argument?

NowNews, although still the most popular magazine covering cultural events in Kalopolis, has recently suffered a significant drop in advertising revenue because of falling circulation. Many readers have begun buying a competing magazine that, at 50 cents per copy, costs less than *NowNews* at $1.50 per copy. In order to boost circulation and thus increase advertising revenue, *NowNews*'s publisher has proposed making it available at no charge. However, this proposal has a serious drawback, since _____.

(A) those Kalopolis residents with the greatest interest in cultural events are regular readers of both magazines.

(B) one reason *NowNews*'s circulation fell was that its competitor's reporting on cultural events was superior.

(C) the newsstands and stores that currently sell *NowNews* will no longer carry it if it is being given away for free.

(D) at present, 10 percent of the total number of copies of each issue of *NowNews* are distributed free to students on college campuses in the Kalopolis area.

(E) *NowNews*'s competitor would begin to lose large amounts of money if it were forced to lower its cover price.

562. Archaeologist: Researchers excavating a burial site in Cyprus found a feline skeleton lying near a human skeleton. Both skeletons were in the same sediment at the same depth and equally well-preserved, suggesting that the feline and human were buried together about 9,500 years ago. This shows that felines were domesticated around the time farming began, when they would have been useful in protecting stores of grain from mice.

Which of the following, if true, would most seriously weaken the archaeologist's argument?

(A) Archaeologists have not found any remains of stores of grain in the immediate vicinity of the burial site.

(B) The burial site in Cyprus is substantially older than any other known burial site in which a feline skeleton and a human skeleton appear to have been buried together.

(C) Paintings found near the burial site seem to show people keeping felines as domestic companions, but do not show felines hunting mice.

(D) In Cyprus, there are many burial sites dating from around 9,500 years ago in which the remains of wild animals appear to have been buried alongside human remains.

(E) Before felines were domesticated, early farmers had no effective way to protect stores of grain from mice.

563. Farmer: Several people in the past few years have claimed to have seen a mountain lion in the suburban outskirts—the latest just last month—and, while mountain lions were thought to have been driven from this entire region about twenty years ago, there is no reason for the people who reported seeing a mountain lion to have deliberately concocted a false report. Therefore, local wildlife managers should begin to urgently address the mountain lion's presence.

Which of the following would, if true, most seriously weaken the farmer's argument?

(A) Farmers in the suburban outskirts mostly raise cattle and hogs, which when fully grown are generally not attacked by mountain lions.

(B) Mountain lions are dissimilar in size and color to other wild animals found near the suburban outskirts.

(C) No person who claimed to have seen a mountain lion had anyone else with them at the purported sighting.

(D) There have been no regional reports in the past year of mountain lions migrating to the area.

(E) Recent surveys show that more than half of the people in the region report that they have never seen a mountain lion before.

564. The heavy traffic in Masana is a growing drain on the city's economy—the clogging of the streets of the central business district alone cost the economy more than $1.2 billion over the past year. In order to address this problem, officials plan to introduce congestion pricing, by which drivers would pay to enter the city's most heavily trafficked areas during the busiest times of the day.

Which of the following, if true, would most strongly indicate that the plan will be a success?

(A) Approximately one-fifth of the vehicles in the central business district are in transit from one side of the city to the other.

(B) Planners expect that, without congestion pricing, traffic in Masana is likely to grow by 6 percent in the next five years.

(C)   In other urban areas, congestion pricing has strongly encouraged carpooling (sharing of rides by private commuters).

(D)   Several studies have shown that a reduction in traffic of 15 percent in Masana could result in 5,500 or more new jobs.

(E)   Over 30 percent of the vehicles in the city's center are occupied by more than one person.

565. Economist: The most economically efficient way to reduce emissions of air pollutants is to tax them in proportion to the damage they are likely to cause. But in Country Y, many serious pollutants are untaxed and unregulated, and policy makers strongly oppose new taxes. Therefore, the best way to achieve a reduction in air pollutant emissions in Country Y would be to institute fixed upper limits on them.

Which of the following is an assumption of the economist's argument?

(A)   Policy makers in Country Y oppose all new taxes equally strongly, regardless of any benefits they may provide.

(B)   Country Y's air pollutant emissions would not fall significantly if they were taxed in proportion to the damage they are likely to cause.

(C)   Policy makers in Country Y strongly favor reductions in air pollutant emissions.

(D)   Country Y's policy makers believe that air pollutant emissions should be reduced with maximum economic efficiency.

(E)   Policy makers in Country Y do not oppose setting fixed upper limits on air pollutant emissions as strongly as they oppose new taxes.

566. Humans get Lyme disease from infected ticks. Ticks get infected by feeding on animals with Lyme disease, but the ease of transmission from host animal to tick varies. With most species of host animal, transmission of Lyme disease to ticks is extremely rare, but white-footed mice are an exception, readily passing Lyme disease to ticks. And white-footed mouse populations greatly expand, becoming the main food source for ticks, in areas where biodiversity is in decline.

The information in the passage most strongly supports which of the following?

(A)   In areas where many humans are infected with Lyme disease, the proportion of ticks infected with Lyme disease is especially high.

(B)   Very few animals that live in areas where there are no white-footed mice are infected with Lyme disease.

(C)   Humans are less at risk of contracting Lyme disease in areas where biodiversity is high.

(D)   Ticks feed on white-footed mice only when other host species are not available to them.

(E)   The greater the biodiversity of an area, the more likely any given host animal in that area is to pass Lyme disease to ticks.

567. Many industrialized nations are trying to reduce atmospheric concentrations of carbon dioxide, a gas released by the burning of fossil fuels. One proposal is to replace conventional cement, which is made with calcium carbonate, by a new "eco-cement." This new cement, made with magnesium carbonate, absorbs large amounts of carbon dioxide when exposed to the atmosphere. Therefore, using eco-cement for new concrete building projects will significantly help reduce atmospheric concentrations of carbon dioxide.

Which of the following, if true, most strengthens the argument?

(A)   The cost of magnesium carbonate, currently greater than the cost of calcium carbonate, probably will fall as more magnesium carbonate is used in cement manufacture.

(B)   Eco-cement is strengthened when absorbed carbon dioxide reacts with the cement.

(C)   Before the development of eco-cement, magnesium-based cement was considered too susceptible to water erosion to be of practical use.

(D)   The manufacture of eco-cement uses considerably less fossil fuel per unit of cement than the manufacture of conventional cement does.

(E)   Most building-industry groups are unaware of the development or availability of eco-cement.

568. Professor: A marine biologist argues that transmission of sea lice from farm salmon to wild salmon is unlikely in the Broughton Archipelago, British Columbia, citing numerous studies suggesting that salinities less than 30 parts per thousand are unfavorable to sea-lice survival. The biologist concludes that the archipelago's 25–30 parts per thousand salinity range between March and June, the critical period for wild salmon migration, tends to suppress sea-lice proliferation. But a review of the literature shows that salinities of 25–30 parts per

thousand in combination with British Columbia's cool spring temperatures favor the flourishing of sea lice.

In this passage, the professor attempts to undermine the biologist's argument by

(A)   pointing out that a condition claimed to be necessary for sea-lice survival is not sufficient for it

(B)   citing studies that suggest that salinity levels were not measured reliably

(C)   claiming that there is evidence showing that one of its premises is false

(D)   questioning the reliability of the biologist's scientific sources

(E)   showing that its conclusion is inconsistent with its premises

569.   Advertisement: When your car's engine is running at its normal operating temperature, any major brand of motor oil will protect it about as well as Tuff does. When the engine is cold, it is a different story: Tuff motor oil flows better at lower temperatures than its major competitors do. So, if you want your car's engine to have maximum protection, you should use Tuff.

Which of the following, if true, most strengthens the argument in the advertisement?

(A)   Tuff motor oil provides above-average protection for engines that happen to overheat.

(B)   Tuff motor oil is periodically supplied free of charge to automobile manufacturers to use in factory-new cars.

(C)   Tuff motor oil's share of the engine oil market peaked three years ago.

(D)   Tuff motor oil, like any motor oil, is thicker and flows less freely at cold temperatures than at hot temperatures.

(E)   Tuff motor oil is manufactured at only one refinery and shipped from there to all markets.

570.   Linguist: In English, the past is described as "behind" and the future "ahead," whereas in Aymara the past is "ahead" and the future "behind." Research indicates that English speakers sway backward when discussing the past and forward when discussing the future. Conversely, Aymara speakers gesture forward with their hands when discussing the past and backward when discussing the future. These bodily movements, therefore, suggest that the language one speaks affects how one mentally visualizes time.

The linguist's reasoning depends on assuming which of the following?

(A)   At least some Aymara speakers sway forward when discussing the past and backward when discussing the future.

(B)   Most people mentally visualize time as running either forward or backward.

(C)   Not all English and Aymara speakers tend to sway or gesture forward or backward when discussing the present.

(D)   How people move when discussing the future correlates to some extent with how they mentally visualize time.

(E)   The researchers also examined the movements of at least some speakers of languages other than English and Aymara discussing the past and the future.

571.   *The Testament of William Thorpe* was published around 1530 as an appendix to Thorpe's longer *Examination*. Many scholars, however, doubt the attribution of the *Testament* to Thorpe because, whereas the *Examination* is dated 1406, the *Testament* is dated 1460. One scholar has recently argued that the 1460 date be amended to 1409, based on the observation that when these numbers are expressed as Roman numerals, MCCCCLX and MCCCCIX, it becomes easy to see how the dates might have become confused through scribal error.

Which of the following, if true, would most support the scholar's hypothesis concerning the date of the *Testament*?

(A)   The sole evidence that historians have had that William Thorpe died no earlier than 1460 was the presumed date of publication of the *Testament*.

(B)   In the preface to the 1530 publication, the editor attributes both works to William Thorpe.

(C)   Few writers in fifteenth-century England marked dates in their works using only Roman numerals.

(D)   The *Testament* alludes to a date, "Friday, September 20," as apparently contemporaneous with the writing of the *Testament*, and September 20 fell on a Friday in 1409 but not in 1460.

(E)   The *Testament* contains few references to historical events that occurred later than 1406.

572. A prominent investor who holds a large stake in the Burton Tool Company has recently claimed that the company is mismanaged, citing as evidence the company's failure to slow down production in response to a recent rise in its inventory of finished products. It is doubtful whether an investor's sniping at management can ever be anything other than counterproductive, but in this case, it is clearly not justified. It is true that **an increased inventory of finished products often indicates that production is outstripping demand**, but in Burton's case it indicates no such thing. Rather, **the increase in inventory is entirely attributable to products that have already been assigned to orders received from customers**.

In the argument given, the two **boldfaced** portions play which of the following roles?

(A) The first states a generalization that underlies the position that the argument as a whole opposes; the second provides evidence to show that the generalization does not apply in the case at issue.

(B) The first states a generalization that underlies the position that the argument as a whole opposes; the second clarifies the meaning of a specific phrase as it is used in that generalization.

(C) The first provides evidence to support the conclusion of the argument as a whole; the second is evidence that has been used to support the position that the argument as a whole opposes.

(D) The first provides evidence to support the conclusion of the argument as a whole; the second states that conclusion.

(E) The first and the second each provide evidence against the position that the argument as a whole opposes.

573. To reduce productivity losses from employees calling in sick, Corporation X implemented a new policy requiring employees to come into work unless they were so sick that they had to go to a doctor. But a year after the policy was implemented, a study found that Corporation X's overall productivity losses due to reported employee illnesses had increased.

Which of the following, if true, would best explain why the policy produced the reverse of its intended effect?

(A) After the policy was implemented, employees more frequently went to the doctor when they felt sick.

(B) Before the policy was implemented, employees who were not sick at all often called in sick.

(C) Employees coming into work when sick often infect many of their coworkers.

(D) Unusually few employees became genuinely sick during the year after the policy was implemented.

(E) There are many other factors besides employee illness that can adversely affect productivity.

574. Advertising by mail has become much less effective, with fewer consumers responding. Because consumers are increasingly overwhelmed by the sheer amount of junk mail they receive, most discard almost all offers without considering them. Thus, an effective way for corporations to improve response rates would be to more carefully target the individuals to whom they mail advertising, thereby cutting down on the amount of junk mail each consumer receives.

Which of the following, if true, would most support the recommendation above?

(A) There are cost-effective means by which corporations that currently advertise by mail could improve response rates.

(B) Many successful corporations are already carefully targeting the individuals to whom they mail advertising.

(C) Any consumer who, immediately after receiving an advertisement by mail, merely glances at it, is very likely to discard it.

(D) Improvements in the quality of the advertising materials used in mail that is carefully targeted to individuals can improve the response rate for such mail.

(E) Response rates to carefully targeted advertisements by mail are considerably higher, on average, than response rates to most other forms of advertising.

575. Petrochemical industry officials have said that the extreme pressure exerted on plant managers during the last five years to improve profits by cutting costs has done nothing to impair the industry's ability to operate safely. However, environmentalists contend that the recent rash of serious oil spills and accidents at petrochemical plants is traceable to cost-cutting measures.

Which of the following, if true, would provide the strongest support for the position held by industry officials?

(A) The petrochemical industry benefits if accidents do not occur, since accidents involve risk of employee injury as well as loss of equipment and product.

(B) Petrochemical industry unions recently demanded that additional money be spent on safety and environmental protection measures, but the unions readily abandoned those demands in exchange for job security.

(C) Despite major cutbacks in most other areas of operation, the petrochemical industry has devoted more of its resources to environmental and safety measures in the last five years than in the preceding five years.

(D) There is evidence that the most damaging of the recent oil spills would have been prevented had cost-cutting measures not been instituted.

(E) Both the large fines and the adverse publicity generated by the most recent oil spill have prompted the petrochemical industry to increase the resources devoted to oil-spill prevention.

576. A company has developed a new sensing device that, according to the company's claims, detects weak, ultralow-frequency electromagnetic signals associated with a beating heart. These signals, which pass through almost any physical obstruction, are purportedly detected by the device even at significant distances. Therefore, if the company's claims are true, their device will radically improve emergency teams' ability to locate quickly people who are trapped within the wreckage of collapsed buildings.

Which of the following, if true, most strengthens the argument?

(A) People trapped within the wreckage of collapsed buildings usually have serious injuries that require prompt medical treatment.

(B) The device gives a distinctive reading when the signals it detects come from human beings rather than from any other living beings.

(C) Most people who have survived after being trapped in collapsed buildings were rescued within two hours of the building's collapse.

(D) Ultralow-frequency signals are not the only electromagnetic signals that can pass through almost any physical obstruction.

(E) Extensive training is required in order to operate the device effectively.

577. Economist: The price of tap water in our region should be raised drastically. **Supplies in local freshwater reservoirs have been declining for years** because water is being used faster than it can be replenished. Since the price of tap water has been low, **few users have bothered to adopt even easy conservation measures**.

The two sections in **boldface** play which of the following roles in the economist's argument?

(A) The first is a conclusion for which support is provided, and which in turn supports the main conclusion; the second is the main conclusion.

(B) The first is an observation for which the second provides an explanation; the second is the main conclusion but not the only conclusion.

(C) The first is a premise supporting the argument's main conclusion; so is the second.

(D) The first is the only conclusion; the second provides an explanation for the first.

(E) The first is the main conclusion; the second is a conclusion for which support is provided, and which in turn supports the first.

578. Politician: Hybrid cars use significantly less fuel per kilometer than nonhybrids. And fuel produces air pollution, which contributes to a number of environmental problems. Motorists can save money by driving cars that are more fuel efficient, and they will be encouraged to drive hybrid cars if we make them aware of that fact. Therefore, we can help reduce the total amount of pollution emitted by cars in this country by highlighting this advantage of hybrid cars.

Which of the following, if true, would most indicate a vulnerability of the politician's argument?

(A) People with more fuel-efficient cars typically drive more than do those with less fuel-efficient cars.

(B) Not all air pollution originates from automobiles.

(C) Hybrid cars have already begun to gain popularity.

(D) Fuel-efficient alternatives to hybrid cars will likely become available in the future.

(E) The future cost of gasoline and other fuel cannot be predicted with absolute precision or certainty.

579. Mayor: False alarms from home security systems waste so much valuable police time that in many communities police have stopped responding to alarms from homes whose systems frequently produce false alarms. This policy reduces wastage of police time but results in a loss of protection for some residents. To achieve a comparable reduction in wastage without reducing protection for residents, the council has enacted a measure to fine residents for repeated false alarms.

Which of the following, if true, casts the most doubt on whether the measure enacted by the council will achieve its goal?

(A) A fine in the amount planned by the council will not cover the expenses police typically incur when they respond to a false alarm.

(B) Homes equipped with security systems are far less likely to be broken into than are homes without security systems.

(C) The threat of fines is likely to cause many residents to deactivate their security systems.

(D) The number of home security systems is likely to increase dramatically over the next five years.

(E) Many home security systems have never produced false alarms.

580. Excavation of the house of a third-century Camarnian official revealed that he had served four magistrates—public officials who administer the law—over his thirty-year public career, in four provincial capital cities. However, given the Camarnian administrative system of that era, it is unclear whether he served them simultaneously, as a traveling administrator living for part of the year in each provincial capital, or else did so sequentially, leaving one magistrate after several years to join another.

Which of the following would, if found in the excavation, most likely help reveal the pattern of the official's administrative service?

(A) Maps and documents describing each of the four provincial capitals

(B) A cache of the official's documents related to work from early in his career

(C) A set of cups of a type made only in the city of the first magistrate whom the official is known to have served

(D) Several pieces of furniture in the styles of two of the provincial capital cities

(E) Heavy clothing appropriate only for the coldest of the four cities

581. In 1563, in Florence's Palazzo Vecchio, Giorgio Vasari built in front of an existing wall a new wall on which he painted a mural. Investigators recently discovered a gap between Vasari's wall and the original, large enough to have preserved anything painted on the original. Historians believe that Leonardo da Vinci had painted, but left unfinished, a mural on the original wall; some historians had also believed that by 1563 the mural had been destroyed. However, it is known that in the late 1560s, when renovating another building, Santa Maria Novella, Vasari built a façade over its frescoes, and the frescoes were thereby preserved. Thus, Leonardo's Palazzo Vecchio mural probably still exists behind Vasari's wall.

Which of the following is an assumption on which the argument depends?

(A) Leonardo rarely if ever destroyed artworks that he left unfinished.

(B) Vasari was likely unaware that the mural in the Palazzo Vecchio had willingly been abandoned by Leonardo.

(C) Vasari probably would not have built the Palazzo Vecchio wall with a gap behind it except to preserve something behind the new wall.

(D) Leonardo would probably have completed the Palazzo Vecchio mural if he had had the opportunity to do so.

(E) When Vasari preserved the frescoes of Santa Maria Novella he did so secretly.

582. Coffee shop owner: A large number of customers will pay at least the fair market value for a cup of coffee, even if there is no formal charge. Some will pay more than this out of appreciation of the trust that is placed in them. And our total number of customers is likely to increase. We could therefore improve our net cash flow by implementing an honor system in which customers pay what they wish for coffee by depositing money in a can.

Manager: We're likely to lose money on this plan. Many customers would cheat the system, paying a very small sum or nothing at all.

Which of the following, if true, would best support the owner's plan, in light of the manager's concern?

(A) The new system, if implemented, would increase the number of customers.

(B) By roasting its own coffee, the shop has managed to reduce the difficulties (and cost) of maintaining an inventory of freshly roasted coffee.

(C) Many customers stay in the cafe for long stretches of time.

(D) The shop makes a substantial profit from pastries and other food bought by the coffee drinkers.

(E) No other coffee shop in the area has such a system.

583. Birds have been said to be descended from certain birdlike dinosaur species with which they share distinctive structural features. The fossil record, however, shows that this cannot be so, since there are bird fossils that are much older than the earliest birdlike dinosaur fossils that have been found.

Which of the following is an assumption on which the argument relies?

(A) The birdlike dinosaurs have no living descendants.

(B) There are no flightless dinosaur species that have the distinctive structural features shared by birds and birdlike dinosaurs.

(C) There are no birdlike dinosaur fossils that are older than the bird fossils but have not yet been unearthed.

(D) It could not have been the case that some birds were descended from one of the birdlike dinosaur species and other birds from another.

(E) Birds cannot have been descended from dinosaur species with which the birds do not share the distinctive structural features.

584. City council member: Demand for electricity has been increasing by 1.5 percent a year, and there simply is no more space to build additional power plants to meet future demand increases. We must therefore begin to curtail usage, which is why I propose passing ordinances requiring energy-conservation measures in all city departments.

The city council member's proposal assumes which of the following?

(A) Existing power plants do not have the capacity to handle all of the projected increase in demand for electricity.

(B) No city departments have implemented energy-conservation measures voluntarily.

(C) Passing ordinances designed to curtail electricity usage will not have negative economic consequences for the city.

(D) Residential consumers are not responsible for the recent increases in demand for electricity.

(E) City departments that successfully conserve energy will set a good example for residential and industrial consumers of electricity.

585. Certain groups of Asian snails include both "left-handed" and "right-handed" species, with shells coiling to the left and right, respectively. Some left-handed species have evolved from right-handed ones. Also, researchers found that snail-eating snakes in the same habitat have asymmetrical jaws, allowing them to grasp right-handed snail shells more easily. If these snakes ate more right-handed snails over time, this would have given left-handed snails an evolutionary advantage over right-handed snails, with the left-handed snails eventually becoming a new species. Thus, the snakes' asymmetrical jaws probably helped drive the emergence of the left-handed snail species.

Which of the following would, if true, most strengthen the argument that asymmetrical snake jaws helped drive left-handed snail evolution?

(A) In one snake species, the snakes with asymmetrical jaws eat snails, while the snakes with symmetrical jaws do not eat snails.

(B) Some species of Asian snails contain either all right-handed snails, or all left-handed snails.

(C) Anatomical differences prevent left-handed snails from mating easily with right-handed snails.

(D) Some right-handed snails in this habitat have shells with a very narrow opening that helps prevent snakes from extracting the snails from inside their shells.

(E) Experiments show that the snail-eating snakes in this habitat fail more often in trying to eat left-handed snails than in trying to eat right-handed snails.

586. A moderately large city is redesigning its central downtown area and is considering a plan that would reduce the number of lanes for automobiles and trucks and increase those for bicycles and pedestrians. The intent is to attract more workers and shoppers to

downtown businesses by making downtown easier to reach and more pleasant to move around in.

Which of the following would, if true, most strongly support the prediction that the plan would achieve its goal?

(A) People who make a habit of walking or bicycling whenever feasible derive significant health benefits from doing so.

(B) Most people who prefer to shop at suburban malls instead of downtown urban areas do so because parking is easier and cheaper at the former.

(C) In other moderately sized cities where measures were taken to make downtowns more accessible for walkers and cyclists, downtown businesses began to thrive.

(D) If the proposed lane restrictions on drivers are rigorously enforced, more people will likely be attracted to downtown businesses than would otherwise be.

(E) Most people who own and frequently ride bicycles for recreational purposes live at a significant distance from downtown urban areas.

587. Previously, Autoco designed all of its cars itself and then contracted with specialized parts suppliers to build parts according to its specifications. Now it plans to include its suppliers in designing the parts they are to build. Since many parts suppliers have more designers with specialized experience than Autoco has, Autoco expects this shift to reduce the overall time and cost of the design of its next new car.

Which of the following, if true, most strongly supports Autoco's expectation?

(A) When suppliers provide their own designs, Autoco often needs to modify its overall design.

(B) In order to provide designs for Autoco, several of the parts suppliers will have to add to their existing staffs of designers.

(C) Parts and services provided by outside suppliers account for more than 50 percent of Autoco's total costs.

(D) When suppliers built parts according to specifications provided by Autoco, the suppliers competed to win contracts.

(E) Most of Autoco's suppliers have on hand a wide range of previously prepared parts designs that can readily be modified for a new car.

588. In response to viral infection, the immune systems of mice typically produce antibodies that destroy the virus by binding to proteins on its surface. Mice infected with the herpesvirus generally develop keratitis, a degenerative disease affecting part of the eye. Since proteins on the surface of cells in this part of the eye closely resemble those on the herpesvirus surface, scientists hypothesize that these cases of keratitis are caused by antibodies to the herpesvirus.

Which of the following, if true, most helps to support the scientists' reasoning?

(A) Other types of virus have surface proteins that closely resemble proteins found in various organs of mice.

(B) Mice that are infected with the herpesvirus but do not develop keratitis produce as many antibodies as infected mice that do develop keratitis.

(C) Mice infected with a new strain of the herpesvirus that has different surface proteins did not develop keratitis.

(D) Mice that have never been infected with the herpesvirus can sometimes develop keratitis.

(E) There are mice that are unable to form antibodies in response to herpes infections, and these mice contract herpes at roughly the same rate as other mice.

589. One might expect that within a particular species, any individuals that managed to slow down the aging process would leave more offspring. Natural selection should therefore favor extreme longevity—but this does not seem to be the case. A possible explanation is that aging is a product of the inevitable wear and tear of living, similar to how household appliances generally accumulate faults that lead to their eventual demise. However, most researchers do not find this analogy satisfactory as an explanation.

Which of the following would, if true, provide the strongest explanation for the researchers' reaction?

(A) Some organisms are capable of living much longer than other organisms.

(B)   Some organisms reproduce very quickly despite having short lifespans.

(C)   There are several ways of defining "extreme longevity," and according to some definitions it occurs frequently.

(D)   Organisms are capable of maintenance and self-repair and can remedy much of the damage that they accumulate.

(E)   Some organisms generate much more wear and tear on their bodies than others.

590.   Last year a record number of new manufacturing jobs were created. Will this year bring another record? Well, **any new manufacturing job is created either within an existing company or by the start-up of a new company**. Within existing firms, new jobs have been created this year at well below last year's record pace. At the same time, there is considerable evidence that the number of new companies starting up this year will be no higher than it was last year and **there is no reason to think that the new companies starting up this year will create more jobs per company than did last year's start-ups**. So clearly, the number of new jobs created this year will fall short of last year's record.

In the argument given, the two portions in **boldface** play which of the following roles?

(A)   The first provides evidence in support of the main conclusion of the argument; the second is a claim that the argument challenges.

(B)   The first is a generalization that the argument seeks to establish; the second is a conclusion that the argument draws in order to support that generalization.

(C)   The first is a generalization that the argument seeks to establish; the second is a judgment that has been advanced in order to challenge that generalization.

(D)   The first is presented as an obvious truth on which the argument is based; the second is a claim that has been advanced in support of a position that the argument opposes.

(E)   The first is presented as an obvious truth on which the argument is based; the second is a judgment advanced in support of the main conclusion of the argument.

591.   Last year a record number of new manufacturing jobs were created. Will this year bring another record? Well, **any new manufacturing job is created either within an existing company or by the start-up of a new company**. Within existing firms, new jobs have been created this year at well below last year's record pace. At the same time, there is considerable evidence that the number of new companies starting up will be no higher this year than it was last year and there is no reason to think that the new companies starting up this year will create more jobs per company than did last year's start-ups. So clearly, **the number of new jobs created this year will fall short of last year's record**.

In the argument given, the two portions in **boldface** play which of the following roles?

(A)   The first is presented as an obvious truth on which the argument is based; the second is the main conclusion of the argument.

(B)   The first is presented as an obvious truth on which the argument is based; the second is a conclusion drawn in order to support the main conclusion of the argument.

(C)   The first and the second each provide evidence in support of the main conclusion of the argument.

(D)   The first is a generalization that the argument seeks to establish; the second is the main conclusion of the argument.

(E)   The first is a generalization that the argument seeks to establish; the second is a conclusion that has been drawn in order to challenge that generalization.

592.   In Stenland, many workers have been complaining that they cannot survive on minimum wage, the lowest wage an employer is permitted to pay. The government is proposing to raise the minimum wage. Many employers who pay their workers the current minimum wage argue that if it is raised, unemployment will increase because they will no longer be able to afford to employ as many workers.

Which of the following, if true in Stenland, most strongly supports the claim that raising the minimum wage there will not have the effects that the employers predict?

(A)   For any position with wages below a living wage, the difficulty of finding and retaining employees adds as much to employment costs as would raising wages.

(B)   Raising the minimum wage does not also increase the amount employers have to contribute in employee benefits.

(C)   When inflation is taken into account, the proposed new minimum wage is not as high as the current one was when it was introduced.

(D)   Many employees currently being paid wages at the level of the proposed new minimum wage will demand significant wage increases.

(E)   Many employers who pay some workers only the minimum wage also pay other workers wages that are much higher than the minimum.

593.   Biologists with a predilection for theory have tried—and largely failed—to define what it is that makes something a living thing. Organisms take in energy-providing materials and excrete waste products, but so do automobiles. Living things replicate and take part in evolution, but so do some computer programs. We must be open to the possibility that there are living things on other planets. Therefore, we will not be successful in defining what it is that makes something a living thing merely by examining living things on Earth—the only ones we know. Trying to do so is analogous to trying to specify _____.

Which of the following most logically completes the passage?

(A)   the laws of physics by using pure mathematics

(B)   what a fish is by listing its chemical components

(C)   what an animal is by examining a plant

(D)   what a machine is by examining a sketch of it

(E)   what a mammal is by examining a zebra

594.   For the period from the eighth century through the eleventh century, the shifting boundaries between Kingdom F and Kingdom G have not been well charted. Although a certain village in a border region between the two kingdoms usually belonged to Kingdom G, ninth-century artifacts found in the village were in the typical Kingdom F style of that time. It is unclear whether the village was actually a part of Kingdom F in the ninth century or whether it was a part of Kingdom G but had merely adopted Kingdom F's artistic styles under Kingdom F's cultural influence.

Which of the following would, if found in ninth-century sites in the village, best help in determining whether the village was a part of Kingdom F or Kingdom G in the ninth century?

(A)   A trading contract written in the Kingdom G dialect

(B)   A drawing of a dwelling complex known to have existed on the border of Kingdom F and Kingdom G in the ninth century

(C)   Knives and other utensils made from metal typical of ninth-century mining sites in Kingdom F

(D)   Some fragments of pottery made in the Kingdom G style from the seventh century out of materials only found in Kingdom F

(E)   Numerous teeth from the ninth century with a chemical signature typical only of teeth from people who had grown up in the heart of Kingdom F

595.   Sammy: For my arthritis, I am going to try my aunt's diet: large amounts of wheat germ and garlic. She was able to move more easily right after she started that diet.

Pat: When my brother began that diet, his arthritis got worse. But he has been doing much better since he stopped eating vegetables in the nightshade family, such as tomatoes and peppers.

Which of the following, if true, would provide a basis for explaining the fact that Sammy's aunt and Pat's brother had contrasting experiences with the same diet?

(A)   A change in diet, regardless of the nature of the change, frequently brings temporary relief from arthritis symptoms.

(B)   The compounds in garlic that can lessen the symptoms of arthritis are also present in tomatoes and peppers.

(C)   Arthritis is a chronic condition whose symptoms improve and worsen from time to time without regard to diet.

(D)   In general, men are more likely to have their arthritis symptoms alleviated by avoiding vegetables in the nightshade family than are women.

(E)   People who are closely related are more likely to experience the same result from adopting a particular diet than are people who are unrelated.

596.   In the 1960s, surveys of Florida's alligator population indicated that the population was dwindling rapidly. Hunting alligators was banned. By the early 1990s, the

alligator population had recovered, and restricted hunting was allowed. Over the course of the 1990s, reports of alligators appearing on golf courses and lawns increased dramatically. Therefore, in spite of whatever alligator hunting went on, the alligator population must have increased significantly over the decade of the 1990s.

Which of the following, if true, most seriously weakens the argument?

(A) The human population of Florida increased significantly during the 1990s.

(B) The hunting restrictions applied to commercial as well as private hunters.

(C) The number of sightings of alligators in lakes and swamps increased greatly in Florida during the 1990s.

(D) Throughout the 1990s, selling alligator products was more strictly regulated than hunting was.

(E) Most of the sightings of alligators on golf courses and lawns in the 1990s occurred at times at which few people were present on those golf courses and lawns.

597. Infotek, a computer manufacturer in Katrovia, has just introduced a new personal computer model that sells for significantly less than any other model. Market research shows, however, that very few Katrovian households without personal computers would buy a computer, regardless of its price. Therefore, introducing the new model is unlikely to increase the number of computers in Katrovian homes.

Which of the following is an assumption on which the argument depends?

(A) Infotek achieved the lower price of the new model by using components of lower quality than those used by other manufacturers.

(B) The main reason cited by consumers in Katrovia for replacing a personal computer is the desire to have an improved model.

(C) Katrovians in households that already have computers are unlikely to purchase the new Infotek model as an additional computer for home use.

(D) The price of other personal computers in Katrovia is unlikely to drop below the price of Infotek's new model in the near future.

(E) Most personal computers purchased in Katrovia are intended for home use.

598. Fast-food restaurants make up 45 percent of all restaurants in Canatria. Customers at these restaurants tend to be young; in fact, studies have shown that the older people get, the less likely they are to eat in fast-food restaurants. Since the average age of the Canatrian population is gradually rising and will continue to do so, the number of fast-food restaurants is likely to decrease.

Which of the following, if true, most seriously weakens the argument?

(A) Fast-food restaurants in Canatria are getting bigger, so each one can serve more customers.

(B) Some older people eat at fast-food restaurants more frequently than the average young person.

(C) Many people who rarely eat in fast-food restaurants nevertheless eat regularly in restaurants.

(D) The overall population of Canatria is growing steadily.

(E) As the population of Canatria gets older, more people are eating at home.

599. Last year a chain of fast-food restaurants, whose menu had always centered on hamburgers, added its first vegetarian sandwich, much lower in fat than the chain's other offerings. Despite heavy marketing, the new sandwich accounts for a very small proportion of the chain's sales. The sandwich's sales would have to quadruple to cover the costs associated with including it on the menu. Since such an increase is unlikely, the chain would be more profitable if it dropped the sandwich.

Which of the following, if true, most seriously weakens the argument?

(A) Although many of the chain's customers have never tried the vegetarian sandwich, in a market research survey most of those who had tried it reported that they were very satisfied with it.

(B) Many of the people who eat at the chain's restaurants also eat at the restaurants of competing chains and report no strong preference among the competitors.

(C) Among fast-food chains in general, there has been little or no growth in hamburger sales over the past several years as the range of competing offerings at other restaurants has grown.

(D) When even one member of a group of diners is a vegetarian or has a preference for low-fat food, the group tends to avoid restaurants that lack vegetarian or low-fat menu options.

(E)   An attempt by the chain to introduce a lower-fat hamburger failed several years ago, since it attracted few new customers and most of the chain's regular customers greatly preferred the taste of the regular hamburgers.

600.   Transportation expenses accounted for a large portion of the total dollar amount spent on trips for pleasure by residents of the United States in 1997, and about half of the total dollar amount spent on transportation was for airfare. However, the large majority of United States residents who took trips for pleasure in 1997 did not travel by airplane but used other means of transportation.

If the statements above are true, which of the following must also be true about United States residents who took trips for pleasure in 1997?

(A)   Most of those who traveled by airplane did so because the airfare to their destination was lower than the cost of other available means of transportation.

(B)   Most of those who traveled by airplane did so because other means of transportation to their destination were unavailable.

(C)   Per mile traveled, those who traveled by airplane tended to spend more on transportation to their destination than did those who used other means of transportation.

(D)   Overall, people who did not travel by airplane had lower average transportation expenses than people who did.

(E)   Those who traveled by airplane spent about as much, on average, on other means of transportation as they did on airfare.

601.   Voters commonly condemn politicians for being insincere, but politicians often must disguise their true feelings when they make public statements. If they expressed their honest views—about, say, their party's policies—then achieving politically necessary compromises would be much more difficult. Clearly, the very insincerity that people decry shows that our government is functioning well.

Which of the following, if true, most seriously undermines this reasoning?

(A)   Achieving political compromises is not all that is necessary for the proper functioning of a government.

(B)   Some political compromises are not in the best long-term interest of the government.

(C)   Voters often judge politicians by criteria other than the sincerity with which they express their views.

(D)   A political party's policies could turn out to be detrimental to the functioning of a government.

(E)   Some of the public statements made by politicians about their party's policies could in fact be sincere.

602.   One summer, floods covered low-lying garlic fields situated in a region with a large mosquito population. Since mosquitoes lay their eggs in standing water, flooded fields would normally attract mosquitoes, yet no mosquitoes were found in the fields. Diallyl sulfide, a major component of garlic, is known to repel several species of insects, including mosquitoes, so it is likely that diallyl sulfide from the garlic repelled the mosquitoes.

Which of the following, if true, most strengthens the argument?

(A)   Diallyl sulfide is also found in onions but at concentrations lower than in garlic.

(B)   The mosquito population of the region as a whole was significantly smaller during the year in which the flooding took place than it had been in previous years.

(C)   By the end of the summer, most of the garlic plants in the flooded fields had been killed by waterborne fungi.

(D)   Many insect species not repelled by diallyl sulfide were found in the flooded garlic fields throughout the summer.

(E)   Mosquitoes are known to be susceptible to toxins in plants other than garlic, such as marigolds.

Questions 603–664 - Difficulty: Hard

603.   Duckbill dinosaurs, like today's monitor lizards, had particularly long tails, which they could whip at considerable speed. Monitor lizards use their tails to strike predators. However, although duckbill tails were otherwise very similar to those of monitor lizards, the duckbill's tailbones were proportionately much thinner and thus more delicate. Moreover, to ward off their proportionately much larger predators, duckbills would have had to whip their tails considerably faster than monitor lizards do.

The information given, if accurate, provides the strongest support for which of the following hypotheses?

(A) If duckbills whipped their tails faster than monitor lizards do, the duckbill's tail would have been effective at warding off the duckbills' fiercest predators.

(B) Duckbills used their tails to strike predators, and their tailbones were frequently damaged from the impact.

(C) Using their tails was not the only means duckbills had for warding off predators.

(D) Duckbills were at much greater risk of being killed by a predator than monitor lizards are.

(E) The tails of duckbills, if used to ward off predators, would have been more likely than the tails of monitor lizards to sustain damage from the impact.

604. In an attempt to produce a coffee plant that would yield beans containing no caffeine, the synthesis of a substance known to be integral to the initial stages of caffeine production was blocked either in the beans, in the leaves, or both. For those plants in which synthesis of the substance was blocked only in the leaves, the resulting beans contained no caffeine.

Any of the following, if true, would provide the basis for an explanation of the observed results EXCEPT:

(A) In coffee plants, the substance is synthesized only in the leaves and then moves to the beans, where the initial stages of caffeine production take place.

(B) In coffee plants, the last stage of caffeine production takes place in the beans using a compound that is produced only in the leaves by the substance.

(C) In coffee plants, the initial stages of caffeine production take place only in the beans, but later stages depend on another substance that is synthesized only in the leaves and does not depend on the blocked substance.

(D) In coffee plants, caffeine production takes place only in the leaves, but the caffeine then moves to the beans.

(E) Caffeine was produced in the beans of the modified coffee plants, but all of it moved to the leaves, which normally produce their own caffeine.

605. Which of the following most logically completes the passage?

Laminated glass is much harder to break than the glass typically used in the windows of cars driven in Relnia. It is more difficult for thieves to break into cars with laminated glass windows than into cars with ordinary glass windows, and laminated glass windows are less likely to break in a collision. Nevertheless, considerations of security and safety do not unambiguously support a proposal to require that in Relnia all glass installed in cars be laminated glass, since _____.

(A) most people cannot visually distinguish laminated glass from the glass typically used for car windows

(B) a significant proportion of cars driven in Relnia are manufactured elsewhere

(C) some cars in Relnia already have laminated glass in their windows

(D) the rates of car theft and of collisions have both fallen slightly in Relnia in recent years

(E) there are times when breaking a car's window is the best way to provide timely help for people trapped inside

606. Consultant: **Ace Repairs ends up having to redo a significant number of the complex repair jobs it undertakes, but when those repairs are redone, they are invariably done right.** Since we have established that there is no systematic difference between the mechanics who are assigned to do the initial repairs and those who are assigned to redo unsatisfactory jobs, we must reject the hypothesis that mistakes made in the initial repairs are due to the mechanics' lack of competence. Rather, it is likely that **complex repairs require a level of focused attention that the company's mechanics apply consistently only to repair jobs that have not been done right on the first try.**

In the consultant's reasoning, the two portions in **boldface** play which of the following roles?

(A) The first is the consultant's main conclusion; the second provides evidence in support of that main conclusion.

(B) The first is evidence that serves as the basis for rejecting one explanation of a certain finding; the second is the consultant's own explanation of that finding.

(C) The first is a claim whose truth is at issue in the reasoning; the second provides evidence to show that the claim is true.

(D) The first presents a contrast whose explanation is at issue in the reasoning; the second is the consultant's explanation of that contrast.

(E) The first presents a contrast whose explanation is at issue in the reasoning; the second is evidence that has been used to challenge the consultant's explanation of that contrast.

607. To reduce waste of raw materials, the government of Sperland is considering requiring household appliances to be broken down for salvage when discarded. To cover the cost of salvage, the government is planning to charge a fee, which would be imposed when the appliance is first sold. Imposing the fee at the time of salvage would reduce waste more effectively, however, because consumers tend to keep old appliances longer if they are faced with a fee for discarding them.

Which of the following, if true, most seriously weakens the argument?

(A) Increasing the cost of disposing of an appliance properly increases the incentive to dispose of it improperly.

(B) The fee provides manufacturers with no incentive to produce appliances that are more durable.

(C) For people who have bought new appliances recently, the salvage fee would not need to be paid for a number of years.

(D) People who sell their used, working appliances to others would not need to pay the salvage fee.

(E) Many nonfunctioning appliances that are currently discarded could be repaired at relatively little expense.

608. When there is less rainfall than normal, the water level of Australian rivers falls and the rivers flow more slowly. Because algae whose habitat is river water grow best in slow-moving water, the amount of algae per unit of water generally increases when there has been little rain. By contrast, however, following a period of extreme drought, algae levels are low even in very slow-moving river water.

Which of the following, if true, does most to explain the contrast described above?

(A) During periods of extreme drought, the populations of some of the species that feed on algae tend to fall.

(B) The more slowly water moves, the more conducive its temperature is to the growth of algae.

(C) When algae populations reach very high levels, conditions within the river can become toxic for some of the other species that normally live there.

(D) Australian rivers dry up completely for short intervals in periods of extreme drought.

(E) Except during periods of extreme drought, algae levels tend to be higher in rivers in which the flow has been controlled by damming than in rivers that flow freely.

609. Increased use of incineration is sometimes advocated as a safe way to dispose of chemical waste. But opponents of incineration point to the 40 incidents involving unexpected releases of dangerous chemical agents that were reported just last year at two existing incinerators commissioned to destroy a quantity of chemical waste material. Since designs for proposed new incinerators include no additional means of preventing such releases, leaks will only become more prevalent if use of incineration increases.

Which of the following, if true, most seriously weakens the argument?

(A) At the two incinerators at which leaks were reported, staff had had only cursory training on the proper procedures for incinerating chemical waste.

(B) Other means of disposing of chemical waste, such as chemical neutralization processes, have not been proven safer than incineration.

(C) The capacity of existing incinerators is sufficient to allow for increased incineration of chemical waste without any need for new incinerators.

(D) The frequency of reports of unexpected releases of chemical agents at newly built incinerators is about the same as the frequency at older incinerators.

(E) In only three of the reported incidents of unexpected chemical leaks did the releases extend outside the property on which the incinerators were located.

610. Public health expert: **Increasing the urgency of a public health message may be counterproductive.** In addition to irritating the majority who already behave responsibly, **it may undermine all government pronouncements on health by convincing people that such messages are overly cautious.** And there is no reason to believe that those who ignore measured voices will listen to shouting.

The two sections in **boldface** play which of the following roles in the public health expert's argument?

(A) The first is a conclusion for which support is provided, but is not the argument's main conclusion; the second is an unsupported premise supporting the argument's main conclusion.

(B) The first is a premise supporting the only explicit conclusion; so is the second.

(C) The first is the argument's main conclusion; the second supports that conclusion and is itself a conclusion for which support is provided.

(D) The first is a premise supporting the argument's only conclusion; the second is that conclusion.

(E) The first is the argument's only explicit conclusion; the second is a premise supporting that conclusion.

611. Several industries have recently switched at least partly from older technologies powered by fossil fuels to new technologies powered by electricity. It is thus evident that less fossil fuel is being used as a result of the operations of these industries than would have been used if these industries had retained their older technologies.

Which of the following, if true, most strengthens the argument above?

(A) Many of the industries that have switched at least partly to the new technologies have increased their output.

(B) Less fossil fuel was used to manufacture the machinery employed in the new technologies than was originally used to manufacture the machinery employed in the older technologies.

(C) More electricity is used by those industries that have switched at least partly to the new technologies than by those industries that have not switched.

(D) Some of the industries that have switched at least partly to the new technologies still use primarily technologies that are powered by fossil fuels.

(E) The amount of fossil fuel used to generate the electricity needed to power the new technologies is less than the amount that would have been used to power the older technologies.

612. The difference in average annual income in favor of employees who have college degrees, compared with those who do not have such degrees, doubled between 1980 and 1990. Some analysts have hypothesized that increased competition between employers for employees with college degrees drove up income for such employees.

Which of the following, if true, most seriously undermines the explanation described above?

(A) During the 1980s a growing percentage of college graduates, unable to find jobs requiring a college degree, took unskilled jobs.

(B) The average age of all employees increased slightly during the 1980s.

(C) The unemployment rate changed very little throughout most of the 1980s.

(D) From 1980 to 1990 the difference in average income between employees with advanced degrees and those with bachelor's degrees also increased.

(E) During the 1980s there were some employees with no college degree who earned incomes comparable to the top incomes earned by employees with a college degree.

613. Which of the following most logically completes the passage?

According to the last pre-election poll in Whippleton, most voters believe that the three problems government needs to address, in order of importance, are pollution, crime, and unemployment. Yet in the election, candidates from parties perceived as strongly against pollution were defeated, while those elected were all from parties with a history of opposing legislation designed to reduce pollution. These results should not be taken to indicate that the poll was inaccurate, however, since _____.

(A) some voters in Whippleton do not believe that pollution needs to be reduced

(B) every candidate who was defeated had a strong antipollution record

(C) there were no issues other than crime, unemployment, and pollution on which the candidates had significant differences of opinion

(D) all the candidates who were elected were perceived as being stronger against both crime and unemployment than the candidates who were defeated

(E) many of the people who voted in the election refused to participate in the poll

614. Manufacturing plants in Arundia have recently been acquired in substantial numbers by investors from abroad. Arundian politicians are proposing legislative action to stop such investment, justifying the proposal by arguing that foreign investors, opportunistically exploiting a recent fall in the value of the Arundian currency, were able to buy Arundian assets at less than their true value.

Which of the following, if true, casts the most serious doubt on the adequacy of the Arundian politicians' justification for the proposed legislation?

(A) The Arundian government originally welcomed the fall in the value of the Arundian currency because the fall made Arundian exports more competitive on international markets.

(B) Foreign investors who acquired Arundian manufacturing plants generally did so with no intention of keeping and running those plants over the long term.

(C) Without the recent fall in the value of the Arundian currency, many of the Arundian assets bought by foreign investors would have been beyond the financial reach of those investors.

(D) In Concordia, a country broadly similar to Arundia, the share of manufacturing assets that is foreign-controlled is 60 percent higher than it is in Arundia.

(E) The true value of an investment is determined by the value of the profits from it, and the low value of the Arundian currency has depressed the value of any profits earned by foreign investors from Arundian assets.

615. Proposal: Carbon dioxide and methane in the atmosphere block the escape of heat into space. So emission of these "greenhouse" gases contributes to global warming. In order to reduce global warming, emission of greenhouse gases needs to be reduced. Therefore, the methane now emitted from open landfills should instead be burned to produce electricity.

Objection: The burning of methane generates carbon dioxide that is released into the atmosphere.

Which of the following, if true, most adequately counters the objection made to the proposal?

(A) Every time a human being or other mammal exhales, there is some carbon dioxide released into the air.

(B) The conversion of methane to electricity would occur at a considerable distance from the landfills.

(C) The methane that is used to generate electricity would generally be used as a substitute for a fuel that does not produce any greenhouse gases when burned.

(D) Methane in the atmosphere is more effective in blocking the escape of heat from the Earth than is carbon dioxide.

(E) The amount of methane emitted from the landfills could be reduced if the materials whose decomposition produces methane were not discarded, but recycled.

616. Proposed new safety rules for Beach City airport would lengthen considerably the minimum time between takeoffs from the airport. In consequence, the airport would be able to accommodate 10 percent fewer flights than currently use the airport daily. The city's operating budget depends heavily on taxes generated by tourist spending, and most of the tourists come by plane. Therefore, the proposed new safety rules, if adopted, will reduce the revenue available for the operating budget.

The argument depends on assuming which of the following?

(A) There are no periods of the day during which the interval between flights taking off from the airport is significantly greater than the currently allowed minimum.

(B) Few, if any, of the tourists who use Beach City airport do so when their main destination is a neighboring community and not Beach City itself.

(C) If the proposed safety rules are adopted, the reduction in tourist numbers will not result mainly from a reduction in the number of tourists who spend relatively little in Beach City.

(D) Increasing the minimum time between takeoffs is the only way to achieve necessary safety improvements without a large expenditure by the city government on airport enhancements.

(E) The response to the adoption of the new safety rules would not include a large increase in the number of passengers per flight.

617. The introduction of new drugs into the market is frequently prevented by a shortage of human subjects for the clinical trials needed to show that the drugs are safe and effective. Since the lives and health of people in future generations may depend on treatments that are currently experimental, practicing physicians are morally in the wrong when, in the absence of any treatment proven to be effective, they fail to encourage suitable patients to volunteer for clinical trials.

Which of the following, if true, casts most doubt on the conclusion of the argument?

(A) Many drugs undergoing clinical trials are intended for the treatment of conditions for which there is currently no effective treatment.

(B) Patients do not share the physician's professional concern for public health, but everyone has a moral obligation to alleviate suffering when able to do so.

(C) Usually, half the patients in a clinical trial serve as a control group and receive a nonactive drug in place of the drug being tested.

(D) An experimental drug cannot legally be made available to patients unless those patients are subjects in clinical trials of the drug.

(E) Physicians have an overriding moral and legal duty to care for the health and safety of their current patients.

618. As a construction material, bamboo is as strong as steel and sturdier than concrete. Moreover, in tropical areas bamboo is a much less expensive construction material than either steel or concrete and is always readily available. In tropical areas, therefore, building with bamboo makes better economic sense than building with steel or concrete, except where land values are high.

Which of the following, if true, most helps to explain the exception noted above?

(A) Buildings constructed of bamboo are less likely to suffer earthquake damage than are steel and concrete buildings.

(B) Bamboo is unsuitable as a building material for multistory buildings.

(C) In order to protect it from being damaged by termites and beetles, bamboo must be soaked, at some expense, in a preservative.

(D) In some tropical areas, bamboo is used to make the scaffolding that is used during large construction projects.

(E) Bamboo growing in an area where land values are increasing is often cleared to make way for construction.

619. The country of Virodia has, until now, been barely self-sufficient in both meat and grain. Greater prosperity there has gone hand in hand with steadily increasing per capita consumption of meat, and it takes several pounds of grain used as feed to produce one pound of meat. Per capita income is almost certain to rise further, yet increases in domestic grain production are unlikely.

Which of the following is most strongly supported by the information given?

(A) Some land in Virodia that is currently used for grain production will soon be turned into pastureland for grazing cattle for meat.

(B) In the future, per capita income in Virodia is unlikely to increase as rapidly as it has in the past.

(C) In Virodia, the amount of grain it takes to produce one pound of meat is likely to increase in coming years.

(D) Grain is soon likely to make up a larger proportion of the average Virodian's diet than ever before.

(E)   Virodia is likely to become an importer of grain or meat or both.

620. Newspaper editors should not allow reporters to write the headlines for their own stories. The reason for this is that, while the headlines that reporters themselves write are often clever, what typically makes them clever is that they allude to little-known information that is familiar to the reporter but that never appears explicitly in the story itself.

Which of the following, if true, most strengthens the argument?

(A)   The reporter who writes a story is usually better placed than the reporter's editor is to judge what the story's most newsworthy features are.

(B)   To write a headline that is clever, a person must have sufficient understanding of the story that the headline accompanies.

(C)   Most reporters rarely bother to find out how other reporters have written stories and headlines about the same events that they themselves have covered.

(D)   For virtually any story that a reporter writes, there are at least a few people who know more about the story's subject matter than does the reporter.

(E)   The kind of headlines that newspaper editors want are those that anyone who has read a reporter's story in its entirety will recognize as clever.

621. Scientists have modified feed corn genetically, increasing its resistance to insect pests. Farmers who tried out the genetically modified corn last season applied less insecticide to their corn fields and still got yields comparable to those they would have gotten with ordinary corn. Ordinary corn seed, however, costs less, and what these farmers saved on insecticide rarely exceeded their extra costs for seed. Therefore, for most feed-corn farmers, switching to genetically modified seed would be unlikely to increase profits.

Which of the following would it be most useful to know in order to evaluate the argument?

(A)   Whether there are insect pests that sometimes reduce feed-corn yields, but against which

commonly used insecticides and the genetic modification are equally ineffective

(B)   Whether the price that farmers receive for feed corn has remained steady over the past few years

(C)   Whether the insecticides typically used on feed corn tend to be more expensive than insecticides typically used on other crops

(D)   Whether most of the farmers who tried the genetically modified corn last season applied more insecticide than was actually necessary

(E)   Whether, for most farmers who plant feed corn, it is their most profitable crop

622. Debater: The average amount of overtime per month worked by an employee in the manufacturing division of the Haglut Corporation is 14 hours. Most employees of the Haglut Corporation work in the manufacturing division. Furthermore, the average amount of overtime per month worked by any employee in the company generally does not fluctuate much from month to month. Therefore, each month, most employees of the Haglut Corporation almost certainly work at least some overtime.

The debater's argument is most vulnerable to criticism on which of these grounds?

(A)   It takes for granted that the manufacturing division is a typical division of the corporation with regard to the average amount of overtime its employees work each month.

(B)   It takes for granted that if a certain average amount of overtime is worked each month by each employee of the Haglut Corporation, then approximately the same amount of overtime must be worked each month by each employee of the manufacturing division.

(C)   It confuses a claim from which the argument's conclusion about the Haglut Corporation would necessarily follow with a claim that would follow from the argument's conclusion only with a high degree of probability.

(D)   It overlooks the possibility that even if, on average, a certain amount of overtime is worked by the members of some group, many members of that group may work no overtime at all.

(E)   It overlooks the possibility that even if most employees of the corporation work some overtime each month, any one corporate employee may, in some months, work no overtime.

623. Proponents of the recently introduced tax on sales of new luxury boats had argued that a tax of this sort would be an equitable way to increase government revenue because the admittedly heavy tax burden would fall only on wealthy people and neither they nor anyone else would suffer any economic hardship. In fact, however, 20 percent of the workers employed by manufacturers of luxury boats have lost their jobs as a direct result of this tax.

The information given, if true, most strongly supports which of the following?

(A) The market for luxury boats would have collapsed even if the new tax on luxury boats had been lower.

(B) The new tax would produce a net gain in tax revenue for the government only if the yearly total revenue that it generates exceeds the total of any yearly tax-revenue decrease resulting from the workers' loss of jobs.

(C) Because many people never buy luxury items, imposing a sales tax on luxury items is the kind of legislative action that does not cost incumbent legislators much popular support.

(D) Before the tax was instituted, luxury boats were largely bought by people who were not wealthy.

(E) Taxes can be equitable only if their burden is evenly distributed over the entire population.

624. In Wareland last year, 16 percent of licensed drivers under 21 and 11 percent of drivers ages 21–24 were in serious accidents. By contrast, only 3 percent of licensed drivers 65 and older were involved in serious accidents. These figures clearly show that the greater experience and developed habits of caution possessed by drivers in the 65-and-older group make them far safer behind the wheel than the younger drivers are.

Which of the following is an assumption on which the argument depends?

(A) Drivers 65 and older do not, on average, drive very many fewer miles per year than drivers 24 and younger.

(B) Drivers 65 and older do not constitute a significantly larger percentage of licensed drivers in Wareland than drivers ages 18–24 do.

(C) Drivers 65 and older are less likely than are drivers 24 and younger to drive during weather conditions that greatly increase the risk of accidents.

(D) The difference between the accident rate of drivers under 21 and of those ages 21–24 is attributable to the greater driving experience of those in the older group.

(E) There is no age bracket for which the accident rate is lower than it is for licensed drivers 65 and older.

625. In the past the country of Malvernia has relied heavily on imported oil. Malvernia recently implemented a program to convert heating systems from oil to natural gas. Malvernia currently produces more natural gas each year than it uses, and oil production in Malvernian oil fields is increasing at a steady pace. If these trends in fuel production and usage continue, therefore, Malvernian reliance on foreign sources for fuel is likely to decline soon.

Which of the following would it be most useful to establish in evaluating the argument?

(A) When, if ever, will production of oil in Malvernia outstrip production of natural gas?

(B) Is Malvernia among the countries that rely most on imported oil?

(C) What proportion of Malvernia's total energy needs is met by hydroelectric, solar, and nuclear power?

(D) Is the amount of oil used each year in Malvernia for generating electricity and fuel for transportation increasing?

(E) Have any existing oil-burning heating systems in Malvernia already been converted to natural-gas-burning heating systems?

626. Exposure to certain chemicals commonly used in elementary schools as cleaners or pesticides causes allergic reactions in some children. Elementary school nurses in Renston report that the proportion of schoolchildren sent to them for treatment of allergic reactions to those chemicals has increased significantly over the past ten years. Therefore, either Renston's schoolchildren have been exposed to greater quantities of the chemicals, or they are more sensitive to them than schoolchildren were ten years ago.

Which of the following is an assumption on which the argument depends?

(A) The number of school nurses employed by Renston's elementary schools has not decreased over the past ten years.

(B) Children who are allergic to the chemicals are no more likely than other children to have allergies to other substances.

(C) Children who have allergic reactions to the chemicals are not more likely to be sent to a school nurse now than they were ten years ago.

(D) The chemicals are not commonly used as cleaners or pesticides in houses and apartment buildings in Renston.

(E) Children attending elementary school do not make up a larger proportion of Renston's population now than they did ten years ago.

627. Lockeport's commercial fishing boats use gill nets, which kill many of the netted fish, including some fish of endangered species. The fishing commission has proposed requiring the use of tent nets, which do not kill fish; boat crews would then throw back fish of endangered species. Profitable commercial fishing boats in similar areas have already switched over to tent nets. The proposal can therefore be implemented without economic harm to Lockeport's commercial fishing boat operators.

Which of the following, if true, casts the most serious doubt on the argument made for the proposal?

(A) In places where the use of tent nets has been mandated, there are typically fewer commercial fishing boats in operation than there were before tent nets came into use.

(B) Even when used properly, gill nets require many more repairs than do tent nets.

(C) Recreational anglers in Lockeport catch more fish of endangered species than do commercial fishing boats.

(D) The endangered species of fish in Lockeport's commercial fishing area did not become endangered as a result of the use of gill nets by fishing fleets.

(E) The endangered species of fish caught by Lockeport's commercial fishing fleet are of no commercial value.

628. Normally, the pineal gland governs a person's sleep-wake cycle by secreting melatonin in response to the daily cycle of light and darkness as detected by the eye. Nonetheless, many people who are totally blind due to lesions in the visual cortex of the brain easily maintain a 24-hour sleep-wake cycle. So the neural pathway by which the pineal gland receives information from the eye probably does not pass through the visual cortex.

For purposes of evaluating the argument it would be most useful to establish which of the following?

(A) Whether melatonin supplements help people who have difficulty maintaining a 24-hour sleep cycle to establish such a pattern

(B) Whether the melatonin levels of most totally blind people who successfully maintain a 24-hour sleep-wake cycle change in response to changes in exposure to light and darkness

(C) Whether melatonin is the only substance secreted by the pineal gland

(D) Whether most people who do not have a 24-hour sleep-wake cycle nevertheless have a cycle of consistent duration

(E) Whether there are any people with normal vision whose melatonin levels respond abnormally to periods of light and darkness

629. **In countries where automobile insurance includes compensation for whiplash injuries sustained in automobile accidents, reports of having suffered such injuries are twice as frequent as they are in countries where whiplash is not covered.** Presently, no objective test for whiplash exists, so it is true that spurious reports of whiplash injuries cannot be readily identified. Nevertheless, these facts do not warrant the conclusion drawn by some commentators that in the countries with the higher rates of reported whiplash injuries, half of the reported cases are spurious. Clearly, **in countries where automobile insurance does not include compensation for whiplash, people often have little incentive to report whiplash injuries that they actually have suffered.**

In the argument given, the two **boldfaced** portions play which of the following roles?

(A) The first is a claim that the argument disputes; the second is a conclusion that has been based on that claim.

(B)   The first is a claim that has been used to support a conclusion that the argument accepts; the second is that conclusion.

(C)   The first is evidence that has been used to support a conclusion for which the argument provides further evidence; the second is the main conclusion of the argument.

(D)   The first is a finding whose implications are at issue in the argument; the second is a claim presented in order to argue against deriving certain implications from that finding.

(E)   The first is a finding whose accuracy is evaluated in the argument; the second is evidence presented to establish that the finding is accurate.

630.   Last year Comfort Airlines had twice as many delayed flights as the year before, but the number of complaints from passengers about delayed flights went up three times. It is unlikely that this disproportionate increase in complaints was rooted in an increase in overall dissatisfaction with the service Comfort Airlines provides, since the airline made a special effort to improve other aspects of its service last year.

Which of the following, if true, most helps to explain the disproportionate increase in customer complaints?

(A)   Comfort Airlines had more flights last year than the year before.

(B)   Last year a single period of unusually bad weather caused a large number of flights to be delayed.

(C)   Some of the improvements that Comfort Airlines made in its service were required by new government regulations.

(D)   The average length of a flight delay was greater last year than it was the year before.

(E)   The average number of passengers per flight was no higher last year than the year before.

631.   Last year a global disturbance of weather patterns disrupted harvests in many of the world's important agricultural areas. Worldwide production of soybeans, an important source of protein for people and livestock alike, was not adversely affected, however. Indeed, last year's soybean crop was actually slightly larger than average. Nevertheless, the weather phenomenon is probably responsible for a recent increase in the world price of soybeans.

Which of the following, if true, provides the strongest justification for the attribution of the increase in soybean prices to the weather phenomenon?

(A)   Last year's harvest of anchovies, which provide an important protein source for livestock, was disrupted by the effects of the weather phenomenon.

(B)   Most countries that produce soybeans for export had above-average harvests of a number of food crops other than soybeans last year.

(C)   The world price of soybeans also rose several years ago, immediately after an earlier occurrence of a similar global weather disturbance.

(D)   Heavy rains attributable to the weather phenomenon improved grazing pastures last year, allowing farmers in many parts of the world to reduce their dependence on supplemental feed.

(E)   Prior to last year, soybean prices had been falling for several years.

632.   Most of the year, the hermit thrush, a North American songbird, eats a diet consisting mainly of insects, but in autumn, as the thrushes migrate to their Central and South American wintering grounds, they feed almost exclusively on wild berries. Wild berries, however, are not as rich in calories as insects, yet thrushes need to consume plenty of calories in order to complete their migration. One possible explanation is that berries contain other nutrients that thrushes need for migration and that insects lack.

Which of the following, if true, most seriously calls into question the explanation given for the thrush's diet during migration?

(A)   Hermit thrushes, if undernourished, are unable to complete their autumn migration before the onset of winter.

(B)   Insect species contain certain nutrients that are not found in wild berries.

(C)   For songbirds, catching insects requires the expenditure of significantly more calories than eating wild berries does.

(D)   Along the hermit thrushes' migration routes, insects are abundant throughout the migration season.

(E)   There are some species of wild berries that hermit thrushes generally do not eat, even though these berry species are exceptionally rich in calories.

633. The kinds of hand and wrist injuries that result from extended use of a computer while maintaining an incorrect posture are common among schoolchildren in Harnville. Computers are important to the school curriculum there, so instead of reducing the amount their students use computers, teachers plan to bring about a sharp reduction in the number of these injuries by carefully monitoring their students' posture when using computers in the classroom.

Which of the following would it be most useful to know in order to assess the likelihood that the teachers' plan will be successful?

(A) Whether extended use of a computer while maintaining incorrect posture can cause injuries other than hand and wrist injuries

(B) Whether hand and wrist injuries not caused by computer use are common among schoolchildren in Harnville

(C) What proportion of schoolchildren in Harnville with hand and wrist injuries use computers extensively outside the classroom

(D) Whether changes in the curriculum could reduce the schools' dependence on computers

(E) What proportion of schoolchildren in Harnville already use correct posture while using a computer

634. A certain cultivated herb is one of a group of closely related plants that thrive in soil with high concentrations of metals that are toxic to most other plants. Agronomists studying the growth of this herb have discovered that it produces large amounts of histidine, an amino acid that, in test-tube solutions, renders these metals chemically inert. Hence, the herb's high histidine production must be the key feature that allows it to grow in metal-rich soils.

In evaluating the argument, it would be most important to determine which of the following?

(A) Whether the herb can thrive in soil that does not have high concentrations of the toxic metals

(B) Whether others of the closely related group of plants also produce histidine in large quantities

(C) Whether the herb's high level of histidine production is associated with an unusually low level of production of some other amino acid

(D) Whether growing the herb in soil with high concentrations of the metals will, over time, reduce their concentrations in the soil

(E) Whether the concentration of histidine in the growing herb declines as the plant approaches maturity

635. Many people suffer an allergic reaction to certain sulfites, including those that are commonly added to wine as preservatives. However, since there are several winemakers who add sulfites to none of the wines they produce, people who would like to drink wine but are allergic to sulfites can drink wines produced by these winemakers without risking an allergic reaction to sulfites.

Which of the following is an assumption on which the argument depends?

(A) These winemakers have been able to duplicate the preservative effect produced by adding sulfites by means that do not involve adding any potentially allergenic substances to their wine.

(B) Not all forms of sulfite are equally likely to produce the allergic reaction.

(C) Wine is the only beverage to which sulfites are commonly added.

(D) Apart from sulfites, there are no substances commonly present in wine that give rise to an allergic reaction.

(E) Sulfites are not naturally present in the wines produced by these winemakers in amounts large enough to produce an allergic reaction in someone who drinks these wines.

636. A new law gives ownership of patents—documents providing exclusive right to make and sell an invention—to universities, not the government, when those patents result from government-sponsored university research. Administrators at Logos University plan to sell any patents they acquire to corporations in order to fund programs to improve undergraduate teaching.

Which of the following, if true, would cast the most doubt on the viability of the college administrators' plan described above?

(A) Profit-making corporations interested in developing products based on patents held by universities are likely to try to serve as exclusive sponsors of ongoing university research projects.

(B) Corporate sponsors of research in university facilities are entitled to tax credits under new federal tax-code guidelines.

(C) Research scientists at Logos University have few or no teaching responsibilities and participate little if at all in the undergraduate programs in their field.

(D) Government-sponsored research conducted at Logos University for the most part duplicates research already completed by several profitmaking corporations.

(E) Logos University is unlikely to attract corporate sponsorship of its scientific research.

637. Since it has become known that **several of a bank's top executives have been buying shares in their own bank,** the bank's depositors, who had been worried by rumors that the bank faced impending financial collapse, have been greatly relieved. They reason that, since top executives evidently have faith in the bank's financial soundness, those worrisome rumors must be false. Such reasoning might well be overoptimistic, however, since **corporate executives have been known to buy shares in their own company in a calculated attempt to dispel negative rumors about the company's health.**

In the argument given, the two **boldfaced** portions play which of the following roles?

(A) The first describes evidence that has been taken as supporting a conclusion; the second gives a reason for questioning that support.

(B) The first describes evidence that has been taken as supporting a conclusion; the second states a contrary conclusion that is the main conclusion of the argument.

(C) The first provides evidence in support of the main conclusion of the argument; the second states that conclusion.

(D) The first describes the circumstance that the argument as a whole seeks to explain; the second gives the explanation that the argument seeks to establish.

(E) The first describes the circumstance that the argument as a whole seeks to explain; the second provides evidence in support of the explanation that the argument seeks to establish.

638. Between 1980 and 2000 the sea otter population of the Aleutian Islands declined precipitously. There were no signs of disease or malnutrition, so there was probably an increase in the number of otters being eaten by predators. Orcas will eat otters when seals, their normal prey, are unavailable, and the Aleutian Islands seal population declined dramatically in the 1980s. Therefore, orcas were most likely the immediate cause of the otter population decline.

Which of the following, if true, most strengthens the argument?

(A) The population of sea urchins, the main food of sea otters, has increased since the sea otter population declined.

(B) Seals do not eat sea otters, nor do they compete with sea otters for food.

(C) Most of the surviving sea otters live in a bay that is inaccessible to orcas.

(D) The population of orcas in the Aleutian Islands has declined since the 1980s.

(E) An increase in commercial fishing near the Aleutian Islands in the 1980s caused a slight decline in the population of the fish that seals use for food.

639. Political Strategist: The domestic policies of our opponents in Party X are contrary to the priorities of many middle-class voters. Yet some of these same voters are supporters of Party X and its candidates due to the party's appeals about foreign policy. In order to win these voters back, we in Party Y must prove to middle-class voters that Party X does not represent their priorities with respect to domestic policy.

Which of the following would, if true, most strongly suggest that the political strategist's plan is unlikely to succeed?

(A) Many in the middle class who support Party X for its foreign policies also support its domestic policies and are fully aware of the implications of those policies.

(B)   Most middle-class supporters of Party X care about foreign policy and know very little about its domestic policies.

(C)   Long-term domestic policy sometimes conflicts with short-term domestic policy.

(D)   There are topics on which Party X and Party Y have significant agreement.

(E)   Some middle-class voters are concerned about both domestic and foreign policy.

640. Studies in restaurants show that the tips left by customers who pay their bill in cash tend to be larger when the bill is presented on a tray that bears a credit-card logo. Consumer psychologists hypothesize that simply seeing a credit-card logo makes many credit-card holders willing to spend more because it reminds them that their spending power exceeds the cash they have immediately available.

Which of the following, if true, most strongly supports the psychologists' interpretation of the studies?

(A)   The effect noted in the studies is not limited to patrons who have credit cards.

(B)   Patrons who are under financial pressure from their credit-card obligations tend to tip less when presented with a restaurant bill on a tray with a credit-card logo than when the tray has no logo.

(C)   In virtually all of the cases in the studies, the patrons who paid bills in cash did not possess credit cards.

(D)   In general, restaurant patrons who pay their bills in cash leave larger tips than do those who pay by credit card.

(E)   The percentage of restaurant bills paid with a given brand of credit card increases when that credit card's logo is displayed on the tray with which the bill is presented.

641. In an experiment, each volunteer was allowed to choose between an easy task and a hard task and was told that another volunteer would do the other task. Each volunteer could also choose to have a computer assign the two tasks randomly. Most volunteers chose the easy task for themselves and under questioning later said they had acted fairly. But when the scenario was described to another group of volunteers, almost all said choosing the easy task would be unfair. This shows that most people apply weaker moral standards to themselves than to others.

Which of the following is an assumption required by this argument?

(A)   At least some volunteers who said they had acted fairly in choosing the easy task would have said that it was unfair for someone else to do so.

(B)   The most moral choice for the volunteers would have been to have the computer assign the two tasks randomly.

(C)   There were at least some volunteers who were assigned to do the hard task and felt that the assignment was unfair.

(D)   On average, the volunteers to whom the scenario was described were more accurate in their moral judgments than the other volunteers were.

(E)   At least some volunteers given the choice between assigning the tasks themselves and having the computer assign them felt that they had made the only fair choice available to them.

642. Country X's recent stock-trading scandal should not diminish investors' confidence in the country's stock market. For one thing, **the discovery of the scandal confirms that Country X has a strong regulatory system**, as the following considerations show. In any stock market, some fraudulent activity is inevitable. If a stock market is well regulated, any significant stock-trading fraud in it will very likely be discovered. This deters potential perpetrators and facilitates improvement in regulatory processes.

In the argument, the portion in **boldface** plays which of the following roles?

(A)   It is the argument's only conclusion.

(B)   It is a conclusion for which the argument provides support and which itself is used to support the argument's main conclusion.

(C)   It is the argument's main conclusion and is supported by another explicitly stated conclusion for which further support is provided.

(D)   It is an assumption for which no explicit support is provided and is used to support the argument's only conclusion.

(E)   It is a compound statement containing both the argument's main conclusion and an assumption used to support that conclusion.

643. **Delta Products Inc. has recently switched at least partly from older technologies using fossil fuels to new technologies powered by electricity.** The question has been raised whether it can be concluded that **for a given level of output Delta's operation now causes less fossil fuel to be consumed than it did formerly.** The answer, clearly, is yes, since the amount of fossil fuel used to generate the electricity needed to power the new technologies is less than the amount needed to power the older technologies, provided level of output is held constant.

In the argument given, the two **boldfaced** portions play which of the following roles?

(A) The first identifies the content of the conclusion of the argument; the second provides support for that conclusion.

(B) The first provides support for the conclusion of the argument; the second identifies the content of that conclusion.

(C) The first states the conclusion of the argument; the second calls that conclusion into question.

(D) The first provides support for the conclusion of the argument; the second calls that conclusion into question.

(E) Each provides support for the conclusion of the argument.

644. A product that represents a clear technological advance over competing products can generally command a high price. Because **technological advances tend to be quickly surpassed** and companies want to make large profits while they still can, many companies charge the greatest price the market will bear when they have such a product. But **large profits on the new product will give competitors a strong incentive to quickly match the new product's capabilities.** Consequently, the strategy to maximize overall profit from a new product is to charge less than the greatest possible price.

In the argument above, the two portions in **boldface** play which of the following roles?

(A) The first is an assumption that forms the basis for a course of action that the argument criticizes; the second presents the course of action endorsed by the argument.

(B) The first is a consideration raised to explain the appeal of a certain strategy; the second is a consideration raised to call into question the wisdom of adopting that strategy.

(C) The first is an assumption that has been used to justify a certain strategy; the second is a consideration that is used to cast doubt on that assumption.

(D) The first is a consideration raised in support of a strategy the argument endorses; the second presents grounds in support of that consideration.

(E) The first is a consideration raised to show that adopting a certain strategy is unlikely to achieve the intended effect; the second is presented to explain the appeal of that strategy.

645. Theater Critic: The play *La Finestrina*, now at Central Theater, was written in Italy in the eighteenth century. The director claims that this production is as similar to the original production as is possible in a modern theater. Although the actor who plays Harlequin the clown gives a performance very reminiscent of the twentieth-century American comedian Groucho Marx, Marx's comic style was very much within the comic acting tradition that had begun in sixteenth-century Italy.

The considerations given best serve as part of an argument that

(A) modern audiences would find it hard to tolerate certain characteristics of a historically accurate performance of an eighteenth-century play

(B) Groucho Marx once performed the part of the character Harlequin in *La Finestrina*

(C) in the United States the training of actors in the twentieth century is based on principles that do not differ radically from those that underlay the training of actors in eighteenth-century Italy

(D) the performance of the actor who plays Harlequin in *La Finestrina* does not serve as evidence against the director's claim

(E) the director of *La Finestrina* must have advised the actor who plays Harlequin to model his performance on comic performances of Groucho Marx

646. Although the discount stores in Goreville's central shopping district are expected to close within five years as a result of competition from a SpendLess discount department store that just opened, those

523

locations will not stay vacant for long. In the five years since the opening of Colson's, a nondiscount department store, a new store has opened at the location of every store in the shopping district that closed because it could not compete with Colson's.

Which of the following, if true, most seriously weakens the argument?

(A) Many customers of Colson's are expected to do less shopping there than they did before the SpendLess store opened.

(B) Increasingly, the stores that have opened in the central shopping district since Colson's opened have been discount stores.

(C) At present, the central shopping district has as many stores operating in it as it ever had.

(D) Over the course of the next five years, it is expected that Goreville's population will grow at a faster rate than it has for the past several decades.

(E) Many stores in the central shopping district sell types of merchandise that are not available at either SpendLess or Colson's.

647. Last year all refuse collected by Shelbyville city services was incinerated. This incineration generated a large quantity of residual ash. In order to reduce the amount of residual ash Shelbyville generates this year to half of last year's total, the city has revamped its collection program. This year city services will separate for recycling enough refuse to reduce the number of truckloads of refuse to be incinerated to half of last year's number.

Which of the following is required for the revamped collection program to achieve its aim?

(A) This year, no materials that city services could separate for recycling will be incinerated.

(B) Separating recyclable materials from materials to be incinerated will cost Shelbyville less than half what it cost last year to dispose of the residual ash.

(C) Refuse collected by city services will contain a larger proportion of recyclable materials this year than it did last year.

(D) The refuse incinerated this year will generate no more residual ash per truckload incinerated than did the refuse incinerated last year.

(E) The total quantity of refuse collected by Shelbyville city services this year will be no greater than that collected last year.

648. Veterinarians generally derive some of their income from selling several manufacturers' lines of pet-care products. Knowing that pet owners rarely throw away mail from their pet's veterinarian unread, one manufacturer of pet-care products offered free promotional materials on its products to veterinarians for mailing to their clients. Very few veterinarians accepted the offer, however, even though the manufacturer's products are of high quality.

Which of the following, if true, most helps to explain the veterinarians' reaction to the manufacturer's promotional scheme?

(A) Most of the veterinarians to whom the free promotional materials were offered were already selling the manufacturer's pet-care products to their clients.

(B) The special promotional materials were intended as a supplement to the manufacturer's usual promotional activities rather than as a replacement for them.

(C) The manufacturer's products, unlike most equally good competing products sold by veterinarians, are also available in pet stores and in supermarkets.

(D) Many pet owners have begun demanding quality in products they buy for their pets that is as high as that in products they buy for themselves.

(E) Veterinarians sometimes recommend that pet owners use products formulated for people when no suitable product specially formulated for animals is available.

649. The average hourly wage of television assemblers in Vernland has long been significantly lower than that in neighboring Borodia. Since Borodia dropped all tariffs on Vernlandian televisions three years ago, the number of televisions sold annually in Borodia has not changed. However, recent statistics show a drop in the number of television assemblers in Borodia. Therefore, updated trade statistics will probably indicate that the number of televisions Borodia imports annually from Vernland has increased.

Which of the following is an assumption on which the argument depends?

(A) The number of television assemblers in Vernland has increased by at least as much as the number of television assemblers in Borodia has decreased.

(B)   Televisions assembled in Vernland have features that televisions assembled in Borodia do not have.

(C)   The average number of hours it takes a Borodian television assembler to assemble a television has not decreased significantly during the past three years.

(D)   The number of televisions assembled annually in Vernland has increased significantly during the past three years.

(E)   The difference between the hourly wage of television assemblers in Vernland and the hourly wage of television assemblers in Borodia is likely to decrease in the next few years.

650. Guidebook writer: I have visited hotels throughout the country and have noticed that in those built before 1930 the quality of the original carpentry work is generally superior to that in hotels built afterward. Clearly carpenters working on hotels before 1930 typically worked with more skill, care, and effort than carpenters who have worked on hotels built subsequently.

Which of the following, if true, most seriously weakens the guidebook writer's argument?

(A)   The quality of original carpentry in hotels is generally far superior to the quality of original carpentry in other structures, such as houses and stores.

(B)   Hotels built since 1930 can generally accommodate more guests than those built before 1930.

(C)   The materials available to carpenters working before 1930 were not significantly different in quality from the materials available to carpenters working after 1930.

(D)   The better the quality of original carpentry in a building, the less likely that building is to fall into disuse and be demolished.

(E)   The average length of apprenticeship for carpenters has declined significantly since 1930.

651. Scientists typically do their most creative work before the age of forty. It is commonly thought that this happens because aging by itself brings about a loss of creative capacity. However, studies show that **of scientists who produce highly creative work beyond the age of forty, a disproportionately large number entered their field at an older age than is usual**. Since by the age of forty the large majority of scientists have been working in their field for at least fifteen years, the studies' finding strongly suggests that the real reason why scientists over forty rarely produce highly creative work is not that they have aged but rather that **scientists over forty have generally spent too long in their field**.

In the argument given, the two portions in **boldface** play which of the following roles?

(A)   The first is a claim, the accuracy of which is at issue in the argument; the second is a conclusion drawn on the basis of that claim.

(B)   The first is an objection that has been raised against a position defended in the argument; the second is that position.

(C)   The first is evidence that has been used to support an explanation that the argument challenges; the second is that explanation.

(D)   The first is evidence that has been used to support an explanation that the argument challenges; the second is a competing explanation that the argument favors.

(E)   The first provides evidence to support an explanation that the argument favors; the second is that explanation.

652. NorthAir charges low fares for its economy-class seats, but it provides very cramped seating and few amenities. Market research shows that economy passengers would willingly pay more for wider seating and better service, and additional revenue provided by these higher ticket prices would more than cover the additional cost of providing these amenities. Even though NorthAir is searching for ways to improve its profitability, it has decided not to make these improvements.

Which of the following, if true, would most help to explain NorthAir's decision in light of its objectives?

(A)   None of NorthAir's competitors offers significantly better seating and service to economy-class passengers than NorthAir does.

(B)   On many of the routes that NorthAir flies, it is the only airline to offer direct flights.

(C)   A few of NorthAir's economy-class passengers are satisfied with the service they receive, given the low price they pay.

(D)   Very few people avoid flying on NorthAir because of the cramped seating and poor service offered in economy class.

(E)   The number of people who would be willing to pay the high fares NorthAir charges for its business-class seats would decrease if its economy-class seating were more acceptable.

653.   Which of the following most logically completes the argument given?

Asthma, a chronic breathing disorder, is significantly more common today among adult competitive swimmers than it is among competitive athletes who specialize in other sports. Although chlorine is now known to be a lung irritant and swimming pool water is generally chlorinated, it would be rash to assume that frequent exposure to chlorine is the explanation of the high incidence of asthma among these swimmers, since _____.

(A)   young people who have asthma are no more likely to become competitive athletes than are young people who do not have asthma

(B)   competitive athletes who specialize in sports other than swimming are rarely exposed to chlorine

(C)   competitive athletes as a group have a significantly lower incidence of asthma than do people who do not participate in competitive athletics

(D)   until a few years ago, physicians routinely recommended competitive swimming to children with asthma, in the belief that this form of exercise could alleviate asthma symptoms

(E)   many people have asthma without knowing they have it and thus are not diagnosed with the condition until they begin engaging in very strenuous activities, such as competitive athletics

654.   In the country of Marut, the Foreign Trade Agency's records were reviewed in 1994 in light of information then newly available about neighboring Goro. The review revealed that in every year since 1963, the agency's projection of what Goro's gross national product (GNP) would be five years later was a serious underestimate. The review also revealed that in every year since 1963, the agency estimated Goro's GNP for the previous year—a Goro state secret—very accurately.

Of the following claims, which is most strongly supported by the statements given?

(A)   Goro's GNP fluctuated greatly between 1963 and 1994.

(B)   Prior to 1995, Goro had not released data intended to mislead the agency in making its five-year projections.

(C)   The amount by which the agency underestimated the GNP it projected for Goro tended to increase over time.

(D)   Even before the new information came to light, the agency had reason to think that at least some of the five-year projections it had made were inaccurate.

(E)   The agency's five-year projections of Goro's GNP had no impact on economic planning in Marut.

655.   Vargonia has just introduced a legal requirement that student-teacher ratios in government-funded schools not exceed a certain limit. All Vargonian children are entitled to education, free of charge, in these schools. When a recession occurs and average incomes fall, the number of children enrolled in government-funded schools tends to increase. Therefore, though most employment opportunities contract in economic recessions, getting a teaching job in Vargonia's government-funded schools will not be made more difficult by a recession.

Which of the following would be most important to determine in order to evaluate the argument?

(A)   Whether in Vargonia there are any schools not funded by the government that offer children an education free of charge

(B)   Whether the number of qualified applicants for teaching positions in government-funded schools increases significantly during economic recessions

(C)   What the current student-teacher ratio in Vargonia's government-funded schools is

(D)   What proportion of Vargonia's workers currently hold jobs as teachers in government-funded schools

(E)   Whether in the past a number of government-funded schools in Vargonia have had student-teacher ratios well in excess of the new limit

656. In Colorado subalpine meadows, nonnative dandelions co-occur with a native flower, the larkspur. Bumblebees visit both species, creating the potential for interactions between the two species with respect to pollination. In a recent study, researchers selected 16 plots containing both species; all dandelions were removed from eight plots; the remaining eight control plots were left undisturbed. The control plots yielded significantly more larkspur seeds than the dandelion-free plots, leading the researchers to conclude that the presence of dandelions facilitates pollination (and hence seed production) in the native species by attracting more pollinators to the mixed plots.

Which of the following, if true, most seriously undermines the researchers' reasoning?

(A) Bumblebees preferentially visit dandelions over larkspurs in mixed plots.

(B) In mixed plots, pollinators can transfer pollen from one species to another to augment seed production.

(C) If left unchecked, nonnative species like dandelions quickly crowd out native species.

(D) Seed germination is a more reliable measure of a species' fitness than seed production.

(E) Soil disturbances can result in fewer blooms, and hence lower seed production.

657. An experiment was done in which human subjects recognize a pattern within a matrix of abstract designs and then select another design that completes that pattern. The results of the experiment were surprising. The lowest expenditure of energy in neurons in the brain was found in those subjects who performed most successfully in the experiments.

Which of the following hypotheses best accounts for the findings of the experiment?

(A) The neurons of the brain react less when a subject is trying to recognize patterns than when the subject is doing other kinds of reasoning.

(B) Those who performed best in the experiment experienced more satisfaction when working with abstract patterns than did those who performed less well.

(C) People who are better at abstract pattern recognition have more energy-efficient neural connections.

(D) The energy expenditure of the subjects' brains increases when a design that completes the initially recognized pattern is determined.

(E) The task of completing a given design is more capably performed by athletes, whose energy expenditure is lower when they are at rest.

658. With seventeen casinos, Moneyland operates the most casinos in a certain state. Although intent on expanding, it was outmaneuvered by Apex Casinos in negotiations to acquire the Eldorado chain. To complete its acquisition of Eldorado, Apex must sell five casinos to comply with a state law forbidding any owner to operate more than one casino per county. Since Apex will still be left operating twenty casinos in the state, it will then have the most casinos in the state.

Which of the following, if true, most seriously undermines the prediction?

(A) Apex, Eldorado, and Moneyland are the only organizations licensed to operate casinos in the state.

(B) The majority of Eldorado's casinos in the state will need extensive renovations if they are to continue to operate profitably.

(C) Some of the state's counties do not permit casinos.

(D) Moneyland already operates casinos in the majority of the state's counties.

(E) Apex will use funds it obtains from the sale of the five casinos to help fund its acquisition of the Eldorado chain.

659. It is widely assumed that people need to engage in intellectual activities such as solving crossword puzzles or mathematics problems in order to maintain mental sharpness as they age. In fact, however, simply talking to other people—that is, participating in social interaction, which engages many mental and perceptual skills—suffices. Evidence to this effect comes from a study showing that the more social contact people report, the better their mental skills.

Which of the following, if true, most seriously weakens the force of the evidence cited?

(A)   As people grow older, they are often advised to keep exercising their physical and mental capacities in order to maintain or improve them.

(B)   Many medical conditions and treatments that adversely affect a person's mental sharpness also tend to increase that person's social isolation.

(C)   Many people are proficient both in social interactions and in solving mathematical problems.

(D)   The study did not itself collect data but analyzed data bearing on the issue from prior studies.

(E)   The tasks evaluating mental sharpness for which data were compiled by the study were more akin to mathematics problems than to conversation.

660.   In the United States, of the people who moved from one state to another when they retired, the percentage who retired to Florida has decreased by three percentage points over the past 10 years. Since many local businesses in Florida cater to retirees, these declines are likely to have a noticeably negative economic effect on these businesses and therefore on the economy of Florida.

Which of the following, if true, most seriously weakens the argument given?

(A)   People who moved from one state to another when they retired moved a greater distance, on average, last year than such people did ten years ago.

(B)   People were more likely to retire to North Carolina from another state last year than people were ten years ago.

(C)   The number of people who moved from one state to another when they retired has increased significantly over the past ten years.

(D)   The number of people who left Florida when they retired to live in another state was greater last year than it was ten years ago.

(E)   Florida attracts more people who move from one state to another when they retire than does any other state.

661.   The spacing of the four holes on a fragment of a bone flute excavated at a Neanderthal campsite is just what is required to play the third through sixth notes of the diatonic scale—the seven-note musical scale used in much of Western music since the Renaissance. Musicologists therefore hypothesize that the diatonic musical scale was developed and used thousands of years before it was adopted by Western musicians.

Which of the following, if true, most strongly supports the hypothesis?

(A)   Bone flutes were probably the only musical instrument made by Neanderthals.

(B)   No musical instrument that is known to have used a diatonic scale is of an earlier date than the flute found at the Neanderthal campsite.

(C)   The flute was made from a cave-bear bone and the campsite at which the flute fragment was excavated was in a cave that also contained skeletal remains of cave bears.

(D)   Flutes are the simplest wind instrument that can be constructed to allow playing a diatonic scale.

(E)   The cave-bear leg bone used to make the Neanderthal flute would have been long enough to make a flute capable of playing a complete diatonic scale.

662.   Which of the following most logically completes the passage?

The figures in portraits by the Spanish painter El Greco (1541–1614) are systematically elongated. In El Greco's time, the intentional distortion of human figures was unprecedented in European painting. Consequently, some critics have suggested that El Greco had an astigmatism, a type of visual impairment, that resulted in people appearing to him in the distorted way that is characteristic of his paintings. However, this suggestion cannot be the explanation, because _____.

(A)   several twentieth-century artists have consciously adopted from El Greco's paintings the systematic elongation of the human form

(B)   some people do have elongated bodies somewhat like those depicted in El Greco's portraits

(C)   if El Greco had an astigmatism, then, relative to how people looked to him, the elongated figures in his paintings would have appeared to him to be distorted

(D)   even if El Greco had an astigmatism, there would have been no correction for it available in the period in which he lived

(E)   there were non-European artists, even in El Greco's time, who included in their works human figures that were intentionally distorted

663.   Museums that house Renaissance oil paintings typically store them in environments that are carefully kept within narrow margins of temperature and humidity to inhibit any deterioration. Laboratory tests have shown that the kind of oil paint used in these paintings actually adjusts to climatic changes quite well. If, as some museum directors believe, **paint is the most sensitive substance in these works**, then by relaxing the standards for temperature and humidity control, **museums can reduce energy costs without risking damage to these paintings**. Museums would be rash to relax those standards, however, since results of preliminary tests indicate that gesso, a compound routinely used by Renaissance artists to help paint adhere to the canvas, is unable to withstand significant variations in humidity.

In the argument above, the two portions in **boldface** play which of the following roles?

(A)   The first is an objection that has been raised against the position taken by the argument; the second is the position taken by the argument.

(B)   The first is the position taken by the argument; the second is the position that the argument calls into question.

(C)   The first is a judgment that has been offered in support of the position that the argument calls into question; the second is a circumstance on which that judgment is, in part, based.

(D)   The first is a judgment that has been offered in support of the position that the argument calls into question; the second is that position.

(E)   The first is a claim that the argument calls into question; the second is the position taken by the argument.

664.   Codex Berinensis, a Florentine copy of an ancient Roman medical treatise, is undated but contains clues to when it was produced. Its first 80 pages are by a single copyist, but the remaining 20 pages are by three different copyists, which indicates some significant disruption. Since a letter in handwriting, identified as that of the fourth copyist, mentions a plague that killed many people in Florence in 1148, Codex Berinensis was probably produced in that year.

Which of the following, if true, most strongly supports the hypothesis that Codex Berinensis was produced in 1148?

(A)   Other than Codex Berinensis, there are no known samples of the handwriting of the first three copyists.

(B)   According to the account by the fourth copyist, the plague went on for 10 months.

(C)   A scribe would be able to copy a page of text the size and style of Codex Berinensis in a day.

(D)   There was only one outbreak of plague in Florence in the 1100s.

(E)   The number of pages of Codex Berinensis produced by a single scribe becomes smaller with each successive change of copyist.

8.9 Answer Key: Critical Reasoning

490. B	525. B	560. B	595. C	630. D
491. B	526. D	561. C	596. A	631. A
492. B	527. D	562. D	597. C	632. C
493. D	528. C	563. C	598. D	633. C
494. D	529. E	564. C	599. D	634. B
495. D	530. B	565. E	600. D	635. E
496. E	531. A	566. C	601. A	636. D
497. C	532. E	567. D	602. D	637. A
498. C	533. B	568. C	603. E	638. C
499. D	534. E	569. A	604. C	639. A
500. A	535. D	570. D	605. E	640. B
501. D	536. E	571. D	606. D	641. A
502. B	537. B	572. A	607. A	642. B
503. C	538. E	573. C	608. D	643. B
504. E	539. D	574. E	609. A	644. B
505. B	540. D	575. C	610. E	645. D
506. B	541. D	576. B	611. E	646. B
507. A	542. B	577. C	612. A	647. D
508. A	543. C	578. A	613. D	648. C
509. B	544. D	579. C	614. E	649. C
510. E	545. D	580. B	615. D	650. D
511. C	546. D	581. C	616. E	651. E
512. E	547. D	582. D	617. E	652. E
513. C	548. D	583. C	618. B	653. D
514. C	549. A	584. A	619. E	654. D
515. A	550. A	585. E	620. E	655. B
516. E	551. E	586. C	621. D	656. E
517. A	552. B	587. E	622. D	657. C
518. D	553. B	588. C	623. B	658. A
519. B	554. B	589. D	624. A	659. B
520. D	555. D	590. E	625. D	660. C
521. E	556. D	591. A	626. C	661. E
522. D	557. E	592. A	627. A	662. C
523. A	558. C	593. E	628. B	663. D
524. C	559. D	594. E	629. D	664. D

8.10 Answer Explanations: Critical Reasoning

The following discussion is intended to familiarize you with the most efficient and effective approaches to Critical Reasoning questions. The particular questions in this chapter are generally representative of the kinds of Critical Reasoning questions you will encounter on the GMAT exam. Remember that it is the problem solving strategy that is important, not the specific details of a particular question.

Questions 490–547 - Difficulty: Easy

490. Arts advocate: Few universities require that students who are specializing in science and technology take many art courses. However, real progress in science and technology requires an element of creativity, which the arts foster. Thus, to help science and technology students succeed in their careers, universities should increase the number of art courses required for them.

Which of the following would, if true, most strengthen the argument above?

(A)   Universities required more art courses for science and technology students in the past.

(B)   Participation in art courses increases students' creative thinking in their science and technology courses.

(C)   More students who are interested in art would specialize in science and technology if the number of art courses required for those programs were increased.

(D)   Some of the most prominent scientists began their careers as artists.

(E)   Discussion of science and technology topics in art courses increases creative thinking among students in those courses.

Argument Evaluation

Situation   The arts advocate argues that universities should increase the number of art courses required for students specializing in science and technology, with the goal of helping these students succeed in their careers. Few universities require students in these fields to take many art courses.

Reasoning   *What piece of information, if true and added to the argument, would most strengthen it?* One of the arts advocate's premises is that progress in science and technology requires creativity. Another premise is that courses in the arts foster creativity. The conclusion is that universities should, for the sake of promoting career success, require students specializing in science and technology to take more courses in art. Suppose that participation in art courses enriches students' participation in the science and technology courses: that would be a further reason for universities to require that the students take more art courses.

A   This does not indicate that increasing art offerings now for science and technology students is the most prudent course of action. Universities' past decision to offer fewer art courses for science and technology students may have resulted from review of data, careful analysis, and prudent policy assumptions. For example, the decision may have been required in order to finance provision of more science and technology courses.

B   **Correct.** This suggests that participation in art courses increases the value of science and technology courses, an additional piece of information that strengthens the argument.

C   The argument does not suggest that the goal of requiring science and technology students to take more art courses is to persuade more students interested in art to specialize in science and technology. This information is therefore largely irrelevant to the arts advocate's Reasoning.

D   This information does not address the role art may have played in the scientists' achievements in science and technology. Several of these scientists may well have been aspiring artists who failed or became disenchanted and discovered that they could better exploit their talents in science and technology.

E   The arts advocate does not advocate that science and technology topics be addressed in art courses. The arts advocate's Reasoning focuses on the value of art courses in fostering creativity.

The correct answer is B.

491. Ramirez: The film industry claims that pirated DVDs, which are usually cheaper than legitimate DVDs and become available well before a film's official DVD release date, adversely affect its bottom line. But the industry should note what the spread of piracy indicates: consumers want lower prices and faster DVD releases. Lowering prices of DVDs and releasing them sooner would mitigate piracy's negative effect on film industry profits.

The argument above relies on which of the following assumptions?

(A)   Releasing legitimate DVDs earlier would not cause any reduction in the revenue the film industry receives from the films' theatrical release.

(B)   Some people who would otherwise purchase pirated DVDs would be willing to purchase legitimate DVDs if they were less expensive and released earlier than they are now.

(C)   The film industry will in the future be able to produce DVDs more cheaply than is currently the case.

(D)   Some current sellers of pirated DVDs would likely discontinue their businesses if legitimate DVDs were released faster and priced lower.

(E)   Current purchasers of pirated DVDs are aware that those DVDs are not authorized by the film industry.

Argument Construction

Situation   Pirated DVDs of films are released earlier than the film's official DVD release day. They are also sold more cheaply. These practices cut into the revenue expected from a film's official DVD sales. According to Ramirez, the prevalence of piracy indicates that consumers want lower prices and earlier releases. Ramirez concludes that if the official DVDs were sold more cheaply and released earlier, the impact of piracy on film industry profits might be reduced.

Reasoning   *What must Ramirez assume for the argument to be logically correct?* To evaluate which answer choice the argument relies on assuming, ask yourself about each answer choice, "If this statement were false, then would the argument's conclusion also have to false?" If the answer is yes, then the argument must be making that assumption. For example, suppose the statement made in answer choice B were false. That would mean that none of the people who would otherwise purchase pirated DVDs would be willing to purchase legitimate DVDs even if these were released earlier and at a significantly lower price. If that were so, then the measures Ramirez suggests would not mitigate piracy.

A   This does not have to be assumed for Ramirez's reasoning to be logically good. Earlier release of the official DVDs at a lower price could somewhat reduce revenue from movie theater showings of the films. But if the revenue from official DVDs released earlier and priced lower were greatly boosted through greatly increased official DVD sales, overall revenue for each film could be higher than would be the case with widespread piracy.

B   **Correct.** If all existing purchasers of pirated film DVDs continued to purchase such DVDs even after implementation of the changes Ramirez advocates, then the changes would not mitigate the destructive consequences of piracy. Thus, Ramirez's reasoning must assume that the recommended changes would cause at least some former purchasers of pirated DVDs to begin purchasing the official DVDs.

C   This might improve profits provided revenue did not also decline. Ramirez's argument does not depend on the assumption that the cost of producing DVDs will decline. Ramirez's reasoning assumes that total sales volume for official DVDs would increase if piracy were reduced.

D   Ideally this would occur with the change Ramirez recommends, but it does not have to be assumed for Ramirez's reasoning to be logically sound. For example, the result Ramirez predicts could occur if all existing sellers of pirated DVDs continued to sell them but sold fewer.

E   This is likely true but is not an assumption that Ramirez needs to make for the reasoning to be logically sound. Even if some DVDs sold by DVD sellers were pirated without the sellers being aware of it, e.g., if they purchased them from a fraudulent wholesaler, the fact that the pirated DVDs are sold more cheaply and before the release of the official DVD would reduce the filmmakers' total revenue.

The correct answer is B.

492. Harunia Province has a relatively dry climate and is attracting a fast-growing population that has put increasing demands on its water supply. The two companies that supply water to the region have struggled to keep up with demand and still remain profitable. Yet now they are asking Harunian authorities to write residential water-use regulations that could reduce their revenues and restrict their future flexibility in supplying water profitably.

Which of the following would, if true, most logically help explain why the water-supply companies are asking the authorities to regulate residential water use?

(A) The companies are planning large water-transportation and irrigation systems that require the approval of neighboring provinces.

(B) The companies believe regulation is inevitable and that having it in place now will allow better planning and thus future profitability.

(C) Few, if any, Harunian government officials have investments in the companies or serve on their boards of directors.

(D) The companies believe that the population is not likely to continue to grow.

(E) Long-term climate projections suggest that greater rainfall will eventually increase the amount of water available.

Argument Construction

Situation   Two water-supply companies are asking the authorities in Harunia Province to regulate residential water use, even though regulation could reduce their revenues and restrict their flexibility in supplying water profitably in the future.

Reasoning   *Which piece of information would most help explain why the companies are advocating water-use regulations that would restrict their operations?* The companies are already struggling to keep up with demand from a fast-growing population in the region. So why would they advocate regulations that could, at least in the immediate term, reduce their profits and restrict them? Is there any advantage that the companies perceive—an advantage that would outweigh any disadvantages—in getting regulations instituted soon?

A   It is unclear how this information bears on the companies' request for regulations in Harunia Province, since neighboring provinces seem primarily involved.

B   **Correct.** The companies presumably must strategically plan their capital investments to cope with increasing water demand in Harunia Province and to receive adequate return on that investment. In that context it seems critically important for the companies to have certainty at the planning stage about future regulatory requirements. Moreover, given possible shortfalls in water supply, the companies would reasonably expect government regulation even if they did not request it.

C   This suggests that, in framing water regulations, Harunian government officials will not be influenced by financial interests, so the companies cannot expect to obtain special favors from the regulatory authorities in the framing of water regulations.

D   If anything, this suggests that the companies could continue to operate without any regulatory regime that might restrict their operations.

E   This would presumably result in a weakening of the case for residential water-use regulation and would also make it easier for the water-supply companies to meet demand.

The correct answer is B.

493. Loss of the Gocha mangrove forests has caused coastal erosion, reducing fish populations and requiring the Gocha Fishing Cooperative (GFC) to partially fund dredging and new shore facilities. However, as part of its subsidiary businesses, the GFC has now invested in a program to replant significant parts of the coast with mangrove trees. Given income from a controlled harvest of wood with continuing replanting, the mangrove regeneration effort makes it more likely that the cooperative will increase its net income.

Which of the following, if true, would most strengthen the argument that mangrove replanting will increase the Gocha cooperative's net income?

(A) The cost of dredging and shore facilities was shared with the local government.

(B) The GFC will be able to hire local workers to assist with the mangrove replanting.

(C) The GFC derives 10 percent of its revenue from salt-production facilities in an area previously cleared of mangroves.

(D) Mangrove forests tend to increase the commercial fish populations in coastal fishing grounds.

(E) A controlled harvesting of mangrove wood by the GFC would have little effect on coastal erosion.

Argument Evaluation

Situation   A subsidiary business of the Gocha Fishing Cooperative (GFC) has invested in a program to replant significant parts of the coast with mangrove trees.

Reasoning   *What additional information, if true, would most strengthen the argument's support for the conclusion that the mangrove regeneration effort will increase the GFC's net income?* If the regeneration effort helped the GFC's fishing operations, this could lead to an increase in GFC's income.

A   If the local government helped with the cost of dredging and shore facilities, that would help reduce the GFC's costs, but that is not directly related to the impact of the GFC's mangrove regeneration effort on GFC's net income.

B   It is unclear whether hiring local workers to assist with mangrove replanting would be less costly than hiring workers from elsewhere, so it is unclear whether this would help the GFC increase its net income.

C   The information provided does not indicate whether the mangrove regeneration effort will have any effect on its salt-production facilities, or any revenue or profit that it derives from these facilities, so this does not strengthen the argument.

D   **Correct.** If the mangrove restoration effort helps increase the commercial fish population in coastal fishing grounds, then there is a good chance that the GFC's income from its fishing operations will increase as a result.

E   The information provided does not indicate what, if any, effect coastal erosion has on GFC's net income, so the fact that controlled harvesting of mangrove wood would have little effect on coastal erosion does not strengthen the argument.

The correct answer is D.

494. Executives at the Fizzles Beverage Company plan to boost profits in Country X on their range of fruit-flavored drinks by introducing new flavors based on tropical fruits that are little known there. The executives reason that since the fruit drinks of other companies have none of these flavors, Fizzles will not have to compete for customers and thus will be able to sell the drinks at a higher price.

Which of the following, if true, presents the most serious potential weakness of the plan?

(A) The new fruit drinks would be priced significantly higher than other Fizzles fruit drinks with more conventional flavors.

(B) In a telephone survey, at least one of the consumers contacted said that they preferred many of the new flavors to all of the more familiar flavors.

(C) To build widespread demand for the new flavors, Fizzles would have to launch an advertising campaign to familiarize consumers with them.

(D) Consumers choosing among fruit-flavored drinks of different brands generally buy on the basis of name recognition and price rather than the specific fruit flavor.

(E) Few consumers who are loyal to a specific brand of fruit-flavored drinks would willingly switch to another brand that costs more.

Evaluation of a Plan

Situation   Fizzle Beverage Company's executives plan to offer drinks with tropical fruit flavors that are little known in Country X in the hope that doing so will boost profits in that country. They reason that because their competitors in that country do not offer drinks with these flavors, Fizzle will be able to sell the drinks at a premium price.

Reasoning   *What casts the most doubt on the claim that the executive's plan will effectively allow them to sell fruit-flavored drinks at a higher price?* The executives believe that the lack of a direct competitor to these drinks will allow the company to sell the drinks for a higher price. But any information indicating that something other than the specific fruit flavor of the drink drives sales of fruit-flavored drinks would cast doubt on the plan.

A   We have already been told that the prices will be higher. The question is whether they will be able to sell the drink successfully at these higher prices as a result of the plan.

B   This provides at least some very slight support for the belief that the plan would succeed (if no one at all preferred the new drinks, then the plan would almost certainly fail); however, the question asks for something that would cast doubt on the effectiveness of the plan.

C   When introducing a new product, companies usually have to launch advertising campaigns, and quite frequently such campaigns effectively create demand for the product, so the fact that Fizzles will have to launch an advertising campaign does not cast doubt on the plan.

D   Correct. The plan depends on consumers wanting the drinks because of their unique, unfamiliar flavors, and being willing to pay a higher price for them because of their uniqueness in the market. If price (presumably a lower one) and name recognition, rather than the specific fruit flavor, are what generally drive sales, then it seems unlikely that the executives' plan will succeed.

E   Nothing in the information provided indicates how many consumers are loyal to any specific brand of fruit-flavored drinks. Perhaps the vast majority of consumers are willing to switch brands. If that is so, then the fact that the very few who are loyal to a specific brand would not be willing to switch would not cast much doubt on the effectiveness of the plan.

The correct answer is D.

495. Economist: In 2015, the average per-person amount paid for goods and services purchased by consumers in Country X was the equivalent of $17,570 in United States dollars, just 30 percent of the corresponding figure of $58,566 for Country Y. Yet in 2015, there was already a substantial middle class in Country X that had discretionary income for middle-class consumer goods such as new vehicles, computers, or major household appliances, while a significant portion of the middle class in Country Y did not have sufficient income to purchase such items.

Which of the following, if true, most helps explain the discrepancy in the relationships described by the economist?

(A) There are many consumer goods, such as household appliances, that are produced in Country X to be sold in the Country Y market.

(B) The volume of trade between Country X and Country Y is increasing rapidly in both directions.

(C) The economy of Country Y is recovering from a downturn that affected both Country Y and Country X.

(D) Country X residents pay much less than their Country Y counterparts for housing, transportation, and child care.

(E) In Country Y as well as in Country X, there are few assembly-line jobs in factories that pay a middle-class wage.

Argument Construction

Situation   An economist points out that even though in 2015 the average per-person amount paid for goods and services in Country X was only 30 percent of the corresponding figure in Country Y, a substantial middle class in Country X had discretionary income for consumer goods whereas a substantial portion of the middle class in Country Y did not.

Reasoning   *What, if true, would most help explain the discrepancies described by the economist?* Information indicating that residents in Country X pay much less for nondiscretionary items than do residents of Country Y would help explain why, even though people in Country Y pay on average three times more for goods and services than people in Country X, Country X has a more substantial middle class capable of buying discretionary goods than does Country Y.

A   That many consumer goods produced in Country X are intended to be sold in Country Y does not help explain why many people in Country Y are not able to afford such goods.

B   An increasing volume of trade between Country X and Country Y—which, for all we know, is perfectly balanced—would not help explain any discrepancies between the two countries.

C   That the economies of both Country X and Country Y both suffered a downturn, and Country Y is recovering, could not plausibly explain why many people in Country Y have trouble paying for discretionary goods unless we had the information that Country Y's recovery was significantly slower than Country X's; but we do not have that information.

D   **Correct.** That people in one nation pay far less for nondiscretionary goods than people in another nation would potentially be helpful in explaining how the people in the former nation would more easily be able to afford discretionary goods.

E   If a claim is true of both Country X and Country Y, it would not help explain a discrepancy between the two countries.

The correct answer is D.

496. Neuroscientist: Memory evolved to help animals react appropriately to situations they encounter by drawing on the past experience of similar situations. But this does not require that animals perfectly recall every detail of all their experiences. Instead, to function well, memory should generalize from past experiences that are similar to the current one.

The neuroscientist's statements, if true, most strongly support which of the following conclusions?

(A) At least some animals perfectly recall every detail of at least some past experiences.

(B) Perfectly recalling every detail of all their past experiences could help at least some animals react more appropriately than they otherwise would to new situations they encounter.

(C) Generalizing from past experiences requires clear memories of most if not all the details of those experiences.

(D) Recalling every detail of all past experiences would be incompatible with any ability to generalize from those experiences.

(E) Animals can often react more appropriately than they otherwise would to situations they encounter if they draw on generalizations from past experiences of similar situations.

Argument Construction

Situation   A neuroscientist claims that memory evolved to help animals learn how to react appropriately by generalizing from past experiences but that this does not require animals to remember all details of those experiences.

Reasoning   *What conclusion would the neuroscientist's theory about memory most strongly support?* The neuroscientist asserts that the evolutionary function of memory is to help animals learn to react appropriately by drawing on generalizations from similar experiences they have had. If memory is to serve this function, drawing on generalizations must actually help animals learn to react more appropriately than they otherwise would, even when they do not remember all the details of past experiences.

A   Even if no animal ever recalls all the details of any past experience, animals could still learn through generalizations, as the neuroscientist claims.

B   This statement could be false even if all of what the neuroscientist says is true. Even if it were never helpful for any animal to recall every detail of all its past experiences, animals could still benefit by learning through generalizations.

C   Generalizations from experiences might be made while the experiences are occurring, so that only the generalizations and not the details need to be remembered.

D   The neuroscientist only claims that remembering perfect details is not required for memory to serve its function, not that such perfect recall is incompatible with memory serving its function.

E   **Correct.** If the evolutionary function of memory is to help animals react more appropriately by drawing on generalizations from past experiences, it follows that animal memories can often successfully serve this function in this manner.

The correct answer is E.

497. In Country X's last election, the Reform Party beat its main opponent, the Conservative Party, although pollsters, employing in-person interviews shortly before the vote, had projected a Conservative Party victory. Afterwards, the pollsters determined that, unlike Conservative Party supporters, Reform Party supporters were less likely to express their party preference during in-person interviews than they were during telephone interviews. Therefore, using only telephone interviews instead would likely result in more accurate projections for the next election.

Which of the following statements, if true, would most support the argument in the passage?

(A) The number of voters in Country X's next election will be significantly larger than the number of voters in the last election.

(B) The Conservative Party will win the next election.

(C) For each person interviewed in telephone polls before the next election, pollsters will be able to reasonably determine the likelihood of that person voting.

(D) People who expressed no party preference during the in-person interviews shortly before Country X's last election did not outnumber the people who expressed a preference for the Conservative Party.

(E) In the next election, pollsters will be able to conduct more in-person interviews than telephone interviews.

Argument Evaluation

Situation   Pollsters, using in-person interviews shortly before the last election in Country X, incorrectly predicted that the Conservative Party would win that election, whereas the Reform Party won instead. The pollsters determined that Reform Party supporters, unlike Conservative Party supporters, are less likely to give their party preference in person than in telephone interviews.

Reasoning   *What additional information, if true, would most strengthen the support, in light of the given information, for the prediction that using only telephone interviews would result in more accurate projections in the next election in Country X?* Even if in telephone interviews pollsters are more likely to get accurate information about which party a person interviewed supports, the pollsters' projections may not be accurate if the pollsters are unable to determine whether that person is actually likely to vote. So, information indicating that pollsters will be able to determine the likelihood that a person will vote would strengthen support for the conclusion.

A   If this larger number of voters in the next election is not anticipated by pollsters, then it may affect the accuracy of their predictions. However, the effect would likely be a decrease, rather than an increase, in accuracy. If the pollsters are able to accurately predict voter turnout, then their predictions for the next election could be more accurate. But we have no indication as to whether their turnout predictions will be accurate.

B   If the Conservative Party will win the next election, an underestimate of Reform Party support will be less important for the accuracy of the projection of which party will win.

C   Correct. It would certainly be helpful if the pollsters were able to determine how likely the person they were interviewing would be to vote.

D   This is irrelevant to the argument. The conclusion concerns the relative accuracy of telephone interviews in predicting voting numbers in the next election.

E   If pollsters are able to do more in-person interviews than telephone interviews for the next election, that at least weakly suggests that they might not be able to conduct a sufficient number of telephone interviews to get a representative sample—which would weaken support for the conclusion, not strengthen it.

The correct answer is C.

498. A company that manufactures plastic products from recyclable plastic is, surprisingly, unconcerned that economic conditions may worsen, despite analysts' belief that consumers would then consider ecofriendly plastic products an expensive luxury. But the company reasons that it will be able to lower its prices because, in a weakened economy, other ecofriendly plastic manufacturers are likely to fail. Demand among manufacturers for recyclable plastics as raw materials would then plummet, creating an oversupply of such materials, making them less expensive for the manufacturer to purchase and thus lowering the company's costs.

Which of the following, if true, most weakens the company's reasoning?

(A) Smaller ecofriendly plastic manufacturers are more likely to fail in a weakened economy than larger ecofriendly manufacturers are.

(B) Some retailers whose sales include various companies' ecofriendly plastic products have struggled in recent years despite the overall good economy.

(C) Consumers would likely soon learn of the oversupply of recyclable plastics and cease recycling them, significantly raising manufacturers' raw-material costs.

(D) Retailers, including retailers that cater to consumers seeking certain types of ecofriendly products, may lose some business if economic conditions worsen.

(E) The plastics used by the company in its products were, after a recent investigation by a regulatory body, declared to be safe for consumers.

Argument Evaluation

Situation   A company that manufactures products from recyclable plastics believes that if economic conditions worsen it will be able to lower its prices. It believes its costs will decline because other ecofriendly plastic manufacturers will fail, thereby reducing the demand for recyclable plastics as raw materials.

Reasoning   *What would most weaken the reasoning?* Suppose the company's costs did not decline and the company consequently could not reduce its prices. Even if demand for recyclable plastics as raw materials weakens in an economic downturn, the company's costs may nonetheless not decline if for some reason the supply of recyclable plastics also declines. If so, then the company may well not be able to lower its prices and stay profitable.

A   We are not told whether the company in question is a smaller ecofriendly plastic manufacturer or a larger one. Given that, the fact that smaller such companies are more likely to fail than larger ones may strengthen the argument rather than weaken it (assuming the company in question is a larger such company).

B   If some retailers whose sales include various companies' ecofriendly plastic products have struggled in a healthy economy, they may well struggle even more in a weak economy. This could help drive the company's competitors out of business, which is what the company argues is likely to happen in an economic downturn; so rather than weakening the argument, this arguably strengthens it.

C   **Correct.** Suppose consumers learn of the oversupply of recyclable plastics and stop recycling them as a result; the oversupply may therefore not last long, and indeed a shortage might arise. This would lead not to lower raw-material costs, as the company argues, but to higher raw-material costs.

D   The information that retailers' lost business might result in a decrease in sales of the competing products does not weaken the argument. A loss of business due to worsening economic conditions is a presupposition of the argument.

E   The fact that the plastics used by the company have been declared safe has probably helped boost demand for the company's products, and perhaps for the competing products as well, yet an economic downturn could still hurt the company's competitors. So, this does little to weaken the company's argument.

The correct answer is C.

499. Researchers asked volunteers to imagine they were running a five-kilometer race against 50 people and then against 500 people, races in each of which the top 10 percent would receive a $1,000 prize. Asked about the effort they would apply in the respective cases, the volunteers indicated, on average, that they would run slower in the race against the greater number of people. A likely explanation of this result is that those of the volunteers who were most *comparatively inclined*—those who most tended to compare themselves with others in the social environment—determined (perhaps unconsciously) that extreme effort would not be worthwhile in the 500-competitor race.

Which of the following would, if known to be true, most help justify the explanation offered above?

(A) The volunteers who were most comparatively inclined were also those that had the greatest desire to win a $1,000 prize.

(B) The volunteers who were the least comparatively inclined had no greater desire to win the $1,000 than those who were the most comparatively inclined.

(C) The volunteers who were most comparatively inclined were likely to indicate that they would run the two races at the same speed.

(D) The most comparatively inclined volunteers believed that they were significantly less likely to finish in the top 10 percent in the race against 500 than in the race against 50.

(E) Volunteers were chosen for participation in the study on the basis of answers to various questions designed to measure the degree to which the volunteers were comparatively inclined.

Argument Construction

Situation Volunteers were asked how much effort they would expend when running a five-kilometer race against 50 people and how much they would expend in such a race against 500 people, when the prize for each race is $1,000 for finishing in the top 10 percent. The volunteers indicated, on average, that they would run more slowly in the race against 500 people than in the race against 50 people. This result is likely because comparatively inclined volunteers believed that extreme effort would not have been worthwhile in the race against 500 competitors.

Reasoning *What would most help to justify the explanation proposed above?* If comparatively inclined volunteers thought it was at least as likely that they would finish in the top 10 percent in the race against 500 as in the race against 50, the proposed explanation would fail. Thus, it would help justify the explanation if we knew that the comparatively inclined volunteers believed they were less likely to win in the race against 500 than in the race against 50.

A If one knew that the volunteers who were most comparatively inclined had the greatest desire to win the $1,000, one might actually be more puzzled about why these volunteers said they would expend less effort against the 500 competitors. If they expended less effort, they would probably be less likely to finish in the top 10 percent.

B If one knew that the volunteers who were more comparatively inclined had no less desire to win a $1,000 prize than those who were least comparatively inclined, one would have at least some reason to think the comparatively inclined volunteers wanted to win the $1,000; this clearly cannot explain why they would not expend as much effort in the 500-competitor race as in the 50-competitor race.

C The claim that one would run the two races at the same speed contradicts the position expressed on average by the group as a whole (that they would run more slowly against the larger group of contestants). Therefore, if the most comparatively inclined volunteers said that they would run the two races at the same speed, their position would be inconsistent with that of the group as a whole. So if this answer choice were true, it would weaken, rather than strengthen, the explanation that the views of the most comparatively inclined volunteers account for the fact that the volunteers said, on average, that they would run more slowly against the greater number of contestants.

D **Correct.** If the most comparatively inclined volunteers believed they would be far less likely to finish in the top 10 percent in the race against 500 than in the race against 50, then they would likely believe that extreme effort would not be worthwhile in the race with more people. This therefore is likely to be at least part of the explanation.

E Even if volunteers were chosen on the basis of answers to questions designed to measure how comparatively inclined they were, we are not told whether the volunteers were chosen because of the degree to which they were comparatively inclined.

The correct answer is D.

500. According to a study, after a week of high-altitude living, twenty men had slimmed down. The men, middle-aged residents of low-altitude areas, had been taken to a research station at 2,650 meters (8,694 feet) above sea level. They had unrestricted access to food and were forbidden vigorous exercise, yet they lost an average of 1.5 kilograms (3.3 pounds) during their one-week stay. Clearly, the lower availability of oxygen at higher altitudes, or hypobaric hypoxia, can be said to have caused the weight loss, since _____.

Which of the following would, if true, most logically complete the argument?

(A) a decrease in oxygen intake has been shown to depress appetite

(B) the men all participated in the same kinds of exercise during their stay

(C) the foods available to the men had fewer calories than the foods they usually ate

(D) exercise at higher altitudes is more difficult than exercise at lower altitudes is

(E) several weeks after returning home, the men still weighed less than they had before the study

Argument Construction

Situation   Twenty middle-aged men lived at a high-altitude research station for one week. They had unrestricted access to food but did no vigorous exercise. By the end of their stay they had lost an average 1.5 kilograms (3.3 pounds) of weight.

Reasoning   *Which additional information, if true, would most help support the claim that lower availability of oxygen at higher altitudes caused the weight loss?* The puzzlement arises from the fact that the twenty men had free access to food and did no vigorous exercise. And consuming less of the types of food they would normally eat would have caused weight loss. But suppose one or both of these behaviors had not occurred?

A   **Correct.** This information helps support the explanatory hypothesis that lower oxygen levels accounted for the weight loss. The men's intake of oxygen certainly decreased at an altitude of 2,650 meters (8694 feet), since they normally lived in low-altitude areas. Moreover, reduced appetite would provide a mechanism by which weight loss could have occurred.

B   The men were forbidden vigorous exercise and we can assume that, in a research context, they followed this restriction. Mild exercise would be unlikely to explain the weight loss.

C   This does not support the explanatory hypothesis concerning the role of oxygen reduction in the weight loss.

D   Even if this is generally true, it does not support the hypothesis that lower oxygen levels accounted for the weight loss.

E   This provides no support for the explanatory hypothesis that lower oxygen levels accounted for the weight loss. It might even cast some doubt on the hypothesis, since over a period of several weeks following the study, the men's weight did not increase with their return to their normal oxygen levels.

The correct answer is A.

501. Editorial: Our city's public transportation agency is facing a budget shortfall. The fastest growing part of the budget has been employee retirement benefits, which are exceptionally generous. Unless the budget shortfall is resolved, transportation service will be cut, and many transportation employees will lose their jobs. Thus, it would be in the employees' best interest for their union to accept cuts in retirement benefits.

Which of the following is an assumption the editorial's argument requires?

(A) The transportation employees' union should not accept cuts in retirement benefits if doing so would not be in the employees' best interest.

(B) The only feasible way for the agency to resolve the budget shortfall would involve cutting transportation service and eliminating jobs.

(C) Other things being equal, it is in the transportation employees' interest to have exceptionally generous retirement benefits.

(D) Cutting the retirement benefits would help resolve the agency's budget shortfall.

(E) The transportation employees' union will not accept cuts in retirement benefits if doing so will not allow more transportation employees to keep their jobs.

Argument Construction

Situation
An editorial indicates that the fastest growing part of a particular city's public transportation agency's budget is employee retirement benefits. The agency's budget has a shortfall. If the shortfall is not resolved, transportation service will be cut and many of the employees will lose their jobs.

Reasoning
What must be true if we are to accept the editorial's conclusion, that it is in the employee's best interest to accept cuts in retirement benefits? If cutting the employees' retirement benefits would not be sufficient to resolve the budget shortfall, then it may well not be in employees' best interest to accept such cuts. The reasons given for accepting the cuts are related to the undesirable consequences of a continued shortfall.

A The argument is about whether the union's accepting the cuts is in fact in the employees' best interest, and does not require any assumption about whether employees should accept what is in their best interest.

B This is incompatible with an assumption made by the argument. The argument assumes that cutting the retirement benefits of the employees would help resolve the budget shortfall.

C The argument would actually be stronger if it were NOT the case that it is in the employees' interest to have exceptionally generous retirement benefits.

D Correct. If cutting retirement benefits would not help resolve the agency's budget shortfall, then cutting those benefits would not help the employees avoid job cuts.

E The argument does not depend on assuming anything regarding what factors would motivate the union's acceptance.

The correct answer is D.

502. Researchers hope to find clues about the A'mk peoples who lived in the Kaumpta region about one thousand years ago but who left few obvious traces. The researchers plan to hire the few remaining shamans of the modern-day indigenous people in Kaumpta, who are believed to be descended from the A'mk, to lead them to ancestral sites that may be the remains of A'mk buildings or ceremonial spaces. The shamans were taught the location of such sites as part of their traditional training as youths, and their knowledge of traditional Kaumpta customs may help determine the nature of any sites the researchers find.

Which of the following is an assumption on which the success of the plan depends?

(A) The researchers have reliable evidence that the A'mk of one thousand years ago built important ceremonial spaces.

(B) The shamans have a reasonably accurate memory of A'mk sites they learned about as youths.

(C) Kaumpta shamans are generally held in high esteem for their traditional knowledge.

(D) Modern technologies available to the researchers are likely to be able to find some A'mk sites easily.

(E) Most or all A'mk sites are likely to be found within the Kaumpta region.

Evaluation of a Plan

Situation   Researchers wish to find sites of an ancient people, the A'mk, who lived in the Kaumpta region one thousand years ago. Indigenous people believed to be descended from the A'mk live in that region today. Their shamans, as youths, were taught about such sites. To discover some of these sites, the researchers plan to hire the shamans.

Reasoning   *What must be true for the success of the researchers' plan to find the sites by relying on the shamans' assistance?* The plan would fail, for example, if there were no such sites in the Kaumpta region. Therefore, the researchers' plan depends on assuming that Kaumpta have some such sites—but not that most of the sites are there. The plan also requires that the shamans collectively have reasonably accurate recall of what they learned about the sites as youths.

A   The researchers hope to find buildings or ceremonial spaces or both. However, the plan does not require ceremonial spaces to be found or that the researchers have evidence of them.

B   **Correct.** If the shamans collectively have no "reasonably accurate memory" of what they learned of the location of such sites, then the researchers' plan is not a useful one and can have no reasonable expectation of success.

C   This is likely to be so if the indigenous group from which they come is still committed to maintaining their traditional knowledge. But the plan does not rely on the shamans being honored among their own people. It must be assumed, of course, that the shamans currently possess "traditional knowledge" and are willing to share it.

D   The researchers' reliance on the shamans' assistance suggests that it is not so easy for the researchers to rely entirely on "modern technologies" in this case.

E   The plan can succeed even if this is not correct. What must be assumed is that at least some of the A'mk sites are within the Kaumpta region; it need not be assumed that most or all are.

The correct answer is B.

503. Astronomer: Most stars are born in groups of thousands, each star in a group forming from the same parent cloud of gas. Each cloud has a unique, homogeneous chemical composition. Therefore, whenever two stars have the same chemical composition as each other, they must have originated from the same cloud of gas.

Which of the following, if true, would most strengthen the astronomer's argument?

(A) In some groups of stars, not every star originated from the same parent cloud of gas.

(B) Clouds of gas of similar or identical chemical composition may be remote from each other.

(C) Whenever a star forms, it inherits the chemical composition of its parent cloud of gas.

(D) Many stars in vastly different parts of the universe are quite similar in their chemical compositions.

(E) Astronomers can at least sometimes precisely determine whether a star has the same chemical composition as its parent cloud of gas.

Argument Evaluation

Situation   Most stars are born in groups, any one of which forms from a parent gas cloud with a unique, homogenous chemical composition.

Reasoning   *What would be additional evidence that any two stars with the same chemical composition originated from the same gas cloud?* The implicit reasoning is that since the chemical composition of each gas cloud is unique and homogenous, any two stars that formed from gas with the same chemical composition must have originated from the same cloud. The astronomer then infers that if two stars have the same composition now, they must have originated from the same cloud. This inference requires the assumption that the composition each star has now depends only on the composition of the cloud in which it originated. Any evidence that supports this assumption will strengthen the argument.

A   Whether or not stars born in different clouds of gas are ever in the same "group" is not clearly relevant to whether or not they ever have the same chemical composition.

B   How remote clouds of similar compositions are from each other is not clearly relevant to whether stars that have the same chemical composition may have formed from different clouds of gas. Also, the suggestion that different gas clouds may have identical compositions conflicts with the astronomer's premise that the composition of each cloud from which stars form is unique.

C   **Correct.** If each star's composition is identical to that of its parent cloud, and each cloud's composition is unique, then any two stars identical in composition must have formed from the same parent cloud.

D   If anything, this would suggest that stars with the same composition might have formed from different clouds, so it would weaken rather than strengthen the argument.

E   If astronomers could do this, they might be able to obtain additional evidence for or against the position taken in the argument, but the mere fact that they can do this does not, in itself, provide any support for the astronomer's argument because it tells us nothing about whether two stars with the same chemical composition as one another actually did originate from the same parent cloud of gas.

The correct answer is C.

504. With employer-paid training, workers have the potential to become more productive not only in their present employment but also in any number of jobs with different employers. To increase the productivity of their workforce, many firms are planning to maintain or even increase their investments in worker training. But some training experts object that if a trained worker is hired away by another firm, the employer that paid for the training has merely subsidized a competitor. They note that such hiring has been on the rise in recent years.

Which of the following would, if true, contribute most to defeating the training experts' objection to the firms' strategy?

(A) Firms that promise opportunities for advancement to their employees get, on average, somewhat larger numbers of job applications from untrained workers than do firms that make no such promise.

(B) In many industries, employees that take continuing-education courses are more competitive in the job market.

(C) More and more educational and training institutions are offering reduced tuition fees to firms that subsidize worker training.

(D) Research shows that workers whose training is wholly or partially subsidized by their employer tend to get at least as much training as do workers who pay for all their own training.

(E) For most firms that invest in training their employees, the value added by that investment in employees who stay exceeds the value lost through other employees' leaving to work for other companies.

Evaluation of a Plan

Situation   Many firms pay to train their workers in order to increase their workforces' productivity. But in recent years firms have been increasingly hiring away from each other workers who have had such training.

Reasoning   *What would most help address the concern that firms that pay to train workers are thereby subsidizing competitors that hire away those workers?* In order for the employer-paid training to be worthwhile for a given firm despite the risk of subsidizing competitors that may hire away the trained workers, that firm has to gain more benefits from the training than it loses by subsidizing such competitors. Any evidence that this is true for most firms would help to address the experts' concern.

A   A typical firm does not necessarily want larger numbers of applications from unqualified workers. And if hired, those workers can still be hired away by competitors after the firm has paid to train them, just as the experts warned.

B   This suggests that in many industries, companies, rather than investing in employee training, prefer to hire employees who already have specifically relevant training (perhaps funded by other companies). If anything, this slightly supports, rather than defeats, the training experts' view. No firm has an interest in making its own employees more competitive in the job market unless the firm is likely to benefit from their being so.

C   Even firms that pay reduced tuition fees for worker training may lose the money they pay for those fees and effectively subsidize competitors that hire the trained employees away. So this does not defeat the training experts' objection.

D   The more highly trained workers—regardless of whether their training was company subsidized or not—would presumably be prime targets for recruitment by competing firms, just as the experts warned. The research finding in question does not help defeat the experts' objection.

E   **Correct.** This explicitly indicates that most firms gain more than they lose from the general practice of firms paying to train their workers.

The correct answer is E.

505. In emerging economies in Africa and other regions, large foreign banks that were set up during the colonial era have long played a major economic role. These institutions have tended to confine their business to the wealthier of banks' potential customers. But development of these countries' economies requires financing of the small businesses that dominate their manufacturing, farming, and services sectors. So economic growth will be likely to occur if local banks take on this portion of the financial services markets, since _____.

Which of the following completions would produce the strongest argument?

(A) local banks tend not to strive as much as large foreign banks to diversify their investments

(B) small farming and manufacturing businesses contribute to economic growth if they obtain adequate investment capital

(C) large foreign banks in emerging economies could, with local employees and appropriate local consultation, profitably expand their business to less wealthy clients

(D) some small businesses are among the wealthier customers of foreign banks in emerging economies

(E) local banks in emerging economies tend to be less risk-averse than foreign banks

Argument Construction

Situation   Large foreign banks have long played an economic role in emerging economies, but they have typically confined their business to wealthier customers. Economic development in these countries requires the financing of small businesses that dominate their manufacturing, farming, and services sectors.

Reasoning   *What would most help support the claim that growth in emerging economies will likely occur if local banks help finance small businesses in the relevant sectors of these emerging markets?* If it were the case that these small businesses would actually be likely to contribute to economic growth, given adequate investment capital, then economic growth would indeed be likely to occur if local banks provided the investment capital.

A   It could be the case that whatever sorts of investments local banks make—diversified or not—economic growth will not tend to occur; for instance, it could be that the businesses they invest in do not use the capital wisely. So, this claim does not help support the conclusion.

B   **Correct.** If small farming and manufacturing businesses will contribute to economic growth if they obtain adequate investment capital, then we have fairly good reason to think that economic growth is likely to occur if local banks take on the financing of such small businesses (we merely need to also assume that they will provide adequate investment capital when they take on this financing).

C   Even if large foreign banks could profitably expand their businesses to less-wealthy clients, we have been given no reason to think they will. Furthermore, the claim in need of support is that economic growth will occur if local, rather than foreign, banks financially support these small businesses.

D   The claim that economic growth will occur if local banks finance small business in certain sectors is not supported by the claim that there are some small businesses supported by foreign banks. If these businesses are already financially supported and yet there is not the sort of economic growth discussed, then that might even suggest that economic growth is unlikely to occur.

E   It could be that, if local banks are less risk-averse than foreign banks, they will invest in risky businesses that fail, which would not tend to support the claim that economic growth will likely result if local banks in emerging counties provide financial support for the relevant sectors.

The correct answer is B.

506. Exporters in Country X are facing lower revenues due to a shortage of the large metal shipping containers in which they send their goods by sea to other countries. Fewer containers arrive in Country X due to reductions in imports. This has meant lost orders, costly delays, and a scramble for alternatives, such as air freight, all of which are costlier. Moreover, the revenues of exporters in Country X will probably continue to decline in the near future. This is because other countries are likely to find it increasingly unprofitable to export their goods to Country X, and because _____.

Which of the following would most logically complete the passage?

(A) production of shipping containers in Country X is growing rapidly as a response to the shortage

(B) shipping companies are willing to move containers from country to country only when the containers are full

(C) the cost of shipping alternatives such as air freight is likely to stabilize in the near future

(D) consumers in Country X are purchasing more products than ever before

(E) the worldwide demand for goods made in Country X has only recently begun to rise after a long decline

Argument Construction

Situation   Exporters in Country X are finding that there is an insufficient number of shipping containers for them to use for their exports, because the number of such containers arriving in Country X has declined because of reduced imports. Also, alternative methods of shipping are relatively costly. Furthermore, other countries will likely find shipping goods to Country X to be less and less profitable.

Reasoning   *What would most support the prediction that Country X's exporters' revenues will likely see further declines in revenue in the near future?* If the number of shipping containers available to exporters is likely to decrease, then the prediction would have further support. We know that other countries exporting to Country X will find it increasingly unprofitable, so there is reason to believe their exports will decline further—meaning there will be fewer imports into Country X, which means fewer shipping containers arriving in Country X carrying imported goods, unless the shipping containers shipped in the future are less full than when they are shipped now. If shipping companies are willing to move such containers to another country only when the containers are full, then that will not occur.

A   If production of shipping containers in Country X were rapidly increasing, then the reason given for the decline in revenue for exporters in Country X—that there is an insufficient number of shipping containers—would be undermined, and so therefore would be the conclusion.

B   **Correct.** If shipping companies are unwilling to move containers from country to country unless the containers are full, then, given Country X's decline in imports, there will likely be fewer shipping containers available to Country X's exporters, which provides support for the claim that their revenues will likely decline.

C   If the cost of shipping alternatives such as air freight is likely to stabilize, then those alternative methods of shipping might become economically viable, which would undermine rather than support the conclusion.

D   The fact that consumers in Country X are purchasing more goods than ever before does not affect how much revenue is generated by exporting goods from Country X.

E   If there is increased demand for goods from Country X, then the price of such goods might increase sufficiently to make alternative methods of shipping economically viable, which would undermine rather than support the conclusion.

The correct answer is B.

507. Candle Corporation's television stations are likely to have more income from advertisers than previously. This is because advertisers prefer to reach people in the 18- to 49-year-old age group and the number of people in that group watching Candle television is increasing. Furthermore, among Candle viewers, the percentage of viewers 18 to 49 years old is increasing.

Which of the following, if true, would most strengthen the argument that Candle Corporation will receive more income from advertisers?

(A) Advertisers carefully monitor the demographic characteristics of television audiences and purchase advertising time to reach the audiences they prefer to reach.

(B) Among people over 49 years old, fewer viewers of Candle stations buy products advertised on television than do viewers of other stations.

(C) There will be increasingly more advertisements on television that are directed at viewers who are over 49 years old.

(D) Candle stations plan to show reruns of television shows during hours when other stations run shows for the first time.

(E) People 18 to 49 years old generally have less disposable income to spend than do people over 49 years old.

Argument Evaluation

Situation Both the number and the percentage of Candle television viewers who are 18 to 49 years old are increasing. Advertisers prefer to reach people in this age group.

Reasoning *What evidence, when combined with the cited facts, would most support the prediction that Candle will receive more income from advertisers?* The argument assumes that the increasing number and percentage of Candle viewers in the age group that advertisers prefer to reach will probably encourage advertisers to spend more on advertising with Candle. This assumption could be supported by evidence that the advertisers realize that Candle is getting more viewers in that preferred age range or by evidence that this awareness will influence the advertisers' purchase of advertising time.

A **Correct.** Advertisers monitoring demographics will probably realize that Candle has increasing numbers of viewers in their preferred age range. If they purchase advertising to reach viewers in that age range, then they will probably purchase more advertising time with Candle.

B This gives advertisers less reason to advertise on Candle to reach viewers over 49 years old. Other things being equal, that makes Candle likely to receive less income from advertisers, not more income.

C Since the percentage of Candle viewers 18 to 49 years old is growing, the percentage over 49 years old is probably shrinking. This could make advertisers seeking to reach older viewers less inclined to advertise on Candle even as they increase their overall television advertising.

D Advertisers are not necessarily inclined to purchase more advertising during showings of reruns than during original airings of television shows and may even be inclined to purchase less advertising during such showings.

E This gives advertisers less incentive to try to reach audiences between 18 and 49 years old and hence less reason to purchase advertising on Candle.

The correct answer is A.

508. A provincial government plans to raise the gasoline tax to give people an incentive to drive less, reducing traffic congestion in the long term. However, skeptics point out that most people in the province live in areas where cars are the only viable transportation to jobs and stores and therefore cannot greatly change their driving habits in response to higher gasoline prices.

In light of the skeptics' objection, which of the following, if true, would most logically support the prediction that the government's plan will achieve its goal of reducing traffic congestion?

(A) The revenue from the tax will be used to make public transportation a viable means of transportation to jobs and stores for far more people.

(B) The tax will encourage many residents to switch to more fuel-efficient cars, reducing air pollution and other problems.

(C) Because gasoline has been underpriced for decades, the province has many neighborhoods where cars are the only viable means of transportation.

(D) Most residents who cannot greatly change their driving habits could compensate for high gasoline prices by reducing other expenses.

(E) Traffic congestion is an especially serious problem for people for whom cars are the only viable means of transportation.

Evaluation of a Plan

Situation   A provincial government plans to raise the gasoline tax in order to reduce traffic congestion by discouraging people from driving. But skeptics point out that most people in the province have no viable form of transportation other than driving.

Reasoning   *What would suggest that raising the gasoline tax will reduce traffic congestion even though most people in the province have no viable form of transportation other than driving?* The skeptics point out that since most people in the province have no way to reach jobs or stores except by car, they will not be able to reduce their driving much even if the gasoline tax increases. Any evidence that raising the gasoline tax would reduce traffic congestion despite this obstacle would help to support the plan in light of the skeptics' objection.

A   **Correct.** If the tax will fund these public transit improvements, then far more people will have a viable means of transportation other than driving, undermining the basis of the skeptics' objection.

B   People switching to fuel-efficient cars would not reduce traffic congestion.

C   This essentially only tends to support the skeptics' objection. Unless the plan somehow helps to alleviate the necessity of driving (by, for example, making alternative transportation available), the information provided gives no reason to suppose that the higher costs would significantly reduce traffic congestion.

D   If residents cannot greatly change their driving habits, then the tax will not reduce traffic congestion.

E   This suggests that many residents in the province could benefit if the plan did reduce traffic congestion, but it does not provide a reason to believe the plan will have that effect.

The correct answer is A.

509. Editorial: The roof of Northtown's municipal equipment-storage building collapsed under the weight of last week's heavy snowfall. The building was constructed recently and met local building-safety codes in every particular, except that the nails used for attaching roof supports to the building's columns were of a smaller size than the codes specify for this purpose. Clearly, this collapse exemplifies how even a single, apparently insignificant departure from safety standards can have severe consequences.

Which of the following, if true, most seriously weakens the editorial's argument?

(A) The only other buildings to suffer roof collapses from the weight of the snowfall were older buildings constructed according to less exacting standards than those in the codes.

(B) The amount of snow that accumulated on the roof of the equipment-storage building was greater than the predicted maximum that was used in drawing up the safety codes.

(C) Because the equipment-storage building was not intended for human occupation, some safety-code provisions that would have applied to an office building did not apply to it.

(D) The municipality of Northtown itself has the responsibility for ensuring that buildings constructed within its boundaries meet the provisions of the building-safety codes.

(E) Because the equipment-storage building was used for storing snow-removal equipment, the building was almost completely empty when the roof collapsed.

Argument Evaluation

Situation   The roof of a recently constructed building collapsed under heavy snowfall. The only way the building did not meet safety standards was that some nails for the roof supports were smaller than prescribed by the building codes.

Reasoning   *What would make it less likely that the building's collapse resulted from a single, apparently minor departure from safety standards?* The building met safety standards except for the size of the nails. So if the collapse exemplifies how a departure from safety standards can have severe consequences, as the conclusion claims, then the size of the nails had to be responsible for the collapse. Thus, evidence that a factor other than the size of the nails could fully account for the collapse would weaken the argument.

A   This suggests that the snow would not have been heavy enough to collapse the roof if the construction had completely met the safety standards, so it strengthens, rather than weakens, the argument.

B   **Correct.** This suggests that the snow could have collapsed the roof even if the nails had met the safety standards, thus casting doubt on the assumption that the nails' inadequacy was responsible for the collapse.

C   The claim that the safety requirements for this building were weaker than some others tends slightly to strengthen, rather than weaken, the hypothesis that the bad consequences resulted partly from a failure to comply. Even if safety-code provisions for an equipment-storage building differ from those for an office building, they may still be adequate to ensure the roof's stability.

D   The question of who was responsible for ensuring compliance with the safety codes is irrelevant to whether a failure to comply was responsible for the roof's collapse.

E   This suggests that the alleged consequences of failing to meet safety standards were less severe than they could have been, but it is irrelevant to determining the cause of the collapse.

The correct answer is B.

510. Political theorist: Even with the best spies, area experts, and satellite surveillance, foreign policy assessments can still lack important information. In such circumstances intuitive judgment is vital. A national leader with such judgment can make good decisions about foreign policy even when current information is incomplete, since _____.

Which of the following, if true, most logically completes the argument?

(A) the central reason for failure in foreign policy decision making is the absence of critical information

(B) those leaders whose foreign policy decisions have been highly ranked have also been found to have good intuitive judgment

(C) both intuitive judgment and good information are required for sound decision making

(D) good foreign policy decisions often lead to improved methods of gathering information

(E) intuitive judgment can produce good decisions based on past experience, even when there are important gaps in current information

Argument Construction

Situation   National leaders sometimes must make foreign policy decisions while lacking important information.

Reasoning   *What would most help support the claim that a national leader with intuitive judgment can make good foreign policy decisions without complete information?* The word *since* preceding the blank indicates that the blank should be filled with a premise supporting the statement immediately before the blank. So an observation that supports the claim that a national leader with intuitive judgment can make good foreign policy decisions without complete information would logically complete the argument.

A   This gives us no reason to suppose that intuitive judgment helps national leaders avoid such failures.

B   This does not specify who ranked the foreign policy decisions, nor how they determined the rankings, so it gives us no reason to accept those rankings. For all we know, the anonymous rankers may have used the dubious rankings they created as the sole evidence for their so-called findings about which leaders have good intuitive judgment.

C   This implies that intuitive judgment alone is inadequate without good information, so it undermines rather than supports the claim that national leaders can make good foreign policy decisions with intuitive judgment while lacking complete information.

D   This gives us no reason to suppose that good foreign policy decisions can be made in the first place by leaders lacking important information.

E   **Correct.** This suggests that national leaders can make good foreign policy decisions using intuitive judgment based on their past foreign policy experience, even without complete information about the current situations they're facing.

The correct answer is E.

511. Supply shortages and signs of growing demand are driving cocoa prices upward. Unusually severe weather in cocoa-producing regions—too much rain in Brazil and too little in West Africa—has limited production. Further, Europe and North America recently reported stronger demand for cocoa. In the first quarter, grinding of cocoa beans—the first stage in processing cocoa for chocolate—rose 8.1 percent in Europe and 16 percent in North America. Analysts have concluded that cocoa's price will continue to rise at least into the near future.

Which of the following would, if true, most strengthen the reasoning above?

(A) Ground cocoa beans can be stored for long periods before they spoil.

(B) Several European and North American manufacturers that use cocoa have recently improved their processing capacity.

(C) It takes new cocoa trees five or six years before they start bearing fruit.

(D) Governments in Europe and North America are likely to change current restrictions on cocoa imports.

(E) Historically, cocoa production has varied widely from year to year.

Argument Evaluation

Situation There has been limited production of cocoa beans due to severe weather and also increased demand for cocoa; as a result, cocoa prices have risen.

Reasoning *What would help support the analysts' inference that cocoa prices will continue to rise at least into the near future?* If the price of cocoa is to continue to rise, then the conditions that have led to the recent increase in price must not be ameliorated. They would be ameliorated if demand for cocoa beans declined, e.g., because price increases made people less likely to want ground cocoa; they would also be ameliorated if supply increased, e.g., because many new cocoa trees were planted and very quickly started bearing fruit. If we had reason to believe that one or more of these ameliorating factors is unlikely to happen, then we have more reason to think that prices might stay high, and possibly even rise further.

A That ground cocoa beans can be stored for long periods without spoiling does not tell us whether supply and demand conditions will stay stable, improve, or get worse.

B The fact that these manufacturers have recently improved their processing capacity might help explain why the grinding of cocoa beans has increased recently; but it does not indicate that this increased capacity will be fully utilized. Often, if end-product demand decreases, industrial capacity will become underutilized.

C **Correct.** If it takes new cocoa trees several years to start bearing fruit, then it is less likely that supply can quickly be increased, which in turn makes it less likely that supply can quickly meet any increased demand and thereby relieve pricing pressures.

D These governments may change current restrictions on cocoa imports, but for all we know they may make them more restrictive rather than less restrictive. If they made them more restrictive, demand might decrease, in which case prices might actually fall.

E If cocoa production varies from year to year, it could be that next year cocoa production increases, in which case, as long as demand does not increase as well, prices might fall.

The correct answer is C.

512. During the earliest period of industrialization in Britain, steam engines were more expensive to build and operate than either windmills or water mills, the other practicable sources of power for factories. Yet despite their significant cost disadvantage, steam-powered factories were built in large numbers well before technical improvements brought their cost down. Furthermore, they were built even in regions where geographical conditions permitted the construction of wind- and water-powered factories close to major markets.

Which of the following, if true, most helps to explain the proliferation of steam-powered factories during the earliest period of industrialization in Britain?

(A) In many areas of Britain, there were fewer steam-powered factories than wind- or water-powered factories in the earliest period of industrialization.

(B) Unlike wind- or water-powered factories, steam-powered factories were fueled with coal, which sometimes had to be transported significant distances from the mine to the site of the factory.

(C) It was both difficult and expensive to convert a factory from wind power or water power to steam power.

(D) In the early period of industrialization, many goods sold in towns and cities could not be mass-produced in factories.

(E) In Britain, the number of sites where a wind- or water-powered factory could be built was insufficient to provide for all of the demand for factory-produced goods at the time.

Argument Construction

Situation   Although steam engines were more expensive than windmills and water mills in early industrial Britain, many steam-powered factories were built even in regions where the construction of wind- and water-powered factories was geographically feasible.

Reasoning   *Why might steam-powered factories have proliferated despite their cost disadvantage?* Early industrialists would have needed some positive reason to choose steam over less expensive power sources for their factories. For example, steam engines might have operated faster or more effectively than windmills or water mills. Or steam engines might have received government subsidies. Or conditions restricting the number or locations of windmills and water mills might have forced industrialists to use steam power instead.

A   This suggests that the steam-powered factories did not initially proliferate as widely as they might have, but it does not explain why they proliferated to the extent that they did.

B   The inconvenience of transporting coal for steam-powered factories would have made those factories less likely to proliferate, not more likely.

C   The difficulty of converting factories to steam power would have made steam-powered factories less likely to proliferate, not more likely.

D   The technological inability to mass-produce popular products in factories would have made factories in general less likely to proliferate, including steam-powered factories.

E   **Correct.** The inadequate number of sites for wind- and water-powered factories might have encouraged early industrialists to build steam-powered factories instead, since the high demand for factory-produced goods could have made these factories profitable despite their cost disadvantage.

The correct answer is E.

513. Snowmaking machines work by spraying a mist that freezes immediately on contact with cold air. Because the sudden freezing kills bacteria, QuickFreeze is planning to market a wastewater purification system that works on the same principle. The process works only when temperatures are cold, however, so municipalities using it will still need to maintain a conventional system.

Which of the following, if true, provides the strongest grounds for a prediction that municipalities will buy QuickFreeze's purification system despite the need to maintain a conventional purification system as well?

(A) Bacteria are not the only impurities that must be removed from wastewater.

(B) Many municipalities have old wastewater purification systems that need to be replaced.

(C) Conventional wastewater purification systems have not been fully successful in killing bacteria at cold temperatures.

(D) During times of warm weather, when it is not in use, QuickFreeze's purification system requires relatively little maintenance.

(E) Places where the winters are cold rarely have a problem of water shortage.

Evaluation of a Plan

Situation   QuickFreeze is planning to market wastewater purification systems that work by spraying a mist that freezes on contact with cold air. The sudden freezing kills bacteria. Because the system works only at cold temperatures, municipalities using it will still need to maintain a conventional system.

Reasoning   *Which statement provides the strongest grounds for thinking that at least some municipalities will buy the purification system despite the need to maintain a conventional purification system as well?* The passage tells us why a municipality using a QuickFreeze wastewater purification system would still need a conventional system. But why would a municipality want the QuickFreeze system in addition to a conventional system? If conventional systems are not fully effective at cold temperatures, the QuickFreeze system would allow municipalities that sometimes experience cold temperatures to purify their wastewater more effectively.

A   This neither weakens nor strengthens the prediction. There is no basis in the passage for determining whether the QuickFreeze system could help remove impurities other than bacteria from wastewater. If it did, the effect of this information would be neutral, because we are already told that the municipalities would be unable to use the QuickFreeze system as a stand-alone purification system. Without further information, the need to remove other impurities would have no effect on the strength of the prediction.

B   The passage states that municipalities using the QuickFreeze system would still need a conventional system. Thus, the old conventional wastewater systems would still need to be replaced with new conventional systems. This answer choice provides no reason to think municipalities would buy the QuickFreeze system.

C   **Correct.** This statement, if true, would strengthen the prediction, because it provides a valid reason why the QuickFreeze system could be needed alongside conventional ones: it is more effective than the conventional systems in cold weather.

D   Although this claim does undercut one reason for thinking municipalities might not be likely to purchase the QuickFreeze system, it provides little reason to think that they will purchase such a system. Perhaps in times of cold weather, the QuickFreeze system is very expensive to maintain.

E   The issue of whether or not there are water shortages in places where winters are cold is not directly relevant. If conventional wastewater systems are sufficient to purify water in such places, municipalities would not need the QuickFreeze system (as they would still need to maintain a conventional purification system).

The correct answer is C.

514. **Plant scientists have used genetic engineering on seeds to produce crop plants that are highly resistant to insect damage**. Unfortunately, the seeds themselves are quite expensive, and the plants require more fertilizer and water to grow well than normal ones. Accordingly, **for most farmers the savings on pesticides would not compensate for the higher seed costs and the cost of additional fertilizer**. However, since consumer demand for grains, fruits, and vegetables grown without the use of pesticides continues to rise, the use of genetically engineered seeds of this kind is likely to become widespread.

In the argument given, the two portions in **boldface** play which of the following roles?

(A) The first supplies a context for the argument; the second is the argument's main conclusion.

(B) The first introduces a development that the argument predicts will have a certain outcome; the second is a state of affairs that, according to the argument, contributes to bringing about that outcome.

(C) The first presents a development that the argument predicts will have a certain outcome; the second acknowledges a consideration that tends to weigh against that prediction.

(D) The first provides evidence to support a prediction that the argument seeks to defend; the second is that prediction.

(E) The first and the second each provide evidence to support the argument's main conclusion.

Argument Construction

Situation   Seeds genetically engineered by plant scientists produce crops that are highly resistant to insect damage, and such crops can be grown with less use of pesticides. The seeds would be costly to use, and the savings on pesticides would not be sufficient, in themselves, to increase most farmers' profitability. Nonetheless, consumer demand for pesticide-free food materials is increasing, so genetically engineered seeds are likely to become widely used.

Reasoning   *What function is served by the statement that plant scientists have used genetic engineering on seeds to produce insect-resistant crop plants? What function is served by the statement that for most farmers the savings on pesticides would not outweigh other associated costs?* The first statement describes an innovation—genetically engineered seeds—that allows crops to be grown with little or no use of pesticides. The second statement notes that savings on pesticide use would not outweigh the higher costs of the genetically engineered seeds. The argument's main conclusion, however, is the prediction, expressed in the second clause of the final sentence of the passage, that use of such genetically engineered seeds will become widespread.

A   The second statement is a not the main conclusion. Instead it is an intermediate conclusion, which is based on the preceding statements. The main conclusion is presented in the final clause of the passage.

B   This correctly characterizes the first statement but not the second. The second statement is not meant to indicate a factor that contributes to the predicted outcome; instead, it indicates a factor that could hypothetically count against the argument's prediction.

C   **Correct.** The first boldface portion reports a development in agricultural technology. In the final sentence, the argument goes on to predict that an outcome of this development will be the widespread adoption of insect-resistant genetically engineered seeds. The second boldface portion acknowledges a financial consideration that would tend to count against that prediction.

D   The first statement does provide partial support for the prediction stated in the argument's main conclusion. The second statement does not provide any support for the prediction that the argument seeks to defend. That prediction is expressed in the final clause of the passage and is the main conclusion of the argument.

E   The second statement cannot accurately be described as giving evidence to support the prediction stated in the argument's main conclusion. Instead, it tangentially acknowledges a consideration that could plausibly be thought to count against the conclusion.

The correct answer is C.

515. Which of the following most logically completes the passage?

Leptin, a protein occurring naturally in the blood, appears to regulate how much fat the body carries by speeding up the metabolism and decreasing the appetite when the body has too much fat. Mice that do not naturally produce leptin have more fat than other mice, but lose fat rapidly when they are given leptin injections. Unfortunately, however, leptin cannot be used as a dietary supplement to control fat, since _____.

(A)　the digestive system breaks down proteins before they can enter the bloodstream

(B)　there are pharmaceuticals already available that can contribute to weight loss by speeding up the metabolism

(C)　people with unusually low levels of leptin in their blood tend to have a high percentage of body fat

(D)　the mice that do not naturally produce leptin were from a specially bred strain of mice

(E)　mice whose bodies did produce leptin also lost some of their body fat when given leptin injections

Argument Construction

Situation　Leptin, a protein naturally occurring in the bloodstream, speeds up metabolism to induce loss of excessive fat. Mice that lack leptin have more fat than other mice, but lose fat when given leptin injections. However, leptin cannot be used as a dietary supplement to control fat.

Reasoning　*What would explain the fact that a dietary supplement of leptin will not help to control fat?* Leptin injected into the bloodstream—but not leptin taken as a dietary supplement—helps control fat. So leptin taken as a dietary supplement is either inactivated in the gastrointestinal system or for some other reason fails to enter the bloodstream.

A　**Correct.** The digestive system breaks down proteins and would therefore break down leptin, which is a protein. This means that leptin given as a dietary supplement would never reach the bloodstream.

B　The question concerns leptin alone, and this new information fails to explain why leptin cannot help control fat if administered as a dietary supplement.

C　It is unsurprising that this would be so, but this information does nothing to explain why leptin consumed as a supplement would fail to control fat.

D　Presumably leptin administered as a dietary supplement was first tested on mice bred to lack leptin. However, the question about leptin does not concern only mice, but presumably humans and other mammals.

E　This suggests that boosting existing normal leptin levels with injections can induce further fat loss. However, this has no obvious relevance to the question raised about why dietary supplements of leptin fail to produce fat loss.

The correct answer is A.

516. Suncorp, a new corporation with limited funds, has been clearing large sections of the tropical Amazon forest for cattle ranching. This practice continues even though greater profits can be made from rubber tapping, which does not destroy the forest, than from cattle ranching, which does destroy the forest.

Which of the following, if true, most helps to explain why Suncorp has been pursuing the less profitable of the two economic activities mentioned above?

(A) The soil of the Amazon forest is very rich in nutrients that are important in the development of grazing lands.

(B) Cattle-ranching operations that are located in tropical climates are more profitable than cattle-ranching operations that are located in cold-weather climates.

(C) In certain districts, profits made from cattle ranching are more heavily taxed than profits made from any other industry.

(D) Some of the cattle that are raised on land cleared in the Amazon are killed by wildcats.

(E) The amount of money required to begin a rubber-tapping operation is twice as high as the amount needed to begin a cattle ranch.

Argument Construction

Situation	Suncorp is a new corporation with limited funds. It has been clearing large sections of the tropical Amazon forest for ranching, even though rubber-tapping would be more profitable.
Reasoning	*What would explain why Suncorp is clearing sections of the rain forest for ranching, even though rubber tapping would be more profitable?* Because Suncorp has limited funds, if rubber tapping has much higher start-up costs, Suncorp might not have enough money to start rubber-tapping operations. If cattle ranching has much lower start-up costs than rubber tapping, Suncorp might be able to afford such an operation.

A   This statement gives a reason why cattle ranching in the Amazon might be more profitable than one might otherwise think it would be. However, we already know from the passage that rubber tapping would be more profitable than cattle ranching. So, this answer choice does not help explain why cattle ranching might be preferable to rubber tapping.

B   The comparison between the profitableness of cattle ranching in tropical climates and in cold-weather climates is irrelevant. The passage only covers cattle ranching in the tropical Amazon forest. This answer choice would at most explain why Suncorp is undertaking cattle ranching in the Amazon rather than in some cold-weather location.

C   This statement makes what needs to be explained harder to understand, for it indicates that cattle ranching in the Amazon might be less profitable than one would otherwise think.

D   Like answer choice C, this statement indicates a disadvantage of cattle ranching in the Amazon. So, it does not explain why cattle ranching would be preferred to some other economic activity.

E   **Correct.** Because it costs less to begin cattle ranching than it does to begin rubber tapping, Suncorp—which has limited funds—would have a reason to pursue cattle ranching over a potentially more profitable activity.

The correct answer is E.

517. Archaeologists use technology to analyze ancient sites. It is likely that this technology will advance considerably in the near future, allowing archaeologists to gather more information than is currently possible. If they study certain sites now, they risk contaminating or compromising them for future studies. Therefore, in order to maximize the potential for gathering knowledge in the long run, a team of archaeologists plans to delay the examination of a newly excavated site.

Which of the following would be most useful to investigate for the purpose of evaluating the plan's prospects for achieving its goal?

(A) Whether any of the contents of the site will significantly deteriorate before the anticipated technology is available

(B) Whether there will continue to be improvements on the relevant technology

(C) Whether the team can study a site other than the newly excavated site for the time being

(D) Whether the site was inhabited by a very ancient culture

(E) Whether the anticipated technology will damage objects under study

Evaluation of a Plan

Situation   To avoid prematurely compromising a newly excavated site, an archaeological team plans to postpone examining it until more advanced technology is developed that will let them gather more information from it. Their goal is to maximize the potential for gathering knowledge.

Reasoning   *What would be most helpful to investigate in order to assess how likely it is that delaying examination of the site will maximize the potential for gathering knowledge from it?* In order to maximize (or even increase) the potential for gathering knowledge from the site by delaying its examination, the risk of compromising the site by examining it now has to be greater than the risk that the site will be compromised as much or more by delaying the examination. The delay might also increase the risk that the site will never be examined at all—for example, the team might lose its funding while it delays, or changes in local political conditions might prevent the site's future examination. Investigating any of these risks could be helpful in assessing the likelihood that the team's plan will achieve its goal.

A   **Correct.** If any of the site's contents will significantly deteriorate before the technology becomes available, that could reduce the ability to gather future information from the site even more than examining and compromising the site now would.

B   The passage already tells us that it is likely the technology *will advance considerably in the near future.* Given this information, further inquiry into whether there will be any ongoing (perhaps minor) improvements is somewhat redundant and probably of minimal value with respect to evaluating the plan's likelihood of success.

C   Even if the team can study a second site in the meanwhile, they might maximize the overall potential for gathering knowledge by delaying the examination of either site, both sites, or neither site until more advanced technology is available.

D   The age of the culture that inhabited the site is irrelevant to assessing the risks of delaying the site's examination until more advanced technology is available.

E   Even if the anticipated technology will damage or destroy the objects under study, it might still maximize the amount of knowledge that can be gathered from those objects. Without any comparison between the damage risk that would be incurred by proceeding with the current technology and the damage risk that would be incurred by waiting, the mere fact that some damage would occur is irrelevant.

The correct answer is A.

518. More and more law firms specializing in corporate taxes are paid on a contingency-fee basis. Under this arrangement, if a case is won, the firm usually receives more than it would have received if it had been paid on the alternate hourly rate basis. If the case is lost, the firm receives nothing. Most firms are likely to make more under the contingency-fee arrangement.

Which of the following, if true, would most strengthen the prediction above?

(A) Firms that work exclusively under the hourly rate arrangement spend, on average, fewer hours on cases that are won than on cases that are lost.

(B) Some litigation can last for years before any decision is reached, and, even then, the decision may be appealed.

(C) Firms under the contingency-fee arrangement still pay their employees on an hourly basis.

(D) Since the majority of firms specialize in certain kinds of cases, they are able to assess accurately their chances of winning each potential case.

(E) Firms working under the contingency-fee arrangement take in fewer cases per year than do firms working under the hourly rate arrangement.

Argument Evaluation

Situation   Law firms of a certain type are increasingly working on a contingency-fee basis, whereby the firm is only paid if the case won. For the individual cases that are thus taken and won, the payments are generally greater than the total payments would have been if the firms had been paid on an hourly basis. Furthermore, although cases taken on a contingency-fee basis present a significant risk of working for many hours on a case and not being paid, the passage claims that most firms are likely to make more money, on average, than they would if they took their cases on an hourly basis.

Reasoning   *What would most strongly indicate that, despite the risks, the law firms working on a contingency fee basis are likely to make more money, on average, than they would have otherwise?* Our task is to find the statement that would most strongly support this prediction. A primary risk of using contingency fees is that a firm might have so many unsuccessful cases that the average revenue (and profit) is less than it would have been with hourly fees. Anything indicating that the firms might be able to reduce that risk would provide some support for the prediction that they would make more money with contingency fees than with hourly fees.

A   Supposing that the firms mentioned in this option changed from working on an hourly-rate basis to working on a contingency-fee basis, we would not have enough information to predict what the results would be. For example, we may have no reason to expect that the firm would accept the same cases that they would have accepted if they were working on an hourly-rate basis. As such, patterns of work on cases taken on an hourly basis may be irrelevant for determining how much the firms would make if they were to take their cases on a contingency-fee basis.

B   This answer choice indicates that firms taking cases on a contingency-fee basis can work on the cases for years without payment. Rather than supporting the point that firms would make more money if they worked on a contingency-fee basis, the option illustrates an aspect of the risks associated with this payment arrangement.

C   This answer choice does not support the prediction that *most firms are likely to make more*, it could mean either that they are likely to have greater total revenue or that they are likely to have a greater amount of profit. With regard to gross revenue, the cost of staff time tells us nothing about how much money the firms are likely to take in. With regard to profits, the need to pay employees even for work on unsuccessful cases slightly weakens the prediction: all else being equal, profits would be higher if employees were not paid for work on such cases. However, we are given no information about whether firms might be able to have some alternative arrangement whereby they pay employees only for successful cases, or about whether they would have to pay considerably more with such arrangements.

D   **Correct.** This answer choice suggests that firms working on a contingency-fee basis would be able to select cases that they would be likely to win and therefore be paid for. Thus, they could mitigate the risk of having too few successful cases to offset the lack of income from the unsuccessful ones. This increases the probability that the firms would be able to bring in more total revenue in the long run with a contingency-fee system than they would if they charged hourly fees. And since we are given no evidence that the ability to select high-win-probability cases would lead to greater costs, this also tends slightly to strengthen the prediction that the firms' profits would be greater in the long run.

E   Although the difference in numbers of cases described in this option could, given certain possible facts, be relevant to the prediction made by the argument, we have not been given any such facts.

The correct answer is D.

519. Pretzel Vendor: The new license fee for operating a pretzel stand outside the art museum is prohibitively expensive. Charging typical prices, I would need to sell an average of 25 pretzels per hour to break even. At my stand outside City Hall, with about as many passers-by as at the art museum, I average only 15 per hour. So I could not break even running a stand outside the art museum, much less turn a profit.

Which of the following, if true, most seriously weakens the pretzel vendor's argument?

(A) The pretzel vendor does not sell anything other than pretzels.

(B) People who visit the art museum are more likely to buy pretzels than are people who go to City Hall.

(C) The license fee for operating a pretzel stand outside City Hall will not increase.

(D) People who buy pretzels at pretzel stands are more likely to do so during the lunch hour than at other times.

(E) The city will grant more licenses for pretzel stands outside the art museum than the number it grants for stands outside City Hall.

Argument Evaluation

Situation   Because of a new license fee for operating a pretzel stand outside the art museum, a pretzel vendor would have to sell on average 25 pretzels per hour to break even, which is 10 more on average than the vendor sells outside City Hall. But the museum would have no more passers-by than City Hall has. The vendor concludes that a pretzel stand outside the museum would not break even.

Reasoning   *What additional information, if true, would most weaken the support, in light of the given information, for the prediction that the vendor would not break even running a stand outside the art museum?* The vendor's prediction that a pretzel stand outside the art museum would not break even is based on the following considerations: (1) the vendor would have to sell 10 more pretzels on average per hour than the vendor sells outside City Hall, and (2) there are no more passers-by outside the museum than outside City Hall. But what matters is not how many *potential* customers pass by the art museum. What matters is how many *actual* customers there will be. If the people who pass by the stand outside the museum are more likely to buy pretzels than the people who pass by the stand at City Hall are, the prediction might fail.

A   This would be more likely to strengthen the argument than weaken it. If the vendor did sell something other than pretzels outside the museum but not outside City Hall, then it is possible that this product would help the vendor at least break even. But this answer choice tells us that the vendor sells only pretzels.

B   Correct. If the people who visit the museum are more likely to buy pretzels than the people who go to City Hall are, then it could be that the vendor will be able to sell 25 pretzels per hour on average. This could be true even if there are not more people outside the art museum than outside City Hall.

C   The vendor's prediction is only about whether a stand outside the art museum could break even, not about whether the business in the current location would continue to break even. For that prediction, it does not matter whether there will be a fee for a stand outside City Hall.

D   The vendor's argument does not include or depend on anything about when the pretzels are sold at the stand. So a claim that more pretzels are sold during the lunch hour than at any other time does not weaken the argument.

E   This claim strengthens the argument instead of weakening it. If there are more pretzel stands outside the art museum than there are outside City Hall, then there would be more competition. That might make it harder to sell even 15 pretzels per hour, let alone 25.

The correct answer is B.

520. Beginning in 1966 all new cars sold in Morodia were required to have safety belts and power steering. Previously, most cars in Morodia were without these features. Safety belts help to prevent injuries in collisions, and power steering helps to avoid collisions in the first place. But even though in 1966 one-seventh of the cars in Morodia were replaced with new cars, the number of car collisions and collision-related injuries did not decline.

Which of the following, if true about Morodia, most helps to explain why the number of collisions and collision-related injuries in Morodia failed to decline in 1966?

(A) Because of a driver-education campaign, most drivers and passengers in cars that did have safety belts used them in 1966.

(B) Most of the new cars bought in 1966 were bought in the months of January and February.

(C) In 1965, substantially more than one-seventh of the cars in Morodia were replaced with new cars.

(D) An excessive reliance on the new safety features led many owners of new cars to drive less cautiously in 1966 than before.

(E) The seat belts and power steering put into new cars sold in 1966 had to undergo strict quality-control inspections by manufacturers, whether the cars were manufactured in Morodia or not.

Argument Construction

Situation Starting in 1966, new cars sold in Morodia were required to have safety belts and power steering. But the numbers of car collisions and collision-related injuries did not decline that year.

Reasoning *What could explain why the newly required safety features did not reduce the numbers of collisions and collision-related injuries in 1966?* The passage says that power steering helps to prevent collisions and that safety belts help to prevent collision-related injuries. Since most Morodian cars previously lacked these features, and one-seventh of them were replaced with new cars in 1966, the proportion of cars with these features must have increased that year. This should have reduced the numbers of collisions and collision-related injuries unless some other factor counteracted the reductions. Evidence of any such countervailing factor would help to explain why the numbers did not decrease.

A Increased usage of safety belts should have reduced the number of collision-related injuries, so it would not help explain why this number did not decrease.

B If the new cars bought in 1966 were mostly purchased early in the year, the increased proportion of cars with the newly required safety features should have started more significantly reducing the numbers of collisions and collision-related injuries early in the year, producing greater reductions for the year as a whole.

C However, many cars were replaced in the year before the safety features were required, in 1966 the replacement of one-seventh of all Morodian cars should still have increased the overall proportion of Morodian cars with the safety features and thus reduced the numbers of collisions and collision-related injuries.

D Correct. If many owners of the cars with the new safety features drove less cautiously, their recklessness could have increased the overall numbers of collisions and collision-related injuries despite any benefits from the safety features.

E Strict quality-control inspections should have made the safety features more reliable, further reducing the numbers of collisions and collision-related injuries.

The correct answer is D.

521. Manufacturers of mechanical pencils make most of their profit on pencil leads rather than on the pencils themselves. The Write Company, which cannot sell its leads as cheaply as other manufacturers can, plans to alter the design of its mechanical pencil so that it will accept only a newly designed Write Company lead, which will be sold at the same price as the Write Company's current lead.

Which of the following, if true, most strongly supports the Write Company's projection that its plan will lead to an increase in its sales of pencil leads?

(A) The new Write Company pencil will be introduced at a price higher than the price the Write Company charges for its current model.

(B) In the foreseeable future, manufacturers of mechanical pencils will probably have to raise the prices they charge for mechanical pencils.

(C) The newly designed Write Company lead will cost somewhat more to manufacture than the Write Company's current lead does.

(D) A rival manufacturer recently announced similar plans to introduce a mechanical pencil that would accept only the leads produced by that manufacturer.

(E) In extensive test marketing, mechanical-pencil users found the new Write Company pencil markedly superior to other mechanical pencils they had used.

Argument Evaluation

Situation   The Write Company makes mechanical pencils and pencil-lead refills. Companies in this type of business make most of their profits from selling the leads, but the Write Company's leads cost more than leads made by other firms, so the refills are not selling well. The company plans to alter the design of its pencil and leads so that only the company's leads will fit. The new leads will be sold at the same price as the existing ones. The company projects that its plan will lead to an increase in the sale of its leads.

Reasoning   *Which of the stated pieces of additional information most strongly supports the company's projection of an increase in sales of leads?* Presumably, because of the price difference, users of Write Company pencils are often refilling them with competitors' cheaper leads instead of Write Company leads. If the number of sales of the company's redesigned pencil did not drop significantly below the number of sales for its original pencil, a likely consequence would be a significant increase in refill sales for the redesigned pencil, because users would no longer have the option of using competitors' leads. The pencil would have to be priced competitively and function well.

A   This slightly weakens support for the company's projection because it suggests that the redesigned pencil might not sell sufficiently well to boost lead sales unless the redesigned pencil is perceived by potential buyers as being worth the higher price.

B   It is not clear whether, if this predicted outcome were to occur, it would help or hinder the Write Company in selling more of its pencil leads. For all we know, the Write Company's pencil and leads could become less price-competitive compared with those of other firms.

C   Since the new lead will cost the same as the current one, the increased unit cost would, all else being equal, tend to reduce profits unless this reduction were compensated for by increased sales volume. Given that the price to consumers would stay the same, the lower profit per lead does not suggest that consumers would buy more of the leads.

D   This provides too little information to tell what the effect of the competitor's action might be. For one thing, we have no information about whether the competitor would continue to sell its leads at a lower price than that of Write Company leads. The competitor's action might create additional competition for the Write Company's new products, increasing the risk that the Write Company's plan will fail. On the other hand, the competitor's pencils would have a similar potential drawback to that of the new Write Company pencils (restriction on the choice of refill leads), so it might tend to reduce the number of consumers who would avoid the new Write Company pencils in favor of the competitor's product.

E   **Correct.** This information suggests that sales of the Write Company's redesigned pencil may increase (or at least will probably not significantly decrease), that many consumers will find the company's pencils worth the additional expense of refilling them with Write Company leads, and that consequently the company's plan to increase lead sales will succeed.

The correct answer is E.

522. Enterprise Bank currently requires customers with checking accounts to maintain a minimum balance or pay a monthly fee. Enterprise plans to offer accounts with no monthly fee and no minimum-balance requirement; to cover their projected administrative costs of $3 per account per month they plan to charge $30 for overdrawing an account. Since each month on average slightly more than 10 percent of Enterprise's customers overdraw their accounts, bank officials predict the new accounts will generate a profit.

Which of the following, if true, most strongly supports the bank officials' prediction?

(A) Some of Enterprise Bank's current checking account customers are expected to switch to the new accounts once they are offered.

(B) One third of Enterprise Bank's revenues are currently derived from monthly fees tied to checking accounts.

(C) Many checking account customers who occasionally pay a fee for not maintaining a minimum balance in their account generally maintain a balance well above the minimum.

(D) Customers whose checking accounts do not have a minimum-balance requirement are more likely than others to overdraw their checking accounts.

(E) Customers whose checking accounts do not have a minimum-balance requirement are more likely than others to write checks for small amounts.

Evaluation of a Plan

Situation Enterprise Bank gives customers checking accounts with no monthly fee provided they maintain a certain minimum balance. However, the bank plans to offer accounts with no minimum-balance requirement and no monthly fee. It plans to cover the bank's $3 per account per month administrative cost by charging a $30 penalty for overdrafts. Only slightly more than 10 percent of customers, on average, overdraw their accounts in a month. The bank officials predict the new accounts will generate a profit.

Reasoning *What new information, if accurate, would most strongly support the prediction?* If about only one customer in ten, on average, currently has an overdraft in a month, and if this trend continues among customers who sign up for the new account, then the proposed $30 penalty per overdraft will cover the $30 cost of maintaining checking accounts for 10 customers per month. Would removing the minimum-balance requirement significantly increase the 10 percent overdraft rate? If so, then significantly more than one in ten customers, on average, would pay a $30 penalty. If this were so, then the new plan would yield a profit, as predicted.

A "Some" might mean only a few, and this would probably not be sufficient to make the new plan significantly profitable.

B This suggests that many customers with the current minimum-balance no-monthly-fee account do not maintain the minimum-balance requirement and pay fees instead. However, this information by itself seems to have little bearing on the new plan.

C Such customers would be likely to overdraw their accounts less frequently. This suggests that if a preponderance of the customers for the proposed new account were such customers, the overdraft rate would decrease, and the proposed new account would be less profitable, or even unprofitable.

D **Correct.** This information provides strong support for the bank officials' prediction. It indicates that the currently roughly 10 percent overdraft rate might increase drastically with the no-minimum-balance account and, on average, cause the imposition of a $30 penalty on significantly more than 10 percent of customers per month. This would make the new account significantly profitable.

E This suggests that a check written by one of these customers is more likely to be for a small amount and is therefore somewhat less likely to cause an overdraft (unless such customers typically have small checking balances, which we are not told). If there were many such customers for the proposed new account, the overdraft rate might be less than 10 percent; this would indicate that the new account might not turn out to be profitable.

The correct answer is D.

523. Highway Official: When resurfacing our concrete bridges, we should use electrically conductive concrete (ECC) rather than standard concrete. In the winter, ECC can be heated by passing an electric current through it, thereby preventing ice buildup. The cost of the electricity needed is substantially lower than the cost of the deicing salt we currently use.

Taxpayer: But ECC is vastly more expensive than standard concrete, so your proposal is probably not justifiable on economic grounds.

Which of the following, if true, could best be used by the highway official to support the official's proposal in the face of the taxpayer's objection?

(A) The use of deicing salt causes corrosion of reinforcing steel in concrete bridge decks and damage to the concrete itself, thereby considerably shortening the useful life of concrete bridges.

(B) Severe icing conditions can cause power outages and slow down the work of emergency crews trying to get power restored.

(C) In weather conditions conducive to icing, ice generally forms on the concrete surfaces of bridges well before it forms on parts of the roadway that go over solid ground.

(D) Aside from its potential use for deicing bridges, ECC might also be an effective means of keeping other concrete structures such as parking garages and airport runways ice free.

(E) If ECC were to be used for a bridge surface, the electric current would be turned on only at times at which ice was likely to form.

Evaluation of a Plan

Situation A highway official recommends using electrically conductive concrete (ECC) for resurfacing concrete bridges. This would allow the transmission of an electric current to prevent ice buildup in winter. The highway official supports the proposal by stating that the cost of the electricity used would be substantially lower than the cost of the deicing salt used at present. A taxpayer objects that ECC is much more expensive than standard concrete.

Reasoning *Which piece of additional information would most logically address the objection of the taxpayer?* Consider whether there could be other, indirect or long-term, costs associated with either of the two deicing methods (salt, electricity). For example, would use of ECC involve installation of additional infrastructure to provide electric power to the bridges—and, if so, how would the total costs compare with total existing costs? What are the cost implications of the current use of deicing salt? Any additional information that addresses these questions will be relevant. Note that the taxpayer's objection primarily concerns the capital cost of ECC bridge surfacing.

A **Correct.** The use of deicing salt causes corrosion that considerably shortens the useful life of the bridge. Clearly, replacement of a bridge would involve a large capital expenditure. This is a major reason for reconsidering the use of deicing salt. Of course, absent additional information about total costs of installation and use of each deicing method, it is not a conclusive reason to discontinue using deicing salt.

B Power outages in severe icing conditions would cause dangerous road-surface conditions on bridges surfaced with ECC, thus requiring a backup method of deicing in such circumstances. This would probably require road maintenance systems to use an auxiliary power backup or deicing salt in rare cases. However, this provides no evidence that the cost of emergency backup measures would exceed the overall savings available with the use of ECC.

C This is a reason for ensuring that deicing of bridges is given priority over deicing other places, but this prioritization can be done whatever method of deicing is used.

D The issues raised by the statements of the highway official and the taxpayer concern only the use of ECC for deicing bridges, so the information in this answer choice has no clear or direct relevance to that issue.

E This most likely offers no relevant additional information, since it is presumably already taken into account in the claim that the cost of electricity for deicing is lower than the cost of deicing salt. So this merely acknowledges one way to help optimize the costs associated with ECC deicing, but it is not, by itself, a substantial refutation of the taxpayer's objection.

The correct answer is A.

524. In virtually any industry, technological improvements increase labor productivity, which is the output of goods and services per person-hour worked. In Parland's industries, labor productivity is significantly higher than it is in Vergia's industries. Clearly, therefore, Parland's industries must, on the whole, be further advanced technologically than Vergia's are.

The argument is most vulnerable to which of the following criticisms?

(A)   It offers a conclusion that is no more than a paraphrase of one of the pieces of information provided in its support.

(B)   It presents as evidence in support of a claim information that is inconsistent with other evidence presented in support of the same claim.

(C)   It takes one possible cause of a condition to be the actual cause of that condition without considering any other possible causes.

(D)   It takes a condition to be the effect of something that happened only after the condition already existed.

(E)   It makes a distinction that presupposes the truth of the conclusion that is to be established.

Argument Evaluation

Situation   Technological improvements in nearly every industry increase labor productivity, which is the output of goods and services per person-hour worked. Because labor productivity is significantly higher in Parland than Vergia, Parland's industries are, in general, more technologically advanced than Vergia's.

Reasoning   *To which criticism is the argument most vulnerable?* Though one factor, such as technological advancements, may lead to greater labor productivity, it may not be the only such factor, or even a necessary factor, leading to great labor productivity. Therefore, the mere fact that one region's labor is more productive than another's is not sufficient to establish that the former region is more technologically advanced than the latter region is.

A   The conclusion is not merely a paraphrase of the pieces of information provided in its support. Indeed, the problem with the argument is that the conclusion goes too far beyond what the premises merit.

B   The premises of the argument are not inconsistent with one another.

C   **Correct.** This accurately describes the flaw in the argument because the reasons given in the argument for its conclusion would be good reasons only if there were no other plausible explanations for Parland's greater labor productivity.

D   The argument does not mention how long Parland has had more productive labor, or when technological improvements would have occurred.

E   Neither of the premises contains anything that presupposes the conclusion to be true. The argument's two premises are *Technological improvements in nearly every industry increase labor productivity* and *Labor productivity is significantly higher in Parland than Vergia*. The argument's conclusion states *Parland's industries must on the whole be further advanced than Vergia's are.* If anything in the premises presupposed that conclusion, the conclusion could not be false if the premises were true. But the conclusion can be false even if both premises are true. Suppose, for instance, that Parland and Vergia engage in different industries and Parland's industries inherently have greater labor productivity. That might not be because Parland's industries are more technologically advanced than Vergia's are, but only because of the nature of the different industries. Yet it can nonetheless be true that technological improvements increase labor productivity.

The correct answer is C.

525. Chaco Canyon, a settlement of the ancient Anasazi culture in North America, had massive buildings. **It must have been a major Anasazi center**. Analysis of wood samples shows that some of the timber for the buildings came from the Chuska and San Mateo mountains, 50 miles from Chaco Canyon. **Only a major cultural center would have the organizational power to import timber from 50 miles away**.

In the argument given, the two portions in **boldface** play which of the following roles?

(A) The first is a premise used to support the argument's main conclusion; the second is the argument's main conclusion.

(B) The first is the argument's main conclusion; the second is a premise used to support that conclusion.

(C) The first is one of two premises used to support the argument's main conclusion; the second is the other of those two premises.

(D) The first is a premise used to support the argument's main conclusion; the second is a premise used to support another conclusion drawn in the argument.

(E) The first is inferred from another statement in the argument; the second is inferred from the first.

Argument Construction

Situation   The ancient Anasazi settlement at Chaco Canyon had massive buildings, for which some of the timber came from mountains 50 miles away.

Reasoning   *What roles do the statement that Chaco Canyon must have been a major Anasazi center and the statement that only a major center would have the organizational power to import timber from 50 miles away play in the argument?* The first and third sentences in the passage are both factual observations. Since no further support is provided for either of them, neither can be a conclusion in the argument. The final sentence (i.e., the second boldface portion of the argument) is a speculative generalization about major cultural centers. None of the other statements gives us any reason to think this generalization is true, so it cannot be a conclusion in the argument, either. However, the third and fourth sentences together imply that Chaco Canyon was a major cultural center, and the first sentence indicates that it was Anasazi. So together, the first, third, and fourth sentences all support the claim that Chaco Canyon was a major Anasazi cultural center and thus more generally a major Anasazi center, as the second sentence asserts. Therefore, the first, third, and fourth sentences are all premises that jointly support the second sentence (i.e., the first **boldface** portion of the argument) as a conclusion.

A   As explained above in the Reasoning section, the first boldface sentence is a conclusion supported by the second boldface sentence, not the other way around.

B   Correct. As explained above in the Reasoning section, the first boldface sentence is the argument's only stated conclusion, and thus is its main conclusion, while all the other sentences are premises used to support it; therefore, the second boldface sentence (*Only a major cultural center . . . 50 miles away*) is a premise used to support the conclusion.

C   As explained above in the Reasoning section, the first boldface sentence is the argument's conclusion, not a premise used to support the conclusion.

D   As explained above in the Reasoning section, the first boldface sentence is the argument's only stated conclusion, and there is no reason to suppose that the argument is intended to lead to any other tacit conclusion that the second boldface sentence is intended to support.

E   As explained above in the Reasoning section, the first boldface sentence is inferred from the three other statements in the argument together, not from any one of them alone. The second boldface sentence is a speculative generalization that cannot be, and is not meant to be, inferred from the first boldface sentence or from any other statement in the argument.

The correct answer is B.

526. The Maxilux car company's design for its new luxury model, the Max 100, included a special design for the tires that was intended to complement the model's image. The winning bid for supplying these tires was submitted by Rubco. Analysts concluded that the bid would only just cover Rubco's costs on the tires, but Rubco executives claim that winning the bid will actually make a profit for the company.

Which of the following, if true, most strongly justifies the claim made by Rubco's executives?

(A) In any Maxilux model, the spare tire is exactly the same make and model as the tires that are mounted on the wheels.

(B) Rubco holds exclusive contracts to supply Maxilux with the tires for a number of other models made by Maxilux.

(C) The production facilities for the Max 100 and those for the tires to be supplied by Rubco are located very near each other.

(D) When people who have purchased a carefully designed luxury automobile need to replace a worn part of it, they almost invariably replace it with a part of exactly the same make and type.

(E) When Maxilux awarded the tire contract to Rubco, the only criterion on which Rubco's bid was clearly ahead of its competitors' bids was price.

Argument Construction

Situation Rubco won a bid for supplying tires for the Max 100, a new luxury model by Maxilux. The bid would barely cover the cost of the tires, but Rubco executives claim that winning the bid will be profitable.

Reasoning *What would support the executives' claim?* Rubco is not expected to make a profit from supplying the tires for the new cars, so we must look for some other way that Rubco could derive a profit as a result of winning the bid. If by winning the bid Rubco created an inevitable market for itself in replacement tires—on which Rubco could earn a profit—then the executives' claim may be justified.

A We have already been told that the bid is expected to barely cover the costs of supplying the tires on the new cars, so the analysts mentioned in the passage have presumably already taken into account that there is a spare tire supplied for the Max 100.

B If winning the bid led Rubco to win more exclusive contracts with the Maxilux, that might help support the executives' claim. But this statement indicates only that Rubco already has several exclusive contracts to supply Maxilux with tires, not that winning the bid has led to, or will lead to, more such contracts, which is what would be needed.

C As in answer choice (A), this is relevant to the costs of supplying the tires for the Max 100, but presumably this was taken into account by the analysts when they concluded that the bid would barely cover Rubco's costs on the tires.

D **Correct.** This indicates that by winning the bid Rubco has created a way to profit from the contract with Maxilux, specifically, by creating a market for replacement tires.

E This is likely one of the reasons that Rubco's bid only just covers Rubco's costs on the tires; it does nothing to justify the executives' claims that the bid will lead to a profit for Rubco.

The correct answer is D.

527. Which of the following most logically completes the passage?

Most bicycle helmets provide good protection for the top and back of the head, but little or no protection for the temple regions on the sides of the head. A study of head injuries resulting from bicycle accidents showed that a large proportion were caused by blows to the temple area. Therefore, if bicycle helmets protected this area, the risk of serious head injury in bicycle accidents would be greatly reduced, especially since _____.

(A) among the bicyclists included in the study's sample of head injuries, only a very small proportion had been wearing a helmet at the time of their accident

(B) even those bicyclists who regularly wear helmets have a poor understanding of the degree and kind of protection that helmets afford

(C) a helmet that included protection for the temples would have to be somewhat larger and heavier than current helmets

(D) the bone in the temple area is relatively thin and impacts in that area are thus very likely to cause brain injury

(E) bicyclists generally land on their arm or shoulder when they fall to the side, which reduces the likelihood of severe impacts on the side of the head

Argument Construction

Situation   Bicycle helmets protect the top and back of the head, but not the sides or temples. A study found that a large proportion of head injuries caused by biking accidents were caused by blows to the temple area.

Reasoning   *Why would the risk of serious head injury in bicycle accidents be greatly reduced if bicycle helmets protected the temple regions?* If for some reason a serious head injury is particularly likely when there is impact to the temple area, then bicycle helmets that protect that area would be apt to reduce the number of serious head injuries from bicycle accidents. One such reason is that the bone in the temple area is relatively thin.

A   This point is irrelevant because it gives us no information about the seriousness or the likelihood of injuries due to impact to the temple area.

B   Whether bicyclists who regularly wear helmets have a good understanding of what protection their helmets afford is not relevant as to whether serious head injuries are particularly likely to occur from impact to the temple area.

C   This point is relevant only to what a helmet that protected the temple area would be like, not to the seriousness of injuries resulting from impact to that area. If anything, this point counts as a reason *against* the conclusion, not *for* it. If such helmets are heavier and larger, they may be used less than they otherwise would be. If fewer helmets are used, then improvements to helmet design will have less of an effect in reducing serious head injuries.

D   **Correct.** This statement provides a reason why the temple area of the rider's head needs protection: impacts to this area are very likely to cause brain injuries.

E   This is largely irrelevant. Even if it suggests that head injuries do not generally result from bicyclists falling to the side, it does not indicate that such injuries are rare or that there is not great risk of serious injury in those cases in which there is impact to the temple area.

The correct answer is D.

528. Which of the following most logically completes the argument?

In a typical year, Innovair's airplanes are involved in 35 collisions while parked or being towed in airports, with a resulting yearly cost of $1,000,000 for repairs.

To reduce the frequency of ground collisions, Innovair will begin giving its ground crews additional training, at an annual cost of $500,000. Although this will cut the number of ground collisions by about half at best, the drop in repair costs can be expected to be much greater, since _____.

(A) most ground collisions happen when ground crews are rushing to minimize the time a delayed airplane spends on the ground

(B) a ground collision typically occurs when there are no passengers on the airplane

(C) the additional training will focus on helping ground crews avoid those kinds of ground collisions that cause the most costly damage

(D) the $500,000 cost figure for the additional training of ground crews includes the wages that those crews will earn during the time spent in actual training

(E) most ground collisions have been caused by the least experienced ground-crew members

Evaluation of a Plan

Situation An airline will give its ground crews additional training to reduce the frequency of the collisions its airplanes are involved in while parked or being towed in airports.

Reasoning *What premise would most logically support the conclusion that the additional training will reduce repair costs from ground collisions much more than it reduces the number of such collisions?* The key word *since* before the blank shows that the argument should be completed with a premise that supports the preceding claim that the *drop in repair costs can be expected to be much greater.* What statement would support that claim? Note that the annual cost of training, $500,000, is half as much as the yearly cost of the repairs needed as a result of ground collisions, $1,000,000. We are told that the training will cut the number of ground collisions by at most about half, so if the drop in repair costs will be much greater than half, which would need to be the case to make the training worthwhile, what would have to be true of the ground collisions that the training will help the ground crews avoid? Presumably, they would have to be among the higher repair cost collisions, as opposed to the less serious collisions that result in lower repair costs. That is, the collisions that are avoided would have to make up more than half of the repair costs, so, they would have to be costlier than average, given that the number of collisions avoided is no more than half. Thus, it would be quite useful to include in the argument a premise providing evidence that the training will help avoid the sorts of ground collisions that lead to above average repair costs.

A We are given no reason to believe that the additional training would affect how much ground crews rush to minimize delays.

B The number of passengers is not clearly relevant to the repair costs resulting from a ground collision and in any case would not be affected by additional ground crew training.

C **Correct.** If the training especially helps the ground crews avoid those kinds of collisions that cause the most costly damage (that is, damage from ground collisions that has higher repair costs than the average repair costs for damage from ground collisions), then it will probably reduce repair costs by more than half.

D Whether the cited expense for training includes wages is irrelevant to whether the training will reduce repair costs more than it reduces the number of collisions.

E This suggests that the additional training may help reduce the number of collisions, not that it will reduce repair costs more than it reduces the number of collisions.

The correct answer is C.

529. Many agriculturally intensive areas of the world are beginning to encounter water scarcity problems. As a result, many farmers in these areas are likely to reduce their output as the water supply they need in order to maintain production shrinks. However, one group of farmers in such a region plans to increase their production by implementing techniques for water conservation.

Which of the following, if true, would most strongly support the prediction that the group's plan will succeed?

(A) Farmers who can gain a larger share of the food market in their regions will be better positioned to control more water resources.

(B) Most agricultural practices in areas with water shortages are water-intensive.

(C) Other regions of the world not facing water shortages are likely to make up for the reduction in agricultural output.

(D) Demand for agricultural products in the group's region is not expected to decline.

(E) More than half the water used for agriculture in the farmers' region is lost to evaporation or leakage from irrigation channels.

Evaluation of a Plan

Situation   Farmers in many agriculturally intensive regions will probably reduce their output because the regions' water supplies are dwindling, but one group of farmers in such a region plans to use water conservation techniques to increase their output.

Reasoning   *What would provide evidence that water conservation techniques will help the farmers increase production despite their region's dwindling water supplies?* In order for the water conservation techniques to be effective, they must result in significantly more water becoming available for the farmers to use. Because overall supplies are shrinking, rather than growing, that can only happen if the farmers are currently losing or wasting a great deal of water in ways that could be prevented with water conservation techniques.

A   This suggests an advantage the farmers will gain if their water conservation plan enables them to increase production, but it provides no evidence that the plan actually will enable them to increase production.

B   This suggests that the plan would have to yield quite a lot of conserved water in order for the farmers to increase production, but it offers no evidence that the plan will do so. Thus, it provides some reason to question whether the plan will succeed.

C   Whether regions without water shortages will increase production is not directly relevant to the question of whether a particular measure would lead to increased production in one region that does have a water shortage.

D   This has some slight, indirect relevance to the question of whether the farmers' plan will succeed: it suggests that if the farmers do manage to increase production, they will continue to have a market for what they produce. However, it does not address the issue of whether they will be able to increase production. Furthermore, even if demand for agricultural products in the group's region were expected to decline, it could still remain high enough to support the farmers' increased output from their water conservation plan.

E   **Correct.** This suggests that the farmers are losing a lot of water in ways that the water conservation techniques might prevent, so it provides evidence that employing some such techniques could enable the farmers to save enough water to increase their output.

The correct answer is E.

530. Hollywood restaurant is replacing some of its standard tables with tall tables and stools. The restaurant already fills every available seat during its operating hours, and the change in seating arrangements will not result in an increase in the restaurant's seating capacity. Nonetheless, the restaurant's management expects revenue to increase as a result of the seating change without any concurrent change in menu, prices, or operating hours.

Which of the following, if true, provides the best reason for the expectation?

(A) One of the taller tables takes up less floor space than one of the standard tables.

(B) Diners seated on stools typically do not linger over dinner as long as diners seated at standard tables.

(C) Since the restaurant will replace only some of its standard tables, it can continue to accommodate customers who do not care for the taller tables.

(D) Few diners are likely to avoid the restaurant because of the new seating arrangement.

(E) The standard tables being replaced by tall tables would otherwise have to be replaced with new standard tables at a greater expense.

Argument Construction

Situation   Hollywood restaurant is replacing some of its tables with taller tables and stools, and the management expects this will increase revenue, despite the fact that the restaurant already fills all of its available seats and that this change will not increase seating capacity. Furthermore, there will not be any change in menu, prices, or operating hours.

Reasoning   *What would strongly support the management's expectation?* Since the new seating will not increase the restaurant's seating capacity, the management's expectations must be based on a belief that the change to taller tables and stools will somehow change diners' behavior, perhaps by leading them to order more food, or to stay at their tables for a shorter time, thereby allowing the restaurant to serve more diners during its operating hours without increasing seating capacity. If diners seated at tall tables and on tall stools spend less time lingering over their dinners, then they will leave sooner, opening up the tables for more diners. Because the restaurant, before the change, already fills every available seat during its operating hours, it is reasonable to think that it will be able to serve more diners than it currently does, thereby selling more food and thus increasing revenue.

A   This would be relevant if we could infer from it that seating capacity will increase. However, the passage indicates that the new seating arrangement will not result in greater capacity.

B   **Correct.** Because the restaurant will be able to serve more meals during its operating hours, the restaurant's revenue can be expected to increase.

C   This may indicate that the restaurant is less likely to alienate customers who do not care for tall tables and stools, but that only supports the claim that the restaurant will not lose customers and therefore lose revenue; it does not indicate that the restaurant will see revenue increase.

D   Again, this merely indicates that there will not be a loss—or much loss—of revenue, not that there will be an increase in revenue.

E   Less expensive tables will decrease the restaurant's costs, but it will not increase the restaurant's revenue.

The correct answer is B.

531. A major network news organization experienced a drop in viewership in the week following the airing of a controversial report on the economy. The network also received a very large number of complaints regarding the report. The network, however, maintains that negative reactions to the report had nothing to do with its loss of viewers.

Which of the following, if true, most strongly supports the network's position?

(A) The other major network news organizations reported similar reductions in viewership during the same week.

(B) The viewers who registered complaints with the network were regular viewers of the news organization's programs.

(C) Major network news organizations publicly attribute drops in viewership to their own reports only when they receive complaints about those reports.

(D) This was not the first time that this network news organization has aired a controversial report on the economy that has inspired viewers to complain to the network.

(E) Most network news viewers rely on network news broadcasts as their primary source of information regarding the economy.

Argument Construction

Situation   A major network news organization aired a controversial report on the economy, and the following week the network's viewership declined. The network claims that the loss of viewers was not connected with negative reactions to the report.

Reasoning   *Which statement most strongly supports the network's position?* If other major news networks had similar drops in viewership, it is implausible to think that the controversial report accounted for the other networks' drops in viewership. On the other hand, it is plausible to suppose that whatever did cause the drop in the viewership experienced by other network news organizations— e.g., holidays, weather, popular non-news programming—also had that effect on the organization that ran the controversial report. This would give some reason to believe that the airing of the report does not account for the organization's drop in viewership.

A   **Correct.** The network's position is that the drop in viewership was not caused by its airing of the controversial report and thus that the drop was caused by something else. This answer choice provides some evidence that there might have been a different cause. If none of the other networks had aired the controversial report, their reductions in viewership were likely due to some other factor; it is implausible to suppose that disapproval of the one network would have caused viewers to avoid all networks. A simultaneous drop in viewership among all the networks would support the hypothesis that a single factor or set of factors caused the drop for all the networks, including the one that aired the report.

B   If anything, this statement tends to undermine the network's claim, because it suggests that the report offended people who otherwise might have continued to watch the organization's programming.

C   Since the network did in fact receive complaints about the report, this statement is irrelevant.

D   The fact that the network has received complaints before about controversial reports on the economy that the network's news organization has aired tells us nothing about whether this recent report caused a subsequent drop in viewership.

E   The fact that viewers turn to network news broadcasts as their primary source of information about the economy tells us nothing about whether viewers might stop watching a particular network news organization's programs as a result of its airing a controversial report on the economy.

The correct answer is A.

532. Only a reduction of 10 percent in the number of scheduled flights using Greentown's airport will allow the delays that are so common there to be avoided. Hevelia airstrip, 40 miles away, would, if upgraded and expanded, be an attractive alternative for fully 20 percent of the passengers using Greentown airport. Nevertheless, experts reject the claim that turning Hevelia into a full-service airport would end the chronic delays at Greentown.

Which of the following, if true, most helps to justify the experts' position?

(A) Turning Hevelia into a full-service airport would require not only substantial construction at the airport itself, but also the construction of new access highways.

(B) A second largely undeveloped airstrip close to Greentown airport would be a more attractive alternative than Hevelia for many passengers who now use Greentown.

(C) Hevelia airstrip lies in a relatively undeveloped area but would, if it became a full-service airport, be a magnet for commercial and residential development.

(D) If an airplane has to wait to land, the extra jet fuel required adds significantly to the airline's costs.

(E) Several airlines use Greentown as a regional hub, so that most flights landing at Greentown have many passengers who then take different flights to reach their final destinations.

Evaluation of a Plan

Situation   To avoid the delays now common at Greentown's airport, the number of scheduled flights there would need to be reduced by 10 percent. If the nearby Hevelia airstrip were expanded and upgraded, it would be an attractive alternative for 20 percent of Greentown airport's passengers. Still, experts do not believe that the delays at Greentown would end even if Hevelia were turned into a full-service airport.

Reasoning   *Which statement most supports the experts' position?* If the number of flights at Greentown's airport did not drop by at least 10 percent, despite the fact that 20 percent of the passengers who currently use Greentown's airport would find nearby Hevelia airstrip an attractive alternative, then the delays would not be avoided. Airlines generally use certain airports as regional hubs—an airport through which an airline routes most of its traffic—so, even if many passengers would be willing to use Hevelia airstrip, the number of flights at Greentown may not decline significantly, or at all.

A   The experts' position concerns what would happen to the flight delays at Greentown airport if the Hevelia airstrip were converted into a full-service airport. So the fact that there are great costs involved in making such a conversion—possibly making such a conversion unlikely—has no bearing on the effects such a conversion would have on flight delays at Greentown if the conversion were to be carried out.

B   This statement indicates that the undeveloped airstrip near Greentown might be a better way to alleviate flight delays at Greentown, but it tells us nothing about the effects that converting the Hevelia airstrip to a full-service airport would have were it to be carried out.

C   This in no way explains why converting the Hevelia airstrip into a full-service airport would not alleviate the problem with flight delays at Greentown.

D   This provides a reason to think that reducing the number of flights at Greentown might make the airport more efficient. But that has no bearing on the effect that converting the Hevelia airstrip to a full-service airport might have on flight delays at Greentown.

E   **Correct.** This statement provides support for the experts' position because it gives a reason for thinking that the number of scheduled flights at Greentown would not be reduced, even if Hevelia airstrip became an attractive alternative for some 20 percent of Greentown's passengers.

The correct answer is E.

533. Farmer: Worldwide, just three grain crops—rice, wheat, and corn—account for most human caloric intake. To maintain this level of caloric intake and also keep pace with global population growth, yields per acre from each of these crops will have to increase at least 1.5 percent every year, given that the supply of cultivated land is diminishing. Therefore, the government should increase funding for research into new ways to improve yields.

Which of the following is an assumption on which the farmer's argument depends?

(A) It is solely the government's responsibility to ensure that the amount of rice, wheat, and corn produced worldwide keeps pace with global population growth.

(B) Increasing government funding for research into new ways to improve the yields per acre of rice, wheat, and corn crops would help to increase total worldwide annual production of food from these crops.

(C) Increasing the yields per acre of rice, wheat, and corn is more important than increasing the yields per acre of other crops.

(D) Current levels of funding for research into ways of improving grain crop yields per acre have enabled grain crop yields per acre to increase by more than 1.5 percent per year worldwide.

(E) In coming decades, rice, wheat, and corn will become a minor part of human caloric intake, unless there is government-funded research to increase their yields per acre.

Argument Construction

Situation   The farmer states that although the worldwide human population is increasing, the supply of cultivated land is decreasing. We thus need to increase yields for the food crops that account for most of human caloric intake—rice, wheat, and corn—if we are to maintain our existing caloric intake. The increase in yields, according to the farmer, would need to be at least 1.5 percent every year.

Reasoning   *What must be true if we are to accept the farmer's conclusion, that the government should increase funding for research into new ways to improve crop yields, on the basis of the above statements?* The farmer uses the above statements as premises of an argument for an increase in government funding for research on crop yields. Supposing that the farmer's statements are true, we need to find in the available options the statement that, if added to the argument, may allow us to accept the farmer's conclusion, based on the argument.

A   Whether or not nongovernmental entities such as NGOs (nongovernmental organizations) are responsible for helping to ensure that humans have an adequate amount of food, governments may or may not also have this responsibility.

B   **Correct.** If government funding of this research does not increase crop yields, then the premises of the argument provide no support for the conclusion that the government should provide such funding. The cogency of the argument thus depends on this statement.

C   Crops in addition to rice, wheat, and corn could also be very important, and perhaps essential for human existence. However, this would not diminish the importance of food crops such as rice, wheat, and corn.

D   This option may suggest that current levels of funding of research into crop yields are sufficient for purposes of our obtaining the necessary crop yields.

E   This option suggests that rice, wheat, and corn may be replaced by other crops, because the other crops have better yields. Because we might thus have a means for increasing crop yields that does not involve an increase in government research funding, this option may actually decrease the support for the conclusion.

The correct answer is B.

534. The air quality board recently informed Coffee Roast, a small coffee roasting firm, of a complaint regarding the smoke from its roaster. Recently enacted air quality regulations require machines roasting more than 10 pounds of coffee to be equipped with expensive smoke-dissipating afterburners. The firm, however, roasts only 8 pounds of coffee at a time. Nevertheless, the company has decided to purchase and install an afterburner.

Which of the following, if true, most strongly supports the firm's decision?

(A) Until settling on the new air quality regulations, the board had debated whether to require afterburners for machines roasting more than 5 pounds of coffee at a time.

(B) Coffee roasted in a machine equipped with an afterburner has its flavor subtly altered.

(C) The cost to the firm of an afterburner is less than the cost of replacing its roaster with a smaller one.

(D) Fewer complaints are reported in areas that maintain strict rules regarding afterburners.

(E) The firm has reason to fear that negative publicity regarding the complaints could result in lost sales.

Evaluation of a Plan

Situation   After being informed of a complaint about smoke from its coffee roaster, a firm decided to purchase and install an afterburner to reduce or eliminate emissions of smoke, even though the roaster roasts too little coffee at a time for an afterburner to be legally required.

Reasoning   *What would have been a good reason for the firm to buy and install the afterburner?* The only factors mentioned that might give the firm reason to buy an afterburner are the complaint about smoke and the regulations requiring an afterburner. Since the regulations do not apply in this case, the complaint is more likely to have motivated the firm's decision. Any serious potential consequences the firm might have faced from failure to address the complaint could have provided a good reason to buy and install the afterburner.

A   If this debate had still been ongoing when the firm made its decision, uncertainty about the pending regulations might have justified the decision. But the debate had already been settled before the firm decided to purchase the afterburner, and the regulations clearly did not require one.

B   An unspecified alteration in flavor is not clearly a good reason to use an afterburner—the afterburner might worsen the flavor.

C   The firm's roaster was already small enough that the regulations did not require it to be replaced, even without an afterburner.

D   This reason relates only to rules regarding afterburners, not to Coffee Roast's purchase of an afterburner, which was not mandated by regulations. Furthermore, it could be that the air quality regulations recently enacted are among the strictest in any region, which could result in fewer complaints regardless of whether Coffee Roast installs an afterburner.

E   **Correct.** Since installing an afterburner is a plausible way to address the complaint and prevent future complaints, the firm has plausible reasons to believe this strategy will help it avoid the negative publicity and lost sales it fears. These considerations could have reasonably justified its decision.

The correct answer is E.

535. People who do regular volunteer work tend to live longer, on average, than people who do not. It has been found that "doing good," a category that certainly includes volunteer work, releases endorphins, the brain's natural opiates, which induce in people a feeling of well-being. Clearly, there is a connection: Regular releases of endorphins must in some way help to extend people's lives.

Which of the following, if true, most seriously undermines the force of the evidence given as support for the hypothesis that endorphins promote longevity?

(A) People who do regular volunteer work are only somewhat more likely than others to characterize the work they do for a living as "doing good."

(B) Although extremely high levels of endorphins could be harmful to health, such levels are never reached as a result of the natural release of endorphins.

(C) There are many people who have done some volunteer work but who do not do such work regularly.

(D) People tend not to become involved in regular volunteer work unless they are healthy and energetic to begin with.

(E) Releases of endorphins are responsible for the sense of well-being experienced by many long-distance runners while running.

Argument Evaluation

Situation   People who volunteer regularly live longer on average than people who do not. Doing good work, including volunteer work, releases endorphins, which induce a feeling of well-being.

Reasoning   *What additional findings would suggest that the cited evidence does not indicate that endorphins increase longevity?* The argument implicitly assumes that the reason regular volunteers tend to live longer is that volunteering lengthens their lives. It further assumes that no factor that is correlated with volunteering, other than the endorphin release, would plausibly explain how volunteering could have this effect. Findings that cast doubt on either of these assumptions would undermine the connection between the cited evidence and the conclusion that endorphins promote longevity.

A   Volunteering might greatly boost volunteers' endorphin levels even if the work the volunteers do for a living is no different from other people's work.

B   Even if unnaturally high endorphin levels could harm health, the levels attainable through volunteer work may promote health.

C   The argument is about an observed correlation in a certain group of people (those who regularly do volunteer work). How many people are outside that group (i.e., do not regularly do volunteer work) is independent of the question of what causes the observed correlation. Even if some people volunteer only occasionally, volunteering regularly may promote longevity by causing regular releases of endorphins.

D   **Correct.** This suggests that the initially better health of people who choose to volunteer could fully explain the cited correlation between volunteering and longevity.

E   Unless we are also given evidence that long-distance runners tend not to live longer than other people, this does not undermine the purported evidence in the argument. Endorphins might promote longevity in both regular volunteers and long-distance runners.

The correct answer is D.

536. A study compared a sample of Swedish people older than 75 who needed in-home assistance with a similar sample of Israeli people. The people in the two samples received both informal assistance, provided by family and friends, and formal assistance, professionally provided. Although Sweden and Israel have equally well-funded and comprehensive systems for providing formal assistance, the study found that the people in the Swedish sample received more formal assistance, on average, than those in the Israeli sample.

Which of the following, if true, does most to explain the difference that the study found?

(A) A companion study found that among children needing special in-home care, the amount of formal assistance they received was roughly the same in Sweden as in Israel.

(B) More Swedish than Israeli people older than 75 live in rural areas where formal assistance services are sparse or nonexistent.

(C) Although in both Sweden and Israel much of the funding for formal assistance ultimately comes from the central government, the local structures through which assistance is delivered are different in the two countries.

(D) In recent decades, the increase in life expectancy of someone who is 75 years old has been greater in Israel than in Sweden.

(E) In Israel, people older than 75 tend to live with their children, whereas in Sweden people of that age tend to live alone.

Argument Construction

Situation
A study of elder care in Israel and Sweden found that in Sweden, of the total amount of care that people older than 75 and needing in-home assistance received, the proportion of care that was formal, i.e., provided by professional care personnel, was greater than in Israel. Both Sweden and Israel had equally good systems for providing formal care, and in both countries, the elderly also received informal care, i.e., care provided by friends and family.

Reasoning
Among the factors given, which would most contribute to explaining the difference the study found between Sweden and Israel with respect to elder care? A good guess would be that there is a difference in some societal factor that affects the difference the study found. For example, perhaps elders in one of the countries regard maintaining independence as a higher priority than elders in the other and consequently try to rely less on friends and family? Perhaps patterns of decline in ability to remain independent are different in the two countries? Or perhaps a greater proportion of elders live alone in one of the countries than in the other?

A   The difference to be explained concerns only elder care, not care of children.

B   The fact that formal elder care is less available in Swedish rural areas than in Israeli rural areas might suggest that there would be a greater reliance on informal care in such areas in Sweden. But this new information throws little light on how the overall proportions of formal and informal care in each country would be affected.

C   This information is not specific enough to help explain the precise difference found in the study. It is reasonable to assume that the study was conducted with sufficient rigor to take account of any relevant structural differences in the delivery of formal elder care.

D   This could suggest either that the greater proportion of informal elder care in Israel contributes to greater life expectancy or that greater life expectancy signals greater fitness during old age that would make it more practical for friends and family to provide informal elder care.

E   **Correct.** The prevalence in Israel of elders living in family settings—in contrast to Sweden, where elders tend to live alone—offers a plausible explanation of the difference that the study found in the patterns of elder care in Israel and Sweden. It seems reasonable to think that, all things being equal, elders living alone would use formal elder care services more often than elders living with friends or family.

The correct answer is E.

537. Film Director: It is true that certain characters and plot twists in my newly released film *The Big Heist* are similar to characters and plot twists in *Thieves*, a movie that came out last year. Pointing to these similarities, the film studio that produced *Thieves* is now accusing me of taking ideas from that film. The accusation is clearly without merit. All production work on *The Big Heist* was actually completed months before *Thieves* was released.

Which of the following, if true, provides the strongest support for the director's position?

(A) Before *Thieves* began production, its script had been circulating for several years among various film studios, including the studio that produced *The Big Heist*.

(B) The characters and plot twists that are most similar in the two films have close parallels in many earlier films of the same genre.

(C) The film studio that produced *Thieves* seldom produces films in this genre.

(D) The director of *Thieves* worked with the director of *The Big Heist* on several earlier projects.

(E) Production work on *Thieves* began before production work on *The Big Heist* was started.

Argument Evaluation

Situation   The director of the film *The Big Heist* has been accused, by the studio that produced the film *Thieves*, of taking ideas from the film. The director responds that the accusation lacks merit, since all production work on *The Big Heist* was completed before *Thieves* appeared last year in theaters.

Reasoning   *Which of the five statements most strongly supports the director's position?* Crime thrillers, as a film genre, are likely to have stock characters and plot lines that reflect a long tradition. So it would be no surprise if some of the characters or plot twists in one such film would resemble, to a greater or lesser extent, the characters and plot twists in another. The studio might be correct in identifying such resemblances between *The Big Heist* and *Thieves*. But it would not necessarily be correct that characters or plot lines in *The Big Heist* were derived from *Thieves*.

A   This undercuts the director's position, since it provides information that indicates an opportunity for the director to copy ideas from the script for *Thieves*.

B   **Correct.** This information strengthens the support for the director's claim that the studio's accusation lacks merit. Since both *Thieves* and *The Big Heist* fall within a long tradition of crime thriller films, the characters and plot lines in both films reflect that tradition, and so any resemblances do not imply deliberate copying of the ideas in *Thieves* by the director of *The Big Heist*.

C   This information seems largely irrelevant to the issue raised and does not strengthen support for the director's conclusion.

D   This does little to indicate that the director's conclusion is correct. For example, the then-future director of *Thieves* might have discussed with the future director of *The Big Heist* specific ideas about character and plot for a planned crime thriller film.

E   This does not support the director's claim. For example, it raises the possibility that information about *Thieves* leaked during the early stages of production—information that could have been exploited in the production of *The Big Heist*.

The correct answer is B.

538. In Mernia commercial fossil hunters often sell important fossils they have found, not to universities or museums, but to individual collectors, who pay much better but generally do not allow researchers access to their collections. To increase the number of fossils available for research, some legislators propose requiring all fossils that are found in Mernia to be sold only to universities or museums.

Which of the following, if true, most strongly indicates that the legislators' proposal will fail to achieve its goal?

(A) Some fossil hunters in Mernia are not commercial fossil hunters, but rather are amateurs who keep the fossils that they find.

(B) Most fossils found in Mernia are common types that have little scientific interest.

(C) Commercial fossil hunters in Mernia currently sell some of the fossils they find to universities and museums.

(D) Many universities in Mernia do not engage in fossil research.

(E) Most fossils are found by commercial fossil hunters, and they would give up looking for fossils if they were no longer allowed to sell to individual collectors.

Evaluation of a Plan

Situation   Fossil hunters in Mernia often sell important fossils to collectors who do not make them accessible to researchers. To increase the number of fossils available for research, some legislators propose requiring all fossils found in Mernia to be sold only to universities or museums.

Reasoning   *What would most strongly suggest that requiring all fossils found in Mernia to be sold only to universities or museums would not increase the number of fossils available for research?* To increase the number of fossils available for research, the proposed requirement will have to be implemented and effectively enforced. It will presumably have to increase the total number of fossils sold to universities and museums. And those institutions will have to make more of the fossils in their collections available to researchers than the private collectors do. Evidence that any of those conditions will not be fulfilled would suggest that the legislators' proposal will fail to achieve its goal.

A   Even if the legislation does not affect fossils kept by amateurs, it might still result in many more fossils being sold to universities or museums rather than to private collectors, and thus might still increase the number of fossils available for research.

B   Even if few Mernian fossils are interesting to researchers, the legislation could still achieve its goal of making more fossils available for research.

C   Even if commercial fossil hunters already sell a few fossils to universities and museums, the legislation could encourage them to sell many more fossils.

D   The universities that do not engage in fossil research presumably will not be interested in buying fossils even if the legislation passes. But the fossil hunters can just sell their fossils to other universities and museums that do engage in fossil research.

E   **Correct.** This suggests that if the legislation passes, fossils will simply be left in the ground rather than sold to private collectors. That would not increase the total number of fossils available for research.

The correct answer is E.

539. Economist: Tropicorp, which constantly seeks profitable investment opportunities, has been buying and clearing sections of tropical forest for cattle ranching, although pastures newly created there become useless for grazing after just a few years. The company has not gone into rubber tapping, even though greater profits can be made from rubber tapping, which leaves the forest intact. Thus, some environmentalists argue that **Tropicorp's actions do not serve even its own economic interest**. However, the initial investment required for a successful rubber-tapping operation is larger than that needed for a cattle ranch; there is a shortage of workers employable in rubber-tapping operations; and taxes are higher on profits from rubber tapping than on profits from cattle ranching. Consequently, **the environmentalists' conclusion is probably wrong**.

In the economist's argument, the two **boldface** portions play which of the following roles?

(A) The first supports the conclusion of the economist's argument; the second calls that conclusion into question.

(B) The first states the conclusion of the economist's argument; the second supports that conclusion.

(C) The first supports the conclusion of the environmentalists' argument; the second states that conclusion.

(D) The first states the conclusion of the environmentalists' argument; the second states the conclusion of the economist's argument.

(E) Each supports the conclusion of the economist's argument.

Argument Construction

Situation
: According to an economist, the firm Tropicorp has been investing in tropical forest that it has cleared for cattle ranching. But its new pastures are useless for grazing after a few years. In contrast, rubber tapping—which would avoid cutting trees—could be more profitable. According to the economist, environmentalists consequently argue that Tropicorp's investment does not serve the firm's economic interest. However, the economist argues, investing in rubber tapping involves some potential costs and risks greater than those that investing in cattle ranching involves. Consequently, the economist argues, the environmentalists' conclusion is probably wrong.

Reasoning
: *What function is served by the statement that Tropicorp's actions do not serve even its own economic interest? What function is served by the statement that the environmentalists' conclusion is probably wrong?* The first statement is a conclusion that the economist attributes to environmentalists. The second statement is the conclusion of an argument presented by the economist.

A The first states the conclusion of the argument that is attributed to environmentalists; it does not support—nor is it meant to—the conclusion of the economist.

B The second statement, not the first, is the conclusion of the economist's argument.

C The first is the conclusion attributed to environmentalists and is not meant merely as support for that conclusion.

D **Correct.** The first states the conclusion of the environmentalists' argument as the economist presents it; the second is the conclusion of the economist's argument.

E Neither statement is meant as support for the economist's conclusion, nor does it offer such support.

The correct answer is D.

540. Brown tides are growths of algae on the sea's surface that prevent sunlight from reaching marine plants below, thereby destroying not only the plants but also the shellfish that live off these plants. Biologists recently isolated a virus that, when added to seawater, kills the algae that cause brown tides. Adding large quantities of this virus to waters affected by brown tides will therefore make it possible to save the populations of shellfish that inhabit those waters.

Which of the following, if true, provides the most support for the conclusion of the argument?

(A) When applied in large quantities, the virus not only kills the algae that cause brown tides but also many harmless kinds of algae.

(B) Marine animals that prey on shellfish avoid areas of the sea in which brown tides are occurring.

(C) The number of different kinds of virus present in seawater is far greater than many marine biologists had, until recently, believed.

(D) The presence of large quantities of the virus in seawater does not adversely affect the growth of marine plants.

(E) The amount of the virus naturally present in seawater in which brown tides occur is neither significantly greater nor significantly less than the amount present in seawater in which brown tides do not occur.

Argument Evaluation

Situation   Brown tides—growths of algae on the sea's surface—kill the marine plants on which certain shellfish depend, by depriving them of sunlight. Biologists have discovered a virus that, if added to seawater in large quantities, can kill the algae. An author argues that this can be a means of saving the shellfish populations.

Reasoning   *Which of the answer choices most strongly supports the conclusion of the argument?* The argument concludes that adding large quantities of the virus to seawater infected by brown tides will help the shellfish survive. Any new information suggesting that the virus would, directly or indirectly, help the shellfish survive supports the conclusion. But the conclusion would be questionable if the virus could directly or indirectly harm the shellfish in a way that would outweigh any benefits the virus provides. New information indicating that this would not occur could provide support for the argument.

A   This information suggests that deployment of the virus could have undesirable side effects, but it neither supports nor casts doubt on the conclusion. We have no information suggesting that killing algae other than those that produce brown tides would, directly or indirectly, help the shellfish survive.

B   This information neither supports nor casts doubt on the conclusion. It indicates a way in which brown tides indirectly provide a benefit to shellfish, even if the indirect harm they cause to shellfish outweighs that benefit.

C   This information indicates that certain viruses can survive in seawater environments, but this information, by itself, neither supports nor casts doubt on the conclusion.

D   Correct. This information indicates that the virus the biologists isolated does not directly harm the marine plants on which shellfish depend. Therefore it provides significant support for the conclusion by indicating that the virus will not harm the shellfish indirectly by harming their food source.

E   This information suggests that only large quantities of the virus the biologists isolated will be effective in eliminating brown tides. But the conclusion of the argument specifies that the virus would need to be added in *large quantities*, so the information given in this answer choice provides no additional support for the conclusion.

The correct answer is D.

541. In persons with astigmatism, the clear outer layer of the eye is deformed in a way that impairs and sometimes distorts vision. The elongated figures in the paintings of El Greco (1541–1614) were so unusual that some critics sought to explain them by hypothesizing that, without knowing it, El Greco had an astigmatism that caused everything to appear to him in the distorted way that was characteristic of his painted figures.

The proposed explanation is most vulnerable to the criticism that it fails to

(A) establish that during the period in which El Greco lived, there was any correction available to those who did realize their vision was distorted

(B) provide evidence that astigmatism was common in the 1500s and 1600s

(C) consider that the critics who proposed the explanation might have suffered from astigmatism

(D) consider the effect of the hypothesized astigmatism on El Greco's perception of his own paintings

(E) allow for the possibility that artists see the world differently than do nonartists

Argument Evaluation

Situation   Figures in the paintings of El Greco are strikingly elongated. Some art critics have hypothesized that this was an unintentional result of his having a type of astigmatism that made things look elongated to him.

Reasoning   *What is a significant weakness in the critics' explanation?* Reasons to doubt the explanation could include any evidence that another explanation is more likely to be true or that the situation envisioned in the explanation may be impossible or inconsistent with the phenomena to be explained. For example, if only human figures in El Greco's paintings were elongated while other similarly shaped objects were not, that observation would be inconsistent with the claim that the elongations were due to a general distortion in his vision. Answer choice D presents a similar reason to think that the proposed explanation is inconsistent with the facts. If El Greco perceived human models as more elongated than they appear to non-astigmatic perceivers, he would also have perceived his depictions of such models as more elongated than those depictions appear to non-astigmatic perceivers. So if he had intended to depict the figures accurately, he would have adjusted his painting accordingly, and his depictions should appear accurately shaped to typical viewers. But they do not. Therefore, the distortions were more likely intentional.

A   The hypothesis of some critics is that El Greco may have had astigmatism without being aware of it. So the explanation does not depend on whether astigmatism could have been corrected during the period in which El Greco lived.

B   The reasoning concerning the hypothesis of some critics does not depend on whether astigmatism was common in the 1500s or 1600s. It is entirely consistent with the hypothesis that astigmatism was rare and that El Greco was one of the few people who had it.

C   Even if the critics who proposed the explanation had astigmatism, the explanation and the reasoning concerning the explanation would not be rendered faulty. The information provided is that the figures in El Greco's paintings were unusually elongated, not merely that they appear elongated to the critics mentioned.

D   Correct. According to the art critics' hypothesis, El Greco did not intend the figures in his paintings to be unnaturally elongated and did not know that they were. But this is the opposite of what one should expect if he had a type of astigmatism that made things look elongated to him. His astigmatism should have made the elongated figures in his paintings appear to him even more elongated than they appear to typical observers. So, regardless of whether he had astigmatism or not, the elongations were most likely intentional. If they were intentional, this feature of his paintings provides no more evidence that he had astigmatism than that he did not.

E   The explanation offered by the critics is entirely compatible with the possibility that artists see the world differently than do nonartists. One might wonder whether this possibility provides an alternative explanation for why El Greco painted elongated figures: he did so because he, like all artists, saw the world differently than nonartists do. But that hypothesis does not offer a coherent alternative to the critics' explanation. If all artists see the world as El Greco did, we should expect them all to depict the world as he did. However, most do not. If, on the other hand, El Greco's way of perceiving the world was only one of many ways in which artists' perceptions differ from those of nonartists, this provides no reason to think that the difference between El Greco's work and others' was not caused by astigmatism.

The correct answer is D.

542. Marketing executive for Magu Corporation: Whenever Magu opens a manufacturing facility in a new city, the company should sponsor, or make donations to, a number of nonprofit organizations in that city. Doing so would improve Magu's image in the community, and thus the money spent on such charitable ventures would lead to increased sales.

Which statement would, if true, point to the most serious weakness in the marketing executive's advice?

(A) Magu sells its products internationally, so sales in any one city represent only a small portion of total revenue.

(B) Spending on charitable ventures would require Magu to decrease direct advertisements, which are the most effective means of reaching its target customers.

(C) If market conditions change, Magu may have to close any such facility or relocate it.

(D) Some nonprofit organizations are poorly organized, so money donated to them would be of little benefit to the community.

(E) If workers at the manufacturing facility believed their wages or working conditions were poor, their complaints would outweigh any good impressions generated by Magu's donations or sponsorships.

Evaluation of a Plan

Situation   A marketing executive for Magu Corporation argues that Magu can increase its sales if it sponsors or donates to nonprofit organizations in any city in which it opens a new manufacturing facility, because doing so would improve its image in that city and increase sales.

Reasoning   *What would most strongly suggest that Magu would not increase sales even if it followed the plan proposed by the marketing executive?* Sponsoring or donating to nonprofit organizations would require the use of financial assets that therefore cannot be spent elsewhere. If as a result Magu had to cut other expenditures that drive sales more effectively than funding nonprofit organizations drives sales, the plan may not succeed.

A   Because Magu sells its products internationally and no one city represents more than a small portion of revenue, any increase in sales in any given city will have only a slight effect on total sales; nonetheless, sales could still rise.

B   Correct. If sponsoring or donating to a nonprofit would require Magu to reduce advertising, and advertising is the most effective means of reaching its target customers, then any positive influence on sales resulting from the charitable venture might be overwhelmed by a decrease in sales because of the advertising cuts.

C   The fact that Magu might have to close or relocate one of these new facilities does not suggest that the marketing executive's plan would not work; Magu's image could, nonetheless, improve and sales could increase as a result.

D   Even if some nonprofit organizations are poorly organized, others may not be, and Magu could limit its support to those.

E   Even if such complaints from workers would outweigh any benefit arising from Magu's support of nonprofit organizations, this does not indicate that the marketing executive's plan will not work, because we have no reason to think that the workers will in fact be dissatisfied with their wages or working conditions.

The correct answer is B.

543. In the last few years, plant scientists have been able to genetically engineer seeds to produce crops highly resistant to insect damage. Farmers growing crops with these seeds will be able to spend significantly less on pesticides. This cost reduction would more than make up for the higher cost of the genetically engineered seeds. Clearly, therefore, farmers who grow crops from genetically engineered seeds will be able to reduce their costs by using them.

Which of the following, if true, most weakens the argument?

(A) Plant scientists have not yet developed insect-resistant strains of every crop that is currently grown commercially.

(B) The cost of several commonly used pesticides is expected to rise in the next few years.

(C) Crops grown from the genetically engineered seeds require significantly more fertilizer and water to grow well than do crops grown from nonengineered seeds.

(D) In the future, the cost of genetically engineered seeds is likely to fall to the level of nonengineered seeds.

(E) The crops that now require the greatest expenditure on pesticides are not the ones for which genetically engineered seeds will become available.

Argument Evaluation

Situation   Farmers who grow crops with seeds that have been genetically engineered to produce crops resistant to insect damage will be able to spend less on pesticides. Though these seeds are more expensive than regular seeds, this greater cost will be more than compensated for by lower expenditures on pesticides.

Reasoning   *What claim most weakens the argument's support for the claim that farmers who grow crops from these genetically engineered seeds will be able to reduce their costs by using them?* The argument gives us good reason to think that even though these seeds are more expensive, the added expense is less than the amount that farmers will save by reducing their pesticide usage. But the argument does not tell us how the use of these seeds affects other costs the farmer might have. If, for instance, crops grown from these seeds require greater use of fertilizer or water, costs may stay stable or even increase.

A   The argument's conclusion is only that farmers who grow crops using these seeds will be able to reduce their costs. The argument does not claim that every farmer will be able to reduce costs for every crop the farmer produces.

B   If the cost of pesticides will increase in the next few years, this gives us some reason to believe that farmers who use these genetically engineered seeds to grow crops will have lower costs than they would have if they used other seeds to grow the same crops. That strengthens rather than weakens the argument's support for its conclusion.

C   **Correct.** As discussed above, if crops grown with the genetically engineered seeds require the use of more fertilizer or water, the farmer who uses such seeds may not see a reduction in costs.

D   If the genetically engineered seeds eventually become no more expensive than regular seeds, then it is more likely that farmers growing crops with these genetically engineered seeds will see their costs reduced.

E   This answer choice indicates that farmers will not be able to reduce costs as much as they might if all crops could be grown using seeds that are genetically engineered to produce crops resistant to insect damage. That, however, is fully consistent with the possibility that if farmers grow crops using the genetically engineered seeds that are available, they will thereby be able to reduce their costs.

The correct answer is C.

544. Educational Theorist: Recent editorials have called for limits on the amount of homework assigned to schoolchildren younger than 12. They point out that free-time activities play an important role in childhood development and that homework in large quantities can severely restrict children's free time, hindering their development. But the actual average homework time for children under 12—little more than 30 minutes per night—leaves plenty of free time. In reality, therefore, the editorials' rationale cannot justify the restriction they advocate.

Which of the following, if true, would most seriously call into question the educational theorist's conclusion?

(A) Some teachers give as homework assignments work of a kind that research suggests is most effective educationally when done in class.

(B) For children younger than 12, regularly doing homework in the first years of school has no proven academic value, but many educators believe that it fosters self-discipline and time management.

(C) Some homework assignments are related to free-time activities that children engage in, such as reading or hobbies.

(D) A substantial proportion of schoolchildren under 12, particularly those in their first few years of school, have less than 10 minutes of homework assigned per night.

(E) Some free-time activities teach children skills or information that they later find useful in their schoolwork.

Argument Evaluation

Situation An educational theorist points out that recent editorials have called for limits on the amount of homework assigned to children under the age of 12, since large amounts of homework can restrict the sort of free-time activities that are crucial to their development. The theorist argues that such restrictions are not justified, because children under 12 spend on average only 30 minutes on homework. That leaves plenty of time for other activities.

Reasoning *What would most seriously call the theorist's conclusion into question?* The theorist gives only the average amount of time children under the age of 12 spend on homework. However, the editorials advocated a limit on the maximum amount of homework assigned, not on the average amount across all schoolchildren. There could be a wide variation among the amounts of time different children spend on homework. While a large number of children may spend only a short amount of time on homework, some children may spend much longer. For those who have the greater amounts of homework, this might leave little time for important free-time activities.

A This claim, if true, may suggest that certain types of homework that teachers assign would be better done in class. It might be best not to give such assignments for homework, but that does not give us much reason to think that the *amount* of homework should be restricted.

B This choice indicates that, despite a possible objection to assigning homework, homework does have value. That does not tell us, though, whether the maximum amount of homework that is assigned is too much, too little, or just right.

C This claim could be true and yet children could still be left with too little time for important free-time activities.

D **Correct.** As explained in the reasoning section above, the educational theorist draws a conclusion regarding whether there should be a limit on the **maximum** amount of homework assigned to children under 12 and bases this conclusion solely on the **average** amount of time children under the age of 12 spend on homework. This conclusion would not be well supported if there is a wide variation in the amount of time children under the age of 12 spend on homework and if some—perhaps in the lower grades—spend only a very short amount of time on it. Suppose, for instance, as this answer choice has, that less than 10 minutes of homework is assigned to some of these children each night. If that were the case, then because the average amount of time schoolchildren under the age of 12 spend on homework each night is 30 minutes, that would mean that many schoolchildren may be spending far more than 30 minutes a night on homework. If so, then those children may not have enough free time for other important activities. That might mean that it would be appropriate to put limits on the amount of homework assigned to children under the age of 12.

E   This claim shows that some free-time activities are important for schoolwork later in life. But that does not tell us whether the maximum amount of homework that is assigned is too much, too little, or just right.

The correct answer is D.

545. Thyrian lawmaker: Thyria's Cheese Importation Board inspects all cheese shipments to Thyria and rejects shipments not meeting specified standards. Yet only one percent is ever rejected. Therefore, since the health consequences and associated economic costs of not rejecting that one percent are negligible, whereas the board's operating costs are considerable, for economic reasons alone the board should be disbanded.

Consultant: I disagree. The threat of having their shipments rejected deters many cheese exporters from shipping substandard product.

The consultant responds to the lawmaker's argument by

(A) rejecting the lawmaker's argument while proposing that the standards according to which the board inspects imported cheese should be raised

(B) providing evidence that the lawmaker's argument has significantly overestimated the cost of maintaining the board

(C) objecting to the lawmaker's introducing into the discussion factors that are not strictly economic

(D) pointing out a benefit of maintaining the board which the lawmaker's argument has failed to consider

(E) shifting the discussion from the argument at hand to an attack on the integrity of the cheese inspectors

Argument Construction

Situation   The Thyrian lawmaker argues that the Cheese Importation Board should be disbanded, because its operating costs are high and it rejects only a small percentage of the cheese it inspects. The consultant disagrees, pointing out that the board's inspections deter those who export cheese to Thyria from shipping substandard cheese.

Reasoning   *What strategy does the consultant use in the counterargument?* The consultant indicates to the lawmaker that there is a reason to retain the board that the lawmaker has not considered. The benefit the board provides is not that it identifies a great deal of substandard cheese and rejects it (thus keeping the public healthy), but that the possibility that their cheese could be found substandard is what keeps exporters from attempting to export low-quality cheese to Thyria.

A   The consultant does reject the lawmaker's argument, but the consultant does not propose higher standards. Indeed, in suggesting that the board should be retained, the consultant implies that the board's standards are appropriate.

B   The consultant does not provide any evidence related to the board's cost.

C   The only point the lawmaker raises that is not strictly economic is about the health consequences of disbanding the board, but the consultant does not address this point at all.

D   **Correct.** This statement properly identifies the strategy the consultant employs in his or her counterargument. The consultant points out that the board provides a significant benefit that the lawmaker did not consider.

E   The consultant does not attack the integrity of the cheese inspectors; to the contrary, the consultant says that their inspections deter the cheese exporters from shipping substandard cheese.

The correct answer is D.

546. The tulu, a popular ornamental plant, does not reproduce naturally, and is only bred and sold by specialized horticultural companies. Unfortunately, the tulu is easily devastated by a contagious fungal rot. The government ministry plans to reassure worried gardeners by requiring all tulu plants to be tested for fungal rot before being sold. However, infected plants less than 30 weeks old have generally not built up enough fungal rot in their systems to be detected reliably. And many tulu plants are sold before they are 24 weeks old.

Which of the following, if performed by the government ministry, could logically be expected to overcome the problem with their plan to test for the fungal rot?

(A) Releasing a general announcement that tulu plants less than 30 weeks old cannot be effectively tested for fungal rot

(B) Requiring all tulu plants less than 30 weeks old to be labeled as such

(C) Researching possible ways to test tulu plants less than 24 weeks old for fungal rot

(D) Ensuring that tulu plants are not sold before they are 30 weeks old

(E) Quarantining all tulu plants from horticultural companies at which any case of fungal rot has been detected until those tulu plants can be tested for fungal rot

Evaluation of a Plan

Situation There is a contagious fungal rot that devastates the tulu, a popular ornamental plant. To reassure worried gardeners, the government ministry plans to require that tulu plants be tested for the rot before being sold. However, many tulu plants are sold before they are 24 weeks old, yet fungal rot in plants less than 30 weeks old generally cannot be detected reliably.

Reasoning *What could the government ministry do to overcome the problem?* The problem arises from the fact that tulu plants are frequently sold before they are 24 weeks old, which is too soon for any fungal rot that is present to have built up enough in their root systems to be detected. Since the goal of the testing is to ensure that infected tulu plants are not sold, an obvious solution would be to make sure that no plants are sold before they are old enough for fungal rot to have built up to a detectable level. Thus, tulu plants should not be sold before they are 30 weeks old.

A Releasing such an announcement would help overcome the problem if it guaranteed that no one would buy or sell tulu plants before the plants were 30 weeks old, but it is far from certain that it would guarantee this.

B Similar to A, introducing such labeling would help overcome the problem if it guaranteed that no one would buy or sell tulu plants before the plants were 30 weeks old, but it is far from certain that it would guarantee this.

C There is no guarantee that such research will be successful at reducing the age at which tulu plants can be reliably tested.

D **Correct.** If the government *ensures* that no tulu plants less than 30 weeks of age are sold, then the specific problem mentioned in the passage would be overcome.

E This will not help overcome the problem. Such a quarantine program might lead horticultural companies to start selling tulu plants *only* if they are less than 24 weeks old, thereby minimizing the chance of quarantine by minimizing the chance of detection.

The correct answer is D.

547. While many people think of genetic manipulation of food crops as being aimed at developing larger and larger plant varieties, some plant breeders have in fact concentrated on discovering or producing dwarf varieties, which are roughly half as tall as normal varieties.

Which of the following would, if true, most help to explain the strategy of the plant breeders referred to above?

(A)   Plant varieties used as food by some are used as ornamentals by others.

(B)   The wholesale prices of a given crop decrease as the supply of it increases.

(C)   Crops once produced exclusively for human consumption are often now used for animal feed.

(D)   Short plants are less vulnerable to strong wind and heavy rains.

(E)   Nations with large industrial sectors tend to consume more processed grains.

Evaluation of a Plan

Situation   Some plant breeders have concentrated on discovering or producing certain species of food crop plants to be roughly half as tall as normal varieties.

Reasoning   *Why would some plant breeders concentrate on discovering or producing smaller varieties of certain food crops?* Presumably these breeders would not seek smaller varieties of plant crops unless the smaller size conveyed some benefit. If short plants were less vulnerable to strong wind and heavy rains, they would be apt to be more productive, other things being equal. Plant breeders would have reason to try to discover or produce such more productive varieties.

A   This statement doesn't indicate whether those who use the plants as ornamentals desire shorter varieties.

B   At most this suggests that higher productivity is not as much of an advantage as it otherwise would be. But there is nothing in the passage that indicates that smaller varieties would be more productive than normal-sized plants.

C   No reason is given for thinking that smaller varieties of plants are more conducive to use for animal feed than are larger varieties.

D   **Correct.** This answer choice is correct because—unlike the other choices—it helps explain why smaller plant varieties could sometimes be preferable to larger varieties. A plant that is less vulnerable to wind and rain is apt to suffer less damage. This is a clear advantage that would motivate plant breeders to try to discover or produce smaller varieties.

E   This has no direct bearing on the question posed. Processed grains are not even mentioned in the passage, let alone linked to smaller plant varieties.

The correct answer is D.

548. Airline Representative: The percentage of flight delays caused by airline error decreased significantly this year. This indicates that airlines listened to complaints about preventable errors and addressed the problems. Although delays caused by weather and other uncontrollable factors will always be part of travel, preventable delays are clearly decreasing.

Which of the following most clearly points to a logical flaw in the representative's reasoning?

(A) Airlines may be motivated by financial concerns to underreport the percentage of flight delays caused by airline error.

(B) The delays caused by uncontrollable factors could have led to an increase in complaints to airlines.

(C) Complaints may not be the most reliable measure of how many errors occurred in a given year.

(D) Delays caused by weather and other uncontrollable factors could have increased dramatically during the year under discussion.

(E) Airline customers might not believe that particular delays were caused by uncontrollable factors rather than airline error.

Argument Evaluation

Situation   According to an airline representative, the percentage of flight delays caused by airline error decreased significantly this year. The representative concludes that airlines have addressed preventable errors reported by travelers.

Reasoning   *Which of the answer choices most clearly suggests a logical flaw in the reasoning of the airline representative?* Flight delays can be caused in many ways: for example, by unpredictable bad weather, mechanical or computer failures, bad management, or some combination of these. Some but not all errors of these kinds—and the flight delays they might cause—are preventable. Note that the argument is focused on *the percentage* of all flight delays that are airline-error (AE) delays. This percentage can decrease by (1) a reduction in the number of AE delays or (2) an increase in the number of non-AE delays, i.e., those delays that the airline could not have prevented. Even if a significant increase occurred in the number of AE delays, such delays could have decreased as a percentage of all flight delays if there had been a large enough increase in non-AE flight delays.

A   The hypothesis stated in this answer choice offers a slight, indirect basis for wondering whether the information on which the representative bases the reasoning is accurate. However, it provides no direct grounds for supposing that the reasoning itself is logically flawed. Even to the extent that this gives any reason to doubt the truth of the purported information, the relevance is very indirect. Even if airlines *may* have a motivation to underreport the percentage of flight delays caused by airline error, there is little reason to suppose that the representative's information may be a result of any airline's acting on such a motivation. And the representative argues on the basis of a decrease in the percentage, not on the basis of any particular percentage. If airlines systematically underreported the percentages, a decrease would still likely be significant.

B   This is only remotely relevant because the representative's quantitative comparison is about a difference in percentage of actual delays due to certain factors, not about a difference in numbers of complaints about such delays. In principle, if the total number of complaints increased and the increase was at least partially attributable to delays caused by uncontrollable factors, this information could suggest that the number of delays caused by uncontrollable factors might have increased. This, in turn, could indirectly suggest the hypothesis stated in answer choice D. But at best the relevance of answer choice B to such a hypothesis is very oblique and conjectural.

C   The issue being discussed primarily concerns flight delays. Airlines could make many kinds of errors that do not lead to flight delays and that generally do not elicit complaints from air travelers.

D   Correct. As explained above, if there is a large enough increase in non-AE flight delays—delays entirely due to factors outside an airline's control—then the overall number of flight delays also increases, provided the number of AE flight delays remains constant or also increases. So even if the number of AE flight delays did not decrease, the percentage of all flight delays that were AE flight delays could decrease.

E   Air travelers who experience flight delays and disbelieve the explanations given by airlines for those delays may be justified in doing so—but in many, or even most, cases also may be mistaken. We have no information as to how this would affect the number of complaints from travelers. Certainly, the general level of trust between airlines and their customers does not affect the facts regarding the rate of AE flight delays or the rate of non-AE flight delays.

The correct answer is D.

549. Although the school would receive financial benefits if it had soft drink vending machines in the cafeteria, we should not allow them. Allowing soft drink machines there would not be in our students' interest. If our students start drinking more soft drinks, they will be less healthy.

The argument depends on which of the following?

(A) If the soft drink vending machines were placed in the cafeteria, students would consume more soft drinks as a result.

(B) The amount of soft drinks that most students at the school currently drink is not detrimental to their health.

(C) Students are apt to be healthier if they do not drink soft drinks at all than if they just drink small amounts occasionally.

(D) Students will not simply bring soft drinks from home if the soft drink vending machines are not placed in the cafeteria.

(E) The school's primary concern should be to promote good health among its students.

Argument Construction

Situation   Allowing soft drink vending machines in a school cafeteria would financially benefit the school, but students who drink more soft drinks would become less healthy.

Reasoning   *What must be true in order for the claim that students drinking more soft drinks would cause them to become less healthy to justify the conclusion that soft drink vending machines should not be allowed in the cafeteria?* The argument is that because drinking more soft drinks would be unhealthy for the students, allowing the vending machines would not be in the students' interest, so the vending machines should not be allowed. This reasoning depends on the implicit factual assumption that allowing the vending machines would result in the students drinking more soft drinks. It also depends on the implicit value judgment that receiving financial benefits should be less important to the school than preventing a situation that would make the students less healthy.

A   **Correct.** If the cafeteria vending machines would not result in students consuming more soft drinks, then allowing the machines would not harm the students' health in the way the argument assumes.

B   Even if the amount of soft drinks the students currently drink were unhealthy, enabling the students to drink more could make them even less healthy.

C   Even if drinking small amounts of soft drinks occasionally would not harm the students, vending machines in the cafeteria could lead the students to drink excessive amounts.

D   Even if students who cannot buy soft drinks in the cafeteria sometimes bring them from home instead, adding vending machines in the cafeteria could increase the students' overall soft drink consumption.

E   A concern does not have to be the primary one in order to be valid and important. It could be held that promoting students' good health should not be the schools' primary concern but should still be a more important concern than the financial benefits from the vending machines.

The correct answer is A.

550. Many athletes inhale pure oxygen after exercise in an attempt to increase muscular reabsorption of oxygen. Measured continuously after exercise, however, the blood lactate levels of athletes who inhale pure oxygen are practically identical, on average, to those of athletes who breathe normal air. The lower the blood lactate level is, the higher the muscular reabsorption of oxygen is.

If the statements above are all true, they most strongly support which of the following conclusions?

(A) Athletes' muscular reabsorption of oxygen is not increased when they inhale pure oxygen instead of normal air.

(B) High blood lactate levels cannot be reduced.

(C) Blood lactate levels are a poor measure of oxygen reabsorption by muscles.

(D) The amount of oxygen reabsorbed by an athlete's muscles always remains constant.

(E) The inhaling of pure oxygen has no legitimate role in athletics.

Argument Construction

Situation   Blood lactate levels after exercise are practically identical in athletes who breathe normal air and in those who inhale pure oxygen after exercise. The lower the blood lactate level, the higher the muscular reabsorption of oxygen.

Reasoning   *What conclusion do the stated facts most strongly support?* We are told that lower blood lactate levels correspond consistently to higher muscular reabsorption of oxygen. Since athletes who breathe pure oxygen after exercise have blood lactate levels practically identical to those in athletes who breathe normal air, probably muscular reabsorption of oxygen does not differ significantly between athletes who breathe pure oxygen and those who breathe pure air.

A   **Correct.** As explained above, the stated facts suggest that muscular reabsorption of oxygen does not differ significantly between athletes who breathe pure oxygen and those who breathe pure air. So breathing pure oxygen instead of normal air after exercise probably does not increase athletes' muscular reabsorption of oxygen.

B   None of the statements indicates that blood lactate levels cannot be reduced by means other than inhaling pure oxygen.

C   We are told that blood lactate levels are negatively correlated with muscular reabsorption of oxygen. This negative correlation might allow muscular reabsorption of oxygen to be precisely determined by measuring blood lactate levels.

D   Muscular reabsorption of oxygen might vary for reasons unrelated to whether an athlete has been inhaling pure oxygen.

E   Inhaling pure oxygen might have some legitimate role unrelated to muscular reabsorption of oxygen.

The correct answer is A.

551. Historian: Fifteenth-century advances in mapmaking contributed to the rise of modern nation-states. In medieval Europe (from the fifth to the fifteenth century), sovereignty centered in cities and towns and radiated outward, with boundaries often ambiguously defined. The conceptual shift toward the modern state began in the late fifteenth century, when mapmakers learned to reflect geography accurately by basing maps on latitude-longitude grids. By the mid-seventeenth century, nearly all maps showed boundary lines.

Which of the following would, if true, most strengthen the historian's reasoning?

(A) Borders did not become codified in Europe until certain treaties were signed in the early nineteenth century.

(B) During the medieval period, various authorities in Europe claimed power over collections of cities and towns, not contiguous territories.

(C) Many members of the political elite collected maps as a hobby during the late sixteenth and early seventeenth centuries.

(D) Seventeenth-century treatises and other sources of political authority describe areas of sovereignty rather than illustrate them using maps.

(E) During the fifteenth century in Europe, mapmakers simplified the borders of sovereignty by drawing clear lines of demarcation between political powers.

Argument Evaluation

Situation   A historian claims that fifteenth-century advances in mapmaking contributed to the rise of modern nation states. In earlier centuries boundaries of sovereignty in Europe were poorly defined but in the fifteenth century maps were made based on grids showing latitude and longitude.

Reasoning   *What additional piece of information, if true and added to the argument, would most improve the support offered for the conclusion that improved mapping contributed to the rise of nation states?* The historian claims that there was a cause–effect relationship between progress in mapmaking and the rise of the nation state. This claim is supported by information that territories of sovereignty were vague and ill-defined before the fifteenth century, when latitude-longitude grids began to allow progressively greater accuracy in the delineation of territories on maps. The argument assumes that the rise of nation states would have required a high degree of clarity about each state's non-overlapping area of sovereignty.

A   This indicates the role of treaties in the evolution of nation states but provides no additional support for the historian's causal claim.

B   This information is consistent with the historian's belief that nothing resembling the modern state existed before the fifteenth century, but it provides no additional support for the historian's causal claim.

C   The relevance of this information to the argument is tenuous at best. There could be many non-political explanations for the interest of political elites in collecting maps. Many people other than political elites may also have collected maps during the period mentioned.

D   This information tends to minimize the role of maps in defining areas of sovereignty and to cast some doubt on the historian's causal claim.

E   **Correct.** This information makes explicit the role of mapmakers in providing clarity about the geographical boundaries of each political entity's sovereignty. It thus provides additional evidence for the historian's causal claim and strengthens the historian's reasoning.

The correct answer is E.

552. Sascha: The attempt to ban parliament's right to pass directed-spending bills—bills that contain provisions specifically funding the favorite projects of some powerful politicians—is antidemocratic. Our nation's constitution requires that money be drawn from our treasury only when so stipulated by laws passed by parliament, the branch of government most directly representative of the citizens. This requirement is based on the belief that exercising the power to spend public resources involves the ultimate exercise of state authority and that therefore _____.

Which of the following most logically completes Sascha's argument?

(A) designating funding specifically for the favorite projects of some powerful politicians should be considered antidemocratic

(B) the right to exercise such a power should belong exclusively to the branch of government most directly representative of the citizens

(C) exercising the power to spend public resources is in most cases—but not all—protected by the constitution

(D) modifications to any spending bills should be considered expenditures authorized by law

(E) only officials who are motivated by concerns for reelection should retain that power

Argument Construction

Situation   According to Sascha, restricting parliament's ability to direct public money to the projects favored by powerful politicians would be undemocratic. Sascha argues that such a restriction on directed spending would be inconsistent with constitutional requirements.

Reasoning   *What piece of information would most logically complete Sascha's argument?* What piece of information would most strongly associate parliament's spending authority with the concept of democracy? A good guess would be: some information that connects parliament's public representation role with its spending authority.

A   Sascha believes that democratic constitutional principles require that parliament remain free to do what is described in this sentence.

B   **Correct.** This statement makes explicit the connection, implicitly relied on by Sascha's argument, between parliament's spending authority and its role in representing the public.

C   This statement may be true but fails to associate parliament's spending authority under the constitution with the notion of democracy.

D   Bills are merely works-in-progress, texts of proposed laws. Modifications of bills do not in themselves provide legal authority for any public spending item.

E   Sascha opposes restrictions on parliament's spending power, and this would seem to imply that Sascha believes every parliamentary representative should be free to vote on such measures regardless of their levels of concern for reelection.

The correct answer is B.

553. Boreal owls range over a much larger area than do other owls of similar size. Scientists have hypothesized that **it is scarcity of prey that leads the owls to range so widely**. This hypothesis would be hard to confirm directly, since it is not possible to produce a sufficiently accurate count of the populations of small mammals inhabiting the forests where boreal owls live. Careful study of owl behavior has, however, shown that **boreal owls do range over larger areas when they live in regions where food of the sort eaten by small mammals is comparatively sparse**. This indicates that the scientists' hypothesis is not sheer speculation.

In the argument given, the two **boldfaced** portions play which of the following roles?

(A) The first presents an explanatory hypothesis; the second states the main conclusion of the argument.

(B) The first presents an explanatory hypothesis; the second presents evidence tending to support this hypothesis.

(C) The first presents an explanatory hypothesis; the second presents evidence to support an alternative explanation.

(D) The first describes a position that the argument opposes; the second presents evidence to undermine the support for the position being opposed.

(E) The first describes a position that the argument opposes; the second states the main conclusion of the argument.

Argument Construction

Situation   Boreal owls range over a much larger area than other owls of similar size. Scientists hypothesize that they do so because of prey scarcity. Counting the owls' prey—small mammals—in the boreal owls' habitat is inherently difficult. This makes the scientists' hypothesis hard to confirm directly. However, it has been found that boreal owls range widely when they inhabit regions that have relatively little food for the small mammals they prey on.

Reasoning   *What function is served by the statement that it is scarcity of prey that leads the owls to range so widely? What function is served by the statement that boreal owls range widely if food for their small-mammal prey is relatively sparse in the region they inhabit?* The first boldface statement expresses an explanatory hypothesis. The passage explicitly says that this is a hypothesis and indicates that scientists have proposed this hypothesis as a tentative explanation for the comparatively wide range of boreal owls. The second boldface statement provides some indirect evidence for the scientists' hypothesis. The final sentence of the passage says that the immediately preceding idea (expressed in the second boldface portion) indicates that the scientists' hypothesis (the first boldface portion) is not mere speculation. The evidence expressed in this second boldface portion is indirect in that it depends heavily on further assumptions and is not sufficient to prove the hypothesis.

A   The main conclusion of the argument is that the scientists' hypothesis is not sheer speculation, i.e., that the scientists have based their hypothesis on some evidence that they have discovered. The first statement presents the scientists' hypothesis. The second statement cites some evidence for the hypothesis and is not the main conclusion of the argument.

B   **Correct.** As explained above, the first statement presents an explanatory hypothesis, while the second cites some indirect evidence for the hypothesis.

C   The second statement cites some indirect evidence for the scientists' hypothesis, not for some other hypothesis.

D   The argument does not oppose the scientists' hypothesis, presented in the first statement; the second statement cites evidence for the hypothesis and does not cite evidence for any position the argument opposes.

E   The second statement does not present the argument's main conclusion. The main conclusion is that the scientists' hypothesis is not mere speculation.

The correct answer is B.

554. Cognitive scientist: Using the pioneering work of comparative psychologist Gordon Gallup as a model, several studies have investigated animals' capacity for mirror self-recognition (MSR). Most animals exposed to a mirror respond only with social behavior, such as aggression. However, in the case of the great apes, repeated exposure to mirrors leads to self-directed behaviors, such as exploring the inside of the mouth, suggesting that these animals recognize the reflection as an image of self. The implication of these studies is that the great apes have a capacity for self-awareness unique among nonhuman species.

The cognitive scientist makes which of the following assumptions in the argument above?

(A) Gallup's work has established that the great apes have a capacity for MSR unique among nonhuman species.

(B) If an animal does not have the capacity for MSR, it does not have the capacity for self-awareness.

(C) If a researcher exposes an animal to a mirror and that animal exhibits social behavior, that animal is incapable of being self-aware.

(D) When exposed to a mirror, all animals display either social behavior or self-directed behavior.

(E) Animals that do not exhibit MSR may demonstrate a capacity for self-awareness in other ways.

Argument Construction

Situation   A cognitive scientist claims that several studies, modeled on Gordon Gallup's work, have investigated animals' capacity for mirror self-recognition (MSR), and found that, whereas most animals exposed to a mirror exhibit only social behavior in response, great apes can come to respond with self-directed behavior. The cognitive scientist infers from this that the great apes, unique among nonhumans, have a capacity for self-awareness.

Reasoning   *What must be true for the studies to support the cognitive scientist's conclusion?* The implicit reasoning is that an animal has self-awareness only if the animal has the capacity for MSR; if the latter is lacking, so is the capacity for self-awareness.

A   The studies the cognitive scientist's inference is based on were not necessarily conducted by Gallup himself. We are told only that they are modeled on his work.

B   **Correct.** If it were possible for an animal to have the capacity for self-awareness even if the animal lacks the capacity for MSR, then the studies would not imply that the great apes have a capacity for self-awareness that other nonhuman animal species lack.

C   The cognitive scientist's reasoning does not require that an animal with the capacity for self-awareness never exhibits social behavior when exposed to a mirror; it merely requires that it does not exhibit only such behavior.

D   The cognitive scientist's reasoning is compatible with an animal's displaying no behavior in response to exposure to a mirror.

E   The cognitive scientist's reasoning is compatible with the claim that an animal that does not exhibit MSR has no capacity at all for self-awareness.

The correct answer is B.

555. Last year a record number of new manufacturing jobs were created. Will this year bring another record? Well, any new manufacturing job is created either within an existing company or by the start-up of a new company. **Within existing firms, new jobs have been created this year at well below last year's record pace**. At the same time, there is considerable evidence that the number of new companies starting up will be no higher this year than it was last year and **there is no reason to think that the new companies starting up this year will create more jobs per company than did last year's start-ups**. So clearly, the number of new jobs created this year will fall short of last year's record.

In the argument given, the two portions in **boldface** play which of the following roles?

(A) The first is a claim that the argument challenges; the second is an explicit assumption on which that challenge is based.

(B) The first is a claim that the argument challenges; the second is a judgment advanced in support of the main conclusion of the argument.

(C) The first provides evidence in support of the main conclusion of the argument; the second is an objection that has been raised against that main conclusion.

(D) The first provides evidence in support of the main conclusion of the argument; the second is a judgment advanced in support of that main conclusion.

(E) The first and the second are each claims that have been advanced in support of a position that the argument opposes.

Argument Construction

Situation   Manufacturing jobs are created either within existing companies or in start-ups. Manufacturing jobs are being created at a much slower rate this year than last year. It seems likely that the number of new start-ups will not exceed last year's number and that the average number of manufacturing jobs per start-up will not exceed last year's number. So fewer manufacturing jobs are likely to be created this year than last year.

Reasoning   *What function is served by the statement that within existing firms, new jobs have been created this year at well below last year's record pace? What function is served by the statement that there is no reason to think that the new companies starting up this year will create more jobs per company than did last year's start-ups? The first statement is one of the statements used as support for the argument's main conclusion (the prediction about this year's job creation). The second statement gives another premise used as support for that prediction.*

A   The argument does not challenge the claim made by the first statement; it uses the first and the second statement as support for the argument's main conclusion, the prediction about this year's job creation.

B   The argument does not challenge the claim made by the first statement, but uses the first and second statements as support for the argument's main conclusion.

C   The first provides evidence in support of the main conclusion of the argument; the second is not an objection that has been raised against the main conclusion.

D   Correct. The first provides evidence in support of the main conclusion of the argument; the second also provides support for the main conclusion.

E   Neither the first nor the second is meant to support a position that the argument opposes; rather, they are both meant to support the argument's main conclusion.

The correct answer is D.

556. A study of ticket sales at a summer theater festival found that people who bought tickets to individual plays had a no-show rate of less than 1 percent, while those who paid in advance for all ten plays being performed that summer had a no-show rate of nearly 30 percent. This may be at least in part because the greater the awareness customers retain about the cost of an item, the more likely they are to use it.

Which of the following would, if true, best serve as an alternative explanation of the results of the study?

(A) The price per ticket was slightly cheaper for those who bought all ten tickets in advance.

(B) Many people who attended the theater festival believed strongly that they should support it financially.

(C) Those who attended all ten plays became eligible for a partial refund.

(D) Usually, people who bought tickets to individual plays did so immediately prior to each performance that they attended.

(E) People who arrived just before the performance began could not be assured of obtaining seats in a preferred location.

Argument Construction

Situation   People who bought tickets to individual plays at a theater festival had a much lower no-show rate than did people who paid in advance for all ten plays.

Reasoning   *What factor other than greater awareness of the ticket costs could explain why people who bought tickets individually were more likely to attend the plays?* The passage suggests that people who bought tickets individually were more likely to attend the plays because they were more vividly aware of what they had paid for each ticket. But there are other possible explanations—perhaps the people who bought the tickets individually were more eager to attend each play for its own sake, or had other characteristics or incentives that made them more likely to attend the plays.

A   A slight price difference would not plausibly explain why the no-show rate was thirty times greater among those who bought all the tickets in advance than among those who bought them individually.

B   This could be true of many people who bought their tickets individually as well as many who bought them in advance.

C   This would provide an added incentive for those who bought tickets in advance to attend all the plays.

D   Correct. If people who bought individual tickets usually did so right before each performance, they would have much less time after buying the tickets to change their minds about whether to attend than would people who bought all the tickets in advance.

E   If anything, this might present an additional difficulty for those who bought individual tickets without advance planning, so it would not help to explain the lower no-show rate among buyers of individual tickets.

The correct answer is D.

557. Although there is no record of poet Edmund Spenser's parentage, we do know that as a youth Spenser attended the Merchant Tailors' School in London for a period between 1560 and 1570. Records from this time indicate that the Merchant Tailors' Guild then had only three members named Spenser: Robert Spenser, listed as a gentleman; Nicholas Spenser, elected the Guild's Warden in 1568; and John Spenser, listed as a "journeyman cloth-maker." Of these, the last was likely the least affluent of the three—and most likely Edmund's father, since school accounting records list Edmund as a scholar who attended the school at a reduced fee.

Which of the following is an assumption on which the argument depends?

(A) Anybody in sixteenth century London who made clothing professionally would have had to be a member of the Merchant Tailors' Guild.

(B) The fact that Edmund Spenser attended the Merchant Tailors' School did not necessarily mean that he planned to become a tailor.

(C) No member of the Guild could become Guild warden in sixteenth century London unless he was a gentleman.

(D) Most of those whose fathers were members of the Merchant Tailors' Guild were students at the Merchant Tailors' School.

(E) The Merchant Tailors' School did not reduce its fees for the children of the more affluent Guild members.

Argument Construction

Situation | Records indicate that the poet Edmund Spenser attended the Merchant Tailors' School for a reduced fee as a youth. There is no record of his parentage, but at the time the Merchant Tailors' Guild had only three members named Spenser, of whom the least affluent was probably John Spenser.

Reasoning | *What must be true in order for the cited facts to support the conclusion that John Spenser was probably Edmund Spenser's father?* The implicit reasoning is that since Edmund Spenser attended the Merchant Tailors' School at a reduced fee, his father must have been poor. And since John Spenser was probably the poorest of the three men named Spenser in the Merchant Tailors' Guild, he was probably Edmund Spenser's father. This reasoning assumes that only the children of poor parents had reduced fees at the Merchant Tailors' School, that the children at the school generally had fathers in the Merchant Tailors' Guild, that children in that time and place generally shared their fathers' surnames, and that the two other Spensers in the Merchant Tailors' Guild were not poor enough for their children to qualify for reduced fees.

A John Spenser, as a tailor and member of the guild, could have been Edmund Spenser's father even if some other professional tailors did not belong to the guild and did not have children at the school.

B Although Edmund Spenser became a poet as an adult, he and all his classmates might have attended the school as children because they planned to become tailors.

C The argument assumes that a Guild's Warden probably would have been wealthier than a journeyman cloth-maker, but that might have been probable even if the Guild's Warden were not a "gentleman."

D Even if most children of fathers in the guild did not attend the school, all the children who did attend the school might have had fathers in the guild.

E **Correct.** If the school reduced its fees for children of wealthier guild members, then the fact that Edmund Spenser's fees were reduced would not provide evidence that his father was the poorest of the three Spensers in the guild, as the argument requires.

The correct answer is E.

558. Hea Sook: One should not readily believe urban legends. Most legends are propagated because the moral lesson underlying them supports a political agenda. People will repeat a tale if it fits their purpose. They may not deliberately spread untruths, but neither are they particularly motivated to investigate deeply to determine if the tale they are telling is true.

Kayla: But people would not repeat stories that they did not believe were true. Therefore, one can safely assume that if a story has been repeated by enough people then it is more likely to be true.

Kayla's reply is most vulnerable to the criticism that it

(A) does not specify how many people need to repeat a story before someone is justified believing it

(B) overstates the significance of political agendas in the retelling of stories

(C) fails to address the claim that people will not verify the truth of a story that fits their purpose

(D) implicitly supports the claim that the people repeating legends are not deliberately spreading untruths

(E) cannot distinguish people's motivations for repeating urban legends from their motivations for repeating other types of story

Argument Evaluation

Situation Hea Sook and Kayla have a difference of opinion on how likely urban legends are to be true.

Reasoning *What criticism is Kayla's reply most vulnerable to?* Hea Sook argues that because urban legends generally are propagated for political purposes, people are not particularly motivated to carefully investigate whether the story they are telling is true. These people may not be deliberately telling an untruth, but they have not taken care to establish whether the story is true. Kayla responds that people would not repeat a story that they did not believe to be true, but Hea Sook not only does not attempt to deny that, but she suggests that it may be true. Kayla ignores the fact that sometimes people believe that something is true without carefully determining whether it actually is true, and that they are less likely to verify whether it is true when the story fits their purposes.

A Kayla does not specify how many people need to repeat a story before one is justified in believing it, but she does not need to. Her claim—that there is some number sufficient for such belief to be justified—could be true even if she does not specify what that number is.

B It is Hea Sook, not Kayla, who asserts that political agendas are a significant factor in whether one retells a story.

C Correct. Kayla does not address whether people are unlikely to verify whether a story is true if the story fits their purpose.

D Kayla does not merely implicitly claim that people who repeat legends are not deliberately spreading untruths; she explicitly states this, but in this she and Hea Sook agree.

E We have no reason to think that Kayla cannot distinguish people's motivations for repeating urban legends from their motivations for repeating other types of stories. She may well be able to do this.

The correct answer is C.

559. Rainwater contains hydrogen of a heavy form called deuterium. The deuterium content of wood reflects the deuterium content of rainwater available to trees during their growth. Wood from trees that grew between 16,000 and 24,000 years ago in North America contains significantly more deuterium than wood from trees growing today. But water trapped in several North American caves that formed during that same early period contains significantly less deuterium than rainwater in North America contains today.

Which of the following, if true, most helps to reconcile the two findings?

(A) There is little deuterium in the North American caves other than the deuterium in the water trapped there.

(B) Exposure to water after a tree has died does not change the deuterium content of the wood.

(C) Industrialization in North America over the past 100 years has altered the deuterium content of rain.

(D) Trees draw on shallow groundwater from rain that falls during their growth, whereas water trapped in caves may have fallen as rainwater thousands of years before the caves formed.

(E) Wood with a high deuterium content is no more likely to remain preserved for long periods than is wood with a low deuterium content.

Argument Construction

Situation   In North America, wood from trees that grew 16,000 to 24,000 years ago contains more deuterium than wood from trees growing today. But water in caves that formed during that same period contains less deuterium than rainwater contains today.

Reasoning   *What could explain the puzzling discrepancy between the observed deuterium levels in wood and in caves?* Since the deuterium content of wood from trees reflects the deuterium content of rainwater available to the trees while they grew, the deuterium levels observed in wood suggests that North American rainwater contained more deuterium 16,000 to 24,000 years ago than it contains today. But this conclusion seems at odds with the low deuterium levels in water in caves that formed 16,000 to 24,000 years ago. Several factors might explain the discrepancy: the water in those caves might not be rainwater from the period when the caves formed; or some natural process might have altered the deuterium levels in the cave water or the wood; or the wood or caves in which deuterium levels were measured might be statistically abnormal somehow.

A   If the caves had absorbed deuterium out of the rainwater trapped in them, there would probably be deuterium in the cave walls. So the observation that there is little deuterium in the caves apart from that in the water eliminates one possible explanation for the oddly low deuterium levels in the cave water.

B   This suggests that the deuterium levels in the wood accurately reflect higher deuterium levels in rainwater that fell 16,000 to 24,000 years ago, but it does not explain why the deuterium levels are so low in water in the caves that formed then.

C   This could explain why deuterium levels in rainwater have changed, but it does not help explain the discrepancy between the high deuterium levels in the wood and the low deuterium levels in the cave water.

D   Correct. If the water in the caves fell as rainwater thousands of years before the caves formed, it may date from a period when rainwater contained much less deuterium than during the period 16,000 to 24,000 years ago, and much less than today.

E   If wood with high deuterium content were more likely to be preserved, then wood from 16,000 to 24,000 years ago might have a high deuterium content even if the rainwater then had a low deuterium content. So the observation that wood with more deuterium is not more likely to be preserved eliminates one possible explanation for the discrepancy.

The correct answer is D.

560. Enforcement of local speed limits through police monitoring has proven unsuccessful in the town of Ardane. In many nearby towns, speed humps (raised areas of pavement placed across residential streets, about 300 feet apart) have reduced traffic speeds on residential streets by 20 to 25 percent. In order to reduce traffic speed and thereby enhance safety in residential neighborhoods, Ardane's transportation commission plans to install multiple speed humps in those neighborhoods.

Which of the following, if true, identifies a potentially serious drawback to the plan for installing speed humps in Ardane?

(A) On residential streets without speed humps, many vehicles travel at speeds more than 25 percent above the posted speed limit.

(B) Because of their high weight, emergency vehicles such as fire trucks and ambulances must slow almost to a stop at speed humps.

(C) The residential speed limit in Ardane is higher than that of the nearby towns where speed humps were installed.

(D) Motorists who are not familiar with the streets in Ardane's residential districts would be likely to encounter the speed humps unawares unless warned by signs and painted indicators.

(E) Bicyclists generally prefer that speed humps be constructed so as to leave a space on the side of the road where bicycles can travel without going over the humps.

Evaluation of a Plan

Situation   Ardane's difficulty in getting compliance with speed limits has led it to propose the installation of speed humps to slow traffic. In nearby towns, speed humps have reduced speeds in residential areas by up to 25 percent.

Reasoning   *Which one of the statements presented identifies a major disadvantage of the proposed installation of speed humps?* Is it possible that they might slow traffic too much? Clearly, there is a general need for traffic to flow smoothly. Would speed humps affect all types of traffic equally? Perhaps not. For example, certain emergency vehicles must sometimes need to travel quickly through residential neighborhoods. A problem with speed humps is that some heavier vehicles must go very slowly over speed humps.

A   This indicates a drawback of not installing speed humps.

B   **Correct.** This information indicates a significant drawback—possibly leading to loss of life and property—of the plan to install the speed humps.

C   This suggests that installing speed humps might lower speeds significantly below the current speed limits. If speeds became very low, the result could be traffic gridlock that would have unforeseen consequences. However, we have insufficient information to evaluate such possibilities.

D   This is unlikely to be a drawback, since such warning signs are typically put in place whenever speed humps are installed.

E   This information provides no evidence of a drawback in Ardane's plan for speed humps, since the design of Ardane's planned speed humps is not indicated.

The correct answer is B.

561. Which of the following most logically completes the argument below?

NowNews, although still the most popular magazine covering cultural events in Kalopolis, has recently suffered a significant drop in advertising revenue because of falling circulation. Many readers have begun buying a competing magazine that, at 50 cents per copy, costs less than *NowNews* at $1.50 per copy. In order to boost circulation and thus increase advertising revenue, *NowNews*'s publisher has proposed making it available at no charge, but this proposal has a serious drawback, since _____.

(A) Those Kalopolis residents with the greatest interest in cultural events are regular readers of both magazines.

(B) One reason *NowNews*'s circulation fell was that its competitor's reporting on cultural events was superior.

(C) The newsstands and stores that currently sell *NowNews* will no longer carry it if it is being given away for free.

(D) At present, 10 percent of the total number of copies of each issue of *NowNews* are distributed free to students on college campuses in the Kalopolis area.

(E) *NowNews*'s competitor would begin to lose large amounts of money if it were forced to lower its cover price.

Argument Construction

Situation   *NowNews* is suffering declines in circulation and advertising revenue due to competition from a lower-priced magazine. The publisher proposes offering *NowNews* for free to reverse these declines.

Reasoning   *What would suggest that the publisher's proposal will fail to increase circulation and advertising revenue?* The proposal's intended effect is simply to increase advertising revenue by increasing circulation. Any evidence that offering the magazine for free will not result in more copies being circulated or will not attract advertisers would therefore be evidence of a drawback in the proposal. So a statement offering such evidence would logically complete the argument.

A   The fact that certain highly motivated Kalopolis residents still read *NowNews* even at a cost of $1.50 per issue leaves open the possibility that providing the magazine free might still boost readership.

B   This suggests that improving its cultural reporting might help *NowNews* increase its circulation, not that the publisher's proposal will fail to do so.

C   **Correct.** If the proposal leads newsstands and stores to stop carrying *NowNews*, circulation and advertising revenue would probably decline as a result.

D   Even if 10 percent of the copies of *NowNews* are already distributed for free, distributing the remaining 90 percent for free could still increase circulation and advertising revenue as the publisher intends.

E   Forcing a competing magazine to lower its cover price and lose lots of money would be an advantage rather than a drawback of the proposal, as far as the publisher of *NowNews* was concerned.

The correct answer is C.

562. Archaeologist: Researchers excavating a burial site in Cyprus found a feline skeleton lying near a human skeleton. Both skeletons were in the same sediment at the same depth and equally well-preserved, suggesting that the feline and human were buried together about 9,500 years ago. This shows that felines were domesticated around the time farming began, when they would have been useful in protecting stores of grain from mice.

Which of the following, if true, would most seriously weaken the archaeologist's argument?

(A) Archaeologists have not found any remains of stores of grain in the immediate vicinity of the burial site.

(B) The burial site in Cyprus is substantially older than any other known burial site in which a feline skeleton and a human skeleton appear to have been buried together.

(C) Paintings found near the burial site seem to show people keeping felines as domestic companions, but do not show felines hunting mice.

(D) In Cyprus, there are many burial sites dating from around 9,500 years ago in which the remains of wild animals appear to have been buried alongside human remains.

(E) Before felines were domesticated, early farmers had no effective way to protect stores of grain from mice.

Argument Evaluation

Situation   A human skeleton and a feline skeleton were apparently buried together in Cyprus about 9,500 years ago.

Reasoning   *What would most strongly suggest that the skeletons do not show that felines were domesticated around the time farming began?* The argument implicitly assumes that farming in Cyprus began around 9,500 years ago, so evidence against that assumption would weaken the argument. The argument could also be weakened by evidence that felines were domesticated much earlier, that the feline skeleton was not from a domesticated cat, or that the two skeletons were not actually buried together around 9,500 years ago.

A   Even if archaeologists searched for evidence of a grain store, the fact that no such evidence was found near the burial site is at best only weak evidence that no grain store existed there or slightly farther away.

B   The lack of corroborating evidence from other burial sites would weaken the argument slightly but would still be compatible with the hypothesis that this site revealed one of the very first burials of a domesticated cat.

C   This would cast doubt on the hypothesis that cats were domesticated mainly to protect stores of grain, but not on the argument's conclusion that cats were domesticated around the time farming began.

D   **Correct.** If many wild animals were buried alongside humans in Cyprus around 9,500 years ago, then the feline skeleton is just as likely to be that of a wild animal than that of a domesticated cat.

E   Since this would provide an additional reason why early farmers might have domesticated the local cats, it would strengthen rather than weaken the argument.

The correct answer is D.

563. Farmer: Several people in the past few years have claimed to have seen a mountain lion in the suburban outskirts—the latest just last month—and, while mountain lions were thought to have been driven from this entire region about twenty years ago, there is no reason for the people who reported seeing a mountain lion to have deliberately concocted a false report. Therefore, local wildlife managers should begin to urgently address the mountain lion's presence.

Which of the following would, if true, most seriously weaken the farmer's argument?

(A) Farmers in the suburban outskirts mostly raise cattle and hogs, which when fully grown are generally not attacked by mountain lions.

(B) Mountain lions are dissimilar in size and color to other wild animals found near the suburban outskirts.

(C) No person who claimed to have seen a mountain lion had anyone else with them at the purported sighting.

(D) There have been no regional reports in the past year of mountain lions migrating to the area.

(E) Recent surveys show that more than half of the people in the region report that they have never seen a mountain lion before.

Argument Evaluation

Situation   A farmer argues that, because several people in recent years, including someone just last month, have claimed to have seen a mountain lion in the suburban outskirts, local wildlife managers need to address the mountain lion's presence. The farmer claims that people would not intentionally create a false story about seeing a mountain lion.

Reasoning   *What would most seriously call into question the farmer's argument that because there have been reports of mountain lion sightings, wildlife managers should address the issue?* Even if it is true that people would not intentionally create a false report of having seen a mountain lion, it is possible that people have mistakenly believed they have seen a mountain lion when in fact what they saw was something else. If some fact called into question the accuracy of the reports of mountain lion sightings, then the farmer's conclusion would have weaker support.

A   Even if most fully grown animals raised by farmers would not be attacked by mountain lions, there could still be good reason to be concerned about the presence of mountain lions in the suburban outskirts. The mountain lion might attack animals before they are fully grown.

B   A dissimilarity in size and color between mountain lions and other wild animals in the area where the mountain lions were purportedly sighted would make it less likely that people mistakenly believed that an animal they spotted was a mountain lion. So, this would strengthen the farmer's argument, not weaken it.

C   **Correct.** If there actually were at least one mountain lion in the area, and several people over a period of a few years accurately claim to have seen one, then it seems likely that on at least some occasions a person would have been in the presence of someone else at the time, given the frequency with which people are in the company of others. So, if there have been no instances of a person reporting seeing a mountain lion when in the company of another, perhaps that is because when someone has mistakenly believed that an animal is a mountain lion, the other person helps correct the mistaken belief. With no one else present, an illusory sighting would be less likely to be corrected.

D   There have been purported sightings of a mountain lion in the area for several years, so presumably, if the sightings are accurate, there has been at least one mountain lion for several years, so the sightings could be accurate even if no mountain lion has migrated to the area in the past year.

E   It might be likely that most people living in the area would not have seen a mountain lion even if one lived in the area. For instance, the mountain lion might intentionally try to avoid people.

The correct answer is C.

564. The heavy traffic in Masana is a growing drain on the city's economy—the clogging of the streets of the central business district alone cost the economy more than $1.2 billion over the past year. In order to address this problem, officials plan to introduce congestion pricing, by which drivers would pay to enter the city's most heavily trafficked areas during the busiest times of the day.

Which of the following, if true, would most strongly indicate that the plan will be a success?

(A) Approximately one-fifth of the vehicles in the central business district are in transit from one side of the city to the other.

(B) Planners expect that, without congestion pricing, traffic in Masana is likely to grow by 6 percent in the next five years.

(C) In other urban areas, congestion pricing has strongly encouraged carpooling (sharing of rides by private commuters).

(D) Several studies have shown that a reduction in traffic of 15 percent in Masana could result in 5,500 or more new jobs.

(E) Over 30 percent of the vehicles in the city's center are occupied by more than one person.

Evaluation of a Plan

Situation Traffic congestion in Masana has been harming the city's economy. To address the problem, officials plan to make drivers pay to enter the city's most heavily trafficked areas during the busiest times of day.

Reasoning *What would most strongly suggest that the plan will reduce the harm to Masana's economy from traffic congestion?* In order to succeed, the plan will have to be implemented and effectively enforced. Furthermore, the prices drivers pay will have to be high enough to significantly change their behavior in ways that reduce the amount of traffic congestion in the city. Finally, the economic benefits from the reduced traffic congestion will have to substantially outweigh any economically damaging side effects of the congestion pricing. Any evidence that any of these conditions will hold would provide at least some support for the prediction that the plan will succeed.

A This provides no evidence that the congestion pricing would affect the behavior of either the one-fifth of drivers whose vehicles traverse the city or of the other four-fifths of drivers, nor does it give any evidence that the plan would produce overriding economic benefits.

B This indicates that the traffic problem will grow worse if the plan is not implemented, but it does not provide any evidence that the plan will help address the problem.

C **Correct.** This indicates that similar plans have successfully changed drivers' behavior in other cities in a way likely to reduce the number of cars on the road in heavily trafficked areas at busy times of day without producing harmful economic side effects. Thus, it provides evidence that the strategy could also be successful in Masana.

D Although this suggests that reducing traffic congestion would be economically beneficial, it doesn't provide any evidence that the plan will succeed in reducing traffic congestion.

E This suggests that many drivers in the city center are already carpooling, which, if anything, indicates that the plan will be less able to further affect those drivers' behavior and thus could be less effective than it might otherwise be.

The correct answer is C.

565. Economist: The most economically efficient way to reduce emissions of air pollutants is to tax them in proportion to the damage they are likely to cause. But in Country Y, many serious pollutants are untaxed and unregulated, and policy makers strongly oppose new taxes. Therefore, the best way to achieve a reduction in air pollutant emissions in Country Y would be to institute fixed upper limits on them.

Which of the following is an assumption of the economist's argument?

(A) Policy makers in Country Y oppose all new taxes equally strongly, regardless of any benefits they may provide.

(B) Country Y's air pollutant emissions would not fall significantly if they were taxed in proportion to the damage they are likely to cause.

(C) Policy makers in Country Y strongly favor reductions in air pollutant emissions.

(D) Country Y's policy makers believe that air pollutant emissions should be reduced with maximum economic efficiency.

(E) Policy makers in Country Y do not oppose setting fixed upper limits on air pollutant emissions as strongly as they oppose new taxes.

Argument Construction

Situation   Although taxing air pollution emissions in proportion to the damage they cause is the most economically efficient way to reduce those emissions, many serious pollutants in Nation Y are untaxed and unregulated, and the nation's policy makers strongly oppose new taxes. Therefore, fixed upper limits on such emissions would more effectively reach this goal.

Reasoning   *What must be true in order for the factors the economist cites to support the claim that fixing upper limits on air pollutant emissions in Nation Y would be the best way to reduce those emissions?* Political opposition to taxation in Nation Y is the only factor the economist cites to support the argument's conclusion that it would be best to institute fixed upper limits on air pollutants. In order for the premise to support the conclusion, there must be less political opposition in Nation Y to instituting such limits than there would be to the proportional taxation approach the economist prefers.

A   Even if the policy makers oppose some new taxes less than others, they could still oppose the proportional taxation approach strongly enough for it to be utterly infeasible.

B   Even if the proportional taxation scheme would significantly reduce emissions, it still might not be the best approach for Nation Y if it would generate too much political opposition to be viable there.

C   Even if policy makers in Nation Y do not strongly favor reducing emissions, fixing upper limits on emissions might still be a better and more politically feasible way to reduce emissions than any alternative is.

D   Since fixing upper emissions limits would be no more economically efficient than the proportional taxation scheme, the policy makers' support for economic efficiency would not make the former approach any more politically feasible than the latter.

E   **Correct.** If the policy makers opposed fixing upper emissions limits as strongly as they oppose new taxes, then their opposition to new taxes would no longer support the conclusion that fixing the emissions limits is a better way to reduce emissions.

The correct answer is E.

566. Humans get Lyme disease from infected ticks. Ticks get infected by feeding on animals with Lyme disease, but the ease of transmission from host animal to tick varies. With most species of host animal, transmission of Lyme disease to ticks is extremely rare, but white-footed mice are an exception, readily passing Lyme disease to ticks. And white-footed mouse populations greatly expand, becoming the main food source for ticks, in areas where biodiversity is in decline.

The information in the passage most strongly supports which of the following?

(A) In areas where many humans are infected with Lyme disease, the proportion of ticks infected with Lyme disease is especially high.

(B) Very few animals that live in areas where there are no white-footed mice are infected with Lyme disease.

(C) Humans are less at risk of contracting Lyme disease in areas where biodiversity is high.

(D) Ticks feed on white-footed mice only when other host species are not available to them.

(E) The greater the biodiversity of an area, the more likely any given host animal in that area is to pass Lyme disease to ticks.

Argument Construction

Situation   White-footed mice readily pass Lyme disease to ticks, which pass it to humans. White-footed mouse populations expand where biodiversity is declining.

Reasoning   *What conclusion do the stated facts support?* Since declining biodiversity causes white-footed mouse populations to increase, and white-footed mice are especially likely to pass Lyme disease to ticks, and ticks pass it to humans, declining biodiversity could reasonably be expected to increase the incidence of Lyme disease in both ticks and humans.

A   In areas where many humans are infected with Lyme disease, the total number of ticks may be unusually high, so even if the number of infected ticks is unusually high, the proportion of infected ticks may not be unusually high

B   Most animals with Lyme disease may get it from sources other than ticks that have fed on infected mice.

C   **Correct.** If biodiversity is high, then any biodiversity decline that has already begun has likely not yet reached a point where white-footed mouse populations have greatly expanded, so the risk of people contracting Lyme disease is still relatively less than in areas where biodiversity is low and where significant decline in biodiversity has likely already occurred.

D   Even if ticks feed on white-footed mice when few other species are available for them to feed on, they may also sometimes feed on white-footed mice when there are many other species for them to feed on.

E   The passage suggests that the overall incidence of Lyme disease is probably lower in more biodiverse areas, so any given host animal in those areas would probably be less likely to pass Lyme disease to a tick.

The correct answer is C.

567. Many industrialized nations are trying to reduce atmospheric concentrations of carbon dioxide, a gas released by the burning of fossil fuels. One proposal is to replace conventional cement, which is made with calcium carbonate, by a new "eco-cement." This new cement, made with magnesium carbonate, absorbs large amounts of carbon dioxide when exposed to the atmosphere. Therefore, using eco-cement for new concrete building projects will significantly help reduce atmospheric concentrations of carbon dioxide.

Which of the following, if true, most strengthens the argument?

(A) The cost of magnesium carbonate, currently greater than the cost of calcium carbonate, probably will fall as more magnesium carbonate is used in cement manufacture.

(B) Eco-cement is strengthened when absorbed carbon dioxide reacts with the cement.

(C) Before the development of eco-cement, magnesium-based cement was considered too susceptible to water erosion to be of practical use.

(D) The manufacture of eco-cement uses considerably less fossil fuel per unit of cement than the manufacture of conventional cement does.

(E) Most building-industry groups are unaware of the development or availability of eco-cement.

Argument Evaluation

Situation   Many nations are trying to reduce atmospheric concentrations of carbon dioxide. One proposed method is to use a new type of "eco-cement" that absorbs carbon dioxide from air.

Reasoning   *What evidence, combined with the cited facts, would most support the prediction that using eco-cement will significantly help reduce atmospheric concentrations of carbon dioxide?* The prediction assumes that the use of eco-cement would be an effective way to reduce carbon dioxide levels. Any evidence supporting this assumption will support the prediction.

A   Since eco-cement uses magnesium carbonate, the prediction that magnesium carbonate prices will fall suggests that a potential financial barrier to widespread eco-cement use will diminish. However, those prices may not fall enough to make eco-cement cost-competitive with regular cement.

B   Even if absorbed carbon dioxide strengthens eco-cement, the strengthened eco-cement might still be much weaker than regular cement and thus might never become widely used, in which case it will not significantly help reduce atmospheric concentrations of carbon dioxide.

C   Even if eco-cement is less susceptible to water erosion than earlier forms of magnesium-based cement were, it might still be much more susceptible to water erosion than regular cement is, and thus might never become widely used.

D   Correct. This suggests that manufacturing eco-cement produces much less carbon dioxide than manufacturing regular cement does, so it supports the claim that widespread use of eco-cement would be an effective way to reduce carbon dioxide levels.

E   If anything, this lack of awareness makes it less likely that eco-cement will become widely used, which in turn makes it less likely that eco-cement will significantly help reduce atmospheric concentrations of carbon dioxide.

The correct answer is D.

568. Professor: A marine biologist argues that transmission of sea lice from farm salmon to wild salmon is unlikely in the Broughton Archipelago, British Columbia, citing numerous studies suggesting that salinities less than 30 parts per thousand are unfavorable to sea-lice survival. The biologist concludes that the archipelago's 25–30 parts per thousand salinity range between March and June, the critical period for wild salmon migration, tends to suppress sea-lice proliferation. But a review of the literature shows that salinities of 25–30 parts per thousand in combination with British Columbia's cool spring temperatures favor the flourishing of sea lice.

In this passage, the professor attempts to undermine the biologist's argument by

(A) pointing out that a condition claimed to be necessary for sea-lice survival is not sufficient for it

(B) citing studies that suggest that salinity levels were not measured reliably

(C) claiming that there is evidence showing that one of its premises is false

(D) questioning the reliability of the biologist's scientific sources

(E) showing that its conclusion is inconsistent with its premises

Argument Evaluation

Situation   A professor gives us information about one biologist's opinion, based on numerous studies, about the low probability of sea-lice transmission from farm salmon to wild salmon in the Broughton Archipelago. The biologist thinks salinities less than 30 parts per thousand (ppt) would make such transmission unlikely; in the archipelago, the salinity is 25–30 ppt between March and June, the period when wild salmon migration occurs. However, the professor challenges the biologist's view, maintaining, based on a literature review, that cool spring temperatures in the archipelago, combined with the lower salinity, do favor flourishing of sea lice.

Reasoning   *In what way does the professor attempt to undermine the biologist's argument?* The professor points out that a premise used by the biologist—that the low spring salinities in the archipelago when the wild salmon migrate suppress sea-lice proliferation—is not correct. The professor claims the academic literature reveals that two conditions—the 25–30 ppt salinities combined with the cool spring temperatures—would be jointly sufficient for the flourishing of sea lice.

A   This does not accurately describe the professor's technique. In effect, the professor points out that salinities of 30 ppt or more are NOT necessary for sea-lice survival; lower salinities combined with lower temperatures are sufficient to enable sea-lice survival.

B   The professor cites no studies that suggest unreliable measurement of salinity levels.

C   **Correct.** As explained in the Reasoning section above, the professor appeals to evidence from the literature to show that one of the biologist's premises is false.

D   The professor primarily questions the conclusion that the biologist draws from the sources; the professor does not question the reliability of the sources.

E   The professor undermines the biologist's argument by claiming that one of its premises is false and thus that the conclusion might not follow. The professor does not claim that if the premises were true the conclusion would have to be false.

The correct answer is C.

569. Advertisement: When your car's engine is running at its normal operating temperature, any major brand of motor oil will protect it about as well as Tuff does. When the engine is cold, it is a different story: Tuff motor oil flows better at lower temperatures than its major competitors do. So, if you want your car's engine to have maximum protection, you should use Tuff.

Which of the following, if true, most strengthens the argument in the advertisement?

(A) Tuff motor oil provides above-average protection for engines that happen to overheat.

(B) Tuff motor oil is periodically supplied free of charge to automobile manufacturers to use in factory-new cars.

(C) Tuff motor oil's share of the engine oil market peaked three years ago.

(D) Tuff motor oil, like any motor oil, is thicker and flows less freely at cold temperatures than at hot temperatures.

(E) Tuff motor oil is manufactured at only one refinery and shipped from there to all markets.

Argument Evaluation

Situation   An advertisement argues that since Tuff motor oil flows better than its major competitors at low temperatures and works about as well as they do at normal temperatures, it provides *maximum protection* for car engines.

Reasoning   *What additional evidence would suggest that Tuff motor oil provides the best available protection for car engines?* The argument requires the assumptions that no type of motor oil other than the "major brands" provides superior protection, that flowing better at lower temperatures ensures superior protection at those temperatures, and that Tuff protects car engines at least as well as its competitors do at above-normal temperatures. Any evidence supporting any of these assumptions would strengthen the argument.

A   **Correct.** If Tuff provides above-average protection when engines overheat, in addition to the solid protection it provides at normal and low temperatures, it may well provide the best available protection overall.

B   The company that makes Tuff might give automobile manufacturers free motor oil as a promotional gimmick even if Tuff is an inferior product.

C   Tuff's sales might have declined over the past three years because consumers have realized that Tuff is an inferior product.

D   The similar responses of Tuff and other motor oils to temperature changes do not suggest that Tuff provides better protection overall than those other motor oils do.

E   Even if Tuff is manufactured at only one refinery, it may still be an inferior product.

The correct answer is A.

570. Linguist: In English, the past is described as "behind" and the future "ahead," whereas in Aymara the past is "ahead" and the future "behind." Research indicates that English speakers sway backward when discussing the past and forward when discussing the future. Conversely, Aymara speakers gesture forward with their hands when discussing the past and backward when discussing the future. These bodily movements, therefore, suggest that the language one speaks affects how one mentally visualizes time.

The linguist's reasoning depends on assuming which of the following?

(A) At least some Aymara speakers sway forward when discussing the past and backward when discussing the future.

(B) Most people mentally visualize time as running either forward or backward.

(C) Not all English and Aymara speakers tend to sway or gesture forward or backward when discussing the present.

(D) How people move when discussing the future correlates to some extent with how they mentally visualize time.

(E) The researchers also examined the movements of at least some speakers of languages other than English and Aymara discussing the past and the future.

Argument Construction

Situation A linguist argues that the language one speaks affects how one mentally visualizes time. The linguist's argument is based on the fact that English speakers, who refer to the past as "behind" and the future as "ahead," display backward and forward bodily movements when speaking of the past and the future, while speakers of Aymara, who refer to the past as "ahead" and the future as "behind" display correspondingly different body movements.

Reasoning *What must be true if we are to accept the linguist's conclusion from the given information that the language one speaks affects how one mentally visualizes time?* The linguist's evidence will support the conclusion only if there is some correlation between people's bodily movements and how they mentally visualize time. So, the linguist's reasoning requires an assumption to that effect.

A The linguist's reasoning is based on the differences in bodily movements discussed in the argument—that is, that Aymara speakers gesture in certain ways and that English speakers sway in certain ways; thus, the linguist's reasoning does not require that Aymara speakers sway in any way whatsoever when they discuss the past or future.

B The linguist's reasoning is based only on speakers of English and Aymara, so no claim related to speakers of other languages—who make up a majority of people—is required.

C The linguist's argument would actually be stronger if all English and Aymara speakers sway or gesture in the ways discussed, so the argument certainly does not depend on assuming that not all such speakers sway or gesture in these ways.

D Correct. The fact that English and Aymara speakers sway or gesture in the ways described would be irrelevant to the linguist's conclusion if how people move when discussing the future does not correlate at least to some extent with how they visualize time.

E It might be helpful to the linguist's argument to examine the movements of speakers of other languages when they discuss the past and the future, but the linguist's argument does not require this.

The correct answer is D.

571. The *Testament of William Thorpe* was published around 1530 as an appendix to Thorpe's longer *Examination*. Many scholars, however, doubt the attribution of the *Testament* to Thorpe because, whereas the *Examination* is dated 1406, the *Testament* is dated 1460. One scholar has recently argued that the 1460 date be amended to 1409, based on the observation that when these numbers are expressed as Roman numerals, MCCCCLX and MCCCCIX, it becomes easy to see how the dates might have become confused through scribal error.

Which of the following, if true, would most support the scholar's hypothesis concerning the date of the *Testament*?

(A) The sole evidence that historians have had that William Thorpe died no earlier than 1460 was the presumed date of publication of the *Testament*.

(B) In the preface to the 1530 publication, the editor attributes both works to William Thorpe.

(C) Few writers in fifteenth-century England marked dates in their works using only Roman numerals.

(D) The *Testament* alludes to a date, "Friday, September 20," as apparently contemporaneous with the writing of the *Testament*, and September 20 fell on a Friday in 1409 but not in 1460.

(E) The *Testament* contains few references to historical events that occurred later than 1406.

Argument Construction

Situation The *Testament of William Thorpe*, dated 1460, was published around 1530 as an appendix to Thorpe's *Examination*, dated 1406. But when expressed in Roman numerals, 1460 could easily be confused with 1409.

Reasoning *Given the facts cited, what would provide additional evidence that Thorpe's Testament dates from 1409 rather than 1460?* The scholar's hypothesis that the work dates from 1409 is based on the observation that in Roman numerals, 1409 might easily have been improperly transcribed as 1460. What evidence would support this hypothesis? Any independent evidence that 1409 is a more likely date for the *Testament* than 1460 would certainly help. For instance, if some event or date that occurred in 1409 but not in 1460 is referred to in the *Testament* as being recent or contemporaneous, this would lend significant support to the hypothesis. For instance, if the *Testament* indicated that some day of the month had just fallen on a given day of the week, and that date fell on that day in 1409 but not in 1460, this would support the hypothesis significantly.

A Suppose there is no reason to think that Thorpe was still alive in 1460 other than the presumption that the *Testament* was published in that year. That gives us no more reason to accept the scholar's hypothesis about a scribal error in reporting the date than to accept the other scholars' hypothesis that the *Testament* is improperly ascribed to Thorpe. Furthermore, it provides very little reason to support either of these hypotheses, because the mere lack of evidence, other than the purported 1460 date of creation, that Thorpe died no earlier than 1460 does not provide us with any evidence that he **did** die earlier than 1460.

B The editor of the 1530 publication could easily have been mistaken about the authorship of one or both works. And even if the editor were correct, Thorpe might have lived long enough to write one work in 1406 and the other in 1460.

C This would cast doubt on the scholar's argument by providing evidence that the original manuscripts were not dated only in Roman numerals.

D Correct. As explained in the Reasoning section above, this provides strong evidence directly supporting the hypothesis that the *Testament* dates from 1409 specifically.

E Even if the *Testament* contained only one reference to a historical event that occurred later than 1406 (for example, one event in 1459), that reference alone could provide strong evidence that the work dates from 1460 rather than 1409.

The correct answer is D.

572. A prominent investor who holds a large stake in the Burton Tool Company has recently claimed that the company is mismanaged, citing as evidence the company's failure to slow down production in response to a recent rise in its inventory of finished products. It is doubtful whether an investor's sniping at management can ever be anything other than counterproductive, but in this case, it is clearly not justified. It is true that **an increased inventory of finished products often indicates that production is outstripping demand**, but in Burton's case it indicates no such thing. Rather, **the increase in inventory is entirely attributable to products that have already been assigned to orders received from customers**.

In the argument given, the two **boldfaced** portions play which of the following roles?

(A) The first states a generalization that underlies the position that the argument as a whole opposes; the second provides evidence to show that the generalization does not apply in the case at issue.

(B) The first states a generalization that underlies the position that the argument as a whole opposes; the second clarifies the meaning of a specific phrase as it is used in that generalization.

(C) The first provides evidence to support the conclusion of the argument as a whole; the second is evidence that has been used to support the position that the argument as a whole opposes.

(D) The first provides evidence to support the conclusion of the argument as a whole; the second states that conclusion.

(E) The first and the second each provide evidence against the position that the argument as a whole opposes.

Argument Construction

Situation   An investor has criticized a company, based on the company's recent increase in inventory and on its not decreasing production as a result of this increase.

Reasoning   *What roles do the two boldfaced statements play in the argument?* The argument suggests that the investor's criticism is based on a principle that increased inventory of finished products often indicates that production is faster than it should be, given the existing demand for a company's products. However, the argument then states that the increase in inventory at the company in question is "entirely attributable" to existing orders of products. The argument thus suggests that the investor's criticism is misplaced, based on a suggestion as to (1) a principle that the investor could be using to support her argument and (2) an explanation as to why the principle does not apply to the company. The two boldfaced portions state these respective elements.

A   **Correct.** The first boldfaced portion states the principle that may provide the basis of the investor's criticism, which the argument as a whole opposes. The second boldfaced portion is a statement that, if true, the generalization would not apply to the company in question.

B   This option correctly describes the first of the boldfaced portions. However, rather than clarifying an aspect of the meaning of the first generalization, the second boldfaced portion indicates why the first generalization may not apply to the company.

C   This option incorrectly describes both of the boldfaced portions. The first boldfaced portion states a general principle that could support the position that the argument *opposes*. The second boldfaced portion then criticizes the application of the principle.

D   Because the second boldfaced portion describes a fundamental premise rather than the conclusion, the description in this option of the second boldfaced portion is incorrect.

E   If we think of an argument as a set of statements that are meant to support, or provide evidence for, a conclusion, then, because the boldfaced statements are indeed part of the argument, they may be seen as providing evidence for the position the argument opposes. However, a description of the roles of the boldfaced statements in this argument would need to provide more detail, such as what option A provides.

The correct answer is A.

573. To reduce productivity losses from employees calling in sick, Corporation X implemented a new policy requiring employees to come into work unless they were so sick that they had to go to a doctor. But a year after the policy was implemented, a study found that Corporation X's overall productivity losses due to reported employee illnesses had increased.

Which of the following, if true, would best explain why the policy produced the reverse of its intended effect?

(A) After the policy was implemented, employees more frequently went to the doctor when they felt sick.

(B) Before the policy was implemented, employees who were not sick at all often called in sick.

(C) Employees coming into work when sick often infect many of their coworkers.

(D) Unusually few employees became genuinely sick during the year after the policy was implemented.

(E) There are many other factors besides employee illness that can adversely affect productivity.

Evaluation of a Plan

Situation   After a company started requiring employees to come to work unless they were sick enough to have to go to a doctor, the company's productivity losses from reported employee illness increased.

Reasoning   *What would explain why the policy increased productivity losses from reported employee illness?* Any factors that could have plausibly caused the policy to increase employee absenteeism from reported illness or to reduce the employees' productivity at work as a result of reported illness could explain why the policy increased productivity losses from reported illness.

A   Even though the policy required sick employees to consult a doctor, there is no reason to think that employees' doing so would have made them less productive than they would otherwise have been when absent from work.

B   This suggests that the policy made it more difficult for employees to falsely claim illness as an excuse for a work absence. Reduction in absences should result in productivity gains rather than losses.

C   **Correct.** This could have been a result of the policy and would have led to productivity losses possibly greater than those seen before the policy was introduced.

D   This would help to explain lower productivity losses from reported illness after the policy was implemented, not higher productivity losses.

E   The question is what could explain how the policy increased productivity losses from reported employee illness specifically, not productivity losses from any other factors.

The correct answer is C.

574. Advertising by mail has become much less effective, with fewer consumers responding. Because consumers are increasingly overwhelmed by the sheer amount of junk mail they receive, most discard almost all offers without considering them. Thus, an effective way for corporations to improve response rates would be to more carefully target the individuals to whom they mail advertising, thereby cutting down on the amount of junk mail each consumer receives.

Which of the following, if true, would most support the recommendation above?

(A) There are cost-effective means by which corporations that currently advertise by mail could improve response rates.

(B) Many successful corporations are already carefully targeting the individuals to whom they mail advertising.

(C) Any consumer who, immediately after receiving an advertisement by mail, merely glances at it is very likely to discard it.

(D) Improvements in the quality of the advertising materials used in mail that is carefully targeted to individuals can improve the response rate for such mail.

(E) Response rates to carefully targeted advertisements by mail are considerably higher, on average, than response rates to most other forms of advertising.

Evaluation of a Plan

Situation Advertising by mail has become less effective because consumers overwhelmed with the amount of junk mail they receive discard almost all of it without considering it.

Reasoning *What would most help to support the claim that making mail advertising more carefully targeted would improve response rates?* The passage recommends targeted advertising, reasoning that since targeted advertising would reduce the total amount of junk mail consumers receive, it would generate higher response rates. Any additional evidence for the claim that carefully targeted advertising would improve response rates would support this recommendation.

A Even if targeted advertising and every other means of improving response rates were too expensive to be cost-effective, targeted advertising could still be effective for any corporation willing to pay the expense.

B If many corporations already mail targeted advertising, and mail advertising is nonetheless yielding declining response rates, that suggests that targeted mail is an ineffective way to increase response rates.

C This could be equally true for targeted and untargeted mail advertising, so it does not suggest that the former is more effective.

D The question under consideration is whether more carefully targeted mail advertising would in itself increase response rates, not whether higher quality advertising would do so.

E **Correct.** This provides some evidence that carefully targeted mail advertising is associated with higher response rates than untargeted mail advertising is, and therefore that targeting mail advertising more carefully would improve response rates.

The correct answer is E.

575. Petrochemical industry officials have said that the extreme pressure exerted on plant managers during the last five years to improve profits by cutting costs has done nothing to impair the industry's ability to operate safely. However, environmentalists contend that the recent rash of serious oil spills and accidents at petrochemical plants is traceable to cost-cutting measures.

Which of the following, if true, would provide the strongest support for the position held by industry officials?

(A) The petrochemical industry benefits if accidents do not occur, since accidents involve risk of employee injury as well as loss of equipment and product.

(B) Petrochemical industry unions recently demanded that additional money be spent on safety and environmental protection measures, but the unions readily abandoned those demands in exchange for job security.

(C) Despite major cutbacks in most other areas of operation, the petrochemical industry has devoted more of its resources to environmental and safety measures in the last five years than in the preceding five years.

(D) There is evidence that the most damaging of the recent oil spills would have been prevented had cost-cutting measures not been instituted.

(E) Both the large fines and the adverse publicity generated by the most recent oil spill have prompted the petrochemical industry to increase the resources devoted to oil-spill prevention.

Argument Evaluation

Situation   Petrochemical industry officials claim that pressure on plant managers to cut costs over the past five years has not made the industry's operations any less safe. Environmentalists claim that recent oil spills and accidents show otherwise.

Reasoning   *What evidence would most strongly suggest that the cost-cutting pressure was not responsible for the recent rash of oil spills and accidents?* Evidence that the plant managers did not cut costs in any specific ways likely to have increased the likelihood of oil spills and accidents would support the industry officials' position that the cost-cutting pressure has not made petrochemical operations any less safe.

A   Even if the petrochemical industry has good reasons to try to prevent accidents, the recent rash of serious accidents suggests that it is failing to do so and that the cost-cutting pressure might be responsible.

B   This suggests that the unions, whose members could directly observe the cost-cutting pressure's effects, share the environmentalists' belief that this pressure contributed to the oil spills and accidents. Because the unions abandoned their demands, their concerns probably have not been addressed.

C   **Correct.** This suggests that, as the industry officials claim, the cost-cutting pressure has not in itself reduced the industry's effectiveness at preventing oil spills and accidents. Thus, it suggests that other factors are probably responsible for the recent problems.

D   This clearly suggests that the cost-cutting measures have indeed caused the industry to operate less safely, as the environmentalists claim.

E   Although this suggests that the industry is now trying to address the recent problems, the cost-cutting measures might nonetheless have caused all those problems.

The correct answer is C.

576. A company has developed a new sensing device that, according to the company's claims, detects weak, ultralow-frequency electromagnetic signals associated with a beating heart. These signals, which pass through almost any physical obstruction, are purportedly detected by the device even at significant distances. Therefore, if the company's claims are true, their device will radically improve emergency teams' ability to locate quickly people who are trapped within the wreckage of collapsed buildings.

Which of the following, if true, most strengthens the argument?

(A) People trapped within the wreckage of collapsed buildings usually have serious injuries that require prompt medical treatment.

(B) The device gives a distinctive reading when the signals it detects come from human beings rather than from any other living beings.

(C) Most people who have survived after being trapped in collapsed buildings were rescued within two hours of the building's collapse.

(D) Ultralow-frequency signals are not the only electromagnetic signals that can pass through almost any physical obstruction.

(E) Extensive training is required in order to operate the device effectively.

Argument Evaluation

Situation   A new sensing device can detect—at significant distances and even behind obstructions such as walls—weak, ultralow-frequency electromagnetic signals that are characteristic of heartbeats. It is predicted, based on this information, that the new device will shorten the time it currently takes to locate people buried under collapsed buildings but still alive.

Reasoning   *What new information, if accurate, would provide further evidence that would support the prediction?* The existing evidence fails to tell us whether the new device can distinguish between human heartbeats and heartbeats from other species. If the device does not allow the user to distinguish between the heartbeats of humans and those of animals of other species, then the prediction might not be correct, because if there are any nonhuman animals in the building, emergency teams may believe they have located a trapped human and begin a rescue effort, when in fact they have merely located an animal of some other species. Any new information that implies the device can help the user to discern between signals associated with a human heartbeat and signals associated with the heartbeats of animals of other species will strengthen support for the prediction.

A   This implies that prompt rescue of people trapped under collapsed buildings is vitally important. The prediction is that the new device will speed rescue of such people, but the new information here does nothing to indicate that the prediction is accurate.

B   **Correct.** As explained in the Reasoning section above, there is a crucial gap in the argument: The argument does not indicate whether the device allows the user to distinguish between signals associated with human heartbeats and signals associated with the heartbeats of other species. This information fills that gap.

C   Even if this is true, shortening the time for locating and rescuing people from collapsed buildings would clearly be beneficial. However, the new information given here does not make it more likely that the prediction is correct.

D   If this is correct, then, if anything, it somewhat undermines the evidence given for the prediction, since it raises the possibility that the detection ability of the device might be impeded by "noise" from irrelevant electromagnetic signals near the collapsed building.

E   This could lead to practical obstacles when using the device even in emergency situations, with the result that the device might never actually be used by competent personnel to "improve emergency teams' ability" because the "extensive training" would cost too much.

The correct answer is B.

577. Economist: The price of tap water in our region should be raised drastically. **Supplies in local freshwater reservoirs have been declining for years** because water is being used faster than it can be replenished. Since the price of tap water has been low, **few users have bothered to adopt even easy conservation measures**.

The two sections in **boldface** play which of the following roles in the economist's argument?

(A) The first is a conclusion for which support is provided, and which in turn supports the main conclusion; the second is the main conclusion.

(B) The first is an observation for which the second provides an explanation; the second is the main conclusion but not the only conclusion.

(C) The first is a premise supporting the argument's main conclusion; so is the second.

(D) The first is the only conclusion; the second provides an explanation for the first.

(E) The first is the main conclusion; the second is a conclusion for which support is provided, and which in turn supports the first.

Argument Construction

Situation   Local water supplies have been declining for years because of excessive water use and low prices. Few users have adopted even easy conservation measures.

Reasoning   *What roles do the two boldface statements play in the argument?* Both are factual observations. Since no further evidence or support is provided for either, neither can be a conclusion in the argument. However, interconnected causal explanations, signaled by *because* and *since*, are provided for both. The observation in the first boldface statement is causally explained by the further observation that water is being used faster than it can be replenished, which in turn is causally explained by the entire final sentence. The observation in the second boldface statement is causally explained by the observation that the price of tap water has been low. The only remaining portion of the argument is the initial sentence, a recommendation supported by these four observations together, and by the causal claims in which they are embedded. Thus, the four observations (including the two boldface statements) and the causal claims containing them are all premises, and the initial statement is the argument's only conclusion.

A   As explained in the Reasoning section above, the two boldface statements are premises of the argument. Although causal explanations are provided for both, no support or evidence is provided for either. Neither statement is inferred from anything else in the argument, so neither can be a conclusion in the argument.

B   As explained in the Reasoning section above, the second boldface statement does provide part of the causal explanation for the observation in the first boldface statement. But the second is not a conclusion. It is not inferred from anything else in the argument, so it cannot be a conclusion in the argument.

C   **Correct.** As explained in the Reasoning section above, each of the statements is a premise that serves along with other claims to support the recommendation in the initial sentence, which is the argument's only conclusion, and in that sense its main conclusion.

D   As explained in the Reasoning section above, the second boldface statement does provide part of the causal explanation for the observation in the first boldface statement. But the first is not a conclusion. It is not inferred from anything else in the argument, so it cannot be a conclusion in the argument.

E   As explained in the Reasoning section above, the two boldface statements are premises of the argument. Although causal explanations are provided for both, no support or evidence is provided for either. Neither statement is inferred from anything else in the argument, so neither can be a conclusion in the argument.

The correct answer is C.

578. Politician: Hybrid cars use significantly less fuel per kilometer than nonhybrids. And fuel produces air pollution, which contributes to a number of environmental problems. Motorists can save money by driving cars that are more fuel efficient, and they will be encouraged to drive hybrid cars if we make them aware of that fact. Therefore, we can help reduce the total amount of pollution emitted by cars in this country by highlighting this advantage of hybrid cars.

Which of the following, if true, would most indicate a vulnerability of the politician's argument?

(A) People with more fuel-efficient cars typically drive more than do those with less fuel-efficient cars.

(B) Not all air pollution originates from automobiles.

(C) Hybrid cars have already begun to gain popularity.

(D) Fuel-efficient alternatives to hybrid cars will likely become available in the future.

(E) The future cost of gasoline and other fuel cannot be predicted with absolute precision or certainty.

Argument Evaluation

Situation   According to a politician, hybrid cars use less fuel per kilometer than nonhybrids, and fuel produces air pollution. Motorists can save money by driving fuel-efficient cars, and will be encouraged to do so if made aware of the fact. The politician concludes that highlighting this fact will result in a reduction in air pollution.

Reasoning   *What would suggest that telling motorists they can save money by driving fuel-efficient cars would not reduce automotive air pollution, despite the facts cited by the politician?* The politician's implicit reasoning is that since hybrid cars use less fuel per kilometer, and fuel produces air pollution, motorists who drive hybrid cars must produce less air pollution than those who drive nonhybrids. The politician concludes that encouraging motorists to drive hybrid cars by telling them they would save money on fuel will therefore reduce automotive air pollution. Evidence that motorists who drive hybrid cars produce just as much automotive air pollution as those who drive nonhybrids would undermine this argument.

A   **Correct.** If drivers of hybrid cars tend to drive more kilometers than drivers of nonhybrids, then they may consume just as much fuel and produce just as much air pollution as the nonhybrid car drivers do, despite their lower fuel use per kilometer.

B   The politician's argument is only about air pollution from cars specifically, not air pollution from all sources.

C   Even if hybrid cars are beginning to gain popularity, informing motorists of the cost savings from fuel efficiency could help these cars become more popular than they would otherwise be.

D   Encouraging motorists to switch to hybrid cars now could reduce fuel use and automotive air pollution in the near future even if other, more fuel-efficient vehicles will become available further in the future.

E   Even if the future cost of fuel cannot be predicted accurately, encouraging motorists to switch to hybrid cars could reduce air pollution as the politician argues.

The correct answer is A.

579. Mayor: False alarms from home security systems waste so much valuable police time that in many communities police have stopped responding to alarms from homes whose systems frequently produce false alarms. This policy reduces wastage of police time but results in a loss of protection for some residents. To achieve a comparable reduction in wastage without reducing protection for residents, the council has enacted a measure to fine residents for repeated false alarms.

Which of the following, if true, casts the most doubt on whether the measure enacted by the council will achieve its goal?

(A) A fine in the amount planned by the council will not cover the expenses police typically incur when they respond to a false alarm.

(B) Homes equipped with security systems are far less likely to be broken into than are homes without security systems.

(C) The threat of fines is likely to cause many residents to deactivate their security systems.

(D) The number of home security systems is likely to increase dramatically over the next five years.

(E) Many home security systems have never produced false alarms.

Evaluation of a Plan

Situation   In many communities, police have been responding to false home-security alarms but have ceased to respond to alarms from homes that often have such false alarms. To reduce wastage of police time without compromising residents' home protection, one town council has enacted a new measure that will fine home residents for repeated false alarms.

Reasoning   *What fact or occurrence would most reduce the likelihood that the town council's newly enacted measure would achieve its goal, which is to reduce wastage of police time without compromising home protection?* Note that the goal is not to eliminate all wastage of police time or to pay all the costs of it; some random wastage is to be expected. But if many residents deactivated their security alarms (even well-functioning systems) because they wish to avoid being fined, this could reduce the level of home protection for those residents.

A   The goal is to reduce wastage of police time resulting from false security-system alarms, not necessarily to cover all the costs in police time for such alarms.

B   This seems obviously true, but it is also irrelevant to the frequency of false home-security alarms. It is therefore irrelevant, also, to whether the council's measure will effectively address wastage of police time stemming from such alarms.

C   **Correct.** If this occurred, it would result in a lower level of home protection for some residents and would mean that the town council's measure would have failed to achieve its goal.

D   This scenario does not make the council's measure more likely to fail to achieve its goal. If the increase in alarm systems occurs, it will likely result in more protection for the homes of more residents. Assuming vigorous enforcement of the new measure, we have no reason to believe that the number of false alarms would increase.

E   This has little bearing on the likelihood of the council's measure succeeding. Any home-security system that has never produced a false alarm could do so tomorrow, for all kinds of reasons.

The correct answer is C.

580. Excavation of the house of a third-century Camarnian official revealed that he had served four magistrates—public officials who administer the law—over his thirty-year public career, in four provincial capital cities. However, given the Camarnian administrative system of that era, it is unclear whether he served them simultaneously, as a traveling administrator living for part of the year in each provincial capital, or else did so sequentially, leaving one magistrate after several years to join another.

Which of the following would, if found in the excavation, most likely help reveal the pattern of the official's administrative service?

(A) Maps and documents describing each of the four provincial capitals

(B) A cache of the official's documents related to work from early in his career

(C) A set of cups of a type made only in the city of the first magistrate whom the official is known to have served

(D) Several pieces of furniture in the styles of two of the provincial capital cities

(E) Heavy clothing appropriate only for the coldest of the four cities

Argument Construction

Situation Evidence from an excavation makes clear that a particular third-century Camarnian official served four magistrates in four provincial capitals over his thirty-year career, but it is unclear whether he served the magistrates simultaneously or sequentially.

Reasoning *What evidence, if it were also found in the excavation, would be most helpful in determining whether the official served the magistrates simultaneously or sequentially?* It would be helpful to find documents from throughout the magistrate's career indicating at what times he worked for each magistrate, or even documents from just one period, as long as there were a large number, because this would likely show whether he was working for just one magistrate or for all four.

A We already know that the official worked in each of the four capitals. The fact that maps and documents describing the capitals were at his house tells us nothing about whether he worked for magistrates in these capitals simultaneously or not.

B **Correct.** Presumably the work-related documents would show whom he was working for at the time, and for how long—and would provide evidence as to whether he was working for multiple magistrates or for just one.

C Merely finding a set of cups made only in one of the cities tells us little. Even if we knew when he acquired the set, he need not have been working for the magistrate of that city at the time he acquired it; perhaps he had simply traveled to that city.

D One frequently moves furniture when moving from one city to another, so the fact that the official had pieces of furniture that may have come from different cities does not give us any indication of whether the official worked for all four magistrates simultaneously or not.

E The fact that heavy clothing appropriate only for the coldest of the four cities was found in the excavation of the official's house does not imply that other clothing, appropriate for one or more of the other cities, was not found. Consistent with the finding of the heavy clothing, the official may have worked exclusively in the city for which that clothing was appropriate, or worked intermittently in this city.

The correct answer is B.

581. In 1563, in Florence's Palazzo Vecchio, Giorgio Vasari built in front of an existing wall a new wall on which he painted a mural. Investigators recently discovered a gap between Vasari's wall and the original, large enough to have preserved anything painted on the original. Historians believe that Leonardo da Vinci had painted, but left unfinished, a mural on the original wall; some historians had also believed that by 1563 the mural had been destroyed. However, it is known that in the late 1560s, when renovating another building, Santa Maria Novella, Vasari built a façade over its frescoes, and the frescoes were thereby preserved. Thus, Leonardo's Palazzo Vecchio mural probably still exists behind Vasari's wall.

Which of the following is an assumption on which the argument depends?

(A) Leonardo rarely if ever destroyed artworks that he left unfinished.

(B) Vasari was likely unaware that the mural in the Palazzo Vecchio had willingly been abandoned by Leonardo.

(C) Vasari probably would not have built the Palazzo Vecchio wall with a gap behind it except to preserve something behind the new wall.

(D) Leonardo would probably have completed the Palazzo Vecchio mural if he had had the opportunity to do so.

(E) When Vasari preserved the frescoes of Santa Maria Novella he did so secretly.

Argument Construction

Situation   Georgio Vasari built a new wall in front of an existing wall in the Palazzo Vecchio that historians believe had had an unfinished mural by Leonardo da Vinci painted on it. Some historians, however, believe the mural had been destroyed by the time Vasari built the new wall. There is a gap between the old and new wall, large enough to have preserved anything painted on it, as there is in Santa Maria Novella, where Vasari also constructed a new wall in front of an old wall; on that wall, the building's frescoes were preserved.

Reasoning   *What claim needs to be true for the cited facts to support the conclusion that Leonardo's Palazzo Vecchio mural likely still exists behind Vasari's wall?* If there are other equally likely reasons that Vasari would have left a gap between the old wall and a new wall, besides preserving any painting on the old wall, the stated facts would not support the conclusion. After all, it may be only fortuitous that the frescoes in the Santa Maria Novella were preserved when Vasari built the new wall with a gap between it and the old wall. Therefore, the argument depends on assuming that it is unlikely that Vasari would have created a gap between the old and new walls unless he had been trying to preserve something painted on the old wall.

A   The argument does not depend on the claim that Leonardo rarely if ever destroyed his unfinished artworks. Obviously, it does depend on the claim that he did not always do so, but even if he fairly regularly destroyed unfinished artworks, this mural could be one of the ones he did not—perhaps the reason the mural was left unfinished was that he died before completing it.

B   The argument does not depend on Vasari knowing that Leonardo had willingly abandoned the mural. Even if Leonardo did willingly leave it unfinished, Vasari could nonetheless have thought the mural was of value and wanted to preserve it.

C   **Correct.** If there had been other likely reasons for Vasari to have built a gap behind the new wall other than to preserve something painted on the old wall, the cited facts would not be a good reason to believe that Vasari built the gap for the purpose of preserving anything painted on it.

D   Leonardo may have had no interest in finishing the mural. Vasari could nevertheless have thought that there was value in preserving it.

E   There is no need to assume that Vasari preserved the frescoes at Santa Maria Novella secretly. Even if he did not do so in this instance, he could have preserved other paintings secretly by the same means, or he may have let others know that he was preserving Leonardo's mural, although there is no historical record that he did let them know.

The correct answer is C.

582. Coffee shop owner: A large number of customers will pay at least the fair market value for a cup of coffee, even if there is no formal charge. Some will pay more than this out of appreciation of the trust that is placed in them. And our total number of customers is likely to increase. We could therefore improve our net cash flow by implementing an honor system in which customers pay what they wish for coffee by depositing money in a can.

Manager: We're likely to lose money on this plan. Many customers would cheat the system, paying a very small sum or nothing at all.

Which of the following, if true, would best support the owner's plan, in light of the manager's concern?

(A) The new system, if implemented, would increase the number of customers.

(B) By roasting its own coffee, the shop has managed to reduce the difficulties (and cost) of maintaining an inventory of freshly roasted coffee.

(C) Many customers stay in the cafe for long stretches of time.

(D) The shop makes a substantial profit from pastries and other food bought by the coffee drinkers.

(E) No other coffee shop in the area has such a system.

Evaluation of a Plan

Situation   The owner and the manager of a coffee shop disagree about whether allowing customers to pay for coffee on an honor system would increase or decrease profits.

Reasoning   *What would be the best evidence that the honor-system plan would increase profits even if many customers cheated the system?* The owner argues that profits would increase because many customers will choose to pay as much or more than before and the total number of customers will likely increase. But the manager points out that many customers would also choose to pay little or nothing. Assuming that the manager is correct about that, what further support could the owner present for the claim that the plan would still be profitable?

A   Since the owner has already basically asserted this, asserting it again would not provide any significant additional support for the plan.

B   This suggests that the shop is already profitable, not that the honor-system plan would make it more profitable.

C   Customers who stay in the cafe for long stretches would not necessarily pay any more per cup on the honor-system plan than other customers would.

D   **Correct.** If the customer base increases (as both the owner and the manager seem to agree), more customers will likely purchase highly profitable pastries and other foods, thus boosting profits.

E   The reason no other coffee shop in the area has an honor system may be that their owners and managers have determined that it would not be profitable.

The correct answer is D.

583. Birds have been said to be descended from certain birdlike dinosaur species with which they share distinctive structural features. The fossil record, however, shows that this cannot be so, since there are bird fossils that are much older than the earliest birdlike dinosaur fossils that have been found.

Which of the following is an assumption on which the argument relies?

(A) The birdlike dinosaurs have no living descendants.

(B) There are no flightless dinosaur species that have the distinctive structural features shared by birds and birdlike dinosaurs.

(C) There are no birdlike dinosaur fossils that are older than the bird fossils but have not yet been unearthed.

(D) It could not have been the case that some birds were descended from one of the birdlike dinosaur species and other birds from another.

(E) Birds cannot have been descended from dinosaur species with which the birds do not share the distinctive structural features.

Argument Construction

Situation   Although birds have been said to be descended from birdlike dinosaurs, some bird fossils predate the earliest known birdlike dinosaur fossils.

Reasoning   *What must be true in order for the premise that some bird fossils predate the earliest known birdlike dinosaur fossils to support the conclusion that birds are not descended from birdlike dinosaurs?* The argument implicitly reasons that since the cited bird fossils predate the earliest known birdlike dinosaur fossils, they must be from birds that lived before the earliest birdlike dinosaurs, and which therefore could not have been descended from birdlike dinosaurs. This reasoning assumes that any birdlike dinosaurs that lived before the first birds would have left fossils that still exist. It also assumes that no undiscovered birdlike dinosaur fossils predate the cited bird fossils.

A   The argument is only about whether birds are descended from birdlike dinosaurs. Whether birdlike dinosaurs have any living descendants other than birds is irrelevant.

B   The argument is only about birds and birdlike dinosaurs. It is not about other types of dinosaurs that were not birdlike.

C   **Correct.** If any undiscovered birdlike dinosaur fossils predate the cited bird fossils, then the latter fossils' age does not support the conclusion that birds are not descended from birdlike dinosaurs.

D   The argument purports to establish that the relative ages of bird fossils and birdlike dinosaur fossils show that birds cannot be descended from any of the known birdlike dinosaur species. In doing this, it acknowledges multiple birdlike dinosaur species and leaves open the question of whether some birds may be descended from one such species and other birds from another such species.

E   The argument does not claim that the known fossil record shows that birds cannot be descended from dinosaurs. It only claims that the record shows that they cannot be descended from the birdlike dinosaurs that shared their distinctive structural features.

The correct answer is C.

584. City council member: Demand for electricity has been increasing by 1.5 percent a year, and there simply is no more space to build additional power plants to meet future demand increases. We must therefore begin to curtail usage, which is why I propose passing ordinances requiring energy-conservation measures in all city departments.

The city council member's proposal assumes which of the following?

(A)   Existing power plants do not have the capacity to handle all of the projected increase in demand for electricity.

(B)   No city departments have implemented energy-conservation measures voluntarily.

(C)   Passing ordinances designed to curtail electricity usage will not have negative economic consequences for the city.

(D)   Residential consumers are not responsible for the recent increases in demand for electricity.

(E)   City departments that successfully conserve energy will set a good example for residential and industrial consumers of electricity.

Argument Construction

Situation   A city council member proposes energy-conservation measures for all city government departments because there is no room to build new power plants to meet future increases in the demand for electricity.

Reasoning   *What must be true in order for the factors the city council member cites to help justify the proposal?* The city council member says electricity usage must be curtailed on account of an increasing demand for electricity and a lack of space for new power plants that could meet future demand increases. In order for this reasoning to help justify the proposal, the cited factors must actually establish a need to curtail electricity usage.

A   **Correct.** If current power plants could satisfy the projected increased demand for electricity, then the increasing demand and the lack of room to build new plants would not establish a need to curtail electricity usage.

B   The proposed ordinances could still be necessary even if one city department had voluntarily implemented energy-conservation measures.

C   Passing the ordinances could still be necessary even if they would have some negative economic effects.

D   No matter who is responsible for the recent increases in demand, curtailing the city government's electricity usage could still help to reduce demand.

E   Ordinances to curtail the city government's energy usage could be economically necessary regardless of whether or not departments that obey the ordinances set a good example.

The correct answer is A.

585. Certain groups of Asian snails include both "left-handed" and "right-handed" species, with shells coiling to the left and right, respectively. Some left-handed species have evolved from right-handed ones. Also, researchers found that snail-eating snakes in the same habitat have asymmetrical jaws, allowing them to grasp right-handed snail shells more easily. If these snakes ate more right-handed snails over time, this would have given left-handed snails an evolutionary advantage over right-handed snails, with the left-handed snails eventually becoming a new species. Thus, the snakes' asymmetrical jaws probably helped drive the emergence of the left-handed snail species.

Which of the following would, if true, most strengthen the argument that asymmetrical snake jaws helped drive left-handed snail evolution?

(A)   In one snake species, the snakes with asymmetrical jaws eat snails, while the snakes with symmetrical jaws do not eat snails.

(B)   Some species of Asian snails contain either all right-handed snails, or all left-handed snails.

(C)   Anatomical differences prevent left-handed snails from mating easily with right-handed snails.

(D)   Some right-handed snails in this habitat have shells with a very narrow opening that helps prevent snakes from extracting the snails from inside their shells.

(E)   Experiments show that the snail-eating snakes in this habitat fail more often in trying to eat left-handed snails than in trying to eat right-handed snails.

Argument Evaluation

Situation   There are both Asian snails with shells that coil to the right and Asian snails with shells that coil to the left, and the latter have evolved from the former; furthermore, there are snakes that have asymmetrical jaws that allow the snakes to grasp the snails with right-coiled shells more easily.

Reasoning   *What fact would help support the claim that the snakes' asymmetrical jaws helped drive the emergence of species of snails with left-coiled shells?* We are told that if over time the snakes with asymmetrical jaws ate more snails with right-coiled shells than snails with left-coiled shells, then this would give snails with left-coiled shells an evolutionary survival advantage. So, if some evidence showed that the snakes with such jaws in fact were more likely to have successfully eaten the snails with the right-coiled shells, then we would have good reason to think the snakes' asymmetrical jaws helped drive the emergence of snails with left-coiled shells.

A   The fact that snakes with asymmetrical jaws eat snails and other snakes do not does not give any indication as to whether snails with left-coiled shells have any evolutionary advantages over snails with right-coiled shells. At best it only tells us that if snakes drove the evolution of snails with left-coiled shells, it would likely have been the snakes with asymmetrical jaws.

B   The fact that some species of Asian snails have no variation in the direction in which their shells coil tells us nothing about what, if any, evolutionary advantages they have relative to other snails, or whether the snakes' asymmetrical jaws had any effect on any such evolutionary advantages.

C   The inability of snails with left-coiled shells to mate easily with snails with right-coiled shells in and of itself tells us nothing about whether the snakes' asymmetrical jaws had any effect on the emergence of snails with left-coiled shells. Although it does suggest a different factor that could have contributed to the emergence of the snail species with left-coiled shells, it does not exclude the possibility that the snakes were also a factor.

D   The fact that snakes cannot extract some snails with right-coiled shells from their shells would suggest that these snails might have an evolutionary advantage; but the argument's conclusion is about an evolutionary advantage that snails with left-coiled shells presumably have, not an advantage that snails with right-coiled shells would have.

E   **Correct.** The fact that experiments show that the snakes are more successful at eating snails with right-coiled shells than they are at eating snails with left-coiled shells would support the claim that these snakes did in fact eat more snails with right-coiled shells, and hence the snails with left-coiled shells would as a result have an evolutionary advantage.

The correct answer is E.

586. A moderately large city is redesigning its central downtown area and is considering a plan that would reduce the number of lanes for automobiles and trucks and increase those for bicycles and pedestrians. The intent is to attract more workers and shoppers to downtown businesses by making downtown easier to reach and more pleasant to move around in.

Which of the following would, if true, most strongly support the prediction that the plan would achieve its goal?

(A) People who make a habit of walking or bicycling whenever feasible derive significant health benefits from doing so.

(B) Most people who prefer to shop at suburban malls instead of downtown urban areas do so because parking is easier and cheaper at the former.

(C) In other moderately sized cities where measures were taken to make downtowns more accessible for walkers and cyclists, downtown businesses began to thrive.

(D) If the proposed lane restrictions on drivers are rigorously enforced, more people will likely be attracted to downtown businesses than would otherwise be.

(E) Most people who own and frequently ride bicycles for recreational purposes live at a significant distance from downtown urban areas.

Evaluation of a Plan

Situation A moderately large city desires to attract more workers and shoppers to downtown businesses by making the downtown area more pleasant and easier to travel to. In light of this goal, the city is considering a plan that would reduce the number of lanes for automobiles and trucks and increase those for bicycles and pedestrians.

Reasoning *What would most strongly support the prediction that reducing the number of lanes for automobiles and trucks and increasing those for bicycles and pedestrians would achieve the goal of attracting more people to downtown businesses?* If other moderately sized cities that have improved the accessibility of their downtown areas to pedestrians and cyclists have seen increased downtown business, then it is reasonable to think that the city in question will have improved downtown business as well.

A If people who make a habit of walking or bicycling derive significant health benefits, that would provide further motivation for trying to encourage people to walk or ride a bicycle, but it does not provide much support for the claim that adding lanes for pedestrians and cyclists will successfully bring people to shop or work more in the city's downtown. Perhaps people will merely use the new lanes for exercise, but not to get to the downtown area to do business.

B Because the plan as described does not provide for additional parking, the fact that parking is a major concern motivating people to shop at suburban malls does not give us good reason to think that the city's plan will help achieve the city's goal.

C **Correct.** If other moderately sized cities that have made their downtown areas more accessible to pedestrians and cyclists have seen their downtown businesses begin to thrive soon afterwards, this is evidence—even if not conclusive—that the changes produced the thriving. Consequently, it is reasonable to think that the same will result for the city in question.

D It might be the case that rigorously enforcing lane restrictions will attract more people to downtown businesses than would otherwise be the case, but the information provided does not indicate how strictly lane restrictions will be enforced.

E The city's plan is aimed at increasing the use of bicycles for the purposes of shopping or getting to work, not only for recreational purposes. And even if people who use their bicycles for recreational purposes would also be likely to use them for shopping or getting to work, the fact that most recreational cyclists live at a significant distance from the city's downtown area may suggest that the city's plan will not be successful, because the cyclists may live too far away to use their bicycles for these purposes, even if it would be somewhat easier for them to do so once the plan has been implemented.

The correct answer is C.

587. Previously, Autoco designed all of its cars itself and then contracted with specialized parts suppliers to build parts according to its specifications. Now it plans to include its suppliers in designing the parts they are to build. Since many parts suppliers have more designers with specialized experience than Autoco has, Autoco expects this shift to reduce the overall time and cost of the design of its next new car.

Which of the following, if true, most strongly supports Autoco's expectation?

(A) When suppliers provide their own designs, Autoco often needs to modify its overall design.

(B) In order to provide designs for Autoco, several of the parts suppliers will have to add to their existing staffs of designers.

(C) Parts and services provided by outside suppliers account for more than 50 percent of Autoco's total costs.

(D) When suppliers built parts according to specifications provided by Autoco, the suppliers competed to win contracts.

(E) Most of Autoco's suppliers have on hand a wide range of previously prepared parts designs that can readily be modified for a new car.

Evaluation of a Plan

Situation   A car manufacturer plans to have its parts suppliers start helping to design the parts they build for the manufacturer. Many parts suppliers have more designers with specialized experience than the manufacturer has.

Reasoning   *What would make it more likely that having the parts suppliers help design the parts will reduce the time and cost of designing the manufacturer's next new car?* In order for the change to reduce the time and cost, the parts suppliers involved in designing the next car will probably have to do their portion of the design process faster and cheaper than the manufacturer would have, and the design collaboration process will have to avoid producing substantial new inefficiencies.

A   The additional need to modify the overall design would probably make the design process slower and more expensive, not faster and cheaper.

B   The additional need to hire more designers would probably increase design costs, not reduce them.

C   Although this suggests that the change is likely to substantially affect the design's expense, it does not indicate whether the expense will increase or decrease.

D   If anything, this competition probably made Autoco's previous design process cheaper. It does not suggest that the new design process, which may involve less competition, will be faster or cheaper than the previous one.

E   **Correct.** Modifying the previously prepared parts designs will probably be faster and cheaper than creating new designs from scratch.

The correct answer is E.

588. In response to viral infection, the immune systems of mice typically produce antibodies that destroy the virus by binding to proteins on its surface. Mice infected with the herpesvirus generally develop keratitis, a degenerative disease affecting part of the eye. Since proteins on the surface of cells in this part of the eye closely resemble those on the herpesvirus surface, scientists hypothesize that these cases of keratitis are caused by antibodies to the herpesvirus.

Which of the following, if true, most helps to support the scientists' reasoning?

(A) Other types of virus have surface proteins that closely resemble proteins found in various organs of mice.

(B) Mice that are infected with the herpesvirus but do not develop keratitis produce as many antibodies as infected mice that do develop keratitis.

(C) Mice infected with a new strain of the herpesvirus that has different surface proteins did not develop keratitis.

(D) Mice that have never been infected with the herpesvirus can sometimes develop keratitis.

(E) There are mice that are unable to form antibodies in response to herpes infections, and these mice contract herpes at roughly the same rate as other mice.

Argument Evaluation

Situation Mice infected with the herpesvirus tend to develop keratitis, an eye disease. The surface of the eye cells have proteins that resemble those on the herpesvirus surface. Based on this finding, scientists have hypothesized that keratitis develops in mice because antibodies that attack herpesvirus surface proteins can also attack eyes.

Reasoning *What other information, if correct, would provide the strongest support for the scientists' hypothesis?* The clue that led the scientists to form their hypothesis was the close resemblance of the proteins on the mouse eye surface to those on the herpesvirus surface. The resemblance could cause antibodies to bind to both types of proteins, in one case eliminating the herpesvirus and in the other case causing keratitis.

A Even if this is correct, we lack information as to whether the antibodies to those other types of virus can damage the organs that display the closely resembling proteins. If such a damage process were confirmed, it could count as evidence—even if not sufficient—to confirm the scientists' hypothesis.

B If anything, this would, absent further information, raise doubts about the correctness of the scientists' proposed explanation.

C **Correct.** This provides strong confirmation of the scientists' hypothesis. The proteins on the new strain of the herpesvirus no longer sufficiently resemble the proteins on the eye surface to cause the antibodies to attack those proteins and cause keratitis.

D For all we know, keratitis may have multiple independent causes and may sometimes be caused by processes other than the protein misidentification hypothesized by the scientists. This information neither confirms nor refutes the scientists' hypothesis.

E The rates at which mice contract herpes is not discussed. We lack any information as to whether mice that lack antibodies to the herpesvirus sometimes contract keratitis along with herpes infection.

The correct answer is C.

589. One might expect that within a particular species, any individuals that managed to slow down the aging process would leave more offspring. Natural selection should therefore favor extreme longevity—but this does not seem to be the case. A possible explanation is that aging is a product of the inevitable wear and tear of living, similar to how household appliances generally accumulate faults that lead to their eventual demise. However, most researchers do not find this analogy satisfactory as an explanation.

Which of the following would, if true, provide the strongest explanation for the researchers' reaction?

(A) Some organisms are capable of living much longer than other organisms.

(B) Some organisms reproduce very quickly despite having short lifespans.

(C) There are several ways of defining "extreme longevity," and according to some definitions it occurs frequently.

(D) Organisms are capable of maintenance and self-repair and can remedy much of the damage that they accumulate.

(E) Some organisms generate much more wear and tear on their bodies than others.

Argument Construction

Situation   One possible explanation for the fact that natural selection does not favor extreme longevity, despite the fact that a slowed-down aging process would leave more offspring, is that aging is the product of wear and tear, much like household appliances eventually no longer function because of wear and tear; most researchers, however, reject this analogy as an explanation.

Reasoning   *What would explain the researchers' rejection of the explanation?* The explanation is based on analogy between organisms and household appliances. If there were a crucial difference between appliances and organisms, such as the fact that organisms are capable of self-repair in a way that household appliances are not, then it would be reasonable for the researchers to reject the explanation.

A   The fact that some organisms can live much longer than other organisms is not a good reason to reject the analogy; after all, some household appliances may last much longer than others, perhaps because they receive a different amount of wear and tear.

B   Even if some organisms reproduce very quickly despite having short lifespans, that does not mean that they would not have even more offspring if they lived longer; also, this is irrelevant as to whether the analogy between the aging process and the wear and tear on household appliances is any good.

C   It is unclear what these different ways of defining "extreme longevity" are—perhaps the definition is merely a relative one; some organisms live much longer than others, and those that do have "extreme longevity." But presumably some household appliances last much longer than others, so this would not indicate a difference, and thus would not explain why most researchers reject the analogy.

D   **Correct.** Household appliances cannot repair themselves as organisms can, so the wear and tear of living is quite different from the wear and tear in household appliances.

E   Presumably some household appliances receive much more wear and tear than other household appliances, so the fact that some organisms generate more wear and tear on their bodies than others does not indicate a difference between appliances and organisms, and thus does not explain why the researchers reject the analogy.

The correct answer is D.

590. Last year a record number of new manufacturing jobs were created. Will this year bring another record? Well, **any new manufacturing job is created either within an existing company or by the start-up of a new company**. Within existing firms, new jobs have been created this year at well below last year's record pace. At the same time, there is considerable evidence that the number of new companies starting up this year will be no higher than it was last year and **there is no reason to think that the new companies starting up this year will create more jobs per company than did last year's start-ups**. So clearly, the number of new jobs created this year will fall short of last year's record.

In the argument given, the two portions in **boldface** play which of the following roles?

(A) The first provides evidence in support of the main conclusion of the argument; the second is a claim that the argument challenges.

(B) The first is a generalization that the argument seeks to establish; the second is a conclusion that the argument draws in order to support that generalization.

(C) The first is a generalization that the argument seeks to establish; the second is a judgment that has been advanced in order to challenge that generalization.

(D) The first is presented as an obvious truth on which the argument is based; the second is a claim that has been advanced in support of a position that the argument opposes.

(E) The first is presented as an obvious truth on which the argument is based; the second is a judgment advanced in support of the main conclusion of the argument.

Argument Construction

Situation   Manufacturing jobs are created either within existing companies or in start-ups. Manufacturing jobs are being created at a much slower rate this year than last year. It seems likely that the number of new start-ups will not exceed last year's number and that the average number of manufacturing jobs per start-up will not exceed last year's number. So fewer manufacturing jobs are likely to be created this year than last year.

Reasoning   *What function is served by the statement that any new manufacturing job is created either within an existing company or by the start-up of a new company? What function is served by the statement that there is no reason to think that the new companies starting up this year will create more jobs per company than did last year's start-ups?* The first statement makes explicit a general background assumption that there are just two ways in which manufacturing jobs are created. This assumption is used, along with other information, to support the argument's main conclusion, i.e., the prediction about job creation this year. The second statement gives a premise meant to help support the prediction about this year's manufacturing-job creation.

A   The first is a general statement making explicit an assumption on which the argument's reasoning depends, but the second is a statement affirmed as part of the argument and does not express a claim that the argument challenges.

B   The first is a generalization that is simply stated, without any support being offered. The second is not a conclusion and is not offered in support of the first.

C   The second is not presented as a challenge to the generalization that is given in the first statement. The argument does not seek to establish the first statement, but merely asserts it.

D   The second is information offered in support of the argument's main conclusion rather than a statement offered in support of a position opposed by the argument.

E   **Correct.** The first, stating a truism, is merely asserted and requires no support in the argument, for which it provides a foundation; the second is a piece of information meant to support the prediction that is the argument's main conclusion.

The correct answer is E.

591. Last year a record number of new manufacturing jobs were created. Will this year bring another record? Well, **any new manufacturing job is created either within an existing company or by the start-up of a new company**. Within existing firms, new jobs have been created this year at well below last year's record pace. At the same time, there is considerable evidence that the number of new companies starting up will be no higher this year than it was last year and there is no reason to think that the new companies starting up this year will create more jobs per company than did last year's start-ups. So clearly, **the number of new jobs created this year will fall short of last year's record**.

In the argument given, the two portions in **boldface** play which of the following roles?

(A) The first is presented as an obvious truth on which the argument is based; the second is the main conclusion of the argument.

(B) The first is presented as an obvious truth on which the argument is based; the second is a conclusion drawn in order to support the main conclusion of the argument.

(C) The first and the second each provide evidence in support of the main conclusion of the argument.

(D) The first is a generalization that the argument seeks to establish; the second is the main conclusion of the argument.

(E) The first is a generalization that the argument seeks to establish; the second is a conclusion that has been drawn in order to challenge that generalization.

Argument Construction

Situation   Manufacturing jobs are created either within existing companies or in start-ups. Manufacturing jobs at existing firms are being created at a much slower rate this year than last year. It seems likely that the number of new start-ups will not exceed last year's number and that the average number of new manufacturing jobs per start-up will not exceed last year's number. So fewer manufacturing jobs are likely to be created this year than last year.

Reasoning   *What function is served by the statement that any new manufacturing job is created either within an existing company or by the start-up of a new company? What function is served by the statement that the number of new jobs created this year will fall short of last year's record number?* The first statement makes explicit a general background assumption that manufacturing jobs are created in just two ways. This assumption is used, along with other information, to support the argument's main conclusion. The second statement gives the argument's main conclusion, a prediction about how this year's manufacturing-job creation will compare with last year's.

A   **Correct.** The first statement expresses a truism: assuming that all manufacturing jobs are created by companies, it is obviously true that all such jobs are created either by companies that already existed or by new companies that did not exist before. The argument then goes on to claim that new-job creation in each of these categories in the current year will be less than in the previous year. Since these two categories are exhaustive (as indicated in the first boldface portion), the argument concludes that new-job creation in the current year will be less than in the previous year. This is the argument's main conclusion (expressed in the second boldface portion).

B   The second statement is the argument's main conclusion, not an intermediate conclusion used to support the argument's main conclusion.

C   The second statement is the main conclusion of the argument, not a statement used as support for the main conclusion.

D   The argument merely asserts, and does not "seek to establish," the first statement. The first statement is a truism that does not need to be supported with evidence.

E   The second statement is the argument's main conclusion and is not meant to present a challenge to the first statement. The first statement serves to provide partial support for the argument's main conclusion.

The correct answer is A.

592. In Stenland, many workers have been complaining that they cannot survive on minimum wage, the lowest wage an employer is permitted to pay. The government is proposing to raise the minimum wage. Many employers who pay their workers the current minimum wage argue that if it is raised, unemployment will increase because they will no longer be able to afford to employ as many workers.

Which of the following, if true in Stenland, most strongly supports the claim that raising the minimum wage there will not have the effects that the employers predict?

(A) For any position with wages below a living wage, the difficulty of finding and retaining employees adds as much to employment costs as would raising wages.

(B) Raising the minimum wage does not also increase the amount employers have to contribute in employee benefits.

(C) When inflation is taken into account, the proposed new minimum wage is not as high as the current one was when it was introduced.

(D) Many employees currently being paid wages at the level of the proposed new minimum wage will demand significant wage increases.

(E) Many employers who pay some workers only the minimum wage also pay other workers wages that are much higher than the minimum.

Argument Evaluation

Situation   Stenland's government proposes to raise the minimum wage because many workers have complained they cannot survive on it. But many employers claim that raising the minimum wage will increase unemployment.

Reasoning   *What evidence would most strongly suggest that raising the minimum wage will not increase unemployment?* The employers with minimum-wage workers implicitly reason that because raising the minimum wage will increase the wages they have to pay each worker, it will reduce the number of workers they can afford to employ, and thus will increase unemployment. Evidence that the increased wage would not actually increase the employers' expenses per employee would cast doubt on their prediction, as would evidence that reducing the number of minimum-wage workers would not increase the nation's overall unemployment rate.

A   **Correct.** This suggests that raising the minimum wage would make it easier for employers to find and retain minimum-wage employees, and that the savings would fully offset the cost of paying the higher wages. If there were such offsetting savings, the employers should still be able to afford to employ as many workers as they currently do.

B   Even if raising the minimum wage does not increase employers' costs for employee benefits, paying the higher wage might still in itself substantially increase employers' overall costs per employee.

C   For all we know, the current minimum wage might have substantially increased unemployment when it was introduced.

D   These additional demands would probably raise employers' overall costs per employee, making it more likely that increasing the minimum wage would increase overall unemployment.

E   Even if some workers receive more than the minimum wage, raising that wage could still raise employers' expenses for employing low-wage workers, making it too expensive for the employers to employ as many workers overall.

The correct answer is A.

593. Biologists with a predilection for theory have tried—and largely failed—to define what it is that makes something a living thing. Organisms take in energy-providing materials and excrete waste products, but so do automobiles. Living things replicate and take part in evolution, but so do some computer programs. We must be open to the possibility that there are living things on other planets. Therefore, we will not be successful in defining what it is that makes something a living thing merely by examining living things on Earth—the only ones we know. Trying to do so is analogous to trying to specify _____.

Which of the following most logically completes the passage?

(A)   the laws of physics by using pure mathematics

(B)   what a fish is by listing its chemical components

(C)   what an animal is by examining a plant

(D)   what a machine is by examining a sketch of it

(E)   what a mammal is by examining a zebra

Argument Construction

Situation   Some biologists have tried, unsuccessfully, to find a theoretically defensible account of what it means for something to be a living thing. Some of the suggested definitions are too broad because they include things that we would not regard as living. To find life on other planets, we must not narrow our conception of life by basing it simply on the kinds of life encountered on Earth.

Reasoning   *Which of the answer choices would be the logically most appropriate completion of the argument?* The argument points out that life-forms elsewhere in the universe may be very different from any of the life-forms on Earth. Both life-forms on Earth and life-forms discovered elsewhere would all qualify as members of a very large class, the class of all life-forms. Taking life-forms on Earth, a mere subset of the class of all life-forms, as representative of all life-forms would be a logical mistake and might not lead to success in defining what it means for something to be a living thing. The correct answer choice, therefore, would involve a case of specifying what some general class of things is by examining the members of only a small, and not necessarily representative, subset of that class of things. In other words, the correct answer choice will involve the logical mistake of taking a subset as representative of a larger class.

A   Pure mathematics is not a subset of the law of physics, so this does not involve the logical mistake of taking a subset as representative of a larger class.

B   The chemical components of a fish are what make up the fish; they are not a small subset of the fish, so this does not involve the logical mistake of taking a subset as representative of a larger class.

C   Plants are not a subset of the class of animals, so this does not involve the logical mistake of taking a subset as representative of a larger class.

D   A sketch of a machine is not a subclass of the machine itself, so this does not involve the logical mistake of taking a subset as representative of a larger class.

E   **Correct.** This involves the logical mistake of taking the class of zebras, a subclass of the class of mammals, as representative of the class of all mammals. Logically, it resembles taking the class of life-forms on Earth as representative of the class of all life-forms.

The correct answer is E.

594. For the period from the eighth century through the eleventh century, the shifting boundaries between Kingdom F and Kingdom G have not been well charted. Although a certain village in a border region between the two kingdoms usually belonged to Kingdom G, ninth-century artifacts found in the village were in the typical Kingdom F style of that time. It is unclear whether the village was actually a part of Kingdom F in the ninth century or whether it was a part of Kingdom G but had merely adopted Kingdom F's artistic styles under Kingdom F's cultural influence.

Which of the following would, if found in ninth-century sites in the village, best help in determining whether the village was a part of Kingdom F or Kingdom G in the ninth century?

(A) A trading contract written in the Kingdom G dialect

(B) A drawing of a dwelling complex known to have existed on the border of Kingdom F and Kingdom G in the ninth century

(C) Knives and other utensils made from metal typical of ninth-century mining sites in Kingdom F

(D) Some fragments of pottery made in the Kingdom G style from the seventh century out of materials only found in Kingdom F

(E) Numerous teeth from the ninth century with a chemical signature typical only of teeth from people who had grown up in the heart of Kingdom F

Argument Construction

Situation   From the eighth century to the eleventh century, the boundaries between two kingdoms, F and G, shifted, but these shifts are not well documented. A certain village in a border region was usually part of Kingdom G, but ninth-century artifacts in the village are typical of the style of ninth-century artifacts from Kingdom F.

Reasoning   *What evidence, if it were found in the ninth-century sites in the village, would be most helpful in determining which of the two kingdoms the village was a part of during that century?* Information strongly indicating that during the ninth century the village was primarily settled by people clearly from Kingdom F would lend support to the claim that the village was part of Kingdom F in the ninth century.

A   A trading contract found at a ninth-century site in the village written in Kingdom G dialect would not settle whether the village was part of Kingdom G, because it could be the case that such a document would be written in that dialect even if the village were part of Kingdom F but regularly traded with Kingdom G.

B   Finding at a ninth-century site in the village a drawing of a dwelling complex known to have been on the border of Kingdom F and Kingdom G would not be useful in determining to which kingdom the village belonged at the time. We are not told in which kingdom that dwelling complex existed, and even if we were told, it could be that a villager in the other kingdom had a drawing of that complex for some reason (e.g., the villager could have had it because that complex was going to be attacked in a skirmish between the kingdoms).

C   Because there could have been trade between Kingdom F and Kingdom G, the fact that utensils made from metal typical of ninth-century mining sites in Kingdom F would not be very helpful in determining to which of the two kingdoms the village belonged in that century.

D   If fragments of pottery from the seventh century made in the Kingdom G style but from materials found only in Kingdom F were discovered, it would be unclear in which kingdom the pottery had been made. Given that the fragments may be from two centuries earlier than the period in question, and that we do not even know what kingdom the pottery was created in, these fragments would be of no use in determining to which kingdom the village belonged in the ninth century.

E   **Correct.** Although the mere presence of people from Kingdom F in the village would not provide strong support for the claim that the village was part of Kingdom F during the ninth century—the village could have shifted from Kingdom F to Kingdom G while maintaining much of its Kingdom F population—the presence of significant numbers of people from the heart of Kingdom F would support the claim that there was widespread migration of people from Kingdom F to the village. This is what one might reasonably expect if the village was part of Kingdom F during the ninth century. The discovery of numerous teeth that clearly belonged to people who grew up in the heart of Kingdom F in the ninth century would support the claim that many such people lived in the village during that century.

The correct answer is E.

595. Sammy: For my arthritis, I am going to try my aunt's diet: large amounts of wheat germ and garlic. She was able to move more easily right after she started that diet.

Pat: When my brother began that diet, his arthritis got worse. But he has been doing much better since he stopped eating vegetables in the nightshade family, such as tomatoes and peppers.

Which of the following, if true, would provide a basis for explaining the fact that Sammy's aunt and Pat's brother had contrasting experiences with the same diet?

(A) A change in diet, regardless of the nature of the change, frequently brings temporary relief from arthritis symptoms.

(B) The compounds in garlic that can lessen the symptoms of arthritis are also present in tomatoes and peppers.

(C) Arthritis is a chronic condition whose symptoms improve and worsen from time to time without regard to diet.

(D) In general, men are more likely to have their arthritis symptoms alleviated by avoiding vegetables in the nightshade family than are women.

(E) People who are closely related are more likely to experience the same result from adopting a particular diet than are people who are unrelated.

Argument Construction

Situation Sammy's aunt's arthritis apparently improved after she consumed large amounts of wheat germ and garlic. Pat's brother's arthritis deteriorated after he followed the same diet. Since he stopped eating vegetables in the nightshade family, such as tomatoes and peppers, his arthritis has improved.

Reasoning *What could account for the fact that Sammy's aunt's arthritis improved and Pat's brother's arthritis got worse after they both followed the wheat germ and garlic diet?* The fact that a person has a health improvement following a diet is, by itself, very weak evidence for the claim that the diet caused the improvement. More generally, the fact that one event follows another is seldom, by itself, evidence that the earlier event caused the later. This applies to both the experience of Sammy's aunt and that of Pat's brother with the wheat germ and garlic diet.

A In theory, this could be somewhat relevant to Sammy's aunt's experience but not to Pat's brother's experience. It is, however, insufficient to explain either.

B Even if this is true, it might be the case that a large quantity of the compounds in question must be consumed in concentrated form to benefit arthritis. No evidence is given to indicate whether this is so. Regardless, the puzzle as to why the wheat germ and garlic diet was followed by arthritis improvement in one case and not in the other remains.

C **Correct.** If we know there are typically fluctuations in the severity of arthritis symptoms and these can occur independent of diet, then the divergent experiences of the two people can be attributed to such fluctuations—even if it is conceded that some diets can affect arthritis symptoms in some manner. The wheat germ and garlic diet may, or may not, be such a diet.

D This could throw light on Pat's brother's experience but not on Sammy's aunt's experience.

E If this is correct, it is still far too general to provide a basis for explaining why the experiences of the two people were different. Does it apply to arthritis? We're not told. Nor are we told that it applies to the wheat germ and garlic diet. Is Pat's brother closely related to Sammy's aunt? We don't know.

The correct answer is C.

596. In the 1960s, surveys of Florida's alligator population indicated that the population was dwindling rapidly. Hunting alligators was banned. By the early 1990s, the alligator population had recovered, and restricted hunting was allowed. Over the course of the 1990s, reports of alligators appearing on golf courses and lawns increased dramatically. Therefore, in spite of whatever alligator hunting went on, the alligator population must have increased significantly over the decade of the 1990s.

Which of the following, if true, most seriously weakens the argument?

(A) The human population of Florida increased significantly during the 1990s.

(B) The hunting restrictions applied to commercial as well as private hunters.

(C) The number of sightings of alligators in lakes and swamps increased greatly in Florida during the 1990s.

(D) Throughout the 1990s, selling alligator products was more strictly regulated than hunting was.

(E) Most of the sightings of alligators on golf courses and lawns in the 1990s occurred at times at which few people were present on those golf courses and lawns.

Argument Evaluation

Situation   In the 1960s, hunting alligators was banned in Florida to allow the alligator population to recover—as it did by the early 1990s. Then restricted hunting was allowed. But over the decade, reports of alligators appearing on golf courses and lawns increased greatly. The author of the argument concludes from this information that the alligator population must have increased significantly during the 1990s.

Reasoning   *What new piece of information would seriously weaken the argument?* Increased sightings of alligators could occur either because there are more alligators or because more people are seeing the ones that are there. Any information indicating an increase in the ratio of people to alligators in locations where the two species coexist could offer an alternative to the hypothesis that the alligator population increased.

A   **Correct.** The argument suggests that Florida is an area in which golf courses and lawns are common. A large rapid increase in the human population of such an area would probably lead to a significant increase in the number of golf courses and lawns, some of which would encroach on the alligators' habitats. Even without any increase in the overall number of alligators, this could lead to an increase in both the percentage of alligators that venture onto golf courses and lawns and the number of people who happen to be in such locations when alligators are present.

B   This information is peripheral to the issue we are being asked to address; it neither weakens nor strengthens the argument.

C   This information tends to strengthen, not weaken, the argument; it suggests that the frequency of reported sightings in other places was reliable and that the sightings indicated a surge in the alligator population.

D   To the extent that this is relevant, it could provide some weak support for the argument. Strictly regulating the sale of alligator products could deter alligator hunting by making it less profitable and could thus allow further increases in the alligator population.

E   Without further evidence, the net effect of this information cannot be reliably determined. On the one hand, if *sightings* is understood as elliptical for *reports of seeing alligators*, this could suggest that some of the reports may be dubious because they are not corroborated by additional observers. On the other hand, it suggests that the alligator population may in fact have increased. Times when few people are present are also times when wildlife such as alligators would be more likely to venture onto lawns and golf courses. Without any evidence that sightings before the 1990s did not typically occur in such conditions, this suggests that the number of alligators observable at those times increased in the 1990s.

The correct answer is A.

597. Infotek, a computer manufacturer in Katrovia, has just introduced a new personal computer model that sells for significantly less than any other model. Market research shows, however, that very few Katrovian households without personal computers would buy a computer, regardless of its price. Therefore, introducing the new model is unlikely to increase the number of computers in Katrovian homes.

Which of the following is an assumption on which the argument depends?

(A) Infotek achieved the lower price of the new model by using components of lower quality than those used by other manufacturers.

(B) The main reason cited by consumers in Katrovia for replacing a personal computer is the desire to have an improved model.

(C) Katrovians in households that already have computers are unlikely to purchase the new Infotek model as an additional computer for home use.

(D) The price of other personal computers in Katrovia is unlikely to drop below the price of Infotek's new model in the near future.

(E) Most personal computers purchased in Katrovia are intended for home use.

Argument Construction

Situation   In Katrovia, a new personal computer model costs less than any other model. But market research shows that very few Katrovian households without personal computers would buy even cheap ones.

Reasoning   *What must be true in order for the stated facts to support the conclusion that introducing the new computer model is unlikely to increase the overall number of computers in Katrovian homes?* The market research supports the conclusion that no new computer model is likely to significantly increase the number of computers in Katrovian homes that currently lack computers. But the overall number of computers in Katrovian homes will still increase if Katrovian homes that already have computers buy additional computers while keeping their existing ones. So the argument has to assume that the new computer model will not increase the number of additional computers purchased for Katrovian homes that already have computers.

A   Even if Infotek used high-quality components in the new computer model, Katrovians might still refuse to buy it.

B   Replacing a personal computer does not change the overall number of personal computers in homes, so Katrovians' motives for replacing their computers are irrelevant to the argument.

C   **Correct.** As explained above, unless computers of the new model are purchased as additional computers for Katrovian homes that already have computers, the new model's introduction is unlikely to increase the overall number of computers in Katrovian homes.

D   The assumption that other personal computer prices would stay relatively high does not help establish the link between its premises and its conclusion. If answer choice D were false, the argument would be no weaker than it is without any consideration of other computers' potential prices.

E   If most personal computers purchased in Katrovia were not intended for home use, then the new model's introduction would be even less likely to increase the number of personal computers in Katrovian homes. So the argument does not depend on assuming that most of the computers purchased are for home use.

The correct answer is C.

598. Fast-food restaurants make up 45 percent of all restaurants in Canatria. Customers at these restaurants tend to be young; in fact, studies have shown that the older people get, the less likely they are to eat in fast-food restaurants. Since the average age of the Canatrian population is gradually rising and will continue to do so, the number of fast-food restaurants is likely to decrease.

Which of the following, if true, most seriously weakens the argument?

(A) Fast-food restaurants in Canatria are getting bigger, so each one can serve more customers.

(B) Some older people eat at fast-food restaurants more frequently than the average young person.

(C) Many people who rarely eat in fast-food restaurants nevertheless eat regularly in restaurants.

(D) The overall population of Canatria is growing steadily.

(E) As the population of Canatria gets older, more people are eating at home.

Argument Evaluation

Situation   In Canatria, the older people get, the less likely they are to eat in fast-food restaurants. The average age of Canatrians is increasing.

Reasoning   *What evidence would most weaken the support provided by the cited facts for the prediction that the number of fast-food restaurants in Canatria is likely to decrease?* The argument implicitly reasons that since studies have shown that Canatrians tend to eat in fast-food restaurants less as they get older, and since Canatrians are getting older on average, the proportion of Canatrians eating in fast-food restaurants will decline. The argument assumes that this means the overall number of fast-food restaurant customers will decline and that demand will decrease enough to reduce the number of fast-food restaurants that can sustain profitability. Consequently, fewer new fast-food restaurants will open or more old ones will close, or both. Thus, the number of fast-food restaurants in Canatria will fall. Any evidence casting doubt on any inference in this chain of implicit reasoning will weaken the argument.

A   This strengthens the argument by providing additional evidence that the total number of fast-food restaurants will decrease. If the average number of customers per fast-food restaurant is increasing, then fewer fast-food restaurants will be needed to serve the same—or a lesser—number of customers.

B   Even if a few individuals do not follow the general trends described, those trends could still reduce the overall demand for and number of fast-food restaurants.

C   The argument is only about fast-food restaurants, not restaurants of other types.

D   Correct. This suggests that even if the proportion of Canatrians eating at fast-food restaurants declines, the total number doing so may not decline. Thus, the total demand for and profitability of fast-food restaurants may not decline either, so the total number of fast-food restaurants in Canatria may not decrease.

E   If anything, this strengthens the argument by pointing out an additional trend likely to reduce the demand for, and thus the number of, fast-food restaurants in Canatria.

The correct answer is D.

599. Last year a chain of fast-food restaurants, whose menu had always centered on hamburgers, added its first vegetarian sandwich, much lower in fat than the chain's other offerings. Despite heavy marketing, the new sandwich accounts for a very small proportion of the chain's sales. The sandwich's sales would have to quadruple to cover the costs associated with including it on the menu. Since such an increase is unlikely, the chain would be more profitable if it dropped the sandwich.

Which of the following, if true, most seriously weakens the argument?

(A) Although many of the chain's customers have never tried the vegetarian sandwich, in a market research survey most of those who had tried it reported that they were very satisfied with it.

(B) Many of the people who eat at the chain's restaurants also eat at the restaurants of competing chains and report no strong preference among the competitors.

(C) Among fast-food chains in general, there has been little or no growth in hamburger sales over the past several years as the range of competing offerings at other restaurants has grown.

(D) When even one member of a group of diners is a vegetarian or has a preference for low-fat food, the group tends to avoid restaurants that lack vegetarian or low-fat menu options.

(E) An attempt by the chain to introduce a lower-fat hamburger failed several years ago, since it attracted few new customers and most of the chain's regular customers greatly preferred the taste of the regular hamburgers.

Argument Evaluation

Situation   Last year a fast-food restaurant chain specializing in hamburgers started offering a low-fat vegetarian sandwich and marketed it heavily. The new sandwich's sales are far too low to cover the costs associated with including it on the menu.

Reasoning   *What evidence would most weaken the support provided by the cited facts for the prediction that it would be more profitable for the chain to drop the sandwich?* The implicit argument is that since the new sandwich's sales are too low to cover the costs associated with including it on the menu, offering the sandwich diminishes the chain's profitability and will continue to do so if the sandwich continues to be offered. This reasoning assumes that the sandwich provides the chain no substantial indirect financial benefits except through its direct sales. It also assumes that the sandwich's sales will not increase sufficiently to make the sandwich a viable product. Any evidence casting doubt on either of these assumptions will weaken the argument.

A   This gives information only about the respondents to the survey who had tried the sandwich (possibly very few), who were probably already more open to liking a vegetarian sandwich than any of the chain's other customers. So their responses are probably unrepresentative of the chain's customers in general and do not suggest that the sandwich has enough market potential.

B   Although the issue of competition with other restaurants is not raised in the information provided, this new information, if anything, strengthens the argument, by suggesting that the introduction of the new sandwich has not significantly enhanced customer preference for eating at the restaurants that offer the new sandwich.

C   This suggests that the cause of stagnation in fast-food restaurants' hamburger sales has been competition from non-fast-food restaurants, but not that the non-fast-food restaurants competed by offering vegetarian options.

D   **Correct.** This suggests that even if the sandwich's sales are low, it may indirectly increase the chain's overall profits by encouraging large groups to eat at the chain.

E   This strengthens the argument by suggesting that the chain's customers are generally not interested in low-fat menu options such as the new sandwich.

The correct answer is D.

600. Transportation expenses accounted for a large portion of the total dollar amount spent on trips for pleasure by residents of the United States in 1997, and about half of the total dollar amount spent on transportation was for airfare. However, the large majority of United States residents who took trips for pleasure in 1997 did not travel by airplane but used other means of transportation.

If the statements above are true, which of the following must also be true about United States residents who took trips for pleasure in 1997?

(A) Most of those who traveled by airplane did so because the airfare to their destination was lower than the cost of other available means of transportation.

(B) Most of those who traveled by airplane did so because other means of transportation to their destination were unavailable.

(C) Per mile traveled, those who traveled by airplane tended to spend more on transportation to their destination than did those who used other means of transportation.

(D) Overall, people who did not travel by airplane had lower average transportation expenses than people who did.

(E) Those who traveled by airplane spent about as much, on average, on other means of transportation as they did on airfare.

Argument Construction

Situation   In 1997, about half of total transportation spending by U.S. residents taking trips for pleasure was for airfare. But the large majority of U.S. residents who took trips for pleasure in 1997 did not travel by airplane.

Reasoning   *What can be deduced from the stated facts?* The information provided indicates that among U.S. residents who took trips for pleasure in 1997, those who traveled by airplane were a small minority. Yet this small minority's spending for airfare accounted for half of all transportation spending among residents taking trips for pleasure. It follows that on average, those who traveled by airplane must have spent far more per person on transportation than those who did not travel by airplane.

A   This does not follow logically from the information given. Most of those who traveled by airplane may have done so even if flying was more expensive than other modes of transportation—for example, because flying was faster or more comfortable.

B   This does not follow from the information given. Most of those who traveled by airplane may have done so even if many other modes of transportation were available—the other modes may all have been less desirable.

C   This does not follow from the information given. Those who traveled by airplane may have traveled much farther on average than those who used other means of transportation, so their transportation spending per mile traveled need not have been greater.

D   Correct. As explained above, those who traveled by airplane must have spent more per person on transportation than those who did not travel by airplane, on average. In other words, those who did not travel by airplane must have had lower average transportation expenses than those who did.

E   This does not follow from the information given. Although half the total dollar spending on transportation was for airfare, much of the transportation spending that was not for airfare was by the large majority of U.S. residents who did not travel by airplane.

The correct answer is D.

601. Voters commonly condemn politicians for being insincere, but politicians often must disguise their true feelings when they make public statements. If they expressed their honest views—about, say, their party's policies—then achieving politically necessary compromises would be much more difficult. Clearly, the very insincerity that people decry shows that our government is functioning well.

Which of the following, if true, most seriously undermines this reasoning?

(A) Achieving political compromises is not all that is necessary for the proper functioning of a government.

(B) Some political compromises are not in the best long-term interest of the government.

(C) Voters often judge politicians by criteria other than the sincerity with which they express their views.

(D) A political party's policies could turn out to be detrimental to the functioning of a government.

(E) Some of the public statements made by politicians about their party's policies could in fact be sincere.

Argument Evaluation

Situation   Politicians must often make insincere public statements because expressing their true feelings would make it harder for them to achieve politically necessary compromises.

Reasoning   *What would suggest that the argument's premises do not establish that politicians' insincerity shows our government is functioning well?* The implicit reasoning is that insincerity helps politicians achieve politically necessary compromises, and these compromises help our government to function well, so insincerity must show that our government is functioning well. Evidence that these necessary compromises do not ensure that our government functions well would undermine the argument's reasoning, as would evidence that politicians' insincerity has other substantial effects that hinder the government's functioning.

A   Correct. If governments may function poorly even when insincerity allows necessary political compromises to be made, then the argument's premises do not establish that politicians' insincerity shows our government is functioning well.

B   The argument does not require that all political compromises help government to function well, only that politically necessary compromises do.

C   Even if voters often judge politicians by criteria other than their sincerity, they may also often decry politicians' insincerity, not realizing or caring that such insincerity helps the government function well.

D   Even if a political party's policies impair the government's functioning, politically necessary compromises by politicians in that party could improve the government's functioning.

E   Even if politicians sometimes speak sincerely about their party's policies, their general willingness to be insincere as needed to achieve politically necessary compromises could be a sign that the government is functioning well.

The correct answer is A.

602. One summer, floods covered low-lying garlic fields situated in a region with a large mosquito population. Since mosquitoes lay their eggs in standing water, flooded fields would normally attract mosquitoes, yet no mosquitoes were found in the fields. Diallyl sulfide, a major component of garlic, is known to repel several species of insects, including mosquitoes, so it is likely that diallyl sulfide from the garlic repelled the mosquitoes.

Which of the following, if true, most strengthens the argument?

(A) Diallyl sulfide is also found in onions but at concentrations lower than in garlic.

(B) The mosquito population of the region as a whole was significantly smaller during the year in which the flooding took place than it had been in previous years.

(C) By the end of the summer, most of the garlic plants in the flooded fields had been killed by waterborne fungi.

(D) Many insect species not repelled by diallyl sulfide were found in the flooded garlic fields throughout the summer.

(E) Mosquitoes are known to be susceptible to toxins in plants other than garlic, such as marigolds.

Argument Evaluation

Situation   When summer floods covered garlic fields in an area with many mosquitoes, no mosquitoes were found in the fields, even though flooded fields would normally attract mosquitoes to lay their eggs in the water. Diallyl sulfide, which is found in garlic, repels mosquitoes and some other insect species, and likely accounts for the lack of mosquitoes in the area.

Reasoning   *Given the facts cited, what would provide additional evidence that diallyl sulfide from the garlic made mosquitoes avoid the flooded fields?* The argument would be strengthened by any independent evidence suggesting that diallyl sulfide pervaded the flooded fields or excluding other factors that might explain the absence of mosquitoes in the fields.

A   This could strengthen the argument if mosquitoes also avoid flooded onion fields, but we do not know whether they do.

B   This would weaken the argument by suggesting that the general mosquito population decline, rather than the diallyl sulfide, could explain the absence of mosquitoes in the fields.

C   It is not clear how this would affect the amount of diallyl sulfide in the flooded fields, so this does not provide evidence that the diallyl sulfide repelled the mosquitoes.

D   Correct. This provides evidence that there was no factor other than diallyl sulfide that reduced insect populations in the flooded garlic fields.

E   If anything, this would weaken the argument, since it is at least possible that some of these toxins were present in the flooded fields.

The correct answer is D.

603. Duckbill dinosaurs, like today's monitor lizards, had particularly long tails, which they could whip at considerable speed. Monitor lizards use their tails to strike predators. However, although duckbill tails were otherwise very similar to those of monitor lizards, the duckbill's tailbones were proportionately much thinner and thus more delicate. Moreover, to ward off their proportionately much larger predators, duckbills would have had to whip their tails considerably faster than monitor lizards do.

The information given, if accurate, provides the strongest support for which of the following hypotheses?

(A)   If duckbills whipped their tails faster than monitor lizards do, the duckbill's tail would have been effective at warding off the duckbills' fiercest predators.

(B)   Duckbills used their tails to strike predators, and their tailbones were frequently damaged from the impact.

(C)   Using their tails was not the only means duckbills had for warding off predators.

(D)   Duckbills were at much greater risk of being killed by a predator than monitor lizards are.

(E)   The tails of duckbills, if used to ward off predators, would have been more likely than the tails of monitor lizards to sustain damage from the impact.

Argument Construction

Situation   Duckbill dinosaur tails were like the tails of contemporary monitor lizards in that they were very long. They differed, though, in that their tailbones were much thinner and more delicate than monitor lizards' tailbones. Monitor lizards use their tails to strike predators. If duckbills did so, they would have had to whip their tails much faster, as their predators were proportionately much larger.

Reasoning   *Which hypothesis is most strongly supported by the given information?* The information states that duckbills would have had to whip their tails much faster than monitor lizards do to ward off their proportionately larger predators, but their tailbones were more delicate. It would be reasonable to conclude, then, that duckbills' tails would have been more likely to sustain damage if used to ward off predators than monitor lizards' tails are.

A   The information gives us little reason to be confident that duckbills would have been effective at warding off their fiercest predators even if they whipped their tails faster than monitor lizards do. Note that we are not even told how effective monitor lizards are at warding off particularly fierce predators.

B   The information gives us both a reason to think that duckbills might have used their tails to strike predators—their tails are similar in length to the tails of monitor lizards, which are used to strike predators—and reasons to think they might not have done so—their tailbones were much thinner and more delicate than monitor lizards' tailbones, and they would have had to whip their tails much faster than monitor lizards whip theirs. Therefore, the support for this answer choice is not very strong.

C   The information does give some modest support for the claim that duckbills' tails would not provide a particularly good defense against their predators. This suggests weakly that they had other defenses against their predators. Note, though, that this answer choice, as worded, entails that duckbills *did* use their tails as a defense; it was simply not the only defense. But the information on which we are to base the hypothesis is compatible with duckbills not having used their tails to ward off predators.

D   The information does not give much support for this answer choice. It could be that duckbills had other effective defenses against their predators. Perhaps they were fast, or had sharp claws.

E   **Correct.** As noted above, duckbills would have had to whip their tails much faster than monitor lizards do to ward off their proportionately larger predators, but their tailbones were more delicate, so duckbills' tails would have been more likely to sustain damage if used to ward off predators than monitor lizards' tails are.

The correct answer is E.

604. In an attempt to produce a coffee plant that would yield beans containing no caffeine, the synthesis of a substance known to be integral to the initial stages of caffeine production was blocked either in the beans, in the leaves, or both. For those plants in which synthesis of the substance was blocked only in the leaves, the resulting beans contained no caffeine.

Any of the following, if true, would provide the basis for an explanation of the observed results EXCEPT:

(A) In coffee plants, the substance is synthesized only in the leaves and then moves to the beans, where the initial stages of caffeine production take place.

(B) In coffee plants, the last stage of caffeine production takes place in the beans using a compound that is produced only in the leaves by the substance.

(C) In coffee plants, the initial stages of caffeine production take place only in the beans, but later stages depend on another substance that is synthesized only in the leaves and does not depend on the blocked substance.

(D) In coffee plants, caffeine production takes place only in the leaves, but the caffeine then moves to the beans.

(E) Caffeine was produced in the beans of the modified coffee plants, but all of it moved to the leaves, which normally produce their own caffeine.

Argument Evaluation

Situation   The synthesis of a substance integral to the initial production of caffeine was blocked only in the beans of some coffee plants, only in the leaves of others, and in both the beans and leaves of yet other coffee plants. No caffeine was found in beans from the plants in which the synthesis of the substance was blocked only in the leaves.

Reasoning   *Which claim would NOT form the basis for an explanation of the observed results?* There are many possible explanations. For instance, the results could be explained by any claim that indicates (1) that the substance integral to the initial production of caffeine is synthesized only in the leaves, or (2) that the substance is also produced in the beans but, when it is blocked from being produced in the leaves, that substance or the caffeine that is produced in the beans is entirely depleted from the beans. However, the observed results would *not* be explained by any claim that (1) indicates that the early stages of caffeine synthesis can occur in the beans, entailing that the crucial substance is present in the beans even when it is blocked in the leaves, and (2) provides no explanation for why blocking the crucial substance in the leaves would prevent the completion of the caffeine synthesis in the beans.

A   If a substance that is integral to the initial production of caffeine is produced only in the leaves, and that production has been blocked, then the observed results are to be expected.

B   If the last stage of caffeine production requires a compound that is produced in the leaves by a substance the synthesis of which is blocked in the leaves, then the observed results are to be expected.

C   **Correct.** Suppose the initial stages of caffeine production take place in the beans. The substance integral to those initial stages must therefore be present in the beans. But this does not tell us whether that substance is synthesized in the beans or elsewhere. It does tell us that some other substance that plays a part in the production of caffeine is synthesized in the leaves, but we are not told that the synthesis of that substance is blocked. Therefore, this answer choice does not give us reason to expect the observed results, and so does not serve as the basis for an explanation of those results.

D   Suppose we know that caffeine production in coffee plants takes place entirely in the leaves but at least some of the caffeine migrates from there to the beans. Then, if the synthesis of a substance that is integral to the initial production of caffeine is blocked in the leaves, it seems reasonable to expect the observed results.

E   If caffeine is normally produced in both the leaves and the beans of a coffee plant, but all the caffeine produced in the beans will migrate from the beans to the leaves if for any reason caffeine is not produced in the leaves, then it is reasonable to expect the observed results.

The correct answer is C.

605. Which of the following most logically completes the passage?

Laminated glass is much harder to break than the glass typically used in the windows of cars driven in Relnia. It is more difficult for thieves to break into cars with laminated glass windows than into cars with ordinary glass windows, and laminated glass windows are less likely to break in a collision. Nevertheless, considerations of security and safety do not unambiguously support a proposal to require that in Relnia all glass installed in cars be laminated glass, since _____.

(A) most people cannot visually distinguish laminated glass from the glass typically used for car windows

(B) a significant proportion of cars driven in Relnia are manufactured elsewhere

(C) some cars in Relnia already have laminated glass in their windows

(D) the rates of car theft and of collisions have both fallen slightly in Relnia in recent years

(E) there are times when breaking a car's window is the best way to provide timely help for people trapped inside

Argument Construction

Situation   Laminated glass is much more difficult to break than the glass that is typically used in car windows in Relnia and, when used in a car window, makes it harder for thieves to break into the car and is less likely to shatter in collisions.

Reasoning   *What claim, despite the given information, most helps support the conclusion that considerations of security and safety do not unambiguously support a proposal to require that in Relnia all glass installed in cars be laminated glass?* If there are any significant safety or security problems that would arise from having laminated glass, this would count against the proposal. For instance, sometimes it is essential to break a car's window to help people trapped in the car.

A   None of the security-or safety-related characteristics of laminated glass discussed in the argument depend on laminated glass being visually distinguishable from the glass typically used for car windows. Therefore, this answer choice does not help justify the conclusion and so would not logically complete the passage.

B   Even if most cars in Relnia are manufactured elsewhere, there may be no reason not to require that all glass installed in cars in Relnia be laminated glass.

C   Whether some cars, no cars, or all cars currently in Relnia have laminated glass in their windows is irrelevant to whether it is a good idea to require that all glass installed in cars in Relnia be laminated glass.

D   Even if rates of car theft and of collision have fallen, that does not mean they could not fall further if laminated glass were required. In fact, we are not told why they fell. Could it be that more cars in Relnia had windows made of laminated glass, and that this led to these reduced rates?

E   **Correct.** This answer choice provides a reason to think that sometimes, for the security or safety of passengers in cars, it might be better not to have all the windows of every car made of laminated glass. Therefore, it logically completes the passage.

The correct answer is E.

606. Consultant: **Ace Repairs ends up having to redo a significant number of the complex repair jobs it undertakes, but when those repairs are redone, they are invariably done right**. Since we have established that there is no systematic difference between the mechanics who are assigned to do the initial repairs and those who are assigned to redo unsatisfactory jobs, we must reject the hypothesis that mistakes made in the initial repairs are due to the mechanics' lack of competence. Rather, it is likely that **complex repairs require a level of focused attention that the company's mechanics apply consistently only to repair jobs that have not been done right on the first try.**

In the consultant's reasoning, the two portions in **boldface** play which of the following roles?

(A) The first is the consultant's main conclusion; the second provides evidence in support of that main conclusion.

(B) The first is evidence that serves as the basis for rejecting one explanation of a certain finding; the second is the consultant's own explanation of that finding.

(C) The first is a claim whose truth is at issue in the reasoning; the second provides evidence to show that the claim is true.

(D) The first presents a contrast whose explanation is at issue in the reasoning; the second is the consultant's explanation of that contrast.

(E) The first presents a contrast whose explanation is at issue in the reasoning; the second is evidence that has been used to challenge the consultant's explanation of that contrast.

Argument Construction

Situation   The following information is attributed to a consultant: Some complex repair jobs done by Ace Repairs have to be redone. The repairs, when redone, are usually successful. But the mechanics who do the initial repairs and any others who redo those repairs are, overall, competent to do the repairs successfully.

Reasoning   *What role in the consultant's reasoning do the boldfaced statements play?* The consultant's first sentence describes a phenomenon that could be puzzling and needs explanation. One might be inclined to argue that the mechanics who redo the repairs are more competent than those who did the initial repairs. But the second boldfaced statement rebuts this explanation by telling us that it has been *established* that there are no systematic differences in competence. The final sentence of the consultant's reasoning puts forward another explanation: that the redoing of a repair elicits from mechanics a higher level of focused attention than did the performance of the initial repair.

A   The first describes a puzzling phenomenon for which the consultant seeks an explanation. It is not presented as a conclusion, i.e., a statement that is asserted on the basis of other statements. The second is not a statement presented *in support of* the first; it gives an explanation offered by the consultant for the puzzling phenomenon described in the first boldfaced portion.

B   The first describes a puzzling phenomenon for which the consultant seeks an explanation, and it is not offered to show that a certain explanation does not fit. The second gives the consultant's own explanation of that finding.

C   The reasoning does not question the accuracy of the first boldfaced portion; that portion is a description of a phenomenon that the consultant believes needs explanation. The second is not meant as evidence to indicate that the first is true; rather, it is offered as an explanation for the puzzling phenomenon described in the first.

D   **Correct.** The first boldfaced portion contrasts the success of repairs that are redone with the failure of those repairs when they were first done. The second gives an explanation proposed by the consultant for the difference.

E   The first contrasts the success of repairs that are redone with the failure of those repairs when they were first done. Rather than giving evidence to challenge the consultant's explanation, the second provides that explanation itself.

The correct answer is D.

607. To reduce waste of raw materials, the government of Sperland is considering requiring household appliances to be broken down for salvage when discarded. To cover the cost of salvage, the government is planning to charge a fee, which would be imposed when the appliance is first sold. Imposing the fee at the time of salvage would reduce waste more effectively, however, because consumers tend to keep old appliances longer if they are faced with a fee for discarding them.

Which of the following, if true, most seriously weakens the argument?

(A) Increasing the cost of disposing of an appliance properly increases the incentive to dispose of it improperly.

(B) The fee provides manufacturers with no incentive to produce appliances that are more durable.

(C) For people who have bought new appliances recently, the salvage fee would not need to be paid for a number of years.

(D) People who sell their used, working appliances to others would not need to pay the salvage fee.

(E) Many nonfunctioning appliances that are currently discarded could be repaired at relatively little expense.

Evaluation of a Plan

Situation   A government is considering requiring household appliances to be broken down for salvage when discarded. To cover the salvage costs, the government plans to charge a fee on appliance sales.

Reasoning   *What would suggest that charging the fee at the time of salvage would less effectively reduce waste than charging the fee at the time of sale would?* The argument is that charging the fee at the time of salvage would reduce waste of raw materials because it would encourage consumers to keep their appliances longer before salvaging them. This argument could be weakened by pointing out other factors that might increase waste if the fee is charged at the time of salvage or reduce waste if the fee is charged at the time of sale.

A   **Correct.** This suggests that charging the fee at the time of salvage rather than the time of sale would encourage consumers to discard their appliances illegally, thereby increasing waste of raw materials by reducing the proportion of discarded appliances that are salvaged.

B   This factor would remain the same regardless of whether the fee was charged at the time of sale or the time of salvage.

C   This might be a reason for consumers to prefer the fee be charged at the time of salvage rather than the time of sale, but it does not suggest that charging the fee at the time of salvage would reduce waste less effectively.

D   This provides an additional reason to expect that charging the fee at the time of salvage would help reduce waste, so it strengthens rather than weakens the argument.

E   This would give consumers an additional reason to keep using their old appliances and postpone paying a fee at the time of salvage, so it strengthens rather than weakens the argument.

The correct answer is A.

608. When there is less rainfall than normal, the water level of Australian rivers falls and the rivers flow more slowly. Because algae whose habitat is river water grow best in slow-moving water, the amount of algae per unit of water generally increases when there has been little rain. By contrast, however, following a period of extreme drought, algae levels are low even in very slow-moving river water.

Which of the following, if true, does most to explain the contrast described above?

(A) During periods of extreme drought, the populations of some of the species that feed on algae tend to fall.

(B) The more slowly water moves, the more conducive its temperature is to the growth of algae.

(C) When algae populations reach very high levels, conditions within the river can become toxic for some of the other species that normally live there.

(D) Australian rivers dry up completely for short intervals in periods of extreme drought.

(E) Except during periods of extreme drought, algae levels tend to be higher in rivers in which the flow has been controlled by damming than in rivers that flow freely.

Argument Construction

Situation   When Australian rivers flow slowly due to little rain, algae populations in those rivers increase. But after periods of extreme drought, algae levels are low even in water moving at speeds that would normally show population increases.

Reasoning   *What would explain the contrast between algae levels in slow-moving water resulting from little rain and slow-moving water after a drought?* There must be some difference between what happens during periods in which there is simply less rainfall than normal and periods in which there is extreme drought, a difference that affects the algae population.

A   This indicates one of the consequences of drought, and slightly suggests that this might be due to a lower algae level. But it does nothing to explain why algae levels might be lower after a drought.

B   This could explain why some rivers that are slow-moving and have little water might have a high algae level—but not why the algae level is low in such rivers after a period of drought.

C   This explains why levels of other species might be low when algae populations are high, not why algae populations are high when there is little rain, but low following a period of extreme drought.

D   Correct. This statement properly identifies something that helps explain the contrast. According to the information given, the habitat of the algae under discussion is river water. If the river dries up, the algae will probably not survive. Then after the drought, algae population levels would likely take a while to rise again.

E   This emphasizes that there is a contrast between what happens to algae during periods of extreme drought and what happens to them at other times, but it does not help explain that contrast.

The correct answer is D.

609. Increased use of incineration is sometimes advocated as a safe way to dispose of chemical waste. But opponents of incineration point to the 40 incidents involving unexpected releases of dangerous chemical agents that were reported just last year at two existing incinerators commissioned to destroy a quantity of chemical waste material. Since designs for proposed new incinerators include no additional means of preventing such releases, leaks will only become more prevalent if use of incineration increases.

Which of the following, if true, most seriously weakens the argument?

(A) At the two incinerators at which leaks were reported, staff had had only cursory training on the proper procedures for incinerating chemical waste.

(B) Other means of disposing of chemical waste, such as chemical neutralization processes, have not been proven safer than incineration.

(C) The capacity of existing incinerators is sufficient to allow for increased incineration of chemical waste without any need for new incinerators.

(D) The frequency of reports of unexpected releases of chemical agents at newly built incinerators is about the same as the frequency at older incinerators.

(E) In only three of the reported incidents of unexpected chemical leaks did the releases extend outside the property on which the incinerators were located.

Argument Evaluation

Situation   Last year, at two chemical waste incinerators, there were forty reported incidents involving unexpected releases of dangerous chemicals. Designs for proposed new incinerators include no additional safeguards against such releases. Therefore, increased use of incineration will likely make such releases more prevalent.

Reasoning   *What would undermine the support provided for the conclusion that leaks will become more prevalent if more chemical waste is disposed of through incineration?* The argument draws a general conclusion about chemical waste incineration from evidence about only two particular incinerators. This reasoning would be undermined by any evidence that the leaks at those two incinerators were the result of something other than insufficient safeguards against such releases.

A   **Correct.** If the staff training at the two incinerators was cursory, then the leaks may have been the results of staff not knowing how to use safeguards with which the incinerators are equipped that, if properly used, would have prevented the release of dangerous chemicals. Therefore, if staff at newer incinerators will be better trained, leaks might not become more prevalent even if chemical waste incineration becomes more common.

B   Other chemical waste disposal methods may be safer than incineration even if no one has proven so; and even if they're not safer overall, they may involve fewer leaks.

C   Continuing to use existing incinerators might well produce just as many leaks as switching to new incinerators would.

D   This suggests that new incinerators produce as many leaks as older incinerators do, a finding that provides additional evidence that increased incineration even with proposed new incinerators would lead to more leaks.

E   The argument is not about how far the releases from leaks extend, only about how many of them are likely to occur.

The correct answer is A.

610. Public health expert: **Increasing the urgency of a public health message may be counterproductive**. In addition to irritating the majority who already behave responsibly, **it may undermine all government pronouncements on health by convincing people that such messages are overly cautious**. And there is no reason to believe that those who ignore measured voices will listen to shouting.

The two sections in **boldface** play which of the following roles in the public health expert's argument?

(A) The first is a conclusion for which support is provided, but is not the argument's main conclusion; the second is an unsupported premise supporting the argument's main conclusion.

(B) The first is a premise supporting the only explicit conclusion; so is the second.

(C) The first is the argument's main conclusion; the second supports that conclusion and is itself a conclusion for which support is provided.

(D) The first is a premise supporting the argument's only conclusion; the second is that conclusion.

(E) The first is the argument's only explicit conclusion; the second is a premise supporting that conclusion.

Argument Construction

Situation   A public health expert argues against increasing the urgency of public health messages by pointing out negative effects that may arise from such an increase, as well as by questioning its efficacy.

Reasoning   *What roles are played in the argument by the two claims in boldface?* The first claim in boldface states that increasing the urgency of public health messages may be counterproductive. After making this claim, the public health expert mentions two specific reasons this could be so: it could irritate people who already behave responsibly, and it could convince people that all public health messages are too cautious. (The latter reason in the second claim in boldface). The phrase [*i*]*n addition to* indicates that neither claim in the second sentence is intended to support or explain the other. However, since each claim in the second sentence gives a reason to believe the claim in the first sentence, each independently supports the first sentence as a conclusion. The word [*a*]*nd* beginning the third sentence reveals that its intended role in the argument is the same as that of the two claims in the second sentence.

A   Everything stated after the first sentence is intended to help support it, so the first sentence is the argument's main conclusion.

B   Everything stated after the first sentence is intended to help support it, so the first sentence is a conclusion, not a premise.

C   Each of the three claims in the second and third sentences is presented as an independent reason to accept the general claim in the first sentence. Therefore, nothing in the passage is intended to support the second statement in boldface as a conclusion.

D   Everything stated after the first sentence is intended to help support it, so the first sentence is a conclusion, not a premise.

E   **Correct.** Each of the three claims in the second and third sentences is presented as an independent reason to accept the general claim in the first sentence. Thus, each of those claims is a premise supporting the claim in the first sentence as the argument's only conclusion.

The correct answer is E.

611. Several industries have recently switched at least partly from older technologies powered by fossil fuels to new technologies powered by electricity. It is thus evident that less fossil fuel is being used as a result of the operations of these industries than would have been used if these industries had retained their older technologies.

Which of the following, if true, most strengthens the argument above?

(A) Many of the industries that have switched at least partly to the new technologies have increased their output.

(B) Less fossil fuel was used to manufacture the machinery employed in the new technologies than was originally used to manufacture the machinery employed in the older technologies.

(C) More electricity is used by those industries that have switched at least partly to the new technologies than by those industries that have not switched.

(D) Some of the industries that have switched at least partly to the new technologies still use primarily technologies that are powered by fossil fuels.

(E) The amount of fossil fuel used to generate the electricity needed to power the new technologies is less than the amount that would have been used to power the older technologies.

Argument Evaluation

Situation   Several industries have now switched, at least partly, to technologies using electricity rather than fossil fuels. Thus, less fossil fuel will be consumed as a result of the operation of these industries than otherwise would have been.

Reasoning   *Which option most strengthens the argument?* One way to strengthen an argument is to eliminate or minimize one of its flaws or weaknesses. Because the conclusion is stated in terms of "fossil fuel consumed as a result of the operation of these industries," the claim would encompass even any fossil fuel that might be used to generate the electricity that the newer technologies use. Yet the premise of the argument does not address this issue. So the argument is strengthened if it turns out that less fossil fuel was used to produce the electricity than would have been used to power the older technologies.

A   In an indirect way, this answer choice slightly weakens rather than strengthens the argument. For if fossil fuels are used to produce the electricity now used by the industries and if it is because of these newer technologies that output has increased, the argument's conclusion is less likely.

B   It does not matter how much fossil fuel was used to manufacture the older technologies originally. That has no bearing on whether more fossil fuel would have been expended as a result of the continued operation of the industries if the partial switch to newer technologies had not occurred.

C   This is what we would expect, but it in no way strengthens the argument.

D   This may seem to weaken the argument by indicating that the switch from older technologies will have less of an impact on fossil fuel consumption by these industries than we might have assumed. But since the conclusion makes no claim about how much consumption has been reduced, it is not clear that this option has any bearing on the strength of the argument one way or the other.

E   **Correct.** As explained in the Reasoning section above, the conclusion is stated in terms of "fossil fuel consumed as a result of the operation of these industries," so the claim would encompass even any fossil fuel that might be used to generate the electricity that the newer technologies use. If at least as much fossil fuel must be used to generate the needed electricity, the conclusion that less fossil fuel is used does not follow. Yet the premise of the argument does not address this issue. So the argument is strengthened if it turns out that less fossil fuel is used to produce the electricity than would have been used to power the older technologies.

The correct answer is E.

612. The difference in average annual income in favor of employees who have college degrees, compared with those who do not have such degrees, doubled between 1980 and 1990. Some analysts have hypothesized that increased competition between employers for employees with college degrees drove up income for such employees.

Which of the following, if true, most seriously undermines the explanation described above?

(A) During the 1980s a growing percentage of college graduates, unable to find jobs requiring a college degree, took unskilled jobs.

(B) The average age of all employees increased slightly during the 1980s.

(C) The unemployment rate changed very little throughout most of the 1980s.

(D) From 1980 to 1990 the difference in average income between employees with advanced degrees and those with bachelor's degrees also increased.

(E) During the 1980s there were some employees with no college degree who earned incomes comparable to the top incomes earned by employees with a college degree.

Argument Evaluation

Situation   The amount by which average annual income for employees with college degrees exceeds that for employees without such degrees doubled between 1980 and 1990.

Reasoning   *What evidence would most strongly suggest that increased competition among employers for employees with college degrees does not explain the relative increase in those employees' incomes?* Such increased competition could not explain the relative increase in income for employees with college degrees if the competition did not actually increase, or if such competition occurred but did not result in employers paying higher wages or salaries, or if the increase in competition to hire employees without college degrees was even greater. So evidence that any of those conditions existed would undermine the analysts' explanation.

A   **Correct.** This suggests that the supply of college graduates grew relative to employers' demand for them, and hence that employers' competition for college-educated employees did not actually increase.

B   The average age might have increased equally for employees with college degrees and for those without them, so the increase is not clearly relevant to explaining why the difference between these two groups' average incomes grew.

C   Even if the overall unemployment rate did not change, competition for college-educated employees could have increased while competition for other employees decreased.

D   This statement gives information comparing income trends among two groups of those with college degrees, and is irrelevant to the comparison of income trends for those with college degrees and those without college degrees.

E   Even if there was strong competition and high pay for certain unusual types of employees without college degrees, increasing competition for employees with college degrees might have explained the overall growing difference in average pay between employees with college degrees and those without.

The correct answer is A.

613. Which of the following most logically completes the passage?

According to the last pre-election poll in Whippleton, most voters believe that the three problems government needs to address, in order of importance, are pollution, crime, and unemployment. Yet in the election, candidates from parties perceived as strongly against pollution were defeated, while those elected were all from parties with a history of opposing legislation designed to reduce pollution. These results should not be taken to indicate that the poll was inaccurate, however, since _____.

(A) some voters in Whippleton do not believe that pollution needs to be reduced

(B) every candidate who was defeated had a strong antipollution record

(C) there were no issues other than crime, unemployment, and pollution on which the candidates had significant differences of opinion

(D) all the candidates who were elected were perceived as being stronger against both crime and unemployment than the candidates who were defeated

(E) many of the people who voted in the election refused to participate in the poll

Argument Construction

Situation   A pre-election poll indicated that most voters believed the three problems government needs to address, in order of importance, are pollution, crime, and unemployment. But in the election, candidates from parties with a history of opposing anti-pollution legislation beat candidates from parties perceived as more strongly against pollution.

Reasoning   *What would most help explain how the poll might have been accurate despite the election results?* Since the poll indicated that voters were most concerned about pollution, it suggested that candidates from anti-pollution parties would be more likely to be elected, other things being equal—and yet those candidates were not elected. There are many possible explanations for this outcome that are compatible with the poll having been accurate. For example, voters might have been swayed by the candidates' personalities, qualifications, or advertising more than by their positions on the issues. Or some candidates might have convinced voters that their personal positions on the issues were different from those of their parties. Or voters might have chosen candidates based on their positions on crime and unemployment, considering those issues together more important than pollution alone. Any statement suggesting that any such factors explained the election results would logically complete the passage by providing a reason to believe that the poll could have been accurate despite those results.

A   If the number of voters who did not believe that pollution needed to be reduced was large enough to explain the election results, then the poll was probably inaccurate. So this does not explain how the poll might have been accurate despite those results.

B   This eliminates the possibility that candidates were defeated for having weak antipollution records conflicting with their parties' antipollution stances, so it eliminates one explanation of how the poll might have been accurate despite the election results. Thus, it slightly weakens the conclusion of the argument instead of providing a premise to support it.

C   This eliminates the possibility that differences of opinion among the candidates on these other issues might explain the election results, but it does not explain how the poll could have been accurate despite the election results.

D   Correct. The poll indicated that voters believed that the government needs to address crime and unemployment as well as pollution. So if the poll was accurate, the election outcome might have resulted from voters considering candidates' positions on crime and unemployment to be jointly more important than their positions on pollution.

E   If anything, this provides a reason to doubt that the poll accurately reflected voters' opinions. It does not explain how the poll might have accurately reflected those opinions despite the election results.

The correct answer is D.

614. Manufacturing plants in Arundia have recently been acquired in substantial numbers by investors from abroad. Arundian politicians are proposing legislative action to stop such investment, justifying the proposal by arguing that foreign investors, opportunistically exploiting a recent fall in the value of the Arundian currency, were able to buy Arundian assets at less than their true value.

Which of the following, if true, casts the most serious doubt on the adequacy of the Arundian politicians' justification for the proposed legislation?

(A) The Arundian government originally welcomed the fall in the value of the Arundian currency because the fall made Arundian exports more competitive on international markets.

(B) Foreign investors who acquired Arundian manufacturing plants generally did so with no intention of keeping and running those plants over the long term.

(C) Without the recent fall in the value of the Arundian currency, many of the Arundian assets bought by foreign investors would have been beyond the financial reach of those investors.

(D) In Concordia, a country broadly similar to Arundia, the share of manufacturing assets that is foreign-controlled is 60 percent higher than it is in Arundia.

(E) The true value of an investment is determined by the value of the profits from it, and the low value of the Arundian currency has depressed the value of any profits earned by foreign investors from Arundian assets.

Argument Evaluation

Situation   After a recent fall in the value of Arundian currency, foreign investors have been acquiring many Arundian manufacturing plants. Arundian politicians are proposing legislation to stop such investment.

Reasoning   *What would most undermine the Arundian politicians' justification for the proposed legislation?* The politicians are justifying their proposal by claiming that foreign investors have been exploiting the fall in the currency's value by buying Arundian assets at less than their *true value* (whatever that means). Any evidence that their claim is false or meaningless would undermine their justification for the proposal, as would any evidence that the claim, even if true, does not provide a good reason to stop the foreign investments.

A   This suggests that the foreign investors got a good deal on the manufacturing plants, since it provides evidence that those plants will now be more competitive and profitable. So, if anything, it supports the politicians' justification for their proposal rather than undermining it.

B   This suggests that the foreign investors generally believe the manufacturing plants are undervalued, and intend to sell them at a profit as soon as the currency rises enough. So it supports the politicians' justification for their proposal rather than undermining it.

C   This suggests that the recent fall in the currency's value made Arundian assets cost less than usual for foreign investors, thus arguably allowing the investors to buy the assets at less than their *true value*. So, if anything, it supports the politicians' justification for their proposal rather than undermining it.

D   The Arundian politicians might consider the example of Concordia to be a warning of the disaster that could befall Arundia unless the legislation is enacted. So the situation in Concordia might be cited as support for the politicians' justification of their proposal.

E   **Correct.** This implies that the fall in the Arundian currency's value has reduced the *true value* of Arundian manufacturing plants and any profits they may make, so it undermines the politicians' claim that the foreign investors exploited the fall in the currency's value to acquire the plants for less than their *true value*.

The correct answer is E.

615. Proposal: Carbon dioxide and methane in the atmosphere block the escape of heat into space. So emission of these "greenhouse" gases contributes to global warming. In order to reduce global warming, emission of greenhouse gases needs to be reduced. Therefore, the methane now emitted from open landfills should instead be burned to produce electricity.

Objection: The burning of methane generates carbon dioxide that is released into the atmosphere.

Which of the following, if true, most adequately counters the objection made to the proposal?

(A) Every time a human being or other mammal exhales, there is some carbon dioxide released into the air.

(B) The conversion of methane to electricity would occur at a considerable distance from the landfills.

(C) The methane that is used to generate electricity would generally be used as a substitute for a fuel that does not produce any greenhouse gases when burned.

(D) Methane in the atmosphere is more effective in blocking the escape of heat from the Earth than is carbon dioxide.

(E) The amount of methane emitted from the landfills could be reduced if the materials whose decomposition produces methane were not discarded, but recycled.

Evaluation of a Plan

Situation   The greenhouse gases methane and carbon dioxide trap heat in Earth's atmosphere and warm the planet. To reduce that global warming, emission of these gases needs to be reduced. For these reasons, someone has proposed that the methane emitted from landfills should be captured and burned to produce electricity. However, an objection to the proposal is that burning methane causes the release of carbon dioxide (another greenhouse gas) into the atmosphere.

Reasoning   *What would be a logically effective response to counter the objection to the proposal?* It is true that burning methane causes the release of carbon dioxide. However, if burning methane from landfills to generate electricity helps reduce net global warming, then the objection would not provide a good reason for rejecting the proposal. It turns out that, as a greenhouse gas, methane has a much more powerful impact on global warming than does carbon dioxide. This fact provides strong support for rejecting the objection to the proposal.

A   Clearly the effects referred to here are unavoidable in the lives of humans and other mammals on Earth. The emissions that must be curtailed to avoid global warming are those that are avoidable as a result of voluntary human activity.

B   This suggests that there could be costs in implementing the proposal, but the possibility of such costs does not, by itself, counter the proposal. Such costs could presumably be reduced by better siting of landfills and electricity-generation plants.

C   This information, if true, would not counter the objection and would provide some support for it. We would still need some reason to believe that allowing carbon dioxide emissions from burning methane would be better than continuing to release methane itself. In the absence of such a reason, we should expect no net greenhouse-gas-related benefit in substituting the landfill-emitted methane for a fuel that produces no greenhouse gases.

D   **Correct.** This information provides a strong rebuttal of the objection. Since methane has more powerful global-warming effects than does carbon dioxide, there is a net greenhouse-gas-reduction benefit in generating electricity by burning methane from landfills even though that burning itself emits the greenhouse gas carbon dioxide.

E   Undoubtedly it would be better to reduce the amount of methane that landfills will generate in the future. However, the possibility of doing so tells us nothing about whether the potential emission of carbon dioxide provides a reason not to burn the methane that is currently emitted from landfills.

The correct answer is D.

616. Proposed new safety rules for the Beach City airport would lengthen considerably the minimum time between takeoffs from the airport. In consequence, the airport would be able to accommodate 10 percent fewer flights than currently use the airport daily. The city's operating budget depends heavily on taxes generated by tourist spending, and most of the tourists come by plane. Therefore, the proposed new safety rules, if adopted, will reduce the revenue available for the operating budget.

The argument depends on assuming which of the following?

(A) There are no periods of the day during which the interval between flights taking off from the airport is significantly greater than the currently allowed minimum.

(B) Few, if any, of the tourists who use the Beach City airport do so when their main destination is a neighboring community and not Beach City itself.

(C) If the proposed safety rules are adopted, the reduction in tourist numbers will not result mainly from a reduction in the number of tourists who spend relatively little in Beach City.

(D) Increasing the minimum time between takeoffs is the only way to achieve necessary safety improvements without a large expenditure by the city government on airport enhancements.

(E) The response to the adoption of the new safety rules would not include an increase in the number of passengers per flight.

Argument Construction

Situation   Proposed safety rules for a city airport would reduce the number of daily flights the airport can accommodate. The city's operating budget depends heavily on taxes generated by tourists, who mostly come by plane. Therefore, adopting the safety rules will result in lower revenue available for the operating budget.

Reasoning   *What must be true in order for the cited facts to support the conclusion that the proposed rules would reduce the revenue for the operating budget?* The implicit reasoning is that since the rules would reduce the number of flights that can be accommodated, they would thereby reduce the number of tourists arriving by plane, which in turn would reduce the tax revenue that tourist spending generates for the operating budget. This assumes that the actual number of daily flights would fall along with the number that the airport can accommodate; that fewer daily flights would mean fewer people flying into the airport; that fewer people flying into the airport would mean fewer tourists flying into the airport; that fewer tourists flying into the airport would mean fewer tourists visiting the city; that fewer tourists visiting the city would mean less taxable spending by tourists; and that less taxable spending by tourists would mean less revenue overall for the operating budget.

A   Even if flights depart the airport less frequently during some periods of the day, increasing the minimum time between flights at busy times of day could reduce the total number of daily flights from the airport.

B   Even if half the tourists flying into the airport were bound for other nearby towns, the other half could still spend enough in town to generate lots of revenue for the operating budget.

C   It is possible that most tourists spend relatively little in the city, but a few spend a lot. In that case, even if a reduction in tourist numbers resulted mainly from a declining number of tourists who spend relatively little, it could also greatly reduce the already small number of tourists who spend a lot.

D   This suggests that the proposed rules might be financially better for the city than any alternative way to improve safety, whereas the argument's conclusion is that the proposed rules are financially disadvantageous.

E   **Correct.** If adopting the proposed rules would result in a large increase in the number of passengers per flight, fewer daily flights would not necessarily mean fewer passengers or fewer tourists overall.

The correct answer is E.

617. The introduction of new drugs into the market is frequently prevented by a shortage of human subjects for the clinical trials needed to show that the drugs are safe and effective. Since the lives and health of people in future generations may depend on treatments that are currently experimental, practicing physicians are morally in the wrong when, in the absence of any treatment proven to be effective, they fail to encourage suitable patients to volunteer for clinical trials.

Which of the following, if true, casts most doubt on the conclusion of the argument?

(A) Many drugs undergoing clinical trials are intended for the treatment of conditions for which there is currently no effective treatment.

(B) Patients do not share the physician's professional concern for public health, but everyone has a moral obligation to alleviate suffering when able to do so.

(C) Usually, half the patients in a clinical trial serve as a control group and receive a nonactive drug in place of the drug being tested.

(D) An experimental drug cannot legally be made available to patients unless those patients are subjects in clinical trials of the drug.

(E) Physicians have an overriding moral and legal duty to care for the health and safety of their current patients.

Argument Evaluation

Situation   A shortage of human subjects for clinical trials needed to show that new drugs are safe and effective often prevents those drugs from being introduced into the market. The lives and health of future generations may depend on treatments that are now experimental.

Reasoning   *What would cast doubt on the judgment that doctors are morally obligated to encourage their patients to volunteer for clinical trials?* Note that the argument's conclusion, unlike its premises, is a moral judgment. This judgment could be cast into doubt by a moral principle that would be likely to conflict with it under the conditions described. For example, a principle suggesting that it is sometimes morally unacceptable for doctors to encourage their patients to volunteer for clinical trials would also suggest that they are not morally obligated to encourage their patients to volunteer for clinical trials, since anything morally obligatory must also be morally acceptable.

A   If anything, this highlights how important it is to ensure that these drugs undergo clinical trials to benefit future generations, so it supports rather than casts doubt on the argument's conclusion.

B   This suggests that patients are morally obligated to volunteer for clinical trials to help prevent suffering in future generations. If anything, this supports the claim that doctors are morally obligated to encourage their patients to volunteer.

C   The clinical trial will probably not harm any patients in the control group, yet their participation will benefit future generations. So, if anything, this supports the claim that doctors should encourage their patients to volunteer.

D   This legal barrier makes it even more essential for the drugs to undergo clinical trials in order to benefit patients, so it supports rather than casts doubt on the argument's conclusion.

E   **Correct.** Since the experimental drugs' safety is being tested during the trials, the drugs may prove unsafe for subjects in the trials. If doctors have an overriding moral duty to keep their current patients safe, then it may be morally unacceptable for them to encourage those patients to volunteer for the trials.

The correct answer is E.

618. As a construction material, bamboo is as strong as steel and sturdier than concrete. Moreover, in tropical areas bamboo is a much less expensive construction material than either steel or concrete and is always readily available. In tropical areas, therefore, building with bamboo makes better economic sense than building with steel or concrete, except where land values are high.

Which of the following, if true, most helps to explain the exception noted above?

(A) Buildings constructed of bamboo are less likely to suffer earthquake damage than are steel and concrete buildings.

(B) Bamboo is unsuitable as a building material for multistory buildings.

(C) In order to protect it from being damaged by termites and beetles, bamboo must be soaked, at some expense, in a preservative.

(D) In some tropical areas, bamboo is used to make the scaffolding that is used during large construction projects.

(E) Bamboo growing in an area where land values are increasing is often cleared to make way for construction.

Argument Construction

Situation   Bamboo is as strong as steel and sturdier than concrete when used as a construction material. In tropical areas, bamboo is much less expensive and is always readily available.

Reasoning   *What explains the exception specified in the conclusion?* The argument's conclusion is that in tropical areas bamboo is a more economical building material than steel or concrete, *except where land values are high.* The information in the passage makes clear why bamboo is a more economical building material in tropical areas than are concrete or steel. So the question is: Why must an exception be made for areas where land values are high? Multistory buildings are particularly desirable in areas where land values are high, but bamboo may not be suitable for such buildings.

A   This explains why bamboo would be preferable to steel or concrete in tropical areas especially prone to earthquakes. However, there is no clear connection to be made between areas where land values are high and areas especially prone to earthquakes.

B   **Correct.** Multistory buildings provide a greater area of floor space for a given site area, and in that sense are more economical. A single-story building with the same floor space will occupy a much bigger site, so the higher the land values, the more likely it is that a multistory building will be built on that land. Thus, given this information, bamboo is less suitable for areas where land values are high.

C   This undermines, to some extent, the claim that bamboo is an economical building material. But it does nothing to explain why it would be less economical specifically in areas where land values are high.

D   This is irrelevant. Bamboo is used to build scaffolding for construction projects and as a building material for permanent structures. There is no way to infer from this that bamboo is less economical specifically in areas where land values are high.

E   The fact that bamboo is cleared from an area to make room for construction in no way implies that bamboo would not be a suitable and economical building material for the area once it has been cleared.

The correct answer is B.

619. The country of Virodia has, until now, been barely self-sufficient in both meat and grain. Greater prosperity there has gone hand in hand with steadily increasing per capita consumption of meat, and it takes several pounds of grain used as feed to produce one pound of meat. Per capita income is almost certain to rise further, yet increases in domestic grain production are unlikely.

Which of the following is most strongly supported by the information given?

(A) Some land in Virodia that is currently used for grain production will soon be turned into pastureland for grazing cattle for meat.

(B) In the future, per capita income in Virodia is unlikely to increase as rapidly as it has in the past.

(C) In Virodia, the amount of grain it takes to produce one pound of meat is likely to increase in coming years.

(D) Grain is soon likely to make up a larger proportion of the average Virodian's diet than ever before.

(E) Virodia is likely to become an importer of grain or meat or both.

Argument Construction

Situation   Virodia has been barely self-sufficient in both meat and grain. Recently per capita meat consumption in Virodia has been increasing. Recent increases in per capita income will probably continue, but production of grain will probably not increase. It takes several pounds of grain to produce each pound of meat.

Reasoning   *What claim is most strongly supported by the given information?* We are told that producing a pound of meat requires several pounds of grain. If (1) more meat is going to be consumed in Virodia, (2) more grain will not be produced, and (3) there is no excess grain, then Virodia will have to import meat, or import grain so it can produce more meat, or both.

A   The information given says nothing about pastureland for grazing cattle, and it provides no evidence that meat producers would be able to produce more meat per area of land by using the land for pasture than by using it for grain production. Furthermore, there is no evidence that the meat in Virodia is produced from cattle rather than from some other types of animals that are fed on grain. Given that the information suggests that there may be an increase in demand for grain, it seems unlikely that there will be a reduction in the amount of land used to produce grain.

B   The information says that per capita income is likely to increase and that greater prosperity correlates positively with greater meat consumption. It provides no reason to think that the correlation between rising income and increasing meat consumption occurs only with more rapid rises in income.

C   Nothing in the information given provides any evidence as to whether the amount of grain needed to produce a pound of meat will change.

D   The information indicates that per capita meat consumption is likely to continue to increase, which actually supports the opposite of what this answer choice states.

E   **Correct.** The information indicates that grain production will probably not increase. We are told however that meat consumption will increase. Meat production in Virodia requires a substantial amount of grain, and we know that Virodia produces no excess grain or meat. This indicates that Virodia will likely have to become an importer of meat, or, if not, it will have to become an importer of grain so that it will be able to produce more meat.

The correct answer is E.

620. Newspaper editors should not allow reporters to write the headlines for their own stories. The reason for this is that, while the headlines that reporters themselves write are often clever, what typically makes them clever is that they allude to little-known information that is familiar to the reporter but that never appears explicitly in the story itself.

Which of the following, if true, most strengthens the argument?

(A) The reporter who writes a story is usually better placed than the reporter's editor is to judge what the story's most newsworthy features are.

(B) To write a headline that is clever, a person must have sufficient understanding of the story that the headline accompanies.

(C) Most reporters rarely bother to find out how other reporters have written stories and headlines about the same events that they themselves have covered.

(D) For virtually any story that a reporter writes, there are at least a few people who know more about the story's subject matter than does the reporter.

(E) The kind of headlines that newspaper editors want are those that anyone who has read a reporter's story in its entirety will recognize as clever.

Argument Evaluation

Situation   The headlines newspaper reporters write for their own stories are often clever only because they allude to little-known information that never appears explicitly in the stories themselves.

Reasoning   *What would most help the argument support the conclusion that newspaper editors should not allow reporters to write headlines for their own stories?* The argument's only explicit premise is that the headlines newspaper reporters write for their own stories are often clever only because they allude to little-known information that never appears explicitly in the stories themselves. In order for this premise to support the conclusion that newspaper editors should not allow reporters to write their own headlines, it would be helpful to be given a reason why editors should avoid headlines alluding to such little-known information.

A   This suggests that reporters are likely to write better headlines for their stories than editors are, so it weakens the argument that editors should not allow reporters to write their own headlines.

B   Since a reporter who wrote a story is likely to understand that story well, this does not provide a reason why editors should not allow reporters to write their own headlines.

C   If most reporters did what is suggested, they could perhaps hone their headline-writing skills—unless almost all reporters are weak in such skills, as suggested in the given information. The fact that they do not bother to do so may help explain why reporters' headline-writing skills are weak. An explanation of why this is so does not provide additional support for the argument's conclusion.

D   The people who know more about a story's subject matter than the reporter writing the story might be just as likely to see the cleverness of allusions to little-known information as the reporters are. So, to the extent that this is relevant at all, it slightly weakens the argument by suggesting that obscurely clever headlines sometimes function as intended.

E   **Correct.** The argument's explicit premise suggests that typically a reporter's headline for his or her own story cannot be recognized as clever by a reader who has read the whole story. So if editors want headlines that anyone who has read the accompanying stories would recognize as clever, they have a reason not to let reporters write the headlines.

The correct answer is E.

621. Scientists have modified feed corn genetically, increasing its resistance to insect pests. Farmers who tried out the genetically modified corn last season applied less insecticide to their corn fields and still got yields comparable to those they would have gotten with ordinary corn. Ordinary corn seed, however, costs less, and what these farmers saved on insecticide rarely exceeded their extra costs for seed. Therefore, for most feed-corn farmers, switching to genetically modified seed would be unlikely to increase profits.

Which of the following would it be most useful to know in order to evaluate the argument?

(A) Whether there are insect pests that sometimes reduce feed-corn yields, but against which commonly used insecticides and the genetic modification are equally ineffective

(B) Whether the price that farmers receive for feed corn has remained steady over the past few years

(C) Whether the insecticides typically used on feed corn tend to be more expensive than insecticides typically used on other crops

(D) Whether most of the farmers who tried the genetically modified corn last season applied more insecticide than was actually necessary

(E) Whether, for most farmers who plant feed corn, it is their most profitable crop

Argument Evaluation

Situation   Farmers who grew feed corn genetically engineered to be pest resistant got yields comparable to those of farmers growing ordinary feed corn, but did so while using less pesticide. Since the amount saved on pesticide was rarely in excess of the extra costs for the genetically modified corn, most farmers will probably not increase profits by choosing the genetically engineered variety.

Reasoning   *Which would be most useful to know in evaluating the argument?* To answer a question such as this, one should look for information that would strengthen or weaken the argument. If one had information that the farmers growing the genetically modified corn could have increased their yields last year at lower cost, this would be helpful in evaluating the argument, because this would show that the argument is weak.

A   It does not matter to the argument whether there are pests against which pesticides and genetic resistance are equally ineffective, because that is compatible with there being pests against which they are not equally effective.

B   Whether prices of feed corn go up or down affects the comparison groups equally.

C   The relative cost of insecticides for other crops has no bearing on the argument because the argument is concerned with only feed corn.

D   Correct. This option provides the information that it would be most useful to know in evaluating the argument. It shows that farmers growing genetically modified corn last year could have attained higher profits than they in fact did.

E   The argument concerns only the relative profitability of growing one variety of feed corn versus another.

The correct answer is D.

622. Debater: The average amount of overtime per month worked by an employee in the manufacturing division of the Haglut Corporation is 14 hours. Most employees of the Haglut Corporation work in the manufacturing division. Furthermore, the average amount of overtime per month worked by any employee in the company generally does not fluctuate much from month to month. Therefore, each month, most employees of the Haglut Corporation almost certainly work at least some overtime.

The debater's argument is most vulnerable to criticism on which of these grounds?

(A) It takes for granted that the manufacturing division is a typical division of the corporation with regard to the average amount of overtime its employees work each month.

(B) It takes for granted that if a certain average amount of overtime is worked each month by each employee of the Haglut Corporation, then approximately the same amount of overtime must be worked each month by each employee of the manufacturing division.

(C) It confuses a claim from which the argument's conclusion about the Haglut Corporation would necessarily follow with a claim that would follow from the argument's conclusion only with a high degree of probability.

(D) It overlooks the possibility that even if, on average, a certain amount of overtime is worked by the members of some group, many members of that group may work no overtime at all.

(E) It overlooks the possibility that even if most employees of the corporation work some overtime each month, any one corporate employee may, in some months, work no overtime.

Argument Evaluation

Situation   Most of the employees of the Haglut Corporation work in the manufacturing division, where employees average 14 hours per month in overtime. The average amount of overtime per month for employees at Haglut does not fluctuate much from month to month.

Reasoning   *What is the argument's greatest weakness?* The argument's conclusion is that almost certainly each month most of the employees of Haglut work at least some overtime. Answer choice (D) identifies the argument's greatest weakness because it points out how the conclusion of the argument could be false even if all of the supporting information were true. For example, it could be that less than half of the employees work any overtime at all, but those that do work overtime work much more than 14 hours per month.

A   The argument leaves open the possibility that in some divisions of the corporation, the average monthly overtime of its employees is quite different from 14 hours, even if (as the argument states) that average does not change much from month to month.

B   The argument does not assume that there is a monthly amount of overtime worked by each employee of the manufacturing division equivalent to the company-wide average monthly overtime per employee.

C   This does not identify a weakness that can be detected in the argument. Since the claims mentioned here are not specified, the passage provides no evidence that clearly indicates that this type of confusion is playing a role in the argument.

D   Correct. The argument ignores the possibility that most of the employees of Haglut work no overtime at all in a particular month—which is quite consistent with the argument's assertion that the average number of monthly overtime hours per employee within the manufacturing division is 14.

E   The possibility described by this is not overlooked by the argument, because this possibility is consistent with the conclusion. It could easily be that most employees of the corporation work some overtime each month—as the conclusion envisions—but that there are always some employees who do not work any overtime.

The correct answer is D.

623. Proponents of the recently introduced tax on sales of new luxury boats had argued that a tax of this sort would be an equitable way to increase government revenue because the admittedly heavy tax burden would fall only on wealthy people and neither they nor anyone else would suffer any economic hardship. In fact, however, 20 percent of the workers employed by manufacturers of luxury boats have lost their jobs as a direct result of this tax.

The information given, if true, most strongly supports which of the following?

(A) The market for luxury boats would have collapsed even if the new tax on luxury boats had been lower.

(B) The new tax would produce a net gain in tax revenue for the government only if the yearly total revenue that it generates exceeds the total of any yearly tax-revenue decrease resulting from the workers' loss of jobs.

(C) Because many people never buy luxury items, imposing a sales tax on luxury items is the kind of legislative action that does not cost incumbent legislators much popular support.

(D) Before the tax was instituted, luxury boats were largely bought by people who were not wealthy.

(E) Taxes can be equitable only if their burden is evenly distributed over the entire population.

Argument Construction

Situation   Proponents of a recently introduced tax on sales of new luxury boats argued that it would be an equitable way to increase government revenue because the tax would fall only on the wealthy and cause no economic hardship. But because of the tax, 20 percent of luxury-boat manufacturing workers have lost their jobs.

Reasoning   *What conclusion do the statements about the proponents' argument and the tax's effects support?* Since the tax caused many workers to lose their jobs, apparently the proponents were incorrect in asserting that it would cause no one to suffer any hardship. Thus, their justification for concluding that the tax is an equitable way to increase government revenue is factually inaccurate, casting doubt on that conclusion.

A   The passage indicates that the tax directly caused a significant decrease (though not necessarily a collapse) in the market for luxury boats. But the passage contains no evidence about whether such a decrease might not have occurred if the new tax had been somewhat lower.

B   **Correct.** Since the tax caused the workers to lose their jobs, it might have made the government lose revenue from payroll taxes that the laid-off workers would have paid if they had kept their jobs. So if the yearly total revenue generated directly and indirectly by the tax were less than those total yearly payroll taxes and any other tax revenue that was lost as a result of the tax, the tax would have caused a net loss in tax revenue.

C   The passage contains no information about what types of legislative actions cost, or do not cost, incumbent legislators popular support.

D   Although the passage suggests that some of the tax proponents' assumptions were wrong, it contains no information suggesting that those proponents were wrong in thinking that luxury boats are purchased mainly by wealthy people.

E   The passage does not provide any basis for determining what makes a tax equitable or about whether the luxury boat tax is equitable. The tax's proponents evidently felt that a tax whose burden falls only on the wealthy rather than evenly on the entire population can be equitable.

The correct answer is B.

624. In Wareland last year, 16 percent of licensed drivers under 21 and 11 percent of drivers ages 21–24 were in serious accidents. By contrast, only 3 percent of licensed drivers 65 and older were involved in serious accidents. These figures clearly show that the greater experience and developed habits of caution possessed by drivers in the 65-and-older group make them far safer behind the wheel than the younger drivers are.

Which of the following is an assumption on which the argument depends?

(A) Drivers 65 and older do not, on average, drive very many fewer miles per year than drivers 24 and younger.

(B) Drivers 65 and older do not constitute a significantly larger percentage of licensed drivers in Wareland than drivers ages 18–24 do.

(C) Drivers 65 and older are less likely than are drivers 24 and younger to drive during weather conditions that greatly increase the risk of accidents.

(D) The difference between the accident rate of drivers under 21 and of those ages 21–24 is attributable to the greater driving experience of those in the older group.

(E) There is no age bracket for which the accident rate is lower than it is for licensed drivers 65 and older.

Argument Evaluation

Situation   Last year in Wareland, a much higher percentage of drivers 24 and under than of drivers 65 and older were in serious accidents.

Reasoning   *What must be true for the observation about the accident rates to support the conclusion that the greater experience and caution of drivers 65 and older make them safer behind the wheel than the younger drivers?* Several factors other than greater experience and caution could explain the lower accident rate among the older drivers. For example, the older drivers might simply drive much less than the younger ones, but still get in just as many accidents per mile driven. Or perhaps because the older drivers are more often retired, their schedules less often lead them to drive at times of day when accident rates are greater for everyone. Or they might be more likely to live in rural areas with less traffic and lower accident rates. The argument depends on assuming that none of these factors fully explains the difference in accident rates.

A   **Correct.** Although we are given no information about the possible extent of any difference in average miles driven, the (somewhat vague) information that drivers 65 and older drive *very many fewer miles per year*, on average, than drivers 24 and younger would cast serious doubt on the statistical argument given. The argument assumes that the difference in miles driven is not sufficiently substantial to undermine the argument.

B   The argument is only about the discrepancy between the percentages of the drivers in two specific age groups who were in serious accidents last year. The percentages of licensed drivers who fall in these age groups are irrelevant.

C   Even if drivers 65 and older are just as likely as younger drivers to drive in inclement weather, they may do so far more carefully than the younger drivers, so the older drivers' greater experience and caution could still explain their lower accident rates.

D   Even if greater experience does not explain the difference between the accident rates of the two younger groups of drivers, it might still explain the differences between the accident rate of those two younger groups taken together and that of drivers aged 65 and older.

E   The accident rate could be lower for drivers in late middle age than for those 65 and older because drivers in late middle age are also cautious and experienced, but their reflexes and vision tend to be less impaired. Even if that were true, the experience and caution of the drivers 65 and older might still make them safer than drivers 24 and under.

The correct answer is A.

625. In the past the country of Malvernia has relied heavily on imported oil. Malvernia recently implemented a program to convert heating systems from oil to natural gas. Malvernia currently produces more natural gas each year than it uses, and oil production in Malvernian oil fields is increasing at a steady pace. If these trends in fuel production and usage continue, therefore, Malvernian reliance on foreign sources for fuel is likely to decline soon.

Which of the following would it be most useful to establish in evaluating the argument?

(A) When, if ever, will production of oil in Malvernia outstrip production of natural gas?

(B) Is Malvernia among the countries that rely most on imported oil?

(C) What proportion of Malvernia's total energy needs is met by hydroelectric, solar, and nuclear power?

(D) Is the amount of oil used each year in Malvernia for generating electricity and fuel for transportation increasing?

(E) Have any existing oil-burning heating systems in Malvernia already been converted to natural-gas-burning heating systems?

Argument Evaluation

Situation   Malvernia has relied heavily on imported oil, but recently began a program to convert heating systems from oil to natural gas. Malvernia produces more natural gas than it uses. Furthermore, Malvernia's oil production is expanding, Therefore, Malvernia will probably reduce its reliance on imported oils if these trends continue.

Reasoning   *Which option provides the information that it would be most useful to know in evaluating the argument?* In other words, we are looking for the option which—depending on whether it was answered yes or no—would either most weaken or most strengthen the argument. The argument indicates that Malvernia will be using less oil for heating and will be producing more oil domestically. But the conclusion that Malvernia's reliance on foreign oil will decline, assuming the current trends mentioned continue, would be undermined if there was something in the works that could offset these trends, for instance, if it turned out that the country's need for oil was going to rise in the coming years.

A   Since both domestic oil production and domestic natural gas production counteract the need for imported oil, it makes little difference to the argument whether domestic oil production exceeds domestic natural gas.

B   Whether there are many countries that rely more on foreign oil than Malvernia would have little impact on whether Malvernia's need for foreign oil can be expected to decline.

C   Since there is no information in the argument about whether Malvernia can expect an increase or decrease from these other energy sources, it does not matter how much they now provide.

D   Correct. This option provides the information that it would be most useful to know in evaluating the argument. As explained in the Reasoning section above, if Malvernia's need for oil rises in the coming years, the conclusion that Malvernia's reliance on foreign oil will decline is undermined.

E   The argument tells us that a program has begun *recently* to convert heating systems from oil to gas. So, even if no such conversions have been completed, the argument still indicates that they can be expected to occur.

The correct answer is D.

626. Exposure to certain chemicals commonly used in elementary schools as cleaners or pesticides causes allergic reactions in some children. Elementary school nurses in Renston report that the proportion of schoolchildren sent to them for treatment of allergic reactions to those chemicals has increased significantly over the past ten years. Therefore, either Renston's schoolchildren have been exposed to greater quantities of the chemicals, or they are more sensitive to them than schoolchildren were ten years ago.

Which of the following is an assumption on which the argument depends?

(A) The number of school nurses employed by Renston's elementary schools has not decreased over the past ten years.

(B) Children who are allergic to the chemicals are no more likely than other children to have allergies to other substances.

(C) Children who have allergic reactions to the chemicals are not more likely to be sent to a school nurse now than they were ten years ago.

(D) The chemicals are not commonly used as cleaners or pesticides in houses and apartment buildings in Renston.

(E) Children attending elementary school do not make up a larger proportion of Renston's population now than they did ten years ago.

Argument Construction

Situation   Some children have allergic reactions to some of the chemicals commonly used in elementary schools as cleaners and pesticides. The number of children sent to elementary school nurses in Renston for allergic reactions to such chemicals has risen significantly over the past ten years.

Reasoning   *What must the argument assume?* The argument's conclusion presents just two alternatives: either the children are exposed to more of the chemicals than children in earlier years *or* they are more sensitive. But there is a third possible explanation for the significant increase in school-nurse visits that the school nurses have reported: that children are just more inclined to go to the school nurse when they experience an allergic reaction than were children several years ago. For the conclusion to follow from its premises, the argument must assume that this is not the correct explanation.

A   If the number of elementary school nurses in Renston elementary schools had decreased over the past ten years, that would in no way explain the rise in the proportion of children reporting to school nurses for allergic reactions.

B   Only school-nurse visits for allergic reactions to the cleaners and pesticides used in elementary schools are in question in the argument. Of course there could be school-nurse visits for allergic reactions to other things, but that issue does not arise in the argument.

C   **Correct.** This can be seen by considering whether the argument would work if we assume that this were false, i.e., that a school-nurse visit *is* more likely in such cases. As noted above, this provides an alternative to the two explanations that the conclusion claims are the sole possibilities.

D   This does not need to be assumed by the argument. The argument's conclusion suggests that children may in recent years have had greater exposure to the chemicals, not that this exposure has occurred exclusively in the schools. The argument does not rely on this latter assumption.

E   The argument does not need to make this assumption. The argument is framed in terms of proportions of children having school-nurse visits for certain allergic reactions. *How many* children there are or what proportion such children are of Renston's total population is not directly relevant to the argument.

The correct answer is C.

627. Lockeport's commercial fishing boats use gill nets, which kill many of the netted fish, including some fish of endangered species. The fishing commission has proposed requiring the use of tent nets, which do not kill fish; boat crews would then throw back fish of endangered species. Profitable commercial fishing boats in similar areas have already switched over to tent nets. The proposal can therefore be implemented without economic harm to Lockeport's commercial fishing boat operators.

Which of the following, if true, casts the most serious doubt on the argument made for the proposal?

(A) In places where the use of tent nets has been mandated, there are typically fewer commercial fishing boats in operation than there were before tent nets came into use.

(B) Even when used properly, gill nets require many more repairs than do tent nets.

(C) Recreational anglers in Lockeport catch more fish of endangered species than do commercial fishing boats.

(D) The endangered species of fish in Lockeport's commercial fishing area did not become endangered as a result of the use of gill nets by fishing fleets.

(E) The endangered species of fish caught by Lockeport's commercial fishing fleet are of no commercial value.

Evaluation of a Plan

Situation   Gill nets, used by Lockeport's commercial fishing boats, kill some fish of endangered species. The fishing commission has proposed requiring the use of tent nets, which do not kill fish. This would allow the fish of endangered species to be thrown back. It is argued that the proposed requirement will not harm commercial fishing boat operators, since commercial fishing boats in other similar places are using tent nets and are profitable.

Reasoning   *What new piece of information would weaken the argument for the proposed requirement?* The crucial support given for the argument is that in other similar places, commercial fishing boats that use tent nets and not gill nets are profitable. But if, in places where only tent nets are now used, the numbers of commercial fishing boats diminished, it would be reasonable to suspect that switching entirely to tent nets may have driven some of the fishing operations out of business or caused them to move to other areas in which there was no expectation that they would use only tent nets.

A   **Correct.** This is new information. As explained above, it would justify doubt about the argument made in favor of the proposal.

B   This suggests that implementation of the proposed requirement could, over time, lower a certain type of operational costs for commercial fishing boats using tent nets. This would provide a new reason in support of the proposed requirement, not a reason to doubt the argument for it.

C   This suggests that perhaps recreational fishing in Lockeport needs to be regulated more strictly, but that is a separate issue from the one addressed in the argument for the proposed tent-net requirement.

D   This information casts no doubt on the relevance of the stated information that using gill nets contributes to undermining populations of at least some of the endangered fish species in Lockeport. If the species are currently endangered, they may need protection regardless of how they became endangered.

E   This information suggests that fish of the endangered species in Lockeport cannot profitably be sold. It does not cast doubt on the argument made in favor of the proposed requirement. Neither does it cast doubt on the practicality or the desirability of the proposed requirement.

The correct answer is A.

628. Normally, the pineal gland governs a person's sleep-wake cycle by secreting melatonin in response to the daily cycle of light and darkness as detected by the eye. Nonetheless, many people who are totally blind due to lesions in the visual cortex of the brain easily maintain a 24-hour sleep-wake cycle. So the neural pathway by which the pineal gland receives information from the eye probably does not pass through the visual cortex.

For purposes of evaluating the argument it would be most useful to establish which of the following?

(A) Whether melatonin supplements help people who have difficulty maintaining a 24-hour sleep cycle to establish such a pattern

(B) Whether the melatonin levels of most totally blind people who successfully maintain a 24-hour sleep-wake cycle change in response to changes in exposure to light and darkness

(C) Whether melatonin is the only substance secreted by the pineal gland

(D) Whether most people who do not have a 24-hour sleep-wake cycle nevertheless have a cycle of consistent duration

(E) Whether there are any people with normal vision whose melatonin levels respond abnormally to periods of light and darkness

Argument Evaluation

Situation   Normally, a person's sleep-wake cycle is governed by the pineal gland secreting melatonin in response to the daily cycle of light and darkness as detected by the eye. Yet many people who are totally blind due to lesions of the visual cortex easily maintain a 24-hour sleep-wake cycle.

Reasoning   *What additional information would be most helpful in evaluating the argument?* The argument's conclusion is that the neural pathway by which the pineal gland receives information probably does not pass through the visual cortex. This is suggested by the fact that people without a well-functioning visual cortex (e.g., people with a certain type of blindness) can nonetheless maintain a 24-hour sleep-wake cycle. Is it by the pineal gland's secretion of melatonin that they do so? The argument tells us that *normally* (i.e., in sighted people), this is the mechanism for sleep regulation. But the argument depends on assuming that a similar mechanism is operating in people who are blind but have well-regulated sleep cycles. The best choice will be the one that helps us decide whether that assumption is correct.

A   This question would not give us an answer that would help in evaluating the argument. A "no" answer would not clarify whether the pineal gland-melatonin mechanism operates in people who are blind. A "yes" answer would do no better. The question refers only to people who have sleep dysfunctions (which the argument does not address).

B   **Correct.** Answering this question would provide the most useful information for evaluating the argument. A "yes" answer would help confirm a key assumption of the argument: that blind people rely on the pineal gland-melatonin mechanism for sleep regulation. A "no" answer would help disconfirm that assumption.

C   Whether or not there are other substances secreted by the pineal gland makes no difference to the reasoning. The argument relies on the premise that the pineal gland governs the sleep cycle *by secreting melatonin*. For example, if the pineal gland sometimes secreted adrenaline, that would still have no bearing on the argument.

D   The consistency or inconsistency of the duration of some people's sleep patterns has no relevance to the reasoning. Their sleep patterns could be due to any of a number of factors.

E   This does not help, for there could be sighted people whose melatonin levels respond abnormally simply because of a pineal-gland abnormality.

The correct answer is B.

629. **In countries where automobile insurance includes compensation for whiplash injuries sustained in automobile accidents, reports of having suffered such injuries are twice as frequent as they are in countries where whiplash is not covered**. Presently, no objective test for whiplash exists, so it is true that spurious reports of whiplash injuries cannot be readily identified. Nevertheless, these facts do not warrant the conclusion drawn by some commentators that in the countries with the higher rates of reported whiplash injuries, half of the reported cases are spurious. Clearly, **in countries where automobile insurance does not include compensation for whiplash, people often have little incentive to report whiplash injuries that they actually have suffered**.

In the argument given, the two **boldfaced** portions play which of the following roles?

(A) The first is a claim that the argument disputes; the second is a conclusion that has been based on that claim.

(B) The first is a claim that has been used to support a conclusion that the argument accepts; the second is that conclusion.

(C) The first is evidence that has been used to support a conclusion for which the argument provides further evidence; the second is the main conclusion of the argument.

(D) The first is a finding whose implications are at issue in the argument; the second is a claim presented in order to argue against deriving certain implications from that finding.

(E) The first is a finding whose accuracy is evaluated in the argument; the second is evidence presented to establish that the finding is accurate.

Argument Evaluation

Situation Reported whiplash injuries are twice as common in countries where car insurance companies pay compensation for such injuries as they are in countries where insurance companies do not. Although there is no objective test for whiplash, this does not mean, as some suggest, that half of the reports of such injuries are fake. It could simply be that where insurance will not pay for such injuries, people are less inclined to report them.

Reasoning *What roles do the two boldfaced portions play in the argument?* The first portion tells us about the correlation between reported cases of whiplash in countries and the willingness of insurance companies in those countries to compensate for whiplash injuries. The argument next states that whiplash is difficult to verify objectively. The argument then asserts that although this last fact, taken together with the first boldfaced portion, has led some to infer that over half of the reported cases in countries with the highest whiplash rates are spurious, such an inference is unwarranted. The second boldfaced portion then helps to explain, by offering an alternative explanation, why such an inference is not necessarily warranted.

A The claim made in the first boldfaced portion is never disputed in the argument. The second is not the argument's conclusion.

B Perhaps the argument uses the first portion to support its conclusion; but there is no indication that it has been used elsewhere to do so. Regardless, the second boldfaced portion is not the argument's conclusion.

C The first portion has been used to support a conclusion that the argument rejects; the second portion is not the argument's conclusion.

D **Correct.** This answer choice correctly identifies the roles played in the argument by the boldfaced portions. As explained in the reasoning section above, the first boldface portion tells us about the correlation between reported cases of whiplash in countries and the willingness of insurance companies in those countries to compensate for whiplash injuries. This is presented as a fact whose implications are at issue in the ensuing portions of the passage. The argument then reports that this fact, considered together with the difficulty of proving whiplash injuries, has led some to infer that over half of the reported cases in countries with the highest whiplash rates are spurious. The conclusion of the argument is that this inference is unwarranted. The second boldface portion expresses the basis for the argument's conclusion: there is a reasonable alternative explanation for the differences in frequency of whiplash injury reports between the two types of countries.

E   The accuracy of the first boldfaced portion is never questioned in the argument; nor is the second intended to somehow help show that the first is accurate. Rather, the argument assumes that the first portion is accurate.

The correct answer is D.

630. Last year Comfort Airlines had twice as many delayed flights as the year before, but the number of complaints from passengers about delayed flights went up three times. It is unlikely that this disproportionate increase in complaints was rooted in an increase in overall dissatisfaction with the service Comfort Airlines provides, since the airline made a special effort to improve other aspects of its service last year.

Which of the following, if true, most helps to explain the disproportionate increase in customer complaints?

(A) Comfort Airlines had more flights last year than the year before.

(B) Last year a single period of unusually bad weather caused a large number of flights to be delayed.

(C) Some of the improvements that Comfort Airlines made in its service were required by new government regulations.

(D) The average length of a flight delay was greater last year than it was the year before.

(E) The average number of passengers per flight was no higher last year than the year before.

Argument Construction

Situation   Last year Comfort Airlines had twice as many delayed flights as it did the year before, but three times as many passenger complaints about delayed flights. The airline made a special effort to improve other aspects of its service last year.

Reasoning   *What could explain why the number of complaints about delayed flights increased disproportionately to the number of delayed flights last year?* In other words, why did the average number of passenger complaints per delayed flight go up last year? One obvious possibility is that the average number of passengers per delayed flight was greater last year than it had been the year before. Another is that the flight delays tended to cause worse problems for passengers last year than they had the year before, so that on average each delay was more upsetting for the passengers.

A   This helps explain why the airline had more delayed flights last year, but not why the increase in complaints about delayed flights was disproportionate to the increase in delayed flights.

B   This helps explain why the airline had more delayed flights last year. But, if anything, the situation should have reduced the number of passenger complaints per delayed flight, since many passengers should have realized that the unusually bad weather was not the airline's fault.

C   If any of the improvements concerned handling of flight delays, for example, and passengers were aware that government regulations addressed this, then passengers might have complained more than previously. But the information we are given here is too general and too vague to explain the disproportionate increase in complaints.

D   **Correct.** Longer flight delays would have more severely inconvenienced passengers and thus would probably have generated more passenger complaints per delay.

E   This rules out the possibility that an increased number of passengers per delayed flight could have caused the disproportionate increase in the number of complaints about delayed flights. But no alternative explanation is offered.

The correct answer is D

631. Last year a global disturbance of weather patterns disrupted harvests in many of the world's important agricultural areas. Worldwide production of soybeans, an important source of protein for people and livestock alike, was not adversely affected, however. Indeed, last year's soybean crop was actually slightly larger than average. Nevertheless, the weather phenomenon is probably responsible for a recent increase in the world price of soybeans.

Which of the following, if true, provides the strongest justification for the attribution of the increase in soybean prices to the weather phenomenon?

(A) Last year's harvest of anchovies, which provide an important protein source for livestock, was disrupted by the effects of the weather phenomenon.

(B) Most countries that produce soybeans for export had above-average harvests of a number of food crops other than soybeans last year.

(C) The world price of soybeans also rose several years ago, immediately after an earlier occurrence of a similar global weather disturbance.

(D) Heavy rains attributable to the weather phenomenon improved grazing pastures last year, allowing farmers in many parts of the world to reduce their dependence on supplemental feed.

(E) Prior to last year, soybean prices had been falling for several years.

Argument Construction

Situation   A weather disturbance last year disrupted harvests worldwide but did not reduce production of soybeans, a protein source for both people and livestock. Soybean prices increased nonetheless, likely a result of the weather.

Reasoning   *What evidence would suggest that the weather disturbance caused the increase in soybean prices even though it did not reduce soybean production?* Prices tend to increase when the supply of a product falls relative to the demand for the product. But the production of soybeans did not fall. Evidence that the weather disturbance either hindered the global distribution of soybeans or increased global demand for soybeans could support the claim that the weather disturbance caused the increase in soybean prices.

A   **Correct.** If the weather disturbance reduced the anchovy harvest, and anchovies provide protein for livestock just as soybeans do, then more soybeans for livestock feed would be needed to compensate for the lack of anchovies. The resulting increase in demand for soybeans could thus have increased global soybean prices.

B   This is not surprising, given that the weather disturbance did not severely affect the soybean-producing countries, but it does not explain how the weather disturbance could have caused soybean prices to increase.

C   The rise in soybean prices after the earlier weather disturbance could easily have been a coincidence. Or, unlike last year's disturbance, the earlier disturbance could have reduced soybean production.

D   This suggests that demand for soybeans should have fallen as a result of the weather disturbance, so it does not explain why soybean prices rose.

E   If soybean prices were unusually low for some temporary reason when the weather disturbance occurred, they might have been likely to rise back to normal levels even without the weather disturbance.

The correct answer is A.

632. Most of the year, the hermit thrush, a North American songbird, eats a diet consisting mainly of insects, but in autumn, as the thrushes migrate to their Central and South American wintering grounds, they feed almost exclusively on wild berries. Wild berries, however, are not as rich in calories as insects, yet thrushes need to consume plenty of calories in order to complete their migration. One possible explanation is that berries contain other nutrients that thrushes need for migration and that insects lack.

Which of the following, if true, most seriously calls into question the explanation given for the thrush's diet during migration?

(A) Hermit thrushes, if undernourished, are unable to complete their autumn migration before the onset of winter.

(B) Insect species contain certain nutrients that are not found in wild berries.

(C) For songbirds, catching insects requires the expenditure of significantly more calories than eating wild berries does.

(D) Along the hermit thrushes' migration routes, insects are abundant throughout the migration season.

(E) There are some species of wild berries that hermit thrushes generally do not eat, even though these berry species are exceptionally rich in calories.

Argument Evaluation

Situation   Hermit thrushes are songbirds that usually eat insects but switch to eating berries when migrating. The thrushes need lots of calories to migrate, but berries contain fewer calories than insects do. Perhaps the berries contain nutrients that insects do not provide.

Reasoning   *What would cast doubt on the claim that the thrushes switch to berries because berries contain nutrients that insects lack and that the thrushes need for their migration?* Evidence that berries do not contain such nutrients or that thrushes do not decrease their net calorie consumption by eating berries would cast doubt on the proposed explanation. So would any evidence that supported an alternative explanation for the diet change during migration—for example, seasonal or regional differences in the amount or quality of berries or insects available for the thrushes to consume.

A   Even if thrushes need to be well-nourished to finish migrating before winter, extra nutrients found in berries but not insects might help provide the nourishment they need.

B   Even if insects contain *certain nutrients* not found in wild berries, those specific nutrients may not be the ones the thrushes need for their migration.

C   Correct. This suggests that the thrushes might gain more net calories from eating berries than from eating insects, which could explain why they switch to eating berries even if the berries contain no extra nutrients.

D   By ruling out a lack of insects to eat while migrating as an alternative explanation for why the thrushes switch to eating berries, this would support the proposed explanation.

E   The calorie-rich species of berries the thrushes do not eat might be poisonous or indigestible for them, even if the species of berries the thrushes do eat contain nutrients they need to migrate.

The correct answer is C.

633. The kinds of hand and wrist injuries that result from extended use of a computer while maintaining an incorrect posture are common among schoolchildren in Harnville. Computers are important to the school curriculum there, so instead of reducing the amount their students use computers, teachers plan to bring about a sharp reduction in the number of these injuries by carefully monitoring their students' posture when using computers in the classroom.

Which of the following would it be most useful to know in order to assess the likelihood that the teachers' plan will be successful?

(A) Whether extended use of a computer while maintaining incorrect posture can cause injuries other than hand and wrist injuries

(B) Whether hand and wrist injuries not caused by computer use are common among schoolchildren in Harnville

(C) What proportion of schoolchildren in Harnville with hand and wrist injuries use computers extensively outside the classroom

(D) Whether changes in the curriculum could reduce the schools' dependence on computers

(E) What proportion of schoolchildren in Harnville already use correct posture while using a computer

Evaluation of a Plan

Situation   Hand and wrist injuries from using computers while maintaining poor posture are common among schoolchildren in Harnville. Teachers plan to greatly reduce the number of such injuries by monitoring their students' posture while the students use computers in the classroom.

Reasoning   *What would be most helpful to know to determine the likelihood that the teachers' plan will succeed?* The primary concern is the *posture* students adopt while using computers. To succeed, the teachers' plan must reduce the time students spend with poor posture while using computers and reduce it enough to greatly reduce the number of injuries. To know how likely this is, it would help to know how effectively the teachers will be able to monitor and improve their students' posture inside the classroom. But how many of the students use computers *outside of school* while maintaining poor posture and how often do they do so? If many students do so quite often, they may develop hand and wrist injuries regardless of what happens in school.

A   The teachers do not plan to reduce any injuries other than hand and wrist injuries, so whether computer use with poor posture causes any such other injuries is irrelevant to the likelihood that their plan will produce its intended effect.

B   The plan being discussed concerns only the reduction of hand and wrist injuries caused specifically by computer use with poor posture, so the frequency of hand and wrist injuries from other causes is irrelevant to the likelihood that the plan will produce its intended effect.

C   Correct. If the students' school use of computers is a large part of their overall computer use, any retraining that accompanies the monitoring might have some effect on their posture and related injury rates overall. However, the greater the proportion of children with hand and wrist injuries who use computers extensively outside the classroom, the more children are likely to keep developing the injuries regardless of any monitoring at school, so the less effective the teachers' plan involving only computer use at school is likely to be.

D   Knowing whether this is the case might help in developing a potential alternative to the teachers' plan, but if it did, this would not help significantly toward assessing the likelihood that the actual plan will succeed. The teachers' actual plan involves monitoring computer use in school without reducing such use. Other possible means of achieving the plan's goal are not part of the plan and are therefore irrelevant to the likelihood that the teachers' actual plan will succeed.

E   The passage indicates that the proportion of the schoolchildren maintaining poor posture while using computers is high enough for many to develop hand and wrist injuries as a result. Whatever the exact proportion is, the teachers' plan may or may not succeed in reducing it.

The correct answer is C.

634. A certain cultivated herb is one of a group of closely related plants that thrive in soil with high concentrations of metals that are toxic to most other plants. Agronomists studying the growth of this herb have discovered that it produces large amounts of histidine, an amino acid that, in test-tube solutions, renders these metals chemically inert. Hence, the herb's high histidine production must be the key feature that allows it to grow in metal-rich soils.

In evaluating the argument, it would be most important to determine which of the following?

(A) Whether the herb can thrive in soil that does not have high concentrations of the toxic metals

(B) Whether others of the closely related group of plants also produce histidine in large quantities

(C) Whether the herb's high level of histidine production is associated with an unusually low level of production of some other amino acid

(D) Whether growing the herb in soil with high concentrations of the metals will, over time, reduce their concentrations in the soil

(E) Whether the concentration of histidine in the growing herb declines as the plant approaches maturity

Argument Evaluation

Situation   A certain herb and closely related species thrive in soil full of metals toxic to most plants. The herb produces much histidine, which makes those metals chemically inert. Histidine production, therefore, is largely what accounts for the herb's thriving in metal-rich soils.

Reasoning   *What evidence would help determine whether the herb's histidine production is what enables it to thrive in metal-rich soils?* The argument is that since the herb's histidine chemically neutralizes the metals that are toxic to most plants, it must explain why the herb can thrive in metal-rich soils. To evaluate this argument, it would be helpful to know about the relationship between other closely related plant species' histidine production and the ability to thrive in metal-rich soils. It would also be helpful to know about any other factors that might plausibly explain why the herb can thrive in those soils.

A   Whether or not the herb thrives in metal-free soils, histidine production could enable it to thrive in soils that contain toxic metals.

B   **Correct.** If the closely related plants do not produce much histidine, whatever other factor allows them to thrive in metal-rich soils would likely account for why the herb thrives in those soils as well.

C   The given information suggests no particular reason to suppose that a low level of some unspecified amino acid would enable a plant to thrive in metal-rich soils.

D   The herb might absorb metals from any metal-rich soil it grows in, regardless of why it thrives in that soil.

E   Whether or not histidine concentrations in the herb decline as it approaches maturity, there could still be enough histidine in the growing herb to neutralize the metals and explain why it can grow in metal-rich soil.

The correct answer is B.

635. Many people suffer an allergic reaction to certain sulfites, including those that are commonly added to wine as preservatives. However, since there are several winemakers who add sulfites to none of the wines they produce, people who would like to drink wine but are allergic to sulfites can drink wines produced by these winemakers without risking an allergic reaction to sulfites.

Which of the following is an assumption on which the argument depends?

(A) These winemakers have been able to duplicate the preservative effect produced by adding sulfites by means that do not involve adding any potentially allergenic substances to their wine.

(B) Not all forms of sulfite are equally likely to produce the allergic reaction.

(C) Wine is the only beverage to which sulfites are commonly added.

(D) Apart from sulfites, there are no substances commonly present in wine that give rise to an allergic reaction.

(E) Sulfites are not naturally present in the wines produced by these winemakers in amounts large enough to produce an allergic reaction in someone who drinks these wines.

Argument Construction

Situation   People who are allergic to certain sulfites can avoid risking an allergic reaction by drinking wine from one of the several producers that does not add sulfites.

Reasoning   *On what assumption does the argument depend?* Drinking wine to which no sulfites have been *added* will not prevent exposure to sulfites if, for instance, sulfites occur naturally in wines. In particular, if the wines that do not have sulfites added have sulfites present naturally in quantities sufficient to produce an allergic reaction, drinking these wines will not result in an allergic reaction. The argument therefore depends on assuming that this is not the case.

A   The argument does not require this because the conclusion does not address allergic reactions to substances other than sulfites.

B   The argument specifically refers to "certain sulfites" producing allergic reactions. It is entirely compatible with certain other forms of sulfites not producing allergic reactions in anyone.

C   This is irrelevant. The argument does not claim that one can avoid having an allergic reaction to sulfites *from any source* just by restricting one's wine consumption to those varieties to which no sulfites have been added.

D   Once again, the argument's conclusion does not address allergic reactions to substances other than sulfites in wine.

E   **Correct.** As explained in the Reasoning section above, the argument relies on the assumption that sulfites are not naturally present, in quantities sufficient to cause allergic reactions, in the wines to which no sulfites are added. If this assumption is not made, then the fact that no sulfites are added to certain wines is not a good reason to believe that people with sulfite allergies who consume the wines will not have an allergic reaction; if there are enough sulfites that naturally occur in the wine, people who consume the wine may well have an allergic reaction despite the fact that no sulfites have been added.

The correct answer is E.

636. A new law gives ownership of patents—documents providing exclusive right to make and sell an invention—to universities, not the government, when those patents result from government-sponsored university research. Administrators at Logos University plan to sell any patents they acquire to corporations in order to fund programs to improve undergraduate teaching.

Which of the following, if true, would cast the most doubt on the viability of the college administrators' plan described above?

(A) Profit-making corporations interested in developing products based on patents held by universities are likely to try to serve as exclusive sponsors of ongoing university research projects.

(B) Corporate sponsors of research in university facilities are entitled to tax credits under new federal tax-code guidelines.

(C) Research scientists at Logos University have few or no teaching responsibilities and participate little if at all in the undergraduate programs in their field.

(D) Government-sponsored research conducted at Logos University for the most part duplicates research already completed by several profit-making corporations.

(E) Logos University is unlikely to attract corporate sponsorship of its scientific research.

Evaluation of a Plan

Situation   Universities own the patents resulting from government-sponsored research at their institutions. One university plans to sell its patents to corporations and use the proceeds to fund a program to improve teaching.

Reasoning   *What would cast doubt on the university's plan?* The plan assumes that the university has been granted, and/or will be granted, patents for its inventions; that there will be a market for its patents; and that corporations will want to buy them. What might make this untrue? For example, the university's inventions might have no practical value or might be useful only for government agencies, and if some of the corporations have already done the same or similar research, they will likely not be prospective buyers of the university's patents.

A   This point is irrelevant to the plan to sell patents in order to fund a program.

B   The university plans to sell the patents to the corporations, not to invite the corporations to sponsor research.

C   This point is irrelevant to the university's plan to sell off patents since the plan does not specify that the research scientists will be involved in the programs to improve undergraduate teaching.

D   Correct. This statement properly identifies a factor that casts doubt on the university's plan. The plan presupposes that corporations will want to buy the rights to the inventions. If some of the corporations have already done the same or similar research, they would likely have developed ways of achieving what the university's inventions promise to achieve. In the case of potential future patents, they might even have already patented the inventions that the university would develop, in which case, the university would be unable to patent them. Or the corporations might have developed similar, but not identical, inventions that serve the same purpose. In such cases, they probably would not need the university's inventions.

E   The plan concerns selling patents resulting from government-sponsored research, not attracting corporate sponsorship for research.

The correct answer is D.

637. Since it has become known that **several of a bank's top executives have been buying shares in their own bank**, the bank's depositors, who had been worried by rumors that the bank faced impending financial collapse, have been greatly relieved. They reason that, since top executives evidently have faith in the bank's financial soundness, those worrisome rumors must be false. Such reasoning might well be overoptimistic, however, since **corporate executives have been known to buy shares in their own company in a calculated attempt to dispel negative rumors about the company's health.**

In the argument given, the two **boldfaced** portions play which of the following roles?

(A)   The first describes evidence that has been taken as supporting a conclusion; the second gives a reason for questioning that support.

(B)   The first describes evidence that has been taken as supporting a conclusion; the second states a contrary conclusion that is the main conclusion of the argument.

(C)   The first provides evidence in support of the main conclusion of the argument; the second states that conclusion.

(D)   The first describes the circumstance that the argument as a whole seeks to explain; the second gives the explanation that the argument seeks to establish.

(E)   The first describes the circumstance that the argument as a whole seeks to explain; the second provides evidence in support of the explanation that the argument seeks to establish.

Argument Evaluation

Situation   Top executives at a bank that has been rumored to be in financial trouble have been buying shares in the bank. Bank depositors see this as a good sign, because they believe that it indicates that the executives have faith in the bank. However, corporate executives sometimes do this just to dispel rumors about a company's health.

Reasoning   *What is the role that the two boldfaced portions play in the argument?* The first boldfaced portion states that bank executives are buying bank shares, which the passage indicates is taken by bank depositors to be evidence of the executives' faith in the bank; in other words, the bank depositors take the fact that the executives are buying shares in the bank as supporting the conclusion that the executives have faith in the bank and thus that the rumors that the bank is facing financial collapse are wrong. The passage then tells us what some have inferred from this (namely, that worrisome rumors about the bank's impending financial collapse are false). Finally, the passage offers in the second boldfaced portion evidence that undermines this inference: Corporate executives have sometimes bought shares in their own companies just to dispel negative rumors, presumably whether the rumors are true or not.

A   **Correct.** This option correctly identifies the roles played by the boldfaced portions. As discussed in the Reasoning section above, the bank depositors have drawn the conclusion from the first boldfaced portion that the bank's finances are sound, but the second boldfaced portion is presented to call their conclusion into question.

B   This correctly describes the first portion's role, but the second portion is not offered as a conclusion— no evidence is given for it; rather it is evidence for something else.

C   The second portion is not offered as a conclusion; no evidence is given for it.

D   The second portion is not itself offered as an explanation of why these bank executives are investing in the bank; if it were, that would mean that the bank executives are doing so *because* corporate executives are known to do such things in a calculated effort to dispel worries. Furthermore the argument does not conclude that this other explanation (which the boldfaced portion points to) is correct, only that the one inferred by depositors may not be.

E   The argument is not so much seeking to establish an explanation of its own as it is trying to undermine that inferred by the depositors.

The correct answer is A.

638. Between 1980 and 2000 the sea otter population of the Aleutian Islands declined precipitously. There were no signs of disease or malnutrition, so there was probably an increase in the number of otters being eaten by predators. Orcas will eat otters when seals, their normal prey, are unavailable, and the Aleutian Islands seal population declined dramatically in the 1980s. Therefore, orcas were most likely the immediate cause of the otter population decline.

Which of the following, if true, most strengthens the argument?

(A) The population of sea urchins, the main food of sea otters, has increased since the sea otter population declined.

(B) Seals do not eat sea otters, nor do they compete with sea otters for food.

(C) Most of the surviving sea otters live in a bay that is inaccessible to orcas.

(D) The population of orcas in the Aleutian Islands has declined since the 1980s.

(E) An increase in commercial fishing near the Aleutian Islands in the 1980s caused a slight decline in the population of the fish that seals use for food.

Argument Evaluation

Situation   A sea otter population declined even though there were no signs of disease or malnutrition. The local seal population also declined. Orcas eat otters when seals are unavailable, and thus are probably the cause of the decline in the otter population.

Reasoning   *What would be evidence that predation by orcas reduced the sea otter population?* Disease and malnutrition are ruled out as alternative explanations of the decline in the sea otter population. The argument could be further strengthened by casting doubt on other possible explanations, such as predation by other animals, or by presenting observations that predation of otters by orcas would help to explain.

A   Regardless of whether or not orcas ate the sea otters, the sea urchin population would most likely have increased when the population of sea otters preying on them decreased.

B   Because the seal population declined during the initial years of the otter population decline, predation by and competition with seals were already implausible explanations of the otter population decline.

C   **Correct.** Orcas eating most of the accessible otters could plausibly explain this observation, which therefore provides additional evidence that orca predation reduced the sea otter population.

D   If the orca population declined at the same time as the sea otter population, it would be less likely that increasing predation by orcas reduced the otter population.

E   Since the sea otters showed no signs of malnutrition, they were probably getting enough fish. But if they were not, commercial fishing rather than orcas might have caused the otter population decline.

The correct answer is C.

639. Political Strategist: The domestic policies of our opponents in Party X are contrary to the priorities of many middle-class voters. Yet some of these same voters are supporters of Party X and its candidates due to the party's appeals about foreign policy. In order to win these voters back, we in Party Y must prove to middle-class voters that Party X does not represent their priorities with respect to domestic policy.

Which of the following would, if true, most strongly suggest that the political strategist's plan is unlikely to succeed?

(A) Many in the middle class who support Party X for its foreign policies also support its domestic policies and are fully aware of the implications of those policies.

(B) Most middle-class supporters of Party X care about foreign policy and know very little about its domestic policies.

(C) Long-term domestic policy sometimes conflicts with short-term domestic policy.

(D) There are topics on which Party X and Party Y have significant agreement.

(E) Some middle-class voters are concerned about both domestic and foreign policy.

Evaluation of a Plan

Situation   A political strategist for Party Y notes that the domestic policies of Party X are contrary to the priorities of middle-class voters. Many middle-class voters nonetheless support Party X because of its foreign policy. The strategist argues that to win these voters back, Party Y should prove to middle-class voters that Party X's domestic policies do not represent their priorities.

Reasoning   *What claim would most strongly suggest that the strategist's plan will not succeed?* Suppose that a large number of the middle-class voters who support Party X's foreign policies also support its domestic policies, despite the fact that the domestic policies are contrary to their priorities. If that were true, then Party Y might well be unable to win back these voters by following the strategist's plan.

A   **Correct.** As noted above, if many middle-class voters who support Party X's foreign policies also support its domestic policies, the strategy of attempting to show these voters that there is a conflict between their priorities and Party X's domestic policies may well fail to get them to vote for Party Y. Presumably these voters are aware of the conflict and support Party X nonetheless—perhaps because Party Y's domestic policies conflict with their priorities even more.

B   If most middle-class supporters of Party X know little about its domestic policies, Party Y may well be able to win them back simply by showing them the inconsistencies between those policies and their own priorities.

C   A conflict between long-term domestic policy and short-term domestic policy tells us nothing about whether educating middle-class voters about conflicts between their priorities and Party X's domestic policies would help win them back to Party Y.

D   The fact that the two parties have significant agreement on certain topics does not suggest the strategist's plan will not succeed. In fact, if the parties agreed on very little, the strategy of pointing only to issues related to domestic policy might be less likely to work. Therefore, this answer choice helps rule out a reason for thinking that the plan might not work.

E   If anything, this would help support the claim that the strategist's plan will succeed.

The correct answer is A.

640. Studies in restaurants show that the tips left by customers who pay their bill in cash tend to be larger when the bill is presented on a tray that bears a credit-card logo. Consumer psychologists hypothesize that simply seeing a credit-card logo makes many credit-card holders willing to spend more because it reminds them that their spending power exceeds the cash they have immediately available.

Which of the following, if true, most strongly supports the psychologists' interpretation of the studies?

(A) The effect noted in the studies is not limited to patrons who have credit cards.

(B) Patrons who are under financial pressure from their credit-card obligations tend to tip less when presented with a restaurant bill on a tray with a credit-card logo than when the tray has no logo.

(C) In virtually all of the cases in the studies, the patrons who paid bills in cash did not possess credit cards.

(D) In general, restaurant patrons who pay their bills in cash leave larger tips than do those who pay by credit card.

(E) The percentage of restaurant bills paid with a given brand of credit card increases when that credit card's logo is displayed on the tray with which the bill is presented.

Argument Evaluation

Situation   Studies have found that restaurant customers give more generous tips when their bills are brought on trays bearing a credit-card logo. Psychologists speculate that this is because the logo reminds customers of their ability to spend more money than they have.

Reasoning   *Which of the options most helps to support the psychologists' explanation of the studies?* The psychologists' hypothesis is that the credit-card logos on the trays bring to the minds of those who tip more the fact that they have more purchasing power than merely the cash that they have at hand. This explanation would not be valid even if those people who are not reminded of their own excess purchasing power—if in fact they have any such power—when they see such a logo nonetheless tip more in such trays. Thus, if restaurant patrons who are under financial pressure from their credit-card obligations do not tip more when their bills are presented on trays bearing credit-card logos, then the psychologists' interpretation of the studies is supported.

A   This undermines the psychologists' interpretation, for it shows that the same phenomenon occurs even when the alleged cause has been removed.

B   **Correct.** If the consumer psychologists' hypothesis is true, it implies that only those who do, in fact, have additional spending power in the form of credit will be influenced by the logos to leave larger tips. If those who do not have such additional spending power are influenced in the same way, the hypothesis is flawed. Answer choice B indicates that the hypothesis is not flawed in this way, so it thereby tends to strengthen the hypothesis. It also strengthens the hypothesis by weakening some alternative hypotheses such as the following: Most of the customers who pay with cash do so because they have excessive credit-card debt and cannot use a credit card. However, seeing a credit-card logo makes them wonder whether credit-card customers may leave larger tips, and to avoid displeasing the server by leaving a small tip, they decide to leave a larger tip than they might otherwise have done.

C   This undermines the psychologists' interpretation by showing that the same phenomenon occurs even when the alleged cause has been removed; patrons cannot be reminded of something that is not there.

D   To the extent that this bears on the interpretation of the study, it weakens it. Patrons using credit cards are surely aware that they have credit, and yet they spend less generously.

E   This does not support the idea that being reminded that one has a credit card induces one to be more generous, only that it induces one to use that credit card.

The correct answer is B.

641. In an experiment, each volunteer was allowed to choose between an easy task and a hard task and was told that another volunteer would do the other task. Each volunteer could also choose to have a computer assign the two tasks randomly. Most volunteers chose the easy task for themselves and under questioning later said they had acted fairly. But when the scenario was described to another group of volunteers, almost all said choosing the easy task would be unfair. This shows that most people apply weaker moral standards to themselves than to others.

Which of the following is an assumption required by this argument?

(A) At least some volunteers who said they had acted fairly in choosing the easy task would have said that it was unfair for someone else to do so.

(B) The most moral choice for the volunteers would have been to have the computer assign the two tasks randomly.

(C) There were at least some volunteers who were assigned to do the hard task and felt that the assignment was unfair.

(D) On average, the volunteers to whom the scenario was described were more accurate in their moral judgments than the other volunteers were.

(E) At least some volunteers given the choice between assigning the tasks themselves and having the computer assign them felt that they had made the only fair choice available to them.

Argument Construction

Situation   In an experiment, most volunteers chose to do an easy task themselves and leave a hard task for someone else. They later said they had acted fairly, but almost all volunteers in another group to which the scenario was described said choosing the easy task would be unfair, indicating that most people apply weaker moral standards to themselves.

Reasoning   *What must be true in order for the facts presented to support the conclusion that most people apply weaker moral standards to themselves than to others?* One set of volunteers said they had acted fairly in taking the easy task, whereas different volunteers said that doing so would be unfair. In neither case did any of the volunteers actually judge their own behavior differently from how they judged anyone else's. So the argument implicitly infers from the experimental results that most of the volunteers would judge their own behavior differently from someone else's if given the chance. This inference assumes that the volunteers in the second group would have applied the same moral standards that those in the first group did if they had been in the first group's position, and vice versa.

A   **Correct.** If none of the volunteers who said their own behavior was fair would have judged someone else's similar behavior as unfair, then their relaxed moral judgment of themselves would not suggest that they applied weaker moral standards to themselves than to others.

B   Even if this is so, the experimental results could still suggest that the volunteers would apply weaker moral standards to themselves than to others.

C   The argument would be equally strong even if volunteers who were assigned the hard task did not know that someone else had gotten an easier task—or even if no volunteers were actually assigned the hard task at all.

D   Even if the moral standards applied by the volunteers who judged themselves were as accurate as those applied by the volunteers to whom the scenario was described, the former standards were still weaker.

E   Even if all the volunteers in the first group had felt that all the choices available to them would have been fair for them to make personally, they might have applied stricter moral standards to someone else in the same position.

The correct answer is A.

642. Country X's recent stock-trading scandal should not diminish investors' confidence in the country's stock market. For one thing, **the discovery of the scandal confirms that Country X has a strong regulatory system**, as the following considerations show. In any stock market, some fraudulent activity is inevitable. If a stock market is well regulated, any significant stock-trading fraud in it will very likely be discovered. This deters potential perpetrators and facilitates improvement in regulatory processes.

In the argument, the portion in **boldface** plays which of the following roles?

(A) It is the argument's only conclusion.

(B) It is a conclusion for which the argument provides support and which itself is used to support the argument's main conclusion.

(C) It is the argument's main conclusion and is supported by another explicitly stated conclusion for which further support is provided.

(D) It is an assumption for which no explicit support is provided and is used to support the argument's only conclusion.

(E) It is a compound statement containing both the argument's main conclusion and an assumption used to support that conclusion.

Argument Construction

Situation   Country X recently had a stock-trading scandal.

Reasoning   *What role does the statement that the scandal's discovery confirms that Country X has a strong regulatory system play in the argument?* In the sentence containing the boldface statement, the phrase *For one thing* indicates that the statement is being used to justify the claim in the preceding sentence. Thus, the boldface statement must support that preceding sentence as a conclusion. Directly after the boldface statement, the phrase as *the following considerations show* indicates that the subsequent sentences are being used to support the boldface statement. Thus, the boldface statement is a conclusion supported by the sentences following it, and this statement itself supports the sentence preceding it, which must be the argument's main conclusion.

A   As explained above, the boldface statement supports the claim in the preceding sentence, so it cannot be the argument's only conclusion.

B   **Correct.** As explained above, the boldface statement is supported by the statements following it and in turn is used to support the argument's main conclusion in the statement preceding it.

C   As explained above, the boldface statement cannot be the argument's main conclusion, because it supports a further conclusion presented in the sentence preceding it.

D   As explained above, the sentences following the boldface statement are the explicit support provided for it.

E   As explained above, the argument's main conclusion is stated only in the first sentence, which precedes the boldface statement. It is not repeated anywhere in the boldface statement.

The correct answer is B.

643. **Delta Products Inc. has recently switched at least partly from older technologies using fossil fuels to new technologies powered by electricity.** The question has been raised whether it can be concluded that, **for a given level of output, Delta's operation now causes less fossil fuel to be consumed than it did formerly.** The answer, clearly, is yes, since the amount of fossil fuel used to generate the electricity needed to power the new technologies is less than the amount needed to power the older technologies, provided level of output is held constant.

In the argument given, the two **boldfaced** portions play which of the following roles?

(A) The first identifies the content of the conclusion of the argument; the second provides support for that conclusion.

(B) The first provides support for the conclusion of the argument; the second identifies the content of that conclusion.

(C) The first states the conclusion of the argument; the second calls that conclusion into question.

(D) The first provides support for the conclusion of the argument; the second calls that conclusion into question.

(E) Each provides support for the conclusion of the argument.

Argument Evaluation

Situation   Delta switched from technologies using fossil fuels to ones using electricity. It has been asked whether this results in less fossil fuel used per level of output. The answer is that it does.

Reasoning   *What roles do the two boldfaced portions play in the argument?* The first boldfaced statement is simply asserted by the passage; no premise, or reason, is given to support it. But the second boldfaced statement, when it is first introduced, is not asserted to be true, but rather is identified as something that might be inferred from the first statement. By the end of the passage the argument concludes that the second statement is true.

A   This option simply reverses the roles that the statements play in the argument.

B   **Correct.** This option identifies the roles the boldfaced portions play: The second statement is not, on its own, the conclusion, because the argument initially merely *asks* whether it can be concluded on the basis of the first statement (that is, it asks whether the first boldface statement provides support for it). The conclusion of the argument is actually the statement *The answer, clearly, is yes.* The word *yes* is elliptical for *Yes, it can be concluded that for a given level of output, Delta's operation now causes less fossil fuel to be consumed than it did formerly.* The boldface portion tells us what can be concluded, and thus it can accurately be described as the content of the conclusion.

C   Nothing in the passage is intended to support the first statement; and the second statement is not supposed to call the first into question.

D   This correctly identifies the role of the first statement, but the second boldfaced portion does not call the argument's conclusion into question—it is part of a sentence that refers to the question whether that conclusion can be drawn from the first statement.

E   Again, this is only half right. The second boldfaced portion is not offered as support for the conclusion; if it were offered as such support, the argument would be guilty of circular reasoning, since the second boldfaced portion states exactly what the argument concludes.

The correct answer is B.

644. A product that represents a clear technological advance over competing products can generally command a high price. Because **technological advances tend to be quickly surpassed** and companies want to make large profits while they still can, many companies charge the greatest price the market will bear when they have such a product. But **large profits on the new product will give competitors a strong incentive to quickly match the new product's capabilities**. Consequently, the strategy to maximize overall profit from a new product is to charge less than the greatest possible price.

In the argument above, the two portions in **boldface** play which of the following roles?

(A) The first is an assumption that forms the basis for a course of action that the argument criticizes; the second presents the course of action endorsed by the argument.

(B) The first is a consideration raised to explain the appeal of a certain strategy; the second is a consideration raised to call into question the wisdom of adopting that strategy.

(C) The first is an assumption that has been used to justify a certain strategy; the second is a consideration that is used to cast doubt on that assumption.

(D) The first is a consideration raised in support of a strategy the argument endorses; the second presents grounds in support of that consideration.

(E) The first is a consideration raised to show that adopting a certain strategy is unlikely to achieve the intended effect; the second is presented to explain the appeal of that strategy.

Argument Evaluation

Situation   Companies generally charge the greatest price the market will bear when they have a product that represents a technological advance. This is because they want to make large profits while they can. But making large profits inspires competition. As a result, profits can be maximized by charging less than the greatest price possible.

Reasoning   *What logical roles do the two portions in boldface play in the argument?* The first sentence of the passage introduces a connection between technological advances and price. The second sentence discusses a pricing strategy related to such advances and offers certain considerations that help explain that strategy. The first boldfaced portion of the passage, which is contained in the second sentence, presents one of these considerations. The third sentence begins with the word "But," which suggests that what follows—the second boldfaced section—presents a consideration that may be at least superficially at odds with the strategy just described. The final sentence of the argument presents an alternative strategy that is supported by the preceding discussion.

A   The course of action endorsed by the argument is described in the passage's fourth and final sentence, not in the second boldfaced portion, which is found in the passage's third sentence.

B   **Correct.** The first boldfaced portion is part of an explanation of why many companies follow the strategy of charging as much as the market will bear when they have a product representing a technological advance. The second boldfaced portion gives a reason not to follow that strategy.

C   The second boldfaced portion does not cast doubt on an assumption used to justify a strategy, but rather casts doubt on the strategy itself.

D   The first boldfaced portion is raised in support of a strategy that the argument calls into question, not a strategy that the argument endorses.

E   The first boldfaced portion helps explain the appeal of adopting a certain strategy; it does not show that the strategy is likely to fail. The second boldfaced portion does not explain the appeal of the strategy, but rather calls the strategy into question.

The correct answer is B.

645. Theater Critic: The play *La Finestrina*, now at Central Theater, was written in Italy in the eighteenth century. The director claims that this production is as similar to the original production as is possible in a modern theater. Although the actor who plays Harlequin the clown gives a performance very reminiscent of the twentieth-century American comedian Groucho Marx, Marx's comic style was very much within the comic acting tradition that had begun in sixteenth-century Italy.

The considerations given best serve as part of an argument that

(A) modern audiences would find it hard to tolerate certain characteristics of a historically accurate performance of an eighteenth-century play

(B) Groucho Marx once performed the part of the character Harlequin in *La Finestrina*

(C) in the United States the training of actors in the twentieth century is based on principles that do not differ radically from those that underlay the training of actors in eighteenth-century Italy

(D) the performance of the actor who plays Harlequin in *La Finestrina* does not serve as evidence against the director's claim

(E) the director of *La Finestrina* must have advised the actor who plays Harlequin to model his performance on comic performances of Groucho Marx

Argument Construction

Situation   The director of the local production of *La Finestrina* says it is as similar to the original production as is possible in a modern theater. The actor playing Harlequin gives a performance reminiscent of Groucho Marx, whose comic style falls within an acting tradition which began in sixteenth-century Italy.

Reasoning   *For which of the options would the consideration given best serve as an argument?* The actor's performance was reminiscent of someone who fell within a tradition going back to sixteenth-century Italy. The play was written, and therefore was likely first performed, in eighteenth-century Italy. All of this suggests that there could be a similarity between the performances of Harlequin in the local production and in the original production. While the two performances *might* have been quite dissimilar, there is nothing *here* that supports that.

A   Regardless of how plausible this option might be on its own merits, the passage provides no support for it because the passage provides no information about the characteristics of a historically accurate performance of an eighteenth-century play.

B   The passage neither says this nor implies it.

C   The passage says nothing about the training of actors, so this option would be supported by the passage only in a very roundabout, indirect way.

D   Correct. This is the option that the considerations most support.

E   That the performance reminded the theater critic of Groucho Marx hardly shows that the similarity was intentional, let alone that it was at the director's instruction.

The correct answer is D.

646. Although the discount stores in Goreville's central shopping district are expected to close within five years as a result of competition from a SpendLess discount department store that just opened, those locations will not stay vacant for long. In the five years since the opening of Colson's, a nondiscount department store, a new store has opened at the location of every store in the shopping district that closed because it could not compete with Colson's.

Which of the following, if true, most seriously weakens the argument?

(A) Many customers of Colson's are expected to do less shopping there than they did before the SpendLess store opened.

(B) Increasingly, the stores that have opened in the central shopping district since Colson's opened have been discount stores.

(C) At present, the central shopping district has as many stores operating in it as it ever had.

(D) Over the course of the next five years, it is expected that Goreville's population will grow at a faster rate than it has for the past several decades.

(E) Many stores in the central shopping district sell types of merchandise that are not available at either SpendLess or Colson's.

Argument Evaluation

Situation   Due to competition from a recently opened SpendLess discount department store, discount stores in Goreville's central shopping district are expected to close within five years. But those locations will not be vacant long, for new stores have replaced all those that closed because of the opening five years ago of a Colson's nondiscount department store.

Reasoning   *Which option would most weaken the argument?* The arguer infers that stores that leave because of the SpendLess will be replaced in their locations by other stores because that is what happened after the Colson's department store came in. Since the reasoning relies on a presumed similarity between the two cases, any information that brings to light a relevant dissimilarity would weaken the argument. If the stores that were driven out by Colson's were replaced mostly by discount stores, that suggests that the stores were replaced because of a need that no longer exists after the opening of SpendLess.

A   The fact that Colson's may be seeing fewer customers does not mean that the discount stores that close will not be replaced; they might be replaced by stores that in no way compete with Colson's or SpendLess.

B   **Correct.** As explained in the Reasoning section above, the reasoning in the argument relies on a presumed similarity between the two cases, so any information that brings to light a relevant dissimilarity would weaken the argument. In the previous five years, the stores that went out of business were apparently direct competitors of Colson's, whereas their replacements were of a different type. In contrast, in the predicted scenario, the stores that are expected to go out of business are apparently direct competitors of the new SpendLess discount store. Furthermore, if there has been a significant increase in the number of discount stores in the shopping district, the market for discount stores may well be nearly saturated, so that few, if any, new ones can survive.

C   If anything, this strengthens the argument by indicating that Goreville's central shopping district is thriving.

D   This strengthens the argument because one is more likely to open a new store in an area with a growing population.

E   Because this statement does not indicate whether any of these stores that offer goods not sold at SpendLess or Colson's will be among those that are closing, it is not possible to determine what effect it has on the strength of the argument.

The correct answer is B.

647. Last year all refuse collected by Shelbyville city services was incinerated. This incineration generated a large quantity of residual ash. In order to reduce the amount of residual ash Shelbyville generates this year to half of last year's total, the city has revamped its collection program. This year city services will separate for recycling enough refuse to reduce the number of truckloads of refuse to be incinerated to half of last year's number.

Which of the following is required for the revamped collection program to achieve its aim?

(A) This year, no materials that city services could separate for recycling will be incinerated.

(B) Separating recyclable materials from materials to be incinerated will cost Shelbyville less than half what it cost last year to dispose of the residual ash.

(C) Refuse collected by city services will contain a larger proportion of recyclable materials this year than it did last year.

(D) The refuse incinerated this year will generate no more residual ash per truckload incinerated than did the refuse incinerated last year.

(E) The total quantity of refuse collected by Shelbyville city services this year will be no greater than that collected last year.

Argument Construction

Situation   To cut in half the residual ash produced at its incinerator, the city will separate, for recycling, enough refuse to cut in half the number of truckloads of refuse going to the incinerator.

Reasoning   *Which option is required if the city's revamped collection program is to achieve its aim?* Cutting the number of truckloads of refuse in half must reduce the amount of residual ash to half last year's level. But if removal of the recycled refuse does not proportionately reduce the amount of ash, this will not happen. So, if the amount of residual ash produced per truckload increases after recycling, then the amount of ash produced will not be cut in half by cutting in half the number of truckloads.

A   This merely indicates that no further reduction of ash through recycling could be achieved this year; it indicates nothing about how much the ash will be reduced.

B   This suggests a further benefit from recycling, but does not bear on the amount of ash that will be produced.

C   Since no information is provided about how much, if any, recyclable materials were removed from the refuse last year, this does not affect the reasoning.

D   **Correct.** This states a requirement for the collection program to achieve its aim. To see why this is required, assume this were not true. Suppose, instead, that the refuse incinerated this year would generate more residual ash per truckload incinerated than the refuse incinerated last year did. If that were the case, then cutting in half the truckloads to be incinerated would not cut in half the amount of residual ash generated by incineration.

E   This is not a requirement because even if the city collects more refuse this year, it could still cut in half the amount of residual ash by cutting in half the number of truckloads going to the incinerator.

The correct answer is D.

648. Veterinarians generally derive some of their income from selling several manufacturers' lines of pet-care products. Knowing that pet owners rarely throw away mail from their pet's veterinarian unread, one manufacturer of pet-care products offered free promotional materials on its products to veterinarians for mailing to their clients. Very few veterinarians accepted the offer, however, even though the manufacturer's products are of high quality.

Which of the following, if true, most helps to explain the veterinarians' reaction to the manufacturer's promotional scheme?

(A) Most of the veterinarians to whom the free promotional materials were offered were already selling the manufacturer's pet-care products to their clients.

(B) The special promotional materials were intended as a supplement to the manufacturer's usual promotional activities rather than as a replacement for them.

(C) The manufacturer's products, unlike most equally good competing products sold by veterinarians, are also available in pet stores and in supermarkets.

(D) Many pet owners have begun demanding quality in products they buy for their pets that is as high as that in products they buy for themselves.

(E) Veterinarians sometimes recommend that pet owners use products formulated for people when no suitable product specially formulated for animals is available.

Evaluation of a Plan

Situation   Veterinarians generally derive some income from selling various manufacturers' pet-care products, but very few veterinarians accepted free promotional materials from one such manufacturer to mail to their clients.

Reasoning   *What would most help explain why so few veterinarians accepted the free promotional materials to mail to their clients?* The passage says that veterinarians generally derive income from selling pet-care products, which suggests that it should have been in many veterinarians' financial interest to accept and mail out the free promotional materials to increase sales. Any evidence that mailing out these specific promotional materials from this manufacturer would not actually have been in many veterinarians' financial interest could help explain why so few veterinarians accepted the materials.

A   This suggests that most of the veterinarians should have had a financial interest in accepting and mailing out the promotional materials in order to increase their sales of the manufacturer's products.

B   Even if the promotional materials supplemented the manufacturer's usual promotional activities, they could still have increased the veterinarians' sales of the manufacturer's products and thus generated more income for the veterinarians.

C   **Correct.** If this manufacturer's products are available in pet stores and supermarkets but most other products sold by veterinarians are not, then distributing the manufacturer's promotional materials could have encouraged customers to buy this manufacturer's products from pet stores and supermarkets rather than to buy competing products from the veterinarians. Thus, the veterinarians may have been concerned that the promotions would reduce their profits.

D   The passage says the manufacturer's products are of high quality, so we have no reason to suppose that clients' demand for quality products would discourage veterinarians from accepting the manufacturer's promotional materials.

E   Presumably the manufacturer's products are specially formulated for pets, so any products veterinarians recommend only when no specially formulated pet-care products are available would not reduce the veterinarians' interest in promoting the manufacturer's products.

The correct answer is C.

649. The average hourly wage of television assemblers in Vernland has long been significantly lower than that in neighboring Borodia. Since Borodia dropped all tariffs on Vernlandian televisions three years ago, the number of televisions sold annually in Borodia has not changed. However, recent statistics show a drop in the number of television assemblers in Borodia. Therefore, updated trade statistics will probably indicate that the number of televisions Borodia imports annually from Vernland has increased.

Which of the following is an assumption on which the argument depends?

(A) The number of television assemblers in Vernland has increased by at least as much as the number of television assemblers in Borodia has decreased.

(B) Televisions assembled in Vernland have features that televisions assembled in Borodia do not have.

(C) The average number of hours it takes a Borodian television assembler to assemble a television has not decreased significantly during the past three years.

(D) The number of televisions assembled annually in Vernland has increased significantly during the past three years.

(E) The difference between the hourly wage of television assemblers in Vernland and the hourly wage of television assemblers in Borodia is likely to decrease in the next few years.

Argument Construction

Situation   Television assemblers in Vernland are paid less than those in neighboring Borodia. The number of televisions sold in Borodia has not dropped since its tariffs on Vernlandian TVs were lowered three years ago, but the number of TV assemblers in Borodia has. So TV imports from Vernland have likely increased.

Reasoning   *What assumption does the argument depend on?* The fact that fewer individuals in Borodia are working as TV assemblers is offered as evidence that TV imports from Vernland into Borodia have likely increased. That piece of evidence is relevant only as an indication that the number of TVs being produced within Borodia has decreased. But a drop in the number of TV assemblers does not indicate a drop in the number of TVs being assembled if the number of TVs an average assembler puts together has increased. Thus, the argument must be assuming that the average time it takes an assembler to put together a TV has not significantly decreased.

A   The argument does not rely on any information about the number of television assemblers in Vernland nor for that matter on the number of TVs assembled in Vernland.

B   The argument need not assume there is any difference in the features of the TVs produced in the two countries. Increased sales of Vernlandian TVs in Borodia could be due to any number of other reasons, such as price or quality.

C   **Correct.** If the average productivity of TV assemblers had increased significantly, the fact that there are fewer Borodian TV assemblers would not strongly support the conclusion that there has been a decrease in the number of TVs assembled in Borodia and an increase in imports; fewer assemblers may be producing just as many TVs as before. Therefore, for the argument to work, it needs to assume that productivity per assembler in Borodia has not decreased significantly.

D   The argument does not depend upon this being so: Vernland's domestic TV sales (or perhaps its exports to countries other than Borodia) may have decreased by more than its exports to Borodia have increased.

E   The argument's conclusion addresses what has happened; the argument in no way relies on any assumptions about what may or may not happen in the coming years.

The correct answer is C.

650. Guidebook writer: I have visited hotels throughout the country and have noticed that in those built before 1930 the quality of the original carpentry work is generally superior to that in hotels built afterward. Clearly carpenters working on hotels before 1930 typically worked with more skill, care, and effort than carpenters who have worked on hotels built subsequently.

Which of the following, if true, most seriously weakens the guidebook writer's argument?

(A) The quality of original carpentry in hotels is generally far superior to the quality of original carpentry in other structures, such as houses and stores.

(B) Hotels built since 1930 can generally accommodate more guests than those built before 1930.

(C) The materials available to carpenters working before 1930 were not significantly different in quality from the materials available to carpenters working after 1930.

(D) The better the quality of original carpentry in a building, the less likely that building is to fall into disuse and be demolished.

(E) The average length of apprenticeship for carpenters has declined significantly since 1930.

Argument Evaluation

Situation The original carpentry in hotels built before 1930 shows superior care, skill, and effort to that in hotels built after 1930. This leads to the conclusion that carpenters working on hotels before 1930 were superior in skill, care, and effort to those that came after.

Reasoning *Which option most seriously weakens the argument?* The argument draws an inference from a comparison between carpentry in hotels of different eras to a judgment about the carpenters working on hotels in those eras. One way to weaken this inference is by finding some way in which the carpentry in the hotels may be unrepresentative of the skill, care, and effort of the carpenters working in the eras. The comparison is between the carpentry evident in hotels of the two eras *that still exist.* Thus, if there is some reason to think that hotels with good carpentry survive longer than those with bad carpentry, then still-existing hotels from the older era will have disproportionately more good carpentry, even assuming no difference between the skill, care, and effort of the carpenters from the two eras.

A This option applies equally to both eras, so it has no bearing on the argument.

B It is not clear whether carpenters working on larger hotels would exercise more, less, or the same skill and care as those working on smaller hotels; thus this option does not weaken the argument.

C The argument does not rely, even implicitly, on there being any difference in the quality of materials used in the two eras, so it does not weaken the argument to point out that no such difference exists.

D Correct. This weakens the reasoning in the argument by showing a respect in which the comparison between *existing* hotels may be unrepresentative. Specifically, the comparison may be unrepresentative in that still-existing hotels that were built prior to 1930 may well have been better built than most hotels built prior to 1930 were; the hotels that did not have unusually high-quality carpentry work may have all fallen into disuse and been demolished.

E The longer a carpenter works as an apprentice, the more skill he or she is apt to have upon becoming a full-fledged carpenter. So this option would tend to slightly strengthen rather than weaken the argument.

The correct answer is D.

651. Scientists typically do their most creative work before the age of forty. It is commonly thought that this happens because aging by itself brings about a loss of creative capacity. However, studies show that **of scientists who produce highly creative work beyond the age of forty, a disproportionately large number entered their field at an older age than is usual.** Since by the age of forty the large majority of scientists have been working in their field for at least fifteen years, the studies' finding strongly suggests that the real reason why scientists over forty rarely produce highly creative work is not that they have aged but rather that **scientists over forty have generally spent too long in their field.**

In the argument given, the two portions in **boldface** play which of the following roles?

(A) The first is a claim, the accuracy of which is at issue in the argument; the second is a conclusion drawn on the basis of that claim.

(B) The first is an objection that has been raised against a position defended in the argument; the second is that position.

(C) The first is evidence that has been used to support an explanation that the argument challenges; the second is that explanation.

(D) The first is evidence that has been used to support an explanation that the argument challenges; the second is a competing explanation that the argument favors.

(E) The first provides evidence to support an explanation that the argument favors; the second is that explanation.

Argument Evaluation

Situation   It is generally thought that the reason scientists tend to do their most creative work before age forty is that creative capacity declines with age. Yet those scientists who do creative work after forty tend, disproportionately, to have started their careers in science later in life. So a better explanation is that many scientists over forty have just been at it too long.

Reasoning   *What roles do the two portions of the argument that are in boldface play?* The argument describes a phenomenon and what is commonly thought to explain it. Then, the first boldfaced statement introduces evidence that suggests that there may be another explanation. After this evidence is further developed, the argument then concludes that there is indeed a better explanation for the phenomenon; that explanation is stated in the second boldfaced portion.

A   The accuracy of the first statement is never called into question by the argument; rather, it is relied upon as the basis for the argument's conclusion.

B   The first statement is not an objection against the position the argument defends; instead, it is a basis for that position.

C   The first statement is not used to support a position the argument challenges, and the second statement is the explanation the argument supports, not the one it challenges.

D   The second statement is indeed an explanation that the argument favors; but the first statement is not used to support a competing explanation that the argument challenges.

E   **Correct.** This option correctly identifies the roles played by the boldfaced portions of the argument.

The correct answer is E.

652. NorthAir charges low fares for its economy-class seats, but it provides very cramped seating and few amenities. Market research shows that economy passengers would willingly pay more for wider seating and better service, and additional revenue provided by these higher ticket prices would more than cover the additional cost of providing these amenities. Even though NorthAir is searching for ways to improve its profitability, it has decided not to make these improvements.

Which of the following, if true, would most help to explain NorthAir's decision in light of its objectives?

(A) None of NorthAir's competitors offers significantly better seating and service to economy-class passengers than NorthAir does.

(B) On many of the routes that NorthAir flies, it is the only airline to offer direct flights.

(C) A few of NorthAir's economy-class passengers are satisfied with the service they receive, given the low price they pay.

(D) Very few people avoid flying on NorthAir because of the cramped seating and poor service offered in economy class.

(E) The number of people who would be willing to pay the high fares NorthAir charges for its business-class seats would decrease if its economy-class seating were more acceptable.

Evaluation of a Plan

Situation   Market research shows that improving some amenities for economy-class passengers would allow NorthAir to raise its economy ticket prices more than enough to cover the additional cost of providing those amenities. But NorthAir has decided not to improve those amenities, even though it is looking for ways to improve its profitability.

Reasoning   *What would most help explain why NorthAir decided not to improve the seating and other amenities, even though the resulting increase in economy-class ticket prices would more than cover the expense?* NorthAir is looking for ways to improve its profitability. Making improvements that would increase ticket prices enough to generate more revenue than they cost should improve profitability, other things being equal. But if improving the amenities would generate side effects that reduced profitability, those side effects would provide a good reason for NorthAir's decision not to improve the amenities and hence would help explain why NorthAir made that decision.

A   The passage says that for NorthAir, the cost of providing better economy seating and other amenities would be more than met by the increased revenue from the higher ticket prices that passengers would be willing to pay. This could give NorthAir a competitive edge, with improved profitability.

B   Even if NorthAir faces little or no competition on certain routes, offering extra amenities might increase passengers' interest in flying those routes. It might also lead passengers to choose NorthAir on other routes that competing airlines also serve. Both of these effects could improve NorthAir's profitability.

C   Even if a few NorthAir economy passengers would not pay more for extra amenities, the market research indicates that most of them would, so offering the amenities could still improve NorthAir's profits attributable to economy-class seating.

D   This suggests that improving the amenities would not increase the total number of NorthAir passengers. But improving the amenities might still enable the airline to increase its ticket prices per passenger enough to improve its profitability.

E   **Correct.** This suggests that improving the economy-class amenities would reduce NorthAir's revenue from sales of business-class tickets, which are likely much more expensive than economy-class tickets. This reduction in revenue could be enough to reduce NorthAir's total profitability despite the increased revenue from economy-class ticket sales.

The correct answer is E.

653. Which of the following most logically completes the argument given?

Asthma, a chronic breathing disorder, is significantly more common today among adult competitive swimmers than it is among competitive athletes who specialize in other sports. Although chlorine is now known to be a lung irritant and swimming pool water is generally chlorinated, it would be rash to assume that frequent exposure to chlorine is the explanation of the high incidence of asthma among these swimmers, since _____.

(A) young people who have asthma are no more likely to become competitive athletes than are young people who do not have asthma

(B) competitive athletes who specialize in sports other than swimming are rarely exposed to chlorine

(C) competitive athletes as a group have a significantly lower incidence of asthma than do people who do not participate in competitive athletics

(D) until a few years ago, physicians routinely recommended competitive swimming to children with asthma, in the belief that this form of exercise could alleviate asthma symptoms

(E) many people have asthma without knowing they have it and thus are not diagnosed with the condition until they begin engaging in very strenuous activities, such as competitive athletics

Argument Construction

Situation   Asthma is more common among competitive swimmers than among other competitive athletes. Chlorine is a lung irritant generally present in swimming pool water.

Reasoning   *What would cast doubt on the hypothesis that exposure to chlorine in swimming pools accounts for the high incidence of asthma among adult competitive swimmers?* Evidence of any other factor that would provide an alternative explanation of why asthma is more common among adult competitive swimmers than among other competitive athletes would make it rash to assume that frequent exposure to chlorine explains the high incidence of asthma among these swimmers, so a statement providing such evidence would logically fill in the blank at the end of the passage to complete the argument.

A   This might help explain why competitive athletes in general are not especially likely to have asthma, but it does not explain why adult competitive swimmers are more likely to have asthma than other competitive athletes are.

B   This provides additional evidence that exposure to chlorine explains why adult competitive swimmers are more likely to have asthma than other competitive athletes are, so it does not cast doubt on that hypothesis.

C   A lower incidence of asthma among competitive athletes than among nonathletes does not help explain the higher incidence of asthma among adult competitive swimmers than among other competitive athletes.

D   Correct. Routinely encouraging children with asthma to take up competitive swimming would likely have made the proportion of adult competitive swimmers with asthma exceed the proportion of other competitive athletes with asthma, even if chlorine in swimming pool water never causes asthma in swimmers.

E   This might help explain why people with asthma are just as likely as other people to become competitive athletes, but it does not help explain why adult competitive swimmers are more likely to have asthma than other competitive athletes are.

The correct answer is D.

654. In the country of Marut, the Foreign Trade Agency's records were reviewed in 1994 in light of information then newly available about neighboring Goro. The review revealed that in every year since 1963, the agency's projection of what Goro's gross national product (GNP) would be five years later was a serious underestimate. The review also revealed that in every year since 1963, the agency estimated Goro's GNP for the previous year—a Goro state secret—very accurately.

Of the following claims, which is most strongly supported by the statements given?

(A) Goro's GNP fluctuated greatly between 1963 and 1994.

(B) Prior to 1995, Goro had not released data intended to mislead the agency in making its five-year projections.

(C) The amount by which the agency underestimated the GNP it projected for Goro tended to increase over time.

(D) Even before the new information came to light, the agency had reason to think that at least some of the five-year projections it had made were inaccurate.

(E) The agency's five-year projections of Goro's GNP had no impact on economic planning in Marut.

Argument Construction

Situation   A review in 1994 revealed that every year since 1963, Marut's Foreign Trade Agency had seriously underestimated what Goro's GNP would be five years later, but accurately estimated what Goro's GNP had been the previous year.

Reasoning   *What conclusion do the stated facts most strongly support?* Goro's GNP in each year at least from 1969 through 1993 had been seriously underestimated by the agency five years in advance, yet was then accurately estimated by the agency one year after the fact. It follows that for each of these years, the agency's earlier projection of Goro's GNP must have been much lower than its later estimate.

A   This is not supported by the information given. The fact that the agency consistently underestimated each year's GNP in its five-year projections and then correctly estimated it after the fact does not indicate that Goro's GNP fluctuated greatly.

B   This is not supported by the information given. The reason the agency's five-year projections were inaccurate might well have been that Goro deliberately released data intended to mislead the agency in making those projections.

C   This is not supported by the information given. The fact that the underestimates remained large throughout the years in question does not indicate that the underestimates increased over time.

D   Correct. As explained above, for many years there were serious discrepancies between the agency's five-year projections of Goro's GNP and its retrospective estimates of each previous year's trade. In any year at least from 1970 through 1993, these discrepancies, if noticed, would have given the agency reason to doubt some of the five-year projections.

E   This is not supported by the information given. Even though at least some of the five-year projections were eventually known to be serious underestimates, they could still have affected Marut's economic planning. The economic planners might have retained an unreasonable faith in the accuracy of the most recent projections.

The correct answer is D.

655. Vargonia has just introduced a legal requirement that student-teacher ratios in government-funded schools not exceed a certain limit. All Vargonian children are entitled to education, free of charge, in these schools. When a recession occurs and average incomes fall, the number of children enrolled in government-funded schools tends to increase. Therefore, though most employment opportunities contract in economic recessions, getting a teaching job in Vargonia's government-funded schools will not be made more difficult by a recession.

Which of the following would be most important to determine in order to evaluate the argument?

(A) Whether in Vargonia there are any schools not funded by the government that offer children an education free of charge

(B) Whether the number of qualified applicants for teaching positions in government-funded schools increases significantly during economic recessions

(C) What the current student-teacher ratio in Vargonia's government-funded schools is

(D) What proportion of Vargonia's workers currently hold jobs as teachers in government-funded schools

(E) Whether in the past a number of government-funded schools in Vargonia have had student-teacher ratios well in excess of the new limit

Argument Evaluation

Situation   During a recession, the number of children in government-funded schools in Vargonia tends to increase. Vargonian children are entitled to a free education in these schools. A new law requires student-teacher ratios in these schools to remain below a certain limit.

Reasoning   *Which of the five questions would provide us with the best information for evaluating the argument?* The argument's conclusion is that recessions do not make teaching jobs in Vargonia's government-funded schools harder to get. During recessions, the reasoning goes, more students will enroll in Vargonia's government-funded schools than in nonrecession times. Implicit in the argument is the thought that, because the new law sets an upper limit on the average number of students per teacher, schools that get an influx of new students would have to hire more teachers. During a recession, however, there might be much more competition in the labor market for teachers because many more qualified people are applying for teaching jobs.

A   This information is not significant in the context of the argument, which does not need to assume that only government-funded schools provide free education.

B   **Correct.** Getting an answer to this question would provide us with specific information useful in evaluating the argument. A "yes" answer to this question would suggest that competition for teaching jobs in Vargonian government-funded schools would be keener during recessions. A "no" answer would suggest that the level of competition would decrease during recessions.

C   Discovering the current student-teacher ratio in Vargonia's schools would be of no value, by itself, in evaluating the argument. We do not know what the new upper limit on the student-teacher ratio is, and we do not know whether Vargonia is currently in a recession.

D   Finding out whether the proportion this refers to is 1 percent, for example, or 4 percent, would tell us nothing about whether getting teaching jobs at government-funded schools in Vargonia becomes more difficult during a recession. Among other things, we do not know whether Vargonia is currently in a recession, and we do not know what proportion of Vargonia's workers would be qualified candidates for teaching jobs.

E   This is of no relevance in evaluating the argument because, presumably, the new limit on student-teacher ratios will be complied with. Thus, even if student-teacher ratios in the past would have exceeded the new limit, the argument concerns whether, *in the future*, getting a teaching job in Vargonia's government-funded schools will be made more difficult by a recession.

The correct answer is B.

656. In Colorado subalpine meadows, nonnative dandelions co-occur with a native flower, the larkspur. Bumblebees visit both species, creating the potential for interactions between the two species with respect to pollination. In a recent study, researchers selected 16 plots containing both species; all dandelions were removed from eight plots; the remaining eight control plots were left undisturbed. The control plots yielded significantly more larkspur seeds than the dandelion-free plots, leading the researchers to conclude that the presence of dandelions facilitates pollination (and hence seed production) in the native species by attracting more pollinators to the mixed plots.

Which of the following, if true, most seriously undermines the researchers' reasoning?

(A) Bumblebees preferentially visit dandelions over larkspurs in mixed plots.

(B) In mixed plots, pollinators can transfer pollen from one species to another to augment seed production.

(C) If left unchecked, nonnative species like dandelions quickly crowd out native species.

(D) Seed germination is a more reliable measure of a species' fitness than seed production.

(E) Soil disturbances can result in fewer blooms, and hence lower seed production.

Argument Evaluation

Situation   Bumblebees visit both larkspur and dandelions in certain meadows. A study found that more larkspur seeds were produced in meadow plots in which both larkspur and dandelions grew than in similar plots from which all dandelions had been removed. The researchers inferred that dandelions facilitate larkspur pollination.

Reasoning   *What evidence would cast the most doubt on the inference from the study's findings to the conclusion that dandelions facilitate larkspur pollination by attracting more pollinators?* The argument assumes that the only relevant difference between the two types of plots was whether dandelions were present. Evidence that the plots differed in some other way that could provide a plausible alternative explanation of why more larkspur seeds were produced in the plots with dandelions would weaken the argument.

A   This would suggest that the larkspur pollination should have been lower in the plots with dandelions, so it does not provide a plausible alternative explanation for the study's findings.

B   This is fully compatible with the claim that the dandelions attracted more pollinators to the mixed plots, and it would also help to support the argument's conclusion that dandelions facilitated larkspur pollination in those plots.

C   Although this suggests that the mixed plots won't remain mixed for long, it does not provide a plausible alternative explanation for the study's finding that larkspur seed production was higher in the mixed plots.

D   The argument is not about how fit larkspurs are as a species, but about why they produced different numbers of seeds in the different plots.

E   **Correct.** This provides a plausible alternative explanation for why larkspur seed production was lower in the plots from which dandelions had been removed, since digging them out would have disturbed the soil.

The correct answer is E.

657. An experiment was done in which human subjects recognize a pattern within a matrix of abstract designs and then select another design that completes that pattern. The results of the experiment were surprising. The lowest expenditure of energy in neurons in the brain was found in those subjects who performed most successfully in the experiments.

Which of the following hypotheses best accounts for the findings of the experiment?

(A) The neurons of the brain react less when a subject is trying to recognize patterns than when the subject is doing other kinds of reasoning.

(B) Those who performed best in the experiment experienced more satisfaction when working with abstract patterns than did those who performed less well.

(C) People who are better at abstract pattern recognition have more energy-efficient neural connections.

(D) The energy expenditure of the subjects' brains increases when a design that completes the initially recognized pattern is determined.

(E) The task of completing a given design is more capably performed by athletes, whose energy expenditure is lower when they are at rest.

Argument Construction

Situation   Experimental subjects worked with pattern recognition and completion. The subjects who performed best showed the lowest expenditure of energy in neurons in the brain.

Reasoning   *Which hypothesis best accounts for the findings?* In order to account for the findings, the hypothesis must suggest a plausible link between successful performance and the energy expenditure of neurons in the brain. Consider each answer choice, and evaluate its plausibility and logic. Where is there a reasonably direct relationship between the given factors and the conclusion that is drawn? Understand that hypotheses based on factors not included in the experiment cannot be used to account for the findings.

A   The experiment did not compare types of reasoning so this hypothesis does not account for the results.

B   No information is provided about subjects' satisfaction, so this hypothesis is not warranted.

C   **Correct.** This statement properly identifies a hypothesis that connects subjects' performance with their energy expenditure and so could account for the experiment's results.

D   The most successful subjects would presumably not have completed fewer patterns than average, so the posited increase in energy would likely lead to higher energy expenditures for them, not lower.

E   No information is offered on the subjects, so no hypothesis about athletes is warranted.

The correct answer is C.

658. With seventeen casinos, Moneyland operates the most casinos in a certain state. Although intent on expanding, it was outmaneuvered by Apex Casinos in negotiations to acquire the Eldorado chain. To complete its acquisition of Eldorado, Apex must sell five casinos to comply with a state law forbidding any owner to operate more than one casino per county. Since Apex will still be left operating twenty casinos in the state, it will then have the most casinos in the state.

Which of the following, if true, most seriously undermines the prediction?

(A) Apex, Eldorado, and Moneyland are the only organizations licensed to operate casinos in the state.

(B) The majority of Eldorado's casinos in the state will need extensive renovations if they are to continue to operate profitably.

(C) Some of the state's counties do not permit casinos.

(D) Moneyland already operates casinos in the majority of the state's counties.

(E) Apex will use funds it obtains from the sale of the five casinos to help fund its acquisition of the Eldorado chain.

Argument Evaluation

Situation   Moneyland operates seventeen casinos, the most in a certain state, and is intent on expanding. Another operator, Apex Casinos, is acquiring the Eldorado casino chain, but must sell five casinos to comply with a state law forbidding any owner to operate more than one casino per county. After these transactions, Apex will operate twenty casinos in the state.

Reasoning   *What observation would cast the most doubt on the prediction that Apex will have the most casinos in the state after the transactions?* Apex will operate twenty casinos, whereas Moneyland now operates just seventeen, and no one else operates even that many. It follows that Apex will operate more casinos after its transactions than Moneyland or any other one owner now operates. However, if Moneyland also acquires three or more casinos during the transactions, then Apex will not have the most casinos in the state afterward. Thus, any observation suggesting that Moneyland is about to acquire several casinos would undermine the prediction.

A   **Correct.** Since Apex is acquiring Eldorado, Moneyland and Apex will be the only remaining licensed casino operators in the state. Therefore, Moneyland is the only likely buyer for the five casinos Apex needs to sell. So Moneyland is likely to acquire the five casinos during the sale and end up with twenty-two casinos—more than Apex.

B   This does not undermine the prediction. Even if the Eldorado casinos cannot operate profitably for long without extensive renovations, Apex will still have twenty casinos immediately after its transactions.

C   This supports rather than undermines the prediction. If fewer counties permit casinos, there will be fewer opportunities for Moneyland or any other operator to acquire more casinos to surpass the twenty Apex will own.

D   This supports rather than undermines the prediction. If Moneyland's seventeen casinos are in most of the state's counties already, then there are fewer counties in which Moneyland could acquire additional casinos to surpass the twenty Apex will own.

E   This supports rather than undermines the prediction. Apex's use of the funds from selling the five casinos to acquire the Eldorado chain will not help anyone else to acquire more casinos to surpass the twenty Apex will own.

The correct answer is A.

659. It is widely assumed that people need to engage in intellectual activities such as solving crossword puzzles or mathematics problems in order to maintain mental sharpness as they age. In fact, however, simply talking to other people—that is, participating in social interaction, which engages many mental and perceptual skills—suffices. Evidence to this effect comes from a study showing that the more social contact people report, the better their mental skills.

Which of the following, if true, most seriously weakens the force of the evidence cited?

(A) As people grow older, they are often advised to keep exercising their physical and mental capacities in order to maintain or improve them.

(B) Many medical conditions and treatments that adversely affect a person's mental sharpness also tend to increase that person's social isolation.

(C) Many people are proficient both in social interactions and in solving mathematical problems.

(D) The study did not itself collect data but analyzed data bearing on the issue from prior studies.

(E) The tasks evaluating mental sharpness for which data were compiled by the study were more akin to mathematics problems than to conversation.

Argument Evaluation

Situation   A study shows that the more social contact people report, the better their mental skills are, so engaging in social interaction is sufficient for maintaining mental sharpness.

Reasoning   *What would suggest that the study does not establish the truth of the conclusion?* The study shows a correlation between mental sharpness and social interaction but does not indicate why this correlation exists. Evidence that mental sharpness contributes to social interaction or that some third factor affects both mental sharpness and social interaction, could provide an alternative explanation for the correlation and thus cast doubt on the explanation that social interaction contributes to mental sharpness.

A   People are often wrongly advised to do things that are not actually beneficial. And even if exercising mental capacities does help to maintain them, the passage says that social interaction provides such exercise.

B   **Correct.** This provides evidence that the correlation observed in the study results from mental sharpness facilitating social interaction, in which case the study results do not indicate that social interaction facilitates mental sharpness.

C   This would be expected, given the argument's conclusion that social interaction helps to maintain better mental skills overall.

D   A study that analyzes data from prior studies can provide evidence just as well as a study that collects its own data can.

E   The argument's conclusion would be compatible with this observation, and would then suggest that social interaction contributes to the mental sharpness needed for tasks similar to math problems.

The correct answer is B.

660. In the United States, of the people who moved from one state to another when they retired, the percentage who retired to Florida has decreased by three percentage points over the past 10 years. Since many local businesses in Florida cater to retirees, these declines are likely to have a noticeably negative economic effect on these businesses and therefore on the economy of Florida.

Which of the following, if true, most seriously weakens the argument given?

(A) People who moved from one state to another when they retired moved a greater distance, on average, last year than such people did ten years ago.

(B) People were more likely to retire to North Carolina from another state last year than people were ten years ago.

(C) The number of people who moved from one state to another when they retired has increased significantly over the past ten years.

(D) The number of people who left Florida when they retired to live in another state was greater last year than it was ten years ago.

(E) Florida attracts more people who move from one state to another when they retire than does any other state.

Argument Evaluation

Situation   Of those people who move to another state when they retire, the percentage moving to Florida has declined. This trend is apt to harm Florida's economy because many businesses there cater to retirees.

Reasoning   *Which of the options most weakens the argument?* The argument draws its conclusion from data about the *proportion* of emigrating retirees moving to Florida. Yet what matters more directly to the conclusion (and to Florida's economy) is the *absolute number* of retirees immigrating to Florida. That number could have remained constant, or even risen, if the absolute number of emigrating retirees itself increased while the proportion going to Florida decreased.

A   This has no obvious bearing on the argument one way or another. It makes it more likely, perhaps, that a person in a distant state will retire to Florida, but less likely that one in a neighboring state will do so.

B   This has no bearing on whether fewer people have been retiring to Florida over the last ten years.

C   **Correct.** This is the option that most seriously weakens the argument.

D   This makes it *more* likely that Florida's economy will be harmed because of decreasing numbers of retirees, but has no real bearing on the argument which concludes specifically that *declines in the proportion of emigrating retirees moving to Florida* will have a negative effect on the state's economy.

E   This is irrelevant. At issue is how the numbers of retirees in Florida from one year compare to the next, not how those numbers compare with numbers of retirees in other states.

The correct answer is C.

661. The spacing of the four holes on a fragment of a bone flute excavated at a Neanderthal campsite is just what is required to play the third through sixth notes of the diatonic scale—the seven-note musical scale used in much of Western music since the Renaissance. Musicologists therefore hypothesize that the diatonic musical scale was developed and used thousands of years before it was adopted by Western musicians.

Which of the following, if true, most strongly supports the hypothesis?

(A) Bone flutes were probably the only musical instrument made by Neanderthals.

(B) No musical instrument that is known to have used a diatonic scale is of an earlier date than the flute found at the Neanderthal campsite.

(C) The flute was made from a cave-bear bone and the campsite at which the flute fragment was excavated was in a cave that also contained skeletal remains of cave bears.

(D) Flutes are the simplest wind instrument that can be constructed to allow playing a diatonic scale.

(E) The cave-bear leg bone used to make the Neanderthal flute would have been long enough to make a flute capable of playing a complete diatonic scale.

Argument Evaluation

Situation   The arrangement of the holes in a bone fragment from a Neanderthal campsite matches part of the scale used in Western music since the Renaissance. Musicologists hypothesize from this that the scale was developed thousands of years before Western musicians adopted it.

Reasoning   *Which of the options, if true, would provide the most support for the musicologists' hypothesis?* One way to approach this question is to ask yourself, "If this option were false, would the hypothesis be *less* likely to be true?" If the Neanderthal bone fragment could *not* have been part of a flute that encompassed *the entire* seven-note diatonic scale, then the bone fragment's existence would not provide strong support for the hypothesis.

A   To the extent that this is even relevant, it tends to weaken the hypothesis; it makes less likely the possibility that Neanderthals used other types of musical instruments employing the diatonic scale.

B   This also weakens the hypothesis because it states that there is no known evidence of a certain type that would support the hypothesis.

C   The fact that the cave-bear bone fragment that was apparently a flute came from a site where many other cave-bear skeletal remains were found has little bearing on the hypothesis, and in no way supports it.

D   This does not strengthen the hypothesis, for even if the option were false—even if a simpler instrument could be constructed that employed the diatonic scale—the existence of a flute employing the diatonic scale would provide no less support for the hypothesis.

E   **Correct.** This option most strongly supports the hypothesis.

The correct answer is E.

662. Which of the following most logically completes the passage?

The figures in portraits by the Spanish painter El Greco (1541–1614) are systematically elongated. In El Greco's time, the intentional distortion of human figures was unprecedented in European painting. Consequently, some critics have suggested that El Greco had an astigmatism, a type of visual impairment, that resulted in people appearing to him in the distorted way that is characteristic of his paintings. However, this suggestion cannot be the explanation, because _____.

(A) several twentieth-century artists have consciously adopted from El Greco's paintings the systematic elongation of the human form

(B) some people do have elongated bodies somewhat like those depicted in El Greco's portraits

(C) if El Greco had an astigmatism, then, relative to how people looked to him, the elongated figures in his paintings would have appeared to him to be distorted

(D) even if El Greco had an astigmatism, there would have been no correction for it available in the period in which he lived

(E) there were non-European artists, even in El Greco's time, who included in their works human figures that were intentionally distorted

Argument Evaluation

Situation   Figures in portraits by the Spanish painter El Greco are elongated. Some critics infer that this was because El Greco suffered from an astigmatism that made people appear elongated to him. But this explanation cannot be correct.

Reasoning   *Which option would most logically complete the argument?* We need something that provides the best reason for thinking that the explanation suggested by critics—astigmatism—cannot be right. The critics' explanation might seem to work because ordinarily an artist would try to paint an image of a person so that the image would have the same proportions as the perceived person. So if people seemed to El Greco to have longer arms and legs than they actually had, the arms and legs of the painted figures should appear to others to be longer than people's arms and legs normally are. This is how the explanation seems to make sense. But if astigmatism were the explanation, then the elongated images in his pictures should have appeared to El Greco to be too long: he would have perceived the images as longer than they actually are—and therefore as inaccurate representations of what he perceived. So astigmatism cannot be a sufficient explanation for the elongated figures in his paintings.

A   Even if subsequent artists intentionally depicted human forms as more elongated than human figures actually are, and they did so to mimic El Greco's painted figures, that does not mean that El Greco's figures were intentionally elongated.

B   Although this option provides another possible explanation for El Greco's elongated figures, it provides no evidence that the people El Greco painted had such elongated figures.

C   **Correct**. El Greco would have perceived the images of people in his paintings as too long, relative to his perception of the people themselves. This means that even if El Greco did have astigmatism, that factor would not provide an answer to the question, Why did El Greco paint images that he knew were distorted?

D   The absence of an ability to correct astigmatism in El Greco's day does not undermine the hypothesis that it was astigmatism that caused El Greco to paint elongated figures.

E   Again, this suggests another possible explanation for the distortion—namely, that El Greco did it deliberately—but it does not provide any reason to think that this is the correct explanation (and that the critics' explanation is actually incorrect).

The correct answer is C.

663. Museums that house Renaissance oil paintings typically store them in environments that are carefully kept within narrow margins of temperature and humidity to inhibit any deterioration. Laboratory tests have shown that the kind of oil paint used in these paintings actually adjusts to climatic changes quite well. If, as some museum directors believe, **paint is the most sensitive substance in these works**, then by relaxing the standards for temperature and humidity control, **museums can reduce energy costs without risking damage to these paintings**. Museums would be rash to relax those standards, however, since results of preliminary tests indicate that gesso, a compound routinely used by Renaissance artists to help paint adhere to the canvas, is unable to withstand significant variations in humidity.

In the argument above, the two portions in **boldface** play which of the following roles?

(A) The first is an objection that has been raised against the position taken by the argument; the second is the position taken by the argument.

(B) The first is the position taken by the argument; the second is the position that the argument calls into question.

(C) The first is a judgment that has been offered in support of the position that the argument calls into question; the second is a circumstance on which that judgment is, in part, based.

(D) The first is a judgment that has been offered in support of the position that the argument calls into question; the second is that position.

(E) The first is a claim that the argument calls into question; the second is the position taken by the argument.

Argument Evaluation

Situation
Museums house Renaissance paintings under strictly controlled climatic conditions to prevent deterioration. This is costly. But the paint in these works actually adjusts well to climate changes. On the other hand, another compound routinely used in these paintings, gesso, does not react well to changes in humidity.

Reasoning
What roles do the two boldfaced statements play in the argument? The first statement is not asserted by the author of the argument, but rather attributed as a belief to some museum directors. What the argument itself asserts is that IF this belief is true THEN the second boldfaced statement is true. But the argument then goes on to offer evidence that the first statement is false and so concludes that museum directors would be ill-advised to assume that the second statement was true.

A This option mistakenly claims that the argument adopts the second statement as its position, when in fact the argument calls this position into question.

B Rather than adopting the first statement, the argument offers evidence that calls it into question.

C This option contends that the first statement is a judgment that is based on the second; in fact the opposite is true.

D Correct. This option properly identifies the roles the two portions in boldface play in the argument.

E While the argument does call the first statement into question, it also calls the second statement into question as well.

The correct answer is D.

664. Codex Berinensis, a Florentine copy of an ancient Roman medical treatise, is undated but contains clues to when it was produced. Its first 80 pages are by a single copyist, but the remaining 20 pages are by three different copyists, which indicates some significant disruption. Since a letter in handwriting, identified as that of the fourth copyist, mentions a plague that killed many people in Florence in 1148, Codex Berinensis was probably produced in that year.

Which of the following, if true, most strongly supports the hypothesis that Codex Berinensis was produced in 1148 ?

(A) Other than Codex Berinensis, there are no known samples of the handwriting of the first three copyists.

(B) According to the account by the fourth copyist, the plague went on for 10 months.

(C) A scribe would be able to copy a page of text the size and style of Codex Berinensis in a day.

(D) There was only one outbreak of plague in Florence in the 1100s.

(E) The number of pages of Codex Berinensis produced by a single scribe becomes smaller with each successive change of copyist.

Argument Evaluation

Situation   The Florentine copy of an ancient Roman work is undated but provides clues as to the time it was produced. The first 80 pages of Codex Berinensis are the work of one copyist. The fact that the last 20 pages are the work of a succession of three different copyists is an indication of serious turmoil at the time the copying was done. Since a letter in the fourth copyist's handwriting reveals that a plague killed many people there in 1148, Codex Berinensis was probably produced in that year.

Reasoning   *Which information supports the hypothesis dating the Codex to 1148?* Consider the basis of the hypothesis: the succession of copyists indicating the work was significantly disrupted, and the fourth copyist's letter indicating the plague of 1148 caused serious loss of life. From this, it is argued that the plague of 1148 was the reason for the multiple copyists and that the work can thus be dated to that year. What if there were multiple plagues?

In that case, Codex Berinensis could have been produced at another time. If, instead, only one plague occurred in the 1100s, the elimination of that possibility supports the hypothesis that the work was done in 1148.

A   Examples of the copyists' handwriting might help date Codex Berinensis; the absence of handwriting samples does not help support 1148 as the date.

B   The length of the plague, while it may account for the succession of copyists, does not help support the particular year the work was done.

C   The amount of work a copyist could achieve each day does not provide any information about the year the work appeared.

D   Correct. This statement properly identifies a circumstance that supports the hypothesis.

E   The productivity or tenure of the various copyists is irrelevant to establishing the date.

The correct answer is D.

9.0 GMAT™ Official Guide Question Index

9.0 GMAT™ Official Guide Question Index

The Official Guide Index is organized by GMAT™ section, difficulty level, and then by mathematical or verbal concept. The question number, page number, and answer explanation page number are listed so that questions within the book can be easily located.

Quantitative Reasoning - Chapter 4 - Page 70

Difficulty	Concept	Question #	Page	Answer Explanation Page
Easy	Algebra Interpretation of Tables; Applied Problems	13	76	114
Easy	Algebraic Expressions	54	82	127
Easy	Algebraic Expressions	62	83	130
Easy	Algebraic Expressions	81	86	138
Easy	Applied Problems	4	75	112
Easy	Applied Problems	5	75	112
Easy	Applied Problems	9	75	113
Easy	Applied Problems	23	77	118
Easy	Applied Problems	25	78	118
Easy	Applied Problems	32	79	120
Easy	Applied Problems	34	79	121
Easy	Applied Problems	41	80	123
Easy	Applied Problems	47	81	125
Easy	Applied Problems	50	81	126
Easy	Applied Problems	57	82	128
Easy	Applied Problems	60	83	129
Easy	Applied Problems	61	83	130
Easy	Applied Problems	64	83	131
Easy	Applied Problems	66	84	132
Easy	Applied Problems	72	85	134
Easy	Applied Problems; First-Degree Equations	85	87	139
Easy	Applied Problems; Percents	33	79	121

(Continued)

Difficulty	Concept	Question #	Page	Answer Explanation Page
Easy	Applied Problems; Percents	49	81	126
Easy	Applied Problems; Percents	67	84	132
Easy	Applied Problems; Properties of Numbers	14	76	115
Easy	Applied Problems; Sequences	68	84	132
Easy	Arithmetic; Simplifying Algebraic Expressions; Percents	31	79	120
Easy	Estimation	28	78	119
Easy	Estimation	46	81	125
Easy	Estimation	48	81	126
Easy	Estimation	51	81	126
Easy	Exponents	38	80	122
Easy	First-Degree Equations	10	75	114
Easy	First-Degree Equations	20	77	117
Easy	First-Degree Equations	22	77	117
Easy	First-Degree Equations	63	83	130
Easy	First-Degree Equations	80	86	137
Easy	Fractions	77	86	136
Easy	Functions	87	87	139
Easy	Inequalities	26	78	118
Easy	Inequalities	55	82	127
Easy	Inequalities	73	85	134
Easy	Inequalities	84	87	138
Easy	Interpretation of Graphs and Tables	45	81	125
Easy	Interpretation of Tables	2	74	111
Easy	Interpretation of Tables	42	80	124
Easy	Measurement Conversion	82	86	138
Easy	Operations on Radical Expressions	65	84	131
Easy	Operations on Rational Numbers	8	75	113
Easy	Operations with Integers	27	78	119

Difficulty	Concept	Question #	Page	Answer Explanation Page
Easy	Operations with Integers	74	85	135
Easy	Operations with Radical Expressions	71	85	134
Easy	Operations with Rational Numbers	11	76	114
Easy	Operations with Rational Numbers	18	77	116
Easy	Operations with Rational Numbers	39	80	123
Easy	Operations with Rational Numbers	40	80	123
Easy	Operations with Rational Numbers	69	84	133
Easy	Percents	7	75	113
Easy	Percents	16	76	116
Easy	Percents	19	77	116
Easy	Percents	59	83	129
Easy	Percents	75	86	136
Easy	Percents	83	87	138
Easy	Percents	86	87	139
Easy	Probability	24	78	118
Easy	Profit and Loss	35	79	121
Easy	Properties of Numbers	52	82	127
Easy	Properties of Numbers	70	84	133
Easy	Properties of Numbers	76	86	136
Easy	Rate	58	83	129
Easy	Ratio and Proportion	12	76	114
Easy	Ratio and Proportion	37	79	122
Easy	Ratio and Proportion	44	80	124
Easy	Sequences	53	82	127
Easy	Simplifying Algebraic Expressions	36	79	122
Easy	Simplifying Algebraic Expressions	78	86	137
Easy	Simultaneous Equations	43	80	124
Easy	Simultaneous First-Degree Equations	29	78	120

(Continued)

Difficulty	Concept	Question #	Page	Answer Explanation Page
Easy	Statistics	1	74	111
Easy	Statistics	3	74	112
Easy	Statistics	6	75	113
Easy	Statistics	15	76	115
Easy	Statistics	17	76	116
Easy	Statistics	21	77	117
Easy	Statistics	30	78	120
Easy	Statistics	56	82	128
Easy	Statistics	79	86	137
Medium	Absolute Value; Number Line	121	92	150
Medium	Algebraic Expressions	92	88	141
Medium	Applied Problems	101	89	144
Medium	Applied Problems	107	90	146
Medium	Applied Problems	118	92	149
Medium	Applied Problems	132	94	154
Medium	Applied Problems	133	94	154
Medium	Applied Problems	135	95	155
Medium	Elementary Combinatorics	145	96	158
Medium	Estimation	134	94	155
Medium	Estimation; Exponents	137	95	156
Medium	Exponents	117	92	149
Medium	First-Degree Equations	104	89	145
Medium	Formulas	91	88	141
Medium	Formulas	95	88	142
Medium	Functions	131	94	154
Medium	Inequalities	122	92	150
Medium	Measurement Conversion	88	87	140
Medium	Measurement Conversion	93	88	141
Medium	Measurement Conversion	106	90	145
Medium	Measurement Conversion	129	94	153

Difficulty	Concept	Question #	Page	Answer Explanation Page
Medium	Operations on Radical Expressions	115	91	148
Medium	Operations with Decimals; Place Value	144	96	158
Medium	Operations with Integers	96	88	142
Medium	Operations with Integers	108	90	146
Medium	Operations with Integers	120	92	150
Medium	Operations with Integers	142	96	158
Medium	Percents	100	89	143
Medium	Percents	110	90	147
Medium	Percents	126	93	152
Medium	Percents	127	93	152
Medium	Percents	139	95	157
Medium	Percents; First-Degree Equations	109	90	146
Medium	Percents; Ratio and Proportion	111	91	147
Medium	Place Value	123	93	151
Medium	Probability	136	95	156
Medium	Properties of Numbers	98	89	143
Medium	Properties of Numbers	128	94	153
Medium	Ratio and Proportion	97	88	142
Medium	Remainders	103	89	144
Medium	Second-Degree Equations	99	89	143
Medium	Second-Degree Equations	114	91	148
Medium	Second-Degree Equations	130	94	154
Medium	Series and Sequences	105	90	145
Medium	Sets	90	88	140
Medium	Sets	116	91	148
Medium	Sets	124	93	151
Medium	Sets	125	93	152
Medium	Sets; Interpretation of Tables	119	92	149
Medium	Simplifying Algebraic Expressions	94	88	141

(*Continued*)

Difficulty	Concept	Question #	Page	Answer Explanation Page
Medium	Simplifying Algebraic Expressions	141	96	157
Medium	Simplifying Algebraic Expressions; Operations on Rational Numbers	113	91	147
Medium	Simultaneous Equations	112	91	147
Medium	Simultaneous Equations; Inequalities	143	96	158
Medium	Statistics	89	87	140
Medium	Statistics	102	89	144
Medium	Statistics	138	95	156
Medium	Statistics	140	96	157
Hard	Applied Problems	146	97	159
Hard	Applied Problems	150	97	160
Hard	Applied Problems	157	98	162
Hard	Applied Problems	163	99	165
Hard	Applied Problems	170	100	168
Hard	Applied Problems	180	102	173
Hard	Applied Problems	184	102	174
Hard	Applied Problems	190	103	177
Hard	Applied Problems	191	103	177
Hard	Applied Problems	199	104	179
Hard	Applied Problems	208	106	183
Hard	Applied Problems	218	107	187
Hard	Applied Problems	219	107	188
Hard	Applied Problems	225	108	191
Hard	Applied Problems; Simultaneous Equations	186	102	175
Hard	Elementary Combinatorics	147	97	159
Hard	Elementary Combinatorics	153	98	161
Hard	Elementary Combinatorics	183	102	174
Hard	Elementary Combinatorics	201	105	180
Hard	Elementary Combinatorics	214	106	185

Difficulty	Concept	Question #	Page	Answer Explanation Page
Hard	Equations	181	102	174
Hard	Estimation	192	103	177
Hard	Inequalities	185	102	175
Hard	Inequalities	193	104	178
Hard	Inequalities	226	108	191
Hard	Interpretation of Graphs and Tables; Statistics	167	100	167
Hard	Negative Exponents	209	106	183
Hard	Negative Exponents	228	108	192
Hard	Operations on Rational Numbers	164	99	166
Hard	Operations on Rational Numbers	166	99	166
Hard	Operations on Rational Numbers	187	103	175
Hard	Operations on Rational Numbers	197	104	179
Hard	Operations on Rational Numbers	202	105	181
Hard	Operations on Rational Numbers	215	107	186
Hard	Operations on Rational Numbers	222	108	189
Hard	Operations on Rational Numbers	223	108	189
Hard	Operations with Integers	176	101	172
Hard	Operations with Integers	204	105	182
Hard	Percents	158	98	163
Hard	Percents	172	100	168
Hard	Percents	175	101	171
Hard	Percents	207	105	182
Hard	Percents	210	106	184
Hard	Percents	216	107	186
Hard	Probability	149	97	160
Hard	Probability	165	99	166
Hard	Probability	173	101	169
Hard	Probability	220	107	188
Hard	Profit and Loss	196	104	179

(Continued)

Difficulty	Concept	Question #	Page	Answer Explanation Page
Hard	Properties of Numbers	148	97	159
Hard	Properties of Numbers	159	99	163
Hard	Properties of Numbers	177	101	172
Hard	Properties of Numbers	178	101	173
Hard	Properties of Numbers	179	102	173
Hard	Properties of Numbers	182	102	174
Hard	Properties of Numbers	189	103	176
Hard	Properties of Numbers	195	104	178
Hard	Properties of Numbers	200	104	180
Hard	Properties of Numbers	213	106	185
Hard	Properties of Numbers; Decimals	152	98	161
Hard	Property of Numbers	168	100	167
Hard	Rate	205	105	182
Hard	Second-Degree Equations	171	100	168
Hard	Second-Degree Equations	188	103	175
Hard	Second-Degree Equations	221	107	188
Hard	Second-Degree Equations	224	108	190
Hard	Second-Degree Equations; Simultaneous Equations	160	99	164
Hard	Sequences	206	105	182
Hard	Sets	227	108	192
Hard	Simplifying Algebraic Expressions	198	104	179
Hard	Simplifying Algebraic Expressions	212	106	185
Hard	Simplifying Expressions; Computation with Integers	203	105	181
Hard	Simultaneous Equations	154	98	161
Hard	Simultaneous Equations; Inequalities	161	99	164
Hard	Statistics	151	97	160
Hard	Statistics	156	98	162
Hard	Statistics	162	99	164

Difficulty	Concept	Question #	Page	Answer Explanation Page
Hard	Statistics	169	100	168
Hard	Statistics	174	101	170
Hard	Statistics	211	106	184
Hard	Statistics; Applied Problems	194	104	178
Hard	Statistics; Applied Problems; Simultaneous Equations	217	107	187
Hard	Systems of Equations	155	98	162

Data Insights - Chapter 6 - Page 214

Difficulty	Concept	Question #	Page	Answer Explanation Page
Easy	Applied Problems	229	226	239
Easy	Applied Problems	231	226	240
Easy	Applied Problems	242	227	245
Easy	Applied Problems	245	227	246
Easy	Applied Problems	246	228	246
Easy	Applied Problems	252	228	248
Easy	Applied Problems	257	229	251
Easy	Applied Problems	260	229	252
Easy	Applied Problems	263	229	253
Easy	Applied Problems; Percents	250	228	248
Easy	Applied Problems; Percents	251	228	248
Easy	Applied Problems; Percents	253	228	249
Easy	Inequalities	261	229	252
Easy	Order	254	228	249
Easy	Order; Ratio	238	227	243
Easy	Percents	259	229	251
Easy	Percents	267	230	254
Easy	Probability	243	227	245

(Continued)

Difficulty	Concept	Question #	Page	Answer Explanation Page
Easy	Probability	258	229	251
Easy	Rate Problem	268	230	255
Easy	Ratio and Proportion	230	226	239
Easy	Ratio and Proportion	233	226	240
Easy	Ratio and Proportion	235	226	241
Easy	Ratio and Proportion	241	227	244
Easy	Ratios	236	227	241
Easy	Sets	249	228	247
Easy	Sets	255	228	250
Easy	Sets	256	229	250
Easy	Sets	262	229	252
Easy	Simultaneous Equations	234	226	241
Easy	Simultaneous Equations	244	227	245
Easy	Simultaneous Equations	248	228	247
Easy	Simultaneous Equations	264	229	253
Easy	Simultaneous Equations	265	229	253
Easy	Simultaneous Equations	266	230	254
Easy	Statistics	232	226	240
Easy	Statistics	237	227	242
Easy	Statistics	239	227	243
Easy	Statistics	240	227	243
Easy	Statistics	247	228	247
Medium	Applied Problems	278	231	259
Medium	Applied Problems	279	231	260
Medium	Applied Problems	284	231	261
Medium	Applied Problems	286	232	262
Medium	Applied Problems	287	232	262
Medium	Applied Problems	291	232	264
Medium	Applied Problems	297	233	267
Medium	Applied Problems	299	233	268

Difficulty	Concept	Question #	Page	Answer Explanation Page
Medium	Applied Problems; Percents	292	232	265
Medium	Applied Problems; Percents	294	233	266
Medium	Applied Problems; Percents	295	233	266
Medium	Applied Problems; Proportions	275	231	257
Medium	Computation with Integers	290	232	264
Medium	Computation with Integers	296	233	266
Medium	First-Degree Equations	281	231	260
Medium	First-Degree Equations	289	232	264
Medium	Inequalities	293	233	265
Medium	Operations with Integers; Order	283	231	261
Medium	Percents	280	231	260
Medium	Probability	285	232	262
Medium	Properties of Integers	301	233	268
Medium	Ratios	273	230	257
Medium	Ratios; Simultaneous Equations	272	230	256
Medium	Sets	288	232	263
Medium	Simultaneous Equations	269	230	255
Medium	Simultaneous Equations	270	230	255
Medium	Simultaneous Equations	271	230	256
Medium	Simultaneous Equations	274	230	257
Medium	Simultaneous Equations	282	231	261
Medium	Statistics	276	231	258
Medium	Statistics	277	231	259
Medium	Statistics	298	233	267
Medium	Statistics	300	233	268
Hard	Applied Problems	306	234	270
Hard	Applied Problems	308	234	271
Hard	Applied Problems	309	234	271
Hard	Applied Problems	314	235	273

(*Continued*)

Difficulty	Concept	Question #	Page	Answer Explanation Page
Hard	Applied Problems	316	235	274
Hard	Applied Problems	320	235	275
Hard	Applied Problems	327	236	279
Hard	Applied Problems	329	237	279
Hard	Applied Problems	331	237	281
Hard	Applied Problems; Estimating	323	236	276
Hard	Computation with Integers	307	234	271
Hard	Inequalities	319	235	275
Hard	Operations on Rational Numbers	324	236	277
Hard	Percents	302	233	269
Hard	Percents	304	234	270
Hard	Percents	310	234	272
Hard	Properties of Numbers	326	236	278
Hard	Probability	305	234	270
Hard	Proportions	332	237	282
Hard	Rate Problems	311	234	272
Hard	Ratio and Proportion	318	235	275
Hard	Sets	303	234	269
Hard	Sets	317	235	274
Hard	Sets	325	236	278
Hard	Simultaneous Equations	312	235	272
Hard	Simultaneous Equations	315	235	274
Hard	Statistics	313	235	273
Hard	Statistics	321	236	276
Hard	Statistics	322	236	276
Hard	Statistics	328	236	279
Hard	Statistics	330	237	280

Verbal Reasoning - Chapter 8 - Page 308

Reading Comprehension - Page 318

Difficulty	Concept	Question #	Page	Answer Explanation Page
Easy	Application	335	319	386
Easy	Application	342	324	391
Easy	Evaluation	339	322	389
Easy	Evaluation	348	327	395
Easy	Evaluation	353	329	398
Easy	Evaluation	356	331	400
Easy	Evaluation	359	332	402
Easy	Evaluation	366	336	406
Easy	Evaluation	370	337	408
Easy	Inference	337	320	387
Easy	Inference	341	324	390
Easy	Inference	344	325	392
Easy	Inference	350	328	396
Easy	Inference	351	329	397
Easy	Inference	352	329	397
Easy	Inference	360	333	402
Easy	Inference	363	334	404
Easy	Inference	364	335	405
Easy	Inference	367	336	407
Easy	Inference	373	337	410
Easy	Inference	376	338	411
Easy	Main Idea	333	318	385
Easy	Main Idea	336	320	387
Easy	Main Idea	347	327	394
Easy	Main Idea	349	328	396
Easy	Main Idea	354	330	399
Easy	Main Idea	372	337	409

(Continued)

Difficulty	Concept	Question #	Page	Answer Explanation Page
Easy	Main Idea	377	338	412
Easy	Supporting Idea	334	318	385
Easy	Supporting Idea	338	321	388
Easy	Supporting Idea	340	323	390
Easy	Supporting Idea	343	325	392
Easy	Supporting Idea	345	326	393
Easy	Supporting Idea	346	326	394
Easy	Supporting Idea	355	330	399
Easy	Supporting Idea	357	331	400
Easy	Supporting Idea	358	332	401
Easy	Supporting Idea	361	333	403
Easy	Supporting Idea	362	334	404
Easy	Supporting Idea	365	335	405
Easy	Supporting Idea	368	337	407
Easy	Supporting Idea	369	337	408
Easy	Supporting Idea	371	337	409
Easy	Supporting Idea	374	338	411
Easy	Supporting Idea	375	338	411
Medium	Application	393	343	422
Medium	Application	398	346	425
Medium	Application	407	350	430
Medium	Application	416	353	435
Medium	Application	421	356	437
Medium	Evaluation	380	339	414
Medium	Evaluation	381	340	414
Medium	Evaluation	383	340	415
Medium	Evaluation	387	341	418
Medium	Evaluation	389	342	419
Medium	Evaluation	399	346	425
Medium	Evaluation	406	349	429

Difficulty	Concept	Question #	Page	Answer Explanation Page
Medium	Evaluation	411	352	432
Medium	Evaluation	417	354	435
Medium	Evaluation	418	354	436
Medium	Evaluation	424	358	439
Medium	Evaluation	428	360	441
Medium	Inference	379	339	413
Medium	Inference	382	340	415
Medium	Inference	385	340	417
Medium	Inference	386	341	417
Medium	Inference	388	342	419
Medium	Inference	392	343	421
Medium	Inference	394	343	423
Medium	Inference	395	344	423
Medium	Inference	404	349	428
Medium	Inference	405	349	429
Medium	Inference	410	351	432
Medium	Inference	414	352	434
Medium	Inference	420	355	437
Medium	Inference	422	357	438
Medium	Inference	427	359	441
Medium	Inference	429	360	442
Medium	Main Idea	384	340	416
Medium	Main Idea	401	347	427
Medium	Main Idea	408	350	430
Medium	Main Idea	409	351	431
Medium	Main Idea	419	355	436
Medium	Main Idea	425	358	440
Medium	Main Idea	426	359	440
Medium	Supporting Idea	378	339	412

(Continued)

Difficulty	Concept	Question #	Page	Answer Explanation Page
Medium	Supporting Idea	390	342	420
Medium	Supporting Idea	391	343	421
Medium	Supporting Idea	396	345	424
Medium	Supporting Idea	397	345	424
Medium	Supporting Idea	400	346	426
Medium	Supporting Idea	402	347	427
Medium	Supporting Idea	403	348	428
Medium	Supporting Idea	412	352	433
Medium	Supporting Idea	413	352	433
Medium	Supporting Idea	415	353	434
Medium	Supporting Idea	423	357	439
Hard	Application	453	370	455
Hard	Application	457	371	458
Hard	Application	466	376	463
Hard	Application	484	381	474
Hard	Evaluation	431	361	443
Hard	Evaluation	437	364	446
Hard	Evaluation	439	365	448
Hard	Evaluation	442	366	449
Hard	Evaluation	448	368	453
Hard	Evaluation	454	370	456
Hard	Evaluation	455	370	456
Hard	Evaluation	458	372	458
Hard	Evaluation	461	373	461
Hard	Evaluation	469	376	465
Hard	Evaluation	476	379	469
Hard	Evaluation	481	380	472
Hard	Evaluation	486	382	475
Hard	Evaluation	487	383	476
Hard	Inference	434	362	445

Difficulty	Concept	Question #	Page	Answer Explanation Page
Hard	Inference	435	362	445
Hard	Inference	436	363	446
Hard	Inference	440	365	448
Hard	Inference	441	366	449
Hard	Inference	444	366	450
Hard	Inference	446	367	452
Hard	Inference	447	368	452
Hard	Inference	451	369	454
Hard	Inference	452	369	455
Hard	Inference	459	372	459
Hard	Inference	462	374	461
Hard	Inference	465	375	463
Hard	Inference	467	376	464
Hard	Inference	470	376	466
Hard	Inference	471	377	466
Hard	Inference	472	377	467
Hard	Inference	473	377	467
Hard	Inference	474	378	468
Hard	Inference	479	380	471
Hard	Inference	480	380	471
Hard	Inference	482	380	473
Hard	Inference	483	381	473
Hard	Inference	488	383	476
Hard	Inference	489	383	477
Hard	Main Idea	430	361	443
Hard	Main Idea	438	364	447
Hard	Main Idea	443	366	450
Hard	Main Idea	445	367	451
Hard	Main Idea	450	369	454
Hard	Main Idea	463	375	462

(Continued)

Difficulty	Concept	Question #	Page	Answer Explanation Page
Hard	Supporting Idea	432	362	444
Hard	Supporting Idea	433	362	444
Hard	Supporting Idea	449	368	453
Hard	Supporting Idea	456	371	457
Hard	Supporting Idea	460	373	460
Hard	Supporting Idea	464	375	462
Hard	Supporting Idea	468	376	465
Hard	Supporting Idea	475	378	468
Hard	Supporting Idea	477	379	470
Hard	Supporting Idea	478	380	470
Hard	Supporting Idea	485	382	475

Critical Reasoning - Page 478

Difficulty	Concept	Question #	Page	Answer Explanation Page
Easy	Argument Construction	491	478	532
Easy	Argument Construction	492	478	533
Easy	Argument Construction	495	479	536
Easy	Argument Construction	496	479	537
Easy	Argument Construction	499	480	540
Easy	Argument Construction	500	481	541
Easy	Argument Construction	501	481	542
Easy	Argument Construction	505	482	546
Easy	Argument Construction	506	483	547
Easy	Argument Construction	510	484	551
Easy	Argument Construction	512	484	553
Easy	Argument Construction	514	485	555
Easy	Argument Construction	515	485	556
Easy	Argument Construction	516	485	557
Easy	Argument Construction	520	486	562

Difficulty	Concept	Question #	Page	Answer Explanation Page
Easy	Argument Construction	525	488	567
Easy	Argument Construction	526	488	568
Easy	Argument Construction	527	488	569
Easy	Argument Construction	530	489	572
Easy	Argument Construction	531	490	573
Easy	Argument Construction	533	490	575
Easy	Argument Construction	536	491	578
Easy	Argument Construction	539	492	581
Easy	Argument Construction	545	494	589
Easy	Argument Evaluation	490	478	531
Easy	Argument Evaluation	493	479	534
Easy	Argument Evaluation	497	480	538
Easy	Argument Evaluation	498	480	539
Easy	Argument Evaluation	503	482	544
Easy	Argument Evaluation	507	483	548
Easy	Argument Evaluation	509	483	550
Easy	Argument Evaluation	511	484	552
Easy	Argument Evaluation	518	486	559
Easy	Argument Evaluation	519	486	561
Easy	Argument Evaluation	521	487	563
Easy	Argument Evaluation	524	488	566
Easy	Argument Evaluation	535	491	577
Easy	Argument Evaluation	537	491	579
Easy	Argument Evaluation	540	492	582
Easy	Argument Evaluation	541	493	583
Easy	Argument Evaluation	543	493	586
Easy	Argument Evaluation	544	493	587
Easy	Evaluation of a Plan	494	479	535
Easy	Evaluation of a Plan	502	481	543

(Continued)

Difficulty	Concept	Question #	Page	Answer Explanation Page
Easy	Evaluation of a Plan	504	482	545
Easy	Evaluation of a Plan	508	483	549
Easy	Evaluation of a Plan	513	485	554
Easy	Evaluation of a Plan	517	486	558
Easy	Evaluation of a Plan	522	487	564
Easy	Evaluation of a Plan	523	487	565
Easy	Evaluation of a Plan	528	489	570
Easy	Evaluation of a Plan	529	489	571
Easy	Evaluation of a Plan	532	490	574
Easy	Evaluation of a Plan	534	490	576
Easy	Evaluation of a Plan	538	492	580
Easy	Evaluation of a Plan	542	493	585
Easy	Evaluation of a Plan	546	494	590
Easy	Evaluation of a Plan	547	494	591
Medium	Argument Construction	549	495	593
Medium	Argument Construction	550	495	594
Medium	Argument Construction	552	496	596
Medium	Argument Construction	553	496	597
Medium	Argument Construction	554	496	598
Medium	Argument Construction	555	497	599
Medium	Argument Construction	556	497	600
Medium	Argument Construction	557	497	601
Medium	Argument Construction	559	498	603
Medium	Argument Construction	561	498	605
Medium	Argument Construction	565	500	609
Medium	Argument Construction	566	500	610
Medium	Argument Construction	570	501	614
Medium	Argument Construction	571	501	615
Medium	Argument Construction	572	502	616
Medium	Argument Construction	577	503	621

Difficulty	Concept	Question #	Page	Answer Explanation Page
Medium	Argument Construction	580	504	624
Medium	Argument Construction	581	504	625
Medium	Argument Construction	583	505	627
Medium	Argument Construction	584	505	628
Medium	Argument Construction	589	506	633
Medium	Argument Construction	590	507	634
Medium	Argument Construction	591	507	635
Medium	Argument Construction	593	508	637
Medium	Argument Construction	594	508	638
Medium	Argument Construction	595	508	640
Medium	Argument Construction	597	509	642
Medium	Argument Construction	600	510	645
Medium	Argument Evaluation	548	495	592
Medium	Argument Evaluation	551	495	595
Medium	Argument Evaluation	558	498	602
Medium	Argument Evaluation	562	499	606
Medium	Argument Evaluation	563	499	607
Medium	Argument Evaluation	567	500	611
Medium	Argument Evaluation	568	500	612
Medium	Argument Evaluation	569	501	613
Medium	Argument Evaluation	575	502	619
Medium	Argument Evaluation	576	503	620
Medium	Argument Evaluation	578	503	622
Medium	Argument Evaluation	585	505	629
Medium	Argument Evaluation	588	506	632
Medium	Argument Evaluation	592	507	636
Medium	Argument Evaluation	596	508	641
Medium	Argument Evaluation	598	509	643
Medium	Argument Evaluation	599	509	644

(Continued)

Difficulty	Concept	Question #	Page	Answer Explanation Page
Medium	Argument Evaluation	601	510	646
Medium	Argument Evaluation	602	510	647
Medium	Evaluation of a Plan	560	498	604
Medium	Evaluation of a Plan	564	499	608
Medium	Evaluation of a Plan	573	502	617
Medium	Evaluation of a Plan	574	502	618
Medium	Evaluation of a Plan	579	504	623
Medium	Evaluation of a Plan	582	504	626
Medium	Evaluation of a Plan	586	505	630
Medium	Evaluation of a Plan	587	506	631
Hard	Argument Construction	603	510	648
Hard	Argument Construction	605	511	650
Hard	Argument Construction	606	511	651
Hard	Argument Construction	608	512	653
Hard	Argument Construction	610	513	655
Hard	Argument Construction	613	513	658
Hard	Argument Construction	616	514	661
Hard	Argument Construction	618	515	663
Hard	Argument Construction	619	515	664
Hard	Argument Construction	623	517	668
Hard	Argument Construction	626	517	671
Hard	Argument Construction	630	519	676
Hard	Argument Construction	631	519	677
Hard	Argument Construction	635	520	681
Hard	Argument Construction	641	522	687
Hard	Argument Construction	642	522	688
Hard	Argument Construction	645	523	691
Hard	Argument Construction	647	524	693
Hard	Argument Construction	649	524	695
Hard	Argument Construction	653	526	699

Difficulty	Concept	Question #	Page	Answer Explanation Page
Hard	Argument Construction	654	526	700
Hard	Argument Construction	657	527	703
Hard	Argument Evaluation	604	511	649
Hard	Argument Evaluation	609	512	654
Hard	Argument Evaluation	611	513	656
Hard	Argument Evaluation	612	513	657
Hard	Argument Evaluation	614	514	659
Hard	Argument Evaluation	617	515	662
Hard	Argument Evaluation	620	516	665
Hard	Argument Evaluation	621	516	666
Hard	Argument Evaluation	622	516	667
Hard	Argument Evaluation	624	517	669
Hard	Argument Evaluation	625	517	670
Hard	Argument Evaluation	628	518	673
Hard	Argument Evaluation	629	518	674
Hard	Argument Evaluation	632	519	678
Hard	Argument Evaluation	634	520	680
Hard	Argument Evaluation	637	521	683
Hard	Argument Evaluation	638	521	684
Hard	Argument Evaluation	640	522	686
Hard	Argument Evaluation	643	523	689
Hard	Argument Evaluation	644	523	690
Hard	Argument Evaluation	646	523	692
Hard	Argument Evaluation	650	525	696
Hard	Argument Evaluation	651	525	697
Hard	Argument Evaluation	655	526	701
Hard	Argument Evaluation	656	527	702
Hard	Argument Evaluation	658	527	704
Hard	Argument Evaluation	659	527	705

(Continued)

Difficulty	Concept	Question #	Page	Answer Explanation Page
Hard	Argument Evaluation	660	528	706
Hard	Argument Evaluation	661	528	707
Hard	Argument Evaluation	662	528	708
Hard	Argument Evaluation	663	529	709
Hard	Argument Evaluation	664	529	710
Hard	Evaluation of a Plan	607	512	652
Hard	Evaluation of a Plan	615	514	660
Hard	Evaluation of a Plan	627	518	672
Hard	Evaluation of a Plan	633	520	679
Hard	Evaluation of a Plan	636	520	682
Hard	Evaluation of a Plan	639	521	685
Hard	Evaluation of a Plan	648	524	694
Hard	Evaluation of a Plan	652	525	698

Appendix A   Answer Sheets

Quantitative Reasoning Answer Sheet

1.	33.	65.	97.	129.
2.	34.	66.	98.	130.
3.	35.	67.	99.	131.
4.	36.	68.	100.	132.
5.	37.	69.	101.	133.
6.	38.	70.	102.	134.
7.	39.	71.	103.	135.
8.	40.	72.	104.	136.
9.	41.	73.	105.	137.
10.	42.	74.	106.	138.
11.	43.	75.	107.	139.
12.	44.	76.	108.	140.
13.	45.	77.	109.	141.
14.	46.	78.	110.	142.
15.	47.	79.	111.	143.
16.	48.	80.	112.	144.
17.	49.	81.	113.	145.
18.	50.	82.	114.	146.
19.	51.	83.	115.	147.
20.	52.	84.	116.	148.
21.	53.	85.	117.	149.
22.	54.	86.	118.	150.
23.	55.	87.	119.	151.
24.	56.	88.	120.	152.
25.	57.	89.	121.	153.
26.	58.	90.	122.	154.
27.	59.	91.	123.	155.
28.	60.	92.	124.	156.
29.	61.	93.	125.	157.
30.	62.	94.	126.	158.
31.	63.	95.	127.	159.
32.	64.	96.	128.	160.

161.	175.	189.	203.	217.
162.	176.	190.	204.	218.
163.	177.	191.	205.	219.
164.	178.	192.	206.	220.
165.	179.	193.	207.	221.
166.	180.	194.	208.	222.
167.	181.	195.	209.	223.
168.	182.	196.	210.	224.
169.	183.	197.	211.	225.
170.	184.	198.	212.	226.
171.	185.	199.	213.	227.
172.	186.	200.	214.	228.
173.	187.	201.	215.	
174.	188.	202.	216.	

Data Insights Answer Sheet

229.	250.	271.	292.	313.
230.	251.	272.	293.	314.
231.	252.	273.	294.	315.
232.	253.	274.	295.	316.
233.	254.	275.	296.	317.
234.	255.	276.	297.	318.
235.	256.	277.	298.	319.
236.	257.	278.	299.	320.
237.	258.	279.	300.	321.
238.	259.	280.	301.	322.
239.	260.	281.	302.	323.
240.	261.	282.	303.	324.
241.	262.	283.	304.	325.
242.	263.	284.	305.	326.
243.	264.	285.	306.	327.
244.	265.	286.	307.	328.
245.	266.	287.	308.	329.
246.	267.	288.	309.	330.
247.	268.	289.	310.	331.
248.	269.	290.	311.	332.
249.	270.	291.	312.	

Reading Comprehension Answer Sheet

333.	365.	397.	429.	461.
334.	366.	398.	430.	462.
335.	367.	399.	431.	463.
336.	368.	400.	432.	464.
337.	369.	401.	433.	465.
338.	370.	402.	434.	466.
339.	371.	403.	435.	467.
340.	372.	404.	436.	468.
341.	373.	405.	437.	469.
342.	374.	406.	438.	470.
343.	375.	407.	430.	471.
344.	376.	408.	440.	472.
345.	377.	409.	441.	473.
346.	378.	410.	442.	474.
347.	379.	411.	443.	475.
348.	380.	412.	444.	476.
349.	381.	413.	445.	477.
350.	382.	414.	446.	478.
351.	383.	415.	447.	479.
352.	384.	416.	448.	480.
353.	385.	417.	449.	481.
354.	386.	418.	450.	482.
355.	387.	419.	451.	483.
356.	388.	420.	452.	484.
357.	389.	421.	453.	485.
358.	390.	422.	454.	486.
359.	391.	423.	455.	487.
360.	392.	424.	456.	488.
361.	393.	425.	457.	489.
362.	394.	426.	458.	
363.	395.	427.	459.	
364.	396.	428.	460.	

Critical Reasoning Answer Sheet

490.	525.	560.	595.	630.
491.	526.	561.	596.	631.
492.	527.	562.	597.	632.
493.	528.	563.	598.	633.
494.	529.	564.	599.	634.
495.	530.	565.	600.	635.
496.	531.	566.	601.	636.
497.	532.	567.	602.	637.
498.	533.	568.	603.	638.
499.	534.	569.	604.	639.
500.	535.	570.	605.	640.
501.	536.	571.	606.	641.
502.	537.	572.	607.	642.
503.	538.	573.	608.	643.
504.	539.	574.	609.	644.
505.	540.	575.	610.	645.
506.	541.	576.	611.	646.
507.	542.	577.	612.	647.
508.	543.	578.	613.	648.
509.	544.	579.	614.	649.
510.	545.	580.	615.	650.
511.	546.	581.	616.	651.
512.	547.	582.	617.	652.
513.	548.	583.	618.	653.
514.	549.	584.	619.	654.
515.	550.	585.	620.	655.
516.	551.	586.	621.	656.
517.	552.	587.	622.	657.
518.	553.	588.	623.	658.
519.	554.	589.	624.	659.
520.	555.	590.	625.	660.
521.	556.	591.	626.	661.
522.	557.	592.	627.	662.
523.	558.	593.	628.	663.
524.	559.	594.	629.	664.

Notes

Notes

Notes